HANDGUNS 2003

15th Annual Edition

Edited by
Ken Ramage

Manuscripts, contributions and inquiries, including first class return postage, should be sent to the HANDGUNS Editorial Offices, Krause Publications, 700 E. State Street, Iola, WI 54990-0001. All materials received will receive reasonable care, but we will not be responsible for their safe return. Material accepted is subject to our requirements for editing and revisions. Author payment covers all rights and title to the accepted material, including photos, drawings and other illustrations. Payment is at our current rates.

CAUTION: Technical data presented here, particularly technical data on the handloading and on firearms adjustment and alteration, inevitably reflects individual experience with particular equipment and components under specific circumstances the reader cannot duplicate exactly. Such data presentations therefore should be used for guidance only and with caution. Krause Publications, Inc., accepts no responsibility for results obtained using this data.

Published by

700 E. State Street • Iola, WI 54990-0001
Telephone: 715/445-2214
Web: www.krause.com

Please call or write for our free catalog of publications.
Our toll-free number to place an order or obtain a free catalog is 800-258-0929
or please use our regular business telephone, 715-445-2214.

Library of Congress Catalog Number: 88-72115
ISBN: 0-87349-486-5

— HANDGUNS STAFF —

Ken Ramage, Editor
HANDGUNS
Firearms & DBI Books

Editorial Comments and Suggestions

We're always looking for feedback on our books. Please let us know what you like about this edition. If you have suggestions for articles you'd like to see in future editions, please contact.

Ken Ramage/Handguns
700 East State St.
Iola, WI 54990
email: ramagek@krause.com

About Our Covers...

Our covers carry two single-action revolvers embellished by Dan Love, a member of the Firearms Engravers Guild of America (FEGA). Engraver Love has met FEGA's requirements for the prestigious rating of 'Certified Professional' and his work is clearly excellent. Photographs of these two revolvers, taken by Alan Richmond, were kindly provided by our friends at FEGA.

On the Front...

A Ruger Bisley-Vaquero 44 Magnum revolver, nicely engraved and gold-inlaid.

On the Back...

This is a Texas Longhorn Arms No. 5 Keith, 44 Magnum revolver. Yes, the loading gate and ejector rod are correctly located on the left side of this particular model. The small lever on the lower front of the revolver's frame serves to lock the cylinder pin in place to keep it from backing out under recoil.

Handguns 2003

Handguns for Sport and Personal Protection

CONTENTS

Page 40

Page 77

Page 81

CATALOG OF TODAY'S HANDGUNS

Page 110

SEMI-CUSTOM HANDGUNS

COMMERCIAL HANDGUNS

Page 132

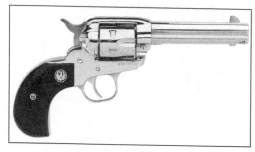

Page 196

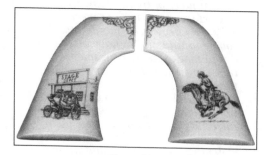

Page 224

HANDGUN NEWS

AUTOLOADING PISTOLS

by John Malloy

FOR MOST OF the year 2001, the firearms industry, in particular the segment that offered autoloading handguns, looked as if it were in trouble.

The anti-gun policies of the previous Clinton administration had brought about a marked decrease in the number of U. S. gun dealers, and restrictions against purchasers had cut down the number of people buying firearms. Lawsuits by municipalities had driven some small manufacturers out of business, and some others stopped offering handguns.

A single event can make a great difference in people's perceptions.

On September 11, 2001, terrorists carried out a devastating attack against the World Trade Center towers in New York and the Pentagon in Washington. Things were very different afterwards, in many ways.

The United States economy, already in a slump, went into a tailspin. The economy made a recovery, but for the first few weeks, the only things selling well were American flags, gas masks, Bibles ...and firearms.

As this is written, the majority of firearms companies seem to have a new, although cautious, optimism. There are still signs of the old uncertainty, though. Some companies that made semiautomatic pistols are now out of business, but some new ones have been started to make similar products.

A number of trends seem evident. Certain states require mechanical safety devices on handguns. So, some manufacturers have introduced new safety arrangements so that they can sell their products in those areas.

The 45 ACP seems to be the leading cartridge for new pistols being introduced. Many of the new pistol offerings are of the time-tested 1911 Colt/Browning design, but some are very different. The 1911 design still interests a vast number of

shooters, and many new variations are available. The military-style 1911A1, as used during World War II, has caught the fancy of many, and several companies have introduced similar pistols.

Pistols chambered for the 22 rimfire are always of interest and several different new concepts, in the general class of plinking pistols, are now offered.

New cartridges for semiautomatic handguns have been introduced. In past years, most new pistol cartridges have been big boomers of 40 to 50 caliber, but now the smaller end of the scale is getting attention. All the recent new cartridges have been small-caliber bottleneck rounds.

The concealed-carry market continues to grow. Reportedly, applications for concealed-weapons licenses reached record levels after the tragedy of September 11, 2001. Almost all handgun manufacturers make something to appeal to those wanting a pistol for personal protection. Polymer frames continue to be popular, and new pistols with polymer frames are now available.

More and more, companies involved with autoloading handguns realize the value of electronic communication, and maintain websites. Websites for the various companies are again included in the following discussion. However, this publication's Web Directory is becoming so useful that this separate listing may well not be needed in the future.

Semiautomatic pistols are of interest to competitive shooters, to plinkers, to hunters, to those who desire personal protection... and to those anti-gun forces who would restrict or ban their possession. In this framework, there is much happening in the world of autoloading handguns.

With all this in mind, let's take a look at what the companies are doing:

Alchemy

The Alchemy Arms Spectre pistol, introduced in 2000 as a new design for personal protection or as a service sidearm, has undergone some modifications. The manual

Malloy tries out a pre-production specimen of Beretta's new plinking 22, the U22 NEOS pistol, on the firing line.

safety has been redesigned for comfort of use, and the safety now will lock the slide.

The new sights are big and wide, allowing the shooter's eye to achieve a sight picture quickly. A new frame incorporates an accessory rail. However, the pistol is also available without a rail.

The Alchemy Spectre was initially available in 45 ACP. The original design had a 4 1/2-inch barrel and measured about 5x7 inches. A new 4-inch "Commander" variant has now joined it. By about August 2002, 9mm and 40 S&W versions were scheduled to be available.

www.alchemy.com

Beretta

Beretta has introduced a number of new pistols. Most are modifications of pistols previously in the line, but one is a completely new offering.

Previously, Beretta had offered a number of 22-caliber pistols, but never one that could really be called a plinking pistol. They were either small pocket pistols or precision target pistols. Now, the brand-new U22 "NEOS" pistol is a new 22-caliber pistol designed as an affordable entry-level plinking pistol that could be put to more precise uses. Its moulded grip with its 'slanty' angle, and its turn-screw barrel removal, will remind long-time shooters of the old High Standard Dura-Matic of the '50s and '60s. However, Beretta has incorporated modern concepts. The magazine release is located on the right, above the trigger, so it can be operated by the right index finger. Thus, the grip frame can be easily replaced with alternate frames to be offered by Beretta. The adjustable sights are contained within a full-length top rail attached to the barrel, a rail that will accept optical or electronic sights. The NEOS is an interesting addition to Beretta's line.

The compact polymer 9000S is now available with a new B-Lok system. This optional key-lock blocks the movement of the hammer.

Recall that the Model 92 pistols are 9mm and the Model 96 pistols are 40 caliber. The new 92/96 Vertec has a reshaped "vertical" *(well, more-nearly vertical)* grip frame. There are a large number of shooters who believe the 1911 Colt has the best 'feel' of any pistol. So, Beretta has shaped their grip frame on these variants to feel more like...well...a 1911. A "short-reach" trigger and thin grip panels add to this effect. Vertec pistols use the same magazines as do the standard 92 and 96 variants.

To commemorate the military operation against terrorism, Beretta has introduced a new Model 92 "Enduring Freedom" variant. It will be manufactured in five versions, honoring the U. S. Army, Marines, Navy, Air Force and Coast Guard.

Many shooters add laser sights to pistols as aftermarket items. Beretta now offers the Model 92 FS, a 9mm pistol that comes from the factory with a laser sight installed. The laser sight, with its battery power and its beam generator, is contained entirely within the grips, and is provided by Crimson Trace. The Crimson Trace company has been building excellent grip-mounted lasers since June 1994, and was a logical choice to provide the laser sight for the new 92 FS.

www.berettausa.com

Bernardelli

Bernardelli, a name in firearms manufacturing since 1721, has been absent from the shooting world for a time. The company has been reorganized and some guns went back into production in November 2001.

All previous lines, including Bernardelli pistols in 22 Short, 22 Long, 22 Long Rifle (22 LR), 25 ACP, 32 ACP, 7.65mm Parabellum, 380, 9mm, 9x21 and 40 S&W, were scheduled for production to be resumed by June 2002. This will be quite a lineup. Some of the former small Bernardellis, however, will not be available in the United States, due to U. S. import restrictions.

A totally new design of 9mm pistol was scheduled for introduction in 2002, but details were not available at the 2002 SHOT Show. However, there were suggestions that it may be a polymer-frame double-action (DA) pistol.

www.bernardelli.com

Browning

What? Did Browning discontinue their 9mm pistols? No, but the 9mm section was inadvertently left out of the 2002 catalog by the printer. Hopefully, revised catalogs will be available by the time you read this.

One item not in the catalog is the "Forest Camper" 22 pistol. It is a variant of the Camper 22 pistol, introduced on these pages several years ago, but with a green anodized frame and multicolored laminated

Those who like the P38 design will be interested in Century International's importation of West German police P1 pistols.

Century International Arms imports the Blue Thunder line of 1911-type 45 pistols. Century has initiated a small change that allows Colt and aftermarket grips to be easily installed.

No surprises—the mechanics of the Century Blue Thunder are straight 1911.

Colt offers a mixture of old and new designs, and has reintroduced its Series 70 Government Model.

grips. It will be made in limited numbers for special distribution.

The 40 S&W chambering is back for the "High Power" pistol. Last year, only the 9mm variant was made.
www.browning.com

Century International

Century International Arms' "Blue Thunder" line of 45-caliber 1911-style pistols was introduced last year and is in full production. One small change has been made in current-production pistols. Early guns had grip screws of shank and head diameters larger than those of original Colt screws. Thus, Colt and most aftermarket grips would not fit without modification. Now they will, for the screws of current pistols are of the correct size to use Colt-type grips. This is a small change, but important to those who want to use different grips, or specialty grips, such as laser-sight grips. A polymer-frame double-stack 45 variant is in the works, but details had not been worked out at press time.

Century is now importing P1 pistols. This is the original Walther P38 design with an aluminum frame, as used by the West German police. The guns come with a holster and an extra magazine. The P38 pistol design is highly

regarded by many who would like to see some company undertake new production. These excellent P1 variants should serve nicely.
www.centuryarms.com

Cobra

Cobra Enterprises is a new name that offers some familiar designs. When Davis Industries, Republic Arms and Talon Industries went out of business recently, Cobra bought all the existing inventory and tooling of the three companies, and set up the new company headquarters in Salt Lake City, Utah.

The Cobra line consists of a polymer-frame double-action-only (DAO) 45 pistol (Republic), a polymer-frame DAO 9mm pistol (Talon) and 32- and 380-caliber single-action semi-auto pistols (Davis). Derringers formerly made under the Davis brand are also included in the Cobra line. It is good to see these affordable pistols continue to be available.

Some small improvements have been made on pistols carrying the Cobra name. Still, Cobra will do warranty and repair work for pistols made by the previous manufacturers.
www.cobrapistols.com

Colt

Colt offers a new Defender Plus pistol, a 45 with a 3-inch barrel and full-size lightweight aluminum frame. Thus, it has full capacity in a lightweight package. The new Colt has a burr hammer, skeletonized trigger, beavertail grip safety and finger-groove rubber grips, things that seem to be in vogue now.

Colt's other new offerings are a mixture of old and new. The Blue Government Model has the construction and slide markings of the old pre-1970 Government Model, with modern niceties such as a burr hammer, ambidextrous safety and skeletonized trigger added.

The Series 70 Government Blue pistol likewise has the slide markings and construction of the original Series 70 guns, and comes with "big diamond" wood grips.

All new Colt 45-caliber semiautomatic pistols now come with two magazines.
www.colt.com

CZ

Too new for their 2002 catalog, CZ-USA has introduced the CZ-P.01 Police pistol. This is a conventional double-action pistol with a nice two-stage decocker. Offered in 9mm, it has an accessory rail. Designed to Czech police specifications, it is tightly fitted, but all parts are completely interchangeable from one specimen to another without additional fitting.
www.cz-usa.com

Dan Wesson

Dan Wesson has introduced a new line of 1911-type pistols as a lower-cost "Patriot" line. The new

Dan Wesson's new Patriot series can be recognized as the company's first pistol with an external extractor.

Bill Jeffery of Dan Wesson introduces the new Patriot pistol at the 2002 SHOT Show.

pistols have a "Series 70" mechanism with a forged slide and frame. Most notable new feature is the external extractor, which makes it obvious something is different from the original 1911 design. Patriot pistols are offered with traditional rounded-top slides, dovetail front sights, Chip McCormick 8-round magazines, and Cocobolo big-diamond grips. At first, they will be available in 45 ACP only, with initial deliveries scheduled for May 2002. Dan Wesson sees the Patriot as a way of getting more new people interested in competition shooting.

The company's mainstay Pointman pistols, introduced in 2000, have the traditional internal extractor. Slides have a solid rib on top, and the front sight is dovetailed into it. Chamberings offered are 9mm, 40 and 10mm, as well as 45. 38 Super may soon be added.

The original Dan Wesson company was founded on the idea of interchangeable components for its revolvers, and a new kit extends this concept to their Pointman autoloaders. The kit contains three 'top ends' in 9mm, 40 S&W and 10mm.

A new Pointman Guardian ("Commander-size"), with a 4 1/4-inch barrel, has also been added to the line.

www.danwessonfirearms.com

Davis

Davis Industries of Chino, CA, the maker of affordable semi-auto pistols and derringers, has gone out of business, after being with us 20 years. Stock and tooling have been acquired by Cobra Enterprises, a company that will continue production of the line. (See Cobra)

DPMS / Panther Arms

This company (Defense Procurement Manufacturing Services), a maker of AR-15-type rifles and accessories, had a prototype 1911A1-type 45 pistol at the February 2002 SHOT Show. It was basically a military-style 1911A1, but with a skeletonized trigger, big-diamond grips and a checkered flat mainspring housing.

The pistol will tentatively be called the Model 45P (Panther 45). Production was scheduled for mid-November 2002.

www.dpmsinc.com

EAA

European American Armory is now handling a line of Israeli-made BUL 1911-style pistols. These will be polymer-frame double-column guns in three barrel sizes—the five-inch "Government," the four-inch "Commander," and the three-inch "Stinger." Slides can be provided with blued or stainless finishes. All variants have a beavertail grip safety, skeletonized trigger and hammer, and extended thumb safety lever.

www.eaacorp.com

Excel Industries

Excel Industries, the maker of the Accu-Tek line of pistols, has brought out two new pistols under the Excel Arms name. The new handguns are both in 45 ACP, a departure from the existing Accu-Tek line of 380 and 9mm chamberings.

The new 45s are single-action subcompacts. Two variants have been introduced. The CP-45 is a stainless-steel gun with a single-column magazine, providing 6+1 capacity. The XP-45 has a polymer frame with a double-column magazine and a 10+1 capacity. This 3 1/2-inch-barrel polymer version tips the scales at 25 ounces.

Pre-production specimens of both types were displayed at the

A new double-action 45-caliber compact pistol has been introduced under the Firestorm name.

February 2002 SHOT Show. Availability of production models was scheduled for May 2002. The new Excel 45s will come with a lock and cleaning kit, and carry a lifetime warranty.

www.accu-tekfirearms.com

Firestorm

A new Firestorm 45 pistol was offered for 2002. A distinct design apart from the existing line of single-action 45s, the new pistol is a conventional double-action, with a decocker. Last year, Firestorm introduced these features in its "Mini-Firestorm" 9mm and 40 DA

One of the new Excel Arms 45 pistols is the XP-45, a 10+1 capacity version with a polymer frame.

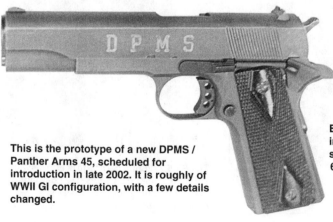

This is the prototype of a new DPMS / Panther Arms 45, scheduled for introduction in late 2002. It is roughly of WWII GI configuration, with a few details changed.

Excel Arms has introduced a new CP-45, a stainless-steel compact with 6+1 capacity. This specimen is serial number *000001*.

pistols. Now, the line is expanded to include the 45 ACP variant. The new Mini-Firestorm 45 is a 7-shot DA pistol. It features an ambidextrous manual safety and—a nice touch— an ambidextrous manual slide release. Finishes are matte black, satin nickel and duo-tone.

www.Firestorm-sgs.com

FNH USA

The formation of a new United States company, FNH USA, Inc., was formally announced in February 2002. This is an American subsidiary of FN Herstal, the Belgian firearms manufacturer, and will produce firearms for U. S. law enforcement and commercial customers, and for the military market.

A number of pistols are in the FNH lineup. Among them are the "High Power" pistols similar to those otherwise available under the Browning name. These include single-action, double-action and double-action-only variants.

Malloy fires a 9mm FN Forty-Nine pistol using a two-handed hold.

Two new pistols are not similar to anything in the Browning line. The FN Model Forty-Nine was anticipated on these pages last year, and is now available in 9mm and 40 S&W. It is a polymer-frame DAO pistol with a revolver-type trigger pulling around 8 to 10 pounds. It weighs 26 ounces, and measures 5 3/4 x 7 3/4 inches, with a 4 1/4-inch barrel. The slide can be furnished in stainless steel or with

The new FN DAO pistol has a cam-actuated tilting-barrel locking system. The captive recoil spring is a flat-coil spring to allow greater compression.

a black semi-gloss finish. It has some interesting features, some hardly noticeable, such as a flat-coil recoil spring to allow greater compression.

The new FN Model Five-seveN is for law-enforcement and military sales only. With a 4.8-inch barrel and 8 1/4-inch overall length, it is a big polymer DAO pistol with a very light weight of only 22 ounces. Perhaps the most interesting feature is the cartridge for which it is chambered. The cartridge is a special 22-caliber bottleneck round, the 5.7x28mm, about

The FN Forty-Nine feels good in the hand, and the DAO pistol is suitable for left-hand use.

This is the FN Five-seveN, a 20-shot polymer pistol for military and law-enforcement sales. Chambering is 5.7x28mm, a high-velocity 22-caliber bottleneck cartridge.

The FN 5.7x28mm cartridge is shown with a 9mm Parabellum cartridge for comparison. The 5.7 is longer, but its small case diameter allows large magazine capacity.

1.6 inches long. It is thus long for a pistol cartridge. *(It is actually the same round used in the FN P90 submachine gun).* However, the cartridge is only .310" in diameter (only slightly wider than a 30-caliber bullet) and, so, 20 rounds can be easily carried in the pistol's magazine. The cartridge is loaded with a 31-grain bullet that achieves 2133 feet per second from the pistol barrel. Because of the light bullet, it is said to have 30 percent less recoil than would be generated shooting a 9mm cartridge in a pistol of equal weight.

It is interesting to note the names of these two pistols feature the letters "FN" and designate the calibers for which the pistols are chambered.

www.fnherstal.com

Glock

Glock had developed prototype specimens of a new safety locking system last year, and final working specimens were on display in February 2002. The system uses a special dimpled key inserted into the rear portion of the grip, behind the magazine well. When locked, a projection extends rearward from the grip and is obvious, by sight or feel, to a shooter gripping the pistol. The new locking system was scheduled for availability in early 2002.

Glock has made a run of "America's Heroes" pistols to commemorate the police and firefighters on the scene during the September 11, 2001 tragedy.

www.glock.com

Heckler & Koch

New in HK's USP line is the USP Compact 40 S&W LEM (Law Enforcement Modification) pistol. The action has been described as a hybrid double-action/single-action system that uses an internal "precock" for reduced trigger pull. The trigger retains the longer DA trigger movement, but it has a fairly light—about 7 pounds—pull. In case of a misfire, the trigger can be pulled again for a second strike. The pistol is available in 40 S&W.

A brand-new pistol, too new for the 2002 catalog, is the P2000, a 9mm offering. The mechanism is said to be similar to that of the 40 S&W LEM, but the 9mm is conventional DA and is equipped with a decocker.

www.hecklerkoch-usa.com

High Standard

A GI Model 45 is new in High Standard's line. The pistols are made in the classic World War II style, and the finish is military-specification Parkerizing. On the left side of the slide, the guns will be marked "Model of 1911 A1." On the right of the slide, "Hi-Standard" will appear.

Each pistol will come with a reprint of an original military instruction manual, "Description of the Automatic Pistol, caliber .45, Model of 1911." All the information in the manual is still valid.

www.highstandard.com

Hi-Point

Hi-Point continues to modify and improve its line of low-cost pistols with little fanfare. The large-frame 40- and 45-caliber Hi-Point pistols will be phasing in polymer frames during 2002. A prototype of the new design was displayed at the 2002 SHOT Show.

The new frame will provide a slightly different grip shape and be slightly lighter than the present aluminum frames. The new pistols will offer an accessory rail, push-button magazine release and last-round hold-open features.

Hi-Point plans to eventually offer adjustable sights on all pistols, and all adjustable-sight models now come with an additional aperture sight.

Hi-Point likes to stress that their guns are made to be shot, and that their No-Questions-Asked warranty covers repairs.

www.hi-pointfirearms.com

Kahr

Kahr got its start with a nicely designed small pistol, and its line has consisted of subcompact 9mm and 40-caliber pistols. At the 2002 SHOT Show, Kahr displayed a larger prototype "Target Model" pistol with a long grip frame and a longer 4-inch barrel. The construction was stainless steel, with wood grips. Most who handled it liked the feel of the pistol—it would be a nice holster gun for those who don't need a subcompact.

For those whose desires run to subcompacts, though, Kahr has added a new model. The new PM9 (Polymer Micro 9mm) is a small (MK9-size) pistol with a shorter polymer grip frame. It has a 3-inch barrel with polygonal rifling. The little gun weighs 15.9 ounces and measures 4 x 5.3 inches. Sights consist of a white ball front and

Kahr's Auto-Ordnance line of full-size 1911 pistols now has a shorter 4 1/4-inch barrel "Mid-Size" variant.

Here is a peek at Kahr's prototype large-frame 40 S&W "Target Model" pistol, exhibited for the first time at the 2002 SHOT Show.

The new Kahr PM9 is a subcompact polymer-frame 9mm with a shortened grip. The new little Kahr has ball-and-bar sights.

white bar rear for fast alignment. The new little Kahr comes with two magazines—a flush 6-rounder or an extension 7-rounder; all Kahr 9mm magazines, however, including the longer ones, will work in the PM9. The frame is black polymer with steel inserts, and the slide is matte stainless steel.

Recall that Kahr now offers the Auto-Ordnance line of 1911-type pistols. New in that line is a "Commander-size" 45 (Kahr calls it a "Mid-size"), with a 4 1/4-inch barrel.

All Kahr pistols come with a lifetime warranty.

www.kahr.com

Kel-Tec

The little 6 1/2-ounce 32 ACP P-32 pistol, introduced in 1999, has been well-received. As of early 2002, well over 70,000 had been made. A new 10-round magazine is now available for the P-32. It adds some bulk, but feels good in the hand. For practice shooting, it provides more grip. I suspect those who carry the P-32 concealed, but also like to carry an extra magazine, may choose to carry the original 7-rounder in the pistol, with the 10-shot as a spare. The P-32 has gained surprising acceptance in the American West—the spring clip allows it to be conveniently carried as a boot pistol.

www.kel-tec.com

Kimber

The Kimber Ultra Ten II was introduced last year, and has been revised slightly. The final version was scheduled for production by the second quarter of 2002. Recall that the "II" designation indicated the new safety locking mechanism.

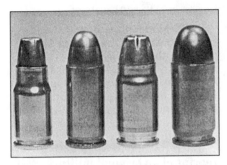

North American Arms' new cartridges and the original rounds from which they were derived: *from left*, the 25 NAA, its parent 32 ACP, the 32 NAA, and the parent 380.

Beginning in 2002, all Kimber pistols will have the lock and are thus considered Series II pistols.

The striking-looking Eclipse pistols—stainless steel, covered black, then the sides polished bright—were Custom Shop items last year. They proved so popular they are now full-time in the line as standard catalog items.

A Stainless Target pistol is now available for the first time chambered in 38 Super.

Kimber is proud to be a sponsor of the U. S. Olympic Shooting Team.

www.kimberamerica.com

Magnum Research

Magnum Research is now handling the new IMI (Israeli Military Industries) Barak 45-caliber pistol. The 30-ounce pistol has a polymer frame with an accessory rail. It is a hammer-fired design and is conventional double-action (DA), with a decocker. Locking is by a cam-actuated tilting-barrel system. The 3.9-

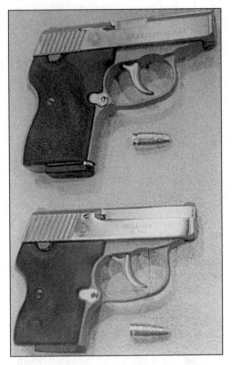

North American Arms has introduced two new Guardian pistols for two new cartridges. The larger-frame Guardian *(top)* uses the 32 NAA, essentially the 380 necked down to 32 caliber. The original smaller-frame version is now offered in 25 NAA, the 32 ACP necked down to 25.

inch barrel has polygonal rifling, and the pistol measures 5.4 x 7.4 inches. Capacity is 10+1. The Barak has a rounded slide that might lead one to suspect that the recoil spring was around the barrel. However, it actually uses two separate springs on rods beneath the barrel.

www.magnumresearch.com

Some people just want to have a pistol with the current 10+1 "legal limit" of cartridges. Kel-Tec now offers a 10-shot magazine for their P-32 that includes a grip extension. Makes the pistol bigger, but feels pretty good.

Malloy examines an Olympic Arms OA-98, a large pistol chambered for the 223 Remington. Parts have been skeletonized to reduce weight.

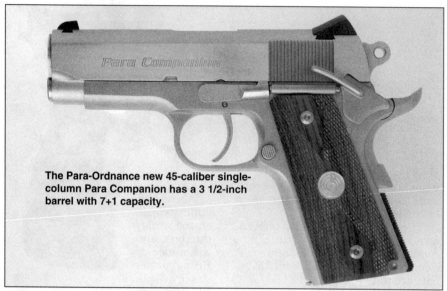

The Para-Ordnance new 45-caliber single-column Para Companion has a 3 1/2-inch barrel with 7+1 capacity.

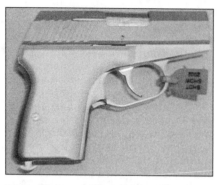

This is the prototype of the new Rohrbaugh 9mm all-metal subcompact pistol. The 14-ounce DAO pistol will be available in a version with a magnetic safety.

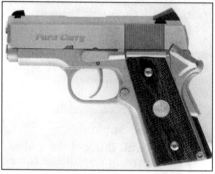

The new Para Carry is a small single-column 45 with a 3-inch barrel, and offers 6+1 capacity.

North American

The little 32 ACP Guardian pistol, introduced a few years ago, proved popular and led North American Arms to introduce a new 380 Guardian last year. Now the company has introduced two new Guardian pistols for two new cartridges.

The new cartridges are the 25 NAA—essentially the 32 ACP necked down to 25 caliber, and the 32 NAA—the 380 necked down to 32 caliber. Cor-Bon will produce the ammunition, and preliminary velocity figures promise to be pretty zippy. The 380-frame Guardian will be offered in the 32 NAA, and the smaller 32-frame Guardian will be available in 25 NAA.

The Guardian pistols will be provided with a new internal safety lock. www.naaminis.com

Olympic

For people who like big pistols, Olympic Arms now offers the OA-98. It is an AR-15 type pistol, chambered for the 223 Remington (5.56mm) cartridge. Pistols of this sort must weigh under 50 ounces to be "civilian legal," so the OA-98 has a skeletonized grip, magazine well and shield to reduce weight.

The OA-98 has been under development for some time, and is now in full production. www.olyarms.com

Para-Ordnance

Para-Ordnance now offers the Para Carry (Model C6.45 LDA) and the Para Companion (Model C7.45 LDA). They are small 45-caliber single-column carry pistols with the company's "Light Double Action" mechanism. These all-steel guns were introduced last year on these pages, and are now in full production.

The Para Carry, with its three-inch barrel, measures 4 3/4 x 6 1/2 inches, weighs 30 ounces and offers 6 + 1 capacity. The Para Companion is slightly larger, with a 3 1/2-inch barrel and measuring about 5 x 7 inches. The slightly longer grip frame gives the pistol a 7 + 1 capacity. www.paraord.com

Republic

Republic Arms, of Chino, California, maker of a 20-ounce polymer 45, has gone out of business. Inventory and tooling have been acquired by Cobra Enterprises, and that new company will continue production of the pistol. *(See Cobra)*

Rohrbaugh

A prototype of the new Rohrbaugh pistol was displayed at the February 2002 SHOT Show. The little gun is an all-metal 14-ounce DAO pistol, chambered for the 9mm cartridge. With a 2.7-inch barrel, it measures 3.6 x 4.9 inches. Thus, it will stick out a little from under a 3x5 note card, but not much. Thick-

Sigarms' limited-production 9mm P226 Sport pistol is a stainless-steel pistol with a heavy barrel, adjustable sights and extended controls, designed for competition shooting.

ness is a little over 3/4-inch. The frame is 7075 aircraft aluminum; all other parts are 17-4 stainless steel. The grips on the prototype were of aluminum, but wood and other materials will be offered.

The little pistol is a short-recoil locked-breech design with a cam-operated tilting-barrel locking system. The barrel is free-bored for a quarter-inch, and the pistol will handle all standard 9mm loads.

Two models will be available. The MS-9 will have a magnetic safety. With this system, the shooter wears a Neodymium magnetic ring that opens an internal block to allow the trigger to operate. Another model, the R-9, will be made without the magnetic safety. Production was scheduled for July 2002.

API380@aol.com

Sarsilmaz

A name generally connected with shotguns, the Turkish Sarsilmaz firm plans to introduce a line of 9mm semiautomatic pistols. The catalog offered in February 2002 featured the pistols, but actual specimens were not available to examine. From the catalog illustrations, the guns looked to be based on the CZ-75 design. A polymer-frame variant may be made under the Bernardelli name. Timing of the introduction of the new pistols was uncertain at press time.

www.sarsilmaz.com

Sigarms

Sigarms has introduced two new handguns. The P226 Sport ST will be made in a limited run for competitive shooters. It is a stainless-steel pistol with a heavy barrel, adjustable sights and extended controls. It will be available in 9mm chambering only.

The P226 ST is now also offered as a stainless-steel duty gun. Availability at present is in 9mm, and versions in 40 S&W and 357 SIG are anticipated.

Sigarms is now handling Sig-Sauer, Sig Pro, Blaser, Sauer, Hammerli and Mauser arms, and is projecting more expansion into the hunting field.

www.sigarms.com

Smith & Wesson

Smith & Wesson has introduced a new pistol, the model 952. The new item is a 9mm target pistol. It is similar to the former Model 52 of long ago, which was chambered for the 38 Special wadcutter cartridge. The 952 barrel bushing is of titanium nitride and is fitted closely. The pistol has a decocker, and uses a "grip safety" device to release the firing pin block, so that trigger pull is unaffected.

Seven models of S&W pistols are now available with the "Saf-T-Trigger" mechanical trigger lock. The American firm, Saf-T-Hammer, originator of the new trigger lock mechanism, is the new owner of Smith &

The new Sphinx Model 3000 pistol.

Wesson. After the bad publicity generated while the company was under British ownership by the Tomkins group, S&W is capitalizing on this with their new "American Made – American Owned" slogan.

All S&W hammers are now made by the Metal Injection Moulding (MIM) process, and are somewhat lighter than previous hammers.

www.smith-wesson.com

Sphinx

We may still think of the Swiss as gunmakers, but Sphinx is the last remaining firearms manufacturer in Switzerland. Sphinx pistols are high-end pistols; made primarily for military, law enforcement and competition use. They are based on the CZ-75 design, and are available in either conventional DA or double-action-only (DAO) configuration. The Swiss Sphinx offerings now include pistols made with titanium frames.

The Model 3000 has an all-titanium frame. It is the top-of-the-line pistol, chambered in 9mm, 9x21, 40 and 45. Barrel options are 4 1/2 or 3 3/4 inches. The CNC-machined titanium frame has a beavertail tang, squared trigger guard and accessory rail.

The Model 2000 now comes with a titanium layer on the frame. It also features an accessory rail on its traditional frame. The same barrel lengths are offered as on the 3000. Cartridges chambered are 9mm, 9x21 and 40; the 45 chambering is not available.

www.sphinxarms.com

Springfield

Big news from Springfield is their new line of X-treme Duty (XD) polymer-frame pistols. The new pistols are available in 4- and 5-inch barrel variants. The chamberings offered

Springfield's new XD pistol (X-treme Duty) is a polymer-frame gun in 9mm and 40 caliber. This is a variant with a 4-inch barrel.

The Taurus PT 145 is here disassembled to show the cam-actuated tilting-barrel system and the two recoil springs; one inside and one outside the guide rod.

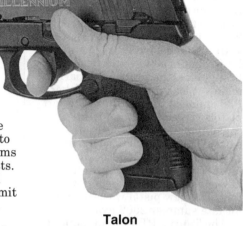

Although the Taurus "Millennium" PT 145 is a DAO pistol, it also features a manually-operated thumb safety, seen just above the shooter's thumb.

are 9mm, 40 S&W and 357 SIG. Safety features include a grip safety *(an uncommon feature on a polymer-frame pistol)*; a trigger safety and an internal firing-pin-block drop safety. The slide will not unlock unless the grip safety is pressed in. The XD pistol also has loaded chamber and cocking indicators. Takedown is simple and essentially foolproof.

Regular readers of these pages will recognize that HS America introduced a similar pistol in 2000. With minor modifications, the pistol is now part of the Springfield line. This nice design should benefit from the company's established distribution system.

In addition, Springfield has introduced the Micro Compact 45. The smallest pistol in the company's 1911 lineup, it has a 3-inch barrel and weighs just 24 ounces. Slimline Cocobolo grips keep the pistol thin, and all sharp edges are rounded off.

All Springfield pistols, including the new XD pistols, are covered by a lifetime warranty.
www.springfield-armory.com

Steyr

Last year, rumors circulated that the plant in which Steyr pistols were being made was being taken over for other uses. By September 2001, Austria's Creditensalt bank, then the owner of Steyr, had apparently sold the land on which the Steyr factory was located to BMW for automotive production.

By February 2002, GSI of Trussville, AL, the U. S. importer for Steyr firearms, confirmed that Steyr was under new ownership,

and that GSI would no longer be the importer. GSI will continue to offer paid service on Steyr firearms as long as their parts supply lasts.

At least some Steyr guns will remain in production, and Dynamit Nobel RWS, Inc, operating from Closter, NJ, will be the new importer. More details could not be had by press time.

The recently-introduced Steyr pistols had begun to develop a following, and we hope this interesting design will continue to be available.
www.dnrws.com

Talon

Talon Industries, of Ennis, MT, had introduced a line of low-cost polymer-frame 380 and 9mm pistols just last year, but now has gone out of business. Inventory and tooling have been acquired by Cobra Enterprises, a company that will continue production. *(See Cobra)*

The Taurus PT 145, a 10+1 compact polymer-frame 45, is now in full production.

Taurus' new Model PT 922 pistol is a nice 22-caliber plinker with a 6-inch barrel.

Taurus

Taurus believes there is always room for a new 22-caliber plinking pistol, and has introduced the PT 922. It is a large-frame 22LR pistol with a 6-inch barrel, based on the PT 92, but is a blowback design. At first glance, the protruding barrel makes it look a bit like a Walther P38 or one of the Walther PP Sport pistols. The PT 922 has 10+1 capacity and a three-position safety. The safety acts as a manual safety and also as a decocking lever. The PT 922 will have the key-operated Taurus Security System. The new pistol was scheduled for late summer 2002 availability.

The Taurus PT 145, announced back in 2000, ran into production delays, only recently resolved. The pistol has now come into full production. This new 45 ACP pistol is the biggest-caliber offering in Taurus' polymer-frame Millennium series. It has a 3 1/4-inch barrel and the locking mechanism is a cam-operated tilting-barrel system. Trigger is DAO, and the pistol also has a manual thumb safety, an uncommon feature on a DAO pistol. Two recoil springs of different diameters operate on the inside and outside of a hollow spring guide. The magazine is a staggered-column type and holds 10 rounds. A Taurus-made magazine loader is provided to get them all in, making the PT 145 a pistol of 10+1 capacity. The PT 145 weighs just 23 ounces and measures 5 x 6 1/4 inches in overall size. All the

A 5-inch "Target" model of the Walther P22 is available. The P22 pistols have 10+1 capacity and weigh about 20 ounces.

The Walther P22 is now in production. This version, with a 3.4-inch barrel, is a compact little plinking pistol.

Taurus Millennium pistols, including the new 45, have the key-lock Taurus Security System. www.taurususa.com

Volquartsen

Volquartsen has made high-grade Custom 22-caliber semi-auto pistols based on the Ruger Mark II for some time. In early 2002, however, Volquartsen introduced a completely new design of rimfire semiautomatic pistol. The new "Cheeta" has a separate rear-mounted grip, and has the magazine forward of the trigger. Designed for long-range shooting, it has an integral scope base.

The barrel is bimetallic—a titanium sleeve over a steel barrel. The grip is ambidextrous, and the safety can be operated from either the right or left side.

Volquartsen reports that the new pistol has produced groups under one inch at 100 yards in tests. In what caliber? Ah, there is an interesting situation. The Cheeta is

scheduled to be available in four rimfire chamberings. As one might expect, the 22 Long Rifle and 22 Winchester Magnum Rimfire are two of them. One of the other two, the 17 Hornady Magnum Rimfire *(essentially the 22 WMR necked down to 17 caliber)* was designed for Marlin and Ruger bolt-action rifles, but Volquartsen has successfully adapted it to the Cheeta autoloading pistol. The 17 Aguila *(the 22 LR necked down to 17 caliber)* was introduced by the Aguila ammunition firm for much the same use, and is on the list for Cheeta chamberings.

The Volquartsen Cheeta was scheduled for April 2002 availablity.

www.volquartsen.com

Volquartsen's new Cheeta pistol will be offered in several rimfire cartridge chamberings. *From the left*, the 22 Long Rifle, the 22 Winchester Magnum Rimfire and the 17 Hornady Magnum Rimfire. The 17 Aguila is also scheduled.

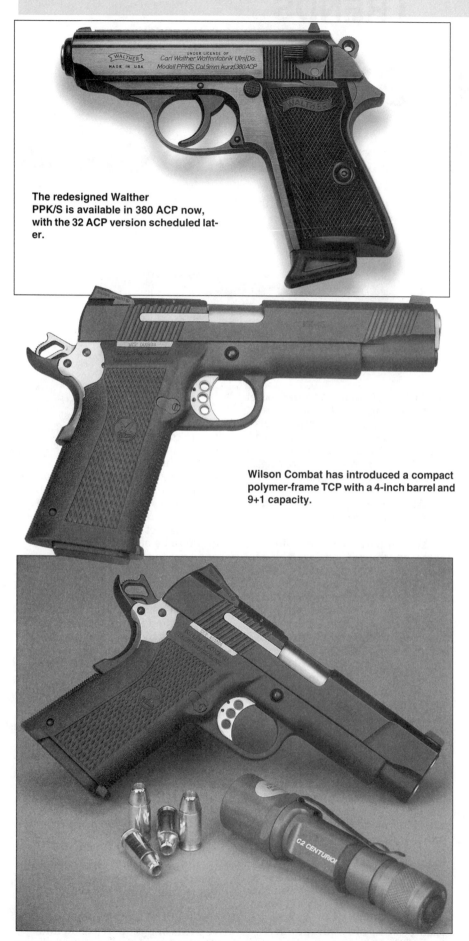

The redesigned Walther PPK/S is available in 380 ACP now, with the 32 ACP version scheduled later.

Wilson Combat has introduced a compact polymer-frame TCP with a 4-inch barrel and 9+1 capacity.

The new Wilson polymer-frame full-size Tactical Carry Pistol is a slim 10+1 pistol.

Walther

As of early 2002, Walther was starting to deliver the neat little P22 pistols it introduced last year. The P22 looks like a small P99, but is a hammer-fired conventional DA blowback. The pistols will be available with interchangeable "backstraps" (rear grip inserts); barrel-length options are 3.4 or 5 inches. The P22 pistols weigh about 20 ounces and have 10+1 capacity.

Recall that the classic PPK/S design was undergoing a slight revision. The new PPK/S in 380 ACP was scheduled for February 2002 availability. The same pistol in 32 ACP will be offered some time later.
www.walther-usa.com

Wilson

Wilson Combat has introduced a new Tactical Carry Pistol (TCP). The new 1911-style pistol has a Kevlar-reinforced polymer frame with stainless-steel inserts. The frame was designed specifically for a staggered 10-round magazine *(not a plugged higher-capacity one)*, which allowed the polymer frame to actually be slightly narrower across the grips than a traditional 1911. The new TCP has been designed with an external extractor.

Two variants are offered, in full-size and compact configurations. The full-size TCP weighs 31 ounces and measures 5 1/2 by 8 5/8 inches, and sports a 5-inch barrel. The compact has a 4.1-inch barrel, an overall size of 5 1/4 by 8 inches and weighs 29 ounces. The shortened grip frame of the compact holds one round less, giving it a 9+1 capacity.

Wilson's TCP pistols are guaranteed to shoot within 1 1/2 inches at 25 yards.
www.wilsoncombat.com

POSTSCRIPT

Many of us remember when the misguided "Assault Weapons" bill was passed into law in 1994. Perhaps the most lasting effect of that act was to restrict firearms magazine capacity to 10 rounds for ordinary citizens, while the police could continue to use high-capacity magazines.

Forgotten by many is that the 1994 law has a 10-year duration and will expire in 2004–not all that long from now. Contact your senators and representatives and line up support to defeat it at the designated time. Then, we can all keep our plugged magazines to remind us to remain active in the future. ●

HANDGUN NEWS

REVOLVERS, SINGLE SHOTS AND OTHERS

by John Taffin

*H*ere's the latest news — and there's plenty of it!

American Derringer

For more than 150 years, a most popular concealed weapon has been the derringer. A multitude of companies have offered both single-shot and double-shot easy-to-hide-away pistols to be used in a time or situation we hope never occurs. Many of these little guns have been poorly made and lacking in accuracy. The derringers from American Derringer go against the grain–being of high-quality and more than adequate accuracy. The lovely Elizabeth Saunders, *aka* Lady Derringer, offers shooters a full line of both single-action and double-action two-shooters in chamberings from 22 rimfire to 380 ACP to 44 Magnum to 45 Colt–even 45-70 (*ouch!*)–and a multiple of calibers in between. The stainless steel M-1, for example is offered in 24 chamberings with the original, and my favorite, being the 45 Colt.

The traditional M-1 looks much like the old 41 Remington, though slightly larger and definitely stronger. In addition to the 24 chamberings currently cataloged, it can also be special-ordered with each of the two barrels in a different chambering. I have used the M-1 45 Colt for over a decade, carried in a Thad Rybka pocket holster which also holds two extra 45 Colt rounds, and

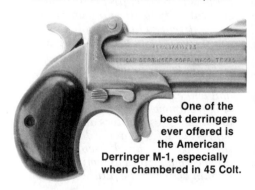

One of the best derringers ever offered is the American Derringer M-1, especially when chambered in 45 Colt.

the M-1 is safe to carry in the pocket as it is equipped with a hammer-block safety that automatically disengages when the hammer is cocked. American Derringer offers a whole line of custom finishes, engraving, holsters, and custom grips.

American Western Arms (AWA)

AWA imports Armi San Marco parts, which are then assembled in this country and the firearms finished–resulting in a beautiful Single Action Army replica, in two basic versions. The standard model is the Longhorn with a color case-hardened frame and hammer, blue finish, and one-piece walnut grips. Both the front sight and hammer checkering are based upon those found on the 19th-century Colt Single Action Army. The top-of-the-line model is the Peacekeeper, which adds a factory-tuned action, 11-degree forcing cone, 1st Generation-style cylinder flutes, and bone/charcoal case-hardened frame.

There is a definite difference between the case coloring found on the Longhorn and the Peacekeeper; the latter's being much more brilliant, and the bluing seems a little deeper, too. Both models feature a beveled ejector-rod housing to keep the metal from digging into the leather on a tight holster, and both models can be had in nickel finish. The Peacekeeper can also be ordered with the "blackpowder frame" that uses an angled screw

A beautiful rendition of the Single Action Army is AWA's Peacekeeper.

in the front of the frame to hold the cylinder pin in place rather than the spring-loaded cross-pin style of the later SAA frame design.

Chamberings include 45 Colt, 44-40, 357 Magnum, and 44 Special. I expect both the 38-40 and 32-20 to be offered eventually. In addition to the Longhorn and Peacekeeper six-guns, American Western Arms also markets a large selection of custom grips and western-style leather.

AWA had a couple of shaky starts but they are now under new ownership and turning out many variations as well as high-grade, fully-engraved, ivory- or pearl-handled six-guns. At Tin Star Ranch in November 2001, I pointed out to Chris Harrison of AWA that they needed to do a better job of radiusing the rounded curve at the backstrap area where it meets the back of the hammer—all three should have the same smooth radius. At the SHOT Show in February 2002, the six-guns on display indicated this problem has been addressed.

Cimarron Firearms

Mike Harvey of Cimarron has been one of the primary forces in upgrading replica six-guns from the "Spaghetti Western-style" of the 1960s to the highly authentic replicas of both percussion and fixed ammunition six-guns we have today. Cimarron's lineup includes the Model P, a near-perfect copy of the 1st Generation Colt Single Action Army, including old model-style frames–often referred to as blackpowder style–that were in use from 1873 to the mid-1880s, and the new model frame that arrived in 1896. Cimarron now offers the Frontier Six-Shooter, totally assembled and finished in this country using European parts. In addition to these authentic "Colt" models, CFA also provides shooters with the Bisley Model, Flat-Top Target Models from the 1890s, and the Thunderer and Lightning–two single actions utilizing the grip shape of Colt's 1877 double actions.

Moving deeper into six-gun history, we find the Model 1872 Open-Top, immediate predecessor of the Colt Single Action Army; the Richards-Mason Conversion (*new this year*), which enabled percussion revolvers to use fixed ammunition–and every cap-and-ball revolver offered by Colt from the original 1836 Paterson through the Walker, Dragoon, Navy, and Army models. Nearly every single action offered by Cimarron is not only available in the original blue and case-colored style but also in what Cimarron refers to as their 'original' finish, a 'distressed' finish that makes the six-gun appear to have been used - but not abused - for over 100 years. Cimarron's custom shop also offers a full line of custom finishes, grips, and engraving.

One of the most spectacular and eye-catching six-guns offered by Cimarron is the Wyatt Earp Buntline. This 10-inch-barreled 45 Colt six-gun is offered in blue/case-coloring, or original finish, and is the same six-gun used by Kurt Russell in his memorable performance as Wyatt Earp in the movie "Tombstone." Each is equipped with authentic one-piece walnut stocks, with a sterling silver shield inlaid in the right-side grip commemorating the presentation of the long-barreled Colt to Wyatt Earp by "the Grateful People of Dodge City." I've ordered mine in the standard blue/case-colored finish.

Colt

Colt has new management once again, and this time it looks good! General William "Bill" Keys is now the president and has pledged to get Colt completely back on track. As a start, the Anaconda is back–not only in the original 44 Magnum and 45

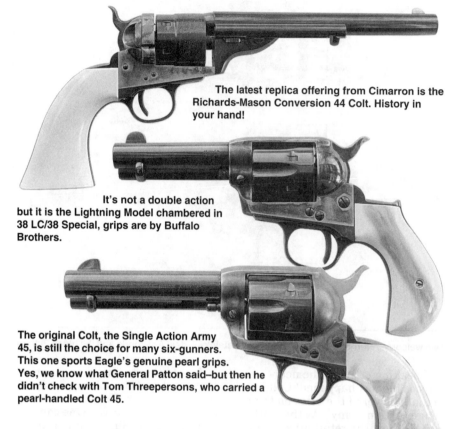

The latest replica offering from Cimarron is the Richards-Mason Conversion 44 Colt. History in your hand!

It's not a double action but it is the Lightning Model chambered in 38 LC/38 Special, grips are by Buffalo Brothers.

The original Colt, the Single Action Army 45, is still the choice for many six-gunners. This one sports Eagle's genuine pearl grips. Yes, we know what General Patton said–but then he didn't check with Tom Threepersons, who carried a pearl-handled Colt 45.

Colt chamberings, but 41 Magnum as well. Colt's 'Cadillac' double-action revolver, the Python, has returned and is available in both stainless steel and the beautiful Royal Blue finish. General Keys also plans to return such longtime favorites as the Detective Special and the Official Police to the product line.

The most stunning announcement – and most welcome – from the General, is his hope to return the New Service to production. This was Colt's large-frame double action produced from the 1890s up to the start of World War II. If Colt can return the New Service, with no major modifications, and having the same look and feel of the magnificent New Service and New Service Target Models of the 1930s chambered in 44 Special, 45 Colt, and 45 ACP–and do so at an affordable price, they will certainly sell all they can produce.

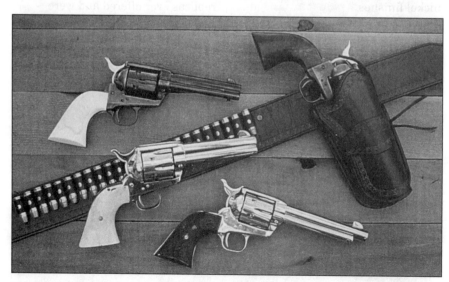

The Colt Single Action has dropped over $400 in suggested retail price and is now offered in blue/case-colored or nickel, 4 3/4- or 5 1/2-inch barrels, and in 45 Colt, 44-40, and 357 Magnum.

Two welcome returnees to the Colt stable, the stainless steel Anaconda and the blued Python.

unique in that they were not manufactured overseas, but actually produced — of all-American parts — in Los Angeles. Great Western disappeared in the 1960s, however. EMF continues to offer a complete line of 19th-century firearms of both fixed ammunition and percussion style.

EMF's top-of-the-line Single Action Army is the Premier Hartford Model with a special deluxe finish, blue and case-colored, Colt-style rubber grips, and chambered in 45 Colt. I have long used several Hartford Models from EMF for *CAS*, including a pair of consecutively-numbered 7 1/2-inch, nickel-plated 44-40s with Colt-style grips. The nickel plating really eases the chore of cleaning up after using blackpowder. One of the most accurate replica six-guns I have ever shot, whether with blackpowder or smokeless, is a 7 1/2-inch Hartford Model in 38-40.

Speaking of price, the near-impossible has happened! Colt has actually lowered the price on their Single Action Army!! At the 2001 SHOT Show the retail price on an SAA was a staggering $1968. One year later the price has been reduced - not by just a few dollars, but by $438 - resulting in a new retail price of $1530. That puts it not all that far above some of the high-dollar replicas being offered. Colt has also added the 357 Magnum as a standard chambering, along with 45 Colt and 44-40. All models are available in both 4 3/4-inch and 5 1/2-inch barrel lengths, and either blue/case-hardened or nickel finishes.

In addition to lowering the price of the Single Action Army, many custom shop services have also been lowered in price. One can now have their Single Action Army converted to 357 Magnum, 38-40, 44-40, 44 Special, or 45 Colt using new barrels and cylinders–at a very reasonable price. Colt is once again listening to shooters.

Early & Modern Firearms (EMF)

EMF holds the distinction of being the first to offer replica Colt Single Actions. 'Way back in the 1950s, EMF was a distributor of the Great Western line of frontier six-shooters. These were the very first replicas ever offered and were

Freedom Arms

For two decades now, Freedom Arms has been offering the finest single actions ever produced by any factory at any time. Beginning with the 454 Casull in 1983, Freedom has gone on to offer their first six-gun, albeit a five-shooter, in 44 Magnum, 357 Magnum, 41 Magnum, 50 Action Express, 22 LR and 22 Magnum, and - quite recently - in 475 Linebaugh. No matter what the caliber, every Freedom Arms revolver is meticulously crafted, with most chamberings available in either a fixed-sight or adjustable-sight version and barrel lengths of 4 3/4, 6, 7 1/2, and 10 inches. The adjustable-sight version also accepts a scope mount. For the first time this year, the Model 83 is offered in a 10-inch 475 Linebaugh. With the advent of the 480 Ruger cartridge, I had a 4 3/4-inch 475 Model 83 fitted with a 480 cylinder. Using Buffalo Bore's 410 Hard Cast load at 1100 fps from this short-barreled revolver, I took a 1200-pound bull bison in December of 2001. Penetration was complete on a broadside shot at 35 yards and, as far as I know, this was the largest game taken with the 480 Ruger up to that time.

In 1997 Freedom Arms downsized their revolver, introducing the Model 97, which is only slightly smaller than the Colt Single Action Army. This mid-framed six-gun was first offered in 357 Magnum, in either fixed or adjustable sight versions, and in barrel lengths of

With the advent of the new Ruger cartridge, this Freedom Arms 475 Linebaugh has been fitted with a second cylinder in 480 Ruger.

5 1/2 or 7 1/2 inches, with a 4 1/4-inch length now added. This was also the first six-shot Freedom Arms revolver and, as such, the first taken to heart by cowboy action shooters. Following the 357 Magnum Model 97 were five-shooters in 45 Colt and 41 Magnum–the latter two chamberings place the Model 97 in the "near-perfect packin' pistol" category. Although smaller than the Colt Single Action Army, the 45 Colt Model 97 will handle loads much heavier than should ever be used in the Colt.

The newest revolver from Freedom Arms is the long-awaited 22 rimfire Model 97. This will be the most expensive - and also the finest - 22 rimfire revolver ever offered to shooters. By the time you read this it will be available in barrel lengths of 4 1/4, 5 1/2, 7 1/2 and 10 inches, with an extra cylinder for 22 Magnum available through the custom shop. Imagine what a tack-driver the 10-inch Model 97 should be!

Magnum Research

Long known for the superbly accurate Desert Eagle semi-auto pistol, Magnum Research also offers hunters a traditionally-styled single-action revolver, the BFR. Previously offered in standard cylinder length versions in 22 Hornet and 454 Casull; and long-frame, long-cylinder five-shooters in 45-70, 444 Marlin, 450 Marlin - and a special 45 Colt that also accepts .410 shotgun shells. The BFR line now includes two of the newest and most powerful six-gun chamberings: 480 Ruger and the 475 Linebaugh.

The BFR is constructed of 17.4 PH stainless-steel with a cut-rifled 416-R stainless-steel barrel; is offered in 6 1/2- and 7 1/2-inch barrel lengths, 10-inch in 22 Hornet, 444 and 450 Marlin, and 45-70; and features a free-wheeling cylinder that rotates forwards or backwards as desired when the loading gate is open. Sights are a fully adjustable rear mated with an orange front, and the revolver is also designed to accept a Leupold scope mount base. Grips are rubber wraparound style. With a suggested retail price of $999, this is the least expensive way to get into a single-action six-gun chambered in 454 or 475, and the only six-gun I know of currently chambered in the lever-gun cartridges: 444 Marlin, 450 Marlin, and 45-70.

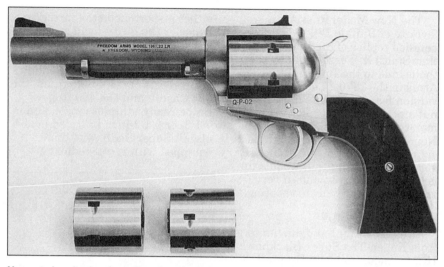

Newest chambering from Freedom Arms is the Model 97 in 22 LR and 22 Magnum.

M.O.A.

For two decades, Richard Mertz of M.O.A. has been offering superbly accurate single-shot pistols of the falling-block style, using a one-piece receiver fitted with a Douglas barrel. Although equipped with precisely adjustable sights, most hunters will opt for the use of scopes and the receivers are drilled and tapped to accept M.O.A. bases.

The M.O.A. Maximum is strong enough to handle about any cartridge that one might wish to hold onto—and some I wouldn't care to shoot, such as the 375 H&H! Any M.O.A. chambered for what is normally a bolt-action rifle cartridge should be fitted with a muzzle brake. Barrels are interchangeable on the M.O.A. action and are free-floating, with no pressure from the forearm. Safety is paramount with the M.O.A. and it can only be loaded or unloaded with the transfer bar button in the "SAFE" position.

Navy Arms

Val Forgett of Navy Arms, who has been providing shooters with quality replicas for nearly a half-century, truly deserves the title "Father of the Modern Replica Firearms Industry." I purchased my first Navy Arms revolver, an 1858 Remington, sometime around 1960. It wasn't the last. Not only can we thank Navy Arms for Colt and Remington centerfire and cap-and-ball replicas, they were the first to bring us a copy of the Smith & Wesson single-action six-gun. First came the Schofield, now offered in a 7-inch Cavalry Model, a 5-inch Wells Fargo Model, and a 3 1/2-inch Hideout Model, all in 45 Colt and 44-40; and now we have the New Model Russian chambered in 44 Russian.

Magnum Research's BFR is offered for rifle cartridges, such as the 444 Marlin and 45-70.

The New Model Russian, a favorite of Buffalo Bill, is a finely-detailed replica of the same six-gun that Smith & Wesson sold by the thousands to the Imperial Russian Army in the 1870s. The Navy Arms version features a blue finish, walnut stocks, and case-colored hammer, trigger, and locking latch. The New Model Russian also features a spur on the rear portion of the trigger guard. Placing your middle finger on this spur provides a very steady hold for accurate shooting.

Ruger

Great news for handgun hunters from Ruger. The Super Blackhawk Hunter model is back! Dropped in 1992 due to the barrel loosening (*rarely*) when a scope was mounted, that problem has been solved and hunters once again reap the benefits. The 7 1/2-inch stainless steel Hunter model differs from the standard Super Blackhawk in having a rounded trigger guard, a heavyweight full-ribbed barrel, scallops on the barrel that accept provided Ruger scope rings, an interchangeable front sight system, and an ejector rod and housing that is approximately 3/4 inch longer for more positive ejection of fired cases. A scope can be mounted without removing the iron sights, making it possible to switch back and forth between scope and iron sights with a tool no more sophisticated than a 50-cent piece to loosen the Ruger scope rings. This is one of the best-designed six-guns ever offered for handgun hunters, and its return is heartily welcomed.

Ruger captured a major portion of the cowboy action market when they introduced the Vaquero 10 years ago. First offered in a 45 Colt blued/case-colored version, it was soon joined by a stainless steel counterpart, as well as those chambered in 44-40, 44 Magnum, and 357 Magnum. Then came the Bisley Vaquero, the same basic six-gun with the Bisley Model grip frame, hammer, and trigger. All versions and calibers have been extremely popular with both CAS participants and outdoorsmen. Last year, Ruger introduced the 45 Colt Vaquero in a "Sheriff's Model" version with 3 3/4-inch barrel and a bird's-head grip frame. This popular offering has now been joined by a smaller version in 32 H&R Magnum. This variation of the Single-Six has fixed sights, blue/case-color or stainless steel finish, and

either a shortened standard grip frame or the bird's-head style. An excellent choice for shooters with small hands.

Ruger's big-bore Super Redhawk trio consists of the 44 Magnum, the 454 Casull, and the 480 Ruger. Scope-ready, stainless steel, and in 7 1/2- or 9 1/2-inch barreled models, all Super Redhawks come equipped with recoil-reducing

cushioned rubber grips. Very popular with hunters, the 454 Super Redhawk sold 15,000 units its first year of production, which has now been equaled by the first year of the 480 Ruger Super Redhawk.

One of most popular Ruger six-guns has been the 22 Bearcat. First made from 1958-1973, it was my son's first handgun, purchased for him on his 10th birthday in

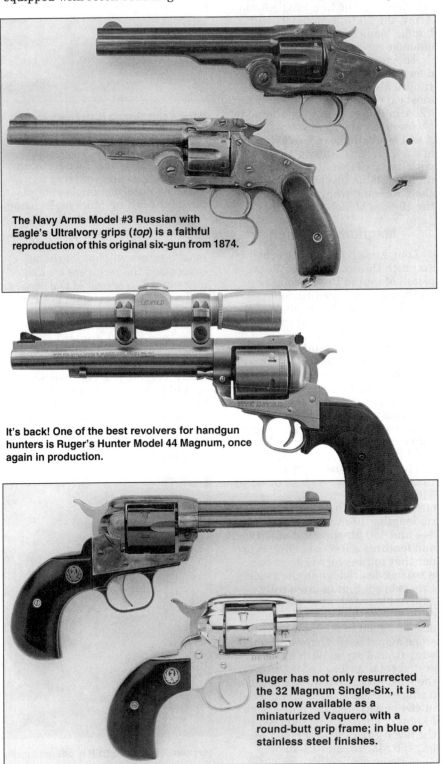

The Navy Arms Model #3 Russian with Eagle's Ultralvory grips (*top*) is a faithful reproduction of this original six-gun from 1874.

It's back! One of the best revolvers for handgun hunters is Ruger's Hunter Model 44 Magnum, once again in production.

Ruger has not only resurrected the 32 Magnum Single-Six, it is also now available as a miniaturized Vaquero with a round-butt grip frame; in blue or stainless steel finishes.

1973. Twenty years later, the Bearcat was reintroduced - only to be dropped again - and then brought back in 1996. Finally, the Bearcat is in production and this year the standard blued model has been joined by the stainless steel version. All new Bearcats feature Ruger's transfer bar system. All the stainless steel version needs to make it the perfect 'kit gun' is adjustable sights.

Smith & Wesson

It looks like a great year! Not only is Colt getting back on track, Smith & Wesson is already there with new ownership and new management. For the first time in several decades Smith & Wesson is once again American-owned. Bob Scott, a former vice-president of S&W, and president of Saf-T-Hammer, is the leader of the group that purchased Smith and is also the new president. Everyone I have talked to at Smith & Wesson is totally upbeat and ready to go forward.

New products abound from Smith & Wesson this year. The old classics–such as the original Model 27, 19, and 29–may be gone; however, a new generation of lightweight revolvers is here. Who would have thought we would ever see an 11 oz. 357 Magnum? It's here–the AirLite Sc series of "J-frames" with major components manufactured of Scandium. These are offered in the 340 Centennial hammerless-style, and the Model 360 with a standard hammer. The 340 Sc is the first five-shot revolver that can be carried in complete comfort in a jeans pocket. For those that prefer a slightly larger - but still lightweight 357 Magnum - there is the 386 MountainLite, a 3 1/8-inch seven-shooter that weighs 18.5 oz. The MountainLite comes equipped with a HiViz fiber-optic front sight, found on many new models and which can be retrofitted by the factory to older models.

Other new revolvers from Smith & Wesson this year include the 6 1/2-inch Model 629 44 Magnum with the HiViz front sight, which Smith & Wesson assured me will stand up to the recoil of the 44 Magnum; and the very popular Model 625 45 ACP is not only available as a standard catalog item with a 4-inch barrel, but is also available through the Performance Center custom-made with a shortened cylinder custom-made to fit the length of the 45 ACP and 45 Auto Rim. Custom gunsmiths built

Introduced in 2000 as the Model 2000 Schofield, the #3 Schofield is also now a regular offering through the S&W Performance Center.

The new twist on the Mountain Gun is the Mountain Lite, an easy-packin' six-gun chambered in 44 Special and 357 Magnum.

It may look strange at first - but it grows on you! Smith & Wesson's "357 MAGNUM-8 TIMES" shoots great and is now a regular offering through the Performance Center.

The future is now at Smith & Wesson with a Scandium 357 Magnum that weighs less than 12 oz. It is controllable, especially with 125-grain JHPs–and the Hogue grips definitely help.

revolvers with shortened cylinders and the barrel extending further back through the frame back in the 1950s. However, this is the first factory offering I've heard of. To complement the short-cylinder 45, the Performance Center also offers the same basic six-gun with a 5 1/2-inch barrel and the cylinder chambering eight 38 Super rounds in a full-moon clip. All Smith & Wesson revolvers now feature an internal lock activated by inserting a special key in a very small opening above the cylinder latch release.

Two S&W revolvers formerly offered exclusively by select dis-

tributors are now standard Performance Center offerings. One is the stainless steel, eight-shot Model 627 with the distinctive, slab-sided 5-inch barrel marked ".357 MAG-8 TIMES." Smith & Wesson had to do some serious modification of the frame and barrel to modify a basic Model 27 to accept an eight-shot cylinder. However, it was accomplished and is one of the better ideas carried out in 357 Magnum. In 2000, Smith & Wesson offered the Model 2000 Schofield on a limited basis. This recreation of the original 1875 Schofield chambered in 45 S&W is now a standard item

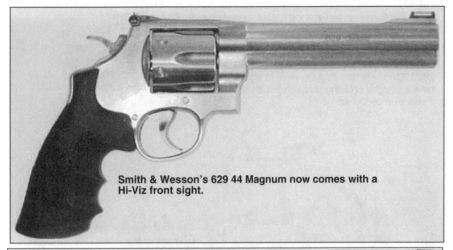

Smith & Wesson's 629 44 Magnum now comes with a Hi-Viz front sight.

An exceptionally attractive little six-gun is the Military & Police Heritage Special version, the McGivern Model.

as the 7-inch-barreled Model 3 Schofield. Thank you, Smith & Wesson - on both counts.

The Schofield started the manufacturing of nostalgic six-guns at Smith & Wesson and it has now been joined by the Heritage Series. The first in this series last year was the HEG, a revolver reminiscent of the old First Model Hand Ejector or, as better known by most shooters, the Triple-Lock. With its slim tapered 6-inch barrel, adjustable sights with a flat black post front sight with a McGivern gold bead and traditional blue finish, the HEG 45 Colt transported us, spiritually speaking in a six-gun sense, back to simpler days.

Now that original Heritage Series offering has been joined by the same basic revolver offered in either 44 Special with a case-colored frame, and a nickel-plated 44 Magnum, both with slim tapered barrels. Rounding out the N-frame Heritage Series is a new rendition of the 1917 Army Model as used in World War I. Beautiful six-guns all, but I have saved the best for last. The latest member of the Heritage Series is the McGivern Model 15.

Ed McGivern's favorite revolver for speed shooting was the Smith & Wesson Military & Police 38 Special. As he set new shooting records, a miniature metal plaque was appropriately inscribed and placed on the sideplate of the M&P 38 Special. This is a faithful recreation of a 1930s Military & Police, complete with a facsimile of the sideplate plaque commemorating the record that was set and, as well, a post front sight with the McGivern gold bead. The only departure of any consequence from the original revolver is the fact that (as on all Heritage Series revolvers) the grip frames are round instead of square. Normally, I reserve round butts for short-barreled revolvers; however, they do feel good on these 5-inch M&Ps. Three finishes are available, Bright Blue, Nickel, or Blue with a case-colored frame. These are beautiful revolvers!

Taurus

Taurus is one company that never lets any grass grow under its feet. While other companies have been touting the 17 Hornady Rimfire Magnum as a rifle cartridge,

Taurus is the first company to offer this new cartridge in a handgun. The latest Tracker from Taurus is an eight-shot 17 HRM. Other new Trackers include a 6-inch 45 Colt and a 4-inch 45 ACP–both holding five rounds. The little Trackers, with their "Ribber" grips, are easy packin' and powerful.

Sometimes six-guns are very serious and other times they simply just need to be fun. The new silhouette guns from Taurus certainly fall into the 'fun' category. These revolvers, with 12-inch barrels, were first offered in 22 LR and 22 Magnum and now have been joined by a 357 Magnum–as well as two "Stingers," the 22 Hornet and 218 Bee.

On a more serious side, at least for big game hunters, is the Taurus Raging Bull. First offered as a six-shot 44 Magnum, it was soon joined by a 5-shot 454 Casull, and then last year by a Raging Bull chambered in 480 Ruger. The Raging Bulls are offered with heavy full-underlug and ported barrels and specially-cushioned rubber finger-grooved grips, all of which help dampen felt recoil. Barrel lengths available are 5 inch, 6 1/2 inch, and 8 3/8 inch - in both blue and stainless finishes.

Fans of the 41 Magnum will be happy to know the Raging Bull is now offered in 41. This cartridge, once pronounced dead by so many "experts," has in recent years been chambered by Freedom Arms and now by both Colt and Taurus. Joining the big-bore Raging Bulls is the Raging Thirty, an eight-shot 30 Carbine. And finally, from Taurus we have the new Protector, in both 38 Special and 357 Magnum. The hammer on the Protector is shrouded on both sides but still allows for manual cocking, and the rear sight - while adjustable - has also been dehorned. This 2-inch pocket pistol is a five-shooter with finger-groove rubber grips and is offered in stainless steel, blue steel, or titanium. All Taurus revolvers feature the built-in security system that allows the action to be locked.

Thompson/Center

Thirty-five years ago Thompson/Center introduced the single-shot Contender to handgunners. First chambered in 22 Long Rifle and 38 Special, it did not take long for Thompson/Center to realize the Contender was capable of handling the pressures normally associated with lever-guns and Magnum revolvers and we soon had

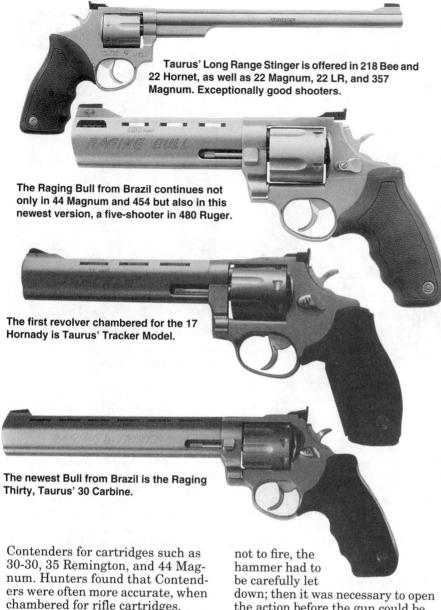

Taurus' Long Range Stinger is offered in 218 Bee and 22 Hornet, as well as 22 Magnum, 22 LR, and 357 Magnum. Exceptionally good shooters.

The Raging Bull from Brazil continues not only in 44 Magnum and 454 but also in this newest version, a five-shooter in 480 Ruger.

The first revolver chambered for the 17 Hornady is Taurus' Tracker Model.

The newest Bull from Brazil is the Raging Thirty, Taurus' 30 Carbine.

Contenders for cartridges such as 30-30, 35 Remington, and 44 Magnum. Hunters found that Contenders were often more accurate, when chambered for rifle cartridges, than many rifles.

The Contender had been offered in dozens of factory chamberings over the years, and J. D. Jones of SSK Industries led the way in wildcatting the Contender with - literally - hundreds of both standard and wildcat offerings. If it can be done safely, Jones has probably offered it. Two of the best (*in my hunting experience*) from SSK have been the 6.5 JDJ and the 375 JDJ. Together, they cover all the bases.

As good as the Contender is, it has two major shortcomings. It is quite often difficult to break open - sometimes requiring two hands to release the action, or worse, requiring one to strike the operating lever sharply karate-style with the edge of the hand. The other "problem" has been that once the Contender was cocked to fire, and one decided

not to fire, the hammer had to be carefully let down; then it was necessary to open the action before the gun could be cocked and ready to fire again.

Thompson/Center addressed both of these problems with the introduction of the Encore single-shot pistol a few years back. In addition to an easy-opening feature and also a hammer safety—which allowed the hammer to be re-cocked without opening the action—the Encore is also a larger, stronger pistol with the ability to handle cartridges normally chambered in bolt-action rifles. Wouldn't it be wonderful if the features of the Encore could be incorporated into the smaller Contender?

The answer is 'yes,' and the new Contender is the G2. Not only has Thompson/Center succeeded in upgrading the original Contender with the easy-opening and hammer safety features of the Encore, they have also ensured the G2 will

accept any T/C barrels. It will also take the same forearm as the original Contender. The grips, however, are not interchangeable and shooters will find the new grip has a slightly different angle - and is more comfortable. A new handgun-hunting chapter begins with the Thompson/Center G2.

Dan Wesson Firearms

In 1968, Dan Wesson brought his better ideas to shooters. Three of his ideas were radical to say the least. Instead of a grip frame, Dan Wesson revolvers featured a stud that accepted a one-piece wooden grip bolted on at the bottom, allowing for great latitude in grip shape and size. Second, all Dan Wesson six-guns came with interchangeable front sights. Both of these features have been picked up by other manufacturers. The most radical of his ideas was the interchangeable barrel system. Instead of a solid barrel, Wesson used a slim barrel within a shroud. A special tool removed a nut at the end of the barrel, which then allowed the shroud to be removed, and the barrel could then be easily unthreaded by hand. What was designed to be a convenient way to change barrel lengths also resulted in superb accuracy.

Dan Wesson revolvers soon became the favorite of six-gun silhouetters and Dan Wesson rode that crest for several years. When that market went down, Dan Wesson experienced financial difficulties and soon closed it's doors. That's the bad news. The good news is that Dan Wesson was purchased by Bob Serva in 1996, moved to New York and equipped with all-new machinery - resulting in the best Dan Wessons ever manufactured. In the past, Dan Wessons were often plagued with rough chambers and a barrel/cylinder gap that was often uneven. All that has changed. The new Dan Wessons, thanks to the all-new machinery, come from the factory with extremely smooth cylinder chambers and perfectly parallel barrel/cylinder spacing.

In addition to all the standard models, Dan Wesson has reintroduced the Alaskan Guide series, a compensated 445 SuperMag with a 4-inch barrel; the rarely-seen 414 SuperMag (*before 1996*) is now a standard model; new chamberings such as the 460 Rowland and 45 WinMag have been introduced; and a totally new cartridge - the 360

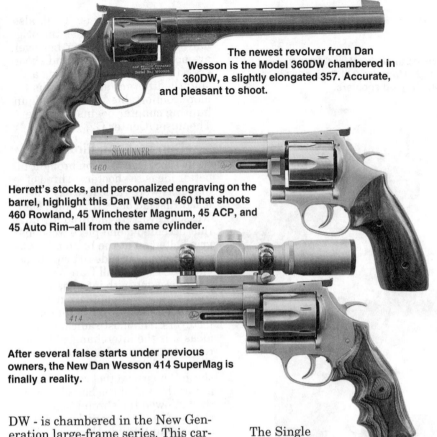

The newest revolver from Dan Wesson is the Model 360DW chambered in 360DW, a slightly elongated 357. Accurate, and pleasant to shoot.

Herrett's stocks, and personalized engraving on the barrel, highlight this Dan Wesson 460 that shoots 460 Rowland, 45 Winchester Magnum, 45 ACP, and 45 Auto Rim–all from the same cylinder.

After several false starts under previous owners, the New Dan Wesson 414 SuperMag is finally a reality.

Raj Singh of Eagle Grips with the new Heritage (S&W "Coke bottle") Grips.

DW - is chambered in the New Generation large-frame series. This cartridge is longer than the 357 Magnum, which is offered on the New Generation small frame, and shorter than the 357 SuperMag, which is found in the New Generation SuperMag frame series.

United States Fire Arms Mfg. Co. (USFA)

From 1873 until 1941, the 1st Generation Colt Single Actions were manufactured in the original Colt factory, under the trademark rampant colt dome. Today, in that same building, USFA is turning out single actions produced and finished as carefully as those original Colts. USFA informs us that all their single actions feature American-made barrels and cylinders and that they provide many of the services and custom touches offered on the originals.

The Contender has been upgraded to the G2. Barrels and forearms interchange with the original, grips do not.

The Single Action Army (or Bisley Model), for example, comes in the three standard barrel lengths of 4 3/4, 5 1/2, and 7 1/2 inches, with other lengths available as a custom feature. Chamberings are 45 Colt, 44 WCF, 38 WCF, 32 WCF, 41 LC, 38 Special, and 44 Special. The metal finish is 'Old Army Bone Case' on frame and hammer, the balance finished in 'Dome Blue,' or full-nickel plating. Standard stocks are one-piece walnut, with hard rubber, pearl, ivory, or stag optional. A 1890s Flat-Top Target revolver is also available, as is a 16-inch barreled Buntline Special, complete with flip-up rear sight and skeleton shoulder stock.

The newest offerings from USFA include the Rodeo, a basic no-frills, satin-finish 45 Colt single action designed for cowboy shooters, and the Omni-Potent, a Bisley-style six-gun with a grip frame reminiscent of the Colt Double Action Model of 1878, complete with a lanyard ring. USFA also offers a complete line of custom features including all levels of engraving, custom stocks, special serial numbers–and even replacement cylinders and barrels for original 1st Generation Colts in the above-mentioned calibers.

Eagle Grips

Eagle has furnished shooters with custom grips of ivory, stag, pearl, and exotic woods for several decades. During that time we have seen grips on factory double-action revolvers go from highly useable wood… to poorly-shaped wood… to rubber. The latter is functional but not aesthetically pleasing. Many of us search the tables at gun shows to find the old Smith & Wesson 'coke-bottle' grips with the diamond in the center for both N- and K-frames. Now Eagle has stepped into the breach and is offering their Heritage Grips, a faithful reproduction of the old Smith grips — right down to the center diamond. Grips are rosewood and feel and look great.

Shooters have had a hard time getting staghorn grips because of the exportation ban, so Eagle has filled a need by offering stag grips of elkhorn. They polish out nicely, with good color. Also from Eagle are the UltraIvory grips that are about one-third the cost of the real thing–and several light-years ahead of the plastics and polymers offered as "ivory." Instead of being molded as one set of grips, UltraIvory comes in large pieces that are first 'slabbed' and then cut into grip shapes. They have good grain and color in them and most folks would have hard time telling them from the real thing.

It looks like a great year for six-gunners! ●

Update:
Handgun Ammunition, Ballistics & Components

by Holt Bodinson

BETTER QUALITY PREMIUM bullets continue to appear across all pistol lines. The quality and selection of sporting ammunition has never been better. Here are the latest developments.

Alliant Powder

Possibly the biggest news of the year was Alliant Technologies' acquisition of Federal Cartridge,

Barnes new reloading manual includes new data for the company's XLC and VLC bullets.

CCI/Speer, Estate Cartridge, RCBS, Weaver, Simmons, Redfield, Ram-Line and Outers from Blount. As the largest supplier of ammunition in the world, Alliant is uniquely positioned to bring its vast resources and experience to bear on the civilian ammunition market. This is a company to watch.

Don't miss Alliant Powder's latest, free "Reloader's Guide" that includes updated data for the short magnums, the full spectrum of shotshells, and additional sections on cowboy action and silhouette loads.

www.alliantpowder.com

Barnes

Barnes new "Reloading Manual #3" is what a reloading manual should be. Pictures of suitable bullets accompany each cartridge together with clear graphic displays of comparative bullet trajectories and energy levels, recommended powder data, and application preferences. In addition, each caliber chapter, such as the 6mms, is followed by a complete ballistics section for all available Barnes bullets. There's even a thread-pitch table for every brand of seating die that equates degrees of seating stem rotation with thousandths of an inch. Neat!

www.barnesbullets.com

Cast Performance Bullet Company

Looking for an LBT bullet design, an odd caliber bullet, a lead bullet sized to different diameters, or a 500-grain Springfield Trap-

door bullet cast from a 20:1 alloy? Cast Performance probably can supply it. These are quality hand-cast products. In fact, they're so good, Cast Performance bullets are factory-loaded by Federal in its Cast Core Premium Handgun Hunting Cartridge line.

www.castperformance.com

CCI-Speer

Now part of the Alliant Ammunition Group, CCI-Speer has developed some intriguing products for the new year. CCI's "Velocitor" is the world's fastest 40-grain 22 LR round. How fast? 1435 fps fast, plus the HP bullet is based on CCI's Gold Dot technology that ensures exacting controlled expansion. With the increasing popularity of the 454 Casull, 50 Action Express, 475 Linebaugh and 480 Ruger in handgun hunting circles, Speer is offering a 300-grain HP .45; 300-grain HP .50; and a 325-grain SP .475 in its Gold Dot component line-up this year. Speer's Gold Dot handgun ammunition line has been expanded with a 124-grain HP 9mm+P at 1220 fps and a 325-grain SP 480 Ruger at 1350 fps. Finally, Speer's truly non-leading, dry-film lubricant has been added to all of their extensive lead bullet designs.

www.cci-ammunition.com & www.speer-bullets.com

Federal

Another member of Alliant's Ammunition Group. In their metallic lines, Federal has added a 125-grain FMJ 357 SIG loading at 1350

fps and a 200-grain expanding FMJ 45 Auto load clocking 1035 fps.
www.federalcartridge.com

Garrett Cartridge

Known for their superior penetrating cast bullet line, Garrett is adding a new 44 Magnum load featuring a 255-grain LBT bullet with a wide flat nose at 1000 fps and a SAAMI pressure-compliant 45-70 loading pushing a 420-grain Hammerhead bullet at 1650 fps, making it ideal for the T/C Contender and the BFR revolver.
www.garrettcartridge.com

Graf & Sons

This popular handloader's heaven is importing a new line of shotgun/pistol powders manufactured in Hungary by Nitrokemia under the trade name "REX." Presently the REX line is available in four burn rates corresponding roughly to Bullseye through Universal.
www.grfs.com

Hodgdon

What powder powers the new 17 HRM? It's Hodgdon's Lil' Gun. If you're into muzzleloading, you'll enjoy Hodgdon's new TRIPLE SEVEN powder that contains no sulfur, is odorless, cleans up completely with one to three water-soaked patches and, volume-for-volume, delivers velocities that exceed all other blackpowder substitutes.
www.hodgdon.com

Hornady

Hornady's novel 17 HRM (Hornady Rimfire Magnum) simply stole the show this year. From its roots in the component business, the company has evolved into a major, innovative ammunition manufacturer. Other new handloading components include a .475 gas check.
www.hornady.com

Huntington

Looking for a unique or hard-to-find reloading component? Huntington is the place to find it. There's also a fresh supply of 8mm Nambu cases on hand. I'm just touching the tip of the iceberg. See them at www.huntingtons.com.

Lyman

Lyman's series of handloading manuals have always been among the most original and invaluable references in the field. Not tied to any particular brand of powder or projectile, Lyman manuals have a breadth of data that is refreshingly unique. This year's release of the *Black Powder Handbook & Loading Manual*, 2nd Edition carries on the tradition, covering not only every possible aspect of muzzleloading but blackpowder cartridges as well. The loading and ballistics data section contains thousands of combinations for every caliber, barrel length

Lyman's *Black Powder Handbook and Loading Manual* is the most comprehensive treatment of the subject ever published.

Responding to the needs of IDPA and Limited competitors, Oregon Trail designed a 185-grain 40-caliber bullet that works flawlessly in the Model 1911.

Hodgdon's TRIPLE SEVEN muzzleloading propellant contains no sulfur, produces high velocities and cleans up quickly with water.

Hornady's 17 Rimfire magnum is quieter and flatter shooting than the 22 Magnum and should prove ideal for varmint hunting in suburbia or densely-populated farming areas.

Winchester is adding 38 Special, 44 Special, 44-40 and 45 Colt, low velocity, lead cowboy action loads to its competitively priced USA line.

"Trueshot" is Oregon Trails' latest line of high quality gas-checked and plain-based handgun and rifle bullets.

and barrel twist typically available. The powders tested include GOEX, Elephant and Pyrodex. Don't miss this manual. It's that good.
www.lymanproducts.com

Oregon Trail/Trueshot

Offering a wide selection of pistol and rifle bullets cast from a great alloy, sized and lubricated correctly, Oregon Trail has earned an enviable reputation in the shooting community. Their former line of "Laser-Cast" gas-checked and plain-based rifle and pistol bullets is now called "Trueshot." It includes such specialized designs as gas-checked 310-grain 44-caliber and 360-grain 45-caliber revolver bullets as well as exceptionally accurate 30- and 32-caliber rifle bullets. Responding to a request from dedicated IDPA and Limited shooters for a 40-caliber bullet that would feed reliably in 1911 autoloaders and meet major power factors with safe pressure margins, Trueshot has developed the solution—the 40-1911 185-grain RN SWC. The new bullet feeds flawlessly in 10mm and 40 S&W guns without having to resort to freeboring. See them at www.trueshotbullets.com.

Schroeder Bullets

Having trouble locating old or odd-size bullets and brass? Then send for Schroeder's new catalog. In it is everything from .287-inch diameter 280 Ross bullets to 6mm Lee Navy brass.
Tel: (619) 423-8124.

Sierra

Periodically, Sierra publishes a very informative and technical newsletter called the "X-Ring" that any handloader will find useful. The current issue, as well as back issues, is available at the company's web site:
www.sierrabullets.com

Taurus

One of the surprise announcements of the year was that Taurus was getting into the handgun ammunition business. Planned for this year are the 9mm, 40 S&W, 45 ACP, 357 Mag., 41 Mag., 44 Mag., 454 Casull, and 480 Ruger. The new brand will appear under the Taurus name and be loaded with a solid copper alloy HP bullet, by Barnes, called the "HEX."
www.taurususa.com

Widener's

This is a great catalog supply house for components and ammunition—some of which are unique. They always stock a wide selection of surplus military bullets, powder, and loaded ammunition with extensive listings of Israel Military Industries products. Excellent prices—good service.
www.wideners.com

Winchester Ammunition

For the cowboy action shooters, Winchester is adding low velocity, lead bullet loads for the 38 Special, 44 Special, 44-40, and 45 Colt to its competitively priced USA line. There are lots of new components this year, including 9x23mm and 454 Casull brass.
www.winchester.com

CENTERFIRE HANDGUN CARTRIDGES — BALLISTICS & PRICES

Notes: Blanks are available in 32 S&W, 38 S&W and 38 Special. "V" after barrel length indicates test barrel was vented to produce ballistics similar to a revolver with a normal barrel-to-cylinder gap. Ammo prices are per 50 rounds except when marked with an ** which signifies a 20 round box; *** signifies a 25-round box. Not all loads are available from all ammo manufacturers. Listed loads are those made by Remington, Winchester, Federal, and others. DISC. is a discontinued load. Prices are rounded to nearest whole dollar and will vary with brand and retail outlet. † = new bullet weight this year; "c" indicates a change in data.

Cartridge	Bullet Wgt. Grs.	VELOCITY (fps)			ENERGY (ft. lbs.)			Mid-Range Traj. (in.)		Bbl. Lgth. (in).	Est. Price/ box
		Muzzle	50 yds.	100 yds.	Muzzle	50 yds.	100 yds.	50 yds.	100 yds.		
221 Rem. Fireball	50	2650	2380	2130	780	630	505	0.2	0.8	10.5"	$15
25 Automatic	35	900	813	742	63	51	43	NA	NA	2"	$18
25 Automatic	45	815	730	655	65	55	40	1.8	7.7	2"	$21
25 Automatic	50	760	705	660	65	55	50	2.0	8.7	2"	$17
7.5mm Swiss	107	1010	NA	NA	240	NA	NA	NA	NA	NA	NEW
7.62mmTokarev	87	1390	NA	NA	365	NA	NA	0.6	NA	4.5"	NA
7.62 Nagant	97	1080	NA	NA	350	NA	NA	NA	NA	NA	NEW
7.63 Mauser	88	1440	NA	NA	405	NA	NA	NA	NA	NA	NEW
30 Luger	93†	1220	1110	1040	305	255	225	0.9	3.5	4.5"	$34
30 Carbine	110	1790	1600	1430	785	625	500	0.4	1.7	10"	$28
30-357 AeT	123	1992	NA	NA	1084	NA	NA	NA	NA	10"	NA
32 S&W	88	680	645	610	90	80	75	2.5	10.5	3"	$17
32 S&W Long	98	705	670	635	115	100	90	2.3	10.5	4"	$17
32 Short Colt	80	745	665	590	100	80	60	2.2	9.9	4"	$19
32 H&R Magnum	85	1100	1020	930	230	195	165	1.0	4.3	4.5"	$21
32 H&R Magnum	95	1030	940	900	225	190	170	1.1	4.7	4.5"	$19
32 Automatic	60	970	895	835	125	105	95	1.3	5.4	4"	$22
32 Automatic	60	1000	917	849	133	112	96			4"	NA
32 Automatic	65	950	890	830	130	115	100	1.3	5.6	NA	NA
32 Automatic	71	905	855	810	130	115	95	1.4	5.8	4"	$19
8mm Lebel Pistol	111	850	NA	NA	180	NA	NA	NA	NA	NA	NEW
8mm Steyr	112	1080	NA	NA	290	NA	NA	NA	NA	NA	NEW
8mm Gasser	126	850	NA	NA	200	NA	NA	NA	NA	NA	NEW
380 Automatic	60	1130	960	NA	170	120	NA	1.0	NA	NA	NA
380 Automatic	85/88	990	920	870	190	165	145	1.2	5.1	4"	$20
380 Automatic	90	1000	890	800	200	160	130	1.2	5.5	3.75"	$10
380 Automatic	95/100	955	865	785	190	160	130	1.4	5.9	4"	$20
38 Super Auto +P	115	1300	1145	1040	430	335	275	0.7	3.3	5"	$26
38 Super Auto +P	125/130	1215	1100	1015	425	350	300	0.8	3.6	5"	$26
38 Super Auto +P	147	1100	1050	1000	395	355	325	0.9	4.0	5"	NA
9x18mm Makarov	95	1000	NA	NA	NA	NA	NA	NA	NA	NA	NEW
9x18mm Ultra	100	1050	NA	NA	240	NA	NA	NA	NA	NA	NEW
9x23mm Largo	124	1190	1055	966	390	306	257	0.7	3.7	4"	NA
9x23mm Win.	125	1450	1249	1103	583	433	338	0.6	2.8	NA	NA
9mm Steyr	115	1180	NA	NA	350	NA	NA	NA	NA	NA	NEW
9mm Luger	88	1500	1190	1010	440	275	200	0.6	3.1	4"	$24
9mm Luger	90	1360	1112	978	370	247	191	NA	NA	4"	$26
9mm Luger	95	1300	1140	1010	350	275	215	0.8	3.4	4"	NA
9mm Luger	100	1180	1080	NA	305	255	NA	0.9	NA	4"	NA
9mm Luger	115	1155	1045	970	340	280	240	0.9	3.9	4"	$21
9mm Luger	123/125	1110	1030	970	340	290	260	1.0	4.0	4"	$23
9mm Luger	140	935	890	850	270	245	225	1.3	5.5	4"	$23
9mm Luger	147	990	940	900	320	290	265	1.1	4.9	4"	$26
9mm Luger +P	90	1475	NA	NA	437	NA	NA	NA	NA	NA	NA
9mm Luger +P	115	1250	1113	1019	399	316	265	0.8	3.5	4"	$27
9mm Federal	115	1280	1130	1040	420	330	280	0.7	3.3	4"V	$24
9mm Luger Vector	115	1155	1047	971	341	280	241	NA	NA	4"	NA
9mm Luger +P	124	1180	1089	1021	384	327	287	0.8	3.8	4"	NA
38 S&W	146	685	650	620	150	135	125	2.4	10.0	4"	$19
38 Short Colt	125	730	685	645	150	130	115	2.2	9.4	6"	$19
39 Special	100	950	900	NA	200	180	NA	1.3	NA	4"V	NA
38 Special	110	945	895	850	220	195	175	1.3	5.4	4"V	$23

Notes: Blanks are available in 32 S&W, 38 S&W and 38 Special. "V" after barrel length indicates test barrel was vented to produce ballistics similar to a revolver with a normal barrel-to-cylinder gap. Ammo prices are per 50 rounds except when marked with an ** which signifies a 20 round box; *** signifies a 25-round box. Not all loads are available from all ammo manufacturers. Listed loads are those made by Remington, Winchester, Federal, and others. DISC. is a discontinued load. Prices are rounded to nearest whole dollar and will vary with brand and retail outlet. † = new bullet weight this year; "c" indicates a change in data.

Cartridge	Bullet Wgt. Grs.	VELOCITY (fps)			ENERGY (ft. lbs.)			Mid-Range Traj. (in.)		Bbl. Lgth. (in).	Est. Price/ box
		Muzzle	50 yds.	100 yds.	Muzzle	50 yds.	100 yds.	50 yds.	100 yds.		
38 Special	110	945	895	850	220	195	175	1.3	5.4	4"V	$23
38 Special	130	775	745	710	175	160	120	1.9	7.9	4"V	$22
38 Special Cowboy	140	800	767	735	199	183	168			7.5" V	NA
38 (Multi-Ball)	140	830	730	505	215	130	80	2.0	10.6	4"V	$10**
38 Special	148	710	635	565	165	130	105	2.4	10.6	4"V	$17
38 Special	158	755	725	690	200	185	170	2.0	8.3	4"V	$18
38 Special +P	95	1175	1045	960	290	230	195	0.9	3.9	4"V	$23
38 Special +P	110	995	925	870	240	210	185	1.2	5.1	4"V	$23
38 Special +P	125	975	929	885	264	238	218	1	5.2	4"	NA
38 Special +P	125	945	900	860	250	225	205	1.3	5.4	4"V	#23
38 Special +P	129	945	910	870	255	235	215	1.3	5.3	4"V	$11
38 Special +P	130	925	887	852	247	227	210	1.3	5.50	4"V	NA
38 Special +P	147/150(c)	884	NA	NA	264	NA	NA	NA	NA	4"V	$27
38 Special +P	158	890	855	825	280	255	240	1.4	6.0	4"V	$20
357 SIG	115	1520	NA	NA	593	NA	NA	NA	NA	NA	NA
357 SIG	124	1450	NA	NA	578	NA	NA	NA	NA	NA	NA
357 SIG	125	1350	1190	1080	510	395	325	0.7	3.1	4"	NA
357 SIG	150	1130	1030	970	420	355	310	0.9	4.0	NA	NA
356 TSW	115	1520	NA	NA	593	NA	NA	NA	NA	NA	NA
356 TSW	124	1450	NA	NA	578	NA	NA	NA	NA	NA	NA
356 TSW	135	1280	1120	1010	490	375	310	0.8	3.50	NA	NA
356 TSW	147	1220	1120	1040	485	410	355	0.8	3.5	5"	NA
357 Mag., Super Clean	105	1650									NA
357 Magnum	110	1295	1095	975	410	290	230	0.8	3.5	4"V	$25
357 (Med.Vel.)	125	1220	1075	985	415	315	270	0.8	3.7	4"V	$25
357 Magnum	125	1450	1240	1090	585	425	330	0.6	2.8	4"V	$25
357 (Multi-Ball)	140	1155	830	665	420	215	135	1.2	6.4	4"V	$11**
357 Magnum	140	1360	1195	1075	575	445	360	0.7	3.0	4"V	$25
357 Magnum	145	1290	1155	1060	535	430	360	0.8	3.5	4"V	$26
357 Magnum	150/158	1235	1105	1015	535	430	360	0.8	3.5	4"V	$25
357 Mag. Cowboy	158	800	761	725	225	203	185				NA
357 Magnum	165	1290	1189	1108	610	518	450	0.7	3.1	8-3/8"	NA
357 Magnum	180	1145	1055	985	525	445	390	0.9	3.9	4"V	$25
357 Magnum	180	1180	1088	1020	557	473	416	0.8	3.6	8"V	NA
357 Mag. CorBon F.A.	180	1650	1512	1386	1088	913	767	1.66	0.0		NA
357 Mag. CorBon	200	1200	1123	1061	640	560	500	3.19	0.0		NA
357 Rem. Maximum	158	1825	1590	1380	1170	885	670	0.4	1.7	10.5"	$14**
40 S&W	135	1140	1070	NA	390	345	NA	0.9	NA	4"	NA
40 S&W	155	1140	1026	958	447	362	309	0.9	4.1	4"	$14***
40 S&W	165	1150	NA	NA	485	NA	NA	NA	NA	4"	$18***
40 S&W	180	985	936	893	388	350	319	1.4	5.0	4"	$14***
40 S&W	180	1015	960	914	412	368	334	1.3	4.5	4"	NA
400 Cor-Bon	135	1450	NA	NA	630	NA	NA	NA	NA	5"	NA
10mm Automatic	155	1125	1046	986	436	377	335	0.9	3.9	5"	$26
10mm Automatic	170	1340	1165	1145	680	510	415	0.7	3.2	5"	$31
10mm Automatic	175	1290	1140	1035	650	505	420	0.7	3.3	5.5"	$11**
10mm Auto. (FBI)	180	950	905	865	361	327	299	1.5	5.4	4"	$16**
10mm Automatic	180	1030	970	920	425	375	340	1.1	4.7	5"	$16**
10mm Auto H.V.	180†	1240	1124	1037	618	504	430	0.8	3.4	5"	$27
10mm Automatic	200	1160	1070	1010	495	510	430	0.9	3.8	5"	$14**
10.4mm Italian	177	950	NA	NA	360	NA	NA	NA	NA	NA	NEW

(left margin tabs: 38 ont., 357, 40, mm)

Notes: Blanks are available in 32 S&W, 38 S&W and 38 Special. "V" after barrel length indicates test barrel was vented to produce ballistics similar to a revolver with a normal barrel-to-cylinder gap. Ammo prices are per 50 rounds except when marked with an ** which signifies a 20 round box; *** signifies a 25-round box. Not all loads are available from all ammo manufacturers. Listed loads are those made by Remington, Winchester, Federal, and others. DISC. is a discontinued load. Prices are rounded to nearest whole dollar and will vary with brand and retail outlet. † = new bullet weight this year; "c" indicates a change in data.

Cartridge	Bullet Wgt. Grs.	VELOCITY (fps)			ENERGY (ft. lbs.)			Mid-Range Traj. (in.)		Bbl. Lgth. (in).	Est. Price/ box
		Muzzle	50 yds.	100 yds.	Muzzle	50 yds.	100 yds.	50 yds.	100 yds.		
41 Action Exp.	180	1000	947	903	400	359	326	0.5	4.2	5"	$13**
41 Rem. Magnum	170	1420	1165	1015	760	515	390	0.7	3.2	4"V	$33
41 Rem. Magnum	175	1250	1120	1030	605	490	410	0.8	3.4	4"V	$14**
41 (Med. Vel.)	210	965	900	840	435	375	330	1.3	5.4	4"V	$30
41 Rem. Magnum	210	1300	1160	1060	790	630	535	0.7	3.2	4"V	$33
44 S&W Russian	247	780	NA	NA	335	NA	NA	NA	NA	NA	NA
44 S&W Special	180	980	NA	NA	383	NA	NA	NA	NA	6.5"	NA
44 S&W Special	180	1000	935	882	400	350	311	NA	NA	7.5"V	NA
44 S&W Special	200†	875	825	780	340	302	270	1.2	6.0	6"	$13**
44 S&W Special	200	1035	940	865	475	390	335	1.1	4.9	6.5"	$13**
44 S&W Special	240/246	755	725	695	310	285	265	2.0	8.3	6.5"	$26
44-40 Win. Cowboy	225	750	723	695	281	261	242				NA
44 Rem. Magnum	180	1610	1365	1175	1035	745	550	0.5	2.3	4"V	$18**
44 Rem. Magnum	200	1400	1192	1053	870	630	492	0.6	NA	6.5"	$20
44 Rem. Magnum	210	1495	1310	1165	1040	805	635	0.6	2.5	6.5"	$18**
44 (Med. Vel.)	240	1000	945	900	535	475	435	1.1	4.8	6.5"	$17
44 R.M. (Jacketed)	240	1180	1080	1010	740	625	545	0.9	3.7	4"V	$18**
44 R.M. (Lead)	240	1350	1185	1070	970	750	610	0.7	3.1	4"V	$29
44 Rem. Magnum	250	1180	1100	1040	775	670	600	0.8	3.6	6.5"V	$21
44 Rem. Magnum	250	1230	1132	1057	840	711	620	0.8	2.9	6.5"V	NA
44 Rem. Magnum	275	1235	1142	1070	931	797	699	0.8	3.3	6.5"	NA
44 Rem. Magnum	300	1200	1100	1026	959	806	702	NA	NA	7.5"	$17
44 Rem. Magnum	330	1385	1297	1220	1406	1234	1090	1.83	0.00	NA	NA
440 CorBon	260	1700	1544	1403	1669	1377	1136	1.58	NA	10"	NA
450 Short Colt/450 Revolver	226	830	NA	NA	350	NA	NA	NA	NA	NA	NEW
45 S&W Schofield	180	730	NA	NA	213	NA	NA	NA	NA	NA	NA
45 S&W Schofield	230	730	NA	NA	272	NA	NA	na			
45 Automatic	165	1030	930	NA	385	315	NA	1.2	NA	5"	NA
45 Automatic	185	1000	940	890	410	360	325	1.1	4.9	5"	$28
45 Auto. (Match)	185	770	705	650	245	204	175	2.0	8.7	5"	$28
45 Auto. (Match)	200	940	890	840	392	352	312	2.0	8.6	5"	$20
45 Automatic	200	975	917	860	421	372	328	1.4	5.0	5"	$18
45 Automatic	230	830	800	675	355	325	300	1.6	6.8	5"	$27
45 Automatic	230	880	846	816	396	366	340	1.5	6.1	5"	NA
45 Automatic +P	165	1250	NA	NA	573	NA	NA	NA	NA	NA	NA
45 Automatic +P	185	1140	1040	970	535	445	385	0.9	4.0	5"	$31
45 Automatic +P	200	1055	982	925	494	428	380	NA	NA	5"	NA
45 Super	185	1300	1190	1108	694	582	504	NA	NA	5"	NA
45 Win. Magnum	230	1400	1230	1105	1000	775	635	0.6	2.8	5"	$14**
45 Win. Magnum	260	1250	1137	1053	902	746	640	0.8	3.3	5"	$16**
45 Win. Mag. CorBon	320	1150	1080	1025	940	830	747	3.47			NA
455 Webley MKII	262	850	NA	NA	420	NA	NA	NA	NA	NA	NA
45 Colt	200	1000	938	889	444	391	351	1.3	4.8	5.5"	$21
45 Colt	225	960	890	830	460	395	345	1.3	5.5	5.5"	$22
45 Colt + P CorBon	265	1350	1225	1126	1073	884	746	2.65	0.0		NA
45 Colt + P CorBon	300	1300	1197	1114	1126	956	827	2.78	0.0		NA
45 Colt	250/255	860	820	780	410	375	340	1.6	6.6	5.5"	$27
454 Casull	250	1300	1151	1047	938	735	608	0.7	3.2	7.5"V	NA
454 Casull	260	1800	1577	1381	1871	1436	1101	0.4	1.8	7.5"V	NA
454 Casull	300	1625	1451	1308	1759	1413	1141	0.5	2.0	7.5"V	NA
454 Casull CorBon	360	1500	1387	1286	1800	1640	1323	2.01	0.0		NA
475 Linebaugh	400	1350	1217	1119	1618	1315	1112	NA	NA	NA	NA
480 Ruger	325	1350	1191	1076	1315	1023	835	2.6	0.0	7.5"	NA
50 Action Exp.	325	1400	1209	1075	1414	1055	835	0.2	2.3	6"	$24**

40, 10m con

44

45, 50

BACK IN TIME FOR YOUR NEXT HUNT...

RUGER
NEW MODEL
SUPER BLACKHAWK HUNTER
KS47NH

.44 Mag.

Suggested retail price of $639.00.

scope rings included

The Ruger New Model Super Blackhawk Hunter is designed to accept your favorite pistol scope. (scope not included)

THE RETURN OF THE HUNTER

Back by popular demand, the New Model Super Blackhawk Hunter offers a no-compromise fusion of traditional single-action style, simplicity and strength with the desirable option of easily mounting your favorite pistol scope. Crafted of heat-treated 400-series stainless steel, the Hunter features a 7 ½" heavy barrel with an integral full-length solid rib, factory machined to accommodate the 1" Ruger stainless scope rings supplied. Fully adjustable Ruger open sights are, of course, standard equipment, so you can choose what's best for your own hunting requirements. Wherever you hunt, whatever the weather, the Hunter is a partner you can always rely on.

instruction manuals for all Ruger firearms available on request. Please specify model for which you require a manual.

STURM, RUGER and Company, Inc.

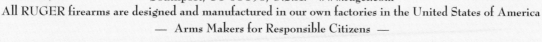

Southport, CT 06490, U.S.A. • www.ruger.com

All RUGER firearms are designed and manufactured in our own factories in the United States of America

— Arms Makers for Responsible Citizens —

Owners of "Old Model" (three screw) single-action revolvers manufactured from 1953-1972, and Bearcats with serial numbers below 93-00000 should contact us for details about FREE safety conversions.

The World's
MOST POWERFUL MAGNUMS
Only from Lazzeroni®

LONG 30 CAL

WARBIRD® 7.82 (.308) — 180gr. — 3,501 fps*

LONG 7mm

FIREBIRD® 7.21 (.284) — 140gr. — 3,687 fps*

No Belts

No Rebated Rims

Just Rock Solid Performance

FOR 2002

The Lazzeroni/ Sako TRG-S is chambered for the red hot Lazzeroni 7.21 (.284) Firebird®, as well as the current 7.82 (.308) Warbird® chambering. This very popular rifle is exclusive to Lazzeroni Arms and features a precision bolt action with three locking lugs, a 26"stainless steel barrel, a three-round detachable magazine box, an injection molded composite stock and Decelerator® recoil pad.

LAZZERONI/SAKO TRG-S

For only $949.99 there is not a better "long range" hunting rifle available anywhere.

Want *real* performance from a short magnum?

SHORT 30 CAL

PATRIOT® 7.82 (.308) — 180gr. — 3,202 fps*

SHORT 7mm

TOMAHAWK® 7.21 (.284) — 140gr. — 3,379 fps*

FOR 2002
The well built and amazingly accurate Lazzeroni/Savage model 16LZ chambered in the Lazzeroni 7.82 (.308) Patriot® short magnum. This all stainless steel rifle is exclusive to Lazzeroni Arms and features a precision bolt action with two locking lugs, heavy duty extractor, a 24" stainless steel barrel, a detachable magazine box and an injection molded composite stock.

LAZZERONI/SAVAGE 16LZ

If you are in the market for a short action magnum with power to spare, this *is* the one...at the introductory price of only $649.99

*Actual muzzle velocity, 26" barrel length at 72° F.

PO Box 26696
Tucson Arizona USA 85726-6696
1-888-492-7247
fax 520-624-4250
arms@lazzeroni.com
www.lazzeroni.com

LAZZERONI®

THE MOST ACCLAIMED REVOLVER IN THE WORLD

FREEDOM ARMS INC.
P.O. BOX 150
FREEDOM, WYOMING 83120
307-883-2468

WEBSITE: WWW.FREEDOMARMS.COM
E-MAIL: FREEDOM@FREEDOMARMS.COM

Model 97 Premier Grade
Caliber's available
.45 Colt
> Optional cylinders in,
> .45 ACP

.41 Magnum
.357 Magnum
> Optional cylinder in,
> .38 Special

.22 Long Rifle
> Optional cylinder in:
> .22 Win. Mag.

Primary uses are Hunting,
Silhouette and Collecting.

Model 83 Premier and Field
Grade Caliber's available
.50 Action Express
.475 Linebaugh
454 Casull
> Optional cylinders in:
> .45 Colt
> .45 ACP
> .45 Win. Mag.

.44 Magnum
.41 Magnum
.357 Magnum
.22 Long Rifle
> Optional cylinder in:
> .22 Win. Mag.

These fine revolvers are
featured on the cover of
"Big Bore Handguns"
by John Taffin.
Get your copy today.

The Right Bullet

TAURUS COPPER BULLETS™

ADVANCED HANDGUN CARTRIDGES

99.95% PURE COPPER

Taurus Copper Bullets are the result of the strategic alliance of Taurus International, Barnes Bullets, Hodgdon Powder and PMC Ammunition.

The Right Gun

ALL NEW .45 ACP STELLAR TRACKER

Featuring The Exclusive Taurus Stellar Clip™

The Perfect Match.

High-Tech Tactical Knives

by James Ayres

WHAT IS A tactical knife? There are folders and fixed blades that are referred to as tactical knives. There are large knives and small ones, plain edges and serrated edges. There are short machetes and daggers that look like Klingon War Knives. All are dubbed "tactical." There seems to be tremendous variation in what is considered a tactical knife, except for one thing. Modern tactical knives all seem to be black.

I know some of the black coatings serve to retard corrosion, and I will stipulate that field conditions can make a plain carbon-steel blade difficult to maintain. But my first sergeant would have heard no excuses from any trooper who failed to maintain his gear. Oil has been around for a long time, and men have gone down to the sea in ships carrying plain steel blades for centuries. Beyond corrosion resistance, I'm not sure what color has to do with function.

The black knife seems to call up visions of Special Ops soldiers on dangerous missions, midnight raids where a knife flashing in the moonlight would spell disaster, or something like that. Once upon a time, long, long ago, when I served with the 82nd Airborne Division and the 7th Special Forces Group (ABN), and that was shortly after the invention of gunpowder, we mostly made do with Randalls and Ka-Bars. No one had a black knife that I knew of, and I never heard of a mission being compromised due to a flashing blade.

Well, I guess things are different today. In any event, black knives rule in this category. Seriously, aside from my curmudgeonly comments regarding black as a fashion choice, these tacticals are, as a group, good sturdy knives that you can depend on for extreme usage. If

a man feels better with a subdued blade, then he should have what gives him confidence. Who knows, it just might make a difference one moonlit night far from home.

In today's world, a tactical folder is well defined as one that has a solid lock, usually in the form of a locking liner, a pocket clip, one-hand-blade-opening capabilities, and one that exhibits strong, robust construction.

As I recall, Bob Terzuola was the first custom maker who combined the locking liner, the pocket clip, a one-hand opener, and aluminum scales to create the first tactical folder. Shortly after the development of Bob's folder, Ernest Emerson and a small number of other custom knifemakers began to create their own versions of the concept. Then Benchmade started production of the first factory versions of the concept. Soon the patterns proliferated,

with virtually every factory and custom knifemaker offering their own interpretation of the idea. Today, the tactical folder dominates the market.

Last year, I tested a group of tactical folders from Benchmade, Chris Reeve, Spyderco and others. The knives were used, and abused, in horrendous conditions by a group of people who were hard on them. None were damaged in the least by extreme usage. This sturdy breed of folder deserves a place in the pocket of anyone who uses and depends on a folder.

▼ The *Model 710* is the first knife Benchmade chose to incorporate the Axis lock, one of the strongest folding-knife locking mechanisms on the market, according to the author.

▶ The proximity of dual thumb studs for opening the blade, and the Axis lock for keeping it open, make for efficient function of the Benchmade *Model 720*.

A new trend emerging is brought to us in the form of tactical folders being "dressed up" with features that are usually reserved for gentlemen's folders. This is a good thing. There is no reason why a folder with all the virtues of the tactical knife cannot be made with a nicer appearance and materials. So far, it's mostly custom knifemakers fancying up tactical folders, but hopefully we will see factories supporting the trend.

The notion of tactical fixed blades is a little more slippery. As in folders, it appears that any knife can become tactical as soon as black coating is applied. Never mind useful design, sharpness or strength, *black* is what matters. There is even a black Marine Combat Knife available. Not a bad thing, just different.

Color commentary aside, what I saw at the 2002 S.H.O.T. (Shooting Hunting Outdoor Trade) Show was the largest selection of well-made, sturdy, sharp, *black* fixed blades I've seen at a trade show. In my not so humble opinion, virtually all of the knives would work equally well if they were done in plain steel—or colored red, for that matter. Never mind this curmudgeon's maundering, let's take a look at some terrific knives.

Benchmade Knife Co.

Most of Benchmade's output is in tactical folders. The company has carved out a place in the market that is uniquely its own. Knives are solidly made, of good quality and good design.

I also particularly appreciate Benchmade's customer service. I bought one of the first locking-liner folders Benchmade manufactured, the Walter Brend folder with a reverse-curved blade and, after many years of hard service in various camps and survival schools, the liner became a little weak. It was used and abused by many students. The blade had been sharpened so many times that the recurve was long gone, and the blade itself was about a third thinner than when it was new. I sent it back to the factory for a new liner, fully expecting to pay a reasonable service charge.

A week later, I got back what amounted to a new knife. The folks at Benchmade had replaced the liner, which I had asked them to do, but their service department also replaced the blade. There was no charge for anything. I was stunned. This kind of service is just not commonly seen today: not in the automobile industry, not in computers, not in any kind of manufactured-product arena. I gave the knife to my son and he is still using it.

Benchmade's Axis lock is one of the strongest folding-knife locks on the market. Bill McHenry and Jason Williams did the first Axis design. This is a great, really great, design, and its execution by Benchmade is equal to the original concept for locking the blade open. The original *Model 710* has a 3.9-inch blade available in M-2 tool steel or 154-CM blade steel.

A group of teenagers in one of the outdoor skills classes I teach used a *Model 710* with M-2 steel and was rougher on it than any folder deserves to be used. Among other chores, they

▲ Other Benchmade models with the Axis lock include the Griptilian, a robust folder with a unique non-slip handle, and a smaller version, the Mini-Griptilian, is now offered in colors other than black.

Boker's Walter Brend Tactical Folder is a handsome, sturdy locking-liner folder with a choice of a G-10 or cocobolo-wood handle. The wood scales make an already handsome knife even more so.

▲ Bud Nealy's handy little fixed blades commissioned for production by Boker are what we used to call boot knives. Nealy's carry system allows the knives to be toted in a pocket, boot, belt—even hanging by a lanyard around the neck.

used a baton (club) to beat the blade through a couple-dozen saplings to build framework for a winter shelter in the Pacific Northwest. There was no damage to the Axis *710* at all. The *710* has an unusual clip point, a re-curved blade and G-10 handle scales with double stainless-steel liners.

The Axis series also includes the *720*, a swooping clip point designed by handmade knifemaker Mel Pardue with aluminum scales. The 3 1/4-inch blade is made of 154CM and is, I'm sure, up to any task the *710* can handle.

Another model with the Axis lock is the Griptilian, a robust folder with a unique non-slip handle. This year, Benchmade has introduced some variations on this proven winner. The Griptilian handle, introduced last year, continues on a smaller version, the Mini-Griptilian, which is now offered in colors other than black. I don't think the colored handles endanger the Griptilian's status as a tactical tough guy. Heck, I once saw Clint Eastwood in a red T-shirt.

Boker USA

Boker's extensive lineup includes tactical folders and fixed blades. The company's Walter Brend Tactical Folder has a 3 1/2-inch 440C stainless steel blade, titanium bolsters and G-10 handle scales over stainless steel liners. This is a handsome, sturdy knife, well suited for the field, and especially handy when clipped onto a belt or pocket.

Boker also offers this model with a cocobolo-wood handle, and the wood scales make an already handsome knife even more so. This year, Boker debuts the Brend Tactical Folder with a full G-10 handle *sans* the titanium bolsters, reducing the weight to 5 1/2 ounces.

Bud Nealy's handy little fixed blades commissioned for production by

◄ Camillus selected American Bladesmith Society master smith Jerry Fisk, one of the world's finest custom knifemakers, to design and test the Fisk Presentation Bowie. It doesn't disappoint.

Boker are what we used to call boot knives. I guess we can still call them boot knives, but Nealy's carry system allows the knives to be toted in a pocket, boot, belt or even hanging by a lanyard around the neck.

The Aikuchi features a hollow-ground 440C tanto blade. The Specialist dons a drop-point blade, and both are available with molded and shaped G-10 handles. The Aikuchi is also offered with a cocobolo-wood grip. These are well-designed, well-made and quite useful little blades. They are so convenient to carry, there's no reason to be without one..

Buck Knives

Buck is one of the old reliables of the American knife industry. Buck makes good knives, has done so for many years, and is now manufacturing a group of tacticals designed in cooperation with Strider Knives. There is one fixed blade and four folders in the series, and they seem to be about as strong as factory knives can be made. None have black blades. The first run will have BG-42 steel and subsequent production runs will include ATS-34 blades.

The Strider Solution has a 4 1/4-inch drop-point blade and a G-10 handle. It is of one-piece

construction, and not only is this a sturdy knife, it is an all-around useful pattern that will serve the outdoorsman and the soldier well.

The Buck Strider folder is offered with a 4-inch spear-point or tanto blade. Both versions have G-10

▲ Becker Knife & Tool, a division of Camillus Cutlery, innovates and motivates with the Combat Utility 7, a knife inspired by the famous Marine combat knife of World War II.

▲ Tactical folders in the Camillus CUDA series include the Quick Action spear point (*top two models*) in plain and semi-serrated blades, and tantos, also plain and serrated.

handle scales, titanium locking liners, and thumb studs for opening the blades. These are large, rugged folders, so Buck also offers Mini-Strider versions with the same blade options. The small folders appear to be just as tough as the larger ones

Camillus

The CUDA series includes the CQB fixed blades designed by Bob Terzuola. These clean, contemporary designs have been in production for some years with original matte-finished blades and black canvas-Micarta® handles. Both sizes, the 5 3/4-inch blade and the 3.95-inch blade, are now offered in basic black. The addition of black blades will undoubtedly increase their appeal.

Tactical folders in the CUDA series include the Quick Action spear point and tanto, and the Darrel Ralph frame-lock EDC, which is now offered in 154CM blade steel. "EDC" stands for *Every Day Carry*, and this is in fact a strong, handy-sized folder suitable for such use. It has a 2.95-inch blade, a pocket clip and weighs only 3 ounces.

Another folder in the lineup is the CUDA Maxx 5.5. This is another Darrel Ralph design with a Crucible AIRDI-150 D-2 semi-stainless steel blade that is, you guessed it, 5 1/2 inches long. The CUDA Maxx 5.5 is one of the largest production folders I have ever seen; not only long but strong. Crafted with titanium handle slabs, one of which also serves as a frame lock, this is an impressive package that should perform as well as it looks. I have not yet had a chance to test one, but knowing Camillus, I expect that there will be no disappointments.

Of course, Camillus continues to produce its Marine Combat Knife and Pilot Survival Knife. These may not be high-tech, but both of them are tactical by any definition.

Becker Knife and Tool, a division of Camillus, makes a series of six fixed blades that embody the tactical virtues. Blade steel is 0170-6C at a Rockwell hardness of 58-59RC (on the Rockwell Hardness Scale).

Handles are GV6H, a tough nylon made in Switzerland. The Companion, with a 5 1/4-inch blade, is the smallest in the group. Like the others in the series, it's a heavyweight, weighing 14.6 ounces. This is an excellent field knife with a margin of strength for extreme use, the kind of knife you would use to field dress a Suburban.

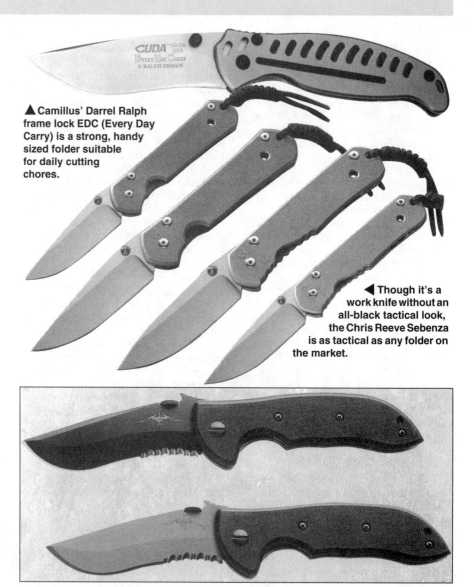

▲ Camillus' Darrel Ralph frame lock EDC (Every Day Carry) is a strong, handy sized folder suitable for daily cutting chores.

◀ Though it's a work knife without an all-black tactical look, the Chris Reeve Sebenza is as tactical as any folder on the market.

Emerson Knives, Inc. produces more than 20 tactical folders, and out of the group, the author's favorite is the Commander.

Other knives in the collection include the following well-proven designs: the TacTool, the Magnum Camp, the Brute, a Patrol Machete and the Machax.

The TacTool is designed to smash, bash, pry, hammer and cut. Basically, it is a forced-entry tool for a tactical team. With a chisel-ground, 7-inch blade, any officer of the law or military can pry open windows and doors, pull hinge pins and smash glass. Oh yeah, it can cut things, too, and comes sharp from the factory.

Jerry Fisk, an award-winning American Bladesmith Society (ABS) master smith, designed the Magnum Camp knife. He meant this to be an all-purpose big knife. With an 8 1/2-inch flat-ground blade, it is an excellent camp and kitchen knife, as well as a super chopper. In the hand, the knife seems quite light, a testimony to its excellent balance.

The Brute, Machax and Patrol machete are all variations on the chopper theme. Each one has a different interpretation of a re-curved blade, and all of them work just like they are designed to do.

New for this year is the Combat Utility 7. The famous Marine combat knife of World War II inspired this new model. The lineage is apparent, but the new interpretation exceeds the original in many ways. It has a full tang for strength, and is flat-ground for cutting efficiency. The 7-inch, clip-point blade will be useful for almost any task. This is a winner and, like the rest of the series, it's reasonably priced. It is also black.

Chris Reeve Knives

The Sebenza is not made in black. Moreover, the word "Sebenza" translates to "work" in

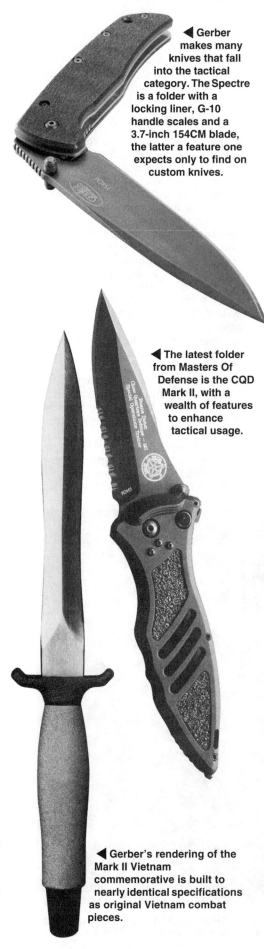

◀ **Gerber makes many knives that fall into the tactical category. The Spectre is a folder with a locking liner, G-10 handle scales and a 3.7-inch 154CM blade, the latter a feature one expects only to find on custom knives.**

◀ **The latest folder from Masters Of Defense is the CQD Mark II, with a wealth of features to enhance tactical usage.**

◀ **Gerber's rendering of the Mark II Vietnam commemorative is built to nearly identical specifications as original Vietnam combat pieces.**

Zulu, a native language from Chris Reeve's home in South Africa. Hardly the stuff of tactical merchandising, to be truly tactical the Sebenza would need to be called "The Great Lion Killer Folding Knife," or something more or less in that vein. This sturdy, all-purpose folder is in fact as tactical as any folder on the market. It is strong. It is sharp. It stays sharp. It does not break. It's a good knife. Good knife, heck, it is a great knife.

Emerson Knives, Inc.

I first met Ernest Emerson at a custom knife show in Solvang many years ago. He had just made his first locking-liner folder, and I bought one of the early models. It was and is a nice knife, and he's a nice guy.

I don't think either of us foresaw the well-deserved success ahead of him. Ernie's booth at the 2002 S.H.O.T. Show was so busy that I was never able to get through the crowd to speak with anyone in spite of visiting three times on two separate days.

Finally, just before I left the show, I did get a look at his current offerings. There were no surprises, and that's a good thing, just well-made, cunningly designed knives on which Emerson has built his reputation. Emerson will tell you that there is more to designing a tactical knife than meets the eye. Ernie has a background in martial arts that forms the foundation of his work. Add to that an artist's eye and well-integrated feedback from serious field users, and you have a group of tactical folders that stand out in any crowd.

Emerson produces more than 20 tactical folders, and out of the group, my favorite is the Commander. It embodies many subtle features that are of importance in such a folder without rendering it useless for utility work. If you haven't tried an Emerson, you should.

Gerber Legendary Blades

Gerber makes many knives that fall into the tactical category. The Spectre is a folder with a locking liner, G-10 handle scales and a 3.7-inch 154CM blade, the latter a feature one only finds on custom knives. Of course, it's all black. In this case, the titanium-nitride coating will do a good job of retarding corrosion.

Of all the knives Gerber produces, the one that caught my eye at the 2002 S.H.O.T. Show was the

Mark II Vietnam Commemorative. I first saw one of these wicked-looking daggers at the Fort Bragg PX. I did not buy it since I already had a Randall and I didn't want such a special-purpose knife.

A friend of mine did buy it, and he came back from Vietnam with a story about the Gerber. It's his story, not mine to tell, yet I know he was glad he bought the distinctive dagger. This version has a 154CM blade, not the original steel, but it does have the original cat's tongue handle. I'm sure there are many men with memories evoked by this knife.

Kershaw

Custom knifemaker Ken Onion and Kershaw have produced a number of attractive folders. Now the twosome has released a fixed blade incorporating Onion's graceful blade shape and a sure-grip handle. It comes with a Kydex® sheath and is all black. Therefore, it is tactical. Seriously, this is a handsome knife. It is 8 5/8 inches long overall and would be a good knife in any color. It's a handy size and looks strong enough for any reasonable, and some not so reasonable, purposes.

Masters Of Defense

Masters Of Defense (MOD) is a specialty knife company solidly in the forefront of all tactical folder production. Indeed, with a few exceptions, folders are what Masters Of Defense is known for making. Massad Ayoob, a well-known self-defense authority, designed MOD's first fixed blade, the Razorback. In fact, knowledgeable users of tactical blades designed each of MOD's folders. The Trident was fashioned by former SEAL Jim Watson, the Hornet by martial artist James Keating, and the Tempest by Michael Janich, another well-known martial artist. The Lady Hawk is the inspiration of famed martial artist and kick boxer Graciela Casillas-Boggs.

All of the models employ 154CM blades, and each incorporates a nested liner that locks up solidly. All but the Razorback feature aluminum handles with insets of checkered non-slip material. All are of top quality, all are black and, even though there isn't much *not* to like about these knives, I wish MOD would make a few with plain, non-black blades.

MOD's latest folder is the CQD Mark II, a small version of the award-winning CQD Special Operation Tactical Folder. Duane Dieter designed both, the large version with a support blade positioned in a groove at the butt. This blade is meant for specialized use such as cutting seat belts and, while the smaller version does not have this feature, it does employ the same robust construction and a wealth of features designed to enhance tactical usage.

The Advanced Tactical Fighter is a fixed blade with more swooping curves, sharp points, serrations and detailed features than any knife I have experienced. Words cannot do it justice. It is a fierce-looking piece and, like all of the MOD knives, it is exceptionally well made.

Ontario Knife Co.

Ontario's Spec Plus Series includes solid, no-frills tactical knives that will get the job done and not break the bank. The blades - most of which exhibit the required black coating - are 1095 carbon steel, but some are in plain steel. In this series is a model for virtually every use.

There is a version of the venerable Marine Combat, the Sp6 Fighter with an 8-inch blade, a modern version of the Marine Raider Bowie, an Air Force Survival Knife, a Divers Probe and more. All of these are essentially updated versions of time-tested designs made with tough, proven, carbon steel.

In the same series are some tantos, a large lock-back folder and one pattern that is even more interesting–the Frontiersman. This is a bowie that seems of about the same design as the bowies fashioned by Bill Bagwell for Ontario's Masters Series.

The Frontiersman has an 11 1/8-inch blade with the same graceful lines, if not the hand-forged qualities, of Bagwell's originals. If you have a need for a large multi-purpose blade, and you do not have a large budget, try this one. It's not designed as a sharpened pry bar. Albeit with a modern look—black and everything—the Frontiersman is a real old-fashioned edged weapon, and that's pretty tactical.

SOG Specialty Knives

Virtually every knife made by SOG fits into the tactical category. From the company's first fixed blade, the SOG Bowie, which has become a signature piece, to the distinctive JetEdge folder, SOG has kept its focus on the tactical market. This year, SOG introduced an attractive little folder named the "Sculptura," and sculptured is just how it looks and feels. This pocket tactical has a solid Arc-Lock, a 2-inch drop-point blade and a clip to secure it to a pocket or to hold some cash together. It only weighs 2.1 ounces and is reasonably priced.

Spyderco

Sal Glesser's company continues to be one of the most, if not the most, innovative knife companies in the world today. Many years ago, Spyderco revolutionized the look and use of folding knives by incorporating the company's patented hole-in-the-blade one-hand opener, complemented by the pocket clip and blade serrations. Today, the legacy of innovation continues.

I had been hearing rumors about some new models before the 2002 S.H.O.T. Show, but I had to wait until I arrived in Las Vegas to see them. I was not disappointed. Spyderco has developed a new term, "Martial Blade Craft (MBC)," to describe bladed combat arts. The company is promoting the notion that one day these arts will become Olympic sports, such as judo and fencing. Well, why not?

Four models from Spyderco's extensive lineup are designed for use in these activities. The group includes the *C60*, designed by

Ontario's Spec Plus Series includes a version of the venerable Marine Combat, the Sp6 Fighter *(top left)* with an 8-inch blade, a modern version of the Marine Raider Bowie *(bottom)*, an Air Force Survival Knife, a Diver's Probe *(second from left)* and more.

A bolo *(top)*, tantos and a fighter *(middle)* and a Spax axe round out the Ontario Spec Plus Series of all-black tactical knives.

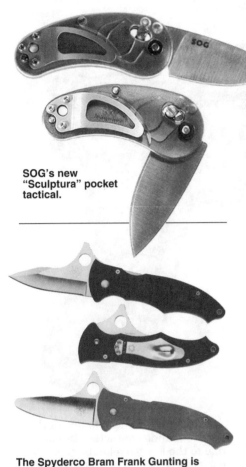

SOG's new "Sculptura" pocket tactical.

The Spyderco Bram Frank Gunting is designed to function as a *Yawara* stick, as well as an edged weapon.

The Lil' Temperance is the most recent addition to Spyderco's group of folders.

New at the 2002 S.H.O.T. Show was Fred Perrin's Temperance fixed blade with an exceptionally comfortable black, molded handle and a flat-ground blade of VG-10 steel.

Massad Ayoob, whose fame precedes him.

The *C60* is a lock-back folder and has a handle that drops deeply below the line of blade. This is meant to position the blade so that it is a natural extension of the hand.

The Bram Frank Gunting is designed to function as a *Yawara* stick, as well as an edged weapon. The Gunting, which is named after an *Escrima* move, enlists Spyderco's Compression Lock. James Keating's Chinook features an upswept bowie blade, and it is a lock-back folder that is so strongly built, it could be used as an impact weapon.

The Lil' Temperance is the most recent addition to this group of folders. The Temperance is a particularly attractive design and available with a modified spear point or a trailing point. Both versions have blades 3 inches long and flat ground. The handles are green G-10 with carved recesses for comfort. The reversible spring pocket clips have indexing holes and are well thought out. Spyderco's nested Compression Lock completes a couple of the most handsome packages.

Also new at the 2002 S.H.O.T. Show were two fixed blades: Fred Perrin's Bowie and the Temperance fixed blade. Both are serious entries in the tactical field. Although they are not black all over, they do have black molded handles that are exceptionally comfortable and seem to mold to your hand. Both have flat-ground blades of VG-10 steel. Perrin's Bowie sports a 5-inch blade, while the Temperance has 4 7/16 inches of steel. These are sensible, usable knives, and I'm sure they would serve the needs of a Tac officer, but they are also good all-around knives. I recommend them both.

Tool Logic

The folks at Tool Logic started business a few years ago with a credit-card-sized tool kit, a useful device that subsequently inspired a legion of similar devices. This year, Tool Logic introduced a folding knife with an integral LED flashlight and whistle. Dubbed "The SL1 Survival Light," it has a 3-inch blade with a

This year, Tool Logic introduced a folding knife with an integral LED flashlight and whistle. Dubbed "The SL1 Survival Light," it has a 3-inch blade with a thumbhole and a few serrations at the base of the edged portion.

thumbhole and a few serrations at the base of the edged portion. It has a clip to secure it to shorts or flotation device, or whatever. Although this combination folder is not as sturdy as some of the heavy-duty folders, it is reasonably priced and has a definite tactical niche.

All kidding about black knives and Klingon daggers aside, these are all pretty great knives. The fixed blades offer more choice in high-quality factory knives than ever before. In times past, you would have needed the budget for a custom knife to equal the features on some of these factory blades.

I am particularly pleased that these excellent folders are available. It was not so many years ago that you had to carry a fixed blade for anything beyond light usage. To carry–conveniently–a folder that will handle extreme tasks that formerly could be done only with a fixed blade is a good thing. It's a good thing because it means that people will more likely have emergency tools when they need them. ●

Editor's Note

This chapter was excerpted from SPORTING KNIVES, 2ND EDITION, *a new annual book from Krause Publications. Contents are organized along the lines of* GUN DIGEST *and* GUNS ILLUSTRATED *, and cover the realm of commercial sporting cutlery. Read about the latest new products, insightful articles from industry authorities – even a website directory – and peruse the extensive illustrated catalog. A valuable reference section is located at the back of the book.* ***This book is available now from your favorite bookseller, or direct from Krause Publications @ 800-258-0929***

This is a cut-away view of the Glock pistol. Notice the small number of moving parts. *Glock photo*

Glock, The Road To Perfection!

by Christopher R. Bartocci

GLOCK PISTOLS HAVE taken the law-enforcement and military communities by storm for more than 15 years now. Not only have they found acceptance with military and law enforcement, they have also become popular with civilian shooters for competition and self-defense. The Glock phenomenon had a very rocky start at its inception. The roadblocks it encountered–and eventually conquered–were primarily caused by media ignorance that, in turn, caused widespread alarm.

An engineer named Gaston Glock founded Glock GmbH in 1963. The plant, located in Deutsch-Wagram, Austria, first produced things such as doorknobs and hinges for the Austrian market. As time went on, it got into military-type products. Glock GmbH began manufacturing knives, entrenching tools, fragmentation grenades, training grenades and non-disintegrating machine-gun belts.

The New Austrian Pistol

In 1980, the Austrian Army began a search for a new pistol—one that was state of the art. Their goal was to issue the new pistol, designated the P-80, to the troops by 1983. Glock decided to enter the competition for Austria's new service pistol.

In 1980, Mr. Glock assembled a panel of Europe's most renowned handgun experts. These experts represented military, law enforcement, and competitive shooters. Their job was to draft a list of the most desired features for a new pistol; 17 criteria resulted. Among them, the following: The pistol should fire the proven 9x19mm service round and have a magazine capacity of at least 8 rounds and no more than 58 parts. This new pistol must be disassembled without tools, and cleaned with standard equipment. The parts must be interchangeable and have a minimum of 25,000 rounds' service life. The pistol can have no more than 20 malfunctions in a 10,000-round endurance test.

The Glock 17

In 1982, the Glock Model 17 was presented to the Austrian Army for trial. Interestingly, a common misconception was that the Glock 17 was given the model designation of '17' because the magazine held 17 rounds. Actually it was Mr. Glock's 17th patent.

The Glock 17 pistol was indeed a revolutionary design. It exceeded all the criteria that Mr. Glock's panel developed. The Glock 17 fired the 9x19mm (9mm NATO) cartridge. The entire frame of the G17 was made of corrosion-resistant polymer material, greatly decreasing weight (22 oz. empty). The polymer frame of the Glock pistol is as much as 86 percent lighter than a conventional steel frame–yet much stronger. The polymer frame absorbs recoil as well as shock/vibrations. The 108-degree natural angle of the grip favors the pistol's aiming characteristics and, due to the low barrel axis, recoil is easier to control. This is especially useful in rapid fire. The pistol had only 34 parts, compared to the maximum of 58 parts set forth by the panel. The pistol could be disassembled with no tools; in fact, the pistol could be totally disassembled with a 3/32-inch pin punch, which eliminated the need for extensive armorers tools. The parts for the G17 are totally interchangeable—so interchangeable that one could disassemble 20 G17 pistols, mix up the parts, re-assemble all 20 pistols, and they would all function at 100 percent!

The new pistol did not have a conventional external safety. However, it had three excellent internal safeties. The Glock 17 is not really double action or single action. It is called "Safe Action." The first of the three safeties is the safety bar that sits in the middle of the trigger. It locks the trigger forward, preventing accidental discharge from rough handling or the trigger snagging on clothing. The only way to disengage this safety is to depress it with the trigger finger.

The second safety is the passive firing-pin block. This is a metal plunger, which is spring-driven in the slide. This plunger locks into the firing-pin/striker cutouts and locks the firing pin in place. The

The newest version of the famous Glock 17. Notice the finger grooves on the front strap of the grip and the accessory rail on the front of the frame. *Glock photo*

only way to fire the pistol, thus disengaging the firing-pin block, is to pull the trigger. An extension of the trigger bar pushes upward on the plunger, clearing the firing-pin channel and allowing the firing pin/striker to strike the primer of the cartridge. The firing-pin block makes it extremely unlikely for the firearm to go off if dropped, thrown, stepped on, or kicked. In fact, Glock has dropped pistols from helicopters to test its durability and reliability–never once did the pistol discharge.

The third and final safety is the Drop Safety. The rear part of the trigger bar, a cruciform shape, rests with its wings in the ready position on the safety ramp (drop) located in the trigger housing. When the trigger is pulled, the trigger bar starts to leave the safety ramp being pushed downward, and when the trigger bar comes into contact with the connector, the trigger bar drops all the way down and releases the striker to fire the round.

These three safeties all function in order: When the trigger is first pulled, the trigger safety is disengaged; as the trigger is being pulled to the rear, the firing pin block is disengaged; then the final safety–the

drop safety–is disengaged at the moment the pistol fires. A common misconception about Glock pistols and the "Safe Action" is that the pistol is carried in the cocked condition. In fact, it is not. The striker is pulled back approximately halfway when the pistol is loaded. When the trigger is pulled, the trigger bar retracts the striker fully to the rear until the trigger bar reaches the connector. The connector/drop safety causes the trigger bar to drop and release the striker, thus allowing the pistol to fire. All three safeties re-engage as soon as the trigger is released.

Is the Glock pistol less safe to carry than a conventional double-action automatic pistol with a manual safety? I guess that is a matter of opinion. For years, revolvers were carried with no manual safety. The reality is the firearm will not discharge unless

the trigger is pulled. The ultimate factor is the operator. You do not pull the trigger until you are ready to fire! The main benefit Safe Action gives the shooter is the consistent trigger-pull weight. The weight of your last trigger pull will be the exact same as your first. Most conventional pistols give the first double-action trigger pull weighing from approximately 8 to 15 pounds, then subsequent single-action shots will have a trigger weight anywhere from 3 to 8 pounds. Unless you are a well-trained shooter, that first shot is often a flyer due to the heavy pull. Safe Action alleviates that. Personal preference plays a big role. No matter how good the design, the operators have to be comfortable with the end product.

The Glock pistol is designed with a cold hammer-forged polygonal rifled barrel, probably one of the most durable barrels in the world. What sets this barrel apart from standard cut-rifling barrels is that the lands and grooves have a rounded, smooth profile instead of the sharp rectangular profile of standard rifling.

Polygonally rifled barrels offer several advantages. First, with the edges being smooth, they do not wear as quickly as conventional barrels, giving an extended barrel life where conventional barrel with sharp edges attract copper deposits, which wears the barrel much faster. The extremely durable polygonal barrel is a tighter overall diameter than conventional barrels giving better bullet to barrel fit. With smooth edges, the bullet obtains a tighter fit and, thus, a better gas seal. With a tighter gas seal, you will have higher velocity. With the

The Glock pistol remains one of the simplest of all firearms. Fewer parts; less to go wrong. Here the Glock is disassembled into its five major components for cleaning. *Lawrence Ventura photo*

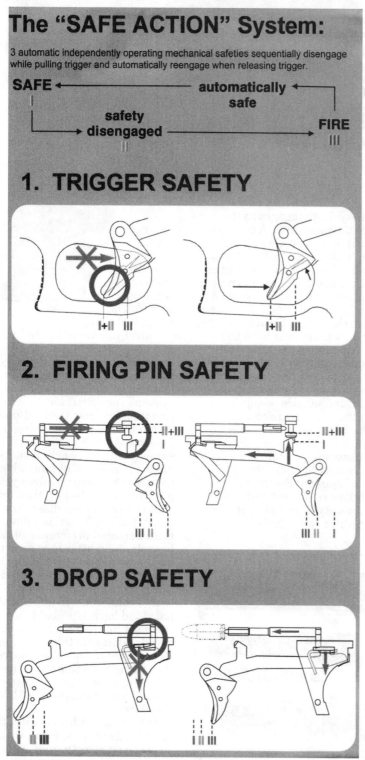

The sequence of Glock's "SAFE ACTION" System. *Glock photo*

barrel having smooth edges, it is much easier to clean and maintain. With the combination of higher velocity and less bore wear, greater extended accuracy is realized.

Glock uses a unique Tenifer finish on metal parts to protect them from corrosion. The Tenifer finish penetrates the metal, providing protection from the elements,

including exposure to saltwater. Even when the black finish appears to wear on the slide, the Tenifer is still working. The black seen on the slide is the surface finish that Glock can re-apply at low cost.

In late 1982, the Glock Model 17 was adopted by the Austrian military as its new P80 pistol. The initial order was for 2,500 pistols. Subse-

quently, in 1984 and '85, the armed forces of Norway and Sweden adopted the Glock pistol. This got the pistol NATO-Classified (*NATO Stock No. 1005/25/133/6775*). The takeover began: The Glock pistol made its worldwide debut.

In 1985, Glock submitted the G17 to the Bureau of Alcohol, Tobacco and Firearms in the United States for an importation evaluation. The American military, law-enforcement, and target-shooting markets were ripe for the taking, and the new state-of-the-art pistol was a sure hit. After BATF completed its evaluation, it required two modifications. The Glock pistols originally had serial numbers just on the right side of the slide and barrel. BATF required a metal serial number plate be attached to the frame, so Glock molded a steel plate in the bottom of the frame just in front of the trigger guard. Another interesting note is that the serial number on the frame is exactly the same as the one on the slide and barrel with the addition of the postfix "US." The second requirement was that the pistol needed to have adjustable "Target" sights. Mr. Glock developed these sights over a weekend. Now the pistol could be imported into the U.S.

In November of 1985, Glock, Inc., was established in Smyrna, Georgia, a suburb of Atlanta. The facility was created to handle but three tasks. First was final assembly of the pistols; the parts would be manufactured in Austria. Second, quality control. Third, all test firing was to be done there.

The New Terrorist Gun

On January 15th, 1985, a *Washington Post* article titled "Qaddafi Buying Austrian Plastic Pistol" appeared. The Glock 17 was referred to variously as the Hijackers Special, Invisible Weapon, Terrorist Special, and, most importantly, as the gun that would pass through a airport X-ray machine because the pistol had polymer components. This was a falsehood of the first order. The slide and barrel are solid steel—not alloys or plastic—and they show up like any other handgun would on an X-ray machine. Glock pistols had been tested thoroughly and repeatedly in X-ray machines and metal detectors throughout Europe, and they react the same as any other handgun. In fact, there are more steel components on a Glock pistol than on some conventional pocket

Not only have Glock pistols been thrown out of buildings, they have been run over, too! Glocks have proven themselves in the harshest of environments: the grueling mud and sand test, frozen in a block of ice, and immersion.

pistols. This hysteria prompted politicians to attempt to ban the Glock pistol in the name of public safety!

On May 16th, 1986, Karl Walter of Glock testified before a U.S. House of Representatives Committee on Judiciary Subcommittee on Crime that Glock at no time had offered, negotiated, or concluded any deal with anyone representing Libya. Glock had even received bad publicity in the movies when the pistol was called a porcelain gun made in Germany that can pass right through an airport metal detector. Glock proven its case and went on with business. Glock was about to shed that image—and in a big way.

Glock Meets American Law Enforcement

In March of 1986, Glock made its first law-enforcement sale in the United States. It was by no means a large department. In fact, it was the two-man police department of Colby, Kansas and soon thereafter, the Flagler County Sheriff's Office in Florida. The first large police department to purchase Glock pistols was St. Paul, Minnesota.

In the fall of 1986, Miami PD contacted Glock regarding the G17 pistol. By May of 1987, there was a pilot program in place where 25 officers tested Glock pistols on the streets. They were one of the first police agencies to put the Glock pistol through grueling testing. This testing included dropping and throwing a Glock 17 pistol against steel and concrete with a primed cartridge case in the chamber at distances up to 60 feet, with no discharge. They then put the pistol—fully loaded—into saltwater for 50 hours, retrieved it, and fired the entire magazine without stoppage. Using Winchester Silvertip ammunition, the G17 was subjected to a 1,000-round endurance test over a 45-minute period–no malfunctions. After testing was completed in the fall of 1987, the Miami Police Department officially became the largest major police department in the U.S. to adopt the new state-of-the-art handgun. Their initial order was for some 1,300 Glock 17 pistols.

The New York State Police were also interested in the new Glock pistol. However, they required an even heavier trigger pull. They wished for the trigger to have more of a revolver feel to it, so in 1990, Glock introduced a replacement leaf spring to replace the standard coiled trigger bar return spring. It was named the "New York State Trigger." There were two variants: the "standard" which was 7.5 to 8.5 pounds and the "+" which was 9 to 11 pounds. As a result, in the winter of 1990, the New York State Police adopted the Glock 17 as its

Since their introduction, Glock has had three generations of pistol frames. First (*right*), the original smooth grip. Second (*middle*), the frame with the checkered front and back strap and third (*left*), the latest frame with the finger groove and accessory rail. *Lawrence Ventura photo*

federal agencies include the U.S. Department of Agriculture, United States Drug Enforcement Administration and Bureau of Indian Affairs.

Many Different Models of Glock

9x19mm (*9mm Luger, 9mm Parabellum and 9mm NATO*)

The Glock model 17 was the pistol that started it all back in 1982. The 9mm pistol was equipped with a polymer 17-round magazine and weighed 22 ounces empty and 31.4 ounces with a full magazine; that is, 2.6 ounces lighter than an empty Beretta model M9/92FS pistol. There is a "+2" magazine extension available that gives an additional 2 rounds in the magazine, giving a capacity of 19 rounds. The pistol is available with night sights, as well as adjustable and fixed sights. The barrel is approximately 4-1/2 inches long with polygonal rifling.

There are three different generations of frames on the G17. First was the original smooth grip, the second was the checkered front and back strap, and the third (*and latest*), the frame has finger grooves in the front strap and an accessory rail on the front of the frame for mounting light sources and laser sights.

In 1988, the second Glock, the Model 19, was introduced. The G19 is the compact version of the Glock 17. The main difference is that the barrel is approximately 4 inches long, approximately 1/2-inch shorter than that of the G17. The pistol grip is shorter, some .43-inch shorter in overall height. The G19 is equipped with a 15-round magazine, and the 17- and 19-round magazine of the G17 will interchange with the G19. The G19 is a very popular duty, as well as under-cover, pistol. The G19 is the pistol of choice of the New York City Police Department.

The Glock Model 17L is the long-barrel competition version. The barrel is approximately 6 inches long. The trigger pull of the G17L is a lighter 3-1/2 pounds compared to the 5-pound standard trigger. Glock does not offer this trigger on any models other than the competition guns. The gun offers an extended magazine release. In October of 1990,

official duty sidearm. By March of 1990, 4,300 guns were delivered to the state troopers.

In January of 1990, SLED (**S**outh Carolina **L**aw **E**nforcement **D**ivision) tested and adopted the G17 as its new semi-automatic pistol. As fate would have it, SLED firearms instructors went to Glock, Inc., for Armorers Training as well as Transitional Instructional Training, where they learned of the brand new 40 S&W Glock Model 22 and 23 pistol. Upon returning to South Carolina, they advised SLED to change the order from the 9mm Glock 17

to the new 40 S&W Glock 22 pistol. So it was, and SLED became the first law-enforcement agency in the world to adopt the new 40 S&W cartridge as well as the newly released Glock 22 pistol.

Federal law enforcement has received Glock pistols with open arms. The Federal Bureau of Investigation has adopted the G22, G23, and G27. The U.S. Marshals issue the G22, and U.S. Customs issue the G17 and 19. Other Glock-issuing

The compact size models 19 (9mm) and 23 (40-cal.) and 32 (357 SIG) are favorites for a concealable duty pistol. *Glock photo*

Glock offers different frame sizes depending on the requirement. From the right, the largest frame (G20 & G21), large frame, compact and mini. *Lawrence Ventura photo*

Armando Valdes took the first-place trophy using a G17L in the 1990 World Shoot IX Championship in Adelaide, Australia.

The Glock Model 26 is the mini-gun of the Glock series, ultra-compact with a barrel length of approximately 3-1/2 inches and a short pistol grip. It features a 10-round magazine. Both the 15-, 17-, and 19-round magazines will function in the G26.

The Mysterious Glock 18

The Glock 18 is the least known of all the Glock pistols. This selective-fire pistol was built in 1986 at the request of the Austrian Cobra (anti-terrorist special operations) unit for an easily concealable submachine gun. The G18 was not imported in the United States until 1989, and only in very limited quantities.

The G18 can be fired either fully automatic (1,100 to 1,200 rounds per minute) or semi-automatic by shifting the selector lever located on the rear left side of the slide. The upper position marked "●" is semi-automatic, and the lower position marked "●●" is fully automatic. The pistol has a special 33-round magazine made for it. However, standard 17- and 19-round magazines interchange.

To be imported into the United States, the BATF required that components must not be interchangeable, thus allowing easy conversion of G17s to the G18 configuration. As a result, the slide and frame dimensions are different. The G18 has higher rails on the frame. To prevent conversions, the trigger bar, trigger mechanism housing, spacer sleeve, and barrel are not interchangeable. By removing the selector lever, you

The Glock 18. The least seen Glock and for good reason. This selective-fire machine pistol fires more than 1,000 rounds per minute. Notice the 33-round extended magazine. *Lawrence Ventura photo*

▼The selector lever on the Glock 18 is located on the left side of the slide. The top position is semi-automatic and the lower position is fully automatic. *Lawrence Ventura photo*

can return the pistol to a semiautomatic-only configuration

In firing the G18, I could not help but be amazed. The pistol was extremely accurate and controllable even with the high rate of fire. I had no difficulty whatsoever holding the trigger, firing all 33 rounds, and keeping them on a silhouette target at 15 yards. After running 100 rounds through the G18 within a minute, the pistol became too hot to touch the slide and barrel. The Glock representative locked the slide open and dipped the gun in a bucket of cold water. Steamed like crazy!! He pulled the pistol out, shook it off, and went back to firing!

The 40-Caliber Glocks

The 40-caliber round (40 S&W) was a joint venture of Smith & Wesson and Winchester/Olin. As a result of the F.B.I. study of the late 1980s with the 10mm, they found two major problems with the 10mm. First was recoil. The 10mm cartridge performance is similar to that of the 41 Remington Magnum. The second was muzzle flash/blast. They ordered some reduced-load 10mm ammunition, and it seemed to alleviate those problems. Lessons learned, Smith & Wesson and Winchester went to work on the '10mm short.'

In 1990, the resultant 40 S&W cartridge was introduced at the SHOT Show. Glock was working on the G20 and G21 at this time, but

▼ Without a doubt the most popular law enforcement pistol Glock produces, the 40-caliber model G22. *Glock photo*

▲ The Glock 17L (9mm) and 24 (40-cal.), Glock's competition pistols. *Glock photo*

▼ The Mini-Glock! The most compact of the Glock line. Shown is the G26 (9mm), also available is the G27 (40-cal.) and the G33 (357 SIG). This is a favorite line for police back-up guns. *Glock photo*

▲ The All-American Glock, the 45 ACP G21. Designed for the American market. This is the largest-frame pistol that Glock produces. The G20, 10mm caliber pistol shares this frame. *Glock photo*

Mr. Glock wasted no time developing a Glock pistol to fire this new round, and halted production of the new G20 and G21. Based on his famous G17, the new Model 22 was chambered for the new 40-caliber cartridge and beat the Smith & Wesson 4006 to the market. The first 40-caliber handgun to enter law-enforcement service was the Glock 22, by far the most popular duty pistol that Glock produces.

Soon to be released was the Model 23, basically a G19 chambered for the 40-caliber round. Many firearm experts claim the G23 is the ultimate weapon to be carried concealed. It has excellent size, weight—and carries 13 rounds of potent 40-caliber ammunition. There is a difference in the 9mm Glocks versus all other calibers. There is a second pin to secure the locking block into place, giving additional strength. Later on, the Model 27, dimensionally the same as the G26 but chambered for the

40-caliber cartridge, was released. The G27 carries 9 rounds in the magazine. For the competitors who liked the G17L, the 40-caliber G24 was released.

The 10mm Glocks

The Glock 20 was the first of Glock's large-frame pistols. At the time, around 1989, there were very few pistols that chambered the powerful 10mm round. Other manufacturers included Colt and Smith & Wesson. The G20 weighed an incredible 26.35 ounces and carried 15 10mm rounds in the magazine. Later, the G29 was introduced. This was a compact version of the G20; the difference being that the barrel of the G20 was approximately 4-1/2 inches and the compact G29 was approximately 3-3/4 inches. The G29 had a shorter grip with a magazine capacity of 10 rounds. These are—without doubt—the least popular of all Glock

models due to the excessive recoil and the high cost of ammunition.

The 45-Caliber Glocks

Without a doubt, the All-American Glock! During the development stages of the G20, there was a great deal of interest in the old 45 ACP cartridge in the United States. The large frame used on the G20 was large enough, so the G21 was born—merely a G20 chambering the 45 Auto cartridge. The G21 had an incredible 13-round magazine and proved to be one of the mildest recoiling of all 45-caliber pistols. Due to the high strength of the pistol, there was no problem firing the high-pressure +P ammunition. With the success of the G21, demand arose for a compact version. The G30 was introduced. Both the G29 and the G30 were introduced at the same time and are built on the same frame. The G30, even with a

Glock's compact 45, the G30. Similar in size to the compact frame, this is a fistful of power carrying 11 rounds of potent 45 Auto ammunition. Glock also offers the G29, which is the identical gun firing the 10mm cartridge. *Glock photo*

Glock's newest Practical/Tactical model 34 (9mm) and G35 (40-cal.). This pistol offers a barrel length between the competition and full-size models, giving extra velocity in a still manageable size. Note the extended slide stop. *Glock photo*

shorter grip, holds 10 rounds and weighs approximately 24 ounces empty and 30 ounces fully loaded. Some, with smaller hands, have difficulty with the large grip. The latest creation by Gaston Glock solved this problem for people with smaller hands: the ultra-compact G36. The G36 is basically a slimmer (the slide is .14-inch narrower) version of the G30. It has a single-column 6-round magazine and weighs approximately 20 ounces empty; approximately 27 ounces fully loaded.

The 35-Caliber Glocks

The 357 SIG is basically a 40 S&W cartridge case necked down to hold a 9mm bullet. In theory, it will deliver ballistics comparable to the 357 Magnum. The new round was developed for the SIG Sauer model P229 and was a joint venture between SIGARMS and the Federal Cartridge Company.

Glock introduced its Models 31, 32, and 33. The G31 was, for all intents and purposes, a G22 with a new barrel. Since the cartridge case is based on the 40 S&W, there was no need to change the frame, slide, or magazine. All that was needed was a barrel, a pretty easy modification. The magazine held 15 rounds of the potent 357 ammunition. Interesting to note, Glock will sell 357 barrels to G22 owners; however, they must have a new-style frame. That is the frame with the finger grooves and accessory rail. The reason is that the new frames are reinforced to deal

Exploded Drawing GLOCK 17

COMPONENT PARTS OF GLOCK PISTOLS

1	Slide	20	Slide lock spring
2	Barrel	21	Slide lock
3	Recoil spring assembly	22	Locking block
4		23	Trigger mechanism housing with ejector
5	Firing pin	24	Connector
6	Spacer sleeve	25	Trigger spring
7	Firing pin spring	25a	New York Trigger Spring 1
8	Spring cups	25b	New York Trigger Spring 2
9	Firing pin safety	26	Trigger with trigger bar
10	Firing pin safety spring	27	Slide stop lever
11	Extractor	28	Trigger pin
12	Extractor depressor plunger	29	Trigger housing pin
13	Extractor depressor plunger spring	30	Follower
14	Spring-loaded bearing	31	Magazine spring
15	Slide cover plate	32	Magazine floor plate
16	Rear sight	32a	Magazine insert
16a	Front sight	33	Magazine tube
17	Receiver	34	Locking block pin:
18	Magazine catch spring		(not for: G 17/17C/17L/19/19C/25)
19	Magazine catch		

Exploded drawing of Glock pistols. Only 33 to 34 parts! *Glock photo*

with the stronger recoil and impact caused by the 357 cartridge. Glock does not recommend the barrels be installed in older guns. The G32 was a 357 version of the G23, and the G33 is the 357 version of the mini G27.

The 357-caliber has not been at all as popular as the other calibers. However, it has slowly gained the interest of law enforcement as well as the shooting community. The New Mexico State Police issue the Glock 31 as its standard sidearm. Ammunition is now available at low cost, and that will certainly boost its popularity.

The 380Auto (9x17, 9mm Kurz) Glocks

The unheard-of Glocks— Most people have not heard of the G25 and G28, and for good reason. These 380 ACP pistols are not imported into the United States because they do not meet the BATF's point system requirements for importation. The G25 is based on the G19, and the G28 is based on the G26. These pistols tend to be popular in countries where citizens are not permitted to own the 9mm military chambering.

Regardless of your cartridge preference, Glock produces pistols in all of the most popular automatic pistol chamberings. They have become the law enforcement's weapon of choice and are very popular with civilian shooters, competitive shooters, and for self-defense. Their simplicity, reliability, and durability have earned them their excellent reputation. The only question is, *"What's next???"* Glock has full-, medium-, and compact-size pistols in all calibers. I can hardly wait! •

Compact 9mm Pistols

Your Best Bet For Concealed Carry?

By Paul Scarlata

Photos by: James Walters & Butch Simpson

THE LAST DECADE and a half has seen momentous changes in the American handgun market. And two of the more notable have been the mass change to autoloading pistols and the growing popularity of small, lightweight handguns.

The first of these is generally attributed to the U.S. Army's adoption of the 9mm M9 Beretta pistol and the subsequent realization, by both police agencies and civilian shooters, of the advantages provided by the self-loading pistol. The latter was aided by gun companies producing (*finally?*) pistols that were reliable with the new breed of high performance, expanding-bullet defensive ammo that was being developed by ammunition makers. The growing market for small handguns was a result of a large number of states passing "*Shall Issue*" laws that made it easier for law-abiding citizens to obtain concealed carry permits.

Ever since the mid-19th century, the most popular type of concealed carry handgun with American police and civilians had been the double-action (DA) snub-nosed revolver. These provided the shooter with a defensive sidearm that combined light weight, compact size, reliability, and simplicity of operation. It is not at all difficult to understand why the snubbie revolver was–and still is–so popular. It begins with the fact that early, compact semi-auto pistols–with few exceptions–incorporated less-than-optimal ergonomics, hard-to-operate controls, finicky functioning, small sights and poor shootability with unimpressive 25, 32 and 380 ACP cartridges. When contrasted to a robust Colt or S&W snubbie chambered for the 38 Special cartridge, it was no contest.

But with the aforementioned growing popularity of semi-autos

Our four 9mm compact pistols included (*clockwise from top, left*) a Glock 26, S&W M908, STI LS-9 and a stainless Kahr 9. All testfiring was done with Cor-Bon's 9x19+P loaded with 115-grain JHP bullets.

and the passage of "*Shall Issue*" laws, it wasn't long before handgun makers realized there was a vast new market out there and set about to capture a share of it. Since the snubbie revolver was so well established, the manufacturers had to develop a self-loading pistol with all the positive attributes of the revolver, plus additional features to make it more attractive to prospective purchasers. Considering what the typical 38-caliber snubbie offered, that was a tall order.

The first generation of so-called "compact" semi-autos consisted of little more than standard pistols with slightly shorter barrels and, in a few cases, shortened grip frames. These early attempts, providing only slight reduction in size and weight, were only moderately successful. Eventually handgun makers began offering purpose-built compact pistols, designed from the ground up for maximum concealment and reliability, chambered for practical cartridges. Of these, I feel the best of the breed are those chambered for the most popular centerfire handgun cartridge in the world - the 9x19mm (*a.k.a. 9mm Luger, 9mm Parabellum, 9mm P*).

Now I'm sure many of you will ask, *"Why the 9x19mm instead of the 40 S&W or the new 357 SIG?"* My answer, which some may scoff at, is simple: the 9x19mm cartridge provides the average person with all the defensive firepower they might need in a compact, light-weight, easy-shooting pistol. The laws of physics are immutable, and they tell us that when you launch a projectile of a certain weight, at a certain velocity from a handgun of a certain mass, a specific level of recoil force will be generated. Firing that same projectile from a lighter handgun will produce greater recoil force. Heavy recoil has a deleterious effect on accuracy, especially with less experienced shooters or for those persons—male and female—of small stature. Since the Second Rule of Defensive Shooting states *"Only those shots that hit the target count,"* we have to ask ourselves: isn't it better to hit with a 9mm than miss with a 45?

Ponder for a moment the reasons for the 38 snubbie's nearly eight decades of popularity. It was capable of doing what needed to be done without undue recoil and muzzle blast and was available in some of the most user-friendly, small-sized handguns to ever to come down the

Handfuls of compact firepower. The STI LS-9 (*left*) and the S&W M908 are slimmer and lighter than most revolvers, making them perfectly suited for concealed carry.

pike. Today's breed of compact 9mm pistols provide the same positive features, plus these additional ones: a flat profile that makes them easier to conceal and carry comfortably; an increase in cartridge capacity of anywhere from two to six rounds; faster and more positive reloading; enhanced recoil control, and—with the proper ammunition—superior on-target performance.

Let us dissect that last statement in detail. Because of the (*mostly undeserved*) "bad press" the 9x19mm cartridge has received over the years, many assume its performance is inferior to rounds such as the 38 Special, 357 Magnum, 40 S&W and 45 ACP. There

are those who will tell you the 38 Spl.+P is a perfectly adequate defensive cartridge and, in the next breath, condemn the 9mm with equal conviction. An examination of the ballistics chart in any ammunition company's catalog will show that even standard velocity 115- and 124-grain 9x19mm loads, when loaded with expanding-type bullets, deliver muzzle energy superior to the 38 Spl.+P loaded with 110-, 125-, 130- and 158-grain bullets. And the difference is even greater when 9mm+P or +P+ loads are included in the equation.

According to the detailed studies of Evan Marshall and Ed Sanow, most 9mm loads with expanding bullets of 115 to 124 grains have one-shot stopping percentages ranging from 81 percent to 93 percent. In fact, several higher-end 9mm loads closely approximate the performance of the more popular 40 S&W and 45 ACP cartridges. These same studies show that even the best 38 Special +P and +P+ loads barely approach lower-end 9mm performance when fired from 4-inch barrels and, when fired from a 2-inch barrel, the 38 Special performance is reduced even further. I believe that with modern, high-performance ammunition, the compact 9mn pistol is clearly capable of doing everything required of a defensive-type handgun—if the shooter does his part.

The four 9x19mm pistols I choose to evaluate for this report share certain features: compact dimensions, light weight, excellent ergonomics, practical sights and easy-to-use controls. But each possesses unique traits that set it apart from the others. The first of our quartet, the

Two of the biggest advantages compact 9mm pistols have over the 38 or 357 snubbie revolvers are their higher capacity (seven to ten rounds) magazines and faster, fumble-free reloading.

Despite their small size, all four pistols displayed excellent recoil control with the fast-stepping Cor-Bon ammunition. Here I fire the Glock 26.

Glock 26, displays those properties that have made the Austrian pistol so famous: polymer frame and magazine, Tenifer finish, squared-off profile and Safe-Action trigger. S&W's **Model 908** has, except for it's eight-round magazine, many of those features connected with the traditional 'Wondernine': a slide-mounted decocker/safety lever, alloy frame paired with a steel slide and a selective DA/SA trigger mechanism. Equally well known is the **Kahr 9**, a relatively new all-steel design whose double-action-only (DAO) trigger is regarded by some as the smoothest on the market. Lastly, the **STI LS-9** provides fans of the single-action 1911-type pistol with today's smallest, purpose-built compact with all the desired features.

So that our four test pistols could be compared fairly, all test firing was conducted with Cor-Bon's 9mm 115-grain +P ammunition. Marshall and Sanow rate this load, whose JHP bullet travels at a rated velocity of 1350 fps for 463 ft/lbs of energy (fpe) at the muzzle, at 90 percent.

Obtaining the able assistance of my friend Butch Simpson, we took advantage of a cool August morning (*a rare occurrence in North Carolina!*) to run out to our gun club to put these little 9mm pistols through their paces. To see if the Cor-Bon

ammo lived up to the factory's claims, we began by chronographing it from each of our test pistols. For comparison we fired some 357 Magnum 110- and 125-grain

While two of the shots I fired with the DAO Kahr 9 mysteriously (?) wandered out into the C and D zones, the rest of my rounds found their way to the proper regions of the target's anatomy.

loads in addition to some 38 Special 125-grain +P ammunition out of a 3-inch S&W M65 revolver. These results, charted nearby, show that when loaded with the Cor-Bon +P ammunition and despite their short barrels, our quartet showed a substantial improvement over the 38 Special+P load, were superior to the 110-grain 357 Magnum–and were closer than I would have imagined to the 125-grain 357 Magnum!

OK, so much for the scientific stuff–pistols of this class are intended as short-range, defensive weapons so we decided to forego the traditional accuracy testing and proceed instead with some off-hand exercises on IPSC targets set out at a distance of seven yards. Needing holsters for this portion of

our test firing, I had earlier contacted Alessi Holsters, M/D Enterprises and Gould & Goodrich–who kindly supplied a selection of their products suitable for each handgun. All four holsters provided comfortable carriage and snag-free presentations and held the pistols high on the belt and close to the body for easy concealment under light vests. As is my usual practice, Simpson and I ran each pistol through the following drills:

1. Draw the pistol; fire six rounds* rapid fire – 'head' shots only.

2. Draw the pistol; perform three sets of rapid-fire 'double taps.'

3. Drill #2 was repeated, firing the pistol one-handed.

4. Draw the pistol; fire six rounds as fast as we could obtain a 'flash' sight picture.

because of varying magazine capacities, each string of fire was limited to six rounds.

After this expenditure of 9mm ammunition you are no doubt wondering about our impressions of the four pistols? Well, all four displayed admirable reliability — in fact we did not experience a single misfire or failure to feed, eject or cycle with any of them. That such reliability nowadays appears to be the norm speaks volumes for today's handgun and ammunition makers. Thanks in great part to the low-recoiling 9x19mm cartridge, all four provided excellent recoil control, fast follow-up shots and accuracy that made them a pleasure to shoot; our test firing ended with all four targets having their higher scoring zones full of tight groups of 0.356-inch holes.

While I have long been an advocate of the 38 Special revolver I must admit these tests were a bit of an eye-opener for me. It is quite evident

Smaller yet! When loaded with high-performance 9mm+P ammunition, pistols such as the Glock 26 and Kahr 9 can equal the stopping power of a 357 Magnum revolver with less recoil and muzzle flash. Truly user-friendly handguns!

Lou Alessi supplied this holster for the little STI LS-9. When paired with well-designed holsters such as these, lightweight compact 9mm pistols may well be the most practical handguns for daily concealed carry.

Our Kahr 9 found a good home in another Gould & Goodrich product, the 805 Standout holster. Their plastic-lined belt held the pistol close to the body and high on the waist.

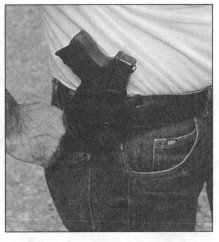

Carrying any of these lightweight 9mm pistols proved a pure pleasure. M/D Enterprises' BS-2 holster was a perfect match for the Glock 26.

Chronograph Results

Ammunition	Model	Velocity (fps)*	Energy (fpe)**
Cor-Bon 9mm+P	Glock 26	1280	410
	S&W 908	1271	404
	STI LS-9	1283	412
	Kahr 9	1267	392
38 Spl+P 125 gr.	S&W M65	956	226
357 Mag 110 gr.	"	1183	350
357 Mag 125 gr.	"	1308	479

* Average of five rounds fired across a Chrony Model-F1 set 15 feet from muzzle.
** Formula 1/2 MV2

Specifications

	Glock 26	S&W Model 908
Chambering	9x19mm	9x19mm
Overall length	6.3"	6 13/16"
Barrel length	3.5"	3.5"
Width (slide)	1.2"	0.92"
Weight (unloaded)	21-3/4 oz.	26 oz.
Construction	steel slide/polymer frame	steel slide/alloy frame
Trigger	Safe Action	selective DA/SA
Magazine	10 rds.	8 rds.
Grips	polymer	Xenoy
Sights front:	white dot	white dot
rear:	white outline	Novak w/dots

	STI LS-9	Kahr 9
Chambering	9x19mm	9x19mm
Overall length	7"	6"
Barrel length	3.4"	3.5"
Width (slide)	0.765"	0.9"
Weight (unloaded)	28 oz.	25 oz.
Construction	all steel	all steel
Trigger	Single action	Double action only
Magazine	7 rds.	7 rds.
Grips	Rosewood	soft polymer
Sights front:	blade	white dot
rear:	Novak low mount	white bar

that the modern compact 9mm pistol offers an excellent combination of shootability, accuracy, rapid reloading, soft recoil and concealability with the enhanced on-target performance of 9mm+P ammunition. There is little doubt in my mind that, under certain circumstances, they may be a much more practical choice than the traditional 38 Special snubbie revolver. And it is comforting to realize that these handy little 9mm pistols don't give up very much to the 357 Magnum snubbie, with its heavy recoil and muzzle flash. This latter point makes them especially suitable for new shooters, those who might have problems handling recoil, women, and shooters of smaller stature. No matter how you look them - they make a lot of sense! •

For further information:

Glock, Inc. - PO Box 369, Smyrna, GA 30081. Tel. 770-432-1202.

Kahr Arms - PO Box 220, Blauvelt, NY 10913. Tel. 914-353-5996.

Smith & Wesson - 2100 Roosevelt Ave., Springfield, MA 01102. Tel. 413-781-8300.

STI International - 114 Halmar Cove, Georgetown, TX 87628. Tel. 800-959-8201.

Alessi Holsters - 2465 Niagra Falls Blvd., Amherst, NY 14228. Tel. 716-691-5615.

Cor-Bon Ammunition - 1311 Industry Rd., Sturgis, SD 57785. Tel. 800-6CORBON.

Gould & Goodrich - 709 E. McNeil St., Lillington, NC 27546. Tel. 910-893-2071.

M/D Enterprises - PO Box 440534, Laredo, TX 78044. Tel. 956-724-4892.

ALL DAY CARRY COMFORT

*Can you carry a full-size combat handgun and its accessories **all** day, **every** day? Sure. Someone who has done so for more than twenty years tells you how.*

by Massad Ayoob

AS I SIT here writing this, there's a Glock 22 on my hip, a full-size service pistol loaded with 16 rounds of Black Hills EXP 165-grain 40 S&W ammunition. It rides in a Mitch Rosen belt scabbard, backed up by two more pre-ban magazines of the same ammo for a total of 46 immediately-available rounds. The mags are in a Safariland synthetic double pouch. Both holster and mag pouch are attached to a dress gunbelt crafted of sharkskin by Rosen.

I don't notice them any more than you notice your pager or belt-mounted cell phone. There are two reasons for this. One is adaptation. The other is careful selection.

Why carry the gun constantly? For the same reason as the pager or the cell phone. For the same reason as a wallet. For the same reason as a watch. For the same reason I always have a flashlight on my person.

You have the pager because someone might need you, even when it's inconvenient for you. You have the cell phone for that reason, and because you might need to reach out to someone unexpectedly. Plans may change, and you may have to drive a car or pay for something when you didn't plan to, and that's why the wallet with the ID and the driver's license and the money and the charge cards should always be with you. On a day off, or a vacation, not wearing the watch is kind of making a statement: "*I don't have to be somewhere at any particular time.*" Even so, we find ourselves keeping a timepiece available because we like some order in our lives, and because we never know when plans will change and hours or minutes - even seconds - might count.

Ever leave home during daytime, planning to be back early and find yourself out after dark? Me, too. Ever have the lights go out unexpectedly? Me, too. Therefore, the constantly carried small flashlight.

Similarly, it can happen that on a day when you did not think you would be involved in a violent, life-threatening confrontation, you will unexpectedly need the where-withal to survive one.

When such days come, we don't have time to go home for our bankbook or our hard-wired phone or our big battery lanterns or our shotguns or AR-15s. We have only what is on our person, immediately available. This is why we carry a wallet, not a little coin purse. Why we have the cell phone, not a quarter or two to activate a pay phone that might or might not be available. Why we have a flashlight, not a book of matches. And, of course, it's why we want to have a handgun that is up to the task of managing a

Today's FBI agents get the choice of a compact Glock 23 or a full-size Glock 22 like this one. Many opt for the latter, knowing they can still conceal it comfortably and well, and shoot the bigger gun a little better under stress.

life-threatening encounter once we realize that, unavoidably, guns are about to start going off.

Now that we have the "why" nailed down, let's talk about the "how."

The Three Key Factors

Attaching a few pounds of stuff to your body that your body isn't used to carrying is going to feel unnatural at first. To make it work, and to make it work without people realizing that you're carrying it, three things have to be dealt with.

First, there's the matter of *body mechanics*. The weight has to be distributed in such a way that it does not cause long-term discomfort, or even physical problems. Police officers have been known to put in for disability because the carrying of the gun and its accompanying duty belt caused them everything from back problems to nerve compression-related disorders. I know people who have been ordered by their doctors to give up wearing ankle holsters because these concealment rigs were interfering with the blood circulation in their lower limbs.

Second, we have to consider *getting accustomed to the gun*. It's no trick to come up with "gunleather" that will distribute the weight and make all-day, every-day carry a doable task. But it's not something we're used to, and there's going to

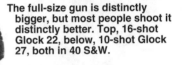

have to be an acclimatization period.

Finally, there is the *discreet concealability* factor. When I'm around other police officers or shooting school students or fellow handgun match competitors, I don't need to wear clothing that conceals my gun. When I'm in police uniform, it doesn't matter, either. Indeed, there are those who would assume that if I was in police uniform and wasn't carrying a gun, that I had breached the rules so horribly that I had been officially disarmed and put on that dreaded list of distrusted officials that

The full-size gun is distinctly bigger, but most people shoot it distinctly better. Top, 16-shot Glock 22, below, 10-shot Glock 27, both in 40 S&W.

NYPD street cops dubbed "the rubber gun squad." But there are times when you and I alike choose to be armed in an environment where most that saw us would panic if they knew we were carrying what they perceived as a "deadly weapon." This means covering garments, and this in turn brings into play some serious concerns about factors ranging from physical comfort to obvious lack of conformity with a certain "dress code norm."

Body Mechanics

As both a young armed citizen and a young cop, I was like most people who need to carry concealed handguns: I put it on when I thought I needed it, and took it off as soon as I didn't. I rarely carried spare ammunition. I would put on a 2-inch barrel small-frame revolver loaded with five or six shots and consider myself armed and ready.

By the time I was 25 I was past that. I was now a police firearms instructor who was actively researching gunfights: both those that involved on- and off-duty cops and those that had befallen armed citizens. I had already learned that (*a*) if you needed a gun, you needed the most powerful, straight-shooting gun you could possibly have accessible, and (*b*) it would be an awfully good idea to have spare ammunition. I was soon to learn that (*c*) it would also be a damn good idea to have a spare gun where you could reach it immediately, too.

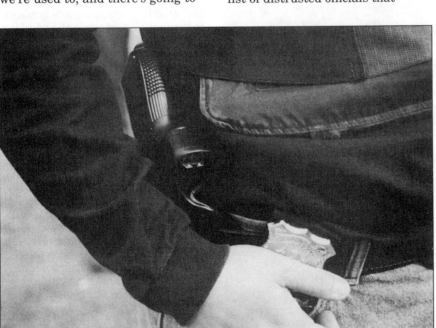

This streetwise NYPD officer carries his uniform duty weapon, a Glock 19, off duty in plainclothes as well.

learned the hard way that cheap holsters that attached to your belt with something resembling the clip of an eyeglass case wouldn't stay attached under such circumstances, either.

I learned that "gunleather" was a system thing. The best gun in a floppy *El Cheapo* holster would hang out from your belt, becoming obvious to anyone near you. I began investing in top-quality, best-design concealment leather. I then learned that a top-quality gun and its top-quality holster were close to worthless if both were attached to a cheap, thin, flimsy belt that would let the whole holster/gun package flop out away from the body. This not only announced to the world that you were carrying a 45, but the outboard weight of the sagging gun was distinctly uncomfortable and it

Wearing a blazer, it is not apparent that Ayoob is wearing…

…not only a full-size Glock 22, but two spare 15-round mags in a Safariland carrier…

I began carrying a full-size Colt Government Model 45 auto. I had worn the same thing as a teenage kid in my dad's jewelry store. Because it was an environment at fairly high risk of armed robbery, the big automatic didn't feel heavy at all. However, as soon as I left the shop I took it off… back then. Not anymore. I now carried all the time when I was out and about, though as soon as I got home I would take the gun off.

I learned that a gun loose in the waistband, carried "Mexican style," was fine so long as you didn't have to run or perform any other sort of strenuous activity. At that point, the gun was at great risk of falling out. I also

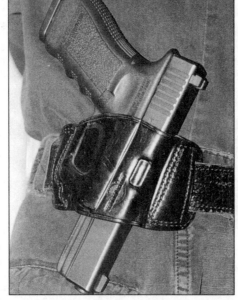

…in a Mitch Rosen belt slide holster, which rides in perfect comfort with discreet concealmen.

slowed the draw to boot, because the gun would stay inside the holster for as long as the holster was attached to the flexible, floppy belt.

Even a good gun in a good holster on a good belt would be noticeable and have a deleterious effect on comfort if all the weight was on one side. As time went on, I discovered that on a concealable dress gunbelt, just as on a police duty belt, the weight had to be balanced. Carrying spare magazines on the opposite side actually seemed to offset the load of the gun itself, and rather than increasing the weight and pull at the hips and on the lumbar spine, it seemed to balance everything. It improved, rather than hurt, the comfort factor.

Lessons of Body Mechanics: A good gun in bad "gunleather" is like an expensive Volvo or Mercedes shod with two-ply retread tires. You thought you had bought the expensive thing to enhance the safety of you and yours, but by shortchanging yourself on the accoutrements, you actually lowered the safety factor. A Chevy with heavy-duty shocks and the best tires is a more roadworthy vehicle than a Volvo or Mercedes with the cheap tires and feeble shocks. Similarly, a bargain-priced second-hand 38 or 357 revolver traded in by a police department and carried in a well-selected top-quality belt/holster combo will get you through the ultimate quick draw contest more safely than a $3,000 Kustom Kombat Special carried in a 'chickenhide' holster on a belt whose institutional memory is the words *"Attention, K-Mart Shoppers."*

The weight of the gun and its accessories must be distributed. The best dress gunbelts will conform to the body, often being seen to have an "orthopedic" curve when laid flat. The gentle, subtle "U"-shape of that curve helps to flare out the lower edge of the belt so it rides flat against the body. The sharp lower edge of a too-straight, too-rigid gunbelt will dig into the hips and the buttocks and turn what should be the peace of mind of the on-board defensive weapon into something close to torture. My friend Clint Smith has been quoted as saying, "Carrying a gun should be comforting, not comfortable." This comes from a seasoned professional who carries a full size Les Baer 45 auto on his hip all day, every day. But take it from whence it comes: Clint Smith carries that professional gun in a professional's leather, and that's why he can wear it comfortably from wake-up to lights-out, along with its spare magazine.

Habituating to the Gun

Guys and gals, remember when you were a youngster and first started carrying a wallet or purse. You felt like a big wallet or purse with a little kid attached. But soon, it became a part of you... and, eventually, the day came when if you *weren't* carrying your wallet or purse, you felt as if something was missing.

It is *exactly* the same way when you carry a gun. At first, you feel like a huge firearm with a small human being attached. But soon, you get used to it. And, inevitably, the day will come when you are acutely aware of its absence when you are someplace where you can't carry it.

Consider the inside the waistband (IWB) holster. Two things struck you when you tried one for the first time. *One*: "This really hides *way* better than a regular belt holster! My concealing garment can come all the way up to the bottom edge of my belt and not reveal that I'm carrying a full size handgun!" *Two*: "This damn thing is *uncomfortable!*"

As my teenage daughter might say, "Well, duh!" You bought the pants to fit *you* around the waist. Now, that same waistband contains you, *and* the gun, and the thickness of the holster that secures that gun in place, and maybe also a spare magazine in its own IWB pouch. Getting crowded? Sure.

Give the IWB concept a chance. For one week, wear a good IWB holster as it should be worn. Just loosen your belt a notch or two, and unbutton the top fastener of the pants. The Fashion Police probably won't notice. But, all of a sudden, you'll find the IWB carry *way* more comfortable than it used to seem. This is Nature's way of telling you that the concept will work for you. All you need to do is let the pants out an inch or two at the waist, or start buying lower body garments that are about two inches larger than you really need in the waist measurement.

A hidden benefit of this is that if you *don't* now carry a gun inside the waistband, that garment will be too big and will start slipping. This encourages you to carry the gun to protect yourself and your family–a good thing.

The two holsters I designed, the LFI Concealment Rig from Ted Blocker Holsters and the ARG (Ayoob Rear Guard) originally produced by Mitch Rosen, are both IWBs. Why? Because the design parameters were all-day, comfort-

Sure, it's easy for gun-trained attorney Penny Dean to carry this baby Glock 27 in her stylish Galco gun purse...

... but that same purse can just as easily carry a full-size Glock 22, with 6 more shots and better hit potential under stress.

able concealed-carry under light concealing garments, with full-size combat handguns. These are still my favorite concealed-carry holsters, for one obvious reason: I designed them for myself. It turns out that what works for me works for a lot of other people who feel the need for constant, comfortable, discreet wear of a full-size sidearm of the type Jeff Cooper called the "fighting handgun."

So, why am I wearing a belt scabbard instead of an IWB as I write this? Because I am getting old and fat, and as I pork up, I discover that there is less room in even the two-inch oversized waistband than there used to be. Could this happen to any of us? Well, let's just say that it may be too late for me, but you still have time to save yourself...

Seriously, when the "love handles" start rolling over the outer edges of the belt, they get in the way of IWB carry. If that is the case, what we need is a belt scabbard that holds the gun tight to our body. As a general rule, the wider *apart the belt slots of the holster*

The choice of size is yours. These Glock 40s are, from top, full-size 16-shot G22, compact 14-shot G-23, subcompact 10-shot G27.

full-size handgun will not work out the concealment thing unless you go with a fanny pack. Form-fitting European-style suits like the Armani aren't conducive to concealed carry, either. Fortunately, there are other options no matter what your dress code.

What tailors call the "American sack suit," the timeless Brooks Brothers or Hart, Schaffner and Marx style, can work with a full-size handgun. You want to bring the holstered gun to an understanding clothier when you get fitted for the suit, however. Allow two more inches in the waist for an inside-the-pants holster. You might want the "body" of the suit jacket to be one size large to allow for fabric drape over the holstered gun. The same is true with slacks and blazers.

If a more casual look is an option, men's fashions have never been better adapted to concealed carry. Straight leg cords, BDUs, and even jeans with "relaxed fit" and boot-cut cuffs are in style. In addition to allowing better concealment with pocket holsters and ankle holsters, they are complemented by looser shirts and by Banana Republic-style photographers' vests. Walt Brewer's Concealed Carry Clothiers vest and

made for gun carriers. Loose fitting multi-pocket vests and BDUs are popular fashions because they conceal belt-mounted cell phones and pagers. What hides a cell phone can hide a service-size pistol or revolver.

The Bottom Line

If you shoot the small gun as well as the big one, fast and under stress – hell, carry the small one! But you know something? Most people don't.

My baby Glock shoots a little tighter at 25 yards than my full-size Glock when I shoot carefully for groups, with all the time in the world. It's an interesting phenomenon that has to do with proportionally more rigid barrels and slides in the shorter guns, and proportionally stronger recoil springs that guarantee holding the gun in battery longer until after the bullet has left the muzzle. The same is true of the slim little S&W Model 39 9mm I carried in hot weather before I gave it to my daughter as a carry gun, when I compared it to my much bigger and heavier S&W Model 5906 service pistol in the same caliber.

But, you know what? While there were days when I carried the small gun and might not have had anything at all because under the circumstances I couldn't conceal a big gun, any time I thought I was going into something dangerous I made damn sure I had a full-size fighting pistol if one was available. The bigger gun holds more rounds, the bigger gun is generally more controllable, and as a rule, if you do have to fire fast under pressure, the full-size gun will deliver the shots closer and faster than the convenient little baby gun. It's not a pure accuracy thing; it's an ergonomics thing.

The decision is yours to make. The purpose of this article is to remind the reader that if you want the maximum potential a full-size defensive handgun can give, it's not impossible to carry one all day, every day, in discreet and comfortable concealment.

The option is there for you. There's a price to pay in equipment selection, in wardrobe—sometimes even in comfort—but the option is there. Empowerment is about options. Whether you choose to carry a full-size pistol, or a compact, or none at all, it's good to know that you had the choice, and that you made a fully informed decision. ●

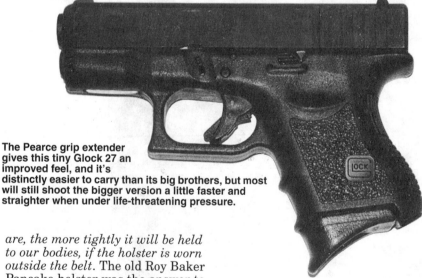

The Pearce grip extender gives this tiny Glock 27 an improved feel, and it's distinctly easier to carry than its big brothers, but most will still shoot the bigger version a little faster and straighter when under life-threatening pressure.

are, the more tightly it will be held to our bodies, if the holster is worn outside the belt. The old Roy Baker Pancake holster was the answer to an overweight person's dream, and the principle holds true with such contemporary holsters as the Bianchi Black Widow and any of the belt-slides such as the one I'm wearing as I type these words.

Wardrobe Factors

If you like to wear skin-tight shirts and go coatless, you and the

Blackie Collins' Toters ™ jeans are both expressly designed for pistol packing. In addition to the specially reinforced pockets, both are designed to help conceal big handguns in IWB holsters or tight-riding belt scabbards.

Dockers set the pace with blousy sport slacks. It's as if they were

'Spring'
Your Handgun for Maximum Efficiency

by Bob Campbell

There are a lot of springs in this gun: recoil spring, slide lock spring, magazine release spring, magazine spring, firing pin spring, hammer (main) spring. These springs are all coil springs. If we included flat springs we might count the extractor!

THE 'SPRINGS' MOST of us know about are the ones on our vehicle. We know that properly-sprung vehicles ride better, and heavily-sprung cars run better on rough roads. We know to replace shocks and struts when they need to be replaced. Handgun springs are no different, so let's take a hard look at pistol springs.

This discussion was spurred by a conversation with a man who once served as a armorer (*gun-smith*) at a military proving ground. He experienced backpressure in suppressed (*silenced*) handguns that led to increased wear; even broken locking wedges. Experimentation with different spring weights and ammunition solved the problem.

This insight applied to my own areas of concern, albeit on a smaller scale. A problem faced by those who modify handguns is the conflict between long- and short-slide handguns, differences in slide mass, compensators, hotter ammunition–and other 'off spec' modifications. Perfect function is the goal. An autoloading handgun must feed, chamber, fire, and eject a wide range of ammunition. It should not batter itself during the firing of many thousand rounds of ammunition.

I find the deviation in allowable ammunition parameters is not as extreme as some think, although it exists. The result is 'battering' at the high end of the spectrum; 'short cycles' at the other. Pistols that depart from the standard (*original type*) often show malfunctions and we must 'tweak' or tune them for reliability.

Understanding the problem is not difficult, and there are only two options–we must increase or reduce the speed of the slide. There are several ideas on the subject, and theories abound. One idea is that heavy slides produce more momentum and, hence, more recoil energy. Short slides, it is said, have less mass and therefore less recoil energy. This can be true if the short slide is properly 'sprung' with a heavy spring that prevents choppy motion. Subjectively, at least, I do not find Commander-length 1911 pistols easier to fire comfortably.

An element in the equation is the use of hotter-than-normal hand-loads and factory +P ammunition. I prefer a gun that does not rattle for ten minutes after firing, but appear to be in the minority. A few friends, pistol competitors, got into trouble with cycle reliability even though they used what they thought were sedate loadings. Pistol powders with slower burning rates than the old standbys (231, Bullseye, and Unique) have become popular.

These slower powders increase lock time, launch the bullet with less of a jolt than faster-burning powders, and produce better accuracy. From a machine rest the difference is noticeable at fifty yards and beyond, I am told. When working with these loads–and I don't have enough experience to comment on them–it is important to *function-test* the gun for the load chosen. Light loads will not properly cycle the gun; heavy loads will batter the gun–or perhaps increase slide velocity to the point where the magazine cannot feed properly (*magazine springs are important, too*).

Powders differ but to say one is better than the other is to say chocolate is better than butter. Each is useful. The heavy slow-burning powders used in magnum revolvers are not suited for autopistol use, although the 10mm and 357 SIG do allow the use of relatively slow-burning powders.

A tragic example of poor powder selection was seen in the Army's early M-16 program. All original testing of the AR-series rifle was done with IMR powder. Even after the Army switched to ball powder-loaded ammunition, Colt tested the rifles with IMR-loaded ammunition. Ball powder produced higher gas pressure and cases stuck in the chamber, as increased pressures did not allow time for the case to 'unstick' for extraction. A number of cures–including heavier buffers and a stronger extractor–were adopted, although the rifle still ran perfectly if fired with IMR-loaded ammunition. Subsequently, Congress found the Army's ammunition program 'bordered on criminal negligence.' Colt rushed to find a solution in light of the Army's refusal to replace stores of ball powder-loaded cartridges. Colt engineers designed a heavier buffer system that had a plurality of internal masses operating in a delayed sequence, opposing the bolt's aggressive rebound. This not only slowed cycling but gave time for chamber pressures to subside, solving the stuck case problem. A Colt designer also fabricated a rubber plug that increased spring forces in the extractor. This was a life-saving stopgap, field-installable.

Experienced gunsmiths later applied this 'operation-assist'

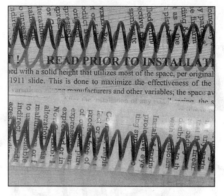

Don't lose the spring packaging–it is difficult to tell one spring from the other without it.

technology to handguns. Full-length guide rods, shock buffers, various recoil reducers and heavy springs were crafted by experienced gunsmiths. I've used a number of special setups over the years, and always had to resist the urge to use a load as hot as I could get away with. In bowling pin matches I tried to take the pin off the table, and in the process discovered that launching 255-grain bullets at 900 fps produces eccentric wear on 1911 parts.

This is when I was first introduced to Wolff springs, and the experience was a good one. 'Snappy' ejection had been slinging empty cases ten feet or more… until I fitted a 22-pound spring to my 1911. Now, the gun functioned normally and recoil was reduced. I never fitted light-duty springs in order to fire light loads–mostly firing hardball, or the equivalent. I quit the bowling pin game a few years before I received a gritty assignment.

As a working cop, I carried a Colt 1911 when possible, although

I was sometimes limited to lesser weapons by administrative fiat. I corresponded with a special agent in Alaska who presented a singular problem. He favored the 1911, but felt that none of the ammunition available gave the performance he needed (*this predates the 45 Super and, I believe, the 45 +P*). He wanted a load that would penetrate the heavy winter clothing often worn by felons in his home state. Protection against large animals was also consideration. Working with a custom loader, we were able to produce a load launching a

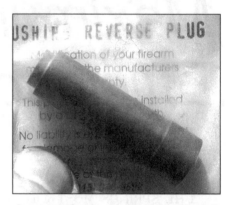

A reverse plug for a full-length guide rod, from Evolution Gun Works, maker of top-quality gear.

250-grain Hornady Extreme Terminal Performance bullet at 938 fps from a five-inch 1911 barrel. There were several false starts, but we were able to apply spring technology to the handgun to make recoil tolerable. Reliability was perfect. A Wilson guide rod, a heavy Wolff spring and Wilson Shok Buff were fitted. The magazines all received Wolff heavy-duty springs. Extraction was not particularly energetic and the gun was reliable with standard hardball loadings.

While the product of bullet weight and velocity is important, bullet weight seems to have more bearing than velocity. A respected gunsmith who services thousands of duty pistols in 9mm Luger tells me that agencies which use the 147-grain 9mm load suffer more wear, especially in locking wedges, than those agencies using high-velocity loads, *including the +P+ loads*. The heavy bullet produces more wear than the 'hotter' round.

I was a bit surprised, but it makes a lot of sense. The first cartridges loaded in 9mm used bullets of 115, 116, 123 and 124 grains.

Small things add up. A premium magazine catch spring makes for a measure of safety.

This Springfield Loaded Model with factory full-length guide rod has proven reliable in action, but is due for spring replacement as it nears 4,000 rounds of ammunition.

115 grains is considered a standard load. Using a 147-grain bullet in the 9mm is similar to using a 270-grain bullet in the 45 ACP. It just doesn't work well. I had to re-examine my ideas on wear. The 9mm +P+ certainly has the muzzle flash and blast, but the heavy-bullet 9mm produced more wear. I recalled the words of my friend the gunsmith. He felt a lighter bullet load in the silenced Beretta would not produce as much wear as the 147-grain 9mm load, in that back-pressure from the heavy bullet load was more severe than from light bullet loads. He realized the accuracy of the 147-grain 9mm is due largely to its long bearing surface. However, he reported excellent results with a special 123-grain subsonic loading.

I looked back on my work with the Colt and the 250-grain loading. This gun, a really nice Series 70 Colt tuned by Teddy Jacobsen, developed a cracked frame after about 600 rounds of the 250-grain loads.

The gun functioned even with the cracked frame, but we chose a fresh Essex frame and transferred and fitted the parts as best we could. The new gun didn't have the crisp trigger the Colt did after Teddy's work but I was a little embarrassed to ask him to redo his work after I broke the frame! This time I went to a 200-grain XTP, a

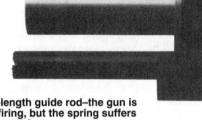

Full-length guide rod–the gun is not firing, but the spring suffers compression.

tough bullet that, if driven faster, expands more and retains penetration. I was able to load the 200-grain XTP to a little over 1150 fps, a load later duplicated by Texas Ammunition. Recoil seemed less and, while I have lost track of my Alaskan correspondent, this load should meet his needs.

Fighting slide momentum is difficult, perhaps impossible. But it can be limited. A 'shok buff' is a simple washer that fits on the recoil spring guide. It is in exactly the right place to absorb some of the battering the gun takes. A properly rated recoil spring is the next requirement. The FBI does not allow 'shok buffs' in bureau-issue pistols because, if not replaced regularly, they could cause a problem as they deteriorate. I'll back up a little on my recommendation of the 'shok buff:' I do like them, but only with a quality recoil spring. They are no substitute for a new-condition spring of proper weight.

An excellent safety precaution in handguns of the 1911 type, which do not incorporate a positive firing pin block, is to use a lightweight firing pin in

combination with a heavy-duty firing pin spring. If the gun will be firing heavy loads a heavy-duty firing pin spring is mandatory to ensure the spring does not take a 'run' and strike the primer before we pull the trigger. Wilson Combat uses this system, reportedly with a shortened firing pin.

While some use full-length guide rods, most gunsmiths feel the gun functions just as well without them. Jim Clark Jr. says they make no difference until really heavy loads are used which "*kink the spring up like a buzz saw chain*."

Recently, I fitted a pair of Accu Match drop-in barrels to two Colt 1911 pistols. One of the barrels required a bit of fitting, not surprising, as 1911s are not the most 'uniform' pistol in existence. One barrel was compensated, and required more fiddling for reliable function. The extra weight on the end of the barrel resulted in taking the link out-of-battery at the wrong time. The link can take battering, and a too-long link will often 'work itself in,' but not always.

Recently, I was asked to examine a malfunctioning 45-caliber 1911 carbine conversion that did not fully chamber the cartridges. The conversion parts involved a

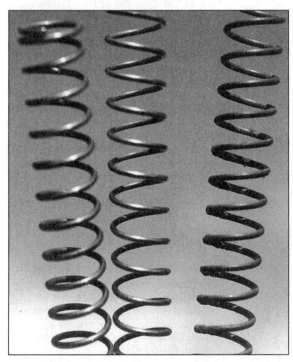

Music wire and alloy springs; a recoil spring (*right*) has succumbed to corrosion.

The 9mm Beretta is reliable with all of these loads: 124 grains/1121 fps; 147 grains/980 fps; 147 grains/1001 fps; 147 grains/978 fps and 115 grains at 1289 fps. Quality springs work with a variety of ammunition.

16-inch barrel and a shoulder stock. The problems in making the gun work were not insurmountable, although there are issues involved in maintaining reliability with both the long and short barrel. (*A rifle is a rifle and a handgun a handgun.*) In this case the added weight of the long barrel required a stronger recoil spring to bring the slide back after each round was fired. Nothing less than hardball ammunition would prove reliable.

Hanging a compensator on the barrel of a 1911 can adversely affect function. I am not partial to low-profile vents or ports but they are superior, in terms of function, to a compensator.

The life of a recoil spring is not necessarily measured in rounds fired, but rather in 'compressions' that occur each time we load and unload the gun, or dry fire it. Once a year recoil spring replacement in a duty gun is a good practice. For the technically minded, when the spring has lost 0.5-inch of free length from 'new' condition it is time to replace the spring.

Most handgun springs are made of music wire, but some makers manufacture handgun springs from various space-age alloys. One of the more successful is Integrated Systems Management, Incorporated. These alloys are claimed to be more resistant to damage by heat. I have used them extensively with excellent luck. ISMI offers magazine springs for both STI and SVI high-capacity pistols, for both 140mm and 170mm magazines.

Even with long experience using the 1911, it is difficult to identify the exact spring weight needed for a specific load. It is important to keep springs marked, if separated from

Wilson 'shok buff' after 1,100 rounds in a CQB Wilson pistol. Still good as new, for all practical purposes.

their packaging, as they are not always visually different, despite greatly varying spring loading.

The three basic divisions of spring weight are those for light, standard, and heavy loads. If you wish to fire light loads, such as the 185-grain SWC in 45 ACP, the proper spring will allow the gun to function at only 750 fps. Remember, start with a heavier weight than anticipated, and work down to lessen the chances of battering. Frankly, quite a few light spring weights are offered for which I've never had the need.

Standard loadings such as the 230-grain bullet at 830 fps can be handled by standard load springs. Premium springs, such as those offered by Wolff, can handle the specification.

For heavy loads, we wish to avoid 'battering,' or the slide's velocity exceeding the magazine's ability to feed. It is asking a lot for a magazine spring to reliably feed from full compression to almost no compression. More recoil and battering result if we do not arrest the slide's momentum.

Spring Load Specifications for the Colt 1911

Ultra Light Duty: 5, 6, 7, 8, and 9 pounds.

I have never used them. The 22-rimfire Colt conversion units are rated at 14 pounds; remember the slide is often lightweight aluminum, takes a quick run and must snap back quickly.

Reduced Power: 7, 8, 9, 10, 11, 12, 13, 14, and 15 pound.

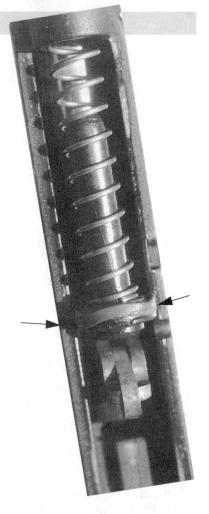

For light target loads such as the 185-grain semi-wadcutter at 750 fps, the 200-grain semi-wadcutter at 800 fps, and 'softball' loads such as a cast 230-grain bullet at 770 fps. All of this follows a logical progression. I have seldom had to go below 11 pounds.

Standard Duty: The factory standard recoil spring for the 1911 is rated at 16 pounds and usually is right on.

Heavy Duty: rated at 17, 18.5, 20, 22, 23, 24 and 26 pounds.

The heaviest I have used is a 22-pound spring with the aforementioned pin loads and 250-grain XTP loads. Function was good. Commanders are supplied with 18-pound springs but light and heavy aftermarket springs run from 12 to 27 pounds. The short slide does take a little more spring for proper function.

When to replace the spring?

There are warning signs that indicate spring replacement is needed. These include an increased ejection distance, improper ejection, light primer strikes, or poor cartridge feeding.

Compact pistols, especially those that use 'spring within a

Government-developed trigger spring for Beretta 92.

This Beretta Elite II has been fitted with heavy-duty Wolff springs for use with +P+ ammunition, also the Wolff trigger module.

EVOLUTION GUN WORKS WORLD CLASS PARTS

BUFF'S

Modification of your firearm may nullify the manufacturer warranty.

This product should be installed by a Qualified Gunsmith.

No liability is expressed or implied for damage or injury which may result from improper installation or use of this product.

(215) 348-9892
4050 B-8 Skyron Drive
Doylestown, PA 18901
FAX (215) 348-1056

Recoil buffers, such as these from EGW, are a good idea.

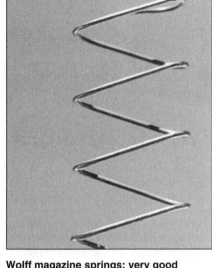

Wolff magazine springs: very good quality; lasts many thousands of compressions.

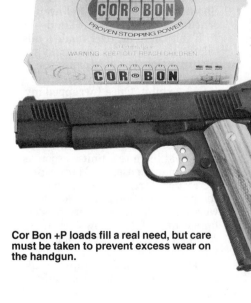

Cor Bon +P loads fill a real need, but care must be taken to prevent excess wear on the handgun.

spring' technology, are brilliant designs that seem to have cured the attendant problems long associated with downsizing. Until recently, I had not met a compact 45 auto that was 100-percent reliable with bullet weights other than 230 grains. The Kimber changed that view, easily digesting 152-grain handloads, 165-grain Federal Personal Defense loads, and Speer +P 200-grain loads. These springs work much harder than those of full-size guns and will need replacing as soon as every 750 rounds, a small price to pay for reliability.

The original compact 45, the Star PD, required replacement of the recoil rod assembly every 500 rounds to ensure reliability.

Think of springs as equivalent to the shocks and springs of your vehicle. They can be adjusted for a harder or softer ride and, when worn, give a rough ride which transfers to other parts. With proper care, the life of the machine – pistol or auto – is extended.

Other springs—

The magazine catch spring can become weak and fail to securely hold the magazine under recoil.

The slide lock spring is an overlooked item that can

weaken and let the slide lock back when we do not wish it to do so. In the case of the Beretta, any gun carried on duty is fitted with a Wolff replacement.

Trigger springs or hammer springs are problematical. They should be replaced with caution. Wolff offers both light 'target' springs and heavy 'duty' springs. An interesting item is the trigger spring developed at the request of the INS for issue and use in Border Patrol Berettas. Absolutely proven in government testing, this trigger addition is coated in rugged NP3 finish. The addition of this unit does indeed add to the smoothness and reliability of the Beretta trigger action. Offered in three weights, I recommend the proven duty weight.

More on magazines—

G. I. magazines have long, straight feed lips that release the cartridge late, allowing it to bump into the ramp and feed. This does not work well with modern jacketed hollowpoint loads, which are shorter. The early-release Wilson magazine has a break in the feed lips and a rounded follower. It works much better.   ●

Sources

Evolution Gun Works
   4050 B 8 Skyron Drive
   Doylestown PA 18901

W. C. Wolff Company
   P O Box 458
   Newton Square PA 19073

Integrated Systems Management, Inc.
   P O Box 204
   7002 West 1000 North
   Carthage IN 46115

More on +P+ use

A Federal agency was very interested in adopting a pistol design that most of us regarded as excellent. It failed in testing after firing less than 3,500 rounds of +P+ 9mm Luger ammunition, but sailed through many proofs with ammunition of lower pressure.

Do different designs react differently to pressure and momentum? Quite possibly this is the case. As time goes by, I am more likely to practice with sedate loads and load the small bore with overpressure loads for serious use. Or simply carry the proven low-pressure big bore with standard ammunition.

Kahr T9

After capturing a big part of the compact pistol market, Kahr Arms has set its sights on something more

by Dave Workman

Some years ago I was wandering down the aisle at the Shooting, Hunting and Outdoor Trade Show in Las Vegas when a fellow stepped out from a small exhibit, introduced himself and offered to show me a new pistol.

That was the first time I'd ever heard of the Kahr semiautomatic, a handsome little 9mm that was simple, tightly built, and felt surprisingly comfortable in my hand. Time went by, there were lots of guns out there to shoot, and in the meantime, Kahr began building a reputation as a reliable compact handgun, the kind a person would buy for concealed carry, or a back-up.

Now and then, at the range someone would show up with a Kahr and invite me to fire a few rounds. I was continually impressed with the quality of these little stainless steel pistols–they seemed almost hand-built. What's more, they shot accurately, and looking at things objectively, what Kahr had was a pistol the size of a typical 380 ACP, but chambered in 9mm, certainly a step up on the power level.

The original K9 Kahr was eventually joined by the MK series, a smaller pistol with shorter grip frame and barrel, but still that same surprising workmanship. Then along came polymer-framed pistols in the P series, and Kahr introduced models chambered in 40 S&W.

So, what could be better than having a lineup of tremendously successful handguns that have been greeted with open arms by an appreciative buying public?

A target pistol. Say *what*?!

Specifications

Model: Kahr T9

Manufacturer: Kahr Arms, 630 Route 303, Blauvelt, NY 10913 (845) 353-7770 / www.kahr.com

Chambering: 9mm

Barrel length: 4 inches

Magazine capacity: 8 rounds

Construction: Stainless steel

Grips: Hogue checkered hardwood

Action: Double action only, striker fired

Sights: Dovetail blade front, MMC adjustable rear

If you're laughing, better bite your lip, because this is one terrific pistol. Called the "T9" (*some might say in keeping with Kahr's tradition of designating their handgun models with a letter and a number that corresponds with the caliber*), this pistol was introduced without much fanfare at the 2002 SHOT Show in Las Vegas, and not even scheduled for release until mid-year.

If this company ever made a mistake in gun building, one might suggest that this was it, because the prototype became a centerpiece of Kahr's exhibit. Once I wrapped my mitts around the gun, I turned to CEO Justin Moon and, as politely as possible, demanded, insisted, cajoled, begged, and pleaded that that I wanted a test unit as soon as was humanly possible. Marketing VP Frank Harris said every one of the pre-production guns – and there were only a handful – were needed for a couple of gun shows, but if he could swing it, I might be able to get a test gun sometime in late March.

"I'll need it ten days, tops, Frank," I distinctly remember promising.

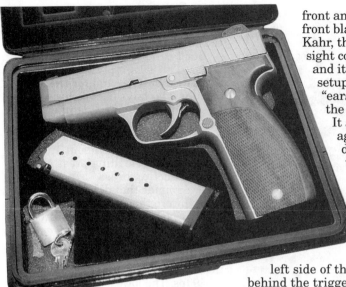

Kahr ships its T9 semi-auto with two magazines and a trigger lock in a padded hard plastic box.

And so I waited. And kept checking via e-mail. And finally, as March was screeching to a halt with some of the worst weather I had seen in weeks, Harris sent me an e-mail that the gun would be in my hands the following day. Good as his word, the Kahr T9 arrived next day at Wade's Bellevue Gun Shop, a top Kahr dealer in western Washington a few blocks from my office.

I rounded up some 9mm ammo from my stores, grabbed my Chrony Delta chronograph, a bunch of Birchwood Shoot-N-C targets and made tracks for the shooting range, in a downpour.

Real Eye-Catcher

Built from stainless steel (*two different stainless steels are used, one for the frame, the other for the slide, to prevent galling on the rails*), the Kahr T9 wears checkered grips from Hogue that are very well-fitted to the pistol. Harris assured me they will be standard on the production gun, and that is good news for anyone who buys one of these pistols, because you won't want to put it down.

My test gun, appropriately serial numbered "PROTO 70," came with two eight-round magazines, a hard plastic box, and a unique trigger lock designed to be mounted behind the trigger and secured with a small padlock.

The barrel measures 4 inches, and overall length just over 7 inches. Finish on the pistol was non-glare satin, and sights were dovetailed

front and rear. While the front blade is made by Kahr, the rear adjustable sight comes from MMC, and it's a rugged little setup with protective "ears" on either side of the actual rear sight. It adjusts for windage by sliding in the dovetail one way or the other, while the elevation adjustment is performed with a hex wrench.

The magazine release button is on the left side of the frame right behind the trigger guard, and it is not ambidextrous.

There is no external manual safety on the T9, and that is one of my pet peeves about many of the striker-fired pistols on today's market. Although Kahr's safety record is a good one, a manual safety is a good feature, despite the long-standing principle that the only reliable "safety" is between your ears. Others may argue that point, suggesting the lack of a safety helps keep this pistol's design simple. No argument there. Like every other Kahr, this T9 is a study in simplicity.

Takedown on this gun was essentially the same as on any other Kahr semi-auto pistol. First, make sure the gun is unloaded with the magazine removed and chamber visually checked clear. Move the slide back and tap out the slide stop bar laterally, pinching the slide stop on the left side of the frame with your fingers and working it out.

My first attempt to fieldstrip this gun spooked me a bit, because the parts were so tightly fitted that the gun did not disassemble as easily as other Kahrs in my past. With a little help from my pal Max De La

Rear sight is an adjustable two-dot from MMC dovetailed into the slide and adjustable for windage and elevation.

Cruz at Wade's, we got the pistol apart and reassembled, in the process discovering just how tight this test gun was engineered and fitted.

Once the slide stop is removed, squeeze the trigger and move the slide forward and off the frame. Pull the recoil spring and guide rod, remove the barrel and the T9 is down to the basics for cleaning and oiling.

Like all other Kahr pistols, the T9 is a recoil-operated self-loader with a striker firing mechanism. The rectangular barrel block locks tight into the ejection port, as on all other Kahr semi-autos, and the patented offset recoil lug is still there. This clever design feature accommodates the trigger mechanism and, according to some Kahr reviews, plays an important part in making this pistol superbly 'shootable.'

If I had one complaint about this gun, it would be the long trigger stroke. For a target pistol, that's a problem (*where it isn't on a gun used for defensive purposes*), but not one that cannot be overcome with a bit of practice.

Kahr T9 with its favorite ammo, Federal Gold Medal 124-grain match. Magazine holds eight rounds. Note those handsome Hogue grips.

On the plus side, the trigger stroke was smooth from start to finish, and the gun broke cleanly. I did not have a trigger weight available for this test, but my best guess is that this gun has a 7- or 8-pound trigger pull, which allowed me to stay on target through three successive late afternoon shooting sessions.

Likes What You Feed It

My 9mm ammo stores may be a little depleted, but there was enough of a cross section that the Kahr was given every opportunity to get finicky, and it did not. The T9 digested everything it was fed, and it did not jam once during three shooting sessions in some pretty crummy conditions.

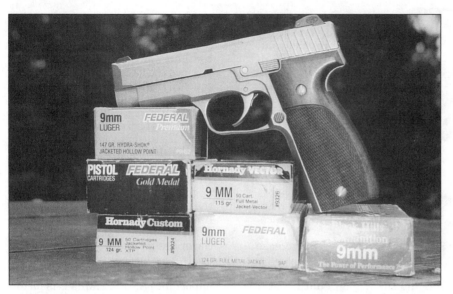

Kahr got a varied diet of ammunition, but author found it preferred the 124-grain pill above all others.

For my initial function firing, I jammed it full of 124-grain Federal Classic FMJ ammo and emptied a couple of magazines as fast as I could squeeze the trigger.

Next, before trotting out my Chrony Delta chronograph, I loaded up with assorted hollow-point rounds, including some rather mediocre handloads I keep around for a 9mm "Baby TZ" that I occasionally like to plink with. These feature Speer JHPs propelled by a dose of HP38 to just over 1,000 fps.

I tossed an empty bean can out about 15 yards and blazed away at it just to get the feel of this pistol. It shot high out of the box, but that was an easy fix.

My next step was to mount a couple of Shoot-N-C 8-inch bullseye centers on a piece of cardboard, march them out to 15 yards and see just how well this gun would hold on a 10-ring. The best groups I got were with Federal 124-grain FMJ match ammo, which roared out the muzzle at 1,116 fps, the second fastest load I tested.

Not to keep anyone in suspense, the hottest pill out the T9 bore was the Black Hills 124-grain FMJ, at a searing 1,177 fps, and as for accuracy, it turned in a pretty good performance the third evening of my testing, plugging a few three-round one-holers that impressed me.

Over the course of three evening shoots, my groups predictably began tightening as I got more used to the trigger pull and adjusted the sights to where they were consistently putting 124-grainers where I wanted them.

As I grew more used to the pistol with each string of shots, I shifted from a two-hand hold to a more classic single-hand target hold. This little Kahr married with the palm of my hand superbly, and I was quite pleased with how there was no sloppy movement with successive recoil and slide cycles. The pistol stayed put, and I don't know whether that's Kahr engineering at work, or

those terrific Hogue checkered grips, or a combination of things including the size and shape of my hand.

But I can say this with confidence: The T9 simply loves those 124-grain bullets, and for the shooter who buys one of these pistols with target shooting in mind, my recommendation would be to use nothing else. Find a comfortable load that clocks about 1,050 fps, set up a reloading press and start collecting brass.

Two rounds that didn't do quite as well were the 147-grain Federal Hydra Shok with a velocity of 1,044 fps (*measured 12 feet from the muzzle*), and the other was the Hornady Vector with a 115-grain bullet moving through my Chrony screens at 1,049 fps. The lowest velocity I clocked was a single 124-grain Hornady Custom XTP moving along at 954.7 fps, which got my attention because every other pill that went out the tube at least nudged the 1,000 fps mark, and the remainder of these particular loads went considerably faster.

I would have liked to find that casing just to check it out, but it flipped off into a corner and mixed with all the other brass.

Regretfully, I could not spend more time with the T9 on this early test

After tossing a trio of shots to the 9- and 8-rings, Workman used (*l-r*) four Hornady Custom 124-grain XTPs, three Federal Gold Medal Match 124s and a pair of Federal Classic 124-grainers to punch those tight little groups at 15 yards.

Author Workman during his first of three range sessions, this one in a downpour. His 15-yard offhand groups, on the targets left and right, were nothing to write home about.

Workman's second range session shows marked improvement. Target at left is the handiwork of Federal Match and Hornady Custom XTPs.

Third time was a charm, as Workman had gotten the full feel of his T9 test model, and began punching sub-1 inch groups with Federal Match ammo, including that six-shot cluster in the X-ring.

run, as I'd promised Kahr the gun would be turned around in ten days. I made that seven, but still managed to get in plenty of shooting; enough to convince me that Kahr designers have come up with a winner.

No excuses here, but had I been able to spend a couple of weeks with the T9, I am quite certain that I could have been shooting nothing but the 10-ring at 25 yards.

One thing I looked for during this test was the kind of wear that the synthetic follower in the Kahr magazine developed after repeated slide locks. It appeared to stand up pretty well, with nary a sign of breakdown, and that's probably because of what looked like a tiny metal pin molded into the follower right where it would pick up the slide stop lever. This should prevent excessive wear and tear on that follower, so I expect these magazines will take thousands of rounds.

The T9 magazine's floorplate is made of an equally tough synthetic, and the couple of times they fell completely to the cement pad of the shooting shed, they didn't appear to get a scratch.

Double Duty

While the T9 is definitely a paper-punching wonder for a compact pistol, it is not so large that it cannot be counted upon to do the kind of duty that Kahr semiautomatics have been providing since that initial introduction in the early 1990s.

I'm talking about personal defense. Any pistol that can shoot this good on the range is going to stack up to any challenge on the street, guaranteed. The addition of that MMC adjustable rear sight certainly enhances the T9's capabilities to put a bullet where it's supposed to go.

Because I only had a few days with this gun, I skipped building a holster for it, but there is no doubt that a good piece of leather wrapped around this piece, and a couple of spare magazines in an offside carrier would put any shooter in pretty good shape for hitting the pavement.

Where enough range time would have provided me with accuracy skills to pepper targets, that same kind of practice will definitely elevate the T9 to street duty.

We're talking about a gun from the same people who build the original K9, and all of its clones. It is rugged beyond expectation for a pistol this size, but the design has established what I consider to be a tremendous track record.

I personally know of only one Kahr pistol that ever suffered a major malfunction, and that was a P9 used as a range gun, and it had a lot of service. De La Cruz estimated that this specific pistol had seen thousands of rounds, and when one of the rails split, it surprised even him.

I saw that pistol, and gave it a good look. The polymer frame split away from the rail on the left side, ahead of the slide stop. Max told me the gun went back to Kahr and was fixed right up, which says plenty about Kahr's customer service.

Bear in mind, this gun most likely saw more ammo through it in a month than the average shooter would put through it in a year, and maybe a lifetime.

As for the T9, I would have no concerns at all about the service life of any part of this gun. From everything I observed during the testing, it is tough as nails.

According to Kahr's Harris, the T9 will hit the market with a manufacturer's suggested retail price of $749, which makes it quite reasonable in this writer's humble opinion.

Kahr is considering a 40-caliber version of this pistol at some point, but there is no production schedule on paper as yet. If that gun becomes a reality, and measures up to the 9mm pistol, it will be a stand-up performer. ●

Ballistics Test Results			
Ammunition	Bullet/grs.	Velocity/fps	Group/in. (@15 yards)
Hornady Custom	124 XTP	1,090	1.75
Federal Match	124 FMJ/SWC	1,116	1.0
Black Hills	124 FMJ	1,177	2.0
Hornady Vector	115 FMJ	1,049	2.8
Federal Classic	124 FMJ	1,097	1.5
Federal Hydra-Shok	147 JHP	1,044	2.75

RUGER'S 44-40 VAQUEROS

by "Doc" O'Meara

IT WAS A Saturday afternoon in 1963. The realization of a vague dream of writing about firearms–and being paid for it–was 20 years ahead, in an unknown future. At that moment I was walking into Ed Agramonte's now long-gone gun shop on Riverdale Avenue, in Yonkers, New York. A few months out of my first hitch in the Navy, I was working for the family plastic packaging business, the main office of which was a few blocks away. Having put in a half-day that Saturday I was already in the neighborhood and, having been paid the day before, I had money burning a hole in my pocket–and my recently-arrived first credit card. Little did I know I was entering into an education and introduction to two aspects of the wonderful world of firearms.

During the previous three years I'd been shooting military rifle and pistol competitions and had acquired appropriate firearms for those activities. Now, interests were expanding. The guns that won the West were piquing my interest and a Model 1873 Winchester was on the agenda. Unfortunately, decent specimens were in short supply in my area–and I'd yet to find one that appealed to me. But there, high on the wall behind the display counter, was another rifle–a Winchester Model 1892. I asked to see it.

Later, I would be told that the $100 I'd paid was too much. I didn't

---

Mismatching their barrel lengths was done deliberately. Using one for close-in speed and the other for long-range precision, together they make a handsome and more versatile pair.

care. Holding it there in the gunshop was like holding a new puppy; you want to fondle it, play with it and just hate to put it down. Nearly all its original blue was intact, the bore of its 24-inch barrel was perfect and the wood had only a few very superficial dings and scratches; about what one would expect from a gently handled season in the deer woods. It was chambered for the 44-40 cartridge, a round about which I knew next to nothing. Soon, that would change, and so would I.

In the months to come, the eight dollars or so, per box, of factory ammunition with which to feed that rifle began to add up. My gunsmith, Art Hoffmeyer, recommended I start reloading the empty cases. In those days, such activity was the province of only the most avid devotees of the shooting game. Gun gurus of the time, like Elmer Keith and Kent Bellah, wrote often of such things, but most ordinary folk regarded home-brewing ammunition as something akin to casting spells, if not outright witchcraft. When the economics involved were explained, however, it seemed almost as if the ammunition would be free.

I parted with about $80 to purchase an RCBS A-2 press and dies, an Ohaus scale, a Forster case trimmer and a Lyman reloading manual; the 42nd Edition. Primers sold for about 50 cents for 100, a can of Unique or 2400 powder cost another two bucks or so, and using the former would give me 875 rounds. A box of 100 JSP bullets was another couple of dollars and change. For around $30 I could feed my rifle 1000 rounds of reloads for less than the price of 200 factory cartridges. With the impatience of youth I set about concocting my own ammunition.

The variety of sounds that emanated from that rifle on my first try of that first batch sent others on the firing line scurrying for shelter. From mild 'pops' to loud 'booms', it was obvious to all (but myself) that those first efforts were not exactly expert. The target told the truth, however. With some sage advice from friends and more attention to detail on my part, I eventually got

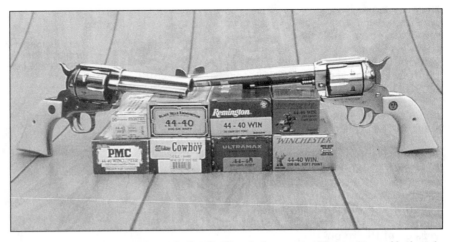

Using six different brands of lead bullet Cowboy Action ammunition and two of jacketed soft points, the 44-40 Ruger Vaqueros received a thorough workout in order to evaluate their accuracy potential.

the hang of it–pretty well. That both the rifle and I survived those early efforts without injury is a tribute to the craftsmen who had built it more than 50 years previously and the guardian angel who watched over me. Just as important, I had been well and truly introduced to the aforementioned two aspects of the wonderful world of firearms: handloading and antique arms.

Four years later, I was a college student with a wife and child. We lived in Montana by then. Money was scarce, but game was plentiful. At first the old 44 seemed enough

to take advantage of nature's bounty, but a more potent rifle was found necessary for the big mule deer, bigger elk and distant antelope on the hunting agenda. That might sound like it would be expensive hunting today, but at that time three dollars would buy a resident license allowing for two deer, an elk, a bear and a turkey. For another dollar and a half generous limits of grouse, pheasant and partridge were there for the taking. Rabbits and squirrels, such as they were, weren't protected at all. We would never go hungry.

On the other hand, tuition, books, rent and utilities did not allow for a comprehensive battery of firearms with which to pursue game. I had to learn to make do. The Winchester 44-40 was among the guns with which I reluctantly had to part in order to afford a more powerful rifle. Family and education came first.

In the years since, many 44-40s, including rifles and handguns, have come and gone. Only a few years ago did a rifle that I could become just as fond of as that first one come to me. It's a Marlin and capable of remarkable accuracy. Among the handguns have been single-action Colts, and Colt and Remington clones, Colt New Service and S&W Frontier DAs. One thing these guns taught me is that the 44-40 is a picky little cartridge. In some instances a description of its performance deserves superlative adjectives. Others are merely mediocre. A few SAA Colts could get you in big trouble, because they have a tendency for the case to set back and freeze the action when

The shorter-barreled revolver doesn't group as tightly as the longer one, but its groups are perfectly acceptable for the intended purpose. In truth, the accuracy of the longer-barreled six-gun is exceptional.

they are fired. It doesn't happen to many six-guns, but that's one reason some of the Old West gunfighters steered clear of handguns made for the cartridge.

For most of its history Ruger has ignored the 44-40 cartridge. Back in the 1980s there was a short run of Super Blackhawks with dual cylinders to shoot both the 44 Magnum and 44-40. A few years ago, with the rapid growth of Cowboy Action shooting, Ruger began to capitalize on that phenomenon and created a fixed-sight version of their venerable Blackhawk revolver, dubbing it the Vaquero.

True to their usual practice, the Vaquero cylinders were chambered precisely to SAAMI standards for the cartridge. However, the barrels were bored the same as those of the 44 Magnum revolvers they've been making for more than four decades. For the uninitiated, that means that using factory ammunition, jacketed bullets of .425-/.426-inch were rattling down a .429-inch bore. Lead bullets of .427-inch diameter did the same, but with slightly better performance in most instances, because gas pressures behind the bullet helped it to swell into the oversize bore.

Using bullets of larger diameter in such an instance is a waste of time, because when fired they will be swaged down to the .427-inch diameter of the chamber throats and still be undersize in the barrel. That is, if they would chamber at all. Complaints of inaccuracy led Ruger's engineers to re-examine the subject. In the end, rather than reduce barrel diameter, they opened the chamber mouths to .4295-inch. Certainly, economics had a great deal to do with that decision. With 44 Magnum revolvers among their most popular, keeping barrels of the name nominal caliber of differing actual bore sizes might prove problematic.

That seems to be the thinking elsewhere. Italian clones of the various frontier era revolvers chambered for the 44-40 all seem to use .429-inch barrels. Using lead bullet factory ammunition in the Ruger 44-40 seems to work out well. Most users, however, will likely handload for their revolvers.

With its longer 7 1/2-inch barrel, the second Vaquero 44-40 proved exceptionally accurate. Some of the groups it delivered would have been worthy of a match target pistol.

The Ruger Vaquero fitted with the 4 5/8-inch barrel shot a little low on target. The front blade turned out to be 1.5mm higher than that of the longer-barreled revolver.

For those who do, it makes better sense to seat .429-inch bullets in their homemade cartridges. To do so without damaging the usually thin brass during the bullet seating operation, the case mouth expander ball from a 44 Magnum die should be used to open the case neck wider than usual.

Basic equipment for the aspiring Cowboy Action shooter consists of two single-action revolvers, a rifle or carbine with an exposed hammer, chambered for a revolver cartridge, and a shotgun of at least 20 gauge, without automatic ejectors if it's a side-by-side double barrel; all of a type in common use around 1912 or earlier. Although it's not required, the usual procedure is to have the rifle and handguns chambered for the same cartridge.

There are lots of suitable revolvers in my safe and a few rifles, as well. No two of the revolvers, however, could be paired by chambering with the Marlin 44-40, which was my first choice for competition. A pair of Ruger Vaqueros for that round seemed the perfect solution. To that end I ordered one with a 7 1/2-inch barrel and another in the 4 5/8-inch length. Both are made of stainless steel and bear the ivory-like white plastic grips, with medallions, available from Ruger.

The reason for ordering the differing barrel lengths was the intent to use one as primary for long-range targets and the other for those that demand more speed. Besides which, I thought they'd look kind of neat together, tucked into one of Kirkpatrick Leather's

The Ruger Vaquero 44-40s are nestled comfortably into an Idaho John double rig, designed for Cowboy Action competition and made by Kirkpatrick Leather of Laredo, Texas. They've been paired with a Marlin Cowboy II rifle chambered for the same cartridge.

"Idaho John" double rigs, with the longer barrel sticking out of the bottom of the crossdraw holster. (If you like it, too, you can reach Kirkpatrick Leather Co. at: 1910 San Bernardino, Laredo, TX 78040.)

The long-barreled Vaquero proved a happy surprise on the range. It actually shot quite respectable groups of less than three inches with both Remington and Winchester factory JSP bullets. Cast bullet factory loads from both Black Hills and Hornady would usually put ten rounds into one ragged hole, about an inch and a half in diameter. Those from PMC, 3D, Ultramax and Winchester's Cowboy Action load did nearly as well; in the neighborhood of two inches. The only fault was that the groups fired over sandbags printed about an inch to the left of center. I could live with that.

The other Vaquero, with its 4 5/8-inch barrel, shot groups more than twice the size of those of its mate, that centered a couple of inches left and more than three inches low, from the same distance. Bore measurements were identical, but the height of the front sight of the shorter-barreled revolver proved to be 1.5 millimeters higher. That would account for the difference in elevation. Chamber mouths of the longer revolver's cylinder were very uniform at .4295-inch, but those of the other varied from the same size to as much as .430-inch. That explained the wider dispersion. Sight height is easily fixed and handloads using .430-inch bullets might shrink the groups and work as well in both revolvers. That remains to be seen.

With only a slight difference in muzzle heaviness to distinguish between them, both revolvers handle pretty much the same. Their triggers release the sears with 4 pounds of pressure and both are just a bit on the mushy side; not as crisp as one would like. The timing is as it should be and there is no end shake or excessive side-to-side play to their cylinders. Both revolvers are well within factory standard tolerances. And each– with allowances made by the user for the difference in bullet placement–is perfectly capable, just as it comes from the box, of doing well in competition. On the other hand, with a little custom work to lighten the hammer draw and make the trigger more crisp, they could be just about perfect for the modern cowboy, to whom "the range" is a place to shoot and have fun, rather than a place to ride horses and work cattle–or where the deer and the antelope play. ●

Kimber Pro Carry II

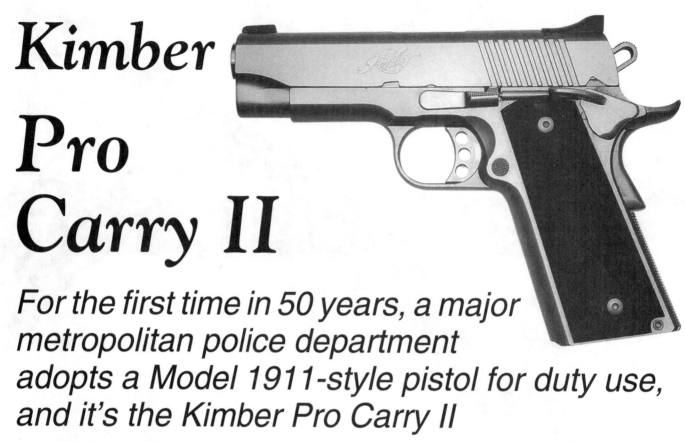

For the first time in 50 years, a major metropolitan police department adopts a Model 1911-style pistol for duty use, and it's the Kimber Pro Carry II

by Dave Workman

IN LATE SPRING 2001, the Tacoma, Washington Police Department caused a tremor in the law enforcement community and firearms industry rivaling the 6.8 earthquake that rattled this city only a few months before, when it disclosed that it had adopted two new duty sidearms.

One of those guns was a no-brainer: The Glock. After all, these "plastic guns" have captured a big share of the law enforcement market over the past ten years, so learning that police in Washington's "City of Destiny" were switching over from their Beretta double-action-only guns to a choice of three different Glocks was hardly news.

What made headlines in the local paper, and the pages of *Gun Week*, (where I am senior editor) was the other option, a Model 1911 platform; the kind of gun that had not been officially adopted by a major metropolitan police agency in a half-century. And the choice from among several 1911 builders really raised eyebrows: Kimber's Pro Carry II and Pro Carry II HD.

The Pro Carry II is a lightweight model with aluminum alloy frame,

and black oxide finish on the stainless slide and anodized finish on the frame, while the Pro Carry II HD is all stainless, with a brushed satin finish. Both guns wear Kimber's black checkered rubber double diamond grips.

What's more, Tacoma cops were going to be trained to pack these pistols cocked and locked, a carry

Specifications

Manufacturer: Kimber, 1 Lawton Street, Yonkers, NY 10705 (406) 758-2222 / www.kimberamerica.com

Model: Pro Carry II and Pro Carry II HD

Finish: Pro Carry II has stainless slide with black oxide finish and anodized aluminum frame. Pro Carry II HD is all-stainless with satin finish.

Barrel length: 4 inches

Chambering: 45 ACP

Magazine capacity: 7 rounds

Overall length: 7.7 inches

Weight: Pro Carry II: 28 ounces; Pro Carry II HD: 35 ounces

Grips: Checkered black rubber double diamond

MSRP: $773 to $879

mode that has been known to give some people heartburn and gun-ignorant liberal politicians a serious case of cold sweats.

According to Tacoma's Sgt. Mark Jenkins, the Kimber platform became the winner after a lengthy testing procedure that involved one of the most exhaustive studies of gun types, ergonomics, human hand dimensions, and a new twist that makes this a very special agency. Jenkins said the first step was to select finalists from over 30 different handgun models. That included every big name in the industry.

Ironically, Jenkins and his colleagues were planning to pick another 1911 manufacturer, but then that company changed its offered sale price to meet Tacoma's design requirements. Jenkins recalled that somebody had suggested Kimber, but at first they had apparently not seemed too interested in submitting guns for the trials.

That changed immediately with a call to Kimber's sales headquarters in Montana, Jenkins said. The next day, four test guns showed up and the department purchased a

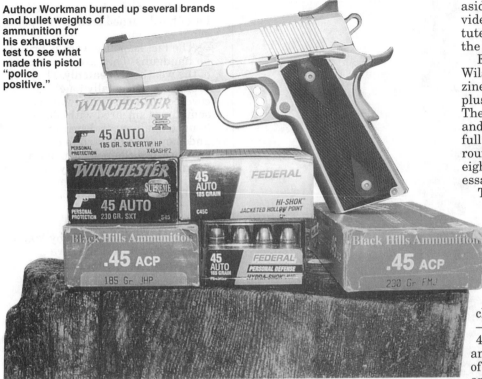

Author Workman burned up several brands and bullet weights of ammunition for his exhaustive test to see what made this pistol "police positive."

fifth gun from a Tacoma gun shop as a "control" for the testing. Every one of those pistols made it through the trials with flying colors, which means very few malfunctions.

The next step was even more unusual, and refreshingly straightforward in today's realm of bean-counting bureaucrats. Every patrol officer in the department – over 500 men and women – were trotted out to the department's range over the course of many days, and given the opportunity to testfire every one of the five finalists, and select the model that they most liked and would prefer to be issued. Everybody's choice was logged, each officer signed that log to confirm his or her specific gun choice, and when all of that was done, approximately 30 percent of Tacoma's police had chosen the Kimber, including one assistant chief and several command officers.

Five weeks before I sat in with Tacoma's first Kimber transition class, I took delivery of Kimber Pro Carry II HD serial #KR19152, a handsome stainless steel number that is Kimber's rendition of a "Commander-size" 45 ACP single-action semi-automatic. It has a 4-inch

bushingless bull barrel with full-length recoil guide rod and a 22-pound recoil spring, checkered rubber grips, black low-mount style sights dovetailed front and rear.

There are three main safety features on this gun: The grip safety, thumb safety and firing pin safety, which is activated when the grip safety is depressed, thus unblocking the firing pin and allowing the pistol to be fired.

This pistol carries a full-length Government Model 7-round magazine, though I immediately set

Tacoma Police Department selected Kimber Pro Carry II HD all-stainless (left) and Pro Carry II with alloy frame.

aside the three Kimber mags provided with the pistol, and substituted several 8-rounders, for which the reason will soon be explained.

Each officer in Tacoma gets five Wilson No. 47 seven-round magazines, so they carry one in the gun plus four spares on their duty belts. These are very reliable magazines, and officers are advised to carry a full magazine in their guns plus one round in the chamber, giving them eight shots out of the holster if necessary, and 28 spare rounds.

Tacoma officers are also issued Safariland SSIII security holsters with built-in retention features. These holsters, incidentally, were specially designed by Safariland for the Kimber Pro Carry II frame, Jenkins disclosed.

In the interest of full disclosure, I tested – and purchased – a Kimber Compact Custom in 45 ACP about four years ago, and I wrote about it in the pages of the HANDGUNS 1999 annual. I am sold on the design, and have found that pistol to be completely reliable.

But that doesn't mean I'm going to give a free ride to everything with the Kimber name stamped in its finish. There are lemons in every industry, and even if Tacoma's cops think this gun is hot stuff, I prefer to see for myself.

First and foremost, the gun that Kimber supplied for my testing was not exactly the same as those purchased by the cops. Their guns come with factory-mounted tritium sights, my test gun had simple black fixed sights.

Also, Tacoma's specifications called for ambidextrous thumb safeties on all of their pistols, while mine came with a standard thumb safety on the left side of the frame only.

Internally, the pistols were identical, because during the three days I spent with the Tacoma transition class, I had a chance to strip a couple of those guns down and look inside. And I found one significant difference: They cleaned their pistols more than I cleaned the test gun.

Stripping down the Kimber Pro Carry II is a snap. First remove the magazine and make cer-

Workman donned the required bullet-proof vest (Tacoma PD range policy) to shoot these groups on department's qualification target, sprained trigger finger and all.

vate citizens who have invested a lot of hard-earned money in a personal carry gun.

The fact is, police work is brutal on handguns. They are in and out of the weather repeatedly. They get dropped, occasionally fought over, covered with dust and road grit, sometimes smeared with blood, banged against car doorframes, and they are subjected to extreme temperature changes, depending upon where you live. They are not fired all the time, but when they are fired, they are fired a lot.

'Give it a bath'

After being introduced by Maule to the eight officers and five instructors as "an old hand with the 1911," it was not long into the first morning session, when instructor Dennis Quilio was explaining the cleaning procedures for this pistol that I offered some much-appreciated advice.

"Before you shoot this gun, strip it down and give it a bath in Hoppe's No. 9," I counseled.

That's exactly what I did when the test gun arrived weeks earlier. This cleans off the shipping oil, which sometimes has a tendency to "bake" and leave a film if the gun is fired while this stuff is still on the metal.

After taking the test pistol home, I tore it apart and applied a generous dose of Hoppe's famous solvent, dried all the surfaces and gave the gun a dab of lithium grease on the rails and other moving parts, and a drop of oil on the barrel lug, slide and barrel link.

Next day, I headed for the range with a big cardboard box filled with a selection of ammunition that ranged from 230-grain ball to 165-grain Federal Hydra Shoks (*which*

tain the chamber is clear, then lock back the slide. Kimber provides a small takedown "L"-shaped pin to insert in a small hole in the guide rod, which stops the forward movement of the recoil spring assembly. Push out the slide stop pin and move the slide forward off the frame. Remove the recoil spring

and guide rod by pulling it out to the rear, and then push the barrel out through the front of the slide.

Not cleaning the test gun was only one deliberate abuse to which I subjected the Pro Carry II HD. Like it or not, cops are famous for not maintaining their duty guns as well as competition shooters or pri-

Ballistics Test Results

Ammunition	Bullet/grs.	Velocity/fps	Group/in. (@15 yards)
Remington Golden Saber	230	788.4	3.0
Winchester Silvertip	185	889.5	7/8-inch
Federal Classic Hi-Shok	185	910.3	2.75
Black Hills FMJ	230	772.2	3.0
Win Clean BEB	230	790.6	3.0
Federal Hydra-Shok	165	957	1.75
Black Hills JHP	185	906.4	3.25
Winchester SXT	230	767.1	3.0

Kimber Pro Carry II HD test gun (*top*) with author's personal Kimber Custom Compact.

Aftermarket Magazine

Torture-Test

ABOUT MIDWAY THROUGH 2001, I asked several magazine companies to supply a couple of their replacement magazines for a diabolical little test.

Because so many shooters who carry the Model 1911 45 ACP fit their guns with replacement 8-round magazines, I wanted to find out what kind of service these could provide.

Wilson, Chip McCormick and Mec-Gar sent samples, and I rounded up a couple of 7-rounders from Metalform. Bare floorplates were fitted with rubber pads.

McCormick not only supplied me with a pair of standard Shooting Stars, they also sent me a Power Mag and one of their 10-rounders for good measure. Wilson sent the requested two, and Mec-Gar sent four, two in stainless and two blued.

First thing I did was spray them all with a rinse to clean out any shipping oil, then let them dry out completely for a couple of days. Afterward, I loaded them up to capacity, and let them sit for three months with the springs compressed. Only then did I put them all in a gun bag and trot down to the gun range, with my Olympic Arms custom "Street Deuce" (see *HAND-GUNS 2001*) and my Springfield 1911A-1 and start shooting.

From the outset, none of these magazines were babied. During speed drills, I simply let the mags drop to the ground, whether on grass, dirt, sand or cement.

This treatment continued off and on for several months, spanning the 2001 hunting season and extending into the spring of 2002. While I typically carry a magnum revolver on my hip during the hunting season, I took the Springfield along with one of each magazine brand, and they endured dust, heat, cold, rain and even snow.

When the opportunity came up to join the Tacoma police for their transition to the Kimber Pro Carry II pistols, which accept the full-length 1911 single-stack magazine, I ignored the three 7-round Kimber mags that had been supplied with my test gun, and stuck to the 8-rounders.

Of all the magazines, I expected the Wilsons to give me the most trouble because of their synthetic followers, but that was not the case. After hundreds of rounds and per-

Springfield, Olympic Arms and Kimber 45 ACPs were used to test replacement magazines from (l-r) McCormick (Power Mag), Mec-Gar, Wilson Combat, Metalform and McCormick (standard 8-rounder).

haps as many insertions and ejections, the two Wilson Combat 8-rounders looked pretty much like new, save for a couple of hardly noticeable scratches on one floorplate. I was impressed.

I've used McCormick Shooting Stars for years, and was duly satisfied with the test magazines that had been supplied to me. That Power Mag has McCormick's metal follower and a synthetic floorplate that closely resembled the ones on Wilson's mags, and proved just as tough.

Only the Mec Gar magazines had a different floorplate, one with a flare that is reminiscent of those on the Walther PPK magazine. Also made from a rugged synthetic, they hit the ground repeatedly and never gave any hint of trouble.

Metalform's 7-rounders took a bruising and continue today as backup magazines for my Street Deuce, as that's what the gun came supplied with from Olympic.

I paid close attention to the magazine lips, and after hundreds of rounds, there is not a sign of weakening or spreading. They all feed into the magazine well today same as they did when they came out of the bag.

My preference for a street gun is the 8-round magazine because it provides one extra shot. That Tacoma has opted for Wilson's No. 47 7-rounder is likely to be a matter of debate for those who like to debate such stuff, but range master Sgt. Mark Jenkins matter-of-factly explained that this is a good magazine, with a good performance record.

There was also some concern that eight-rounders might have a greater tendency to malfunction, but I ve never seen it, and my little experiment offered no evidence that any of these aftermarket 8-round magazines would fail.

Quite the contrary, every one of the test magazines has taken a pounding, far more than one would expect to dish out during the "normal" service life of a pistol.

I did, however, notice some feeding problems with the McCormick 10-rounder, after having spent the winter fully loaded in a pouch on the seat of my pickup.

Shooters who select any of these magazines as replacements for their factory-supplied models will be well equipped, in this writer's opinion. You may spend up to $25 to $28 apiece for them; just consider it a very wise investment.

turned in the best performance of all during my earlier test of the Compact Custom). I also grabbed a box of handloads.

It should be noted for the record that none of my test loads were the same ammo used by Tacoma during its range sessions or for street duty. There's a reason for this: My test gun would be subjected to a very wide range of ammo, and everybody knows that police agencies do not always stick with the same brand of ammunition when they get a better price from another supplier.

Thus began Workman's version of "Celebrity Death Match," in this case the celebrity being a Kimber, and the challenger being every rotten thing I could think of to do to it, before, during and after shooting.

My local gun range has a sandy loam in the pistol pit, and quite by accident, I dropped the Kimber on this stuff early in the range test. This mishap was actually a lucky

On the line, officers learned fast that they can handle the recoil of a 45 ACP.

stroke, because it's a cinch that I did not get all the grit out of the gun when I touched off the first few rounds, something that would never happen to a cop, right? Add this notation: Something that would never happen to an armed private citizen who has a close encounter of the worst kind outside the confines of his home or business, right? Fortunately during the early phase of my field test, it snowed, and I let it. The Kimber just kept on working. A few days later, the sun shined, the temperature climbed about 20 degrees, and I let it do that, too. Again, the Kimber just kept shooting away, all the while without any serious effort to clean it. Then came Washington state's notoriously cold seasonal rains, and you bet I let it do that! The Pro Carry kept eating up ammunition, never suffering a single jam or other malfunction, even when soaking wet and dirty.

I shot the gun with dirty, muddy hands. I shot it with wet and sweaty hands. Even with some grease on my hands. I shot it cold, I shot it hot. Even shot it with gloves on.

You guessed it. The Kimber's ability to handle weather changes

Steve O'Keefe was one of two officers in the first class who selected the alloy-framed Pro Carry II, and he took to it like a natural.

was a non-issue, but the fact that with all the shooting I did, this gun did not fail to feed or eject even once got my attention. But, then again, it took nearly 1,000 rounds through my personal Kimber before I had a failure to feed malfunction, so none of this came as a surprise.

By the time the police class rolled around, my test gun had seen a few months worth of wear and tear in as many weeks.

Accuracy assured

Being a creature of dumb luck, most of it bad, ten days before I joined the cops in Tacoma, I went firewood cutting. During the course of that misadventure, while bucking up a tree, I slipped and fell, suffering a sprain in the worst possible place: my trigger finger.

Ever try to fire a 45 auto with a sprained trigger finger? As a result, I pretty much lost trigger control, and began shooting a little to the left. Thereafter, everything that happened to the accuracy of this pistol was my fault and not the Kimber's. I make that note because this pistol turned out to be a superbly accurate model, and better still, every one of the guns issued to the officers in that first class shot to point of aim time after time. My early testing involved punching holes in paper, but at the police range, we shot at falling steel plates, bowling pins, human silhouettes and a diabolical series of metal targets that rise and drop

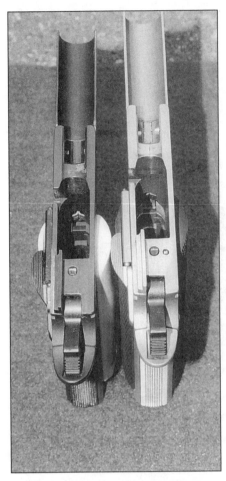

Note that Workman's personal Kimber Compact Custom (*left*) has no firing pin safety, while the Pro Carry II HD (*right*) does have that safety feature (top right, frame).

by compressed air to simulate bad guys using hostages as shields.

After my first day of shooting with the police, that trigger finger was beginning to swell anew and throb, so the second day, I sat things out and the only trigger I pressed was on my camera.

Some of the guns ran poorly the first day out because during the initial field-stripping session in class, the officers neglected to lube their slide rails. Once they were oiled properly, they worked like champs.

The only other problem suffered with two of the pistols was that the ambi-safety worked loose. I discussed this with Van Brunt, who immediately contacted the police, and they worked through the issue, which actually had to do with the size of the right rubber grip and its bearing surface on the off-side thumb safety latch.

Over the chronograph

As I expected with a variety of ammunition, I got a variety of velocities shooting test rounds over my Chrony Delta, placed 10 yards from the muzzle. The fastest velocity I clocked came with the 165-grain Hydra Shok, moving along at 957 fps. Not far behind that were the Federal 185-grain Hi Shok at 910.3 fps, followed closely by the Black Hills 185-grain JHP (using the Speer Gold Dot bullet) at 906.4

fps, and the Winchester 185-grain Silvertip at 889.5 fps.

Rounding out my test loads was a Black Hills 230-grain Gold Dot JHP clocking 797.8 fps, the Winchester WinClean 230-grain BEB at 790.6 fps, trailed by the Black Hills 230-grain FMJ ball round at 772.2 fps and the Winchester 230-grain SXT at 767.1 fps.

The tightest groups came with the 185-grain Hi Shok and the Winchester 185-grain Silvertip, the latter which occasionally put three- and five-shot strings into a single ragged hole.

But what about Tacoma's duty round, the Remington 230-grain Golden Saber bonded? For that test, conducted at the Tacoma police range with my test gun and pistols I borrowed from officers Brian Garrison and Steve O'Keefe (*two of the better shooters in the class*), I ran five-shot strings over the chronograph with the following results: O'Keefe's gun booted them out at an average 778.2 fps with a high velocity of 798.4 fps. Rounds from Garrison's pistol averaged 777.6 fps with a high of 790.8 fps. Surprisingly, out of my test gun, the Remingtons turned in an average of 788.4 fps, with a high speed of 811.6 fps, about 10-12 fps faster than either officer's sidearm. Nothing to be alarmed about, as all of these velocities are right about where they should be from a 4-inch 45 ACP, and spot-on when it comes to anticipated performance of this particular cartridge.

A 'semi-custom' gun

Quilio told his fellow officers that these new Kimbers are "semi-custom" pistols, built to satisfy Tacoma's specs, but that does not mean private citizens cannot get their hands on exactly the same gun. Just order one with the same ambi-safety and night sights, and you're in business.

Depending upon the gun shop, I've found them listed in the $773 to $879 range with no frills, which is the manufacturer's suggested retail pricing. They will be worth every penny, too. My testing proved that beyond any doubt, and I'm confident their performance will be meticulously tracked and recorded by Jenkins and his crew of Kimber-certified armorers. Kimber pistols have been pleasing *pistoleros* for several years, now. It speaks well of the design and engineering that they have now pinned on a badge. ●

Takedown of Pro Carry II is simple, and the gun comes apart fast to its basic components.

CAST BULLETS IN THE 380 ACP CARTRIDGE

by Mike Thomas

MORE HANDLOADERS ARE concocting their own 380 ACP ammunition these days despite the fact that 380 loading dies are not selling at exactly the same brisk pace as those for the 38 Special or the 9mm Luger. Compared to just ten or twenty years ago, however, the diminutive 380 is gaining stature within the handloading realm.

It was once rare indeed to run across anyone who handloaded for this round. Why the turnaround in the last few years? The proliferation of concealed-carry laws in this country is one explanation, and likely the most significant. I am not implying handloaders are making their own ammo for defensive use.

I am, however, assuming that many enthusiasts who already handload will buy dies, components, etc. each time they purchase a firearm chambered for a new cartridge. It's the nature of the hobby, I suppose.

To many of us the very term "concealed carry" is synonymous with lightweight, compact handguns. Most 380s fit this description, though some better than others. And, virtually all of these

---

Pistols used by the author in developing cast bullet load data for the 380 ACP cartridge. Baikal Makarov IJ70-17 (top) and Walther PPK/S. While there are 380 ACP pistols slightly lighter and smaller, author doubts any are more accurate or reliable than these two.

are semi-automatic pistols of either single- or double-action design. Noted exceptions are the few double-action-only models from Smith & Wesson and Colt.

There are many excellent 380 ACP pistols available today. My total experience with the 380 cartridge has been with four different handguns, all of which have reputations for quality.

Nevertheless, there may be some real junk out there that is also chambered for this round, so beware.

Modern technology and design features have evolved to the point that many 380 automatics can truly be called accurate, seldom the case just a few years back.

Obviously I am not speaking of serious target-grade accuracy, but groups under four or five inches at 25 yards. Some might question why I would test a short-barreled pocket auto with a less-than-ideal trigger pull and crude sights at such a distance, rather than at 7, 10, or 15 yards as is commonly done. And, yes, it is a fact that nearly any time a handgun is used in a defensive situation, the range is short—very short. I have more confidence in a gun that is not only 100 percent reliable, but accurate as well. No one should have to settle for "washtub" accuracy at 10 yards. Poor accuracy may not only have an effect on the confidence factor, it may be also be indicative of ill-fitting parts and sloppy workmanship. No one should have to settle for that.

With some experimentation and reasonable attention to detail, cast bullets can absolutely equal, in all respects, their jacketed bullet counterparts. The term, *"in all respects"* refers here to accuracy, velocity, terminal performance, and feeding reliability. As a bonus, handloaders who use cast bullets in the 380 ACP quickly find it a very forgiving round since the small case capacity limits velocity so that leading is seldom a problem.

Top muzzle velocities with maximum loads (*and bullets of around 90 grains*) will rarely exceed 1,000 feet per second (fps). In fact, the author's speediest handloads fall

Author fires the Walther PPK/S from the bench. The Makarov 380 lies nearby. All test work is done at 25 yards, rather than the shorter distances such "pocket pistols" are often restricted to.

shy of this mark. A word of caution regarding maximum loads: Many 380 autos are not of "locked breech" design; rather they have relatively simple "blowback" actions. Such a design lacks the strength of a locked breech, but this feature is considered rather academic by many and contributes to the compact dimensions shared by many small pistols. The reason for this is that the powder capacity of the 380 case is so small that even very slight increases in charge weight can increase chamber pressures quite dramatically. Of course, the same can be said for seating bul-

lets too deeply. Consequently, neither action style will handle overloads well. For comparison purposes we may note that an empty 380 case has a water capacity of just under 9 grains while a 38 Special hull will hold just over 20 grains of the same liquid.

For this handloading project I used two very common double-action semi-automatic pistols: an imported Baikal Makarov IJ70-17A and a Walther PPK/S. The Makarov is a well-made and surprisingly accurate pistol that is also quite reasonably priced. Unloaded weight is around 25 ounces; barrel length is 3-3/4 inches. The Walther is the 23-ounce American-made stainless steel version with a 3 1/3-inch barrel. Both pistols have the typically heavy double-action trigger pull of "pocket" automatics. Some criticize this feature, perhaps because they can find no other shortcomings to talk about. It's a moot point at best with these handguns, and no handicap.

Three bullet moulds were selected which adequately cover the weight range spectrum of bullets suitable for use in the 380 cartridge. All are of a plain-base design. While gas-checked bullets could certainly be used in the 380, they offer no practical advantage, again due to the modest muzzle velocities attainable with this cartridge. Bullet moulds include the RCBS 38-90-RN (93-grain round-

While there are many suitable powders available for loading the 380 ACP, these were used in the author's test work and represent the burning rates suitable for the cartridge. From 'fast' to 'slow' (*left to right*): Winchester 231, Alliant Unique, Alliant Herco (*old Hercules container shown*), and Alliant Blue Dot. Slow-burning powders like Blue Dot reduce the chance of a double-charged case going unnoticed.

Handloaded 380 ACP cartridge (*left*) with 106-grain flat-nose bullet cast from Lyman mould #356632. For comparison is a Winchester factory round loaded with the 85-grain SilverTip bullet. Overall cartridge length of handloads must be kept in line with factory ammo to ensure reliable feeding from the magazine.

nose), the Lyman #356632 (106-grain flat-nose), and the SAECO / Redding #377 (124-grain flat-nose). These moulds are of double-cavity design. Bullets were cast from a soft wheel-weight alloy that registered a Brinell hardness (bhn) of 8 on an LBT (Lead Bullet Technology) bullet hardness gauge.

Bullet lubricants. Many cast bullet enthusiasts (*including myself*) have found that differences in type, brand, and firmness of lubricants quite often mean little or nothing in practical terms when muzzle velocities are limited to around 1,000 fps. Simply put, any lubricant that promotes accuracy and prevents bore leading is the "best." I used two lubes, both of which are soft and do not require heating to flow in a lubricator/sizer: GAR half-and-half NRA formula Alox and beeswax and Lyman's Super Moly. These were applied to bullets in a SAECO / Redding lubrisizer fitted with a .356-inch bullet sizing die. Both lubes worked well and I could detect no discernible difference between them in terms of overall bullet performance. There was no bore leading with either lubricant during this project.

Components. I used Winchester brass, CCI-500 (standard small pistol) primers, and four powders: Winchester 231 and Alliant's Unique, Herco, and Blue Dot. There are a number of other suitable propellants, of course, but those listed are representative of the fast- to slow-burning rates that are compatible with the 380

ACP. RCBS loading dies were installed in a 1960's-vintage Texan turret press.

At the risk of appearing overly cautious, I emphasize once again that the 380 case–despite its very small capacity–can be easily overcharged with the faster powders. If for no reason other than the safety aspect, the slower powders have an advantage here.

Overall cartridge length: This may require a bit of experimentation depending on the particular handgun and magazine combination. Normally, magazine dimensions usually dictate maximum OAL. Making up two or three dummy rounds and trying them is the best route to follow here. *Don't*

do this with live ammo! I have found it unnecessary to crimp my handloads as all bullets are securely held in place following the bullet seating process. However, different combinations of dies, brass, and bullets may add enough dimensional variables that a tight "grip" may not be possible without crimping. If so, a taper crimp die should solve the problem. Roll crimps are unsuitable for the 380 ACP.

I see no point in going into great detail regarding loading data as the accompanying table is straightforward and self-explanatory. I will, however, touch on a few high points that do require further comment. All bullets demonstrated

380 ACP CAST BULLET LOADING DATA

Bullet	Powder	Charge	MV (fps)	Comments
RCBS 38-090-RN 93 grs. OAL= .980"	Win. 231	2.5 grs.	685	velocity too low
	Win. 231	3.0 grs.	850	
	Win. 231	3.3 grs.	N/C	
	Unique	3.0 grs.	790	
	Unique	3.5 grs.	845	
	Unique	3.7 grs.	N/C	
	Herco	3.5 grs.	865	accurate
	Herco	4.0 grs. MAX.	920	accurate
	Blue Dot	4.5 grs.	745	
	Blue Dot	5.0 grs.	795	
	Blue Dot	5.3 grs.	860	accurate
Lyman #356632 106 grs. OAL=.950"	Win. 231	2.5 grs.	735	accurate
	Win. 231	3.0 grs. MAX.	895	accurate
	Unique	2.5 grs.	730	
	Unique	3.0 grs.	N/C	
	Herco	3.5 grs.	880	
	Herco	4.0 grs.	N/C	
	Herco	4.3 grs. MAX.	N/C	accurate
	Blue Dot	3.5 grs.	600	barely works action
	Blue Dot	4.5 grs.	790	accurate
	Blue Dot	5.0 grs. MAX.	900	accurate
SAECO/Redding #377 124 gr. FN OAL=.960"	Win. 231	2.5 grs.	795	accurate
	Win. 231	2.8 grs.	835	
	Win. 231	3.0 grs. MAX.	870	
	Unique	2.5 grs.	N/C	
	Unique	2.8 grs.	790	accurate
	Herco	3.0 grs.	810	
	Blue Dot	4.0 grs.	755	accurate
	Blue Dot	4.5 grs.	840	accurate

NOTES: Ambient temperatures varied from 85º to 95º Fahrenheit during the load testing process. All loads chronographed ten feet from gun muzzle using a PACT PC chronograph. Velocities rounded off to the nearest five feet-per-second. All velocities recorded using the Makarov pistol. Walther PPK / S velocities were very close to Makarov figures, often varying only a few feet-per-second. Winchester brass and CCI-500 primers were used exclusively for all load development. All starting loads should be reduced by 10 percent before increasing powder charge and all loads should be carefully monitored for signs of excessive pressure. If the overall cartridge length (OAL) is increased or decreased, or ANY component is substituted for those shown in the tables, a further initial charge reduction is required pursuant to prudent and safe handloading procedures. *N/C*= not chronographed.

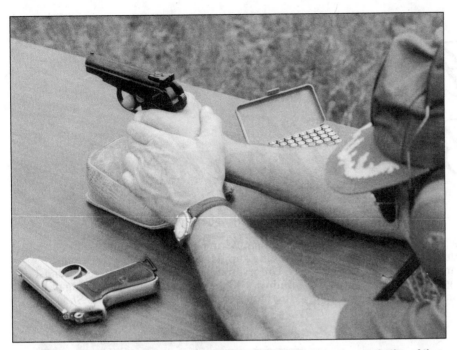

Author fires the Makarov off the benchrest. While this pistol lacks the aesthetics of the Walther, it is well-made, rugged, accurate—and a great value. What more is needed? The PPK/S lies left of the bag.

Sources

Alliant Techsystems Smokeless Powder Group, 200 Valley Rd., Suite #305, Mt. Arlington, New Jersey, 07856/ 800-276-9337 (smokeless powders)

CCI / Speer, P.O. Box 856, Lewiston, Idaho 83501/ 800-627-3240   (primers, bullets, loaded ammunition)

GAR, 590 McBride Ave., West Paterson, New Jersey 07424/ 201-754-1114 (GAR bullet lubricants, bullet moulds, loading and casting equipment)

Walther America, 2100 Roosevelt Avenue, Springfield MA 01102/ 800-372-6454 (Walther pistols)

LBT (Lead Bullet Technology), HCR 62, Box 145, Moyie Springs, Idaho 83845/ 208-267-3588 (custom-made bullet moulds, bullet lubricants, etc.)

Lyman Products Corp. 475 Smith St., Middletown, CT 06457/ 800-22-LYMAN (loading and casting equipment, bullet moulds, lubricants, etc.)

PACT, Inc., P.O. Box 531525, Grand Prairie, Texas 75053/ 214-641-0049 (chronographs, electronic scales, timers, etc.)

RCBS, 605 Oro Dam Rd., Oroville, CA 95965-5792/ 800-533-5000 (loading and casting equipment, bullet moulds, scales, measures, dies, etc.)

Redding Reloading Equipment, 1089 Starr Rd., Cortland, NY 13045/ 607-753-3331 (loading dies and presses, scales, measures, SAECO cast bullet moulds, lubrisizer, etc.)

Winchester Division, Olin Corporation, 427 N. Shamrock, E. Alton, Illinois 62024/ 618-258-3566 (loading components: powders, primers, cartridge cases, etc., all types loaded ammunition)

decent accuracy with at least two of the four powders used. I initially tried bullets sized in a .358-inch die; they were far less accurate than .356-inch bullets. All bullets fed reliably in both pistols. I am inclined to go with one of the lighter bullets for all-around use in the Walther. With its fixed sights, the lighter bullets print closer to the point-of-aim at 25 yards. The heavy 124-grain SAECO/Redding bullet shoots at least 4 inches high with most loads. The Makarov, with an adjustable rear sight, has no such limitation.

A final note: While cast bullets are inexpensive, practical, and accurate in the 380 ACP cartridge, their use should be confined to paper targets, plinking, and small game or pests at very short ranges. We all need to be aware that commercially manufactured ammunition is the only type that should be considered for use in any firearm that may be employed in a defensive role. Potential civil liability concerns come into play here and such issues are far outside the scope of this article. •

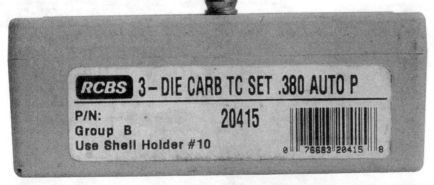

RCBS 3–DIE CARB TC SET .380 AUTO P

P/N: **20415**
Group B
Use Shell Holder #10

0   76683 20415   8

RCBS dies were used by the author for load development work. The 380 ACP is no more difficult to load for than any other pistol cartridge but the restricted case capacity can cause dangerously high pressures far more quickly than a larger capacity case if safe powder charges are exceeded by careless handloading!

A Tribute to Ben Shostle

by Tom Turpin

THIS IS A tribute to former FEGA President and fellow Kentuckian by birth, Ben Shostle. Like me, Ben left his native Bluegrass state; unlike me, he set up shop in Indiana. He is a self-taught engraver who learned his engraving skills to complement his exper-tise as a gunsmith and custom stockmaker. Eventually, the engraving supplanted the other skills almost entirely. Unfortunately, today ill health–and almost total blindness–has forever stilled the tapping of his engraving hammer. *Photos courtesy of Ben Shostle.*

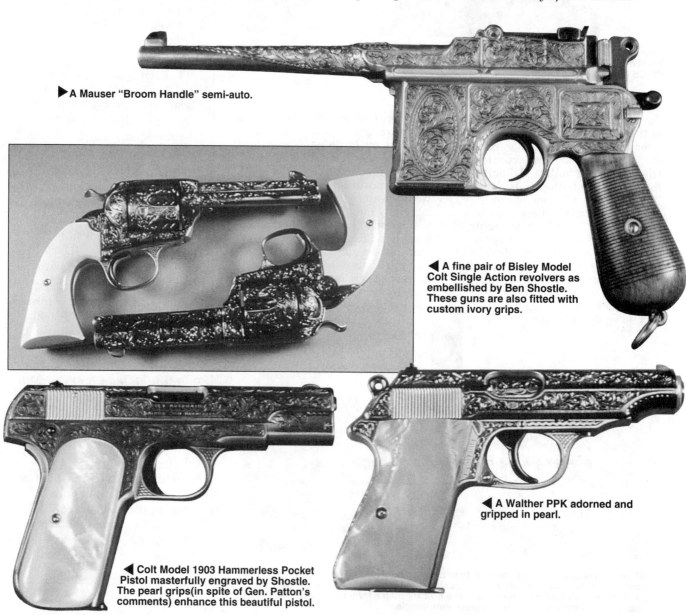

▶ A Mauser "Broom Handle" semi-auto.

◀ A fine pair of Bisley Model Colt Single Action revolvers as embellished by Ben Shostle. These guns are also fitted with custom ivory grips.

◀ A Walther PPK adorned and gripped in pearl.

◀ Colt Model 1903 Hammerless Pocket Pistol masterfully engraved by Shostle. The pearl grips(in spite of Gen. Patton's comments) enhance this beautiful pistol.

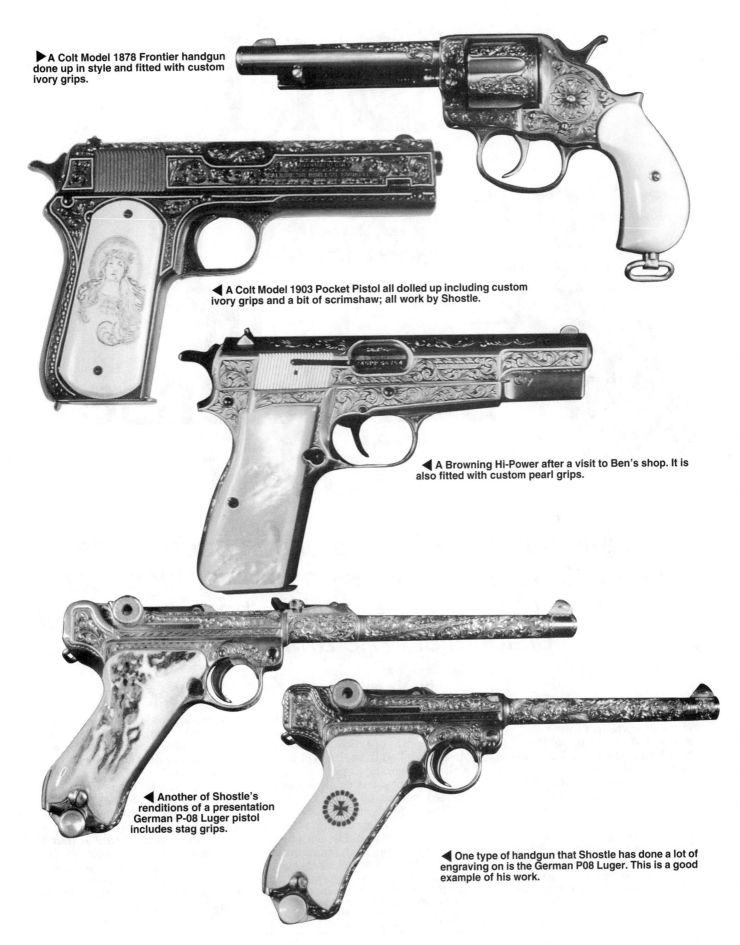

▶A Colt Model 1878 Frontier handgun done up in style and fitted with custom ivory grips.

◀A Colt Model 1903 Pocket Pistol all dolled up including custom ivory grips and a bit of scrimshaw; all work by Shostle.

◀A Browning Hi-Power after a visit to Ben's shop. It is also fitted with custom pearl grips.

◀Another of Shostle's renditions of a presentation German P-08 Luger pistol includes stag grips.

◀One type of handgun that Shostle has done a lot of engraving on is the German P08 Luger. This is a good example of his work.

The 1911

In Self-defense Today

Some say the 1911 pistol has been made obsolete for self-defense by newer high-tech handguns. Others say it's still the best gunfighting pistol ever. The answer is…

by Massad Ayoob

The 1911 has a long and proven history in the battlefield and on the street. This is the 1911A1 currently produced by Colt to mirror WWII production guns.

THE 1911 PISTOL had staunch advocates from the moment of its inception. For the first half of the twentieth century, however, its fans consisted primarily of war veterans who had learned to trust it in the service, and target shooters who had to fire a 45 auto for at least a third of the only handgun game in town, NRA bullseye. For home defense, most recommended a service revolver just like the cops carried, and for concealed carry, it was either a "snub-nose 38" or a small pocket auto.

In the 1950s, a prophet rose in the West. Jeff Cooper's incisively written series of articles in *Guns & Ammo* extolled the virtues of the Colt 45 automatic as proven in genuine gunfights, and easily demonstrated on demand at the replicated gunfights he hosted, called 'Leatherslaps.' From this seminal period would be born two important defensive handgunning trends. One was practical shooting

competition, as we know it today. The other was the renaissance of the 1911 pistol–not only for those matches, but also for general defensive use.

Police were taking notice, too. A handful of forward-thinking agencies, primarily in southern California, had dumped the six-shooter with its impotent 38-caliber round-nose lead bullets, and adopted the 45 auto as a standard issue duty gun. Splendid results were reported. Gun writer Mason Williams convinced the prestigious law enforcement professional journal

Law and Order to publish The Heene Report, an exhaustive study of the 1911 pistol's advantages for cops. More agencies adopted–or at least approved–the gun.

This opened the door to other auto pistol concepts. In 1967, the Illinois State Police became the first major PD in the nation to adopt the Smith & Wesson Model 39, a 9mm auto pistol with double-action first shot. Chiefs who were leery about cocked and locked weapons in the holsters of the rank and file felt more comfortable with the hammer-down design. S&W followed up with a higher capacity version, the Model 59. Even the strongest advocates of the 45 auto had to stop sneering at double-action autos when SIG introduced their P-220 (originally as the Browning BDA) and it was proven on the streets by such police departments as that of Huntington Beach, California. S&W followed suit in 1983 with their first 45 auto, the Model 645, to warm response from police departments.

By now, chiefs were weathering major civil liability storms and for the most part were not at all inclined to let the troops walk the streets with cocked guns that went off with short, easy pulls of the trigger. The double-action auto became the 'gold' standard. Then

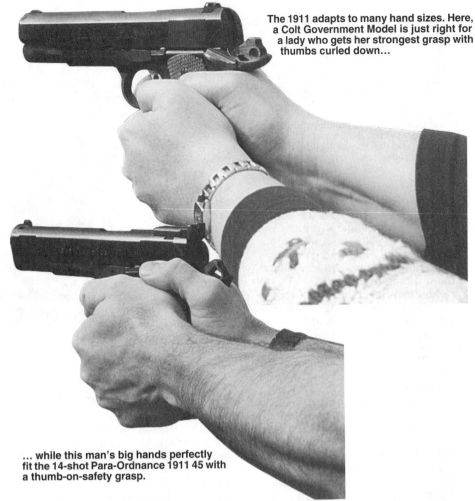

The 1911 adapts to many hand sizes. Here, a Colt Government Model is just right for a lady who gets her strongest grasp with thumbs curled down...

... while this man's big hands perfectly fit the 14-shot Para-Ordnance 1911 45 with a thumb-on-safety grasp.

The 1911 is quick into action. Here, Dave DiFabio awaits the draw signal at an LFI-I class...

...and on the signal, he executes a perfect draw, taking the safety off and letting the finger into the trigger guard only when his Wilson 45 comes up on target...

...and then delivers a fast sequence of perfect center hits.

Today's 1911s are better than ever. This stainless Kimber, reasonably priced, delivers ample accuracy and flawless reliability with superb ergonomics.

came the Glock, determined "double-action-only" by BATF itself. Glock sales roared past the entire pack of "traditional" DA autos and by the late 1990s the Austrian pistol was solidly ensconced as the leader of the American law enforcement handgun market.

Meanwhile, an old trend continued. Where cops went, armed citizens followed in terms of widespread defensive handgun tastes. Civilians had been hotter for 1911s than cops for most of the latter half of the 20th century, and while they too bought SIGs and Berettas and S&W autos and Glocks in droves, the 1911 remained on *their* best-seller list.

This does not mean that the cops have abandoned the 1911 entirely. There are still entire departments that carry them, and many more agencies where they remain optional. Personally owned 1911 pistols are on patrol in some

officers' holsters in the streets of Salt Lake City, Denver, Houston, and Tacoma among others. But I know more cops who carry 1911s off-duty than on, and a much larger proportion of civilians have chosen the old warhorse as their personal carry or home defense gun.

Let's look at why.

Defensive Advantages

One reason the 1911 was quickly eclipsed by the high-capacity "wondernine" was that cops originally bought into autoloaders for one reason: firepower. Where an eight-shot Government Model gave a one-third increase over a six-shooter, a sixteen-shot 9mm doubled *that*. In many versions,

however, the price was high: a fat, square grip and a long-reach trigger that made accurate shooting more difficult for anyone who didn't have large hands.

The 1911, by contrast, had been a standard of ergonomics in handgun design since before the word came into common usage. If you have short fingers, get one with a short trigger and the fit is perfect. Need more bulk? 1911s with longer-reach triggers, and fatter after-market grips, are only as far away as your local gun shop.

If you want firepower in the 1911, you can have it. Kimber, Para-Ordnance, STI and Wilson are among the purveyors of high-capacity, "fat grip" pistols in this format, available in chamberings from 9mm to 38 Super to 40 S&W to 45 ACP. But many civilians – and many police departments – have found that firepower isn't necessarily the first item on the list of desirable attributes for a defensive semiautomatic pistol.

Once the shooting starts, it's usually (not always, but *usually*) over in less than six rounds per survivor. Yes, there are those other times, but firepower is still down to about third on the list of priorities.

First and foremost is *hit potential*. The bullet has to hit–and hit *center*–to stop the fight. One reason so many hi-cap guns have become self-fulfilling prophecies and been run to *slide-lock* with the fight still on is that some people find them difficult to hit with under stress. The 1911 has a bore axis that sits low to the hand, minimizing recoil. It points well. The trigger is usually the right distance from the finger to minimize chances of jerking the shot off-target when firing fast under very high stress.

Once appropriately familiarized with the gun, countless people over many generations have discovered that they shoot a 1911 better than anything else, particularly under pressure. For some the difference is huge. For others, the 1911 only lets them shoot a tiny bit better. But, when you're fighting for your life, that tiny bit can make all the difference.

The second, and perhaps most overlooked, advantage of the 1911 is *proprietary nature to the user*. This gun, when fully loaded, is properly carried cocked and locked. A lot of police chiefs never got past

Jonathan Ciener's conversion unit makes cheap 22 rimfire practice easy with a 1911. This unit is on a Colt Commander frame.

the scary-looking "cocked" part to the life-saving "locked" part. *Anyone* in a confrontation with a violent opponent is at risk of a disarming attempt. When they get your modern, high-tech, point-and-shoot gun away from you, all *they* have to do is point it and shoot it.

By contrast, there are numerous cases on record where the bad guy got the 'on-safe' gun away from the good guy and couldn't figure out which little lever or button "turned it on," buying the good guy time to rectify the situation and bring about a happy ending. Several of these documented incidents have involved cocked and locked 1911 pistols.

There are lots of different safety catch designs, but the frame-mounted lever of the 1911 sets the gold standard. It is perfectly placed for operation by the knowledgeable shooter's thumb as the hand naturally closes into firing position. It is also very easy to flip back to the 'on-safe' position when that becomes necessary. Thanks to the late, great Armand Swenson, we've had functional ambidextrous safety levers for 1911s for decades, so our southpaw brothers and sisters aren't left out.

Notes on Daily Carry

When you carry a powerful handgun all day, every day, you discover that the 1911 is a forgiving design. The most concealable of fast-draw hip holsters is the inside-the-waistband design, and this puts a premium on gun thickness, though the thinner gun will always conceal better and more

The 1911 lends itself to customizing for match shooting. Years ago, Mike Plaxco built this Springfield 45 for the author, fitting his own compensator and BoMar sights. Ayoob won many matches with it.

The 1911 is available in assorted hi-tech forms. This is the author's pet Springfield Tactical Response Pistol in the Operator model, with flashlight attachment rail, loaded with 10-round extended Wilson 45 magazine. Grips are "Burners" by Jerry Barnhart.

comfortably no matter what the holster style. There is no slimmer 45 auto than the 1911.

If the full-size Government Model is a tad long for you, we've had the popular Commander length since Colt introduced it around 1950. The Officers length came along later, popularized first by custom gunsmiths like George Sheldon, Armand Swenson, and Lyn Alexiou, but today available in almost every maker's catalog. The

If a single-stack magazine isn't enough, you can get a higher capacity 45. This well-worn ParaOrdnance P-14 holds 14 rounds.

Government barrel length is 5 inches, a Commander barrel measures 4-1/4 inches, while the Officers tube runs 3-1/2 inches. Today we're all the way down to 3-inch barrels. It was master pistolsmith Bill Laughridge who first made this shortest length work, and such stubby 45s are now available out of the box as the Colt Defender, Springfield Micro, and Kimber Ultra-Carry. Like the Officers, they also have shorter butts, improving concealability still further at the sacrifice of only one round of cartridge capacity. There are guns like the Colt CCO that mix and match the concepts. The CCO has a Commander-length barrel/slide assembly on the short Officers gripframe. Ray Ordorica, former editor of this publication, called the CCO the ideal concealed-carry 1911. Argument was notable by its absence.

As a general rule, if you need to carry a gun you need to carry spare ammo. Like the pistols themselves, standard 1911 magazines are slim and flat, comfortable to carry and easy to conceal. Many find that it's as comfortable to carry two single-

A 1911 doesn't have to be big anymore. This is Springfield Armory's aptly-named Micro Compact 45.

The 1911 is an all-around gun. Author's old favorite Colt National Match 45 with BoMar sights has served him at bullseye matches, the IPSC Nationals, Bianchi Cup and Second Chance, and as a uniform service pistol, concealed carry weapon, and home defense gun.

stack 1911 magazines as to carry one big double-stack, and this helps to ease the disparity in round count.

Finally, all the best concealment holsters are made for the 1911, in all its shapes and sizes. You have the widest selection to pick from. The same is true for accessories like sights, stocks, and other options.

Overcoming Problems

The 1911 is not without its faults. Not all were created equal. Some early Colts, and some cheap clones, were made of softer metals that didn't stand up well. Stay with the major brands and you'll be fine on that score. The gun was not built with the brutal recoil of 10mm or +P 45 in mind, and if you start shooting those hot loads in the thousands you'll start breaking parts (*usually slide stops*).

The most popular 1911 cartridge is the 45 ACP. It needs a hollow-point bullet to keep it from overpenetrating, and historically, conventional jacketed hollowpoints have had a certain velocity floor beneath which they would not expand reliably. This has been largely resolved by the coming of high-tech hollowpoint designs. The 230-grain CCI Gold Dot, Federal Hydra-Shok, PMC Starfire, Remington Golden Saber, and Winchester SXT were all designed to expand even when fired from shorter-barrel pistols.

For most of the 20th century, the 1911 was plagued with a reputation for sloppy shooting unless it had been accurized by a custom gunsmith. That's pretty much over. With today's CNC machining, you can expect a brand new 1911 from a quality maker to put five shots in somewhere between two and three inches at 25 yards. You'll find the occasional out-of-the-box specimen that, with ammo it likes, may shoot as tight as one inch at that distance.

A greater concern is the whole cocked and locked thing. Some people are simply not comfortable with a cocked gun. There are countless concealment holsters that will intersperse a safety strap between the cocked hammer and the firing pin of your 1911. If that is not enough, Para-Ordnance offers the excellent LDA series of 1911s rendered with double-action-only trigger systems. The pull is amazingly smooth and light, and the LDA models are available in configurations ranging from flat single-stack subcompacts to the full-size, high-capacity service gun with 5-inch barrel.

Another answer to cocked hammer concerns is Bill Laughridge's SFS (*Safe Fast Shooting*) kit. The hammer rides safely down on a live round with this conversion, but the standard release movement of the thumb safety causes that hammer to fly back to the cocked position. (*For info call the Cylinder & Slide Shop at 800-448-1713.*)

If *cocked and locked* puts you off, the 1911 is available in double-action-only as the Para-Ordnance LDA. This is the compact 7-shot 45 model.

Colt's Concealed Carry Officers (CCO) has been called the ideal personal protection 45 auto. This one belongs to the author, who agrees.

For the rare person who doesn't think the 1911 is sufficiently powerful, consider the LAR Grizzly in 45 Winchester Magnum. D. R. Middlebrooks customized this one for the author with a JetComp recoil compensator.

The 1911 dresses up nicely. This is the author's engraved Les Baer/Gunsite Custom 45, presented to him after being voted National Tactical Advocate in 1995 at the National Tactical Invitational.

For many, though, the concern is not so much the cocked hammer as the relatively short, easy trigger pull that unleashes each shot (*and particularly the first*) from the 1911. John Browning built this great gun to be a battle pistol, something a soldier would resort to when the sappers were through the wire and he had to swiftly draw, fire, and hit center with a powerful bullet. It was never designed for holding people at gunpoint under high stress, which is exactly the job of the home defense gun, the concealed-carry handgun, and the police service pistol most of the time.

The standard answer is, *"keeping the finger off the trigger is a training issue."* It's always tempting to go with a pat answer, but we can't get past the fact that it takes a cool hand under stress to keep that finger from making its way to the trigger. We wouldn't be pointing the gun at the suspect in the first place unless we were in danger from him, and when we are in danger we want to be ready to shoot. This is why the 1911, for the "threat management" function of the typical cop or armed citizen in most situations, tends to work best in the hands of a seasoned expert handgunner who is already proven to be cool under pressure.

Does this mean that you should follow the conventional wisdom of all those nervous police chiefs and avoid carrying a 1911? Not necessarily. If you have very short fingers, the 1911's easy trigger reach may make the first shot so much more accurate for you, especially under stress, that it can be a deciding factor in gun selection. Remember, *any element of gun design that allows the shooter to hit more accurately under stress, concomitantly reduces the danger of a wild shot that could strike a bystander.* Thus, the 1911's choice could be strongly defended under the principle of competing harms, which in this case would be a reasonable belief that the danger of a wild shot from the supposedly safer double-action pistol outweighed the danger of a short-trigger-stroke pistol going off by accident, particularly when the documentable training and coolness under pressure of the shooter in question minimized the chances of an accident in the first place.

Are you an old vet trained in the 1911 and qualified with it over many years of military service? It makes sense not to throw that competence away, and to carry a gun that the record will show Uncle Sam paid good taxpayer dollars to train you to skillfully employ.

You are a competitive shooter who fires 30,000 rounds a year from 1911 match guns in training, practice, and practical shooting matches? A jury of reasonable, prudent men and women will understand why you chose to carry a gun that would allow you to directly transfer those hard-earned skills to management of a real world encounter, if a knowledgeable defense lawyer gets it across to them in a common sense way.

Bottom Line

The 1911 is not for everyone. That said, there are certain people for whom it is the ideal defensive handgun. So many people have decided that they fit this profile that it's a safe bet the 1911 won't be considered obsolete for real world self-defense any time soon. ●

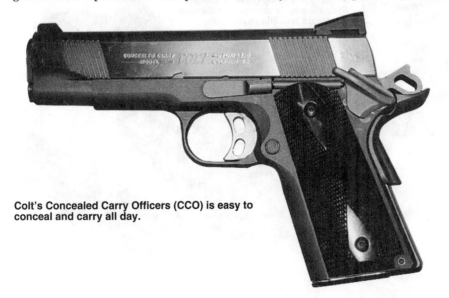

Colt's Concealed Carry Officers (CCO) is easy to conceal and carry all day.

Knives With Multi-Carry Options

by Roger Combs

▶ The *Model 100* River/Rescue is a Benchmade fixed blade that can be toted on webbing or a belt, or tied on with cord.

DAY IN AND day out, those who use and appreciate knives become accustomed to carrying them in such places as a pocket or purse, in a belt sheath or clipped directly onto a belt or pocket. There are plenty of other caches, and some knives are made (*or their sheaths are designed*) for special locations, concealed or carried openly. Other knives are simply tied, lashed or strapped to a convenient spot, quick to grab.

There are neck knives, boot knives, sleeve knives, knives to be carried on a backpack strap, along the small of the back, horizontally near a belt buckle, in a shoulder rig, even under a hat or helmet. The locations are limited only by the imagination.

A word of caution: since Sept. 11, 2001, no knife of any kind may be carried on a commercial aircraft, or through security checkpoints in airports and many train stations, government buildings, schools and other locations. There was a time, not so long ago, when it was acceptable to carry a small pocketknife or wear a neck knife aboard an airplane, but not anymore. Whether or not those days will ever return, nobody knows, but it should not be counted as likely. The knives described here have many uses at different times, but all must be carried with care and in accordance with current laws.

Many custom knifemakers can and do produce excellent neck, boot or sleeve knives on order. But we are concerned here with readily available factory production. That said, let us take a look at knives with multi-carry options available from manufacturers.

Benchmade

For years, Benchmade has been best known for its innovative folding-knife designs. Lately, the fertile minds in Oregon City have come up with several interesting fixed-blade knives with multiple-carry options for spe-

Sharing the same style of special Kydex® sheath are the Benchmade Nimravus and Nimravus Cub.

A small, lightweight knife, the Benchmade Tether's neck lanyard is designed to easily break, a safety measure.

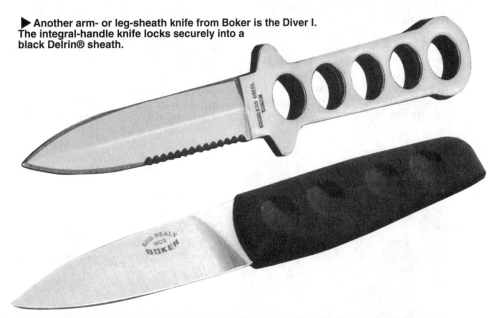

▶ **Benchmade's Rescue Hook can be attached to a harness, shoulder strap or worn around the neck.**

Handles on either model are made of a textured, non-slip, black G-10 material.

The *Model 100* River/Rescue is another Benchmade fixed blade that can be toted on webbing or a belt, but the Kydex® sheath is designed similar to the Nimravus with cord holes for lashing it to the outside of a sleeve or to a tab on a Personal Flotation Device. The 3.23-inch blade is 440C stainless steel, with a choice of an all-plain or partly-serrated edge.

The blade may be employed as with any other knife, but the shape is specifically designed to be less prone to accidental puncturing of a life raft if dropped. Handle material is black non-slip G-10.

Moving to a couple of neck knives, the *Model 160* TK-1 Tether is a small, lightweight knife hardly noticeable when worn. The knife material is 440C stainless steel,

5 3/4 inches long overall, with a *skeletonized* handle. The non-slip handle coating is available in black, gray or green. The blade, plain edge or partly serrated, stretches 2 inches. Knife and Kydex sheath weigh a slight 3 ounces.

The *Model 5* Rescue Hook is worn attached to a harness or shoulder strap or, in its tiny Delrin® sheath, around the neck. This little device is primarily a sharpened rescue hook for firefighters, EMTs and police. The entire package weighs little more than an ounce and is slightly less than 3 inches long. The sharpened hook design is intended to cut through seat belts, lanyards, straps, boots and other such things in emergencies. Benchmade says the latest design refinement is a hole in the handle engineered to fit snugly over oxygen bottle valves. It's proving popular with rescue personnel.

Boker

Many of the knives Boker USA markets are the result of collabora-

cial uses. The fixed-blade *models 140* Nimravus and *145* Nimravus Cub share the same style of Kydex® sheath. The sheath design has provisions for lashing or taping it to a backpack or load-carrying strap, with the blade tip pointed up or tip down. When carried with the handle downward, the thumb-toggle secure and release system holds the knife securely in place until it is drawn, a one-hand operation.

Blade material for both Nimravus models is 154CM stainless steel or M-2 high-speed steel, both with non-reflective BT2 finishes. Blade lengths are 4 1/2 inches for the Nimravus and 3.65 inches for the Cub. Blades come in plain or combination plain/serrated edges.

▶ **Another arm- or leg-sheath knife from Boker is the Diver I. The integral-handle knife locks securely into a black Delrin® sheath.**

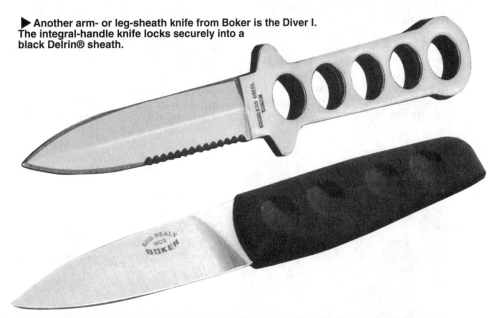

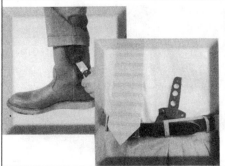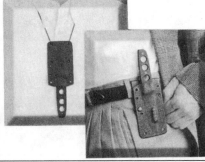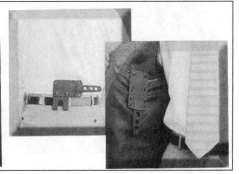

The Boker Escort knife is designed by Bud Nealy and features his patented nine-position sheath system.

In the city, there's no better knife to have attached to a key ring than the Buck Metro with a 1 1/8-inch blade, and a bottle and can opener. You can even accessorize with black-, blue- or purple-handle versions.

tions with well-known custom makers. Take the company's Escort knife, for example, designed by Bud Nealy who has made knives for federal, state and local law enforcement agencies, as well as for personal bodyguards.

The Escort features Nealy's patented nine-position sheath system that can position the knife in a boot, around the neck with lanyard, vertically or horizontally on the belt, on the front or back of the torso, in a jacket breast pocket, or lashed to a pack strap. The knife has a 3 1/4-inch blade of Solingen stainless steel, a fiberglass-reinforced Delrin handle with indexing finger indentations, and Nealy's Multi-Concealment Kydex sheath.

Overall, the knife is 7 inches long and weighs 2.3 ounces.

Another arm- or leg-sheath knife from Boker is the Diver I. This integral-handle knife is all 440 stainless steel with a 4-inch, partly serrated, double-edged blade. The locking sheath is made of black Delrin material.

Buck

Buck Knives observed its 100th anniversary in 2002 with a number of commemorative knives and events. One of the new designs is the little Buck Metro; a knife intended to be carried on a key chain, among other places. This 1 1/2-ounce tool features a 1 1/8-inch knife blade, and a bottle and can opener. Handle-color choices include black, blue or purple. The Metro is egg-shaped and features one-hand opening and closing. Closed, the knife is 2 3/8 inches long.

The Buck Tiburon is, as the name might imply, a water sports knife that was designed in collaboration with well-known kayaker Ed Gillet. The 3 3/4-inch 17-7PH stainless steel blade features a serrated edge and chisel point that is less likely to puncture boat hulls or flotation devices. The handle is *skeletonized*, reducing the overall weight to 6 ounces. The molded sheath is designed specifically for belt wear, lashed to a pack strap or on either arm. Both the knife and the sheath have provisions for safety lanyards.

Camillus

A couple of the Camillus CUDA fixed-blade knives, designed by custom knifemaker Bob Terzuola, fit the category. The Close Quarters Battle (CQB) knives feature multi-position Kydex sheaths with Tek-Lok to hold everything secure. They may be worn or lashed in any of several positions and locations. The regular CUDA CQB has a 5 3/4-inch ATS-34 stainless steel blade, while the Jr. CQB features a 4-inch blade of the same material. The knives are available with plain or partly serrated edges, and handles are non-slip, black canvas Micarta®.

Case

Three Case knives qualify as knives with multi-carry options other than worn on a belt sheath or in a pocket. The Camper's Knife, Camper's Knife With Pliers and Electrician's Knife are each equipped with a bail on one end of

The molded sheath of the Buck Tiburon water sports knife looks great on a belt, lashed to a pack strap, or on either arm.

The Camillus CUDA Close Quarters Battle (CQB) knives feature multi-position Kydex® sheaths.

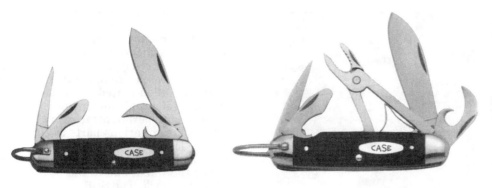

The Case Camper's Knife, Camper's Knife With Pliers, and Electrician's Knife.

Cold Steel's Mini Culloden is patterned after the Scottish *Sgian Dhub* knife.

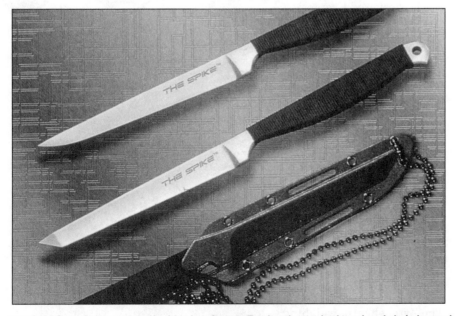

The Cold Steel Spike neck knife rides in a Secure-Ex sheath attached to a bead chain lanyard.

the handle to easily hook the individual knife to a key ring. This keeps it handy, and makes for a quick-to-access folder when needed.

The stainless steel blades on are each 3 3/4 inches long, and brown, jigged-synthetic handle slabs give the knives traditional appearances. The Camper's Knife adds a can opener, cap lifter/screwdriver, and punch, with one model including pliers. The Electrician's Knife features a screwdriver blade and a pruning blade for specialized cutting.

Coast Cutlery

Coast imports a little pocket/key chain knife the company designates "CG1204." The folder has a 2-inch stainless steel blade and a Zytel® handle, and weighs just over a half ounce with key chain and ring attached.

Cold Steel

Cold Steel may lead the pack in the number of knives with multi-carry options. The Mini Culloden is patterned after the Scottish *Sgian Dhub* knife, and the name "Culloden" is in honor of a famous 1746 Scottish battle. The Mini Culloden showcases an AUS-8A stainless steel blade that is 3 1/2 inches long in a plain or serrated edge. The handle is equally lengthy and composed of diamond-patterned Kraton® for a good grip. Weight is listed at 2.3 ounces, and the knife comes with Cold Steel's Concealex® neck sheath.

Next, a couple of push knives feature sheaths designed to carry the T-handle Safe Keeper II and Safe Keeper III on belts, in coat pockets, tucked in boots, attached to web gear, or strapped to ankles or wrists. The Safe Keeper II has a 420 blade measuring 3 3/4 inches, while the Safe Keeper III employs a 2 1/2-inch 420 blade. With checkered-Kraton handles, each weighs about 3 1/2 ounces.

Knifemaker Barry Dawson designed the Spike neck knife to be slung from a Secure-Ex sheath attached to a bead chain lanyard. The sheath also involves slots and eyelets in the sides so that it might be lashed inside a sleeve, or hooked to a D-ring or on a pack strap. The Spike features a slender, 4-inch 420 steel blade and a Kraton handle for an overall length of 8 inches. The Spike is available in a tapered, upswept blade, or in a tanto blade shape.

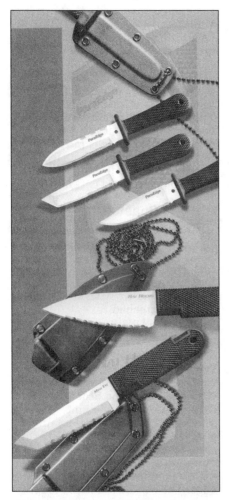

Three Cold Steel Para Edge neck knives are delivered with Concealex® sheaths and partly serrated, double-edge *tanto* and clip-point blades.

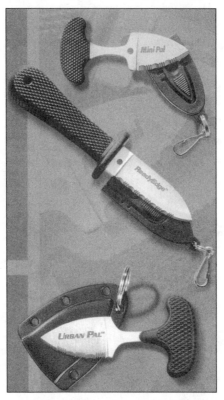

Small and smaller might describe the Cold Steel Ready Edge, with a 2-inch blade, and the Mini Pal, which relies on just 1 inch of steel. The Urban Pal has a 1 1/2-inch serrated blade.

but 1 1/2 ounces, may be worn around the neck with *paracord* (a parachute-type cord), employed as a boot knife, attached to a belt, in a jacket pocket or rigged to a harness with a two-position, detachable, black-Teflon-plated stainless steel clip. Holes and slots molded into the sheath permit attachment to other gear or various parts of the body. The Zytel belt adapter allows the knife to be worn above or below the waist, and in the small of the back. The Stiff K.I.S.S. is held in the sheath by a molded detent, which is released by pushing the thumb against the top of the sheath for a smooth, silent draw or, more abruptly and loudly, with a sharp pull. *Paracord*, steel clip, Zytel belt adapter and screws are provided with the sheath.

Emerson Knives, Inc.

Ernest Emerson's designs are mostly large, rugged tactical folders, but the "La Griffe" (literally "*the claw*"), introduced a few years ago, has proven a popular model. The neck knife was designed by French knifemaker Fredric Perrin and features a 1 3/4-inch curved blade and *skeletonized* handle. Overall, the 154-CM

Small and smaller might describe the next two Cold Steel knives. The Ready Edge has a 2-inch blade and the Mini Pal relies on just 1 inch of steel. Both feature fully serrated edges to easily cut through aluminum cans, cardboard, nylon line, carpet and other tough materials. They incorporate Kraton handles and tiny Zytel sheaths that lock the knives safely in place for tip-up carry. The ends of the sheaths have metal clips for snapping onto key chains, belt loops, jacket zippers or lanyards.

A bit larger, Cold Steel neck knives include three Para Edge models. Each available 3-inch blade—clip point, tanto or double-edge spear point—is made of AUS-6A stainless steel and partly serrated. Handles are non-slip checkered Kraton, and a hard Concealex neck sheath is included.

The Urban Pal, with a 1 1/2-inch blade, and the slightly larger Super

Edge are little serrated-edge neck knives packaged with Kraton sheaths. Larger still is the Hai Hocho knife with a 4-inch, serrated-edge, AUS-6A blade weighing 2.2 ounces, including neck sheath with beaded-steel lanyard. Handle material is checkered Kraton.

The Mini Tac neck knives come with 4-inch, plain or all-serrated AUS 6A tanto blades and checkered-Kraton 3 1/2-inch handles. The Concealex neck sheaths feature friction-fit retainer systems to prevent loss.

Columbia River Knife & Tool

The Columbia River Knife & Tool Stiff K.I.S.S.(*Keep It Super Simple*) knife is certainly designed for a variety of carry modes and locations. Ed Halligan conceived the Stiff K.I.S.S. fixed blade to be 7 1/4 inches long and .12-inch thick, weighing 2 ounces. The AUS-6M stainless steel blade is 3 1/2 inches long, available with plain or serrated edge. The Zytel sheath, weighing

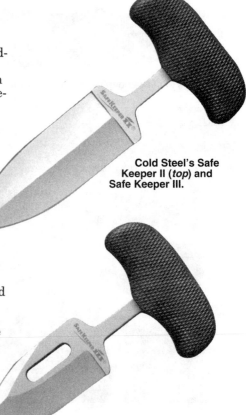

Cold Steel's Safe Keeper II (*top*) and Safe Keeper III.

stainless steel, black-oxide-coated knife is 4.9 inches long and weighs 1 1/2 ounces. The Kydex sheath holds the little knife firmly in place. Many of Emerson's law enforcement customers carry La Griffe models as backup knives.

Gerber Legendary Blades

There are four models in Gerber's Expedition Series I and II that are offered for wear on the arm, sleeve, leg or pack strap. In fact, the four similarly designed knives are sold with adjustable rubber leg straps appropriate for wear while rafting or diving. The stainless steel blades are each 3 1/4 inches long, and the knives are offered with either yellow- or black-rubber handles. Each knife weighs 8 ounces and is 8 1/4

inches long overall. Lanyard holes complete the packages and are located at the ends of the handles.

The Gerber Guardian Back-Up is sold as a boot knife with a sheath that has a clip and lash loops. The sheath is designed to hold the knife handle up or down. The design, from famed custom knifemaker Bob Loveless, features a 3 1/4 inch stainless steel blade, with a nylon handle covered with Santoprene® for a non-slip grip. Draw tension is adjustable.

Gutmann Cutlery

The large Gutmann Cutlery fixed-blade Walther Solace knife may be worn on the belt, to be sure, but the molded Kydex sheath is designed to carry the knife around the neck on a lanyard, at the top of a boot, or lashed to a belt strap, tip up or tip down. The Solace features a 3 1/2-inch 440A stainless steel blade and is 8 1/4 inches overall with a *paracord*-wrapped handle. Built with a slim profile, it weighs only 4 ounces.

The new Gutmann Special Forces knife is designed for concealed wear and includes a covert carrying harness rig. The 3 15/16-inch blade is made of ATS-34 steel coated with a matte Teflon® finish. The Kraton handle is deeply checkered for a non-slip grip. The black nylon sheath includes a belt- or boot-

Three Cold Steel Para Edge neck knives are delivered with Concealex® sheaths and partly serrated, double-edge *tanto* and clip-point blades.

▲ **A Kydex® sheath holds the Fredric Perrin-designed Emerson Knives La Griffe neck knife firmly in place.**

Four models of the Gerber Expedition Series I and II knives are worn on the arm, sleeve, leg or pack strap, and sold with adjustable rubber leg straps appropriate for wear while rafting or diving.

▲ **The Columbia River Knife & Tool Stiff K.I.S.S. is held in the sheath by a molded detent.**

carrying clip for additional wear options. The Special Forces knife weighs 5.4 ounces.

Ka-Bar Knives

Many folks might categorize the Ka-Bar military/fighting knives as just that, military/fighting knives, but include the company's Kydex sheath with several of the fixed-blade models, and you have carry-anywhere tools. The Kydex sheath has four slots and eight eyelet holes so it may be lashed, strapped or corded to a pack strap, lower leg or arm, tip up or tip down. A safety strap that snaps is included in the design. No doubt, the Ka-Bar name is one of the best known in fighting knives, dating back to World War II days. Modern versions of that knife are available, but order the Kydex sheath for carrying options.

Katz

The Katz Avenger boot/diver/paratrooper knife may be ordered with leather or nylon boot sheath, or a diving quick-release ABS sheath with harness. The Avenger, or its similar partner the Saber-Tooth Avenger with serrated edge, features a 4 1/2-inch blade of XT70 stainless steel. The handle is non-slip checkered Kraton with a slight palm swell to the design. At 8 3/4 inches overall, the knife weighs 6 1/2 ounces and includes a lanyard hole through the butt of the handle.

Kershaw

Kershaw's Sea Hunters feature blunt-tip or regular double-edge blades, cord-cutting hooks, neon and black designs for visibility, and diver's sheaths with adjustable straps and quick-release buckles. The blunt-tip version has a 3 1/2-inch blade, while the double-edge, tipped model's blade is 3 3/4 inches long. Each knife weighs about three ounces.

In the boot-knife category, the Amphibian has a double-edge blade, open-tang handle to reduce weight and includes an optional boot or diver's sheath. The Amphibian's blade is 3 3/4 inches long, and the knife weighs 3.2 ounces.

Masters Of Defense

The Masters Of Defense Scorpion neck knife has a short, convex-edged blade and skeletonized handle for lightweight carrying. Furthermore,

The Gerber Guardian Back-Up is sold as a boot knife with a sheath that has clip and lash loops designed to hold the knife handle up or down.

▶ The large Gutmann Cutlery fixed-blade Walther Solace knife may be worn in a variety of ways.

The Katz Avenger boot/diver/paratrooper knife may be ordered with a leather, nylon, or ABS sheath with harness.

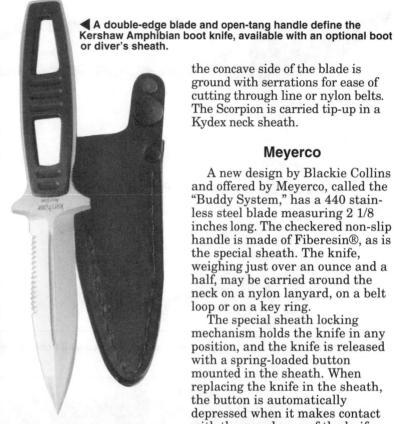

◀ A double-edge blade and open-tang handle define the Kershaw Amphibian boot knife, available with an optional boot or diver's sheath.

▲ Diver's sheaths with adjustable straps and quick-release buckles are included with the Kershaw Sea Hunters.

the concave side of the blade is ground with serrations for ease of cutting through line or nylon belts. The Scorpion is carried tip-up in a Kydex neck sheath.

Meyerco

A new design by Blackie Collins and offered by Meyerco, called the "Buddy System," has a 440 stainless steel blade measuring 2 1/8 inches long. The checkered non-slip handle is made of Fiberesin®, as is the special sheath. The knife, weighing just over an ounce and a half, may be carried around the neck on a nylon lanyard, on a belt loop or on a key ring.

The special sheath locking mechanism holds the knife in any position, and the knife is released with a spring-loaded button mounted in the sheath. When replacing the knife in the sheath, the button is automatically depressed when it makes contact with the guard area of the knife. Edge options are plain or serrated.

Outdoor Edge

Two versions of the Outdoor Edge Wedge are available, the original with a 2 3/8-inch blade, and the Wedge II with a 3-inch blade. Both Outdoor Edge knives are meant for carry in skeleton sheaths with corded-loop lanyards, or clipped to belt loops or D-rings by swivel clips. The 6M stainless steel blades are hand ground, and the handles are of black non-slip Delrin. A positive lock button keeps each knife in its sheath until the release is pressed.

Schrade

The Schrade Cliphanger Silhouette and larger Viper folders may be carried in pockets, but also clipped to belt loops or D-rings via their clips and extended fobs. Each clip strap fits into the knife handle and locks in place with a safety-release button. The handle material is deeply checkered non-slip Zytel. The Silhouette has a 3 1/4-inch blade, while the Viper's blade is 4 1/2 inches long, both with partially serrated, stainless steel edges.

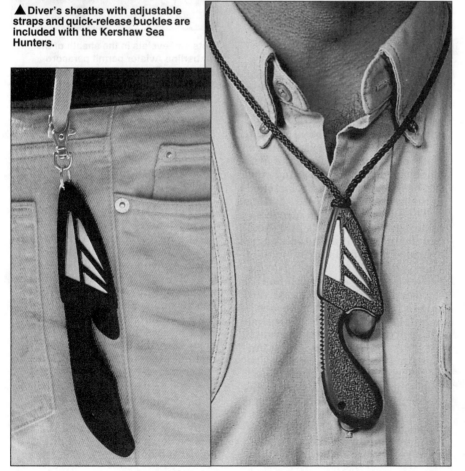

◀ The Outdoor Edge Wedge and Wedge II knives.

The Masters Of Defense Scorpion neck knife.

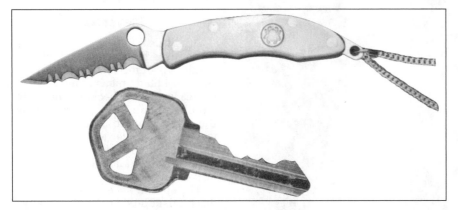

"A necklace that cuts" is a good way to describe the Spyderco Mini Police Necklace.

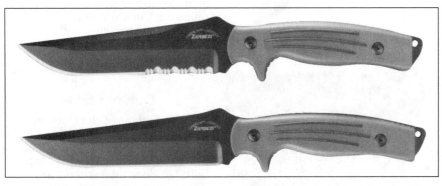

The Timberline Zambezi fixed-blade knife is a real worker.

Slots and eyelets in the sheath of the Timberline Aviator permit paracord attachment to various straps, belts or other equipment where required.

For those involved in water sports, the Schrade Water Rat Delrin sheath may be strapped to the arm or leg, as well as attached to a vest or D-ring using the PFD (Personal Flotation Device) clip. The Water Rat is available with a black or a bright-orange handle. The stainless steel blade is 7 3/8 inches long, partially serrated along its edge. It has a blunt tip to reduce puncturing accidents on rafts, canoes or kayaks. A safety release button is pressed to release the knife from the sheath, and it withdraws smoothly.

SOG Specialty Knives

SOG has introduced a couple of new neck knives in recent months. The SOG Duo has a 2 3/4-inch AUS-6A stainless steel blade but, by loosening the blade from the handle with a screw, the rest of the blade is unveiled from within the grip, with a second, serrated-edge blade pointing away from the first blade tip. The double-pointed steel can be flipped over and refastened to the handle for two blade options.

The Duo is carried in a special Kydex sheath that folds into the handle, making it an interesting hybrid of a fixed-blade and folding knife. The little neck knife weighs two ounces, and the sheath has a removable clip as well as a lanyard hole for a variety of carry modes.

Smaller yet, is the SOG Outline with a Kydex sheath that permits the knife to be worn on a neck lanyard, in a boot, or in a pocket. The 2 1/2-inch blade is 440A stainless steel adjoined to a skeleton handle. The Outline weighs only 1 ounce and is slightly more than 4 1/2 inches long. The blade edge is serrated, except on a modified tanto-tip version.

Spyderco

The little Spyderco Mini Police Necklace is just as the name implies, a neck knife. It also is a working lock-back folding knife with a 1 5/16-inch ATS-34 stainless steel blade. The blade features SpyderEdge serrations for ease of cutting.

The SpyderCard is a credit-card-size knife in length, width and thickness with a 2 13/16-inch AUS-6 steel blade. It might be carried in a wallet or purse, but will have to be checked through before boarding a commercial airliner. It weighs 3 1/4 ounces and the blade locks open with the liner. Blade options include plain or 50/50 serrated.

Timberline

Greg Lightfoot designed the Timberline Zambezi fixed-blade knife as a real worker, and the custom Kydex sheath system allows it be carried on the belt, boot, leg or arm, or strapped to other equipment. The 6-inch 440C steel blade is powder coated with a non-glare finish. Edge choices are either plain or a combination plain and serrated. The handle is non-glare Zytel with Kraton slip-resistant ribs, and the grip is secured with stainless steel removable fasteners for easy cleaning. The extended tang butt has a lanyard hole for additional carry options.

Another Lightfoot design is the Mini Pit Bull. The Timberline sheath with Timber-Clip offers options of carrying the 3-inch-blade knife on its bead neck chain, and tip-up or tip-down on the belt or in a boot. The blade is made of AUS-6 stainless steel in an all-plain or combo edge. The Zytel handle is textured for a non-slip grip and the full tang extends beyond the butt with a lanyard hole for other options.

Vaughn Neeley designed the Timberline Aviator pilot survival knife to include a Kydex sheath. The sheath has a detachable ballistic belt loop and web assembly to be attached with four hex fasteners. Slots and eyelets in the sheath permit *paracord* attachment to various straps, belts or other equipment where required. A safety thumb snap securely holds the knife no matter the carry mode.

The Aviator features a 3.4-inch bead-blasted blade with a chisel-ground tanto shape, available in plain or combo edge. The knife weighs 7.8 ounces and is 8.75 inches long overall. It is certainly a military/survival knife design, but with many carrying options.

United Cutlery

One of the biggest knives one might carry is the United Cutlery Black Ronin Tanto with shoulder harness. The Black Ronin is really a short sword with a 9 1/2-inch stainless steel blade. Overall, it is more than 14 inches long with a sturdy grip wrapped in black-nylon *paracord*, and the edge is partially serrated.

For something smaller, look to the T-Handle Combo knife fashioned for back-of-the-belt carry, or to be strapped on an arm or leg. The sheath actually contains two small T-handle knives, one at each end of the sheath. One blade has a plain edge, while the other is serrated. A slightly different sheath contains one of the T-handle knives

Try out the United T-Handle Combo knife for back-of-the-belt carry, or strapped on an arm or leg.

and is just right for neck wear using a nylon lanyard.

The United Black Sentry has a 5-inch tanto blade, a knuckle-guard handle and comes with a special shoulder harness. The sheath also includes a belt loop, boot clip and a quick-release blade insert, reversible for left or right-hand wear. The edge is one-third serrated.

United's Undercover Dagger is a 7 1/4-inch knife carried in a special nylon PVC-reinforced sheath designed to be worn horizontally on the back of a belt. The blade, 3 7/16 inches long, is made of 420 stainless steel ground to a modified tanto shape.

Custom maker Fred Carter designed the United Guardian and Mini Guardian neck knives. They use bead-blasted AUS-8 stainless steel for the blades, and checkered ABS material for the handles and sheaths. A nylon lanyard cord is

included. The Guardian has a 4-inch tanto blade, while the Mini Guardian's similarly shaped blade is 2 5/16 inches long. ●

Editor's Note

This chapter was excerpted from SPORTING KNIVES, 2ND EDITION, *a new annual book from Krause Publications. Contents are organized along the lines of* GUN DIGEST *and* GUNS ILLUSTRATED *, and cover the realm of commercial sporting cutlery. Read about the latest new products, insightful articles from industry authorities – even a website directory – and peruse the extensive illustrated catalog. A valuable reference section is located at the back of the book.* ***This book is available now from your favorite bookseller, or direct from Krause Publications @ 800-258-0929***

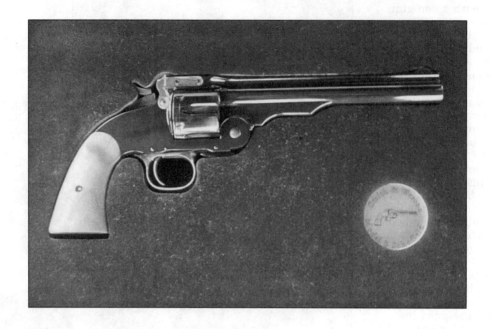

THE
RETURN OF
SMITH & WESSON'S
SCHOFIELD REVOLVER

by "Doc" O'Meara

ONE OF THE stars of last year's SHOT Show was Smith & Wesson's Schofield revolver. The firm's announcement that it was returning the antique design to it's catalog more than 120 years after initial production ceased came as a surprise to most in the industry. The news was met with joy by many shooters and collectors. Among cowboy action shooters, who had been making do with replicas to meet their needs for a distinctly un-SAA Colt-like revolver for several years, it was a particularly noteworthy event. Here, for them, was an opportunity to have the real thing, rather than a counterfeit of uncertain quality.

The problem with the replicas has been that they were modified to accept cartridges longer than those for which the originals were made. The first of them were chambered for the 45 Colt, then some later production revolvers were made to shoot the 44-40 Winchester round. This required that the frames and cylinders be extended, resulting in mechanical reliability problems that took several years to completely correct.

Restored to production after an absence of more than 120 years, S&W's modern reincarnation of the antique Schofield revolver is provided in a blue, plush-lined, wooden presentation case.

The replica makers made those alterations because, at the time, there was almost no commercially available factory-loaded 45 Schofield ammunition. The sole source was Fiocchi, of Italy, and few dealers stocked the brand. Of course, it is a relatively simple matter for the experienced handloader to modify existing brass, but few manufacturers are willing to produce firearms for which no ammunition is readily available, except by special order. Now that the original cartridge for the S&W Schofield can be procured from several sources, including Black Hills Ammunition, Cor-Bon, Ultramax– and fresh brass from both Starline and Bertram Bullets–the Smith & Wesson revolver could be made to its original dimensions and chambered for the original cartridge.

What makes the Schofield significantly different from other S&W Model Number 3 variants of the period is placement of the latch used to open the top-break revolver on the frame, just above the hammer slot, rather than on the barrel assembly. Major (brevet Lt. Colonel) George W. Schofield, from whom the revolver derives its name, was a U.S. Army officer assigned to the 10th Cavalry, of Buffalo Soldier fame. The modification he designed and patented was subsequently adopted for production by Smith & Wesson. It allowed a mounted trooper to open the revolver, eject the spent cartridges, reload and close it–ready once again to do battle; all with one hand, on a moving horse, without taking his other hand from the reins.

As compared with its primary competition, the 1860 Army Colt, which was being phased from service at that time, and Colt's New Model Metallic Cartridge Revolving Pistol, as the Single Action Army revolver was first known, the Schofield's rate of fire was amazing for its time. An experienced horseman could load, fire and reload the S&W two or three times for each such evolution done with the SAA Colt. In timed tests the Hartford-made revolver required 60 seconds to extract the empties and reload while the shooter was riding a horse at the gallop. It could be done in 26 seconds with the S&W. Acceptance trials also demonstrated that, when dismounted, it was possible to do it all as many as seven

Shooting from a rest, using two hands, the Schofield proved capable of delivering several very tight groups from a distance of 15 yards. They measured less than two inches.

times with the S&W while the Colt was reloaded just once.

Why, then, did the Colt remain in service for decades, while the last military purchase of the Schofield was in 1878–to be declared surplus shortly after and removed from service? Quite simply, the less complicated construction of the Colt allowed it to hold up better under the stress to which a combat arm is subjected and which was much easier to repair when it did fail. A few springs and a screwdriver kept in one's kit would allow a soldier to fix his revolver in the field (*probably against regulations, but better you should be caught doing so than having your scalp lifted if you didn't*). Repairing the S&W required the services of a skilled armorer. By the time production was halted in 1879, there had only been 8,969 sold to the military and to civilian consumers.

Modern cowboy action shooters strive, for the most part, for authenticity of dress and armament as a part of the "spirit of the game." Certainly, there were lots of other makers' guns in the holsters of Western men (and women) than the seemingly ubiquitous SAA Colt. For that reason, many competitors want something out of the ordinary for their use. The Schofield fills that role nicely.

It's taken Smith & Wesson several years to join the fray. The

success of the replica makers, coupled with consistent pressure from customers, eventually got through to the decision-makers in Springfield. The Performance Center, in consultation with S&W Historian Roy Jinks who also provided samples of the original from his personal collection for the project, began a detailed examination of the revolver's design and function characteristics. Their analysis found that, with modern metallurgy, it could be made sufficiently strong to withstand the increased pressures of reasonable smokeless powder loads. It would, after all, not be a firearm used for police or military service in today's world, and would not appeal to hunters, who require game-stopping power. Its sole use would be in the hands of collectors and competitors, most of who would specifically prefer the use of the mildest loads permissible for their target games.

Enter the lawyers: As originally designed, the Schofield relied upon a half-cock safety to prevent contact between the firing pin and the primer of the chambered cartridge. Our self-reliant and personally responsible great-grandfathers found such an arrangement perfectly satisfactory, but in this litigious age a passive safety was considered necessary. Wisely so. No factor involved with firearms use is

The sole factory load with which we tested the new Schofield was Black Hills 230-grain Cowboy Action load.

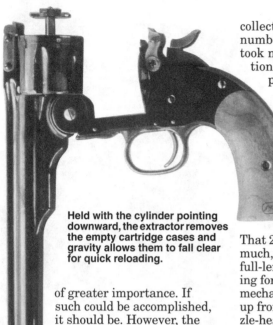

Held with the cylinder pointing downward, the extractor removes the empty cartridge cases and gravity allows them to fall clear for quick reloading.

of greater importance. If such could be accomplished, it should be. However, the integrity of the appearance of the original had to be maintained.

With the help of computer models, two significant changes were made. The first was removing the firing pin from the hammer and mounting a rebounding firing pin assembly on the frame. This reduces the already-minimal risk of piercing a primer and permits safer use of ammunition generating smokeless powder pressures, which are greater than those of the original blackpowder loads. The other was the internal addition of a hammer-block safety that prevents the hammer from striking the firing pin, should it suffer a blow or the firearm be dropped. Only the absence of an exposed firing pin on the cocked hammer alters the cosmetics of the new Schofield.

The first of these revolvers were reserved for

The frame-mounted firing pin, visible here, makes use of smokeless powder ammunition safer. Hidden within the frame is a passive hammer-block safety mechanism designed by computer to work without interfering with the revolver's other mechanical functions.

collectors who bid for specific serial numbers in an on-line auction. It took more than a year for production to catch up and the general public is beginning to see these revolvers become available. The question before us is, have they been worth the wait? While our answer is very much affirmative, it is a qualified *yes*.

The Schofield is a large revolver, weighing 40 ounces. That 2-1/2 pounds doesn't sound like much, but the 7-inch barrel with its full-length rib and the integral housing for the extractor activation mechanism puts most of the weight up front, giving it a distinctly muzzle-heavy feel that is much better controlled with two hands than one, when fast shooting is necessary.

The crude rear sight notch makes sight acquisition relatively slow, particularly for those with aging eyes. As well, the thin half-moon post front sight at the end of the full-length sighting channel of that heavy barrel tends to wave about a bit. Again, something best controlled with two hands.

The final criticism, in terms of the Schofield revolver's handling qualities, is the shape of the grip frame. Its acute curvature tends to cause it to slide in the hand under recoil somewhat more than do some other revolvers of the period. This too, is best managed by using two hands to shoot it.

So, we have established the Schofield is at a relative disadvantage when shot with a single hand. Still, the cocking stroke of the hammer is fast, smooth and short. The weight of pull of the trigger, which is very crisp, is a perfectly acceptable 4 pounds, 2 ounces as measured with the RCBS trigger-pull scale. And, of course, its speed of loading, extraction and reloading is on par with the more modern swing-out cylinder revolvers commonly available.

Fit and finish of the Schofield test revolver from S&W's Performance Center is excellent. The external parts are mated perfectly. The blue finish is deep and luxurious, but without the high shine for which some of S&W's premium

revolvers have been so justly famous. The hammer, trigger, trigger guard, rear sight and latch mechanism are color case-hardened with the predominantly gray tones typical of these revolvers in their first incarnation. The stocks, made of straight-grained walnut, fit so precisely that one wonders how it can be done so well. In style, this is a faithful reproduction of the 1st Model Schofields.

At the time of our test, Black Hills Ammunition's excellent 230-grain load was the sole ammunition variant at hand. Because the revolver's most frequent use is expected to be within the relatively close distances encountered in cowboy action competitions, we limited our shooting to 15 yards. First, we wanted to know what the revolver was capable of providing in terms of pure precision. That turned out to be a series of gratifyingly tight clusters measuring less than two inches, firing from a two-handed rest. Shooting as rapidly as grip correction and sight realignment permitted, our groups were kept to less than three inches from the same distance; a respectable result by any standard, especially so considering our relative lack of familiarity with the particular revolver used for these tests and its antique design characteristics.

There were no malfunctions of any sort during the tests. As long as one turns the barrel assembly over, so that extraction is downward, the fired cases clear the mechanism completely as they fall to the ground. If held up, however, just as would be the case with any modern revolver relying upon a star extractor, a case may slip away and fall back into the chamber. This is easily fixed, but can slow one down severely in competition.

Each of these revolvers is individually crafted in S&W's Performance Center to be handsomely finished and functionally reliable. They are also surprisingly accurate, in spite of the relatively crude sights. They come to the purchaser in a beautifully-crafted wooden presentation case, fitted into a plush blue lining. The 21st century version of Smith & Wesson's classic Model Number 3 Schofield revolver is certain to be prized by collectors and shooters alike, and will look as much at home in the holster of a cowboy action competitor as it did during the Frontier era of the Old West. ●

Six-Guns & Loads For

WINCHESTER
.45
COWBOY
650
FPS

Cowboy Action Shooting

by John Taffin

WE ALL KNOW that history takes some strange twists and turns but who could have foreseen what took place in the 1990s? At the beginning of the decade the 10mm and 40 S&W arrived, and many semi-automatics were quickly chambered for them, especially the 40 S&W. The "experts" proclaimed the revolver, the single-action six-gun in particular, was dead. The future would be black plastic guns; high-capacity black plastic guns, at that. We all know what happened to those evil high-cap magazines and the single-action six-gun–far from being dead–is more popular than ever. In fact single-action six-guns and everything connected with them are an important part, perhaps even the most important part, of the business 'engine' driving the firearms industry today.

Today cowboy action shooting is the fastest-growing shooting sport in the country. The founding (*and largest of several today*) organization, the Single Action Shooting Society (SASS), was founded in southern California by a group of single-action six-gun enthusiasts who christened themselves 'The Wild Bunch' after the 1969 movie with the same title. In the movie, the Wild Bunch was a group of 19th-century desperados who found themselves–in 1912–facing the realization they outlived their time. Nothing works for them until they redeem themselves by fighting for good and going out in a blaze of glory, wielding six-guns and wreathed in gunsmoke.

Cimarron's Flattop Target Model and Winchester's 45 Colt cowboy load is definitely a winning combination.

What started in southern California has now spread across the country, with matches being held in every state. It is a rare shooter that cannot find a local monthly match within easy driving distance of home. There are also CAS matches held in many foreign countries. Cowboy action shooting is based on the premise that *"our heroes have always been cowboys"* and there is nothing like wearing cowboy clothes and shooting cowboy guns, single-action six-guns.

Cowboy action shooting matches are generally set up in stages, each of which requires the use of a lever-gun, shotgun, and most importantly, a pair of single-action six-guns. The rules simply state the firearms used must be those that were available prior to 1899, or replicas or types thereof. When it comes to six-guns, this means that

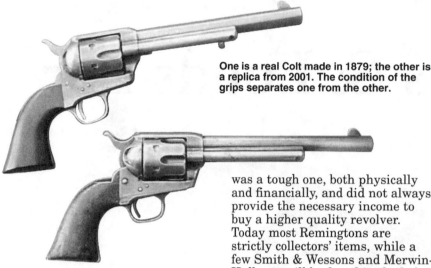

One is a real Colt made in 1879; the other is a replica from 2001. The condition of the grips separates one from the other.

any functionally-safe single-action revolver (cap and ball or fixed ammunition type) holding six rounds, of which only five are loaded since the rules require an empty chamber for safety. Most matches also require the wearing of pre-1899 clothes, or B-western clothes, or cowboy clothes, or.... there is a lot of leeway here but tennis shoes and ball caps are definitely out!

Any CAS match, and especially the large regional matches and championship matches, will reveal a large variety of costuming, belts, holsters, and six-guns. These matches are a true feast for the eyes of anyone who loves six-guns and anything Western. Those six-guns on display can usually be separated into three main categories: the original, or real six-guns of the frontier period; modern replicas of the original six-guns; and single-action six-guns from Ruger. Finally, there are those remaining six-guns that do not fit into any of these categories, but still have applications in cowboy action shooting. Along with the six-guns, we will look at the generous offerings of cowboy action shooting ammunition from several manufacturers—especially those that specialize in loading the cast bullet rounds to muzzle velocities under 1,000 fps as required by CAS rules.

THE REAL SIX-GUNS: Hollywood to the contrary, every cowboy and character on the Western frontier did not pack a Colt Single Action Army. In addition to the legendary Colt, there were single-action six-guns from Merwin-Hulbert, Remington, and Smith & Wesson—in addition to many cheaper revolvers. The cowboy life

was a tough one, both physically and financially, and did not always provide the necessary income to buy a higher quality revolver. Today most Remingtons are strictly collectors' items, while a few Smith & Wessons and Merwin-Hulberts will be found in the holsters of cowboy action shooters—but when it comes to desirable original six-guns from the frontier times, the Colt Single Action Army remains '*King*.'

The Colt Single Action Army, officially known as the Model P, appeared in 1873, chambered for the 45 Colt. The SAA was originally designed for military use, with the first guns being the U.S. Cavalry Model, the 7 1/2-inch Peacemaker. This is the model favored by most early lawmen who easily made the transition from the 7 1/2-inch Colt 1851 Navy 36 or the 8-inch Colt 1860 Army 44. The Single Action Army was soon offered in other barrel lengths, standardizing two of them: the 5 1/2-inch Artillery Model, and the 4 3/4-inch Civilian (*or Gunfighter*) Model. Some have credited lawman Bat Masterson with popularizing the short 4 3/4-inch barrel length. Colt records show that Masterson used saloon stationery to order "... *a nickel-plated 45 Colt with the barrel even with the ejecting rod.*" However, a closer look at Colt records reveals the short barrel appeared at least three years before Masterson ordered it.

Gunfighters on both sides of the law carried the Colt Single Action Army. History records the likes of Jesse James, Cole Younger, Wyatt Earp, Doc Holliday, Bill Tilghman, and Jeff Milton—to name

a few. In the 1880s, a young New Yorker, Theodore Roosevelt, went out to the Badlands of the Dakota Territory to become a rancher. He carried a 7 1/2-inch Colt Single Action Army; fully engraved with carved ivory stocks, in a fully engraved Cheyenne-style holster that he wore on the left side, butt to the front. Not only is TR my political hero of all time, I also deeply admire his taste in six-guns, grips, and leather. The most visible general in World War II, George S. Patton, was also known for his trademark handgun, a fully engraved, nickel-plated, ivory-stocked 4 3/4-inch Colt Single Action Army, carried in an S. D. Myres Border Patrol holster.

Can you imagine Western movies without the Colt Single Action Army? My earliest recollection of any gun in the movies goes back to 1947. The movie was "*Angel and the Badman*," with John Wayne as the gunfighter Quirt Evans who was about to be tamed by the Angel, the lovely Quaker lass played by Gail Russell. At the age of eight I not only fell in love with Miss Russell, but also recorded a lasting impression of Quirt's plain 4 3/4-inch Colt Single Action Army with hard rubber grips. One year later, the Duke would use that same Colt in "*Tall in the Saddle*." At the ripe old age of nine I knew that someday I, too, would have a Colt like John Wayne's!

In the early days we had the great old "B" Western movies from the 1930s and 1940s; then came television. The true star of all these shows was the Colt Single Action Army. Then one evening

Real and replica: (*top*) current production Smith & Wesson Model 3 Schofield 45 S&W; (*bottom*) Navy Arms replica of the Model 3 Russian in 44 Russian. Grips are Ultra Ivory by Eagle Grips.

(Saturday night in most parts of the country), a new young star emerged–James Arness as 'Matt Dillon, U.S. Marshall' who, for several decades would hand out *"Gunsmoke"* from his 7 1/2-inch Single Action Army. Notice I did not say 'Colt' as Matt's revolver was actually a Great Western!

The basic design of the Colt goes all the way back to 1836 and the Paterson model. As this is written, the Colt Single Action Army is nearly 130 years old and still in production! From the 1873 to 1941, more than 350,000 Colt Single Actions (in more than 30 chamberings) were manufactured at the Hartford plant. Half were chambered for the ever-popular 45 Colt; half of the remainder was the *"Frontier Sixshooter;"* the name found on the barrel instead of the chambering mark of 44-40. The three next most popular chamberings were 38-40, 32-20, and strangely enough, 41 Long Colt.

Although Colt introduced a double-action model in 1877, the Lightning 38 Long Colt and the Thunderer 41 Long Colt, followed by the full-sized double-action Model 1878 in 45 Colt one year later, most six-gunners stayed with their single actions. This would change after the turn-of-the-century as Americans discovered the new Smith & Wesson double actions and Colt's new 45, the Model 1911 autoloader. It would take the advent of the Model 1911 and a world war before the Texas Rangers would trade their beloved Colt Single Action 45 Colt for the 1911 Government Model 45 ACP.

These two blackpowder Colts, an 1879 44-40 Frontier Six-Shooter and an 1881 45 Colt were purchased for much less than the cost of one new Colt Single Action Army.

Sales of the Model P continued to decline after the turn of the century and this market fact, coupled with worn-out machinery and the effects of World War II, ended production of the now-legendary Colt Single Action Army. After the war, Colt announced the Single Action Army was dead and buried–never to be seen again. However, the popularity of TV westerns in the 1950s created demand for the old Colt once again. In 1956 the Single Action Army was resurrected and the Second Generation Single Action era began. Materials used were stronger, and the only chamberings offered would be 38 Special, 357 Magnum, 44 Special and 45 Colt–but it was still the same basic beloved six-gun.

By the 1970s history repeated itself as the Colt production

machinery and tooling was again wearing out and the SAA was again removed from production. However, it is impossible to withhold such a great gun from six-gunners and, in 1979, the Third Generation Single Action Army arrived with some design changes. The hand, and the ratchet on the back to the cylinder were changed for easier assembly, the full-length cylinder bushing was replaced by a short 'button' bushing in the front of the cylinder, and for some strange reason the barrel threads were changed. By the end of the 1980s, production of the Third Generation SAA seemingly ended after having been offered in 45 Colt, 44 Special, 44-40, and 357 Magnum. Colt resurrected the Model P as a custom shop model available in 45 Colt, 44-40, and wonder of wonders (*not been seen since the 1930s*), 38-40!

Today the Colt Single Action Army remains in production (*and, as of 2002, costs substantially less*) in both 45 Colt and 44-40, with the barrel lengths of 4-3/4 and 5-1/2 inches. A longer barrel and selected optional chamberings are also available. For nearly 130 years the Colt Single Action Army has been a survivor. This year's price reduction ensures an even longer life.

Just what is so special about a Colt Single Action Army, especially when one considers the high-quality replicas available for less than half the money? This may be one of those situations where *"If one understands, no explanation is necessary; if one doesn't, no explanation is possible."* I do know that no other six-gun stirs my heart, soul, and spirit like a genuine Single Action Army. No other six-gun has the aesthetic value of the old Colt. Look at the graceful lines, suggesting that this six-gun was not 'invented,' rather 'discovered' as if it was delivered supernaturally. Pull back the hammer, listening as it spells C-O-L-T on the way back to full cock. Close your eyes as you hold the Colt and you will hear the tinkling of a piano at the Long Branch, feel hundreds of miles of trail dust on your clothes, smell bacon and beans sizzling over an open campfire.

You have decided that 'authenticity' is the way to go in participating in cowboy action shooting. Where do you find authentic six-guns? The easiest way is to simply order a brand new Colt. However, there is an easier and less expensive–and

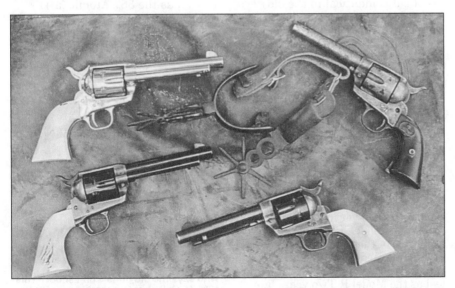

Three generations of Colt Single Action Armys for cowboy action shooting, in 45 Colt, 44 Special, and 44-40.

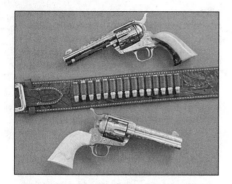

Two Colt SAAs 'fancied' for CAS: Third Generation 44-40 engraved by Dale Miller, and Second Generation 45 engraved by Jim Riggs. Grips, ram's horn and ivory, are by Paul Persinger; leather by El Paso Saddlery.

The classic Colt Single Action Army, a truly authentic six-gun for CAS.

even more authentic way to go–buy used. One place to look is local gun shops; another to search the pages of *Gun List*, that always has many Colt Single Actions from the First, Second, and Third Generation runs listed for sale; gun shows are a good place to find Colts; and do not neglect the classified advertising section in your local newspaper. In the past year I found four First Generation Colt Single Actions in excellent shooting shape for less than the cost of two brand new Custom Shop Single Actions. Two of those Colts were 7-1/2 inch black-powder guns; one an 1879 44-40, the other a 45 Colt made in 1881. The other two were 4-3/4 inch civilian models, a 1907-vintage 32-20, and a 1917 specimen in 45 Colt. The key is to be patient and watchful. The wonderful old six-guns are there and can be found at relatively reasonable prices.

Until this past year the only original single action still in production was the Colt Single Action. Beginning in the year 2000, and in celebration of the 125th anniversary of the introduction of the original Model 3 Schofield, Smith & Wesson reintroduced their 19th century single action adopted by the U.S. Cavalry in 1875.

In 1871 a young cavalry officer, Lt. Col. George W. Schofield, received one of the new Smith and Wesson Model No. 3s that had been adopted by United States Army. Note this was two years before the 1873 Colt Single Action Army became the official sidearm. Schofield worked with Smith & Wesson to improve the break-top 44-caliber six-gun. His main concern was the barrel latch. By moving it from the barrel to the frame it would be possible to fire the

improved revolver with one hand and to unload and reload in 26 seconds while on horseback! This was accomplished easily–one simply pushed on the frame-mounted latch with the thumb of the shooting hand, the barrel then rotated downwards, the cartridges were automatically ejected, and the revolver was ready for reloading. Try to accomplish this in 26 seconds with a Colt Single Action Army!

In 1874, the United States Army accepted the new Smith & Wesson Single Action Model 3 Schofield chambered in a new cartridge: the 45 S&W, or 45 Schofield. The new cartridge was shorter than the 45 Colt and could be used in either the Colt or the Smith & Wesson. The first 3000 Model 3 Schofields were delivered in July of 1875.

Now the original Schofield is back as a Smith and Wesson Performance Center revolver. Yes, it is pricey but now similar in cost to a new Colt Single Action Army. There are some interior design changes that were necessary to meet both current manufacturing processes and safety requirements, but on the outside, the new Schofield is identical to the old Schofield… and it is a real–not a replica–six-gun.

THE REPLICA SIX-GUNS: In the 1950s, thanks to television and the many hours of Western programming, the demand grew for single-action six-guns. Two new companies were there to scratch the itch. Sturm, Ruger had started in 1949, offering an inexpensive but accurate 22 semi-automatic pistol. Four years later, Bill Ruger went against prevailing wisdom and began producing what has become one of the most popular revolvers of all time, the Single-Six revolver in 22 rimfire. To create this model, Ruger downsized the frame of the Colt Single Action, but maintained the full-sized grip frame of the Colt to provide the same feel as the Model P. Two years later Ruger introduced the Blackhawk,

first in 357 Magnum and one year later in 44 Magnum. As they say, the rest is history.

A Single-Six 22 is not a true replica, however, and while Bill Ruger was building his new Single-Six in Connecticut, another Bill–Bill Wilson–offered a full-sized replica of the Colt Single Action Army from a new plant in Los Angeles, California. Many of the parts of the Great Western Frontier Revolver were interchangeable with Colt SAA parts; however, the Great Western used a frame-mounted firing pin such as offered by the old Christy Gun Works before World War II. Great Westerns were offered in standard barrel lengths of 4-3/4, 5-1/2, 7-1/2, and 12 inches, in the following chamberings: 45 Colt, 44 Special, 38 Special, 357 Magnum, as well as the 357 Atomic (a +P+

Who says the old guns won't shoot? This 1881 45 Colt shoots superbly with Black Hills Ammunition's Cowboy load.

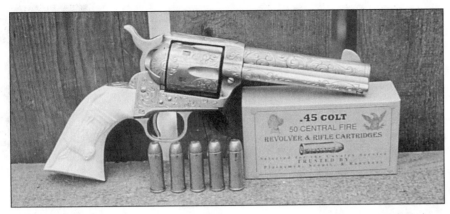

The legendary Colt Single Action Army 45 Colt, engraved by Jim Riggs, stocked with carved ivory by Paul Persinger. Even if you don't win the match you can still look good.

357 Magnum) and 44 Magnum. The standard finish was blue with a case-colored frame; full blue and nickel were also offered. Standard grips were imitation stag, as seen on the six-guns of many Western movie heroes in the 1930s and 1940s. Great Westerns disappeared in the 1960s but they can still be found at gun shows; unfortunately the very low-priced examples seem to have disappeared. They do, however, represent a great choice and great value for cowboy action shooters.

Thanks to the efforts of people like Boyd Davis of Early and Modern Firearms (EMF), Val Forgett of Navy Arms, and Mike Harvey at Cimarron Firearms Co., we now have truly authentic replica six-guns and our choices are almost limitless. We can have authentically-crafted "Single Action Armys" from such companies as AWA (American Western Arms), CFA (Cimarron Firearms Co.), EMF, Navy Arms, and USFA (United States Firearms Mfg. Co.). These are available in various finishes, such as blue with case-colored frames, brilliantly colored fireblue, nickel, and even engraved models with one-piece ivory stocks. The standard barrel lengths are 4-3/4, 5-1/2, and 7-1/2 inches as with the originals, plus we can also choose 3- and 4-inch barreled Sheriff's Models, even 10- and 12-inch Buntline Specials.

The Bisley Model is back in the three standard barrel lengths, and both the Single Action Army and the Bisley Model are available in the Flat-Top Target version offered to target shooters by Colt in the 1890s. Want a Remington instead of a Colt? Both the 1875 Remington with the web under the barrel, as well as the 1890 Model

with the cut-away web, can be had. The Remington has a different feel than the Colt Single Action Army but many frontier citizens considered it a superior design.

The Colts and Remingtons are both solid-frame six-guns, while Smith & Wesson built all of their single actions in the top-break style, hinged at the bottom front of the frame with a latch at the top rear of the frame. Smith & Wesson's Model 3 Schofield and Model 3 Russian are the fastest reloading single-action six-guns offered to cowboy action shooters.

Colt was caught by surprise when Smith & Wesson introduced the first centerfire big-bore single-action six-gun in 1869. Colt could not bring out a new cartridge revolver until the patent ran out in 1872, so they converted their 1851 Navy and 1860 Army Models to fixed ammunition with the Colt Cartridge Conversions, followed by the 1872 Open-Top, a revolver that looked like

a cartridge conversion model but was actually produced as a cartridge firing six-gun. One year later the Open-Top would be totally redesigned, chambered in the 45 Colt and become the Model of 1873, the Model P... the Peacemaker... the legendary Colt Single Action Army.

We can also have 'replicas' of the single actions that never existed, including the Lightning and New Thunderer from Cimarron that are single actions, but with grip frames reminiscent of the old double-action Colt Lightning. The replica Lightning is built on a 22-rimfire frame and chambered in 38 Special and 38 Long Colt, while the New Thunderer is a full-sized single action offered in all the standard calibers. EMF's single action 'that never was,' is the Pinkerton Model with a bird's-head grip frame.

No matter who the importer, virtually all replica single actions are made by either Uberti or Armi San Marco. At least this has been the case in the past. However, American Western Arms now owns Armi San Marco and all ASM production goes exclusively to AWA. This means all the other importers now depend upon Uberti (*now owned by Beretta*) for their needs. While Cimarron, EMF, and Navy Arms are all importers of completed six-guns; AWA brings in parts and assembles and finishes the guns in this country. USFA, which started doing the same thing using Uberti parts, has been steadily working towards using all American-

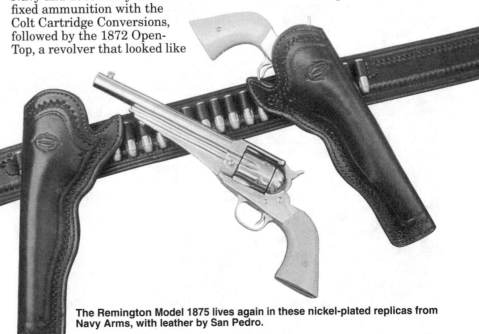

The Remington Model 1875 lives again in these nickel-plated replicas from Navy Arms, with leather by San Pedro.

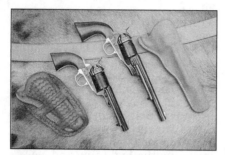

The Colt Cartridge Conversions are back in replica form such as these examples from Cimarron: an 1860 in 44 Colt and an 1851 in 38 Long Colt. Leather by Thad Rybka.

Excellent sixguns for blackpowder competition are these nickel-plated Hartford Model 44-40s from EMF. Leather by San Pedro.

made parts. Current reports say their six-guns are almost totally American-made, but still use forged main frames from Uberti.

Replicas are great bargains with prices running between $400 and $500 for standard single actions, $750 for Smith and Wesson single actions, the same price for the top-line Peacekeepers from AWA, and around $1000 for USFA six-guns.

THE RUGER SIX-GUNS:
Ruger offers a complete line of centerfire single-action six-guns for cowboy action shooters. When the original rules were set by SASS they were wise enough to include a Modern Class for those who owned Ruger Blackhawks. This class differs in that it allows the use of single-action six-guns with adjustable sights. Shooters in the Modern Class can use Ruger's Blackhawk, Super Blackhawk, and Bisley models, as well as the New Frontier from Colt. Many shooters got their start in cowboy action shooting matches by using their Ruger Blackhawks.

When I first started shooting in the 1950s, First Generation Colt Single Action Armys were readily available at reasonable prices, and Ruger's new Blackhawk had just arrived in 357 Magnum and 44 Magnum. I soon realized that while the Colt had it all over the Ruger Blackhawk aesthetically, the

Ruger's answer to the Colt single Action Army is this 45 Vaquero.

Blackhawk was vastly superior, mechanically speaking. The Colt was powered by a flat main spring, a flat bolt spring, and a flat hand spring. Springs in un-tuned Colts broke on a regular basis, while the Ruger was virtually unbreakable. Even with the scant youthful experience I realized the ideal six-gun would be a Colt Single Action Army with Ruger Blackhawk lockwork.

Thanks to cowboy action shooting we are now close, or at least as close as we will ever get, to a traditional styled Single Action Army with Ruger's indestructible lockwork. For 40 years Ruger's Blackhawk with its adjustable sights has been a workhorse single action for outdoorsmen and hunters. In the mid-1990s Ruger looked at the cowboy action shooting market and 'modernized' their Blackhawk by taking a giant step backwards and turning it into a classic-looking, traditionally-styled, fixed-sighted single action for competing in the Traditional or Black Powder classes in cowboy action shooting. The Vaquero, as Ruger calls their new 19th-century single action, has been a tremendous success. It is bull strong and virtually indestructible, while still keeping the Colt Single Action Army look. And though it looks traditional on the outside it has Ruger's transfer bar safety making it the safest of all single-action six-guns.

The Vaquero is about 10 percent heavier and larger than a similarly chambered Colt Single Action Army, the Blackhawk's flat-top frame has been contoured and rounded

off very nicely to provide a CAS single action-style look, and the traditional 'hog-wallow' rear sight sets high enough that one can sight down the top of a Vaquero without cocking the hammer. Vaqueros are available in either stainless steel or blue with a case-colored frame. Due to the Vaquero's larger size and modern lockwork, it does not have quite the same marvelous balance and feel as the Colt Single Action Army–but at one-fourth the price most shooters will heed the words spoken at the end of the *Wild Bunch* movie by of one of the survivors: *"It ain't like it used to be, but it will have to do."*

Vaqueros are offered by Ruger in the three standard barrel lengths, 4-5/8, 5-1/2, and 7-1/2 inches, chambered in 45 Colt, 44-40, 44 Magnum, and 357 Magnum (*Please bring out a 38-40 version!*). There is also a Bisley Vaquero version with the larger grip frame, and target-style hammer and trigger from the Bisley Model Blackhawk. The Bisley Vaquero is only available in the two shorter barrel lengths, as is the 357 Magnum in both models.

THE REMAINING SIX-GUNS:
Finally we come to the remaining six-guns for cowboy action shooting that do not fit in any of the three main categories of *Real*, *Replica*, and *Ruger*. The six-guns are the Colt Cowboy, the European American Armory Bounty Hunter, and the Freedom Arms Model 97.

That Colt Cowboy could be described as a cross between the Colt Single Action Army and the Ruger Vaquero. Frame-size is slightly smaller than a Ruger Vaquero but slightly larger than a Colt Single Action, and it has a

Navy Arms supplies replicas of the Smith & Wesson Schofield in both the 7-inch Military Model and the 5-inch Wells Fargo Model, in either 45 Colt or 44-40.

transfer bar safety like that found in all Rugers. Unlike the Ruger Vaquero, opening the loading gate on the Colt Cowboy does not allow the cylinder to rotate freely. The hammer must still be placed in the half-cock notch to rotate the cylinder. Costing about one-third as much as the original Colt SAA, and available only as a 5-1/2 inch 45 Colt, the Colt Cowboy is not nearly as nicely finished, the case coloring is not as vivid, and the grip frame, while being the same size as the original Single Action Army, is not fitted as well to the frame or the black hard rubber grips. The trigger, as in the Ruger Vaquero, rides farther forward in the trigger guard than does the trigger of a Colt Single Action Army.

The sights are very easy to see with a square-notch rear sight mated with a front sight that is almost square. The Cowboy shoots very well and, with CAS loads, will stay at one inch or less at 50 feet. The one great advantage the Colt Cowboy has over all the others is that it is a real Colt, marked "Colt's Patent F.A. Mfg. Co." on the barrel.

The Bounty Hunter, imported by EAA, is produced in the Weihrauch factory in Mellrichstadt, Germany, and as such is one of the few imported single actions not produced in Italy. As with the Colt Cowboy, the Bounty Hunter has a transfer bar safety, and a Colt-style top trap, however it is larger and heavier than a Colt Single Action Army, being built on a 44 Magnum frame; in fact, some measurements are larger than the Ruger Vaquero. One nice touch, rarely seen anymore, is the recessing of the cartridge case rims in the cylinder.

All Bounty Hunters I have used lock up tightly and shoot well. They are available in 357 Magnum, 44 Magnum, and 45 Colt with barrel lengths of 4-3/4 and 7-1/2 inches, nickeled or blued with a case-colored frame, and with one-piece walnut grips standard and ivory polymer available as an option. The Bounty Hunter represents excellent value and is the least expensive way to get into cowboy action shooting.

When you are already building the finest six-guns ever made, what do you do for an encore? Freedom Arms is also now into cowboy action

shooting with their Model 97. Their Model 83, chambered in 454 Casull since 1983, is a superb five-shot single action designed primarily for hunters. It has since been chambered in 44 Magnum, 357 Magnum, 41 Magnum, and two really big bores: the 50 Action Express and the 475 Linebaugh. To accommodate cowboy action shooters, Freedom Arms essentially reduced their Model 83 to about 90 percent size, chambered it in 357 Magnum (*with auxiliary 38 Special cylinders available*), and transformed it into a six-shot revolver as well.

The Model 97 Mid-Frame is slightly smaller than a Colt single action and will fit leather made for the old Colt. Although it operates like a traditional single action with a half-cock notch on the hammer, the Model 97 is fitted with a sliding safety in the face of the hammer. This single-action six-gun is safe to carry fully loaded with six rounds but, of course, CAS rules mandate carrying of only five rounds, with the hammer down on an empty chamber. The grip shape of the Model 97 is unlike any other and, to my hand, feels much like the old Colt Bisley.

Model 97s are available in standard barrel lengths of 5-1/2 and 7-1/2 inches, with fixed or adjustable sights. It just doesn't get any better than this for cowboy action shooting!

THE AMMUNITION MAKERS:

Cowboy action shooting requires ammunition with cast or swaged bullets with a muzzle

velocity of less than 1000 fps when fired from a six-gun. The standard bullet design for CAS competition is the round-nosed flat-point (RNFP). Of the long-established major ammunition manufacturers, I know of only two that are producing ammunition specifically for CAS use. Hornady offers both 45 Colt and 44-40 for cowboy action shooting, while Winchester does the same, plus 38 Special and 44 Special. Three companies that specialize in CAS loads are Black Hills Ammunition (*the first to really do so as far as I know*), Ten-X, and Ultramax.

Jeff Hoffman of Black Hills picked up on cowboy action shooting early, introducing ammunition in the major frontier calibers, and has been the driving force in bringing back many of the long-forgotten cartridges. First came the most popular round, 45 Colt, followed by 44 Special, 38 Special, and 357 Magnum. Black Hills

Freedom Arms 7 1/2-inch Model 97 and typical groups with Black Hills Ammunition.

Test Firing Black Hills Cowboy Ammunition

Cartridge /Wgt.	Make/Model/ Bbl Length	MV	Group*
45 Colt/250	Ruger Vaquero 7 1/2"	845	1.5"
	Ruger Vaquero 5 1/2"	780	1.5"
	Ruger Vaquero 4 5/8"	770	1.9"
45 Schofield/230	Ruger Vaquero 7 1/2"	790	1.0"
	Ruger Vaquero 5 1/2"	775	1.5"
	Ruger Vaquero 4 5/8"	780	1.9"
	CFA Schofield 7"	645	1.8"
	CFA Schofield 5"	610	1.9"
	Navy Arms Schofield 7"	705	1.0
	Navy Arms Schofield 5"	675	2.5"
44-40/200	Ruger Vaquero 5 1/2"	850	1.8"
	Colt SAA 5 1/2"	830	1.8"
44 Russian/210	Colt SAA 7 1/2"	745	1.5"
	Colt SAA 5 1/2"	710	1.5"
	Colt SAA 4 3/4"	670	1.6"
	CFA 1860 Conversion 8"	700	1.5"
44 Colt/230	Colt SAA 7 1/2"	750	1.5"
	Colt SAA 5 1/2"	700	2.5"
	Colt SAA 4 3/4"	680	2.0"
	CFA 1860 Conversion 8"	690	2.3"
38-40/180	Colt SAA 4 3/4''	895	1.6"
	EMF Hartford 4 3/4"	830	2.1"
	EMF Hartford 7 1/2"	930	1.9"
38 Long Colt/150	CFA 1851 Conversion 5"	670	1.4"
	Colt SAA 5 1/2"	675	1.5"
	Great Western 5 1/2"	690	2.0"
	Great Western 71/2"	680	1.1"
32-20/115	CFA 7 1/2"	825	1.4"
	CFA 4 3/4"	690	1.4"
38 Special/158	CFA 1851 Conversion 5"	695	0.9"
	Colt SAA 5 1/2"	725	1.8"
	Great Western 7 1/2"	690	1.3"
	Great Western 5 1/2"	775	2.5"
44 Special/210	Colt SAA 7 1/2"	775	1.6"
	Colt SAA 5 1/2"	765	2.9"
	Colt SAA 4 3/4"	720	1.8"
357 Magnum/158	FA M97 7 1/2"	855	0.6"
	FA M97 5 1/2"	770	1.1"
	Colt New Frontier 5 1/2"	735	0.9"
	Ruger Black Hawk 4 5/8"	770	1.6"

Groups fired at a cowboy action shooting distance of 50 feet.

Test Firing Ultramax Cowboy Ammunition

Cartridge /Wgt.	Make/Model/ Bbl Length	MV	Group*
45 Colt/250	CFA Model P 7 /2"	775	0.8"
	CFA U.S. Cavalry 7 1/2"	755	2.1"
	Ruger Blackhawk 7 1/2"	800	0.9"
45 Colt/200	CFA Model P 7 1/2 "	725	1.3"
	CFA U.S. Cavalry 7 1/2"	710	1.5"
	Ruger Blackhawk 7 1/2"	750	0.8"
45 Schofield/230	CFA Model P 7 1/2"	685	1.5"
	CFA U.S. Cavalry 7 1/2"	690	2.5"
	Ruger Bisley 7 1/2"	725	1.5"
45 Schofield/180	CFA Model P 7 1/2"	730	1.0"
	CFA U.S. Cavalry 7 1/2"	710	1.3"
	Ruger Bisley 7 1/2"	745	1.6"
44-40/200	Colt SAA 7 1/2"	790	1.9"
	Colt New Frontier 7 1/2"	835	1.3"
	CFA Model P 7 1/2"	765	2.4"
	EMF Hartford 7 1/2"	705	1.8"
38-40/180	EMF Hartford 7 1/2"	600	2.0"
	Ruger Blackhawk 4 3/4"	810	1.6"
44 Special/200	Colt SAA 7 1/2"	805	1.0"
	Colt New Frontier 71/2"	760	1.3"
	Ruger Bisley 7 1/2"	770	1.4"
357 Magnum/158	FA M97 7 1/2"	805	1.0"
	Ruger Blackhawk 6 1/2"	705	1.5"
357 Magnum/125	FA M97 7 1/2"	965	1.5"
	Ruger Blackhawk 6 1/2"	855	1.6"
38 Special/158	FA M97 7 1/2"	840	1.5"
	Ruger Blackhawk 6 1/2"	750	1.6"
38 Special/125	FA M97 7 1/2"	815	1.0"
	Ruger Bisley 7 1/2"	765	1.5"

Groups fired at a cowboy action shooting distance of 50 feet.

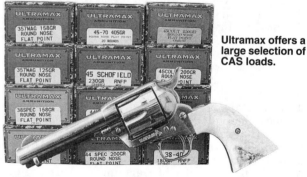

Ultramax offers a large selection of CAS loads.

then worked with companies like as Starline, Cimarron, and AA Bullets to provide the brass, the six-guns, and the bullets for cowboy action shooting.

Then, Black Hills and Starline worked together to give us cowboy-loaded 38-40 and 44-40 ammo, followed by the 32-20 and the long-gone and forgotten 45 Schofield. And they did not stop there. We now have 44 Russian, 44 Colt, and 38 Long Colt. The 44 Colt is actually a new version of an old cartridge made by trimming the diameter of the rims of 44 Special brass so six rounds will fit in the smaller cylinders of a Cartridge Conversion or Open-Top. The 44 Special brass is also shortened slightly to become a 44 Colt, which is now lengthwise in between the 44 Russian and 44 Special.

Ken McKenzie of Ten-X is not only a life member of SASS, his number 4444 is that double 44 brand found on his Ten-X ammunition. Being a cowboy action shooter, it is no problem for McKenzie to offer the most complete line of cowboy ammunition in the industry. For six-gunners, Ten-X offers 45 Colt, 45 Schofield, 44-40, 44 Russian, 44 Colt, 44 Special, 38-40, 32-20, 38 Long Colt as well as cowboy-loaded 357 and 44 Magnums—and if that is not enough, would you believe 32 S&W, 38 S&W and, that most rare of all Cowboy cartridges, the 41 Long Colt.

Ten-X doesn't stop there as they offer many rifle cartridges for lever guns and single shots, including 25-20, 25-35, 30-30, 32-40, 38-55, 38-56, 40-50, 40-60, 40-82, 45-60,

45-70, and 50-70. You want more? How about blackpowder loads in the 38 Special, 357 Magnum, 44 Colt, 44 Magnum, 44-40, 45 Colt... and even 12-gauge shotgun rounds.

Ken McKenzie of Ten-X says his reason for starting the company was to provide the best possible loads for cowboy shooters. In addition, he provides the most extensive line of both smokeless and black-powder-substitute loads. Such top competitors as Bounty Hunter, China Camp, and Island Girl all use and endorse Ten-X ammunition.

Roger Braunstein of Ultramax started the company in 1986 to provide remanufactured handgun and rifle ammunition. With the growth of cowboy action shooting, Ultramax added CAS loads including 45 Colt, 45 Schofield, 44-40, 44

Ruger is heavily into the CAS market with their traditionally styled Vaquero (blue or stainless) in barrel lengths of 4-5/8, 5-1/2, and 7-1/2 inches.

Freedom Arms offers CAS competitors both fixed and adjustable-sighted models, with 5 1/2 or 7 1/2-inch barrels.

Russian, 38-40, 32-20, 44 Special, 38 Special, 357 Magnum, 44 Magnum, and for lever-gun users 45-70, 38-55, and 30-30. Ultramax also has a line of cowboy action shooting loads for women that features a 200-grain bullet in 45 Colt, a 180-grain bullet in the 45 Schofield, and a 125-grain bullet in both 38 Special and 357 Magnum—all of which feature lower recoil than standard CAS loads. They also feature some of the best-looking packaging in the industry. ●

Cowboy Ammunition Manufacturers:

Black Hills Ammunition, *PO Box 3090, Rapid City SD 57709; 1-605-343-5150*

Ten-X Ammunition, *201 S. Winneville #E, Ontario CA 91761; 1-909-605-1617*

Ultramax, *2112 Elk Vale Rd., Rapid City SD 57701; 1-605-342-4141*

Six-Gun Manufacturers And Importers:

American Western Arms *(AWA), 1450 SW 10th St., Suite #3B, Delray Beach FL 33444; 1-877-292-4867*

Cimarron F.A. Co., *PO Box 906, Fredericksburg TX 78624; 1-210-997-9090*

Colt's Mfg. Co., *PO Box 1868, Hartford CT 06144; 1-800-962-COLT*

European American Armory *(EAA), PO Box 1299, Sharpes FL 32959; 1-407-639-4842*

E.M.F. Company, Inc., *1900 E. Warner Ave., Suite 1-D, Santa Ana CA 92705; 1-714-261-6611*

Freedom Arms, *PO Box 150, Freedom WY 83120; 1-307-883-2468*

Navy Arms, *689 Bergen Blvd., Ridgefield NJ 07657; 1-201-945-2500*

Sturm, Ruger & Co., *200 Ruger Rd., Prescott AZ; 1-520-541-8820*

United States Firearms Manufacturing Company, Inc. *(USFA), 55 Van Dyke Ave., Hartford CT; 1-877-227-6901*

Test Firing Ten-X Cowboy Ammunition

Cartridge/Wgt.	Make/Model/Bbl Length	MV	Group*
45 Colt/250	Colt New Frontier 7 1/2 "	695	1.1"
	Ruger BlackHawk 7 1/2"	800	0.9"
44-40/200	Colt New Frontier 7 1/2"	680	1.9"
44 Special/200	Colt New Frontier 7 1/2"	635	1.4"
	Ruger Blackhawk 7 1/2"	705	1.1"
44 Russian/200	Colt New Frontier 7 1/2"	700	1.0"
	Ruger Blackhawk 7 1/2"	760	1.6"
44 Colt/200	Colt New Frontier 7 1/2"	675	1.6"
	Ruger Blackhawk 7 1/2"	680	1.1"
	1860 Cartridge Conversion 8"	660	1.3"
	1872 Open-Top 8"	610	1.3"
44 Colt BP/200	1860 Cartridge Conversion 8"	640	1.5"

Groups fired at a cowboy action shooting distance of 50 feet.

Handgunning Dangerous Game

by Chuck Taylor

WITH THE FOCUS of hunting stories being on the hunt and actual kill, it's all too easy to forget how we got there in the first place. Months, sometimes years, go into building knowledge, skill and experience, all for the purpose of being at the right place at the right time. And when that synchronicity of time and place come together, we bet it all on a tiny piece of time within which success or failure – and sometimes life itself – hangs in precarious balance.

With dangerous game, there is little margin for error – these animals can seriously injure, even kill, you with surprising ease. Out "in the boonies," you're in their back yard, not yours, and you're playing their game, too, not your own. It's a game at which they excel because they have to–or they die. So, with stakes that high being played on a daily basis, they become very, very good.

Most game we label dangerous are predators. Some are big and some not, but they all have one thing in common – they hunt for a

living and kill their prey, whatever it may be, with astonishing speed and savagery. They're canny and fast, tough and strong; they have to be or they can't outperform the prey upon which they depend for their very survival.

Here in North America, the bear reigns supreme. He's big, strong and fast, smart, agile and temperamental, making him a genuine handful, especially at close quarters. He's tough to stop once he gets rolling and he can appear and disappear like a wisp of smoke, making him difficult to hunt.

Wild boar, though a relative newcomer to North America, is also thought by many to be at least as dangerous. Weighing in the 350-lb.-plus class, a mature male will almost always attack when encountered up close, making his speed, power and tenacity as seri-

The largest of North American feline predators, a mature male mountain lion can weigh up to 200-lbs. and the female 150-lbs. Canny, fast and agile, they present an excellent challenge to any handgun hunter.

ous hazard. Moreover, he's smart – at least as smart as a bear, maybe smarter – and his ears, eyes and nose make sneaking up on him to within handgun range a challenging proposition.

The mountain lion is another nasty North American critter. Weighing in the 150-200 lb. range, he's fast, very canny, tenacious as heck and extremely agile. Even with dogs, a close encounter with him is a highly stimulating experience. Without them, it can be exceptionally dangerous.

However, the term *dangerous* has far-reaching implications. Implications that may be broader than you think. The truth is that nearly *all* wild animals are dangerous. It's just the definition of circumstances in which they become dangerous that's hard to understand. Size really doesn't matter (*annoy a badger or wolverine and watch what happens next*), nor does species. Given the wrong situation, everything that walks in the woods can be quite dangerous indeed.

Two of Taylor's favorites – Smith & Wesson Model 24 44 Spls. with 6 1/2- and 4-inch barrels. Loaded with 16 grains of 2400 and a hard-cast Keith 250-grain SWC, they rival the 44 Magnum's performance on dangerous game.

I remember a number of experiences in which this lesson was driven home to me. Once while hunting javelina in the brushy hills south of Prescott, Arizona, I found myself quite unintentionally in the middle of a herd of about thirty of them. I was stuck, unable to move, with what seemed like the world's supply of these toothy little critters within spitting distance all around me. Confused, I froze, figuring that one would catch my scent and they'd all run off in a panic.

But I was wrong. One did catch my scent all right, but he didn't run. Instead, from less than ten feet, he attacked. I got him—probably because I already had my heavy-loaded 6 1/2-inch 44 Special S&W Model 24 at 'Ready.' The hard-cast 250-grain Keith SWC struck him almost dead-center between the eyes and dropped him. Yet, had that not been the case, I doubt if I would have had time to react quickly enough. As it was, I only had time for that one shot.

If I had misplaced it, that little critter's 2-inch canine fangs would have been sunk deeply into one of my legs and he would have dragged me to the ground and invited his friends to join in. Then, with violent headshakes, they would have opened me up like a can of chili.

Don't believe it? Ask anyone whose been nailed by one. It's an experience one never forgets! They also have the interesting habit of coming to each other's aid, so generally when one javelina attacks,

he gets help from his or her buddies within a few seconds. Once they get you down, you're in their world and in big, potentially even terminal, trouble.

And what about those varmints – raccoons, coyotes, bobcats, foxes and so on – we all take great delight in calling? I've had a raccoon come out of nowhere, then see my partner move and jump right into my lap, apparently thinking I was a tree or something. I've also had coyotes and foxes rush me from less than ten feet when they charge in to my call and then realize they've been had.

Not three months ago, I called in a young bobcat, which approached from behind me in a wide circle, moving downwind. He then came straight in to the call speaker, which was beneath a juniper tree about 15 feet from me. I was first amused as I watched him stalk his presumed prey (a distressed jackrabbit), then realized he'd gotten too close, too quickly. I needed to nail this fellow quickly, but as I raised my 6-inch Colt Python 357 Magnum to shoot, he spun around and came straight for me.

Fortunately, I was able to get off one shot, it's 110-grain Hornady XTP JHP (1579 fps) striking him full in the chest. Nonetheless, before he expired, he was able to reach my boots, proceeding to chew heck out of one of them. Afraid to fire again for fear of hitting my own foot, I jumped up and lashed outward with him still attached. Luckily, he let go and went spinning through the air, coming to earth about ten meters away, whereupon he promptly got a sec-

ond 110-grain XTP in the chops to hasten his demise.

Even deer can be extremely dangerous. Hunting Texas whitetail bucks down on the Y-O Ranch some years ago, I'd taken down a great buck from just under 100 meters with my pet 6-inch S&W Model 29, loaded with 180-grain *Super Vel* JHPs (1550 fps). My guide was so tickled at the successful shot that he took off like a kid, running with complete abandon to the spot on the hillside where the buck had fallen.

The trouble was that, though both his shoulders were broken, the deer was still very much alive. As I arrived puffing behind the

High visibility sights are a must. Adjustable sights allow precise zeroing of the weapon with a specific load, improving shot placement.

guide, I could see the buck tensing his hindquarters to spring and lower his head. My guide, oblivious to the fact that (*a*) he was too close and (*b*) the buck was preparing to nail him, turned to me and shouted, "*What a great sh....*"

He never finished the sentence because as I arrived, I knocked him down with my best football tackle. It proved to be just in the nick of time – the buck took his shot, sailed right through the spot in which the guide had been standing a heartbeat before, and fell to the ground dead.

Once while I was scouting for elk during the rut, I was charged by a big bull that took offense to my presence and decided to teach me a lesson. After unsuccessfully trying to outrun him for 50 meters or so, I realized I had only one option left. So I turned, drew my heavy-loaded 4-inch S&W Model 24 44 Special

7 1/2-inch Colt New Frontier (*top*) and Ruger Blackhawk in 45 Colt are also great handguns for dangerous game.

and–from not more than twenty feet away–shot him between the eyes, downing him. Once again, the lesson was learned–anything in the woods can be dangerous if it wants to be. All you have to do is be in the wrong place at the wrong time under the wrong circumstances.

I've encountered mountain lions while rock climbing, foxes and wolves while walking up narrow ravines, and javelina while checking out caves. I've had bears come into my camp at night and been chased by a badger who was annoyed that I had inadvertently disturbed him. In every case, had I not been armed and realized that all animals are potentially dangerous, I would have been, at the very least, seriously injured. In the cases where larger animals were involved, I could have – and very likely would have – been killed.

Still, as invigorating as such events might be, I've chosen to limit the handguns and calibers I use for hunting to standard types. For me, the whole point of hunting with a handgun is to use superior woodcraft skills, thus allowing me to get the animal close enough to use a regular handgun. The fact there are optically-sighted "carbines-without-a-buttstock" chambered for ultra-potent rifle-class cartridges is, to me, unworthy. I want the limitations of the handgun to be a primary factor. The increased difficulty those limitations present are, to me, the whole point.

This being the case, I recommend nothing less than a heavy-loaded 357 Magnum or 10mm Auto. A heavy-loaded 44 Special, 45 Auto Rim or 45 Colt is better and a 41 or 44 Mag is just about right. Generally speaking, I prefer a hard-cast (pure Linotype) SWC bullet for maximum penetration, bone-breaking ability and full-caliber wound channel. Velocities should be relatively high, as high as both safety and weapon-controllability dictate, with the 1000-1500 fps range being ideal.

There are instances where a JHP or JSP bullet can be utilized effectively, but in my experience, they should be limited to the smaller species. In the 357 Magnum, for instance, I like the 110-grain Hornady XTP JHP and 19.0 grains of 2400 for small 'nasties' like bobcats, lynxes, coyotes and javelina. To give a better chance of quickly stopping larger animals bent upon your destruction (*wounded deer, elk, livestock, et al*), a 160-grain hard-cast Keith SWC and 15.0 grains of 2400 is as good as the 357 gets.

If you like the 10mm Auto, a hard-cast 190-grain SWC and 6.5 grains of Unique will give you right at 1100 fps, good accuracy and reliable mechanical function. And it will penetrate like the dickens, too.

For the 41 Mag, try a hard-cast 210-grain SWC and 14.0 grains of 2400 or H-110. It'll give you about 1100 fps from a 6-inch barreled Model 57, good accuracy and excellent penetration. If you prefer a frangible bullet, Speer's 220-grain JSP and 19.0 grains of 2400 will give you 1300 fps, with good stopping power.

At the top, we have the venerable 44 Magnum, which I prefer above all. For a frangible bullet load, I like the Remington 180-grain JHP and 26.0 grains of H-110 (1550 fps from 6-inch barrel), but my all-time favorite for dangerous game is a hard-cast Keith 250-grain SWC and 21.0 grains of 2400 (1270 fps from 6-inch barrel). Both are very accurate and offer excellent stopping power at ranges under 50-meters, but the 250-grain Keith bullet load is as good as is possible with a normal handgun.

Between service pistol cartridges (9mm, 40 S&W, 45 ACP, et al), and the true magnums (357, 10mm, 41 and 44), we have what I call the "mid-range" cartridges – the 44 Spl., 45 Auto Rim and 45 Colt. With healthy loads, they produce near-magnum performance,

Even the venerable elk can be highly dangerous, especially during the rut. Taylor was once charged by a large bull in heavy timber while scouting and was forced to kill him at less than ten meters with a head shot from heavy-loaded 44 Spl.

Author with record-book wild boar taken at point-blank range in heavy brush with 6-inch S&W Model 29, loaded with 250-grain Keith hard-cast SWCs. The first shot stopped the boar, then the author moved in and finished him.

but are nearly as controllable as service cartridges. For example, a 180-grain Sierra JHP and 19.0 grains of 2400 will give you nearly 1300 fps from a 6-inch barreled Model 24 44 Spl., while a hard-cast Keith 250-grain SWC and 16.0 grains gives you 1150. There is even a heavier frangible bullet option in Hornady's 240-grain XTP JHP and the same powder charge. It opens up well, yet because of its weight, also delivers good penetration.

Often overlooked, the 45 Auto Rim is a genuine winner, producing nearly 1100 fps from a 5-inch S&W Model 625 with a hard-cast Keith 250-grain SWC and 14.5 grains of 2400. If you want a lighter JHP load, try Hornady's 185-grain XTP JHP and 8.5 grains of Unique for 1100 fps. Both shoot into an inch at 25 meters and exhibit only moderate recoil.

Though it's been with us for over a hundred years, the 45 Colt has yet to see its full potential. For over thirty years, I've been loading it with a hard-cast Keith SWC and had excellent results. Ruger's 7 1/2-inch Blackhawk is nearly ideal for the 45 Colt. It's an exceptionally strong handgun, so 20.0 grains of 2400 (1150 fps) isn't at all out of line. Colt's 7 1/2-inch New Frontier isn't quite as strong, but 17.0 grains of 2400 with that same Keith SWC hits very hard, nonetheless.

Longer barrels mean higher velocities, thus giving frangible bul-

lets a better chance to expand, and enhanced penetration to non-frangible ones. Heavy loads can also mean increased recoil, so muzzle brakes like the Keeper System or Magnaport are worth considering to minimize recoil and muzzle flip.

Since weapon control is obviously critical, stocks that fit your hands, yet absorb as much recoil energy as possible are also a good idea. However, be certain they allow quick used of a speed loader because a fast reload is something often needed when dangerous game is involved. To further enhance control, narrow, round and polish the trigger. It gives you much better "feel" for those fast DA shots in an emergency.

To allow fastest sight acquisition, high-visibility sights are a must, often with colored inserts for use in low light. And since the loads are tailored to the weapon and kind of animal you're hunting, adjustable sights offer more flexibility.

Even the best equipment doesn't matter much if you can't use it well, so zero the weapon carefully (*I've found 50 meters to be the best*), then train extensively with it before you even considering taking it into the field. Learn quick, yet stable field shooting positions (*like Kneeling*) to further increase your field efficiency and don't forget the low-light work, either. The odds are high that you'll have to make the telling shot while in the shade or during the dawn/dusk period when most animals are active.

Remove the ultra-violet reflection and scent from your clothing and wear gloves and a facemask to cover exposed skin. Approach critters and/or stands from downwind and as you do, move very, *very* slowly. Once on site, don't talk and stay as still as possible. Even animals thought to have only mediocre vision (bears and boars, for example) seem to have no problem whatsoever in detecting movement and responding accordingly.

Also often overlooked—with potentially dire consequences—is the need to be able to hit small, angled or partially obscured targets at close range. Typically, dangerous

encounters occur at very close range, often in places where mobility is severely limited. Such events happen fast, with the animal in a less-than-optimum position for a telling shot. In order to avoid being caught short (*which will usually get you hurt!*), train on targets showing the animal in different body positions, so you know how to get that bullet to vitals from any angle.

When on my first trip to Africa, I learned three hard lessons about dangerous game. Subsequent trips back to Africa and to Alaska confirmed them, as did further hunting in North America proper. They are:

1. Get as close as you can...then get five meters closer!

2. The three most important characteristics for dangerous game cartridges are penetration, penetration and penetration!

3. Forget the one-shot kill. Put 'em down and keep 'em from getting to you, then kill them.

I've found that all three are of even more importance with handguns, by nature far less powerful than even a middle-range centerfire rifle. You've got to put that first shot where it will disable the animal—destroy its ability to charge—then you can move in and finish the job with little or no danger. Generally, breaking one or both shoulders is the best way to accomplish this goal (*depending upon the animal's body angle when the shot is taken*), with a cranial coup de grace shot following shortly thereafter.

These, then, are the most common-sense ways to handgun dangerous animals. Yes, they're smart, tough, fast and agile, but they're not invulnerable. Pick the best gun, cartridge and load for your needs, learn to shoot it well under all circumstances, refine and perfect your woodcraft skills to give you the best possible shot and have the patience, once in the field, to let things run their course. Once on site, stay quiet, don't move and wait. Then, once the animal is in proximity, wait some more until you can get the best shot.

Chasing around in the bushes after wounded dangerous animals is not much fun and, with the application of a little common sense, is completely avoidable. *Don't shoot if the angles are wrong and when the moment of truth comes, concentrate on marksmanship fundamentals.* Otherwise, you're courting potential disaster. ●

SHOOTER'S MARKETPLACE

INTERESTING PRODUCT NEWS
FOR THE ACTIVE SHOOTING SPORTSMAN

The companies represented on the following pages will be happy to provide additional information – feel free to contact them.

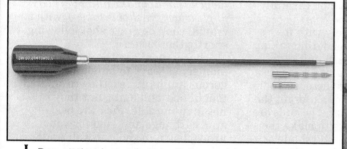

SHOOTER'S MARKETPLACE

COMBINATION RIFLE AND OPTICS REST

The Magna-Pod weighs less than two pounds, yet firmly supports more than most expensive tripods. It will hold 50 pounds at its low 9-inch height and over 10 pounds extended to 17 inches. It sets up in seconds where there is neither time nor space for a tripod and keeps your expensive equipment safe from knock-overs by kids, pets, pedestrians, or even high winds. It makes a great mono-pod for camcorders, etc., and its carrying box is less than 13" x 13" x 3 1/4" high for easy storage and access.

Attached to its triangle base it becomes an extremely stable table pod or rifle bench rest. The rifle yoke pictured in photo is included.

It's 5 pods in 1: Magna-Pod, Mono-Pod, Table-Pod, Shoulder-Pod and Rifle Rest. Send for free catalog.

SHEPHERD ENTERPRISES, INC.
Box 189, Waterloo, NE 68069
Phone: 402-779-2424 • Fax: 402-779-4010
E-mail: shepherd@shepherdscopes.com • Web: www.shepherdscopes.com

RUGGED TOMMI & JOUNI FOLDER

From a harsh and challenging environment, Finns have learned to make tools they can rely on for their survival. In this tradition, Kellam Knives Co. continues to provide knives today – reliable and razor sharp.

Jouni Kellokoski, president of Kellam Knives, designed the FJ1 knife as his optimal personal carry folder. Custom made quality. From tuxedo to jeans, it's handsome and elegant, yet ready for many rugged tasks. Cocobolo wood and ivory micarta handle with an AUS-8 stainless 2.5" blade. Razor sharp.

Since 1610 the KP Smithy family has been hammering with the ultimate knowledge of knifemaking. The smith pounds steel hundreds of times with a hammer to make razor sharp knives. The tradition still continues. No compromise is made with workmanship or materials. Hand hammered and progression tempered razor sharp blades up to 62 Rc hardness with handles of rare root burl of raita wood.

902 S. Dixie Hwy., Lantana, FL 33462
Phone: 561-588-3185
or 800-390-6918
Fax: 561-588-3186
Web: www.kellamknives.com
Email: info@kellamknives.com

6x18x40 VARMINT/TARGET SCOPE

Send for
Free Catalog

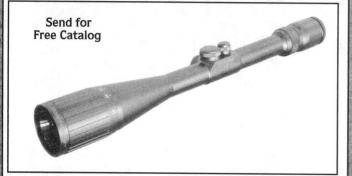

The Shepherd 6x18x40 Varmint/Target Scope makes long-range varmint and target shooting child's play. Just pick the ranging circle that best fits your target (be it prairie dogs, coyotes or paper varmints) and Shepherd's exclusive, patented Dual Reticle Down Range System does the rest. You won't believe how far you can accurately shoot, even with rimfire rifles.

Shepherd's superior lens coating mean superior light transmission and tack-sharp resolution.

This new shockproof, waterproof scope features 1/4 minute-of-angle clicks on the ranging circles and friction adjustments on the crosshairs that allow fine-tuning to 0.001 MOA. A 40mm adjustable objective provides a 5.5-foot field of view at 100 yards (16x setting). 16.5 FOV @ 6X.

SHEPHERD ENTERPRISES, INC.
Box 189, Waterloo, NE 68069
Phone: 402-779-2424 • Fax: 402-779-4010
E-mail: shepherd@shepherdscopes.com • Web: www.shepherdscopes.com

PRESSURE ♦ VELOCITY ♦ ACCURACY

You must know all three. For over thirty years, Oehler ballistic test equipment and software have been the standard for precision measurements. We invite comparison. and even make our systems compare to themselves. The patented *Proof Channel*™ uses three screens to make two velocity measurements on each shot. The Model 43 Personal Ballistics Lab provides shooters with accurate measurements of pressure, velocity, ballistic coefficient, and target information. Oehler instruments are used by military proving grounds and all major ammunition makers.

Phone for free catalog or technical help.

OEHLER RESEARCH, INC.
P.O. Box 9135, Austin, TX 78766
Phone: 800-531-5125 or 512-327-6900
Web: www.oehler-research.com

SHOOTER'S MARKETPLACE

CUSTOM KNIVES

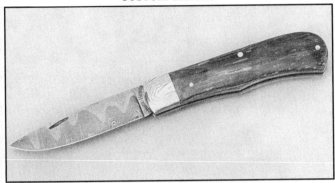

Knife pictured has Damascus blade made of 480 layers of 1095-203E steels in Mr. Hawes' shimmed ladder pattern. Bolster made of mokume from Sakmar. Handles are mammoth ivory. Truly a one-of-a-kind gem that will also function as a utility knife if you desire.

Hawes Forge specializes in high carbon, Damascus steel that are not just for show, they are made to stand up to use and will hold a superior edge. Let Hawes Forge provide you with a knife you can be proud of from their designs or yours.

HAWES FORGE

P.O. Box 176, Weldon, IL 61882
Phone: 217-736-2479

FOR THE SERIOUS RELOADER...

Rooster Labs' line of top-quality, innovative products...for individual and commercial reloaders...now includes:
- **ZAMBINI** 220° Pistol Bullet Lubricant (1x4 & 2x6)
- **HVR** 220° High Velocity Rifle Bullet Lube (1x4)
- **ROOSTER JACKET** Water-based Liquid Bullet Film Lube
- **ROOSTER BRIGHT** Brass Case Polish...Brilliant!
- **CFL-56** Radical Case Forming Lube...for the Wildcatter
- **PDQ-21** Spray Case Sizing Lube...quick, no contamination
- **BP-7 BLACK POWDER** Bullet Lube (1x4 hollow)

Rooster LABORATORIES®

P.O. Box 414605, Kansas City, MO 64141
Phone: 816-474-1622 • Fax: 816-474-7622
E-mail: roosterlabs@aol.com

RUGER 10-22® COMPETITION HAMMER

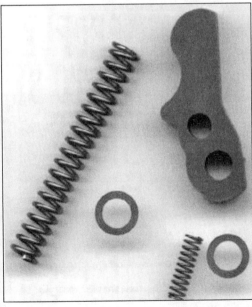

Precision EDM/CNC machined custom hammer for your Ruger 10-22®. Machined from a solid billet of steel. Case hardened to RC-58-60. Drop in designed to lighten your trigger pull to a crisp 2-1/4 lbs. Precision ground with Vapor hand honed engagement surfaces. Includes Wolff Extra Power hammer spring, replacement trigger return spring, and 2 hammer shims.

Price $29.99 plus $3.85 Priority mail.

POWER CUSTOM, INC.

29739 Hwy. J, Dept. KP, Gravois Mills, MO 65037
Phone: 1-573-372-5684 • Fax: 1-573-372-5799
Web: www.powercustom.com • E-mail: rwpowers@laurie.net

FOLDING BIPODS

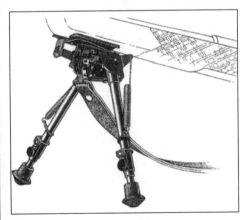

Harris Bipods clamp securely to most stud-equipped bolt-action rifles and are quick-detachable. With adapters, they will fit some other guns. On all models except the Model LM, folding legs have completely adjustable spring-return extensions. The sling swivel attaches to the clamp. This time-proven design is manufactured with heat-treated steel and hard alloys and has a black anodized finish.

Series S Bipods rotate 35° for instant leveling on uneven ground. Hinged base has tension adjustment and buffer springs to eliminate tremor or looseness in crotch area of bipod. They are otherwise similar to non-rotating Series 1A2.

Thirteen models are available from Harris Engineering; literature is free.

HARRIS ENGINEERING INC.

Dept: GD54, Barlow, KY 42024
Phone: 270-334-3633 • Fax: 270-334-3000

SWIFT EXTENDS THE HUNT FROM DAWN TO DUSK

Swift Instruments, Inc., extends the hunt with three new illuminated reticle rifle scopes. All three are waterproof, shock tested and have multi-coated lenses that provide for a brighter, sharper, glare-free image from dawn to dusk. Add to this variable intensity illuminated red cross hairs in the center of the reticle that adjust to increase or decrease to your needs to make getting on target easier in low light situations. All three of these new rifle scopes offer fast focusing with Swift *Speed Focus* feature.

Model 680M Swift: 3-9X, 40mm
Model 681M Swift: 1.5-6X, 40mm
Model 682M Swift: 4-12X, 50mm

SWIFT INSTRUMENTS, INC.
952 Dorchester Avenue, Boston, MA 02125
Phone: 617-436-2960 • Fax: 617-436-3232
Web: www.swift-optics.com

ALASKAN HUNTER

Gary Reeder Custom Guns, builder of full custom guns, including custom cowboy guns, hunting handguns, African hunting rifles, custom Encores and Encore barrels, has a free brochure available or you can check out the large Web site at www.reedercustomguns.com. One of our most popular series is our Alaskan Hunter. This beefy 5-shot 454 Casull is for the serious handgun hunter and joins our 475 Linebaugh and 500 Linebaugh as our most popular hunting handguns. For more information contact:

GARY REEDER CUSTOM GUNS
2601 E. 7th Avenue, Flagstaff, AZ 86004
Phone: 928-527-4100 or 928-526-3313

BLACK HILLS GOLD AMMUNITION

Black Hills Ammunition has introduced a new line of premium performance rifle ammunition. Calibers available in the Black Hills Gold Line are .243, .270, .308, .30-06, and .300 Win Mag. This line is designed for top performance in a wide range of hunting situations. Bullets used in this ammunition are the Barnes X-Bullet with XLC coating and the highly accurate Nosler Ballistic-Tip™.

Black Hills Ammunition is sold dealer direct. The Gold line is packaged in 20 rounds per box, 10 boxes per case. Black Hills pays all freight to dealers in the continental United States. Minimum dealer order is only one case.

BLACK HILLS AMMUNITION
P.O. Box 3090, Rapid City, SD 57709
Phone: 1-605-348-5150 • Fax: 1-605-348-9827
Web: www.black-hills.com

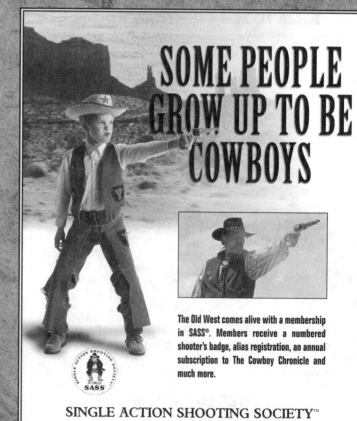

SOME PEOPLE GROW UP TO BE COWBOYS

The Old West comes alive with a membership in SASS®. Members receive a numbered shooter's badge, alias registration, an annual subscription to The Cowboy Chronicle and much more.

SINGLE ACTION SHOOTING SOCIETY™
Toll Free: **1-877-411-SASS**
WWW.SASSNET.COM

SHOOTER'S MARKETPLACE

828 SWIFT HHS

RUBBER ARMORED — WATERPROOF BINOCULAR
8.5x,44 HCF - (336 FT.) — 23.4 OZ. — R.I.E. 44.2

The new 8.5x,44mm Swift model 828 HHS offers world-class optical performance in a light (23.4 oz.) strong, magnesium body. It features twist-up eyecups with a click-stop action on the right diopter for a precise setting that won't go out of adjustment. It is both fully multi-coated and phase-coated in order to provide bright, crisp, high definition viewing, with enhanced contrast in low light situations. Its body is rubber clad for a sure grip and as a cushion against shocks. This nitrogen purged, waterproof and fogproof, roof prism binoculars focus adjustment is both smooth and precise. It will close focus to 9 feet. Complete with lined soft leather grain case and a comfortable Swift broad woven neck strap.

Limited Lifetime Warranty.

SWIFT INSTRUMENTS, INC.

952 Dorchester Avenue, Boston, MA 02125
Phone: 617-436-2960
Fax: 617-436-3232
Web: www.swift-optics.com

BEAR TRACK CASES

Designed by an Alaskan bush pilot! Polyurethane coated, zinc plated corners and feet, zinc plated— spring loaded steel handles, stainless steel hinges, high density urethane foam inside with a neoprene seal. Aluminum walls are standard at .070 with riveted ends. Committed to quality that will protect your valuables regardless of the transportation method you use. Exterior coating also protects other items from acquiring "aluminum black." Many styles, colors and sizes available. Wheels come on large cases and special orders can be accommodated. Call for a brochure or visit online.

Bear Track Cases when top quality protection is a must.

BEAR TRACK CASES

314 Highway 239, Freedom, WY 83120
Phone: 307-883-2468 • Fax: 307-883-2005
Web: www.beartrackcases.com

FINE GUN STOCKS

Manufacturing custom and production gunstocks for hundreds of models of rifles and shotguns—made from the finest stock woods and available in all stages of completion.

Visit www.gunstocks.com to view their bargain list of fine custom gunstocks. Each displayed in full color.

GREAT AMERICAN GUNSTOCK COMPANY

3420 Industrial Drive
Yuba City, CA 95993
Phone: 530-671-4570
Fax: 530-671-3906
Gunstock Hotline: 800-784-GUNS (4867)
Web: www.gunstocks.com
E-mail: gunstox@oro.net

CATALOG #24

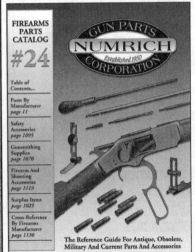

Catalog #24 is our newest edition. This 1152 page catalog features more than 400 schematics for use in identifying commercial, military, antique, and foreign guns. Edition #24 contains 180,000 individual items from our inventory of over 650 million parts and accessories and is necessary for any true gunsmith or hobbyish. It has been the industry's reference book for firearm parts and identification for over 50 years.

Order Item #UY-24 $12.95
U.S. Orders: Bulk Mail (Shipping charges included)
Foreign Orders: Air Mail-30 day delivery
or Surface Mail-90 day delivery. (Shipping charges additional).

NUMRICH GUN PARTS CORPORATION

226 Williams Lane, West Hurley, NY 12491
Orders: (845) 679-2417 • Customer Service: (845) 679-4867
Toll-Free Fax: (877) Gun Parts
e-GunParts.com • E-mail: info@gunpartscorp.com

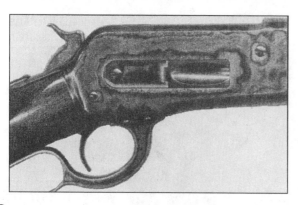

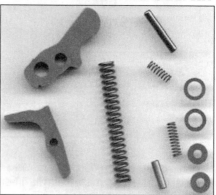

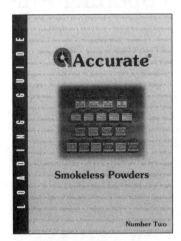

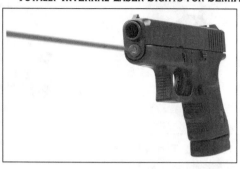
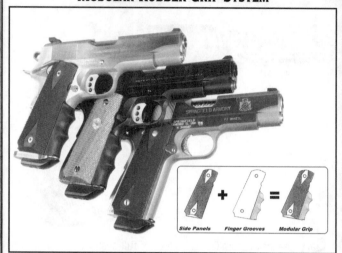

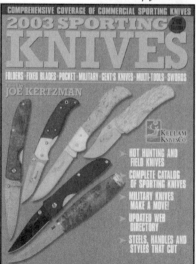

COMPLETE COMPACT CATALOG

HANDGUNS 2003

GUNDEX

Numbers

GUNDEX

GUNDEX

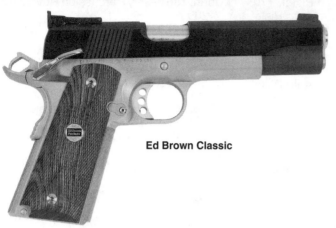

Ed Brown Classic

Ed Brown Classic Class A

BRILEY 1911-STYLE AUTO PISTOLS

Caliber: 9mm Para., 38 Super, 40 S&W, 10-shot magazine; 45 ACP, 8-shot magazine. **Barrel:** 3.6" or 5". **Weight:** NA. **Length:** NA. **Grips:** rosewood or rubber. **Sights:** Bo-Mar adjustable rear, Briley dovetail blade front. **Features:** Modular or Caspian alloy, carbon steel or stainless steel frame; match barrel and trigger group; lowered and flared ejection port; front and rear serrations on slide; beavertail grip safety; hot blue, hard chrome or stainless steel finish. Introduced 2000. Made in U.S. From Briley Manufacturing Inc.

Price: Fantom (3.6" bbl., fixed low-mount rear sight, armor coated
lower receiver) . . . . from **$1,895.00**
Price: Fantom with two-port compensator . . . . from **$2,245.00**
Price: Advantage (5" bbl., adj. low-mount rear sight, checkered
mainspring housing) . . . . from **$1,650.00**
Price: Versatility Plus (5" bbl., adj. low-mount rear sight,
modular or Caspian frame) . . . . from **$1,850.00**
Price: Signature Series (5" bbl., adj. low-mount rear sight,
40 S&W only) . . . . from **$2,250.00**
Price: Plate Master (5" bbl. with compensator, lightened slide,
Briley scope mount) . . . . from **$1,895.00**
Price: El Presidente (5" bbl. with Briley quad compensator,
Briley scope mount) . . . . from **$2,500.00**

ED BROWN CLASSIC CUSTOM
AND CLASS A LIMITED 1911-STYLE AUTO PISTOLS

Caliber: 45 ACP; 7-shot magazine; 40 S&W, 400 Cor-Bon, 38 Super, 9x23, 9mm Para. **Barrel:** 4.25", 5", 6". **Weight:** NA. **Length:** NA. **Grips:** Hogue exotic checkered wood. **Sights:** Bo-Mar or Novak rear, blade front. **Features:** Blued or stainless steel frame; ambidextrous safety; beavertail grip safety; checkered forestrap and mainspring housing; match-grade barrel; slotted hammer; long lightweight or Videki short steel trigger. Many options offered. Made in U.S. by Ed Brown Products.

Price: Classic Custom (45 ACP, 5" barrel) . . . . from **$2,895.00**
Price: Class A Limited (all calibers; several bbl. lengths in
competition and carry forms) . . . . from **$2,250.00**

EUROPEAN AMERICAN ARMORY WITNESS AUTO PISTOLS

Caliber: 9mm Para., 9x21, 38 Super, 40 S&W, 45 ACP, 10mm; 10-shot magazine. **Barrel:** 3.55", 3.66", 4.25", 4.5", 4.75", 5.25". **Weight:** 26 to 38 oz. **Length:** 7.25" to 10.5" overall. **Grips:** Black rubber, smooth walnut, checkered walnut, ivory polymer. **Sights:** three-dot, windage-adjustable or fully adjustable rear, blade front. **Features:** Single and double action; polymer or forged steel frame; forged steel slide; field strips without tools; ergonomic grip angle; front and rear serrations on slide; matte blue and stainless steel finish. Frame can be converted to other calibers. Imported from Italy by European American Armory.

Price: Witness Full Size (4.5" bbl., three-dot sights, 8.1" overall)
. . . . from **$399.00**
Price: Witness Compact (3.66" bbl., three-dot sights, 7.25" overall)
. . . . from **$399.00**

Kimber Custom Compact CDP

Price: Carry-Comp (4.25" bbl. with compensator, three-dot sights,
8.1" overall) . . . . from **$439.00**
Price: Gold Team (5.25" bbl. with compensator, adjustable sights,
10.5" overall) . . . . from **$2,195.00**
Price: Silver Team (5.25" bbl. with compensator, adjustable sights,
9.75" overall) . . . . from **$999.00**
Price: Limited Class (4.75" barrel, adj. sights and trigger,
drilled for scope mount) . . . . from **$999.00**
Price: P-Series (4.55" bbl., polymer frame, black,
porting and sight options wonder finish) . . . . from **$379.00**

KIMBER CUSTOM 1911-STYLE AUTO PISTOLS

Caliber: 9mm Para., 38 Super, 9-shot magazines; 40 S&W, 8-shot magazine; 45 ACP, 7-shot magazine. **Barrel:** 5". **Weight:** 38 oz. **Length:** 8.7" overall. **Grips:** Black synthetic, smooth or double-diamond checkered rosewood, or double-diamond checkered walnut. **Sights:** McCormick low profile or Kimber adjustable rear, blade front. **Features:** Machined steel slide, frame and barrel; front and rear beveled slide serrations; cut and button-rifled, match-grade barrel; adjustable aluminum trigger; full-length guide rod; Commander-style hammer; high-ride beavertail safety; beveled magazine well. Other models available. Made in U.S. by Kimber Mfg. Inc.

Price: Custom (black matte finish) **$730.00**
Price: Custom Royal (polished blue finish, checkered
rosewood grips) **$886.00**
Price: Custom Stainless (satin-finished stainless steel frame
and slide) **$832.00**
Price: Custom Target (matte black or stainless finish,
Kimber adj. sight) **$837.00**

Kimber Custom Pro CDP

Kimber Ultra CDP

North American Arms Guardian

Price: Custom Compact CDP (4" bbl., alum. frame, tritium three-dot sights, 28 oz.) **$1,084.00**

Price: Custom Pro CDP (4" bbl., alum. frame, tritium sights, full-length grip, 28 oz.) **$1,084.00**

Price: Ultra CDP (3" bbl., aluminum frame, tritium sights, 25 oz.). **$1,084.00**

Price: Gold Match (polished blue finish, hand-fitted barrel, ambid. safety) **$1,169.00**

Price: Stainless Gold Match (stainless steel frame and slide, hand-fitted bbl., amb. safety) **$1,315.00**

Price: Gold Combat (hand-fitted, stainless barrel; KimPro black finish, tritium sights) **$1,682.00**

Price: Gold Combat Stainless (stainless frame and slide, satin silver finish, tritium sights) **$1,623.00**

Price: Super Match (satin stainless frame, KimPro black finished, stainless slide) **$1,927.00**

LES BAER CUSTOM 1911-STYLE AUTO PISTOLS
Caliber: 9mm Para., 38 Super, 40 S&W, 45 ACP, 400 Cor-Bon; 7- or 8-shot magazine. **Barrel:** 4-1/4", 5", 6". **Weight:** 28 to 40 oz. **Length:** NA. **Grips:** Checkered cocobolo. **Sights:** Low-mount combat fixed, combat fixed with tritium inserts or low-mount adjustable rear, dovetail front. **Features:** Forged steel or aluminum frame; slide serrated front and rear; lowered and flared ejection port; beveled magazine well; speed trigger with

4-pound pull; beavertail grip safety; ambidextrous safety. Other models available. Made in U.S. by Les Baer Custom.

Price: Baer 1911 Premier II 5" Model (5" bbl., optional stainless steel frame and slide) .... from **$1,428.00**

Price: Premier II 6" Model (6" barrel) .... from **$1,595.00**

Price: Premier II LW1 (forged aluminum frame, steel slide and barrel) .... from **$1,740.00**

Price: Custom Carry (4" or 5" barrel, steel frame) ...... from **$1,640.00**

Price: Custom Carry (4" barrel, aluminum frame) ...... from **$1,923.00**

Price: Swift Response Pistol (fixed tritium sights, Bear Coat finish). .... from **$2,240.00**

Price: Monolith (5" barrel and slide with extra-long dust cover) .... from **$1,599.00**

Price: Stinger (4-1/4" barrel, steel or aluminum frame) ... from **$1,491.00**

Price: Thunder Ranch Special (tritium fixed combat sight, Thunder Ranch logo) .... from **$1,620.00**

Price: National Match Hardball (low-mount adj. sight; meets DCM rules). .... from **$1,335.00**

Price: Bullseye Wadcutter Pistol (Bo-Mar rib w/ adj. sight, guar. 2-1/2" groups) .... from **$1,495.00**

Price: Ultimate Master Combat (5" or 6" bbl., adj. sights, checkered front strap). .... from **$2,376.00**

Price: Ultimate Master Combat Compensated (four-port compensator, adj. sights) .... from **$2,476.00**

NORTH AMERICAN ARMS GUARDIAN AUTO PISTOL
Caliber: 32 ACP, 6-shot magazine. **Barrel:** 2.18". **Weight:** 13.57 oz. **Length:** 4.36" overall. **Grips:** Checkered or smooth; cocobolo, kingwood, winewood, goncalo alves, pau ferro, white or black simulated mother of pearl. **Sights:** White dot, fiber optics or tritium (nine models). **Features:** Double action only; stainless steel frame and slide; barrel porting; frame stippling; forward striped or scalloped slide serrations; meltdown (rounded edges) treatment; slide/frame finishes available in combinations that include black titanium, stainless steel, gold titanium and highly polished or matte choices. From North American Arms Custom Shop.

Price: NAA-32 Guardian. **$408.00**

Price: Full matte .... add **$50.00**

Price: High-polish finish .... add **$150.00**

Price: Ported barrel .... add **$90.00**

North American Arms Guardian with high polish finish

North American Arms Guardian with matte finish

Rock River Arms Elite Commando

Rock River Arms Standard Match

Rock River Arms National Match Hardball

ROCK RIVER ARMS 1911-STYLE AUTO PISTOLS

Caliber: 9mm Para., 38 Super, 40 S&W, 45 ACP. **Barrel:** 4" or 5". **Weight:** NA. **Length:** NA. **Grips:** Double-diamond, checkered cocobolo or black synthetic. **Sights:** Bo-Mar low-mount adjustable, Novak fixed with tritium inserts, Heine fixed or Rock River scope mount; dovetail front blade. **Features:** Chrome-moly, machined steel frame and slide; slide serrated front and rear; aluminum speed trigger with 3.5-4 lb. pull; national match KART barrel; lowered and flared ejection port; tuned and polished extractor; beavertail grip safety; beveled mag. well. Other frames offered. Made in U.S. by Rock River Arms Inc.

Price: Elite Commando (4" barrel, Novak tritium sights) **$1,395.00**
Price: Standard Match (5" barrel, Heine fixed sights). **$1,150.00**
Price: National Match Hardball (5" barrel, Bo-Mar adj. sights)
. . . . from **$1,275.00**
Price: Bullseye Wadcutter (5" barrel, Rock River slide scope
mount) . . . . from **$1,380.00**
Price: Basic Limited Match (5" barrel, Bo-Mar adj. sights)
. . . . from **$1,395.00**
Price: Limited Match (5" barrel, guaranteed 1-1/2" groups
at 50 yards). . . . . from **$1,795.00**
Price: Hi-Cap Basic Limited (5" barrel, four frame choices)
. . . . from **$1,895.00**
Price: Ultimate Match Achiever (5" bbl. with compensator,
mount and Aimpoint) . . . . from **$2,255.00**
Price: Match Master Steel (5" bbl. with compensator,
mount and Aimpoint) **$5,000.00**

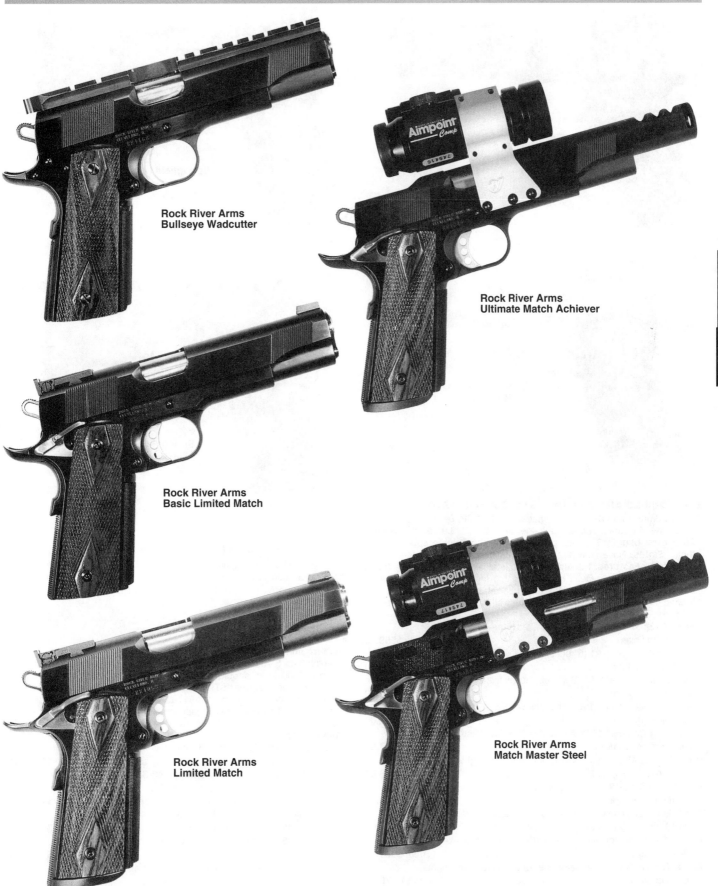

Rock River Arms
Bullseye Wadcutter

Rock River Arms
Ultimate Match Achiever

Rock River Arms
Basic Limited Match

Rock River Arms
Limited Match

Rock River Arms
Match Master Steel

HANDGUNS

Springfield Pro

Springfield Loaded Operator

Springfield Micro Compact Mil-Spec

Springfield
Tactical Response Pistol

SPRINGFIELD ARMORY 1911-STYLE AUTO PISTOLS

Caliber: 9mm Para., 8- or 9-shot magazine; 45 ACP, 6-, 7-, 8- or 10-shot magazine; 45 Super, 7-shot magazine. **Barrel:** 3.5", 3.9", 5", 6". **Weight:** 25 to 41 oz. **Length:** 7" to 9.5" overall. **Grips:** Checkered cocobolo or synthetic. **Sights:** Novak low-profile, Novak tritium or adjustable target rear; blade front. **Features:** Parkerized, blued, stainless steel or bi-tone frame and slide; lightweight Delta hammer; match trigger; front and rear slide serrations; hammer-forged, air-gauged barrel; beavertail grip safety; extended thumb safety; beveled magazine well. Made in U.S. From Springfield Inc.

Price: Mil-Spec 1911-A1 (5" barrel, fixed three-dot sights,
parkerized finish) .... from **$559.00**
Price: Full-Size 1911-A1 (5" bbl., Novak fixed or adj. sights,
steel or alum. frame)................................ from **$799.00**
Price: Champion 1911-A1 (3.9" bbl., Novak fixed sights,
steel or alum. frame)................................ from **$856.00**
Price: Compact 1911-A1 (3.9" bbl., Novak fixed sights,
alum. frame) .... from **$782.00**
Price: Ultra-Compact 1911-A1 (3.5" bbl., Novak fixed sights,
steel or alum. frame)................................ from **$817.00**
Price: Trophy Match 1911-A1 (5" or 6" bbl., adj. sights,
blued or stainless) .... from **$1,148.00**
Price: Long Slide 1911-A1 (6." bbl., adj. sights, stainless,
45 ACP or 45 Super) .... from **$1,049.00**
Price: Full Size High Capacity (5" bbl., Mil-spec fixed sights,
two 10-shot magazines) .... from **$807.00**
Price: Ultra Compact High Capacity (3.5" bbl., Novak fixed sights,
10-shot mag.) .... from **$909.00**
Price: Tactical Response Pistol (3.9" or 5", Novak fixed sights,
Teflon or stain.). .... from **$1,370.00**

Price: Professional Model (5" bbl., Novak three-dot tritium sights,
Black-T finish), Nowlin barrel. .... from **$2,395.00**
Price: Micro compact .... from **$749.00**
Price: Operator 1911-A1 (lightrail on frame in Mil-spec) **$756.00**
Price: Loaded **$836.00**
Price: Tactical Response **$1,473.00**

STI 2011 AUTO PISTOLS

Caliber: 9mm Para., 9x23, 38 Super, 40 S&W, 40 Super, 10mm, 45 ACP. **Barrel:** 3.4", 5", 5.5", 6". **Weight:** 28 to 44 oz. **Length:** 7" to 9-5/8" overall. **Grips:** Checkered, double-diamond rosewood or glass-filled nylon polymer (six colors). **Sights:** STI, Novak or Heine adjustable rear, blade front. **Features:** Updated version of 1911-style auto pistol; serrated slide, front and rear; STI skeletonized trigger; ambidextrous or single-sided thumb safety; blue or hard-chrome finish; etched logo and model name. From STI International.

Price: Competitor (38 Super, 5.5" barrel, C-More Rail Scope
and mount) .... from **$2,499.00**
Price: Trojan (9mm, 45 ACP, 40 Super, 40 S&W; 5" or 6" barrel)
.... from **$970.00**
Price: Edge 5.0" (40 S&W or 45 ACP; 5" barrel) .... from **$1,776.00**
Price: Eagle 5.0" (9mm, 9x23, 38 Super, 40 S&W, 10mm,
40 Super, 45 ACP; 5" bbl.) .... from **$1,699.00**
Price: Eagle 6.0" (9mm, 38 Super, 40 S&W, 10mm, 40 Super,
45 ACP; 6" bbl.) .... from **$1,795.40**
Price: BLS9/BLS40 (9mm, 40 S&W; 3.4" barrel, full-length grip)
.... from **$843.70**

HANDGUNS

Vektor SP2 Ultra

Volquartsen 3.5 Compact

Volquartsen Deluxe

Volquartsen Masters

Volquartsen Olympic

STI COMPACT AUTO PISTOLS

Caliber: 9mm Para., 40 S&W. **Barrel:** 3.4". **Weight:** 28 oz. **Length:** 7" over-all. **Grips:** Checkered double-diamond rosewood. **Sights:** Heine Low Mount fixed rear, slide integral front. **Features:** Similar to STI 2011 models except has compact frame, 7-shot magazine in 9mm (6-shot in 40 cal.), single-sided thumb safety, linkless barrel lockup system, matte blue finish. From STI International.
Price: (9mm Para. or 40 S&W) . . . . from **$746.50**

VOLQUARTSEN CUSTOM 22 CALIBER AUTO PISTOLS

Caliber: 22 LR; 10-shot magazine. **Barrel:** 3.5" to 10"; stainless steel air gauge. **Weight:** 2-1/2 to 3 lbs. 10 oz. **Length:** NA. **Grips:** Finger-grooved plastic or walnut. **Sights:** Adjustable rear and blade front or Weaver-style scope mount. **Features:** Conversions of Ruger Mk. II Auto pistol. Variety of configurations featuring compensators, underlug barrels, etc. Stainless steel finish; black Teflon finish available for additional $85; target hammer, trigger. Made in U.S. by Volquartsen Custom.
Price: 3.5 Compact (3.5" barrel, T/L adjustable rear sight, scope base optional) **$640.00**
Price: Deluxe (barrel to 10", T/L adjustable rear sight) **$675.00**
Price: Deluxe with compensator **$745.00**
Price: Masters (6.5" barrel, finned underlug, T/L adjustable rear sight, compensator) **$950.00**
Price: Olympic (7" barrel, recoil-reducing gas chamber, T/L adjustable rear sight) **$870.00**
Price: Stingray (7.5" ribbed, ported barrel; red-dot sight) **$995.00**
Price: Terminator (7.5" ported barrel, grooved receiver, scope rings) **$730.00**
Price: Ultra-Light Match (6" tensioned barrel, Weaver mount, weighs 2-1/2 lbs.) **$885.00**
Price: V-6 (6", triangular, ventilated barrel with underlug, T/L adj. sight) **$1,030.00**
Price: V-2000 (6" barrel with finned underlug, T/L adj. sight) . . . **$1,095.00**
Price: V-Magic II (7.5" barrel, red-dot sight) **$1,055.00**

HANDGUNS

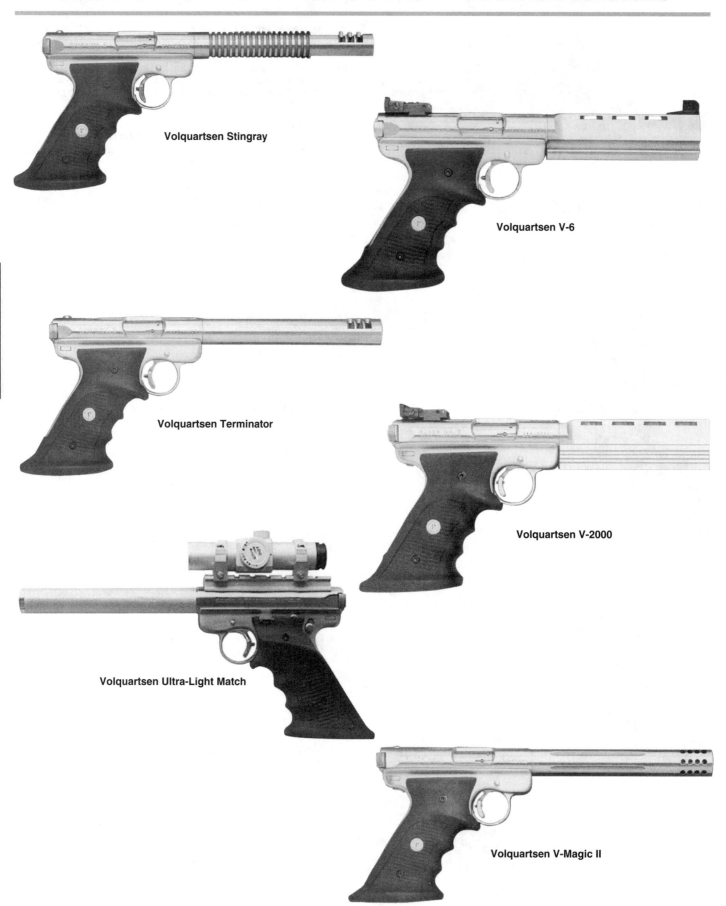

Volquartsen Stingray

Volquartsen V-6

Volquartsen Terminator

Volquartsen V-2000

Volquartsen Ultra-Light Match

Volquartsen V-Magic II

500 Linebaugh

44 Linebaugh Long

500 Linebaugh Long

475 Linebaugh

500 Linebaugh

500 Linebaugh

HANDGUNS

LINEBAUGH CUSTOM SIXGUNS REVOLVERS

Caliber: 45 Colt, 44 Linebaugh Long, 458 Linebaugh, 475 Linebaugh, 500 Linebaugh, 500 Linebaugh Long, 445 Super Mag. **Barrel:** 4-3/4", 5-1/2", 6", 7-1/2"; other lengths available. **Weight:** NA. **Length:** NA. **Grips:** Dustin Linebaugh Custom made to customer's specs. **Sights:** Bowen steel rear or factory Ruger; blade front. **Features:** Conversions using customer's Ruger Blackhawk Bisley and Vaquero Bisley frames. Made in U.S. by Linebaugh Custom Sixguns.

Price: Small 45 Colt conversion (rechambered cyl., new barrel)
.... from **$1,200.00**

Price: Large 45 Colt conversion (oversized cyl., new barrel, 5- or 6-shot) .... from **$1,800.00**

Price: 475 Linebaugh, 500 Linebaugh conversions ...... from **$1,800.00**

Price: Linebaugh and 445 Super Mag calibers on 357 Maximum frame .... from **$3,000.00**

GARY REEDER CUSTOM GUNS REVOLVERS

Caliber: 357 Magnum, 45 Colt, 44-40, 41 Magnum, 44 Magnum, 454 Casull, 475 Linebaugh, 500 Linebaugh. **Barrel:** 2-1/2" to 12". **Weight:** Varies by model. **Length:** Varies by model. **Grips:** Black Cape buffalo horn, laminated walnut, simulated pearl, others. **Sights:** Notch fixed or adjustable rear, blade or ramp front. **Features:** Custom conversions of Ruger Vaquero, Blackhawk Bisley and Super Blackhawk frames. Jeweled hammer and trigger, tuned action, model name engraved on barrel, additional engraving on frame and cylinder, integral muzzle brake, finish available in high-

polish or satin stainless steel or black Chromex finish. Also available on customer's gun at reduced cost. Other models available. Made in U.S. by Gary Reeder Custom Guns.

Price: Gamblers Classic (2-1/2" bbl., engraved cards and dice, no ejector rod housing) .... from **$995.00**

Price: Tombstone Classic (3-1/2" bbl. with gold bands, notch sight, birdshead grips) .... from **$995.00**

Price: Doc Holliday Classic (3-1/2" bbl., engraved cards and dice, white pearl grips) .... from **$995.00**

Price: Ultimate Vaquero (engraved barrel, frame and cylinder, made to customer specs) .... from **$995.00**

Price: Black Widow (4-5/8" bbl., black Chromex finish, black widow spider engraving) .... from **$1,095.00**

Price: Cowboy Classic (stainless finish, cattle brand engraved, limited to 100 guns) .... from **$995.00**

Price: African Hunter (6" bbl., with or without muzzle brake, 475 or 500 Linebaugh) .... (on your gun from) **$1,295.00**

Price: Alaskan Survivalist (3" bbl., Redhawk frame, engraved bear, 45 Colt or 44 Magnum) .... from **$1,095.00**

Price: Ultimate Back-Up (3-1/2" bbl., fixed sights, choice of animal engraving, 475 Linebaugh, 500 Linebaugh)
.... (on your gun from) **$1,295.00**

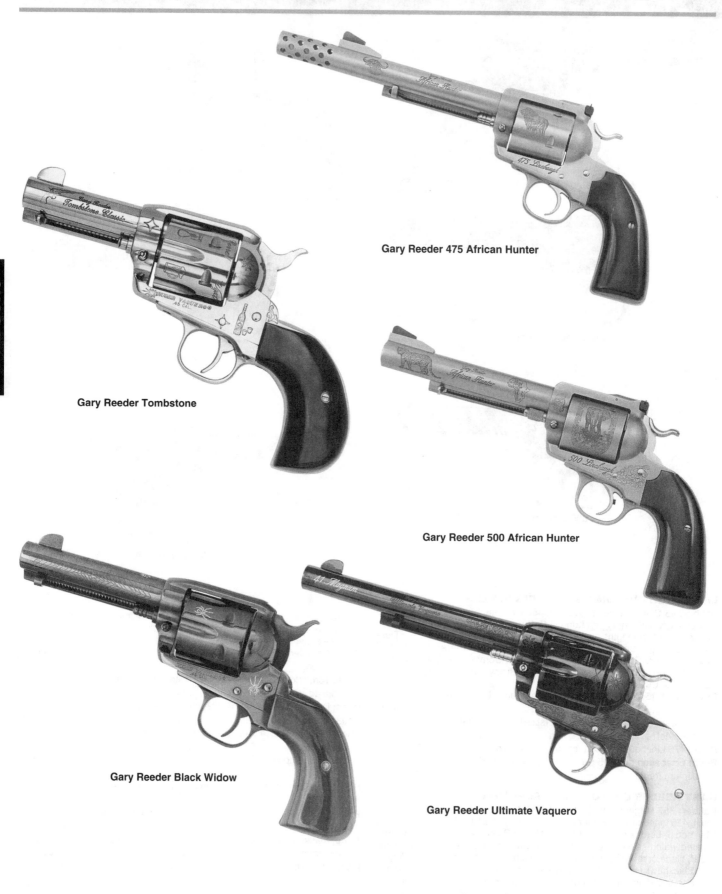

Gary Reeder 475 African Hunter

Gary Reeder Tombstone

Gary Reeder 500 African Hunter

Gary Reeder Black Widow

Gary Reeder Ultimate Vaquero

HANDGUNS

**United State Fire-Arms
Single Action Army**

**United States Fire-Arms
SAA Flat Top Target**

**United States Fire-Arms
SAA Bisley**

**United States Fire-Arms
Omni-Snubnose**

**United States Fire-Arms
Omni-Potent Six Shooter**

UNITED STATES FIRE-ARMS SINGLE-ACTION REVOLVERS

Caliber: 32 WCF, 38 Special, 38 WCF, 41 Colt, 44 WCF, 44 Special, 45 Colt, **Barrel:** 2", 3", 4-3/4", 5-1/2", 7-1/2", 16". **Weight:** NA. **Length:** NA. **Grips:** Hard rubber, rosewood, stag, pearl, ivory, ivory Micarta, smooth walnut, burled walnut and checkered walnut. **Sights:** Notch rear, blade front. **Features:** Hand-fitted replicas of Colt single-action revolvers. Full Dome Blue, Dome Blue, Armory Blue (gray-blue), Old Armory Bone Case (color casehardened) and nickel plate finishes. Carved and scrimshaw grips, engraving and gold inlays offered. Made in U.S. From United States Fire-Arms Mfg. Co.

Price: Single Action Army (32 WCF, 38 Spec., 38 WCF, 41 Colt, 45 Colt, 44 Spec., 44 WCF) **$1,250.00**

Price: SAA Flat Top Target (extended blade front, drift-adj. rear sights . . . . from **$1,450.00**

Price: SAA Bisley (Bisley grip and hammer) . . . . from **$1,525.00**

Price: Omni-Snubnose (2" or 3" barrel, lanyard loop, 45 Colt only) . . . . from **$1,325.00**

Price: Omni-Potent Six Shooter (lanyard loop on grip). . . . from **$1,325.00**

Price: New Buntline Special (16" bbl., skeleton shoulder stock, case, scabbard) . . . . from **$2,299.00**

Price: China Camp Cowboy Action Gun (4-3/4", 5-1/2" or 7-1/2" bbl., Silver Steel finish). . . . . from **$1,200.00**

Price: Henry Nettleton Cavalry Revolver (5-1/2" or 7-1/2" bbl., 45 Colt only) . . . . from **$1,125.00**

Price: U.S. 1851 Navy Conversion (7-1/2" bbl., color casehardened frame, 38 Spec. only). . . . . from **$1,499.00**

Price: U.S. Pre-War (SAA, Old Armory Bone Case or Armory Blue finish) . . . . from **$1,525.00**

SEMI-CUSTOM HANDGUNS — REVOLVERS

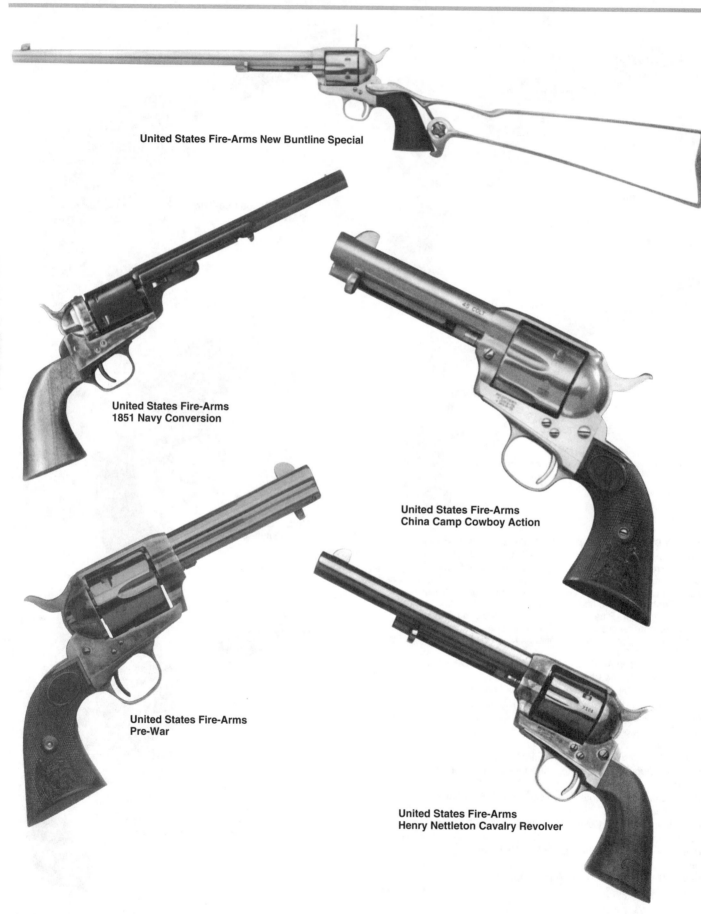

United States Fire-Arms New Buntline Special

United States Fire-Arms
1851 Navy Conversion

United States Fire-Arms
China Camp Cowboy Action

United States Fire-Arms
Pre-War

United States Fire-Arms
Henry Nettleton Cavalry Revolver

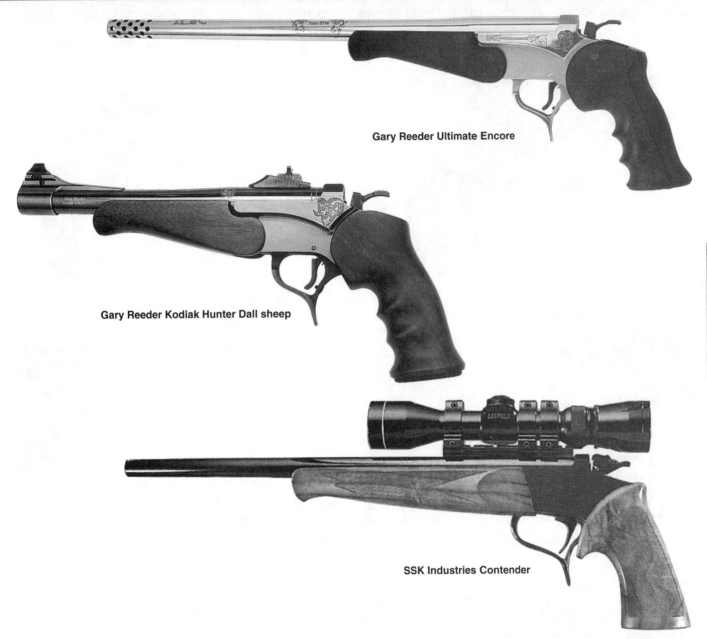

Gary Reeder Ultimate Encore

Gary Reeder Kodiak Hunter Dall sheep

SSK Industries Contender

GARY REEDER CUSTOM GUNS
CONTENDER AND ENCORE PISTOLS

Caliber: 22 Cheetah, 218 Bee, 22 K-Hornet, 22 Hornet, 218 Mashburn Bee, 22-250 Improved, 6mm/284, 7mm STW, 7mm GNR, 30 GNR, 338 GNR, 300 Win. Magnum, 338 Win. Magnum, 350 Rem. Magnum, 358 STA, 375 H&H, 378 GNR, 416 Remington, 416 GNR, 450 GNR, 475 Linebaugh, 500 Linebaugh, 50 Alaskan, 50 AE, 454 Casull; others available. **Barrel:** 8" to 15" (others available). **Weight:** NA. **Length:** Varies with barrel length. **Grips:** Walnut fingergroove. **Sights:** Express-style adjustable rear and barrel band front (Kodiak Hunter); none furnished most models. **Features:** Offers complete guns and barrels in the T/C Contender and Encore. Integral muzzle brake, engraved animals and model name, tuned action, high-polish or satin stainless steel or black Chromex finish. Made in U.S. by Gary Reeder Custom Guns.

Price: Kodiak Hunter (50 AE or 454 Casull, Kodiak bear and Dall sheep engravings) . . . . from **$995.00**

Price: Ultimate Encore (15" bbl. with muzzle brake, grizzly bear engraving) . . . . from **$995.00**

SSK INDUSTRIES CONTENDER AND ENCORE PISTOLS

Caliber: More than 200, including most standard pistol and rifle calibers, as well as 226 JDJ, 6mm JDJ, 257 JDJ, 6.5mm JDJ, 7mm JDJ, 6.5mm Mini-Dreadnaught, 30-06 JDJ, 280 JDJ, 375 JDJ, 6mm Whisper, 300 Whisper and 338 Whisper. **Barrel:** 10" to 26"; blued or stainless; variety of configurations. **Weight:** Varies with barrel length and features. **Length:** Varies with barrel length. **Grips:** Pachmayr, wood models available. **Features:** Offers frames, barrels and complete guns in the T/C Contender and Encore. Fluted, diamond, octagon and round barrels; flatside Contender frames; chrome-plating; muzzle brakes; trigger jobs; variety of stocks and forends; sights and optics. Made in U.S. by SSK Industries.

Price: Blued Contender frame	from **$390.00**
Price: Stainless Contender frame	from **$390.00**
Price: Blued Encore frame	from **$290.00**
Price: Stainless Encore frame	from **$318.00**
Price: Contender barrels	from **$315.00**
Price: Encore barrels	from **$340.00**

Includes models suitable for several forms of competition and other sporting purposes.

Accu-Tek AT-380

Accu-Tek HC-380

Accu-Tek XL-9

ACCU-TEK MODEL AT-380 AUTO PISTOL

Caliber: 380 ACP, 5-shot magazine. **Barrel:** 2.75". **Weight:** 20 oz. **Length:** 5.6" overall. **Grips:** Grooved black composition. **Sights:** Blade front, rear adjustable for windage. **Features:** Stainless steel frame and slide. External hammer; manual thumb safety; firing pin block, trigger disconnect. Introduced 1991. Price includes cleaning kit and gun lock. Made in U.S.A. by Accu-Tek.
Price: Satin stainless **$239.00**

Accu-Tek Model AT-32SS Auto Pistol

Same as the AT-380SS except chambered for 32 ACP. Introduced 1991. Price includes cleaning kit and gun lock.
Price: Satin stainless **$239.00**

ACCU-TEK MODEL HC-380 AUTO PISTOL

Caliber: 380 ACP, 10-shot magazine. **Barrel:** 2.75". **Weight:** 26 oz. **Length:** 6" overall. **Grips:** Checkered black composition. **Sights:** Blade front, rear adjustable for windage. **Features:** External hammer; manual thumb safety with firing pin and trigger disconnect; bottom magazine release. Stainless steel construction. Introduced 1993. Price includes cleaning kit and gun lock. Made in U.S.A. by Accu-Tek.
Price: Satin stainless **$249.00**

ACCU-TEK XL-9 AUTO PISTOL

Caliber: 9mm Para., 5-shot magazine. **Barrel:** 3". **Weight:** 24 oz. **Length:** 5.6" overall. **Grips:** Black pebble composition. **Sights:** Three-dot system; rear adjustable for windage. **Features:** Stainless steel construction; double-action-only mechanism. Introduced 1999. Price includes cleaning kit and gun lock, two magazines. Made in U.S.A. by Accu-Tek.
Price: **$267.00**

AMERICAN ARMS MATEBA AUTO/REVOLVER

Caliber: 357 Mag., 6-shot. **Barrel:** 4", 6", 8". **Weight:** 2.75 lbs. **Length:** 8.77" overall. **Grips:** Smooth walnut. **Sights:** Blade on ramp front, adjustable rear. **Features:** Double or single action. Cylinder and slide recoil together upon firing. All-steel construction with polished blue finish. Introduced 1995. Imported from Italy by American Arms, Inc.
Price: **$1,295.00**
Price: 6" **$1,349.00**

AMT AUTOMAG II AUTO PISTOL

Caliber: 22 WMR, 9-shot magazine (7-shot with 3-3/8" barrel). **Barrel:** 3-3/8", 4-1/2", 6". **Weight:** About 32 oz. **Length:** 9-3/8" overall. **Grips:** Grooved carbon fiber. **Sights:** Blade front, adjustable rear. **Features:** Made of stainless steel. Gas-assisted action. Exposed hammer. Slide flats have brushed finish, rest is sandblast. Squared trigger guard. Introduced 1986. From Galena Industries, Inc.
Price: **$429.00**

AMT AUTOMAG III PISTOL

Caliber: 30 Carbine, 8-shot magazine. **Barrel:** 6-3/8". **Weight:** 43 oz. **Length:** 10-1/2" overall. **Grips:** Carbon fiber. **Sights:** Blade front, adjustable rear. **Features:** Stainless steel construction. Hammer-drop safety. Slide flats have brushed finish, rest is sandblasted. Introduced 1989. From Galena Industries, Inc.
Price: **$529.00**

AMT AUTOMAG IV PISTOL

Caliber: 45 Winchester Magnum, 6-shot magazine. **Barrel:** 6.5". **Weight:** 46 oz. **Length:** 10.5" overall. **Grips:** Carbon fiber. **Sights:** Blade front, adjustable rear. **Features:** Made of stainless steel with brushed finish. Introduced 1990. Made in U.S.A. by Galena Industries, Inc.
Price: **$599.00**

AMT 45 ACP HARDBALLER II

Caliber: 45 ACP. **Barrel:** 5". **Weight:** 39 oz. **Length:** 8-1/2" overall. **Grips:** Wrap-around rubber. **Sights:** Adjustable. **Features:** Extended combat safety, serrated matte slide rib, loaded chamber indicator, long grip safety, beveled magazine well, adjustable target trigger. All stainless steel. From Galena Industries, Inc.
Price: **$425.00**
Price: Government model (as above except no rib, fixed sights) . **$399.00**
Price: 400 Accelerator (400 Cor-Bon, 7" barrel) **$549.00**
Price: Commando (40 S&W, Government Model frame) **$435.00**

AMT 45 ACP HARDBALLER LONG SLIDE

Caliber: 45 ACP. **Barrel:** 7". **Length:** 10-1/2" overall. **Grips:** Wrap-around rubber. **Sights:** Fully adjustable rear sight. **Features:** Slide and barrel are 2" longer than the standard 45, giving less recoil, added velocity, longer sight radius. Has extended combat safety, serrated matte rib, loaded chamber indicator, wide adjustable trigger. From Galena Industries, Inc.
Price: **$529.00**

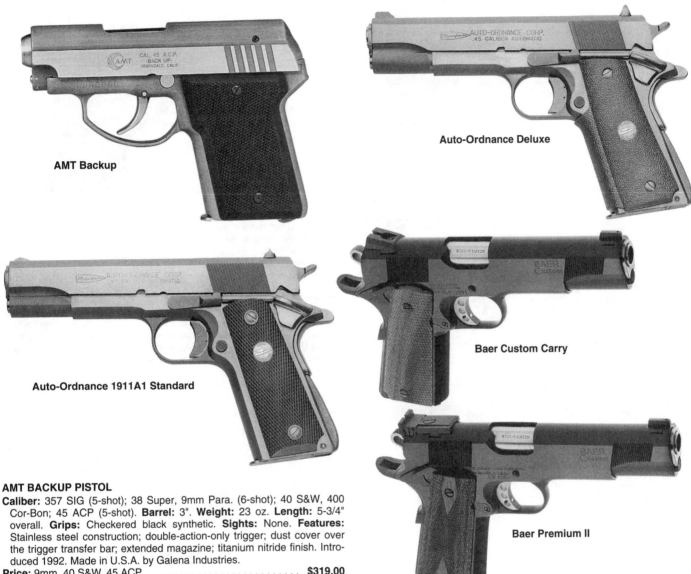

AMT Backup

Auto-Ordnance Deluxe

Auto-Ordnance 1911A1 Standard

Baer Custom Carry

Baer Premium II

AMT BACKUP PISTOL

Caliber: 357 SIG (5-shot); 38 Super, 9mm Para. (6-shot); 40 S&W, 400 Cor-Bon; 45 ACP (5-shot). **Barrel:** 3". **Weight:** 23 oz. **Length:** 5-3/4" overall. **Grips:** Checkered black synthetic. **Sights:** None. **Features:** Stainless steel construction; double-action-only trigger; dust cover over the trigger transfer bar; extended magazine; titanium nitride finish. Introduced 1992. Made in U.S.A. by Galena Industries.

Price: 9mm, 40 S&W, 45 ACP **$319.00**
Price: 38 Super, 357 SIG, 400 Cor-Bon **$369.00**

AMT 380 DAO Small Frame Backup

Similar to DAO Backup except smaller frame, 2-1/2" barrel, weighs 18 oz., and is 5" overall. Has 5-shot magazine, matte/stainless finish. Made in U.S.A. by Galena Industries.

Price: **$319.00**

AUTO-ORDNANCE 1911A1 AUTOMATIC PISTOL

Caliber: 45 ACP, 7-shot magazine. **Barrel:** 5". **Weight:** 39 oz. **Length:** 8-1/2" overall. **Grips:** Checkered plastic with medallion. **Sights:** Blade front, rear adjustable for windage. **Features:** Same specs as 1911A1 military guns—parts interchangeable. Frame and slide blued; each radius has non-glare finish. Made in U.S.A. by Auto-Ordnance Corp.

Price: 45 ACP, blue. **$511.00**
Price: 45 ACP, Parkerized **$515.00**
Price: 45 ACP Deluxe (three-dot sights, textured rubber
wraparound grips) **$525.00**

AUTAUGA 32 AUTO PISTOL

Caliber: 32 ACP, 6-shot magazine. **Barrel:** 2". **Weight:** 11.3 oz. **Length:** 4.3" overall. **Grips:** Black polymer. **Sights:** Fixed. **Features:** Double-action-only mechanism. Stainless steel construction. Uses Winchester Silver Tip ammunition.

Price: . . . . **NA**

BAER 1911 CUSTOM CARRY AUTO PISTOL

Caliber: 45 ACP, 7- or 10-shot magazine. **Barrel:** 5". **Weight:** 37 oz. **Length:** 8.5" overall. **Grips:** Checkered walnut. **Sights:** Baer improved ramp-style dovetailed front, Novak low-mount rear. **Features:** Baer forged NM frame, slide and barrel with stainless bushing; fitted slide to frame; double serrated slide (full-size only); Baer speed trigger with 4-lb. pull; Baer deluxe hammer and sear, tactical-style extended ambidextrous safety, beveled magazine well; polished feed ramp and throated barrel; tuned extractor; Baer extended ejector, checkered slide stop; lowered and flared ejection port, full-length recoil guide rod; recoil buff. Partial listing shown. Made in U.S.A. by Les Baer Custom, Inc.

Price: Standard size, blued **$1,640.00**
Price: Standard size, stainless **$1,690.00**
Price: Comanche size, blued **$1,640.00**
Price: Comanche size, stainless **$1,690.00**
Price: Comanche size, aluminum frame, blued slide **$1,923.00**
Price: Comanche size, aluminum frame, stainless slide **$1,995.00**

BAER 1911 PREMIER II AUTO PISTOL

Caliber: 9x23, 38 Super, 400 Cor-Bon, 45 ACP, 7- or 10-shot magazine. **Barrel:** 5". **Weight:** 37 oz. **Length:** 8.5" overall. **Grips:** Checkered rosewood, double diamond pattern. **Sights:** Baer dovetailed front, low-mount

Beretta 92 Billennium

Beretta 950 Jetfire

Beretta 96

Bo-Mar rear with hidden leaf. **Features:** Baer NM forged steel frame and barrel with stainless bushing; slide fitted to frame; double serrated slide; lowered, flared ejection port; tuned, polished extractor; Baer extended ejector, checkered slide stop, aluminum speed trigger with 4-lb. pull, deluxe Commander hammer and sear, beavertail grip safety with pad, beveled magazine well, extended ambidextrous safety; flat mainspring housing; polished feed ramp and throated barrel; 30 lpi checkered front strap. Made in U.S.A. by Les Baer Custom, Inc.
Price: Blued **$1,428.00**
Price: Stainless **$1,558.00**
Price: 6" model, blued, from **$1,595.00**

BAER 1911 S.R.P. PISTOL
Caliber: 45 ACP. **Barrel:** 5". **Weight:** 37 oz. **Length:** 8.5" overall. **Grips:** Checkered walnut. **Sights:** Trijicon night sights. **Features:** Similar to the F.B.I. contract gun except uses Baer forged steel frame. Has Baer match barrel with supported chamber, Wolff springs, complete tactical action job. All parts Mag-na-fluxed; deburred for tactical carry. Has Baer Ultra Coat finish. Tuned for reliability. Contact Baer for complete details. Introduced 1996. Made in U.S.A. by Les Baer Custom, Inc.
Price: Government or Comanche length **$2,240.00**

BERETTA MODEL 92 BILLENNIUM LIMITED EDITION
Caliber: 9mm. **Grips:** Carbon fiber. **Sights:** 3 dot. **Features:** Single action. Semiauto. Steel frame, frame mounted safety. Only 2000 made worldwide.
Price: **$1,357.00**

BERETTA MODEL 92FS PISTOL
Caliber: 9mm Para., 10-shot magazine. **Barrel:** 4.9". **Weight:** 34 oz. **Length:** 8.5" overall. **Grips:** Checkered black plastic. **Sights:** Blade front, rear adjustable for windage. Tritium night sights available. **Features:** Double action. Extractor acts as chamber loaded indicator, squared trigger guard, grooved front- and backstraps, inertia firing pin. Matte or blued finish. Introduced 1977. Made in U.S.A. and imported from Italy by Beretta U.S.A.
Price: With plastic grips **$676.00**
Price: Vertech with access rail **$712.00**
Price: Vertech Inox **$762.00**

Beretta Model 92FS/96 Brigadier Pistols
Similar to the Model 92FS/96 except with a heavier slide to reduce felt recoil and allow mounting removable front sight. Wrap-around rubber grips. Three-dot sights dovetailed to the slide, adjustable for windage. Weighs 35.3 oz. Introduced 1999.
Price: 9mm or 40 S&W, 10-shot **$716.00**
Price: Inox models (stainless steel) **$771.00**

Beretta Model 92FS Compact and Compact Type M Pistol
Similar to the Model 92FS except more compact and lighter: overall length 7.8"; 4.3" barrel; weighs 30.9 oz. Has Bruniton finish, chrome-lined bore, combat trigger guard, ambidextrous safety/decock lever. Single column 8-shot magazine (Type M), or double column 10-shot (Compact), 9mm only. Introduced 1998. Imported from Italy by Beretta U.S.A.
Price: Compact (10-shot) **$676.00**
Price: Compact Type M (8-shot) **$676.00**
Price: Compact Inox (stainless) **$734.00**
Price: Compact Type M Inox (stainless) **$721.00**

Beretta Model 96 Pistol
Same as the Model 92FS except chambered for 40 S&W. Ambidextrous safety mechanism with passive firing pin catch, slide safety/decocking lever, trigger bar disconnect. Has 10-shot magazine. Available with three-dot sights. Introduced 1992.
Price: Model 96, plastic grips **$676.00**
Price: Stainless, rubber grips **$734.00**
Price: Vertech with access rail **$712.00**
Price: Vertech Inox **$762.00**

BERETTA MODEL 80 CHEETAH SERIES DA PISTOLS
Caliber: 380 ACP, 10-shot magazine (M84); 8-shot (M85); 22 LR, 7-shot (M87). **Barrel:** 3.82". **Weight:** About 23 oz. (M84/85); 20.8 oz. (M87). **Length:** 6.8" overall. **Grips:** Glossy black plastic (wood optional at extra cost). **Sights:** Fixed front, drift-adjustable rear. **Features:** Double action, quick takedown, convenient magazine release. Introduced 1977. Imported from Italy by Beretta U.S.A.
Price: Model 84 Cheetah, plastic grips **$589.00**
Price: Model 84 Cheetah, wood grips, nickel finish **$652.00**
Price: Model 85 Cheetah, plastic grips, 8-shot **$556.00**
Price: Model 85 Cheetah, wood grips, nickel, 8-shot **$609.00**
Price: Model 87 Cheetah, wood, 22 LR, 7-shot **$589.00**
Price: Model 87 Target, plastic grips **$669.00**

Beretta Model 86 Cheetah
Similar to the 380-caliber Model 85 except has tip-up barrel for first-round loading. Barrel length is 4.4", overall length of 7.33". Has 8-shot magazine, walnut grips. Introduced 1989.
Price: **$591.00**

BERETTA MODEL 950 JETFIRE AUTO PISTOL
Caliber: 25 ACP, 8-shot. **Barrel:** 2.4". **Weight:** 9.9 oz. **Length:** 4.7" overall. **Grips:** Checkered black plastic or walnut. **Sights:** Fixed. **Features:** Single action, thumb safety; tip-up barrel for direct loading/unloading, cleaning. From Beretta U.S.A.
Price: Jetfire plastic, matte finish **$226.00**
Price: Jetfire plastic, stainless **$267.00**

Beretta M8000/8040 Cougar

Beretta U22 Neos

Bersa Thunder 380

Beretta Model 21 Bobcat Pistol

Similar to the Model 950 BS. Chambered for 22 LR or 25 ACP. Both double action. Has 2.4" barrel, 4.9" overall length; 7-round magazine on 22 cal.; 8 rounds in 25 ACP, 9.9 oz., available in nickel, matte, engraved or blue finish. Plastic grips. Introduced in 1985.

Price: Bobcat, 22 or 25, blue **$285.00**
Price: Bobcat, 22, stainless **$307.00**
Price: Bobcat, 22 or 25, matte **$252.00**

BERETTA MODEL 3032 TOMCAT PISTOL

Caliber: 32 ACP, 7-shot magazine. **Barrel:** 2.45". **Weight:** 14.5 oz. **Length:** 5" overall. **Grips:** Checkered black plastic. **Sights:** Blade front, drift-adjustable rear. **Features:** Double action with exposed hammer; tip-up barrel for direct loading/unloading; thumb safety; polished or matte blue finish. Imported from Italy by Beretta U.S.A. Introduced 1996.

Price: Blue $370.00
Price: Matte $340.00
Price: Stainless. $418.00
Price: Titanium $572.00

BERETTA MODEL 8000/8040/8045 COUGAR PISTOL

Caliber: 9mm Para., 10-shot, 40 S&W, 10-shot magazine; 45 ACP, 8-shot. **Barrel:** 3.6". **Weight:** 33.5 oz. **Length:** 7" overall. **Grips:** Checkered plastic. **Sights:** Blade front, rear drift adjustable for windage. **Features:** Slide-mounted safety; rotating barrel; exposed hammer. Matte black Bruniton finish. Announced 1994. Imported from Italy by Beretta U.S.A.

Price: $709.00
Price: D model, 9mm, 40 S&W. $739.00
Price: D model, 45 ACP $739.00

BERETTA MODEL 9000S COMPACT PISTOL

Caliber: 9mm Para., 40 S&W; 10-shot magazine. **Barrel:** 3.4". **Weight:** 26.8 oz. **Length:** 6.6". **Grips:** Soft polymer. **Sights:** Windage-adjustable white-dot rear, white-dot blade front. **Features:** Glass-reinforced polymer frame; patented tilt-barrel, open-slide locking system; chrome-lined barrel; external serrated hammer; automatic firing pin and manual safeties. Introduced 2000. Imported from Italy by Beretta USA.

Price: 9000S Type F (single and double action, external
hammer) $551.00
Price: 9000S Type D (double-action only, no external
hammer or safety). $551.00

Beretta Model 8000/8040/8045 Mini Cougar

Similar to the Model 8000/8040 Cougar except has shorter grip frame and weighs 27.6 oz. Introduced 1998. Imported from Italy by Beretta U.S.A.

Price: 9mm or 40 S&W. $709.00
Price: 9mm or 40 S&W, DAO $739.00
Price: 45 ACP, 6-shot $739.00
Price: 45 ACP DAO $739.00

BERETTA MODEL U22 NEOS

Caliber: 22 LR, 10-shot magazine. **Barrel:** 4.2"; 6". **Weight:** 32 oz.; 36 oz. **Length:** 8.8"; 10.3". **Sights:** Target. **Features:** Intregral rail for standard scope mounts, light, perfectly weighted, 100% American made by Beretta.

Price: $256.00
Price: Inox $299.00

BERSA THUNDER 380 AUTO PISTOLS

Caliber: 380 ACP, 7-shot (Thunder 380 Lite), 9-shot magazine (Thunder 380 DLX). **Barrel:** 3.5". **Weight:** 23 oz. **Length:** 6.6" overall. **Grips:** Black polymer. **Sights:** Blade front, notch rear adjustable for windage; three-dot system. **Features:** Double action; firing pin and magazine safeties. Available in blue or nickel. Introduced 1995. Distributed by Eagle Imports, Inc.

Price: Thunder 380, 7-shot, deep blue finish $256.95
Price: Thunder 380 Deluxe, 9-shot, satin nickel. $291.95

BLUE THUNDER/COMMODORE 1911-STYLE AUTO PISTOLS

Caliber: 45 ACP, 7-shot magazine. **Barrel:** 4-1/4", 5". **Weight:** NA. **Length:** NA. **Grips:** Checkered hardwood. **Sights:** Blade front, drift-adjustable rear. **Features:** Extended slide release and safety, spring guide rod, skeletonized hammer and trigger, magazine bumper, beavertail grip safety. Imported from the Philippines by Century International Arms Inc.

Price: . . . . **$464.80 to $484.80**

BROWNING HI-POWER 9mm AUTOMATIC PISTOL

Caliber: 9mm Para.,10-shot magazine. **Barrel:** 4-21/32". **Weight:** 32 oz. **Length:** 7-3/4" overall. **Grips:** Walnut, hand checkered, or black Polyamide. **Sights:** 1/8" blade front; rear screw-adjustable for windage and elevation. Also available with fixed rear (drift-adjustable for windage). **Features:** External hammer with half-cock and thumb safeties. A blow on the hammer cannot discharge a cartridge; cannot be fired with magazine removed. Fixed rear sight model available. Includes gun lock. Imported from Belgium by Browning.

Price: Fixed sight model, walnut grips $680.00
Price: Fully adjustable rear sight, walnut grips $730.00
Price: Mark III, standard matte black finish, fixed sight, moulded grips,
ambidextrous safety $662.00

Browning Micro Buck Mark Standard

Calico M-110

Browning Buck Mark Challenge

Carbon-15

Browning Hi-Power Practical Pistol

Similar to the standard Hi-Power except has silver-chromed frame with blued slide, wrap-around Pachmayr rubber grips, round-style serrated hammer and removable front sight, fixed rear (drift-adjustable for windage). Available in 9mm Para. Includes gun lock. Introduced 1991.

Price: **$717.00**

BROWNING BUCK MARK STANDARD 22 PISTOL

Caliber: 22 LR, 10-shot magazine. **Barrel:** 5-1/2". **Weight:** 32 oz. **Length:** 9-1/2" overall. **Grips:** Black moulded composite with checkering. **Sights:** Ramp front, Browning Pro Target rear adjustable for windage and elevation. **Features:** All steel, matte blue finish or nickel, gold-colored trigger. Buck Mark Plus has laminated wood grips. Includes gun lock. Made in U.S.A. Introduced 1985. From Browning.

Price: Buck Mark Standard, blue **$286.00**
Price: Buck Mark Nickel, nickel finish with contoured rubber grips **$338.00**
Price: Buck Mark Plus, matte blue with laminated wood grips . . . **$350.00**
Price: Buck Mark Plus Nickel, nickel finish, laminated wood grips **$383.00**

Browning Buck Mark Camper

Similar to the Buck Mark except 5-1/2" bull barrel. Weight is 34 oz. Matte blue finish, molded composite grips. Introduced 1999. From Browning.

Price: **$258.00**
Price: Camper Nickel, nickel finish, molded composite grips **$287.00**

Browning Buck Mark Challenge

Similar to the Buck Mark except has a lightweight barrel and smaller grip diameter. Barrel length is 5-1/2", weight is 25 oz. Introduced 1999. From Browning.

Price: **$320.00**

Browning Buck Mark Micro

Same as the Buck Mark Standard and Buck Mark Plus except has 4" barrel. Available in blue or nickel. Has 16-click Pro Target rear sight. Introduced 1992.

Price: Micro Standard, matte blue finish. **$286.00**
Price: Micro Nickel, nickel finish **$338.00**
Price: Buck Mark Micro Plus, matte blue, lam. wood grips. **$350.00**
Price: Buck Mark Micro Plus Nickel **$383.00**

Browning Buck Mark Bullseye

Same as the Buck Mark Standard except has 7-1/4" fluted barrel, matte blue finish. Weighs 36 oz.

Price: Bullseye Standard, molded composite grips **$420.00**
Price: Bullseye Target, contoured rosewood grips **$541.00**

Browning Buck Mark 5.5

Same as the Buck Mark Standard except has a 5-1/2" bull barrel with integral scope mount, matte blue finish.

Price: 5.5 Field, Pro-Target adj. rear sight, contoured walnut grips **$459.00**
Price: 5.5 Target, hooded adj. target sights, contoured walnut grips

. . . . **$459.00**

Buck Mark Commemorative

Same as the Buck Mark Standard except has a 6-3/4" Challenger-style barrel, matte blue finish and scrimshaw-style, bonded ivory grips. Includes pistol rug. Limited to 1,000 guns.

Price: Commemorative. **$437.00**

CALICO M-110 AUTO PISTOL

Caliber: 22 LR. **Barrel:** 6". **Weight:** 3.7 lbs. (loaded). **Length:** 17.9" overall. **Grips:** Moulded composition. **Sights:** Adjustable post front, notch rear. **Features:** Aluminum alloy frame; compensator; pistol grip compartment; ambidextrous safety. Uses same helical-feed magazine as M-100 Carbine. Introduced 1986. Made in U.S.A. From Calico.

Price: **$570.00**

CARBON-15 (Type 97) PISTOL

Caliber: 223, 10-shot magazine. **Barrel:** 7.25". **Weight:** 46 oz. **Length:** 20" overall. **Stock:** Checkered composite. **Sights:** Ghost ring. **Features:** Semi-automatic, gas-operated, rotating bolt action. Carbon fiber upper and lower receiver; chromemoly bolt carrier; fluted stainless match barrel; mil. spec. optics mounting base; uses AR-15-type magazines. Introduced 1992. From Professional Ordnance, Inc.

Price: **$1,600.00**
Price: Type 20 pistol (light-profile barrel, no compensator, weighs 40 oz.). **$1,500.00**

Charles Daly M-1911-A1P

Colt XSE Model O Commander

Colt 1991 Model O Compact

Colt XSE Lightweight Commander

Colt Lightweight Commander

CHARLES DALY M-1911-A1P AUTOLOADING PISTOL

Caliber: 45 ACP, 7- or 10-shot magazine. **Barrel:** 5". **Weight:** 38 oz. **Length:** 8-3/4" overall. **Grips:** Checkered. **Sights:** Blade front, rear drift adjustable for windage; three-dot system. **Features:** Skeletonized combat hammer and trigger; beavertail grip safety; extended slide release; over-size thumb safety; Parkerized finish. Introduced 1996. Imported from the Philippines by K.B.I., Inc.
Price: **$469.95**

COLT MODEL 1991 MODEL O AUTO PISTOL

Caliber: 45 ACP, 7-shot magazine. **Barrel:** 5". **Weight:** 38 oz. **Length:** 8.5" overall. **Grips:** Checkered black composition. **Sights:** Ramped blade front, fixed square notch rear, high profile. **Features:** Matte finish. Continuation of serial number range used on original G.I. 1911 A1 guns. Comes with one magazine and moulded carrying case. Introduced 1991.
Price: **$645.00**
Price: Stainless. **$800.00**

Colt Model 1991 Model O Commander Auto Pistol

Similar to the Model 1991 A1 except has 4-1/4" barrel. Overall length is 7-3/4". Comes with one 7-shot magazine, molded case.
Price: Blue **$645.00**
Price: Stainless steel **$800.00**

COLT XSE SERIES MODEL O AUTO PISTOLS

Caliber: 45 ACP, 8-shot magazine. **Barrel:** 4.25", 5". **Grips:** Checkered, double diamond rosewood. **Sights:** Drift-adjustable three-dot combat. **Features:** Brushed stainless finish; adjustable, two-cut aluminum trigger; extended ambidextrous thumb safety; upswept beavertail with palm swell; elongated slot hammer; beveled magazine well. Introduced 1999. From Colt's Manufacturing Co., Inc.
Price: XSE Government (5" barrel) **$950.00**
Price: XSE Commander (4.25" barrel) **$950.00**

COLT XSE LIGHTWEIGHT COMMANDER AUTO PISTOL

Caliber: 45 ACP, 8-shot. **Barrel:** 4-1/4". **Weight:** 26 oz. **Length:** 7-3/4" overall. **Grips:** Double diamond checkered rosewood. **Sights:** Fixed, glare-proofed blade front, square notch rear; three-dot system. **Features:** Brushed stainless slide, nickeled aluminum frame; McCormick elongated-slot enhanced hammer, McCormick two-cut adjustable aluminum hammer. Made in U.S.A. by Colt's Mfg. Co., Inc.
Price: 45, stainless **$950.00**

COLT DEFENDER

Caliber: 40 S&W, 45 ACP, 7-shot magazine. **Barrel:** 3". **Weight:** 22-1/2 oz. **Length:** 6-3/4" overall. **Grips:** Pebble-finish rubber wraparound with finger grooves. **Sights:** White dot front, snag-free Colt competition rear. **Features:** Stainless finish; aluminum frame; combat-style hammer; Hi Ride grip safety, extended manual safety, disconnect safety. Introduced 1998. Made in U.S.A. by Colt's Mfg. Co.
Price: **$773.00**

Colt Defender

Coonan 357 Magnum

CZ 75B 9mm

CZ 75B Decocker

CZ 75D Compact

COONAN 357 MAGNUM, 41 MAGNUM PISTOLS

Caliber: 357 Mag., 41 Magnum, 7-shot magazine. **Barrel:** 5". **Weight:** 42 oz. **Length:** 8.3" overall. **Grips:** Smooth walnut. **Sights:** Interchangeable ramp front, rear adjustable for windage. **Features:** Stainless steel construction. Unique barrel hood improves accuracy and reliability. Link-less barrel. Many parts interchange with Colt autos. Has grip, hammer, half-cock safeties, extended slide latch. Made in U.S.A. by Coonan Arms, Inc.

Price: 5" barrel, from **$735.00**
Price: 6" barrel, from **$768.00**
Price: With 6" compensated barrel **$1,014.00**
Price: Classic model (Teflon black two-tone finish, 8-shot magazine, fully adjustable rear sight, integral compensated barrel) **$1,400.00**
Price: 41 Magnum Model, from **$825.00**

Coonan Compact Cadet 357 Magnum Pistol

Similar to the 357 Magnum full-size gun except has 3.9" barrel, shorter frame, 6-shot magazine. Weight is 39 oz., overall length 7.8". Linkless bull barrel, full-length recoil spring guide rod, extended slide latch. Introduced 1993. Made in U.S.A. by Coonan Arms, Inc.

Price: **$855.00**

CZ 75B AUTO PISTOL

Caliber: 9mm Para., 40 S&W, 10-shot magazine. **Barrel:** 4.7". **Weight:** 34.3 oz. **Length:** 8.1" overall. **Grips:** High impact checkered plastic. **Sights:** Square post front, rear adjustable for windage; three-dot system. **Features:** Single action/double action design; firing pin block safety; choice of black polymer, matte or high-polish blue finishes. All-steel frame. Imported from the Czech Republic by CZ-USA.

Price: Black polymer **$472.00**
Price: Glossy blue **$486.00**
Price: Dual tone or satin nickel **$486.00**
Price: 22 LR conversion unit **$279.00**

CZ 75B Decocker

Similar to the CZ 75B except has a decocking lever in place of the safety lever. All other specifications are the same. Introduced 1999. Imported from the Czech Republic by CZ-USA.

Price: 9mm, black polymer **$467.00**
New! **Price:** 40 S&W **$481.00**

CZ 75B Compact Auto Pistol

Similar to the CZ 75 except has 10-shot magazine, 3.9" barrel and weighs 32 oz. Has removable front sight, non-glare ribbed slide top. Trigger guard is squared and serrated; combat hammer. Introduced 1993. Imported from the Czech Republic by CZ-USA.

Price: 9mm, black polymer **$499.00**
Price: Dual tone or satin nickel **$513.00**
Price: D Compact, black polymer **$526.00**

HANDGUNS

CZ 85

CZ 97B

CZ 83B

CZ 75/85 Kadet

CZ 75M IPSC Auto Pistol

Similar to the CZ 75B except has a longer frame and slide, slightly larger grip to accommodate new heavy-duty magazine. Ambidextrous thumb safety, safety notch on hammer; two-port in-frame compensator; slide racker; frame-mounted Firepoint red dot sight. Introduced 2001. Imported from the Czech Republic by CZ USA.

Price: 40 S&W, 10-shot mag. **$1,498.00**
Price: CZ 75 Standard IPSC (40 S&W, adj. sights) **$1,038.00**

CZ 85B Auto Pistol

Same gun as the CZ 75 except has ambidextrous slide release and safety-levers; non-glare, ribbed slide top; squared, serrated trigger guard; trigger stop to prevent overtravel. Introduced 1986. Imported from the Czech Republic by CZ-USA.

Price: Black polymer. **$483.00**
Price: Combat, black polymer. **$540.00**
Price: Combat, dual tone **$487.00**
Price: Combat, glossy blue. **$499.00**

CZ 85 Combat

Similar to the CZ 85B (9mm only) except has an adjustable rear sight, adjustable trigger for overtravel, free-fall magazine, extended magazine catch. Does not have the firing pin block safety. Introduced 1999. Imported from the Czech Republic by CZ-USA.

Price: 9mm, black polymer **$540.00**
Price: 9mm, glossy blue **$561.00**
Price: 9mm, dual tone or satin nickel **$561.00**

CZ 83B DOUBLE-ACTION PISTOL

Caliber: 9mm Makarov, 32 ACP, 380 ACP, 10-shot magazine. **Barrel:** 3.8". **Weight:** 26.2 oz. **Length:** 6.8" overall. **Grips:** High impact checkered plastic. **Sights:** Removable square post front, rear adjustable for windage;

three-dot system. **Features:** Single action/double action; ambidextrous magazine release and safety. Blue finish; non-glare ribbed slide top. Imported from the Czech Republic by CZ-USA.

Price: Blue **$378.00**
Price: Nickel **$378.00**

CZ 97B AUTO PISTOL

Caliber: 45 ACP, 10-shot magazine. **Barrel:** 4.85". **Weight:** 40 oz. **Length:** 8.34" overall. **Grips:** Checkered walnut. **Sights:** Fixed. **Features:** Single action/double action; full-length slide rails; screw-in barrel bushing; linkless barrel; all-steel construction; chamber loaded indicator; dual transfer bars. Introduced 1999. Imported from the Czech Republic by CZ-USA.

Price: Black polymer. **$607.00**
Price: Glossy blue **$621.00**

CZ 75/85 KADET AUTO PISTOL

Caliber: 22 LR, 10-shot magazine. **Barrel:** 4.88". **Weight:** 36 oz. **Grips:** High impact checkered plastic. **Sights:** Blade front, fully adjustable rear. **Features:** Single action/double action mechanism; all-steel construction. Duplicates weight, balance and function of the CZ 75 pistol. Introduced 1999. Imported from the Czech Republic by CZ-USA.

Price: Black polymer. **$486.00**

CZ 100 AUTO PISTOL

Caliber: 9mm Para., 40 S&W, 10-shot magazine. **Barrel:** 3.7". **Weight:** 24 oz. **Length:** 6.9" overall. **Grips:** Grooved polymer. **Sights:** Blade front with dot, white outline rear drift adjustable for windage. **Features:** Double action only with firing pin block; polymer frame, steel slide; has laser sight mount. Introduced 1996. Imported from the Czech Republic by CZ-USA.

Price: 9mm Para. **$405.00**
Price: 40 S&W **$405.00**

CZ 100

Davis P-380

Davis P-32

Desert Eagle Mark XIX

Desert Eagle Baby Eagle

DAVIS P-380 AUTO PISTOL

Caliber: 380 ACP, 5-shot magazine. **Barrel:** 2.8". **Weight:** 22 oz. **Length:** 5.4" overall. **Grips:** Black composition. **Sights:** Fixed. **Features:** Choice of chrome or black Teflon finish. Introduced 1991. Made in U.S.A. by Davis Industries.
Price: **$98.00**

DAVIS P-32 AUTO PISTOL

Caliber: 32 ACP, 6-shot magazine. **Barrel:** 2.8". **Weight:** 22 oz. **Length:** 5.4" overall. **Grips:** Laminated wood. **Sights:** Fixed. **Features:** Choice of black Teflon or chrome finish. Announced 1986. Made in U.S.A. by Davis Industries.
Price: **$107.00**

DESERT EAGLE MARK XIX PISTOL

Caliber: 357 Mag., 9-shot; 44 Mag., 8-shot; 50 Magnum, 7-shot. **Barrel:** 6", 10", interchangeable. **Weight:** 357 Mag.—62 oz.; 44 Mag.—69 oz.; 50 Mag.— 72 oz. **Length:** 10-1/4" overall (6" bbl.). **Grips:** Rubber. **Sights:** Blade on ramp front, combat-style rear. Adjustable available. **Features:** Interchangeable barrels; rotating three-lug bolt; ambidextrous safety; adjustable trigger. Military epoxy finish. Satin, bright nickel, hard chrome, polished and blued finishes available. 10" barrel extra. Imported from Israel by Magnum Research, Inc.
Price: 357, 6" bbl., standard pistol **$1,199.00**
Price: 44 Mag., 6", standard pistol **$1,199.00**
Price: 50 Magnum, 6" bbl., standard pistol. **$1,199.00**

DESERT EAGLE BABY EAGLE PISTOLS

Caliber: 9mm Para., 40 S&W, 45 ACP, 10-round magazine. **Barrel:** 3.5", 3.7", 4.72". **Weight:** NA. **Length:** 7.25" to 8.25" overall. **Grips:** Polymer. **Sights:** Drift-adjustable rear, blade front. **Features:** Steel frame and slide; polygonal rifling to reduce barrel wear; slide safety; decocker. Reintroduced in 1999. Imported from Israel by Magnum Research Inc.
Price: Standard (9mm or 40 cal.; 4.72" barrel, 8.25" overall) . . . **$499.00**
Price: Semi-Compact (9mm, 40 or 45 cal.; 3.7" barrel,
7.75" overall) **$499.00**
Price: Compact (9mm or 40 cal.; 3.5" barrel, 7.25" overall) **$499.00**
Price: Polymer (9mm or 40 cal; polymer frame; 3.25" barrel,
7.25" overall) **$499.00**

EAA WITNESS DA AUTO PISTOL

Caliber: 9mm Para., 10-shot magazine; 38 Super, 40 S&W, 10-shot magazine; 45 ACP, 10-shot magazine. **Barrel:** 4.50". **Weight:** 35.33 oz. **Length:** 8.10" overall. **Grips:** Checkered rubber. **Sights:** Undercut blade front, open rear adjustable for windage. **Features:** Double-action trigger system; round trigger guard; frame-mounted safety. Introduced 1991. Imported from Italy by European American Armory.

HANDGUNS

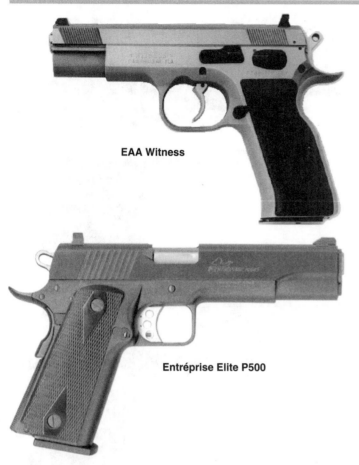

EAA Witness

Entréprise Boxer P500

Entréprise Elite P500

Entréprise Tactical 500

Price: 9mm, blue. $449.00
Price: 9mm, Wonder finish $459.00
Price: 9mm Compact, blue, 10-shot. $449.00
Price: As above, Wonder finish $459.60
Price: 40 S&W, blue $449.60
Price: As above, Wonder finish $459.60
Price: 40 S&W Compact, 9-shot, blue $449.60
Price: As above, Wonder finish $459.60
Price: 45 ACP, blue. $449.00
Price: As above, Wonder finish $459.60
Price: 45 ACP Compact, 8-shot, blue. $449.00
Price: As above, Wonder finish $459.60

EAA EUROPEAN MODEL AUTO PISTOLS
Caliber: 32 ACP or 380 ACP, 7-shot magazine. **Barrel:** 3.88". **Weight:** 26 oz. **Length:** 7-3/8" overall. **Grips:** European hardwood. **Sights:** Fixed blade front, rear drift-adjustable for windage. **Features:** Chrome or blue finish; magazine, thumb and firing pin safeties; external hammer; safety-lever takedown. Imported from Italy by European American Armory.
Price: Blue $132.60
Price: Wonder finish $163.80

EAA/BUL 1911 AUTO PISTOL
Caliber: 45 ACP. **Barrel:** 3", 4", 5". **Weight:** 24-30 oz. **Length:** 7-10". **Grips:** Full checkered. **Sights:** Tactical rear, dove tail front. **Features:** Lightweight polymer frame, extended beavertail, skeletonized trigger and hammer, beveled mag well.
Price: Blue $559.00
Price: Chrome. $599.00

ENTRÉPRISE ELITE P500 AUTO PISTOL
Caliber: 45 ACP, 10-shot magazine. **Barrel:** 5". **Weight:** 40 oz. **Length:** 8.5" overall. **Grips:** Black ultra-slim, double diamond, checkered synthetic. **Sights:** Dovetailed blade front, rear adjustable for windage;

three-dot system. **Features:** Reinforced dust cover; lowered and flared ejection port; squared trigger guard; adjustable match trigger; bolstered front strap; high grip cut; high ride beavertail grip safety; steel flat mainspring housing; extended thumb lock; skeletonized hammer, match grade sear, disconnector; Wolff springs. Introduced 1998. Made in U.S.A. by Entréprise Arms.
Price: $739.90

Entréprise Boxer P500 Auto Pistol
Similar to the Medalist model except has adjustable Competizione "melded" rear sight with dovetailed Patridge front; high mass chiseled slide with sweep cut; machined slide parallel rails; polished breech face and barrel channel. Introduced 1998. Made in U.S.A. by Entréprise Arms.
Price: $1,399.00

Entréprise Medalist P500 Auto Pistol
Similar to the Elite model except has adjustable Competizione "melded" rear sight with dovetailed Patridge front; machined slide parallel rails with polished breech face and barrel channel; front and rear slide serrations; lowered and flared ejection port; full-length one-piece guide rod with plug; National Match barrel and bushing; stainless firing pin; tuned match extractor; oversize firing pin stop; throated barrel and polished ramp; slide lapped to frame. Introduced 1998. Made in U.S.A. by Entréprise Arms.
Price: 45 ACP. $979.00
Price: 40 S&W $1,099.00

Entréprise Tactical P500 Auto Pistol
Similar to the Elite model except has Tactical2 Ghost Ring sight or Novak lo-mount sight; ambidextrous thumb safety; front and rear slide serrations; full-length guide rod; throated barrel, polished ramp; tuned match extractor; fitted barrel and bushing; stainless firing pin; slide lapped to frame; dehorned. Introduced 1998. Made in U.S.A. by Entréprise Arms.
Price: $979.90
Price: Tactical Plus (full-size frame, Officer's slide) $1,049.00

FEG PJK-9HP

Firestorm Mini

Felk MTF 450

Firestorm Compact

Firestorm 45 Gov't

ERMA KGP68 AUTO PISTOL
Caliber: 32 ACP, 6-shot, 380 ACP, 5-shot. **Barrel:** 4". **Weight:** 22-1/2 oz. **Length:** 7-3/8" overall. **Grips:** Checkered plastic. **Sights:** Fixed. **Features:** Toggle action similar to original "Luger" pistol. Action stays open after last shot. Has magazine and sear disconnect safety systems.
Price: **$499.95**

FEG PJK-9HP AUTO PISTOL
Caliber: 9mm Para., 10-shot magazine. **Barrel:** 4.75". **Weight:** 32 oz. **Length:** 8" overall. **Grips:** Hand-checkered walnut. **Sights:** Blade front, rear adjustable for windage; three dot system. **Features:** Single action; polished blue or hard chrome finish; rounded combat-style serrated hammer. Comes with two magazines and cleaning rod. Imported from Hungary by K.B.I., Inc.
Price: Blue **$259.95**
Price: Hard chrome. **$259.95**

FEG SMC-380 AUTO PISTOL
Caliber: 380 ACP, 6-shot magazine. **Barrel:** 3.5". **Weight:** 18.5 oz. **Length:** 6.1" overall. **Grips:** Checkered composition with thumbrest. **Sights:** Blade front, rear adjustable for windage. **Features:** Patterned after the PPK pistol. Alloy frame, steel slide; double action. Blue finish. Comes with two magazines, cleaning rod. Imported from Hungary by K.B.I., Inc.
Price: **$224.95**

FELK MTF 450 AUTO PISTOL
Caliber: 9mm Para. (10-shot); 40 S&W (8-shot); 45 ACP (9-shot magazine). **Barrel:** 3.5". **Weight:** 19.9 oz. **Length:** 6.4" overall. **Grips:** Checkered. **Sights:** Blade front; adjustable rear. **Features:** Double-action-only trigger, striker fired; polymer frame; trigger safety, firing pin safety, trigger bar safety; adjustable trigger weight; fully interchangeable slide/barrel to change calibers. Introduced 1998. Imported by Felk Inc.
Price: **$395.00**
Price: 45 ACP pistol with 9mm and 40 S&W slide/barrel
assemblies **$999.00**

FIRESTORM AUTO PISTOL
Features: 7 or 10 rd. double action pistols with matte, duotone or nickel finish. Distributed by SGS Importers International.
Price: 22 LR 10 rd, 380 7 rd. matte **$248.95**
Price: Duotone **$273.95**
Price: Mini 9mm, 40 S&W, 10 rd. matte **$366.95**
Price: Duotone **$374.95**
Price: Nickel **$391.95**
Price: Mini 9mm, 7 rd. matte **$374.95**
Price: Duotone **$387.95**
Price: Nickel **$399.95**
Price: 45 Government, Compact, 7 rd. matte. **$314.95**
Price: Duotone **$324.95**
Price: Extra magazines **$29.95-49.95**

HANDGUNS

Glock 17C

Glock 22

Glock 26

Glock 30

GLOCK 17 AUTO PISTOL

Caliber: 9mm Para., 10-shot magazine.
Barrel: 4.49". **Weight:** 22.04 oz. (without magazine). **Length:** 7.32" overall. **Grips:** Black polymer. **Sights:** Dot on front blade, white outline rear adjustable for windage. **Features:** Polymer frame, steel slide; double-action trigger with "Safe Action" system; mechanical firing pin safety, drop safety; simple takedown without tools; locked breech, recoil operated action. Adopted by Austrian armed forces 1983. NATO approved 1984. Imported from Austria by Glock, Inc.
Price: Fixed sight, with extra magazine, magazine loader, cleaning kit

.... **$641.00**
Price: Adjustable sight **$671.00**
Price: Model 17L (6" barrel) **$800.00**
Price: Model 17C, ported barrel (compensated) **$646.00**

Glock 19 Auto Pistol

Similar to the Glock 17 except has a 4" barrel, giving an overall length of 6.85" and weight of 20.99 oz. Magazine capacity is 10 rounds. Fixed or adjustable rear sight. Introduced 1988.
Price: Fixed sight **$641.00**
Price: Adjustable sight **$671.00**
Price: Model 19C, ported barrel **$646.00**

Glock 20 10mm Auto Pistol

Similar to the Glock Model 17 except chambered for 10mm Automatic cartridge. Barrel length is 4.60", overall length is 7.59", and weight is 26.3 oz. (without magazine). Magazine capacity is 10 rounds. Fixed or adjustable rear sight. Comes with an extra magazine, magazine loader, cleaning rod and brush. Introduced 1990. Imported from Austria by Glock, Inc.
Price: Fixed sight **$700.00**
Price: Adjustable sight **$730.00**

Glock 21 Auto Pistol

Similar to the Glock 17 except chambered for 45 ACP, 10-shot magazine. Overall length is 7.59", weight is 25.2 oz. (without magazine). Fixed or adjustable rear sight. Introduced 1991.
Price: Fixed sight **$700.00**
Price: Adjustable sight **$730.00**

Glock 22 Auto Pistol

Similar to the Glock 17 except chambered for 40 S&W, 10-shot magazine. Overall length is 7.28", weight is 22.3 oz. (without magazine). Fixed or adjustable rear sight. Introduced 1990.
Price: Fixed sight **$641.00**
Price: Adjustable sight **$671.00**
Price: Model 22C, ported barrel **$646.00**

Glock 23 Auto Pistol

Similar to the Glock 19 except chambered for 40 S&W, 10-shot magazine. Overall length is 6.85", weight is 20.6 oz. (without magazine). Fixed or adjustable rear sight. Introduced 1990.
Price: Fixed sight **$641.00**
Price: Model 23C, ported barrel **$646.00**
Price: Adjustable sight **$671.00**

GLOCK 26, 27 AUTO PISTOLS

Caliber: 9mm Para. (M26), 10-shot magazine; 40 S&W (M27), 9-shot magazine. **Barrel:** 3.46". **Weight:** 21.75 oz. **Length:** 6.29" overall. **Grips:** Integral. Stippled polymer. **Sights:** Dot on front blade, fixed or fully adjustable white outline rear. **Features:** Subcompact size. Polymer frame, steel slide; double-action trigger with "Safe Action" system, three safeties. Matte black Tenifer finish. Hammer-forged barrel. Imported from Austria by Glock, Inc. Introduced 1996.
Price: Fixed sight **$641.00**
Price: Adjustable sight **$671.00**

GLOCK 29, 30 AUTO PISTOLS

Caliber: 10mm (M29), 45 ACP (M30), 10-shot magazine. **Barrel:** 3.78". **Weight:** 24 oz. **Length:** 6.7" overall. **Grips:** Integral. Stippled polymer. **Sights:** Dot on front, fixed or fully adjustable white outline rear. **Features:** Compact size. Polymer frame steel slide; double-recoil spring reduces recoil; Safe Action system with three safeties; Tenifer finish. Two magazines supplied. Introduced 1997. Imported from Austria by Glock, Inc.
Price: Fixed sight **$700.00**
Price: Adjustable sight **$730.00**

HANDGUNS

Glock 31

Hammerli Trailside PL 22

Glock 35

Heckler & Koch USP Compact

GLOCK 36 AUTO PISTOL

Caliber: 45 ACP, 6-shot magazine. **Barrel:** 3.78". **Weight:** 20.11 oz. **Length:** 6.77" overall. **Grips:** Integral. Stippled polymer. **Sights:** Dot on front, fully adjustable white outline rear. **Features:** Polymer frame, steel slide; double-action trigger with "Safe Action" system; three safeties; Tenifer finish. Imported from Austria by Glock, Inc.

Price: Fixed sight	**$700.00**
Price: Adj. sight	**$730.00**

HAMMERLI "TRAILSIDE" TARGET PISTOL

Caliber: 22 LR. **Barrel:** 4.5", 6". **Weight:** 28 oz. **Grips:** Synthetic. **Sights:** Fixed. **Features:** 10-shot magazine. Imported from Switzerland by Sigarms. Distributed by Hammerli U.S.A.

Price:	**$549.00**

HECKLER & KOCH USP AUTO PISTOL

Caliber: 9mm Para., 10-shot magazine, 40 S&W, 10-shot magazine. **Barrel:** 4.25". **Weight:** 28 oz. (USP40). **Length:** 6.9" overall. **Grips:** Non-slip stippled black polymer. **Sights:** Blade front, rear adjustable for windage. **Features:** New HK design with polymer frame, modified Browning action with recoil reduction system, single control lever. Special "hostile environment" finish on all metal parts. Available in SA/DA, DAO, left- and right-hand versions. Introduced 1993. Imported from Germany by Heckler & Koch, Inc.

Price: Right-hand	**$699.00**
Price: Left-hand	**$714.00**
Price: Stainless steel, right-hand	**$749.00**
Price: Stainless steel, left-hand	**$799.00**

Heckler & Koch USP Compact Auto Pistol

Similar to the USP except has 3.58" barrel, measures 6.81" overall, and weighs 1.60 lbs. (9mm). Available in 9mm Para. 357 SIG or 40 S&W with 10-shot magazine. Introduced 1996. Imported from Germany by Heckler & Koch, Inc.

Price: Blue	**$786.00**
Price: Blue with control lever on right	**$821.00**
Price: Stainless steel	**$849.00**
Price: Stainless steel with control lever on right	**$874.00**
New! Price: Same as USP Compact DAO, enhanced trigger performance	**$821.00**

Glock 31/31C Auto Pistols

Similar to the Glock 17 except chambered for 357 Auto cartridge; 10-shot magazine. Overall length is 7.32", weight is 23.28 oz. (without magazine). Fixed or adjustable sight. Imported from Austria by Glock, Inc.

Price: Fixed sight	**$641.00**
Price: Adjustable sight	**$671.00**
Price: Model 31C, ported barrel	**$646.00**

Glock 32/32C Auto Pistols

Similar to the Glock 19 except chambered for the 357 Auto cartridge; 10-shot magazine. Overall length is 6.85", weight is 21.52 oz. (without magazine). Fixed or adjustable sight. Imported from Austria by Glock, Inc.

Price: Fixed sight	**$616.00**
Price: Adjustable sight	**$644.00**
Price: Model 32C, ported barrel	**$646.00**

Glock 33 Auto Pistol

Similar to the Glock 26 except chambered for the 357 Auto cartridge; 9-shot magazine. Overall length is 6.29", weight is 19.75 oz. (without magazine). Fixed or adjustable sight. Imported from Austria by Glock, Inc.

Price: Fixed sight	**$641.00**
Price: Adjustable sight	**$671.00**

GLOCK 34, 35 AUTO PISTOLS

Caliber: 9mm Para. (M34), 40 S&W (M35), 10-shot magazine. **Barrel:** 5.32". **Weight:** 22.9 oz. **Length:** 8.15" overall. **Grips:** Integral. Stippled polymer. **Sights:** Dot on front, fully adjustable white outline rear. **Features:** Polymer frame, steel slide; double-action trigger with "Safe Action" system; three safeties; Tenifer finish. Imported from Austria by Glock, Inc.

Price: Model 34, 9mm.	**$770.00**
Price: Model 35, 40 S&W	**$770.00**

HANDGUNS

Heckler & Koch USP45

Heckler & Koch USP Expert

Heckler & Koch USP45 Tactical

Heckler & Koch P7M8

Heckler & Koch USP45 Auto Pistol

Similar to the 9mm and 40 S&W USP except chambered for 45 ACP, 10-shot magazine. Has 4.13" barrel, overall length of 7.87" and weighs 30.4 oz. Has adjustable three-dot sight system. Available in SA/DA, DAO, left- and right-hand versions. Introduced 1995. Imported from Germany by Heckler & Koch, Inc.

Price: Right-hand **$827.00**
Price: Left-hand **$862.00**
Price: Stainless steel right-hand **$888.00**
Price: Stainless steel left-hand **$923.00**

Heckler & Koch USP45 Compact

Similar to the USP45 except has stainless slide; 8-shot magazine; modified and contoured slide and frame; extended slide release; 3.80" barrel, 7.09" overall length, weighs 1.75 lbs.; adjustable three-dot sights. Introduced 1998. Imported from Germany by Heckler & Koch, Inc.

Price: With control lever on left, stainless. **$909.00**
Price: As above, blue **$857.00**
Price: With control lever on right, stainless. **$944.00**
Price: As above, blue **$892.00**

HECKLER & KOCH USP45 TACTICAL PISTOL

Caliber: 45 ACP, 10-shot magazine. **Barrel:** 4.92". **Weight:** 2.24 lbs. **Length:** 8.64" overall. **Grips:** Non-slip stippled polymer. **Sights:** Blade front, fully adjustable target rear. **Features:** Has extended threaded barrel with rubber O-ring; adjustable trigger; extended magazine floorplate; adjustable trigger stop; polymer frame. Introduced 1998. Imported from Germany by Heckler & Koch, Inc.

Price: **$1,124.00**

HECKLER & KOCH MARK 23 SPECIAL OPERATIONS PISTOL

Caliber: 45 ACP, 10-shot magazine. **Barrel:** 5.87". **Weight:** 43 oz. **Length:** 9.65" overall. **Grips:** Integral with frame; black polymer. **Sights:** Blade front, rear drift adjustable for windage; three-dot. **Features:** Polymer frame; double action; exposed hammer; short recoil, modified Browning action. Civilian version of the SOCOM pistol. Introduced 1996. Imported from Germany by Heckler & Koch, Inc.

Price: **$2,444.00**

Heckler & Koch USP Expert Pistol

Combines features of the USP Tactical and HK Mark 23 pistols with a new slide design. Chambered for 45 ACP; 10-shot magazine. Has adjustable target sights, 5.20" barrel, 8.74" overall length, weighs 1.87 lbs. Match-grade single- and double-action trigger pull with adjustable stop; ambidextrous control levers; elongated target slide; barrel O-ring that seals and centers barrel. Suited to IPSC competition. Introduced 1999. Imported from Germany by Heckler & Koch, Inc.

Price: **$1,533.00**

HECKLER & KOCH P7M8 AUTO PISTOL

Caliber: 9mm Para., 8-shot magazine. **Barrel:** 4.13". **Weight:** 29 oz. **Length:** 6.73" overall. **Grips:** Stippled black plastic. **Sights:** Blade front, adjustable rear; three dot system. **Features:** Unique "squeeze cocker" in frontstrap cocks the action. Gas-retarded action. Squared combat-type trigger guard. Blue finish. Compact size. Imported from Germany by Heckler & Koch, Inc.

Price: P7M8, blued. **$1,472.00**

Hi-Point 45 ACP

Hi-Point 9MM Comp

Kahr K9

HI-POINT FIREARMS 40 S&W AUTO
Caliber: 40 S&W, 8-shot magazine. **Barrel:** 4.5".
Weight: 39 oz. **Length:** 7.72" overall. **Grips:**
Checkered acetal resin. **Sights:** Adjustable; low
profile. **Features:** Internal drop-safe mechanism; al-
loy frame. Introduced 1991. From MKS Supply, Inc.
Price: Matte black. $159.00

HI-POINT FIREARMS 45 CALIBER PISTOL
Caliber: 45 ACP, 7-shot magazine. **Barrel:** 4.5". **Weight:** 39 oz. **Length:**
7.95" overall. **Grips:** Checkered acetal resin. **Sights:** Adjustable; low profile. **Features:** Internal drop-safe mechanism; alloy frame. Introduced
1991. From MKS Supply, Inc.
Price: Matte black. $159.00
Price: Chrome slide, black frame $169.00

HI-POINT FIREARMS 9MM COMP PISTOL
Caliber: 9mm, Para., 10-shot magazine. **Barrel:** 4". **Weight:** 39 oz.
Length: 7.72" overall. **Grips:** Textured acetal plastic. **Sights:** Adjustable;
low profile. **Features:** Single-action design. Scratch-resistant, non-glare
blue finish, alloy frame. Muzzle brake/compensator. Compensator is slot-
ted for laser or flashlight mounting. Introduced 1998. From MKS Supply,
Inc.
Price: Matte black. $159.00

HI-POINT FIREARMS MODEL 9MM COMPACT PISTOL
Caliber: 9mm Para., 8-shot magazine. **Barrel:** 3.5". **Weight:** 29 oz.
Length: 6.7" overall. **Grips:** Textured acetal plastic. **Sights:** Combat-
style adjustable three-dot system; low profile. **Features:** Single-action de-
sign; frame-mounted magazine release; polymer or alloy frame. Scratch-
resistant matte finish. Introduced 1993. Made in U.S.A. by MKS Supply,
Inc.
Price: Black, alloy frame $137.00
Price: With polymer frame (29 oz.), non-slip grips $137.00
Price: Aluminum with polymer frame $137.00

Hi-Point Firearms Model 380 Polymer Pistol
Similar to the 9mm Compact model except chambered for 380 ACP, 8-
shot magazine, adjustable three-dot sights. Weighs 29 oz. Polymer
frame. Introduced 1998. Made in U.S.A. by MKS Supply.
Price: $99.95

Hi-Point Firearms 380 Comp Pistol
Similar to the 380 Polymer Pistol except has a 4"
barrel with muzzle compensator; action locks open after last shot. In-
cludes a 10-shot and an 8-shot magazine; trigger lock. Introduced 2001.
Made in U.S.A. by MKS Supply Inc.
Price: $125.00
Price: With laser sight. $190.00

HS AMERICA HS 2000 PISTOL
Caliber: 9mm Para., 357 SIG, 40 S&W, 10-shot magazine. **Barrel:** 4.08".
Weight: 22.88 oz. **Length:** 7.2" overall. **Grips:** Integral black polymer.
Sights: Drift-adjustable white dot rear, white dot blade front. **Features:** Incorporates trigger, firing pin, grip and out-of-battery safeties; firing-pin status and loaded chamber indicators; ambidextrous magazine release; dual-
tension recoil spring with stand-off device; polymer frame; black finish with
chrome-plated magazine. Imported from Croatia by HS America.
Price: $419.00

IAI M-2000 PISTOL
Caliber: 45 ACP, 8-shot. **Barrel:** 5", (Compact 4.25"). **Weight:** 36 oz.
Length: 8.5", (6" Compact). **Grips:** Plastic or wood. **Sights:** Fixed. **Fea-
tures:** 1911 Government U.S. Army-style. Steel frame and slide parker-
ized. GI grip safety. Beveled feed ramp barrel. By IAI, Inc.
Price: $465.00

KAHR K9, K40 DA AUTO PISTOLS
Caliber: 9mm Para., 7-shot, 40 S&W, 6-shot magazine. **Barrel:** 3.5".
Weight: 25 oz. **Length:** 6" overall. **Grips:** Wrap-around textured soft poly-
mer. **Sights:** Blade front, rear drift adjustable for windage; bar-dot combat
style. **Features:** Trigger-cocking double-action mechanism with passive
firing pin block. Made of 4140 ordnance steel with matte black finish. Con-
tact maker for complete price list. Introduced 1994. Made in U.S.A. by
Kahr Arms.
Price: E9, black matte finish. $425.00
Price: Matte black, night sights 9mm $668.00
Price: Matte stainless steel, 9mm. $638.00
Price: 40 S&W, matte black $580.00
Price: 40 S&W, matte black, night sights $668.00
Price: 40 S&W, matte stainless $638.00
Price: K9 Elite 98 (high-polish stainless slide flats, Kahr combat
trigger), from $694.00
Price: As above, MK9 Elite 98, from. $694.00
Price: As above, K40 Elite 98, from $694.00
Price: Covert, black, stainless slide, short grip. $599.00
Price: Covert, black, tritium nite sights $689.00

Kahr K9 9mm Compact Polymer Pistol
Similar to K9 steel frame pistol except has polymer frame, matte stainless
steel slide. Barrel length 3.5"; overall length 6"; weighs 17.9 oz. Includes
two 7-shot magazines, hard polymer case, trigger lock. Introduced 2000.
Made in U.S.A. by Kahr Arms.
Price: $599.00

Kahr MK40

Kel-Tec P-32

Kel-Tec P-11

Kimber Custom II

Kahr MK9/MK40 Micro Pistol

Similar to the K9/K40 except is 5.5" overall, 4" high, has a 3" barrel. Weighs 22 oz. Has snag-free bar-dot sights, polished feed ramp, dual recoil spring system, DA-only trigger. Comes with 6- and 7-shot magazines. Introduced 1998. Made in U.S.A. by Kahr Arms.

Price: Matte stainless **$638.00**
Price: Elite 98, polished stainless, tritium night sights **$791.00**

KAHR PM9 PISTOL

Caliber: 9x19. **Barrel:** 3", 1:10 twist. **Weight:** 15.9 oz. **Length:** 5.3" overall. **Features:** Lightweight black polymer frame, polygonal rifling, stainless steel slide, DAO with passive striker block, trigger lock, hard case, 6 and 7 rd. mags.

Price: Matte stainless slide **$622.00**
Price: Tritium night sights **$719.00**

KEL-TEC P-11 AUTO PISTOL

Caliber: 9mm Para., 10-shot magazine. **Barrel:** 3.1". **Weight:** 14 oz. **Length:** 5.6" overall. **Grips:** Checkered black polymer. **Sights:** Blade front, rear adjustable for windage. **Features:** Ordnance steel slide, aluminum frame. Double-action-only trigger mechanism. Introduced 1995. Made in U.S.A. by Kel-Tec CNC Industries, Inc.

Price: Blue **$314.00**
Price: Hard chrome. **$368.00**
Price: Parkerized **$355.00**

KEL-TEC P-32 AUTO PISTOL

Caliber: 32 ACP, 7-shot magazine. **Barrel:** 2.68". **Weight:** 6.6 oz. **Length:** 5.07" overall. **Grips:** Checkered composite. **Sights:** Fixed. **Features:** Double-action-only mechanism with 6-lb. pull; internal slide stop. Textured composite grip/frame. Made in U.S.A. by Kel-Tec CNC Industries, Inc.

Price: Blue **$300.00**
Price: Hard chrome **$340.00**
Price: Parkerized **$355.00**

KIMBER CUSTOM II AUTO PISTOL

Caliber: 45 ACP, 40 S&W, .38 Super. **Barrel:** 5", match grade, .40 S&W, .38 Super barrels ramped. **Weight:** 38 oz. **Length:** 8.7" overall. **Grips:** Checkered black rubber, walnut, rosewood. **Sights:** Dovetail front and rear, Kimber adjustable or fixed three dot (green) Meptrolight night sights. **Features:** Slide, frame and barrel machined from steel or stainless steel forgings. Match grade barrel, chamber and trigger group. Extended thumb safety, beveled magazine well, beveled front and rear slide serrations, high ride beavertail grip safety, checkered flat mainspring housing, kidney cut under trigger guard, high cut grip, match grade stainless steel berrel bushing, polished breech face, Commander-style hammer, lowered and flared ejection port, Wolff springs, bead blasted black oxide finish. Introduced in 1996. Made in U.S.A. by Kimber Mfg., Inc.

Price: Custom **$730.00**
Price: Custom Walnut (double-diamond walnut grips) **$752.00**
Price: Custom Stainless **$832.00**
Price: Custom Stainless 40 S&W **$870.00**
Price: Custom Stainless Target 45 ACP (stainless, adj. sight) . . . **$945.00**
Price: Custom Stainless Target 38 Super **$974.00**

Kimber Custom II Auto Pistol

Similar to Compact II, 4" bull barrel fitted directly to the stainless steel slide without a bushing, grip is .400" shorter than standard, no front serrations. Weighs 34 oz. 45 ACP only. Introduced in 1998. Made in U.S.A. by Kimber Mfg., Inc.

Price: **$870.00**

Kimber Compact II Custom

Kimber Ten II High Capacity Polymer

Kimber Ultra Carry II

Kimber CDP II

Kimber Pro Carry II Auto Pistol

Similar to Custom II, has aluminum frame, 4" bull barrel fitted directly to the slide without bushing. HD with stainless steel frame. Introduced 1998. Made in U.S.A. by Kimber Mfg., Inc.

Price: 45 ACP **$773.00**
Price: HD II **$879.00**
Price: Pro Carry HD II Stainless 45 ACP **$845.00**
Price: Pro Carry HD II Stainless 38 Spec. **$917.00**

Kimber Ultra Carry II Auto Pistol

Similar to Compact Stainless II, lightweight aluminum frame, 3" match grade bull barrel fitted to slide without bushing. Grips .400" shorter. Special slide stop. Low effort recoil. Weighs 25 oz. Introduced in 1999. Made in U.S.A. by Kimber Mfg., Inc.

Price: **$767.00**
Price: Stainless **$841.00**
Price: Stainless 40 S&W **$884.00**

Kimber Ten II High Capacity Polymer Pistol

Similar to Custom II, Pro Carry II and Ultra Carry II depending on barrel length. Ten-round magazine capacity (double stack and flush fitting). Polymer grip frame molded over stainless steel or aluminum (Ultra Ten II only) frame insert. Checkered front strap and belly of trigger guard. All models have fixed sights except Gold Match Ten II, which has adjustable sight. Frame grip dimensions approximate that of the standard 1911 for natural aiming and better recoil control. Ultra Ten II weight is 24 oz. Others 32-34 oz. Additional 14-round magazines available where legal. All new for 2002. Much-improved version of the Kimber Polymer series. Made in U.S.A. by Kimber Mfg., Inc.

Price: Ultra Ten II **$850.00**
Price: Pro Carry Ten II **$828.00**
Price: Stainless Ten II **$812.00**

Kimber Gold Match II Auto Pistol

Similar to Custom II models. Includes stainless steel barrel with match grade chamber and barrel bushing, ambidextrous thumb safety, adjustable sight, premium aluminum trigger, hand-checkered double diamond rosewood grips. Barrel hand-fitted to bushing and slide for target accuracy. Made in U.S.A. by Kimber Mfg., Inc.

Price: Gold Match II **$1,169.00**
Price: Gold Match Stainless II 45 ACP **$1,315.00**
Price: Gold Match Stainless II 40 S&W **$1,345.00**

Kimber Gold Match Ten II Polymer Auto Pistol

Similar to Stainless Gold Match II. High capacity polymer frame with ten-round magazine. No ambi thumb safety. Polished flats add elegant look. Introduced 1999. Made in U.S.A. by Kimber Mfg., Inc.

Price: **$1,118.00**

Kimber Gold Combat II Auto Pistol

Similar to Gold Match II except designed for concealed carry. Extended and beveled magazine well, Meprolight tritium night sights; premium aluminum trigger; 30 lpi front strap checkering; special Custom Shop markings; Kim Pro premium finish. Introduced 1999. Made in U.S.A. by Kimber Mfg., Inc.

Price: 45 ACP **$1,682.00**
Price: Gold Combat Stainless (satin-finished stainless frame and slide, special Custom Shop markings) **$1,623.00**

Kimber CDP II Series Auto Pistol

Similar to Custom II, but designed for concealed carry. Aluminum frame. Standard features include stainless steel slide, Meprolight tritium three dot (green) dovetail-mounted night sights, match grade barrel and chamber, 30 LPI front strap checkering, two tone finish, ambidextrous thumb safety, hand-checkered double diamond rosewood grips. Introduced in 2000. Made in U.S.A. by Kimber Mfg., Inc.

Price: Ultra CDP II 40 S&W **$1,120.00**
Price: Ultra CDP II (3 barrel, short grip) **$1,084.00**
Price: Compact CDP II (4 barrel, short grip) **$1,084.00**
Price: Pro CDP II (4 barrel, full length grip) **$1,084.00**
Price: Custom CDP II (5 barrel, full length grip) **$1,084.00**

Kimber Eclipse II

Kimber Eclipse Target II

Kimber LTP II

Llama Micromax

Llama Minimax

Kimber Eclipse II Series Auto Pistol

Similar to Custom II and other stainless Kimber pistol.s Stainless slide and frame, black anodized, two tone finish. Gray/black laminated grips. 30 LPI front strap checkering. All have night sights, with Target versions having Meprolight adjustable Bar/Dot version. New for 2002. Made in U.S.A. by Kimber Mfg., Inc.

Price: Eclipse Ultra II (3 barrel, short grip) **$1,052.00**
Price: Eclipse Pro II (4 barrel, full length grip) **$1,052.00**
Price: Eclipse Pro Target II (4 barrel, full length grip,
  adjustable sight) **$1,153.00**
Price: Eclipse Custom II (5 barrel, full length grip) **$1,071.00**
Price: Eclipse Target II (5 barrel, full length grip,
  adjustable sight) **$1,153.00**

Kimber LTP II Polymer Auto Pistol

Similar to Gold Match II. Built for Limited Ten competition. First Kimber pistol with new, innovative Kimber external extractor. KimPro premium finish. Stainless steel match grade barrel. Extended and beveled magazine well. Checkered front strap and trigger guard belly. Tungsten full length guide rod. Premium aluminum trigger. Ten-round single stack magazine. Wide ambidextrous thumb safety. New for 2002. Made in U.S.A. by Kimber Mfg., Inc.
Price: **$2,036.00**

Kimber Super Match II Auto Pistol

Similar to Gold Match II. Built for target and action shotting competition. Tested for accuracy. Target included. Stainless steel barrel and chamber. KimPro finish on stainless steel slide. Stainless steel frame. 30 LPI checkered front strap, premium aluminum trigger, Kimber adjustable sight. Introduced in 1999.
Price: **$1,926.00**

LLAMA MICROMAX 380 AUTO PISTOL

Caliber: 32 ACP, 8-shot, 380 ACP, 7-shot magazine. **Barrel:** 3-11/16". **Weight:** 23 oz. **Length:** 6-1/2" overall. **Grips:** Checkered high impact polymer. **Sights:** 3-dot combat. **Features:** Single-action design. Mini custom extended slide release; mini custom extended beavertail grip safety; combat-style hammer. Introduced 1997. Distributed by Import Sports, Inc.
Price: Matte blue **$281.95**
Price: Satin chrome (380 only) **$298.95**

LLAMA MINIMAX SERIES

Caliber: 40 S&W, 7-shot; 45 ACP, 6-shot magazine. **Barrel:** 3-1/2". **Weight:** 35 oz. **Length:** 7-1/3" overall. **Grips:** Checkered rubber. **Sights:** Three-dot combat. **Features:** Single action, skeletonized combat-style hammer, extended slide release, cone-style barrel, flared ejection port. Introduced 1996. Distributed by Import Sports, Inc.
Price: Blue **$324.95**
Price: Duo-Tone finish (45 only) **$333.95**
Price: Satin chrome **$341.95**

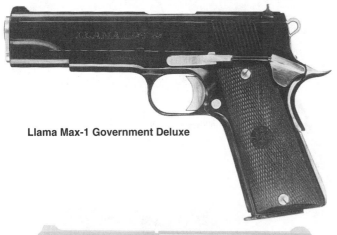

Llama Max-1 Government Deluxe

Para-Ordnance P12.45

North American Arms Guardian

Para-Ordnance LDA

Llama Minimax Sub-Compact Auto Pistol

Similar to the Minimax except has 3.14" barrel, weighs 31 oz.; 6.8" overall length; has 10-shot magazine with finger extension; beavertail grip safety. Introduced 1999. Distributed by Import Sports, Inc.
Price: 45 ACP, matte blue **$341.95**
Price: As above, satin chrome **$358.95**
Price: Duo-Tone finish (45 only) **$349.95**

LLAMA MAX-I AUTO PISTOLS

Caliber: 45 ACP, 7-shot. **Barrel:** 5-1/8". **Weight:** 36 oz. **Length:** 8-1/2" overall. **Grips:** Black rubber. **Sights:** Blade front, rear adjustable for windage; three-dot system. **Features:** Single-action trigger; skeletonized combat-style hammer; steel frame; extended manual and grip safeties. Introduced 1995. Distributed by Import Sports, Inc.
Price: 45 ACP, 7-shot, Government model **$310.95**

NORTH AMERICAN ARMS GUARDIAN PISTOL

Caliber: 32 ACP, 6-shot magazine. **Barrel:** 2.1". **Weight:** 13.5 oz. **Length:** 4.36" overall. **Grips:** Black polymer. **Sights:** Fixed. **Features:** Double-action-only mechanism. All stainless steel construction; snag-free. Introduced 1998. Made in U.S.A. by North American Arms.
Price: **$359.00**

OLYMPIC ARMS OA-96 AR PISTOL

Caliber: 223. **Barrel:** 6", 8", 4140 chrome-moly steel. **Weight:** 5 lbs. **Length:** 15-3/4" overall. **Grips:** A2 stowaway pistol grip; no buttstock or receiver tube. **Sights:** Flat-top upper receiver, cut-down front sight base. **Features:** AR-15-type receivers with special bolt carrier; short aluminum hand guard; Vortex flash hider. Introduced 1996. Made in U.S.A. by Olympic Arms, Inc.
Price: **$858.00**

Olympic Arms OA-98 AR Pistol

Similar to the OA-93 except has removable 7-shot magazine, weighs 3 lbs. Introduced 1999. Made in U.S.A. by Olympic Arms, Inc.
Price: **$990.00**

PARA-ORDNANCE P-SERIES AUTO PISTOLS

Caliber: 9mm Para., 40 S&W, 45 ACP, 10-shot magazine. **Barrel:** 3", 3-1/2", 4-1/4", 5". **Weight:** From 24 oz. (alloy frame). **Length:** 8.5" overall. **Grips:** Textured composition. **Sights:** Blade front, rear adjustable for windage. High visibility three-dot system. **Features:** Available with alloy, steel or stainless steel frame with black finish (silver or stainless gun). Steel and stainless steel frame guns weigh 40 oz. (P14.45), 36 oz. (P13.45), 34 oz. (P12.45). Grooved match trigger, rounded combat-style hammer. Beveled magazine well. Manual thumb, grip and firing pin lock safeties. Solid barrel bushing. Contact maker for full details. Introduced 1990. Made in Canada by Para-Ordnance.
Price: Steel frame **$795.00**
Price: Alloy frame **$765.00**
Price: Stainless steel **$865.00**

Para-Ordnance Limited Pistols

Similar to the P-Series pistols except with full-length recoil guide system; fully adjustable rear sight; tuned trigger with overtravel stop; beavertail grip safety; competition hammer; front and rear slide serrations; ambidextrous safety; lowered ejection port; ramped match-grade barrel; dovetailed front sight. Introduced 1998. Made in Canada by Para-Ordnance.
Price: 9mm, 40 S&W, 45 ACP . . . . **$945.00 to $999.00**

Para-Ordnance LDA Auto Pistols

Similar to P-series except has double-action trigger mechanism. Steel frame with matte black finish, checkered composition grips. Available in 9mm Para., 40 S&W, 45 ACP. Introduced 1999. Made in Canada by Para-Ordnance.
Price: **$775.00**

**Para-Ordnance C5
45 LDA Para Carry**

Peters Stahl High Capacity

**Para-Ordnance C7
45 LDA Para Companion**

Peters Stahl Trophy Master

Peters Stahl Millenium

Para-Ordnance LDA Limited Pistols

Similar to LDA, has ambidextrous safety, adjustable rear sight, front slide serrations and full-length recoil guide system. Made in Canada by Para-Ordnance.
Price: Black finish $975.00
Price: Stainless. $1,049.00

PARA-ORDNANCE P-SERIES AUTO PISTOLS

Caliber: 45 ACP. **Barrel:** 3", 6+1 shot. **Weight:** 30 oz. **Length:** 6.5". **Grips:** Double diamond checkered Cocobolo. **Features:** Stainless finish and receiver, "World's Smallest DAO .45 Auto." Major performance in micro package with Para LDA trigger system and safeties.
Price: $899.00

PARA-ORDNANCE C5 45 LDA PARA CARRY

Caliber: 45 ACP. **Barrel:** 3", 6+1 shot. **Weight:** 30 oz. **Length:** 6.5". **Grips:** Double diamond checkered Cocobolo. **Features:** Stainless finish and receiver, "world's smallest DAO 45 auto." Major performance in micro package wtih Para LDA trigger system and safeties.
Price: $899.00

PARA-ORDNANCE C7 45 LDA PARA COMPANION

Caliber: 45 ACP. **Barrel:** 3.5", 7+1 shot. **Weight:** 32 oz. **Length:** 7". **Grips:** Double diamond checkered Cocobolo. **Features:** Para LDA trigger system with Para LDA 3 safeties (slide lock, firing pin block and grip safety). Lightning speed, full size capacity.
Price: $899.00

PETERS STAHL AUTOLOADING PISTOLS

Caliber: 9mm Para., 45 ACP. **Barrel:** 5" or 6". **Grips:** Walnut or walnut with rubber wrap. **Sights:** Fully adjustable rear, blade front. **Features:** Stainless steel extended slide stop, safety and extended magazine release button; speed trigger with stop and approx. 3-lb. pull; polished ramp. Introduced 2000. Imported from Germany by Phillips & Rogers.
Price: High Capacity (accepts 15-shot magazines in 45 cal.; includes 10-shot magazine) $1,695.00
Price: Trophy Master (blued or stainless, 7-shot in 45, 8-shot in 9mm) $1,995.00
Price: Millenium Model (titanium coating on receiver and slide) $2,195.00

HANDGUNS

Phoenix Arms HP22

Republic Patriot

PSA-25 Auto

Rock River Standard Match

PHOENIX ARMS HP22, HP25 AUTO PISTOLS

Caliber: 22 LR, 10-shot (HP22), 25 ACP, 10-shot (HP25). **Barrel:** 3". **Weight:** 20 oz. **Length:** 5-1/2" overall. **Grips:** Checkered composition. **Sights:** Blade front, adjustable rear. **Features:** Single action, exposed hammer; manual hold-open; button magazine release. Available in satin nickel, polished blue finish. Introduced 1993. Made in U.S.A. by Phoenix Arms.

Price: With gun lock and cable lanyard **$128.00**
Price: HP Rangemaster kit with 5" bbl., locking case
and assessories **$169.00**
Price: HP Deluxe Rangemaster kit with 3" and 5" bbls.,
2 mags., case **$199.00**

PSA-25 AUTO POCKET PISTOL

Caliber: 25 ACP, 6-shot magazine. **Barrel:** 2-1/8". **Weight:** 9.5 oz. **Length:** 4-1/8" overall. **Grips:** Checkered black polymer, ivory, checkered transparent carbon fiber-filled polymer. **Sights:** Fixed. **Features:** All steel construction; striker fired; single action only; magazine disconnector; cocking indicator. Introduced 1987. Made in U.S.A. by Precision Small Arms, Inc.

Price: Traditional (polished black oxide) **$269.00**
Price: Nouveau-Satin (brushed nickel) **$269.00**
Price: Nouveau-Mirror (highly polished nickel) **$309.00**
Price: Featherweight (aluminum frame, nickel slide) **$405.00**
Price: Diplomat (black oxide with gold highlights, ivory grips) . . . **$625.00**
Price: Montreaux (gold plated, ivory grips) **$692.00**
Price: Renaissance (hand engraved nickel, ivory grips) **$1,115.00**
Price: Imperiale (inlaid gold filigree over blue, scrimshawed
ivory grips) **$3,600.00**

REPUBLIC PATRIOT PISTOL

Caliber: 45 ACP, 6-shot magazine. **Barrel:** 3". **Weight:** 20 oz. **Length:** 6" overall. **Grips:** Checkered. **Sights:** Blade front, drift-adjustable rear. **Features:** Black polymer frame, stainless steel slide; double-action-only trigger system; squared trigger guard. Introduced 1997. Made in U.S.A. by Republic Arms, Inc.

Price: About **$325.00**

ROCK RIVER ARMS STANDARD MATCH AUTO PISTOL

Caliber: 45 ACP. **Barrel:** NA. **Weight:** NA. **Length:** NA. **Grips:** Cocobolo, checkered. **Sights:** Heine fixed rear, blade front. **Features:** Chrome-moly steel frame and slide; beavertail grip safety with raised pad; checkered slide stop; ambidextrous safety; polished feed ramp and extractor; aluminum speed trigger with 3.5 lb. pull. Made in U.S.A. From Rock River Arms.

Price: **$1,025.00**

ROCKY MOUNTAIN ARMS PATRIOT PISTOL

Caliber: 223, 10-shot magazine. **Barrel:** 7", with muzzle brake. **Weight:** 5 lbs. **Length:** 20.5" overall. **Grips:** Black composition. **Sights:** None furnished. **Features:** Milled upper receiver with enhanced Weaver base; milled lower receiver from billet plate; machined aluminum National Match handguard. Finished in DuPont Teflon-S matte black or NATO green. Comes with black nylon case, one magazine. Introduced 1993. From Rocky Mountain Arms, Inc.

Price: With A-2 handle top . . . . **$2,500.00 to $2,800.00**
Price: Flat top model . . . . **$3,000.00 to $3,500.00**

RUGER P89 AUTOLOADING PISTOL

Caliber: 9mm Para., 10-shot magazine. **Barrel:** 4.50". **Weight:** 32 oz. **Length:** 7.84" overall. **Grips:** Grooved black synthetic composition. **Sights:** Square post front, square notch rear adjustable for windage, both with white dot inserts. **Features:** Double action, ambidextrous slide-mounted safety-levers. Slide 4140 chrome-moly steel or 400-series stainless steel, frame lightweight aluminum alloy. Ambidextrous magazine release. Blue, stainless steel. Introduced 1986; stainless 1990.

Price: P89, blue, extra mag and mag loader, plastic case locks . **$475.00**
Price: KP89, stainless, extra mag and mag loader,
plastic case locks **$525.00**

Ruger P89

Ruger P93D

Ruger P90

Ruger KP95DAO

Ruger P89D Decocker Autoloading Pistol

Similar to standard P89 except has ambidextrous decocking levers in place of regular slide-mounted safety. Decocking levers move firing pin inside slide where hammer can not reach, while simultaneously blocking firing pin from forward movement—allows shooter to decock cocked pistol without manipulating trigger. Conventional thumb decocking procedures are therefore unnecessary. Blue, stainless steel. Introduced 1990.

Price: P89D, blue, extra mag and mag loader, plastic case locks **$475.00**

Price: KP89D, stainless, extra mag and mag loader,

plastic case locks **$525.00**

Ruger P89 Double-Action-Only Autoloading Pistol

Same as KP89 except operates only in double-action mode. Has spurless hammer, gripping grooves on each side of rear slide; no external safety or decocking lever. Internal safety prevents forward movement of firing pin unless trigger is pulled. Available 9mm Para., stainless steel only. Introduced 1991.

Price: Lockable case, extra mag and mag loader **$525.00**

RUGER P90 MANUAL SAFETY MODEL AUTOLOADING PISTOL

Caliber: 45 ACP, 8-shot magazine. **Barrel:** 4.50". **Weight:** 33.5 oz. **Length:** 7.75" overall. **Grips:** Grooved black synthetic composition. **Sights:** Square post front, square notch rear adjustable for windage, both with white dot. **Features:** Double action ambidextrous slide-mounted safety-levers move firing pin inside slide where hammer can not reach, simultaneously blocking firing pin from forward movement. Stainless steel only. Introduced 1991.

Price: KP90 with extra mag, loader, case and gunlock **$565.00**

Price: P90 (blue). **$525.00**

Ruger KP90 Decocker Autoloading Pistol

Similar to the P90 except has a manual decocking system. The ambidextrous decocking levers move the firing pin inside the slide where the hammer can not reach it, while simultaneously blocking the firing pin from forward movement—allows shooter to decock a cocked pistol without manipulating the trigger. Available only in stainless steel. Overall length 7.75", weighs 33.5 oz. Introduced 1991.

Price: KP90D with case, extra mag and mag loading tool **$565.00**

RUGER P93 COMPACT AUTOLOADING PISTOL

Caliber: 9mm Para., 10-shot magazine. **Barrel:** 3.9". **Weight:** 31 oz. **Length:** 7.25" overall. **Grips:** Grooved black synthetic composition. **Sights:** Square post front, square notch rear adjustable for windage. **Features:** Front of slide crowned with convex curve; slide has seven finger grooves; trigger guard bow higher for better grip; 400-series stainless slide, lightweight alloy frame; also blue. Decocker-only or DAO-only. Includes hard case and lock. Introduced 1993. Made in U.S.A. by Sturm, Ruger & Co.

Price: KP93DAO, double-action-only **$575.00**

Price: KP93D ambidextrous decocker, stainless **$575.00**

Price: P93D, ambidextrous decocker, blue **$495.00**

Ruger KP94 Autoloading Pistol

Sized midway between full-size P-Series and compact P93. 4.25" barrel, 7.5" overall length, weighs about 33 oz. KP94 manual safety model; KP94DAO double-action-only (both 9mm Para., 10-shot magazine); KP94D is decocker-only in 40-caliber with 10-shot magazine. Slide gripping grooves roll over top of slide. KP94 has ambidextrous safety-levers; KP94DAO has no external safety, full-cock hammer position or decocking lever; KP94D has ambidextrous decocking levers. Matte finish stainless slide, barrel, alloy frame. Also blue. Includes hard case and lock. Introduced 1994. Made in U.S.A. by Sturm, Ruger & Co.

Price: P94, P944, blue (manual safety) **$495.00**

Price: KP94 (9mm), KP944 (40-caliber) (manual

safety-stainless) **$575.00**

Price: KP94DAO (9mm), KP944DAO (40-caliber) **$575.00**

Price: KP94D (9mm), KP944D (40-caliber)-decock only **$575.00**

HANDGUNS

Ruger KMK 4

Ruger KP512

Ruger 22/45-P4

RUGER P95 AUTOLOADING PISTOL

Caliber: 9mm Para., 10-shot magazine. **Barrel:** 3.9". **Weight:** 27 oz. **Length:** 7.25" overall. **Grips:** Grooved; integral with frame. **Sights:** Blade front, rear drift adjustable for windage; three-dot system. **Features:** Moulded polymer grip frame, stainless steel or chrome-moly slide. Suitable for +P+ ammunition. Safety model, decocker or DAO. Introduced 1996. Made in U.S.A. by Sturm, Ruger & Co. Comes with lockable plastic case, spare magazine, loader and lock.
Price: P95 DAO double-action-only **$425.00**
Price: P95D decocker only **$425.00**
Price: KP95D stainless steel decocker only **$475.00**
Price: KP95DAO double-action only, stainless steel **$475.00**
Price: KP95 safety model, stainless steel. **$475.00**
Price: P95 safety model, blued finish **$425.00**

RUGER P97 AUTOLOADING PISTOL

Caliber: 45ACP 8-shot magazine. **Barrel:** 4-1/8". **Weight:** 30-1/2 oz. **Length:** 7-1/4" overall. Grooved: Integral with frame. **Sights:** Blade front, rear drift adjustable for windage; three dot system. **Features:** Moulded polymer grip frame, stainless steel slide. Decocker or DAO. Introduced 1997. Made in U.S.A. by Sturm, Ruger & Co. Comes with lockable plastic case, spare magaline, loading tool.
Price: KP97D decocker only. **$495.00**
Price: KP97DAO double-action only **$495.00**
Price: P97D decocker only, blued **$460.00**

RUGER MARK II STANDARD AUTOLOADING PISTOL

Caliber: 22 LR, 10-shot magazine. **Barrel:** 4-3/4" or 6". **Weight:** 35 oz. (4-3/4" bbl.). **Length:** 8-5/16" (4-3/4" bbl.). **Grips:** Checkered composition grip panels. **Sights:** Fixed, wide blade front, fixed rear. **Features:** Updated design of original Standard Auto. New bolt hold-open latch. 10-shot magazine, magazine catch, safety, trigger and new receiver contours. Introduced 1982.
Price: Blued (MK 4, MK 6) **$289.00**
Price: In stainless steel (KMK 4, KMK 6) **$379.00**

Ruger 22/45 Mark II Pistol

Similar to other 22 Mark II autos except has grip frame of Zytel that matches angle and magazine latch of Model 1911 45 ACP pistol. Available in 4" bull, 4-3/4" standard and 5-1/2" bull barrels. Comes with extra magazine, plastic case, lock. Introduced 1992.
Price: P4, 4" bull barrel, adjustable sights **$275.00**
Price: KP 4 (4-3/4" barrel), stainless steel, fixed sights **$305.00**
Price: KP512 (5-1/2" bull barrel), stainless steel, adj. sights **$359.00**
Price: P512 (5-1/2" bull barrel, all blue), adj. sights **$275.00**

SAFARI ARMS ENFORCER PISTOL

Caliber: 45 ACP, 6-shot magazine. **Barrel:** 3.8", stainless. **Weight:** 36 oz. **Length:** 7.3" overall. **Grips:** Smooth walnut with etched black widow spider logo. **Sights:** Ramped blade front, LPA adjustable rear. **Features:** Extended safety, extended slide release; Commander-style hammer; beavertail grip safety; throated, polished, tuned. Parkerized matte black or satin stainless steel finishes. Made in U.S.A. by Safari Arms.
Price: **$630.00**

SAFARI ARMS GI SAFARI PISTOL

Caliber: 45 ACP, 7-shot magazine. **Barrel:** 5", 416 stainless. **Weight:** 39.9 oz. **Length:** 8.5" overall. **Grips:** Checkered walnut. **Sights:** G.I.-style blade front, drift-adjustable rear. **Features:** Beavertail grip safety; extended thumb safety and slide release; Commander-style hammer. Parkerized finish. Reintroduced 1996.
Price: **$439.00**

SAFARI ARMS CARRIER PISTOL

Caliber: 45 ACP, 7-shot magazine. **Barrel:** 6", 416 stainless steel. **Weight:** 30 oz. **Length:** 9.5" overall. **Grips:** Wood. **Sights:** Ramped blade front, LPA adjustable rear. **Features:** Beavertail grip safety; extended controls; full-length recoil spring guide; Commander-style hammer. Throated, polished and tuned. Satin stainless steel finish. Introduced 1999. Made in U.S.A. by Safari Arms, Inc.
Price: **$714.00**

SAFARI ARMS COHORT PISTOL

Caliber: 45 ACP, 7-shot magazine. **Barrel:** 3.8", 416 stainless. **Weight:** 37 oz. **Length:** 8.5" overall. **Grips:** Smooth walnut with laser-etched black widow logo. **Sights:** Ramped blade front, LPA adjustable rear. **Features:** Combines the Enforcer model, slide and MatchMaster frame. Beavertail grip safety; extended thumb safety and slide release; Commander-style hammer. Throated, polished and tuned. Satin stainless finish. Introduced 1996. Made in U.S.A. by Safari Arms, Inc.
Price: **$654.00**

SAFARI ARMS MATCHMASTER PISTOL

Caliber: 45 ACP, 7-shot. **Barrel:** 5" or 6", 416 stainless steel. **Weight:** 38 oz. (5" barrel). **Length:** 8.5" overall. **Grips:** Smooth walnut. **Sights:** Ramped blade, LPA adjustable rear. **Features:** Beavertail grip safety; extended controls; Commander-style hammer; throated, polished, tuned. Parkerized matte-black or satin stainless steel. Made in U.S.A. by Olympic Arms, Inc.
Price: 5" barrel **$594.00**
Price: 6" barrel **$654.00**

SIG Sauer P220

SIG Arms Pro 2009

SIG Arms P245 Compact

Safari Arms Carry Comp Pistol

Similar to the Matchmaster except has Wil Schueman-designed hybrid compensator system. Made in U.S.A. by Olympic Arms, Inc.
Price: **$1,067.00**

SEECAMP LWS 32 STAINLESS DA AUTO

Caliber: 32 ACP Win. Silvertip, 6-shot magazine. **Barrel:** 2", integral with frame. **Weight:** 10.5 oz. **Length:** 4-1/8" overall. **Grips:** Glass-filled nylon. **Sights:** Smooth, no-snag, contoured slide and barrel top. **Features:** Aircraft quality 17-4 PH stainless steel. Inertia-operated firing pin. Hammer fired double-action-only. Hammer automatically follows slide down to safety rest position after each shot—no manual safety needed. Magazine safety disconnector. Polished stainless. Introduced 1985. From L.W. Seecamp.
Price: **$425.00**

SIG SAUER P220 SERVICE AUTO PISTOL

Caliber: 45 ACP, (7- or 8-shot magazine). **Barrel:** 4-3/8". **Weight:** 27.8 oz. **Length:** 7.8" overall. **Grips:** Checkered black plastic. **Sights:** Blade front, drift adjustable rear for windage. Optional Siglite nightsights. **Features:** Double action. Decocking lever permits lowering hammer onto locked firing pin. Squared combat-type trigger guard. Slide stays open after last shot. Imported from Germany by SIGARMS, Inc.
Price: Blue SA/DA or DAO **$790.00**
Price: Blue, Siglite night sights **$880.00**
Price: K-Kote or nickel slide **$830.00**
Price: K-Kote or nickel slide with Siglite night sights **$930.00**

SIG Sauer P220 Sport Auto Pistol

Similar to the P220 except has 4.9" barrel, ported compensator, all-stainless steel frame and slide, factory-tuned trigger, adjustable sights, extended competition controls. Overall length is 9.9", weighs 43.5 oz. Introduced 1999. From SIGARMS, Inc.
Price: **$1,320.00**

SIG Sauer P245 Compact Auto Pistol

Similar to the P220 except has 3.9" barrel, shorter grip, 6-shot magazine, 7.28" overall length, and weighs 27.5 oz. Introduced 1999. From SIG-ARMS, Inc.
Price: Blue **$780.00**
Price: Blue, with Siglite sights **$850.00**
Price: Two-tone **$830.00**
Price: Two-tone with Siglite sights **$930.00**
Price: With K-Kote finish. **$830.00**
Price: K-Kote with Siglite sights **$930.00**

SIG Sauer P229 DA Auto Pistol

Similar to the P228 except chambered for 9mm Para., 40 S&W, 357 SIG. Has 3.86" barrel, 7.08" overall length and 3.35" height. Weight is 30.5 oz. Introduced 1991. Frame made in Germany, stainless steel slide assembly made in U.S.; pistol assembled in U.S. From SIGARMS, Inc.
Price: **$795.00**
Price: With nickel slide **$890.00**
Price: Nickel slide Siglite night sights **$935.00**

SIG PRO AUTO PISTOL

Caliber: 9mm Para., 40 S&W, 10-shot magazine. **Barrel:** 3.86". **Weight:** 27.2 oz. **Length:** 7.36" overall. **Grips:** Composite and rubberized one-piece. **Sights:** Blade front, rear adjustable for windage. Optional Siglite night sights. **Features:** Polymer frame, stainless steel slide; integral frame accessory rail; replaceable steel frame rails; left- or right-handed magazine release. Introduced 1999. From SIGARMS, Inc.
Price: SP2340 (40 S&W) **$596.00**
Price: SP2009 (9mm Para.) **$596.00**
Price: As above with Siglite night sights **$655.00**

SIG Sauer P226 Service Pistol

Similar to the P220 pistol except has 4.4" barrel, and weighs 28.3 oz. 357 SIG or 40 S&W. Imported from Germany by SIGARMS, Inc.
Price: Blue SA/DA or DAO **$830.00**
Price: With Siglite night sights **$930.00**
Price: Blue, SA/DA or DAO 357 SIG **$830.00**
Price: With Siglite night sights **$930.00**
Price: K-Kote finish, 40 S&W only or nickel slide **$830.00**
Price: K-Kote or nickel slide Siglite night sights **$930.00**
Price: Nickel slide 357 SIG. **$875.00**
Price: Nickel slide, Siglite night sights **$930.00**

SIG Sauer P229 Sport Auto Pistol

Similar to the P229 except available in 357 SIG only; 4.8" heavy barrel; 8.6" overall length; weighs 40.6 oz.; vented compensator; adjustable target sights; rubber grips; extended slide latch and magazine release. Made of stainless steel. Introduced 1998. From SIGARMS, Inc.
Price: **$1,320.00**

HANDGUNS — AUTOLOADERS, SERVICE & SPORT

SIG Sauer P229S

Smith & Wesson 457

SIG Sauer P232

Smith & Wesson 4013 TSW

SIG SAUER P232 PERSONAL SIZE PISTOL
Caliber: 380 ACP, 7-shot. **Barrel:** 3-3/4". **Weight:** 16 oz. **Length:** 6-1/2" overall. **Grips:** Checkered black composite. **Sights:** Blade front, rear adjustable for windage. **Features:** Double action/single action or DAO. Blowback operation, stationary barrel. Introduced 1997. Imported from Germany by SIGARMS, Inc.
Price: Blue SA/DA or DAO **$505.00**
Price: In stainless steel.................................. **$545.00**
Price: With stainless steel slide, blue frame **$525.00**
Price: Stainless steel, Siglite night sights, Hogue grips **$585.00**

SIG SAUER P239 PISTOL
Caliber: 9mm Para., 8-shot, 357 SIG 40 S&W, 7-shot magazine. **Barrel:** 3.6". **Weight:** 25.2 oz. **Length:** 6.6" overall. **Grips:** Checkered black composite. **Sights:** Blade front, rear adjustable for windage. Optional Siglite night sights. **Features:** SA/DA or DAO; blackened stainless steel slide, aluminum alloy frame. Introduced 1996. Made in U.S.A. by SIGARMS, Inc.
Price: SA/DA or DAO **$620.00**
Price: SA/DA or DAO with Siglite night sights **$720.00**
Price: Two-tone finish.................................. **$665.00**
Price: Two-tone finish, Siglite sights...................... **$765.00**

SMITH & WESSON MODEL 22A SPORT PISTOL
Caliber: 22 LR, 10-shot magazine. **Barrel:** 4", 5-1/2", 7". **Weight:** 29 oz. **Length:** 8" overall. **Grips:** Two-piece polymer. **Sights:** Patridge front, fully adjustable rear. **Features:** Comes with a sight bridge with Weaver-style integral optics mount; alloy frame; .312" serrated trigger; stainless steel slide and barrel with matte blue finish. Introduced 1997. Made in U.S.A. by Smith & Wesson.
Price: 4" **$264.00**
Price: 5-1/2" **$292.00**
Price: 7" **$331.00**

SMITH & WESSON MODEL 457 TDA AUTO PISTOL
Caliber: 45 ACP, 7-shot magazine. **Barrel:** 3-3/4". **Weight:** 29 oz. **Length:** 7-1/4" overall. **Grips:** One-piece Xenoy, wrap-around with straight backstrap.

Sights: Post front, fixed rear, three-dot system. **Features:** Aluminum alloy frame, matte blue carbon steel slide; bobbed hammer; smooth trigger. Introduced 1996. Made in U.S.A. by Smith & Wesson.
Price: **$591.00**

SMITH & WESSON MODEL 908 AUTO PISTOL
Caliber: 9mm Para., 8-shot magazine. **Barrel:** 3-1/2". **Weight:** 26 oz. **Length:** 6-13/16". **Grips:** One-piece Xenoy, wrap-around with straight backstrap. **Sights:** Post front, fixed rear, three-dot system. **Features:** Aluminum alloy frame, matte blue carbon steel slide; bobbed hammer; smooth trigger. Introduced 1996. Made in U.S.A. by Smith & Wesson.
Price: **$535.00**

SMITH & WESSON MODEL 4013, 4053 TSW AUTOS
Caliber: 40 S&W, 9-shot magazine. **Barrel:** 3-1/2". **Weight:** 26.4 oz. **Length:** 6-7/8" overall. **Grips:** Xenoy one-piece wrap-around. **Sights:** Novak three-dot system. **Features:** Traditional double-action system; stainless slide, alloy frame; fixed barrel bushing; ambidextrous decocker; reversible magazine catch, equipment rail. Introduced 1997. Made in U.S.A. by Smith & Wesson.
Price: Model 4013 TSW **$886.00**
Price: Model 4053 TSW, double-action-only **$886.00**

Smith & Wesson Model 22S Sport Pistols
Similar to the Model 22A Sport except with stainless steel frame. Available only with 5-1/2" or 7" barrel. Introduced 1997. Made in U.S.A. by Smith & Wesson.
Price: 5-1/2" standard barrel.......................... **$358.00**
Price: 5-1/2" bull barrel, wood target stocks with thumbrest..... **$434.00**
Price: 7" standard barrel.............................. **$395.00**
Price: 5-1/2" bull barrel, two-piece target stocks with thumbrest . **$353.00**

Smith & Wesson 3913 TSW

Smith & Wesson
3913 LadySmith

Smith & Wesson 4006

SMITH & WESSON MODEL 410 DA AUTO PISTOL

Caliber: 40 S&W, 10-shot magazine. **Barrel:** 4". **Weight:** 28.5 oz. **Length:** 7.5 oz. **Grips:** One-piece Xenoy, wrap-around with straight backstrap. **Sights:** Post front, fixed rear; three-dot system. **Features:** Aluminum alloy frame; blued carbon steel slide; traditional double action with left-side slide-mounted decocking lever. Introduced 1996. Made in U.S.A. by Smith & Wesson.
Price: Model 410 . . . . **$591.00**
Price: Model 410, HiViz front sight **$612.00**

SMITH & WESSON MODEL 910 DA AUTO PISTOL

Caliber: 9mm Para., 10-shot magazine. **Barrel:** 4". **Weight:** 28 oz. **Length:** 7-3/8" overall. **Grips:** One-piece Xenoy, wrap-around with straight backstrap. **Sights:** Post front with white dot, fixed two-dot rear. **Features:** Alloy frame, blue carbon steel slide. Slide-mounted decocking lever. Introduced 1995.
Price: Model 910. . . . . **$535.00**
Price: Model 410, HiViz front sight **$535.00**

SMITH & WESSON MODEL 3913 TRADITIONAL DOUBLE ACTION

Caliber: 9mm Para., 8-shot magazine. **Barrel:** 3-1/2". **Weight:** 26 oz. **Length:** 6-13/16" overall. **Grips:** One-piece Delrin wrap-around, textured surface. **Sights:** Post front with white dot, Novak LoMount Carry with two dots. **Features:** Aluminum alloy frame, stainless slide (M3913) or blue steel slide (M3914). Bobbed hammer with no half-cock notch; smooth .304" trigger with rounded edges. Straight backstrap. Equipment rail. Extra magazine included. Introduced 1989.
Price: **$760.00**

Smith & Wesson Model 3913-LS LadySmith Auto

Similar to the standard Model 3913 except has frame that is upswept at the front, rounded trigger guard. Comes in frosted stainless steel with matching gray grips. Grips are ergonomically correct for a woman's hand. Novak LoMount Carry rear sight adjustable for windage, smooth edges for snag resistance. Extra magazine included. Introduced 1990.
Price: **$782.00**

Smith & Wesson Model 3953 DAO Pistol

Same as the Model 3913 except double-action-only. Model 3953 has stainless slide with alloy frame. Overall length 7"; weighs 25.5 oz. Extra magazine included. Equipment rail. Introduced 1990.
Price: **$760.00**

Smith & Wesson Model 3913TSW/3953TSW Auto Pistols

Similar to the Model 3913 and 3953 except TSW guns have tighter tolerances, ambidextrous manual safety/decocking lever, flush-fit magazine, delayed-unlock firing system; magazine disconnector. Compact alloy frame, stainless steel slide. Straight backstrap. Introduced 1998. Made in U.S.A. by Smith & Wesson.
Price: Single action/double action **$760.00**
Price: Double action only **$760.00**

SMITH & WESSON MODEL 4006 TDA AUTO

Caliber: 40 S&W, 10-shot magazine. **Barrel:** 4". **Weight:** 38.5 oz. **Length:** 7-7/8" overall. **Grips:** Xenoy wrap-around with checkered panels. **Sights:** Replaceable post front with white dot, Novak LoMount Carry fixed rear with two white dots, or micro. click adjustable rear with two white dots. **Features:** Stainless steel construction with non-reflective finish. Straight backstrap, quipment rail. Extra magazine included. Introduced 1990.
Price: With adjustable sights **$944.00**
Price: With fixed sight. **$907.00**
Price: With fixed night sights **$1,040.00**
Price: With Saf-T-Trigger, fixed sights **$927.00**

SMITH & WESSON MODEL 4006 TSW

Caliber: 40, 10-shot. **Barrel:** 4". **Grips:** Straight back strap grip. **Sights:** Fixed Novak LoMount Carry. **Features:** Traditional double action, ambidextrous safety, Saf-T-Trigger, equipment rail, satin stainless.
Price: **$927.00**

Smith & Wesson Model 4043, 4046 DA Pistols

Similar to the Model 4006 except is double-action-only. Has a semi-bobbed hammer, smooth trigger, 4" barrel; Novak LoMount Carry rear sight, post front with white dot. Overall length is 7-1/2", weighs 28 oz. Model 4043 has alloy frame, equipment rail. Extra magazine included. Introduced 1991.
Price: Model 4043 (alloy frame) **$886.00**
Price: Model 4046 (stainless frame). **$907.00**
Price: Model 4046 with fixed night sights **$1,040.00**

SMITH & WESSON MODEL 4500 SERIES AUTOS

Caliber: 45 ACP, 8-shot magazine. **Barrel:** 5" (M4506). **Weight:** 41 oz. (4506). **Length:** 8-1/2" overall. **Grips:** Xenoy one-piece wrap-around, arched or straight backstrap. **Sights:** Post front with white dot, adjustable or fixed Novak LoMount Carry on M4506. **Features:** M4506 has serrated hammer spur, equipment rail. All have two magazines. Contact Smith & Wesson for complete data. Introduced 1989.
Price: Model 4566 (stainless, 4-1/4", traditional DA, ambidextrous safety, fixed sight) **$942.00**
Price: Model 4586 (stainless, 4-1/4", DA only) **$942.00**
New!!! Price: Model 4566 (stainless, 4-1/4" with Saf-T-Trigger, fixed sight) **$961.00**

Smith & Wesson 4566 TSW

Smith & Wesson Sigma SW40V

Smith & Wesson 4553 TSW

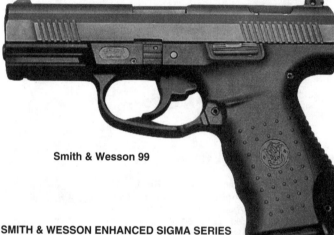

Smith & Wesson 99

SMITH & WESSON MODEL 4513TSW/4553TSW PISTOLS

Caliber: 45 ACP, 7-shot magazine. **Barrel:** 3-3/4". **Weight:** 28 oz. (M4513TSW). **Length:** 6-7/8 overall. **Grips:** Checkered Xenoy; straight backstrap. **Sights:** White dot front, Novak LoMount Carry 2-Dot rear. **Features:** Model 4513TSW is traditional double action, Model 4553TSW is double action only. TSW series has tighter tolerances, ambidextrous manual safety/decocking lever, flush-fit magazine, delayed-unlock firing system; magazine disconnector. Compact alloy frame, stainless steel slide, equipment rail. Introduced 1998. Made in U.S.A. by Smith & Wesson.
Price: Model 4513TSW. **$924.00**
Price: Model 4553TSW. **$924.00**

SMITH & WESSON MODEL 4566 TSW

Caliber: 45 ACP. **Barrel:** 4-1/4", 8-shot . **Grips:** Straight back strap grip. **Sights:** Fixed Novak LoMount Carry. **Features:** Ambidextrous safety, equipment rail, Saf-T-Trigger, satin stainless finish. Traditional double action.
Price: **$961.00**

SMITH & WESSON MODEL 5900 SERIES AUTO PISTOLS

Caliber: 9mm Para., 10-shot magazine. **Barrel:** 4". **Weight:** 28-1/2 to 37-1/2 oz. (fixed sight); 38 oz. (adjustable sight). **Length:** 7-1/2" overall. **Grips:** Xenoy wrap-around with curved backstrap. **Sights:** Post front with white dot, fixed or fully adjustable with two white dots. **Features:** All stainless, stainless and alloy or carbon steel and alloy construction. Smooth .304" trigger, .260" serrated hammer. Equipment rail. Introduced 1989.
Price: Model 5906 (stainless, traditional DA, adjustable sight, ambidextrous safety). **$904.00**
Price: As above, fixed sight **$841.00**
Price: With fixed night sights **$995.00**
Price: With Saf-T-Trigger **$882.00**
Price: Model 5946 DAO (as above, stainless frame and slide) . . **$863.00**

SMITH & WESSON ENHANCED SIGMA SERIES DAO PISTOLS

Caliber: 9mm Para., 40 S&W, 10-shot magazine. **Barrel:** 4". **Weight:** 26 oz. **Length:** 7.4" overall. **Grips:** Integral. **Sights:** White dot front, fixed rear; three-dot system. Tritium night sights available. **Features:** Ergonomic polymer frame; low barrel centerline; internal striker firing system; corrosion-resistant slide; Teflon-filled, electroless-nickel coated magazine, equipment rail. Introduced 1994. Made in U.S.A. by Smith & Wesson.
Price: SW9E, 9mm, 4" barrel, black finish, fixed sights **$447.00**
Price: SW9V, 9mm, 4" barrel, satin stainless, fixed night sights. . **$447.00**
Price: SW9VE, 4" barrel, satin stainless, Saf-T-Trigger, fixed sights **$466.00**
Price: SW40E, 40 S&W, 4" barrel, black finish, fixed sights. **$657.00**
Price: SW40V, 40 S&W, 4" barrel, black polymer, fixed sights. . . **$447.00**
Price: SW40VE, 4" barrel, satin stainless, Saf-T-Trigger, fixed sights **$466.00**

SMITH & WESSON MODEL CS9 CHIEF'S SPECIAL AUTO

Caliber: 9mm Para., 7-shot magazine. **Barrel:** 3". **Weight:** 20.8 oz. **Length:** 6-1/4" overall. **Grips:** Hogue wrap-around rubber. **Sights:** White dot front, fixed two-dot rear. **Features:** Traditional double-action trigger mechanism. Alloy frame, stainless or blued slide. Ambidextrous safety. Introduced 1999. Made in U.S.A. by Smith & Wesson.
Price: Blue or stainless. **$680.00**

Smith & Wesson Model CS40 Chief's Special Auto

Similar to CS9, chambered for 40 S&W (7-shot magazine), 3-1/4" barrel, weighs 24.2 oz., measures 6-1/2" overall. Introduced 1999. Made in U.S.A. by Smith & Wesson.
Price: Blue or stainless. **$717.00**

Springfield 1911A1 Standard

Springfield Full-Size 1911A1

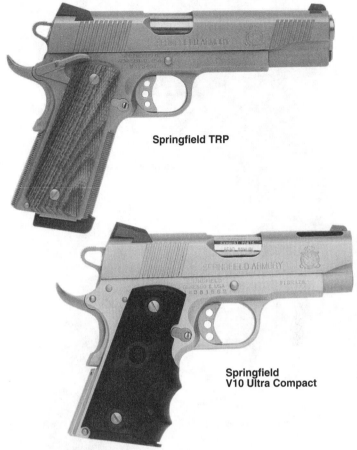

Springfield TRP

Springfield
V10 Ultra Compact

Smith & Wesson Model CS45 Chief's Special Auto

Similar to CS40, chambered for 45 ACP, 6-shot magazine, weighs 23.9 oz. Introduced 1999. Made in U.S.A. by Smith & Wesson.
Price: Blue or stainless **$717.00**

SMITH & WESSON MODEL 99

Caliber: 9mm Para. 4" barrel; 40 S&W 4-1/8" barrel; 10-shot, adj. sights.
Features: Traditional double action satin stainless, black polymer frame, equipment rail, Saf-T-Trigger.
Price: 4" barrel **$648.00**
Price: 4-1/8" barrel **$648.00**

SPRINGFIELD, INC. FULL-SIZE 1911A1 AUTO PISTOL

Caliber: 9mm Para., 9-shot; 38 Super, 9-shot; 40 S&W, 9-shot; 45 ACP, 7-shot. **Barrel:** 5". **Weight:** 35.6 oz. **Length:** 8-5/8" overall. **Grips:** Cocobolo. **Sights:** Fixed three-dot system. **Features:** Beveled magazine well; lowered and flared ejection port. All forged parts, including frame, barrel, slide. All new production. Introduced 1990. From Springfield, Inc.
Price: Mil-Spec 45 ACP, Parkerized **$559.00**
Price: Standard, 45 ACP, blued, Novak sights **$824.00**
Price: Standard, 45 ACP, stainless, Novak sights **$828.00**
Price: Lightweight 45 ACP (28.6 oz., matte finish, night sights) . . **$877.00**
Price: 40 S&W, stainless **$860.00**
Price: 9mm, stainless **$837.00**

Springfield, Inc. TRP Pistols

Similar to 1911A1 except 45 ACP only, checkered front strap and mainspring housing, Novak Night Sight combat rear sight and matching dovetailed front sight, tuned, polished extractor, oversize barrel link; lightweight speed trigger and combat action job, match barrel and bushing, extended ambidextrous thumb safety and fitted beavertail grip safety. Carry bevel on entire pistol; checkered cocobolo wood grips, comes with two Wilson 7-shot magazines. Frame is engraved "Tactical," both sides of frame with "TRP." Introduced 1998. From Springfield, Inc.
Price: Standard with Armory Kote finish **$1,395.00**
Price: Standard, stainless steel **$1,370.00**

Springfield, Inc. 1911A1 High Capacity Pistol

Similar to Standard 1911A1, available in 45 ACP with 10-shot magazine. Commander-style hammer, walnut grips, beveled magazine well, plastic carrying case. Introduced 1993. From Springfield, Inc.
Price: Mil-Spec 45 ACP **$807.00**
Price: 45 ACP Ultra Compact (3-1/2" bbl.) **$909.00**

Springfield, Inc. 1911A1 V-Series Ported Pistols

Similar to standard 1911A1, scalloped slides with 10, 12 or 16 matching barrel ports to redirect powder gasses and reduce recoil and muzzle flip. Adjustable rear sight, ambi thumb safety, Videki speed trigger, and beveled magazine well. Checkered walnut grips standard. Available in 45 ACP, stainless or bi-tone. Introduced 1992.
Price: V-16 Long Slide, stainless **$1,121.00**
Price: Target V-12, stainless **$878.00**
Price: V-10 (Ultra-Compact, bi-tone) **$853.00**
Price: V-10 stainless **$863.00**

Springfield, Inc. 1911A1 Champion Pistol

Similar to standard 1911A1, slide is 4". Novak Night Sights. Delta hammer and cocobolo grips. Available in 45 ACP only; Parkerized or stainless. Introduced 1989.
Price: Parkerized **$856.00**
Price: Stainless **$870.00**

Springfield Inc. Ultra Compact Pistol

Similar to 1911A1 Compact, shorter slide, 3.5" barrel, beavertail grip safety, beveled magazine well, Novak Low Mount or Novak Night Sights, Videki speed trigger, flared ejection port, stainless steel frame, blued slide, match grade barrel, rubber grips. Introduced 1996. From Springfield, Inc.
Price: Parkerized 45 ACP, Night Sights **$817.00**
Price: Stainless 45 ACP, Night Sights **$884.00**
Price: Lightweight, 9mm, stainless **$870.00**

Springfield X-Treme Duty

Taurus PT92B

Taurus PT 22

Springfield Inc. Long Slide 1911 A1 Pistol

Similar to Full Size model, 6" barrel and slide for increased sight radius and higher velocity, fully adjustable sights, muzzle-forward weight distribution for reduced recoil and quicker shot-to-shot recovery. From Springfield Inc.

Price: Target, 45 ACP, stainless with Night Sights **$1,049.00**
Price: Trophy Match, stainless with adj. sights **$1,452.00**

SPRINGFIELD, INC. MICRO-COMPACT 1911A1 PISTOL

NEW! Caliber: 45 ACP, 6+1 capacity. **Barrel:** 3" 1:16 LH. **Weight:** 24 oz. **Length:** 5.7". **Sights:** Novak LoMount tritium. **Features:** Forged frame and slide, ambi thumb safety, extreme carry bevel treatment, lockable plastic case, 2 magazines.
Price: **$1,060.00**

SPRINGFIELD, INC. X-TREME DUTY

NEW! Caliber: 9mm, 40 S&W, 357 Sig. **Barrel:** 4.08". **Weight:** 22.88 oz. **Length:** 7.2". **Sights:** Dovetail front and rear. **Features:** Lightweight, ultra high-impact polymer frame. Trigger, firing pink and grip safety. Two 10-rod steel easy glide magazines
Price: **$489.00**

STEYR M & S SERIES AUTO PISTOLS

Caliber: 9mm Para., 40 S&W, 357 SIG; 10-shot magazine. **Barrel:** 4" (3.58" for Model S). **Weight:** 28 oz. (22.5 oz. for Model S). **Length:** 7.05" overall (6.53" for Model S). **Grips:** Ultra-rigid polymer. **Sights:** Drift-adjustable, white-outline rear; white-triangle blade front. **Features:** Polymer frame; trigger-drop firing pin, manual and key-lock safeties; loaded chamber indicator; 5.5-lb. trigger pull; 111-degree grip angle enhances natural pointing. Introduced 2000. Imported from Austria by GSI Inc.
Price: Model M (full-sized frame with 4" barrel) **$609.95**
Price: Model S (compact frame with 3.58" barrel) **$609.95**
Price: Extra 10-shot magazines (Model M or S) **$39.00**

TAURUS MODEL PT 22/PT 25 AUTO PISTOLS

Caliber: 22 LR, 8-shot (PT 22); 25 ACP, 9-shot (PT 25). **Barrel:** 2.75". **Weight:** 12.3 oz. **Length:** 5.25" overall. **Grips:** Smooth rosewood or mother-of-pearl. **Sights:** Fixed. **Features:** Double action. Tip-up barrel for loading, cleaning. Blue, nickel, duotone or blue with gold accents. Introduced 1992. Made in U.S.A. by Taurus International.
Price: 22 LR, 25 ACP, blue, nickel or with duo-tone finish
with rosewood grips **$215.00**
Price: 22 LR, 25 ACP, blue with gold trim, rosewood grips **$230.00**
Price: 22 LR, 25 ACP, blue, nickel or duotone finish with checkered
wood grips. **$190.00**
Price: 22 LR, 25 ACP, blue with gold trim, mother of pearl grips . **$230.00**

TAURUS MODEL PT92B AUTO PISTOL

Caliber: 9mm Para., 10-shot mag. **Barrel:** 5". **Weight:** 34 oz. **Length:** 8.5" overall. **Grips:** Checkered rubber, rosewood, mother-of-pearl. **Sights:** Fixed notch rear. Three-dot sight system. Also offered with micrometer-click adjustable night sights. **Features:** Double action, ambidextrous 3-way hammer drop safety, allows cocked & locked carry. Blue, stainless steel, blue with gold highlights, stainless steel with gold highlights, forged aluminum frame, integral key-lock.
Price: Blue . . . . **$575.00 to $670.00**

Taurus Model PT99 Auto Pistol

Similar to PT92, fully adjustable rear sight.
Price: Blue . . . . **$575.00 to $670.00**
Price: 22 Conversion kit for PT 92 and PT99 (includes barrel and slide)
. . . . **$266.00**

TAURUS MODEL PT-100/101 AUTO PISTOL

Caliber: 40 S&W, 10-shot mag. **Barrel:** 5". **Weight:** 34 oz. **Length:** 8-1/2". **Grips:** Checkered rubber, rosewood, mother-of-pearl. **Sights:** 3-dot fixed or adjustable; night sights available. **Features:** Single/double action with three-position safety/decocker. Re-introduced in 2001. Imported by Taurus International.
Price: PT100. . . . . **$575.00 to $670.00**
Price: PT101. . . . . **$595.00 to $610.00**

TAURUS MODEL PT-111 MILLENNIUM AUTO PISTOL

Caliber: 9mm Para., 10-shot mag. **Barrel:** 3.25". **Weight:** 18.7 oz. **Length:** 6.0" overall. **Grips:** Polymer. **Sights:** 3-dot fixed; night sights available. Low profile, three-dot combat. **Features:** Double action only, polymer frame, matte stainless or blue steel slide, manual safety, integral key-lock. Deluxe models with wood grip inserts.
Price: . . . . **$425.00 to $550.00**

Taurus Model PT-111 Millennium Titanium Pistol

Similar to PT-111, titanium slide, night sights.
Price: **$585.00**

TAURUS PT-132 MILLENIUM AUTO PISTOL

Caliber: 32 ACP, 10-shot mag. **Barrel:** 3.25". **Weight:** 18.7 oz. **Grips:** Polymer. **Sights:** 3-dot fixed; night sights available. **Features:** Double action only, polymer frame, matte stainless or blue steel slide, manual safety, integral key-lock action. Introduced 2001.
Price: . . . . **$425.00 to $435.00**

Taurus PT-911

Taurus PT-940

Taurus PT-938

Taurus PT-945

Taurus PT-957

TAURUS PT-138 MILLENIUM SERIES
Caliber: 380 ACP, 10-shot mag. **Barrel:** 3.25". **Weight:** 18.7 oz. **Grips:** Polymer. **Sights:** Fixed 3-dot fixed. **Features:** Double action only, polymer frame, matte stainless or blue steel slide, manual safety, integral key-lock.
Price: . . . . $425.00 to $520.00

TAURUS PT-140 MILLENIUM AUTO PISTOL
Caliber: 40 S&W, 10-shot mag. **Barrel:** 3.25". **Weight:** 18.7 oz. **Grips:** Checkered polymer. **Sights:** 3-dot fixed; night sights available. **Features:** Double-action only; matte stainless or blue steel slide, black polymer frame, manual safety, integral key-lock action. From Taurus International.
Price: . . . . $455.00 to $605.00

TAURUS PT-145 MILLENIUM AUTO PISTOL
Caliber: 45 ACP, 10-shot mag. **Barrel:** 3.27". **Weight:** 23 oz. **Stock:** Checkered polymer. **Sights:** 3-dot fixed; night sights available. **Features:** Double-action only, matte stainless or blue steel slide, black polymer frame, manual safety, integral key-lock. From Taurus International.
Price: . . . . $490.00 to $575.00

TAURUS MODEL PT-911 AUTO PISTOL
Caliber: 9mm Para., 10-shot mag. **Barrel:** 4". **Weight:** 28.2 oz. **Length:** 7" overall. **Grips:** Checkered rubber, rosewood, mother-of-pearl. **Sights:** Fixed, three-dot blue or stainless; night sights optional. **Features:** Double action, semi-auto ambidextrous 3-way hammer drop safety, allows cocked and locked carry. Blue, stainless steel, blue with gold highlights, or stainless steel with gold highlights, forged aluminum frame, integral key-lock.
Price: . . . . $525.00 to $620.00

TAURUS MODEL PT-938 AUTO PISTOL
Caliber: 380 ACP, 10-shot mag. **Barrel:** 3.72". **Weight:** 27 oz. **Length:** 6.5" overall. **Grips:** Checkered rubber. **Sights:** Fixed, three-dot. **Features:** Double action, ambidextrous 3-way hammer drop allows cocked & locked carry. Forged aluminum frame. Integral key-lock. Imported by Taurus International.
Price: Blue $500.00
Price: Stainless. $530.00

TAURUS MODEL PT-940 AUTO PISTOL
Caliber: 40 S&W, 10-shot mag. **Barrel:** 4". **Weight:** 28.2 oz. **Length:** 7.05" overall. **Grips:** Checkered rubber, rosewood or mother-of-pearl. **Sights:** Fixed, three-dot blue or stainless; night sights optional. **Features:** Double action, semi-auto ambidextrous 3-way hammer drop safety, allows cocked & locked carry. Blue, stainless steel, blue with gold highlights, or stainless steel with gold hightlights, forged aluminum frame, integral key-lock.
Price: . . . . $525.00 to $620.00

TAURUS MODEL PT-945 SERIES
Caliber: 45 ACP, 8-shot mag. **Barrel:** 4.25". **Weight:** 28.2/29.5 oz. **Length:** 7.48" overall. **Grips:** Checkered rubber, rosewood or mother-of-pearl. **Sights:** Fixed, three-dot; night sights optional. **Features:** Double-action with ambidextrous 3-way hammer drop safety allows cocked & locked carry. Forged aluminum frame, PT-945C has poarted barrel/slide. Blue, stainless, blue with gold highlights, stainless with gold highlights, integral key-lock. Introduced 1995. Imported by Taurus International.
Price: . . . . $560.00 to $655.00

HANDGUNS

Vektor SP1

Walther PP

Vektor Ultra with Tasco Scope

Walther PPK/S

TAURUS MODEL PT-957 AUTO PISTOL

Caliber: 357 SIG, 10-shot mag. **Barrel:** 4". **Weight:** 28 oz. **Length:** 7" overall. **Grips:** Checkered rubber, rosewood or mother-of-pearl. **Sights:** Fixed, three-dot blue or stainless; night sights optional. **Features:** Double-action, blue, stainless steel, blue with gold accents or stainless with gold accents, ported barrel/slide, three-position safety with decocking lever and ambidextrous safety. Forged aluminum frame, integral key-lock. Introduced 1999. Imported by Taurus International.
Price: . . . . **$525.00 to $620.00**
NEW! Price: Non-ported. . . . . **$525.00 to $535.00**

VEKTOR SP1 SPORT PISTOL

Caliber: 9mm Para., 10-shot mag. **Barrel:** 5 ".**Weight:** 38 oz. **Length:** 9-3/8" overall. **Grips:** Checkered black composition. **Sights:** Combat-type blade front, adjustable rear. **Features:** Single action only with adjustable trigger stop; three-chamber compensator; extended magazine release. Introduced 1999. Imported from South Africa by Vektor USA.
Price: **$829.95**

Vektor SP1 Tuned Sport Pistol

Similar to Vektor Sport, fully adjustable straight trigger, LPA three-dot sight system, and hard nickel finish. Introduced 1999. Imported from South Africa by Vektor USA.
Price: **$1,199.95**

Vektor SP1 Target Pistol

Similar to the Vektor Sport except has 5-7/8" barrel without compensator; weighs 40-1/2 oz.; has fully adjustable straight match trigger; black slide, bright frame. Introduced 1999. Imported from South Africa by Vektor USA.
Price: **$1,299.95**

Vektor SP1, SP2 Ultra Sport Pistols

Similar to the Vektor Target except has three-chamber compensator with three jet ports; strengthened frame with integral beavertail; lightweight polymer scope mount (Weaver rail). Overall length is 11", weighs 41-1/2 oz. Model SP2 is in 40 S&W. Introduced 1999. Imported from South Africa by Vektor USA.
Price: SP1 (9mm). **$2,149.95**
Price: SP2 (40 S&W) **$2,149.95**

VEKTOR SP1 AUTO PISTOL

Caliber: 9mm Para., 40 S&W (SP2), 10-shot magazine. **Barrel:** 4-5/8". **Weight:** 35 oz. **Length:** 8-1/4" overall. **Grips:** Checkered black composition. **Sights:** Combat-type fixed. **Features:** Alloy frame, steel slide; traditional double-action mechanism; matte black finish. Introduced 1999. Imported from South Africa by Vektor USA.
Price: SP1 (9mm). **$599.95**
Price: SP1 with nickel finish **$629.95**
Price: SP2 (40 S&W) **$649.95**

Vektor SP1, SP2 Compact General's Model Pistol

Similar to the 9mm Para. Vektor SP1 except has 4" barrel, weighs 31-1/2 oz., and is 7-1/2" overall. Recoil operated. Traditional double-action mechanism. SP2 model is chambered for 40 S&W. Introduced 1999. Imported from South Africa by Vektor USA.
Price: SP1 (9mm Para.) **$649.95**
Price: SP2 (40 S&W) **$649.95**

VEKTOR CP-1 COMPACT PISTOL

Caliber: 9mm Para., 10-shot magazine. **Barrel:** 4". **Weight:** 25.4 oz. **Length:** 7" overall. **Grips:** Textured polymer. **Sights:** Blade front adjustable for windage, fixed rear; adjustable sight optional. **Features:** Ergonomic grip frame shape; stainless steel barrel; delayed gas-buffered blowback action. Introduced 1999. Imported from South Africa by Vektor USA.
Price: With black slide **$479.95**
Price: With nickel slide **$499.95**
Price: With black slide, adjustable sight **$509.95**
Price: With nickel slide, adjustable sight **$529.95**

WALTHER PP AUTO PISTOL

Caliber: 380 ACP, 7-shot magazine. **Barrel:** 3.86". **Weight:** 23-1/2 oz. **Length:** 6.7" overall. **Grips:** Checkered plastic. **Sights:** Fixed, white markings. **Features:** Double action; manual safety blocks firing pin and drops hammer; chamber loaded indicator on 32 and 380; extra finger rest magazine provided. Imported from Germany by Carl Walther USA.
Price: 380 . . . . **$999.00**

Walther PPK/S American Auto Pistol

Similar to Walther PP except made entirely in the United States. Has 3.27" barrel with 6.1" length overall. Introduced 1980.
Price: 380 ACP only, blue. **$540.00**
Price: As above, 32 ACP or 380 ACP, stainless. **$540.00**

HANDGUNS

Walther PPK

Walther P99

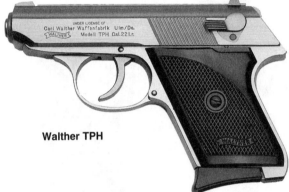

Walther TPH

**Dan Wesson Firearms
Pointman Major**

Walther PPK American Auto Pistol

Similar to Walther PPK/S except weighs 21 oz., has 6-shot capacity. Made in the U.S. Introduced 1986.
Price: Stainless, 32 ACP or 380 ACP **$540.00**
Price: Blue, 380 ACP only **$540.00**

WALTHER MODEL TPH AUTO PISTOL

Caliber: 22 LR, 25 ACP, 6-shot magazine. **Barrel:** 2-1/4". **Weight:** 14 oz. **Length:** 5-3/8" overall. **Grips:** Checkered black composition. **Sights:** Blade front, rear drift-adjustable for windage. **Features:** Made of stainless steel. Scaled-down version of the Walther PP/PPK series. Made in U.S.A. Introduced 1987. From Carl Walther USA.
Price: Blue or stainless steel, 22 or 25 . . . . **$440.00**

WALTHER P88 COMPACT PISTOL

Caliber: 9mm Para., 10-shot magazine. **Barrel:** 3.93". **Weight:** 28 oz. **Grips:** Checkered black polymer. **Sights:** Blade front, drift adjustable rear. **Features:** Double action with ambidextrous decocking lever and magazine release; alloy frame; loaded chamber indicator; matte blue finish. Imported from Germany by Carl Walther USA.
Price: **$900.00**

WALTHER P99 AUTO PISTOL

Caliber: 9mm Para., 9x21, 40 S&W, 10-shot magazine. **Barrel:** 4". **Weight:** 25 oz. **Length:** 7" overall. **Grips:** Textured polymer. **Sights:** Blade front (comes with three interchangeable blades for elevation adjustment), micrometer rear adjustable for windage. **Features:** Double-action mechanism with trigger safety, decock safety, internal striker safety; chamber loaded indicator; ambidextrous magazine release levers; polymer frame with interchangeable backstrap inserts. Comes with two magazines. Introduced 1997. Imported from Germany by Carl Walther USA.
Price: **$799.00**

Walther P990 Auto Pistol

Similar to the P99 except is double action only. Available in blue or silver tenifer finish. Introduced 1999. Imported from Germany by Carl Walther USA.
Price: **$749.00**

WALTHER P-5 AUTO PISTOL

Caliber: 9mm Para., 8-shot magazine. **Barrel:** 3.62". **Weight:** 28 oz. **Length:** 7.10" overall. **Grips:** Checkered plastic. **Sights:** Blade front, adjustable rear. **Features:** Uses the basic Walther P-38 double-action mechanism. Blue finish. Imported from Germany by Carl Walther USA.
Price: **$900.00**

DAN WESSON FIREARMS POINTMAN MAJOR AUTO PISTOL

Caliber: 45 ACP. **Barrel:** 5". **Grips:** Rosewood checkered. **Sights: Features:** Blued or stainless steel frame and serrated slide; Chip McCormick match-grade trigger group, sear and disconnect; match-grade barrel; high-ride beavertail safety; checkered slide release; high rib; interchangeable sight system; laser engraved. Introduced 2000. Made in U.S.A. by Dan Wesson Firearms.
Price: Model PM1-B (blued) **$799.00**
Price: Model PM1-S (stainless) **$799.00**

Dan Wesson Firearms Pointman Seven Auto Pistols

Similar to Pointman Major, dovetail adjustable target rear sight and dovetail target front sight. Available in blued or stainless finish. Introduced 2000. Made in U.S.A. by Dan Wesson Firearms.
Price: PM7 (blued frame and slide) **$999.00**
Price: PM7S (stainless finish). **$1,099.00**

Dan Wesson Firearms Pointman Guardian Auto Pistols

Similar to Pointman Major, more compact frame with 4.25" barrel. Available in blued or stainless finish with fixed or adjustable sights. Introduced 2000. Made in U.S.A. by Dan Wesson Firearms.
Price: PMG-FS, all new frame (fixed sights) **$769.00**
Price: PMG-AS (blued frame and slide, adjustable sights) **$799.00**
Price: PMGD-FS Guardian Duce, all new frame (stainless frame and blued slide, fixed sights) **$829.00**
Price: PMGD-AS Guardian Duce (stainless frame and blued slide, adj. sights). **$799.00**

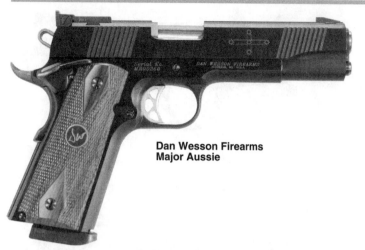

Dan Wesson Firearms Major Aussie

Dan Wesson Firearms Patriot Marksman

Wilkinson Sherry

Dan Wesson Firearms Major Tri-Ops Packs

Similar to Pointman Major. Complete frame assembly fitted to 3 match grade complete slide assemblied (9mm, 10mm, 40 S&W). Includes recoil springs and magazines that come in hard cases fashioned after high-grade European rifle case. Constructed of navy blue cordura stretched over hardwood with black leather trim and comfortable black leather wrapped handle. Brass corner protectors, dual combination locks, engraved presentation plate on the lid. Inside, the Tri-Ops Pack components are nested in precision die-cut closed cell foam and held securely in place by convoluted foam in the inside of the lid. Introduced 2002. Made in U.S.A. by Dan Wesson Firearms.
Price: TOP1B (blued), TOP1-S (stainless) **$2.459.00**

Dan Wesson Firearms Major Aussie

Similar to Pointman Major. Available in 45 ACP. Features Bomar-style adjustable rear target sight, unique slide top configuration exclusive to this model (features radius from the flat side surfaces of the slide to a narrow flat on top and then a small redius and reveal ending in a flat, low (1/16" high) sight rib 3/8" wide with lengthwise serrations). Clearly identified by the Southern Cross flag emblem laser engraved on the sides of the slide (available in 45 ACP only). Introduced 2002. Made in U.S.A. by Dan Wesson Firearms.
Price: PMA-B (blued) **$999.00**
Price: PMA-S (stainless). **$1,099.00**

Dan Wesson Firearms Pointman Minor Auto Pistol

Similar to Pointman Major. Full size (5") entry level IDPA or action pistol model with blued carbon alloy frame and round top slide, bead blast matte finish on frame and slide top and radius, satin-brushed polished finish on sides of slide, chromed barrel, dovetail mount fixed rear target sight and tactical/target ramp front sight, match trigger, skeletonized target hammer, high ride beavertail, fitted extractor, serrations on thumb safety, slide release and mag release, lowered and relieved ejection port, beveled mag well, exotic hardwood grips, serrated mainspring housing, laser engraved. Introduced 2000. Made in U.S.A. by Dan Wesson Firearms.
Price: Model PM2-P **$599.00**

Dan Wesson Firearms Pointman Hi-Cap Auto Pistol

Similar to Pointman Minor, full-size high-capacity (10-shot) magazine with 5" chromed barrel, blued finish and dovetail fixed rear sight. Match adjustable trigger, ambidextrous extended thumb safety, beavertail safety. Introduced 2001. From Dan Wesson Firearms.
Price: PMHC (Pointman High-Cap) **$689.00**

Dan Wesson Firearms Pointman Dave Pruitt Signature Series

Similar to other full-sized Pointman models, customized by Master Pistol-smith and IDPA Grand Master Dave Pruitt. Alloy carbon-steel with black oxide bluing and bead-blast matte finish. Front and rear chevron cocking serrations, dovetail mount fixed rear target sight and tactical/target ramp front sight, ramped match barrel with fitted match bushing and link, Chip McCormick (or equivalent) match grade trigger group, serrated ambidextrous tactical/carry thumb safety, high ride beavertail, serrated slide release and checkered mag release, match grade sear and hammer, fitted

extractor, lowered and relieved ejection port, beveled mag well, full length 2-piece recoil spring guide rod, cocobolo double diamond checkered grips, serrated steel mainspring housing, special laser engraving. Introduced 2001. From Dan Wesson Firearms.
Price: PMDP (Pointman Dave Pruitt) **$899.00**

DAN WESSON FIREARMS PATRIOT 1911 PISTOL

Caliber: 45 ACP. **Grips:** Exotic exhibition grade cocobolo, double diamond hand cut checkering. **Sights:** New innovative combat/carry rear sight that completely encloses the dovetail. **Features:** The new Patriot Expert and Patriot Marksman are full size match grade series 70 1911s machined from steel forgings. Available in blued chome moly steel or stainless steel. Beveled mag well, lowered and flared ejection port, high sweep beavertail safety. Delivery begins in June 2002.
Price: Model PTM-B (blued) **$797.00**
Price: Model PTM-S (stainless) **$898.00**
Price: Model PTE-B (blued) **$864.00**
Price: Model PTE-S (stainless) **$971.00**

WILKINSON SHERRY AUTO PISTOL

Caliber: 22 LR, 8-shot magazine. **Barrel:** 2-1/8". **Weight:** 9-1/4 oz. **Length:** 4-3/8" overall. **Grips:** Checkered black plastic. **Sights:** Fixed, groove. **Features:** Cross-bolt safety locks the sear into the hammer. Available in all blue finish or blue slide and trigger with gold frame. Introduced 1985.
Price: **$280.00**

WILKINSON LINDA AUTO PISTOL

Caliber: 9mm Para. **Barrel:** 8-5/16". **Weight:** 4 lbs., 13 oz. **Length:** 12-1/4" overall. **Grips:** Checkered black plastic pistol grip, walnut forend. **Sights:** Protected blade front, aperture rear. **Features:** Fires from closed bolt. Semi-auto only. Straight blowback action. Cross-bolt safety. Removable barrel. From Wilkinson Arms.
Price: **$675.00**

Includes models suitable for several forms of competition and other sporting purposes.

Baer 1911 Ultimate Master

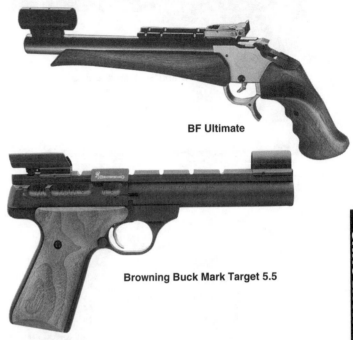

BF Ultimate

Baer 1911 Bullseye Wadcutter

Browning Buck Mark Target 5.5

BAER 1911 ULTIMATE MASTER COMBAT PISTOL

Caliber: 9x23, 38 Super, 400 Cor-Bon 45 ACP (others available), 10-shot magazine. **Barrel:** 5", 6"; Baer NM. **Weight:** 37 oz. **Length:** 8.5" overall. **Grips:** Checkered rosewood. **Sights:** Baer dovetail front, low-mount Bo-Mar rear with hidden leaf. **Features:** Full-house competition gun. Baer forged NM blued steel frame and double serrated slide; Baer triple port, tapered cone compensator; fitted slide to frame; lowered, flared ejection port; Baer reverse recoil plug; full-length guide rod; recoil buff; beveled magazine well; Baer Commander hammer, sear; Baer extended ambidextrous safety, extended ejector, checkered slide stop, beavertail grip safety with pad, extended magazine release button; Baer speed trigger. Made in U.S.A. by Les Baer Custom, Inc.

Price: Compensated, open sights. $2,476.00
Price: 6" Model 400 Cor-Bon $2,541.00

BAER 1911 NATIONAL MATCH HARDBALL PISTOL

Caliber: 45 ACP, 7-shot magazine. **Barrel:** 5". **Weight:** 37 oz. **Length:** 8.5" overall. **Grips:** Checkered walnut. **Sights:** Baer dovetail front with undercut post, low-mount Bo-Mar rear with hidden leaf. **Features:** Baer NM forged steel frame, double serrated slide and barrel with stainless bushing; slide fitted to frame; Baer match trigger with 4-lb. pull; polished feed ramp, throated barrel; checkered front strap, arched mainspring housing; Baer beveled magazine well; lowered, flared ejection port; tuned extractor; Baer extended ejector, checkered slide stop; recoil buff. Made in U.S.A. by Les Baer Custom, Inc.

Price: $1,335.00

Baer 1911 Bullseye Wadcutter Pistol

Similar to National Match Hardball except designed for wadcutter loads only. Polished feed ramp and barrel throat; Bo-Mar rib on slide; full-length recoil rod; Baer speed trigger with 3-1/2-lb. pull; Baer deluxe hammer and sear; Baer beavertail grip safety with pad; flat mainspring housing checkered 20 lpi. Blue finish; checkered walnut grips. Made in U.S.A. by Les Baer Custom, Inc.

Price: From $1,495.00
Price: With 6" barrel, from $1,690.00

BF ULTIMATE SILHOUETTE HB SINGLE SHOT PISTOL

Caliber: 7mm U.S., 22 LR Match and 100 other chamberings. **Barrel:** 10.75" Heavy Match Grade with 11-degree target crown. **Weight:** 3 lbs., 15 oz. **Length:** 16" overall. **Grips:** Thumbrest target style. **Sights:** Bo-Mar/Bond ScopeRib I Combo with hooded post front adjustable for height and width, rear notch available in .032", .062", .080" and .100" widths; 1/2-MOA clicks. **Features:** Designed to meet maximum rules for IHMSA Production Gun. Falling block action gives rigid barrel-receiver mating. Hand fitted and headspaced. Etched receiver; gold-colored trigger. Introduced 1988. Made in U.S.A. by E. Arthur Brown Co. Inc.

Price: $669.00

Classic BF Hunting Pistol

Similar to BF Ultimate Silhouette HB Single Shot Pistol, except no sights; drilled and tapped for scope mount. Barrels from 8 to 15". Variety of options offered. Made in U.S.A. by E. Arthur Brown Co. Inc.

Price: $599.00

BROWNING BUCK MARK SILHOUETTE

Caliber: 22 LR, 10-shot magazine. **Barrel:** 9-7/8". **Weight:** 53 oz. **Length:** 14" overall. **Grips:** Smooth walnut stocks and forend, or finger-groove walnut. **Sights:** Post-type hooded front adjustable for blade width and height; Pro Target rear fully adjustable for windage and elevation. **Features:** Heavy barrel with .900" diameter; 12-1/2" sight radius. Special sighting plane forms scope base. Introduced 1987. Made in U.S.A. From Browning.

Price: $448.00

Browning Buck Mark Target 5.5

Same as Buck Mark Silhouette, 5-1/2" barrel with .900" diameter. Hooded sights mounted on scope base that accepts optical or reflex sight. Rear sight is Browning fully adjustable Pro Target, front sight is adjustable post that customizes to different widths, can be adjusted for height. Contoured walnut grips with thumbrest, or finger-groove walnut. Matte blue finish. Overall length is 9-5/8", weighs 35-1/2 oz. Has 10-shot magazine. Introduced 1990. From Browning.

Price: $425.00
Price: Target 5.5 Gold (as above with gold anodized frame and top rib) $477.00
Price: Target 5.5 Nickel (as above with nickel frame and top rib) $477.00

HANDGUNS

Browning Buck Mark Bullseye

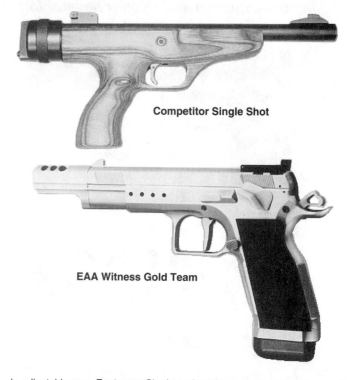

Competitor Single Shot

Colt Gold Cup Trophy

EAA Witness Gold Team

Browning Buck Mark Field 5.5

Same as Target 5.5, hoodless ramp-style front sight and low profile rear sight. Matte blue finish, contoured or finger-groove walnut stocks. Introduced 1991.

Price: **$425.00**

Browning Buck Mark Bullseye

Similar to Buck Mark Silhouette, 7-1/4" heavy barrel with three flutes per side; trigger adjusts from 2-1/2 to 5 lbs.; specially designed rosewood target or three-finger-groove stocks with competition-style heel rest, or with contoured rubber grip. Overall length 11-5/16", weighs 36 oz. Introduced 1996. Made in U.S.A. From Browning.

Price: With ambidextrous moulded composite stocks **$389.00**
Price: With rosewood stocks, or wrap-around finger groove **$500.00**

COLT GOLD CUP MODEL O PISTOL

Caliber: 45 ACP, 8-shot magazine. **Barrel:** 5", with new design bushing. **Weight:** 39 oz. **Length:** 8-1/2". **Grips:** Checkered rubber composite with silver-plated medallion. **Sights:** Patridge-style front, Bomar-style rear adjustable for windage and elevation, sight radius 6-3/4". **Features:** Arched or flat housing; wide, grooved trigger with adjustable stop; ribbed-top slide, hand fitted, with improved ejection port.

Price: Blue **$1,050.00**
Price: Stainless. **$1,116.00**

COMPETITOR SINGLE SHOT PISTOL

Caliber: 22 LR through 50 Action Express, including belted magnums. **Barrel:** 14" standard; 10.5" silhouette; 16" optional. **Weight:** About 59 oz. (14" bbl.). **Length:** 15.12" overall. **Grips:** Ambidextrous; synthetic (standard) or laminated or natural wood. **Sights:** Ramp front, adjustable rear. **Features:** Rotary canon-type action cocks on opening; cammed ejector; interchangeable barrels, ejectors. Adjustable single stage trigger, sliding thumb safety and trigger safety. Matte blue finish. Introduced 1988. From Competitor Corp., Inc.

Price: 14", standard calibers, synthetic grip **$414.95**
Price: Extra barrels, from **$159.95**

CZ 75 CHAMPION COMPETITION PISTOL

Caliber: 9mm Para., 9x21, 40 S&W, 10-shot mag. **Barrel:** 4.49". **Weight:** 35 oz. **Length:** 9.44" overall. **Grips:** Black rubber. **Sights:** Blade front, ful-

ly adjustable rear. **Features:** Single-action trigger mechanism; three-port compensator (40 S&W, 9mm have two port) full-length guide rod; extended magazine release; ambidextrous safety; flared magazine well; fully adjustable match trigger. Introduced 1999. Imported from the Czech Republic by CZ USA.

Price: 9mm Para., 9x21, 40 S&W, dual-tone finish **$1,484.00**

CZ 75 ST IPSC AUTO PISTOL

Caliber: 40 S&W, 10-shot magazine. **Barrel:** 5.12". **Weight:** 2.9 lbs. **Length:** 8.86" overall. **Grips:** Checkered walnut. **Sights:** Fully adjustable rear. **Features:** Single-action mechanism; extended slide release and ambidextrous safety; full-length slide rail; double slide serrations. Introduced 1999. Imported from the Czech Republic by CZ-USA.

Price: Dual-tone finish **$1,038.00**

EAA/BAIKAL IZH35 AUTO PISTOL

Caliber: 22 LR, 5-shot mag. **Barrel:** 6". **Grips:** Walnut; fully adjustable right-hand target-style. **Sights:** Fully adjustable rear, blade front; detachable scope mount. **Features:** Hammer-forged target barrel; machined steel receiver; adjustable trigger; manual slide hold back, grip and manual trigger-bar disconnect safeties; cocking indicator. Introduced 2000. Imported from Russia by European American Armory.

Price: Blued finish. **$539.00**

EAA WITNESS GOLD TEAM AUTO

Caliber: 9mm Para., 9x21, 38 Super, 40 S&W, 45 ACP. **Barrel:** 5.1". **Weight:** 41.6 oz. **Length:** 9.6" overall. **Grips:** Checkered walnut, competition style. **Sights:** Square post front, fully adjustable rear. **Features:** Triple-chamber cone compensator; competition SA trigger; extended safety and magazine release; competition hammer; beveled magazine well; beavertail grip. Hand-fitted major components. Hard chrome finish. Match-grade barrel. From E.A.A. Custom Shop. Introduced 1992. From European American Armory.

Price: **$2,150.00**

EAA Witness Silver Team Auto

Similar to Witness Gold Team, double-chamber compensator, oval magazine release, black rubber grips, double-dip blue finish. Super Sight and drilled and tapped for scope mount. Built for the intermediate competition shooter. Introduced 1992. From European American Armory Custom Shop.

Price: 9mm Para., 9x21, 38 Super, 40 S&W, 45 ACP **$968.00**

Freedom Arms 8322 Silhouette Class

Hammerli SP 20

High Standard Trophy

High Standard Victor

ENTRÉPRISE TOURNAMENT SHOOTER MODEL I

Caliber: 45 ACP, 10-shot mag. **Barrel:** 6". **Weight:** 40 oz. **Length:** 8.5" overall. **Grips:** Black ultra-slim double diamond checkered synthetic. **Sights:** Dovetailed Patridge front, adjustable Competizione "melded" rear. **Features:** Oversized magazine release button; flared magazine well; fully machined parallel slide rails; front and rear slide serrations; serrated top of slide; stainless ramped bull barrel with fully supported chamber; full-length guide rod with plug; stainless firing pin; match extractor; polished ramp; tuned match extractor; black oxide. Introduced 1998. Made in U.S.A. by Entréprise Arms.
Price: **$2,300.00**
Price: TSMIII (Satin chrome finish, two-piece guide rod) **$2,700.00**

EXCEL INDUSTRIES CP-45, XP-45 AUTO PISTOL

Caliber: 45 ACP, 6-shot & 10-shot mags. **Barrel:** 3-1/4". **Weight:** 31 oz. & 25 oz. **Length:** 6-3/8" overall. **Grips:** Checkered black nylon. **Sights:** Fully adjustable rear. **Features:** Stainless steel frame and slide; single action with external hammer and firing pin block, manual thumb safety; last-shot hold open. Includes gun lock and cleaning kit. Introduced 2001. Made in U.S.A. by Excel Industries Inc.
Price: CP-45. . . . . **$425.00**
Price: XP-45 . . . . **$465.00**

FEINWERKEBAU AW93 TARGET PISTOL

Caliber: 22. **Barrel:** 6". **Grips:** Fully adjustable orthopaedic. **Sights:** Fully adjustable micrometer. **Features:** Advanced Russian design with German craftmanship. Imported from Germany by Nygord Precision Products.
Price: **$1,495.00**

FREEDOM ARMS MODEL 8322 FIELD GRADE SILHOUETTE CLASS

Caliber: 22 LR, 5-shot cylinder. **Barrel:** 10". **Weight:** 63 oz. **Length:** 15.5" overall. **Grips:** Black Micarta. **Sights:** Removable patridge front blade; Iron Sight Gun Works silhouette rear, click adjustable for windage and elevation (optional adj. front sight and hood). **Features:** Stainless steel, matte finish, manual sliding-bar safety system; dual firing pins, lightened hammer for fast lock time, pre-set trigger stop. Introduced 1991. Made in U.S.A. by Freedom Arms.
Price: Silhouette Class. **$1,901.75**
Price: Extra fitted 22 WMR cylinder **$264.00**

FREEDOM ARMS MODEL 83 CENTERFIRE SILHOUETTE MODELS

Caliber: 357 Mag., 41 Mag., 44 Mag.; 5-shot cylinder. **Barrel:** 10", 9" (357 Mag. only). **Weight:** 63 oz. (41 Mag.). **Length:** 15.5", 14-1/2" (357 only). **Grips:** Pachmayr Presentation. **Sights:** Iron Sight Gun Works silhouette rear sight, replaceable adjustable front sight blade with hood. **Features:** Stainless steel, matte finish, manual sliding-bar safety system. Made in U.S.A. by Freedom Arms.
Price: Silhouette Models. **$1,634.85**

GAUCHER GP SILHOUETTE PISTOL

Caliber: 22 LR, single shot. **Barrel:** 10". **Weight:** 42.3 oz. **Length:** 15.5" overall. **Grips:** Stained hardwood. **Sights:** Hooded post on ramp front, open rear adjustable for windage and elevation. **Features:** Matte chrome barrel, blued bolt and sights. Other barrel lengths available on special order. Introduced 1991. Imported by Mandall Shooting Supplies.
Price: **$425.00**

HAMMERLI SP 20 TARGET PISTOL

Caliber: 22 LR, 32 S&W. **Barrel:** 4.6". **Weight:** 34.6-41.8 oz. **Length:** 11.8" overall. **Grips:** Anatomically shaped synthetic Hi-Grip available in five sizes. **Sights:** Integral front in three widths, adjustable rear with changeable notch widths. **Features:** Extremely low-level sight line; anatomically shaped trigger; adjustable JPS buffer system for different recoil characteristics. Receiver available in red, blue, gold, violet or black. Introduced 1998. Imported from Switzerland by SIGARMS, Inc and Hammerli Pistols USA.
Price: Hammerli 22 LR **$1,668.00**
Price: Hammerli 32 S&W **$1,743.00**

HARRIS GUNWORKS SIGNATURE JR. LONG RANGE PISTOL

Caliber: Any suitable caliber. **Barrel:** To customer specs. **Weight:** 5 lbs. **Stock:** Gunworks fiberglass. **Sights:** None furnished; comes with scope rings. **Features:** Right- or left-hand benchrest action of titanium or stainless steel; single shot or repeater. Comes with bipod. Introduced 1992. Made in U.S.A. by Harris Gunworks, Inc.
Price: **$2,700.00**

HIGH STANDARD TROPHY TARGET PISTOL

Caliber: 22 LR, 10-shot mag. **Barrel:** 5-1/2" bull or 7-1/4" fluted. **Weight:** 44 oz. **Length:** 9.5" overall. **Stock:** Checkered hardwood with thumbrest. **Sights:** Undercut ramp front, frame-mounted micro-click rear adjustable for windage and elevation; drilled and tapped for scope mounting. **Features:** Gold-plated trigger, slide lock, safety-lever and magazine release; stippled front grip and backstrap; adjustable trigger and sear. Barrel weights optional. From High Standard Manufacturing Co., Inc.
Price: 5-1/2", scope base **$540.00**
Price: 7.25" **$689.00**
Price: 7.25", scope base **$625.00**

HIGH STANDARD VICTOR TARGET PISTOL

Caliber: 22 LR, 10-shot magazine. **Barrel:** 4-1/2" or 5-1/2"; push-button takedown. **Weight:** 46 oz. **Length:** 9.5" overall. **Stock:** Checkered hardwood with thumbrest. **Sights:** Undercut ramp front, micro-click rear adjustable for windage and elevation. Also available with scope mount, rings, no sights. **Features:** Stainless steel construction. Full-length vent rib. Gold-plated trigger, slide lock, safety-lever and magazine release; stippled front grip and backstrap; polished slide; adjustable trigger and sear. Comes with barrel weight. From High Standard Manufacturing Co., Inc.
Price: 4-1/2" scope base **$564.00**
Price: 5-1/2", sights **$625.00**
Price: 5-1/2" scope base **$564.00**

Ruger Mark II Bull Barrel - MK10

Safari Arms Big Deuce

KIMBER SUPER MATCH AUTO PISTOL
Caliber: 45 ACP, 7-shot magazine. **Barrel:** 5". **Weight:** 38 oz. **Length:** 18.7" overall. **Sights:** Blade front, Kimber fully adjustable rear. **Features:** Guaranteed to have shot 3" group at 50 yards. Stainless steel frame, black KimPro slide; two-piece magazine well; premium aluminum match-grade trigger; 30 lpi front strap checkering; stainless match-grade barrel; ambidextrous safety; special Custom Shop markings. Introduced 1999. Made in U.S.A. by Kimber Mfg., Inc.
Price: **$1,927.00**

MORINI MODEL 84E FREE PISTOL
Caliber: 22 LR, single shot. **Barrel:** 11.4". **Weight:** 43.7 oz. **Length:** 19.4" overall. **Grips:** Adjustable match type with stippled surfaces. **Sights:** Interchangeable blade front, match-type fully adjustable rear. **Features:** Fully adjustable electronic trigger. Introduced 1995. Imported from Switzerland by Nygord Precision Products.
Price: **$1,450.00**

PARDINI MODEL SP, HP TARGET PISTOLS
Caliber: 22 LR, 32 S&W, 5-shot magazine. **Barrel:** 4.7". **Weight:** 38.9 oz. **Length:** 11.6" overall. **Grips:** Adjustable; stippled walnut; match type. **Sights:** Interchangeable blade front, interchangeable, fully adjustable rear. **Features:** Fully adjustable match trigger. Introduced 1995. Imported from Italy by Nygord Precision Products.
Price: Model SP (22 LR) **$950.00**
Price: Model HP (32 S&W) **$1,050.00**

PARDINI GP RAPID FIRE MATCH PISTOL
Caliber: 22 Short, 5-shot magazine. **Barrel:** 4.6". **Weight:** 43.3 oz. **Length:** 11.6" overall. **Grips:** Wrap-around stippled walnut. **Sights:** Interchangeable post front, fully adjustable match rear. **Features:** Model GP Schuman has extended rear sight for longer sight radius. Introduced 1995. Imported from Italy by Nygord Precision Products.
Price: Model GP **$1,095.00**
Price: Model GP Schuman **$1,595.00**
New! Price: Model GP-E Electronic, has special parts **$1,595.00**

PARDINI K22 FREE PISTOL
NEW! **Caliber:** 22 LR, single shot. **Barrel:** 9.8". **Weight:** 34.6 oz. **Length:** 18.7" overall. **Grips:** Wrap-around walnut; adjustable match type. **Sights:** Interchangeable post front, fully adjustable match open rear. **Features:** Removable, adjustable match trigger. Toggle bolt pushes cartridge into chamber. Barrel weights mount above the barrel. New upgraded model introduced in 2002. Imported from Italy by Nygord Precision Products.
Price: **$1,295.00**

PARDINI GT45 TARGET PISTOL
Caliber: 45, 9mm, 40 S&W. **Barrel:** 5", 6". **Grips:** Checkered fore strap. **Sights:** Interchangeable post front, fully adjustable match open rear. **Features:** Ambi-safeties, trigger pull adjustable. Fits Helweg Glock holsters for defense shooters. Imported from Italy by Nygord Precision Products.
Price: 5" **$1,050.00**
Price: 6" **$1,125.00**
Price: Frame mount available . . . . **$75.00 extra**
Price: Slide mount available . . . . **$35.00 extra**

PARDINI/NYGORD "MASTER" TARGET PISTOL
Caliber: 22 cal. **Barrel:** 5-1/2". **Grips:** Semi-wrap-around. **Sights:** Micrometer rear and red dot. **Features:** Elegant NRA "Bullseye" pistol. Superior balance of Pardini pistols. Revolutionary recirpcating internal weight barrel shroud. Imported from Italy by Nygord Precision Products.
Price: **$1,095.00**

RUGER MARK II TARGET MODEL AUTOLOADING PISTOL
Caliber: 22 LR, 10-shot magazine. **Barrel:** 6-7/8". **Weight:** 42 oz. **Length:** 11-1/8" overall. **Grips:** Checkered composition grip panels. **Sights:** .125" blade front, micro-click rear, adjustable for windage and elevation. Sight radius 9-3/8". Plastic case with lock included.
Features: Introduced 1982.
Price: Blued (MK-678) **$349.00**
Price: Stainless (KMK-678) **$439.00**

Ruger Mark II Government Target Model
Same gun as Mark II Target Model except has 6-7/8" barrel, higher sights and is roll marked "Government Target Model" on right side of receiver below rear sight. Identical in all aspects to military model used for training U.S. Armed Forces except for markings. Comes with factory test target, also lockable plastic case. Introduced 1987.
Price: Blued (MK-678G) **$425.00**
Price: Stainless (KMK-678G) **$509.00**

Ruger Stainless Competition Model Pistol
Similar to Mark II Government Target Model stainless pistol, 6-7/8" slab-sided barrel; receiver top is fitted with Ruger scope base of blued, chrome moly steel; has Ruger 1" stainless scope rings for mounting variety of optical sights; checkered laminated grip panels with right-hand thumbrest. Blued open sights with 9-1/4" radius. Overall length 11-1/8", weight 45 oz. Case and lock included. Introduced 1991.
Price: KMK-678GC **$529.00**

Ruger Mark II Bull Barrel
Same gun as Target Model except has 5-1/2" or 10" heavy barrel (10" meets all IHMSA regulations). Weight with 5-1/2" barrel is 42 oz., with 10" barrel, 51 oz. Case with lock included.
Price: Blued (MK-512) **$349.00**
Price: Blued (MK-10) **$357.00**
Price: Stainless (KMK-10) **$445.00**
Price: Stainless (KMK-512) **$439.00**

SAFARI ARMS BIG DEUCE PISTOL
Caliber: 45 ACP, 7-shot magazine. **Barrel:** 6", 416 stainless steel. **Weight:** 40.3 oz. **Length:** 9.5" overall. **Grips:** Smooth walnut. **Sights:** Ramped blade front, LPA adjustable rear. **Features:** Beavertail grip safety; extended thumb safety and slide release; Commander-style hammer. Throated, polished and tuned. Parkerized matte black slide with satin stainless steel frame. Introduced 1995. Made in U.S.A. by Safari Arms, Inc.
Price: **$714.00**

SMITH & WESSON MODEL 41 TARGET
Caliber: 22 LR, 10-shot clip. **Barrel:** 5-1/2", 7". **Weight:** 44 oz. (5-1/2" barrel). **Length:** 9" overall (5-1/2" barrel). **Grips:** Checkered walnut with modified thumbrest, usable with either hand. **Sights:** 1/8" Patridge on ramp base; micro-click rear adjustable for windage and elevation. **Features:** 3/8" wide, grooved trigger; adjustable trigger stop drilled and tapped.
Price: S&W Bright Blue, either barrel **$958.00**

HANDGUNS

Smith & Wesson Model 41

Springfield 1911A1 Trophy Match

Thompson/Center Super 14 Contender

SMITH & WESSON MODEL 22A TARGET PISTOL

Caliber: 22 LR, 10-shot magazine. **Barrel:** 5-1/2" bull. **Weight:** 38.5 oz. **Length:** 9-1/2" overall. **Grips:** Dymondwood with ambidextrous thumbrests and flared bottom or rubber soft touch with thumbrest. **Sights:** Patridge front, fully adjustable rear. **Features:** Sight bridge with Weaver-style integral optics mount; alloy frame, stainless barrel and slide; blue finish. Introduced 1997. Made in U.S.A. by Smith & Wesson.

Price: $367.00
Price: HiViz front sight $387.00

Smith & Wesson Model 22S Target Pistol

Similar to the Model 22A except has stainless steel frame. Introduced 1997. Made in U.S.A. by Smith & Wesson.

Price: $434.00
Price: HiViz front sight $453.00

Springfield, Inc. 1911A1 Trophy Match Pistol

Similar to the 1911A1 except factory accurized, Videki speed trigger, delta hammer; has 4- to 5-1/2-lb. trigger pull, click adjustable rear sight, match-grade barrel and bushing. Comes with cocobolo grips. Introduced 1994. From Springfield, Inc.

Price: Blue $1,148.00
Price: Stainless steel $1,219.00

Springfield, Inc. Expert Pistol

Similar to the Competition Pistol except has triple-chamber tapered cone compensator on match barrel with dovetailed front sight; lowered and flared ejection port; fully tuned for reliability; fitted slide to frame; extended ambidextrous thumb safety, extended magazine release button; beavertail grip safety; Pachmayr wrap-around grips. Comes with two magazines, plastic carrying case. Introduced 1992. From Springfield, Inc.

Price: 45 ACP, Duotone finish $1,724.00
Price: Expert Ltd. (non-compensated) $1,624.00

Springfield, Inc. Distinguished Pistol

Has all the features of the 1911A1 Expert except is full-house pistol with deluxe Bo-Mar low-mounted adjustable rear sight; full-length recoil spring guide rod and recoil spring retainer; checkered frontstrap; S&A magazine well; walnut grips. Hard chrome finish. Comes with two magazines with slam pads, plastic carrying case. From Springfield, Inc.

Price: 45 ACP $2,445.00
Price: Distinguished Limited (non-compensated) $2,345.00

SPRINGFIELD, INC. 1911A1 BULLSEYE WADCUTTER PISTOL

Caliber: 38 Super, 45 ACP. **Barrel:** 5". **Weight:** 45 oz. **Length:** 8.59" overall (5" barrel). **Grips:** Checkered walnut. **Sights:** Bo-Mar rib with undercut blade front, fully adjustable rear. **Features:** Built for wadcutter loads only. Has full-length recoil spring guide rod, fitted Videki speed trigger with 3.5-lb. pull; match Commander hammer and sear; beavertail grip safety; lowered and flared ejection port; tuned extractor; fitted slide to frame; recoil buffer system; beveled and polished magazine well; checkered front strap and steel mainspring housing (flat housing standard); polished and throated National Match barrel and bushing. Comes with two magazines with slam pads, plastic carrying case, test target. Introduced 1992. From Springfield, Inc.

Price: $1,499.00

Springfield, Inc. Basic Competition Pistol

Has low-mounted Bo-Mar adjustable rear sight, undercut blade front; match throated barrel and bushing; polished feed ramp; lowered and flared ejection port; fitted Videki speed trigger with tuned 3.5-lb. pull; fitted slide to frame; recoil buffer system; checkered walnut grips; serrated, arched mainspring housing. Comes with two magazines with slam pads, plastic carrying case. Introduced 1992. From Springfield, Inc.

Price: 45 ACP, blue, 5" only $1,295.00

Springfield, Inc. 1911A1 N.M. Hardball Pistol

Has Bo-Mar adjustable rear sight with undercut front blade; fitted match Videki trigger with 4-lb. pull; fitted slide to frame; throated National Match barrel and bushing, polished feed ramp; recoil buffer system; tuned extractor; Herrett walnut grips. Comes with two magazines, plastic carrying case, test target. Introduced 1992. From Springfield, Inc.

Price: 45 ACP, blue $1,336.00

STI EAGLE 5.0 PISTOL

Caliber: 9mm, 38 & 40 Super, 40 S&W, 10mm, 45 ACP, 45 HP, 10-shot magazine. **Barrel:** 5", bull. **Weight:** 34.5 oz. **Length:** 8.62" overall. **Grips:** Checkered polymer. **Sights:** STI front, Novak or Heine rear. **Features:** Standard frames plus 7 others; adjustable match trigger; skeletonized hammer; extended grip safety with locator pad; match-grade fit of all parts. Many options available. Introduced 1994. Made in U.S.A. by STI International.

Price: $1,794.00

THOMPSON/CENTER SUPER 14 CONTENDER

Caliber: 22 LR, 222 Rem., 223 Rem., 7-30 Waters, 30-30 Win., 357 Rem. Maximum, 44 Mag., single shot. **Barrel:** 14". **Weight:** 45 oz. **Length:** 17-1/4" overall. **Grips:** T/C "Competitor Grip" (walnut and rubber). **Sights:** Fully adjustable target-type. **Features:** Break-open action with auto safety. Interchangeable barrels for both rimfire and centerfire calibers. Introduced 1978.

Price: Blued $520.24
Price: Stainless steel $578.40
Price: Extra barrels, blued $251.06
Price: Extra barrels, stainless steel $278.68

Thompson/Center Super 16 Contender

Same as the T/C Super 14 Contender except has 16-1/4" barrel. Rear sight can be mounted at mid-barrel position (10-3/4" radius) or moved to the rear (using scope mount position) for 14-3/4" radius. Overall length is 20-1/4". Comes with T/C Competitor Grip of walnut and rubber. Available in, 223 Rem., 45-70 Gov't. Also available with 16" vent rib barrel with internal choke, caliber 45 Colt/410 shotshell.

Unique D.E.S. 69U

Wichita Silhouette

Price: Blue $525.95
Price: 45-70 Gov't., blue $531.52
Price: Super 16 Vent Rib, blued $559.70
Price: Extra 16" barrel, blued $245.61
Price: Extra 45-70 barrel, blued $251.08
Price: Extra Super 16 vent rib barrel, blue $278.73

TOZ-35 FREE MATCH PISTOL

Caliber: 22 cal. **Barrel:** 11-1/2". **Grips:** Morini grips. **Sights:** Fully adjustable micrometer. **Features:** Pistol of choice for "Olympic Free Pistol" event. Single shot in wooden case with all tools and spare parts. No longer being made. Imported from Russia by Nygord Precision Products.
Price: $950.00

UNIQUE D.E.S. 32U TARGET PISTOL

Caliber: 32 S&W Long wadcutter. **Barrel:** 5.9". **Weight:** 40.2 oz. **Grips:** Anatomically shaped, adjustable stippled French walnut. **Sights:** Blade front, micrometer click rear. **Features:** Trigger adjustable for weight and position; dry firing mechanism; slide stop catch. Optional sleeve weights. Introduced 1990. Imported from France by Nygord Precision Products.
Price: Right-hand, about $1,350.00
Price: Left-hand, about $1,380.00

UNIQUE D.E.S. 69U TARGET PISTOL

Caliber: 22 LR, 5-shot magazine. **Barrel:** 5.91". **Weight:** 35.3 oz. **Length:** 10.5" overall. **Grips:** French walnut target-style with thumbrest and adjustable shelf; hand-checkered panels. **Sights:** Ramp front, micro. adjustable rear mounted on frame; 8.66" sight radius. **Features:** Meets U.I.T. standards. Comes with 260-gram barrel weight; 100, 150, 350-gram weights available. Fully adjustable match trigger; dry-firing safety device. Imported from France by Nygord Precision Products.
Price: Right-hand, about $1,250.00
Price: Left-hand, about $1,290.00

UNIQUE MODEL 96U TARGET PISTOL

Caliber: 22 LR, 5- or 6-shot magazine. **Barrel:** 5.9". **Weight:** 40.2 oz. **Length:** 11.2" overall. **Grips:** French walnut. Target style with thumbrest and adjustable shelf. **Sights:** Blade front, micrometer rear mounted on frame. **Features:** Designed for Sport Pistol and Standard U.I.T. shooting. External hammer; fully adjustable and movable trigger; dry-firing device. Introduced 1997. Imported from France by Nygord Precision Products.
Price: $1,350.00

WALTHER GSP MATCH PISTOL

Caliber: 22 LR, 32 S&W Long (GSP-C), 5-shot magazine. **Barrel:** 4.22". **Weight:** 44.8 oz. (22 LR), 49.4 oz. (32). **Length:** 11.8" overall. **Grips:** Walnut. **Sights:** Post front, match rear adjustable for windage and elevation. **Features:** Available with either 2.2-lb. (1000 gm) or 3-lb. (1360 gm) trigger. Spare magazine, barrel weight, tools supplied. Imported from Germany by Nygord Precision Products.
Price: GSP, with case $1,495.00
Price: GSP-C, with case $1,595.00

HANDGUNS

Includes models suitable for hunting and competitive courses of fire, both police and international.

Armscor M-200DC

Comanche III

Medusa Model 47

ARMSCOR M-200DC REVOLVER

Caliber: 38 Spec., 6-shot cylinder. **Barrel:** 2-1/2", 4". **Weight:** 22 oz. (2-1/2" barrel). **Length:** 7-3/8" overall (2-1/2" barrel). **Grips:** Checkered rubber. **Sights:** Blade front, fixed notch rear. **Features:** All-steel construction; floating firing pin, transfer bar ignition; shrouded ejector rod; blue finish. Reintroduced 1996. Imported from the Philippines by K.B.I., Inc.

Price: 2-1/2" **$199.99**
Price: 4" **$205.00**

ARMSPORT MODEL 4540 REVOLVER

Caliber: 38 Special. **Barrel:** 4". **Weight:** 32 oz **Length:** 9" overall. **Sights:** Fixed rear, blade front. **Features:** Ventilated rib; blued finish. Imported from Argentina by Armsport Inc.

Price: **$140.00**

COMANCHE I, II, III DA REVOLVERS

Features: Adjustable sights. Blue or stainless finish. Distributed by SGS Importers.

Price: I 22 LR, 6" bbl, 9-shot, blue **$231.95**
Price: I 22LR, 6" bbl, 9-shot, stainless **$248.95**
Price: II 38 Special, 4" bbl, 6-shot, blue **$214.95**
Price: II 38 Special, 4" bbl, 6-shot, stainless **$231.95**
Price: III 357 Mag, 3", 4", 6" bbl, 6-shot, blue **$248.95**
Price: III 357 Mag, 3", 4", 6" bbl, 6-shot, stainless **$264.95**

EAA STANDARD GRADE REVOLVERS

Caliber: 38 Spec., 6-shot; 357 magnum, 6-shot. **Barrel:** 2", 4". **Weight:** 38 oz. (22 rimfire, 4"). **Length:** 8.8" overall (4" bbl.). **Grips:** Rubber with finger grooves. **Sights:** Blade front, fixed or adjustable on rimfires; fixed only on 32, 38. **Features:** Swing-out cylinder; hammer block safety; blue finish. Introduced 1991. Imported from Germany by European American Armory.

Price: 38 Special 2" **$249.00**
Price: 38 Special, 4" **$259.00**
Price: 357 Magnum, 2" **$259.00**
Price: 357 Magnum, 4" **$279.00**

MEDUSA MODEL 47 REVOLVER

Caliber: Most 9mm, 38 and 357 caliber cartridges; 6-shot cylinder. **Barrel:** 2-1/2", 3", 4", 5", 6"; fluted. **Weight:** 39 oz. **Length:** 10" overall (4" barrel). **Grips:** Gripper-style rubber. **Sights:** Changeable front blades, fully adjustable rear. **Features:** Patented extractor allows gun to chamber, fire and extract over 25 different cartridges in the .355 to .357 range, without half-moon clips. Steel frame and cylinder; match quality barrel. Matte blue finish. Introduced 1996. Made in U.S.A. by Phillips & Rogers, Inc.

Price: **$899.00**

ROSSI MODEL 351/352 REVOLVERS

Caliber: 38 Special +P, 5-shot. **Barrel:** 2". **Weight:** 24 oz. **Length:** 6-1/2" overall. **Grips:** Rubber. **Sights:** Blade front, fixed rear. **Features:** Patented key-lock Taurus Security System; forged steel frame handles +P ammunition. Introduced 2001. Imported by BrazTech/Taurus.

Price: Model 351 (blued finish) **$298.00**
Price: Model 352 (stainless finish) **$345.00**

ROSSI MODEL 461/462 REVOLVERS

Caliber: 357 Magnum +P, 6-shot. **Barrel:** 2". **Weight:** 26 oz. **Length:** 6-1/2" overall. **Grips:** Rubber. **Sights:** Fixed. **Features:** Single/double action. Patented key-lock Taurus Security System; forged steel frame handles +P ammunition. Introduced 2001. Imported by BrazTech/Taurus.

Price: Model 461 (blued finish) **$298.00**
Price: Model 462 (stainless finish) **$345.00**

ROSSI MODEL 971/972 REVOLVERS

Caliber: 357 Magnum +P, 6-shot. **Barrel:** 4" , 6". **Weight:** 40-44 oz. **Length:** 8-1/2" or 10-1/2" overall. **Grips:** Rubber. **Sights:** Fully adjustable. **Features:** Single/double action. Patented key-lock Taurus Security System; forged steel frame handles +P ammunition. Introduced 2001. Imported by BrazTech/Taurus.

Price: Model 971 (blued finish, 4" barrel) **$345.00**
Price: Model 972 (stainless steel finish, 6" barrel) **$391.00**

Rossi Model 851

Similar to Model 971/972, chambered for 38 Special +P. Blued finish, 4" barrel. Introduced 2001. From BrazTech/Taurus.

Price: **$298.00**

RUGER GP-100 REVOLVERS

Caliber: 38 Spec., 357 Mag., 6-shot. **Barrel:** 3", 3" full shroud, 4", 4" full shroud, 6", 6" full shroud. **Weight:** 3" barrel—35 oz., 3" full shroud—36 oz., 4" barrel—37 oz., 4" full shroud—38 oz. **Sights:** Fixed; adjustable on 4" full shroud, all 6" barrels. **Grips:** Ruger Santoprene Cushioned Grip with Goncalo Alves inserts. **Features:** Uses action, frame incorporating improvements and features of both the Security-Six and Redhawk revolvers. Full length, short ejector shroud. Satin blue and stainless steel.

Ruger GP161

Ruger KSRH-7

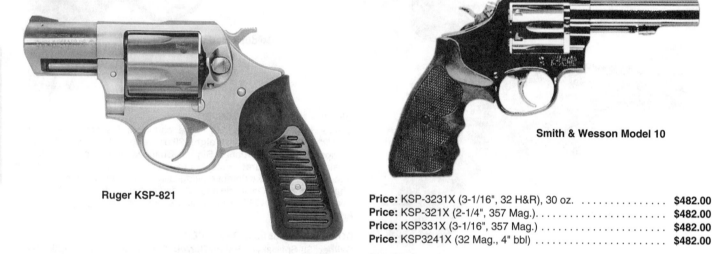

Ruger KSP-821

Smith & Wesson Model 10

Price: GP-141 (357, 4" full shroud, adj. sights, blue) **$499.00**
Price: GP-160 (357, 6", adj. sights, blue) **$499.00**
Price: GP-161 (357, 6" full shroud, adj. sights, blue), 46 oz. **$499.00**
Price: GPF-331 (357, 3" full shroud) **$489.00**
Price: GPF-340 (357, 4") **$489.00**
Price: GPF-341 (357, 4" full shroud) **$489.00**
Price: KGP-141 (357, 4" full shroud, adj. sights, stainless) **$539.00**
Price: KGP-160 (357, 6", adj. sights, stainless), 43 oz. **$539.00**
Price: KGP-161 (357, 6" full shroud, adj. sights, stainless) 46 oz. **$539.00**
Price: KGPF-330 (357, 3", stainless) **$529.00**
Price: KGPF-331 (357, 3" full shroud, stainless) **$529.00**
Price: KGPF-340 (357, 4", stainless), KGPF-840 (38 Special) . . **$529.00**
Price: KGPF-341 (357, 4" full shroud, stainless) **$529.00**
Price: KGPF-840 (38 Special, 4", stainless) **$529.00**

Ruger SP101 Double-Action-Only Revolver
Similar to standard SP101 except double-action-only with no single-action sear notch. Spurless hammer for snag-free handling, floating firing pin and Ruger's patented transfer bar safety system. Available with 2-1/4" barrel in 357 Magnum. Weighs 25 oz., overall length 7.06". Natural brushed satin, high-polish stainless steel. Introduced 1993.
Price: KSP321XL (357 Mag.) **$482.00**

RUGER SP101 REVOLVERS
Caliber: 22 LR, 32 H&R Mag., 6-shot; 38 Spec. +P, 357 Mag., 5-shot. **Barrel:** 2-1/4", 3-1/16", 4". **Weight:** (38 & 357 mag models) 2-1/4"—25 oz.; 3-1/16"—27 oz. **Sights:** Adjustable on 22, 32, fixed on others. **Grips:** Ruger Cushioned Grip with inserts. **Features:** Incorporates improvements and features found in the GP-100 revolvers into a compact, small frame, double-action revolver. Full-length ejector shroud. Stainless steel only. Introduced 1988.
Price: KSP-821X (2-1/4", 38 Spec.) **$482.00**
Price: KSP-831X (3-1/16", 38 Spec.) **$482.00**
Price: KSP-241X (4" heavy bbl., 22 LR), 34 oz. **$482.00**

Price: KSP-3231X (3-1/16", 32 H&R), 30 oz. **$482.00**
Price: KSP-321X (2-1/4", 357 Mag.) **$482.00**
Price: KSP331X (3-1/16", 357 Mag.) **$482.00**
Price: KSP3241X (32 Mag., 4" bbl) **$482.00**

RUGER REDHAWK
Caliber: 44 Rem. Mag., 45 Colt, 6-shot. **Barrel:** 5-1/2", 7-1/2". **Weight:** About 54 oz. (7-1/2" bbl.). **Length:** 13" overall (7-1/2" barrel). **Grips:** Square butt cushioned grip panels. **Sights:** Interchangeable Patridge-type front, rear adjustable for windage and elevation. **Features:** Stainless steel, brushed satin finish, blued ordnance steel. 9-1/2" sight radius. Introduced 1979.
Price: Blued, 44 Mag., 5-1/2" RH-445, 7-1/2" RH-44 . . . . **$585.00**
Price: Blued, 44 Mag., 7-1/2" RH44R, with scope mount, rings . . **$625.00**
Price: Stainless, 44 Mag., KRH445, 5-1/2", 7-1/2" KRH-44 . . . . . **$645.00**
Price: Stainless, 44 Mag., 7-1/2", with scope mount, rings
KRH-44R. **$685.00**
Price: Stainless, 45 Colt, KRH455, 5-1/2", 7-1/2" KRH-45 . . . . . . **$645.00**
Price: Stainless, 45 Colt, 7-1/2", with scope mount and rings
KRH-45R. **$685.00**

Ruger Super Redhawk Revolver
Similar to standard Redhawk except has heavy extended frame with Ruger Integral Scope Mounting System on wide topstrap. Also available 454 Casull and 480 Ruger. Wide hammer spur lowered for better scope clearance. Incorporates mechanical design features and improvements of GP-100. Choice of 7-1/2" or 9-1/2" barrel, both ramp front sight base with Redhawk-style Interchangeable Insert sight blades, adjustable rear sight. Comes with Ruger "Cushioned Grip" panels with wood panels. Target gray stainless steel. Introduced 1987.
Price: KSRH-7 (7-1/2"), KSRH-9 (9-1/2"), 44 Mag **$685.00**
Price: KSRH-7454 (7-1/2") 454 Casull, 9-1/2 KSRH-9454 . . . . . . **$775.00**
Price: KSRH-7480 (7-1/2") 480 Ruger **$775.00**
Price: KSRH-9480 (9-1/2") 480 Ruger **$775.00**

SMITH & WESSON MODEL 10 M&P HB REVOLVER
Caliber: 38 Spec., 6-shot. **Barrel:** 4". **Weight:** 33.5 oz. **Length:** 9-5/16" overall. **Grips:** Uncle Mike's Combat soft rubber; square butt. **Sights:** Fixed; ramp front, square notch rear.
Price: Blue **$496.00**

Smith & Wesson Model 14

Smith & Wesson Model 36LS

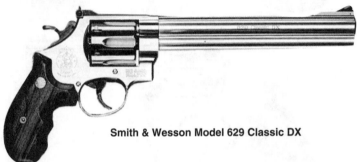

Smith & Wesson Model 629 Classic DX

Smith & Wesson Model 65LS

SMITH & WESSON COMMEMORATIVE MODEL 29

Features: Reflects original Model 29: 6-1/2" barrel, four-screw side plate, over-sized target grips, red vamp front and black blade rear sights, 150th Anniversary logo, engraved, gold-plated, blue, in wood presentation case. Limited.
Price: . . . . **NA**

SMITH & WESSON MODEL 629 REVOLVERS

Caliber: 44 Magnum, 44 S&W Special, 6-shot. **Barrel:** 5", 6", 8-3/8". **Weight:** 47 oz. (6" bbl.). **Length:** 11-3/8" overall (6" bbl.). **Grips:** Soft rubber; wood optional. **Sights:** 1/8" red ramp front, white outline rear, internal lock, adjustable for windage and elevation.
Price: Model 629, 4" **$717.00**
Price: Model 629, 6" **$739.00**
Price: Model 629, 8-3/8" barrel **$756.00**

Smith & Wesson Model 629 Classic Revolver

Similar to standard Model 629, full-lug 5", 6-1/2" or 8-3/8" barrel, chamfered front of cylinder, interchangeable red ramp front sight with adjustable white outline rear, Hogue grips with S&W monogram, frame is drilled and tapped for scope mounting. Factory accurizing and endurance packages. Overall length with 5" barrel is 10-1/2"; weighs 51 oz. Introduced 1990.
Price: Model 629 Classic (stainless), 5", 6-1/2" **$768.00**
Price: As above, 8-3/8" **$793.00**
Price: Model 629 with HiViz front sight **$814.00**

Smith & Wesson Model 629 Classic DX Revolver

Similar to Model 629 Classic, offered only with 6-1/2" or 8-3/8" full-lug barrel, five front sights: red ramp, black Patridge, black Patridge with gold bead, black ramp, black Patridge with white dot, white outline rear sight, adjustable sight, internal lock. Hogue combat-style and wood round butt grip. Introduced 1991.
Price: Model 629 Classic DX, 6-1/2" **$986.00**
Price: As above, 8-3/8" **$1,018.00**

SMITH & WESSON MODEL 37 CHIEF'S SPECIAL & AIRWEIGHT

Caliber: 38 Spec. +P, 5-shot. **Barrel:** 1-7/8". **Weight:** 19-1/2 oz. (2" bbl.); 13-1/2 oz. (Airweight). **Length:** 6-1/2" (round butt). **Grips:** Round butt soft rubber. **Sights:** Fixed, serrated ramp front, square notch rear. Glass beaded finish.
Price: Model 37 . . . . **$523.00**

Smith & Wesson Model 36LS, 60LS LadySmith

Similar to standard Model 36. 1-7/8" barrel, 38 Special. Smooth, contoured rosewood grips with S&W monogram. Speedloader cutout. Comes in a fitted carry/storage case. Introduced 1989.
Price: Model 36LS **$518.00**
Price: Model 60LS, 2-1/8" barrel stainless, 357 Magnum **$566.00**

SMITH & WESSON MODEL 60 CHIEF'S SPECIAL

Caliber: 357 Magnum, 5-shot. **Barrel:** 2-1/8" or 3". **Weight:** 24 oz. **Length:** 7-1/2 overall (3" barrel). **Grips:** Rounded butt synthetic grips. **Sights:** Fixed, serrated ramp front, square notch rear. **Features:** Stainless steel construction. 3" full lug barrel, adjustable sights, internal lock. Made in U.S.A. by Smith & Wesson.
Price: 2-1/8" barrel **$541.00**
Price: 3" barrel **$574.00**

SMITH & WESSON MODEL 65

Caliber: 357 Mag. and 38 Spec., 6-shot. **Barrel:** 4". **Weight:** 34 oz. **Length:** 9-5/16" overall (4" bbl.). **Grips:** Uncle Mike's Combat. **Sights:** 1/8" serrated ramp front, fixed square notch rear. **Features:** Heavy barrel. Stainless steel construction. Internal lock.
Price: **$531.00**

SMITH & WESSON
MODEL 317 AIRLITE, 317 LADYSMITH REVOLVERS

Caliber: 22 LR, 8-shot. **Barrel:** 1-7/8" 3". **Weight:** 9.9 oz. **Length:** 6-3/16" overall. **Grips:** Dymondwood Boot or Uncle Mike's Boot. **Sights:** Serrated ramp front, fixed notch rear. **Features:** Aluminum alloy, carbon and stainless steels, and titanium construction. Short spur hammer, smooth combat trigger. Clear Cote finish. Introduced 1997. Made in U.S.A. by Smith & Wesson.
Price: With Uncle Mike's Boot grip **$550.00**
Price: With DymondWood Boot grip, 3" barrel, HiViz front sight, internal lock **$600.00**
Price: Model 317 LadySmith (DymondWood only, comes with display case) **$596.00**

**Smith & Wesson
Model 317 AirLite**

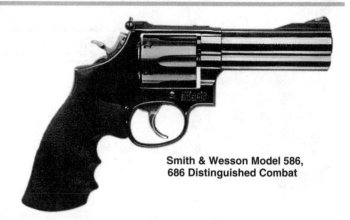

**Smith & Wesson Model 586,
686 Distinguished Combat**

Smith & Wesson Model 637 Airweight Revolver

Similar to the Model 37 Airweight except has alloy frame, stainless steel barrel, cylinder and yoke; rated for 38 Spec. +P; Uncle Mike's Boot Grip. Weighs 15 oz. Introduced 1996. Made in U.S.A. by Smith & Wesson.

Price: **$548.00**

SMITH & WESSON MODEL 64 STAINLESS M&P

Caliber: 38 Spec. +P, 6-shot. **Barrel:** 2", 3", 4". **Weight:** 34 oz. **Length:** 9-5/16" overall. **Grips:** Soft rubber. **Sights:** Fixed, 1/8" serrated ramp front, square notch rear. **Features:** Satin finished stainless steel, square butt.

Price: 2" **$522.00**
Price: 3", 4" **$532.00**

SMITH & WESSON MODEL 65LS LADYSMITH

Caliber: 357 Magnum, 38 Spec. +P, 6-shot. **Barrel:** 3". **Weight:** 31 oz. **Length:** 7.94" overall. **Grips:** Rosewood, round butt. **Sights:** Serrated ramp front, fixed notch rear. **Features:** Stainless steel with frosted finish. Smooth combat trigger, service hammer, shrouded ejector rod. Comes with case. Introduced 1992.

Price: **$584.00**

SMITH & WESSON MODEL 66 STAINLESS COMBAT MAGNUM

Caliber: 357 Mag. and 38 Spec. +P, 6-shot. **Barrel:** 2-1/2", 4", 6". **Weight:** 36 oz. (4" barrel). **Length:** 9-9/16" overall. **Grips:** Soft rubber. **Sights:** Red ramp front, micro-click rear adjustable for windage and elevation. **Features:** Satin finish stainless steel. Internal lock.

Price: 2-1/2" **$590.00**
Price: 4" **$579.00**
Price: 6" **$608.00**

SMITH & WESSON MODEL 67 COMBAT MASTERPIECE

Caliber: 38 Special, 6-shot. **Barrel:** 4". **Weight:** 32 oz. **Length:** 9-5/16" overall. **Grips:** Soft rubber. **Sights:** Red ramp front, micro-click rear adjustable for windage and elevation. **Features:** Stainless steel with satin finish. Smooth combat trigger, semi-target hammer. Introduced 1994.

Price: **$585.00**

Smith & Wesson Model 686 Magnum PLUS Revolver

Similar to the Model 686 except has 7-shot cylinder, 2-1/2", 4" or 6" barrel. Weighs 34-1/2 oz., overall length 7-1/2" (2-1/2" barrel). Hogue rubber grips. Internal lock. Introduced 1996. Made in U.S.A. by Smith & Wesson.

Price: 2-1/2" barrel **$631.00**
Price: 4" barrel **$653.00**
Price: 6" barrel **$663.00**

SMITH & WESSON MODEL 625 REVOLVER

Caliber: 45 ACP, 6-shot. **Barrel:** 5". **Weight:** 46 oz. **Length:** 11.375" overall. **Grips:** Soft rubber; wood optional. **Sights:** Patridge front on ramp, S&W micrometer click rear adjustable for windage and elevation. **Features:** Stainless steel construction with .400" semi-target hammer, .312" smooth combat trigger; full lug barrel. Glass beaded finish. Introduced 1989.

Price: 5" **$745.00**
Price: 4" with internal lock **$745.00**

SMITH & WESSON MODEL 640 CENTENNIAL DA ONLY

Caliber: 357 Mag., 38 Spec. +P, 5-shot. **Barrel:** 2-1/8". **Weight:** 25 oz. **Length:** 6-3/4" overall. **Grips:** Uncle Mike's Boot Grip. **Sights:** Serrated

Smith & Wesson Model 625

ramp front, fixed notch rear. **Features:** Stainless steel. Fully concealed hammer, snag-proof smooth edges. Internal lock. Introduced 1995 in 357 Magnum.

Price: **$599.00**

SMITH & WESSON MODEL 617 K-22 MASTERPIECE

Caliber: 22 LR, 6- or 10-shot. **Barrel:** 4", 6", 8-3/8". **Weight:** 42 oz. (4" barrel). **Length:** NA. **Grips:** Soft rubber. **Sights:** Patridge front, adjustable rear. Drilled and tapped for scope mount. **Features:** Stainless steel with satin finish; 4" has .312" smooth trigger, .375" semi-target hammer; 6" has either .312" combat or .400" serrated trigger, .375" semi-target or .500" target hammer; 8-3/8" with .400" serrated trigger, .500" target hammer. Introduced 1990.

Price: 4" **$644.00**
Price: 6", target hammer, target trigger **$625.00**
Price: 6", 10-shot **$669.00**
Price: 8-3/8", 10 shot **$679.00**

SMITH & WESSON MODEL 610 CLASSIC HUNTER REVOLVER

Caliber: 10mm, 40 S&W, 6-shot cylinder. **Barrel:** 6-1/2" full lug. **Weight:** 52 oz. **Length:** 12" overall. **Grips:** Hogue rubber combat. **Sights:** Interchangeable blade front, micro-click rear adjustable for windage and elevation. **Features:** Stainless steel construction; target hammer, target trigger; unfluted cylinder; drilled and tapped for scope mounting. Introduced 1998.

Price: **$785.00**

SMITH & WESSON MODEL 340 PD AIRLITE Sc CENTENNIAL

Caliber: 357 Magnum, 38 Spec. +P, 5-shot. **Barrel:** 1-7/8". **Grips:** Rounded butt grip. **Sights:** HiViz front. **Features:** Synthetic grip, internal lock. Blue.

Price: **$799.00**

SMITH & WESSON MODEL 360 PD AIRLITE Sc CHIEF'S SPECIAL

Caliber: 357 Magnum, 38 Spec. +P, 5-shot. **Barrel:** 1-7/8". **Grips:** Rounded butt grip. **Sights:** Fixed. **Features:** Synthetic grip, internal lock. Stainless.

Price: Red ramp front **$767.00**
Price: HiViz front **$781.00**

Smith & Wesson
Model 340 PD Airlite Sc

Smith & Wesson Model
386 PD Airlite SC

Smith & Wesson Model 360 PD
Airlite SC Chief's Special

Smith & Wesson Model 442

SMITH & WESSON MODEL 386 PD AIRLITE Sc

Caliber: 357 Magnum, 38 Spec. +P, 7-shot. **Barrel:** 2-1/2". **Grips:** Rounded butt grip. **Sights:** Adjustable, HiViz front. **Features:** Synthetic grip, internal lock.
Price: Blue $815.00

SMITH & WESSON MODEL 331, 332 AIRLITE Ti REVOLVERS

Caliber: 32 H&R Mag., 6-shot. **Barrel:** 1-7/8". **Weight:** 11.2 oz. (with wood grip). **Length:** 6-15/16" overall. **Grips:** Uncle Mike's Boot or Dymondwood Boot. **Sights:** Black serrated ramp front, fixed notch rear. **Features:** Aluminum alloy frame, barrel shroud and yoke; titanium cylinder; stainless steel barrel liner. Matte finish. Introduced 1999. Made in U.S.A. by Smith & Wesson.
Price: Model 331 Chiefs $716.00
Price: Model 332, internal lock $734.00

SMITH & WESSON MODEL 337 CHIEF'S SPECIAL AIRLITE Ti

Caliber: 38 Spec. +P, 5-shot. **Barrel:** 1-7/8". **Weight:** 11.2 oz. (Dymondwood grips). **Length:** 6-5/16" overall. **Grips:** Uncle Mike's Boot or Dymondwood Boot. **Sights:** Black serrated front, fixed notch rear. **Features:** Aluminum alloy frame, barrel shroud and yoke; titanium cylinder; stainless steel barrel liner. Matte finish. Introduced 1999. Made in U.S.A. by Smith & Wesson.
Price: $716.00

SMITH & WESSON MODEL 342 CENTENNIAL AIRLITE Ti

Caliber: 38 Spec. +P, 5-shot. **Barrel:** 1-7/8". **Weight:** 11.3 oz. (Dymondwood stocks). **Length:** 6-15/16" overall. **Grips:** Uncle Mike's Boot or Dymondwood Boot. **Sights:** Black serrated ramp front, fixed notch rear. **Features:** Aluminum alloy frame, barrel shroud and yoke; titanium cylinder; stainless steel barrel liner. Shrouded hammer. Matte finish. Internal lock. Introduced 1999. Made in U.S.A. by Smith & Wesson.
Price: $734.00

Smith & Wesson Model 442 Centennial Airweight

Similar to Model 640 Centennial, alloy frame giving weighs 15.8 oz. Chambered for 38 Special +P, 1-7/8" carbon steel barrel; carbon steel cylinder; concealed hammer; Uncle Mike's Boot grip. Fixed square notch rear sight, serrated ramp front. DA only, glass beaded finish. Introduced 1993.
Price: Blue $547.00

SMITH & WESSON MODEL 638 AIRWEIGHT BODYGUARD

Caliber: 38 Spec. +P, 5-shot. **Barrel:** 1-7/8". **Weight:** 15 oz. **Length:** 6-15/16" overall. **Grips:** Uncle Mike's Boot grip. **Sights:** Serrated ramp front, fixed notch rear. **Features:** Alloy frame, stainless cylinder and barrel; shrouded hammer. Glass beaded finish. Introduced 1997. Made in U.S.A. by Smith & Wesson.
Price: With Uncle Mike's Boot grip $564.00

Smith & Wesson Model 642 Airweight Revolver

Similar to Model 442 Centennial Airweight, stainless steel barrel, cylinder and yoke with matte finish; Uncle Mike's Boot Grip; DA only; weighs 15.8 oz. Introduced 1996. Made in U.S.A. by Smith & Wesson.
Price: $571.00

Smith & Wesson Model 642LS LadySmith Revolver

Same as Model 642 except has smooth combat wood grips, comes with deluxe soft case; Dymondwood grip; aluminum alloy frame, stainless cylinder, barrel and yoke; frosted matte finish. Weighs 15.8 oz. Introduced 1996. Made in U.S.A. by Smith & Wesson.
Price: 1-7/8" $597.00

SMITH & WESSON MODEL 649 BODYGUARD REVOLVER

Caliber: 357 Mag., 38 Spec. +P, 5-shot. **Barrel:** 2-1/8". **Weight:** 20 oz. **Length:** 6-5/16" overall. **Grips:** Uncle Mike's Combat. **Sights:** Black pinned ramp front, fixed notch rear. **Features:** Stainless steel construction; shrouded hammer; smooth combat trigger. Internal lock. Made in U.S.A. by Smith & Wesson.
Price: $594.00

HANDGUNS

Smith & Wesson Model 649

Smith & Wesson Model 696

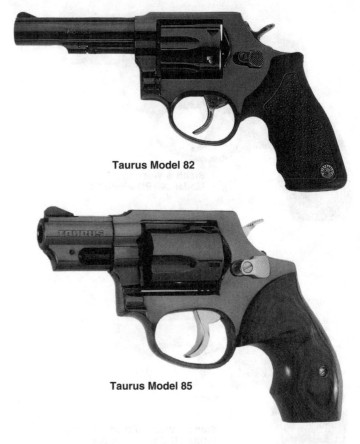

Taurus Model 82

Taurus Model 85

SMITH & WESSON MODEL 657 REVOLVER
Caliber: 41 Mag., 6-shot. **Barrel:** 7-1/2" full lug. **Weight:** 48 oz. **Grips:** Soft rubber. **Sights:** Pinned 1/8" red ramp front, micro-click rear adjustable for windage and elevation. Target hammer, drilled and tapped, unfluted cylinder. **Features:** Stainless steel construction.
Price: **$706.00**

SMITH & WESSON MODEL 696 REVOLVER
Caliber: 44 Spec., 5-shot. **Barrel:** 3". **Weight:** 35.5 oz. **Length:** 8-1/4" overall. **Grips:** Uncle Mike's Combat. **Sights:** Red ramp front, click adjustable white outline rear. **Features:** Stainless steel construction; round butt frame; satin finish. Introduced 1997. Made in U.S.A. by Smith & Wesson.
Price: **$620.00**

NEW! TAURUS MODEL 17 "TRACKER"
Caliber: 17 HMR, 7-shot. **Barrel:** 6". **Weight:** 45.8 oz. **Grips:** Rubber. **Sights:** Adjustable. **Features:** Double action, matte stainless, integral key-lock.
Price: **$391.00**

NEW! TAURUS MODEL 17-12 TARGET "SILHOUETTE"
Caliber: 17 HMR, 7-shot. **Barrel:** 12". **Weight:** 57.8 oz. **Grips:** Rubber. **Sights:** Adjustable. **Features:** Vent rib, double action, adjustable main spring and trigger stop. Matte stainless, integral key-lock.
Price: **$414.00**

NEW! TAURUS MODEL 63
Caliber: 22 LR, 10 + 1 shot. **Barrel:** 23". **Weight:** 97.9 oz. **Grips:** Premium hardwood. **Sights:** Adjustable. **Features:** Auto loading action, round barrel, manual firing pin block, integral security system lock, trigger guard mounted safety, blue or stainless finish.
Price: . . . . **$295.00 to $310.00**

TAURUS MODEL 65 REVOLVER
Caliber: 357 Mag., 6-shot. **Barrel:** 4". **Weight:** 38 oz. **Length:** 10-1/2" overall. **Grips:** Soft rubber. **Sights:** Fixed. **Features:** Double action, integral key-lock. Imported by Taurus International.
Price: Blue or matte stainless. . . . . **$345.00 to $435.00**

Taurus Model 66 Revolver
Similar to Model 65, 4" or 6" barrel, 7-shot cylinder, adjustable rear sight. Integral key-lock action. Imported by Taurus International.
Price: Blue or matte stainless. . . . . **$345.00 to $495.00**

Taurus Model 66 Silhouette Revolver
Similar to Model 6, 12" barrel, 7-shot cylinder, adjustable sight. Integral key-lock action, blue or matte stainless steel finish, rubber grips. Introduced 2001. Imported by Taurus International.
Price: . . . . **$414.00 to $461.00**

TAURUS MODEL 82 HEAVY BARREL REVOLVER
Caliber: 38 Spec., 6-shot. **Barrel:** 4", heavy. **Weight:** 36.5 oz. **Length:** 9-1/4" overall (4" bbl.). **Grips:** Soft black rubber. **Sights:** Serrated ramp front, square notch rear. **Features:** Double action, solid rib, integral key-lock. Imported by Taurus International.
Price: Blue or matte stainless. . . . . **$325.00 to $375.00**

TAURUS MODEL 85 REVOLVER
Caliber: 38 Spec., 5-shot. **Barrel:** 2". **Weight:** 17-24.5 oz., titanium 13.5-15.4 oz. **Grips:** Rubber, rosewood or mother-of-pearl. **Sights:** Ramp front, square notch rear. **Features:** Blue, matte stainless, blue with gold accents, stainless with gold accents; rated for +P ammo. Integral key-lock. Introduced 1980. Imported by Taurus International.
Price: . . . . **$345.00 to $460.00**
Price: Total Titanium. **$530.00**

TAURUS MODEL 94 REVOLVER
Caliber: 22 LR, 9-shot cylinder. **Barrel:** 2", 4", 5". **Weight:** 18.5-27.5 oz. **Grips:** Soft black rubber. **Sights:** Serrated ramp front, click-adjustable rear. **Features:** Double action, integral key-lock. Introduced 1989. Imported by Taurus International.
Price: Blue **$325.00**
Price: Matte stainless **$375.00**
Price: Model 94 UL, forged aluminum alloy, 18-18.5 oz. **$365.00**
Price: As above, stainless **$410.00**

Taurus Model 94UL

Taurus Model 44

Taurus Model 22H Raging Hornet

Taurus Model 415

TAURUS MODEL 22H RAGING HORNET REVOLVER
Caliber: 22 Hornet, 8-shot. **Barrel:** 10". **Weight:** 50 oz. **Length:** 6.5" overall. **Grips:** Soft black rubber. **Sights:** Fully adjustable, scope mount base included. **Features:** Ventilated rib, stainless steel construction with matte finish. Double action, integral key-lock. Introduced 1999. Imported by Taurus International.
Price: **$898.00**

TAURUS MODEL 30C RAGING THIRTY
Caliber: 30 carbine, 8-shot. **Barrel:** 10". **Weight:** 72.3 oz. **Grips:** Soft black rubber. **Sights:** Adjustable. **Features:** Double action, ventilated rib, matte stainless, comes with five "Stellar" full-moon clips, integral key-lock.
Price: **$898.00**

TAURUS MODEL 44 REVOLVER
Caliber: 44 Mag., 6-shot. **Barrel:** 4", 6-1/2", 8-3/8". **Weight:** 44-3/4 oz. **Grips:** Rubber. **Sights:** Adjustable. **Features:** Double action. Integral key-lock. Introduced 1994. Imported by Taurus International.
Price: Blue or stainless steel . . . . **$445.00 to $575.00**

TAURUS MODEL 217 TARGET "SILHOUETTE"
Caliber: 218 Bee, 8-shot. **Barrel:** 12". **Weight:** 52.3 oz. **Grips:** Rubber. **Sights:** Adjustable. **Features:** Double action, ventilated rib, adjustable mainspring and trigger stop, matte stainless, integral key-lock.
Price: **$461.00**

TAURUS MODEL 218 RAGING BEE
Caliber: 218 Bee, 7-shot. **Barrel:** 10". **Weight:** 74.9 oz. **Grips:** Rubber. **Sights:** Adjustable rear. **Features:** Ventilated rib, adjustable action, matte stainless, integral key-lock.
Price: **$898.00**

TAURUS MODEL 415 REVOLVER
Caliber: 41 Mag., 5-shot. **Barrel:** 2-1/2". **Weight:** 30 oz. **Length:** 7-1/8" overall. **Grips:** Rubber. **Sights:** Fixed. **Features:** Stainless steel construction; matte finish; ported barrel. Double action. Integral key-lock. Introduced 1999. Imported by Taurus International.
Price: **$475.00**
Price: Total Titanium **$600.00**

TAURUS MODEL 425/627 TRACKER REVOLVERS
Caliber: 357 Mag., 7-shot; 41 Mag., 5-shot. **Barrel:** 4" and 6". **Weight:** 28.8-40 oz. (titanium) 24.3-28. (6"). **Grips:** Rubber. **Sights:** Fixed front, adjustable rear. **Features:** Double action stainless steel, Shadow Gray or Total Titanium; vent rib (steel models only); integral key-lock action. Imported by Taurus International.
Price: **$500.00**
Price: Total Titanium **$690.00**

TAURUS MODEL 445
Caliber: 44 Special, 5-shot. **Barrel:** 2". **Weight:** 20.3-28.25 oz. **Length:** 6-3/4" overall. **Grips:** Rubber. **Sights:** Ramp front, notch rear. **Features:** Blue or stainless steel. Standard or DAO concealed hammer, optional porting. Introduced 1997. Imported by Taurus International.
Price: . . . . **$345.00 to $500.00**
Price: Total Titanium 19.8 oz. **$600.00**

TAURUS MODEL 455 "STELLAR TRACKER"
Caliber: 45 ACP, 5-shot. **Barrel:** 2", 4", 6". **Weight:** 28/33/38.4 oz. **Grips:** Rubber. **Sights:** Adjustable. **Features:** Double action, matte stainless, includes five "Stellar" full-moon clips, integral key-lock.
Price: **$525.00**

TAURUS MODEL 460 "TRACKER"
Caliber: 45 Colt, 5-shot. **Barrel:** 4" or 6". **Weight:** 33/38.4 oz. **Grips:** Rubber. **Sights:** Adjustable. **Features:** Double action, ventilated rib, matte stainless steel, comes with five "Stellar" full-moon clips.
Price: **$525.00**

TAURUS MODEL 605 REVOLVER
Caliber: 357 Mag., 5-shot. **Barrel:** 2". **Weight:** 24 oz. **Grips:** Rubber. **Sights:** Fixed. **Features:** Double action, blue or stainless, concealed hammer models DAO, porting optional, integral key-lock. Introduced 1995. Imported by Taurus International.
Price: . . . . **$345.00 to $405.00**

HANDGUNS

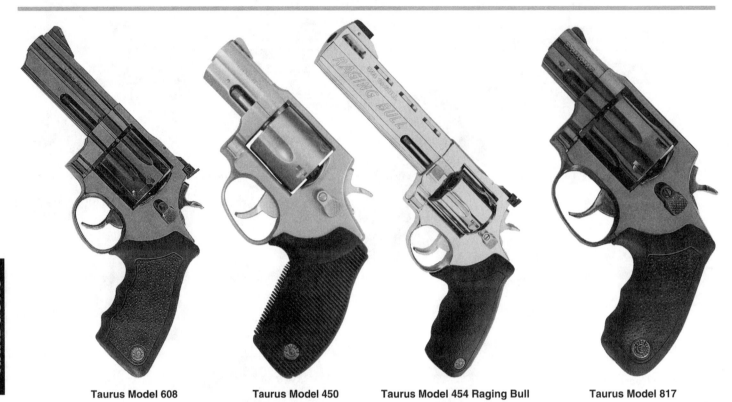

Taurus Model 608   Taurus Model 450   Taurus Model 454 Raging Bull   Taurus Model 817

TAURUS MODEL 608 REVOLVER

Caliber: 357 Mag. 38 Spec., 8-shot. **Barrel:** 4", 6-1/2", 8-3/8". **Weight:** 44-57 oz. **Length:** 9-3/8" overall. **Grips:** Soft black rubber. **Sights:** Adjustable. **Features:** Double action, integral key-lock action. Available in blue or stainless. Introduced 1995. Imported by Taurus International.
Price: . . . . **$445.00 to $575.00**

TAURUS MODEL 650CIA REVOLVER

Caliber: 357 Magnum, 5-shot. **Barrel:** 2". **Weight:** 24.5 oz. **Grips:** Rubber. **Sights:** Ramp front, square notch rear. **Features:** Double-action only, blue or matte stainless steel, integral key-lock, internal hammer. Introduced 2001. From Taurus International.
Price: . . . . **$375.00 to $422.00**

TAURUS MODEL 651CIA REVOLVER

Caliber: 357 Magnum, 5-shot. **Barrel:** 2". **Weight:** 17-24.5 oz. **Grips:** Rubber. **Sights:** Fixed. **Features:** Concealed single action/double action design. Shrouded cockable hammer, blue, matte stainless, Shadow Gray, Total Titanium, integral key-lock.
Price: . . . . **$375.00 to $563.00**

TAURUS MODEL 450 REVOLVER

Caliber: 45 Colt, 5-shot. **Barrel:** 2". **Weight:** 21.2-22.3 oz. **Length:** 6-5/8" overall. **Grips:** Rubber. **Sights:** Ramp front, notch rear. **Features:** Double action, blue or stainless, ported, integral key-lock. Introduced 1999. Imported by Taurus International.
Price: **$470.00**
Price: Ultra-Lite (alloy frame) **$525.00**
Price: Total Titanium, 19.2 oz. **$600.00**

TAURUS MODEL 444/454/480 RAGING BULL REVOLVERS

Caliber: 44 Mag., 45 LC, 454 Casull, 480 Ruger, 5-shot. **Barrel:** 5", 6-1/2", 8-3/8". **Weight:** 53-63 oz. **Length:** 12" overall (6-1/2" barrel). **Grips:** Soft black rubber. **Sights:** Patridge front, adjustable rear. **Features:** Double action, ventilated rib, ported, integral key-lock. Introduced 1997. Imported by Taurus International.
Price: Blue **$785.00**
Price: Matte stainless **$855.00**

TAURUS RAGING BULL MODEL 416

Caliber: 41 Magnum, 6-shot. **Barrel:** 6-1/2". **Weight:** 61.9 oz. **Grips:** Rubber. **Sights:** Adjustable. **Features:** Double action, ported, ventilated rib, matte stainless, integral key-lock.
Price: **$630.00**

TAURUS MODEL 617 REVOLVER

Caliber: 357 Magnum, 7-shot. **Barrel:** 2". **Weight:** 28.3 oz. **Length:** 6-3/4" overall. **Grips:** Soft black rubber. **Sights:** Fixed. **Features:** Double action, blue or matte stainless steel, integral key-lock. Available with porting, concealed hammer. Introduced 1998. Imported by Taurus International.
Price: . . . . **$375.00 to $440.00**
Price: Total Titanium, 19.9 oz. **$600.00**

Taurus Model 617ULT Revolver

Similar to Model 617 except aluminum alloy and titanium components, matte stainless finish, integral key-lock action. Weighs 18.5 oz. Available ported or non-ported. Introduced 2001. Imported by Taurus International.
Price: (5-shot cylinder) . . . . **$530.00 to $545.00**

TAURUS MODEL 817 ULTRA-LITE REVOLVER

Caliber: 38 Spec., 7-shot. **Barrel:** 2". **Weight:** 21 oz. **Length:** 6-1/2" overall. **Grips:** Soft rubber. **Sights:** Fixed. **Features:** Double action, integral key-lock. Introduced 1999. Imported by Taurus International.
Price: Blue **$375.00**
Price: Blue, ported **$395.00**
Price: Matte, stainless **$420.00**
Price: Matte, stainless, ported **$440.00**

TAURUS MODEL 850CIA REVOLVER

Caliber: 38 Special, 5-shot. **Barrel:** 2". **Weight:** 17-24.5 oz. **Grips:** Rubber. **Sights:** Ramp front, square notch rear. **Features:** Double action only, blue or matte stainless steel, rated for +P ammo, integral key-lock, internal hammer. Introduced 2001. From Taurus International.
Price: . . . . **$375.00 to $422.00**
Price: Total Titanium **$563.00**

Taurus Model 941

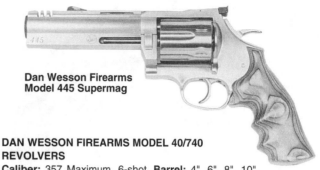

**Dan Wesson Firearms
Model 445 Supermag**

TAURUS MODEL 851CIA REVOLVER
Caliber: 38 Spec., 5-shot. **Barrel:** 2". **Weight:** 17-24.5 oz. **Grips:** Rubber. **Sights:** Fixed-UL/ULT adjustable. **Features:** Concealed single action/double action design. Shrouded cockable hammer, blue, matte stainless, Total Titanium, blue or stainless UL and ULT, integral key-lock. Rated for +P ammo.
Price: . . . . **$375.00 to $563.00**

TAURUS MODEL 941 REVOLVER
Caliber: 22 WMR, 8-shot. **Barrel:** 2", 4", 5". **Weight:** 27.5 oz. (4" barrel). **Grips:** Soft black rubber. **Sights:** Serrated ramp front, rear adjustable. **Features:** Double action, integral key-lock. Introduced 1992. Imported by Taurus International.
Price: Blue **$345.00**
Price: Stainless (matte) **$395.00**
Price: Model 941 Ultra Lite, forged aluminum alloy, 2" **$375.00**
Price: As above, stainless **$425.00**

TAURUS MODEL 970/971 TRACKER REVOLVERS
Caliber: 22 LR (Model 970), 22 Magnum (Model 971); 7-shot. **Barrel:** 6". **Weight:** 53.6 oz. **Grips:** Rubber. **Sights:** Adjustable. **Features:** Double barrel, heavy barrel with ventilated rib; matte stainless finish, integral key-lock. Introduced 2001. From Taurus International.
Price: . . . . **$375.00 to $391.00**

TAURUS MODEL 980/981 SILHOUETTE REVOLVERS
Caliber: 22 LR (Model 980), 22 Magnum (Model 981); 7-shot. **Barrel:** 12". **Weight:** 68 oz. **Grips:** Rubber. **Sights:** Adjustable. **Features:** Double action, heavy barrel with ventilated rib and scope mount, matte stainless finish, integral key-lock. Introduced 2001. From Taurus International.
Price: (Model 980) **$398.00**
Price: (Model 981) **$414.00**

DAN WESSON FIREARMS MODEL 722 SILHOUETTE REVOLVER
Caliber: 22 LR, 6-shot. **Barrel:** 10", vent heavy. **Weight:** 53 oz. **Grips:** Combat style. **Sights:** Patridge-style front, .080" narrow notch rear. **Features:** Single action only. Satin brushed stainless finish. Reintroduced 1997. Made in U.S.A. by Dan Wesson Firearms.
Price: 722 VH10 (vent heavy 10" bbl.) **$888.00**
Price: 722 VH10 SRS1 (Super Ram Silhouette , Bo-Mar sights, front hood, trigger job) **$1,164.00**

DAN WESSON FIREARMS MODEL 3220/73220 TARGET REVOLVER
Caliber: 32-20, 6-shot. **Barrel:** 2.5", 4", 6", 8", 10" standard vent, vent heavy. **Weight:** 47 oz. (6" VH). **Length:** 11.25" overall. **Grips:** Hogue Gripper rubber (walnut, exotic hardwoods optional). **Sights:** Red ramp interchangeable front, fully adjustable rear. **Features:** Bright blue (3220) or stainless (73220). Reintroduced 1997. Made in U.S.A. by Dan Wesson Firearms.
Price: 3220 VH2.5 (blued, 2.5" vent heavy bbl.) **$643.00**
Price: 73220 VH10 (stainless 10" vent heavy bbl.) **$873.00**

DAN WESSON FIREARMS MODEL 40/740 REVOLVERS
Caliber: 357 Maximum, 6-shot. **Barrel:** 4", 6", 8", 10". **Weight:** 72 oz. (8" bbl.). **Length:** 14.3" overall (8" bbl.). **Grips:** Hogue Gripper rubber (walnut or exotic hardwood optional). **Sights:** 1/8" serrated front, fully adjustable rear. **Features:** Blue or stainless steel. Made in U.S.A. by Dan Wesson Firearms.
Price: Blue, 4" **$702.00**
Price: Blue, 6" **$749.00**
Price: Blue, 8" **$795.00**
Price: Blue, 10" **$858.00**
Price: Stainless, 4" **$834.00**
Price: Stainless, 6" **$892.00**
Price: Stainless, 8" slotted **$1,024.00**
Price: Stainless, 10" **$998.00**
Price: 4", 6", 8" Compensated, blue . . . . **$749.00 to $885.00**
Price: As above, stainless . . . . **$893.00 to $1,061.00**

Dan Wesson Firearms Model 414/7414 and 445/7445 SuperMag Revolvers
Similar size and weight as Model 40 revolvers. Chambered for 414 SuperMag or 445 SuperMag cartridge. Barrel lengths of 4", 6", 8", 10". Contact maker for complete price list. Reintroduced 1997. Made in the U.S by Dan Wesson Firearms.
Price: 4", vent heavy, blue or stainless. **$904.00**
Price: 8", vent heavy, blue or stainless. **$1,026.00**
Price: 10", vent heavy, blue or stainless. **$1,103.00**
Price: Compensated models . . . . **$965.00 to $1,149.00**

DAN WESSON FIREARMS MODEL 22/722 REVOLVERS
Caliber: 22 LR, 22 WMR, 6-shot. **Barrel:** 2-1/2", 4", 6", 8" or 10"; interchangeable. **Weight:** 36 oz. (2-1/2"), 44 oz. (6"). **Length:** 9-1/4" overall (4" barrel). **Grips:** Hogue Gripper rubber (walnut, exotic woods optional). **Sights:** 1/8" serrated, interchangeable front, white outline rear adjustable for windage and elevation. **Features:** Built on the same frame as the Wesson 357; smooth, wide trigger with over-travel adjustment, wide spur hammer, with short double-action travel. Available in blue or stainless steel. Reintroduced 1997. Contact Dan Wesson Firearms for complete price list.
Price: 22 VH2.5/722 VH2.5 (blued or stainless 2-1/2" bbl.) **$551.00**
Price: 22VH10/722 VH10 (blued or stainless 10" bbl.) **$750.00**

Dan Wesson 722M Small Frame Revolver
Similar to Model 22/722 except chambered for 22 WMR. Blued or stainless finish, 2-1/2", 4", 6", 8" or 10" barrels.
Price: Blued or stainless finish . . . . **$643.00 to $873.00**

DAN WESSON FIREARMS MODEL 15/715 and 32/732 REVOLVERS
Caliber: 32-20, 32 H&R Mag. (Model 32), 357 Mag. (Model 15). **Barrel:** 2-1/2", 4", 6", 8" (M32), 2-1/2", 4", 6", 8", 10" (M15); vent heavy. **Weight:** 36 oz. (2-1/2" barrel). **Length:** 9-1/4" overall (4" barrel). **Grips:** Checkered, interchangeable. **Sights:** 1/8" serrated front, fully adjustable rear. **Features:** New Generation Series. Interchangeable barrels; wide, smooth trigger, wide hammer spur; short double-action travel. Available in blue or stainless. Reintroduced 1997. Made in U.S.A. by Dan Wesson Firearms. Contact maker for full list of models.
Price: Model 15/715, 2-1/2" (blue or stainless) **$551.00**
Price: Model 15/715, 8" (blue or stainless) **$612.00**
Price: Model 15/715, compensated . . . . **$704.00 to $827.00**
Price: Model 32/732, 4" (blue or stainless) **$674.00**
Price: Model 32/732, 8" (blue or stainless) **$766.00**

Dan Wesson Firearms Model 744 VH8

**Dan Wesson Firearms
Super Ram Silhouette**

Dan Wesson Firearms Alaskan Guide Special

DAN WESSON FIREARMS MODEL 41/741, 44/744 and 45/745 REVOLVERS

Caliber: 41 Mag., 44 Mag., 45 Colt, 6-shot. **Barrel:** 4", 6", 8", 10"; interchangeable; 4", 6", 8" Compensated. **Weight:** 48 oz. (4"). **Length:** 12" overall (6" bbl.) **Grips:** Smooth. **Sights:** 1/8" serrated front, white outline rear adjustable for windage and elevation. **Features:** Available in blue or stainless steel. Smooth, wide trigger with adjustable over-travel, wide hammer spur. Available in Pistol Pac set also. Reintroduced 1997. Contact Dan Wesson Firearms for complete price list.

Price: 41 Mag., 4", vent heavy (blue or stainless) **$643.00**
Price: 44 Mag., 6", vent heavy (blue or stainless) **$689.00**
Price: 45 Colt, 8", vent heavy (blue or stainless) **$766.00**
Price: Compensated models (all calibers) . . . . **$812.00 to $934.00**

DAN WESSON FIREARMS LARGE FRAME SERIES REVOLVERS

Caliber: 41, 741/41 Magnum; 44, 744/44 Magnum; 45, 745/45 Long Colt; 360, 7360/357; 460, 7460/45. **Barrel:** 2"-10". **Weight:** 49 oz.-69 oz. **Grips:** Standard, Hogue rubber Gripper Grips. **Sights:** Standard front, serrated ramp with color insert. Standard rear, adustable wide notch. Other sight options available. **Features:** Available in blue or stainless steel. Smooth, wide trigger with overtravel, wide hammer spur. Double and single action.

Price: . . . . **$769.00 to $889.00**

DAN WESSON FIREARMS MODEL 360/7360 REVOLVERS

Caliber: 357 Mag. **Barrel:** 4", 6", 8", 10"; vent heavy. **Weight:** 64 oz. (8" barrel). **Grips:** Hogue rubber finger groove. **Sights:** Interchangeable ramp or Patridge front, fully adjustable rear. **Features:** New Generation Large Frame Series. Interchangeable barrels and grips; smooth trigger, wide hammer spur. Blue (360) or stainless (7360). Introduced 1999. Made in U.S.A. by Dan Wesson Firearms.

Price: 4" bbl., blue or stainless **$735.00**
Price: 10" bbl., blue or stainless **$873.00**
Price: Compensated models . . . . **$858.00 to $980.00**

DAN WESSON FIREARMS MODEL 460/7460 REVOLVERS

Caliber: 45 ACP, 45 Auto Rim, 45 Super, 45 Winchester Magnum and 460 Rowland. **Barrel:** 4", 6", 8", 10"; vent heavy. **Weight:** 49 oz. (4" barrel). **Grips:** Hogue rubber finger groove; interchangeable. **Sights:** Interchangeable ramp or Patridge front, fully adjustable rear. **Features:** New Generation Large Frame Series. Shoots five cartridges (45 ACP, 45 Auto Rim, 45 Super, 45 Winchester Magnum and 460 Rowland; six half-moon clips for auto cartridges included). Interchangeable barrels and grips. Available with non-fluted cylinder and Slotted Lightweight barrel shroud. Introduced 1999. Made in U.S.A. by Dan Wesson Firearms.

Price: 4" bbl., blue or stainless **$735.00**
Price: 10" bbl., blue or stainless **$888.00**
Price: Compensated models . . . . **$919.00 to $1,042.00**

DAN WESSON FIREARMS STANDARD SILHOUETTE REVOLVERS

Caliber: 357 SuperMag/Maxi, 41 Mag., 414 SuperMag, 445 SuperMag. **Barrel:** 8", 10". **Weight:** 64 oz. (8" barrel). **Length:** 14.3" overall (8" barrel). **Grips:** Hogue rubber finger groove; interchangeable. **Sights:** Patridge front, fully adjustable rear. **Features:** Interchangeable barrels and grips, fluted or non-fluted cylinder, satin brushed stainless finish. Introduced 1999. Made in U.S.A. by Dan Wesson Firearms.

Price: 357 SuperMag/Maxi, 8" **$1,057.00**
Price: 41 Mag., 10" **$888.00**
Price: 414 SuperMag., 8" **$1,057.00**
Price: 445 SuperMag., 8" **$1,057.00**

Dan Wesson Firearms Super Ram Silhouette Revolver

Similar to Standard Silhouette except has 10 land and groove Laser Coat barrel, Bo-Mar target sights with hooded front, special laser engraving. Fluted or non-fluted cylinder. Introduced 1999. Made in U.S.A. by Dan Wesson Firearms.

Price: 357 SuperMag/Maxi, 414 SuperMag., 445 SuperMag., 8", blue or stainless **$1,364.00**
Price: 41 Magnum, 44 Magnum, 8", blue or stainless **$1,241.00**
Price: 41 Magnum, 44 Magnum, 10", blue or stainless **$1,333.00**

DAN WESSON FIREARMS ALASKAN GUIDE SPECIAL

Caliber: 445 SuperMag, 44 Magnum. **Barrel:** Compensated 4" vent heavy barrel assembly. **Features:** Stainless steel with baked on, non-glare, matte black coating, special laser engraving.

Price: Model 7445 VH4C AGS **$995.00**
Price: Model 744 VH4C AGS **$855.00**

Both classic six-shooters and modern adaptations for hunting and sport.

American Frontier 1871-1872 Open-Top

Century Model 100

American Frontier 1851 Mason

Cimarron 1873 Model P

AMERICAN FRONTIER 1851 NAVY CONVERSION

Caliber: 38, 44. **Barrel:** 5-1/2", 7-1/2", octagon. **Grips:** Varnished walnut, Navy size. **Sights:** Blade front, fixed rear. **Features:** Shoots metallic cartridge ammunition. Non-rebated cylinder; blued steel backstrap and trigger guard; color case-hardened hammer, trigger, ramrod, plunger; no ejector rod assembly. Introduced 1996.
Price: $795.00

AMERICAN FRONTIER 1871-1872 OPEN-TOP REVOLVERS

Caliber: 38, 44. **Barrel:** 5-1/2", 7-1/2", 8" round. **Grips:** Varnished walnut. **Sights:** Blade front, fixed rear. **Features:** Reproduction of the early cartridge conversions from percussion. Made for metallic cartridges. High polish blued steel, silver-plated brass backstrap and trigger guard, color case-hardened hammer; straight non-rebated cylinder with naval engagement engraving; stamped with original patent dates. Does not have conversion breechplate.
Price: $795.00

AMERICAN FRONTIER RICHARDS 1860 ARMY

Caliber: 38, 44. **Barrel:** 5-1/2", 7-1/2", round. **Grips:** Varnished walnut, Army size. **Sights:** Blade front, fixed rear. **Features:** Shoots metallic cartridge ammunition. Rebated cylinder; available with or without ejector assembly; high-polish blue including backstrap; silver-plated trigger guard; color case-hardened hammer and trigger. Introduced 1996.
Price: $795.00

American Frontier 1851 Navy Richards & Mason Conversion

Similar to 1851 Navy Conversion except has Mason ejector assembly. Introduced 1996. Imported from Italy by American Frontier Firearms Mfg.
Price: $695.00

CABELA'S MILLENNIUM REVOLVER

Caliber: 45 Colt. **Barrel:** 4-3/4". **Weight:** NA. **Length:** 10" overall. **Grips:** Hardwood. **Sights:** Blade front, hammer notch rear. **Features:** Matte black finish; unpolished brass accents. Introduced 2001. From Cabela's.
Price: $219.99

CENTURY GUN DIST. MODEL 100 SINGLE-ACTION

Caliber: 30-30, 375 Win., 444 Marlin, 45-70, 50-70. **Barrel:** 6-1/2" (standard), 8", 10". **Weight:** 6 lbs. (loaded). **Length:** 15" overall (8" bbl). **Grips:** Smooth walnut. **Sights:** Ramp front, Millett adjustable square notch rear. **Features:** Highly polished high tensile strength manganese bronze frame, blue cylinder and barrel; coil spring trigger mechanism. Contact maker for full price information. Introduced 1975. Made in U.S.A. From Century Gun Dist., Inc.
Price: 6-1/2" barrel, 45-70 . . . . $2,000.00

CIMARRON LIGHTNING SA

Caliber: 38 Special. **Barrel:** 3-1/2", 4-3/4", 5-1/2". **Grips:** Checkered walnut. **Sights:** Blade front. **Features:** Replica of the Colt 1877 Lightning DA. Similar to Cimarron Thunderer™, except smaller grip frame to fit smaller hands. Blue finish with color-case hardened frame. Introduced 2001. From Cimarron F.A. Co.
Price: . . . . $389.00 to $449.00

CIMARRON MODEL "P" JR.

Caliber: 38 Special. **Barrel:** 3-1/2", 4-3/4", 5-1/2". **Grips:** Checkered walnut. **Sights:** Blade front. **Features:** Styled after 1873 Colt Peacemaker, except 20 percent smaller. Blue finish with color-case hardened frame; Cowboy Comp® action. Introduced 2001. From Cimarron F.A. Co.
Price: . . . . $389.00 to $449.00

CIMARRON U.S. CAVALRY MODEL SINGLE-ACTION

Caliber: 45 Colt. **Barrel:** 7-1/2". **Weight:** 42 oz. **Length:** 13-1/2" overall. **Grips:** Walnut. **Sights:** Fixed. **Features:** Has "A.P. Casey" markings; "U.S." plus patent dates on frame, serial number on backstrap, trigger guard, frame and cylinder, "APC" cartouche on left grip; color case-hardened frame and hammer, rest charcoal blue. Exact copy of the original. Imported by Cimarron F.A. Co.
Price: . . . . $499.00 to $539.00

Cimarron Rough Rider Artillery Model Single-Action

Similar to U.S. Cavalry model, 5-1/2" barrel, weighs 39 oz., is 11-1/2" overall. U.S. markings and cartouche, case-hardened frame and hammer; 45 Colt only.
Price: . . . . $499.00 to $539.00

CIMARRON 1872 OPEN TOP REVOLVER

Caliber: 38, 44 Special, 45 S&W Schofield. **Barrel:** 5-1/2" and 7-1/2". **Grips:** Walnut. **Sights:** Blade front, fixed rear. **Features:** Replica of first cartridge-firing revolver. Blue, charcoal blue, nickel or Original® finish; Navy-style brass or steel Army-style frame. Introduced 2001 by Cimarron F.A. Co.
Price: . . . . $469.00 to $509.00

CIMARRON 1873 MODEL P

Caliber: 38 WCF, 357 Mag., 44 WCF, 44 Spec., 45 Colt. **Barrel:** 4-3/4", 5-1/2", 7-1/2". **Weight:** 39 oz. **Length:** 10" overall (4" barrel). **Grips:** Walnut. **Sights:** Blade front, fixed or adjustable rear. **Features:** Uses "old model" blackpowder frame with "Bullseye" ejector or New Model frame. Imported by Cimarron F.A. Co.
Price: . . . . $469.00 to $509.00

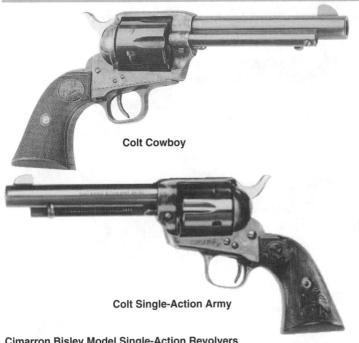

Colt Cowboy

EAA Bounty Hunter

Colt Single-Action Army

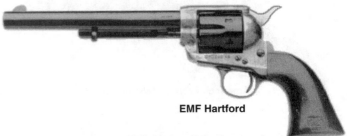

EMF Hartford

Cimarron Bisley Model Single-Action Revolvers

Similar to 1873 Frontier Six Shooter, special grip frame and trigger guard, knurled wide-spur hammer, curved trigger. Available in 357 Mag., 44 WCF, 45 Schofield, 45 Colt. Introduced 1999. Imported by Cimarron F.A. Co.

Price: **$499.00**

Cimarron Flat Top Single-Action Revolvers

Similar to 1873 Frontier Six Shooter, flat top strap with windage-adjustable rear sight, elevation-adjustable front sight. Available in 357 Mag., 44 WCF, 45 Schofield, 45 Colt; 4-3/4", 5-1/2", 7-1/2" barrel. Introduced 1999. Imported by Cimarron F.A. Co.

Price: **$499.00**

Cimarron Bisley Flat Top Revolver

Similar to Flat Top revolver, special grip frame and trigger guard, wide spur hammer, curved trigger. Introduced 1999. Imported by Cimarron F.A. Co.

Price: **$509.00**

CIMARRON THUNDERER REVOLVER

Caliber: 357 Mag., 44 WCF, 45 Colt, 6-shot. **Barrel:** 3-1/2", 4-3/4", 5-1/2", 7-1/2", with ejector. **Weight:** 38 oz. (3-1/2" barrel). **Grips:** Smooth walnut. **Sights:** Blade front, notch rear. **Features:** Thunderer grip; color case-hardened frame with balance blued. Introduced 1993. Imported by Cimarron F.A. Co.

Price: 3-1/2", 4-3/4", smooth grips **$489.00**
Price: As above, checkered grips **$524.00**
Price: 5-1/2", 7-1/2", smooth grips **$529.00**
Price: As above, checkered grips **$564.00**

CIMARRON 1872 OPEN-TOP REVOLVER

Caliber: 38 Spec., 38 Colt, 44 Colt, 44 Russian, 45 Schofield. **Barrel:** 7-1/2". **Grips:** Smooth walnut. **Sights:** Blade front, fixed rear. **Features:** Replica of the original production. Color case-hardened frame, rest blued, including grip frame. Introduced 1999. Imported from Italy by Cimarron F.A. Co.

Price: . . . . **$469.00 to $509.00**

COLT COWBOY SINGLE-ACTION REVOLVER

Caliber: 45 Colt, 6-shot. **Barrel:** 5-1/2". **Weight:** 42 oz. **Grips:** Black composition, first generation style. **Sights:** Blade front, notch rear. **Features:** Dimensional replica of Colt's original Peacemaker with medium-size color case-hardened frame; transfer bar safety system; half-cock loading. Introduced 1998. Made in U.S.A. by Colt's Mfg. Co.

Price: About **$670.00**

COLT SINGLE-ACTION ARMY REVOLVER

Caliber: 44-40, 45 Colt, 6-shot. **Barrel:** 4-3/4", 5-1/2", 7-1/2". **Weight:** 40 oz. (4-3/4" barrel). **Length:** 10-1/4" overall (4-3/4" barrel). **Grips:** Black Eagle composite. **Sights:** Blade front, notch rear. **Features:** Available in full nickel finish with nickel grip medallions, or Royal Blue with color case-hardened frame, gold grip medallions. Reintroduced 1992.

Price: **$1,938.00**

EAA BOUNTY HUNTER SA REVOLVERS

Caliber: 22 LR/22 WMR, 357 Mag., 44 Mag., 45 Colt, 6-shot. **Barrel:** 4-1/2", 7-1/2". **Weight:** 2.5 lbs. **Length:** 11" overall (4-5/8" barrel). **Grips:** Smooth walnut. **Sights:** Blade front, grooved topstrap rear. **Features:** Transfer bar safety; three position hammer; hammer forged barrel. Introduced 1992. Imported by European American Armory.

Price: Blue or case-hardened **$369.00**
Price: Nickel **$399.00**
Price: 22LR/22WMR, blue **$269.00**
Price: As above, nickel **$299.00**

EMF HARTFORD SINGLE-ACTION REVOLVERS

Caliber: 357 Mag., 32-20, 38-40, 44-40, 44 Spec., 45 Colt. **Barrel:** 4-3/4", 5-1/2", 7-1/2". **Weight:** 45 oz. **Length:** 13" overall (7-1/2" barrel). **Grips:** Smooth walnut. **Sights:** Blade front, fixed rear. **Features:** Identical to the original Colts with inspector cartouche on left grip, original patent dates and U.S. markings. All major parts serial numbered using original Colt-style lettering, numbering. Bullseye ejector head and color case-hardening on frame and hammer. Introduced 1990. From E.M.F.

Price: **$500.00**
Price: Cavalry or Artillery **$390.00**
Price: Nickel plated, add **$125.00**
Price: Casehardened New Model frame **$365.00**

EMF 1894 Bisley Revolver

Similar to the Hartford single-action revolver except has special grip frame and trigger guard, wide spur hammer; available in 38-40 or 45 Colt, 4-3/4", 5-1/2" or 7-1/2" barrel. Introduced 1995. Imported by E.M.F.

Price: Casehardened/blue **$400.00**
Price: Nickel **$525.00**

EMF Hartford Pinkerton Single-Action Revolver

Same as the regular Hartford except has 4" barrel with ejector tube and birds head grip. Calibers: 357 Mag., 45 Colt. Introduced 1997. Imported by E.M.F.

Price: **$375.00**

EMF 1894 Bisley

Freedom Arms Model 83 Premier Grade

EMF 1875 Outlaw

Freedom Arms Model 83 Field Grade

EMF 1890 Police

Freedom Arms Model 83 475 Linebaugh

EMF Hartford Express Single-Action Revolver

Same as the regular Hartford model except uses grip of the Colt Lightning revolver. Barrel lengths of 4", 4-3/4", 5-1/2". Introduced 1997. Imported by E.M.F.

Price: **$375.00**

EMF 1875 OUTLAW REVOLVER

Caliber: 357 Mag., 44-40, 45 Colt. **Barrel:** 7-1/2". **Weight:** 46 oz. **Length:** 13-1/2" overall. **Grips:** Smooth walnut. **Sights:** Blade front, fixed groove rear. **Features:** Authentic copy of 1875 Remington with firing pin in hammer; color case-hardened frame, blue cylinder, barrel, steel backstrap and brass trigger guard. Also available in nickel, factory engraved. Imported by E.M.F.

Price: All calibers **$575.00**
Price: Nickel **$735.00**

EMF 1890 Police Revolver

Similar to the 1875 Outlaw except has 5-1/2" barrel, weighs 40 oz., with 12-1/2" overall length. Has lanyard ring in butt. No web under barrel. Calibers 357, 44-40, 45 Colt. Imported by E.M.F.

Price: All calibers **$590.00**
Price: Nickel **$750.00**

FREEDOM ARMS MODEL 83 PREMIER GRADE REVOLVER

Caliber: 357 Mag., 41 Mag., 44 Mag., 454 Casull, 475 Linebaugh, 50 AE, 5-shot. **Barrel:** 4-3/4", 6", 7-1/2", 9" (357 Mag. only), 10". **Weight:** 52.8 oz. **Length:** 13" (7-1/2" bbl.). **Grips:** Impregnated hardwood. **Sights:** Blade front, notch or adjustable rear. **Features:** All stainless steel construction; sliding bar safety system. Lifetime warranty. Made in U.S.A. by Freedom Arms, Inc.

Price: 454 Casull, 475 Linebaugh, 50 AE. **$2,058.00**
Price: 454 Casull, fixed sight **$1,979.00**
Price: 357 Mag., 41 Mag., 44 Mag. **$1,976.00**
Price: 44 Mag., fixed sight **$1,911.00**

Freedom Arms Model 83 Field Grade Revolver

Model 83 frame. Weighs 52-56 oz. Adjustable rear sight, replaceable front blade, matte finish, Pachmayr grips. All stainless steel. Introduced 1992. Made in U.S.A. by Freedom Arms Inc.

Price: 454 Casull, 475 Linebaugh, 50 AE, adj. sights **$1,591.00**
Price: 454 Casull, fixed sights **$1,553.00**
Price: 357 Mag., 41 Mag., 44 Mag. **$1,527.00**

FREEDOM ARMS MODEL 83 VARIMINT CLASS REVOLVERS

Caliber: 22 LR, 5-shot. **Barrel:** 5-1/8, 7-1/2". **Weight:** 58 oz. (7-1/2" bbl.). **Length:** 11-1/2" (7-1/2" bbl.). **Grips:** Impregnated hardwood. **Sights:** Steel base adjustable "V" notch rear sight and replaceable brass bead front sight. **Features:** Stainless steel, matte finish, manual sliding-bar system, dual firing pins, pre-set trigger stop. One year limited warranty to original owner. Made in U.S.A. by Freedom Arms, Inc.

Price: Varmint Class **$1,828.00**
Price: Extra fitted 22 WMR cylinder **$264.00**

Freedom Arms Model 83 Varmint Class

IAR Model 1873 Six Shooter

Freedom Arms Model 97 Premier Grade

IAR Model 1873 Frontier

Heritage Rough Rider

FREEDOM ARMS MODEL 97 PREMIER GRADE REVOLVER
Caliber: 22 LR, 357 Mag., 41 Mag., 45 Colt, 5-shot. **Barrel:** 4-1/2", 5-1/2", 7-1/2", 10". **Weight:** 37 oz. (45 Colt 5-1/2"). **Length:** 10-3/4" (5-1/2" bbl.). **Grips:** Impregnated hardwood. **Sights:** Adjustable rear, replaceable blade front. **Features:** Stainless steel, brushed finish, automatic transfer bar safety system. Introduced in 1997. Made in U.S.A. by Freedom Arms.
Price: 357 Mag., 41 Mag., 45 Colt **$1,668.00**
Price: 357 Mag., 45 Colt, fixed sight **$1,576.00**
Price: Extra fitted cylinders 38 Special, 45 ACP **$264.00**
Price: 22 LR with sporting chambers **$1,732.00**
Price: Extra fitted 22 WMR cylinder **$264.00**
Price: Extra fitted 22 LR match grade cylinder **$476.00**
Price: 22 match grade chamber instead of 22 LR sport chamber
. . . . **$214.00**

HERITAGE ROUGH RIDER REVOLVER
Caliber: 22 LR, 22 LR/22 WMR combo, 6-shot. **Barrel:** 2-3/4", 3-1/2", 4-3/4", 6-1/2", 9". **Weight:** 31 to 38 oz. **Length:** NA. **Grips:** Exotic hardwood, laminated wood or mother of pearl; bird's head models offered. **Sights:** Blade front, fixed rear. Adjustable sight on 6-1/2" only. **Features:** Hammer block safety. High polish blue or nickel finish. Introduced 1993. Made in U.S.A. by Heritage Mfg., Inc.
Price: . . . . **$184.95 to $239.95**

IAR MODEL 1873 SIX SHOOTER
Caliber: 22 LR/22 WMR combo. **Barrel:** 5-1/2". **Weight:** 36-1/2" oz. **Length:** 11-3/8" overall. **Grips:** One-piece walnut. **Sights:** Blade front, notch rear. **Features:** A 3/4-scale reproduction. Color case-hardened frame, blued barrel. All-steel construction. Made by Uberti. Imported from Italy by IAR, Inc.
Price: **$360.00**

IAR Model 1873 Frontier Marshal

IAR MODEL 1873 FRONTIER REVOLVER
Caliber: 22 RL, 22 LR/22 WMR. **Barrel:** 4-3/4". **Weight:** 45 oz. **Length:** 10-1/2" overall. **Grips:** One-piece walnut with inspector's cartouche. **Sights:** Blade front, notch rear. **Features:** Color case-hardened frame, blued barrel, black nickel-plated brass trigger guard and backstrap. Bright nickel and engraved versions available. Introduced 1997. Imported from Italy by IAR, Inc.
Price: **$380.00**
Price: Nickel-plated **$425.00**
Price: 22 LR/22WMR combo **$420.00**

IAR MODEL 1873 FRONTIER MARSHAL
Caliber: 357 Mag., 45 Colt. **Barrel:** 4-3/4", 5-1/2, 7-1/2". **Weight:** 39 oz. **Length:** 10-1/2" overall. **Grips:** One-piece walnut. **Sights:** Blade front, notch rear. **Features:** Bright brass trigger guard and backstrap, color case-hardened frame, blued barrel and cylinder. Introduced 1998. Imported from Italy by IAR, Inc.
Price: **$395.00**

HANDGUNS

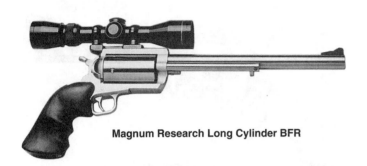

Magnum Research Long Cylinder BFR

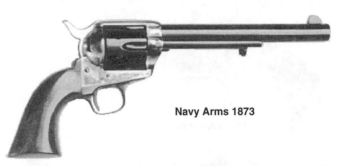

Navy Arms 1873

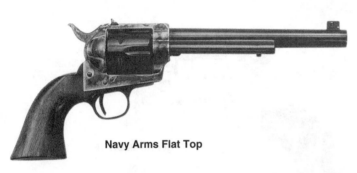

Navy Arms Flat Top

Navy Arms 1875 Schofield

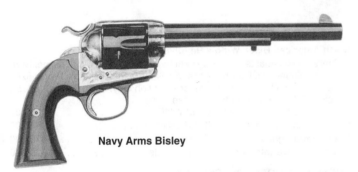

Navy Arms Bisley

Navy Arms New Model Russian

MAGNUM RESEARCH BFR SINGLE-ACTION REVOLVER

(Long cylinder) Caliber: 45/70 Government, 444 Marlin, 45 LC/410, 450 Marlin. **Barrel:** 7.5", 10". **Weight:** 4 lbs., 4.36 lbs. **Length:** 15", 17.5".
(Short cylinder) Caliber: 454 Casull, 22 Hornet, BFR 480/475. **Barrel:** 6.5", 7.5", 10". **Weight:** 3.2 lbs, 3.5 lbs., 4.36 lbs. (10"). **Length:** 12.75 (6"), 13.75", 16.25"
Sights: All have fully adjustable rear, orange blade ramp front. **Features:** Stainless steel construction, all 5-shot (except 45 LC/410 & 22 Hornet are 6-shot). 45 LC/410 with modified choke and wrench, 410 shot shellslug incompatible with 45/70 caliber. Barrels are stress-relieved and cut rifled. Made in U.S.A. From Magnum Research, Inc.
Price: **$999.00**

MAGNUM RESEARCH BFR REVOLVER

Caliber: 22 Hornet, 444 Marlin, 45 LC/410, 450 Marlin, 454 Casull, 45/70, 480 Ruger/475 Linebaugh. **Barrel:** 6-1/2", 7-1/2", 10". **Weight:** 3.2-4.36 lbs. **Length:** 12.75"-17.5". **Grips:** Rubber. **Sights:** Ramp front, adjustable rear. **Features:** Single action, stainless steel construction. Announced 1998. Made in U.S.A. from Magnum Research.
Price: **$999.00**

NAVY ARMS FLAT TOP TARGET MODEL REVOLVER

Caliber: 45 Colt, 6-shot cylinder. **Barrel:** 7-1/2". **Weight:** 40 oz. **Length:** 13-1/4" overall. **Grips:** Smooth walnut. **Sights:** Spring-loaded German silver front, rear adjustable for windage. **Features:** Replica of Colt's Flat Top Frontier target revolver made from 1888 to 1896. Blue with color case-hardened frame. Introduced 1997. Imported by Navy Arms.
Price: **$450.00**

NAVY ARMS BISLEY MODEL SINGLE-ACTION REVOLVER

Caliber: 44-40 or 45 Colt, 6-shot cylinder. **Barrel:** 4-3/4", 5-1/2", 7-1/2". **Weight:** 40 oz. **Length:** 12-1/2" overall (7-1/2" barrel). **Grips:** Smooth walnut. **Sights:** Blade front, notch rear. **Features:** Replica of Colt's Bisley Model. Polished blue finish, color case-hardened frame. Introduced 1997. Imported by Navy Arms.
Price: . . . . **$425.00 to $460.00**

NAVY ARMS 1873 SINGLE-ACTION REVOLVER

Caliber: 357 Mag., 44-40, 45 Colt, 6-shot cylinder. **Barrel:** 4-3/4", 5-1/2", 7-1/2". **Weight:** 36 oz. **Length:** 10-3/4" overall (5-1/2" barrel). **Grips:** Smooth walnut. **Sights:** Blade front, notch rear. **Features:** Blue with color case-hardened frame. Introduced 1991. Imported by Navy Arms.
Price: **$405.00**

NAVY ARMS 1875 SCHOFIELD REVOLVER

Caliber: 44-40, 45 Colt, 6-shot cylinder. **Barrel:** 3-1/2", 5", 7". **Weight:** 39 oz. **Length:** 10-3/4" overall (5" barrel). **Grips:** Smooth walnut. **Sights:** Blade front, notch rear. **Features:** Replica of Smith & Wesson Model 3 Schofield. Single-action, top-break with automatic ejection. Polished blue finish. Introduced 1994. Imported by Navy Arms.
Price: Hideout Model, 3-1/2" barrel **$695.00**
Price: Wells Fargo, 5" barrel. **$695.00**
Price: U.S. Cavalry model, 7" barrel, military markings **$695.00**

NAVY ARMS NEW MODEL RUSSIAN REVOLVER

Caliber: 44 Russian, 6-shot cylinder. **Barrel:** 6-1/2". **Weight:** 40 oz. **Length:** 12" overall. **Grips:** Smooth walnut. **Sights:** Blade front, notch rear. **Features:** Replica of the S&W Model 3 Russian Third Model revolver. Spur trigger guard, polished blue finish. Introduced 1999. Imported by Navy Arms.
Price: **$769.00**

HANDGUNS

HANDGUNS — SINGLE ACTION REVOLVERS

North American Mini

North American Mini-Master

North American Black Widow

Ruger Blackhawk

Ruger KSSMBH-4F

NAVY ARMS 1851 NAVY CONVERSION REVOLVER
Caliber: 38 Spec., 38 Long Colt. **Barrel:** 5-1/2", 7-1/2". **Weight:** 44 oz. **Length:** 14" overall (7-1/2" barrel). **Grips:** Smooth walnut. **Sights:** Bead front, notch rear. **Features:** Replica of Colt's cartridge conversion revolver. Polished blue finish with color case-hardened frame, silver plated trigger guard and backstrap. Introduced 1999. Imported by Navy Arms.
Price: **$165.00**

NAVY ARMS 1860 ARMY CONVERSION REVOLVER
Caliber: 38 Spec., 38 Long Colt. **Barrel:** 5-1/2", 7-1/2". **Weight:** 44 oz. **Length:** 13-1/2" overall (7-1/2" barrel). **Grips:** Smooth walnut. **Sights:** Blade front, notch rear. **Features:** Replica of Colt's conversion revolver. Polished blue finish with color case-hardened frame, full-size 1860 Army grip with blued steel backstrap. Introduced 1999. Imported by Navy Arms.
Price: **$190.00**

NORTH AMERICAN MINI-REVOLVERS
Caliber: 22 Short, 22 LR, 22 WMR, 5-shot. **Barrel:** 1-1/8", 1-5/8". **Weight:** 4 to 6.6 oz. **Length:** 3-5/8" to 6-1/8" overall. **Grips:** Laminated wood. **Sights:** Blade front, notch fixed rear. **Features:** All stainless steel construction. Polished satin and matte finish. Engraved models available. From North American Arms.
Price: 22 Short, 22 LR **$176.00**
Price: 22 WMR, 1-5/8" bbl. **$194.00**
Price: 22 WMR, 1-1/8" or 1-5/8" bbl. with extra 22 LR cylinder .. **$231.00**

NORTH AMERICAN MINI-MASTER
Caliber: 22 LR, 22 WMR, 5-shot cylinder. **Barrel:** 4". **Weight:** 10.7 oz. **Length:** 7.75" overall. **Grips:** Checkered hard black rubber. **Sights:** Blade front, white outline rear adjustable for elevation, or fixed. **Features:** Heavy vent barrel; full-size grips. Non-fluted cylinder. Introduced 1989.
Price: Adjustable sight, 22 WMR or 22 LR **$299.00**
Price: As above with extra WMR/LR cylinder **$336.00**
Price: Fixed sight, 22 WMR or 22 LR **$281.00**
Price: As above with extra WMR/LR cylinder **$318.00**

North American Black Widow Revolver
Similar to Mini-Master, 2" heavy vent barrel. Built on 22 WMR frame. Non-fluted cylinder, black rubber grips. Available with Millett Low Profile fixed sights or Millett sight adjustable for elevation only. Overall length 5-7/8", weighs 8.8 oz. From North American Arms.
Price: Adjustable sight, 22 LR or 22 WMR **$269.00**
Price: As above with extra WMR/LR cylinder **$306.00**
Price: Fixed sight, 22 LR or 22 WMR **$251.00**
Price: As above with extra WMR/LR cylinder **$288.00**

RUGER NEW MODEL BLACKHAWK
AND BLACKHAWK CONVERTIBLE
Caliber: 30 Carbine, 357 Mag./38 Spec., 41 Mag., 45 Colt, 6-shot. **Barrel:** 4-5/8" or 5-1/2", either caliber; 7-1/2" (30 Carbine and 45 Colt). **Weight:** 42 oz. (6-1/2" bbl.). **Length:** 12-1/4" overall (5-1/2" bbl.). **Grips:** American walnut. **Sights:** 1/8" ramp front, micro-click rear adjustable for windage and elevation. **Features:** Ruger transfer bar safety system, independent firing pin, hardened chrome-moly steel frame, music wire springs throughout. Case and lock included.
Price: Blue 30 Carbine, 7-1/2" (BN31) **$435.00**
Price: Blue, 357 Mag., 4-5/8", 6-1/2" (BN34, BN36) **$435.00**
Price: As above, stainless (KBN34, KBN36) **$530.00**
Price: Blue, 357 Mag./9mm Convertible, 4-5/8", 6-1/2" (BN34X, BN36X) includes extra cylinder **$489.00**
Price: Blue, 41 Mag., 4-5/8", 6-1/2" (BN41, BN42) **$435.00**
Price: Blue, 45 Colt, 4-5/8", 5-1/2", 7-1/2" (BN44, BN455, BN45) **$435.00**
Price: Stainless, 45 Colt, 4-5/8", 7-1/2" (KBN44, KBN45) **$530.00**
Price: Blue, 45 Colt/45 ACP Convertible, 4-5/8", 5-1/2" (BN44X, BN455X) includes extra cylinder **$489.00**

RUGER NEW MODEL SINGLE REVOLVER
Caliber: 32 H&R. **Barrel:** 4-5/8", 6-shot. **Grips:** Black Micarta "birds head", rosewood with color case. **Sights:** Fixed. **Features:** Instruction manual, high impact case, gun lock standard.
Price: Stainless, KSSMBH-4F, birds head **$576.00**
Price: color case, SSMBH-4F, birds head **$576.00**
Price: color case, SSM-4F-S, rosewood **$576.00**

Ruger SSMBH-4F

Ruger Super Blackhawk Hunter

Ruger Bisley Vaquero

Ruger Bisley Single-Action

Ruger New Bearcat

HANDGUNS

Price: 357 Mag. BNV34, KBNV34 (4-5/8"),
BNV35, KBNV35 (5-1/2") **$535.00**
Price: 44-40 BNV40, KBNV40 (4-5/8"). BNV405,
KBNV405 (5-1/2"). BNV407, KBNV407 (7-1/2") **$535.00**
Price: 44 Mag., BNV474, KBNV474 (4-5/8"). BNV475,
KBNV475 (5-1/2"). BNV477, KBNV477 (7-1/2") **$535.00**
Price: 45 LC, BN444, KBNV44 (4-5/8"). BNV455,
KBNV455 (5-1/2"). BNV45, KBNV45 (7-1/2") **$535.00**
New!!! Price: 45 LC, BNVBH453, KBNVBH453
3-3/4" with "birds head" grip **$576.00**
Price: 357 Mag., RBNV35 (5-1/2") **$535.00**; KRBNV35 (5-1/2") . **$555.00**
Price: 45 LC, RBNV44 (4-5/8"), RBNV455 (5-1/2") **$535.00**
Price: 45 LC, KRBNV44 (4-5/8"), KRBNV455 (5-1/2") **$555.00**

Ruger Bisley-Vaquero Single-Action Revolver

Similar to Vaquero, Bisley-style hammer, grip and trigger, available in 357 Magnum, 44 Magnum and 45 LC only, 4-5/8" or 5-1/2" barrel. Smooth rosewood grips with Ruger medallion. Roll-engraved, unfluted cylinder. Introduced 1997. From Sturm, Ruger & Co.
Price: Color case-hardened frame, blue grip frame, barrel and cylinder,
RBNV-475, RBNV-474, 44 Mag. **$535.00**
Price: High-gloss stainless steel, KRBNV-475, KRBNV-474 . . . . **$555.00**
Price: For simulated ivory grips add . . . . **$41.00 to $44.00**

RUGER NEW BEARCAT SINGLE-ACTION

Caliber: 22 LR, 6-shot. **Barrel:** 4". **Weight:** 24 oz. **Length:** 8-7/8" overall. **Grips:** Smooth rosewood with Ruger medallion. **Sights:** Blade front, fixed notch rear. **Features:** Reintroduction of the Ruger Bearcat with slightly lengthened frame, Ruger patented transfer bar safety system. Available in blue only. Introduced 1993. With case and lock. From Sturm, Ruger & Co.
Price: SBC4, blue **$379.00**
New Price: KSBC-4, ss **$429.00**

RUGER MODEL SINGLE-SIX REVOLVER

Caliber: 32 H&R Magnum. **Barrel:** 4-5/8", 6-shot. **Weight:** 33 oz. **Length:** 10-1/8". **Grips:** Blue, rosewood, stainless, simulated ivory. **Sights:** Blade front, notch rear fixed. **Features:** Transfer bar and loading gate interlock safety, instruction manual, high impact case and gun lock.
Price: **$576.00**
Price: Blue, SSM4FS **$576.00**
Price: SS, KSSM4FSI **$576.00**

RUGER NEW MODEL SUPER BLACKHAWK

Caliber: 44 Mag., 6-shot. Also fires 44 Spec. **Barrel:** 4-5/8", 5-1/2", 7-1/2", 10-1/2" bull. **Weight:** 48 oz. (7-1/2" bbl.), 51 oz. (10-1/2" bbl.). **Length:** 13-3/8" overall (7-1/2" bbl.). **Grips:** American walnut. **Sights:** 1/8" ramp front, micro-click rear adjustable for windage and elevation. **Features:** Ruger transfer bar safety system, fluted or un-fluted cylinder, steel grip and cylinder frame, round or square back trigger guard, wide serrated trigger, wide spur hammer. With case and lock.
Price: Blue, 4-5/8", 5-1/2", 7-1/2" (S458N, S45N, S47N) **$519.00**
Price: Blue, 10-1/2" bull barrel (S411N) **$529.00**
Price: Stainless, 4-5/8", 5-1/2", 7-1/2" (KS458N, KS45N,
KS47N) **$535.00**
Price: Stainless, 10-1/2" bull barrel (KS411N) **$545.00**

RUGER NEW MODEL SUPER BLACKHAWK HUNTER

Caliber: 44 Mag., 6-shot. **Barrel:** 7-1/2", full-length solid rib, unfluted cylinder. **Weight:** 52 oz. **Length:** 13-5/8". **Grips:** Black laminated wood. **Sights:** Adjustable rear, replaceable front blade. **Features:** Reintroduced Ultimate SA revolver. Includes instruction manual, high-impact case, set 1" medium scope rings, gun lock, ejector rod as standard.
Price: **$639.00**

RUGER VAQUERO SINGLE-ACTION REVOLVER

Caliber: 357 Mag., 44-40, 44 Mag., 45 LC, 6-shot. **Barrel:** 4-5/8", 5-1/2", 7-1/2". **Weight:** 38-41 oz. **Length:** 13-1/8" overall (7-1/2" barrel). **Grips:** Smooth rosewood with Ruger medallion. **Sights:** Blade front, fixed notch rear. **Features:** Uses Ruger's patented transfer bar safety system and loading gate interlock with classic styling. Blued model color case-hardened finish on frame, rest polished and blued. Stainless has high-gloss. Introduced 1993. From Sturm, Ruger & Co.

Ruger Super Single-Six

Uberti Cattleman

Uberti 1875 Army

Uberti 1890 Army

RUGER SINGLE-SIX AND SUPER SINGLE-SIX CONVERTIBLE

Caliber: 22 LR, 6-shot; 22 WMR in extra cylinder. **Barrel:** 4-5/8", 5-1/2", 6-1/2", 9-1/2" (6-groove). **Weight:** 35 oz. (6-1/2" bbl.). **Length:** 11-13/16" overall (6-1/2" bbl.). **Grips:** Smooth American walnut. **Sights:** Improved Patridge front on ramp, fully adjustable rear protected by integral frame ribs (super single-six); or fixed sight (single six). **Features:** Ruger transfer bar safety system, loading gate interlock, hardened chrome-moly steel frame, wide trigger, music wire springs throughout, independent firing pin.
Price: 4-5/8", 5-1/2", 6-1/2", 9-1/2" barrel, blue, adjustable sight NR4, NR5, NR6, NR9 . . . . **$389.00**
Price: 5-1/2", 6-1/2" bbl. only, stainless steel, adjustable sight KNR5, KNR6 . . . . **$469.00**
Price: 5-1/2", 6-1/2" barrel, blue fixed sights **$379.00**

Ruger Bisley Small Frame Revolver

Similar to Single-Six, frame is styled after classic Bisley "flat-top." Most mechanical parts are unchanged. Hammer is lower and smoothly curved with deeply checkered spur. Trigger is strongly curved with wide smooth surface. Longer grip frame designed with hand-filling shape, and trigger guard is a large oval. Adjustable dovetail rear sight; front sight base accepts interchangeable square blades of various heights and styles. Unfluted cylinder and roll engraving. Weighs 41 oz. Chambered for 22 LR, 6-1/2" barrel only. Plastic lockable case. Introduced 1985.
Price: RB-22AW **$422.00**

Ruger Bisley Single-Action Revolver

Similar to standard Blackhawk, hammer is lower with smoothly curved, deeply checkered wide spur. The trigger is strongly curved with wide smooth surface. Longer grip frame has hand-filling shape. Adjustable rear sight, ramp-style front. Unfluted cylinder and roll engraving, adjustable sights. Chambered for 357, 44 Mags. and 45 Colt; 7-1/2" barrel; overall length of 13"; weighs 48 oz. Plastic lockable case. Introduced 1985.
Price: RB-35W, 357Mag, RBD-44W, 44Mag, RB-45W, 45 Colt . . **$535.00**

SMITH & WESSON COMMEMORATIVE MODEL 2000

Caliber: 45 S&W Schofield. **Barrel:** 7". **Features:** 150th Anniversary logo, engraved, gold-plated, walnut grips, blue, original style hammer, trigger, and barrel latch. Wood presentation case. Limited.
Price: . . . . **NA**

TRISTAR/UBERTI REGULATOR REVOLVER

Caliber: 45 Colt. **Barrel:** 4-3/4", 5-1/2", 7-1/2". **Weight:** 32-38 oz. **Length:** 8-1/4" overall (4-3/4" bbl.) **Grips:** One-piece walnut. **Sights:** Blade front, notch rear. **Features:** Uberti replica of 1873 Colt Model "P" revolver. Color-case hardened steel frame, brass backstrap and trigger guard, hammer-block safety. Imported from Italy by Tristar Sporting Arms.
Price: Regulator **$335.00**
Price: Regulator Deluxe (blued backstrap, trigger guard) **$367.00**

UBERTI 1873 CATTLEMAN SINGLE-ACTION

Caliber: 22 LR/22 WMR, 38 Spec., 357 Mag., 44 Spec., 44-40, 45 Colt/45 ACP, 6-shot. **Barrel:** 4-3/4", 5-1/2", 7-1/2"; 44-40, 45 Colt also with 3", 3-1/2", 4". **Weight:** 38 oz. (5-1/2" bbl.). **Length:** 10-3/4" overall (5-1/2" bbl.). **Grips:** One-piece smooth walnut. **Sights:** Blade front, groove rear; fully adjustable rear available. **Features:** Steel or brass backstrap, trigger guard; color case-hardened frame, blued barrel, cylinder. Imported from Italy by Uberti U.S.A.
Price: Steel backstrap, trigger guard, fixed sights **$410.00**
Price: Brass backstrap, trigger guard, fixed sights **$359.00**
Price: Bisley model **$435.00**

Uberti 1873 Buckhorn Single-Action

A slightly larger version of the Cattleman revolver. Available in 44 Magnum or 44 Magnum/44-40 convertible, otherwise has same specs.
Price: Steel backstrap, trigger guard, fixed sights **$410.00**

UBERTI 1875 SA ARMY OUTLAW REVOLVER

Caliber: 357 Mag., 44-40, 45 Colt, 45 Colt/45 ACP convertible, 6-shot. **Barrel:** 5-1/2", 7-1/2". **Weight:** 44 oz. **Length:** 13-3/4" overall. **Grips:** Smooth walnut. **Sights:** Blade front, notch rear. **Features:** Replica of the 1875 Remington S.A. Army revolver. Brass trigger guard, color case-hardened frame, rest blued. Imported by Uberti U.S.A.
Price: **$483.00**
Price: 45 Colt/45 ACP convertible **$525.00**

UBERTI 1890 ARMY OUTLAW REVOLVER

Caliber: 357 Mag., 44-40, 45 Colt, 45 Colt/45 ACP convertible, 6-shot. **Barrel:** 5-1/2", 7-1/2". **Weight:** 37 oz. **Length:** 12-1/2" overall. **Grips:** American walnut. **Sights:** Blade front, groove rear. **Features:** Replica of the 1890 Remington single-action. Brass trigger guard, rest is blued. Imported by Uberti U.S.A.
Price: **$483.00**

UBERTI NEW MODEL RUSSIAN REVOLVER

Caliber: 44 Russian, 6-shot cylinder. **Barrel:** 6-1/2". **Weight:** 40 oz. **Length:** 12" overall. **Grips:** Smooth walnut. **Sights:** Blade front, notch rear. **Features:** Replica of the S&W Model 3 Russian Third Model revolver. Spur trigger guard, polished blue finish. Introduced 1999. Imported by Uberti USA.
Price: **$800.00**

HANDGUNS

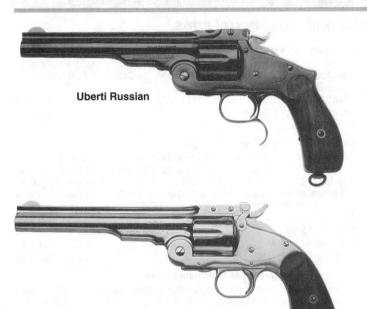

Uberti Russian

Uberti Schofield

Uberti Bisley

Uberti Bisley Flat Top

UBERTI 1875 SCHOFIELD-STYLE BREAK-TOP REVOLVER

Caliber: 44-40, 45 Colt, 6-shot cylinder. **Barrel:** 5", 7". **Weight:** 39 oz. **Length:** 10-3/4" overall (5" barrel). **Grips:** Smooth walnut. **Sights:** Blade front, notch rear. **Features:** Replica of Smith & Wesson Model 3 Schofield. Single-action, top-break with automatic ejection. Polished blue finish. Introduced 1994. Imported by Uberti USA.
Price: **$750.00**

UBERTI BISLEY MODEL SINGLE-ACTION REVOLVER

Caliber: 38-40, 357 Mag., 44 Spec., 44-40 or 45 Colt, 6-shot cylinder. **Barrel:** 4-3/4", 5-1/2", 7-1/2". **Weight:** 40 oz. **Length:** 12-1/2" overall (7-1/2" barrel). **Grips:** Smooth walnut. **Sights:** Blade front, notch rear. **Features:** Replica of Colt's Bisley Model. Polished blue finish, color case-hardened frame. Introduced 1997. Imported by Uberti USA.
Price: **$435.00**

Uberti Bisley Model Flat Top Target Revolver

Similar to standard Bisley model, flat top strap, 7-1/2" barrel only, spring-loaded German silver front sight blade, standing leaf rear sight adjustable for windage. Polished blue finish, color case-hardened frame. Introduced 1998. Imported by Uberti USA.
Price: **$435.00**

U.S. FIRE-ARMS SINGLE ACTION ARMY REVOLVER

Caliber: 44 Russian, 38-40, 44-40, 45 Colt, 6-shot cylinder. **Barrel:** 4-3/4", 5-1/2", 7-1/2", 10". **Weight:** 37 oz. **Length:** NA. **Grips:** Hard rubber. **Sights:** Blade front, notch rear. **Features:** Recreation of original guns; 3" and 4" have no ejector. Available with all-blue, blue with color case-hardening, or full nickel-plate finish. Made in U.S.A. by United States Fire-Arms Mfg. Co.
Price: 4-3/4", blue/cased-colors **$1,250.00**
Price: 7-1/2", carbonal blue/case-colors **$1,450.00**
Price: 7-1/2" nickel **$1,350.00**

U.S. Fire-Arms Flattop Target Revolver

Similar to Single Action Army, 4-3/4", 5-1/2" or 7-1/2" barrel, two-piece hard rubber stocks, flat top frame, adjustable rear sight. Made in U.S.A. by United States Fire-Arms Mfg. Co.
Price: Dome Blue **$1,175.00**
Price: Armory Blue/bone case **$1,450.00**

U.S. FIRE-ARMS BISLEY MODEL REVOLVER

Caliber: 4 Colt, 6-shot cylinder. **Barrel:** 4-3/4", 5-1/2", 7-1/2", 10". **Weight:** 38 oz. (5-1/2" barrel). **Length:** NA. **Grips:** Two-piece hard rubber. **Sights:** Blade front, notch rear. **Features:** Available in all blue, blue with color case-hardening, or full nickel plate finish. Made in U.S.A. by United States Patent Fire-Arms Mfg. Co.
Price: Dome Blue/Armory Blue, bone case **$1,525.00**
Price: Armory Blue/bone case **$1,852.00**
Price: Nickel **$1,900.00**

U.S. Fire-Arms "China Camp" Cowboy Action Revolver

Similar to Single Action Army revolver, available in Silver Steel finish only. Offered in 4-3/4", 5-1/2", 7-1/2" barrels. Made in U.S.A. by United States Fire-Arms Mfg. Co.
Price: **$1,200.00**

U.S. Fire-Arms "Buntline Special"

Similar to Single Action Army revolver except has 16" barrel, flip-up rear peep sight, 45 Colt only. Bone case frame, Armory Blue or nickel finish. Made in U.S.A. by United States Fire-Arms Mfg. Co.
Price: Cased, deluxe set **$2,895.00**
Price: Nickel/rubber **$2,795.00**

U.S. Fire-Arms Omni-Potent Six Shooter

Similar to Single Action Army revolver, bird's head grip with lanyard ring and hump in backstrap. Offered in 4-3/4", 5-1/2" and 7-1/2" barrels. Made in U.S.A. by United States Fire-Arms Mfg. Co.
Price: Armory Blue/bone case **$1,325.00**
Price: Nickel **$1,375.00**
Price: Snubnose, 2", 3", 4", Armory Blue/case. **$1,325.00**
Price: Snubnose, 2", 3", 4", nickel **$1,375.00**
Price: Target, armory blue/case **$1,365.00**
Price: Target, nickel **$1,500.00**

U.S. FIRE-ARMS NEW RODEO COWBOY ACTION REVOLVER

Caliber: 45 Colt. **Barrel:** 4-3/4", 5-1/2". **Grips:** Rubber. **Features:** Historically correct armory bone case hammer, blue satin finish, transfer bar safety system, correct solid firing pin. Entry level basic cowboy SASS gun for beginner or expert.
Price: **$505.00**

Specially adapted single-shot and multi-barrel arms.

AMERICAN DERRINGER MODEL 1

American Derringer Model 1

Caliber: 22 LR, 22 WMR, 30 Carbine, 30 Luger, 30-30 Win., 32 H&R Mag., 32-20, 380 ACP, 38 Super, 38 Spec., 38 Spec. shotshell, 38 Spec. +P, 9mm Para., 357 Mag., 357 Mag./45/410, 357 Maximum, 10mm, 40 S&W, 41 Mag., 38-40, 44-40 Win., 44 Spec., 44 Mag., 45 Colt, 45 Win. Mag., 45 ACP, 45 Colt/410, 45-70 single shot. **Barrel:** 3". **Weight:** 15-1/2 oz. (38 Spec.). **Length:** 4.82" overall. **Grips:** Rosewood, Zebra wood. **Sights:** Blade front. **Features:** Made of stainless steel with high-polish or satin finish. Two-shot capacity. Manual hammer block safety. Introduced 1980. Available in almost any pistol caliber. Contact the factory for complete list of available calibers and prices. From American Derringer Corp.

Price: 22 LR	**$320.00**
Price: 38 Spec.	**$320.00**
Price: 357 Maximum	**$345.00**
Price: 357 Mag.	**$335.00**
Price: 9mm, 380	**$320.00**
Price: 40 S&W	**$335.00**
Price: 44 Spec.	**$398.00**
Price: 44-40 Win.	**$398.00**
Price: 45 Colt	**$385.00**
Price: 30-30, 45 Win. Mag.	**$460.00**
Price: 41, 44 Mags.	**$470.00**
Price: 45-70, single shot	**$387.00**
Price: 45 Colt, 410, 2-1/2"	**$385.00**
Price: 45 ACP, 10mm Auto	**$340.00**

American Derringer Model 4

Similar to the Model 1 except has 4.1" barrel, overall length of 6", and weighs 16-1/2 oz.; chambered for 357 Mag., 357 Maximum, 45-70, 3" 410-bore shotshells or 45 Colt or 44 Mag. Made of stainless steel. Manual hammer block safety. Introduced 1985.

Price: 3" 410/45 Colt	**$425.00**
Price: 45-70	**$560.00**
Price: 44 Mag. with oversize grips	**$515.00**
Price: Alaskan Survival model (45-70 upper barrel, 410 or 45 Colt lower)	**$475.00**

American Derringer Model 6

Similar to the Model 1 except has 6" barrel chambered for 3" 410 shotshells or 22 WMR, 357 Mag., 45 ACP, 45 Colt; rosewood stocks; 8.2" o.a.l. and weighs 21 oz. Shoots either round for each barrel. Manual hammer block safety. Introduced 1986.

Price: 22 WMR	**$440.00**
Price: 357 Mag.	**$440.00**
Price: 45 Colt/410	**$450.00**
Price: 45 ACP	**$440.00**

American Derringer Model 7 Ultra Lightweight

Similar to Model 1 except made of high strength aircraft aluminum. Weighs 7-1/2 oz., 4.82" o.a.l., rosewood stocks. Available in 22 LR, 22 WMR, 32 H&R Mag., 380 ACP, 38 Spec., 44 Spec. Introduced 1986.

Price: 22 LR, WMR	**$325.00**
Price: 38 Spec.	**$325.00**
Price: 380 ACP	**$325.00**
Price: 32 H&R Mag/32 S&W Long	**$325.00**
Price: 44 Spec.	**$565.00**

American Derringer Model 10 Lightweight

Similar to the Model 1 except frame is of aluminum, giving weight of 10 oz. Stainless barrels. Available in 38 Spec., 45 Colt or 45 ACP only. Matte gray finish. Introduced 1989.

Price: 45 Colt	**$385.00**
Price: 45 ACP	**$330.00**
Price: 38 Spec.	**$305.00**

American Derringer Lady Derringer

Same as the Model 1 except has tuned action, is fitted with scrimshawed synthetic ivory grips; chambered for 32 H&R Mag. and 38 Spec.; 357 Mag., 45 Colt, 45/410. Deluxe Grade is highly polished; Deluxe Engraved is engraved in a pattern similar to that used on 1880s derringers. All come in a French fitted jewelry box. Introduced 1991.

Price: 32 H&R Mag.	**$375.00**
Price: 357 Mag.	**$405.00**
Price: 38 Spec.	**$360.00**
Price: 45 Colt, 45/410	**$435.00**

American Derringer Texas Commemorative

A Model 1 Derringer with solid brass frame, stainless steel barrel and rosewood grips. Available in 38 Spec., 44-40 Win., or 45 Colt. Introduced 1987.

Price: 38 Spec.	**$365.00**
Price: 44-40	**$420.00**
Price: Brass frame, 45 Colt	**$450.00**

AMERICAN DERRINGER DA 38 MODEL

Caliber: 22 LR, 9mm Para., 38 Spec., 357 Mag., 40 S&W. **Barrel:** 3". **Weight:** 14.5 oz. **Length:** 4.8" overall. **Grips:** Rosewood, walnut or other hardwoods. **Sights:** Fixed. **Features:** Double-action only; two-shots. Manual safety. Made of satin-finished stainless steel and aluminum. Introduced 1989. From American Derringer Corp.

Price: 22 LR	**$435.00**
Price: 38 Spec.	**$460.00**
Price: 9mm Para.	**$445.00**
Price: 357 Mag.	**$450.00**
Price: 40 S&W	**$475.00**

ANSCHUTZ MODEL 64P SPORT/TARGET PISTOL

Caliber: 22 LR, 22 WMR, 5-shot magazine. **Barrel:** 10". **Weight:** 3 lbs., 8 oz. **Length:** 18-1/2" overall. **Stock:** Choate Rynite. **Sights:** None furnished; grooved for scope mounting. **Features:** Right-hand bolt; polished blue finish. Introduced 1998. Imported from Germany by AcuSport.

Price: 22 LR	**$455.95**
Price: 22 WMR	**$479.95**

BOND ARMS DEFENDER DERRINGER

Caliber: 410 Buckshot or slug, 45 Colt/45 Schofield (2.5" chamber), 45 Colt (only), 450 Bond Super/45 ACP/45 Super, 44 Mag./44 Special/44 Russian, 10mm, 40 S&W, 357 SIG, 357 Maximum/357 Mag./38 Special, 357 Mag/38 Special & 38 Special, 38 Short Colt, 9mm Luger (9x19), 32 H&R Mag./38 S&W Long/32 Colt New Police, 22 LR., 22 WMR, 38-40, 44-40. **Barrel:** 3", 3-1/2". **Weight:** 20-21 oz. **Length:** 5"-5-1/2". **Grips:** Exotic woods or animal horn. **Sights:** Blade front, fixed rear. **Features:** Interchangeable barrels, retracting and rebounding firing pins, cross-bolt safety, automatic extractor for rimmed calibers. Stainless steel construction. Right or left hand.

Price: Texas (with TG) 3" bbl.	**$359.00**
Price: Super (with TG) 3" bbl., 450 Bond Super and 45 ACP	**$359.00**
Price: Cowboy (no TG)	**$359.00**
Price: Century 2000 (with TG), Cowboy Century 2000 (no TG), 3-1/2" bbls., 410/45 Colt	**$379.00**

Price: additional calibers available separately

BROWN CLASSIC SINGLE SHOT PISTOL

Caliber: 17 Ackley Hornet through 45-70 Govt. **Barrel:** 15" airgauged match grade. **Weight:** About 3 lbs., 7 oz. **Grips:** Walnut; thumbrest target style. **Sights:** None furnished; drilled and tapped for scope mounting. **Features:** Falling block action gives rigid barrel-receiver mating; hand-fitted and headspaced. Introduced 1998. Made in U.S.A. by E.A. Brown Mfg.

Price:	**$499.00**

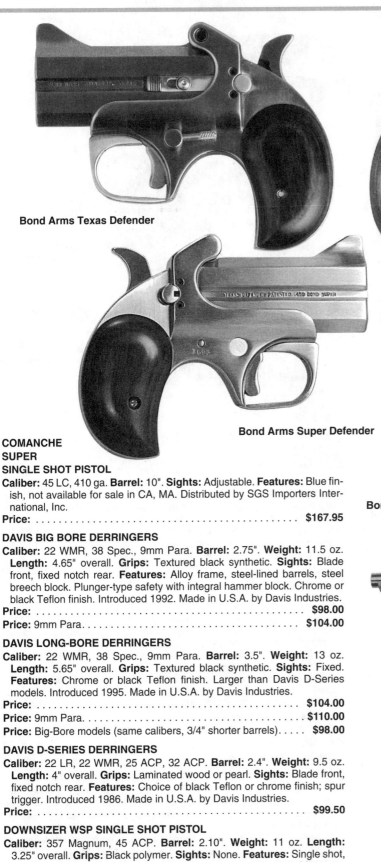

Bond Arms Texas Defender

Bond Arms Cowboy Defender

Bond Arms Super Defender

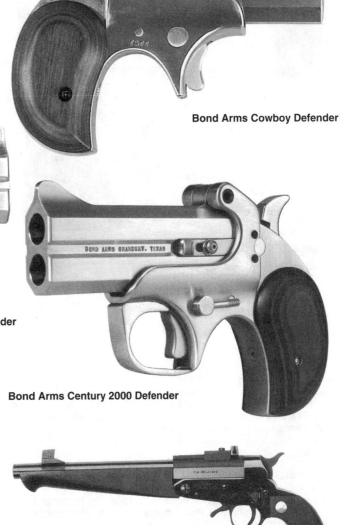

Bond Arms Century 2000 Defender

HANDGUNS

COMANCHE SUPER SINGLE SHOT PISTOL
Caliber: 45 LC, 410 ga. **Barrel:** 10". **Sights:** Adjustable. **Features:** Blue finish, not available for sale in CA, MA. Distributed by SGS Importers International, Inc.
Price: **$167.95**

DAVIS BIG BORE DERRINGERS
Caliber: 22 WMR, 38 Spec., 9mm Para. **Barrel:** 2.75". **Weight:** 11.5 oz. **Length:** 4.65" overall. **Grips:** Textured black synthetic. **Sights:** Blade front, fixed notch rear. **Features:** Alloy frame, steel-lined barrels, steel breech block. Plunger-type safety with integral hammer block. Chrome or black Teflon finish. Introduced 1992. Made in U.S.A. by Davis Industries.
Price: **$98.00**
Price: 9mm Para. **$104.00**

DAVIS LONG-BORE DERRINGERS
Caliber: 22 WMR, 38 Spec., 9mm Para. **Barrel:** 3.5". **Weight:** 13 oz. **Length:** 5.65" overall. **Grips:** Textured black synthetic. **Sights:** Fixed. **Features:** Chrome or black Teflon finish. Larger than Davis D-Series models. Introduced 1995. Made in U.S.A. by Davis Industries.
Price: **$104.00**
Price: 9mm Para. **$110.00**
Price: Big-Bore models (same calibers, 3/4" shorter barrels) **$98.00**

DAVIS D-SERIES DERRINGERS
Caliber: 22 LR, 22 WMR, 25 ACP, 32 ACP. **Barrel:** 2.4". **Weight:** 9.5 oz. **Length:** 4" overall. **Grips:** Laminated wood or pearl. **Sights:** Blade front, fixed notch rear. **Features:** Choice of black Teflon or chrome finish; spur trigger. Introduced 1986. Made in U.S.A. by Davis Industries.
Price: **$99.50**

DOWNSIZER WSP SINGLE SHOT PISTOL
Caliber: 357 Magnum, 45 ACP. **Barrel:** 2.10". **Weight:** 11 oz. **Length:** 3.25" overall. **Grips:** Black polymer. **Sights:** None. **Features:** Single shot, tip-up barrel. Double action only. Stainless steel construction. Measures .900" thick. Introduced 1997. From Downsizer Corp.
Price: **$499.00**

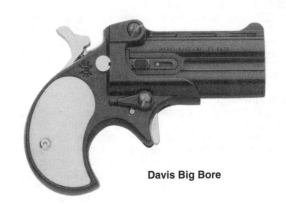

Comanche Super Single Shot

Davis Big Bore

Davis Long-Bore

IAR Model 1872 Derringer

Downsizer Single Shot

IAR Model 1888 Derringer

Gaucher GN1 Silhouette

Maximum Single Shot

GAUCHER GN1 SILHOUETTE PISTOL

Caliber: 22 LR, single shot. **Barrel:** 10". **Weight:** 2.4 lbs. **Length:** 15.5" overall. **Grips:** European hardwood. **Sights:** Blade front, open adjustable rear. **Features:** Bolt action, adjustable trigger. Introduced 1990. Imported from France by Mandall Shooting Supplies.

Price: About **$525.00**
Price: Model GP Silhouette **$425.00**

IAR MODEL 1872 DERRINGER

Caliber: 22 Short. **Barrel:** 2-3/8". **Weight:** 7 oz. **Length:** 5-1/8" overall. **Grips:** Smooth walnut. **Sights:** Blade front, notch rear. **Features:** Gold or nickel frame with blue barrel. Reintroduced 1996 using original Colt designs and tooling for the Colt Model 4 Derringer. Made in U.S.A. by IAR, Inc.

Price: **$109.00**
Price: Single cased gun **$125.00**
Price: Double cased set **$215.00**

IAR MODEL 1866 DOUBLE DERRINGER

Caliber: 38 Special. **Barrel:** 2-3/4". **Weight:** 16 oz. **Grips:** Smooth walnut. **Sights:** Blade front, notch rear. **Features:** All steel construction. Blue barrel, color case-hardened frame. Uses original designs and tooling for the Uberti New Maverick Derringer. Introduced 1999. Made in U.S.A. by IAR, Inc.

Price: **$395.00**

MAXIMUM SINGLE SHOT PISTOL

Caliber: 22 LR, 22 Hornet, 22 BR, 22 PPC, 223 Rem., 22-250, 6mm BR, 6mm PPC, 243, 250 Savage, 6.5mm-35M, 270 MAX, 270 Win., 7mm TCU, 7mm BR, 7mm-35, 7mm INT-R, 7mm-08, 7mm Rocket, 7mm Super-Mag., 30 Herrett, 30 Carbine, 30-30, 308 Win., 30x39, 32-20, 350 Rem. Mag., 357 Mag., 357 Maximum, 358 Win., 375 H&H, 44 Mag., 454 Casull. **Barrel:** 8-3/4", 10-1/2", 14". **Weight:** 61 oz. (10-1/2" bbl.); 78 oz. (14" bbl.). **Length:** 15", 18-1/2" overall (with 10-1/2" and 14" bbl., respectively). **Grips:** Smooth walnut stocks and forend. Also available with 17" finger

groove grip. **Sights:** Ramp front, fully adjustable open rear. **Features:** Falling block action; drilled and tapped for M.O.A. scope mounts; integral grip frame/receiver; adjustable trigger; Douglas barrel (interchangeable). Introduced 1983. Made in U.S.A. by M.O.A. Corp.

Price: Stainless receiver, blue barrel **$799.00**
Price: Stainless receiver, stainless barrel.................... **$883.00**
Price: Extra blued barrel................................. **$254.00**
Price: Extra stainless barrel **$317.00**
Price: Scope mount **$60.00**

RPM XL SINGLE SHOT PISTOL

Caliber: 22 LR through 45-70. **Barrel:** 8", 10-3/4", 12", 14". **Weight:** About 60 oz. **Grips:** Smooth Goncalo Alves with thumb and heel rests. **Sights:** Hooded front with interchangeable post, or Patridge; ISGW rear adjustable for windage and elevation. **Features:** Barrel drilled and tapped for scope mount. Visible cocking indicator. Spring-loaded barrel lock, positive hammer-block safety. Trigger adjustable for weight of pull and over-travel. Contact maker for complete price list. Made in U.S.A. by RPM.

Price: XL Hunter model (action only) **$1,045.00**
Price: Extra barrel, 8" through 10-3/4" **$407.50**
Price: Extra barrel, 12" through 14" **$547.50**
Price: Muzzle brake **$160.00**
Price: Left hand action, add **$50.00**

SAVAGE STRIKER BOLT-ACTION HUNTING HANDGUN

Caliber: 223, 243, 7mm-08, 308, 300 WSM 2-shot mag. **Barrel:** 14". **Weight:** About 5 lbs. **Length:** 22-1/2" overall. **Stock:** Black composite ambidextrous mid-grip; grooved forend; "Dual Pillar" bedding. **Sights:** None furnished; drilled and tapped for scope mounting. **Features:** Short left-hand bolt with right-hand ejection; free-floated barrel; uses Savage Model 110 rifle scope rings/bases. Introduced 1998. Made in U.S.A. by Savage Arms, Inc.

Price: Model 510F (blued barrel and action) **$425.00**
Price: Model 516FSS (stainless barrel and action) **$462.00**

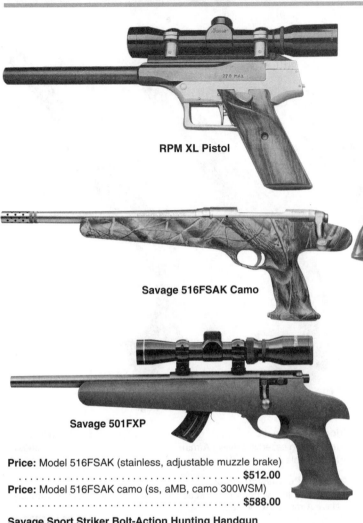

RPM XL Pistol

T/C Encore

Savage 516FSAK Camo

Weatherby Mark V CFP

Savage 501FXP

Price: Model 516FSAK (stainless, adjustable muzzle brake)
.... **$512.00**
Price: Model 516FSAK camo (ss, aMB, camo 300WSM)
.... **$588.00**

Savage Sport Striker Bolt-Action Hunting Handgun
Similar to Striker, but chambered in 22 LR and 22 WMR. Detachable, 10-shot magazine (5-shot magazine for 22 WMR). Overall length 19", weighs 4 lbs. Ambidextrous fiberglass/graphite composite rear grip. Drilled and tapped, scope mount installed. Introduced 2000. Made in U.S.A. by Savage Arms Inc.

Price: Model 501F (blue finish, 22LR) **$216.00**
New!!! Price: Model 501FXP with soft case, 1.25-4x28 scope .. **$258.00**
Price: Model 502F (blue finish, 22 WMR)................. **$238.00**

THOMPSON/CENTER ENCORE PISTOL
Caliber: 22-250, 223, 260 Rem., 7mm-08, 243, 308, 270, 30-06, 44 Mag., 454 Casull, 480 Ruger, 444 Marlin single shot, 450 Marlin with muzzle tamer, no sights. **Barrel:** 12", 15", tapered round. **Weight:** NA. **Length:** 21" overall with 12" barrel. **Grips:** American walnut with finger grooves, walnut forend. **Sights:** Blade on ramp front, adjustable rear, or none. **Features:** Interchangeable barrels; action opens by squeezing the trigger guard; drilled and tapped for scope mounting; blue finish. Announced 1996. Made in U.S.A. by Thompson/Center Arms.

Price: **$561.00**
Price: Extra 12" barrels.................................. **$250.00**
Price: Extra 15" barrels.................................. **$258.00**
Price: 45 Colt/410 barrel, 12" **$274.00**
Price: 45 Colt/410 barrel, 15" **$292.00**

Thompson/Center Stainless Encore Pistol
Similar to blued Encore, made of stainless steel, available with 15" barrel in 223, 22-250, 243 Win., 7mm-08, 308, 30/06 Sprgfld., 45/70 Gov't., 45/410 VR. With black rubber grip and forend. Made in U.S.A. by Thompson/Center Arms.
Price: **$619.00**

Thompson/Center Stainless Super 14
Same as standard Super 14 and Super 16 except made of stainless steel with blued sights. Both models have black Rynite forend and finger-groove, ambidextrous grip with a built-in rubber recoil cushion with sealed-in air pocket. Receiver has different cougar etching. Available in 22 LR Match, .223 Rem., 30-30 Win., 35 Rem. (Super 14), 45 Colt/410. Introduced 1993.
Price: **$578.40**
Price: 45 Colt/410, 14" **$613.94**

Thompson/Center Contender Shooter's Package
Package contains a 14" barrel without iron sights (10" for the 22 LR Match); Weaver-style base and rings; 2.5x-7x Recoil Proof pistol scope; and a soft carrying case. Calibers 22 LR, 223, 7-30 Waters, 30-30. Frame and barrel are blued; grip and forend are black composite. Introduced 1998. Made in U.S.A. by Thompson/Center Arms.
Price: **$735.00**

THOMPSON/CENTER CONTENDER
Caliber: 7mm TCU, 30-30 Win., 22 LR, 22 WMR, 22 Hornet, 223 Rem., 270 Rem., 7-30 Waters, 32-20 Win., 357 Mag., 357 Rem. Max., 44 Mag., 10mm Auto, 445 SuperMag., 45/410, single shot. **Barrel:** 10", bull barrel and vent. rib. **Weight:** 43 oz. (10" bbl.). **Length:** 13-1/4" (10" bbl.). **Stock:** T/C "Competitor Grip." Right or left hand. **Sights:** Under-cut blade ramp front, rear adjustable for windage and elevation. **Features:** Break-open action with automatic safety. Single-action only. Interchangeable bbls., both caliber (rim & centerfire), and length. Drilled and tapped for scope. Engraved frame. See T/C catalog for exact barrel/caliber availability.
Price: Blued (rimfire cals.) **$509.03**
Price: Blued (centerfire cals.)........................... **$509.03**
Price: Extra bbls. **$229.02**
Price: 45/410, internal choke bbl. **$235.11**

Thompson/Center Stainless Contender
Same as standard Contender except made of stainless steel with blued sights, black Rynite forend and ambidextrous finger-groove grip with built-in rubber recoil cushion with sealed-in air pocket. Receiver has different cougar etching. Available with 10" bull barrel in 22 LR, 22 LR Match, 22 Hornet, 223 Rem., 30-30 Win., 357 Mag., 44 Mag., 45 Colt/410. Introduced 1993.
Price: **$566.59**
Price: 45 Colt/410.................................... **$590.44**
Price: With 22 LR match chamber **$578.40**

UBERTI ROLLING BLOCK TARGET PISTOL
Caliber: 22 LR, 22 WMR, 22 Hornet, 357 Mag., 45 Colt, single shot. **Barrel:** 9-7/8", half-round, half-octagon. **Weight:** 44 oz. **Length:** 14" overall. **Stock:** Walnut grip and forend. **Sights:** Blade front, fully adjustable rear. **Features:** Replica of the 1871 rolling block target pistol. Brass trigger guard, color case-hardened frame, blue barrel. Imported by Uberti U.S.A.
Price: **$410.00**

HANDGUNS

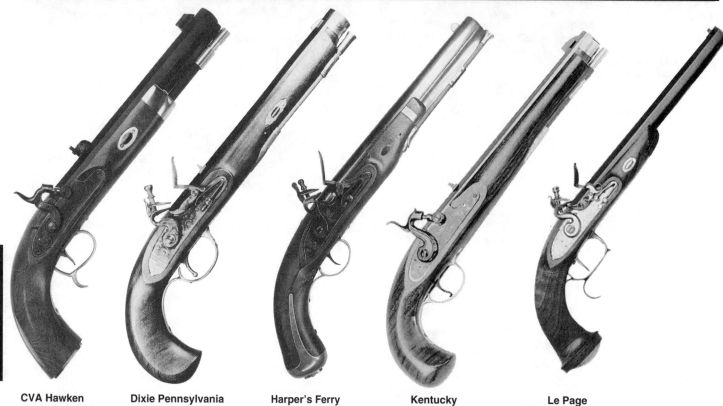

CVA Hawken   Dixie Pennsylvania   Harper's Ferry   Kentucky   Le Page

CVA HAWKEN PISTOL

Caliber: 50. **Barrel:** 9-3/4"; 15/16" flats. **Weight:** 50 oz. **Length:** 16-1/2" overall. **Stocks:** Select hardwood. **Sights:** Beaded blade front, fully adjustable open rear. **Features:** Color case-hardened lock, polished brass wedge plate, instep, ramrod thimble, trigger guard, grip cap. Imported by CVA.
Price: **$167.95**
Price: Kit **$127.95**

DIXIE PENNSYLVANIA PISTOL

Caliber: 44 (.430" round ball). **Barrel:** 10", (7/8" octagon). **Weight:** 2-1/2 labs. **Stocks:** Walnut-stained hardwood. **Sights:** Blade front, open rear drift-adjustable for windage; brass. **Features:** Available in flint only. Brass trigger guard, thimbles, instep, wedge plates; high-luster blue barrel. Imported from Italy by Dixie Gun Works.
Price: Finished **$215.00**
Price: Kit **$195.00**

FRENCH-STYLE DUELING PISTOL

Caliber: 44. **Barrel:** 10". **Weight:** 35 oz. **Length:** 15-3/4" overall. **Stocks:** Carved walnut. **Sights:** Fixed. **Features:** Comes with velvet-lined case and accessories. Imported by Mandall Shooting Supplies.
Price: **$295.00**

HARPER'S FERRY 1806 PISTOL

Caliber: 58 (.570" round ball). **Barrel:** 10". **Weight:** 40 oz. **Length:** 16" overall. **Stocks:** Walnut. **Sights:** Fixed. **Features:** Case-hardened lock, brass-mounted browned barrel. Replica of the first U.S. Gov't.-made flintlock pistol. Imported by Navy Arms, Dixie Gun Works.
Price: .... **$275.00 to $405.00**
Price: Kit (Dixie) **$249.00**

KENTUCKY FLINTLOCK PISTOL

Caliber: 44, 45. **Barrel:** 10-1/8". **Weight:** 32 oz. **Length:** 15-1/2" overall. **Stocks:** Walnut. **Sights:** Fixed. **Features:** Specifications, including caliber, weight and length may vary with importer. Case-hardened lock, blued barrel; available also as brass barrel flint Model 1821. Imported by Navy Arms, The Armoury.
Price: .... **$145.00 to $235.00**

Price: In kit form, from .... **$90.00 to $112.00**
Price: Single cased set (Navy Arms) **$360.00**
Price: Double cased set (Navy Arms) **$590.00**

Kentucky Percussion Pistol

Similar to flint version but percussion lock. Imported by The Armoury, Navy Arms, CVA (50-cal.).
Price: .... **$129.95 to $225.00**
Price: Blued steel barrel (CVA) **$167.95**
Price: Kit form (CVA) **$119.95**
Price: Steel barrel (Armoury) **$179.00**
Price: Single cased set (Navy Arms) **$355.00**
Price: Double cased set (Navy Arms) **$600.00**

LE PAGE PERCUSSION DUELING PISTOL

Caliber: 44. **Barrel:** 10", rifled. **Weight:** 40 oz. **Length:** 16" overall. **Stocks:** Walnut, fluted butt. **Sights:** Blade front, notch rear. **Features:** Double-set triggers. Blued barrel; trigger guard and buttcap are polished silver. Imported by Dixie Gun Works.
Price: **$395.00**

LYMAN PLAINS PISTOL

Caliber: 50 or 54. **Barrel:** 8"; 1:30" twist, both calibers. **Weight:** 50 oz. **Length:** 15" overall. **Stocks:** Walnut half-stock. **Sights:** Blade front, square notch rear adjustable for windage. **Features:** Polished brass trigger guard and ramrod tip, color case-hardened coil spring lock, spring-loaded trigger, stainless steel nipple, blackened iron furniture. Hooked patent breech, detachable belt hook. Introduced 1981. From Lyman Products.
Price: Finished **$244.95**
Price: Kit **$189.95**

PEDERSOLI MANG TARGET PISTOL

Caliber: 38. **Barrel:** 10.5", octagonal; 1:15" twist. **Weight:** 2.5 lbs. **Length:** 17.25" overall. **Stocks:** Walnut with fluted grip. **Sights:** Blade front, open rear adjustable for windage. **Features:** Browned barrel, polished breech plug, rest color case-hardened. Imported from Italy by Dixie Gun Works.
Price: **$825.00**

Lyman Plains Pistol **Pedersoli Mang** **Queen Anne** **Thompson/Center Encore** **Traditions Pioneer** **Traditions William Parker**

QUEEN ANNE FLINTLOCK PISTOL

Caliber: 50 (.490" round ball). **Barrel:** 7-1/2", smoothbore. **Stocks:** Walnut. **Sights:** None. **Features:** Browned steel barrel, fluted brass trigger guard, brass mask on butt. Lockplate left in the white. Made by Pedersoli in Italy. Introduced 1983. Imported by Dixie Gun Works.

Price: $225.00
Price: Kit $175.00

THOMPSON/CENTER ENCORE 209x50 MAGNUM PISTOL

Caliber: 50. **Barrel:** 15"; 1:20" twist. **Weight:** About 4 lbs. **Grips:** American walnut grip and forend. **Sights:** Click-adjustable, steel rear, ramp front. **Features:** Uses 209 shotgun primer for closed-breech ignition; accepts charges up to 110 grains of FFg black powder or two, 50-grain Pyrodex pellets. Introduced 2000.

Price: $310.00

TRADITIONS BUCKHUNTER PRO IN-LINE PISTOL

Caliber: 50. **Barrel:** 9-1/2", round. **Weight:** 48 oz. **Length:** 14" overall. **Stocks:** Smooth walnut or black epoxy-coated hardwood grip and forend. **Sights:** Beaded blade front, folding adjustable rear. **Features:** Thumb safety; removable stainless steel breech plug; adjustable trigger, barrel drilled and tapped for scope mounting. From Traditions.

Price: With walnut grip $229.00
Price: Nickel with black grip $239.00
Price: With walnut grip and 12-1/2" barrel $239.00
Price: Nickel with black grip, muzzle brake and 14-3/4" fluted barrel. $289.00
Price: 45 cal. nickel w/bl. grip, muzzlebrake and 14-3/4" fluted bbl.
.... $289.00

TRADITIONS KENTUCKY PISTOL

Caliber: 50. **Barrel:** 10"; octagon with 7/8" flats; 1:20" twist. **Weight:** 40 oz. **Length:** 15" overall. **Stocks:** Stained beech. **Sights:** Blade front, fixed rear. **Features:** Birds-head grip; brass thimbles; color case-hardened lock. Percussion only. Introduced 1995. From Traditions.

Price: Finished $139.00
Price: Kit $109.00

TRADITIONS PIONEER PISTOL

Caliber: 45. **Barrel:** 9-5/8"; 13/16" flats, 1:16" twist. **Weight:** 31 oz. **Length:** 15" overall. **Stocks:** Beech. **Sights:** Blade front, fixed rear. **Features:** V-type mainspring. Single trigger. German silver furniture, blackened hardware. From Traditions.

Traditions Buckhunter Pro

Price: $139.00
Price: Kit $119.00

TRADITIONS TRAPPER PISTOL

Caliber: 50. **Barrel:** 9-3/4"; 7/8" flats; 1:20" twist. **Weight:** 2-3/4 lbs. **Length:** 16" overall. **Stocks:** Beech. **Sights:** Blade front, adjustable rear. **Features:** Double-set triggers; brass buttcap, trigger guard, wedge plate, forend tip, thimble. From Traditions.

Price: Percussion $189.00
Price: Flintlock $209.00
Price: Kit $149.00

TRADITIONS VEST-POCKET DERRINGER

Caliber: 31. **Barrel:** 2-1/4"; brass. **Weight:** 8 oz. **Length:** 4-3/4" overall. **Stocks:** Simulated ivory. **Sights:** Beed front. **Features:** Replica of riverboat gamblers' derringer; authentic spur trigger. From Traditions.

Price: $109.00

TRADITIONS WILLIAM PARKER PISTOL

Caliber: 50. **Barrel:** 10-3/8"; 15/16" flats; polished steel. **Weight:** 37 oz. **Length:** 17-1/2" overall. **Stocks:** Walnut with checkered grip. **Sights:** Brass blade front, fixed rear. **Features:** Replica dueling pistol with 1:20" twist, hooked breech. Brass wedge plate, trigger guard, cap guard; separate ramrod. Double-set triggers. Polished steel barrel, lock. Imported by Traditions.

Price: $269.00

Army 1860

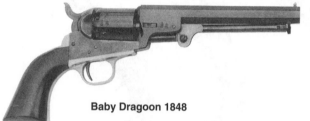

Baby Dragoon 1848

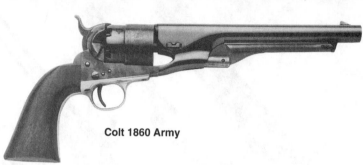

Colt 1860 Army

ARMY 1860 PERCUSSION REVOLVER

Caliber: 44, 6-shot. **Barrel:** 8". **Weight:** 40 oz. **Length:** 13-5/8" overall. **Stocks:** Walnut. **Sights:** Fixed. **Features:** Engraved Navy scene on cylinder; brass trigger guard; case-hardened frame, loading lever and hammer. Some importers supply pistol cut for detachable shoulder stock, have accessory stock available. Imported by Cabela's (1860 Lawman), E.M.F., Navy Arms, The Armoury, Cimarron, Dixie Gun Works (half-fluted cylinder, not roll engraved), Euroarms of America (brass or steel model), Armsport, Traditions (brass or steel), Uberti U.S.A. Inc., United States Patent Fire-Arms.

Price: About $190.00
Price: Hartford model, steel frame, German silver trim,
cartouches (E.M.F.) $215.00
Price: Single cased set (Navy Arms) $300.00
Price: Double cased set (Navy Arms) $490.00
Price: 1861 Navy: Same as Army except 36-cal., 7-1/2" bbl., weighs 41 oz., cut for shoulder stock; round cylinder (fluted available), from Cabela's, CVA (brass frame, 44-cal.), United States Patent Fire-Arms
.... $99.95 to $385.00
Price: Steel frame kit (E.M.F., Euroarms) .... $125.00 to $216.25
Price: Colt Army Police, fluted cyl., 5-1/2", 36-cal. (Cabela's) ... $124.95
Price: With nickeled frame, barrel and backstrap, gold-tone fluted cylinder, trigger and hammer, simulated ivory grips (Traditions) $199.00

BABY DRAGOON 1848, 1849 POCKET, WELLS FARGO

Caliber: 31. **Barrel:** 3", 4", 5", 6"; seven-groove; RH twist. **Weight:** About 21 oz. **Stocks:** Varnished walnut. **Sights:** Brass pin front, hammer notch rear. **Features:** No loading lever on Baby Dragoon or Wells Fargo models. Unfluted cylinder with stagecoach holdup scene; cupped cylinder pin; no grease grooves; one safety pin on cylinder and slot in hammer face; straight (flat) mainspring. From Armsport, Cimarron F.A. Co., Dixie Gun Works, Uberti U.S.A. Inc.

Price: 6" barrel, with loading lever (Dixie Gun Works) $254.95
Price: 4" (Uberti USA Inc.) $335.00

COLT 1860 ARMY PERCUSSION REVOLVER

Caliber: 44. **Barrel:** 8", 7-groove, left-hand twist. **Weight:** 42 oz. **Stocks:** One-piece walnut. **Sights:** German silver front sight, hammer notch rear. **Features:** Steel backstrap cut for shoulder stock; brass trigger guard. Cylinder has Navy scene. Color case-hardened frame, hammer, loading lever. Reproduction of original gun with all original markings. From Colt Blackpowder Arms Co.

Price: $190.00

COLT 1848 BABY DRAGOON REVOLVER

Caliber: 31, 5-shot. **Barrel:** 4". **Weight:** About 21 oz. **Stocks:** Smooth walnut. **Sights:** Brass pin front, hammer notch rear. **Features:** Color case-hardened frame; no loading lever; square-back trigger guard; round bolt cuts; octagonal barrel; engraved cylinder scene. Imported by Colt Blackpowder Arms Co.

Price: $429.95

Colt 1860 "Cavalry Model" Percussion Revolver

Similar to the 1860 Army except has fluted cylinder. Color case-hardened frame, hammer, loading lever and plunger; blued barrel, backstrap and cylinder, brass trigger guard. Has four-screw frame cut for optional shoulder stock. From Colt Blackpowder Arms Co.

Price: $399.95

COLT 1851 NAVY PERCUSSION REVOLVER

Caliber: 36. **Barrel:** 7-1/2", octagonal; 7-groove left-hand twist. **Weight:** 40-1/2 oz. **Stocks:** One-piece oiled American walnut. **Sights:** Brass blade front, hammer notch rear. **Features:** Faithful reproduction of the original gun. Color case-hardened frame, loading lever, plunger, hammer and latch. Blue cylinder, trigger, barrel, screws, wedge. Silver-plated brass backstrap and square-back trigger guard. From Colt Blackpowder Arms Co.

Price: $449.95

COLT 1861 NAVY PERCUSSION REVOLVER

Caliber: 36. **Barrel:** 7-1/2". **Weight:** 42 oz. **Length:** 13-1/8" overall. **Stocks:** One-piece walnut. **Sights:** Blade front, hammer notch rear. **Features:** Color case-hardened frame, loading lever, plunger; blued barrel, backstrap, trigger guard; roll-engraved cylinder and barrel. From Colt Blackpowder Arms Co.

Price: $449.95

COLT 1849 POCKET DRAGOON REVOLVER

Caliber: 31. **Barrel:** 4". **Weight:** 24 oz. **Length:** 9-1/2" overall. **Stocks:** One-piece walnut. **Sights:** Fixed. Brass pin front, hammer notch rear. **Features:** Color case-hardened frame. No loading lever. Unfluted cylinder with engraved scene. Exact reproduction of original. From Colt Blackpowder Arms Co.

Price: $429.95

COLT 1862 POCKET POLICE "TRAPPER MODEL" REVOLVER

Caliber: 36. **Barrel:** 3-1/2". **Weight:** 20 oz. **Length:** 8-1/2" overall. **Stocks:** One-piece walnut. **Sights:** Blade front, hammer notch rear. **Features:** Has separate 4-5/8" brass ramrod. Color case-hardened frame and hammer; silver-plated backstrap and trigger guard; blued semi-fluted cylinder, blued barrel. From Colt Blackpowder Arms Co., Navy Arms.

Price: (Colt Blackpowder Arms) $429.95
Price: "New" Pocket Police, Navy Arms $315.00

COLT THIRD MODEL DRAGOON

Caliber: 44. **Barrel:** 7-1/2". **Weight:** 66 oz. **Length:** 13-3/4" overall. **Stocks:** One-piece walnut. **Sights:** Blade front, hammer notch rear. **Features:** Color case-hardened frame, hammer, lever and plunger; round trigger guard; flat mainspring; hammer roller; rectangular bolt cuts. From Colt Blackpowder Arms Co.

Price: Three-screw frame with brass grip straps $499.95
Price: First Dragoon (oval bolt cuts in cylinder, square-back
trigger guard) $499.95
Price: Second Dragoon (rectangular bolt cuts in cylinder,
square-back trigger guard) $499.95

HANDGUNS

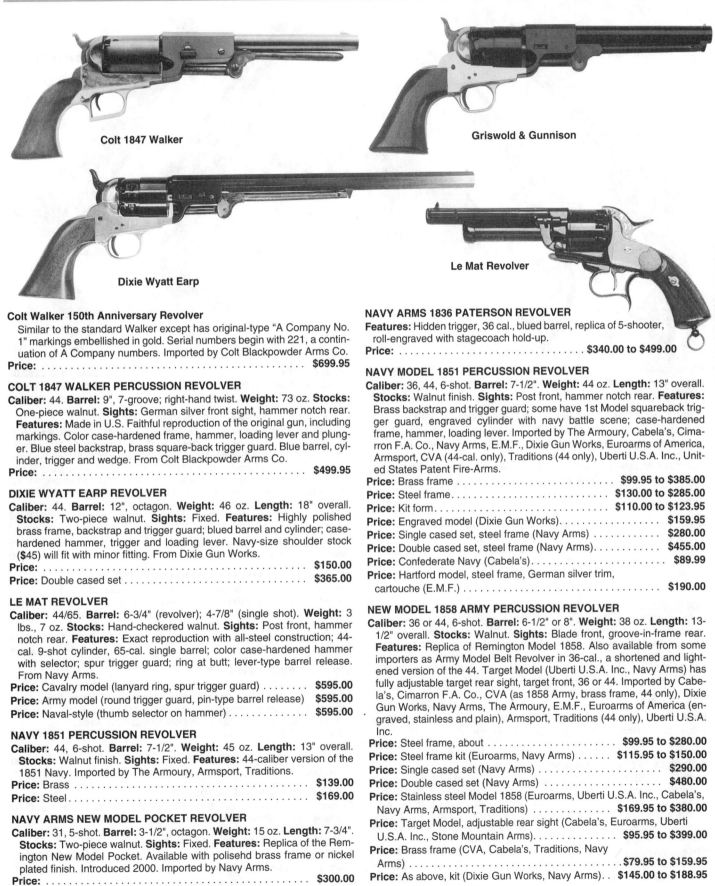

Colt 1847 Walker

Griswold & Gunnison

Dixie Wyatt Earp

Le Mat Revolver

Colt Walker 150th Anniversary Revolver

Similar to the standard Walker except has original-type "A Company No. 1" markings embellished in gold. Serial numbers begin with 221, a continuation of A Company numbers. Imported by Colt Blackpowder Arms Co.
Price: **$699.95**

COLT 1847 WALKER PERCUSSION REVOLVER

Caliber: 44. **Barrel:** 9", 7-groove; right-hand twist. **Weight:** 73 oz. **Stocks:** One-piece walnut. **Sights:** German silver front sight, hammer notch rear. **Features:** Made in U.S. Faithful reproduction of the original gun, including markings. Color case-hardened frame, hammer, loading lever and plunger. Blue steel backstrap, brass square-back trigger guard. Blue barrel, cylinder, trigger and wedge. From Colt Blackpowder Arms Co.
Price: **$499.95**

DIXIE WYATT EARP REVOLVER

Caliber: 44. **Barrel:** 12", octagon. **Weight:** 46 oz. **Length:** 18" overall. **Stocks:** Two-piece walnut. **Sights:** Fixed. **Features:** Highly polished brass frame, backstrap and trigger guard; blued barrel and cylinder; case-hardened hammer, trigger and loading lever. Navy-size shoulder stock ($45) will fit with minor fitting. From Dixie Gun Works.
Price: **$150.00**
Price: Double cased set **$365.00**

LE MAT REVOLVER

Caliber: 44/65. **Barrel:** 6-3/4" (revolver); 4-7/8" (single shot). **Weight:** 3 lbs., 7 oz. **Stocks:** Hand-checkered walnut. **Sights:** Post front, hammer notch rear. **Features:** Exact reproduction with all-steel construction; 44-cal. 9-shot cylinder, 65-cal. single barrel; color case-hardened hammer with selector; spur trigger guard; ring at butt; lever-type barrel release. From Navy Arms.
Price: Cavalry model (lanyard ring, spur trigger guard) **$595.00**
Price: Army model (round trigger guard, pin-type barrel release) **$595.00**
Price: Naval-style (thumb selector on hammer) **$595.00**

NAVY 1851 PERCUSSION REVOLVER

Caliber: 44, 6-shot. **Barrel:** 7-1/2". **Weight:** 45 oz. **Length:** 13" overall. **Stocks:** Walnut finish. **Sights:** Fixed. **Features:** 44-caliber version of the 1851 Navy. Imported by The Armoury, Armsport, Traditions.
Price: Brass **$139.00**
Price: Steel **$169.00**

NAVY ARMS NEW MODEL POCKET REVOLVER

Caliber: 31, 5-shot. **Barrel:** 3-1/2", octagon. **Weight:** 15 oz. **Length:** 7-3/4". **Stocks:** Two-piece walnut. **Sights:** Fixed. **Features:** Replica of the Remington New Model Pocket. Available with polishd brass frame or nickel plated finish. Introduced 2000. Imported by Navy Arms.
Price: **$300.00**

NAVY ARMS 1836 PATERSON REVOLVER

Features: Hidden trigger, 36 cal., blued barrel, replica of 5-shooter, roll-engraved with stagecoach hold-up.
Price: . . . . **$340.00 to $499.00**

NAVY MODEL 1851 PERCUSSION REVOLVER

Caliber: 36, 44, 6-shot. **Barrel:** 7-1/2". **Weight:** 44 oz. **Length:** 13" overall. **Stocks:** Walnut finish. **Sights:** Post front, hammer notch rear. **Features:** Brass backstrap and trigger guard; some have 1st Model squareback trigger guard, engraved cylinder with navy battle scene; case-hardened frame, hammer, loading lever. Imported by The Armoury, Cabela's, Cimarron F.A. Co., Navy Arms, E.M.F., Dixie Gun Works, Euroarms of America, Armsport, CVA (44-cal. only), Traditions (44 only), Uberti U.S.A. Inc., United States Patent Fire-Arms.
Price: Brass frame . . . . **$99.95 to $385.00**
Price: Steel frame . . . . **$130.00 to $285.00**
Price: Kit form . . . . **$110.00 to $123.95**
Price: Engraved model (Dixie Gun Works) **$159.95**
Price: Single cased set, steel frame (Navy Arms) **$280.00**
Price: Double cased set, steel frame (Navy Arms) **$455.00**
Price: Confederate Navy (Cabela's) **$89.99**
Price: Hartford model, steel frame, German silver trim, cartouche (E.M.F.) **$190.00**

NEW MODEL 1858 ARMY PERCUSSION REVOLVER

Caliber: 36 or 44, 6-shot. **Barrel:** 6-1/2" or 8". **Weight:** 38 oz. **Length:** 13-1/2" overall. **Stocks:** Walnut. **Sights:** Blade front, groove-in-frame rear. **Features:** Replica of Remington Model 1858. Also available from some importers as Army Model Belt Revolver in 36-cal., a shortened and lightened version of the 44. Target Model (Uberti U.S.A. Inc., Navy Arms) has fully adjustable target rear sight, target front, 36 or 44. Imported by Cabela's, Cimarron F.A. Co., CVA (as 1858 Army, brass frame, 44 only), Dixie Gun Works, Navy Arms, The Armoury, E.M.F., Euroarms of America (engraved, stainless and plain), Armsport, Traditions (44 only), Uberti U.S.A. Inc.
Price: Steel frame, about . . . . **$99.95 to $280.00**
Price: Steel frame kit (Euroarms, Navy Arms) . . . . . . **$115.95 to $150.00**
Price: Single cased set (Navy Arms) **$290.00**
Price: Double cased set (Navy Arms) **$480.00**
Price: Stainless steel Model 1858 (Euroarms, Uberti U.S.A. Inc., Cabela's, Navy Arms, Armsport, Traditions) . . . . **$169.95 to $380.00**
Price: Target Model, adjustable rear sight (Cabela's, Euroarms, Uberti U.S.A. Inc., Stone Mountain Arms) . . . . **$95.95 to $399.00**
Price: Brass frame (CVA, Cabela's, Traditions, Navy Arms) . . . . **$79.95 to $159.95**
Price: As above, kit (Dixie Gun Works, Navy Arms) . . **$145.00 to $188.95**

Uberti 1858

Rogers & Spencer

North American Companion

Pocket Police 1862

Ruger Old Army

Price: Buffalo model, 44-cal. (Cabela's) **$119.99**
Price: Hartford model, steel frame, German silver trim,
 cartouche (E.M.F.). **$215.00**

NORTH AMERICAN COMPANION PERCUSSION REVOLVER
Caliber: 22. **Barrel:** 1-1/8". **Weight:** 5.1 oz. **Length:** 4-5/10" overall.
Stocks: Laminated wood. **Sights:** Blade front, notch fixed rear. **Features:**
All stainless steel construction. Uses standard #11 percussion caps.
Comes with bullets, powder measure, bullet seater, leather clip holster,
gun rug. Long Rifle or Magnum frame size. Introduced 1996. Made in U.S.
by North American Arms.
Price: Long Rifle frame **$191.00**

North American Magnum Companion Percussion Revolver
 Similar to the Companion except has larger frame. Weighs 7.2 oz., has
1-5/8" barrel, measures 5-7/16" overall. Comes with bullets, powder mea-
sure, bullet seater, leather clip holster, gun rag. Introduced 1996. Made in
U.S. by North American Arms.
Price: **$209.00**

POCKET POLICE 1862 PERCUSSION REVOLVER
Caliber: 36, 5-shot. **Barrel:** 4-1/2", 5-1/2", 6-1/2", 7-1/2". **Weight:** 26 oz.
Length: 12" overall (6-1/2" bbl.). **Stocks:** Walnut. **Sights:** Fixed. **Fea-
tures:** Round tapered barrel; half-fluted and rebated cylinder; case-hard-
ened frame, loading lever and hammer; silver or brass trigger guard and
backstrap. Imported by Dixie Gun Works, Navy Arms (5-1/2" only), Uberti
U.S.A. Inc. (5-1/2", 6-1/2" only), United States Patent Fire-Arms and Cima-
rron F.A. Co.
Price: About . . . . **$139.95 to $335.00**
Price: Single cased set with accessories (Navy Arms) **$365.00**
Price: Hartford model, steel frame, German silver trim,
 cartouche (E.M.F.). **$215.00**

ROGERS & SPENCER PERCUSSION REVOLVER
Caliber: 44. **Barrel:** 7-1/2". **Weight:** 47 oz. **Length:** 13-3/4" overall.
Stocks: Walnut. **Sights:** Cone front, integral groove in frame for rear.
Features: Accurate reproduction of a Civil War design. Solid frame; extra
large nipple cut-out on rear of cylinder; loading lever and cylinder easily
removed for cleaning. From Dixie Gun Works, Euroarms of America (stan-
dard blue, engraved, burnished, target models), Navy Arms.
Price: . . . . **$160.00 to $299.95**
Price: Nickel-plated. **$215.00**
Price: Engraved (Euroarms) **$287.00**

Price: Kit version . . . . **$245.00 to $252.00**
Price: Target version (Euroarms) . . . . **$239.00 to $270.00**
Price: Burnished London Gray (Euroarms) . . . . **$245.00 to $270.00**

RUGER OLD ARMY PERCUSSION REVOLVER
Caliber: 45, 6-shot. Uses .457" dia. lead bullets or 454 conical. **Barrel:** 7-
1/2" (6-groove; 1:16" twist). **Weight:** 2-7/8 lbs. **Length:** 13-1/2" overall.
Stocks: Rosewood. **Sights:** Ramp front, rear adjustable for windage and
elevation; or fixed (groove). **Features:** Stainless steel; standard size nip-
ples, chrome-moly steel cylinder and frame, same lockwork as original Su-
per Blackhawk. Also stainless steel. Includes hard case and lock. Made in
USA. From Sturm, Ruger & Co.
Price: Stainless steel (Model KBP-7) **$535.00**
Price: Blued steel (Model BP-7) **$499.00**
Price: Blued steel, fixed sight (BP-7F) **$499.00**
Price: Stainless steel, fixed sight (KBP-7F) **$535.00**

SHERIFF MODEL 1851 PERCUSSION REVOLVER
Caliber: 36, 44, 6-shot. **Barrel:** 5". **Weight:** 40 oz. **Length:** 10-1/2" overall.
Stocks: Walnut. **Sights:** Fixed. **Features:** Brass backstrap and trigger
guard; engraved navy scene; case-hardened frame, hammer, loading le-
ver. Imported by E.M.F.
Price: Steel frame. **$169.95**
Price: Brass frame **$140.00**

SPILLER & BURR REVOLVER
Caliber: 36 (.375" round ball). **Barrel:** 7", octagon. **Weight:** 2-1/2 lbs.
Length: 12-1/2" overall. **Stocks:** Two-piece walnut. **Sights:** Fixed. **Fea-
tures:** Reproduction of the C.S.A. revolver. Brass frame and trigger guard.
Also available as a kit. From Dixie Gun Works, Navy Arms.
Price: **$145.00**
Price: Kit form (Dixie) **$149.95**
Price: Single cased set (Navy Arms) **$270.00**
Price: Double cased set (Navy Arms) **$430.00**

TEXAS PATERSON 1836 REVOLVER
Caliber: 36 (.375" round ball). **Barrel:** 7-1/2". **Weight:** 42 oz. **Stocks:** One-
piece walnut. **Sights:** Fixed. **Features:** Copy of Sam Colt's first commercial-
ly-made revolving pistol. Has no loading lever but comes with loading tool.
From Cimarron F.A. Co., Dixie Gun Works, Navy Arms, Uberti U.S.A. Inc.
Price: About . . . . **$310.00 to $395.00**
Price: With loading lever (Uberti U.S.A. Inc.) **$450.00**
Price: Engraved (Navy Arms). **$485.00**

HANDGUNS

BLACKPOWDER REVOLVERS

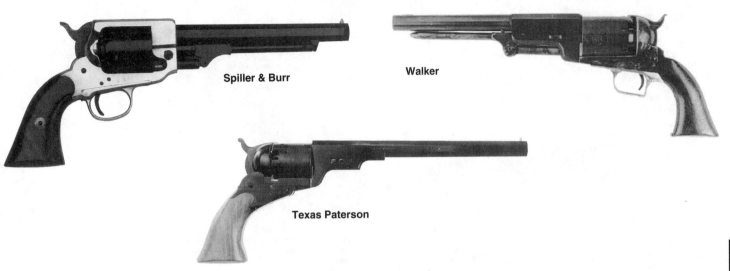

Spiller & Burr

Walker

Texas Paterson

Uberti 1861 Navy Percussion Revolver
Similar to Colt 1851 Navy except has round 7-1/2" barrel, rounded trigger guard, German silver blade front sight, "creeping" loading lever. Available with fluted or round cylinder. Imported by Uberti U.S.A. Inc.
Price: Steel backstrap, trigger guard, cut for stock **$265.00**

1ST U.S. MODEL DRAGOON
Caliber: 44. **Barrel:** 7-1/2", part round, part octagon. **Weight:** 64 oz.
Stocks: One-piece walnut. **Sights:** German silver blade front, hammer notch rear. **Features:** First model has oval bolt cuts in cylinder, square-back flared trigger guard, V-type mainspring, short trigger. Ranger and Indian scene roll-engraved on cylinder. Color case-hardened frame, loading lever, plunger and hammer; blue barrel, cylinder, trigger and wedge. Available with old-time charcoal blue or standard blue-black finish. Polished brass backstrap and trigger guard. From Cimarron F.A. Co., Dixie Gunworks, Uberti U.S.A. Inc., United States Patent Fire-Arms, Navy Arms.
Price: . . . . **$295.00 to $435.00**

2nd U.S. Model Dragoon Revolver
Similar to the 1st Model except distinguished by rectangular bolt cuts in the cylinder. From Cimarron F.A. Co., Uberti U.S.A. Inc., United States Patent Fire-Arms, Navy Arms, Dixie Gunworks.
Price: . . . . **$295.00 to $435.00**

3rd U.S. Model Dragoon Revolver
Similar to the 2nd Model except for oval trigger guard, long trigger, modifications to the loading lever and latch. Imported by Cimarron F.A. Co., Uberti U.S.A. Inc., United States Patent Fire-Arms, Dixie Gunworks.
Price: Military model (frame cut for shoulder stock,
steel backstrap) . . . .**$295.00 to $435.00**
Price: Civilian (brass backstrap, trigger guard). . . . . . **$295.00 to $325.00**

1862 POCKET NAVY PERCUSSION REVOLVER
Caliber: 36, 5-shot. **Barrel:** 5-1/2", 6-1/2", octagonal, 7-groove, LH twist.
Weight: 27 oz. (5-1/2" barrel). **Length:** 10-1/2" overall (5-1/2" bbl.).

Stocks: One-piece varnished walnut. **Sights:** Brass pin front, hammer notch rear. **Features:** Rebated cylinder, hinged loading lever, brass or silver-plated backstrap and trigger guard, color-cased frame, hammer, loading lever, plunger and latch, rest blued. Has original-type markings. From Cimarron F.A. Co., Uberti U.S.A. Inc., Dixie Gunworks.
Price: With brass backstrap, trigger guard . . . . **$260.00 to $310.00**

1861 Navy Percussion Revolver
Similar to Colt 1851 Navy except has round 7-1/2" barrel, rounded trigger guard, German silver blade front sight, "creeping" loading lever. Fluted or round cylinder. Imported by Cimarron F.A. Co., Uberti U.S.A. Inc., Dixie Gunworks.
Price: Steel backstrap, trigger guard, cut for stock. . . **$255.00 to $300.00**

U.S. PATENT FIRE-ARMS 1862 POCKET NAVY
Caliber: 36. **Barrel:** 4-1/2", 5-1/2", 6-1/2". **Weight:** 27 oz. (5-1/2" barrel).
Length: 10-1/2" overall (5-1/2" barrel). **Stocks:** Smooth walnut. **Sights:** Brass pin front, hammer notch rear. **Features:** Blued barrel and cylinder, color case-hardened frame, hammer, lever; silver-plated backstrap and trigger guard. Imported from Italy; available from United States Patent Fire-Arms Mfg. Co.
Price: **$335.00**

WALKER 1847 PERCUSSION REVOLVER
Caliber: 44, 6-shot. **Barrel:** 9". **Weight:** 84 oz. **Length:** 15-1/2" overall.
Stocks: Walnut. **Sights:** Fixed. **Features:** Case-hardened frame, loading lever and hammer; iron backstrap; brass trigger guard; engraved cylinder. Imported by Cabela's, Cimarron F.A. Co., Navy Arms, Dixie Gun Works, Uberti U.S.A. Inc., E.M.F., Cimarron, Traditions, United States Patent Fire-Arms.
Price: About . . . . **$225.00 to $445.00**
Price: Single cased set (Navy Arms) **$405.00**
Price: Deluxe Walker with French fitted case (Navy Arms) **$540.00**
Price: Hartford model, steel frame, German silver trim,
cartouche (E.M.F.) **$295.00**

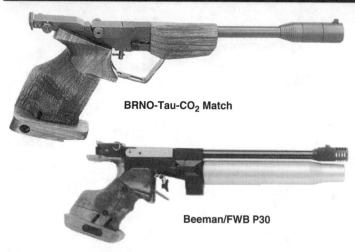

BRNO-Tau-CO₂ Match

Beeman/FWB P30

Benjamin Sheridan CO₂

BEEMAN P1 MAGNUM AIR PISTOL

Caliber: 177, 5mm, single shot. **Barrel:** 8.4". **Weight:** 2.5 lbs. **Length:** 11" overall. **Power:** Top lever cocking; spring-piston. **Stocks:** Checkered walnut. **Sights:** Blade front, square notch rear with click micrometer adjustments for windage and elevation. Grooved for scope mounting. **Features:** Dual power for 177 and 20-cal.: low setting gives 350-400 fps; high setting 500-600 fps. Rearward expanding mainspring simulates firearm recoil. All Colt 45 auto grips fit gun. Dry-firing feature for practice. Optional wooden shoulder stock. Introduced 1985. Imported by Beeman.
Price: 177, 5mm... $415.00

Beeman P2 Match Air Pistol

Similar to the Beeman P1 Magnum except shoots only 177 pellets; completely recoilless single-stroke pneumatic action. Weighs 2.2 lbs. Choice of thumbrest match grips or standard style. Introduced 1990.
Price: 177, 5mm, standard grip............................ $385.00
Price: 177, match grip.................................... $455.00

BEEMAN P3 AIR PISTOL

Caliber: 177 pellet, single shot. **Barrel:** N/A. **Weight:** 1.7 lbs. **Length:** 9.6" overall. **Power:** Single-stroke pneumatic; overlever barrel cocking. **Grips:** Reinforced polymer. **Sights:** Adjustable rear, blade front. **Features:** Velocity 410 fps. Polymer frame; automatic safety; two-stage trigger; built-in muzzle brake. Introduced 1999 by Beeman.
Price: $159.00

BEEMAN/FEINWERKBAU 65 MKII AIR PISTOL

Caliber: 177, single shot. **Barrel:** 6.1", removable bbl. wgt. available. **Weight:** 42 oz. **Length:** 13.3" overall. **Power:** Spring, sidelever cocking. **Stocks:** Walnut, stippled thumbrest; adjustable or fixed. **Sights:** Front, interchangeable post element system, open rear, click adjustable for windage and elevation and for sighting notch width. Scope mount available. **Features:** New shorter barrel for better balance and control. Cocking effort 9 lbs. Two-stage trigger, four adjustments. Quiet firing, 525 fps. Programs instantly for recoil or recoilless operation. Permanently lubricated. Steel piston ring. Imported by Beeman.
Price: Right-hand...................................... $1,070.00

BEEMAN/FEINWERKBAU 103 PISTOL

Caliber: 177, single shot. **Barrel:** 10.1", 12-groove rifling. **Weight:** 2.5 lbs. **Length:** 16.5" overall. **Power:** Single-stroke pneumatic, underlever cocking. **Stocks:** Stippled walnut with adjustable palm shelf. **Sights:** Blade front, open rear adjustable for windage and elevation. Notch size adjustable for width. Interchangeable front blades. **Features:** Velocity 510 fps. Fully adjustable trigger. Cocking effort of 2 lbs. Imported by Beeman.
Price: Right-hand...................................... $1,195.00
Price: Left-hand....................................... $1,235.00

BEEMAN/FWB P30 MATCH AIR PISTOL

Caliber: 177, single shot. **Barrel:** 10-5/16", with muzzlebrake. **Weight:** 2.4 lbs. **Length:** 16.5" overall. **Power:** Pre-charged pneumatic. **Stocks:** Stippled walnut; adjustable match type. **Sights:** Undercut blade front, fully adjustable match rear. **Features:** Velocity to 525 fps; up to 200 shots per CO₂ cartridge. Fully adjustable trigger; built-in muzzlebrake. Introduced 1995. Imported from Germany by Beeman.
Price: Right-hand...................................... $1,275.00
Price: Left-hand....................................... $1,350.00

BEEMAN/FWB C55 CO2 RAPID FIRE PISTOL

Caliber: 177, single shot or 5-shot magazine. **Barrel:** 7.3". **Weight:** 2.5 lbs. **Length:** 15" overall. **Power:** Special CO₂ cylinder. **Sights:** Anatomical, adjustable. **Sights:** Interchangeable front, fully adjustable open micro-click rear with adjustable notch size. **Features:** Velocity 510 fps. Has 11.75" sight radius. Built-in muzzlebrake. Introduced 1993. Imported by Beeman Precision Airguns.
Price: Right-hand...................................... $1,460.00
Price: Left-hand....................................... $1,520.00

BEEMAN HW70A AIR PISTOL

Caliber: 177, single shot. **Barrel:** 6-1/4", rifled. **Weight:** 38 oz. **Length:** 12-3/4" overall. **Power:** Spring, barrel cocking. **Stocks:** Plastic, with thumbrest. **Sights:** Hooded post front, square notch rear adjustable for windage and elevation. Comes with scope base. **Features:** Adjustable trigger, 31-lb. cocking effort, 440 fps MV; automatic barrel safety. Imported by Beeman.
Price: $185.00
Price: HW70S, black grip, silver finish $210.00

BEEMAN/WEBLEY TEMPEST AIR PISTOL

Caliber: 177, 22, single shot. **Barrel:** 6-7/8". **Weight:** 32 oz. **Length:** 8.9" overall. **Power:** Spring-piston, break barrel. **Stocks:** Checkered black plastic with thumbrest. **Sights:** Blade front, adjustable rear. **Features:** Velocity to 500 fps (177), 400 fps (22). Aluminum frame; black epoxy finish; manual safety. Imported from England by Beeman.
Price: $180.00

Beeman/Webley Hurricane Air Pistol

Similar to the Tempest except has extended frame in the rear for a click-adjustable rear sight; hooded front sight; comes with scope mount. Imported from England by Beeman.
Price: $225.00

BENJAMIN SHERIDAN CO2 PELLET PISTOLS

Caliber: 177, 20, 22, single shot. **Barrel:** 6-3/8", rifled brass. **Weight:** 29 oz. **Length:** 9.8" overall. **Power:** 12-gram CO₂ cylinder. **Stocks:** Walnut. **Sights:** High ramp front, fully adjustable notch rear. **Features:** Velocity to 500 fps. Turn-bolt action with cross-bolt safety. Gives about 40 shots per CO₂ cylinder. Black or nickel finish. Made in U.S. by Benjamin Sheridan Co.
Price: Black finish, EB17 (177), EB20 (20), about $115.23

BENJAMIN SHERIDAN PNEUMATIC PELLET PISTOLS

Caliber: 177, 20, 22, single shot. **Barrel:** 9-3/8", rifled brass. **Weight:** 38 oz. **Length:** 13-1/8" overall. **Power:** Underlever pnuematic, hand pumped. **Stocks:** Walnut stocks and pump handle. **Sights:** High ramp front, fully adjustable notch rear. **Features:** Velocity to 525 fps (variable). Bolt action with cross-bolt safety. Choice of black or nickel finish. Made in U.S. by Benjamin Sheridan Co.
Price: Black finish, HB17 (177), HB20 (20), HB22 (22), about........... $129.50

BERETTA 92 FS/CO2 AIR PISTOLS

Caliber: 177 pellet, 8-shot magazine. **Barrel:** 4.9". **Weight:** 44.4 oz. **Length:** 8.2" (10.2" with compensator). **Power:** CO₂ cartridge. **Grips:** Plastic or wood. **Sights:** Adjustable rear, blade front. **Features:** Velocity 375 fps. Replica of Beretta 92 FS pistol. Single- and double-action trigger; ambidextrous safety; black or nickel-plated finish. Made by Umarex for Beretta USA.
Price: .... $200.00 to $465.00

BRNO TAU-7 CO2 MATCH PISTOL

Caliber: 177. **Barrel:** 10.24". **Weight:** 37 oz. **Length:** 15.75" overall. **Power:** 12.5-gram CO₂ cartridge. **Stocks:** Stippled hardwood with adjustable palm rest. **Sights:** Blade front, open fully adjustable rear. **Features:** Comes with extra seals and counterweight. Blue finish. Imported by Great Lakes Airguns.
Price: About $299.50

BSA 240 MAGNUM AIR PISTOL

Caliber: 177, 22, single shot. **Barrel:** 6". **Weight:** 2 lbs. **Length:** 9" overall. **Power:** Spring-air, top-lever cocking. **Stocks:** Walnut. **Sights:** Blade front, micrometer adjustable rear. **Features:** Velocity 510 fps (177), 420 fps (22); crossbolt safety. Combat autoloader styling. Imported from U.K. by Precision Sales International, Inc.
Price: $259.99

COLT GOVERNMENT 1911 A1 AIR PISTOL

Caliber: 177, 8-shot cylinder magazine. **Barrel:** 5", rifled. **Weight:** 38 oz. **Length:** 8-1/2" overall. **Power:** CO₂ cylinder. **Stocks:** Checkered black plastic or smooth wood. **Sights:** Post front, adjustable rear. **Features:** Velocity to 393 fps. Quick-loading cylinder magazine; single and double action; black or silver finish. Introduced 1998. Imported by Colt's Mfg. Co., Inc.
Price: Black finish.. $199.00
Price: Silver finish... $209.00

HANDGUNS

Crosman Model 1377

Daisy/Power Line 717

CROSMAN BLACK VENOM PISTOL
Caliber: 177 pellets, BB, 17-shot magazine; darts, single shot. **Barrel:** 4.75" smoothbore. **Weight:** 16 oz. **Length:** 10.8" overall. **Power:** Spring. **Stocks:** Checkered. **Sights:** Blade front, adjustable rear. **Features:** Velocity to 270 fps (BBs), 250 fps (pellets). Spring-fed magazine; cross-bolt safety. Introduced 1996. Made in U.S. by Crosman Corp.
Price: About **$20.00**

CROSMAN BLACK FANG PISTOL
Caliber: 177 BB, 17-shot magazine. **Barrel:** 4.75" smoothbore. **Weight:** 10 oz. **Length:** 10.8" overall. **Power:** Spring. **Stocks:** Checkered. **Sights:** Blade front, fixed notch rear. **Features:** Velocity to 250 fps. Spring-fed magazine; cross-bolt safety. Introduced 1996. Made in U.S. by Crosman Corp.
Price: About **$16.00**

CROSMAN MODEL 1377 AIR PISTOLS
Caliber: 177 (M1377), single shot. **Barrel:** 8", rifled steel. **Weight:** 39 oz. **Length:** 13-5/8". **Power:** Hand pumped. **Sights:** Blade front, rear adjustable for windage and elevation. **Features:** Bolt action moulded plastic grip, hand size pump forearm. Cross-bolt safety. From Crosman.
Price: About **$60.00**

CROSMAN AUTO AIR II PISTOL
Caliber: BB, 17-shot magazine, 177 pellet, single shot. **Barrel:** 8-5/8" steel, smoothbore. **Weight:** 13 oz. **Length:** 10-3/4" overall. **Power:** CO2 Powerlet. **Stocks:** Grooved plastic. **Sights:** Blade front, adjustable rear; highlighted system. **Features:** Velocity to 480 fps (BBs), 430 fps (pellets). Semi-automatic action with BBs, single shot with pellets. Black. Introduced 1991. From Crosman.
Price: About **$38.00**

CROSMAN MODEL 357 SERIES AIR PISTOL
Caliber: 177 10-shot pellet clips. **Barrel:** 4" (Model 3574W), 6" (Model 3576W). **Weight:** 32 oz. (6"). **Length:** 11-3/8" overall (357-6). **Power:** CO2 Powerlet. **Stocks:** Grip, wrap-around style. **Sights:** Ramp front, fully adjustable rear. **Features:** Average 430 fps (Model 3574W). Break-open barrel for easy loading. Single or double action. Vent. rib barrel. Wide, smooth trigger. Black finish. From Crosman.
Price: 4" or 6", about **$65.00**

CROSMAN MODEL 1008 REPEAT AIR
Caliber: 177, 8-shot pellet clip. **Barrel:** 4.25", rifled steel. **Weight:** 17 oz. **Length:** 8.625" overall. **Power:** CO2 Powerlet. **Stocks:** Checkered black plastic. **Sights:** Post front, adjustable rear. **Features:** Velocity about 430 fps. Break-open barrel for easy loading; single or double semi-automatic action; two 8-shot clips included. Optional carrying case available. Introduced 1992. From Crosman.
Price: About **$60.00**
Price: With case, about **$70.00**
Price: Model 1008SB (silver and black finish), about **$60.00**

DAISY MODEL 2003 PELLET PISTOL
Caliber: 177 pellet, 35-shot clip. **Barrel:** Rifled steel. **Weight:** 2.2 lbs. **Length:** 11.7" overall. **Power:** CO2. **Stocks:** Checkered plastic. **Sights:** Blade front, open rear. **Features:** Velocity to 400 fps. Crossbolt trigger-block safety. Made in U.S. by Daisy Mfg. Co.
Price: About **$67.95**

DAISY MODEL 454 AIR PISTOL
Caliber: 177 BB, 20-shot clip. **Barrel:** Smoothbore steel. **Weight:** 1.6 lbs. **Length:** 10.4" overall. **Power:** CO2. **Stocks:** Moulded black, ribbed composition. **Sights:** Blade front, fixed rear. **Features:** Velocity to 420 fps. Semi-automatic action; cross-bolt safety; black finish. Introduced 1998. Made in U.S. by Dairy Mfg. Co.
Price: **$61.95**

DAISY/POWERLINE 717 PELLET PISTOL
Caliber: 177, single shot. **Barrel:** 9.61". **Weight:** 2.25 lbs. **Length:** 13-1/2" overall. **Stocks:** Moulded wood-grain plastic, with thumbrest. **Sights:** Blade and ramp front, micro-adjustable notch rear. **Features:** Single pump pneumatic pistol. Rifled steel barrel. Cross-bolt trigger block. Muzzle velocity 385 fps. From Daisy Mfg. Co. Introduced 1979.
Price: About **$71.95**

Daisy/PowerLine 747 Pistol
Similar to the 717 pistol except has a 12-groove rifled steel barrel by Lothar Walther, and adjustable trigger pull weight. Velocity of 360 fps. Manual cross-bolt safety.
Price: About **$140.00**

DAISY/POWERLINE 1140 PELLET PISTOL
Caliber: 177, single shot. **Barrel:** Rifled steel. **Weight:** 1.3 lbs. **Length:** 11.7" overall. **Power:** Single-stroke barrel cocking. **Stocks:** Checkered resin. **Sights:** Hooded post front, open adjustable rear. **Features:** Velocity to 325 fps. Made of black lightweight engineering resin. Introduced 1995. From Daisy.
Price: About **$38.95**

DAISY/POWERLINE 44 REVOLVER
Caliber: 177 pellets, 6-shot. **Barrel:** 6", rifled steel; interchangeable 4" and 8". **Weight:** 2.7 lbs. **Length:** 13.1" overall. **Power:** CO2. **Stocks:** Moulded plastic with checkering. **Sights:** Blade on ramp front, fully adjustable notch rear. **Features:** Velocity up to 400 fps. Replica of 44 Magnum revolver. Has swingout cylinder and interchangeable barrels. Introduced 1987. From Daisy Mfg. Co.
Price: **$59.95**

DAISY/POWERLINE 1270 CO2 AIR PISTOL
Caliber: BB, 60-shot magazine. **Barrel:** Smoothbore steel. **Weight:** 17 oz. **Length:** 11.1" overall. **Power:** CO2 pump action. **Stocks:** Moulded black polymer. **Sights:** Blade on ramp front, adjustable rear. **Features:** Velocity to 420 fps. Crossbolt trigger block safety; plated finish. Introduced 1997. Made in U.S. by Daisy Mfg. Co.
Price: About **$39.95**

EAA/BAIKAL IZH-46 TARGET AIR PISTOL
Caliber: 177, single shot. **Barrel:** 11.02". **Weight:** 2.87 lbs. **Length:** 16.54" overall. **Power:** Underlever single-stroke pneumatic. **Grips:** Adjustable wooden target. **Sights:** Micrometer fully adjustable rear, blade front. **Features:** Velocity about 420 fps. Hammer-forged, rifled barrel. Imported from Russia by European American Armory.
Price: **$319.00**

EAA/BAIKAL MP-654K AIR PISTOL
Caliber: 177 BB, detachable 13-shot magazine. **Barrel:** 3.75". **Weight:** 1.6 lbs. **Length:** 6.34". **Power:** CO2 cartridge. **Grips:** Black checkered plastic. **Sights:** Notch rear, blade front. **Features:** Velocity about 380 fps. Double-action trigger; slide safety; metal slide and frame. Replica of Makarov pistol. Imported from Russia by European American Armory.
Price: **$119.00**

EAA/BAIKAL MP-651K AIR PISTOL/RIFLE
Caliber: 177 pellet (8-shot magazine); 177 BB (23-shot). **Barrel:** 5.9" (17.25" with rifle attachment). **Weight:** 1.54 lbs. (3.3 lbs. with rifle attachment). **Length:** 9.4" (31.3" with rifle attachment) **Power:** CO2 cartridge, semi-automatic. **Stock:** Plastic. **Sights:** Notch rear/blade front (pistol); periscopic sighting system (rifle). **Features:** Velocity 328 fps. Unique pistol/rifle combination allows the pistol to be inserted into the rifle shell. Imported from Russia by European American Armory.
Price: **$99.00**

"GAT" AIR PISTOL
Caliber: 177, single shot. **Barrel:** 7-1/2" cocked, 9-1/2" extended. **Weight:** 22 oz. **Power:** Spring-piston. **Stocks:** Cast checkered metal. **Sights:** Fixed. **Features:** Shoots pellets, corks or darts. Matte black finish. Imported from England by Stone Enterprises, Inc.
Price: **$24.95**

HAMMERLI 480 MATCH AIR PISTOL
Caliber: 177, single shot. **Barrel:** 9.8". **Weight:** 37 oz. **Length:** 16.5" overall. **Power:** Air or CO2. **Stocks:** Walnut with 7-degree rake adjustment. Stippled grip area. **Sights:** Undercut blade front, fully adjustable open match rear. **Features:** Underbarrel cannister charges with air or CO2 for power supply; gives 320 shots per filling. Trigger adjustable for position. Introduced 1994. Imported from Switzerland by Hammerli Pistols U.S.A.
Price: **$1,391.00**

Hammerli 480K2 Match Air Pistol
Similar to 480 except short, detachable aluminum air cylinder for use only with compressed ai, can be filled while on gun or off; special adjustable barrel weights. Muzzle velocity of 470 fps, gives about 180 shots. Stippled black composition grip with adjustable palm shelf and rake angle. Case and cylinder. Introduced 1996. Imported from Switzerland by SIGARMS, Inc.
Price: **$1,218.00**

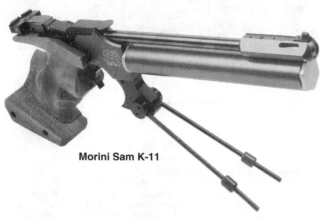

Morini Sam K-11

HAMMERLI AP40 AIR PISTOL
Caliber: 177. **Barrel:** 10". **Stocks:** Adjustable orthopaedic. **Sights:** Fully adjustable micrometer. **Features:** Sleek, light, well balanced and accurate. Imported from Switzerland by Nygord Precision Products.
Price: $985.00

MARKSMAN 1010 REPEATER PISTOL
Caliber: 177, 18-shot BB repeater. **Barrel:** 2-1/2", smoothbore. **Weight:** 24 oz. **Length:** 8-1/4" overall. **Power:** Spring. **Features:** Velocity to 200 fps. Thumb safety. Black finish. Uses BBs, darts, bolts or pellets. Repeats with BBs only. From Marksman Products.
Price: Matte black finish $26.00
Price: Model 2000 (as above except silver-chrome finish). $27.00

MARKSMAN 2005 LASERHAWK SPECIAL EDITION AIR PISTOL
Caliber: 177, 24-shot magazine. **Barrel:** 3.8", smoothbore. **Weight:** 22 oz. **Length:** 10.3" overall. **Power:** Spring-air. **Sights:** Checkered. **Sights:** Fixed fiber optic front sight. **Features:** Velocity to 300 fps with Hyper-Velocity pellets. Square trigger guard with skeletonized trigger; extended barrel for greater velocity and accuracy. Shoots BBs, pellets, darts or bolts. Made in the U.S. From Marksman Products.
Price: $32.00

MORINI 162E MATCH AIR PISTOL
Caliber: 177, single shot. **Barrel:** 9.4". **Weight:** 32 oz. **Length:** 16.1" overall. **Power:** Scuba air. **Stocks:** Adjustable match type. **Sights:** Interchangeable blade front, fully adjustable match-type rear. **Features:** Power mechanism shuts down when pressure drops to a pre-set level. Adjustable electronic trigger. Introduced 1995. Imported from Switzerland by Nygord Precision Products.
Price: $995.00
Price: 162M mechanical trigger $975.00

MORINI SAM K-11 AIR PISTOL
Caliber: 177. **Barrel:** 10". **Weight:** 38 oz. **Stocks:** Fully adjustable. **Sights:** Fully adjustable. **Features:** Improved trigger, more angle adjustment on grip. Sophisticated counter balance system. Deluxe aluminum case, two cylinders and manometer. Imported from Switzerland by Nygord Precision Products.
Price: $995.00

PARDINI K58 MATCH AIR PISTOL
Caliber: 177, single shot. **Barrel:** 9". **Weight:** 37.7 oz. **Length:** 15.5" overall. **Power:** Pre-charged compressed air; single-stroke cocking. **Stocks:** Adjustable match type; stippled walnut. **Sights:** Interchangeable post front, fully adjustable match rear. **Features:** Fully adjustable trigger. Short version K-2 available. Imported from Italy by Nygord Precision Products.
Price: $750.00
Price: K2 model, precharged air pistol, introduced in 1998 . . . . $895.00

RWS 9B/9N AIR PISTOLS
Caliber: 177, single shot. **Grips:** Plastic with thumbrest. **Sights:** Adjustable. **Features:** Spring-piston powered; 550 fps. Black or nickel finish. Introduced 2001. Imported from Germany by Dynamit Nobel-RWS.
Price: 9B $169.00
Price: 9N $185.00

RWS C-225 AIR PISTOLS
Caliber: 177, 8-shot rotary magazine. **Barrel:** 4", 6". **Power:** CO2. **Stocks:** Checkered black plastic. **Sights:** Post front, rear adjustable for windage. **Features:** Velocity to 385 fps. Semi-automatic fire; decocking lever. Imported from Germany by Dynamit Nobel-RWS.
Price: 4", blue. $210.00
Price: 4", nickel. $220.00
Price: 6", blue. $220.00

STEYR LP 5CP MATCH AIR PISTOL
Caliber: 177, 5-shot magazine. **Weight:** 40.7 oz. **Length:** 15.2" overall. **Power:** Pre-charged air cylinder. **Stocks:** Adjustable match type. **Sights:** Interchangeable blade front, fully adjustable match rear. **Features:** Adjustable sight radius; fully adjustable trigger. Barrel compensator. One-shot magazine available. Introduced 1995. Imported from Austria by Nygord Precision Products.
Price: $1,150.00

STEYR LP10P MATCH PISTOL
Caliber: 177, single shot. **Barrel:** 9". **Weight:** 38.7 oz. **Length:** 15.3" overall. **Power:** Scuba air. **Stocks:** Fully adjustable Morini match, palm shelf, stippled walnut. **Sights:** Interchangeable blade in 4mm, 4.5mm or 5mm widths, fully adjustable open rear, interchangeable 3.5mm or 4mm leaves. **Features:** Velocity about 500 fps. Adjustable trigger, adjustable sight radius from 12.4" to 13.2". With compensator. New "aborber" eliminates recoil. Imported from Austria by Nygord Precision Products.
Price: $1,125.00

TECH FORCE SS2 OLYMPIC COMPETITION AIR PISTOL
Caliber: 177 pellet, single shot. **Barrel:** 7.4". **Weight:** 2.8 lbs. **Length:** 16.5" overall. **Power:** Spring piston, sidelever. **Grips:** Hardwood. **Sights:** Extended adjustable rear, blade front accepts inserts. **Features:** Velocity 520 fps. Recoilless design; adjustments allow duplication of a firearm's feel. Match-grade, adjustable trigger; includes carrying case. Imported from China by Compasseco Inc.
Price: $295.00

TECH FORCE 35 AIR PISTOL
Caliber: 177 pellet, single shot. **Barrel:** 7.4". **Weight:** 2.86 lbs. **Length:** 14.9" overall. **Power:** Spring piston, underlever. **Grips:** Hardwood. **Sights:** Micrometer adjustable rear, blade front. **Features:** Velocity 400 fps. Grooved for scope mount; trigger safety. Imported from China by Compasseco Inc.
Price: $49.95

Tech Force 8 Air Pistol
Similar to Tech Force 35, but with break-barrel action, ambidextrous polymer grips. From Compasseco Inc.
Price: $59.95

Tech Force S2-1 Air Pistol
Similar to Tech Force 8, more basic grips and sights for plinking. From Compasseco Inc.
Price: $29.95

WALTHER CP88 PELLET PISTOL
Caliber: 177, 8-shot rotary magazine. **Barrel:** 4", 6". **Weight:** 37 oz. (4" barrel) **Length:** 7" (4" barrel). **Power:** CO2. **Stocks:** Checkered plastic. **Sights:** Blade front, fully adjustable rear. **Features:** Faithfully replicates size, weight and trigger pull of the 9mm Walther P88 compact pistol. Has SA/DA trigger mechanism; ambidextrous safety, levers. Comes with two magazines, 500 pellets, one CO2 cartridge. Introduced 1997. Imported from Germany by Interarms.
Price: Blue $179.00
Price: Nickel $189.00

WALTHER LP201 MATCH PISTOL
Caliber: 177, single shot. **Barrel:** 8.66". **Weight:** NA. **Length:** 15.1" overall. **Power:** Scuba air. **Stocks:** Orthopaedic target type. **Sights:** Undercut blade front, open match rear fully adjustable for windage and elevation. **Features:** Adjustable velocity; matte finish. Introduced 1995. Imported from Germany by Nygord Precision Products.
Price: $1,095.00

Walther CP88 Competition Pellet Pistol
Similar to the standard CP88 except has 6" match-grade barrel, muzzle weight, wood or plastic stocks. Weighs 41 oz., has overall length of 9". Introduced 1997. Imported from Germany by Interarms.
Price: Blue, plastic grips. $170.00
Price: Nickel, plastic grips $195.00
Price: Blue, wood grips $205.00
Price: Nickel, wood grips $232.00

WALTHER CP99 AIR PISTOL
Caliber: 177 pellet, 8-shot rotary magazine. **Barrel:** 3". **Weight:** 26 oz. **Length:** 7.1" overall. **Power:** CO2 cartridge. **Grip:** Polymer. **Sights:** Drift-adjustable rear, blade front. **Features:** Velocity 320 fps. Replica of Walther P99 pistol. Trigger allows single and double action; ambidextrous magazine release; interchangeable backstraps to fit variety of hand sizes. Introduced 2000. From Walther USA.
Price: .... NA

WALTHER PPK/S AIR PISTOL
Caliber: 177 BB. **Barrel:** N/A. **Weight:** 20 oz. **Length:** 6.3" overall. **Power:** CO2 cartridge. **Grip:** Plastic. **Sights:** Fixed rear, blade front. **Features:** Replica of Walther PPK pistol. Blow back system moves slide when fired; trigger allows single and double action. Introduced 2000. From Walther USA.
Price: .... NA

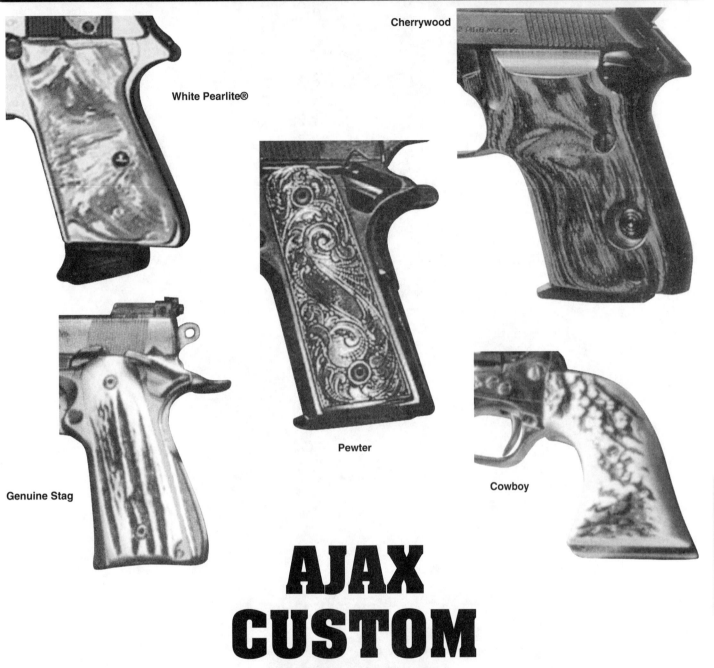

White Pearlite®

Cherrywood

Pewter

Genuine Stag

Cowboy

AJAX CUSTOM GRIPS

Grip materials include ivory polymer, ivory, white and black Pearlite, Indian Sambar stag, walnut, cherrywood, black silverwood, simulated buffalo horn and pewter. Smooth, fingergroove and checkered designs offered for some models. Available for most single- and double-action revolvers and automatics. Made in U.S. by Ajax Custom Grips Inc.

Prices: $35 to $145 (ivory is by special order only)

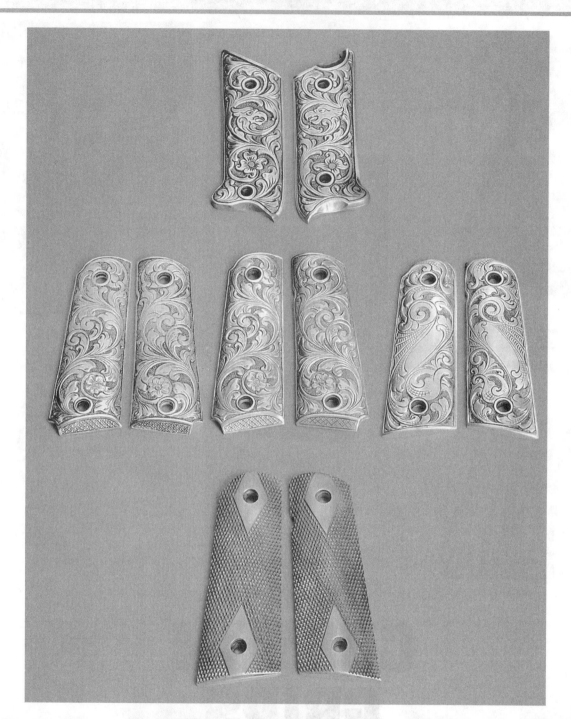

ALL AMERICA SALES

All America Sales offers pewter grips in a variety of patterns, including scrollwork, checkering, "the right to keep and bear arms" eagle and others. Some models feature a gold finish. Grips available for Colt Government, Gold Cup and Commander models; Ruger Mark II pistol; and some single-action revolvers. From All America Sales Inc.

Prices: $49.95 to $59.95

ACCESSORIES

ALL AMERICA SALES *(continued)*

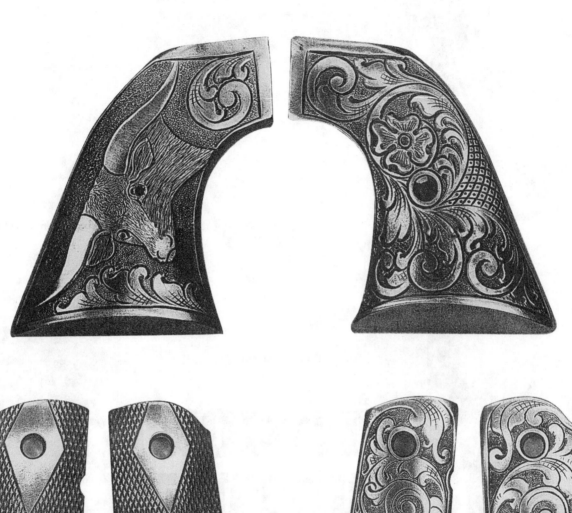

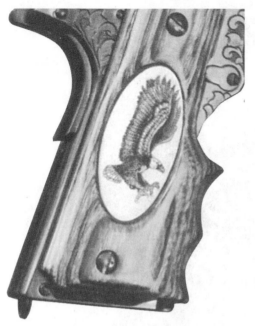

Colt Government Model Landing Eagle

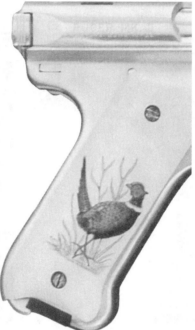

Ruger Pheasant

Colt Single Action Army Classic Panel

Colt Government Model Facing Buck

ALTAMONT CUSTOM GRIPS

Beretta Super Rosewood

Grip materials include bonded ivory, laminated rosewood, fancy walnut, laminated walnut, laminated silver-black hardwood, black ebony, bocote, rosewood, hard black epoxy, imitation pearl, Asian Sambar stag and ivory. Scrimshaw designs, inlays, carvings and personalization available. Smooth, fingergroove and checkered designs offered. Grips made for most single- and double-action revolvers and automatics. Made in U.S. by Altamont.

Prices: $21 to $85 (ivory and other exotics at additional cost)

GRIPS

Slip-on Grips for Autoloaders

Boot Grips for Revolvers

Grips for Pistols

BUTLER CREEK (UNCLE MIKE'S)

CUSTOM GRADE SYNTHETIC MOLDED GRIPS

These Uncle Mike's polymer grips are designed by custom handgun grip maker Craig Spegel. They are designed to fill the hand without a spongy feel. Double-action revolver grips feature finger grooves for improved control. From Butler Creek.

Price: Revolver Grips (for most Ruger, Smith & Wesson and Taurus single- and double-action revolvers) **$20.95**
Price: Revolver Boot Grips (for small-frame Ruger, Smith & Wesson and Taurus double-action revolvers) **$20.95**
Price: Slip-on Grips (for most small, medium, compact large-frame and full-size large frame automatics that do not have grip safeties) ...**$10.95**
Price: Pistol Grips (for most Ruger, Smith & Wesson Beretta, Colt, Sig-Sauer, Taurus and CZ-75 autos) **$20.95**

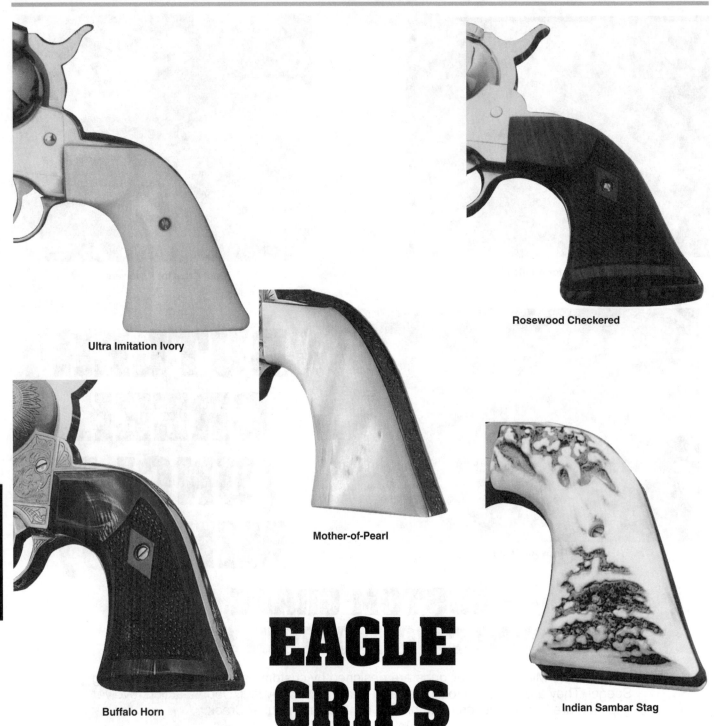

Ultra Imitation Ivory

Rosewood Checkered

Mother-of-Pearl

Buffalo Horn

EAGLE GRIPS

Indian Sambar Stag

Grip materials include imitation ivory, rosewood, buffalo horn, ebony, mother of pearl and Indian Sambar stag. Smooth, fingergroove and checkered designs offered. Grips made for most single- and double-action revolvers and automatics. Made in U.S. by Eagle Grips.

Prices: From $39.95 (checkering at additional cost)

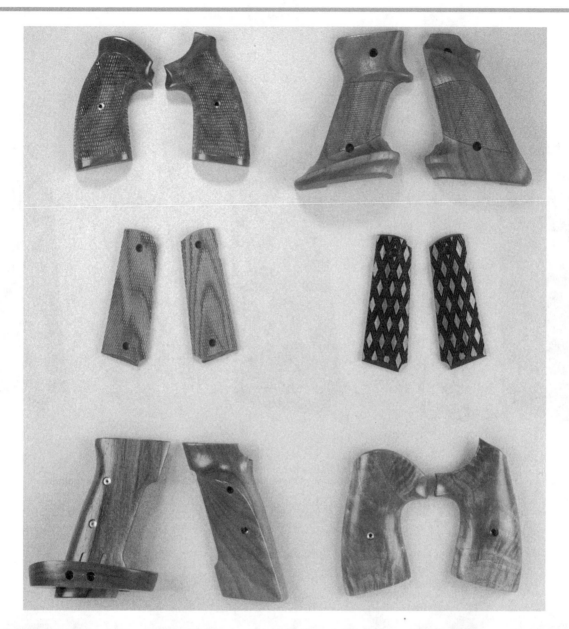

HERRETT STOCKS INC.

Herrett Stocks Inc. of Twin Falls, Idaho, has been producing high-quality handgun grips (and rifle stocks) for more than 40 years. Models are available to fit nearly every pistol and revolver in production — and even a few that are no longer made. The company specializes in American walnut grips, but also offers cocobolo, bubinga and other exotic woods. Grips are available with a variety of options, including smooth, checkered or finger grooved; double-diamond pattern; black lacquer finish for contrast of the diamond pattern; and many models custom-fitted to the shooter's hand, including the famous Shooting Star design. Herrett grips are made in the U.S.

Prices: $19.95 to $329.95

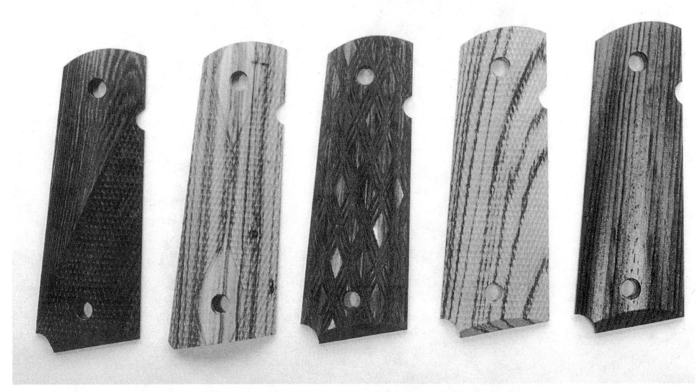

From left to right: 1911-style in camiteo; 1911-style in tulipwood;
1911-style in red raspberry Dymondwood; 1911-style in zebrawood; and 1911-style in cocobolo

AHRENDS INC.

Ahrends Inc. specializes in grips for Colt and Browning pistols, but also offers grips for Beretta, Smith & Wesson, Walther and many other handguns. Woods available include bubinga, cocobolo, Gaboon ebony, kingwood, Madagascar rosewood, Moradillo, tulipwood, cordia, camiteo, padauk, Iowa black walnut, African blackwood, and others. Laminated Dymondwood is offered in 10 colors, including winewood, red raspberry, indigo royal blue, French green, charcoal ruby and apple jack. Offered in smooth, fully checkered, tactical and diamond patterns. Made in U.S. by Ahrends Inc.

Prices: $36 to $86
(skip checkering and other options offered at additional cost)

AHRENDS INC. *(continued)*

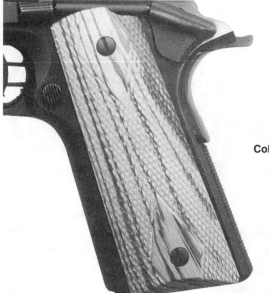

Colt 1911 Government model in zebrawood

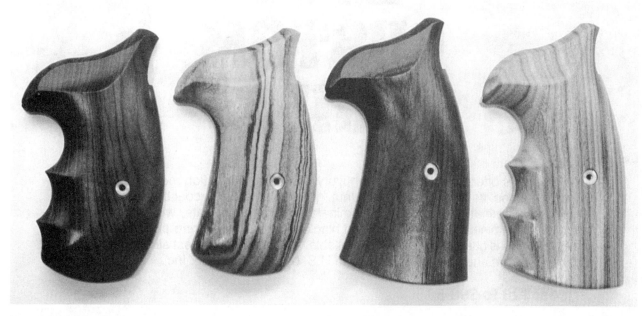

From left to right: S&W revolver in cocobolo; S&W revolver in cordia; S&W revolver in cocobolo; and S&W revolver in moradillo

GRIPS

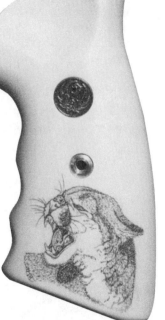

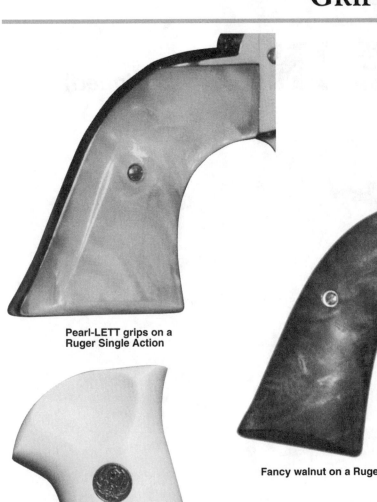

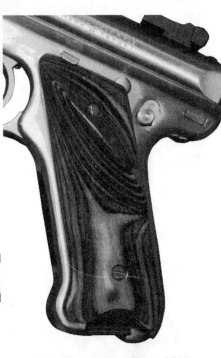

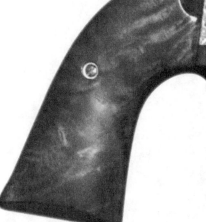

Pearl-LETT grips on a
Ruger Single Action

Genuine India stag on a Ruger Single Action

Fancy walnut on a Ruger Bisley

Scrimshaw on micarta
for Ruger Double Action

Wood laminate on Ruger MK II

LETT CUSTOM GRIPS

Grip materials offered include imitation ivory, Pearl-Lett (imitation mother of pearl), Bolivian rosewood, zebrawood, fancy walnut, goncalo alves, charcoal burgundy laminate, silver black laminate, charcoal ruby laminate, hawkeye laminate, winewood laminate, camouflage laminate, ivory micarta and black micarta. Checkering and scrimshaw designs, as well as custom scrimshaw, available. Grips made for most single- and double-action revolvers and automatics. Made in U.S. by W.F. Lett Mfg. Inc.

Prices: $26 to $98.50

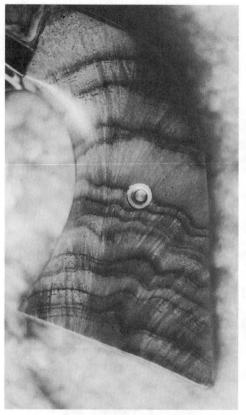

Hi-Grade French Walnut

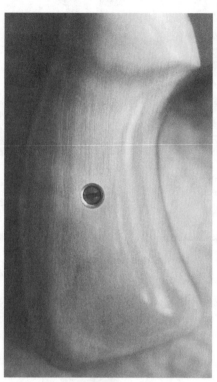

Alaskan Dall Ram's Horn

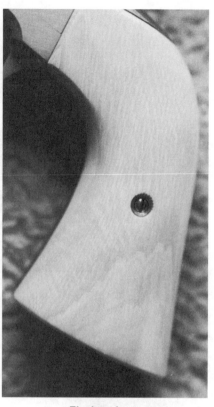

Elephant Ivory

ROY'S CUSTOM GRIPS

This Lynchburg Va., company offers handgun grips in more than 44 materials, including cocobolo, ebony, flamewood, curly koa, pau ferro, rosewood, snakewood, tulipwood, walnut, bubinga, briar burl, zebrawood, Alaskan Dall ram horn, European red stag and genuine ivory. Several finishes are offered. Each set of grips is handmade and fitted to the individual firearm. Made in U.S. by Roy's Custom Grips.

Prices: Wood: $100 to $300
Prices: Ivory: $400 to $750

ACCESSORIES

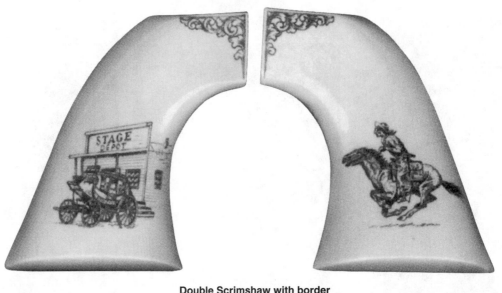

Double Scrimshaw with border

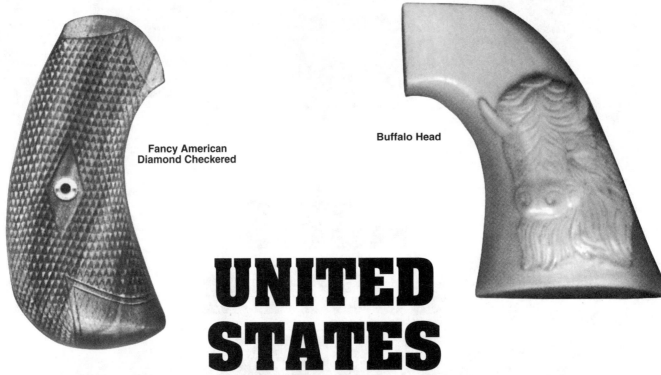

Fancy American
Diamond Checkered

Buffalo Head

UNITED STATES FIRE-ARMS GRIPS

Grip materials include hard rubber, American walnut, Turkish burl, bastone burl, English burl, African rosewood, pearl, bone, ivory micarta and ivory. Checkering, scrimshaw and carved figuring also available. Grips available for single-action revolvers. Made in U.S. by United States Fire-Arms Manu. Co. Inc.

Prices: $65 to $625

CH4D Heavyduty Champion

Frame: Cast iron
Frame Type: O-frame
Die Thread: 7/8-14 or 1-14
Avg. Rounds Per Hour: NA
Ram Stroke: 3-1/4"
Weight: 26 lbs.
Features: 1.185" diameter ram with 16 square inches of bearing surface; ram drilled to allow passage of spent primers; solid steel handle; toggle that slightly breaks over the top dead center. Includes universal primer arm with large and small punches. From CH Tool & Die/4D Custom Die.
Price: $220.00

CH4D No. 444 4-Station "H" Press

Frame: Aluminum alloy
Frame Type: H-frame
Die Thread: 7/8-14
Avg. Rounds Per Hour: 200
Ram Stroke: 3-3/4"
Weight: 12 lbs.
Features: Two 7/8" solid steel shaft "H" supports; platen rides on permanently lubed bronze bushings; loads smallest pistol to largest magnum rifle cases and has strength to full-length resize. Includes four rams, large and small primer arm and primer catcher. From CH Tool & Die/4D Custom Die, Co.
Price: $195.00

CH4D No. 444-X Pistol Champ

Frame: Aluminum alloy
Frame Type: H-frame
Die Thread: 7/8-14
Avg. Rounds Per Hour: 200
Ram Stroke: 3-3/4"
Weight: 12 lbs.
Features: Tungsten carbide sizing die; Speed Seater seating die with tapered entrance to automatically align bullet on case mouth; automatic primer feed for large or small primers; push-button powder measure with easily changed bushings for 215 powder/load combinations; taper crimp die. Conversion kit for caliber changeover available. From CH Tool & Die/4D Custom Die, Co.
Price: .... $292.00-$316.50

FORSTER Co-Ax Press B-2

Frame: Cast iron
Frame Type: Modified O-frame
Die Thread: 7/8-14
Avg. Rounds Per Hour: 120
Ram Stroke: 4"
Weight: 18 lbs.
Features: Snap in/snap out die change; spent primer catcher with drop tube threaded into carrier below shellholder; automatic, handle-activated, cammed shellholder with opposing spring-loaded jaws to contact extractor groove; floating guide rods for alignment and reduced friction; no torque on the head due to design of linkage and pivots; shellholder jaws that float with die permitting case to center in the die; right- or left-hand operation; priming device for seating to factory specifications. "S" shellholder jaws included. From Forster Products.
Price: $298.00
Price: Extra shellholder jaws $26.00

HOLLYWOOD Senior Press

Frame: Ductile iron
Frame Type: O-frame
Die Thread: 7/8-14
Avg. Rounds Per Hour: 50-100
Ram Stroke: 6-1/2"
Weight: 50 lbs.
Features: Leverage and bearing surfaces ample for reloading cartridges or swaging bullets. Precision ground one-piece 2-1/2" pillar with base; operating

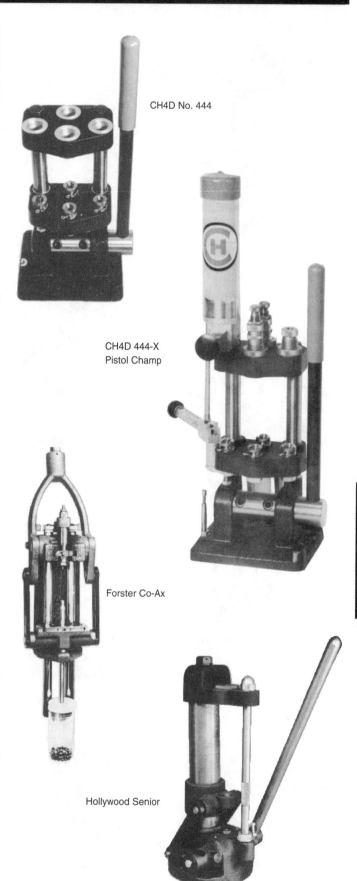

CH4D No. 444

CH4D 444-X
Pistol Champ

Forster Co-Ax

Hollywood Senior

ACCESSORIES

METALLIC CARTRIDGE PRESSES

Hollywood Senior Turret

Lee Hand Press

Hornady Lock-N-Load Classic

Lee Challenger

handle of 3/4" steel and 15" long; 5/8" steel tie-down rod fro added strength when swaging; heavy steel toggle and camming arms held by 1/2" steel pins in reamed holes. The 1-1/2" steel die bushing takes standard threaded dies; removed, it allows use of Hollywood shotshell dies. From Hollywood Engineering.

Price: **$500.00**

HOLLYWOOD Senior Turret Press

Frame: Ductile iron
Frame Type: H-frame
Die Thread: 7/8-14
Avg. Rounds Per Hour: 50-100
Ram Stroke: 6-1/2"
Weight: 50 lbs.
Features: Same features as Senior press except has three-position turret head; holes in turret may be tapped 1-1/2" or 7/8" or four of each. Height, 15". Comes complete with one turret indexing handle; one 1-1/2" to 7/8" die hole bushing; one 5/8" tie down bar for swaging. From Hollywood Engineering.

Price: **$600.00**

HORNADY Lock-N-Load Classic

Frame: Die cast heat-treated aluminum alloy
Frame Type: O-frame
Die Thread: 7/8-14
Avg. Rounds Per Hour: NA
Ram Stroke: 3-5/8"
Weight: 14 lbs.
Features: Features Lock-N-Load bushing system that allows instant die changeovers. Solid steel linkage arms that rotate on steel pins; 30° angled frame design for improved visibility and accessibility; primer arm automatically moves in and out of ram for primer pickup and solid seating; two primer arms for large and small primers; long offset handle for increased leverage and unobstructed reloading; lifetime warranty. Comes as a package with primer catcher, PPS automatic primer feed and three Lock-N-Load die bushings. Dies and shellholder available separately or as a kit with primer catcher, positive priming system, automatic primer feed, three die bushings and reloading accessories. From Hornady Mfg. Co.

Price: Press and Three Die Bushings **$99.95**
Price: Classic Reloading Kit. **$259.95**

LEE Hand Press

Frame: ASTM 380 aluminum
Frame Type: NA
Die Thread: 7/8-14
Avg. Rounds Per Hour: 100
Ram Stroke: 3-1/4"
Weight: 1 lb., 8 oz.
Features: Small and lightweight for portability; compound linkage for handling up to 375 H&H and case forming. Dies and shellholder not included. From Lee Precision, Inc.

Price: **$22.98**

LEE Challenger Press

Frame: ASTM 380 aluminum
Frame Type: O-frame
Die Thread: 7/8-14
Avg. Rounds Per Hour: 100
Ram Stroke: 3-1/2"
Weight: 4 lbs., 1 oz.
Features: Larger than average opening with 30° offset for maximum hand clearance; steel connecting pins; spent primer catcher; handle adjustable for start and stop positions; handle repositions for left- or right-hand use; shortened handle travel to prevent springing the frame from alignment. Dies and shellholders not included. From Lee Precision, Inc.

Price: **$45.00**

ACCESSORIES

METALLIC CARTRIDGE PRESSES

LEE Loader

Kit consists of reloading dies to be used with mallet or soft hammer. Neck sizes only. Comes with powder charge cup. From Lee Precision, Inc.
Price: $19.98

LEE Reloader Press

Frame: ASTM 380 aluminum
Frame Type: C-frame
Die Thread: 7/8-14
Avg. Rounds Per Hour: 100
Ram Stroke: 3"
Weight: 1 lb., 12 oz.
Features: Balanced lever to prevent pinching fingers; unlimited hand clearance; left- or right-hand use. Dies and shellholders not included. From Lee Precision, Inc.
Price: $24.98

Lee Reloader

LEE Turret Press

Frame: ASTM 380 aluminum
Frame Type: O-frame
Die Thread: 7/8-14
Avg. Rounds Per Hour: 300
Ram Stroke: 3"
Weight: 7 lbs., 2 oz.
Features: Replaceable turret lifts out by rotating 30˚; T-primer arm reverses for large or small primers; built-in primer catcher; adjustable handle for right- or left-hand use or changing angle of down stroke; accessory mounting hole for Lee Auto-Disk powder measure. Optional Auto-Index rotates die turret to next station for semi-progressive use. Safety override prevents overstressing should turret not turn. From Lee Precision, Inc.
Price: $69.98
Price: With Auto-Index $83.98
Price: Four-Hole Turret with Auto-Index $85.98

Lee Turret

LYMAN 310 Tool

Frame: Stainless steel
Frame Type: NA
Die Thread: 7/8-14
Avg. Rounds Per Hour: NA
Ram Stroke: NA
Weight: 10 oz.
Features: Compact, portable reloading tool for pistol or rifle cartridges. Adapter allows loading rimmed or rimless cases. Die set includes neck resizing/decapping die; primer seating chamber; neck expanding die; bullet seating die; and case head adapter. From Lyman Products Corp.
Price: Dies $45.95
Price: Press $47.50
Price: Carrying pouch $9.95

LYMAN AccuPress

Frame: Die cast
Frame Type: C-frame
Die Thread: 7/8-14
Avg. Rounds Per Hour: 75
Ram Stroke: 3.4"
Weight: 4 lbs.
Features: Reversible, contoured handle for bench mount or hand-held use; for rifle or pistol; compound leverage; Delta frame design. Accepts all standard powder measures. From Lyman Products Corp.
Price: $34.95

Lyman 310

METALLIC CARTRIDGE PRESSES

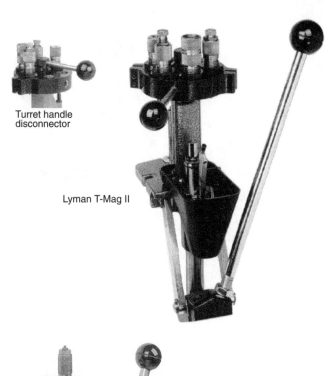

Turret handle disconnector

Lyman T-Mag II

Lyman Crusher II

Ponsness/Warren
Metal-Matic P-200

LYMAN Crusher II

Frame: Cast iron
Frame Type: O-frame
Die Thread: 7/8-14
Avg. Rounds Per Hour: 75
Ram Stroke: 3-7/8"
Weight: 19 lbs.
Features: Reloads both pistol and rifle cartridges; 1" diameter ram; 4-1/2" press opening for loading magnum cartridges; direct torque design; right- or left-hand use. New base design with 14 square inches of flat mounting surface with three bolt holes. Comes with priming arm and primer catcher. Dies and shellholders not included. From Lyman Products Corp.
Price:.. **$116.50**

LYMAN T-Mag II

Frame: Cast iron with silver metalflake powder finish
Frame Type: Turret
Die Thread: 7/8-14
Avg. Rounds Per Hour: 125
Ram Stroke: 3-13/16"
Weight: 18 lbs.
Features: Reengineered and upgraded with new turret system for ease of indexing and tool-free turret removal for caliber changeover; new flat machined base for bench mounting; new nickel-plated non-rust handle and links; and new silver hammertone powder coat finish for durability. Right- or left-hand operation; handles all rifle or pistol dies. Comes with priming arm and primer catcher. Dies and shellholders not included. From Lyman Products Corp.
Price:.. **$164.95**
Price: Extra turret **$37.50**

PONSNESS/WARREN Metal-Matic P-200

Frame: Die cast aluminum
Frame Type: Unconventional
Die Thread: 7/8-14
Avg. Rounds Per Hour: 200+
Weight: 18 lbs.
Features: Designed for straight-wall cartridges; die head with 10 tapped holes for holding dies and accessories for two calibers at one time; removable spent primer box; pivoting arm moves case from station to station. Comes with large and small primer tool. Optional accessories include primer feed, extra die head, primer speed feeder, powder measure extension and dust cover. Dies, powder measure and shellholder not included. From Ponsness/Warren.
Price:.. **$215.00**
Price: Extra die head....................................... **$44.95**
Price: Powder measure extension **$29.95**
Price: Primer feed... **$44.95**
Price: Primer speed feed.................................. **$14.50**
Price: Dust cover.. **$21.95**

RCBS Partner

Frame: Aluminum
Frame Type: O-frame
Die Thread: 7/8-14
Avg. Rounds Per Hour: 50-60
Ram Stroke: 3-5/8"
Weight: 5 lbs.
Features: Designed for the beginning reloader. Comes with primer arm equipped with interchangeable primer plugs and sleeves for seating large and small primers. Shellholder and dies not included. Available in kit form (see Metallic Presses—Accessories). From RCBS.
Price:.. **$61.95**

RCBS AmmoMaster Single

Frame: Aluminum base; cast iron top plate connected by three steel posts.
Frame Type: NA
Die Thread: 1-1/4"-12 bushing; 7/8-14 threads
Avg. Rounds Per Hour: 50-60
Ram Stroke: 5-1/4"
Weight: 19 lbs.
Features: Single-stage press convertible to progressive. Will form cases or swage bullets. Case detection system to disengage powder measure when no case is present in powder charging station; five-station shellplate; Uniflow Powder measure with clear powder measure adaptor to make bridged powders visible and correctable. 50-cal. conversion kit allows reloading 50 BMG. Kit includes top plate to accommodate either 1-3/8" x 12 or 1-1/2" x 12 reloading dies. Piggyback die plate for quick caliber change-overs available. Reloading dies not included. From RCBS.
Price: $206.95
Price: 50 conversion kit $96.95
Price: Piggyback/AmmoMaster die plate $25.95
Price: Piggyback/AmmoMaster shellplate $25.95
Price: Press cover $10.95

RCBS Reloader Special-5

Frame: Aluminum
Frame Type: 30˚ offset O-frame
Die Thread: 1-1/4"-12 bushing; 7/8-14 threads
Avg. Rounds Per Hour: 50-60
Ram Stroke: 3-1/16"
Weight: 7.5 lbs.
Features: Single-stage press convertible to progressive with RCBS Piggyback II. Primes cases during resizing operation. Will accept RCBS shotshell dies. From RCBS.
Price: $112.95

RCBS Rock Chucker

Frame: Cast iron
Frame Type: O-frame
Die Thread: 1-1/4"-12 bushing; 7/8-14 threads
Avg. Rounds Per Hour: 50-60
Ram Stroke: 3-1/16"
Weight: 17 lbs.
Features: Designed for heavy-duty reloading, case forming and bullet swaging. Provides 4" of ram-bearing surface to support 1" ram and ensure alignment; ductile iron toggle blocks; hardened steel pins. Comes standard with Universal Primer Arm and primer catcher. Can be converted from single-stage to progressive with Piggyback II conversion unit. From RCBS.
Price: $141.95

REDDING Turret Press

Frame: Cast iron
Frame Type: Turret
Die Thread: 7/8-14
Avg. Rounds Per Hour: NA
Ram Stroke: 3.4"
Weight: 23 lbs., 2 oz.
Features: Strength to reload pistol and magnum rifle, case form and bullet swage; linkage pins heat-treated, precision ground and in double shear; hollow ram to collect spent primers; removable turret head for caliber changes; progressive linkage for increased power as ram nears die; slight frame tilt for comfortable operation; rear turret support for stability and precise alignment; six-station turret head; priming arm for both large and small primers. Also available in kit form with shellholder, primer catcher and one die set. From Redding Reloading Equipment.
Price: $298.50
Price: Kit $336.00

RCBS Partner

RCBS AmmoMaster Single

RCBS Reloader Special-5

RCBS Rock Chucker

ACCESSORIES

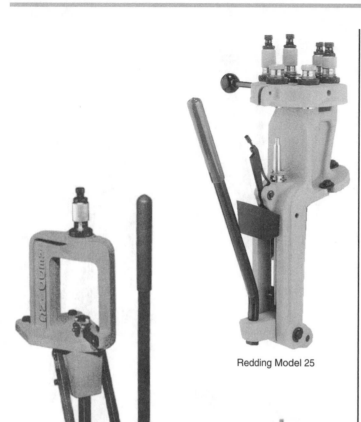

Redding Model 25

Redding Boss

Rock Crusher

Redding Ultramag

REDDING Boss

Frame: Cast iron
Frame Type: O-frame
Die Thread: 7/8-14
Avg. Rounds Per Hour: NA
Ram Stroke: 3.4"
Weight: 11 lbs., 8 oz.
Features: 36˚ frame offset for visibility and accessibility; primer arm positioned at bottom ram travel; positive ram travel stop machined to hit exactly top-dead-center. Also available in kit form with shellholder and set of Redding A dies. From Redding Reloading Equipment.
Price: **$135.00**
Price: Kit **$172.00**

REDDING Ultramag

Frame: Cast iron
Frame Type: Non-conventional
Die Thread: 7/8-14
Avg. Rounds Per Hour: NA
Ram Stroke: 4-1/8"
Weight: 23 lbs., 6 oz.
Features: Unique compound leverage system connected to top of press for tons of ram pressure; large 4-3/4" frame opening for loading outsized cartridges; hollow ram for spent primers. Kit available with shellholder and one set Redding A dies. From Redding Reloading Equipment.
Price: **$298.50**
Price: Kit **$336.00**

ROCK CRUSHER Press

Frame: Cast iron
Frame Type: O-frame
Die Thread: 2-3/4"-12 with bushing reduced to 1-1/2"-12
Avg. Rounds Per Hour: 50
Ram Stroke: 6"
Weight: 67 lbs.
Features: Designed to load and form ammunition from 50 BMG up to 23x115 Soviet. Frame opening of 8-1/2"x3-1/2"; 1-1/2"x12"; bushing can be removed and bushings of any size substituted; ram pressure can exceed 10,000 lbs. with normal body weight; 40mm diameter ram. Angle block for bench mounting and reduction bushing for RCBS dies available. Accessories for Rock Crusher include powder measure, dies, shellholder, bullet puller, priming tool, case gauge and other accessories found elsewhere in this catalog. From The Old Western Scrounger.
Price: **$795.00**
Price: Angle block **$57.95**
Price: Reduction bushing **$21.00**
Price: Shellholder **$47.25**
Price: Priming tool, 50 BMG, 20 Lahti **$65.10**

PROGRESSIVE PRESSES

CORBIN BENCHREST S-PRESS

Frame: All steel
Frame Type: O-Frame
Die Thread: 7/8-14 and
  T-slot adapter
Avg. Rounds Per Hour: NA
Ram Stroke: 4'
Weight: 22 lbs.
Features: Roller bearing linkage, removeable head, right- or left-hand mount.
Price: **$269.50**

DILLON AT 500

Frame: Aluminum alloy
Frame Type: NA
Die Thread: 7/8-14
Avg. Rounds Per Hour: 200-300

ACCESSORIES

Ram Stroke: 3-7/8"
Weight: NA
Features: Four stations; removable tool head to hold dies in alignment and allow caliber changes without die adjustment; manual indexing; capacity to be upgraded to progressive RL 550B. Comes with universal shellplate to accept 223, 22-250, 243, 30-06, 9mm, 38/357, 40 S&W, 45 ACP. Dies not included. From Dillon Precision Products.
Price: $193.95

DILLON RL 550B

Frame: Aluminum alloy
Frame Type: NA
Die Thread: 7/8-14
Avg. Rounds Per Hour: 500-600
Ram Stroke: 3-7/8"
Weight: 25 lbs.
Features: Four stations; removable tool head to hold dies in alignment and allow caliber changes without die adjustment; auto priming system that emits audible warning when primer tube is low; a 100-primer capacity magazine contained in DOM steel tube for protection; new auto powder measure system with simple mechanical connection between measure and loading platform for positive powder bar return; a separate station for crimping with star-indexing system; 220 ejected-round capacity bin; 3/4-lb. capacity powder measure. Height above bench, 35"; requires 3/4" bench overhang. Will reload 120 different rifle and pistol calibers. Comes with one caliber conversion kit. Dies not included. From Dillon Precision Products, Inc.
Price: $325.95

DILLON RL 1050

Frame: Ductile iron
Frame Type: Platform type
Die Thread: 7/8-14
Avg. Rounds Per Hour: 1000-1200
Ram Stroke: 2-5/16"
Weight: 62 lbs.
Features: Eight stations; auto case feed; primer pocket swager for military cartridge cases; auto indexing; removable tool head; auto prime system with 100-primer capacity; low primer supply alarm; positive powder bar return; auto powder measure; 515 ejected round bin capacity; 500-600 case feed capacity; 3/4-lb. capacity powder measure. Loads all pistol rounds as well as 30 M1 Carbine, 223, and 7.62x39 rifle rounds. Height above the bench, 43". Dies not included. From Dillon Precision Products, Inc.
Price: $1,199.95

DILLON Super 1050

Similar to RL1050, but has lengthened frame and short-stroke crank to accommodate long calibers.
Price: $1,299.95

DILLON Square Deal B

Frame: Zinc alloy
Frame Type: NA
Die Thread: None (unique Dillon design)
Avg. Rounds Per Hour: 400-500
Ram Stroke: 2-5/16"
Weight: 17 lbs.
Features: Four stations; auto indexing; removable tool head; auto prime system with 100-primer capacity; low primer supply alarm; auto powder measure; positive powder bar return; 170 ejected round capacity bin; 3/4-lb. capacity powder measure. Height above the bench, 34". Comes complete with factory adjusted carbide die set. From Dillon Precision Products, Inc.
Price: $252.95

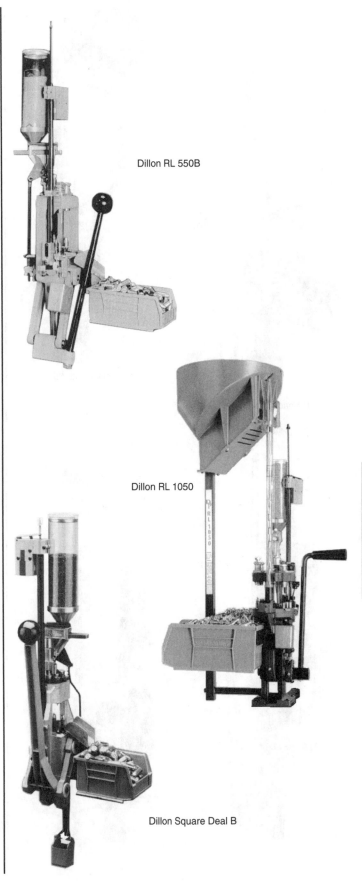

Dillon RL 550B

Dillon RL 1050

Dillon Square Deal B

ACCESSORIES

METALLIC CARTRIDGE PRESSES

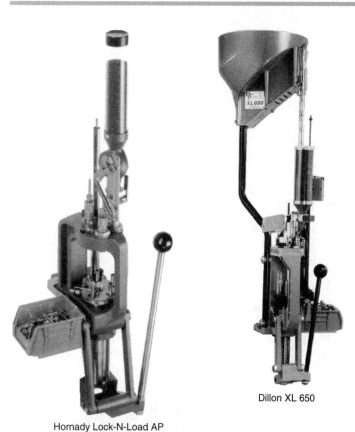

Hornady Lock-N-Load AP

Dillon XL 650

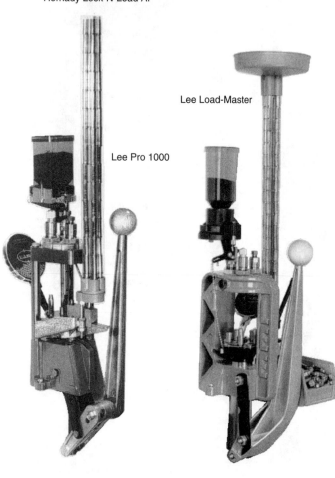

Lee Pro 1000

Lee Load-Master

DILLON XL 650

Frame: Aluminum alloy
Frame Type: NA
Die Thread: 7/8-14
Avg. Rounds Per Hour: 800-1000
Ram Stroke: 4-9/16"
Weight: 46 lbs.
Features: Five stations; auto indexing; auto case feed; removable tool head; auto prime system with 100-primer capacity; low primer supply alarm; auto powder measure; positive powder bar return; 220 ejected round capacity bin; 3/4-lb. capacity powder measure. 500-600 case feed capacity with optional auto case feed. Loads all pistol/rifle calibers less than 3-1/2" in length. Height above the bench, 44"; 3/4" bench overhang required. From Dillon Precision Products, Inc.
Price: Less dies **$443.95**

HORNADY Lock-N-Load AP

Frame: Die cast heat-treated aluminum alloy
Frame Type: O-frame
Die Thread: 7/8-14
Avg. Rounds Per Hour: NA
Ram Stroke: 3-3/4"
Weight: 26 lbs.
Features: Features Lock-N-Load bushing system that allows instant die changeovers; five-station die platform with option of seating and crimping separately or adding taper-crimp die; auto prime with large and small primer tubes with 100-primer capacity and protective housing; brass kicker to eject loaded rounds into 80-round capacity cartridge catcher; offset operating handle for leverage and unobstructed operation; 2" diameter ram driven by heavy-duty cast linkage arms rotating on steel pins. Comes with five Lock-N-Load die bushings, shellplate, deluxe powder measure, auto powder drop, and auto primer feed and shut-off, brass kicker and primer catcher. Lifetime warranty. From Hornady Mfg. Co.
Price: **$367.65**

LEE Load-Master

Frame: ASTM 380 aluminum
Frame Type: O-frame
Die Thread: 7/8-14
Avg. Rounds Per Hour: 600
Ram Stroke: 3-1/4"
Weight: 8 lbs., 4 oz.
Features: Available in kit form only. A 1-3/4" diameter hard chrome ram for handling largest magnum cases; loads rifle or pistol rounds; five station press to factory crimp and post size; auto indexing with wedge lock mechanism to hold one ton; auto priming; removable turrets; four-tube case feeder with optional case collator and bullet feeder (late 1995); loaded round ejector with chute to optional loaded round catcher; quick change shellplate; primer catcher. Dies and shellholder for one caliber included. From Lee Precision, Inc.
Price: Rifle **$320.00**
Price: Pistol **$330.00**
Price: Extra turret **$10.98**
Price: Adjustable charge bar **$9.98**

LEE Pro 1000

Frame: ASTM 380 aluminum and steel
Frame Type: O-frame
Die Thread: 7/8-14
Avg. Rounds Per Hour: 600
Ram Stroke: 3-1/4"
Weight: 8 lbs., 7 oz.
Features: Optional transparent large/small or rifle case feeder; deluxe auto-disk case-activated powder measure; case sensor for primer feed. Comes complete with carbide die set (steel dies for rifle) for one caliber. Optional accessories include: case feeder for large/small pistol cases or rifle cases; shell plate carrier with auto prime, case ejector, auto-index and spare parts; case collator for case feeder. From Lee Precision, Inc.
Price: **$199.98**

PONSNESS/WARREN Metallic II

Frame: Die cast aluminum
Frame Type: H-frame
Die Thread: 7/8-14
Avg. Rounds Per Hour: 150+
Ram Stroke: NA
Weight: 32 lbs.
Features: Die head with five tapped 7/8-14 holes for dies, powder measure or other accessories; pivoting die arm moves case from station to station; depriming tube for removal of spent primers; auto primer feed; interchangeable die head. Optional accessories include additional die heads, powder measure extension tube to accommodate any standard powder measure, primer speed feeder to feed press primer tube without disassembly. Comes with small and large primer seating tools. Dies, powder measure and shellholder not included. From Ponsness/Warren.
Price: $375.00
Price: Extra die head $56.95
Price: Primer speed feeder $14.50
Price: Powder measure extension $29.95
Price: Dust cover $27.95

RCBS AmmoMaster-Auto

Frame: Aluminum base; cast iron top plate connected by three steel posts
Frame Type: NA
Die Thread: 1-1/4-12 bushing; 7/8-14 threads
Avg. Rounds Per Hour: 400-500
Ram Stroke: 5-1/4"
Weight: 19 lbs.
Features: Progressive press convertible to single-stage. Features include: 1-1/2" solid ram; automatic indexing, priming, powder charging and loaded round ejection. Case detection system disengages powder measure when no case is present in powder charging station. Comes with five-station shellplate and Uniflow powder measure with clear powder measure adaptor to make bridged powders visible and correctable. Piggyback die plate for quick caliber change-over available. Reloading dies not included. From RCBS.
Price: $394.95
Price: Piggyback/AmmoMaster die plate $22.95
Price: Piggyback/AmmoMaster shellplate $27.95
Price: Press cover $10.95

RCBS Pro 2000™

Frame: Cast iron
Frame Type: H-Frame
Die Thread: 7/8 x 14
Avg. Rounds Per Hour: NA
Ram Stroke: NA
Weight: NA
Features: Five-station manual indexing; full-length sizing; removable die plate; fast caliber conversion. Uses APS Priming System. From RCBS.
Price: $468.95

STAR Universal Pistol Press

Frame: Cast iron with aluminum base
Frame Type: Unconventional
Die Thread: 11/16-24 or 7/8-14
Avg. Rounds Per Hour: 300
Ram Stroke: NA
Weight: 27 lbs.
Features: Four or five-station press depending on need to taper crimp; handles all popular handgun calibers from 32 Long to 45 Colt. Comes completely assembled and adjusted with carbide dies (except 30 Carbine) and shellholder to load one caliber. Prices slightly higher for 9mm and 30 Carbine. From Star Machine Works.
Price: With taper crimp $1,055.00

RCBS AmmoMaster

Fully-automated Star Universal

Price: Without taper crimp $1,025.00
Price: Extra tool head, taper crimp................... $425.00
Price: Extra tool head, w/o taper crimp $395.00

METALLIC SIGHTS

Misc. Handgun Sights

MILLETT SCOPE-SITE Open, adjustable or fixed rear sights dovetail into a base integral with the top scope-mounting ring. Blaze orange front ramp sight is integral with the front ring half. Rear sights have white outline aperture. Provides fast, short-radius, Patridge-type open sights on the top of the scope. Can be used with all Millett rings, Weaver-style bases, Ruger 77 (also fits Redhawk), Ruger Ranch Rifle, No. 1, No. 3, Rem. 870, 1100; Burris, Leupold and Redfield bases.
Price: Scope-Site top only, windage only.................. **$31.15**
Price: As above, fully adjustable......................... **$66.10**
Price: Scope-Site Hi-Turret, fully adjustable, low, medium,
   high. **$66.10**

WICHITA MULTI RANGE SIGHT SYSTEM Designed for silhouette shooting. System allows you to adjust the rear sight to four repeatable range settings, once it is pre-set. Sight clicks to any of the settings by turning a serrated wheel. Front sight is adjustable for weather and light conditions with one adjustment. Specify gun when ordering.
Price: Rear sight.................................... **$120.00**
Price: Front sight.................................... **$90.00**

WILLIAMS DOVETAIL OPEN SIGHT (WDOS) Open rear sight with windage and elevation adjustment. Furnished "U" notch or choice of blades. Slips into dovetail and locks with gib lock. Heights from .281" to .531".
Price:With blade...................................... **$17.95**
Price:Less blade...................................... **$11.05**
Price:Rear sight blades, each......................... **$6.29**

Globe Target Front Sights

Lyman No. 17A Target

LYMAN No. 17A TARGET Includes seven interchangeable inserts: four apertures, one transparent amber and two posts .50" and .100" in width.
Price: **$28.25**
Price: Insert set..................................... **$13.25**

Handgun Sights

AO Adjustable

AO Pro Express

AO Express Big Dot

North American
Arms Guardian
Custom Front/Rear
AO Big Dot Tritium

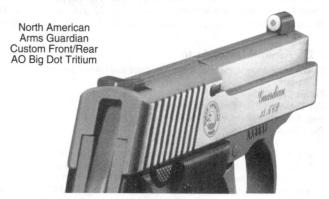

Springfield
V10 Compact
Small Custom Express
AO Big Dot Tritium

AO EXPRESS SIGHTS Low-profile, snag-free express-type sights. Shallow V rear with white vertical line, white dot front. All-steel, matte black finish. Rear is available in different heights. Made for most pistols, many with double set-screws. From AO Sight Systems, Inc.
Price: Standard Set, front and rear. **$60.00**
Price: Big Dot Set, front and rear...................... **$60.00**
Price: Tritium Set, Standard or Big Dot. **$90.00**
Price: 24/7 Pro Express, Std. or Big Dot Tritium **$120.00**

BO-MAR DELUXE BMCS Gives 3/8" windage and elevation adjustment at 50 yards on Colt Gov't 45; sight radius under 7". For GM and Commander models only. Uses existing dovetail slot. Has shield-type rear blade.
Price:.. **$65.95**
Price: BMCS-2 (for GM and 9mm)........................ **$68.95**
Price: Flat bottom.................................... **$65.95**
Price: BMGC (for Colt Gold Cup), angled serrated blade, rear. . **$68.95**
Price: BMGC front sight............................... **$12.95**
Price: BMCZ-75 (for CZ-75,TZ-75, P-9 and most clones).
   Works with factory front. **$68.95**

METALLIC SIGHTS

Heinie Slant Pro

BO-MAR FRONT SIGHTS Dovetail style for S&W 4506, 4516, 1076; undercut style (.250", .280", 5/16" high); Fast Draw style (.210", .250", .230" high).
Price: **$12.95**

BO-MAR BMU XP-100/T/C CONTENDER No gunsmithing required; has .080" notch.
Price: **$77.00**

BO-MAR BMML For muzzleloaders; has .062" notch, flat bottom.
Price: **$65.95**
Price: With 3/8" dovetail. **$65.95**

BO-MAR RUGER "P" ADJUSTABLE SIGHT Replaces factory front and rear sights.
Price: Rear sight. **$65.95**
Price: Front sight. **$12.00**

BO-MAR BMR Fully adjustable rear sight for Ruger MKI, MKII Bull barrel autos.
Price: Rear. **$65.95**
Price: Undercut front sight. **$12.00**

BO-MAR GLOCK Fully adjustable, all-steel replacement sights. Sight fits factory dovetail. Longer sight radius. Uses Novak Glock .275" high, .135" wide front, or similar.
Price: Rear sight. **$68.95**
Price: Front sight. **$20.95**

BO-MAR LOW PROFILE RIB & ACCURACY TUNER Streamlined rib with front and rear sights; 7 1/8" sight radius. Brings sight line closer to the bore than standard or extended sight and ramp. Weight 5 oz. Made for Colt Gov't 45, Super 38, and Gold Cup 45 and 38.
Price: **$140.00**

BO-MAR COMBAT RIB For S&W Model 19 revolver with 4" barrel. Sight radius 5 3/4", weight 5 1/2 oz.
Price: **$127.00**

BO-MAR WINGED RIB For S&W 4" and 6" length barrels—K-38, M10, HB 14 and 19. Weight for the 6" model is about 7 1/4 oz.
Price: **$140.00**

BO-MAR COVER-UP RIB Adjustable rear sight, winged front guards. Fits right over revolver's original front sight. For S&W 4" M-10HB, M-13, M-58, M-64 & 65, Ruger 4" models SDA-34, SDA-84, SS-34, SS-84, GF-34, GF-84.
Price: **$130.00**

CHIP MCCORMICK "DROP-IN" A low mount sight that fits any 1911-style slide with a standard military-type dovetail sight cut (60x.290"). Dovetail front sights also available. From Chip McCormick Corp.
Price: **$47.95**

CHIP MCCORMICK FIXED SIGHTS Same sight picture (.110" rear - .110" front) that's become the standard for pro combat shooters. Low mount design with rounded edges. For 1911-style pistols. May require slide machining for installation. From Chip McCormick Corp.
Price: **$24.95**

C-MORE SIGHTS Replacement front sight blades offered in two types and five styles. Made of Du Pont Acetal, they come in a set of five high-contrast colors: blue, green, pink, red and yellow. Easy to install. Patridge style for Colt Python (all barrels), Ruger Super Blackhawk (7 1/2"), Ruger Blackhawk (4 5/8"); ramp style for Python (all barrels), Blackhawk (4 5/8"), Super Blackhawk (7 1/2" and 10 1/2"). From C-More Systems.
Price: Per set. **$19.95**

G.G. & G. GHOST RINGS Replaces the factory rear sight without gunsmithing. Black phosphate finish. Available for Colt M1911 and Commander, Beretta M92F, Glock, S&W, SIG Sauer.
Price: **$65.00**

HEINIE SLANT PRO Made with a slight forward slant, the unique design of these rear sights is snag free for unimpeded draw from concealment. The combination of the slant and the rear serrations virtually eliminates glare. Made for most popular handguns. From Heinie Specialty Products.
Price: . . . . **$50.35 to $122.80**

HEINIE STRAIGHT EIGHT SIGHTS Consists of one tritium dot in the front sight and a slightly smaller Tritium dot in the rear sight. When aligned correctly, an elongated 'eight' is created. The Tritium dots are green in color. Designed with the belief that the human eye can correct vertical alignment faster than horizontal. Available for most popular handguns. From Heinie Specialty Products.
Price: . . . . **$104.95 to $122.80**

HEINIE CROSS DOVETAIL FRONT SIGHTS Made in a variety of heights, the standard dovetail is 60 degrees x .305" x .062" with a .002 taper. From Heinie Specialty Products.
Price: . . . . **$20.95 to $47.20**

JP GHOST RING Replacement bead front, ghost ring rear for Glock and M1911 pistols. From JP Enterprises.
Price: **$79.95**
Price: Bo-Mar replacement leaf with JP dovetail front bead. . . . **$99.95**

LES BAER CUSTOM ADJUSTABLE LOW MOUNT REAR SIGHT Considered one of the top adjustable sights in the world for target shooting with 1911-style pistols. Available with Tritium inserts. From Les Baer Custom.
Price: . . . . **$49.00** (standard); **$99.00** (tritium)

LES BAER DELUXE FIXED COMBAT SIGHT A tactical-style sight with a very low profile. Incorporates a no-snag design and has serrations on sides. For 1911-style pistols. Available with Tritium inserts for night shooting. From Les Baer Custom.
Price: . . . . **$26.00** (standard); **$67.00** (with Tritium)

LES BAER DOVETAIL FRONT SIGHT Blank dovetail sight machined from bar stock. Can be contoured to many different configurations to meet user's needs. Available with Tritium insert. From Les Baer Custom.
Price: . . . . **$17.00** (standard); **$47.00** (with Tritium insert)

LES BAER FIBER OPTIC FRONT SIGHT Dovetail .330x65 degrees, .125" wide post, .185" high, .060" diameter. Red and green fiber optic. From Les Baer Custom.
Price: **$24.00**

LES BAER PPC-STYLE ADJUSTABLE REAR SIGHT Made for use with custom built 1911-style pistols, allows the user to preset three elevation adjustments for PPC-style shooting. Milling required for installation. Made from 4140 steel. From Les Baer Custom.
Price: **$120.00**

LES BAER DOVETAIL FRONT SIGHT WITH TRITIUM INSERT This fully contoured and finished front sight comes ready for gunsmith installation. From Les Baer Custom.
Price: **$47.00**

MMC TACTICAL ADJUSTABLE SIGHTS Low-profile, snag free design. Twenty-two click positions for elevation, drift adjustable for windage. Machined from 4140 steel and heat treated to 40 RC. Tritium and non-tritium. Ten different configurations and colors. Three different finishes. For 1911s, all Glock, HK USP, S&W, Browning Hi-Power.
Price: Sight set, tritium. **$144.92**
Price: Sight set, white outline or white dot. **$99.90**
Price: Sight set, black. **$93.90**

MEPROLIGHT TRITIUM NIGHT SIGHTS Replacement sight assemblies for use in low-light conditions. Available for rifles, shotguns, handguns and bows. TRU-DOT models carry a 12-year warranty on the useable illumination, while non-TRU-DOT have a 5-year warranty. Contact Hesco, Inc. for complete list of available models.
Price: Kahr K9, K40, fixed, TRU-DOT. **$100.00**
Price: Ruger P85, P89, P94, adjustable, TRU-DOT. **$156.00**
Price: Ruger Mini-14R sights. **$140.00**
Price: SIG Sauer P220, P225, P226, P228, adjustable, TRU-DOT. **$156.00**
Price: Smith&Wesson autos, fixed or adjustable, TRU-DOT. . **$100.00**
Price: Taurus PT92, PT100, adjustable, TRU-DOT. **$156.00**
Price: Walther P-99, fixed, TRU-DOT. **$100.00**
Price: Shotgun bead. **$32.00**
Price: Beretta M92, Cougar, Brigadier, fixed, TRU-DOT. . . . **$100.00**
Price: Browning Hi-Power, adjustable, TRU-DOT. **$156.00**
Price: Colt M1911 Govt., adjustable, TRU-DOT. **$156.00**

MILLETT SERIES 100 REAR SIGHTS All-steel highly visible, click adjustable. Blades in white outline, target black, silhouette, 3-dot, and tritium bars. Fit most popular revolvers and autos.
Price: . . . . **$49.30 to $80.00**

ACCESSORIES

METALLIC SIGHTS

Meprolight Night Sights

Glock Pistol

Beretta Pistol

Colt 1911 Govt. Commander Pistol

Ruger P85, P85MKII & P89 Pistol

H&K USP

Taurus Model 44 & 608 Revolvers

Millett Series 100

Millett Glock Series 100 Sight

MILLETT BAR-DOT-BAR TRITIUM NIGHT SIGHTS Replacement front and rear combos fit most automatics. Horizontal tritium bars on rear, dot front sight.
Price: **$145.00**

MILLETT BAR/DOT Made with orange or white bar or dot for increased visibility. Available for Beretta 84, 85, 92S, 92SB, Browning, Colt Python & Trooper, Ruger GP 100, P85, Redhawk, Security Six.
Price: . . . . **$14.99 to $24.99**

MILLETT 3-DOT SYSTEM SIGHTS The 3-Dot System sights use a single white dot on the front blade and two dots flanking the rear notch. Fronts available in Dual-Crimp and Wide Stake-On styles, as well as special applications. Adjustable rear sight available for most popular auto pistols and revolvers including Browning Hi-Power, Colt 1911 Government and Ruger P85.
Price: Front, from. **$16.00**
Price: Adjustable rear. **$55.60**

MILLETT REVOLVER FRONT SIGHTS All-steel replacement front sights with either white or orange bar. Easy to install. For Ruger GP-100, Redhawk, Security-Six, Police-Six, Speed-Six, Colt Trooper, Diamondback, King Cobra, Peacemaker, Python, Dan Wesson 22 and 15-2.
Price: . . . . **$13.60 to $16.00**

MILLETT DUAL-CRIMP FRONT SIGHT Replacement front sight for automatic pistols. Dual-Crimp uses an all-steel two-point hollow rivet system. Available in eight heights and four styles. Has a skirted base that covers the front sight pad. Easily installed with the Millett Installation Tool

Set. Available in Blaze Orange Bar, White Bar, Serrated Ramp, Plain Post. Available in heights of .185", .200", .225", .275", .312", .340" and .410".
Price: **$16.00**

MILLETT STAKE-ON FRONT SIGHT Replacement front sight for automatic pistols. Stake-On sights have skirted base that covers the front sight pad. Easily installed with the Millet Installation Tool Set. Available in seven heights and four styles—Blaze Orange Bar, White Bar, Serrated Ramp, Plain Post. Available for Glock 17L and 24, others.
Price: **$16.00**

MILLETT ADJUSTABLE TARGET Positive light-deflection serration and slant to eliminate glare and sharp edge sight notch. Audible "click" adjustments. For AMT Hardballer, Beretta 84, 85, 92S, 92SB, Browning Hi-Power, Colt 1911 Government and Gold Cup, Colt revolvers, Dan Wesson 15, 41, 44, Ruger revolvers, Glock 17, 17L, 19, 20, 21, 22, 23.
Price: **$44.99**

MILLETT ADJUSTABLE WHITE OUTLINE Similar to the Target sight, except has a white outline on the blade to increase visibility. Available for the same handguns as the Target model, plus BRNO CZ-75/TZ-75/TA-90 without pin on front sight, and Ruger P85.
Price: . . . . **$44.99 to $49.99**

OMEGA OUTLINE SIGHT BLADES Replacement rear sight blades for Colt and Ruger single action guns and the Interarms Virginian Dragoon. Standard Outline available in gold or white notch outline on blue metal. From Omega Sales, Inc.
Price: **$8.95**

OMEGA MAVERICK SIGHT BLADES Replacement "peep-sight" blades for Colt, Ruger SAs, Virginian Dragoon. Three models available—No. 1, Plain; No. 2, Single Bar; No. 3, Double Bar Rangefinder. From Omega Sales, Inc.
Price: Each. **$6.95**

ONE RAGGED HOLE Replacement rear sight ghost ring sight for Ruger handguns. Fits Blackhawks, Redhawks, Super Blackhawks, GP series and Mk. II target pistols with adjustable sights. From One Ragged Hole, Tallahassee, Florida.
Price: . . . . **NA**

PACHMAYR ACCU-SET Low-profile, fully adjustable rear sight to be used with existing front sight. Available with target, white outline or 3-dot blade. Blue finish. Uses factory dovetail and locking screw. For Browning, Colt, Glock, SIG Sauer, S&W and Ruger autos. From Pachmayr.
Price: **$59.98**

Pachmayr Accu-Set

P-T TRITIUM NIGHT SIGHTS Self-luminous tritium sights for most popular handguns, Colt AR-15, H&K rifles and shotguns. Replacement handgun sight sets available in 3-Dot style

ACCESSORIES

(green/green, green/yellow, green/orange) with bold outlines around inserts; Bar-Dot available in green/green with or without white outline rear sight. Functional life exceeds 15 years. From Innovative Weaponry, Inc.

Price: Handgun sight sets. $99.95
Price: Rifle sight sets. $99.95
Price: Rifle, front only. $49.95
Price: Shotgun, front only. $49.95

TRIJICON NIGHT SIGHTS Three-dot night sight system uses tritium lamps in the front and rear sights. Tritium "lamps" are mounted in silicone rubber inside a metal cylinder. A polished crystal sapphire provides protection and clarity. Inlaid white outlines provide 3-dot aiming in daylight also. Available for most popular handguns including Glock 17, 19, 20, 21, 23, 24, 25, 26, 29, 30, H&K USP, Ruger P94, SIG P220, P225, 226, Colt 1911. Front and rear sets available. From Trijicon, Inc.

Price: . . . . $80.00 to $299.00

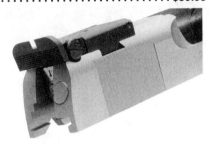

Trijicon Night Sights

TRIJICON 3-DOT Self-luminous front iron night sight for the Ruger SP101.
Price: $39.99

Wichita Series 70/80

WICHITA SERIES 70/80 SIGHT Provides click windage and elevation adjustments with precise repeatability of settings. Sight blade is grooved and angled back at the top to reduce glare. Available in Low Mount Combat or Low Mount Target styles for Colt 45s and their copies, S&W 645, Hi-Power, CZ 75 and others.

Price: Rear sight, target or combat. $75.00
Price: Front sight, Patridge or ramp. $15.00

WICHITA GRAND MASTER DELUXE RIBS Ventilated rib has wings machined into it for better sight acquisition and is relieved for Mag-Na-Porting. Milled to accept Weaver see-thru-style rings. Made of stainless or blued steel; front and rear sights blued. Has Wichita Multi-Range rear sight system, adjustable front sight. Made for revolvers with 6" barrel.

Price: Model 301S, 301B (adj. sight K frames with custom bbl. of 1" to 1.032" dia. L and N frame with 1.062" to 1.100" dia. bbl.). . . $189.00
Price: Model 303S, 303B (adj. sight K, L, N frames with factory barrel). $189.00

Williams Fire Sight Ruger MKII Sights

WILLIAMS FIRE SIGHT SETS Red fiber optic metallic sight replaces the original. Rear sight has two green fiber optic elements. Made of CNC-machined aluminum. Fits all Glocks, Ruger P-Series (except P-85),

S&W 910, Colt Gov't. Model Series 80, Ruger GP 100 and Redhawk, and SIG Sauer (front only).
Price: Front and rear set $39.95
Price: SIG Sauer front $19.95

Williams Fire Sight Set

WILSON ADJUSTABLE REAR SIGHTS Machined from steel, the click adjustment design requires simple cuts and no dovetails for installation. Available in several configurations: matte black standard blade with .128" notch; with .110" notch; with Tritium dots and .128" square or "U" shaped notch; and Combat Pyramid. From Wilson Combat.
Price: . . . . $24.95 to $69.95

WILSON NITE-EYES SIGHTS Low-profile, snag free design with green and yellow Tritium inserts. For 1911-style pistols. From Wilson Combat.
Price: $119.95

WILSON TACTICAL COMBAT SIGHTS Low-profile and snag-free in design, the sight employs the Combat Pyramid shape. For many 1911-style pistols and some Glock models. From Wilson Combat.
Price: $139.95

Sight Attachments

Merit Target Discs

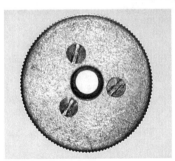

Open   Closed

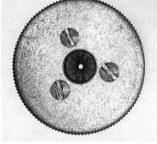

Merit Master Disc

ACCESSORIES

METALLIC SIGHTS

MERIT ADJUSTABLE APERTURES Eleven clicks give 12 different apertures. No. 3 Disc and Master, primarily target types, 0.22" to .125"; No. 4, 1/2" dia. hunting type, .025" to .155". Available for all popular sights. The Master, with flexible rubber light shield, is particularly adapted to extension, scope height, and tang sights. All models have internal click springs; are hand fitted to minimum tolerance.

Price: No. 3 Master Disk. **$66.00**
Price: No. 3 Target Disc (Plain Face). **$56.00**
Price: No. 4 Hunting Disc. **$48.00**

MERIT LENS DISC Similar to Merit Iris Shutter (Model 3 or Master) but incorporates provision for mounting prescription lens integrally. Lens may be obtained locally from your optician. Sight disc is 7/16" wide (Model 3), or 3/4" wide (Master).

Price: No. 3 Target Lens Disk **$68.00**
Price: No. 3 Master Lens Disk. **$78.00**

MERIT OPTICAL ATTACHMENT For iron sight shooting with handgun or rifle. Instantly attached by rubber suction cup to prescription or shooting glasses. Swings aside. Aperture adjustable from .020" to .156".

Price: **$65.00**

WILLIAMS APERTURES Standard thread, fits most sights. Regular series 3/8" to 1/2" O.D., .050" to .125" hole. "Twilight" series has white reflector ring.

Price: Regular series. **$4.97**

Price: Twilight series. **$6.79**
Price: Wide open 5/16" aperture for shotguns fits 5-D or Foolproof sights (specify model). **$8.77**

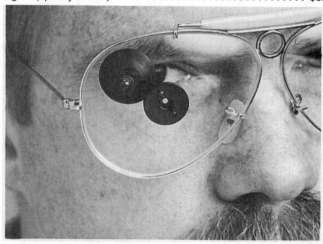

Merit Optical Attachment

MUZZLE BRAKES

Gentry Quiet Muzzle Brake

Developed by gunmaker David Gentry, the "Quiet Muzzle Brake" is said to reduce recoil by up to 85 percent with no loss of accuracy or velocity. There is no increase in noise level because the noise and gases are directed away from the shooter. The barrel is threaded for installation and the unit is blued to match the barrel finish. Price, installed, is **$150.00**. Add **$15.00** for stainless steel, **$45.00** for knurled cap to protect threads. Shipping extra.

JP Muzzle Brake

Designed for single shot handguns, AR-15, Ruger Mini-14, Ruger Mini Thirty and other sporting rifles, the JP Muzzle Brake redirects high pressure gases against a large frontal surface which applies forward thrust to the gun. All gases are directed up, rearward and to the sides. Priced at **$79.95** (AR-15 or sporting rifles), **$89.95** (bull barrel and SKS, AK models), **$89.95** (Ruger Minis), Dual Chamber model **$79.95**. From JP Enterprises, Inc.

JP Muzzle Brake

KDF Slim Line Muzzle Brake

This threaded muzzle brake has 30 pressure ports that direct combustion gases in all directions to reduce felt recoil up to a claimed 80 percent without affecting accuracy or ballistics. It is said to reduce felt recoil of a 30-06 to that of a 243. Price, installed, is **$179.00**. From KDF, Inc.

Mag-Na-Port

Electrical Discharge Machining works on any firearm except those having non-conductive shrouded barrels. EDM is a metal erosion technique using carbon electrodes that control the area to be processed. The Mag-Na-Port venting process utilizes small trapezoidal openings to direct powder gases upward and outward to reduce recoil. No effect is had on bluing or nickeling outside the Mag-Na-Port area so no refinishing is needed. Rifle-style porting on single shot or large caliber handguns with barrels 7 1/2" or longer is **$110.00**; Dual Trapezoidal porting on most handguns with minimum barrel length of 3",

$100.00; standard revolver porting, **$78.50**; porting through the slide and barrel for semi-autos, **$115.00**; traditional rifle porting, **$125.00**. Prices do not include shipping, handling and insurance. From Mag-Na-Port International.

Mag-Na-Brake

A screw-on brake under 2" long with progressive integrated exhaust chambers to neutralize expanding gases. Gases dissipate with an opposite twist to prevent the brake from unscrewing, and with a 5-degree forward angle to minimize sound pressure level. Available in blue, satin blue, bright or satin stainless. Standard and Light Contour installation cost **$179.00** for bolt-action rifles, many single action and single shot handguns. A knurled thread protector supplied at extra cost. Also available in Varmint style with exhaust chambers covering 220 degrees for prone-position shooters. From Mag-Na-Port International.

SSK Arrestor Brake

This is a true muzzle brake with an expansion chamber. It takes up about 1" of barrel and reduces velocity accordingly. Some Arrestors are added to a barrel, increasing its length. Said to reduce the felt recoil of a 458 to that approaching a 30-06. Can be set up to give zero muzzle rise in any caliber, and can be added to most guns. For handgun or rifle. Prices start at **$95.00**. Contact SSK Industries for full data.

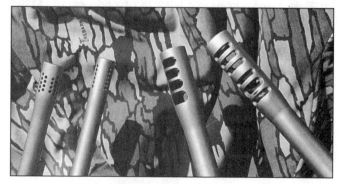

SSK Arrestor Muzzle Brakes

Maker and Model	Magn.	Field at 100 Yds. (feet)	Eye Relief (in.)	Length (in.)	Tube Dia. (in.)	W & E Adjustments	Weight (ozs.)	Price	Other Data
ADCO									
Magnum 50 mm[5]	0	—	—	4.1	45 mm	Int.	6.8	$269.00	[1]Multi-Color Dot system changes from red to green. [2]For air-guns, paintball, rimfires. Uses common lithium water battery. [3]Comes with standard dovetail mount. [4].75" dovetail mount; poly body; adj. intensity diode. [5]10 MOA dot; black or nickel. [6]Square format; with mount battery. From ADCO Sales.
MIRAGE Ranger 1"	0	—	—	5.2	1	Int.	3.9	159.00	
MIRAGE Ranger 30mm	0	—	—	5.5	30mm	Int.	5	159.00	
MIRAGE Competitor	0	—	—	5.5	30mm	Int.	5.5	229.00	
IMP Sight[2]	0	—	—	4.5	—	Int.	1.3	17.95	
Square Shooter 2[3]	0	—	—	5	—	Int.	5	99.00	
MIRAGE Eclipse[1]	0	—	—	5.5	30mm	Int.	5.5	229.00	
Champ Red Dot	0	—	—	4.5	—	Int.	2	33.95	
Vantage 1"	0	—	—	3.9	1	Int.	3.9	129.00	
Vantage 30mm	0	—	—	4.2	30mm	Int.	4.9	132.00	
Vision 2000[6]	0	60	—	4.7	—	Int.	6.2	79.00	
e-dot ESB[1]	0	—	—	4.12	1	Int.	3.7	139.00	
e-dot E1B	0	—	—	4.12	1	Int.	3.7	119.00	
e-dot ECB	0	—	—	3.8	30mm	Int.	6.4	119.00	
e-dot E30B	0	—	—	4.3	30mm	Int.	4.6	119.00	
AIMPOINT									
Comp	0	—	—	4.6	30mm	Int.	4.3	331.00	Illuminates red dot in field of view. Noparallax (dot does not need to be centered). Unlimited field of view and eye relief. On/off, adj. intensity. Dot covers 3" @100 yds. [1]Comes with 30mm rings, battery, lense cloth. [2]Requires 1" rings. Black finish. AP Comp avail. in black, blue, SS, camo. [3]Black finish (AP 5000-B) ; avail. with regular 3-min. or 10-min. Mag Dot as B2 or S2. [4]Band pass reflection coating for compatibility with night vision equipment; U.S. Army contract model; with anti-reflex coated lenses (Comp ML), $359.00. From Aimpoint U.S.A.
Comp M[4]	0	—	—	5	30mm	Int.	6.1	409.00	
Series 5000[3]	0	—	—	6	30mm	Int.	6	297.00	
Series 3000 Universal[2]	0	—	—	6.25	1	Int.	6	232.00	
Series 5000/2x[1]	2	—	—	7	30mm	Int.	9	388.00	
ARMSON O.E.G.									
Standard	0	—	—	5.125	1	Int.	4.3	202.00	Shown red dot aiming point. No batteries needed. Standard model fits 1" ring mounts (not incl.). From Trijicon, Inc.
BEEMAN									
Pistol Scopes									
5021	2	19	10-24	9.1	1	Int.	7.4	85.50	All scopes have 5 point reticle, all glass fully coated lenses. Imported by Beeman.
5020	1.5	14	11-16	8.3	.75	Int.	3.6	NA	
BSA									
Pistol									
P52x20	2	N/A	N/A	N/A	N/A	Int.	N/A	79.95	[1]Red dot sights also available in 42mm and 50mm versions. [2]Includes Universal Bow Mount. [3]Five other models offered. From BSA.
P54x28	4	N/A	N/A	N/A	N/A	Int.	N/A	89.95	
Red Dot									
RD30[1]	0	—	—	3.8	30mm	Int.	5	59.95	
PB30[1]	0	—	—	3.8	30mm	Int.	4.5	79.95	
Bow30[2]	0	—	—	N/A	30mm	Int.	5	89.95	
BigCat[3]	3.5-10	30-11	5	9.7	1	Int.	16.8	219.95	
BURRIS									
Speeddot 135[1]									[1]Dot reticle on some models. [2]Matte satin finish. [3]Available with parallax adjustment (standard on 10x, 12x, 4-12x, 6-12x, 6-18x, 6x HBR and 3-12x Signature). [4]Silver matte finish extra. [5]Target knobs extra, standard on silhouette models. LER and XER with P.A., 6x HBR. [6]Available with Heavy Plex reticle. [7]Available with Posi-Lock. **Speeddot 135:** [1]Waterproof, fogproof, coated lenses, 11 brightness settings; 3-MOA or 11-MOA dot size; includes Weaver-style rings and battery. **Partial listing shown.** Contact Burris for complete details.
Red Dot	1	—	—	4.85	35mm	Int.	5	291.00	
Handgun									
1.50-4x LER[1, 4, 7]	1.6-3.	16-11	11-25	10.25	1	Int.	11	363.00	
2-7x LER[2, 3, 4, 7]	2-6.5	21-7	7-27	9.5	1	Int.	12.6	401.00	
3-9x LER[3, 4, 7]	3.4-8.4	12-5	22-14	11	1	Int.	14	453.00	
2x LER[3, 4, 5]	1.7	21	10-24	8.75	1	Int.	6.8	265.00	
4x LER[1, 3, 4, 5, 7]	3.7	11	10-22	9.625	1	Int.	9	296.00	
10x LER[1, 3, 5]	9.5	4	8-12	13.5	1	Int.	14	460.00	

SCOPES / HUNTING, TARGET & VARMINT

Maker and Model	Magn.	Field at 100 Yds. (feet)	Eye Relief (in.)	Length (in.)	Tube Dia. (in.)	W & E Adjustments	Weight (ozs.)	Price	Other Data
Scout Scope									
1xXER[2, 6]	1.5	32	4-24	9	1	Int.	7.0	**290.00**	
2.75x[2, 6]	2.7	15	7-14	9.375	1	Int.	7.0	**319.00**	

Plex	Fine Plex	Heavy Plex & Electro-Dot Plex	Peep Plex	Ballistic Mil-Dot	Target Dot	Mil-Dot

BUSHNELL (Bausch & Lomb Elite rifle scopes now sold under Bushnell brand)

Maker and Model	Magn.	Field at 100 Yds. (feet)	Eye Relief (in.)	Length (in.)	Tube Dia. (in.)	W & E Adjustments	Weight (ozs.)	Price	Other Data
Elite 3200 Handgun RainGuard									(Bushnell) [1,2]Also silver finish. [2]Also silver finish. [3]Variable intesity; fits Weaver-style base.
32-2632M[1]	2-6	10-4	20	9	1	Int.	10	**444.95**	
32-2632G	2-6	10-4	20	9	1	Int.	10	**444.95**	
HOLOsight Model[3]	1	—	—	6	—	Int.	8.7	**444.95**	
Trophy Handgun									
73-0232[1]	2	20	9-26	8.7	1	Int.	7.7	**218.95**	
73-2632[2]	2-6	21-7	9-26	9.1	1	Int.	10.9	**287.95**	

HOLOSIGHT RETICLE

Standard

KILHAM

Maker and Model	Magn.	Field at 100 Yds. (feet)	Eye Relief (in.)	Length (in.)	Tube Dia. (in.)	W & E Adjustments	Weight (ozs.)	Price	Other Data
Hutson Handgunner II	1.7	8	—	5.5	.875	Int.	5.1	**119.95**	Unlimited eye relief; internal click adjustments; crosshair reticle. Fits Thompson/Center rail mounts, for S&W K, N, Ruger Blackhawk, Super, Super Single-Six, Contender.
Hutson Handgunner	3	8	10-12	6	.875	Int.	5.3	**119.95**	

LEUPOLD

Maker and Model	Magn.	Field at 100 Yds. (feet)	Eye Relief (in.)	Length (in.)	Tube Dia. (in.)	W & E Adjustments	Weight (ozs.)	Price	Other Data
Vari-X III 3.5x10 Tactical	3.5-10	29.5-10.7	3.6-4.6	12.5	1	Int.	13.5	**801.80**	Constantly centered reticles, choice of Duplex, tapered CPC, Leupold Dot, Crosshair and Dot. CPC and Dot reticles extra. [1]2x and 4x scopes have from 12"-24" of eye relief and are suitable for handguns, top ejection arms and muzzleloaders. Partial listing shown. **Contact Leupold for complete details.** *Models available with illuminated reticle for additional cost.
M8-2X EER[1]	1.7	21.2	12-24	7.9	1	Int.	6	**312.50**	
M8-2X EER Silver[1]	1.7	21.2	12-24	7.9	1	Int.	6	**337.50**	
M8-2.5x28 IER Scout	2.3	22	9.3	10.1	1	Int.	7.5	**408.90**	
M8-4X EER[1]	3.7	9	12-24	8.4	1	Int.	7	**425.00**	
M8-4X EER Silver[1]	3.7	9	12-24	8.4	1	Int.	7	**425.00**	
Vari-X 2.5-8 EER	2.5-8	13-4.3	11.7-12	9.7	1	Int.	10.9	**608.90**	

Duplex	CPC	Post & Duplex	Leupold Dot	Dot

MEPROLIGHT

Maker and Model	Magn.	Field at 100 Yds. (feet)	Eye Relief (in.)	Length (in.)	Tube Dia. (in.)	W & E Adjustments	Weight (ozs.)	Price	Other Data
Meprolight Reflex Sights 14-21 5.5 MOA 1x30[1]	1	—	—	4.4	30mm	Int.	5.2	**335.00**	[1]Also available with 4.2 MOA dot. Uses tritium and fiber optics- no batteries required. From Hesco, Inc.

MILLETT

Maker and Model	Magn.	Field at 100 Yds. (feet)	Eye Relief (in.)	Length (in.)	Tube Dia. (in.)	W & E Adjustments	Weight (ozs.)	Price	Other Data
SP-1 Compact[1] Red Dot	1	36.65	—	4.1	1	Int.	3.2	**149.95**	[1]3-MOA dot. [2]5-MOA dot. [3]3-, 5-, 8-, 10-MOA dots. [4]10-MOA dot. All have click adjustments; waterproof, shockproof; 11 dot intensity settings. All avail. in matte/black or silver finish. From Millett Sights.
SP-2 Compact[2] Red Dot	1	58	—	4.5	30mm	Int.	4.3	**149.95**	
MultiDot SP[3]	1	50	—	4.8	30mm	Int.	5.3	**289.95**	
30mm Wide View[4]	1	60	—	5.5	30mm	Int.	5	**289.95**	

NIKON

Maker and Model	Magn.	Field at 100 Yds. (feet)	Eye Relief (in.)	Length (in.)	Tube Dia. (in.)	W & E Adjustments	Weight (ozs.)	Price	Other Data
Monarch UCC									Super multi-coated lenses and blackening of all internal metal parts for maximum light gathering capability; positive .25-MOA; fogproof; waterproof; shockproof; luster and matte finish. [1]Also available in matte silver finish. [2]Available in silver matte finish. [3]Available with TurkeyPro or Nikoplex reticle. From Nikon, Inc.
2x20 EER	2	22	26.4	8.1	1	Int.	6.3	**169.99**	

ACCESSORIES

Maker and Model	Magn.	Field at 100 Yds. (feet)	Eye Relief (in.)	Length (in.)	Tube Dia. (in.)	W & E Adjustments	Weight (ozs.)	Price	Other Data
SIGHTRON									
Pistol									[1]Satin black; also stainless. Electronic Red Dot scopes come with ring mount, front and rear extension tubes, polarizing filter, battery, haze filter caps, wrench. Lifetime warranty. From Sightron, Inc.
SII 1x28P[1]	1	30	9-24	9.49	1	Int.	8.46	212.95	
SII 2x28P[1]	2	16-10	9-24	9.49	1	Int.	8.28	212.95	
SIMMONS									
Prohunter Handgun									[1]Black matte finish; also available in silver. [2]With dovetail rings. [3]With 3V lithium battery, extension tube, polarizing filter, Weaver rings. Contact Simmons Outdoor Corp. for complete details.
77732[1]	2	22	9-17	8.75	1	Int.	7	139.99	
77738[1]	4	15	11.8-17.6	8.5	1	Int.	8	149.99	
Red Dot									
51004[2]	1	—	—	4.8	25mm	Int.	4.7	59.99	
51112[3]	1	—	—	5.25	30mm	Int.	6	99.99	
SWIFT									
Pistol									All Swift scopes have Quadraplex reticles and are fogproof and waterproof. Available in regular matte black or silver finish. [1]Comes with ring mounts, wrench, lens caps, extension tubes, filter, battery. From Swift Instruments.
679M 1.25-4x28	1.25-4	23-9	23-15	9.3	1	Int.	8.2	250.00	
Pistol Scopes									
661 4x32	4	90	10-22	9.2	1	Int.	9.5	130.00	
663 2x20[1]	2	18.3	9-21	7.2	1	Int.	8.4	130.00	
THOMPSON/CENTER RECOIL PROOF SERIES									
Pistol Scopes									[1]Black; lighted reticle. From Thompson/Center Arms.
8315[1]	2.5-7	15-5	8-21, 8-11	9.25	1	Int.	9.2	343.00	
8326	2.5-7	15-5	8-21, 8-11	9.25	1	Int.	10.5	408.00	
TRIJICON									
ReflexII 1x24	1	—	—	4.25	—	Int.	4.2	425.00	All models feature tritium and fiber optics dual lighting system that requires no batteries. From Trijicon, Inc.
ULTRA DOT									
Ultra-Dot Sights[1]									[1]Ultra Dot sights include rings, battery, polarized filter, and 5-year warranty. All models available in black or satin finish. [2]Illuminated red dot has eleven brightness settings. Shock-proof aluminum tube. From Ultra Dot Distribution.
Ultra-Dot 25[2]	1	—	—	5.1	1	Int.	3.9	159.00	
Ultra-Dot 30[2]	1	—	—	5.1	30mm	Int.	4	179.00	
WEAVER									
Handgun									[1]Gloss black. [2]Matte black. [3]Silver. All scopes are shock-proof, waterproof, and fogproof. From Weaver Products.
H2[1-3]	2	21	4-29	8.5	1	Int.	6.7	212.99-224.99	
H4[1-3]	4	18	11.5-18	8.5	1	Int.	6.7	234.99	
VH4[1-3]	1.5-4	13.6-5.8	11-17	8.6	1	Int.	8.1	289.99	
VH8[1-2-3]	2.5-8	8.5-3.7	12.16	9.3	1	Int.	8.3	299.99	

ACCESSORIES

LASER SIGHTS

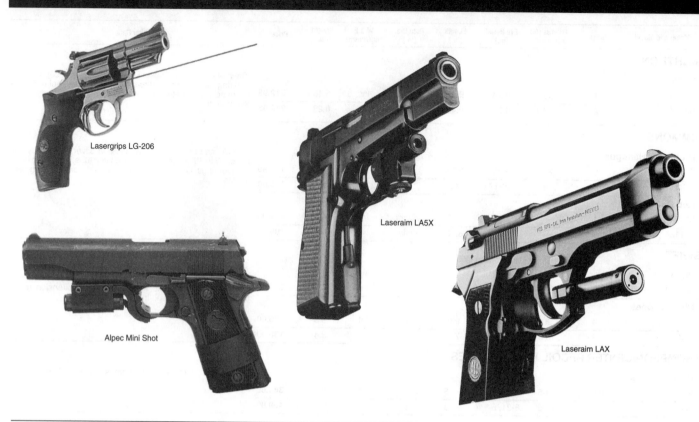

Lasergrips LG-206

Laseraim LA5X

Alpec Mini Shot

Laseraim LAX

Maker and Model	Wavelength (nm)	Beam Color	Lens	Operating Temp. (degrees F.)	Weight (ozs.)	Price	Other Data
ALPEC							[1]Range 1000 yards. [2]Range 300 yards. Mini Shot II range 500 yards, output 650mm, **$129.95**. [3]Range 300 yards; Laser Shot II 500 yards; Super Laser Shot 1000 yards. Black or stainless finish aluminum; removable pressure or push-button switch. Mounts for most handguns, many rifles and shotguns. From Alpec Team, Inc.
Power Shot[1]	635	Red	Glass	NA	2.5	$199.95	
Mini Shot[2]	670	Red	Glass	NA	2.5	99.95	
Laser Shot[3]	670	Red	Glass	NA	3.0	99.95	
BEAMSHOT							[1]Black or silver finish; adj. for windage and elevation; 300-yd. range; also M1000/S (500-yd. range), M1000/u (800-yd.). [2]Black finish; 300-, 500-, 800-yd. models. All come with removable touch pad switch, 5" cable. Mounts to fit virtually any firearm. From Quarton USA Co.
1000[1]	670	Red	Glass	—	3.8	NA	
3000[2]	635/670	Red	Glass	—	2	NA	
1001/u	635	Red	Glass	—	3.8	NA	
780	780	Red	Glass	—	3.8	NA	
BSA							[1]Comes with mounts for 22/air rifle and Weaver-style bases.
LS650[1]	N/A	Red	N/A	N/A	N/A	69.95	
LASERAIM							[1]1.5-mile range; 1" dot at 100 yds.; 20+ hrs. batt. life. [2]Laser projects 2" dot at 100 yds.: with rotary switch; with Hotdot **$237.00**; with Hotdot touch switch **$357.00**. [3]For Glock 17-27; G1 Hotdot **$299.00**; price installed. All have w&e adj.; black or satin silver finish. From Laseraim Technologies, Inc.
LA5X Handgun Sight[1]	—	Red	—	—	1 oz.	129.95	
LAX[1]	—	Red	—	—	2 oz.	79.00	
LA10 Hotdot[1]	—	—	—	—	NA	199.00	
MA-35RB Mini Aimer[2]	—	—	—	—	1.0	129.00	
G1 Laser[3]	—	—	—	—	2.0	229.00	
LASER DEVICES							[1]For S&W P99 semi-auto pistols; also BA-2, 5 oz., **$339.00**. [2]For revolvers. [3]For HK, Walther P99. [4]For semi-autos. [5]For rifles; also FA-4/ULS, 2.5 oz., **$325.00**. [6]For HK sub guns. [7]For military rifles. [8]For shotguns. [9]For SIG-Pro pistol. [10]Universal, semi-autos. [11]For AR-15 variants. All avail. with Magnum Power Point (650nM) or daytime-visible Super Power Point (632nM) diode. Infrared diodes avail. for law enforcement. From Laser Devices, Inc.
BA-1[1]	632	Red	Glass	—	2.4	372.00	
BA-3[2]	632	Red	Glass	—	3.3	332.50	
BA-5[3]	632	Red	Glass	—	3.2	372.00	
Duty-Grade[4]	632	Red	Glass	—	3.5	372.00	
FA-4[5]	632	Red	Glass	—	2.6	358.00	

ACCESSORIES

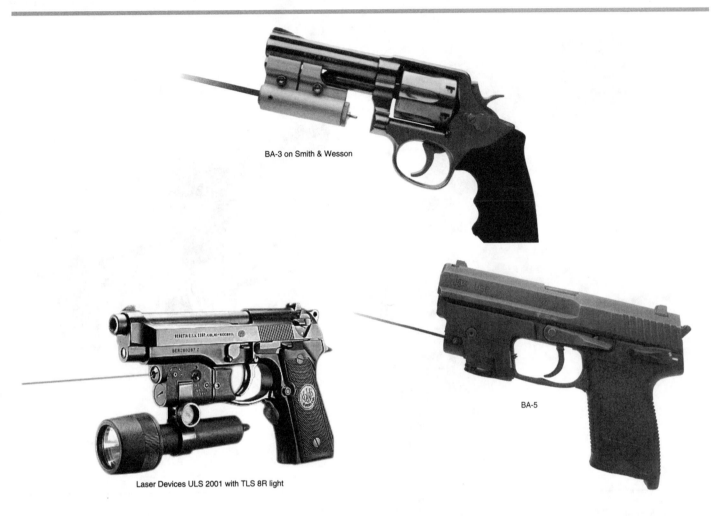

BA-3 on Smith & Wesson

Laser Devices ULS 2001 with TLS 8R light

BA-5

Maker and Model	Wavelength (nm)	Beam Color	Lens	Operating Temp. (degrees F.)	Weight (ozs.)	Price	Other Data
LASER DEVICES (cont.)							
LasTac[1]	632	Red	Glass	—	5.5	298.00 to 477.00	
MP-5 [6]	632	Red	Glass	—	2.2	495.00	
MR-2[7]	632	Red	Glass	—	6.3	485.00	
SA-2[8]	632	Red	Glass	—	3.0	360.00	
SIG-Pro[9]	632	Red	Glass	—	2.6	372.00	
ULS-2001[10]	632	Red	Glass	—	4.5	210.95	
Universal AR-2A	632	Red	Glass	—	4.5	445.00	
LASERGRIPS							Replaces existing grips with built-in laser high in the right grip panel. Integrated pressure sensitive pad in grip activates the laser. Also has master on/off switch. [1]For Beretta 92, 96, Colt 1911/Commander, Ruger MkII, S&W J-frames, SIG Sauer P228, P229. [2]For all Glock models. Option on/off switch. Requires factory installation. [3]For S&W K, L, N frames, round or square butt (LG-207); [4]For Taurus small-frame revolvers. [5]For Ruger SP-101. [6]For SIG Sauer P226. From Crimson Trace Corp.
LG-201[1]	633	Red-Orange	Glass	NA	—	349.00	
LG-206[3]	633	Red-Orange	Glass	NA	—	289.00	
LG-085[4]	633	Red-Orange	Glass	NA	—	279.00	
LG-101[5]	633	Red-Orange	Glass	NA	—	289.00	
LG-226[6]	633	Red-Orange	Glass	NA	—	379.00	
GLS-630[2]	633	Red-Orange	Glass	NA	—	595.00	

LASER SIGHTS

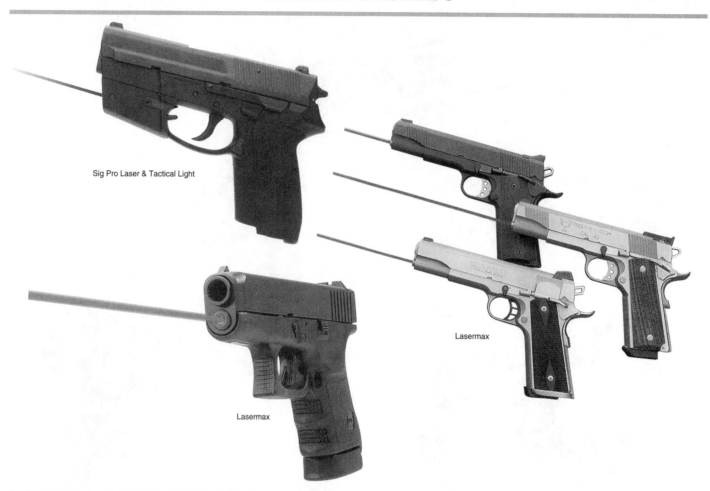

Sig Pro Laser & Tactical Light

Lasermax

Lasermax

Maker and Model	Wavelength (nm)	Beam Color	Lens	Operating Temp. (degrees F.)	Weight (ozs.)	Price	Other Data
LASERLYTE							[1]Dot/circle or dot/crosshair projection; black or stainless. [2]Also 635/645mm model. From TacStar Laserlyte.
LLX-0006-140/090[1]	635/645	Red	—	—	1.4	**159.95**	
WPL-0004-140/090[2]	670	Red	—	—	1.2	**109.95**	
TPL-0004-140/090[2]	670	Red	—	—	1.2	**109.95**	
T7S-0004-140[2]	670	Red	—	—	0.8	**109.95**	
LASERMAX							Replaces the recoil spring guide rod; includes a customized takedown lever that serves as the laser's instant on/off switch. For Glock, Smith & Wesson, Sigarms, Beretta and select Taurus models. Installs in most pistols without gunsmithing. Battery life 1/2 hour to 2 hours in continuous use. From LaserMax.
LMS-1000 Internal Guide Rod	635	Red-Orange	Glass	40-120	.25	**From 394.95**	
NIGHT STALKER							Waterproof; LCD panel displays power remaining; programmable blink rate; constant or memory on. From Wilcox Industries Corp.
S0 Smart	635	Red	NA	NA	2.46	**515.00**	

SCOPE RINGS & BASES

Maker, Model, Type	Adjust.	Scopes	Price
AIMTECH			
Handguns			
AMT Auto Mag II .22 Mag.	No	Weaver rail	$56.99
Astra .44 Mag Revolver	No	Weaver rail	63.25
Beretta/Taurus 92/99	No	Weaver rail	63.25
Browning Buckmark/Challenger II	No	Weaver rail	56.99
Browning Hi-Power	No	Weaver rail	63.25
Glock 17, 17L, 19, 23, 24 etc. no rail	No	Weaver rail	63.25
Glock 20, 21 no rail	No	Weaver rail	63.25
Glock 9mm and .40 with access. rail	No	Weaver rail	74.95
Govt. 45 Auto/.38 Super	No	Weaver rail	63.25
Hi-Standard (Mitchell version) 107	No	Weaver rail	63.25
H&K USP 9mm/40 rail mount	No	Weaver rail	74.95
Rossi 85/851/951 Revolvers	No	Weaver rail	63.25
Ruger Mk I, Mk II	No	Weaver rail	49.95
Ruger P85/P89	No	Weaver rail	63.25
S&W K, L, N frames	No	Weaver rail	63.25
S&W K. L, N with tapped top strap*	No	Weaver rail	69.95
S&W Model 41 Target 22	No	Weaver rail	63.25
S&W Model 52 Target 38	No	Weaver rail	63.25
S&W Model 99 Walther frame rail mount	No	Weaver rail	74.95
S&W 2nd Gen. 59/459/659 etc.	No	Weaver rail	56.99
S&W 3rd Gen. full size 5906 etc.	No	Weaver rail	69.95
S&W 422, 622, 2206	No	Weaver rail	56.99
S&W 645/745	No	Weaver rail	56.99
S&W Sigma	No	Weaver rail	64.95
Taurus PT908	No	Weaver rail	63.25
Taurus 44 6.5" bbl.	No	Weaver rail	69.95
Walther 99	No	Weaver rail	74.95

All mounts no-gunsmithing, iron sight usable. Rifle mounts are solid see-through bases. All mounts accommodate standard Weaver-style rings of all makers. From Aimtech division, L&S Technologies, Inc. *3-blade sight mount combination. **Replacement handguard and mounting rail.

B-SQUARE

Maker, Model, Type	Adjust.	Scopes	Price
Pistols (centerfire)			
Beretta 92, 96/Taurus 99	No	Weaver rail	69.95
Colt M1911	E only	Weaver rail	69.95
Desert Eagle	No	Weaver rail	69.95

Maker, Model, Type	Adjust.	Scopes	Price
B-SQUARE (cont.)			
Glock	No	Weaver rail	69.95
H&K USP, 9mm and 40 S&W	No	Weaver rail	69.95
Ruger P85/89	E only	Weaver rail	69.95
SIG Sauer P226	E only	Weaver rail	69.95
Pistols (rimfire)			
Browning Buck Mark	No	Weaver rail	32.95
Colt 22	No	Weaver rail	49.95
Ruger Mk I/II, bull or taper	No	Weaver rail	32.95-49.95
Smith & Wesson 41, 2206	No	Weaver rail	36.95-49.95
Revolvers			
Colt Anaconda/Python	No	Weaver rail	35.95-74.95
Ruger Single-Six	No	Weaver rail	64.95
Ruger GP-100	No	Weaver rail	64.95
Ruger Blackhawk, Super	No	Weaver rail	64.95
Ruger Redhawk, Super	No	Weaver rail	64.95
Smith & Wesson K, L, N	No	Weaver rail	36.95-74.95
Taurus 66, 669, 607, 608	No	Weaver rail	64.95

Prices shown for anodized black finish; add $10 for stainless finish. Partial listing of mounts shown here. Contact B-Square for complete listing and details.

BURRIS

Maker, Model, Type	Adjust.	Scopes	Price
L.E.R. (LU) Mount Bases[1]	W only	1" split rings	24.00-52.00
L.E.R. No Drill-No Tap Bases[1, 2, 3]	W only	1" split rings	48.00-52.00

[1]Universal dovetail; accepts Burris, Universal, Redfield, Leupold rings. For Dan Wesson, S&W, Virginian, Ruger Blackhawk, Win. 94. [2]Selected rings and bases available with matte Safari or silver finish. [3]For S&W K, L, N frames, Colt Python, Dan Wesson with 6" or longer barrels.

CATCO

Maker, Model, Type	Adjust.	Scopes	Price
Glock	No	Weaver rail	69.95

Uses Weaver-style rings (not incl.). No gunsmithing required. See-Thru design. From CATCO.

CONETROL

Maker, Model, Type	Adjust.	Scopes	Price
Pistol Bases, 2-or 3-ring[1]	W only	—	NA

[1]For XP-100, T/C Contender, Colt SAA, Ruger Blackhawk, S&W and others.

KRIS MOUNTS

Maker, Model, Type	Adjust.	Scopes	Price
One Piece (T)[1]	No	1", 26mm split rings	12.98

[1]Blackhawk revolver. Mounts have oval hole to permit use of iron sights.

ACCESSORIES

NOTES
(S)—Side Mount; (T)—Top Mount; 22mm = .866"; 25.4mm = 1.024"; 26.5mm = 1.045"; 30mm = 1.81".

SCOPE RINGS & BASES

Maker, Model, Type	Adjust.	Scopes	Price
LASER AIM	No	Laser Aim	**19.99-69.00**

Mounts Laser Aim above or below barrel. Avail. for most popular handguns, rifles, shotguns, including militaries. From Laser Aim Technologies, Inc.

Maker, Model, Type	Adjust.	Scopes	Price
LEUPOLD			
STD Bases[1]	W only	One- or two-piece bases	24.60
STD Rings[2]	—	1" super low, low, medium, high	32.40
DD RBH Handgun Mounts[2]	No	—	59.40

[1]Base and two rings; Casull, Ruger, S&W, T/C; add $5.00 for silver finish. [2]Rem. 700, Win. 70-type actions.

Maker, Model, Type	Adjust.	Scopes	Price
MILLETT			
One-Piece Bases[2]	Yes	1"	23.95
Universal Two-Piece Bases			
Handgun Bases, Rings[1]	—	1"	34.60-69.15
30mm Rings[3]	—	30mm	37.75-42.95

[1]Two- and three-ring sets for Colt Python, Trooper, Diamondback, Peacekeeper, Dan Wesson, Ruger Redhawk, Super Redhawk. [2]Turn-in bases and Weaver-style for most popular rifles and T/C Contender, XP-100 pistols. [3]Both Weaver and turn-in styles; three heights. From Millett Sights.

Maker, Model, Type	Adjust.	Scopes	Price
THOMPSON/CENTER			
Duo-Ring Mount[1]	No	1"	61.99-62.99
Weaver-Style Bases	No	—	10.28-33.36
Weaver-Style Rings[2]	No	1"	27.74-42.13

[1]Attaches directly to T/C Contender bbl., no drilling/tapping; also for T/C M/L rifles, needs base adapter; blue or stainless. [2]Medium and high; blue or silver finish. From Thompson/Center.

Maker, Model, Type	Adjust.	Scopes	Price
WARNE			
Premier Series (all steel)			
T.P.A. (Permanently Attached)	No	1", 4 heights 30mm, 2 heights	87.75 98.55
Premier Series Rings fit Premier Series Bases			
Premier Series (all-steel Q.D. rings)			
Premier Series (all steel) Quick detachable lever	No	1", 4 heights 26mm, 2 heights 30mm, 3 heights	131.25 129.95 142.00
All-Steel One-Piece Base, ea.			38.50
All-Steel Two-Piece Base, ea.			14.00
Maxima Series (fits all Weaver-style bases)			
Permanently Attached[1]	No	1", 3 heights 30mm, 3 heights	25.50 36.00

Maker, Model, Type	Adjust.	Scopes	Price
WARNE *(cont.)*			
Adjustable Double Lever[2]	No	1", 3 heights 30mm, 3 heights	72.60 80.75
Thumb Knob	No	1", 3 heights 30mm, 3 heights	59.95 68.25
Stainless-Steel Two-Piece Base, ea.			15.25

Vertically split rings with dovetail clamp, precise return to zero. Fit most popular rifles, handguns. Regular blue, matte blue, silver finish. [1]All-Steel, non-Q.D. rings. [2]All-steel, Q.D. rings. From Warne Mfg. Co.

Maker, Model, Type	Adjust.	Scopes	Price
WEAVER			
Complete Mount Systems			
Pistol	No	1"	75.00-105.00

Nearly all modern rifles, pistols, and shotguns. Detachable rings in standard, See-Thru, and extension styles, in Low, Medium, High or X-High heights; gloss (blued), silver and matte finishes to match scopes. Extension rings are only available in 1" High style and See-Thru X-tensions only in gloss finish. No Drill & Tap Pistol systems in gloss or silver for: Colt Python, Trooper, 357, Officer's Model; Ruger Single-Six, Security-Six (gloss finish only), Blackhawk, Super Blackhawk, Blackhawk SRM 357, Redhawk, Ruger 22 Auto Pistols, Mark II; Smith & Wesson I- and current K-frames with adj. rear sights. From Weaver.

Maker, Model, Type	Adjust.	Scopes	Price
WEIGAND			
Browning Buck Mark[1]	No	—	29.95
Colt 22 Automatic[1]	No	—	19.95
Integra Mounts[2]	No	—	39.95-69.00
S&W Revolver[3]	No	—	29.95
Ruger 10/22[4]	No	—	14.95-39.95
Ruger Revolver[5]	No	—	29.95
Taurus Revolver[4]	No	—	29.95-65.00
T/C Encore Monster Mount	No	—	69.00
T/C Contender Monster Mount	No	—	69.00
Lightweight Rings	No	1", 30mm	29.95-39.95
1911, P-9 Scopemounts			
SM3[6]	No	Weaver rail	99.95
SRS 1911-2[7]	No	30mm	59.95
APCMNT[8]	No	—	69.95

[1]No gunsmithing. [2]S&W K, L, N frames; Taurus vent rib models; Colt Anaconda/Python; Ruger Redhawk; Ruger 10/22. [3]K, L, N frames. [4]Three models. [5]Redhawk, Blackhawk, GP-100. [6]3rd Gen.; drill and tap; without slots **$59.95**. [7]Ringless design, silver only. [8]For Aimpoint Comp. Red Dot scope, silver only. From Weigand Combat Handguns, Inc.

Maker, Model, Type	Adjust.	Scopes	Price
WIDEVIEW			
Desert Eagle Pistol Mount	No	1", 30mm	34.95-44.95

[1]For Weaver-type base. From Wideview Scope Mount Corp.

NOTES
(S)—Side Mount; (T)—Top Mount; 22mm = .866"; 25.4mm = 1.024"; 26.5mm = 1.045"; 30mm = 1.81".

Swift M700T Scout

BAUSCH & LOMB DISCOVERER 15x to 60x zoom, 60mm objective. Constant focus throughout range. Field at 1000 yds. 38 ft (60x), 150 ft. (15x). Comes with lens caps. Length 17 1/2"; weight 48.5 oz.
Price:.. **$391.95**

BAUSCH & LOMB ELITE 15x to 45x zoom, 60mm objective. Field at 1000 yds., 125-65 ft. Length is 12.2"; weight, 26.5 oz. Waterproof, armored. Tripod mount. Comes with black case.
Price:.. **$766.95**

BAUSCH & LOMB ELITE ZOOM 20x-60x, 70mm objective. Roof prism. Field at 1000 yds. 90-50 ft. Length is 16"; weight 40 oz. Waterproof, armored. Tripod mount. Comes with black case.
Price: **$921.95**

BAUSCH & LOMB 80MM ELITE 20x-60x zoom, 80mm objective. Field of view at 1000 yds. 98-50 ft. (zoom). Weight 51 oz. (20x, 30x), 54 oz. (zoom); length 17". Interchangeable bayonet-style eyepieces. Built-in peep sight.
Price: With EDPrime Glass **$1,276.95**

BUSHNELL TROPHY 63mm objective, 20x-60x zoom. Field at 1000 yds. 90ft. (20x), 45 ft. (60x). Length 12.7"; weight 20 oz. Black rubber armored, waterproof. Case included.
Price: **$421.95**

BUSHNELL COMPACT TROPHY 50mm objective, 20x-50x zoom. Field at 1000 yds. 92 ft. (20x), 52 ft. (50x). Length 12.2"; weight 17 oz. Black rubber armored, waterproof. Case included.
Price:.. **$337.95**

BUSHNELL SENTRY 16-32 zoom, 50mm objective. Field at 1000 yds. 140-65 ft. Length 8.7", weight 21.5 oz. Black rubber armored. Built-in peep sight. Comes with tripod and hardcase.
Price:.. **$205.95**

BUSHNELL SPACEMASTER 20x-45x zoom. Long eye relief. Rubber armored, prismatic. 60mm objective. Field at 1000 yds. 90-58 ft. Minimum focus 20 ft. Length 12.7".
Price: With tripod, carrying case and 20x-45x LER eyepiece. **$560.95**

BUSHNELL SPORTVIEW 12x-36x zoom, 50mm objective. Field at 100 yds. 160 ft. (12x), 90 ft. (36x). Length 14.6"; weight 25 oz.
Price: With tripod and carrying case **$159.95**

BUSHNELL XTRA-WIDE® 15-45x zoom, 60mm objective. Field at 1000 yds. 160-87 ft. Length 13"; weight 35 oz.
Price: **$640.95**

HERMES 1 70mm objective, 16x, 25x, 40x. Field at 1000 meters 160 ft. (16x), 75ft. (40x). Length 12.2"; weight 33 oz. From CZ-USA.
Price: Body **$359.00**
Price: 25x eyepiece **$86.00**
Price: 40x eyepiece **$128.00**

KOWA TS-500 SERIES Offset 45° or straight body. Comes with 20-40x zoom eyepiece or 20x fixed eyepiece. 50mm obj. Field at 1000 yds.: 171 ft. (20x fixed), 132-74 ft. (20-40x zoom). Length 8.9-10.4", weight 13.4-14.8 oz.
Price: TS-501 (offset 45° body w/20x fixed eyepiece) **$258.00**
Price: TS-502 (straight body w/20x fixed eyepiece) **$231.00**
Price: TS-501Z (offset 45° body w/20-40x zoom eyepiece) **$321.00**
Price: TS-502Z (straight body w/20-40x zoom eyepiece).................... **$290.00**

KOWA TS-610 SERIES Offset 45° or straight body. Available with fluorite lens. Sunshade. 60mm obj. Field of view at 1000 yds.: 177 ft. (20xW), 154 ft. (22xW), 102 ft. (25x), 92 ft. (25xLER), 62 ft. (40x), 102-56 ft. (20-60x zoom). Length 11.2"; weight 27 oz. Note: Eyepieces for TSN 7mm series, TSN-660 series, and TS-610 series are interchangeable.
Price: TS-611 body (45° offset) **$530.00**
Price: TS-612 body (straight)...................................... **$489.00**
Price: TS-614 body (straight, fluorite lens) **$1,010.00**
Price: TSE-Z2M (20-60x zoom eyepiece) **$231.00**
Price: TSE-17HB (25x long eye relief eyepiece) **$240.00**
Price: TSE-15WM (27x wide angle eyepiece) **$182.00**
Price: TSE-21WB (20x wide angle high-grade eyepiece) **$230.00**
Price: TSE-10PM (40x eyepiece) **$108.00**

Price: TSE-16PM (25x eyepiece) **$108.00**
Price: TSN-DA1 (digital photo adapter) **$105.00**
Price: Adapter rings for DA1 .... **$43.00**
Price: TSN-PA2 (800mm photo adapter) **$269.00**
Price: TSN-PA4 (1200mm photo adapter) **$330.00**
Price: Camera mounts (for use with photo adapter) **$30.00**

KOWA TSN-660 SERIES Offset 45° or straight body. Fully waterproof. Available with fluorite lens. Sunshade and rotating tripod mount. 66mm obj., field of view at 1000 yds.: 177 ft. (20x@), 154 ft. (27xW), 131 ft. (30xW), 102 ft. (25x), 92 ft. (25xLER), 62 ft. (40x), 108-79 ft. (20-40x Multi-Coated Zoom), 102-56 ft. (20-60x Zoom), 98-62 ft. (20-60x High Grade Zoom). Length 12.3"; weight 34.9-36.7 oz. Note: Eyepieces for TSN 77mm Series, TSN-660 Series, and TSN610 Series are interchangeable.
Price: TSN-661 body (45° offset) **$660.00**
Price: TSN-662 body (straight) **$610.00**
Price: TSN-663 body (45° offset, fluorite lens)......................**$1,070.00**
Price: TSN-664 body (straight, fluorite lens) **$1,010.00**
Price: TSE-Z2M (20-60x zoom eyepiece) **$231.00**
Price: TSE-Z4 (20-60x high-grade zoom eyepiece)...................... **$378.00**
Price: TSE-Z6 (20-40x multi-coated zoom eyepiece) **$250.00**
Price: TSE-17HB (25x long eye relief eyepiece) **$240.00**
Price: TSE-14W (30x wide angle eyepiece) **$288.00**
Price: TSE-21WB (20x wide angle eyepiece) **$230.00**
Price: TSE-15PM (27x wide angle eyepiece)........................... **$182.00**
Price: TSE-10PM (40x eyepiece) **$108.00**
Price: TSE-16PM (25x eyepiece) **$108.00**
Price: TSNE5B (77x eyepiece) **$235.00**
Price: TSNE7B (60x eyepiece)....................................... **$230.00**
Price: TSN-DA1 (digital photo adapter) **$105.00**
Price: Adapter rings for DA1 .... **$43.00**
Price: TSN-PA2 (800mm photo adapter) **$269.00**
Price: TSN-PA4 (1200mm photo adapter) **$330.00**
Price: Camera mounts (for use with photo adapter) **$30.00**

KOWA TSN-820 SERIES Offset 45 or straight body. Fully waterproof. Available with fluorite lens. Sunshade and rotating tripod mount. 82mm obj., field of view at 1000 yds: 75 ft (27xLER, 50xW), 126 ft. (32xW), 115-58 ft. (20-60xZoom). Length 15"; weight 49.4-52.2 oz.
Price: TSN-821M body (45° offset) **$850.00**
Price: TSN-822M body (straight) **$770.00**
Price: TSN-823M body (45° offset, fluorite lens) **$1,850.00**
Price: TSN-824M body (straight, fluorite lens) **$1,730.00**
Price: TSE-Z7 (20-60x zoom eyepiece) **$433.00**
Price: TSE-9W (50x wide angle eyepiece)............................. **$345.00**
Price: TSE-14WB (32x wide angle eyepiece) **$366.00**
Price: TSE-17HC (27x long eye relief eyepiece) **$248.00**
Price: TSN-Da1 (digital photo adapter) **$105.00**
Price: Adapter rings for DA1 .... **$43.00**
Price: TSN-PA2C (850mm photo adapter)............................. **$300.00**
Price: Camera mounts (for use with photo adapter) **$30.00**

LEUPOLD 12-40x60 VARIABLE 60mm objective, 12-40x. Field at 100 yds. 17.5-5.3 ft.; eye relief 1.2" (20x). Overall length 11.5", weight 32 oz. Rubber armored.
Price: **$1,217.90**

LEUPOLD 25x50 COMPACT 50mm objective, 25x. Field at 100 yds. 8.3 ft.; eye relief 1"; length overall 9.4"; weight 20.5 oz.
Price: Armored model **$848.20**
Price: Packer Tripod **$96.40**

MEOPTA HA 70 (Hermes I) Spotting scope 70mm objective, 16x, 25xWA, 40x, 50x or 20-45x. Length 12.2"; weight 32.5 oz.
Price: .... **NA**

MIRADOR TTB SERIES Draw tube armored spotting scopes. Available with 75mm or 80mm objective. Zoom model (28x-62x, 80mm) is 11 7/8" (closed), weighs 50 oz. Field at 1000 yds. 70-42 ft. Comes with lens covers.
Price: 28-62x80mm **$1,133.95**
Price: 32x80mm **$971.95**
Price: 26-58x75mm **$989.95**
Price: 30x75mm **$827.95**

MIRADOR SSD SPOTTING SCOPES 60mm objective, 15x, 20x, 22x, 25x, 40x, 60x, 20-60x; field at 1000 yds. 37 ft.; length 10 1/4"; weight 33 oz.
Price: 25x **$575.95**
Price: 22x Wide Angle... **$593.95**
Price: 20-60x Zoom **$746.95**
Price: As above, with tripod, case.................................. **$944.95**

MIRADOR SIA SPOTTING SCOPES Similar to the SSD scopes except with 45° eyepiece. Length 12 1/4"; weight 39 oz.
Price: 25x **$809.95**
Price: 22x Wide Angle... **$827.95**
Price: 20-60x Zoom **$980.95**

MIRADOR SSR SPOTTING SCOPES 50mm or 60mm objective. Similar to SSD except rubber armored in black or camouflage. Length 11 1/8"; weight 31 oz.
Price: Black, 20x **$521.95**
Price: Black, 18x Wide Angle **$539.95**
Price: Black, 16-48x Zoom **$692.95**
Price: Black, 20x, 60mm, EER **$692.95**
Price: Black, 22x Wide Angle, 60mm **$701.95**
Price: Black, 20-60x Zoom **$854.95**

MIRADOR SSF FIELD SCOPES Fixed or variable power, choice of 50mm, 60mm, 75mm objective lens. Length 9 3/4"; weight 20 oz. (15-32x50).
Price: 20x50mm **$359.95**

Spotting Scopes

Price: 25x60mm **$440.95**
Price: 30x75mm **$584.95**
Price: 15-32x50mm Zoom **$548.95**
Price: 18-40x60mm Zoom **$629.95**
Price: 22-47x75mm Zoom **$773.95**

MIRADOR SRA MULTI ANGLE SCOPES Similar to SSF Series except eyepiece head rotates for viewing from any angle.
Price: 20x50mm **$503.95**
Price: 25x60mm **$647.95**
Price: 30x75mm **$764.95**
Price: 15-32x50mm Zoom **$692.95**
Price: 18-40x60mm Zoom **$836.95**
Price: 22-47x75mm Zoom **$953.95**

MIRADOR SIB FIELD SCOPES Short-tube, 45° scopes with porro prism design. 50mm and 60mm objective. Length 10 1/4"; weight 18.5 oz. (15-32x50mm); field at 1000 yds. 129-81 ft.
Price: 20x50mm **$386.95**
Price: 25x60mm **$449.95**
Price: 15-32x50mm Zoom **$575.95**
Price: 18-40x60mm Zoom **$638.95**

NIKON FIELDSCOPES 60mm and 78mm lens. Field at 1000 yds. 105 ft. (60mm, 20x), 126 ft. (78mm, 25x). Length 12.8" (straight 60mm), 12.6" (straight 78mm); weight 34.5-47.5 oz. Eyepieces available separately.
Price: 60mm straight body **$499.99**
Price: 60mm angled body **$519.99**
Price: 60mm straight ED body **$779.99**
Price: 60mm angled ED body **$849.99**
Price: 78mm straight ED body **$899.99**
Price: 78mm angled ED body **$999.99**
Price: Eyepieces (15x to 60x) . . . . . . **$146.95** to **$324.95**
Price: 20-45x eyepiece (25-56x for 78mm) **$320.55**

NIKON SPOTTING SCOPE 60mm objective, 20x fixed power or 15-45x zoom. Field at 1000 yds. 145 ft. (20x). Gray rubber armored. Straight or angled eyepiece. Weighs 44.2 oz., length 12.1" (20x).
Price: 20x60 fixed (with eyepiece) **$290.95**
Price: 15-45x zoom (with case, tripod, eyepiece) **$578.95**

PENTAX PF-80ED spotting scope 80mm objective lens available in 18x, 24x, 36x, 48x, 72x and 20-60x. Length 15.6", weight 11.9 to 19.2 oz.
Price: **$1,320.00**

SIGHTRON SII 2050X63 63mm objective lens, 20x-50x zoom. Field at 1000 yds 91.9 ft. (20x), 52.5 ft. (50x). Length 14"; weight 30.8 oz. Black rubber finish. Also available with 80mm objective lens.
Price: 63mm or 80mm **$339.95**

SIMMONS 1280 50mm objective, 15-45x zoom. Black matte finish. Ocular focus. Peep finder sight. Waterproof. FOV 95-51 ft. @ 1000 yards. Wgt. 33.5 oz., length 12".
Price: With tripod **$267.99**

SIMMONS 1281 60mm objective, 20-60x zoom. Black matte finish. Ocular focus. Peep finder sight. Waterproof. FOV 78-43 ft. @ 1000 yards. Wgt. 34.5 oz. Length 12".
Price: With tripod **$295.99**

SIMMONS 77206 PROHUNTER 50mm objectives, 25x fixed power. Field at 1000 yds. 113 ft.; length 10.25"; weighs 33.25 oz. Black rubber armored.
Price: With tripod case **$160.60**

SIMMONS 41200 REDLINE 50mm objective, 15x-45x zoom. Field at 1000 yds. 104-41 ft.; length 16.75"; weighs 32.75 oz.
Price: With hard case and tripod **$99.99**
Price: 20-60x, Model 41201 . . . . . . **$129.99**

STEINER FIELD TELESCOPE 24x, 80mm objective. Field at 1000 yds. 105 ft. Weight 44 oz. Tripod mounts. Rubber armored.
Price: **$1,299.00**

SWAROVSKI CT EXTENDIBLE SCOPES 75mm or 85mm objective, 20-60x zoom, or fixed 15x, 22x, 30x, 32x eyepieces. Field at 1000 yds. 135 ft. (15x), 99 ft. (32x); 99 ft. (20x), 5.2 ft. (60x) for zoom. Length 12.4" (closed), 17.2" (open) for the CT75; 9.7"/17.2" for CT85. Weight 40.6 oz. (CT75), 49.4 oz. (CT85). Green rubber armored.
Price: CT75 body **$765.56**
Price: CT85 body **$1,094.44**
Price: 20-60x eyepiece **$343.33**
Price: 15x, 22x eyepiece **$232.22**
Price: 30x eyepiece **$265.55**

SWAROVSKI AT-80/ST-80 SPOTTING SCOPES 80mm objective, 20-60x zoom, or fixed 15x, 22x, 30x, 32x eyepieces. Field at 1000 yds. 135 ft. (15x), 99 ft. (32x); 99 ft. (20x), 52.5 ft. (60x) for zoom. Length 16" (AT-80), 15.6" (ST-80); weight 51.8 oz. Available with HD (high density) glass.
Price: AT-80 (angled) body **$1,094.44**
Price: ST-80 (straight) body **$1,094.44**
Price: With HD glass **$1,555.00**
Price: 20-60x eyepiece **$343.33**
Price: 15x, 22x eyepiece **$232.22**
Price: 30x eyepiece **$265.55**

SWIFT LYNX M836 15x-45x zoom, 60mm objective. Weight 7 lbs., length 14". Has 45° eyepiece, sunshade.
Price: **$315.00**

SWIFT NIGHTHAWK M849U 80mm objective, 20x-60x zoom, or fixed 19, 25x, 31x, 50x, 75x eyepieces. Has rubber armored body, 1.8x optical finder, retractable lens hood, 45° eyepiece. Field at 1000 yds. 60 ft. (28x), 41 ft. (75x). Length 13.4 oz.; weight 39 oz.
Price: Body only **$870.00**
Price: 20-68x eyepiece **$370.00**
Price: Fixed eyepieces . . . . . . **$130.00** to **$240.00**
Price: Model 849 (straight) body **$795.00**

SWIFT NIGHTHAWK M850U 65mm objective, 16x-48x zoom, or fixed 19x, 20x, 25x, 40x, 60x eyepieces. Rubber armored with a 1.8x optical finder, retractable lens hood. Field at 1000 yds. 83 ft. (22x), 52 ft. (60x). Length 12.3"; weight 30 oz. Has 45° eyepiece.
Price: Body only **$650.00**
Price: 16x-48x eyepiece **$370.00**
Price: Fixed eyepieces . . . . . . **$130.00** to **$240.00**
Price: Model 850 (straight) body **$575.00**

SWIFT LEOPARD M837 50mm objective, 25x. Length 9 11/16" to 10 1/2". Weight with tripod 28 oz. Rubber armored. Comes with tripod.
Price: **$160.00**

SWIFT TELEMASTER M841 60mm objective. 15x to 60x variable power. Field at 1000 yds. 160 feet (15x) to 40 feet (60x). Weight 3.25 lbs.; length 18" overall.
Price: **$399.50**

SWIFT PANTHER M844 15x-45x zoom or 22x WA, 15x, 20x, 40x. 60mm objective. Field at 1000 yds. 141 ft. (15x), 68 ft. (40x), 95-58 ft. (20x-45x).
Price: Body only **$380.00**
Price: 15x-45x zoom eyepiece **$120.00**
Price: 20x-45x zoom (long eye relief) eyepiece **$140.00**
Price: 15x, 20x, 40x eyepiece **$65.00**
Price: 22x WA eyepiece **$80.00**

SWIFT M700T 12x-36x, 50mm objective. Field of view at 100 yds. 16 ft. (12x), 9 ft. (36x). Length 14"; weight with tripod 3.22 lbs.
Price: **$225.00**

SWIFT SEARCHER M839 60mm objective, 20x, 40x. Field at 1000 yds. 118 ft. (30x), 59 ft. (40x). Length 12.6"; weight 3 lbs. Rotating eyepiece head for straight or 45° viewing.
Price: **$580.00**
Price: 30x, 50x eyepieces, each **$67.00**

TASCO 29TZBWP WATERPROOF SPOTTER 60mm objective lens, 20x-60x zoom. Field at 100 yds. 7 ft., 4 in. to 3 ft., 8 in. Black rubber armored. Comes with tripod, hard case.
Price: **$356.50**

TASCO WC28TZ WORLD CLASS SPOTTING SCOPE 50mm objective, 12-36x zoom. Field at 100 yds. World Class. 13-3.8 ft. Comes with tripod and case.
Price: **$220.00**

TASCO CW5001 COMPACT ZOOM 50mm objective, 12x-36x zoom. Field at 100 yds. 16 ft., 9 in. Includes photo adapter tube, tripod with panhead lever, case.
Price: **$280.00**

TASCO 3700WP WATERPROOF SPOTTER 50mm objective, 18x-36x zoom. Field at 100 yds. 12ft., 6 in. to 7 ft., 9 in. Black rubber armored. Comes with tripod, hard case.
Price: **$288.60**

TASCO 3700, 3701 SPOTTING SCOPE 50mm objective. 18x-36x zoom. Field at 100 yds. 12 ft., 6 in. to 7 ft., 9 in. Black rubber armored.
Price: Model 3700 (black, with tripod, case) **$237.00**
Price: Model 3701 (as above, brown camo) **$237.00**

TASCO 21EB ZOOM 50mm objective lens, 15x-45x zoom. Field at 100 yds. 11 ft. (15x). Weight 22 oz.; length 18.3" overall. Comes with panhead lever tripod.
Price: **$119.00**

TASCO 22EB ZOOM 60mm objective lens, 20x-60x zoom. Field at 100 yds. 7 ft., 2 in. (20x). Weight 28 oz.; length 21.5" overall. Comes with micro-adjustable tripod.
Price: **$183.00**

UNERTL "FORTY-FIVE" 54mm objective. 20x (single fixed power). Field at 100 yds. 10',10"; eye relief 1"; focusing range infinity to 33 ft. Weight about 32 oz.; overall length 15 3/4". With lens covers.
Price: With multi-layer lens coating **$662.00**
Price: With mono-layer magnesium coating **$572.00**

UNERTL STRAIGHT PRISMATIC 63.5mm objective, 24x. Field at 100 yds., 7 ft. Relative brightness, 6.96. Eye relief 1/2". Weight 40 oz.; length closed 19". Push-pull and screw-focus eyepiece. 16x and 32x eyepieces **$125.00** each.
Price: **$515.00**

UNERTL 20x STRAIGHT PRISMATIC 54mm objective, 20x. Field at 100 yds. 8.5 ft. Relative brightness 6.1. Eye relief 1/2". Weight 36 oz.; length closed 13 1/2". Complete with lens covers.
Price: **$477.00**

UNERTL TEAM SCOPE 100mm objective. 15x, 24x, 32x eyepieces. Field at 100 yds. 13 to 7.5 ft. Relative brightness, 39.06 to 9.79. Eye relief 2" to 1 1/2". Weight 13 lbs.; length 29 7/8" overall. Metal tripod, yoke and wood carrying case furnished (total weight 80 lbs.).
Price: **$2,810.00**

WEAVER 20x50 50mm objective. Field of view 124 ft. at 100 yds. Eye relief .85"; weighs 21 oz.; overall length 10". Waterproof, armored.
Price: **$368.99**

WEAVER 15-40x60 ZOOM 60mm objective. 15x-40x zoom. Field at 100 yds. 119 ft. (15x), 66 ft. (60x). Overall length 12.5", weighs 26 oz. Waterproof, armored.
Price: **$551.99**

COMPENDIUM OF STATE LAWS GOVERNING FIREARMS

The following chart lists the main provisions of state firearms laws as of the date of publication. In addition to the state provisions, the purchase, sale, and, in certain circumstances, the possession and interstate transportation of firearms are regulated by the Federal Gun Control Act of 1968 as amended by the Firearms Owners' Protection Act of 1986. Also, cities and localities may have their own gun ordinances in addition to federal and state restrictions. Details may be obtained by contacting local law enforcement authorities or by consulting your state's firearms law digest compiled by the NRA Institute for Legislative Action.

STATE	GUN BAN	EXEMPTIONS TO NICS$_2$	STATE WAITING PERIOD - NUMBER OF DAYS		LICENSE OR PERMIT TO PURCHASE		REGISTRATION		RECORD OF SALE REPORTED TO STATE OR LOCAL GOVT.
			HANDGUNS	LONG GUNS	HANDGUNS	LONG GUNS	HANDGUNS	LONG GUNS	
Alabama	—	—	—	—	—	—	—	—	X
Alaska	—	RTC	—	—	—	—	—	—	—
Arizona	—	RTC	—	—	—	—	—	—	—
Arkansas	—	RTC	—	—	—	—	—	—	—
California	X_{20}	—	10	10	—	—	X	—	X
Colorado	—	—	—	—	—	—	—	—	—
Connecticut	X_{20}	GRTC	$14_{14, 15}$	$14_{14, 15}$	X_{16}	—	—	—	X
Delaware	—	GRTC	—	—	—	—	—	—	—
Florida	—	GRTC	$3_{14, 15}$	—	—	—	—	—	—
Georgia	—	RTC	—	—	—	—	—	—	—
Hawaii	X_{20}	L, RTC	—	—	X_{16}	X_{16}	X_{12}	X_{12}	X
Idaho	—	RTC	—	—	—	—	—	—	—
Illinois	20	L	3	1	X_{16}	X_{16}	—$_4$	—$_4$	X
Indiana	—	RTC, O_3	—	—	—	—	—	—	X
Iowa	—	L, RTC	—	—	X_{16}	—	—	—	X
Kansas	—	—	1	—	1	—	—$_1$	—	1
Kentucky	—	RTC	—	—	—	—	—	—	—
Louisiana	—	GRTC	—	—	—	—	—	—	—
Maine	—	—	—	—	—	—	—	—	—
Maryland	X_{20}	GRTC	7	7_9	8	—	—	—	X
Massachusetts	X_{20}	L, RTC	7	—	X_{16}	X_{16}	—	—	X
Michigan	—	L	—	—	X_{16}	—	X	—	X
Minnesota	—	L, GRTC	7_{16}	16	X_{16}	X_{16}	—	—	X
Mississippi	—	RTC_3	—	—	—	—	—	—	—
Missouri	—	—	7	—	X_{16}	—	—	—	X
Montana	—	RTC	—	—	—	—	—	—	—
Nebraska	—	L	—	—	X	—	—	—	—
Nevada	—	RTC	1	—	—	—	1	—	—
New Hampshire	—	—	—	—	—	—	—	—	X
New Jersey	X_{20}	—	—	—	X_{16}	X_{16}	—	—	X
New Mexico	—	—	—	—	—	—	—	—	—
New York	X_{20}	L, RTC	—	—	X_{16}	16	X	7	X
North Carolina	—	L, RTC	—	—	X_{16}	—	—	—	X
North Dakota	—	RTC	—	—	—	—	—	—	X
Ohio	X_{20}	—	1	—	16	—	1	—	1
Oklahoma	—	RTC	—	—	—	—	—	—	—
Oregon	—	—	—	—	—	—	—	—	X
Pennsylvania	—	—	—	—	—	—	—	—	X
Rhode Island	—	—	7	7	—	—	—	—	X
South Carolina	—	RTC	8	—	8	—	—	—	X
South Dakota	—	GRTC	2	—	—	—	—	—	X
Tennessee	—	RTC	—	—	—	—	—	—	X
Texas	—	RTC_3	—	—	—	—	—	—	—
Utah	—	RTC	—	—	—	—	—	—	—
Vermont	—	—	—	—	—	—	—	—	—
Virginia	X_{20}	—	1, 8	—	1,8	—	—	—	1
Washington	—	RTC	5_{10}	—	—	—	—	—	X
West Virginia	—	—	—	—	—	—	—	—	—
Wisconsin	—	—	2	—	—	—	—	—	X
Wyoming	—	RTC	—	—	—	—	—	—	—
District of Columbia	X_{20}	L	—	—	X_{16}	X_{16}	X_{16}	X	X

REFERENCE

COMPENDIUM OF STATE LAWS GOVERNING FIREARMS

Since state laws are subject to frequent change, this chart is not to be considered legal advice or a restatement of the law.
All fifty states have sportsmen's protections laws to halt harrassment.

Compiled by
NRA INSTITUTE FOR LEGISLATIVE ACTION
11250 WAPLES MILL ROAD
FAIRFAX, VIRGINIA 22030
www.nraila.org

STATE	STATE PROVISION FOR RIGHT-TO-CARRY CONCEALED[15]	CARRYING OPENLY PROHIBITED	OWNER ID CARDS OR LICENSING	FIREARM RIGHTS CONSTITUTIONAL PROVISION	STATE FIREARMS PREEMPTION LAWS	RANGE PROTECTION LAW
Alabama	R	X[11]	—	X	X	—
Alaska	R	—	—	X	—	X
Arizona	R	—	—	X	X	—
Arkansas	R	X[5]	—	X	X	X
California	L	X[6]	—	—	X	X
Colorado	L	1	—	X	—	X
Connecticut	R	X	—	X	X[17]	X
Delaware	L	—	—	X	X	X
Florida	R	X	—	X	X	X
Georgia	R	X	—	X	X	X
Hawaii	L	X	X	X	—	—
Idaho	R	—	—	X	X	X
Illinois	D	X	X	X	—	X
Indiana	R	X	—	X	X[18]	X
Iowa	L	X	—	—	X	X
Kansas	D	1	—	X	—	—
Kentucky	R	—	—	X	X	X
Louisiana	R	—	—	X	X	X
Maine	R	—	—	X	X	X
Maryland	L	X	—	—	X	X
Massachusetts	L	X	X	X	X[17]	X
Michigan	L	X[11]	—	X	X	X
Minnesota	L	X	—	—	X	—
Mississippi	R	—	—	X	X	—
Missouri	D	—	—	X	X	X
Montana	R	—	—	X	X	X
Nebraska	D	—	—	X	—	—
Nevada	R	—	—	X	X	X
New Hampshire	R	—	—	X	—	X
New Jersey	L	X	X	—	X[17]	X
New Mexico	D	—	—	X	X	—
New York	L	X	X	—	X[22]	X
North Carolina	R	—	—	X	X	X
North Dakota	R	X[6]	—	X	X	X
Ohio	D	1	16	X	—	X
Oklahoma	R	X[6]	—	X	X	X
Oregon	R	—	—	X	X	X
Pennsylvania	R	X[11]	—	X	X	X
Rhode Island	L	X	—	X	X	X
South Carolina	R	X	—	X	X	—
South Dakota	R	—	—	X	X	X
Tennessee	R	X[5]	—	X	X	—
Texas	R	X	—	X	X	—
Utah	R	X[6]	—	X	X	X
Vermont	R[19]	X[5]	—	X	X	X
Virginia	R	—	—	X	X	X
Washington	R	X[21]	—	X	X	—
West Virginia	R	—	—	X	X	X
Wisconsin	D	—	—	X	X	X
Wyoming	R	—	—	X	X	X
District of Columbia	L	X	X	NA	—	—

REFERENCE

With over 20,000 "gun control" laws on the books in America, there are two challenges facing every gun owner. First, you owe it to yourself to become familiar with the federal laws on gun ownership. Only by knowing the laws can you avoid innocently breaking one.

Second, while federal legislation receives much more media attention, state legislatures and city councils make many more decisions regarding your right to own and carry firearms. NRA members and all gun owners must take extra care to be aware of anti-gun laws and ordinances at the state and local levels.

Notes:

1. In certain cities or counties.

2. **National Instant Check System (NICS) exemption codes:**
   RTC-Carry Permit Holders Exempt From NICS
   GRTC-Holders of RTC Permits issued before November 30, 1998 exempt from NICS. Holders of more recent permits are not exempt.
   L-Holders of state licenses to possess or purchase or firearms ID cards exempt from NICS.
   O-Other, See Note 3.

3. **NICS exemptions notes: Indiana:** Personal protection and hunting and target permits; **Mississippi:** Permit issued to security guards does **not** qualify.; **Texas:** Texas Peace Officer license, TCLEOSE Card, is grandfathered only.

4. Chicago only. No handgun not already registered may be possessed.

5. **Arkansas** prohibits carrying a firearm "with a purpose to employ it as a weapon against a person." **Tennessee** prohibits carrying "with the intent to go armed." **Vermont** prohibits carrying a firearm "with the intent or purpose of injuring another."

6. Loaded.

7. New York City only.

8. A permit is required to acquire another handgun before 30 days have elapsed following the acquisition of a handgun.

9. **Maryland** subjects purchases of "assault weapons" to a 7-day waiting period.

10. May be extended by police to 30 days in some circumstances. An individual not holding a driver's license must wait 90 days.

11. Carrying a handgun openly in a motor vehicle requires a license.

12. Every person arriving in **Hawaii** is required to register any firearm(s) brought into the State within 3 days of arrival of the person or firearm(s), whichever occurs later. Handguns purchased from licensed dealers must be registered within 5 days.

13. Concealed carry laws vary significantly between the states. Ratings reflect the real effect a state's particular laws have on the ability of citizens to carry firearms for self-defense.

14. Purchases from licensed dealers only.

15. The state waiting period does not apply to a person holding a valid permit or license to carry a firearm. In **Connecticut,** a hunting license also exempts the holder, for long gun purchases. In **Indiana,** only persons with unlimited carry permits are exempt.

16. **Connecticut:** A permit to purchase or a carry permit is required to obtain a handgun and a carry permit is required to transport a handgun outside your home. **District of Columbia:** No handgun may be possessed unless it was registered prior to Sept. 23, 1976 and re-registered by Feb. 5, 1977. A permit to purchase is required for a rifle or shotgun. **Hawaii:** Purchase permits, required for all firearms, may not be issued until 14 days after application. A handgun purchase permit is valid for 10 days, for one handgun; a long gun permit is valid for one year, for multiple long guns. **Illinois:** A Firearm Owner's Identification Card (FOI) is required to possess or purchase a firearm, must be issued to qualified applicants within 30 days, and is valid for 5 years. **Iowa:** A purchase permit is required for handguns, and is valid for one year, beginning three days after issuance. **Massachusetts:** Firearms and feeding devices for firearms are divided into classes. Depending on the class, a firearm identification card (FID) or class A license or class B license is required to possess, purchase, or carry a firearm, ammunition therefore, or firearm feeding device, or "large capacity feeding device." **Michigan:** A handgun purchaser must obtain a license to purchase from local law enforcement, and within 10 days present the license and handgun to obtain a certificate of inspection. **Minnesota:** A handgun transfer or carrying permit, or a 7-day waiting period and handgun transfer report, is required to purchase handguns or "assault weapons" from a dealer. A permit or transfer report must be issued to qualified applicants within 7 days. A permit is valid for one year, a transfer report for 30 days. **Missouri:** A purchase permit is required for a handgun, must be issued to qualified applicants within 7 days, and is valid for 30 days. **New Jersey:** Firearm owners must possess an FID, which must be issued to qualified applicants within 30 days. To purchase a handgun, an FID and a purchase permit, which must be issued within 30 days to qualified applicants, is valid for 90 days, are required. An FID is required to purchase long guns. **New York:** Purchase, possession and/or carrying of a handgun require a single license, which includes any restrictions made upon the bearer. New York City also requires a license for long guns. **North Carolina:** To purchase a handgun, a license or permit is required, which must be issued to qualified applicants within 30 days. **Ohio**: Some cities require a permit-to-purchase or firearm owner ID card.

17. Preemption through judicial ruling. Local regulation may be instituted in **Massachusetts** if ratified by the legislature.

18. Except Gary and East Chicago and local laws enacted before January, 1994.

19. **Vermont** law respects your right to carry without a permit.

20. **California prohibits** "assault weapons" and commencing January 1, 2001, any "unsafe handgun." **Connecticut, New Jersey, New York City,** and other local jurisdictions in **New York,** and some local jurisdictions in **Ohio** prohibit "assault weapons." **Hawaii** prohibits "assault pistols." **Illinois:** Chicago, Evanston, Oak Park, Morton Grove, Winnetka, Wilmette, and Highland Park prohibit handguns; some cities prohibit other kinds of firearms. **Maryland** prohibits several small, low-caliber, inexpensive handguns and "assault pistols." **Massachusetts:** It is unlawful to sell, transfer or possess "any assuait weapon or large capacity feeding device" [more than 10 rounds] that was not legally possessed on September 13, 1994. **Ohio:** some cities prohibit handguns of certain magazine capacities." **Virginia** prohibits "Street Sweeper" shotguns. The **District of Columbia** prohibits new acquisition of handguns and any semi-automatic firearm capable of using a detachable ammunition magazine of more than 12 rounds capacity. (With respect to some of these laws and ordinances, individuals may retain prohibited firearms owned previously, with certain restrictions.)

21. Local jurisdictions may opt out of prohibition.

22. Preemption only applies to handguns.

Concealed carry codes:

R: Right-to-Carry: "shall issue" or less restrictive discretionary permit system (Ala., Conn.) (See also note #21.)
L: Right-to-Carry Limited by local authority's discretion over permit issuance.
D: Right-to-Carry Denied, no permit system exists; concealed carry is prohibited.

Rev.3/2001 5m

REFERENCE

- **The right to self-defense neither begins nor ends at a state border.**

- **A law-abiding citizen does not suffer a character change by crossing a state line.**

- **An "unalienable right" is not determined by geographical boundaries.**

- **A patchwork of state laws regarding the carrying of firearms can make criminals out of honest folks, especially those who frequently must travel the states to earn a living.**

- **Using data for all 3,054 U.S. counties from 1977 to 1994, University of Chicago Prof. John Lott finds that for each additional year a concealed handgun law is in effect the murder rate declines by 3%, robberies by over 2%, and the rape rate by 2%.**

In spite of the truth of these statements and the fact that nearly half of all Americans live in states that allow a law-abiding citizen to carry a firearm concealed for personal protection, it has not been commonplace that these same citizens could carry their firearm across states lines. NRA-ILA is working to pass right-to-carry reciprocity laws granting permit holders the ability to carry their firearms legally while visiting or traveling beyond their home state.

In order to assist NRA Members in determining which states recognize their permits, NRA-ILA has created this guide. **This guide is not to be considered as legal advice or a restatement of the law. It is important to remember that state carry laws vary considerably. Be sure to check with state and local authorities outside your home state for a complete listing of restrictions on carrying concealed in that state.** Many states restrict carrying in bars, restaurants (where alcohol is served), establishments where packaged alcohol is sold, schools, colleges, universities, churches, parks, sporting events, correctional facilities, courthouses, federal and state government offices/buildings, banks, airport terminals, police stations, polling places, any posted private property restricting the carrying of concealed firearms, etc. In addition to state restrictions, federal law prohibits carrying on military bases, in national parks and the sterile area of airports. National Forests usually follow laws of the state wherein the forest is located.

NOTE: Vermont does not issue permits, but allows carrying of concealed firearms if there is no intent to commit a crime. Vermont residents traveling to other states must first obtain a non-resident permit from that state—if available—prior to carrying concealed. Utah will honor any permit issued by another state or county for 60 consecutive days.

NOTE TO READERS: Right To Carry reciprocity and recognition between the various states is subject to frequent change through legislative action and regulatory interpretation. This information is the best available at the time of publication. This summary is not intended as legal advice or restatement of law.

•• **Last Revised 6/2002** ••

NRA - RIGHT-TO-CARRY RECIPROCITY GUIDE

Alabama
Right-to-Carry Law Type
Shall Issue

Issuing Authority:
County Sheriff
These states also recognize your permit:
Alaska, Florida, Georgia, Idaho, Indiana, Kentucky, Michigan, Mississippi, Montana, North Dakota, Utah, Vermont, Wyoming
Contact agency for non-resident permits if granted:
Permits not granted.
http://www.dps.state.al.us

Alaska
Right-to-Carry Law Type
Shall Issue

Issuing Authority:
State Trooper
These states also recognize your permit:
Alabama, Arizona, Florida, idaho, Indiana, Kentucky, Michigan, Montana, North Dakota, Oklahoma, Texas, Vermont, Wyoming
Contact agency for non-resident permits if granted:
Permits not granted.
http://www.dps.state.ak.us/ast/achp/

Arizona
Right-to-Carry Law Type
Shall Issue

Issuing Authority:
Arizona Department of Public Safety
These states also recognize your permit:
Alaska, Arkansas, Idaho, Indiana, Kentucky, Michigan, Montana, Texas, Utah, Vermont
Contact agency for non-resident permits if granted:
Arizona Department of Public Safety
http://www.dps.state.az.us/ccw/welcome.htm

Arkansas
Right-to-Carry Law Type
Shall Issue

Issuing Authority:
State Police
These states also recognize your permit:
Alaska, Arizona, Florida, Idaho, Indiana, Kentucky, Michigan, Montana, Oklahoma, South Carolina, Tennessee, Texas, Utah, Vermont, Wyoming
Contact agency for non-resident permits if granted:
Permits not granted.
http://www.state.ar.us/asp/handgun.html

California
Right-to-Carry Law Type
Discretionary Issue

Issuing Authority:
County Sheriff
These states also recognize your permit:
Idaho, Indiana, Kentucky, Michigan, Montana, Utah, Vermont
Contact agency for non-resident permits if granted:
Permits not granted.
http://caag.state.ca.us/

Colorado
Right-to-Carry Law Type
Discretionary Issue

Issuing Authority:
City Chief of Police/County Sheriff
These states also recognize your permit:
Idaho, Indiana, Kentucky, Michigan, Utah, Vermont
Contact agency for non-resident permits if granted:
Permits not granted.
http://www.state.co.us/gov_dir/cdps/csp.htm

Connecticut
Right-to-Carry Law Type
Shall Issue

Issuing Authority:
Department of Public Safety, Special Licenses & Firearms Unit
These states also recognize your permit:
Idaho, Indiana, Kentucky, Michigan, Montana, Utah, Vermont
Contact agency for non-resident permits if granted:
Dept. of Public Safety, Special Licenses Unit; (860) 685-8000
http://www.state.ct.us/dps/CSP.htm

Delaware
Right-to-Carry Law Type
Discretionary Issue

Issuing Authority:
Prothonotary of Superior Court
These states also recognize your permit:
Idaho, Indiana, Kentucky, Michigan, Montana, Utah, Vermont
Contact agency for non-resident permits if granted:
Permits not granted.
http://www.state.de.us/dsp/

Florida
Right-to-Carry Law Type
Shall Issue

Issuing Authority:
Department of State, Division of Licensing
These states also recognize your permit:
Alabama, Alaska, Arkansas, Georgia, Idaho, Indiana, Kentucky, Louisiana, Michigan, Mississippi, Montana, New Hampshire, North Dakota, Pennsylvania, Tennessee, Texas, Utah, Vermont, Wyoming
Contact agency for non-resident permits if granted:
Dept. of State, Division of Licensing; (850) 488-5381
http://licgweb.dos.state.fl.us/

Georgia
Right-to-Carry Law Type
Shall Issue

Issuing Authority:
County Probate Judge
These states also recognize your permit:
Alabama, Florida, Idaho, Indiana, Kentucky, Michigan, Montana, New Hampshire, Tennessee, Utah, Vermont
Contact agency for non-resident permits if granted:
Permits not granted.
http://www.ganet.org/ago/

NRA - RIGHT-TO-CARRY RECIPROCITY GUIDE

Hawaii
Right-to-Carry Law Type
Discretionary Issue

Issuing Authority:
Chief of Police
These states also recognize your permit:
Idaho, Indiana, Kentucky, Michigan, Montana, Utah, Vermont
Contact agency for non-resident permits if granted:
Permits not granted.
http://www.hawaii.gov/ag/index.html

Kansas
Right-to-Carry Law Type
Non-Issue

Issuing Authority:
Permits not available.
These states also recognize your permit:
None
Contact agency for non-resident permits if granted:
Permits not granted.
http://www.ink.org/public/ksag/

Idaho
Right-to-Carry Law Type
Shall Issue

Issuing Authority:
County Sheriff
These states also recognize your permit:
Alabama, Alaska, Florida, Georgia, Indiana, Kentucky, Michigan, Montana, North Dakota, Utah, Vermont, Wyoming
Contact agency for non-resident permits if granted:
Any Sheriffs' Department
http://www./state.id.us/dle/dle.htm

Kentucky
Right-to-Carry Law Type
Shall Issue

Issuing Authority:
State Police
These states also recognize your permit:
Alabama, Alaska, Arizona, Arkansas, Florida, Georgia, Idaho, Indiana, Louisiana, Michigan, Mississippi, Montana, N. Dakota, Pennsylvania, Tennessee, Texas, Utah, W. Virginia, Vermont, Wyoming
Contact agency for non-resident permits if granted:
Permits not granted.
http://www.state.ky.us/agencies/ksp/ksphome.htm#menu

Illinois
Right-to-Carry Law Type
Non-Issue

Issuing Authority:
Permits not available.
These states also recognize your permit:
None.
Contact agency for non-resident permits if granted:
Permits not granted.
http://www.state.il.us/isp/isphpage.htm

Louisiana
Right-to-Carry Law Type
Shall Issue

Issuing Authority:
Department of Public Safety & Corrections
These states also recognize your permit:
Alaska, Florida, Idaho, Indiana, Kentucky, Michigan, Montana, Tennessee, Texas, Utah, Vermont, Virginia
Contact agency for non-resident permits if granted:
Permits not granted.
http://www.dps.state.la.us/stpolice.html

Indiana
Right-to-Carry Law Type
Shall Issue

Issuing Authority:
Chief Law Enforcement Officer of Municipality
These states also recognize your permit:
Alabama, Alaska, Florida, Georgia, Idaho, Kentucky, Michigan, Montana, Utah, Vermont, Wyoming
Contact agency for non-resident permits if granted:
Permits not granted.
http://www.state.in.us/isp/

Maine
Right-to-Carry Law Type
Shall Issue

Issuing Authority:
Dept. of Public Safety, Maine State Police, Licensing Division
These states also recognize your permit:
Idaho, Indiana, Kentucky, Michigan, Montana, Utah, Vermont
Contact agency for non-resident permits if granted:
Chief of State Police; (207) 624-8775

Iowa
Right-to-Carry Law Type
Discretionary Issue

Issuing Authority:
(resident) Sheriff (non-resident) Commissioner of Public Safety
These states also recognize your permit:
Idaho, Indiana, Kentucky, Michigan, Montana, Utah, Vermont
Contact agency for non-resident permits if granted:
Commissioner of Public Safety; (515) 281-3211
http://www.state.ia.us/government/dps/index.html

Maryland
Right-to-Carry Law Type
Discretionary Issue

Issuing Authority:
Superintendent of State Police
These states also recognize your permit:
Alaska, Idaho, Indiana, Kentucky, Michigan, Montana, Utah, Vermont
Contact agency for non-resident permits if granted:
Superintendent of State Police
http://www.inform.umd.edu/UMS+State/MD_Resources/MDSP/handgun.html

REFERENCE

NRA - RIGHT-TO-CARRY RECIPROCITY GUIDE

Massachusetts
Right-to-Carry Law Type
Discretionary Issue

Issuing Authority:
Department of State Police, Firearms Record Bureau
These states also recognize your permit:
Alaska, Idaho, Indiana, Kentucky, Michigan, Montana, Utah, Vermont
Contact agency for non-resident permits if granted:
Permits are technically available for non-residents, but are rarely granted
http://www.state.ma.us/msp/firearms/index.htm

Michigan
Right-to-Carry Law Type
Shall Issue

Issuing Authority:
County Gun Board/Sheriff
These states also recognize your permit:
Alabama, Alaska, Florida, Georgia, Idaho, Indiana, Kentucky, Montana, New Hampshire, North Dakota, Utah, Vermont, Wyoming
Contact agency for non-resident permits if granted:
Permits not granted.
http://www.msp.state.mi.us

Minnesota
Right-to-Carry Law Type
Discretionary Issue

Issuing Authority:
Chief of Police/County Sheriff
These states also recognize your permit:
Idaho, Indiana, Kentucky, Michigan, Montana, Utah, Vermont
Contact agency for non-resident permits if granted:
Permits not granted.
http://www.dps.state.mn.us/

Mississippi
Right-to-Carry Law Type
Shall Issue

Issuing Authority:
Department of Public Safety
These states also recognize your permit:
Alabama, Florida, Idaho, Indiana, Kentucky, Michigan, Montana, Tennessee, Utah, Vermont, Wyoming
Contact agency for non-resident permits if granted:
Permits not granted.
http://www.dps.state.ms.us/

Missouri
Right-to-Carry Law Type
Non-Issue

Issuing Authority:
Permits not available.
These states also recognize your permit:
None.
Contact agency for non-resident permits if granted:
Permits not granted.
http://www.dps.state.mo.us/home/dpshome.htm

Montana
Right-to-Carry Law Type
Shall Issue

Issuing Authority:
County Sheriff
These states also recognize your permit:
Alaska, Florida, Idaho, Indiana, Kentucky, Michigan, North Dakota, Utah, Vermont, Wyoming
Contact agency for non-resident permits if granted:
Permits not granted.
http://www.doj.state.mt.us/ls/weaponslist.htm

Nebraska
Right-to-Carry Law Type
Non-Issue

Issuing Authority:
Permits not available.
These states also recognize your permit:
None.
Contact agency for non-resident permits if granted:
Permits not granted.
http://www.nebraska-state-patrol.org/

Nevada
Right-to-Carry Law Type
Shall Issue

Issuing Authority:
County Sheriff
These states also recognize your permit:
Alaska, Idaho, Indiana, Kentucky, Michigan, Montana, Utah, Vermont
Contact agency for non-resident permits if granted:
In person with any County Sheriff
http://www.state.nv.us/ag

New Hampshire
Right-to-Carry Law Type
Shall Issue

Issuing Authority:
Selectman/Mayor or Chief of Police
These states also recognize your permit:
Alabama, Alaska, Florida, Georgia, Idaho, Indiana, Kentucky, Michigan, North Dakota, Utah, Vermont, Wyoming
Contact agency for non-resident permits if granted:
Director of State Police; (603) 271-3575
http://www.state.nh.us.nhsp.index.html

New Jersey
Right-to-Carry Law Type
Discretionary Issue

Issuing Authority:
Chief of Police/Superintendent of State Police
These states also recognize your permit:
Idaho, Indiana, Kentucky, Michigan, Montana, Utah, Vermont
Contact agency for non-resident permits if granted:
Superintendent of State Police; (609) 882-2000 ext. 2664 (technically available but rarely granted)
http://www.njsp.org/front.html

REFERENCE

NRA - Right-To-Carry Reciprocity Guide

New Mexico
Right-to-Carry Law Type
Non-Issue

Issuing Authority:
Permits not available.
These states also recognize your permit:
None
Contact agency for non-resident permits if granted:
Permits not granted.
http://www.dps.nm.org/

New York
Right-to-Carry Law Type
Discretionary Issue

Issuing Authority:
Varies by county
These states also recognize your permit:
Idaho, Indiana, Michigan, Montana, Utah, Vermont
Contact agency for non-resident permits if granted:
Permits not granted.
http://www.troopers.state.ny.us/

North Carolina
Right-to-Carry Law Type
Shall Issue

Issuing Authority:
County Sheriff
These states also recognize your permit:
Alaska, Idaho, Indiana, Kentucky, Michigan, Montana, Utah,
Vermont, Virginia
Contact agency for non-resident permits if granted:
Permits not granted.
http://www.jus.state.nc.us

North Dakota
Right-to-Carry Law Type
Shall Issue

Issuing Authority:
Chief of the Bureau of Criminal Investigation
These states also recognize your permit:
Alabama, Alaska, Florida, Kentucky, Michigan, Montana, New
Hampshire, Wyoming
Contact agency for non-resident permits if granted:
Chief of the Bureau of Criminal Investigation
http://www.ag.state.nd.us/BCI/BCI.html

Ohio
Right-to-Carry Law Type
Non-Issue

Issuing Authority:
Permits not available.
These states also recognize your permit:
None.
Contact agency for non-resident permits if granted:
Permits not granted.
http://www.ag.state.oh.us/

Oklahoma
Right-to-Carry Law Type
Shall Issue

Issuing Authority:
State Bureau of Investigation
These states also recognize your permit:
Alaska, Arkansas, Idaho, Indiana, Kentucky, Michigan, Montana,
Texas, Utah, Virginia, Vermont, Wyoming
Contact agency for non-resident permits if granted:
Permits not granted.
http://www.osbi.state.ok.us/

Oregon
Right-to-Carry Law Type
Shall Issue

Issuing Authority:
County Sheriff
These states also recognize your permit:
Alaska, Idaho, Indiana, Kentucky, Michigan, Montana, Utah, Vermont
Contact agency for non-resident permits if granted:
Discretionary to residents of contiguous states only
http://www.osp.state.or.us/html/index_high.html

Pennsylvania
Right-to-Carry Law Type
Shall Issue

Issuing Authority:
County Sheriff or Chief of Police
These states also recognize your permit:
Florida, Idaho, Indiana, Kentucky, Michigan, Montana, Utah,
Vermont
Contact agency for non-resident permits if granted:
Any Sheriff's Department
http://www.state.pa.us/PA_Exec/State_Police/

Rhode Island
Right-to-Carry Law Type
Discretionary Issue

Issuing Authority:
Attorney General
These states also recognize your permit:
Idaho, Indiana, Kentucky, Michigan, Montana, Utah, Vermont
Contact agency for non-resident permits if granted:
Attorney General by mail only (no phone calls) send self-addressed
stamped envelope to: Dept. of Attorney General 150 South Main
Street Providence, RI 02903 Attn: Bureau of Criminal Identification
http://www.riag.state.ri.us

South Carolina
Right-to-Carry Law Type
Shall Issue

Issuing Authority:
S.C. Law Enforcement Division
These states also recognize your permit:
Alaska, Arkansas, Idaho, Indiana, Kentucky, Michigan, Montana,
Tennessee, Utah, Vermont, Virginia, Wyoming
Contact agency for non-resident permits if granted:
Permits not granted.

REFERENCE

South Dakota

Right-to-Carry Law Type
Shall Issue

Issuing Authority:
Chief of Police/County Sheriff
These states also recognize your permit:
Idaho, Indiana, Kentucky, Michigan, Utah, Vermont
Contact agency for non-resident permits if granted:
Permits not granted.
http://www.state.sd.us/state/executive/dcr/hp/page1sdh.htm

Tennessee

Right-to-Carry Law Type
Shall Issue

Issuing Authority:
Department of Public Safety
These states also recognize your permit:
Alaska, Arkansas, Florida, Georgia, Idaho, Indiana, Kentucky,
Louisiana, Michigan, Mississippi, Montana, South Carolina, Texas,
Utah, Virginia, Vermont
Contact agency for non-resident permits if granted:
Permits not granted.
http://www.state.tn.us/safety/

Texas

Right-to-Carry Law Type
Shall Issue

Issuing Authority:
Department of Public Safety
These states also recognize your permit:
Arizona, Arkansas, Florida, Idaho, Indiana, Kentucky, Louisiana,
Michigan, Montana, Oklahoma, Tennessee, Utah, Virginia, Vermont
Contact agency for non-resident permits if granted:
Department of Public Safety. Call (800) 224-5744 or (512) 424-7293.
http://www.txdps.state.tx.us./administration/crime_records/chl/
reciprocity.htm

Utah

Right-to-Carry Law Type
Shall Issue

Issuing Authority:
Department of Public Safety
These states also recognize your permit:
Alabama, Alaska, Arizona, Florida, Idaho, Indiana, Kentucky,
Michigan, Montana, Oklahoma, South Carolina, Vermont, Wyoming
Contact agency for non-resident permits if granted:
Department of Public Safety; (801) 965-4484
http://www.bci.state.ut.us/

Vermont

Right-to-Carry Law Type
Shall Issue

Issuing Authority:
Permits not required.
These states also recognize your permit:
None
Contact agency for non-resident permits if granted:
Permits not required
http://www.state.vt.us/atg/

Virginia

Right-to-Carry Law Type
Shall Issue

Issuing Authority:
State Circuit Court of residence
These states also recognize your permit:
Idaho, Indiana, Kentucky, Michigan, Montana, Tennessee, Utah, West
Virginia, Vermont
Contact agency for non-resident permits if granted:
Permits not granted.
http://www.vsp.state.va.us/vsp.html

Washington

Right-to-Carry Law Type
Shall Issue

Issuing Authority:
Chief of Police/Sheriff
These states also recognize your permit:
Idaho, Indiana, Kentucky, Michigan, Montana, Utah, Vermont,
Virginia
Contact agency for non-resident permits if granted:
Permits not granted.
http://www.wa.gov/wsp/wsphome.htm

West Virginia

Right-to-Carry Law Type
Shall Issue

Issuing Authority:
County Sheriff
These states also recognize your permit:
Alaska, Idaho, Indiana, Kentucky, Michigan, Montana, Utah,
Virginia, Vermont
Contact agency for non-resident permits if granted:
Permits not granted.
http://www.wvstatepolice.com/legal/legal.shtml

Wisconsin

Right-to-Carry Law Type
Non-Issue

Issuing Authority:
Permits not available.
These states also recognize your permit:
None.
Contact agency for non-resident permits if granted:
Permits not granted.
http://www.doj.state.wi.us/

Wyoming

Right-to-Carry Law Type
Shall Issue

Issuing Authority:
Attorney General
These states also recognize your permit:
Alabama, Alaska, Florida, Georgia, Idaho, Indiana, Kentucky,
Michigan, Mississippi, Montana, North Dakota, Oklahoma, South
Carolina, Utah, Vermont
Contact agency for non-resident permits if granted:
Permits not granted.
http://www.state.wy.us/~ag/index.html

REFERENCE

UNITED STATES

ALABAMA
Alabama Gun Collectors Assn.
Secretary, P.O. Box 70965, Tuscaloosa, AL 35407

ALASKA
Alaska Gun Collectors Assn., Inc.
C.W. Floyd, Pres., 5240 Little Tree, Anchorage, AK 99507

ARIZONA
Arizona Arms Assn.
Don DeBusk, President, 4837 Bryce Ave., Glendale, AZ 85301

CALIFORNIA
California Cartridge Collectors Assn.
Rick Montgomery, 1729 Christina, Stockton, CA 95204/209-463-7216 evs.
California Waterfowl Assn.
4630 Northgate Blvd., #150, Sacramento, CA 95834
Greater Calif. Arms & Collectors Assn.
Donald L. Bullock, 8291 Carburton St., Long Beach, CA 90808-3302
Los Angeles Gun Ctg. Collectors Assn.
F.H. Ruffra, 20810 Amie Ave., Apt. #9, Torrance, CA 90503
Stock Gun Players Assn.
6038 Appian Way, Long Beach, CA, 90803

COLORADO
Colorado Gun Collectors Assn.
L.E.(Bud) Greenwald, 2553 S. Quitman St., Denver, CO 80219/303-935-3850
Rocky Mountain Cartridge Collectors Assn.
John Roth, P.O. Box 757, Conifer, CO 80433

CONNECTICUT
Ye Connecticut Gun Guild, Inc.
Dick Fraser, P.O. Box 425, Windsor, CT 06095

FLORIDA
Unified Sportsmen of Florida
P.O. Box 6565, Tallahassee, FL 32314

GEORGIA
Georgia Arms Collectors Assn., Inc.
Michael Kindberg, President, P.O. Box 277, Alpharetta, GA 30239-0277

ILLINOIS
Illinois State Rifle Assn.
P.O. Box 637, Chatsworth, IL 60921
Mississippi Valley Gun & Cartridge Coll. Assn.
Bob Filbert, P.O. Box 61, Port Byron, IL 61275/309-523-2593
Sauk Trail Gun Collectors
Gordell M. Matson, P.O. Box 1113, Milan, IL 61264
Wabash Valley Gun Collectors Assn., Inc.
Roger L. Dorsett, 2601 Willow Rd., Urbana, IL 61801/217-384-7302

INDIANA
Indiana State Rifle & Pistol Assn.
Thos. Glancy, P.O. Box 552, Chesterton, IN 46304
Southern Indiana Gun Collectors Assn., Inc.
Sheila McClary, 309 W. Monroe St., Boonville, IN 47601/812-897-3742

IOWA
Beaver Creek Plainsmen Inc.
Steve Murphy, Secy., P.O. Box 298, Bondurant, IA 50035
Central States Gun Collectors Assn.
Dennis Greischar, Box 841, Mason City, IA 50402-0841

KANSAS
Kansas Cartridge Collectors Assn.
Bob Linder, Box 84, Plainville, KS 67663

KENTUCKY
Kentuckiana Arms Collectors Assn.
Charles Billips, President, Box 1776, Louisville, KY 40201
Kentucky Gun Collectors Assn., Inc.
Ruth Johnson, Box 64, Owensboro, KY 42302/502-729-4197

LOUISIANA
Washitaw River Renegades
Sandra Rushing, P.O. Box 256, Main St., Grayson, LA 71435

MARYLAND
Baltimore Antique Arms Assn.
Mr. Cillo, 1034 Main St., Darlington, MD 21304

MASSACHUSETTS
Bay Colony Weapons Collectors, Inc.
John Brandt, Box 111, Hingham, MA 02043
Massachusetts Arms Collectors
Bruce E. Skinner, P.O. Box 31, No. Carver, MA 02355/508-866-5259

MICHIGAN
Association for the Study and Research of .22 Caliber Rimfire Cartridges
George Kass, 4512 Nakoma Dr., Okemos, MI 48864

MINNESOTA
Sioux Empire Cartridge Collectors Assn.
Bob Cameron, 14597 Glendale Ave. SE, Prior Lake, MN 55372

MISSISSIPPI
Mississippi Gun Collectors Assn.
Jack E. Swinney, P.O. Box 16323, Hattiesburg, MS 39402

MISSOURI
Greater St. Louis Cartridge Collectors Assn.
Don MacChesney, 634 Scottsdale Rd., Kirkwood, MO 63122-1109
Mineral Belt Gun Collectors Assn.
D.F. Saunders, 1110 Cleveland Ave., Monett, MO 65708
Missouri Valley Arms Collectors Assn., Inc.
L.P Brammer II, Membership Secy., P.O. Box 33033, Kansas City, MO 64114

MONTANA
Montana Arms Collectors Assn.
Dean E. Yearout, Sr., Exec. Secy., 1516 21st Ave. S., Great Falls, MT 59405
Weapons Collectors Society of Montana
R.G. Schipf, Ex. Secy., 3100 Bancroft St., Missoula, MT 59801/406-728-2995

NEBRASKA
Nebraska Cartridge Collectors Club
Gary Muckel, P.O. Box 84442, Lincoln, NE 68501

NEW HAMPSHIRE
New Hampshire Arms Collectors, Inc.
James Stamatelos, Secy., P.O. Box 5, Cambridge, MA 02139

NEW JERSEY
Englishtown Benchrest Shooters Assn.
Michael Toth, 64 Cooke Ave., Carteret, NJ 07008
Jersey Shore Antique Arms Collectors
Joe Sisia, P.O. Box 100, Bayville, NJ 08721-0100
New Jersey Arms Collectors Club, Inc.
Angus Laidlaw, Vice President, 230 Valley Rd., Montclair, NJ 07042/201-746-0939; e-mail: acclaidlaw@juno.com

NEW YORK
Iroquois Arms Collectors Assn.
Bonnie Robinson, Show Secy., P.O. Box 142, Ransomville, NY 14131/716-791-4096
Mid-State Arms Coll. & Shooters Club
Jack Ackerman, 24 S. Mountain Terr., Binghamton, NY 13903

NORTH CAROLINA
North Carolina Gun Collectors Assn.
Jerry Ledford, 3231-7th St. Dr. NE, Hickory, NC 28601

OHIO
Ohio Gun Collectors Assn.
P.O. Box 9007, Maumee, OH 43537-9007/419-897-0861; Fax:419-897-0860
Shotshell Historical and Collectors Society
Madeline Bruemmer, 3886 Dawley Rd., Ravenna, OH 44266
The Stark Gun Collectors, Inc.
William I. Gann, 5666 Waynesburg Dr., Waynesburg, OH 44688

OREGON
Oregon Arms Collectors Assn., Inc.
Phil Bailey, P.O. Box 13000-A, Portland, OR 97213-0017/503-281-6864; off.:503-281-0918
Oregon Cartridge Collectors Assn.
Boyd Northrup, P.O. Box 285, Rhododendron, OR 97049

PENNSYLVANIA
Presque Isle Gun Collectors Assn.
James Welch, 156 E. 37 St., Erie, PA 16504

SOUTH CAROLINA
Belton Gun Club, Inc.
Attn. Secretary, P.O. Box 126, Belton, SC 29627/864-369-6767

Gun Owners of South Carolina
Membership Div.: William Strozier, Secretary, P.O. Box 70, Johns Island, SC 29457-0070/803-762-3240; Fax:803-795-0711; e-mail:76053.222@compuserve. com

SOUTH DAKOTA
Dakota Territory Gun Coll. Assn., Inc.
Curt Carter, Castlewood, SD 57223

TENNESSEE
Smoky Mountain Gun Coll. Assn., Inc.
Hugh W. Yabro, President, P.O. Box 23225, Knoxville, TN 37933

Tennessee Gun Collectors Assn., Inc.
M.H. Parks, 3556 Pleasant Valley Rd., Nashville, TN 37204-3419

TEXAS
Houston Gun Collectors Assn., Inc.
P.O. Box 741429, Houston, TX 77274-1429
Texas Gun Collectors Assn.
Bob Eder, Pres., P.O. Box 12067, El Paso, TX 79913/915-584-8183
Texas State Rifle Assn.
1131 Rockingham Dr., Suite 101, Richardson, TX 75080-4326

VIRGINIA
Virginia Gun Collectors Assn., Inc.
Addison Hurst, Secy., 38802 Charlestown Height, Waterford, VA 20197/540-882-3543

WASHINGTON
Association of Cartridge Collectors on the Pacific Northwest
Robert Jardin, 14214 Meadowlark Drive KPN, Gig Harbor, WA 98329
Washington Arms Collectors, Inc.
Joyce Boss, P.O. Box 389, Renton, WA, 98057-0389/206-255-8410

WISCONSIN
Great Lakes Arms Collectors Assn., Inc.
Edward C. Warnke, 2913 Woodridge Lane, Waukesha, WI 53188
Wisconsin Gun Collectors Assn., Inc.
Lulita Zellmer, P.O. Box 181, Sussex, WI 53089

WYOMING
Wyoming Weapons Collectors
P.O. Box 284, Laramie, WY 82073/307-745-4652 or 745-9530

NATIONAL ORGANIZATIONS
Amateur Trapshooting Assn.
David D. Bopp, Exec. Director, 601 W. National Rd., Vandalia, OH 45377/937-898-4638; Fax:937-898-5472
American Airgun Field Target Assn.
5911 Cherokee Ave., Tampa, FL 33604
American Coon Hunters Assn.
Opal Johnston, P.O. Cadet, Route 1, Box 492, Old Mines, MO 63630
American Custom Gunmakers Guild
Jan Billeb, Exec. Director, 22 Vista View Drive, Cody, WY 82414-9606 (307) 587-4297 (phone/fax). Email: acgg@acgg.org Website: www.acgg.org
American Defense Preparedness Assn.
Two Colonial Place, 2101 Wilson Blvd., Suite 400, Arlington, VA 22201-3061
American Paintball League
P.O. Box 3561, Johnson City, TN 37602/800-541-9169
American Pistolsmiths Guild
Alex B. Hamilton, Pres., 1449 Blue Crest Lane, San Antonio, TX 78232/210-494-3063
American Police Pistol & Rifle Assn.
3801 Biscayne Blvd., Miami, FL 33137

American Single Shot Rifle Assn.
Charles Kriegel, Secy., 1346C Whispering Woods Drive, West Carrollton OH 45449/937-866-9064. Website: www.assra.com
American Society of Arms Collectors
George E. Weatherly, P.O. Box 2567, Waxahachie, TX 75165
American Tactical Shooting Assn.(A.T.S.A.)
c/o Skip Gochenour, 2600 N. Third St., Harrisburg, PA 17110/717-233-0402; Fax:717-233-5340
Association of Firearm and Tool Mark Examiners
Lannie G. Emanuel, Secy., Southwest Institute of Forensic Sciences, P.O. Box 35728, Dallas, TX 75235/214-920-5979; Fax:214-920-5928; Membership Secy., Ann D. Jones, VA Div. of Forensic Science, P.O. Box 999, Richmond, VA 23208/804-786-4706; Fax:804-371-8328
Boone & Crockett Club
250 Station Dr., Missoula, MT 59801-2753
Browning Collectors Assn.
Secretary:Scherrie L. Brennac, 2749 Keith Dr., Villa Ridge, MO 63089/314-742-0571
The Cast Bullet Assn., Inc.
Ralland J. Fortier, Editor, 4103 Foxcraft Dr., Traverse City, MI 49684
Citizens Committee for the Right to Keep and Bear Arms
Natl. Hq., Liberty Park, 12500 NE Tenth Pl., Bellevue, WA 98005
Colt Collectors Assn.
25000 Highland Way, Los Gatos, CA 95030/408-353-2658.
Ducks Unlimited, Inc.
Natl. Headquarters, One Waterfowl Way, Memphis, TN 38120/901-758-3937
Fifty Caliber Shooters Assn.
PO Box 111, Monroe UT 84754-0111
Firearms Coalition/Neal Knox Associates
Box 6537, Silver Spring, MD 20906/301-871-3006
Firearms Engravers Guild of America
Rex C. Pedersen, Secy., 511 N. Rath Ave., Lundington, MI 49431/616-845-7695(Phone and Fax)
Foundation for North American Wild Sheep
720 Allen Ave., Cody, WY 82414-3402/web site: http://iigi.com/os/non/fnaws/fnaw s.htm; e-mail: fnaws@wyoming.com
Freedom Arms Collectors Assn.
P.O. Box 160302, Miami, FL 33116-0302
Garand Collectors Assn.
P.O. Box 181, Richmond, KY 40475
Glock Shooting Sports Foundation
PO Box 309, Smyrna GA 30081 770-432-1202 Website: www.gssfonline.com
Golden Eagle Collectors Assn. (G.E.C.A.)
Chris Showler, 11144 Slate Creek Rd., Grass Valley, CA 95945
Gun Owners of America
8001 Forbes Place, Suite 102, Springfield, VA 22151/703-321-8585

ARMS ASSOCIATION

Handgun Hunters International
J.D. Jones, Director, P.O. Box 357 MAG, Bloomingdale, OH 43910

Harrington & Richardson Gun Coll. Assn.
George L. Cardet, 330 S.W. 27th Ave., Suite 603, Miami, FL 33135

High Standard Collectors' Assn.
John J. Stimson, Jr., Pres., 540 W. 92nd St., Indianapolis, IN 46260 Website: www.highstandard.org

Hopkins & Allen Arms & Memorabilia Society (HAAMS)
P.O. Box 187, 1309 Pamela Circle, Delphos, OH 45833

International Ammunition Association, Inc.
C.R. Punnett, Secy., 8 Hillock Lane, Chadds Ford, PA 19317/610-358-1285;Fax:610-3 58-1560

International Benchrest Shooters
Joan Borden, RR1, Box 250BB, Springville, PA 18844/717-965-2366

International Blackpowder Hunting Assn.
P.O. Box 1180, Glenrock, WY 82637/307-436-9817

IHMSA (Intl. Handgun Metallic Silhouette Assn.)
PO Box 368, Burlington, IA 52601 Website: www.ihmsa.org

International Society of Mauser Arms Collectors
Michael Kindberg, Pres., P.O. Box 277, Alpharetta, GA 30239-0277

Jews for the Preservation of Firearms Ownership (JPFO) 501(c)(3)
2872 S. Wentworth Ave., Milwaukee, WI 53207/414-769-0760; Fax:414-483-8435

The Mannlicher Collectors Assn.
Membership Office: P.O. Box1249, The Dalles, Oregon 97058

Marlin Firearms Collectors Assn., Ltd.
Dick Paterson, Secy., 407 Lincoln Bldg., 44 Main St., Champaign, IL 61820

Merwin Hulbert Association,
2503 Kentwood Ct., High Point, NC 27265

Miniature Arms Collectors/Makers Society, Ltd.
Ralph Koebbeman, Pres., 4910 Kilburn Ave., Rockford, IL 61101/815-964-2569

M1 Carbine Collectors Assn. (M1-CCA)
623 Apaloosa Ln., Gardnerville, NV 89410-7840

National Association of Buckskinners (NAB)
Territorial Dispatch—1800s Historical Publication, 4701 Marion St., Suite 324, Livestock Exchange Bldg., Denver, CO 80216/303-297-9671

The National Association of Derringer Collectors
P.O. Box 20572, San Jose, CA 95160

National Assn. of Federally Licensed Firearms Dealers
Andrew Molchan, 2455 E. Sunrise, Ft. Lauderdale, FL 33304

National Association to Keep and Bear Arms
P.O. Box 78336, Seattle, WA 98178

National Automatic Pistol Collectors Assn.
Tom Knox, P.O. Box 15738, Tower Grove Station, St. Louis, MO 63163

National Bench Rest Shooters Assn., Inc.
Pat Ferrell, 2835 Guilford Lane, Oklahoma City, OK 73120-4404/405-842-9585; Fax: 405-842-9575

National Muzzle Loading Rifle Assn.
Box 67, Friendship, IN 47021 / 812-667-5131. Website: www.nmlra@nmlra.org

National Professional Paintball League (NPPL)
540 Main St., Mount Kisco, NY 10549/914-241-7400

National Reloading Manufacturers Assn.
One Centerpointe Dr., Suite 300, Lake Oswego, OR 97035

National Rifle Assn. of America
11250 Waples Mill Rd., Fairfax, VA 22030 / 703-267-1000. Website: www.nra.org

National Shooting Sports Foundation, Inc.
Robert T. Delfay, President, Flintlock Ridge Office Center, 11 Mile Hill Rd., Newtown, CT 06470-2359/203-426-1320; FAX: 203-426-1087

National Skeet Shooting Assn.
Dan Snyuder, Director, 5931 Roft Road, San Antonio, TX 78253-9261/800-877-5338. Website: nssa-nsca.com

National Sporting Clays Association
Ann Myers, Director, 5931 Roft Road, San Antonio, TX 78253-9261/800-877-5338. Website: nssa-nsca.com

National Wild Turkey Federation, Inc.
P.O. Box 530, 770 Augusta Rd., Edgefield, SC 29824

North American Hunting Club
P.O. Box 3401, Minnetonka, MN 55343/612-936-9333; Fax: 612-936-9755

North American Paintball Referees Association (NAPRA)
584 Cestaric Dr., Milpitas, CA 95035

North-South Skirmish Assn., Inc.
Stevan F. Meserve, Exec. Secretary, 507 N. Brighton Court, Sterling, VA 20164-3919

Old West Shooter's Association
712 James Street, Hazel TX 76020 817-444-2049

Remington Society of America
Gordon Fosburg, Secretary, 11900 North Brinton Road, Lake, MI 48623

Rocky Mountain Elk Foundation
P.O. Box 8249, Missoula, MT 59807-8249/406-523-4500;Fax: 406-523-4581 Website: www.rmef.org

Ruger Collector's Assn., Inc.
P.O. Box 240, Greens Farms, CT 06436

Safari Club International
4800 W. Gates Pass Rd., Tucson, AZ 85745/520-620-1220

Sako Collectors Assn., Inc.
Jim Lutes, 202 N. Locust, Whitewater, KS 67154

Second Amendment Foundation
James Madison Building, 12500 NE 10th Pl., Bellevue, WA 98005

Single Action Shooting Society (SASS)
23255-A La Palma Avenue, Yorba Linda, CA 92887/714-694-1800; FAX: 714-694-1815/email: sasseot@aol.com Website: www.sassnet.com

Smith & Wesson Collectors Assn.
Cally Pletl, Admin. Asst.,PO Box 444, Afton, NY 13730

The Society of American Bayonet Collectors
P.O. Box 234, East Islip, NY 11730-0234

Southern California Schuetzen Society
Dean Lillard, 34657 Ave. E., Yucaipa, CA 92399

Sporting Arms and Ammunition Manufacturers' Institute (SAAMI)
Flintlock Ridge Office Center, 11 Mile Hill Rd., Newtown, CT 06470-2359/203-426-4358; FAX: 203-426-1087

Sporting Clays of America (SCA)
Ron L. Blosser, Pres., 9257 Buckeye Rd., Sugar Grove, OH 43155-9632/614-746-8334; Fax: 614-746-8605

Steel Challenge
23234 Via Barra, Valencia CA 91355 Website: www.steelchallenge.com

The Thompson/Center Assn.
Joe Wright, President, Box 792, Northboro, MA 01532/508-845-6960

U.S. Practical Shooting Assn./IPSC
Dave Thomas, P.O. Box 811, Sedro Woolley, WA 98284/360-855-2245 Website: www.uspsa.org

U.S. Revolver Assn.
Brian J. Barer, 40 Larchmont Ave., Taunton, MA 02780/508-824-4836

U.S.A. Shooting
U.S. Olympic Shooting Center, One Olympic Plaza, Colorado Springs, CO 80909/719-578-4670. Website: wwwusashooting.org

The Varmint Hunters Assn., Inc.
Box 759, Pierre, SD 57501/Member Services 800-528-4868

Weatherby Collectors Assn., Inc.
P.O. Box 478, Pacific, MO 63069 Website: www.weatherbycollectors.com Email: WCAsecretary@aol.com

The Wildcatters
P.O. Box 170, Greenville, WI 54942

Winchester Arms Collectors Assn.
P.O. Box 230, Brownsboro, TX 75756/903-852-4027

The Women's Shooting Sports Foundation (WSSF)
4620 Edison Avenue, Ste. C, Colorado Springs, CO 80915/719-638-1299; FAX: 719-638-1271/email: wssf@worldnet.att.net

ARGENTINA

Asociacion Argentina de Coleccionistas de Armes y Municiones
Castilla de Correos No. 28, Succursal I B, 1401 Buenos Aires, Republica Argentina

AUSTRALIA

Antique & Historical Arms Collectors of Australia
P.O. Box 5654, GCMC Queensland 9726, Australia

The Arms Collector's Guild of Queensland Inc.
Ian Skennerton, P.O. Box 433, Ashmore City 4214, Queensland, Australia

Australian Cartridge Collectors Assn., Inc.
Bob Bennett, 126 Landscape Dr., E. Doncaster 3109, Victoria, Australia

Sporting Shooters Assn. of Australia, Inc.
P.O. Box 2066, Kent Town, SA 5071, Australia

CANADA

ALBERTA
Canadian Historical Arms Society
P.O. Box 901, Edmonton, Alb., Canada T5J 2L8

National Firearms Assn.
Natl. Hq: P.O. Box 1779, Edmonton, Alb., Canada T5J 2P1

BRITISH COLUMBIA
The Historical Arms Collectors of B.C. (Canada)
Harry Moon, Pres., P.O. Box 50117, South Slope RPO, Burnaby, BC V5J 5G3, Canada/604-438-0950; Fax:604-277-3646

ONTARIO
Association of Canadian Cartridge Collectors
Monica Wright, RR 1, Millgrove, ON, LOR IVO, Canada

Tri-County Antique Arms Fair
P.O. Box 122, RR #1, North Lancaster, Ont., Canada K0C 1Z0

EUROPE

BELGIUM
European Cartridge Research Assn.
Graham Irving, 21 Rue Schaltin, 4900 Spa, Belgium/32.87.77.43.40; Fax:32.87.77.27.51

CZECHOSLOVAKIA
Spolecnost Pro Studium Naboju (Czech Cartridge Research Assn.)
JUDr. Jaroslav Bubak, Pod Homolko 1439, 26601 Beroun 2, Czech Republic

DENMARK
Aquila Dansk Jagtpatron Historic Forening (Danish Historical Cartridge Collectors Club)
Steen Elgaard Møller, Ulriksdalsvej 7, 4840 Nr. Alslev, Denmark 10045-53846218;Fax:00455384 6209

ENGLAND
Arms and Armour Society
Hon. Secretary A. Dove, P.O. Box 10232, London, 5W19 2ZD, England

Dutch Paintball Federation
Aceville Publ., Castle House 97 High Street, Colchester, Essex C01 1TH, England/011-44-206-564840

European Paintball Sports Foundation
c/o Aceville Publ., Castle House 97 High St., Colchester, Essex, C01 1TH, England

Historical Breechloading Smallarms Assn.
D.J. Penn M.A., Secy., P.O. Box 12778, London SE1 6BX, England. Journal and newsletter are $23 a yr., including airmail.

National Rifle Assn.
(Great Britain) Bisley Camp, Brookwood, Woking Surrey GU24 OPB, England/01483.797777; Fax: 014730686275

United Kingdom Cartridge Club
Ian Southgate, 20 Millfield, Elmley Castle, Nr. Pershore, Worcestershire, WR10 3HR, England

FRANCE
STAC-Western Co.
3 Ave. Paul Doumer (N.311); 78360 Montesson, France/01.30.53-43-65; Fax: 01.30.53.19.10

GERMANY
Bund Deutscher Sportschützen e.v. (BDS)
Borsigallee 10, 53125 Bonn 1, Germany

Deutscher Schützenbund
Lahnstrasse 120, 65195 Wiesbaden, Germany

SPAIN
Asociacion Espanola de Colleccionistas de Cartuchos (A.E.C.C.)
Secretary: Apdo. Correos No. 1086, 2880-Alcala de Henares (Madrid), Spain. President: Apdo. Correos No. 682, 50080 Zaragoza, Spain

SWEDEN
Scandinavian Ammunition Research Assn.
c/o Morten Stoen, Annerudstubben 3, N-1383 Asker, Norway

NEW ZEALAND
New Zealand Cartridge Collectors Club
Terry Castle, 70 Tiraumea Dr., Pakuranga, Auckland, New Zealand

New Zealand Deerstalkers Assn.
P.O. Box 6514 TE ARO, Wellington, New Zealand

SOUTH AFRICA
Historical Firearms Soc. of South Africa
P.O. Box 145, 7725 Newlands, Republic of South Africa

Republic of South Africa Cartridge Collectors Assn.
Arno Klee, 20 Eugene St., Malanshof Randburg, Gauteng 2194, Republic of South Africa

S.A.A.C.A. (Southern Africa Arms and Ammunition Assn.)
Gauteng office: P.O. Box 7597, Weltevreden Park, 1715, Republic of South Africa/011-679-1151; Fax: 011-679-1131; e-mail: saaaca@iafrica.com. Kwa-Zulu Natal office: P.O. Box 4065, Northway, Kwazulu-Natal 4065, Republic of South Africa

SAGA (S.A. Gunowners' Assn.)
P.O. Box 35203, Northway, Kwazulu-Natal 4065, Republic of South Africa

PERIODICAL PUBLICATIONS

AAFTA News (M)
5911 Cherokee Ave., Tampa, FL 33604. Official newsletter of the American Airgun Field Target Assn.

Action Pursuit Games Magazine (M)
CFW Enterprises, Inc., 4201 W. Vanowen Pl., Burbank, CA 91505 818-845-2656. $4.99 single copy U.S., $5.50 Canada. Editor: Dan Reeves. World's leading magazine of paintball sports.

Air Gunner Magazine
4 The Courtyard, Denmark St., Wokingham, Berkshire RG11 2AZ, England/011-44-734-771677. $U.S. $44 for 1 yr. Leading monthly airgun magazine in U.K.

Airgun Ads
Box 33, Hamilton, MT 59840/406-363-3805; Fax: 406-363-4117. $35 1 yr. (for first mailing; $20 for second mailing; $35 for Canada and foreign orders.) Monthly tabloid with extensive For Sale and Wanted airgun listings.

The Airgun Letter
Gapp, Inc., 4614 Woodland Rd., Ellicott City, MD 21042-6329/410-730-5496; Fax: 410-730-9544; e-mail: staff@airgnltr.net; http://www.airgunletter.com. $21 U.S., $24 Canada, $27 Mexico and $33 other foreign orders, 1 yr. Monthly newsletter for airgun users and collectors.

Airgun World
4 The Courtyard, Denmark St., Wokingham, Berkshire RG40 2AZ, England/011-44-734-771677. Call for subscription rates. Oldest monthly airgun magazine in the U.K., now a sister publication to Air Gunner.

Alaska Magazine
Morris Communications, 735 Broad Street, Augusta, GA 30901/706-722-6060. Hunting, Fishing and Life on the Last Frontier articles of Alaska and western Canada.

American Firearms Industry
Nat'l. Assn. of Federally Licensed Firearms Dealers, 2455 E. Sunrise Blvd., Suite 916, Ft. Lauderdale, FL 33304. $35.00 yr. For firearms retailers, distributors and manufacturers.

American Guardian
NRA, 11250 Waples Mill Rd., Fairfax, VA 22030. Publications division. $15.00 1 yr. Magazine features personal protection; home-self-defense; family recreation shooting; women's issues; etc.

American Gunsmith
Belvoir Publications, Inc., 75 Holly Hill Lane, Greenwich, CT 06836-2626/203-661-6111. $49.00 (12 issues). Technical journal of firearms repair and maintenance.

American Handgunner*
Publisher's Development Corp., 591 Camino de la Reina, Suite 200, San Diego, CA 92108/800-537-3006 $16.95 yr. Articles for handgun enthusiasts, competitors, police and hunters.

American Hunter (M)
National Rifle Assn., 11250 Waples Mill Rd., Fairfax, VA 22030 (Same address for both.) Publications Div. $35.00 yr. Wide scope of hunting articles.

American Rifleman (M)
National Rifle Assn., 11250 Waples Mill Rd., Fairfax, VA 22030 (Same address for both). Publications Div. $35.00 yr. Firearms articles of all kinds.

American Survival Guide
McMullen Angus Publishing, Inc., 774 S. Placentia Ave., Placentia, CA 92670-6846. 12 issues $19.95/714-572-2255; FAX: 714-572-1864.

Armes & Tir*
c/o FABECO, 38, rue de Trévise 75009 Paris, France. Articles for hunters, collectors, and shooters. French text.

Arms Collecting (Q)
Museum Restoration Service, P.O. Box 70, Alexandria Bay, NY 13607-0070. $22.00 yr.; $62.00 3 yrs.; $112.00 5 yrs.

Australian Shooter (formerly Australian Shooters Journal)
Sporting Shooters' Assn. of Australia, Inc., P.O. Box 2066, Kent Town SA 5071, Australia. $60.00 yr. locally; $65.00 yr. overseas surface mail. Hunting and shooting articles.

The Backwoodsman Magazine
P.O. Box 627, Westcliffe, CO 81252. $16.00 for 6 issues per yr.; $30.00 for 2 yrs.; sample copy $2.75. Subjects include muzzle-loading, woodslore, primitive survival, trapping, homesteading, blackpowder cartridge guns, 19th century how-to.

Black Powder Cartridge News (Q)
SPG, Inc., P.O. Box 761, Livingston, MT 59047/Phone/Fax: 406-222-8416. $17 yr. (4 issues) ($6 extra 1st class mailing). For the blackpowder cartridge enthusiast.

Blackpowder Hunting (M)
Intl. Blackpowder Hunting Assn., P.O. Box 1180Z, Glenrock, WY 82637/307-436-9817. $20.00 1 yr., $36.00 2 yrs. How-to and where-to features by experts on hunting; shooting; ballistics; traditional and modern blackpowder rifles, shotguns, pistols and cartridges.

Black Powder Times
P.O. Box 234, Lake Stevens, WA 98258. $20.00 yr.; add $5 per year for Canada, $10 per year other foreign. Tabloid newspaper for blackpowder activities; test reports.

Blade Magazine
Krause Publications, 700 East State St., Iola, WI 54990-0001. $25.98 for 12 issues. Foreign price (including Canada-Mexico) $50.00. A magazine for all enthusiasts of handmade, factory and antique knives.

Caliber
GFI-Verlag, Theodor-Heuss Ring 62, 50668 K"ln, Germany. For hunters, target shooters and reloaders.

The Caller (Q) (M)
National Wild Turkey Federation, P.O. Box 530, Edgefield, SC 29824. Tabloid newspaper for members; 4 issues per yr. (membership fee $25.00)

Cartridge Journal (M)
Robert Mellichamp, 907 Shirkmere, Houston, TX 77008/713-869-0558. Dues $12 for U.S. and Canadian members (includes the newsletter); 6 issues.

The Cast Bullet*(M)
Official journal of The Cast Bullet Assn. Director of Membership, 203 E. 2nd St., Muscatine, IA 52761. Annual membership dues $14, includes 6 issues.

COLTELLI, che Passione (Q)
Casella postale N.519, 20101 Milano, Italy/Fax:02-48402857. $15 1 yr., $27 2 yrs. Covers all types of knives—collecting, combat, historical. Italian text.

Combat Handguns*
Harris Publications, Inc., 1115 Broadway, New York, NY 10010.

Deer & Deer Hunting Magazine
Krause Publications, 700 E. State St., Iola, WI 54990-0001. $19.95 yr. (9 issues). For the serious deer hunter. Website: www.krause.com

The Derringer Peanut (M)
The National Association of Derringer Collectors, P.O. Box 20572, San Jose, CA 95160. A newsletter dedicated to developing the best derringer information. Write for details.

Deutsches Waffen Journal
Journal-Verlag Schwend GmbH, Postfach 100340, D-74503 Schwäbisch Hall, Germany/0791-404-500; FAX:0791-404-505 and 404-424. DM102 p. yr. (interior); DM125.30 (abroad), postage included. Antique and modern arms and equipment. German text.

Double Gun Journal
P.O. Box 550, East Jordan, MI 49727/800-447-1658. $35 for 4 issues.

Ducks Unlimited, Inc. (M)
1 Waterfowl Way, Memphis, TN 38120

The Engraver (M) (Q)
P.O. Box 4365, Estes Park, CO 80517/970-586-2388; Fax: 970-586-0394. Mike Dubber, editor. The journal of firearms engraving.

The Field
King's Reach Tower, Stamford St., London SE1 9LS England. £36.40 U.K. 1 yr.; 49.90 (overseas, surface mail) yr.; £82.00 (overseas, air mail) yr. Hunting and shooting articles, and all country sports.

Field & Stream
Time4 Media, Two Park Ave., New York, NY 10016/212-779-5000. Monthly shooting column. Articles on hunting and fishing.

Field Tests
Belvoir Publications, Inc., 75 Holly Hill Lane; P.O. Box 2626, Greenwich, CT 06836-2626/203-661-6111; 800-829-3361 (subscription line). U.S. & Canada $29 1 yr., $58 2 yrs.; all other countries $45 1 yr., $90 2 yrs. (air).

Fur-Fish-Game
A.R. Harding Pub. Co., 2878 E. Main St., Columbus, OH 43209. $15.95 yr. Practical guidance regarding trapping, fishing and hunting.

The Gottlieb-Tartaro Report
Second Amendment Foundation, James Madison Bldg., 12500 NE 10th Pl., Bellevue, WA 98005/206-454-7012;Fax:206-451-3959. $30 for 12 issues. An insiders guide for gun owners.

Gray's Sporting Journal
Gray's Sporting Journal, P.O. Box 1207, Augusta, GA 30903. $36.95 per yr. for 6 issues. Hunting and fishing journals. Expeditions and Guides Book (Annual Travel Guide).

Gun List†
700 E. State St., Iola, WI 54990. $36.98 yr. (26 issues); $65.98 2 yrs. (52 issues). Indexed market publication for firearms collectors and active shooters; guns, supplies and services. Website: www.krause.com

Gun News Digest (Q)
Second Amendment Fdn., P.O. Box 488, Station C, Buffalo, NY 14209/716-885-6408;Fax:716-884-4471. $10 U.S.; $20 foreign.

The Gun Report
World Wide Gun Report, Inc., Box 38, Aledo, IL 61231-0038. $33.00 yr. For the antique and collectable gun dealer and collector.

Gunmaker (M) (Q)
ACGG, P.O. Box 812, Burlington, IA 52601-0812. The journal of custom gunmaking.

The Gunrunner
Div. of Kexco Publ. Co. Ltd., Box 565G, Lethbridge, Alb., Canada T1J 3Z4. $23.00 yr., sample $2.00. Monthly newspaper, listing everything from antiques to artillery.

Gun Show Calendar (Q)
700 E. State St., Iola, WI 54990. $14.95 yr. (4 issues). Gun shows listed; chronologically and by state. Website: www.krause.com

Gun Tests
11 Commerce Blvd., Palm Coast, FL 32142. The consumer resource for the serious shooter. Write for information.

Gun Trade News
Bruce Publishing Ltd., P.O. Box 82, Wantage, Ozon OX12 7A8, England/44-1-235-771770; Fax: 44-1-235-771848. Britain's only "trade only" magazine exclusive to the gun trade.

Gun Week†
Second Amendment Foundation, P.O. Box 488, Station C, Buffalo, NY 14209. $35.00 yr. U.S. and possessions; $45.00 yr. other countries. Tabloid paper on guns, hunting, shooting and collecting (36 issues).

Gun World
Y-Visionary Publishing, LP 265 South Anita Drive, Ste. 120, Orange, CA 92868. $21.97 yr.; $34.97 2 yrs. For the hunting, reloading and shooting enthusiast.

Guns & Ammo
Primedia, 6420 Wilshire Blvd., Los Angeles, CA 90048/213-782-2780. $23.94 yr. Guns, shooting, and technical articles.

Guns
Publishers Development Corporation, P.O. Box 85201, San Diego, CA 92138/800-537-3006. $19.95 yr. In-depth articles on a wide range of guns, shooting equipment and related accessories for gun collectors, hunters and shooters.

Guns Review
Ravenhill Publishing Co. Ltd., Box 35, Standard House, Bonhill St., London EC 2A 4DA, England. £20.00 sterling (approx. U.S. $38 USA & Canada) yr. For collectors and shooters.

H.A.C.S. Newsletter (M)
Harry Moon, Pres., P.O. Box 50117, South Slope RPO, Burnaby BC, V5J 5G3, Canada/604-438-0950; Fax:604-277-3646. $25 p. yr. U.S. and Canada. Official newsletter of The Historical Arms Collectors of B.C. (Canada).

Handgunner*
Richard A.J. Munday, Seychelles house, Brightlingsen, Essex CO7 ONN, England/012063-305201. £18.00 (sterling).

Handguns
Primedia, 6420 Wilshire Blvd., Los Angeles, CA 90048/323-782-2868. $23/94 yr. For the handgunning and shooting enthusiast.

Handloader*
Wolfe Publishing Co., 2626 Stearman Road, Ste. A, Prescott, AZ 86301/520-445-7810;Fax:520-778-5124. $22.00 yr. The journal of ammunition reloading.

INSIGHTS*
NRA, 11250 Waples Mill Rd., Fairfax, VA 22030. Editor, John E. Robbins. $15.00 yr., which includes NRA junior membership; $10.00 for adult subscriptions (12 issues).

Plenty of details for the young hunter and target shooter; emphasizes gun safety, marksmanship training, hunting skills.

International Arms & Militaria Collector (Q)
Arms & Militaria Press, P.O. Box 80, Labrador, Qld. 4215, Australia. A$39.50 yr. (U.S. & Canada), 2 yrs. A$77.50; A$37.50 (others), 1 yr., 2 yrs. $73.50 all air express mail; surface mail is less. Editor: Ian D. Skennerton.

International Shooting Sport*/UIT Journal
International Shooting Union (UIT), Bavariaring 21, D-80336 Munich, Germany. Europe: (Deutsche Mark) DM44.00 yr., 2 yrs. DM83.00; outside Europe: DM50.00 yr., 2 yrs. DM95.00 (air mail postage included.) For international sport shooting.

Internationales Waffen-Magazin
Habegger-Verlag Zürich, Postfach 9230, CH-8036 Zürich, Switzerland. SF 105.00 (approx. U.S. $73.00) surface mail for 10 issues. Modern and antique arms, self-defense. German text; English summary of contents.

The Journal of the Arms & Armour Society (M)
A. Dove, P.O. Box 10232, London, SW19 2ZD England. £15.00 surface mail; £20.00 airmail sterling only yr. Articles for the historian and collector.

Journal of the Historical Breechloading Smallarms Assn.
Published annually. P.O. Box 12778, London, SE1 6XB, England. $21.00 yr. Articles for the collector plus mailings of short articles on specific arms, reprints, newsletters, etc.

Knife World
Knife World Publications, P.O. Box 3395, Knoxville, TN 37927. $15.00 yr.; $25.00 2 yrs. Published monthly for knife enthusiasts and collectors. Articles on custom and factory knives; other knife-related interests, monthly column on knife identification, military knives.

Man At Arms*
P.O. Box 460, Lincoln, RI 02865. $27.00 yr., $52.00 2 yrs. plus $8.00 for foreign subscribers. The N.R.A. magazine of arms collecting-investing, with excellent articles for the collector of antique arms and militaria.

The Mannlicher Collector (Q)(M)
Mannlicher Collectors Assn., Inc., P.O. Box 7144, Salem Oregon 97303. $20/ yr. subscription included in membership.

MAN/MAGNUM
S.A. Man (Pty) Ltd., P.O. Box 35204, Northway, Durban 4065, Republic of South Africa. SA Rand 200.00 for 12 issues. Africa's only publication on hunting, shooting, firearms, bushcraft, knives, etc.

PERIODICAL PUBLICATIONS

The Marlin Collector (M)
R.W. Paterson, 407 Lincoln Bldg., 44 Main St., Champaign, IL 61820.

Muzzle Blasts (M)
National Muzzle Loading Rifle Assn., P.O. Box 67, Friendship, IN 47021/812-667-5131. $35.00 yr. annual membership. For the blackpowder shooter.

Muzzleloader Magazine*
Scurlock Publishing Co., Inc., Dept. Gun, Route 5, Box 347-M, Texarkana, TX 75501. $18.00 U.S.; $22.50 U.S./yr. for foreign subscribers. The publication for blackpowder shooters.

National Defense (M)*
American Defense Preparedness Assn., Two Colonial Place, Suite 400, 2101 Wilson Blvd., Arlington, VA 22201-3061/703-522-1820; FAX: 703-522-1885. $35.00 yr. Articles on both military and civil defense field, including weapons, materials technology, management.

National Knife Magazine (M)
Natl. Knife Coll. Assn., 7201 Shallowford Rd., P.O. Box 21070, Chattanooga, TN 37424-0070. Membership $35 yr.; $65.00 International yr.

National Rifle Assn. Journal (British) (Q)
Natl. Rifle Assn. (BR.), Bisley Camp, Brookwood, Woking, Surrey, England. GU24, OPB. £24.00 Sterling including postage.

National Wildlife*
Natl. Wildlife Fed., 1400 16th St. NW, Washington, DC 20036, $16.00 yr. (6 issues); International Wildlife, 6 issues, $16.00 yr. Both, $22.00 yr., includes all membership benefits. Write attn.: Membership Services Dept., for more information.

New Zealand GUNS*
Waitekauri Publishing, P.O. 45, Waikino 3060, New Zealand. $NZ90.00 (6 issues) yr. Covers the hunting and firearms scene in New Zealand.

New Zealand Wildlife (Q)
New Zealand Deerstalkers Assoc., Inc., P.O. Box 6514, Wellington, N.Z. $30.00 (N.Z.). Hunting, shooting and firearms/game research articles.

North American Hunter* (M)
P.O. Box 3401, Minnetonka, MN 55343/612-936-9333; e-mail: huntingclub@pclink.com. $18.00 yr. (7 issues). Articles on all types of North American hunting.

Outdoor Life
Time4 Media, Two Park Ave., New York, NY 10016. $16.95/yr. Extensive coverage of hunting and shooting. Shooting column by Jim Carmichel.

La Passion des Courteaux (Q)
Phenix Editions, 25 rue Mademoiselle, 75015 Paris, France. French text.

Paintball Games International Magazine
Aceville Publications, Castle House, 97 High St., Colchester, Essex, England CO1 1TH/011-44-206-564840. Write for subscription rates. Leading magazine in the U.K. covering competitive paintball activities.

Paintball News
PBN Publishing, P.O. Box 1608, 24 Henniker St., Hillsboro, NH 03244/603-464-6080. $35 U.S. 1 yr. Bi-weekly. Newspaper covering the sport of paintball, new product reviews and industry features.

Paintball Sports (Q)
Paintball Publications, Inc., 540 Main St., Mount Kisco, NY 10549/941-241-7400. $24.75 U.S. 1 yr., $32.75 foreign. Covering the competitive paintball scene.

Performance Shooter
Belvoir Publications, Inc., 75 Holly Hill Lane, Greenwich, CT 06836-2626/203-661-6111. $45.00 yr. (12 issues). Techniques and technology for improved rifle and pistol accuracy.

Petersen's HUNTING Magazine
Primedia, 6420 Wilshire Blvd., Los Angeles, CA 90048. $19.94 yr.; Canada $29.34 yr.; foreign countries $29.94 yr. Hunting articles for all game; test reports.

P.I. Magazine
America's Private Investigation Journal, 755 Bronx Dr., Toledo, OH 43609. Chuck Klein, firearms editor with column about handguns.

Pirsch
BLV Verlagsgesellschaft mbH, Postfach 400320, 80703 Munich, Germany/089-12704-0;Fax:089-12705-354. German text.

Point Blank
Citizens Committee for the Right to Keep and Bear Arms (sent to contributors), Liberty Park, 12500 NE 10th Pl., Bellevue, WA 98005

POINTBLANK (M)
Natl. Firearms Assn., Box 4384 Stn. C, Calgary, AB T2T 5N2, Canada. Official publication of the NFA.

The Police Marksman*
6000 E. Shirley Lane, Montgomery, AL 36117. $17.95 yr. For law enforcement personnel.

Police Times (M)
3801 Biscayne Blvd., Miami, FL 33137/305-573-0070.

Popular Mechanics
Hearst Corp., 224 W. 57th St., New York, NY 10019. Firearms, camping, outdoor oriented articles.

Precision Shooting
Precision Shooting, Inc., 222 McKee St., Manchester, CT 06040. $37.00 yr. U.S. Journal of the International Benchrest Shooters, and target shooting in general. Also considerable coverage of varmint shooting, as well as big bore, small bore, schuetzen, lead bullet, wildcats and precision reloading.

Rifle*
Wolfe Publishing Co., 2626 Stearman Road, Ste. A, Prescott, AZ 86301/520-445-7810; Fax: 520-778-5124. $19.00 yr. The sporting firearms journal.

Rifle's Hunting Annual
Wolfe Publishing Co., 2626 Stearman Road, Ste. A, Prescott, AZ 86301/520-445-7810; Fax: 520-778-5124. $4.99 Annual. Dedicated to the finest pursuit of the hunt.

Rod & Rifle Magazine
Lithographic Serv. Ltd., P.O. Box 38-138, Wellington, New Zealand. $50.00 yr. (6 issues). Hunting, shooting and fishing articles.

Safari* (M)
Safari Magazine, 4800 W. Gates Pass Rd., Tucson, AZ 85745/602-620-1220. $55.00 (6 times). The journal of big game hunting, published by Safari Club International. Also publish Safari Times, a monthly newspaper, included in price of $55.00 national membership.

Second Amendment Reporter
Second Amendment Foundation, James Madison Bldg., 12500 NE 10th Pl., Bellevue, WA 98005. $15.00 yr. (non-contributors).

Shoot! Magazine*
Shoot! Magazine Corp., 1770 West State Stret PMB 340, Boise ID 83702/208-368-9920; Fax: 208-338-8428. Website: www.shootmagazine.com $32.95 (6 times/yr.). Articles of interest to the cowboy action shooter, or others interested the Western-era firearms and ammunition.

Shooter's News
23146 Lorain Rd., Box 349, North Olmsted, OH 44070/216-979-5258;Fax:216-979-5259. $29 U.S. 1 yr., $54 2 yrs.; $52 foreign surface. A journal dedicated to precision riflery.

Shooting Industry
Publisher's Dev. Corp., 591 Camino de la Reina, Suite 200, San Diego, CA 92108. $50.00 yr. To the trade. $25.00.

Shooting Sports USA
National Rifle Assn. of America, 11250 Waples Mill Road, Fairfax, VA 22030. Annual subscriptions for NRA members are $5 for classified shooters and $10 for non-classified shooters. Non-NRA member subscriptions are $15. Covering events, techniques and personalities in competitive shooting.

PERIODICAL PUBLICATIONS

Shooting Sportsman*
P.O. Box 11282, Des Moines, IA 50340/800-666-4955 (for subscriptions). Editorial: P.O. Box 1357, Camden, ME 04843. $19.95 for six issues. The magazine of wingshooting and fine guns.

The Shooting Times & Country Magazine (England)†
IPC Magazines Ltd., King's Reach Tower, Stamford St, 1 London SE1 9LS, England/0171-261-6180;Fax:0171-261-7179. £65 (approx. $98.00) yr.; £79 yr. overseas (52 issues). Game shooting, wild fowling, hunting, game fishing and firearms articles. Britain's best selling field sports magazine.

Shooting Times
Primedia, 2 News Plaza, P.O. Box 1790, Peoria, IL 61656/309-682-6626. $16.97 yr. Guns, shooting, reloading; articles on every gun activity.

The Shotgun News‡
Primedia, 2 News Plaza, P.O. Box 1790, Peoria, IL 61656/800-495-8362. $28.95 yr.; foreign subscription call for rates. Sample copy $4.00. Gun ads of all kinds.

SHOT Business
National Shooting Sports Foundation, Flintlock Ridge Office Center, 11 Mile Hill Rd., Newtown, CT 06470-2359/203-426-1320; FAX: 203-426-1087. For the shooting, hunting and outdoor trade retailer.

Shotgun Sports
P.O. Box 6810, Auburn, CA 95604/916-889-2220; FAX:916-889-9106. $31.00 yr. Trapshooting how-to's, shotshell reloading, shotgun patterning, shotgun tests and evaluations, Sporting Clays action, waterfowl/upland hunting. Call 1-800-676-8920 for a free sample copy.

The Single Shot Exhange Magazine
PO box 1055, York SC 29745/803-628-5326 phone/fax. $31.50/yr., monthly. Articles of interest to the blackpowder cartridge shooter and antique arms collector.
Single Shot Rifle Journal* (M)
Editor John Campbell, PO Box 595, Bloomfield Hills, MI 48303/248-458-8415. Email: jcampbel@dmbb.com Annual dues $35 for 6 issues. Journal of the American Single Shot Rifle Assn.

The Sixgunner (M)
Handgun Hunters International, P.O. Box 357, MAG, Bloomingdale, OH 43910

The Skeet Shooting Review
National Skeet Shooting Assn., 5931 Roft Rd., San Antonio, TX 78253. $20.00 yr. (Assn. membership includes mag.)

Competition results, personality profiles of top Skeet shooters, how-to articles, technical, reloading information.

Soldier of Fortune
Subscription Dept., P.O. Box 348, Mt. Morris, IL 61054. $29.95 yr.; $39.95 Canada; $50.95 foreign.

Sporting Clays Magazine
Patch Communications, 5211 South Washington Ave., Titusville, FL 32780/407-268-5010; FAX: 407-267-7216. $29.95 yr. (12 issues). Official publication of the National Sporting Clays Association.

Sporting Goods Business
Miller Freeman, Inc., One Penn Plaza, 10th Fl., New York, NY 10119-0004. Trade journal.

Sporting Goods Dealer
Two Park Ave., New York, NY 10016. $100.00 yr. Sporting goods trade journal.

Sporting Gun
Bretton Court, Bretton, Peterborough PE3 8DZ, England. £27.00 (approx. U.S. $36.00), airmail £35.50 yr. For the game and clay enthusiasts.

The Squirrel Hunter
P.O. Box 368, Chireno, TX 75937. $14.00 yr. Articles about squirrel hunting.

Stott's Creek Calendar
Stott's Creek Printers, 2526 S 475 W, Morgantown, IN 46160/317-878-5489. 1 yr (3 issues) $11.50; 2 yrs. (6 issues) $20.00. Lists all gun shows everywhere in convenient calendar form; call for information.

Super Outdoors
2695 Aiken Road, Shelbyville, KY 40065/502-722-9463; 800-404-6064; Fax: 502-722-8093. Mark Edwards, publisher. Contact for details.

TACARMI
Via E. De Amicis, 25; 20123 Milano, Italy. $100.00 yr. approx. Antique and modern guns. (Italian text.)

Territorial Dispatch—1800s Historical Publication (M)
National Assn. of Buckskinners, 4701 Marion St., Suite 324, Livestock Exchange Bldg., Denver, CO 80216. Michael A. Nester & Barbara Wyckoff, editors. 303-297-9671.

Trap & Field
1000 Waterway Blvd., Indianapolis, IN 46202. $25.00 yr. Official publ. Amateur Trapshooting Assn. Scores, averages, trapshooting articles.

Turkey Call* (M)
Natl. Wild Turkey Federation, Inc., P.O. Box 530, Edgefield, SC 29824. $25.00 with membership (6 issues per yr.)

Turkey & Turkey Hunting*
Krause Publications, 700 E. State St., Iola, WI 54990-0001. $13.95 (6 issue p. yr.). Magazine with leading-edge articles on all aspects of wild turkey behavior, biology and the successful ways to hunt better with that info. Learn the proper techniques to calling, the right equipment, and more.

The Accurate Rifle
Precisions Shooting, Inc., 222 Mckee Street, Manchester CT 06040. $37 yr. Dedicated to the rifle accuracy enthusiast.

The U.S. Handgunner* (M)
U.S. Revolver Assn., 40 Larchmont Ave., Taunton, MA 02780. $10.00 yr. General handgun and competition articles. Bi-monthly sent to members.

U.S. Airgun Magazine
P.O. Box 2021, Benton, AR 72018/800-247-4867; Fax: 501-316-8549. 10 issues a yr. Cover the sport from hunting, 10-meter, field target and collecting. Write for details.

The Varmint Hunter Magazine (Q)
The Varmint Hunters Assn., Box 759, Pierre, SD 57501/800-528-4868. $24.00 yr.

Waffenmarkt-Intern
GFI-Verlag, Theodor-Heuss Ring 62, 50668 K"ln, Germany. Only for gunsmiths, licensed firearms dealers and their suppliers in Germany, Austria and Switzerland.

Wild Sheep (M) (Q)
Foundation for North American Wild Sheep, 720 Allen Ave., Cody, WY 82414. Website: http://iigi.com/os/non/fnaws/fnaws.htm; e-mail: fnaws@wyoming.com. Official journal of the foundation.

Wisconsin Outdoor Journal
Krause Publications, 700 E. State St., Iola, WI 54990-0001. $17.97 yr. (8 issues). For Wisconsin's avid hunters and fishermen, with features from all over that state with regional reports, legislative updates, etc. Website: www.krause.com

Women & Guns
P.O. Box 488, Sta. C, Buffalo, NY 14209. $24.00 yr. U.S.; $72.00 foreign (12 issues). Only magazine edited by and for women gun owners.

World War II*
Cowles History Group, 741 Miller Dr. SE, Suite D-2, Leesburg, VA 20175-8920. Annual subscriptions $19.95 U.S.; $25.95 Canada; 43.95 foreign. The title says it— WWII; good articles, ads, etc.

*Published bi-monthly
† Published weekly
‡Published three times per month. All others are published monthly.

IMPORTANT NOTICE TO BOOK BUYERS

Books listed here may be bought from Ray Riling Arms Books Co., 6844 Gorsten St., P.O. Box 18925, Philadelphia, PA 19119, Phone 215/438-2456; FAX: 215-438-5395. E-Mail: sales@rayrilingarms-books.com. Joe Riling is the researcher and compiler of "The Handgunner's Library" and a seller of gun books for over 34 years. The Riling stock includes books classic and modern, many hard-to-find items, and many not obtainable elsewhere. These pages list a portion of the current stock. They offer prompt, complete service, with delayed shipments occurring only on out-of-print or out-of-stock books.

Visit our web site at **www.rayrilingarmsbooks.com** and order all of your favorite titles on line from our secure site.

NOTICE FOR ALL CUSTOMERS: Remittance in U.S. funds must accompany all orders. For your convenience we now accept VISA, Master-Card & American Express. For shipments in the U.S. add $7.00 for the 1st book and $2.00 for each additional book for postage and insurance. Mini-

mum order $10.00. International Orders add $13.00 for the 1st book and $5.00 for each additional book. All International orders are shipped at the buyer's risk unless an additional $5 for insurance is included. USPS does not offer insurance to all countries unless shipped Air-Mail please e-mail or call for pricing.

Payments in excess of order or for "Backorders" are credited or fully refunded at request. Books "As-Ordered" are not returnable except by permission and a handling charge on these of 10% or $2.00 per book which ever is greater is deducted from refund or credit. Only Pennsylvania customers must include current sales tax.

A full variety of arms books also available from Rutgers Book Center, 127 Raritan Ave., Highland Park, NJ 08904/908-545-4344; FAX: 908-545-6686 or I.D.S.A. Books, 1324 Stratford Drive, Piqua, OH 45356/937-773-4203; FAX: 937-778-1922.

BALLISTICS AND HANDLOADING

ABC's of Reloading, 6th Edition, by C. Rodney James and the editors of Handloader's Digest, DBI Books, a division of Krause Publications, Iola, WI, 1997. 288 pp., illus. Paper covers. $21.95
The definitive guide to every facet of cartridge and shotshell reloading.

Accurate Arms Loading Guide Number 2, by Accurate Arms. McEwen, TN: Accurate Arms Company, Inc., 2000. Paper Covers. $18.95
Includes new data on smokeless powders XMR4064 and XMP5744 as well as a special section on Cowboy Action Shooting. The new manual includes 50 new pages of data. An appendix includes nominal rotor charge weights, bullet diameters.

The American Cartridge, by Charles Suydam, Borden Publishing Co. Alhambra, CA, 1986. 184 pp., illus. $24.95
An illustrated study of the rimfire cartridge in the United States.

Ammo and Ballistics, by Robert W. Forker, Safari Press, Inc., Huntington Beach, CA., 1999. 252 pp., illustrated. Paper covers. $18.95
Ballistic data on 125 calibers and 1,400 loads out to 500 yards.

Ammunition: Grenades and Projectile Munitions, by Ian V. Hogg, Stackpole Books, Mechanicsburg, PA, 1998. 144 pp., illus. $22.95
Concise guide to modern ammunition. International coverage with detailed specifications and illustrations.

Barnes Reloading Manual #2, Barnes Bullets, American Fork, UT, 1999. 668 pp., illus. $24.95
Features data and trajectories on the new weight X, XBT and Solids in calibers from .22 to .50 BMG.

Big Bore Rifles And Cartridges, Wolfe Publishing Co., Prescott, AZ, 1991. Paper covers. $26.00
This book covers cartridges from 8mm to .600 Nitro with loading tables.

Black Powder Guide, 2nd Edition, by George C. Nonte, Jr., Stoeger Publishing Co., So. Hackensack, NJ, 1991. 288 pp., illus. Paper covers. $14.95
How-to instructions for selection, repair and maintenance of muzzleloaders, making your own bullets, restoring and refinishing, shooting techniques.

Blackpowder Loading Manual, 3rd Edition, by Sam Fadala, DBI Books, a division of Krause Publications, Iola, WI, 1995. 368 pp., illus. Paper covers. $20.95
Revised and expanded edition of this landmark blackpowder loading book. Covers hundreds of loads for most of the popular blackpowder rifles, handguns and shotguns.

Cartridges of the World, 9th Edition, by Frank Barnes, Krause Publications, Iola, WI, 2000. 512 pp., illus. Paper covers. $27.95
Completely revised edition of the general purpose reference work for which collectors, police, scientists and laymen reach first for answers to cartridge identification questions.

Cartridge Reloading Tools of the Past, by R.H. Chamberlain and Tom Quigley, Tom Quigley, Castle Rock, WA, 1998. 167 pp., illustrated. Paper covers. $25.00
A detailed treatment of the extensive Winchester and Ideal line of handloading tools and bullet molds, plus Remington, Marlin, Ballard, Browning, Maynard, and many others.

Cast Bullets for the Black Powder Rifle, by Paul A. Matthews, Wolfe Publishing Co., Prescott, AZ, 1996. 133 pp., illus. Paper covers. $22.50
The tools and techniques used to make your cast bullet shooting a success.

Complete Blackpowder Handbook, 3rd Edition, by Sam Fadala, DBI Books, a division of Krause Publications, Iola, WI, 1997. 400 pp., illus. Paper covers. $21.95
Expanded and completely rewritten edition of the definitive book on the subject of blackpowder.

Complete Reloading Guide, by Robert & John Traister, Stoeger Publishing Co., Wayne, NJ, 1997. 608 pp., illus. Paper covers. $34.95
Perhaps the finest, most comprehensive work ever published on the subject of reloading.

Complete Reloading Manual, One Book / One Caliber. California: Load Books USA, 2000. $7.95 Each
Containing unabridged information from U. S. Bullet and Powder Makers. With thousands of proven and tested loads, plus dozens of various bullet designs and different powders. Spiral bound. Available in all Calibers.

Early Loading Tools & Bullet Molds, Pioneer Press, 1988. 88 pages, illustrated. Softcover. $7.50

European Sporting Cartridges: Volume 1, by Brad Dixon, Seattle, WA: Armory Publications, 1997. 1st edition. 250 pp., Illus. $60.00
Photographs and drawings of over 550 centerfire cartridge case types in 1,300 illustrations produced in Germany and Austria from 1875-1995.

European Sporting Cartridges: Volume 2, by Brad Dixon, Seattle, WA: Armory Publications, 2000. 1st edition. 240 pages. $60.00
An illustrated history of centerfire hunting and target cartridges produced in Czechoslovakia, Switzerland, Norway, Sweden, Finland, Russia, Italy, Denmark, Belguim from 1875 to 1998. Adds 50 specimens to volume 1, Germany-Austria. Also, illustrates 40 small arms magazine experiments during the late 19th Century, and includes the English-Language export ammunition catalogue of Kovo (Povaszke Strojarne), Prague, Czeck. from the 1930's.

Game Loads and Practical Ballistics for the American Hunter, by Bob Hagel, Wolfe Publishing Co., Prescott, AZ, 1992. 310 pp., illus. $27.90
Hagel's knowledge gained as a hunter, guide and gun enthusiast is gathered in this informative text.

German 7.9MM Military Ammunition 1888-1945, by Daniel Kent, Ann Arbor, MI: Kent, 1990. 153 pp., plus appendix. illus., b&w photos. $35.00

Handbook for Shooters and Reloaders, by P.O. Ackley, Salt Lake City, UT, 1998, (Vol. I), 567 pp., illus. Includes a separate exterior ballistics chart. $21.95
(Vol. II), a new printing with specific new material. 495 pp., illus. $20.95

Handgun Muzzle Flash Tests: How Police Cartridges Compare, by Robert Olsen, Paladin Press, Boulder, CO.Fully illustrated. 133 pages. Softcover. $20.00
Tests dozens of pistols and revolvers for the brightness of muzzle flash, a critical factor in the safety of law enforcement personnel.

Handgun Stopping Power; The Definitive Study, by Marshall & Sandow. Boulder, CO: Paladin Press, 1992. 240 pages. $45.00
Offers accurate predictions of the stopping power of specific loads in calibers from .380 Auto to .45 ACP, as well as such specialty rounds as the Glaser Safety Slug, Federal Hydra-Shok, MagSafe, etc. This is the definitive methodology for predicting the stopping power of handgun loads, the first to take into account what really happens when a bullet meets a man.

REFERENCE

THE HANDGUNNER'S LIBRARY

Handloader's Digest, 17th Edition, edited by Bob Bell. DBI Books, a division of Krause Publications, Iola, WI, 1997. 480 pp., illustrated. Paper covers. $27.95

Top writers in the field contribute helpful information on techniques and components. Greatly expanded and fully indexed catalog of all currently available tools, accessories and components for metallic, blackpowder cartridge, shotgun reloading and swaging.

Handloader's Manual of Cartridge Conversions, by John J. Donnelly, Stoeger Publishing Co., So. Hackensack, NJ, 1986. Unpaginated. $39.95

From 14 Jones to 70-150 Winchester in English and American cartridges, and from 4.85 U.K. to 15.2x28R Gevelot in metric cartridges. Over 900 cartridges described in detail.

Hatcher's Notebook, by S. Julian Hatcher, Stackpole Books, Harrisburg, PA, 1992. 488 pp., illus. $39.95

A reference work for shooters, gunsmiths, ballisticians, historians, hunters and collectors.

History and Development of Small Arms Ammunition; Volume 2 Centerfire: Primitive, and Martial Long Arms. by George A. Hoyem. Oceanside, CA: Armory Publications, 1991. 303 pages, illustrated. $60.00

Covers the blackpowder military centerfire rifle, carbine, machine gun and volley gun ammunition used in 28 nations and dominions, together with the firearms that chambered them.

History and Development of Small Arms Ammunition; Volume 4, American Military Rifle Cartridges. Oceanside, CA: Armory Publications, 1998. 244pp., illus. $60.00

Carries on what Vol. 2 began with American military rifle cartridges. Now the sporting rifle cartridges are at last organized by their originators-235 individual case types designed by eight makers of single shot rifles and four of magazine rifles from .50-140 Winchester Express to .22-15-60 Stevens. plus experimentals from .70-150 to .32-80. American Civil War enthusiasts and European collectors will find over 150 primitives in Appendix A to add to those in Volumes One and Two. There are 16 pages in full color of 54 box labels for Sharps, Remington and Ballard cartridges. There are large photographs with descriptions of 15 Maynard, Sharps, Winchester, Browning, Freund, Remington-Hepburn, Farrow and other single shot rifles, some of them rare one of a kind specimens.

Hodgdon Powder Data Manual #27, Hodgdon Powder Co., Shawnee Mission, KS, 1999. 800 pp. $27.95

Reloading data for rifle and pistol loads.

Hodgdon Shotshell Data Manual, Hodgdon Powder Co., Shawnee Mission, KS, 1999. 208 pp. $19.95

Contains hundreds of loads for lead shot, buck shot, slugs, bismuth shot and steel shot plus articles on ballistics, patterning, special reloads and much more.

Home Guide to Cartridge Conversions, by Maj. George C. Nonte Jr., The Gun Room Press, Highland Park, NJ, 1976. 404 pp., illus. $24.95

Revised and updated version of Nonte's definitive work on the alteration of cartridge cases for use in guns for which they were not intended.

Hornady Handbook of Cartridge Reloading, 5th Edition, Vol. I and II, Edited by Larry Steadman, Hornady Mfg. Co., Grand Island, NE, 2000., illus. $49.95

2 Volumes; Volume 1, 773 pp.; Volume 2, 717 pp. New edition of this famous reloading handbook covers rifle and handgun reloading data and ballistic tables.

Latest loads, ballistic information, etc.

How-To's for the Black Powder Cartridge Rifle Shooter, by Paul A. Matthews, Wolfe Publishing Co., Prescott, AZ, 1995. 45 pp. Paper covers. $22.50

Covers lube recipes, good bore cleaners and over-powder wads. Tips include compressing powder charges, combating wind resistance, improving ignition and much more.

The Illustrated Reference of Cartridge Dimensions, edited by Dave Scovill, Wolfe Publishing Co., Prescott, AZ, 1994. 343 pp., illus. Paper covers. $19.00

A comprehensive volume with over 300 cartridges. Standard and metric dimensions have been taken from SAAMI drawings and/or fired cartridges.

Kynock, by Dale J. Hedlund, Armory Publications, Seattle, WA, 2000. 130 pages, illus. 9" x 12" with four color dust jacket. $59.95

A comprehensive review of Kynoch shotgun cartridges covering over 50 brand names and case types, and over 250 Kynoch shotgun cartridge headstamps. Additional information on Kynoch metallic ammunition including the identity of the mysterious .434 Seelun.

Lee Modern Reloading, by Richard Lee, 350 pp. of charts and data and 85 illustrations. 512 pp. $24.95

Bullet casting, lubricating and author's formula for calculating proper charges for cast bullets. Includes virtually all current load data published by the powder suppliers. Exclusive source of volume measured loads.

Loading the Black Powder Rifle Cartridge, by Paul A Matthews, Wolfe Publishing Co., Prescott, AZ, 1993. 121 pp., illus. Paper covers. $22.50

Author Matthews brings the blackpowder cartridge shooter valuable information on the basics, including cartridge care, lubes and moulds, powder charges and developing and testing loads in his usual authoritative style.

Loading the Peacemaker—Colt's Model P, by Dave Scovill, Wolfe Publishing Co., Prescott, AZ, 1996. 227 pp., illus. $24.95

A comprehensive work about the history, maintenance and repair of the most famous revolver ever made, including the most extensive load data ever published.

Lyman Cast Bullet Handbook, 3rd Edition, edited by C. Kenneth Ramage, Lyman Publications, Middlefield, CT, 1980. 416 pp., illus. Paper covers. $19.95

Information on more than 5000 tested cast bullet loads and 19 pages of trajectory and wind drift tables for cast bullets.

Lyman Black Powder Handbook, edited by C. Kenneth Ramage, Lyman Products for Shooters, Middlefield, CT, 1975. 239 pp., illus. Paper covers. $14.95

Comprehensive load information for the modern blackpowder shooter.

Lyman Pistol & Revolver Handbook, 2nd Edition, edited by Thomas J. Griffin, Lyman Products Co., Middlefield, CT, 1996. 287 pp., illus. Paper covers. $18.95

The most up-to-date loading data available including the hottest new calibers, like 40 S&W, 9x21, 9mm Makarov, 9x25 Dillon and 454 Casull.

Lyman Reloading Handbook No. 47, edited by Edward A. Matunas, Lyman Publications, Middlefield, CT, 1992. 480 pp., illus. Paper covers. $24.95

A comprehensive reloading manual complete with "How to Reload" information. Expanded data section with all the newest rifle and pistol calibers.

Lyman Shotshell Handbook, 4th Edition, edited by Edward A. Matunas, Lyman Products Co., Middlefield, CT, 1996. 330 pp., illus. Paper covers. $24.95

Has 9000 loads, including slugs and buckshot, plus feature articles and a full color I.D. section.

Lyman's Guide to Big Game Cartridges & Rifles, by Edward Matunas, Lyman Publishing Corporation, Middlefield, CT, 1994. 287 pp., illus. Paper covers. $17.95

A selection guide to cartridges and rifles for big game—antelope to elephant.

Making Loading Dies and Bullet Molds, by Harold Hoffman, H & P Publishing, San Angelo, TX, 1993. 230 pp., illus. Paper covers. $24.95

A good book for learning tool and die making.

Metallic Cartridge Reloading, 3rd Edition, by M.L. McPherson, DBI Books, a division of Krause Publications, Iola, WI., 1996. 352 pp., illus. Paper covers. $21.95

A true reloading manual with over 10,000 loads for all popular metallic cartridges and a wealth of invaluable technical data provided by a recognized expert.

Military Rifle and Machine Gun Cartridges, by Jean Huon, Alexandria, VA: Ironside International, 1995. 1st edition. 378 pages, over 1,000 photos. $34.95

Superb reference text.

Modern Combat Ammunition, by Duncan Long, Paladin Press, Boulder, CO, 1997, soft cover, photos, illus., 216 pp. $34.00

Now, Paladin's leading weapons author presents his exhaustive evaluation of the stopping power of modern rifle, pistol, shotgun and machine gun rounds based on actual case studies of shooting incidents. He looks at the hot new cartridges that promise to dominate well into the next century .40 S&W, 10mm auto, sub-sonic 9mm's - as well as the trusted standbys. Find out how to make your own exotic tracers, fléchette and sabot rounds, caseless ammo and fragmenting bullets.

Modern Exterior Ballistics, by Robert L. McCoy, Schiffer Publishing Co., Atglen, PA, 1999. 128 pp. $95.00

Advanced students of exterior ballistics and flight dynamics will find this comprehensive textbook on the subject a useful addition to their libraries.

Modern Handloading, by Maj. Geo. C. Nonte, Winchester Press, Piscataway, NJ, 1972. 416 pp., illus. $15.00

Covers all aspects of metallic and shotshell ammunition loading, plus more loads than any book in print.

Modern Reloading, by Richard Lee, Inland Press, 1996. 510 pp., illus. $24.98

The how-to's of rifle, pistol and shotgun reloading plus load data for rifle and pistol calibers.

Modern Sporting Rifle Cartridges, by Wayne van Zwoll, Stoeger Publishing Co., Wayne, NJ, 1998. 310 pp., illustrated. Paper covers. $21.95

Illustrated with hundreds of photos and backed up by dozens of tables and schematic drawings, this four-part book tells the story of how rifle bullets and cartridges were developed and, in some cases, discarded.

Modern Practical Ballistics, by Art Pejsa, Pejsa Ballistics, Minneapolis, MN, 1990. 150 pp., illus. $29.95

Covers all aspects of ballistics and new, simplified methods. Clear examples illustrate new, easy but very accurate formulas.

Mr. Single Shot's Cartridge Handbook, by Frank de Haas, Mark de Haas, Orange City, IA, 1996. 116 pp., illus. Paper covers. $21.50

This book covers most of the cartridges, both commercial and wildcat, that the author has known and used.

THE HANDGUNNER'S LIBRARY

Nick Harvey's Practical Reloading Manual, by Nick Harvey, Australian Print Group, Maryborough, Victoria, Australia, 1995. 235 pp., illus. Paper covers. $24.95

Contains data for rifle and handgun including many popular wildcat and improved cartridges. Tools, powders, components and techniques for assembling optimum reloads with particular application to North America.

Nosler Reloading Manual #4, edited by Gail Root, Nosler Bullets, Inc., Bend, OR, 1996. 516 pp., illus. $26.99

Combines information on their Ballistic Tip, Partition and Handgun bullets with traditional powders and new powders never before used, plus trajectory information from 100 to 500 yards.

The Paper Jacket, by Paul Matthews, Wolfe Publishing Co., Prescott, AZ, 1991. Paper covers. $13.50

Up-to-date and accurate information about paper-patched bullets.

Reloading Tools, Sights and Telescopes for S/S Rifles, by Gerald O. Kelver, Brighton, CO, 1982. 163 pp., illus. Softcover. $15.00

A listing of most of the famous makers of reloading tools, sights and telescopes with a brief description of the products they manufactured.

Reloading for Shotgunners, 4th Edition, by Kurt D. Fackler and M.L. McPherson, DBI Books, a division of Krause Publications, Iola, WI, 1997. 320 pp., illus. Paper covers. $19.95

Expanded reloading tables with over 11,000 loads. Bushing charts for every major press and component maker. All new presentation on all aspects of shotshell reloading by two of the top experts in the field.

The Rimfire Cartridge in the United States and Canada, Illustrated history of rimfire cartridges, manufacturers, and the products made from 1857-1984. by John L. Barber, Thomas Publications, Gettysburg, PA 2000. 1st edition. Profusely illustrated. 221 pages. $50.00

The author has written an encyclopedia of rimfire cartridges from the .22 to the massive 1.00 in. Gatling. Fourteen chapters, six appendices and an excellent bibliography make up a reference volume that all cartridge collectors should aquire.

Sierra 50th Anniversary, 4th Edition Rifle Manual, edited by Ken Ramage, Sierra Bullets, Santa Fe Springs, CA, 1997. 800 pp., illus. $26.99

New cartridge introductions, etc.

Sierra 50th Anniversary, 4th Edition Handgun Manual, edited by Ken Ramage, Sierra Bullets, Santa Fe, CA, 1997. 700 pp., illus. $21.99

Histories, reloading recommendations, bullets, powders and sections on the reloading process, etc.

Sixgun Cartridges and Loads, by Elmer Keith, The Gun Room Press, Highland Park, NJ, 1986. 151 pp., illus. $24.95

A manual covering the selection, uses and loading of the most suitable and popular revolver cartridges. Originally published in 1936. Reprint.

Speer Reloading Manual No. 13, edited by members of the Speer research staff, Omark Industries, Lewiston, ID, 1999. 621 pp., illustrated. $24.95

With thirteen new sections containing the latest technical information and reloading trends for both novice and expert in this latest edition. More than 9,300 loads are listed, including new propellant powders from Accurate Arms, Alliant, Hodgdon and Vihtavuori.

Street Stoppers, The Latest Handgun Stopping Power Street Results, by Marshall & Lanow. Boulder, CO, Paladin Press, 1996. 374 pages, illus. Softcover. $42.95

Street Stoppers is the long-awaited sequel to Handgun Stopping Power. It provides the latest results of real-life shootings in all of the major handgun calibers, plus more than 25 thought-provoking chapters that are vital to anyone interested in firearms, would ballistics, and combat shooting. This book also covers the street results of the hottest new caliber to hit the shooting world in years, the .40 Smith & Wesson. Updated street results of the latest exotic ammunition including Remington Golden Saber and CCI-Speer Gold Dot, plus the venerable offerings from MagSafe, Glaser, Cor-Bon and others. A fascinating look at the development of Hydra-Shok ammunition is included.

Understanding Ballistics, Revised 2nd Edition by Robert A. Rinker, Mulberry House Publishing Co., Corydon, IN, 2000. 430 pp., illus Paper covers. New, Revised and Expanded. 2nd Edition. $24.95

Explains basic to advanced firearm ballistics in understandable terms.

Why Not Load Your Own?, by Col. T. Whelen, Gun Room Press, Highland Park, NJ 1996, 4th ed., rev. 237 pp., illus. $20.00

A basic reference on handloading, describing each step, materials and equipment. Includes loads for popular cartridges.

Wildcat Cartridges Volumes 1 & 2 Combination, by the editors of Handloaders magazine, Wolfe Publishing Co., Prescott, AZ, 1997. 350 pp., illus. Paper covers. $39.95

A profile of the most popular information on wildcat cartridges that appeared in the Handloader magazine.

COLLECTORS

A Glossary of the Construction, Decoration and Use of Arms and Armor in All Countries and in All Times. By George Cameron Stone., Dover Publishing, New York 1999. Softcover. $39.95

An exhaustive study of arms and armor in all countries through recorded history - from the stone age up to the second world war. With over 4500 Black & White Illustrations. This Dover edition is an unabridged republication of the work originally published in 1934 by the Southworth Press, Portland MA. A new Introduction has been specially prepared for this edition.

Accoutrements of the United States Infantry, Riflemen, and Dragoons 1834-1839. by R.T. Huntington, Historical Arms Series No. 20. Canada: Museum Restoration. 58 pp. illus. Softcover. $8.95

Although the 1841 edition of the U.S. Ordnance Manual provides ample information on the equipment that was in use during the 1840s, it is evident that the patterns of equipment that it describes were not introduced until 1838 or 1839. This guide is intended to fill this gap in our knowledge by providing an overview of what we now know about the accoutrements that were issued to the regular infantryman, rifleman, and dragoon, in the 1830's with excursions into earlier and later years.

Age of the Gunfighter; Men and Weapons on the Frontier 1840-1900, by Joseph G. Rosa, University of Oklahoma Press, Norman, OK, 1999. 192 pp., illustrated. Paper covers. $21.95

Stories of gunfighters and their encounters and detailed descriptions of virtually every firearm used in the old West.

Air Guns, by Eldon G. Wolff, Duckett's Publishing Co., Tempe, AZ, 1997. 204 pp., illus Paper covers. $35.00

Historical reference covering many makers, European and American guns, canes and more.

Allied and Enemy Aircraft: May 1918; Not to be Taken from the Front Lines, Historical Arms Series No. 27. Canada: Museum Restoration. Softcover. $8.95

The basis for this title is a very rare identification manual published by the French government in 1918 that illustrated 60 aircraft with three or more views: French, English American, German, Italian, and Belgian, which might have been seen over the trenches ofFrance. Each is describe in a text translated from the original French. This is probably the most complete collection of illustrations of WW1 aircraft which has survived.

American Beauty; The Prewar Colt National Match Government Model Pistol, by Timothy J. Mullin, Collector Grade Publications, Cobourg, Ontario, Canada. 72 pp., illustrated. $34.95

Includes over 150 serial numbers, and 20 spectacular color photos of factory engraved guns and other authenticated upgrades, including rare "double-carved" ivory grips.

The American Military Saddle, 1776-1945, by R. Stephen Dorsey & Kenneth L. McPheeters, Collector's Library, Eugene, OR, 1999. 400 pp., illustrated. $59.95

The most complete coverage of the subject ever writeen on the American Military Saddle. Nearly 1000 actual photos and official drawings, from the major public and private collections in the U.S. and Great Britain.

American Police Collectibles; Dark Lanterns and Other Curious Devices, by Matthew G. Forte, Turn of the Century Publishers, Upper Montclair, NJ, 1999. 248 pp., illustrated. $24.95

For collectors of police memorabilia (handcuffs, police dark lanterns, mechanical and chain nippers, rattles, billy clubs and nightsticks) and police historians.

Ammunition; Small Arms, Grenades, and Projected Munitions, by Greenhill Publishing. 144 pp., Illustrated. $22.95 The best concise guide to modern ammunition available today. Covers ammo for small arms, grenades, and projected munitions. 144 pp., Illustrated. As NEW – Hardcover.

Antique Guns, the Collector's Guide, 2nd Edition, edited by John Traister, Stoeger Publishing Co., So. Hackensack, NJ, 1994. 320 pp., illus. Paper covers. $19.95

Covers a vast spectrum of pre-1900 firearms: those manufactured by U.S. gunmakers as well as Canadian, French, German, Belgian, Spanish and other foreign firms.

Arming the Glorious Cause; Weapons of the Second War for Independence, by James B. Whisker, Daniel D. Hartzler and Larry W. Tantz, Old Bedford Village Press, Bedford, PA., 1998. 175 pp., illustrated. $45.00

A photographic study of Confederate weapons.

Arms & Accoutrements of the Mounted Police 1873-1973, by Roger F. Phillips and Donald J. Klancher, Museum Restoration Service, Ont., Canada, 1982. 224 pp., illus. $49.95

A definitive history of the revolvers, rifles, machine guns, cannons, ammunition, swords, etc. used by the NWMP, the RNWMP and the RCMP during the first 100 years of the Force.

Arms and Armor In Antiquity and The Middle Ages. By Charles Boutell, Combined Books Inc., PA 1996. 296 pp., w/ b/w illus. Also a descriptive Notice of Modern Weapons. Translated from the French of M.P. Lacombe, and with a preface, notes, and one additional chapter on Arms and Armour in England. $14.95

Arms and Armor in the Art Institute of Chicago. By Waltler J. Karcheski, Bulfinch, New York 1999. 128 pp., 103 color photos, 12 black & white illustrations. $50.00

The George F. Harding Collection of arms and armor is the most visited installation at the Art Institute of Chicago - a testament to the enduring appeal of swords, muskets and the other paraphernalia of medieval and early modern war. Organized both chronologically and by type of weapon, this book captures the best of this astonishing collection in 115 striking photographs - most in color - accompanied by illuminating text. Here are intricately filigreed breastplates and ivory-handled crossbows, samurai katana and Toledo-steel scimitars, elaborately decorated maces and beautifully carved flintlocks - a treat for anyone who has ever been beguiled by arms, armor and the age of chivalry.

Arms and Armor in Colonial America 1526-1783. by Harold Peterson, Dover Publishing, New York, 2000. 350 pages with over 300 illustrations, index, bibliography & appendix. Softcover. $29.95

Over 200 years of firearms, ammunition, equipment & edged weapons.

Arms and Armor: The Cleveland Museum of Art. By Stephen N. Fliegel, Abrams, New York, 1998. 172 color photos, 17 halftones. 181 pages. $49.50

Intense look at the culture of the warrior and hunter, with an intriguing discussion of the decorative arts found on weapons and armor, set against the background of political and social history. Also provides information on the evolution of armor, together with manufacture and decoration, and weapons as technology and art.

Arms and Equipment of the Civil War, by Jack Coggins, Barnes & Noble, Rockleight, N.J., 1999. 160 pp., illustrated. $12.98

This unique encyclopedia provides a new perspective on the war. It provides lively explanations of how ingenious new weapons spelled victory or defeat for both sides. Aided by more than 500 illustrations and on-the-scene comments by Union and Confederate soldiers.

Arms Makers of Colonial America, by James B. Whisker, Selinsgrove, PA:, 1992: Susquehanna University Press. 1st edition. 217 pages, illustrated. $45.00

A comprehensively documented historial survey of the broad spectrum of arms makers in America who were active before 1783.

Arms Makers of Maryland, by Daniel D. Hartzler, George Shumway, York, PA, 1975. 200 pp., illus. $50.00

A thorough study of the gunsmiths of Maryland who worked during the late 18th and early 19th centuries.

Arms Makers of Pennsylvania, by James B. Whisker, Selinsgrove, PA, Susquehanna Univ. Press, 1990. 1st edition. 218 pages, illustrated in black and white and color. $45.00

Concentrates primarily on the cottage industry gunsmiths & gun makers who worked in the Keystone State from it's early years through 1900.

Arms Makers of Western Pennsylvania, by James B. Whisker, Old Bedford Village Press. 1st edition. This deluxe hard bound edition has 176 pages, $45.00

Printed on fine coated paper, with many large photographs, and detailed text describing the period, lives, tools, and artistry of the Arms Makers of Western Pennsylvania.

Arsenal Of Freedom: The Springfield Armory 1890-1948, by Lt. Col. William Brophy, Andrew Mowbray, Inc., Lincoln, RI,1997. 20 pgs. of photos. 400 pages. As new - Softcover. $29.95

A year by year account drawn from offical records. Packed with reports, charts, tables, line drawings, and 20 page photo section.

Artistic Ingredients of the Longrifle, by George Shumway Publisher, 1989 102 pp., with 94 illus. $20.00

After a brief review of Pennsylvania-German folk art and architecture, to establish the artistic enviroment in which the longrifle was made, the author demonstrates that the sophisticated rococo decoration on the many of the finer longrifles is comparable to the best rococo work of Philadelphia cabinet makers and silversmiths.

The Art of Gun Engraving, by Claude Gaier and Pietro Sabatti, Knickerbocker Press, N.Y., 1999. 160 pp., illustrated. $34.95

The richness and detail lavished on early firearms represents a craftmanship nearly vanished. Beginning with crossbows in the 100's, hunting scenes, portraits, or mythological themes are intricately depicted within a few square inches of etched metal. The full-color photos contained herein recaptures this lost art with exquisite detail.

Astra Automatic Pistols, by Leonardo M. Antaris, FIRAC Publishing Co., Sterling, CO, 1989. 248 pp., illus. $55.00

Charts, tables, serial ranges, etc. The definitive work on Astra pistols.

Basic Documents on U.S. Martial Arms, commentary by Col. B. R. Lewis, reissue by Ray Riling, Phila., PA, 1956 and 1960. *Rifle Musket Model 1855.* The first issue rifle of musket caliber, a muzzle loader equipped with the Maynard Primer, 32 pp. *Rifle Musket Model 1863.* The typical Union muzzle-loader of the Civil War, 26 pp. *Breech-Loading Rifle Musket Model 1866.* The first of our 50-caliber breechloading rifles, 12 pp. *Remington Navy Rifle Model 1870.* A commercial type breech-loader made at Springfield, 16 pp. *Lee Straight Pull Navy Rifle Model 1895.* A magazine cartridge arm of 6mm caliber. 23 pp. *Breech-Loading Arms* (five models) 27 pp. *Ward-Burton Rifle Musket 1871*-16 pp. Each $10.00.

Battle Weapons of the American Revolution, by George C. Neuman, Scurlock Publishing Co., Texarkana, TX, 2001. 400 pp. Illus. Softcovers. $34.95

The most extensive photographic collection of Revolutionary War weapons ever in one volume. More than 1,600 photos of over 500 muskets, rifles, swords, bayonets, knives and other arms used by both sides in America's War for Independence.

The Bedford County Rifle and Its Makers, by George Shumway. 40pp. illustrated, Softcover. $10.00

The authors study of the graceful and distinctive muzzle-loading rifles made in Bedford County, Pennsylvania. Stands as a milestone on the long path to the understanding of America's longrifles.

Behold the Longrifle Again, by James B. Whisker, Old Bedford Village Press, Bedford, PA, 1997. 176 pp., illus. $45.00

Excellent reference work for the collector profusely illustrated with photographs of some of the finest Kentucky rifles showing front and back profiles and overall view.

The Belgian Rattlesnake; The Lewis Automatic Machine Gun, by William M. Easterly, Collector Grade Publications, Cobourg, Ontario, Canada, 1998. 584 pp., illustrated. $79.95

The most complete account ever published on the life and times of Colonel Isaac Newton Lewis and his crowning invention, the Lewis Automatic machine gun.

Beretta Automatic Pistols, by J.B. Wood, Stackpole Books, Harrisburg, PA, 1985. 192 pp., illus. $24.95

Only English-language book devoted to the Beretta line. Includes all important models.

The Big Guns, Civil War Siege, Seacoast, and Naval Cannon, by Edwin Olmstead, Wayne E. Stark, and Spencer C. Tucker, Museum Restoration Service, Bloomfield, Ontario, Canada, 1997. 360 pp., illustrated. $80.00

This book is designed to identify and record the heavy guns available to both sides by the end of the Civil War.

Birmingham Gunmakers, by Douglas Tate, Safari Press, Inc., Huntington Beach, CA, 1997. 300 pp., illus. $50.00

An invaluable work for anybody interested in the fine sporting arms crafted in this famous British gunmakers' city.

Blue Book of Gun Values, 22nd Edition, edited by S.P. Fjestad, Blue Book Publications, Inc. Minneapolis, MN 2001. $34.95

This new 22nd Edition simply contains more firearms values and information than any other single publication. Expanded to over 1,600 pages featuring over 100,000 firearms prices, the new Blue Book of Gun Values also contains over million words of text – no other book is even close! Most of the information contained in this publication is simply not available anywhere else, for any price!

Blue Book of Modern Black Powder Values, by Dennis Adler, Blue Book Publications, Inc. Minneapolis, MN 2000. 200 pp., illustrated. 41 color photos. Softcover. $14.95

This new title contains more up-to-date black powder values and related information than any other single publication. With 120 pages, this new book will keep you up to date on modern black powder models and prices, including most makes & models introduced this year! .

The Blunderbuss 1500-1900, by James D. Forman, Historical Arms Series No. 32. Canada: Museum Restoration, 1994. An excellent and authoritative booklet giving tons of information on the Blunderbuss, a very neglected subject. 40 pages, illustrated. Softcover. $8.95

Boarders Away I: With Steel-Edged Weapons & Polearms, by William Gilkerson, Andrew Mowbray, Inc. Publishers, Lincoln, RI, 1993. 331 pages. $48.00

Contains the essential 24 page chapter 'War at Sea' which sets the historical and practical context for the arms discussed. Includeds chapters on, Early Naval Weapons, Boarding Axes, Cutlasses, Officers Fighting Swords and Dirks, and weapons at hand of Random Mayhem.

Boarders Away, Volume II: Firearms of the Age of Fighting Sail, by William Gilkerson, Andrew Mowbray, Inc. Publishers, Lincoln, RI, 1993. 331 pp., illus. $65.00

Covers the pistols, muskets, combustibles and small cannon used aboard American and European fighting ships, 1626-1826.

The Book of Colt Firearms, by R. L. Wilson, Blue Book Publications, Inc, Minneapolis, MN, 1993. 616 pp., illus. $158.00

A complete Colt library in a single volume. In over 1,250.000 words, over 1,250 black and white and 67 color photographs, this mammoth work tells the Colt story from 1832 throught the present.

Boothroyd's Revised Directory Of British Gunmakers, by Geoffrey Boothroyd, Long Beach, CA: Safari Press, 2000. Revised edition. 412pp, photos. $39.95

Over a 30 year period Geoffrey Boothroyd has accumulated information on just about every sporting gun maker that ever has existed in the British Isles from 1850 onward. In this magnificent reference work he has placed all the gun makers he has found over the years (over 1000 entries) in an alphabetical listing with as much information as he has been able to unearth. One of the best reference sources on all British makers (including Wales, Scotland and Ireland) in which you can find data on the most obscure as well as the most famous. Contains starting date of the business, addresses, proprietors, what they made and how long they operated with other interesting details for the collector of fine British guns.

THE HANDGUNNER'S LIBRARY

Boston's Gun Bible, by Boston T. Party, Ignacio, CO: Javelin Press, August 2000. Expanded Edition.Softcover. $28.00

This mammoth guide for gun owners everywhere is a completely updated and expanded edition (more than 500 new pages!) of Boston T. Party's classic Boston on Guns and Courage. Pulling no punches, Boston gives new advice on which shoulder weapons and handguns to buy and why before exploring such topics as why you should consider not getting a concealed carry permit, what guns and gear will likely be outlawed next, how to spend within your budget, why you should go to a quality defensive shooting academy now, which guns and gadgets are inferior and why, how to stay off illegal government gun registration lists, how to spot an undercover agent trying to entrap law-abiding gun owners and much more.

Breech-Loading Carbines of the United States Civil War Period, by Brig. Gen. John Pitman, Armory Publications, Tacoma, WA, 1987. 94 pp., illus. $29.95

The first in a series of previously unpublished manuscripts originated by the late Brigadier General John Putnam. Exploded drawings showing parts actual size follow each sectioned illustration.

The Breech-Loading Single-Shot Rifle, by Major Ned H. Roberts and Kenneth L. Waters, Wolfe Publishing Co., Prescott, AZ, 1995. 333 pp., illus. $28.50

A comprehensive and complete history of the evolution of the Schutzen and single-shot rifle.

The Bren Gun Saga, by Thomas B. Dugelby, Collector Grade Publications, Cobourg, Ontario, Canada, 1999, revised and expanded edition. 406 pp., illustrated. $65.95

A modern, definitive book on the Bren in this revised expanded edition, which in terms of numbers of pages and illustrations is nearly twice the size of the original.

British Board of Ordnance Small Arms Contractors 1689-1840, by De Witt Bailey, Rhyl, England: W. S. Curtis, 2000. 150 pp. $18.00

Thirty years of research in the Archives of the Ordnance Board in London has identified more than 600 of these suppliers. The names of many can be found marking the regulation firearms of the period. In the study, the contractors are identified both alphabetically and under a combination of their date period together with their specialist trade.

The British Enfield Rifles, Volume 1, The SMLE Mk I and Mk III Rifles, by Charles R. Stratton, North Cape Pub. Tustin, CA, 1997. 150 pp., illus. Paper covers. $16.95

A systematic and thorough examination on a part-by-part basis of the famous British battle rifle that endured for nearly 70 years as the British Army's number one battle rifle.

British Enfield Rifles, Volume 2, No.4 and No.5 Rifles, by Charles R. Stratton, North Cape Publications, Tustin, CA, 1999. 150 pp., illustrated. Paper covers. $16.95

The historical background for the development of both rifles describing each variation and an explanation of all the "marks", "numbers" and codes found on most parts.

British Enfield Rifles, Volume 4, The Pattern 1914 and U. S. Model 1917 Rifles, by Charles R. Stratton, North Cape Publications, Tustin, CA, 2000. Paper covers. $16.95

One of the lease know American and British collectible military rifles is analyzed on a part by part basis. All markings and codes, refurbishment procedures and WW 2 upgrade are included as are the varios sniper rifle versions.

The British Falling Block Breechloading Rifle from 1865, by Jonathan Kirton, Tom Rowe Books, Maynardsville, TN, 2nd edition, 1997. 380 pp., illus. $70.00

Expanded 2nd edition of a comprehensive work on the British falling block rifle.

British Gun Engraving, by Douglas Tate, Safari Press, Inc., Huntington Beach, CA, 1999. 240 pp., illustrated. Limited, signed and numbered edition, in a slipcase. $80.00

A historic and photographic record of the last two centuries.

British Service Rifles and Carbines 1888-1900, by Alan M. Petrillo, Excaliber Publications, Latham, NY, 1994. 72 pp., illus, Paper covers. $11.95

A complete review of the Lee-Metford and Lee-Enfield rifles and carbines.

British Single Shot Rifles, Volume 1, Alexander Henry, by Wal Winfer, Tom Rowe, Maynardsville, TN, 1998, 200 pp., illus. $50.00

Detailed Study of the single shot rifles made by Henry. Illustrated with hundreds of photographs and drawings.

British Single Shot Rifles Volume 2, George Gibbs, by Wal Winfer, Tom Rowe, Maynardsville, TN, 1998. 177 pp., illus. $50.00

Detailed study of the Farquharson as made by Gibbs. Hundreds of photos.

British Single Shot Rifles, Volume 3, Jeffery, by Wal Winfer, Rowe Publications, Rochester, N.Y., 1999. 260 pp., illustrated. $60.00

The Farquharson as made by Jeffery and his competitors, Holland & Holland, Bland, Westley, Manton, etc. Large section on the development of nitro cartridges including the .600.

British Single Shot Rifles, Vol. 4; Westley Richards, by Wal Winfer, Rowe Publications, Rochester, N.Y., 2000. 265 pages, illustrated, photos. $60.00

In his 4th volume Winfer covers a detailed study of the Westley Richards single shot rifles, including Monkey Tails, Improved Martini, 1872,1873, 1878,1881, 1897 Falling Blocks. He also covers Westley Richards Cartridges, History and Reloading information.

British Small Arms Ammunition, 1864-1938 (Other than .303 inch), by Peter Labbett, Armory Publications, Seattle, WA. 1993, 358 pages, illus. Four-color dust jacket. $79.00

A study of British military rifle, handgun, machine gun, and aiming tube ammunition through 1 inch from 1864 to 1938. Photo-illustrated including the firearms that chambered the cartridges.

The British Soldier's Firearms from Smoothbore to Rifled Arms, 1850-1864, by Dr. C.H. Roads, R&R Books, Livonia, NY, 1994. 332 pp., illus. $49.00

A reprint of the classic text covering the development of British military hand and shoulder firearms in the crucial years between 1850 and 1864.

British Sporting Guns & Rifles, compiled by George Hoyem, Armory Publications, Coeur d'Alene, ID, 1997. 1024 pp., illus. In two volumes. $250.00

Eighteen old sporting firearms trade catalogs and a rare book reproduced with their color covers in a limited, signed and numbered edition.

Browning Dates of Manufacture, compiled by George Madis, Art and Reference House, Brownsboro, TX, 1989. 48 pp. $10.00

Gives the date codes and product codes for all models from 1824 to the present.

Browning Sporting Arms of Distinction 1903-1992, by Matt Eastman, Matt Eastman Publications, Fitzgerald, GA, 1995. 450 pp., illus. $49.95

The most recognized publication on Browning sporting arms; covers all models.

Buffalo Bill's Wild West: An American Legend, by R.L. Wilson and Greg Martine, Random House, N.Y., 1999. 3,167 pp., illustrated. $60.00

Over 225 color plates and 160 black-and-white illustrations, with in-depth text and captions, the colorful arms, posters, photos, costumes, saddles, accoutrement are brought to life.

Bullard Arms, by G. Scott Jamieson, The Boston Mills Press, Ontario, Canada, 1989. 244 pp., illus. $35.00

The story of a mechanical genius whose rifles and cartridges were the equal to any made in America in the 1880s.

Burning Powder, compiled by Major D.B. Wesson, Wolfe Publishing Company, Prescott, AZ, 1992. 110 pp. Soft cover. $10.95

A rare booklet from 1932 for Smith & Wesson collectors.

The Burnside Breech Loading Carbines, by Edward A. Hull, Andrew Mowbray, Inc., Lincoln, RI, 1986. 95 pp., illus. $16.00

No. 1 in the "Man at Arms Monograph Series." A model-by-model historical/technical examination of one of the most widely used cavalry weapons of the American Civil War based upon important and previously unpublished research.

Camouflage Uniforms of European and NATO Armies; 1945 to the Present, by J. F. Borsarello, Atglen, PA: Schiffer Publications. Over 290 color and b/w photographs, 120 pages. Softcover. $29.95

This full-color book covers nearly all of the NATO, and other European armies' camouflaged uniforms, and not only shows and explains the many patterns, but also their efficacy of design. Described and illustrated are the variety of materials tested in over forty different armies, and includes the history of obsolete trial tests from 1945 to the present time. More than two hundred patterns have been manufactured since World War II using various landscapes and seasonal colors for their look. The Vietnam and Gulf Wars, African or South American events, as well as recent Yugoslavian independence wars have been used as experimental terrains to test a variety of patterns. This book provides a superb reference for the historian, reenactor, designer, and modeler.

Camouflage Uniforms of the Waffen-SS A Photographic Reference, by Michael Beaver, Schiffer Publishing, Atglen, PA. Over 1,000 color and b/w photographs and illustrations, 296 pages. $69.95

Finally a book that unveils the shroud of mystery surrounding Waffen-SS camouflage clothing. Illustrated here, both in full color and in contemporary black and white photographs, this unparalleled look at Waffen-SS combat troops and their camouflage clothing will benefit both the historian and collector.

Canadian Gunsmiths from 1608: A Checklist of Tradesmen, by John Belton, Historical Arms Series No. 29. Canada: Museum Restoration, 1992. 40 pp., 17 illustrations. Softcover. $8.95

This Checklist is a greatly expanded version of HAS No. 14, listing the names, occupation, location, and dates of more than 1,500 men and women who worked as gunmakers, gunsmiths, armorers, gun merchants, gun patent holders, and a few other gun related trades. A collection of contemporary gunsmiths' letterhead have been provided to add color and depth to the study.

Cap Guns, by James Dundas, Schiffer Publishing, Atglen, PA, 1996. 160 pp., illus. Paper covers. $29.95

Over 600 full-color photos of cap guns and gun accessories with a current value guide.

Carbines of the Civil War, by John D. McAulay, Pioneer Press, Union City, TN, 1981. 123 pp., illus. Paper covers. $12.95

A guide for the student and collector of the colorful arms used by the Federal cavalry.

THE HANDGUNNER'S LIBRARY

Carbines of the U.S. Cavalry 1861-1905, by John D. McAulay, Andrew Mowbray Publishers, Lincoln, RI, 1996. $35.00
Covers the crucial use of carbines from the beginning of the Civil War to the end of the cavalry carbine era in 1905.

Cartridge Carbines of the British Army, by Alan M. Petrillo, Excalibur Publications, Latham, NY, 1998. 72 pp., illustrated. Paper covers. $11.95
Begins with the Snider-Enfield which was the first regulation cartridge carbine introduced in 1866 and ends with the .303 caliber No.5, Mark 1 Enfield.

Cartridge Catalogues, compiled by George Hoyem, Armory Publications, Coeur d'Alene, ID, 1997. 504 pp., illus.
Fourteen old ammunition makers' and designers' catalogs reproduced with their color covers in a limited, signed and numbered edition. Completely revised edition of the general purpose reference work for which collectors, police, scientists and laymen reach first for answers to cartridge identification questions. Available October, 1996.

Cartridge Reloading Tools of the Past, by R.H. Chamberlain and Tom Quigley, Tom Quigley, Castle Rock, WA, 1998. 167 pp., illustrated. Paper covers. $25.00
A detailed treatment of the extensive Winchester and Ideal lines of handloading tools and bulletmolds plus Remington, Marlin, Ballard, Browning and many others.

Cartridges for Collectors, by Fred Datig, Pioneer Press, Union City, TN, 1999. In three volumes of 176 pp. each. Vol.1 (Centerfire); Vol.2 (Rimfire and Misc.) types;
Vol.3 (Additional Rimfire, Centerfire, and Plastic.). All illustrations are shown in full-scale drawings. Volume 1, softcover only, $19.95. Volumes 2 & 3, Hardcover $19.95

Civil War Arms Makers and Their Contracts, edited by Stuart C. Mowbray and Jennifer Heroux, Andrew Mowbray Publishing, Lincoln, RI, 1998. 595 pp. $39.50
A facsimile reprint of the Report by the Commissioner of Ordnance and Ordnance Stores, 1862.

Civil War Arms Purchases and Deliveries, edited by Stuart C. Mowbray, Andrew Mowbray Publishing, Lincoln, RI, 1998. 300pp., illus. $39.50
A facsimile reprint of the master list of Civil War weapons purchases and deliveries including Small Arms, Cannon, Ordnance and Projectiles.

Civil War Breech Loading Rifles, by John D. McAulay, Andrew Mowbray, Inc., Lincoln, RI, 1991. 144 pp., illus. Paper covers. $15.00
All the major breech-loading rifles of the Civil War and most, if not all, of the obscure types are detailed, illustrated and set in their historical context.

Civil War Cartridge Boxes of the Union Infantryman, by Paul Johnson, Andrew Mowbray, Inc., Lincoln, RI, 1998. 352 pp., illustrated. $45.00
There were four patterns of infantry cartridge boxes used by Union forces during the Civil War. The author describes the development and subsequent pattern changes to these cartridge boxes.

Civil War Commanders, by Dean Thomas, Thomas Publications, Gettysburg, PA. 1998. 72 pages, illustrated, photos. Paper Covers. $9.95
138 photographs and capsule biographies of Union and Confederate officers. A convenient personalities reference guide.

Civil War Firearms, by Joseph G. Bilby, Combined Books, Conshohocken, PA, 1996. 252 pp., illus. $34.95
A unique work combining background data on each firearm including its battlefield use, and a guide to collecting and firing surviving relics and modern reproductions.

Civil War Guns, by William B. Edwards, Thomas Publications, Gettysburg, PA, 1997. 444 pp., illus. $40.00
The complete story of Federal and Confederate small arms; design, manufacture, identifications, procurement issue, employment, effectiveness, and postwar disposal by the recognized expert.

Civil War Infantryman: In Camp, On the March, And in Battle, by Dean Thomas, Thomas Publications, Gettysburg, PA. 1998. 72 pages, illustrated, Softcovers. $12.95
Uses first-hand accounts to shed some light on the "common soldier" of the Civil War from enlistment to muster-out, including camp, marching, rations, equipment, fighting, and more.

Civil War Pistols, by John D. McAulay, Andrew Mowbray Inc., Lincoln, RI, 1992. 166 pp., illus. $38.50
A survey of the handguns used during the American Civil War.

Civil War Sharps Carbines and Rifles, by Earl J. Coates and John D. McAulay, Thomas Publications, Gettysburg, PA, 1996. 108 pp., illus. Paper covers. $12.95
Traces the history and development of the firearms including short histories of specific serial numbers and the soldiers who received them.

Civil War Small Arms of the U.S. Navy and Marine Corps, by John D. McAulay, Mowbray Publishing, Lincoln, RI, 1999. 186 pp., illustrated. $39.00
The first reliable and comprehensive guide to the firearms and edged weapons of the Civil War Navy and Marine Corps.

The W.F. Cody Buffalo Bill Collector's Guide with Values, by James W. Wojtowicz, Collector Books, Paducah, KY, 1998. 271 pp., illustrated. $24.95
A profusion of colorful collectibles including lithographs, programs, photographs, books, medals, sheet music, guns, etc. and today's values.

Col. Burton's Spiller & Burr Revolver, by Matthew W. Norman, Mercer University Press, Macon, GA, 1997. 152 pp., illus. $22.95
A remarkable archival research project on the arm together with a comprehensive story of the establishment and running of the factory.

Collector's Guide to Colt .45 Service Pistols Models of 1911 and 1911A1, Enlarged and revised edition. Clawson Publications, Fort Wayne, IN, 1998. 130 pp., illustrated. $45.00
From 1911 to the end of production in 1945 with complete military identification including all contractors.

A Collector's Guide to United States Combat Shotguns, by Bruce N. Canfield, Andrew Mowbray Inc., Lincoln, RI, 1992. 184 pp., illus. Paper covers. $24.00
This book provides full coverage of combat shotguns, from the earliest examples right up to the Gulf War and beyond.

A Collector's Guide to Winchester in the Service, by Bruce N. Canfield, Andrew Mowbray, Inc., Lincoln, RI, 1991. 192 pp., illus. Paper covers. $22.00
The firearms produced by Winchester for the national defense. From Hotchkiss to the M14, each firearm is examined and illustrated.

A Collector's Guide to the '03 Springfield, by Bruce N. Canfield, Andrew Mowbray Inc., Lincoln, RI, 1989. 160 pp., illus. Paper covers. $22.00
A comprehensive guide follows the '03 through its unparalleled tenure of service. Covers all of the interesting variations, modifications and accessories of this highly collectible military rifle.

Collector's Illustrated Encyclopedia of the American Revolution, by George C. Neumann and Frank J. Kravic, Rebel Publishing Co., Inc., Texarkana, TX, 1989. 286 pp., illus. $36.95
A showcase of more than 2,300 artifacts made, worn, and used by those who fought in the War for Independence.

Colonial Frontier Guns, by T.M. Hamilton, Pioneer Press, Union City, TN, 1988. 176 pp., illus. Paper covers. $17.50
A complete study of early flint muskets of this country.

Colt: An American Legend, by R.L. Wilson, Artabras, New York, 1997. 406 pages, fully illustrated, most in color. $60.00
A reprint of the commemorative album celebrates 150 years of the guns of Samuel Colt and the manufacturing empire he built, with expert discussion of every model ever produced, the innovations of each model and variants, updated model and serial number charts and magnificent photographic showcases of the weapons.

The Colt Armory, by Ellsworth Grant, Man-at-Arms Bookshelf, Lincoln, RI, 1996. 232 pp., illus. $35.00
A history of Colt's Manufacturing Company.

Colt Blackpowder Reproductions & Replica: A Collector's and Shooter's Guide, by Dennis Miller, Blue Book Publications, Minneapolis, MN, 1999. 288 pp., illustrated. Paper covers. $29.95
The first book on this important subject, and a must for the investor, collector, and shooter.

Colt Heritage, by R.L. Wilson, Simon & Schuster, 1979. 358 pp., illus. $75.00
The official history of Colt firearms 1836 to the present.

Colt Memorabilia Price Guide, by John Ogle, Krause Publications, Iola, WI, 1998. 256 pp., illus. Paper covers. $29.95
The first book ever compiled about the vast array of non-gun merchandise produced by Sam Colt's companies, and other companies using the Colt name.

The Colt Model 1905 Automatic Pistol, by John Potocki, Andrew Mowbray Publishing, Lincoln, RI, 1998. 191 pp., illus. $28.00
Covers all aspects of the Colt Model 1905 Automatic Pistol, from its invention by the legendary John Browning to its numerous production variations.

Colt Peacemaker British Model, by Keith Cochran, Cochran Publishing Co., Rapid City, SD, 1989. 160 pp., illus. $35.00
Covers those revolvers Colt squeezed in while completing a large order of revolvers for the U.S. Cavalry in early 1874, to those magnificent cased target revolvers used in the pistol competitions at Bisley Commons in the 1890s.

Colt Peacemaker Encyclopedia, by Keith Cochran, Keith Cochran, Rapid City, SD, 1986. 434 pp., illus. $65.00
A must book for the Peacemaker collector.

Colt Peacemaker Encyclopedia, Volume 2, by Keith Cochran, Cochran Publishing Co., SD, 1992. 416 pp., illus. $60.00
Included in this volume are extensive notes on engraved, inscribed, historical and noted revolvers, as well as those revolvers used by outlaws, lawmen, movie and television stars.

Colt Percussion Accoutrements 1834-1873, by Robin Rapley, Robin Rapley, Newport Beach, CA, 1994. 432 pp., illus. Paper covers. $39.95
The complete collector's guide to the identification of Colt percussion accoutrements; including Colt conversions and their values.

Colt Pocket Hammerless Pistols, by Dr. John W. Brunner, Phillips Publications, Williamstown, NJ, 1998. 212 pp., illustrated. $59.95
You will never again have to question a .25, .32 or .380 with this well illustrated, definitive reference guide at hand.

THE HANDGUNNER'S LIBRARY

Colt Revolvers and the Tower of London, by Joseph G. Rosa, Royal Armouries of the Tower of London, London, England, 1988. 72 pp., illus. Soft covers. $15.00

Details the story of Colt in London through the early cartridge period.

Colt Rifles and Muskets from 1847-1870, by Herbert Houze, Krause Publications, Iola, WI, 1996. 192 pp., illus. $34.95

Discover previously unknown Colt models along with an extensive list of production figures for all models.

Colt's SAA Post War Models, by George Garton, The Gun Room Press, Highland Park, NJ, 1995. 166 pp., illus. $39.95

Complete facts on the post-war Single Action Army revolvers. Information on calibers, production numbers and variations taken from factory records.

Colt Single Action Army Revolvers: The Legend, the Romance and the Rivals, by "Doc" O'Meara, Krause Publications, Iola, WI, 2000. 160 pp., illustrated with 250 photos in b&w and a 16 page color section. $34.95

Production figures, serial numbers by year, and rarities.

Colt Single Action Army Revolvers and Alterations, by C. Kenneth Moore, Mowbray Publishers, Lincoln, RI, 1999. 112 pp., illustrated. $35.00

A comprehensive history of the revolvers that collectors call "Artillery Models." These are the most historical of all S.A.A. Colts, and this new book covers all the details.

Colt Single Action Army Revolvers and the London Agency, by C. Kenneth Moore, Andrew Mowbray Publishers, Lincoln, RI, 1990. 144 pp., illus. $35.00

Drawing on vast documentary sources, this work chronicles the relationship between the London Agency and the Hartford home office.

The Colt U.S. General Officers' Pistols, by Horace Greeley IV, Andrew Mowbray Inc., Lincoln, RI, 1990. 199 pp., illus. $38.00

These unique weapons, issued as a badge of rank to General Officers in the U.S. Army from WWII onward, remain highly personal artifacts of the military leaders who carried them. Includes serial numbers and dates of issue.

Colts from the William M. Locke Collection, by Frank Sellers, Andrew Mowbray Publishers, Lincoln, RI, 1996. 192 pp., illus. $55.00

This important book illustrates all of the famous Locke Colts, with captions by arms authority Frank Sellers.

Colt's Dates of Manufacture 1837-1978, by R.L. Wilson, published by Maurie Albert, Coburg, Australia; N.A. distributor I.D.S.A. Books, Hamilton, OH, 1983. 61 pp. $6.00

An invaluable pocket guide to the dates of manufacture of Colt firearms up to 1978.

Colt's 100th Anniversary Firearms Manual 1836-1936: A Century of Achievement, Wolfe Publishing Co., Prescott, AZ, 1992. 100 pp., illus. Paper covers. $12.95

Originally published by the Colt Patent Firearms Co., this booklet covers the history, manufacturing procedures and the guns of the first 100 years of the genius of Samuel Colt.

Colt's Pocket '49: Its Evolution Including the Baby Dragoon and Wells Fargo, by Robert Jordan and Darrow Watt, privately printed, Loma Mar, CA 2000. 304 pages, with 984 color photos, illus. Beautifully bound in a deep blue leather like case. $125.00

Detailed information on all models and covers engaving, cases, accoutrements, holsters, fakes, and much more. Included is a summary booklet containing information such as serial numbers, production ranges & identifing photos. This book is a masterpiece on its subject.

Complete Guide to all United States Military Medals 1939 to Present, by Colonel Frank C. Foster, Medals of America Press, Fountain Inn, SC, 2000. 121 pp,.illustrated, photos. $29.95

Complete criteria for every Army, Navy, Marines, Air Force, Coast Guard, and Merchant Marine awards since 1939. All decorations, service medals, and ribbons shown in full-color and accompanied by dates and campaigns as well as detailed descriptions on proper wear and display.

Complete Guide to the M1 Garand and the M1 Carbine, by Bruce N. Canfield, 2nd printing, Andrew Mowbray Inc., Lincoln, RI, 1999. 296 pp., illus. $39.50

Expanded and updated coverage of both the M1 Garand and the M1 Carbine, with more than twice as much information as the author's previous book on this topic.

The Complete Guide to U.S. Infantry Weapons of the First War, by Bruce Canfield, Andrew Mowbray, Publisher, Lincoln, RI, 2000. 304 pp., illus. $39.95

The definitive study of the U.S. Infantry weapons used in WW1.

The Complete Guide to U.S. Infantry Weapons of World War Two, by Bruce Canfield, Andrew Mowbray, Publisher, Lincoln, RI, 1995. 303 pp., illus. $39.95

A definitive work on the weapons used by the United States Armed Forces in WWII.

A Concise Guide to the Artillery at Gettysburg, by Gregory Coco, Thomas Publications, Gettysburg, PA, 1998. 96 pp., illus. Paper Covers. $10.00

Coco's tenth book on Gettysburg is a beginner's guide to artillery and its use at the battle. It covers the artillery batteries describing the types of cannons, shells, fuses, etc.using interesting narrative and human interest stories.

Cooey Firearms, Made in Canada 1919-1979, by John A. Belton, Museum Restoration, Canada, 1998. 36pp., with 46 illus. Paper Covers. $8.95

More than 6 million rifles and at least 67 models, were made by this small Canadian riflemaker. They have been identified from the first 'Cooey Canuck' through the last variations made by the 'Winchester-Cooey'. Each is descibed and most are illustrated in this first book on The Cooey.

Cowboy Collectibles and Western Memorabilia, by Bob Bell and Edward Vebell, Schiffer Publishing, Atglen, PA, 1992. 160 pp., illus. Paper covers. $29.95

The exciting era of the cowboy and the wild west collectibles including rifles, pistols, gun rigs, etc.

Cowboy Culture: The Last Frontier of American Antiques, by Michael Friedman, Schiffer Publishing, Ltd., West Chester, PA, 1992. 300 pp., illustrated.

Covers the artful aspects of the old west, the antiques and collectibles. Illustrated with clear color plates of over 1,000 items such as spurs, boots, guns, saddles etc.

Cowboy and Gunfighter Collectible, by Bill Mackin, Mountain Press Publishing Co., Missoula, MT, 1995. 178 pp., illus. Paper covers. $25.00

A photographic encyclopedia with price guide and makers' index.

Cowboys and the Trappings of the Old West, by William Manns and Elizabeth Clair Flood, Zon International Publishing Co., Santa Fe, NM, 1997, 1st edition. 224 pp., illustrated. $45.00

A pictorial celebration of the cowboys dress and trappings.

Cowboy Hero Cap Pistols, by Rudy D'Angelo, Antique Trader Books, Dubuque, IA, 1998. 196 pp., illus. Paper covers. $34.95

Aimed at collectors of cap pistols created and named for famous film and television cowboy heros, this in-depth guide hits all the marks. Current values are given.

Custom Firearms Engraving, by Tom Turpin, Krause Publications, Iola, WI, 1999. 208 pp., illustrated. $49.95

Over 200 four-color photos with more than 75 master engravers profiled. Engravers Directory with addresses in the U.S. and abroad.

The Decorations, Medals, Ribbons, Badges and Insignia of the United States Army; World War 2 to Present, by Col. Frank C. Foster, Medals of America Press, Fountain Inn, SC. 2001. 145 pages, illustrated. $29.95

The most complete guide to United States Army medals, ribbons, rank, insignia nad patches from WWII to the present day. Each medal and insignia shown in full color. Includes listing of respective criteria and campaigns.

The Decorations, Medals, Ribbons, Badges and Insignia of the United States Navy; World War 2 to Present, by James G. Thompson, Medals of America Press, Fountain Inn, SC. 2000. 123 pages, illustrated. $29.95

The most complete guide to United States Army medals, ribbons, rank, insignia nad patches from WWII to the present day. Each medal and insignia shown in full color. Includes listing of respective criteria and campaigns.

The Derringer in America, Volume 1, The Percussion Period, by R.L. Wilson and L.D. Eberhart, Andrew Mowbray Inc., Lincoln, RI, 1985. 271 pp., illus. $48.00

A long awaited book on the American percussion deringer.

The Derringer in America, Volume 2, The Cartridge Period, by L.D. Eberhart and R.L. Wilson, Andrew Mowbray Inc., Publishers, Lincoln, RI, 1993. 284 pp., illus. $65.00

Comprehensive coverage of cartridge deringers organized alphabetically by maker. Includes all types of deringers known by the authors to have been offered to the American market.

The Devil's Paintbrush: Sir Hiram Maxim's Gun, by Dolf Goldsmith, 3rd Edition, expanded and revised, Collector Grade Publications, Toronto, Canada, 2000. 384 pp., illus. $79.95

The classic work on the world's first true automatic machine gun.

Dr. Josephus Requa Civil War Dentist and the Billinghurst-Requa Volley Gun, by John M. Hyson, Jr., & Margaret Requa DeFrancisco, Museum Restoration Service, Bloomfield, Ont., Canada, 1999. 36 pp., illus. Paper covers. $8.95

The story of the inventor of the first practical rapid-fire gun to be used during the American Civil War.

The Duck Stamp Story, by Eric Jay Dolin and Bob Dumaine, Krause Publications, Iola, WI, 2000. 208 pp., illustrated with color throughout. Paper covers. $29.95; Hardbound. $49.95.

Detailed information on the value and rarity of every federal duck stamp. Outstanding art and illustrations.

The Dutch Luger (Parabellum) A Complete History, by Bas J. Martens and Guus de Vries, Ironside International Publishers, Inc., Alexandria, VA, 1995. 268 pp., illus. $49.95.

The history of the Luger in the Netherlands. An extensive description of the Dutch pistol and trials and the different models of the Luger in the Dutch service.

The Eagle on U.S. Firearms, by John W. Jordan, Pioneer Press, Union City, TN, 1992. 140 pp., illus. Paper covers. $17.50.

Stylized eagles have been stamped on government owned or manufactured firearms in the U.S. since the beginning of our country. This book lists and illustrates these various eagles in an informative and refreshing manner.

Encyclopedia of Rifles & Handguns; A Comprehensive Guide to Firearms, edited by Sean Connolly, Chartwell Books, Inc., Edison, NJ., 1996. 160 pp., illustrated. $26.00.

A lavishly illustrated book providing a comprehensive history of military and civilian personal firepower.

Eprouvettes: A Comprehensive Study of Early Devices for the Testing of Gunpowder, by R.T.W. Kempers, Royal Armouries Museum, Leeds, England, 1999. 352 pp., illustrated with 240 black & white and 28 color plates. $125.00.

The first comprehensive study of eprouvettes ever attempted in a single volume.

European Firearms in Swedish Castles, by Kaa Wennberg, Bohuslaningens Boktryckeri AB, Uddevalla, Sweden, 1986. 156 pp., illus. $50.00.

The famous collection of Count Keller, the Ettersburg Castle collection, and others. English text.

European Sporting Cartridges, Part 1, by W.B. Dixon, Armory Publications, Inc., Coeur d'Alene, ID, 1997. 250 pp., illus. $63.00

Photographs and drawings of over 550 centerfire cartridge case types in 1,300 illustrations produced in German and Austria from 1875 to 1995.

European Sporting Cartridges, Part 2, by W.B. Dixon, Armory Publications, Inc., Coeur d'Alene, ID, 2000. 240 pp., illus. $63.00

An illustrated history of centerfire hunting and target cartridges produced in Czechoslovakia, Switzerland, Norway, Sweden, Finland, Russia, Italy, Denmark, Belguim from 1875 to 1998. Adds 50 specimens to volume 1 (Germany-Austria). Also, illustrates 40 small arms magazine experiments during the late 19th Century, and includes the English-Language export ammunition catalogue of Kovo (Povazske Strojarne), Prague, Czech. from the, 1930's.

Fifteen Years in the Hawken Lode, by John D. Baird, The Gun Room Press, Highland Park, NJ, 1976. 120 pp., illus. $24.95.

A collection of thoughts and observations gained from many years of intensive study of the guns from the shop of the Hawken brothers.

'51 Colt Navies, by Nathan L. Swayze, The Gun Room Press, Highland Park, NJ, 1993. 243 pp., illus. $59.95.

The Model 1851 Colt Navy, its variations and markings.

Fighting Iron, by Art Gogan, Andrew Mowbray, Inc., Lincoln, R.I., 1999. 176 pp., illustrated. $28.00.

It doesn't matter whether you collect guns, swords, bayonets or accountrement—sooner or later you realize that it all comes down to the metal. If you don't understand the metal you don't understand your collection.

Fine Colts, The Dr. Joseph A. Murphy Collection, by R.L. Wilson, Sheffield Marketing Associates, Inc., Doylestown, PA, 1999. 258 pp., illustrated. Limited edition signed and numbered. $99.00.

This lavish new work covers exquisite, deluxe and rare Colt arms from Paterson and other percussion revolvers to the cartridge period and up through modern times.

Firearms, by Derek Avery, Desert Publications, El Dorado, AR, 1999. 95 pp., illustrated. $9.95.

The firearms included in this book are by necessity only a selection, but nevertheless one that represents the best and most famous weapons seen since the Second World War.

Firearms and Tackle Memorabilia, by John Delph, Schiffer Publishing, Ltd., West Chester, PA, 1991. 124 pp., illus. $39.95.

A collector's guide to signs and posters, calendars, trade cards, boxes, envelopes, and other highly sought after memorabilia. With a value guide.

Firearms of the American West 1803-1865, Volume 1, by Louis A. Garavaglia and Charles Worman, University of Colorado Press, Niwot, CO, 1998. 402 pp., illustrated. $59.95.

Traces the development and uses of firearms on the frontier during this period.

Firearms of the American West 1866-1894, by Louis A. Garavaglia and Charles G. Worman, University of Colorado Press, Niwot, CO, 1998. 416 pp., illus. $59.95.

A monumental work that offers both technical information on all of the important firearms used in the West during this period and a highly entertaining history of how they were used, who used them, and why.

Firearms from Europe, by David Noe, Larry W. Yantz, Dr. James B. Whisker, Rowe Publications, Rochester, N.Y., 1999. 192 pp., illustrated. $45.00.

A history and description of firearms imported during the American Civil War by the United States of America and the Confederate States of America.

Firepower from Abroad, by Wiley Sword, Andrew Mowbray Publishing, Lincoln, R.I., 2000. 120 pp., illustrated. $23.00.

The Confederate Enfield and the LeMat revolver and how they reached the Confederate market.

Flayderman's Guide to Antique American Firearms and Their Values, 7th Edition, edited by Norm Flayderman, DBI books, a division of Krause Publications, Iola, WI, 1998. 656 pp., illus. Paper covers. $32.95.

A completely updated and new edition with more than 3,600 models and variants extensively described with all marks and specifications necessary for quick identification.

The FN-FAL Rifle, et al, by Duncan Long, Paladin Press, Boulder, CO, 1999. 144 pp., illustrated. Paper covers. $18.95.

Detailed descriptions of the basic models produced by Fabrique Nationale and the myriad variants that evolved as a result of the firearms universal acceptance.

The .45-70 Springfield, by Joe Poyer and Craig Riesch, North Cape Publications, Tustin, CA, 1996. 150 pp., illus. Paper covers. $16.95.

A revised and expanded second edition of a best-selling reference work organized by serial number and date of production to aid the collector in identifying popular "Trapdoor" rifles and carbines.

The French 1935 Pistols, by Eugene Medlin and Colin Doane, Eugene Medlin, El Paso, TX, 1995. 172 pp., illus. Paper covers. $25.95.

The development and identification of successive models, fakes and variants, holsters and accessories, and serial numbers by dates of production.

Freund & Bro. Pioneer Gunmakers to the West, by F.J. Pablo Balentine, Graphic Publishers, Newport Beach, CA, 1997. 380 pp., illustrated $69.95.

The story of Frank W. and George Freund, skilled German gunsmiths who plied their trade on the Western American frontier during the final three decades of the nineteenth century.

From the Kingdom of Lilliput: The Miniature Firearms of David Kucer, by K. Corey Keeble and **The Making of Miniatures,** by David Kucer, Museum Restoration Service, Ontario, Canada, 1994. 51 pp., illus, $25.00.

An overview of the subject of miniatures in general combined with an outline by the artist himself on the way he makes a miniature firearm.

Frontier Pistols and Revolvers, by Dominique Venner, Book Sales Inc., Edison, N.J., 1998. 144 pp., illus. $19.95.

Colt, Smith & Wesson, Remington and other early-brand revolvers which tamed the American frontier are shown amid vintage photographs, etchings and paintings to evoke the wild West.

The Fusil de Tulole in New France, 1691-1741, by Russel Bouchard, Museum Restorations Service, Bloomfield, Ontario, Canada, 1997. 36 pp., illus. Paper covers. $8.95

The development of the company and the identification of their arms.

Game Guns & Rifles: Percussion to Hammerless Ejector in Britain, by Richard Akehurst, Trafalgar Square, N. Pomfret, VT, 1993. 192 pp., illus. $39.95.

Long considered a classic this important reprint covers the period of British gunmaking between 1830-1900.

The Gas Trap Garand, by Billy Pyle, Collector Grade Publications, Cobourg, Ontario, Canada, 1999 316 pp., illustrated. $59.95.

The in-depth story of the rarest Garands of them all, the initial 80 Model Shop rifles made under the personal supervision of John Garand himself in 1934 and 1935, and the first 50,000 plus production "gas trap" M1's manufactured at Springfield Armory between August, 1937 and August, 1940.

George Schreyer, Sr. and Jr., Gunmakers of Hanover, Pennsylvania, by George Shumway, George Shumway Publishers, York, PA, 1990. 160pp., illus. $50.00.

This monograph is a detailed photographic study of almost all known surviving long rifles and smoothbore guns made by highly regarded gunsmiths George Schreyer, Sr. and Jr.

The German Assault Rifle 1935-1945, by Peter R. Senich, Paladin Press, Boulder, CO, 1987. 328 pp., illus. $60.00.

A complete review of machine carbines, machine pistols and assault rifles employed by Hitler's Wehrmacht during WWII.

The German K98k Rifle, 1934-1945: The Backbone of the Wehrmacht, by Richard D. Law, Collector Grade Publications, Toronto, Canada, 1993. 336 pp., illus. $69.95.

The most comprehensive study ever published on the 14,000,000 bolt-action K98k rifles produced in Germany between 1934 and 1945.

German Machine Guns, by Daniel D. Musgrave, revised edition, Ironside International Publishers, Inc. Alexandria, VA, 1992. 586 pp., 650 illus. $49.95.

The most definitive book ever written on German machineguns. Covers the introduction and development of machineguns in Germany from 1899 to the rearmament period after WWII.

German Military Rifles and Machine Pistols, 1871-1945, by Hans Dieter Gotz, Schiffer Publishing Co., West Chester, PA, 1990. 245 pp., illus. $35.00.

This book portrays in words and pictures the development of the modern German weapons and their ammunition including the scarcely known experimental types.

The German MP40 Maschinenpistole, by Frank Iannamico, Moose Lake Publishing, Harmony, ME, 1999. 185 pp., illustrated. Paper covers. $19.95.

The history, development and use of this famous gun of World War 2.

German 7.9mm Military Ammunition, by Daniel W. Kent, Daniel W. Kent, Ann Arbor, MI, 1991. 244 pp., illus. $35.00.

The long-awaited revised edition of a classic among books devoted to ammunition.

The Golden Age of Remington, by Robert W.D. Ball, Krause publications, Iola, WI, 1995. 194 pp., illus. $29.95.

For Remington collectors or firearms historians, this book provides a pictorial history of Remington through World War I. Includes value guide.

THE HANDGUNNER'S LIBRARY

The Government Models, by William H.D. Goddard, Andrew Mowbray Publishing, Lincoln, RI, 1998. 296 pp., illustrated. $58.50.
The most authoritative source on the development of the Colt model of 1911.

Grasshoppers and Butterflies, by Adrian B. Caruana, Museum Restoration Service, Alexandria, Bay, N.Y., 1999. 32 pp., illustrated. Paper covers. $8.95.
No.39 in the Historical Arms Series. The light 3 pounders of Pattison and Townsend.

The Greener Story, by Graham Greener, Quiller Press, London, England, 2000. 256 pp., illustrated with 32 pages of color photos. $64.50.
W.W. Greener, his family history, inventions, guns, patents, and more.

A Guide to American Trade Catalogs 1744-1900, by Lawrence B. Romaine, Dover Publications, New York, NY. 422 pp., illus. Paper covers. $12.95

A Guide to Ballard Breechloaders, by George J. Layman, Pioneer Press, Union City, TN, 1997. 261 pp., illus. Paper covers. $19.95
Documents the saga of this fine rifle from the first models made by Ball & Williams of Worcester, to its production by the Marlin Firearms Co, to the cessation of 19th century manufacture in 1891, and finally to the modern reproductions made in the 1990's.

A Guide to the Maynard Breechloader, by George J. Layman, George J. Layman, Ayer, MA, 1993. 125 pp., illus. Paper covers. $11.95.
The first book dedicated entirely to the Maynard family of breech-loading firearms. Coverage of the arms is given from the 1850s through the 1880s.

A Guide to U. S. Army Dress Helmets 1872-1904, by Kasal and Moore, North Cape Publications, 2000. 88 pp., illus. Paper covers. $15.95
This thorough study provides a complete description of the Model 1872 & 1881 dress helmets worn by the U.S. Army. Including all componets from bodies to plates to plumes & shoulder cords and tells how to differentiate the originals from reproductions. Extensively illustrated with photographs, '8 pages in full color' of complete helmets and their components.

Gun Collecting, by Geoffrey Boothroyd, Sportsman's Press, London, 1989. 208 pp., illus. $29.95.
The most comprehensive list of 19th century British gunmakers and gunsmiths ever published.

Gunmakers of London 1350-1850, by Howard L. Blackmore, George Shumway Publisher, York, PA, 1986. 222 pp., illus. $35.00.
A listing of all the known workmen of gun making in the first 500 years, plus a history of the guilds, cutlers, armourers, founders, blacksmiths, etc. 260 gunmarks are illustrated.

Gunmakers of London Supplement 1350-1850, by Howard L. Blackmore, Museum Restoration Service, Alexandria Bay, NY, 1999. 156 pp., illustrated. $60.00.
Begins with an introductory chapter on "foreighn" gunmakers followed by records of all the new information found about previously unidentified armourers, gunmakers and gunsmiths.

The Guns that Won the West: Firearms of the American Frontier, 1865-1898, by John Walter, Stackpole Books, Inc., Mechanicsburg, PA.,1999. 256 pp., illustrated. $34.95.
Here is the story of the wide range of firearms from pistols to rifles used by plainsmen and settlers, gamblers, native Americans and the U.S. Army.

Gunsmiths of Illinois, by Curtis L. Johnson, George Shumway Publishers, York, PA, 1995. 160 pp., illus. $50.00.
Genealogical information is provided for nearly one thousand gunsmiths. Contains hundreds of illustrations of rifles and other guns, of handmade origin, from Illinois.

The Gunsmiths of Manhattan, 1625-1900: A Checklist of Tradesmen, by Michael H. Lewis, Museum Restoration Service, Bloomfield, Ont., Canada, 1991. 40 pp., illus. Paper covers. $8.95.
This listing of more than 700 men in the arms trade in New York City prior to about the end of the 19th century will provide a guide for identification and further research.

The Guns of Dagenham: Lanchester, Patchett, Sterling, by Peter Laidler and David Howroyd, Collector Grade Publications, Inc., Cobourg, Ont., Canada, 1995. 310 pp., illus. $39.95.
An in-depth history of the small arms made by the Sterling Company of Dagenham, Essex, England, from 1940 until Sterling was purchased by British Aerospace in 1989 and closed.

Guns of the Western Indian War, by R. Stephen Dorsey, Collector's Library, Eugene, OR, 1997. 220 pp., illus. Paper covers. $30.00.
The full story of the guns and ammunition that made western history in the turbulent period of 1865-1890.

Gun Powder Cans & Kegs, by Ted & David Bacyk and Tom Rowe, Rowe Publications, Rochester, NY, 1999. 150 pp., illus. $65.00.
The first book devoted to powder tins and kegs. All cans and kegs in full color. With a price guide and rarity scale.

The Guns of Remington: Historic Firearms Spanning Two Centuries, compiled by Howard M. Madaus, Biplane Productions, Publisher, in cooperation with Buffalo Bill Historical Center, Cody, WY, 1998. 352 pp., illustrated with over 800 color photos. $79.95.
A complete catalog of the firearms in the exhibition, "It Never Failed Me: The Arms & Art of Remington Arms Company" at the Buffalo Bill Historical Center, Cody, Wyoming.

Gun Tools, Their History and Identification by James B. Shaffer, Lee A. Rutledge and R. Stephen Dorsey, Collector's Library, Eugene, OR, 1992. 375 pp., illus. $30.00.
Written history of foreign and domestic gun tools from the flintlock period to WWII.

Gun Tools, Their History and Identifications, Volume 2, by Stephen Dorsey and James B. Shaffer, Collectors' Library, Eugene, OR, 1997. 396 pp., illus. Paper covers. $30.00.
Gun tools from the Royal Armouries Museum in England, Pattern Room, Royal Ordnance Reference Collection in Nottingham and from major private collections.

Gunsmiths of the Carolinas 1660-1870, by Daniel D. Hartzler and James B. Whisker, Old Bedford Village Press, Bedford, PA, 1998. 176 pp., illustrated. $40.00.
This deluxe hard bound edition of 176 pages is printed on fine coated paper, with about 90 pages of large photographs of fine longrifles from the Carolinas, and about 90 pages of detailed research on the gunsmiths who created the highly prized and highly collectable longrifles. Dedicated to serious students of original Kentucky rifles, who may seldom encounter fine longrifles from the Carolinas.

Gunsmiths of Maryland, by Daniel D. Hartzler and James B. Whisker, Old Bedford Village Press, Bedford, PA, 1998. 208 pp., illustrated. $45.00.
Covers firelock Colonial period through the breech-loading patent models. Featuring longrifles.

Gunsmiths of Virginia, by Daniel D. Hartzler and James B. Whisker, Old Bedford Village Press, Bedford, PA, 1992. 206 pp., illustrated. $45.00.
A photographic study of American longrifles.

Gunsmiths of West Virginia, by Daniel D. Hartzler and James B. Whisker, Old Bedford Village Press, Bedford, PA, 1998. 176 pp., illustrated. $40.00.
A photographic study of American longrifles.

Gunsmiths of York County, Pennsylvania, by Daniel D. Hartzler and James B. Whisker, Old Bedford Village Press, Bedford, PA, 1998. 160 pp., illustrated. $40.00.
160 pages of photographs and research notes on the longrifles and gunsmiths of York County, Pennsylvania. Many longrifle collectors and gun builders have noticed that York County style rifles tend to be more formal in artistic decoration than some other schools of style. Patriotic themes, and folk art were popular design elements.

Hall's Military Breechloaders, by Peter A. Schmidt, Andrew Mowbray Publishers, Lincoln, RI, 1996. 232 pp., illus. $55.00.
The whole story behind these bold and innovative firearms.

The Handgun, by Geoffrey Boothroyd, David and Charles, North Pomfret, VT, 1989. 566 pp., illus. $60.00.
Every chapter deals with an important period in handgun history from the 14th century to the present.

Handgun of Military Rifle Marks 1866-1950, by Richard A. Hoffman and Noel P. Schott, Mapleleaf Militaria Publishing, St. Louis, MO, 1999, second edition. 60 pp., illustrated. Paper covers. $20.00.
An illustrated guide to identifying military rifle and marks.

Handguns & Rifles: The Finest Weapons from Around the World, by Ian Hogg, Random House Value Publishing, Inc., N.Y., 1999. 128 pp., illustrated. $18.98.
The serious gun collector will welcome this fully illustrated examination of international handguns and rifles. Each entry covers the history of the weapon, what purpose it serves, and its advantages and disadvantages.

The Hawken Rifle: Its Place in History, by Charles E. Hanson, Jr., The Fur Press, Chadron, NE, 1979. 104 pp., illus. Paper covers. $15.00.
A definitive work on this famous rifle.

Hawken Rifles, The Mountain Man's Choice, by John D. Baird, The Gun Room Press, Highland Park, NJ, 1976. 95 pp., illus. $29.95.
Covers the rifles developed for the Western fur trade. Numerous specimens are described and shown in photographs.

High Standard: A Collector's Guide to the Hamden & Hartford Target Pistols, by Tom Dance, Andrew Mowbray, Inc., Lincoln, RI, 1991. 192 pp., illus. Paper covers. $24.00.
From Citation to Supermatic, all of the production models and specials made from 1951 to 1984 are covered according to model number or series.

Historic Pistols: The American Martial Flintlock 1760-1845, by Samuel E. Smith & Edwin W. Bitter, The Gun Room Press, Highland Park, NJ, 1986. 353 pp., illus. $45.00.
Covers over 70 makers and 163 models of American martial arms.

Historical Hartford Hardware, by William W. Dalrymple, Colt Collector Press, Rapid City, SD, 1976. 42 pp., illus. Paper covers. $10.00.
Historically associated Colt revolvers.

The History and Development of Small Arms Ammunition, Volume 2, by George A. Hoyem, Armory Publications, Oceanside, CA, 1991. 303 pp., illus. $65.00.
Covers the blackpowder military centerfire rifle, carbine, machine gun and volley gun ammunition used in 28 nations and dominions, together with the firearms that chambered them.

The History and Development of Small Arms Ammunition, Volume 4, by George A. Hoyem, Armory Publications, Seattle, WA, 1998. 200 pp., illustrated $65.00.

A comprehensive book on American black powder and early smokeless rifle cartridges.

The History of Colt Firearms, by Dean Boorman, Lyons Press, New York, NY, 2001. 144 pp., illus. $29.95.

Discover the fascinating story of the world's most famous revolver, complete with more than 150 stunning full-color photographs.

History of Modern U.S. Military Small Arms Ammunition. Volume 1, 1880-1939, revised by F.W. Hackley, W.H. Woodin and E.L. Scranton, Thomas Publications, Gettysburg, PA, 1998. 328 pp., illus. $49.95.

This revised edition incorporates all publicly available information concerning military small arms ammunition for the period 1880 through 1939 in a single volume.

History of Modern U.S. Military Small Arms Ammunition. Volume 2, 1940-1945 by F.W. Hackley, W.H. Woodin and E.L. Scranton. Gun Room Press, Highland Park, NJ. 300 + pages, illustrated. $39.95.

Based on decades of original research conducted at the National Archives, numerous military, public and private museums and libraries, as well as individual collections, this edition incorporates all publicly available information concerning military small arms ammunition for the period 1940 through 1945.

The History of Winchester Rifles, by Dean Boorman, Lyons Press, New York, NY, 2001. 144 pp., illus. $29.95.

A captivating and wonderfully photographed history of one of the most legendary names in gun lore. 150 full-color photos.

The History of Winchester Firearms 1866-1992, sixth edition, updated, expanded, and revised by Thomas Henshaw, New Win Publishing, Clinton, NJ, 1993. 280 pp., illus. $27.95.

This classic is the standard reference for all collectors and others seeking the facts about any Winchester firearm, old or new.

History of Winchester Repeating Arms Company, by Herbert G. Houze, Krause Publications, Iola, WI, 1994. 800 pp., illus. $50.00.

The complete Winchester history from 1856-1981.

Honour Bound: The Chauchat Machine Rifle, by Gerard Demaison and Yves Buffetaut, Collector Grade Publications, Inc., Cobourg, Ont., Canada, 1995. $39.95.

The story of the CSRG (Chauchat) machine rifle, the most manufactured automatic weapon of World War One.

Hopkins & Allen Revolvers & Pistols, by Charles E. Carder, Avil Onze Publishing, Delphos, OH, 1998, illustrated. Paper covers. $24.95.

Covers over 165 photos, graphics and patent drawings.

How to Buy and Sell Used Guns, by John Traister, Stoeger Publishing Co., So. Hackensack, NJ, 1984. 192 pp., illus. Paper covers. $10.95.

A new guide to buying and selling guns.

Hunting Weapons From the Middle Ages to the Twentieth Century, by Howard L. Blackmore, Dover Publications, Meneola, NY, 2000. 480 pp., illustrated. Paper covers. $16.95.

Dealing mainly with the different classes of weapons used in sport—swords, spears, crossbows, guns, and rifles—from the Middle Ages until the present day.

Identification Manual on the .303 British Service Cartridge, No. 1-Ball Ammunition, by B.A. Temple, I.D.S.A. Books, Piqua, OH, 1986. 84 pp., 57 illus. $12.50

Identification Manual on the .303 British Service Cartridge, No. 2-Blank Ammunition, by B.A. Temple, I.D.S.A. Books, Piqua, OH, 1986. 95 pp., 59 illus. $12.50

Identification Manual on the .303 British Service Cartridge, No. 3-Special Purpose Ammunition, by B.A. Temple, I.D.S.A. Books, Piqua, OH, 1987. 82 pp., 49 illus. $12.50

Identification Manual on the .303 British Service Cartridge, No. 4-Dummy Cartridges Henry 1869-c.1900, by B.A. Temple, I.D.S.A. Books, Piqua, OH, 1988. 84 pp., 70 illus. $12.50

Identification Manual on the .303 British Service Cartridge, No. 5-Dummy Cartridges (2), by B.A. Temple, I.D.S.A. Books, Piqua, OH, 1994. 78 pp. $12.50

The Illustrated Book of Guns, by David Miller, Salamander Books, N.Y., N.Y., 2000. 304 pp., illustrated in color. $34.95.

An illustrated directory of over 1,000 military and sporting firearms.

The Illustrated Encyclopedia of Civil War Collectibles, by Chuck Lawliss, Henry Holt and Co., New York, NY, 1997. 316 pp., illus. Paper covers. $22.95.

A comprehensive guide to Union and Confederate arms, equipment, uniforms, and other memorabilia.

Illustrations of United States Military Arms 1776-1903 and Their Inspector's Marks, compiled by Turner Kirkland, Pioneer Press, Union City, TN, 1988. 37 pp., illus. Paper covers. $7.00.

Reprinted from the 1949 Bannerman catalog. Valuable information for both the advanced and beginning collector.

Indian War Cartridge Pouches, Boxes and Carbine Boots, by R. Stephen Dorsey, Collector's Library, Eugene, OR, 1993. 156 pp., illus. Paper Covers. $20.00.

The key reference work to the cartridge pouches, boxes, carbine sockets and boots of the Indian War period 1865-1890.

An Introduction to the Civil War Small Arms, by Earl J. Coates and Dean S. Thomas, Thomas Publishing Co., Gettysburg, PA, 1990. 96 pp., illus. Paper covers. $10.00.

The small arms carried by the individual soldier during the Civil War.

Japanese Rifles of World War Two, by Duncan O. McCollum, Excalibur Publications, Latham, NY, 1996. 64 pp., illus. Paper covers. $18.95.

A sweeping view of the rifles and carbines that made up Japan's arsenal during the conflict.

Kalashnikov Arms, compiled by Alexei Nedelin, Design Military Parade, Ltd., Moscow, Russia, 1997. 240 pp., illus. $49.95.

Weapons versions stored in the St. Petersburg Military Historical Museum of Artillery, Engineer Troops and Communications and in the Izhmash JSC.

Kalashnikov "Machine Pistols, Assault Rifles, and Machine Guns, 1945 to the Present", by John Walter, Paladin Press, Boulder, CO, 1999, hardcover, photos, illus., 146 pp. $22.95

This exhaustive work published by Greenhill Military Manuals features a gun-by-gun directory of Kalashnikov variants. Technical specifications and illustrations are provided throughout, along with details of sights, bayonets, markings and ammunition. A must for the serious collector and historian.

The Kentucky Pistol, by Roy Chandler and James Whisker, Old Bedford Village Press, Bedford, PA, 1997. 225 pp., illus. $60.00

A photographic study of Kentucky pistols from famous collections.

The Kentucky Rifle, by Captain John G.W. Dillin, George Shumway Publisher, York, PA, 1993. 221 pp., illus. $50.00.

This well-known book was the first attempt to tell the story of the American longrifle. This edition retains the original text and illustrations with supplemental footnotes provided by Dr. George Shumway.

Know Your Broomhandle Mausers, by R.J. Berger, Blacksmith Corp., Southport, CT, 1985. 96 pp., illus. Paper covers. $12.95.

An interesting story on the big Mauser pistol and its variations.

Krag Rifles, by William S. Brophy, The Gun Room Press, Highland Park, NJ, 1980. 200 pp., illus. $35.00.

The first comprehensive work detailing the evolution and various models, both military and civilian.

The Krieghoff Parabellum, by Randall Gibson, Midland, TX, 1988. 279 pp., illus. $40.00.

A comprehensive text pertaining to the Lugers manufactured by H. Krieghoff Waffenfabrik.

Las Pistolas Espanolas Tipo "Mauser," by Artemio Mortera Perez, Quiron Ediciones, Valladolid, Spain, 1998. 71 pp., illustrated. Paper covers. $34.95.

This book covers in detail Spanish machine pistols and C96 copies made in Spain. Covers all Astra "Mauser" pistol series and the complete line of Beistegui C96 type pistols. Spanish text.

Law Enforcement Memorabilia Price and Identification Guide, by Monty McCord, DBI Books a division of Krause Publications, Inc. Iola, WI, 1999. 208 pp., illustrated. Paper covers. $19.95.

An invaluable reference to the growing wave of law enforcement collectors. Hundreds of items are covered from miniature vehicles to clothes, patches, and restraints.

Legendary Sporting Guns, by Eric Joly, Abbeville Press, New York, N.Y., 1999. 228 pp., illustrated. $65.00.

A survey through the ages and relates how many different types of firearms were created and refined for use afield.

Legends and Reality of the AK, by Val Shilin and Charlie Cutshaw, Paladen Press, Boulder, CO, 2000. 192 pp., illustrated. Paper covers. $35.00.

A behind-the-scenes look at history, design and impact of the Kalashnikov family of weapons.

LeMat, the Man, the Gun, by Valmore J. Forgett and Alain F. and Marie-Antoinette Serpette, Navy Arms Co., Ridgefield, NJ, 1996. 218 pp., illus. $49.95.

The first definitive study of the Confederate revolvers invention, development and delivery by Francois Alexandre LeMat.

Les Pistolets Automatiques Francaise 1890-1990, by Jean Huon, Combined Books, Inc., Conshohocken, PA, 1997. 160 pp., illus. French text. $34.95

French automatic pistols from the earliest experiments through the World Wars and Indo-China to modern security forces.

Levine's Guide to Knives And Their Values, 4th Edition, by Bernard Levine, DBI Books, a division of Krause Publications, Iola, WI, 1997. 512 pp., illus. Paper covers. $27.95

All the basic tools for identifying, valuing and collecting folding and fixed blade knives.

The Light 6-Pounder Battalion Gun of 1776, by Adrian Caruana, Museum Restoration Service, Bloomfield, Ontario, Canada, 2001. 76 pp., illus. Paper covers. $8.95

REFERENCE

THE HANDGUNNER'S LIBRARY

The London Gun Trade, 1850-1920, by Joyce E. Gooding, Museum Restoration Service, Bloomfield, Ontario, Canada, 2001. 48 pp., illus. Paper covers. $8.95

Names, dates and locations of London gunmakers working between 1850 and 1920 are listed. Compiled from the original Kelly's Post Office Directories of the City of London.

The London Gunmakers and the English Duelling Pistol, 1770-1830, by Keith R. Dill, Museum Restoration Service, Bloomfield, Ontario, Canada, 1997. 36 pp., illus. Paper covers. $8.95

Ten gunmakers made London one of the major gunmaking centers of the world. This book examines how the design and construction of their pistols contributed to that reputation and how these characteristics may be used to date flintlock arms.

Longrifles of North Carolina, by John Bivens, George Shumway Publisher, York, PA, 1988. 256 pp., illus. $50.00.

Covers art and evolution of the rifle, immigration and trade movements. Committee of Safety gunsmiths, characteristics of the North Carolina rifle.

Longrifles of Pennsylvania, Volume 1, Jefferson, Clarion & Elk Counties, by Russel H. Harringer, George Shumway Publisher, York, PA, 1984. 200 pp., illus. $50.00.

First in series that will treat in great detail the longrifles and gunsmiths of Pennsylvania.

The Luger Handbook, by Aarron Davis, Krause Publications, Iola, WI, 1997. 112 pp., illus. Paper covers. $9.95.

Quick reference to classify Luger models and variations with complete details including proofmarks.

Lugers at Random, by Charles Kenyon, Jr., Handgun Press, Glenview, IL, 1990. 420 pp., illus. $59.95.

A new printing of this classic, comprehensive reference for all Luger collectors.

The Luger Story, by John Walter, Stackpole Books, Mechanicsburg, PA, 2001. 256 pp., illus. Paper Covers $29.95.

The standard history of the world's most famous handgun.

M1 Carbine, by Larry Ruth, Gun room Press, Highland Park, NJ, 1987. 291 pp., illus. Paper $19.95.

The origin, development, manufacture and use of this famous carbine of World War II.

The M1 Carbine: Owner's Guide, by Scott A. Duff, Scott A. Duff, Export, PA, 1997. 126 pp., illus. Paper covers. $19.95.

This book answers the questions M1 owners most often ask concerning maintenance activities not encounted by military users.

The M1 Garand: Owner's Guide, by Scott A. Duff, Scott A. Duff, Export, PA, 1998. 132 pp., illus. Paper covers. $19.95.

This book answers the questions M1 owners most often ask concerning maintenance activities not encounted by military users.

The M1 Garand Serial Numbers and Data Sheets, by Scott A. Duff, Export, PA, 1995. 101 pp., illus. Paper covers. $11.95.

Provides the reader with serial numbers related to dates of manufacture and a large sampling of data sheets to aid in identification or restoration.

The M1 Garand 1936 to 1957, by Joe Poyer and Craig Riesch, North Cape Publications, Tustin, CA, 1996. 216 pp., illus. Paper covers. $19.95.

Describes the entire range of M1 Garand production in text and quick-scan charts.

The M1 Garand: Post World War, by Scott A. Duff, Scott A. Duff, Export, PA, 1990. 139 pp., illus. Soft covers. $19.95.

A detailed account of the activities at Springfield Armory through this period. International Harvester, H&R, Korean War production and quantities delivered. Serial numbers.

The M1 Garand: World War 2, by Scott A. Duff, Scott A. Duff, Export, PA, 1993. 210 pp., illus. Paper covers. $39.95.

The most comprehensive study available to the collector and historian on the M1 Garand of World War II.

Maine Made Guns and Their Makers, by Dwight B. Demeritt Jr., Maine State Museum, Augusta, ME, 1998. 209 pp., illustrated. $55.00.

An authoritative, biographical study of Maine gunsmiths.

Marlin Firearms: A History of the Guns and the Company That Made Them, by Lt. Col. William S. Brophy, USAR, Ret., Stackpole Books, Harrisburg, PA, 1989. 672 pp., illus. $75.00.

The definitive book on the Marlin Firearms Co. and their products.

Martini-Henry .450 Rifles & Carbines, by Dennis Lewis, Excalibur Publications, Latham, NY, 1996. 72 pp., illus. Paper covers. $11.95.

The stories of the rifles and carbines that were the mainstay of the British soldier through the Victorian wars.

Mauser Bolt Rifles, by Ludwig Olson, F. Brownell & Son, Inc., Montezuma, IA, 1999. 364 pp., illus. $59.95.

The most complete, detailed, authoritative and comprehensive work ever done on Mauser bolt rifles. Completely revised deluxe 3rd edition.

Mauser Military Rifles of the World, 2nd Edition, by Robert Ball, Krause Publications, Iola, WI, 2000. 304 pp., illustrated with 1,000 b&w photos and a 48 page color section. $44.95.

This 2nd edition brings more than 100 new photos of these historic rifles and the wars in which they were carried.

Mauser Smallbores Sporting, Target and Training Rifles, by Jon Speed, Collector Grade Publications, Cobourg, Ontario, Canada 1998. 349 pp., illustrated. $67.50.

A history of all the smallbore sporting, target and training rifles produced by the legendary Mauser-Werke of Obendorf Am Neckar.

Military Holsters of World War 2, by Eugene J. Bender, Rowe Publications, Rochester, NY, 1998. 200 pp., illustrated. $45.00.

A revised edition with a new price guide of the most definitive book on this subject.

Military Pistols of Japan, by Fred L. Honeycutt, Jr., Julin Books, Palm Beach Gardens, FL, 1997. 168 pp., illus. $42.00.

Covers every aspect of military pistol production in Japan through WWII.

The Military Remington Rolling Block Rifle, by George Layman, Pioneer Press, TN, 1998. 146 pp., illus. Paper covers. $24.95.

A standard reference for those with an interest in the Remington rolling block family of firearms.

Military Rifles of Japan, 5th Edition, by F.L. Honeycutt, Julin Books, Lake Park, FL, 1999. 208 pp., illus. $42.00.

A new revised and updated edition. Includes the early Murata-period markings, etc.

Military Small Arms Data Book, by Ian V. Hogg, Stackpole Books, Mechanicsburg, PA, 1999. $44.95. 336 pp., illustrated.

Data on more than 1,500 weapons. Covers a vast range of weapons from pistols to anti-tank rifles. Essential data, 1870-2000, in one volume.

Modern Beretta Firearms, by Gene Gangarosa, Jr., Stoeger Publishing Co., So. Hackensack, NJ, 1994. 288 pp., illus. Paper covers. $16.95.

Traces all models of modern Beretta pistols, rifles, machine guns and combat shotguns.

Modern Gun Values, The Gun Digest Book of, 10th Edition, by the Editors of Gun Digest, DBI Books, a division of Krause Publications, Iola, WI., 1996. 560 pp. illus. Paper covers. $21.95.

Greatly updated and expanded edition describing and valuing over 7,000 firearms manufactured from 1900 to 1996. The standard for valuing modern firearms.

Modern Gun Identification & Value Guide, 13th Edition, by Russell and Steve Quertermous, Collector Books, Paducah, KY, 1998. 504 pp., illus. Paper covers. $14.95.

Features current values for over 2,500 models of rifles, shotguns and handguns, with over 1,800 illustrations.

More Single Shot Rifles, by James C. Grant, The Gun Room Press, Highland Park, NJ, 1976. 324 pp., illus. $35.00.

Details the guns made by Frank Wesson, Milt Farrow, Holden, Borchardt, Stevens, Remington, Winchester, Ballard and Peabody-Martini.

Mortimer, the Gunmakers, 1753-1923, by H. Lee Munson, Andrew Mowbray Inc., Lincoln, RI, 1992. 320 pp., illus. $65.00.

Seen through a single, dominant, English gunmaking dynasty this fascinating study provides a window into the classical era of firearms artistry.

The Mosin-Nagant Rifle, by Terence W. Lapin, North Cape Publications, Tustin, CA, 1998. 30 pp., illustrated. Paper covers. $19.95.

The first ever complete book on the Mosin-Nagant rifle written in English. Covers every variation.

The Navy Luger, by Joachim Gortz and John Walter, Handgun Press, Glenview, IL, 1988. 128 pp., illus. $24.95.

The 9mm Pistole 1904 and the Imperial German Navy. A concise illustrated history.

The New World of Russian Small Arms and Ammunition, by Charlie Cutshaw, Paladin Press, Boulder, CO, 1998. 160 pp., illustrated. $42.95.

Detailed descriptions, specifications and first-class illustrations of the AN-94, PSS silent pistol, Bizon SMG, Saifa-12 tactical shotgun, the GP-25 grenade launcher and more cutting edge Russian weapons.

The Number 5 Jungle Carbine, by Alan M. Petrillo, Excalibur Publications, Latham, NY, 1994. 32 pp., illus. Paper covers. $7.95.

A comprehensive treatment of the rifle that collectors have come to call the "Jungle Carbine"—the Lee-Enfield Number 5, Mark 1.

The '03 Era: When Smokeless Revolutionized U.S. Riflery, by Clark S. Campbell, Collector Grade Publications, Inc., Ontario, Canada, 1994. 334 pp., illus. $44.50.

A much-expanded version of Campbell's *The '03 Springfields*, representing forty years of in-depth research into "all things '03."

Observations on Colt's Second Contract, November 2, 1847, by G. Maxwell Longfield and David T. Basnett, Museum Restoration Service, Bloomfield, Ontario, Canada, 1997. 36 pp., illus. Paper covers. $6.95.

This study traces the history and the construction of the Second Model Colt Dragoon supplied in 1848 to the U.S. Cavalry.

Official Guide to Gunmarks, 3rd Edition, by Robert H. Balderson, House of Collectibles, New York, NY, 1996. 367 pp., illus. Paper covers. $15.00.

Identifies manufacturers' marks that appear on American and foreign pistols, rifles and shotguns.

THE HANDGUNNER'S LIBRARY

Official Price Guide to Gun Collecting, by R.L. Wilson, Ballantine/House of Collectibles, New York, NY, 1998. 450 pp., illus. Paper covers. $21.50.

Covers more than 30,000 prices from Colt revolvers to Winchester rifles and shotguns to German Lugers and British sporting rifles and game guns.

Official Price Guide to Military Collectibles, 6th Edition, by Richard J. Austin, Random House, Inc., New York, NY, 1998. 200 pp., illus. Paper cover. $20.00.

Covers weapons and other collectibles from wars of the distant and recent past. More than 4,000 prices are listed. Illustrated with 400 black & white photos plus a full-color insert.

The Official Soviet SVD Manual, by Major James F. Gebhardt (Ret.) Paladin Press, Boulder, CO, 1999. 112 pp., illustrated. Paper covers. $15.00.

Operating instructions for the 7.62mm Dragunov, the first Russian rifle developed from scratch specifically for sniping.

Old Gunsights: A Collector's Guide, 1850 to 2000, by Nicholas Stroebel, Krause Publications, Iola, WI, 1998. 320 pp., illus. Paper covers. $29.95

An in-depth and comprehensive examination of old gunsights and the rifles on which they were used to get accurate feel for prices in this expanding market.

Old Rifle scopes, by Nicholas Stroebel, Krause Publications, Iola, WI, 2000. 400 pp., illustrated. Paper covers. $31.95.

This comprehensive collector's guide takes aim at more than 120 scope makers and 60 mount makers and features photos and current market values for 300 scopes and mounts manufactured from 1950-1985.

The P-08 Parabellum Luger Automatic Pistol, edited by J. David McFarland, Desert Publications, Cornville, AZ, 1982. 20 pp., illus. Paper covers. $11.95.

Covers every facet of the Luger, plus a listing of all known Luger models.

Packing Iron, by Richard C. Rattenbury, Zon International Publishing, Millwood, NY, 1993. 216 pp., illus $45.00.

The best book yet produced on pistol holsters and rifle scabbards. Over 300 variations of holster and scabbards are illustrated in large, clear plates.

Parabellum: A Technical History of Swiss Lugers, by Vittorio Bobba, Priuli & Verlucca, Editori, Torino, Italy, 1996. Italian and English text. Illustrated. $100.00.

Patents for Inventions, Class 119 (Small Arms), 1855-1930. British Patent Office, Armory Publications, Oceanside, CA, 1993. 7 volume set. $250.00.

Contains 7980 abridged patent descriptions and their sectioned line drawings, plus a 37-page alphabetical index of the patentees.

Pattern Dates for British Ordnance Small Arms, 1718-1783, by DeWitt Bailey, Thomas Publications, Gettysburg, PA, 1997. 116 pp., illus. Paper covers. $20.00

The weapons discussed in this work are those carried by troops sent to North America between 1737 and 1783, or shipped to them as replacement arms while in America.

The Pitman Notes on U.S. Martial Small Arms and Ammunition, 1776-1933, Volume 2, Revolvers and Automatic Pistols, by Brig. Gen. John Pitman, Thomas Publications, Gettysburg, PA, 1990. 192 pp., illus. $29.95.

A most important primary source of information on United States military small arms and ammunition.

The Plains Rifle, by Charles Hanson, Gun Room Press, Highland Park, NJ, 1989. 169 pp., illus. $35.00.

All rifles that were made with the plainsman in mind, including pistols.

Powder and Ball Small Arms, by Martin Pegler, Windrow & Green, London, 1998. 128 pp., illus. $39.95.

Part of the new "Live Firing Classic Weapons" series featuring full color photos of experienced shooters dressed in authentic costumes handling, loading and firing historic weapons.

The Powder Flask Book, by Ray Riling, R&R Books, Livonia, NY, 1993. 514 pp., illus. $69.95.

The complete book on flasks of the 19th century. Exactly scaled pictures of 1,600 flasks are illustrated.

Proud Promise: French Autoloading Rifles, 1898-1979, by Jean Huon, Collector Grade Publications, Inc., Cobourg, Ont., Canada, 1995. 216 pp., illus. $39.95.

The author has finally set the record straight about the importance of French contributions to modern arms design.

E. C. Prudhomme's Gun Engraving Review, by E. C. Prudhomme, R&R Books, Livonia, NY, 1994. 164 pp., illus. $60.00.

As a source for engravers and collectors, this book is an indispensable guide to styles and techniques of the world's foremost engravers.

Purdey Gun and Rifle Makers: The Definitive History, by Donald Dallas, Quiller Press, London, 2000. 245 pp., illus. Color throughout. $100.00

A limited edition of 3,000 copies. Signed and Numbered. With a PURDEY book plate.

Reloading Tools, Sights and Telescopes for Single Shot Rifles, by Gerald O. Kelver, Brighton, CO, 1982. 163 pp., illus. Paper covers. $13.95.

A listing of most of the famous makers of reloading tools, sights and telescopes with a brief description of the products they manufactured.

The Remington-Lee Rifle, by Eugene F. Myszkowski, Excalibur Publications, Latham, NY, 1995. 100 pp., illus. Paper covers. $22.50.

Features detailed descriptions, including serial number ranges, of each model from the first Lee Magazine Rifle produced for the U.S. Navy to the last Remington-Lee Small Bores shipped to the Cuban Rural Guard.

Revolvers of the British Services 1854-1954, by W.H.J. Chamberlain and A.W.F. Taylerson, Museum Restoration Service, Ottawa, Canada, 1989. 80 pp., illus. $27.50.

Covers the types issued among many of the United Kingdom's naval, land or air services.

Rhode Island Arms Makers & Gunsmiths, by William O. Archibald, Andrew Mowbray, Inc., Lincoln, RI, 1990. 108 pp., illus. $16.50.

A serious and informative study of an important area of American arms making.

Rifles of the World, by Oliver Achard, Chartwell Books, Inc., Edison, NJ, 141 pp., illus. $24.95.

A unique insight into the world of long guns, not just rifles, but also shotguns, carbines and all the usual multi-barreled guns that once were so popular with European hunters, especially in Germany and Austria.

The Rock Island '03, by C.S. Ferris, C.S. Ferris, Arvada, CO, 1993. 58 pp., illus. Paper covers. $12.50.

A monograph of interest to the collector or historian concentrating on the U.S. M1903 rifle made by the less publicized of our two producing facilities.

Round Ball to Rimfire, Vol. 1, by Dean Thomas, Thomas Publications, Gettysburg, PA, 1997. 144 pp., illus. $40.00.

The first of a two-volume set of the most complete history and guide for all small arms ammunition used in the Civil War. The information includes data from research and development to the arsenals that created it.

Ruger and his Guns, by R.L. Wilson, Simon & Schuster, New York, NY, 1996. 358 pp., illus. $65.00.

A history of the man, the company and their firearms.

Russell M. Catron and His Pistols, by Warren H. Buxton, Ucross Books, Los Alamos, NM, 1998. 224 pp., illustrated. Paper covers. $49.50.

An unknown American firearms inventor and manufacturer of the mid twentieth century. Military, commerical, ammunition.

The SAFN-49 and The FAL, by Joe Poyer and Dr. Richard Feirman, North Cape Publications, Tustin, CA, 1998. 160 pp., illus. Paper covers. $14.95.

The first complete overview of the SAFN-49 battle rifle, from its pre-World War 2 beginnings to its military service in countries as diverse as the Belgian Congo and Argentina. The FAL was "light" version of the SAFN-49 and it became the Free World's most adopted battle rifle.

Sam Colt's Own Record 1847, by John Parsons, Wolfe Publishing Co., Prescott, AZ, 1992. 167 pp., illus. $24.50.

Chronologically presented, the correspondence published here completes the account of the manufacture, in 1847, of the Walker Model Colt revolver.

J. P. Sauer & Sohn, Sauer "Dein Waffenkamerad" Volume 2, by Cate & Krause, Walsworth Publishing, Chattanooga, TN, 2000. 440 pp., illus. $79.00.

A historical study of Sauer automatic pistols. This new volume includes a great deal of new knowledge that has surfaced about the firm J.P. Sauer. You will find new photos, documentation, serial number ranges and historial facts which will expand the knowledge and interest in the oldest and best of the German firearms companies.

Scottish Firearms, by Claude Blair and Robert Woosnam-Savage, Museum Restoration Service, Bloomfield, Ont., Canada, 1995. 52 pp., illus. Paper covers. $8.95.

This revision of the first book devoted entirely to Scottish firearms is supplemented by a register of surviving Scottish long guns.

The Scottish Pistol, by Martin Kelvin. Fairleigh Dickinson University Press, Dist. By Associated University Presses, Cranbury, NJ, 1997. 256 pp., illus. $49.50.

The Scottish pistol, its history, manufacture and design.

Sharps Firearms, by Frank Seller, Frank M. Seller, Denver, CO, 1998. 358 pp., illus. $55.00.

Traces the development of Sharps firearms with full range of guns made including all martial variations.

Simeon North: First Official Pistol Maker of the United States, by S. North and R. North, The Gun Room Press, Highland Park, NJ, 1972. 207 pp., illus. $15.95.

Reprint of the rare first edition.

The SKS Carbine, by Steve Kehaya and Joe Poyer, North Cape Publications, Tustin, CA, 1997. 150 pp., illus. Paper covers. $16.95.

The first comprehensive examination of a major historical firearm used through the Vietnam conflict to the diamond fields of Angola.

The SKS Type 45 Carbines, by Duncan Long, Desert Publications, El Dorado, AZ, 1992. 110 pp., illus. Paper covers. $19.95

Covers the history and practical aspects of operating, maintaining and modifying this abundantly available rifle.

Smith & Wesson 1857-1945, by Robert J. Neal and Roy G. Jinks, R&R Books, Livonia, NY, 1996. 434 pp., illus. $50.00.

The bible for all existing and aspiring Smith & Wesson collectors.

Sniper Variations of the German K98k Rifle, by Richard D. Law, Collector Grade Publications, Ontario, Canada, 1997. 240 pp., illus. $47.50.

Volume 2 of "Backbone of the Wehrmacht" the author's in-depth study of the German K98k rifle. This volume concentrates on the telescopic-sighted rifle of choice for most German snipers during World War 2.

Southern Derringers of the Mississippi Valley, by Turner Kirkland, Pioneer Press, Tenn., 1971. 80 pp., illus., paper covers. $4.00.

A guide for the collector, and a much-needed study.

Soviet Russian Postwar Military Pistols and Cartridges, by Fred A. Datig, Handgun Press, Glenview, IL, 1988. 152 pp., illus. $29.95.

Thoroughly researched, this definitive sourcebook covers the development and adoption of the Makarov, Stechkin and the new PSM pistols. Also included in this source book is coverage on Russian clandestine weapons and pistol cartridges.

Soviet Russian Tokarev "TT" Pistols and Cartridges 1929-1953, by Fred Datig, Graphic Publishers, Santa Ana, CA, 1993. 168 pp., illus. $39.95.

Details of rare arms and their accessories are shown in hundreds of photos. It also contains a complete bibliography and index.

Soviet Small-Arms and Ammunition, by David Bolotin, Handgun Press, Glenview, IL, 1996. 264 pp., illus. $49.95.

An authoritative and complete book on Soviet small arms.

Sporting Collectibles, by Jim and Vivian Karsnitz, Schiffer Publishing Ltd., West Chester, PA, 1992. 160 pp., illus. Paper covers. $29.95.

The fascinating world of hunting related collectibles presented in an informative text.

The Springfield 1903 Rifles, by Lt. Col. William S. Brophy, USAR, Ret., Stackpole Books Inc., Harrisburg, PA, 1985. 608 pp., illus. $75.00.

The illustrated, documented story of the design, development, and production of all the models, appendages, and accessories.

Springfield Armory Shoulder Weapons 1795-1968, by Robert W.D. Ball, Antique Trader Books, Dubuque, IA, 1998. 264 pp., illus. $34.95.

This book documents the 255 basic models of rifles, including test and trial rifles, produced by the Springfield Armory. It features the entire history of rifles and carbines manufactured at the Armory, the development of each weapon with specific operating characteristics and procedures.

Springfield Model 1903 Service Rifle Production and Alteration, 1905-1910, by C.S. Ferris and John Beard, Arvada, CO, 1995. 66 pp., illus. Paper covers. $12.50.

A highly recommended work for any serious student of the Springfield Model 1903 rifle.

Springfield Shoulder Arms 1795-1865, by Claud E. Fuller, S. & S. Firearms, Glendale, NY, 1996. 76 pp., illus. Paper covers. $17.95.

Exact reprint of the scarce 1930 edition of one of the most definitive works on Springfield flintlock and percussion muskets ever published.

Standard Catalog of Firearms, 11th Edition, by Ned Schwing, Krause Publications, Iola, WI, 2001. 1328 Pages, illustrated. 6,000+ b&w photos plus a 16-page color section. Paper covers. $32.95.

This is the largest, most comprehensive and best-selling firearm book of all time! And this year's edition is a blockbuster for both shooters and firearm collectors. More than 12,000 firearms are listed and priced in up to six grades of condition. That's almost 80,000 prices! Gun enthusiasts will love the new full-color section of photos highlighting the finest firearms sold at auction this past year –including the new record for an American historical firearm: $684,000!

Standard Catalog of Winchester, 1st Edition, edited by David D. Kowalski, Krause Publications, Iola, WI, 2000. 704 pp., illustrated with 2,000 B&W photos and 75 color photos. Paper covers. $39.95.

This book identifies and values more than 5,000 collectibles, including firearms, cartridges shotshells, fishing tackle, sporting goods and tools manufactured by Winchester Repeating Arms Co.

Steel Canvas: The Art of American Arms, by R.L. Wilson, Random House, NY, 1995, 384 pp., illus. $65.00.

Presented here for the first time is the breathtaking panorama of America's extraordinary engravers and embellishers of arms, from the 1700s to modern times.

Stevens Pistols & Pocket Rifles, by K.L. Cope, Museum Restoration Service, Alexandria Bay, NY, 1992. 114 pp., illus. $24.50.

This is the story of the guns and the man who designed them and the company which he founded to make them.

A Study of Colt Conversions and Other Percussion Revolvers, by R. Bruce McDowell, Krause Publications, Iola, WI, 1997. 464 pp., illus. $39.95.

The ultimate reference detailing Colt revolvers that have been converted from percussion to cartridge.

The Sumptuous Flaske, by Herbert G. Houze, Andrew Mowbray, Inc., Lincoln, RI, 1989. 158 pp., illus. Soft covers. $35.00.

Catalog of a recent show at the Buffalo Bill Historical Center bringing together some of the finest European and American powder flasks of the 16th to 19th centuries.

The Swedish Mauser Rifles, by Steve Kehaya and Joe Poyer, North Cape Publications, Tustin, CA, 1999. 267 pp., illustrated. Paper covers. $19.95.

Every known variation of the Swedish Mauser carbine and rifle is described including all match and target rifles and all sniper fersions. Includes serial number and production data.

Televisions Cowboys, Gunfighters & Cap Pistols, by Rudy A. D'Angelo, Antique Trader Books, Norfolk, VA, 1999. 287 pp., illustrated in color and black and white. Paper covers. $31.95.

Over 850 beautifully photographed color and black and white images of cap guns, actors, and the characters they portrayed in the "Golden Age of TV Westerns. With accurate descriptions and current values.

Thompson: The American Legend, by Tracie L. Hill, Collector Grade Publications, Ontario, Canada, 1996. 584 pp., illus. $85.00.

The story of the first American submachine gun. All models are featured and discussed.

Toys That Shoot and Other Neat Stuff, by James Dundas, Schiffer Books, Atglen, PA, 1999. 112 pp., illustrated. Paper covers. $24.95.

Shooting toys from the twentieth century, especially 1920's to 1960's, in over 420 color photographs of BB guns, cap shooters, marble shooters, squirt guns and more. Complete with a price guide.

The Trapdoor Springfield, by M.D. Waite and B.D. Ernst, The Gun Room Press, Highland Park, NJ, 1983. 250 pp., illus. $39.95.

The first comprehensive book on the famous standard military rifle of the 1873-92 period.

Treasures of the Moscow Kremlin: Arsenal of the Russian Tsars, A Royal Armories and the Moscow Kremlin exhibition. HM Tower of London 13, June 1998 to 11 September, 1998. BAS Printers, Over Wallop, Hampshire, England. xxii plus 192 pp. over 180 color illustrations. Text in English and Russian. $65.00.

For this exhibition catalog each of the 94 objects on display are photographed and described in detail to provide a most informative record of this important exhibition.

U.S. Breech-Loading Rifles and Carbines, Cal. 45, by Gen. John Pitman, Thomas Publications, Gettysburg, PA, 1992. 192 pp., illus. $29.95.

The third volume in the Pitman Notes on U.S. Martial Small Arms and Ammunition, 1776-1933. This book centers on the "Trapdoor Springfield" models.

U.S. Handguns of World War 2: The Secondary Pistols and Revolvers, by Charles W. Pate, Andrew Mowbray, Inc., Lincoln, RI, 1998. 515 pp., illus. $39.00.

This indispensable new book covers all of the American military handguns of World War 2 except for the M1911A1 Colt automatic.

United States Martial Flintlocks, by Robert M. Reilly, Mowbray Publishing Co., Lincoln, RI, 1997. 264 pp., illus. $40.00.

A comprehensive history of American flintlock longarms and handguns (mostly military) c. 1775 to c. 1840.

U.S. Martial Single Shot Pistols, by Daniel D. Hartzler and James B. Whisker, Old Bedford Village Pess, Bedford, PA, 1998. 128 pp., illus. $45.00.

A photographic chronicle of military and semi-martial pistols supplied to the U.S. Government and the several States.

U.S. Military Arms Dates of Manufacture from 1795, by George Madis, David Madis, Dallas, TX, 1989. 64 pp. Soft covers. $6.00.

Lists all U.S. military arms of collector interest alphabetically, covering about 250 models.

U.S. Military Small Arms 1816-1865, by Robert M. Reilly, The Gun Room Press, Highland Park, NJ, 1983. 270 pp., illus. $39.95.

Covers every known type of primary and secondary martial firearms used by Federal forces.

U.S. M1 Carbines: Wartime Production, by Craig Riesch, North Cape Publications, Tustin, CA, 1994. 72 pp., illus. Paper covers. $16.95.

Presents only verifiable and accurate information. Each part of the M1 Carbine is discussed fully in its own section; including markings and finishes.

U.S. Naval Handguns, 1808-1911, by Fredrick R. Winter, Andrew Mowbray Publishers, Lincoln, RI, 1990. 128 pp., illus. $26.00.

The story of U.S. Naval Handguns spans an entire century—included are sections on each of the important naval handguns within the period.

Walther: A German Legend, by Manfred Kersten, Safari Press, Inc., Huntington Beach, CA, 2000. 400 pp., illustrated. $85.00.

This comprehensive book covers, in rich detail, all aspects of the company and its guns, including an illustrious and rich history, the WW2 years, all the pistols (models 1 through 9), the P-38, P-88, the long guns, .22 rifles, centerfires, Wehrmacht guns, and even a gun that could shoot around a corner.

Walther Pistols: Models 1 Through P99, Factory Variations and Copies, by Dieter H. Marschall, Ucross Books, Los Alamos, NM. 2000. 140 pages, with 140 b & w illustrations, index. Paper Covers. $19.95.

This is the English translation, revised and updated, of the highly successful and widely acclaimed German language edition. This book provides the collector with a reference guide and overview of the entire line of the Walther military, police, and self-defense pistols from the very first to the very latest. Models 1-9, PP, PPK, MP, AP, HP, P.38, P1, P4, P38K, P5, P88, P99 and the Manurhin models. Variations, where issued, serial ranges, calibers, marks, proofs, logos, and design aspects in an astonishing quantity and variety are crammed into this very well researched and highly regarded work.

The Walther Handgun Story: A Collector's and Shooter's Guide, by Gene Gangarosa, Steiger Publications, 1999. 300., illustrated. Paper covers. $21.95.

Covers the entire history of the Walther empire. Illustrated with over 250 photos.

Walther P-38 Pistol, by Maj. George Nonte, Desert Publications, Cornville, AZ, 1982. 100 pp., illus. Paper covers. $11.95.

Complete volume on one of the most famous handguns to come out of WWII. All models covered.

Walther Models PP & PPK, 1929-1945 – Volume 1, by James L. Rankin, Coral Gables, FL, 1974. 142 pp., illus. $40.00

Complete coverage on the subject as to finish, proofmarks and Nazi Party inscriptions.

Walther Volume II, Engraved, Presentation and Standard Models, by James L. Rankin, J.L. Rankin, Coral Gables, FL, 1977. 112 pp., illus. $40.00.

The new Walther book on embellished versions and standard models. Has 88 photographs, including many color plates.

Walther, Volume III, 1908-1980, by James L. Rankin, Coral Gables, FL, 1981. 226 pp., illus. $40.00.

Covers all models of Walther handguns from 1908 to date, includes holsters, grips and magazines.

Winchester: An American Legend, by R.L. Wilson, Random House, New York, NY, 1991. 403 pp., illus. $65.00.

The official history of Winchester firearms from 1849 to the present.

Winchester Bolt Action Military & Sporting Rifles 1877 to 1937, by Herbert G. Houze, Andrew Mowbray Publishing, Lincoln, RI, 1998. 295 pp., illus. $45.00.

Winchester was the first American arms maker to commercially manufacture a bolt action repeating rifle, and this book tells the exciting story of these Winchester bolt actions.

The Winchester Book, by George Madis, David Madis Gun Book Distributor, Dallas, TX, 1986. 650 pp., illus. $49.50.

A new, revised 25th anniversary edition of this classic book on Winchester firearms. Complete serial ranges have been added.

Winchester Dates of Manufacture 1849-1984, by George Madis, Art & Reference House, Brownsboro, TX, 1984. 59 pp. $9.95.

A most useful work, compiled from records of the Winchester factory.

Winchester Engraving, by R.L. Wilson, Beinfeld Books, Springs, CA, 1989. 500 pp., illus. $135.00.

A classic reference work of value to all arms collectors.

The Winchester Handbook, by George Madis, Art & Reference House, Lancaster, TX, 1982. 287 pp., illus. $24.95.

The complete line of Winchester guns, with dates of manufacture, serial numbers, etc.

The Winchester-Lee Rifle, by Eugene Myszkowski, Excalibur Publications, Tucson, AZ 2000. 96 pp., illustrated. Paper Covers. $22.95

The development of the Lee Straight Pull, the cartridge and the approval for military use. Covers details of the inventor and memorabilia of Winchester-Lee related material.

Winchester Lever Action Repeating Firearms, Vol. 1, The Models of 1866, 1873 and 1876, by Arthur Pirkle, North Cape Publications, Tustin, CA, 1995. 112 pp., illus. Paper covers. $19.95.

Complete, part-by-part description, including dimensions, finishes, markings and variations throughout the production run of these fine, collectible guns.

Winchester Lever Action Repeating Rifles, Vol. 2, The Models of 1886 and 1892, by Arthur Pirkle, North Cape Publications, Tustin, CA, 1996. 150 pp., illus. Paper covers. $19.95.

Describes each model on a part-by-part basis by serial number range complete with finishes, markings and changes.

Winchester Lever Action Repeating Rifles, Volume 3, The Model of 1894, by Arthur Pirkle, North Cape Publications, Tustin, CA, 1998. 150 pp., illus. Paper covers. $19.95.

The first book ever to provide a detailed description of the Model 1894 rifle and carbine.

The Winchester Lever Legacy, by Clyde "Snooky" Williamson, Buffalo Press, Zachary, LA, 1988. 664 pp., illustrated. $75.00

A book on reloading for the different calibers of the Winchester lever action rifle.

The Winchester Model 94: The First 100 Years, by Robert C. Renneberg, Krause Publications, Iola, WI, 1991. 208 pp., illus. $34.95.

Covers the design and evolution from the early years up to the many different editions that exist today.

Winchester Rarities, by Webster, Krause Publications, Iola, WI, 2000. 208 pp., with over 800 color photos, illus. $49.95.

This book details the rarest of the rare; the one-of-a-kind items and the advertising pieces from years gone by. With nearly 800 full color photos and detailed pricing provided by experts in the field, this book gives collectors and enthusiasts everything they need.

Winchester Shotguns and Shotshells, by Ronald W. Stadt, Krause Publications, Iola, WI, 1995. 256 pp., illus. $34.95.

The definitive book on collectible Winchester shotguns and shotshells manufactured through 1961.

The Winchester Single-Shot- Volume 1; A History and Analysis, by John Campbell, Andrew Mowbray, Inc., Lincoln RI, 1995. 272 pp., illus. $55.00.

Covers every important aspect of this highly-collectible firearm.

The Winchester Single-Shot- Volume 2; Old Secrets and New Discoveries, by John Campbell, Andrew Mowbray, Inc., Lincoln RI, 2000. 280 pp., illus. $55.00.

An exciting follow-up to the classic first volume.

Winchester Slide-Action Rifles, Volume 1: Model 1890 & 1906, by Ned Schwing, Krause Publications, Iola, WI, 1992. 352 pp., illus. $39.95.

First book length treatment of models 1890 & 1906 with over 50 charts and tables showing significant new information about caliber style and rarity.

Winchester Slide-Action Rifles, Volume 2: Model 61 & Model 62, by Ned Schwing, Krause Publications, Iola, WI, 1993. 256 pp., illus. $34.95.

A complete historic look into the Model 61 and the Model 62. These favorite slide-action guns receive a thorough presentation which takes you to the factory to explore receivers, barrels, markings, stocks, stampings and engraving in complete detail.

Winchester's North West Mounted Police Carbines and other Model 1876 Data, by Lewis E. Yearout, The author, Great Falls, MT, 1999. 224 pp., illustrated. Paper covers. $38.00

An impressive accumulation of the facts on the Model 1876, with particular empasis on those purchased for the North West Mounted Police.

Worldwide Webley and the Harrington and Richardson Connection, by Stephen Cuthbertson, Ballista Publishing and Distributing Ltd., Gabriola Island, Canada, 1999. 259 pp., illus. $50.00

A masterpiece of scholarship. Over 350 photographs plus 75 original documents, patent drawings, and advertisements accompany the text.

GENERAL

Action Shooting: Cowboy Style, by John Taffin, Krause Publications, Iola, WI, 1999. 320 pp., illustrated. $39.95.

Details on the guns and ammunition. Explanations of the rules used for many events. The essential cowboy wardrobe.

Advanced Muzzleloader's Guide, by Toby Bridges, Stoeger Publishing Co., So. Hackensack, NJ, 1985. 256 pp., illus. Paper covers. $14.95.

The complete guide to muzzle-loading rifles, pistols and shotguns—flintlock and percussion.

Aids to Musketry for Officers & NCOs, by Capt. B.J. Friend, Excalibur Publications, Latham, NY, 1996. 40 pp., illus. Paper covers. $7.95.

A facsimile edition of a pre-WWI British manual filled with useful information for training the common soldier.

Air Gun Digest, 3rd Edition, by J.I. Galan, DBI Books, a division of Krause Publications, Iola, WI, 1995. 258 pp., illus. Paper covers. $19.95

Everything from A to Z on air gun history, trends and technology.

American and Imported Arms, Ammunition and Shooting Accessories, Catalog No. 18 of the Shooter's Bible, Stoeger, Inc., reprinted by Fayette Arsenal, Fayetteville, NC, 1988. 142 pp., illus. Paper covers. $10.95.

A facsimile reprint of the 1932 Stoeger's Shooter's Bible.

America's Great Gunmakers, by Wayne van Zwoll, Stoeger Publishing Co., So. Hackensack, NJ, 1992. 288 pp., illus. Paper covers. $16.95.

This book traces in great detail the evolution of guns and ammunition in America and the men who formed the companies that produced them.

Ammunition: Small Arms, Grenades and Projected Munitions, by Ian V. Hogg, Greenhill Books, London, England, 1998. 144 pp., illustrated. $22.95.

The best concise guide to modern ammunition. Wide-ranging and international coverage. Detailed specifications and illustrations.

Armed and Female, by Paxton Quigley, E.P. Dutton, New York, NY, 1989. 237 pp., illus. $16.95.

The first complete book on one of the hottest subjects in the media today, the arming of the American woman.

Arming the Glorious Cause: Weapons of the Second War for Independence, by James B. Whisker, Daniel D. Hartzler and Larry W. Yantz, R & R Books, Livonia, NY, 1998. 175 pp., illustrated. $45.00.

A photographic study of Confederate weapons.

Arms and Armour in Antiquity and the Middle Ages, by Charles Boutell, Stackpole Books, Mechanicsburg, PA, 1996. 352 pp., illus. $22.95.

Detailed descriptions of arms and armor, the development of tactics and the outcome of specific battles.

Arms & Armor in the Art Institute of Chicago, by Walter J. Karcheski, Jr., Bulfinch Press, Boston, MA, 1995. 128 pp., illus. $35.00.

Now, for the first time, the Art Institute of Chicago's arms and armor collection is presented in the visual delight of 103 color illustrations.

Arms for the Nation: Springfield Longarms, edited by David C. Clark, Scott A. Duff, Export, PA, 1994. 73 pp., illus. Paper covers. $9.95.

A brief history of the Springfield Armory and the arms made there.

Arsenal of Freedom, The Springfield Armory, 1890-1948: A Year-by-Year Account Drawn from Official Records, compiled and edited by Lt. Col. William S. Brophy, USAR Ret., Andrew Mowbray, Inc., Lincoln, RI, 1991. 400 pp., illus. Soft covers. $29.95.

A "must buy" for all students of American military weapons, equipment and accoutrements.

Assault Pistols, Rifles and Submachine Guns, by Duncan Long, Paladin Press, Boulder, CO, 1997, 8 1/2 x 11, soft cover, photos, illus. 152 pp. $21.95.

This book offers up-to-date, practical information on how to operate and field-strip modern military, police and civilian combat weapons. Covers new developments and trends such as the use of fiber optics, liquid-recoil systems and lessening of barrel length are covered. Troubleshooting procedures, ballistic tables and a list of manufacturers and distributors are also included.

Assault Weapons, 5th Edition, The Gun Digest Book of, edited by Jack Lewis and David E. Steele, DBI Books, a division of Krause Publications, Iola, WI, 2000. 256 pp., illustrated. Paper covers. $21.95.

This is the latest word on true assault weaponry in use today by international military and law enforcement organizations.

The Belgian Rattlesnake: The Lewis Automatic Machine Gun, by William M. Easterly, Collector Grade Publications, Inc., Cobourg, Ont. Canada, 1998. 542 pp., illus. $79.95.

A social and technical biography of the Lewis automatic machine gun and its inventors.

The Big Guns: Civil War Siege, Seacoast, and Naval Cannon, by Edwin Olmstead, Wayne E. Stark and Spencer C. Tucker, Museum Restoration Service, Bloomfield, Ontario, Canada, 1997. 360 pp., illus. $80.00.

This book is designed to identify and record the heavy guns available to both sides during the Civil War.

Blackpowder Loading Manual, 3rd Edition, by Sam Fadala, DBI Books, a division of Krause Publications, Iola, WI, 1995. 368 pp., illus. Paper covers. $20.95.

Revised and expanded edition of this landmark blackpowder loading book. Covers hundreds of loads for most of the popular blackpowder rifles, handguns and shotguns.

Bolt Action Rifles, 3rd Edition, by Frank de Haas, DBI Books, a division of Krause Publications, Iola, WI, 1995. 528 pp., illus. Paper covers. $24.95.

A revised edition of the most definitive work on all major bolt-action rifle designs.

The Book of the Crossbow, by Sir Ralph Payne-Gallwey, Dover Publications, Mineola, NY, 1996. 416 pp., illus. Paper covers. $14.95.

Unabridged republication of the scarce 1907 London edition of the book on one of the most devastating hand weapons of the Middle Ages.

Bows and Arrows of the Native Americans, by Jim Hamm, Lyons & Burford Publishers, New York, NY, 1991. 156 pp., illus. $19.95.

A complete step-by-step guide to wooden bows, sinew-backed bows, composite bows, strings, arrows and quivers.

British Small Arms of World War 2, by Ian D. Skennerton, I.D.S.A. Books, Piqua, OH, 1988. 110 pp., 37 illus. $25.00.

"Carbine," the Story of David Marshall Williams, by Ross E. Beard, Jr. Phillips Publications, Williamstown, NJ, 1999. 225 pp., illus. $29.95.

The story of the firearms genius, David Marshall "Carbine" Williams. From prison to the pinnacles of fame, the tale of this North Carolinian is inspiring. The author details many of Williams' firearms inventions and developments.

Combat Handgunnery, 4th Edition, The Gun Digest Book of, by Chuck Taylor, DBI Books, a division of Krause Publications, Iola, WI, 1997. 256 pp., illus. Paper covers. $18.95.

This edition looks at real world combat handgunnery from three different perspectives—military, police and civilian.

The Complete Blackpowder Handbook, 3rd Edition, by Sam Fadala, DBI Books, a division of Krause Publications, Iola, WI, 1997. 400 pp., illus. Paper covers. $21.95.

Expanded and completely rewritten edition of the definitive book on the subject of blackpowder.

The Complete Guide to Game Care and Cookery, 3rd Edition, by Sam Fadala, DBI Books, a division of Krause Publications, Iola, WI, 1994. 320 pp., illus. Paper covers. $18.95.

Over 500 photos illustrating the care of wild game in the field and at home with a separate recipe section providing over 400 tested recipes.

The Complete .50-caliber Sniper Course, by Dean Michaelis, Paladin Press, Boulder, CO, 2000. 576 pp., illustrated. $60.00.

The history from German Mauser T-Gewehr of World War 1 to the Soviet PTRD and beyond. Includes the author's Program of Instruction for Special Operations Hard-Target Interdiction Course.

Complete Guide to Guns & Shooting, by John Malloy, DBI Books, a division of Krause Publications, Iola, WI, 1995. 256 pp., illus. Paper covers. $18.95.

What every shooter and gun owner should know about firearms, ammunition, shooting techniques, safety, collecting and much more.

Cowboy Action Shooting, by Charly Gullett, Wolfe Publishing Co., Prescott, AZ, 1995. 400 pp., illus. Paper covers. $24.50.

The fast growing of the shooting sports is comprehensively covered in this text—the guns, loads, tactics and the fun and flavor of this Old West era competition.

Crossbows, edited by Roger Combs, DBI Books, a division of Krause Publications, Iola, WI, 1986. 192 pp., illus. Paper covers. $15.95.

Complete, up-to-date coverage of the hottest bow going—and the most controversial.

Custom Firearms Engraving, by Tom Turpin, Krause Publications, Iola, WI, 1999. 208 pp., illustrated. $49.95.

Provides a broad and comprehensive look at the world of firearms engraving. The exquisite styles of more than 75 master engravers are shown on beautiful examples of handguns, rifles, shotguns, and other firearms, as well as knives.

Dead On, by Tony Noblitt and Warren Gabrilska, Paladin Press, Boulder, CO, 1998. 176 pp., illustrated. Paper covers. $22.00

The long-range marksman's guide to extreme accuracy.

Death from Above: The German FG42 Paratrooper Rifle, by Thomas B. Dugelby and R. Blake Stevens, Collector Grade Publications, Toronto, Canada, 1990. 147 pp., illus. $39.95.

The first comprehensive study of all seven models of the FG42.

Early American Flintlocks, by Daniel D. Hartzler and James B. Whisker, Bedford Valley Press, Bedford, PA 2000. 192 pp., Illustrated.

Covers early Colonial Guns, New England Guns, Pennsylvania Guns and Souther Guns.

Encyclopedia of Modern Firearms, Vol. 1, compiled and publ. by Bob Brownell, Montezuma, IA, 1959. 1057 pp. plus index, illus. $70.00. Dist. By Bob Brownell, Montezuma, IA 50171.

Massive accumulation of basic information of nearly all modern arms pertaining to "parts and assembly." Replete with arms photographs, exploded drawings, manufacturers' lists of parts, etc.

Encyclopedia of Native American Bows, Arrows and Quivers, by Steve Allely and Jim Hamm, The Lyons Press, N.Y., 1999. 160 pp., illustrated. $29.95.

A landmark book for anyone interested in archery history, or Native Americans.

The Exercise of Armes, by Jacob de Gheyn, edited and with an introduction by Bas Kist, Dover Publications, Inc., Mineola, NY, 1999. 144 pp., illustrated. Paper covers. $12.95.

Republications of all 117 engravings from the 1607 classic military manual. A meticulously accurate portrait of uniforms and weapons of the 17th century Netherlands.

Exploded Long Gun Drawings, The Gun Digest Book of, edited by Harold A. Murtz, DBI Books, a division of Krause Publications, Iola, WI, 512 pp., illus. Paper covers. $20.95.

Containing almost 500 rifle and shotgun exploded drawings.

Fighting Iron; A Metals Handbook for Arms Collectors, by Art Gogan, Mowbray Publishers, Inc., Lincoln, RI, 1999. 176 pp., illustrated. $28.00.

A guide that is easy to use, explains things in simple English and covers all of the different historical periods that we are interested in.

The Fighting Submachine Gun, Machine Pistol, and Shotgun, a Hands-On Evaluation, by Timothy J. Mullin, Paladin Press, Boulder, CO, 1999. 224 pp., illustrated. Paper covers. $35.00.

An invaluable reference for military, police and civilian shooters who may someday need to know how a specific weapon actually performs when the targets are shooting back and the margin of errors is measured in lives lost.

Fireworks: A Gunsight Anthology, by Jeff Cooper, Paladin Press, Boulder, CO, 1998. 192 pp., illus. Paper cover. $27.00

A collection of wild, hilarious, shocking and always meaningful tales from the remarkable life of an American firearms legend.

Frank Pachmayr: The Story of America's Master Gunsmith and his Guns, by John Lachuk, Safari Press, Huntington Beach, CA, 1996. 254 pp., illus. First edition, limited, signed and slipcased. $85.00; Second printing trade edition. $50.00.

The colorful and historically significant biography of Frank A. Pachmayr, America's own gunsmith emeritus.

From a Stranger's Doorstep to the Kremlin Gate, by Mikhail Kalashnikov, Ironside International Publishers, Inc., Alexandria, VA, 1999. 460 pp., illustrated. $34.95.

A biography of the most influential rifle designer of the 20th century. His AK-47 assault rifle has become the most widely used (and copied) assault rifle of this century.

The Frontier Rifleman, by H.B. LaCrosse Jr., Pioneer Press, Union City, TN, 1989. 183 pp., illus. Soft covers. $17.50.

The Frontier rifleman's clothing and equipment during the era of the American Revolution, 1760-1800.

The Gatling Gun: 19th Century Machine Gun to 21st Century Vulcan, by Joseph Berk, Paladin Press, Boulder, CO, 1991. 136 pp., illus. $34.95.

Here is the fascinating on-going story of a truly timeless weapon, from its beginnings during the Civil War to its current role as a state-of-the-art modern combat system.

THE HANDGUNNER'S LIBRARY

German Artillery of World War Two, by Ian V. Hogg, Stackpole Books, Mechanicsburg, PA, 1997. 304 pp., illus. $44.95.

Complete details of German artillery use in WWII.

Grand Old Lady of No Man's Land: The Vickers Machine Gun, by Dolf L. Goldsmith, Collector Grade Publications, Cobourg, Canada, 1994. 600 pp., illus. $79.95.

Goldsmith brings his years of experience as a U.S. Army armourer, machine gun collector and shooter to bear on the Vickers, in a book sure to become a classic in its field.

The Grenade Recognition Manual, Volume 1, U.S. Grenades & Accessories, by Darryl W. Lynn, Service Publications, Ottawa, Canada, 1998. 112 pp., illus. Paper covers. $29.95.

This new book examines the hand grenades of the United States beginning with the hand grenades of the U.S. Civil War and continues through to the present.

The Grenade Recognition Manual, Vol. 2, British and Commonwealth Grenades and Accessories, by Darryl W. Lynn, Printed by the Author, Ottawa, Canada, 2001. 201 pp., illustrated with over 200 photos and drawings. Paper covers. $29.95.

Covers British, Australian, and Canadian Grenades. It has the complete British Numbered series, most of the L series as well as the Australian and Canadian grenades in use. Also covers Launchers, fuzes and lighters, launching cartridges, fillings, and markings.

Gun Digest Treasury, 7th Edition, edited by Harold A. Murtz, DBI Books, a division of Krause Publications, Iola, WI, 1994. 320 pp., illus. Paper covers. $17.95.

A collection of some of the most interesting articles which have appeared in Gun Digest over its first 45 years.

Gun Digest 2002, 56th Edition, edited by Ken Ramage, DBI Books a division of Krause Publications, Iola, WI, 2001. 544 pp., illustrated. Paper covers. $24.95.

This all new 56th edition continues the editorial excellence, quality, content and comprehensive cataloguing that firearms enthusiasts have come to know and expect. The most read gun book in the world for the last half century.

Gun Engraving, by C. Austyn, Safari Press Publication, Huntington Beach, CA, 1998. 128 pp., plus 24 pages of color photos. $50.00.

A well-illustrated book on fine English and European gun engravers. Includes a fantastic pictorial section that lists types of engravings and prices.

Gun Notes, Volume 1, by Elmer Keith, Safari Press, Huntington Beach, CA, 1995. 219 pp., illustrated Limited Edition, Slipcased. $75.00

A collection of Elmer Keith's most interesting columns and feature stories that appeared in "Guns & Ammo" magazine from 1961 to the late 1970's.

Gun Notes, Volume 2, by Elmer Keith, Safari Press, Huntington Beach, CA, 1997. 292 pp., illus. Limited 1st edition, numbered and signed by Keith's son. Slipcased. $75.00. Trade edition. $35.00.

Covers articles from Keith's monthly column in "Guns & Ammo" magazine during the period from 1971 through Keith's passing in 1982.

Gun Talk, edited by Dave Moreton, Winchester Press, Piscataway, NJ, 1973. 256 pp., illus. $9.95.

A treasury of original writing by the top gun writers and editors in America. Practical advice about every aspect of the shooting sports.

The Gun That Made the Twenties Roar, by Wm. J. Helmer, rev. and enlarged by George C. Nonte, Jr., The Gun Room Press, Highland Park, NJ, 1977. Over 300 pp., illus. $24.95.

Historical account of John T. Thompson and his invention, the infamous "Tommy Gun."

Gun Trader's Guide, 23rd Edition, published by Stoeger Publishing Co., Wayne, NJ, 1999. 592 pp., illus. Paper covers. $23.95.

Complete specifications and current prices for used guns. Prices of over 5,000 handguns, rifles and shotguns both foreign and domestic.

Gun Writers of Yesteryear, compiled by James Foral, Wolfe Publishing Co., Prescott, AZ, 1993. 449 pp. $35.00.

Here, from the pre-American rifleman days of 1898-1920, are collected some 80 articles by 34 writers from eight magazines.

The Gunfighter, Man or Myth? by Joseph G. Rosa, Oklahoma Press, Norman, OK, 1969. 229 pp., illus. (including weapons). Paper covers. $14.95.

A well-documented work on gunfights and gunfighters of the West and elsewhere. Great treat for all gunfighter buffs.

Gunfitting: The Quest for Perfection, by Michael Yardley, Safari Press, Huntington Beach, CA, 1995. 128 pp., illus. $24.95.

The author, a very experienced shooting instructor, examines gun stocks and gunfitting in depth.

Guns Illustrated 2002, 3rd Edition, edited by Ken Ramage, DBI Books a division of Krause Publications, Iola, WI, 1999. 352 pp., illustrated. Paper covers. $22.95.

Highly informative, technical articles on a wide range of shooting topics by some of the top writers in the industry. A catalog section lists more than 3,000 firearms currently manufactured in or imported to the U.S.

Guns & Shooting: A Selected Bibliography, by Ray Riling, Ray Riling Arms Books Co., Phila., PA, 1982. 434 pp., illus. Limited, numbered edition. $75.

A limited edition of this superb bibliographical work, the only modern listing of books devoted to guns and shooting.

Guns, Bullets, and Gunfighters, by Jim Cirillo, Paladin Press, Boulder, CO, 1996. 119 pp., illus. Paper covers. $16.00.

Lessons and tales from a modern-day gunfighter.

Guns, Loads, and Hunting Tips, by Bob Hagel, Wolfe Publishing Co., Prescott, AZ, 1986. 509 pp., illus. $19.95.

A large hardcover book packed with shooting, hunting and handloading wisdom.

Handgun Digest, 3rd Edition, edited by Chris Christian, DBI Books, a division of Krause Publications, Iola, WI, 1995. 256 pp., illus. Paper covers. $18.95.

Full coverage of all aspects of handguns and handgunning from a highly readable and knowledgeable author.

Hidden in Plain Sight, "A Practical Guide to Concealed Handgun Carry" (Revised 2nd Edition), by Trey Bloodworth and Mike Raley, Paladin Press, Boulder, CO, 1997, 5 1/2 x 8 1/2, softcover, photos, 176 pp. $20.00

Concerned with how to comfortably, discreetly and safely exercise the privileges granted by a CCW permit? This invaluable guide offers the latest advice on what to look for when choosing a CCW, how to dress for comfortable, effective concealed carry, traditional and more unconventional carry modes, accessory holsters, customized clothing and accessories, accessibility data based on draw-time comparisons and new holsters on the market. Includes 40 new manufacturer listings.

HK Assault Rifle Systems, by Duncan Long, Paladin Press, Boulder, CO, 1995. 110 pp., illus. Paper covers. $27.95.

The little known history behind this fascinating family of weapons tracing its beginnings from the ashes of World War Two to the present time.

The Hunter's Table, by Terry Libby/Recipes of Chef Richard Blondin, Countrysport Press, Selma, AL, 1999. 230 pp. $30.00.

The Countrysport book of wild game guisine.

I Remember Skeeter, compiled by Sally Jim Skelton, Wolfe Publishing Co., Prescott, AZ, 1998. 401 pp., illus. Paper covers. $19.95.

A collection of some of the beloved storyteller's famous works interspersed with anecdotes and tales from the people who knew best.

In The Line of Fire, "A Working Cop's Guide to Pistol Craft", by Michael E. Conti, Paladin Press, Boulder, CO, 1997, soft cover, photos, illus., 184 pp. $30.00

As a working cop, you want to end your patrol in the same condition you began: alive and uninjured. Improve your odds by reading and mastering the information in this book on pistol selection, stopping power, combat reloading, stoppages, carrying devices, stances, grips and Conti's "secrets" to accurate shooting.

Joe Rychertinik Reflects on Guns, Hunting, and Days Gone By, by Joe Rychertinik, Precision Shooting, Inc., Manchester, CT, 1999. 281 pp., illustrated. Paper covers. $16.95.

Thirty articles by a master story-teller.

Kill or Get Killed, by Col. Rex Applegate, Paladin Press, Boulder, CO, 1996. 400 pp., illus. $39.95.

The best and longest-selling book on close combat in history.

Larrey: Surgeon to Napoleon's Imperial Guard, by Robert G. Richardson, Quiller Press, London, 2000. 269 pp., illus. B & W photos, maps and drawings. $23.95

Not a book for the squeamish, but one full of interest, splendidly researched, bringing both the character of the Napoleonic wars and Larrey himself vividly to life. Authenticity of detail is preserved throughout.

The Long-Range War: Sniping in Vietnam, by Peter R. Senich, Paladin Press, Boulder, CO, 1994. 280 pp., illus. $49.95.

The most complete report on Vietnam-era sniping ever documented.

Manual for H&R Reising Submachine Gun and Semi-Auto Rifle, edited by George P. Dillman, Desert Publications, El Dorado, AZ, 1994. 81 pp., illus. Paper covers. $12.95.

A reprint of the Harrington & Richardson 1943 factory manual and the rare military manual on the H&R submachine gun and semi-auto rifle.

The Manufacture of Gunflints, by Sydney B.J. Skertchly, facsimile reprint with new introduction by Seymour de Lotbiniere, Museum Restoration Service, Ontario, Canada, 1984. 90 pp., illus. $24.50.

Limited edition reprinting of the very scarce London edition of 1879.

Master Tips, by J. Winokur, Potshot Press, Pacific Palisades, CA, 1985. 96 pp., illus. Paper covers. $11.95.

Basics of practical shooting.

The Military and Police Sniper, by Mike R. Lau, Precision Shooting, Inc., Manchester, CT, 1998. 352 pp., illustrated. Paper covers. $44.95.

Advanced precision shooting for combat and law enforcement.

Military Rifle & Machine Gun Cartridges, by Jean Huon, Paladin Press, Boulder, CO, 1990. 392 pp., illus. $34.95.

Describes the primary types of military cartridges and their principal loadings, as well as their characteristics, origin and use.

Military Small Arms of the 20ᵗʰ Century, 7ᵗʰ Edition, by Ian V. Hogg and John Weeks, DBI Books, a division of Krause Publications, Iola, WI, 2000. 416 pp., illustrated. Paper covers. $24.95.
Cover small arms of 46 countries. Over 800 photographs and illustrations.

Modern Custom Guns, Walnut, Steel, and Uncommon Artistry, by Tom Turpin, Krause Publications, Iola, WI, 1997. 206 pp., illus. $49.95.
From exquisite engraving to breathtaking exotic woods, the mystique of today's custom guns is expertly detailed in word and awe-inspiring color photos of rifles, shotguns and handguns.

Modern Guns Identification & Values, 13th Edition, by Russell & Steve Quertermous, Collector Books, Paducah, KY, 1999. 516 pp., illus. Paper covers. $12.95.
A standard reference for over 20 years. Over 1,800 illustrations of over 2,500 models with their current values.

Modern Law Enforcement Weapons & Tactics, 2nd Edition, by Tom Ferguson, DBI Books, a division of Krause Publications, Iola, WI, 1991. 256 pp., illus. Paper covers. $18.95.
An in-depth look at the weapons and equipment used by law enforcement agencies of today.

Modern Machine Guns, by John Walter, Stackpole Books, Inc. Mechanicsburg, PA, 2000. 144 pp., with 146 illustrations. $22.95.
A compact and authoritative guide to post-war machine-guns. A gun-by-gun directory identifying individual variants and types including detailed evaluations and technical data.

Modern Sporting Guns, by Christopher Austyn, Safari Press, Huntington Beach, CA, 1994. 128 pp., illus. $40.00.
A discussion of the "best" English guns; round action, over-and-under, boxlocks, hammer guns, bolt action and double rifles as well as accessories.

The More Complete Cannoneer, by M.C. Switlik, Museum & Collectors Specialties Co., Monroe, MI, 1990. 199 pp., illus. $19.95.
Compiled agreeably to the regulations for the U.S. War Department, 1861, and containing current observations on the use of antique cannons.

The MP-40 Machine Gun, Desert Publications, El Dorado, AZ, 1995. 32 pp., illus. Paper covers. $11.95.
A reprint of the hard-to-find operating and maintenance manual for one of the most famous machine guns of World War II.

Naval Percussion Locks and Primers, by Lt. J. A. Dahlgren, Museum Restoration Service, Bloomfield, Canada, 1996. 140 pp., illus. $35.00
First published as an Ordnance Memoranda in 1853, this is the finest existing study of percussion locks and primers origin and development.

The Official Soviet AKM Manual, translated by Maj. James F. Gebhardt (Ret.), Paladin Press, Boulder, CO, 1999. 120 pp., illustrated. Paper covers. $18.00.
This official military manual, available in English for the first time, was originally published by the Soviet Ministry of Defence. Covers the history, function, maintenance, assembly and disassembly, etc. of the 7.62mm AKM assault rifle.

The One-Round War: U.S.M.C. Scout-Snipers in Vietnam, by Peter Senich, Paladin Press, Boulder, CO, 1996. 384 pp., illus. Paper covers $59.95.
Sniping in Vietnam focusing specifically on the Marine Corps program.

Pin Shooting: A Complete Guide, by Mitchell A. Ota, Wolfe Publishing Co., Prescott, AZ, 1992. 145 pp., illus. Paper covers. $14.95.
Traces the sport from its humble origins to today's thoroughly enjoyable social event, including the mammoth eight-day Second Chance Pin Shoot in Michigan.

Powder and Ball Small Arms, by Martin Pegler, Windrow & Greene Publishing, London, 1998. 128 pp., illustrated with 200 color photos. $39.95.
Part of the new "Live Firing Classic Weapons" series. Full-color photos of experienced shooters dressed in authentic costumes handling, loading and firing historic weapons.

Principles of Personal Defense, by Jeff Cooper, Paladin Press, Boulder, CO, 1999. 56 pp., illustrated. Paper covers. $14.00.
This revised edition of Jeff Cooper's classic on personal defense offers great new illustrations and a new preface while retaining the timeliness theory of individual defense behavior presented in the original book.

E.C. Prudhomme, Master Gun Engraver, A Retrospective Exhibition: 1946-1973, intro. by John T. Amber, The R. W. Norton Art Gallery, Shreveport, LA, 1973. 32 pp., illus. Paper covers. $9.95.
Examples of master gun engravings by Jack Prudhomme.

The Quotable Hunter, edited by Jay Cassell and Peter Fiduccia, The lyons Press, N.Y., 1999. 224 pp., illustrated. $20.00.
This collection of more than three hundred memorable quotes from hunters through the ages captures the essence of the sport, with all its joys idiosyncrasies, and challenges.

A Rifleman Went to War, by H. W. McBride, Lancer Militaria, Mt. Ida, AR, 1987. 398 pp., illus. $29.95.
The classic account of practical marksmanship on the battlefields of World War I.

Sharpshooting for Sport and War, by W.W. Greener, Wolfe Publishing Co., Prescott, AZ, 1995. 192 pp., illus. $30.00.
This classic reprint explores the *first* expanding bullet; service rifles; shooting positions; trajectories; recoil; external ballistics; and other valuable information.

The Shooter's Bible 2002, No. 93, edited by William S. Jarrett, Stoeger Publishing Co., Wayne, NJ, 2001. 576 pp., illustrated. Paper covers. $23.95.
Over 3,000 firearms currently offered by major American and foreign gunmakers. Represented are handguns, rifles, shotguns and black powder arms with complete specifications and retail prices.

Shooting To Live, by Capt. W. E. Fairbairn & Capt. E. A. Sykes, Paladin Press, Boulder, CO, 1997, 4 1/2 x 7, soft cover, illus., 112 pp. $14.00
Shooting to Live is the product of Fairbairn's and Sykes' practical experience with the handgun. Hundreds of incidents provided the basis for the first true book on life-or-death shootouts with the pistol. Shooting to Live teaches all concepts, considerations and applications of combat pistol craft.

Shooting Sixguns of the Old West, by Mike Venturino, MLV Enterprises, Livingston, MT, 1997. 221 pp., illus. Paper covers. $26.50.
A comprehensive look at the guns of the early West: Colts, Smith & Wesson and Remingtons, plus blackpowder and reloading specs.

Sniper Training, FM 23-10, Reprint of the U.S. Army field manual of August, 1994, Paladin Press, Boulder, CO, 1995. 352pp., illus. Paper covers. $30.00
The most up-to-date U.S. military sniping information and doctrine.

Sniping in France, by Major H. Hesketh-Prichard, Lancer Militaria, Mt. Ida, AR, 1993. 224 pp., illus. $24.95.
The author was a well-known British adventurer and big game hunter. He was called upon in the early days of "The Great War" to develop a program to offset an initial German advantage in sniping. How the British forces came to overcome this advantage.

Special Warfare: Special Weapons, by Kevin Dockery, Emperor's Press, Chicago, IL, 1997. 192 pp., illus. $29.95.
The arms and equipment of the UDT and SEALS from 1943 to the present.

Sporting Collectibles, by Dr. Stephen R. Irwin, Stoeger Publishing Co., Wayne, NJ, 1997. 256 pp., illus. Paper covers. $19.95.
A must book for serious collectors and admirers of sporting collectibles.

The Sporting Craftsmen: A Complete Guide to Contemporary Makers of Custom-Built Sporting Equipment, by Art Carter, Countrysport Press, Traverse City, MI, 1994. 240 pp., illus. $35.00.
Profiles leading makers of centerfire rifles; muzzleloading rifles; bamboo fly rods; fly reels; flies; waterfowl calls; decoys; handmade knives; and traditional longbows and recurves.

Sporting Rifle Takedown & Reassembly Guide, 2nd Edition, by J.B. Wood, DBI Books, a division of Krause Publications, Iola, WI, 1997. 480 pp., illus. $19.95.
An updated edition of the reference guide for anyone who wants to properly care for their sporting rifle. (Available September 1997)

2001 Standard Catalog of Firearms, the Collector's Price & Reference Guide, 11th Edition, by Ned Schwing, Krause Publications, Iola, WI, 2000. 1,248 pp., illus. Paper covers. $32.95.
Packed with more than 80,000 real world prices with more than 5,000 photos. Easy to use master index listing every firearm model.

The Street Smart Gun Book, by John Farnam, Police Bookshelf, Concord, NH, 1986. 45 pp., illus. Paper covers. $11.95.
Weapon selection, defensive shooting techniques, and gunfight-winning tactics from one of the world's leading authorities.

Stress Fire, Vol. 1: Stress Fighting for Police, by Massad Ayoob, Police Bookshelf, Concord, NH, 1984. 149 pp., illus. Paper covers. $9.95.
Gunfighting for police, advanced tactics and techniques.

Survival Guns, by Mel Tappan, Desert Publications, El Dorado, AZ, 1993. 456 pp., illus. Paper covers. $21.95.
Discusses in a frank and forthright manner which handguns, rifles and shotguns to buy for personal defense and securing food, and the ones to avoid.

The Tactical Advantage, by Gabriel Suarez, Paladin Press, Boulder, CO, 1998. 216 pp., illustrated. Paper covers. $22.00.
Learn combat tactics that have been tested in the world's toughest schools.

Tactical Marksman, by Dave M. Lauch, Paladin Press, Boulder, CO, 1996. 165 pp., illus. Paper covers. $35.00.
A complete training manual for police and practical shooters.

Thompson Guns 1921-1945, Anubis Press, Houston, TX, 1980. 215 pp., illus. Paper covers. $15.95.
Facsimile reprinting of five complete manuals on the Thompson submachine gun.

To Ride, Shoot Straight, and Speak the Truth, by Jeff Cooper, Paladin Press, Boulder, CO, 1997, 5 1/2 x 8 1/2, soft-cover, illus., 384 pp. $32.00
Combat mind-set, proper sighting, tactical residential architecture, nuclear war - these are some of the many subjects explored by Jeff Cooper in this illustrated anthology. The author discusses various arms, fighting skills and the importance of knowing how to defend oneself, and one's honor, in our rapidly changing world.

Trailriders Guide to Cowboy Action Shooting, by James W. Barnard, Pioneer Press, Union City, TN, 1998. 134 pp., plus 91 photos, drawings and charts. Paper covers. $24.95.
Covers the complete spectrum of this shooting discipline, from how to dress to authentic leather goods, which guns are legal, calibers, loads and ballistics.

The Ultimate Sniper, by Major John L. Plaster, Paladin Press, Boulder, CO, 1994. 464 pp., illus. Paper covers. $42.95.

An advanced training manual for military and police snipers.

Unrepentant Sinner, by Col. Charles Askins, Paladin Press, Boulder, CO, 2000. 322 pp., illustrated. $29.95.

The autobiography of Colonel Charles Askins.

U.S. Marine Corp Rifle and Pistol Marksmanship, 1935, reprinting of a government publication, Lancer Militaria, Mt. Ida, AR, 1991. 99 pp., illus. Paper covers. $11.95.

The old corps method of precision shooting.

U.S. Marine Corps Scout/Sniper Training Manual, Lancer Militaria, Mt. Ida, AR, 1989. Soft covers. $19.95.

Reprint of the original sniper training manual used by the Marksmanship Training Unit of the Marine Corps Development and Education Command in Quantico, Virginia.

U.S. Marine Corps Scout-Sniper, World War II and Korea, by Peter R. Senich, Paladin Press, Boulder, CO, 1994. 236 pp., illus. $44.95.

The most thorough and accurate account ever printed on the training, equipment and combat experiences of the U.S. Marine Corps Scout-Snipers.

U.S. Marine Corps Sniping, Lancer Militaria, Mt. Ida, AR, 1989. Irregular pagination. Soft covers. $17.95.

A reprint of the official Marine Corps FMFM1-3B.

Weapons of the Waffen-SS, by Bruce Quarrie, Sterling Publishing Co., Inc., 1991. 168 pp., illus. $24.95.

An in-depth look at the weapons that made Hitler's Waffen-SS the fearsome fighting machine it was.

Weatherby: The Man, The Gun, The Legend, by Grits and Tom Gresham, Cane River Publishing Co., Natchitoches, LA, 1992. 290 pp., illus. $24.95.

A fascinating look at the life of the man who changed the course of firearms development in America.

The Winchester Era, by David Madis, Art & Reference House, Brownsville, TX, 1984. 100 pp., illus. $19.95.

Story of the Winchester company, management, employees, etc.

Winchester Repeating Arms Company by Herbert Houze, Krause Publications, Iola, WI. 512 pp., illus. $50.00.

With British Snipers to the Reich, by Capt. C. Shore, Lander Militaria, Mt. Ida, AR, 1988. 420 pp., illus. $29.95.

One of the greatest books ever written on the art of combat sniping.

The World's Machine Pistols and Submachine Guns - Vol. 2a 1964 to 1980, by Nelson & Musgrave, Ironside International, Alexandria, VA, 2000. 673 pages, illustrated. $59.95.

Containing data, history and photographs of over 200 weapons. With a special section covering shoulder stocked automatic pistols, 100 additional photos.

The World's Submachine Guns - Vol. 1 1918 to 1963, by Nelson & Musgrave, Ironside International, Alexandria, VA, 2001. 673 pages, illustrated. $59.95.

A revised edition covering much new material that has come to light since the book was originally printed in 1963.

The World's Sniping Rifles, by Ian V. Hogg, Paladin Press, Boulder, CO, 1998. 144 pp., illustrated. $22.95.

A detailed manual with descriptions and illustrations of more than 50 high-precision rifles from 14 countries and a complete analysis of sights and systems.

GUNSMITHING

Accurizing the Factory Rifle, by M.L. McPhereson, Precision Shooting, Inc., Manchester, CT, 1999. 335 pp., illustrated. Paper covers. $44.95.

A long-awaited book, which bridges the gap between the rudimentary (mounting sling swivels, scope blocks and that general level of accomplishment) and the advanced (precision chambering, barrel fluting, and that general level of accomplishment) books that are currently available today.

Advanced Rebarreling of the Sporting Rifle, by Willis H. Fowler, Jr., Willis H. Fowler, Jr., Anchorage, AK, 1994. 127 pp., illus. Paper covers. $32.50.

A manual outlining a superior method of fitting barrels and doing chamber work on the sporting rifle.

The Art of Engraving, by James B. Meek, F. Brownell & Son, Montezuma, IA, 1973. 196 pp., illus. $38.95.

A complete, authoritative, imaginative and detailed study in training for gun engraving. The first book of its kind—and a great one.

Artistry in Arms, The R. W. Norton Gallery, Shreveport, LA, 1970. 42 pp., illus. Paper covers. $9.95.

The art of gunsmithing and engraving.

Barrels & Actions, by Harold Hoffman, H&P Publishers, San Angelo, TX, 1990. 309 pp., illus. Spiral bound. $29.95.

A manual on barrel making.

Black Powder Hobby Gunsmithing, by Sam Fadala and Dale Storey, DBI Books, a division of Krause Publications, Iola, WI., 1994. 256 pp., illus. Paper covers. $18.95.

A how-to guide for gunsmithing blackpowder pistols, rifles and shotguns from two men at the top of their respective fields.

Checkering and Carving of Gun Stocks, by Monte Kennedy, Stackpole Books, Harrisburg, PA, 1962. 175 pp., illus. $39.95.

Revised, enlarged cloth-bound edition of a much sought-after, dependable work.

The Complete Metal Finishing Book, by Harold Hoffman, H&P Publishers, San Angelo, TX, 1992. 364 pp., illus. Paper covers. $29.95.

Instructions for the different metal finishing operations that the normal craftsman or shop will use. Primarily firearm related.

Exploded Handgun Drawings, The Gun Digest Book of, edited by Harold A. Murtz, DBI Books, a division of Krause Publications, Iola, WI. 1992. 512 pp., illus. Paper covers. $20.95.

Exploded or isometric drawings for 494 of the most popular handguns.

Exploded Long Gun Drawings, The Gun Digest Book of, edited by Harold A. Murtz, DBI Books, a division of Krause Publications, Iola, WI. 512 pp., illus. Paper covers. $20.95.

Containing almost 500 rifle and shotgun exploded drawings. An invaluable aid to both professionals and hobbyists.

The Finishing of Gun Stocks, by Harold Hoffman, H&P Publishers, San Angelo, TX, 1994. 98 pp., illus. Paper covers. $17.95.

Covers different types of finishing methods and finishes.

Firearms Assembly/Disassembly, Part I: Automatic Pistols, 2nd Revised Edition, The Gun Digest Book of, by J.B. Wood, DBI Books, a division of Krause Publications, Iola, WI, 1999. 480 pp., illus. Paper covers. $24.95.

Covers 58 popular autoloading pistols plus nearly 200 variants of those models integrated into the text and completely cross-referenced in the index.

Firearms Assembly/Disassembly Part II: Revolvers, Revised Edition, The Gun Digest Book of, by J.B. Wood, DBI Books, a division of Krause Publications, Iola, WI, 1990. 480 pp., illus. Paper covers. $19.95.

Covers 49 popular revolvers plus 130 variants. The most comprehensive and professional presentation available to either hobbyist or gunsmith.

Firearms Assembly/Disassembly Part III: Rimfire Rifles, Revised Edition, The Gun Digest Book of, by J. B. Wood, DBI Books, a division of Krause Publications, Iola, WI., 1994. 480 pp., illus. Paper covers. $19.95.

Greatly expanded edition covering 65 popular rimfire rifles plus over 100 variants all completely cross-referenced in the index.

Firearms Assembly/Disassembly Part IV: Centerfire Rifles, Revised Edition, The Gun Digest Book of, by J.B. Wood, DBI Books, a division of Krause Publications, Iola, WI, 1991. 480 pp., illus. Paper covers. $19.95.

Covers 54 popular centerfire rifles plus 300 variants. The most comprehensive and professional presentation available to either hobbyist or gunsmith.

Firearms Assembly/Disassembly, Part V: Shotguns, Revised Edition, The Gun Digest Book of, by J.B. Wood, DBI Books, a division of Krause Publications, Iola, WI, 1992. 480 pp., illus. Paper covers. $19.95.

Covers 46 popular shotguns plus over 250 variants with step-by-step instructions on how to dismantle and reassemble each. The most comprehensive and professional presentation available to either hobbyist or gunsmith.

Firearms Assembly/Disassembly Part VI: Law Enforcement Weapons, The Gun Digest Book of, by J.B. Wood, DBI Books, a division of Krause Publications, Iola, WI, 1981. 288 pp., illus. Paper covers. $16.95.

Step-by-step instructions on how to completely dismantle and reassemble the most commonly used firearms found in law enforcement arsenals.

Firearms Assembly 3: The NRA Guide to Rifle and Shotguns, NRA Books, Wash., DC, 1980. 264 pp., illus. Paper covers. $13.95.

Text and illustrations explaining the takedown of 125 rifles and shotguns, domestic and foreign.

Firearms Assembly 4: The NRA Guide to Pistols and Revolvers, NRA Books, Wash., DC, 1980. 253 pp., illus. Paper covers. $13.95.

Text and illustrations explaining the takedown of 124 pistol and revolver models, domestic and foreign.

Firearms Bluing and Browning, By R.H. Angier, Stackpole Books, Harrisburg, PA. 151 pp., illus. $19.95.

A world master gunsmith reveals his secrets of building, repairing and renewing a gun, quite literally, lock, stock and barrel. A useful, concise text on chemical coloring methods for the gunsmith and mechanic.

Firearms Disassembly—With Exploded Views, by John A. Karns & John E. Traister, Stoeger Publishing Co., S. Hackensack, NJ, 1995. 320 pp., illus. Paper covers. $19.95.

Provides the do's and don'ts of firearms disassembly. Enables owners and gunsmiths to disassemble firearms in a professional manner.

Guns and Gunmaking Tools of Southern Appalachia, by John Rice Irwin, Schiffer Publishing Ltd., 1983. 118 pp., illus. Paper covers. $9.95.

The story of the Kentucky rifle.

Gunsmithing: Pistols & Revolvers, by Patrick Sweeney, DBI Books, a division of Krause Publications, Iola, WI, 1998. 352 pp., illus. Paper covers. $24.95.

Do-it-Yourself projects, diagnosis and repair for pistols and revolvers.

Gunsmithing: Rifles, by Patrick Sweeney, Krause Publications, Iola, WI, 1999. 352 pp., illustrated. Paper covers. $24.95.

Tips for lever-action rifles. Building a custom Ruger 10/22. Building a better hunting rifle.

Gunsmithing Tips and Projects, a collection of the best articles from the *Handloader* and *Rifle* magazines, by various authors, Wolfe Publishing Co., Prescott, AZ, 1992. 443 pp., illus. Paper covers. $25.00.

Includes such subjects as shop, stocks, actions, tuning, triggers, barrels, customizing, etc.

Gunsmith Kinks, by F.R. (Bob) Brownell, F. Brownell & Son, Montezuma, IA, 1st ed., 1969. 496 pp., well illus. $22.98.

A widely useful accumulation of shop kinks, short cuts, techniques and pertinent comments by practicing gunsmiths from all over the world.

Gunsmith Kinks 2, by Bob Brownell, F. Brownell & Son, Publishers, Montezuma, IA, 1983. 496 pp., illus. $22.95.

A collection of gunsmithing knowledge, shop kinks, new and old techniques, shortcuts and general know-how straight from those who do them best—the gunsmiths.

Gunsmith Kinks 3, edited by Frank Brownell, Brownells Inc., Montezuma, IA, 1993. 504 pp., illus. $24.95.

Tricks, knacks and "kinks" by professional gunsmiths and gun tinkerers. Hundreds of valuable ideas are given in this volume.

Gunsmith Kinks 4, edited by Frank Brownell, Brownells Inc., Montezuma, IA, 2001. 564 pp., illus. $27.75

332 detailed illustrations. 560+ pages with 706 separate subject headings and over 5000 cross-indexed entries. An incredible gold mine of information.

Gunsmithing, by Roy F. Dunlap, Stackpole Books, Harrisburg, PA, 1990. 742 pp., illus. $34.95.

A manual of firearm design, construction, alteration and remodeling. For amateur and professional gunsmiths and users of modern firearms.

Gunsmithing at Home: Lock, Stock and Barrel, by John Traister, Stoeger Publishing Co., Wayne, NJ, 1997. 320 pp., illus. Paper covers. $19.95.

A complete step-by-step fully illustrated guide to the art of gunsmithing.

The Gunsmith's Manual, by J.P. Stelle and Wm. B. Harrison, The Gun Room Press, Highland Park, NJ, 1982. 376 pp., illus. $19.95.

For the gunsmith in all branches of the trade.

Home Gunsmithing the Colt Single Action Revolvers, by Loren W. Smith, Ray Riling Arms Books, Co., Phila., PA, 2001. 119 pp., illus. $29.95.

Affords the Colt Single Action owner detailed, pertinent information on the operating and servicing of this famous and historic handgun.

How to Convert Military Rifles, Williams Gun Sight Co., Davision, MI, new and enlarged seventh edition, 1997. 76 pp., illus. Paper covers. $13.95.

This latest edition updated the changes that have occured over the past thirty years. Tips, instructions and illustratons on how to convert popular military rifles as the Enfield, Mauser 96 nad SKS just to name a few are presented.

Mauser M98 & M96, by R.A. Walsh, Wolfe Publishing Co., Prescott, AR, 1998. 123 pp., illustrated. Paper covers. $32.50.

How to build your own favorite custom Mauser rifle from two of the best bolt action rifle designs ever produced—the military Mauser Model 1898 and Model 1896 bolt rifles.

Mr. Single Shot's Gunsmithing-Idea-Book, by Frank de Haas, Mark de Haas, Orange City, IA, 1996. 168 pp., illus. Paper covers. $21.50.

Offers easy to follow, step-by-step instructions for a wide variety of gunsmithing procedures all reinforced by plenty of photos.

Pistolsmithing, by George C. Nonte, Jr., Stackpole Books, Harrisburg, PA, 1974. 560 pp., illus. $34.95.

A single source reference to handgun maintenance, repair, and modification at home, unequaled in value.

Practical Gunsmithing, by the editors of American Gunsmith, DBI Books, a division of Krause Publications, Iola, WI, 1996. 256 pp., illus. Paper covers. $19.95.

A book intended primarily for home gunsmithing, but one that will be extremely helpful to professionals as well.

Professional Stockmaking, by D. Wesbrook, Wolfe Publishing Co., Prescott AZ, 1995. 308 pp., illus. $54.00.

A step-by-step how-to with complete photographic support for every detail of the art of working wood into riflestocks.

Recreating the American Longrifle, by William Buchele, et al, George Shumway Publisher, York, Pa, 5th edition, 1999. 175 pp., illustrated. $40.00.

Includes full size plans for building a Kentucky rifle.

Riflesmithing, The Gun Digest Book of, by Jack Mitchell, DBI Books, a division of Krause Publications, Iola, WI, 1982. 256 pp., illus. Paper covers. $16.95.

The art and science of rifle gunsmithing. Covers tools, techniques, designs, finishing wood and metal, custom alterations.

Shotgun Gunsmithing, The Gun Digest Book of, by Ralph Walker, DBI Books, a division of Krause Publications, Iola, WI, 1983. 256 pp., illus. Paper covers. $16.95.

The principles and practices of repairing, individualizing and accurizing modern shotguns by one of the world's premier shotgun gunsmiths.

Sporting Rifle Take Down & Reassembly Guide, 2nd Edition, by J.B. Wood, Krause Publications, Iola, WI, 1997. 480 pp., illus. Paper covers. $19.95.

Hunters and shooting enthusiasts must have this reference featuring 52 of the most popular and widely used sporting centerfire and rimfire rifles.

The Story of Pope's Barrels, by Ray M. Smith, R&R Books, Livonia, NY, 1993. 203 pp., illus. $39.00.

A reissue of a 1960 book whose author knew Pope personally. It will be of special interest to Schuetzen rifle fans, since Pope's greatest days were at the height of the Schuetzen-era before WWI.

Survival Gunsmithing, by J.B. Wood, Desert Publications, Cornville, AZ, 1986. 92 pp., illus. Paper covers. $11.95.

A guide to repair and maintenance of the most popular rifles, shotguns and handguns.

The Tactical 1911, by Dave Lauck, Paladin Press, Boulder, CO, 1998. 137 pp., illus. Paper covers. $20.00.

Here is the only book you will ever need to teach you how to select, modify, employ and maintain your Colt.

HANDGUNS

Advanced Master Handgunning, by Charles Stephens, Paladin Press, Boulder, CO., 1994. 72 pp., illus. Paper covers. $14.00.

Secrets and surefire techniques for winning handgun competitions.

American Beauty: The Prewar Colt National Match Government Model Pistol, by Timothy Mullin, Collector Grade Publications, Canada, 1999. 72 pp., 69 illus. $34.95

69 illustrations, 20 in full color photos of factory engraved guns and other authenticated upgrades, including rare 'double-carved' ivory grips.

Axis Pistols: WORLD WAR TWO 50 YEARS COMMEMORATIVE ISSUE, by Jan C. Stills, Walsworth Publishing, 1989. 360 pages, illus. $59.95

The Ayoob Files: The Book, by Massad Ayoob, Police Bookshelf, Concord, NH, 1995. 223 pp., illus. Paper covers. $14.95.

The best of Massad Ayoob's acclaimed series in American Handgunner magazine.

Big Bore Sixguns, by John Taffin, Krause Publications, Iola, WI, 1997. 336 pp., illus. $39.95.

The author takes aim on the entire range of big bores from .357 Magnums to .500 Maximums, single actions and cap-and-ball sixguns to custom touches for big bores..

The Browning High Power Automatic Pistol (Expanded Edition), by Blake R. Stevens, Collector Grade Publications, Canada, 1996. 310 pages, with 313 illus. $49.95

An in-depth chronicle of seventy years of High Power history, from John M Browning's original 16-shot prototypes to the present. Profusely illustrated with rare original photos and drawings from the FN Archive to describe virtually every sporting and military version of the High Power. The numerous modifications made to the basic design over the years are, for the first time, accurately arranged in chronological order, thus permitting the dating of any High Power to within a few years of its production. Full details on the WWII Canadian-made Inglis Browning High Power pistol. The Expanded Edition contains 30 new pages on the interesting Argentine full-auto High Power, the latest FN 'MK3' and BDA9 pistols, plus FN's revolutionary P90 5.7x28mm Personal Defence Weapon, and more!

Browning Hi-Power Pistols, Desert Publications, Cornville, AZ, 1982. 20 pp., illus. Paper covers. $11.95.

Covers all facets of the various military and civilian models of the Browning Hi-Power pistol.

Canadian Military Handguns 1855-1985, by Clive M. Law, Museum Restoration Service, Bloomfield, Ont. Canada, 1994. 130pp., illus. $40.00.

A long-awaited and important history for arms historians and pistol collectors.

The Colt .45 Auto Pistol, compiled from U.S. War Dept. Technical Manuals, and reprinted by Desert Publications, Cornville, AZ, 1978. 80 pp., illus. Paper covers. $11.95.

Covers every facet of this famous pistol from mechanical training, manual of arms, disassembly, repair and replacement of parts.

Colt Automatic Pistols, by Donald B. Bady, Pioneer Press, Union City, TN, 1999. 368 pp., illustrated. Softcover. $19.95.

A revised and enlarged edition of a key work on a fascinating subject. Complete information on every Colt automatic pistol.

Combat Handgunnery, 4th Edition, by Chuck Taylor, DBI Books, a division of Krause Publications, Iola, WI, 1997. 256 pp., illus. Paper covers. $18.95.

This all-new edition looks at real world combat handgunnery from three different perspectives—military, police and civilian. Available, October, 1996.

Combat Revolvers, by Duncan Long, Paladin Press, Boulder, CO, 1999, 8 1/2 x 11, soft cover, 115 photos, 152 pp. $21.95

This is an uncompromising look at modern combat revolvers. All the major foreign and domestic guns are covered: the Colt Python, S&W Model 29, Ruger GP 100 and hundreds more. Know the gun that you may one day stake your life on.

The Complete Book of Combat Handgunning, by Chuck Taylor, Desert Publications, Cornville, AZ, 1982. 168 pp., illus. Paper covers. $20.00.

Covers virtually every aspect of combat handgunning.

Complete Guide to Compact Handguns, by Gene Gangarosa, Jr., Stoeger Publishing Co., Wayne, NJ, 1997. 228 pp., illus. Paper covers. $22.95.

Includes hundreds of compact firearms, along with text results conducted by the author.

Complete Guide to Service Handguns, by Gene Gangarosa, Jr., Stoeger Publishing Co., Wayne, NJ, 1998. 320 pp., illus. Paper covers. $22.95.

The author explores the revolvers and pistols that are used around the globe by military, law enforcement and civilians.

The Custom Government Model Pistol, by Layne Simpson, Wolfe Publishing Co., Prescott, AZ, 1994. 639 pp., illus. Paper covers. $24.50.

The book about one of the world's greatest firearms and the things pistolsmiths do to make it even greater.

The CZ-75 Family: The Ultimate Combat Handgun, by J.M. Ramos, Paladin Press, Boulder, CO, 1990. 100 pp., illus. Soft covers. $25.00.

An in-depth discussion of the early-and-late model CZ-75s, as well as the many newest additions to the Czech pistol family.

Encyclopedia of Pistols & Revolvers, by A.E. Hartnik, Knickerbocker Press, New York, NY, 1997. 272 pp., illus. $19.95.

A comprehensive encyclopedia specially written for collectors and owners of pistols and revolvers.

Experiments of a Handgunner, by Walter Roper, Wolfe Publishing Co., Prescott, AZ, 1989. 202 pp., illus. $37.00.

A limited edition reprint. A listing of experiments with functioning parts of handguns, with targets, stocks, rests, handloading, etc.

The Farnam Method of Defensive Handgunning, by John S. Farnam, Police Bookshelf, 1999. 191 pp., illus. Paper covers. $25.00

A book intended to not only educate the new shooter, but also to serve as a guide and textbook for his and his instructor's training courses.

Fast and Fancy Revolver Shooting, by Ed. McGivern, Anniversary Edition, Winchester Press, Piscataway, NJ, 1984. 484 pp., illus. $18.95.

A fascinating volume, packed with handgun lore and solid information by the acknowledged dean of revolver shooters.

.45 ACP Super Guns, by J.M. Ramos, Paladin Press, Boulder, CO, 1991. 144 pp., illus. Paper covers. $24.00.

Modified .45 automatic pistols for competition, hunting and personal defense.

The .45, The Gun Digest Book of, by Dean A. Grennell, DBI Books, a division of Krause Publications, Iola, WI, 1989. 256 pp., illus. Paper covers. $17.95.

Definitive work on one of America's favorite calibers.

Glock: The New Wave in Combat Handguns, by Peter Alan Kasler, Paladin Press, Boulder, CO, 1993. 304 pp., illus. $27.00.

Kasler debunks the myths that surround what is the most innovative handgun to be introduced in some time.

Glock's Handguns, by Duncan Long, Desert Publications, El Dorado, AR, 1996. 180 pp., illus. Paper covers. $18.95.

An outstanding volume on one of the world's newest and most successful firearms of the century.

Hand Cannons: The World's Most Powerful Handguns, by Duncan Long, Paladin Press, Boulder, CO, 1995. 208 pp., illus. Paper covers. $22.00.

Long describes and evaluates each powerful gun according to their features.

The Handgun, by Geoffrey Boothroyd, Safari Press, Inc., Huntington Beach, CA, 1999. 566 pp., illustrated. $50.00.

A very detailed history of the handgun. Now revised and a completely new chapter written to take account of developments since the 1970 edition.

Handguns 2002, 13th Edition, edited by Ken Ramage, DBI Books a division of Krause Publications, Iola, WI, 1999. 352 pp., illustrated. Paper covers. $22.95.

Top writers in the handgun industry give you a complete report on new handgun developments, testfire reports on the newest introductions and previews on what's ahead.

Handgun Digest, 3rd Edition, edited by Chris Christian, DBI Books, a division of Krause Publications, Iola, WI, 1995. 256 pp., illus. Paper covers. $18.95.

Full coverage of all aspects of handguns and handgunning from a highly readable and knowledgeable author.

Handgun Reloading, The Gun Digest Book of, by Dean A. Grennell and Wiley M. Clapp, DBI Books, a division of Krause Publications, Iola, WI, 1987. 256 pp., illus. Paper covers. $16.95.

Detailed discussions of all aspects of reloading for handguns, from basic to complex. New loading data.

Handgun Stopping Power "The Definitive Study", by Evan P. Marshall & Edwin J. Sanow, Paladin Press, Boulder, CO, 1997, soft cover, photos, 240 pp. $45.00

Dramatic first-hand accounts of the results of handgun rounds fired into criminals by cops, storeowners, cabbies and others are the heart and soul of this long-awaited book. This is the definitive methodology for predicting the stopping power of handgun loads, the first to take into account what really happens when a bullet meets a man.

Heckler & Koch's Handguns, by Duncan Long, Desert Publications, El Dorado, AR, 1996. 142 pp., illus. Paper covers. $19.95.

Traces the history and the evolution of H&K's pistols from the company's beginning at the end of WWII to the present.

Hidden in Plain Sight, by Trey Bloodworth & Mike Raley, Professional Press, Chapel Hill, NC, 1995. Paper covers. $19.95.

A practical guide to concealed handgun carry.

High Standard Automatic Pistols 1932-1950, by Charles E. Petty, The Gunroom Press, Highland Park, NJ, 1989. 124 pp., illus. $19.95.

A definitive source of information for the collector of High Standard arms.

Hi-Standard Pistols and Revolvers, 1951-1984, by James Spacek, James Spacek, Chesire, CT, 1998. 128 pp., illustrated. Paper covers. $12.50.

Technical details, marketing features and instruction/parts manual of every model High Standard pistol and revolver made between 1951 and 1984. Most accurate serial number information available.

The Hi-Standard Pistol Guide, by Burr Leyson, Duckett's Sporting Books, Tempe AZ, 1995. 128 pp., illus. Paper covers. $22.00.

Complete information on selection, care and repair, ammunition, parts, and accessories.

How to Become a Master Handgunner: The Mechanics of X-Count Shooting, by Charles Stephens, Paladin Press, Boulder, CO, 1993. 64 pp., illus. Paper covers. $14.00.

Offers a simple formula for success to the handgunner who strives to master the technique of shooting accurately.

Hunting for Handgunners, by Larry Kelly and J.D. Jones, DBI Books, a division of Krause Publications, Iola, WI, 1990. 256 pp., illus. Paper covers. $16.95.

Covers the entire spectrum of hunting with handguns in an amusing, easy-flowing manner that combines entertainment with solid information.

Illustrated Encyclopedia of Handguns, by A.B. Zhuk, Stackpole Books, Mechanicsburg, PA, 1994. 256 pp., illus. Cloth cover, $49.95

Identifies more than 2,000 military and commercial pistols and revolvers with details of more than 100 popular handgun cartridges.

The Inglis Diamond: The Canadian High Power Pistol, by Clive M. Law, Collector Grade Publications, Canada, 2001. 312 pp., illustrated. $49.95

This definitive work on Canada's first and indeed only mass produced handgun, in production for a very brief span of time and consequently made in relatively few numbers, the venerable Inglis-made Browning High Power covers the pistol's initial history, the story of Chinese and British adoption, use post-war by Holland, Australia, Greece, Belgium, New Zealand, Peru, Brasil and other countries. All new information on the famous light-weights and the Inglis Diamond variations. Completely researched through official archives in a dozen countries. Many of the bewildering variety of markings have never been satisfactorily explained until now. Also included are many photos of holsters and accessories.

Instinct Combat Shooting, by Chuck Klein, The Goose Creek, IN, 1989. 49 pp., illus. Paper covers. $12.00.

Defensive handgunning for police.

Know Your Czechoslovakian Pistols, by R.J. Berger, Blacksmith Corp., Chino Valley, AZ, 1989. 96 pp., illus. Soft covers. $12.95.

A comprehensive reference which presents the fascinating story of Czech pistols.

Know Your 45 Auto Pistols—Models 1911 & A1, by E.J. Hoffschmidt, Blacksmith Corp., Southport, CT, 1974. 58 pp., illus. Paper covers. $12.95.

A concise history of the gun with a wide variety of types and copies.

Know Your Walther P38 Pistols, by E.J. Hoffschmidt, Blacksmith Corp., Southport, CT, 1974. 77 pp., illus. Paper covers. $12.95.

Covers the Walther models Armee, M.P., H.P., P.38—history and variations.

Know Your Walther PP & PPK Pistols, by E.J. Hoffschmidt, Blacksmith Corp., Southport, CT, 1975. 87 pp., illus. Paper covers. $12.95.

A concise history of the guns with a guide to the variety and types.

La Connaissance du Luger, Tome 1, by Gerard Henrotin, H & L Publishing, Belguim, 1996. 144 pages, illustrated. $45.00.

(The Knowledge of Luger, Volume 1, translated.) B&W and Color photo's. French text.

The Luger Handbook, by Aarron Davis, Krause Publications, Iola, WI, 1997. 112 pp., illus. Paper covers. $9.95.

Now you can identify any of the legendary Luger variations using a simple decision tree. Each model and variation includes pricing information, proof marks and detailed attributes in a handy, user-friendly format. Plus, it's fully indexed. Instantly identify that Luger!

REFERENCE

Lugers of Ralph Shattuck, by Ralph Shattuck, Peoria, AZ, 2000. 49 pages, illus. Hardcover. $29.95.

49 pages, illustrated with maps and full color photos of here to now never before shown photos of some of the rarest lugers ever. Written by one of the world's renowned collectors. A MUST have book for any Luger collector.

Lugers at Random (Revised Format Edition), by Charles Kenyon, Jr., Handgun Press, Glenview, IL, 2000. 420 pp., illus. $59.95.

A new printing of this classic, comprehensive reference for all Luger collectors.

The Luger Story, by John Walter, Stackpole Books, Mechanicsburg, PA, 2001. 256 pp., illus. Paper Covers. $29.95.

The standard history of the world's most famous handgun.

The Mauser Self-Loading Pistol, by Belford & Dunlap, Borden Publ. Co., Alhambra, CA. Over 200 pp., 300 illus., large format. $29.95.

The long-awaited book on the "Broom Handles," covering their inception in 1894 to the end of production. Complete and in detail: pocket pistols, Chinese and Spanish copies, etc.

9mm Handguns, 2nd Edition, The Gun Digest Book of, edited by Steve Comus, DBI Books, a division of Krause Publications, Iola, WI, 1993. 256 pp., illus. Paper covers. $18.95.

Covers the 9mm cartridge and the guns that have been made for it in greater depth than any other work available.

9mm Parabellum; The History & Development of the World's 9mm Pistols & Ammunition, by Klaus-Peter Konig and Martin Hugo, Schiffer Publishing Ltd., Atglen, PA, 1993. 304 pp., illus. $39.95.

Detailed history of 9mm weapons from Belguim, Italy, Germany, Israel, France, USA, Czechoslovakia, Hungary, Poland, Brazil, Finland and Spain.

The Official 9mm Markarov Pistol Manual, translated into English by Major James Gebhardt, U.S. Army (Ret.), Desert Publications, El Dorado, AR, 1996. 84 pp., illus. Paper covers. $12.95.

The information found in this book will be of enormous benefit and interest to the owner or a prospective owner of one of these pistols.

The Official Soviet 7.62mm Handgun Manual, by Translation by Maj. James F. Gebhardt Ret.), Paladin Press, Boulder, CO, 1997, soft cover, illus., 104 pp. $20.00.

This Soviet military manual, now available in English for the first time, covers instructions for use and maintenance of two side arms, the Nagant 7.62mm revolver, used by the Russian tsarist armed forces and later the Soviet armed forces, and the Tokarev7.62mm semi-auto pistol, which replaced the Nagant.

P-38 Automatic Pistol, by Gene Gangarosa, Jr., Stoeger Publishing Co., S. Hackensack, NJ, 1993. 272 pp., illus. Paper covers. $16.95

This book traces the origins and development of the P-38, including the momentous political forces of the World War II era that caused its near demise and, later, its rebirth.

The P-38 Pistol: The Walther Pistols, 1930-1945. Volume 1. by Warren Buxton, Ucross Books, Los Alamos, MN 1999. $68.50

A limited run reprint of this scarce and sought-after work on the P-38 Pistol. 328 pp. with 160 illustrations.

The P-38 Pistol: The Contract Pistols, 1940-1945. Volume 2. by Warren Buxton, Ucross Books, Los Alamos, MN 1999. 256 pp. with 237 illustrations. $68.50

The P-38 Pistol: Postwar Distributions, 1945-1990. Volume 3. by Warren Buxton, Ucross Books, Los Alamos, MN 1999. $68.50

Plus an addendum to Volumes 1 & 2. 272 pp. with 342 illustrations.

PARABELLUM - A Technical History of Swiss Lugers, by V. Bobba, Italy.1998. 224pp, profuse color photos, large format. $100.00.

The is the most beautifully illustrated and well-documented book on the Swiss Lugers yet produced. This splendidly produced book features magnificent images while giving an incredible amount of detail on the Swiss Luger. In-depth coverage of key issues include: the production process, pistol accessories, charts with serial numbers, production figures, variations, markings, patent drawings, etc. Covers the Swiss Luger story from 1894 when the first Bergmann-Schmeisser models were tested till the commercial model 1965. Shows every imaginable production variation in amazing detail and full color! A must for all Luger collectors. This work has been produced in an extremely attractive package using quality materials throughout and housed in a protective slipcase.

Pistols and Revolvers, by Jean-Noel Mouret, Barns and Noble, Rockleigh, N.J., 1999. 141 pp., illustrated. $12.98.

Here in glorious display is the master guidebook to flintlocks, minatures, the Sig P-210 limited edition, the Springfield Trophy Master with Aimpoint 5000 telescopic sight, every major classic and contemporary handgun, complete with their technical data.

Report of Board on Tests of Revolvers and Automatic Pistols, From the Annual Report of the Chief of Ordnance, 1907. Reprinted by J.C. Tillinghast, Marlow, NH, 1969. 34 pp., 7 plates, paper covers. $9.95.

A comparison of handguns, including Luger, Savage, Colt, Webley-Fosbery and other makes.

Ruger Automatic Pistols and Single Action Revolvers, by Hugo A. Lueders, edited by Don Findley, Blacksmith Corp., Chino Valley, AZ, 1993. 79 pp., illus. Paper covers. $14.95.

The definitive work on Ruger automatic pistols and single action revolvers.

The Ruger "P" Family of Handguns, by Duncan Long, Desert Publications, El Dorado, AZ, 1993. 128 pp., illus. Paper covers. $14.95.

A full-fledged documentary on a remarkable series of Sturm Ruger handguns.

The Ruger .22 Automatic Pistol, Standard/Mark I/Mark II Series, by Duncan Long, Paladin Press, Boulder, CO, 1989. 168 pp., illus. Paper covers. $16.00.

The definitive book about the pistol that has served more than 1 million owners so well.

The Semiautomatic Pistols in Police Service and Self Defense, by Massad Ayoob, Police Bookshelf, Concord, NH, 1990. 25 pp., illus. Soft covers. $9.95.

First quantitative, documented look at actual police experience with 9mm and 45 police service automatics.

The Sharpshooter—How to Stand and Shoot Handgun Metallic Silhouettes, by Charles Stephens, Yucca Tree Press, Las Cruces, NM, 1993. 86 pp., illus. Paper covers. $10.00.

A narration of some of the author's early experiences in silhouette shooting, plus how-to information.

Shooting Colt Single Actions, by Mike Venturino, Livingston, MT, 1997. 205 pp., illus. Paper covers. $25.00

A definitive work on the famous Colt SAA and the ammunition it shoots.

Sig/Sauer Handguns, by Duncan Long, Desert Publications, El Dorado, AZ, 1995. 150 pp., illus. Paper covers. $16.95.

The history of Sig/Sauer handguns, including Sig, Sig-Hammerli and Sig/Sauer variants.

Sixgun Cartridges and Loads, by Elmer Keith, reprint edition by The Gun Room Press, Highland Park, NJ, 1984. 151 pp., illus. $24.95.

A manual covering the selection, use and loading of the most suitable and popular revolver cartridges.

Sixguns, by Elmer Keith, Wolfe Publishing Company, Prescott, AZ, 1992. 336 pp. Paper covers. $29.95. Hardcover $35.00

The history, selection, repair, care, loading, and use of this historic frontiersman's friend—the one-hand firearm.

Smith & Wesson's Automatics, by Larry Combs, Desert Publications, El Dorado, AZ, 1994. 143 pp., illus. Paper covers. $19.95.

A must for every S&W auto owner or prospective owner.

Spanish Handguns: The History of Spanish Pistols and Revolvers, by Gene Gangarosa, Jr., Stoeger Publishing Co., Accokeek, MD, 2001. 320 pp., illustrated. B & W photos. Paper covers. $21.95

Street Stoppers: The Latest Handgun Stopping Power Street Results, by Evan P. Marshall & Edwin J. Sandow, Paladin Press, Boulder, CO, 1997. 392 pp., illus. Paper covers. $42.95.

Compilation of the results of real-life shooting incidents involving every major handgun caliber.

The Tactical 1911, by Dave Lauck, Paladin Press, Boulder, CO, 1999. 152 pp., illustrated. Paper covers. $22.00.

The cop's and SWAT operator's guide to employment and maintenance.

The Tactical Pistol, by Gabriel Suarez with a foreword by Jeff Cooper, Paladin Press, Boulder, CO, 1996. 216 pp., illus. Paper covers. $25.00.

Advanced gunfighting concepts and techniques.

The Thompson/Center Contender Pistol, by Charles Tephens, Paladin Press, Boulder, CO, 1997. 58 pp., illus. Paper covers. $14.00.

How to tune and time, load and shoot accurately with the Contender pistol.

The .380 Enfield No. 2 Revolver, by Mark Stamps and Ian Skennerton, I.D.S.A. Books, Piqua, OH, 1993. 124 pp., 80 illus. Paper covers. $19.95.

The Truth About Handguns, by Duane Thomas, Paladin Press, Boulder, CO, 1997. 136 pp., illus. Paper covers. $18.00.

Exploding the myths, hype, and misinformation about handguns.

Walther Pistols: Models 1 Through P99, Factory Variations and Copies, by Dieter H. Marschall, Ucross Books, Los Alamos, NM. 2000. 140 pages, with 140 b & w illustrations, index. Paper Covers. $19.95.

This is the English translation, revised and updated, of the highly successful and widely acclaimed German language edition. This book provides the collector with a reference guide and overview of the entire line of the Walther military, police, and self-defense pistols from the very first to the very latest. Models 1-9, PP, PPK, MP, AP, HP, P.38, P1, P4, P38K, P5, P88, P99 and the Manurhin models. Variations, where issued, serial ranges, calibers, marks, proofs, logos, and design aspects in an astonishing quantity and variety are crammed into this very well researched and highly regarded work.

U.S. Handguns of World War 2, The Secondary Pistols and Revolvers, by Charles W. Pate, Mowbray Publishers, Lincoln, RI, 1997. 368 pp., illus. $39.00.

This indispensable new book covers all of the American military handguns of W.W.2 except for the M1911A1.

PRODUCT & SERVICE DIRECTORY...286-296

MANUFACTURERS' DIRECTORY 297-318

AMMUNITION, COMMERCIAL

"Su-Press-On",Inc.
3-D Ammunition & Bullets
3-Ten Corp.
A.W. Peterson Gun Shop, Inc.
Ace Custom 45's, Inc.
Ad Hominem
Air Arms
American Ammunition
Arizona Ammunition, Inc.
Arms Corporation of the Philippines
Arundel Arms & Ammunition, Inc., A.
A-Square Company, Inc.
Atlantic Rose, Inc.
Badger Shooters Supply, Inc.
Ballistic Product, Inc.
Ben William's Gun Shop
Benjamin/Sheridan Co., Crossman
Big Bear Arms & Sporting Goods, Inc.
Black Hills Ammunition, Inc.
Blammo Ammo
Blount, Inc., Sporting Equipment Div.
Brenneke KG, Wilhelm
Buffalo Bullet Co., Inc..
Bull-X, Inc.
Cabela's
Cambos Outdoorsman
Casull Arms Corp.
CBC
Champion's Choice, Inc.
Cor-Bon Bullet & Ammo Co.
Crosman Airguns
Cubic Shot Shell Co., Inc.
Cumberland States Arsenal
Daisy Mfg. Co.
Dead Eye's Sport Center
Delta Arms Ltd.
Delta Frangible Ammunition LLC
Diana
   (See U.S. Importer - Dynamit Nobel-RWS, Inc.)
Dynamit Nobel-RWS, Inc.
Effebi SNC-Dr. Franco Beretta
Eley Ltd.
Elite Ammunition
Estate Cartridge, Inc.
Federal Cartridge Co.
Fiocchi of America Inc.
Fish Mfg. Gunsmith Sptg. Co., Marshall
Garcia National Gun Traders, Inc.
Garrett Cartridges Inc.
Garthwaite Pistolsmith, Inc., Jim
Gibbs Rifle Co., Inc.
Gil Hebard Guns Inc.
Glaser Safety Slug, Inc.
GOEX Inc.
Goodwin's Gun Shop
Gun Accessories
   (See Glaser Safety Slug, Inc.)
Gun City
Hansen & Co.
   (See Hansen Cartridge Co.)
Hart & Son, Inc.
Hi-Performance Ammunition Company
Hirtenberger Aktiengesellschaft
Hornady Mfg. Co.
Hunters Supply, Inc.
IMX, LLC
Intercontinental Distributors, Ltd.
Ion Industries, Inc
Keng's Firearms Specialty, Inc. / US Tactical Systems
Kent Cartridge America, Inc
Kent Cartridge Mfg. Co. Ltd.
Knight Rifles
Lapua Ltd.
Lethal Force Institute
   (See Police Bookshelf)

Lock's Philadelphia Gun Exchange
Magnum Research, Inc.
MagSafe Ammo Co.
Magtech Ammunition Co. Inc.
Maionchi-L.M.I.
Mandall Shooting Supplies Inc.
Markell,Inc.
McBros Rifle Co.
Men-Metallwerk Elisenhuette GmbH
Mullins Ammunition
New England Ammunition Co.
Oklahoma Ammunition Co.
Omark Industries,Div. of Blount,Inc.
Outdoor Sports Headquarters, Inc.
P.S.M.G. Gun Co.
Pacific Cartridge, Inc.
Paragon Sales & Services, Inc.
Parker & Sons Shooting Supply
Peterson Gun Shop, Inc., A.W.
PMC / Eldorado Cartridge Corp.
Police Bookshelf
Polywad, Inc.
Pony Express Reloaders
Precision Delta Corp.
Pro Load Ammunition, Inc.
R.E.I.
Ravell Ltd.
Remington Arms Co., Inc.
Rucker Dist. Inc.
RWS
   (See US Importer-Dynamit Nobel-RWS, Inc.)
Sellier & Bellot, USA Inc
Southern Ammunition Co., Inc.
Speer Bullets
SSK Industries
TCCI
The A.W. Peterson Gun Shop, Inc.
The BulletMakers Workshop
The Gun Room Press
The Gun Works
Thompson Bullet Lube Co.
USAC
Valor Corp.
VAM Distribution Co LLC
Victory USA
Vihtavuori Oy/Kaltron-Pettibone
Visible Impact Targets
Voere-KGH m.b.H.
Vom Hoffe
   (See Old Western Scrounger, Inc., The)
Weatherby, Inc.
Westley Richards & Co.
Whitestone Lumber Corp.
Widener's Reloading & Shooting Supply, Inc.
Wilhelm Brenneke KG
Winchester Div. Olin Corp.
Zero Ammunition Co., Inc.

AMMUNITION, CUSTOM

3-D Ammunition & Bullets
3-Ten Corp.
A.W. Peterson Gun Shop, Inc.
Accuracy Unlimited
AFSCO Ammunition
Allred Bullet Co.
American Derringer Corp.
American Products, Inc.
Arizona Ammunition, Inc.
Arms Corporation of the Philippines
Atlantic Rose, Inc.
Ballard Rifle & Cartridge Co., LLC
Bear Arms
Belding's Custom Gun Shop
Berger Bullets Ltd.
Big Bore Bullets of Alaska
Black Hills Ammunition, Inc.
Blue Mountain Bullets
Brynin, Milton

Buckskin Bullet Co.
CBC
CFVentures
Cubic Shot Shell Co., Inc.
Custom Tackle and Ammo
Dakota Arms, Inc.
Dead Eye's Sport Center
Delta Frangible Ammunition LLC
DKT, Inc.
Elite Ammunition
Estate Cartridge, Inc.
GDL Enterprises
GOEX Inc.
Gonzalez Guns, Ramon B
Grayback Wildcats
Hirtenberger Aktiengesellschaft
Hobson Precision Mfg. Co.
Hoelscher, Virgil
Horizons Unlimited
Hornady Mfg. Co.
Hunters Supply, Inc.
IMX, LLC
James Calhoon Mfg.
James Calhoon Varmint Bullets
Jensen Bullets
Jensen's Custom Ammunition
Jensen's Firearms Academy
Kaswer Custom, Inc.
Keeler, R. H.
Kent Cartridge Mfg. Co. Ltd.
L E Jurras & Assoc.
L.A.R. Mfg., Inc.
Lethal Force Institute
   (See Police Bookshelf)
Lindsley Arms Cartridge Co.
Linebaugh Custom Sixguns
Loch Leven Industries / Convert-A-Pell
MagSafe Ammo Co.
MAST Technology
McBros Rifle Co.
McMurdo, Lynn
   (See Specialty Gunsmithing)
Men-Metallwerk Elisenhuette GmbH
Milstor Corp.
Mullins Ammunition
Oklahoma Ammunition Co.
Old Western Scrounger,Inc.
P.S.M.G. Gun Co.
Peterson Gun Shop, Inc., A.W.
Phillippi Custom Bullets, Justin
Police Bookshelf
Power Plus Enterprises, Inc.
Precision Delta Corp.
Precision Munitions, Inc.
Professional Hunter Supplies
   (See Star Custom Bull)
R.E.I.
Ramon B. Gonzalez Guns
Sandia Die & Cartridge Co.
SOS Products Co.
   (See Buck Stix-SOS Products Co.)
Specialty Gunsmithing
Spencer's Custom Guns
SSK Industries
Star Custom Bullets
State Arms Gun Co.
Stewart's Gunsmithing
The A.W. Peterson Gun Shop, Inc.
The BulletMakers Workshop
The Country Armourer
Unmussig Bullets, D. L.
Vitt/Boos
Vom Hoffe
   (See Old Western Scrounger, Inc., The)
Vulpes Ventures, Inc. Fox Cartridge Division
Warren Muzzleloading Co., Inc.
Weaver Arms Corp. Gun Shop
Worthy Products, Inc.
Zero Ammunition Co., Inc.

AMMUNITION, FOREIGN

A.W. Peterson Gun Shop, Inc.

Ad Hominem
AFSCO Ammunition
Armscorp USA, Inc.
Atlantic Rose, Inc.
Atlantic Rose, Inc.
B & P America
Beeman Precision Airguns
Cape Outfitters
CBC
Cheddite France S.A.
Cubic Shot Shell Co., Inc.
Dead Eye's Sport Center
Diana
   (See U.S. Importer - Dynamit Nobel-RWS, Inc.)
DKT, Inc.
Dynamit Nobel-RWS, Inc.
E. Arthur Brown Co.
Fiocchi of America Inc.
First Inc., Jack
Gamebore Division, Polywad Inc
Gibbs Rifle Co., Inc.
GOEX Inc.
Goodwin's Gun Shop
Gunsmithing, Inc.
Hansen & Co.
   (See Hansen Cartridge Co.)
Heidenstrom Bullets
Hirtenberger Aktiengesellschaft
Hornady Mfg. Co.
IMX, LLC
Intrac Arms International
K.B.I. Inc
MagSafe Ammo Co.
Maionchi-L.M.I.
Mandall Shooting Supplies Inc.
Marksman Products
MAST Technology
Merkuria Ltd.
Mullins Ammunition
Navy Arms Company
Oklahoma Ammunition Co.
Old Western Scrounger,Inc.
P.S.M.G. Gun Co.
Paragon Sales & Services, Inc.
Peterson Gun Shop, Inc., A.W.
Petro-Explo Inc.
Precision Delta Corp.
R.E.T. Enterprises
Ramon B. Gonzalez Guns
RWS
   (See US Importer-Dynamit Nobel-RWS, Inc.)
Samco Global Arms, Inc.
Sentinel Arms
Southern Ammunition Co., Inc.
Speer Bullets
Stratco, Inc.
T.F.C. S.p.A.
The A.W. Peterson Gun Shop, Inc.
The BulletMakers Workshop
The Paul Co.
Victory Ammunition
Vihtavuori Oy/Kaltron-Pettibone
Vom Hoffe
   (See Old Western Scrounger, Inc., The)

AMMUNITION COMPONENTS-- BULLETS, POWDER, PRIMERS, CASES

3-D Ammunition & Bullets
A.W. Peterson Gun Shop, Inc.
Acadian Ballistic Specialties
Accuracy Unlimited
Accurate Arms Co., Inc.
Action Bullets & Alloy Inc
ADCO Sales, Inc.
Alaska Bullet Works, Inc.
Alliant Techsystems Smokeless Powder Group
Allred Bullet Co.
Alpha LaFranck Enterprises
American Products, Inc.
Arizona Ammunition, Inc.

Armfield Custom Bullets
A-Square Company, Inc.
Atlantic Rose, Inc.
Baer's Hollows
Ballard Rifle & Cartridge Co., LLC
Barnes
Barnes Bullets, Inc.
Beartooth Bullets
Bell Reloading, Inc.
Berger Bullets Ltd.
Berry's Mfg., Inc.
Big Bore Bullets of Alaska
Big Bore Express
Bitterroot Bullet Co.
Black Belt Bullets
   (See Big Bore Express)
Black Hills Shooters Supply
Black Powder Products
Blount, Inc., Sporting Equipment Div.
Blue Mountain Bullets
Brenneke KG, Wilhelm
Briese Bullet Co., Inc.
Brown Co, E. Arthur
Brown Dog Ent.
BRP, Inc. High Performance Cast Bullets
Buck Stix--SOS Products Co.
Buckeye Custom Bullets
Buckskin Bullet Co.
Buffalo Arms Co.
Buffalo Bullet Co., Inc..
Buffalo Rock Shooters Supply
Bullseye Bullets
Bull-X, Inc.
Butler Enterprises
Cambos Outdoorsman
Canyon Cartridge Corp.
Cascade Bullet Co., Inc.
Cast Performance Bullet Company
Casull Arms Corp.
CCI Ammunition
Champion's Choice, Inc.
Cheddite France S.A.
CheVron Bullets
Chuck's Gun Shop
Clean Shot Technologies
Colorado Sutlers Arsenal
   (See Cumberland States
Competitor Corp. Inc.
Cook Engineering Service
Cor-Bon Bullet & Ammo Co.
Cumberland States Arsenal
Cummings Bullets
Curtis Cast Bullets
Curtis Gun Shop
   (See Curtis Cast Bullets)
Custom Bullets by Hoffman
D&J Bullet Co. & Custom Gun Shop, Inc.
Dakota Arms, Inc.
Davide Pedersoli and Co.
DKT, Inc.
Dohring Bullets
Eichelberger Bullets, Wm.
Eldorado Cartridge Corp
   (See PMC/Eldorado
Federal Cartridge Co.
Fiocchi of America Inc.
Fish Mfg. Gunsmith Sptg. Co., Marshall
Forkin, Ben (See Belt MTN Arms)
Forkin Arms
Fowler Bullets
Fowler, Bob
   (See Black Powder Products)
Foy Custom Bullets
Freedom Arms, Inc.
Garcia National Gun Traders, Inc.
Gehmann, Walter
   (See Huntington Die Specialties)
GOEX Inc.
Golden Bear Bullets
Gotz Bullets
Grayback Wildcats

Green Mountain Rifle Barrel Co., Inc.
Grier's Hard Cast Bullets
GTB
Gun City
Hammets VLD Bullets
Hardin Specialty Dist.
Harris Enterprises
Harrison Bullets
Hart & Son, Inc.
Hawk Laboratories, Inc.
   (See Hawk, Inc.)
Hawk, Inc.
Haydon Shooters Supply, Russ
Heidenstrom Bullets
Hercules, Inc.
   (See Alliant Techsystems, Smokeless)
Hi-Performance Ammunition Company
Hirtenberger Aktiengesellschaft
Hobson Precision Mfg. Co.
Hodgdon Powder Co.
Hornady Mfg. Co.
HT Bullets
Hunters Supply, Inc.
Impact Case Co.
Imperial Magnum Corp.
IMR Powder Co.
Intercontinental Distributors, Ltd.
J&D Components
J&L Superior Bullets
   (See Huntington Die Special)
J.R. Williams Bullet Co.
James Calhoon Mfg.
James Calhoon Varmint Bullets
Jensen Bullets
Jensen's Firearms Academy
Jericho Tool & Die Co., Inc.
Jester Bullets
JLK Bullets
JRP Custom Bullets
Ka Pu Kapili
Kaswer Custom, Inc.
Keith's Bullets
Keng's Firearms Specialty, Inc. / US Tactical Systems
Ken's Kustom Kartridges
Kent Cartridge Mfg. Co. Ltd.
KLA Enterprises
Knight Rifles
Knight Rifles
   (See Modern Muzzle Loading, Inc.)
Lapua Ltd.
Lawrence Brand Shot
   (See Precision Reloading)
Legend Products Corp.
Liberty Shooting Supplies
Lightning Performance Innovations, Inc.
Lindsley Arms Cartridge Co.
Littleton, J. F.
Lomont Precision Bullets
Loweth, Richard H.R.
Lyman Products Corp.
Magnus Bullets
Maine Custom Bullets
Maionchi-L.M.I.
Marchmon Bullets
Markesbery Muzzle Loaders, Inc.
MarMik, Inc.
MAST Technology
McMurdo, Lynn
   (See Specialty Gunsmithing)
Meister Bullets
   (See Gander Mountain)
Men-Metallwerk Elisenhuette GmbH
Merkuria Ltd.
Michael's Antiques
Mitchell Bullets, R.F.
MI-TE Bullets
Montana Precision Swaging
Mountain State Muzzleloading Supplies, Inc.
Mulhern, Rick
Murmur Corp.
Nagel's Custom Bullets

National Bullet Co.
Naval Ordnance Works
Necromancer Industries, Inc.
North American Shooting
 Systems
North Devon Firearms Services
Northern Precision Custom
 Swaged Bullets
Nosler, Inc.
OK Weber,Inc.
Oklahoma Ammunition Co.
Old Wagon Bullets
Old Western Scrounger,Inc.
Oregon Trail Bullet Company
Pacific Cartridge, Inc.
Pacific Rifle Co.
Page Custom Bullets
Pease Accuracy
Penn Bullets
Peterson Gun Shop, Inc., A.W.
Petro-Explo Inc.
Phillippi Custom Bullets, Justin
Pinetree Bullets
PMC / Eldorado Cartridge Corp.
Polywad, Inc.
Power Plus Enterprises, Inc.
Precision Delta Corp.
Precision Munitions, Inc.
Prescott Projectile Co.
Price Bullets, Patrick W.
PRL Bullets, c/o Blackburn
 Enterprises
Professional Hunter Supplies
 (See Star Custom Bull)
Proofmark Corp.
R.I.S. Co., Inc.
Rainier Ballistics Corp.
Ramon B. Gonzalez Guns
Ravell Ltd.
Redwood Bullet Works
Reloading Specialties, Inc.
Remington Arms Co., Inc.
Rhino
Robinson H.V. Bullets
Rubright Bullets
Russ Haydon Shooters' Supply
SAECO
 (See Redding Reloading
 Equipment)
Scharch Mfg., Inc.
Schneider Bullets
Schroeder Bullets
Schumakers Gun Shop
Scot Powder
Seebeck Assoc., R.E.
Shappy Bullets
Sharps Arms Co., Inc., C.
Shilen, Inc.
Sierra Bullets
SOS Products Co.
 (See Buck Stix-SOS
 Products Co.)
Southern Ammunition Co., Inc.
Specialty Gunsmithing
Speer Bullets
Spencer's Custom Guns
Stanley Bullets
Star Ammunition, Inc.
Star Custom Bullets
Starke Bullet Company
Starline, Inc.
Stewart's Gunsmithing
Swift Bullet Co.
T.F.C. S.p.A.
Taracorp Industries, Inc.
TCCI
TCSR
The A.W. Peterson Gun Shop,
 Inc.
The Ordnance Works
Thompson Bullet Lube Co.
Thompson Precision
TMI Products
 (See Haselbauer Products,
 Jerry)
Traditions Performance
 Firearms
Trico Plastics
True Flight Bullet Co.
Tucson Mold, Inc.
Unmussig Bullets, D. L.

USAC
Vann Custom Bullets
Vihtavuori Oy/Kaltron-
 Pettibone
Vincent's Shop
Viper Bullet and Brass Works
Vom Hoffe
 (See Old Western Scrounger,
 Inc., The)
Warren Muzzleloading Co., Inc.
Watson Trophy Match Bullets
Weatherby, Inc.
Western Nevada West Coast
 Bullets
Widener's Reloading &
 Shooting Supply, Inc.
Winchester Div. Olin Corp.
Winkle Bullets
Woodleigh
 (See Huntington Die
 Specialties)
Worthy Products, Inc.
Wyant Bullets
Wyoming Custom Bullets
Zero Ammunition Co., Inc.

ANTIQUE ARMS DEALER

Ackerman & Co.
Ad Hominem
Antique American Firearms
Antique Arms Co.
Aplan Antiques & Art, James O.
Armoury, Inc., The
Arundel Arms & Ammunition,
 Inc., A.
Ballard Rifle & Cartridge Co.,
 LLC
Bear Mountain Gun & Tool
Bob's Tactical Indoor Shooting
 Range & Gun Shop
British Antiques
Buckskin Machine Works, A.
 Hunkeler
Buffalo Arms Co.
Cape Outfitters
Carlson, Douglas R, Antique
 American Firearms
CBC-BRAZIL
Chadick's Ltd.
Chambers Flintlocks Ltd., Jim
Champlin Firearms, Inc.
Chuck's Gun Shop
Clements' Custom Leathercraft,
 Chas
Cole's Gun Works
D&D Gunsmiths, Ltd.
David R. Chicoine
Dixie Gun Works
Dixie Gun Works
Dixon Muzzleloading Shop, Inc.
Duffy, Charles E
 (See Guns Antique & Modern
 DBA)
Ed's Gun House
Enguix Import-Export
Fagan & Co.Inc
Fish Mfg. Gunsmith Sptg. Co.,
 Marshall
Flayderman & Co., Inc.
Frielich Police Equipment
Fulmer's Antique Firearms,
 Chet
Getz Barrel Co.
Glass, Herb
Goergen's Gun Shop, Inc.
Golden Age Arms Co.
Goodwin's Gun Shop
Gun Hunter Books
 (See Gun Hunter Trading Co)
Gun Hunter Trading Co.
Guns Antique & Modern DBA /
 Charles E. Duffy
Hallowell & Co.
Hammans, Charles E.
HandCrafts Unltd
 (See Clements' Custom
 Leather)
Handgun Press

Hansen & Co.
 (See Hansen Cartridge Co.)
Hunkeler, A
 (See Buckskin Machine
 Works
Imperial Miniature Armory
James Wayne Firearms for
 Collectors and Investors
Kelley's
Knight's Mfg. Co.
Ledbetter Airguns, Riley
LeFever Arms Co., Inc.
Lever Arms Service Ltd.
Lock's Philadelphia Gun
 Exchange
Log Cabin Sport Shop
Logdewood Mfg.
Mandall Shooting Supplies Inc.
Martin's Gun Shop
Michael's Antiques
Montana Outfitters, Lewis E.
 Yearout
Muzzleloaders Etcetera, Inc.
Navy Arms Company
New England Arms Co.
Peter Dyson & Son Ltd.
Pony Express Sport Shop
Powder Horn Ltd.
Ravell Ltd.
Reno, Wayne
Retting, Inc., Martin B
Robert Valade Engraving
Rutgers Book Center
Samco Global Arms, Inc.
Sarco, Inc.
Scott Fine Guns Inc., Thad
 Shootin' Shack, Inc.
Sportsmen's Exchange &
 Western Gun Traders, Inc.
Steves House of Guns
Stott's Creek Armory, Inc.
The Gun Room
The Gun Room Press
The Gun Shop
The Gun Works
Turnbull Restoration, Doug
Vic's Gun Refinishing
Vintage Arms, Inc.
Wallace, Terry
Westley Richards & Co.
Wild West Guns
William Fagan & Co.
Winchester Consultants
Winchester Sutler, Inc., The
Wood, Frank (See Classic
 Guns, Inc.)
Yearout, Lewis E.
 (See Montana Outfitters)

APPRAISER - GUNS, ETC.

A.W. Peterson Gun Shop, Inc.
Ackerman & Co.
Antique Arms Co.
Armoury, Inc., The
Arundel Arms & Ammunition,
 Inc., A.
Barta's Gunsmithing
Beitzinger, George
Blue Book Publications, Inc.
Bob Rogers Gunsmithing
Bob's Tactical Indoor Shooting
 Range & Gun Shop
British Antiques
Bullet N Press
Butterfield's
Cannon's
Cape Outfitters
Chadick's Ltd.
Champlin Firearms, Inc.
Christie's East
Chuilli, Stephen
Clark Firearms Engraving
Clements' Custom Leathercraft,
 Chas
Cole's Gun Works
Colonial Arms, Inc.
Colonial Repair
Corry, John
Custom Tackle and Ammo

D&D Gunsmiths, Ltd.
David R. Chicoine
DGR Custom Rifles
Dixie Gun Works
Dixon Muzzleloading Shop, Inc.
Duane's Gun Repair
 (See DGR Custom Rifles)
Ed's Gun House
Eversull Co., Inc.
Fagan & Co.Inc
Ferris Firearms
Fish Mfg. Gunsmith Sptg. Co.,
 Marshall
Flayderman & Co., Inc.
Forty Five Ranch Enterprises
Francotte & Cie S.A. Auguste
Frontier Arms Co.,Inc.
Gene's Custom Guns
George E. Mathews & Son, Inc.
Gerald Pettinger Books, see
 Pettinger Books
Getz Barrel Co.
Gillmann, Edwin
Gilmore Sports Concepts
Goergen's Gun Shop, Inc.
Golden Age Arms Co.
Gonzalez Guns, Ramon B
Goodwin's Gun Shop
Griffin & Howe, Inc.
Groenewold, John
Gun City
Gun Hunter Books
 (See Gun Hunter Trading Co)
Gun Hunter Trading Co.
Guncraft Books
 (See Guncraft Sports Inc.)
Guncraft Sports Inc.
Guns
Gunsmithing, Inc.
Hallowell & Co.
Hammans, Charles E.
HandCrafts Unltd
 (See Clements' Custom
 Leather)
Handgun Press
Hank's Gun Shop
Hansen & Co.
 (See Hansen Cartridge Co.)
Hughes, Steven Dodd
Irwin, Campbell H.
Island Pond Gun Shop
Ithaca Classic Doubles
Jackalope Gun Shop
James Wayne Firearms for
 Collectors and Investors
Jensen's Custom Ammunition
Kelley's
L.L. Bean, Inc.
Lampert, Ron
LaRocca Gun Works
Ledbetter Airguns, Riley
LeFever Arms Co., Inc.
Lock's Philadelphia Gun
 Exchange
Log Cabin Sport Shop
Logdewood Mfg.
Lomont Precision Bullets
Long, George F.
Mahony, Philip Bruce
Mandall Shooting Supplies Inc.
Martin's Gun Shop
Mathews & Son, Inc., George E.
McCann Industries
McCann's Machine & Gun Shop
Mercer Custom Guns
Montana Outfitters, Lewis E.
 Yearout
Muzzleloaders Etcetera, Inc.
Navy Arms Company
New England Arms Co.
Nitex Gun Shop
Pasadena Gun Center
Pentheny de Pentheny
Peterson Gun Shop, Inc., A.W.
Pettinger Books, Gerald
Pony Express Sport Shop
Powder Horn Ltd.
R.A. Wells Custom Gunsmith
R.E.T. Enterprises
Ramon B. Gonzalez Guns
Retting, Inc., Martin B

River Road Sporting Clays
Robert Valade Engraving
Rutgers Book Center
Scott Fine Guns Inc., Thad
 Shootin' Shack, Inc.
Spencer Reblue Service
Sportsmen's Exchange &
 Western Gun Traders, Inc.
Stott's Creek Armory, Inc.
Stratco, Inc.
Ten-Ring Precision, Inc.
The A.W. Peterson Gun Shop,
 Inc.
The Gun Room Press
The Gun Shop
The Gun Shop
The Gun Works
The Orvis Co.
The Swampfire Shop
 (See Peterson Gun Shop,
 Inc.)
Thurston Sports, Inc.
Valade Engraving, Robert
Vic's Gun Refinishing
Walker Arms Co., Inc.
Wallace, Terry
Wasmundt, Jim
Weber & Markin Custom
 Gunsmiths
Werth, T. W.
Whidin & Sons Ltd, E.H.
Whitestone Lumber Corp.
Wichita Arms, Inc.
Wild West Guns
William Fagan & Co.
Williams Shootin' Iron Service,
 The Lynx-Line
Winchester Consultants
Winchester Sutler, Inc., The
Wood, Frank (See Classic
 Guns, Inc.)
Yearout, Lewis E.
 (See Montana Outfitters)

BOOKS & MANUALS (PUBLISHERS & DEALERS)

"Su-Press-On", Inc.
Alpha 1 Drop Zone
American Handgunner
 Magazine
Armory Publications
Arms & Armour Press
Ballistic Product, Inc.
Ballistic Product, Inc.
Barnes Bullets, Inc.
Bauska Barrels
Beartooth Bullets
Beeman Precision Airguns
Blacksmith Corp.
Blacktail Mountain Books
Blue Book Publications, Inc.
Blue Ridge Machinery & Tools,
 Inc.
Boone's Custom Ivory Grips,
 Inc.
Brown Co, E. Arthur
Brownells, Inc.
Bullet N Press
C. Sharps Arms Co.
 Inc./Montana Armory
Calibre Press, Inc.
Cape Outfitters
Cheyenne Pioneer Products
Colonial Repair
Colorado Sutlers Arsenal
 (See Cumberland States
 Arsenal)
Corbin Mfg. & Supply, Inc.
Cumberland States Arsenal
DBI Books Division of Krause
 Publications
Dixon Muzzleloading Shop, Inc.
Executive Protection Institute
Flores Publications Inc, J
 (See Action Direct Inc.)
Galati International
Gerald Pettinger Books, see
 Pettinger Books
Golden Age Arms Co.

Gun City
Gun List (See Krause
 Publications)
Guncraft Books
 (See Guncraft Sports Inc.)
Guncraft Sports Inc.
Gunnerman Books
GUNS Magazine
Gunsmithing, Inc.
H&P Publishing
Handgun Press
Harris Publications
Hawk Laboratories, Inc.
 (See Hawk, Inc.)
Hawk, Inc.
Heritage / VSP Gun Books
Hodgdon Powder Co.
Home Shop Machinist The
 Village Press Publications
Hornady Mfg. Co.
Hungry Horse Books
Huntington Die Specialties
I.D.S.A. Books
Info-Arm
Ironside International
 Publishers, Inc.
Jantz Supply
Kelley's
King & Co.
Koval Knives
Krause Publications, Inc.
L.B.T.
Lapua Ltd.
Lethal Force Institute
 (See Police Bookshelf)
Lyman Products Corp.
Madis Books
Magma Engineering Co.
Mandall Shooting Supplies Inc.
MarMik, Inc.
Montana Armory, Inc
 (See C. Sharps Arms Co.
 Inc.)
Mountain South
Mountain State Muzzleloading
 Supplies, Inc.
Mulberry House Publishing
Navy Arms Company
OK Weber,Inc.
Outdoor Sports Headquarters,
 Inc.
Paintball Games International
 Magazine Aceville
Pejsa Ballistics
Petersen Publishing Co.
 (See Emap USA)
Pettinger Books, Gerald
PFRB Co.
Police Bookshelf
Precision Shooting, Inc.
Professional Hunter Supplies
 (See Star Custom Bull)
Ravell Ltd.
Ray Riling Arms Books Co.
Remington Double Shotguns
Russ Haydon Shooters' Supply
Rutgers Book Center
S&S Firearms
Safari Press, Inc.
Sanders Gun and Machine
 Shop
Saunders Gun & Machine Shop
Scharch Mfg., Inc.
Scharch Mfg., Inc.
Semmer, Charles
 (See Remington Double
 Shotguns)
Sharps Arms Co., Inc., C.
Shotgun Sports Magazine, dba
 Shootin' Accessories Ltd.
Sierra Bullets
Speer Bullets
SPG LLC
Stackpole Books
Star Custom Bullets
Stewart Game Calls, Inc.,
 Johnny
Stoeger Industries
Stoeger Publishing Co.
 (See Stoeger Industries)
Swift Bullet Co.

The A.W. Peterson Gun Shop, Inc.
The Gun Parts Corp.
The Gun Room Press
The Gun Works
The NgraveR Co.
Thomas, Charles C.
Track of the Wolf, Inc.
Trafalgar Square
Trotman, Ken
Tru-Balance Knife Co.
Vega Tool Co.
Vintage Industries, Inc.
VSP Publishers
    (See Heritage/VSP Gun Books)
W.E. Brownell Checkering Tools
WAMCO--New Mexico
Wells Creek Knife & Gun Works
Wilderness Sound Products Ltd.
Williams Gun Sight Co.
Wolfe Publishing Co.
Wolf's Western Traders

BULLET, CASE & DIE LUBRICANTS

Beartooth Bullets
Bonanza (See Forster Products)
Brown Co, E. Arthur
Buckskin Bullet Co.
Buffalo Arms Co.
Camp-Cap Products
CFVentures
Cooper-Woodward
CVA
E-Z-Way Systems
Ferguson, Bill
Forster Products
GAR
Guardsman Products
Heidenstrom Bullets
Hollywood Engineering
Hornady Mfg. Co.
Imperial (See E-Z-Way Systems)
Knoell, Doug
L.B.T.
Le Clear Industries
    (See E-Z-Way Systems)
Lee Precision, Inc.
Lithi Bee Bullet Lube
MI-TE Bullets
Paco's
    (See Small Custom Mould & Bullet Co)
RCBS Div. of Blount
Reardon Products
Rooster Laboratories
Shay's Gunsmithing
Small Custom Mould & Bullet Co.
Tamarack Products, Inc.
Uncle Mike's
    (See Michaels of Oregon Co.)
Warren Muzzleloading Co., Inc.
Widener's Reloading & Shooting Supply, Inc.
Young Country Arms

CARTRIDGES FOR COLLECTORS

"Gramps" Antiques
Ackerman & Co.
Ad Hominem
Armory Publications
British Antiques
Cameron's
Campbell, Dick
Cartridge Transfer Group, Pete de Coux
Cherry Creek State Park Shooting Center
Cole's Gun Works
Colonial Repair
Cubic Shot Shell Co., Inc.

de Coux, Pete
    (See Cartridge Transfer Group)
Duane's Gun Repair
    (See DGR Custom Rifles)
Ed's Gun House
Ed's Gun House
Enguix Import-Export
Epps, Ellwood/Isabella (See Gramps)
First Inc., Jack
Fitz Pistol Grip Co.
Forty Five Ranch Enterprises
Goergen's Gun Shop, Inc.
Goodwin's Gun Shop
Grayback Wildcats
Gun City
Gun Hunter Books
    (See Gun Hunter Trading Co)
Gun Hunter Trading Co.
Kelley's
Liberty Shooting Supplies
Mandall Shooting Supplies Inc.
MAST Technology
Michael's Antiques
Montana Outfitters, Lewis E. Yearout
Pasadena Gun Center
Samco Global Arms, Inc.
SOS Products Co.
    (See Buck Stix-SOS Products Co.)
Stone Enterprises Ltd.
The Country Armourer
The Gun Parts Corp.
The Gun Room Press
Vom Hoffe
    (See Old Western Scrounger, Inc., The)
Ward & Van Valkenburg
Winchester Consultants
Yearout, Lewis E.
    (See Montana Outfitters)

CASES, CABINETS, RACKS & SAFES - GUN

All Rite Products, Inc.
Allen Co., Bob
Allen Co., Inc.
Allen Sportswear, Bob
    (See Allen Co., Bob)
Alumna Sport by Dee Zee
American Display Co.
American Security Products Co.
Americase
Art Jewel Enterprises Ltd.
Ashby Turkey Calls
Bagmaster Mfg., Inc.
Barramundi Corp.
Berry's Mfg., Inc.
Big Sky Racks, Inc.
Big Spring Enterprises "Bore Stores"
Bill's Custom Cases
Bison Studios
Black Sheep Brand
Brauer Bros.
Brown, H. R.
    (See Silhouette Leathers)
Browning Arms Co.
Bushmaster Hunting & Fishing
Cannon Safe, Inc.
Chipmunk (See Oregon Arms, Inc.)
Cobalt Mfg., Inc.
CONKKO
Connecticut Shotgun Mfg. Co.
D&L Industries (See D.J. Marketing)
D.J. Marketing
Dara-Nes, Inc.
    (See Nesci Enterprises, Inc.)
Deepeeka Exports Pvt. Ltd.
Doskocil Mfg. Co., Inc.
DTM International, Inc.
Elk River, Inc.
EMF Co., Inc.
English, Inc., A.G.

Enhanced Presentations, Inc.
Eversull Co., Inc.
Fort Knox Security Products
Freedom Arms, Inc.
Frontier Safe Co.
Galati International
GALCO International Ltd.
Gun-Ho Sports Cases
Hall Plastics, Inc., John
Hastings Barrels
Homak
Hoppe's Div. Penguin Industries, Inc.
Hugger Hooks Co.
Hunter Co., Inc.
Hydrosorbent Products
Impact Case Co.
Johanssons Vapentillbehor, Bert
Johnston Bros.
    (See C&T Corp. TA Johnson Brothers)
Kalispel Case Line
Kane Products, Inc.
KK Air International
    (See Impact Case Co.)
Knock on Wood Antiques
Kolpin Mfg., Inc.
Lakewood Products LLC
Liberty Safe
Mandall Shooting Supplies Inc.
Marsh, Mike
McWelco Products
Morton Booth Co.
MPC
MTM Molded Products Co., Inc.
Nalpak
Necessary Concepts, Inc.
Nesci Enterprises Inc.
Oregon Arms, Inc.
    (See Rogue Rifle Co., Inc.)
Outa-Site Gun Carriers
Pflumm Mfg. Co.
Poburka, Philip (See Bison Studios)
Powell & Son (Gunmakers) Ltd., William
Prototech Industries, Inc.
Quality Arms, Inc.
Rogue Rifle Co., Inc.
Schulz Industries
Southern Security
Sportsman's Communicators
Sun Welding Safe Co.
Sweet Home, Inc.
Talmage, William G.
The Outdoor Connection,Inc.
The Surecase Co.
Tinks & Ben Lee Hunting Products (See Wellington)
Trulock Tool
Universal Sports
W. Waller & Son, Inc.
Whitestone Lumber Corp.
Wilson Case, Inc.
Woodstream
Zanotti Armor, Inc.
Ziegel Engineering

CHRONOGRAPHS & PRESSURE TOOLS

Air Rifle Specialists
Brown Co, E. Arthur
C.W. Erickson's L.L.C.
Canons Delcour
Clearview Products
Competition Electronics, Inc.
Custom Chronograph, Inc.
D&H Precision Tooling
Hege Jagd-u. Sporthandels GmbH
Hutton Rifle Ranch
Kent Cartridge Mfg. Co. Ltd.
Mac-1 Airgun Distributors
Oehler Research,Inc.
P.A.C.T., Inc.
Romain's Custom Guns, Inc.
Savage Arms, Inc.

Shooting Chrony, Inc.
Spencer's Custom Guns
Stratco, Inc.
Tepeco

CLEANING & REFINISHING SUPPLIES

AC Dyna-tite Corp.
Alpha 1 Drop Zone
American Gas & Chemical Co., Ltd
Answer Products Co.
Armite Laboratories
Atlantic Mills, Inc.
Atsko/Sno-Seal, Inc.
Barnes Bullets, Inc.
Battenfeld Technologies
Beeman Precision Airguns
Belltown Ltd.
Bill's Gun Repair
Birchwood Casey
Blount, Inc., Sporting Equipment Div.
Blount/Outers
Blue and Gray Products Inc
    (See Ox-Yoke Originals)
Break-Free, Inc.
Bridgers Best
Brown Co, E. Arthur
Brownells, Inc.
C.S. Van Gorden & Son, Inc.
Cambos Outdoorsman
Cambos Outdoorsman
Camp-Cap Products
Chem-Pak Inc.
CONKKO
Connecticut Shotgun Mfg. Co.
Creedmoor Sports, Inc.
CRR, Inc./Marble's Inc.
Custom Products
    (See Jones Custom Products)
Cylinder & Slide, Inc., William R. Laughridge
D&H Prods. Co., Inc.
Dara-Nes, Inc.
    (See Nesci Enterprises, Inc.)
Decker Shooting Products
Deepeeka Exports Pvt. Ltd.
Desert Mountain Mfg.
Dewey Mfg. Co., Inc., J.
Du-Lite Corp.
Dykstra, Doug
E&L Mfg., Inc.
Eezox, Inc.
Ekol Leather Care
Faith Associates
Felk Oil Gun Lube
Flitz International Ltd.
Fluoramics, Inc.
Frontier Products Co.
G96 Products Co., Inc.
Golden Age Arms Co.
Guardsman Products
Gunsmithing, Inc.
Hafner World Wide, Inc.
Half Moon Rifle Shop
Heatbath Corp.
Hoppe's Div. Penguin Industries, Inc.
Hornady Mfg. Co.
Hydrosorbent Products
Iosso Products
James Calhoon Varmint Bullets
Jantz Supply
Jantz Supply
Johnston Bros.
    (See C&T Corp. TA Johnson Brothers)
Jonad Corp.
K&M Industries, Inc.
Kellogg's Professional Products
Kent Cartridge Mfg. Co. Ltd.
Kesselring Gun Shop
Kleen-Bore,Inc.
Knight Rifles
Laurel Mountain Forge
Lee Supplies, Mark

LEM Gun Specialties Inc. The Lewis Lead Remover
List Precision Engineering
LPS Laboratories, Inc.
Lyman Products Corp.
Mac-1 Airgun Distributors
Mandall Shooting Supplies Inc.
Marble Arms
    (See CRR, Inc./Marble's Inc.)
Mark Lee Supplies
Micro Sight Co.
Minute Man High Tech Industries
Mountain State Muzzleloading Supplies, Inc.
Mountain View Sports, Inc.
MTM Molded Products Co., Inc.
Muscle Products Corp.
Nesci Enterprises Inc.
Northern Precision Custom Swaged Bullets
Now Products, Inc.
October Country Muzzleloading
Old World Oil Products
Omark Industries,Div. of Blount,Inc.
Original Mink Oil, Inc.
Otis Technology, Inc.
Outers Laboratories Div. of Blount, Inc. Sporting
Ox-Yoke Originals, Inc.
Parker & Sons Shooting Supply
Parker Gun Finishes
Pendleton Royal, c/o Swingler Buckland Ltd.
Perazone-Gunsmith, Brian
Pete Rickard, Inc.
Peter Dyson & Son Ltd.
Precision Airgun Sales, Inc.
PrOlixrr Lubricants
Pro-Shot Products, Inc.
R&S Industries Corp.
Radiator Specialty Co.
Rickard, Inc., Pete
Rooster Laboratories
Russ Haydon Shooters' Supply
Rusty Duck Premium Gun Care Products
Saunders Gun & Machine Shop
Schumakers Gun Shop
Sheffield Knifemakers Supply, Inc.
Shiloh Creek
Shooter's Choice Gun Care
Shotgun Sports Magazine, dba Shootin' Accessories Ltd.
Silencio/Safety Direct
Sinclair International, Inc.
Sno-Seal, Inc. (See Atsko/Sno-Seal)
Southern Bloomer Mfg. Co.
Spencer's Custom Guns
Splitfire Sporting Goods, L.L.C.
Starr Trading Co., Jedediah
Stoney Point Products, Inc.
Svon Corp.
T.F.C. S.p.A.
TDP Industries, Inc.
Tetra Gun Lubricants (See FTI, Inc.)
Texas Platers Supply Co.
The A.W. Peterson Gun Shop, Inc.
The Dutchman's Firearms, Inc.
The Gun Works
The Lewis Lead Remover
    (See LEM Gun Specialties)
The Paul Co.
Track of the Wolf, Inc.
United States Products Co.
Van Gorden & Son Inc., C. S.
Venco Industries, Inc.
    (See Shooter's Choice)
VibraShine, Inc.
Volquartsen Custom Ltd.
Vom Hoffe
    (See Old Western Scrounger, Inc., The)
Warren Muzzleloading Co., Inc.
Watson Trophy Match Bullets

WD-40 Co.
Wick, David E.
Willow Bend
Wolf's Western Traders
Young Country Arms

COMPUTER SOFTWARE - BALLISTICS

Action Target, Inc.
AmBr Software Group Ltd.
Arms Software
Arms, Programming Solutions
    (See Arms Software)
Barnes Bullets, Inc.
Canons Delcour
Corbin Mfg. & Supply, Inc.
Data Tech Software Systems
Hodgdon Powder Co.
J.I.T. Ltd.
Jensen Bullets
Kent Cartridge Mfg. Co. Ltd.
Maionchi-L.M.I.
Oehler Research,Inc.
Outdoor Sports Headquarters, Inc.
P.A.C.T., Inc.
Pejsa Ballistics
Powley Computer
    (See Hutton Rifle Ranch)
RCBS Div. of Blount
Sierra Bullets
The Ballistic Program Co., Inc.
The Country Armourer
Tioga Engineering Co., Inc.
Vancini, Carl (See Bestload, Inc.)
W. Square Enterprises

CUSTOM GUNSMITH

A&W Repair
A.A. Arms, Inc.
Acadian Ballistic Specialties
Accuracy Unlimited
Ace Custom 45's, Inc.
Acra-Bond Laminates
Adair Custom Shop, Bill
Ahlman Guns
Al Lind Custom Guns
Aldis Gunsmithing & Shooting Supply
Alpha Gunsmith Division
Alpha Precision, Inc.
Alpine Indoor Shooting Range
Amrine's Gun Shop
Answer Products Co.
Antique Arms Co.
Armament Gunsmithing Co., Inc.
Arms Craft Gunsmithing
Arms Ingenuity Co.
Armscorp USA, Inc.
Arnold Arms Co., Inc.
Artistry in Wood
Art's Gun & Sport Shop, Inc.
Arundel Arms & Ammunition, Inc., A.
Autauga Arms, Inc.
Baelder, Harry
Baer Custom, Inc, Les
Bain & Davis, Inc.
Bansner's Ultimate Rifles, LLC
Barnes Bullets, Inc.
Baron Technology
Barta's Gunsmithing
Bear Arms
Bear Mountain Gun & Tool
Beaver Lodge (See Fellowes, Ted)
Behlert Precision, Inc.
Beitzinger, George
Belding's Custom Gun Shop
Ben William's Gun Shop
Bengtson Arms Co., L.
Biesen, Al
Biesen, Roger
Bill Adair Custom Shop
Billings Gunsmiths Inc.

REFERENCE

BlackStar AccuMax Barrels
BlackStar Barrel Accurizing
(See BlackStar AccuMax)
Bob Rogers Gunsmithing
Bond Custom Firearms
Borden Ridges Rimrock Stocks
Borovnik KG, Ludwig
Bowen Classic Arms Corp.
Brace, Larry D.
Briese Bullet Co., Inc.
Briganti, A.J.
Briley Mfg. Inc.
Broad Creek Rifle Works, Ltd.
Brockman's Custom
Gunsmithing
Broken Gun Ranch
Brown Precision, Inc.
Brown Products, Inc., Ed
Buchsenmachermeister
Buckhorn Gun Works
Buckskin Machine Works, A.
Hunkeler
Budin, Dave
Bull Mountain Rifle Co.
Bullberry Barrel Works, Ltd.
Burkhart Gunsmithing, Don
Cache La Poudre Rifleworks
Cambos Outdoorsman
Cambos Outdoorsman
Cannon's
Carolina Precision Rifles
Carter's Gun Shop
Caywood, Shane J.
CBC-BRAZIL
Chambers Flintlocks Ltd., Jim
Chicasaw Gun Works
Chuck's Gun Shop
Chuilli, Stephen
Clark Custom Guns, Inc.
Clark Firearms Engraving
Classic Arms Company
Classic Arms Corp.
Clearview Products
Cleland's Outdoor World, Inc
Cloward's Gun Shop
Coffin, Charles H.
Cogar's Gunsmithing
Cole's Gun Works
Colonial Arms, Inc.
Colonial Repair
Colorado Gunsmithing
Academy
Colorado School of Trades
Colt's Mfg. Co., Inc.
Conrad, C. A.
Corkys Gun Clinic
Cox, Ed. C.
Craig Custom Ltd., Research &
Development
Cullity Restoration
Curtis Custom Shop
Custom Gun Products
Custom Gun Stocks
Custom Single Shot Rifles
Cylinder & Slide, Inc., William
R. Laughridge
D&D Gunsmiths, Ltd.
D&J Bullet Co. & Custom Gun
Shop, Inc.
Dangler, Homer L.
D'Arcy Echols & Co.
Darlington Gun Works, Inc.
Dave's Gun Shop
David Miller Co.
David R. Chicoine
David W. Schwartz Custom
Guns
Davis, Don
Delorge, Ed
Del-Sports, Inc.
DGR Custom Rifles
DGS, Inc., Dale A. Storey
Dilliott Gunsmithing, Inc.
Donnelly, C. P.
Duane A. Hobbie Gunsmithing
Duane's Gun Repair
(See DGR Custom Rifles)
Duffy, Charles E
(See Guns Antique & Modern
DBA)
Duncan's Gun Works, Inc.

E. Arthur Brown Co.
Eckelman Gunsmithing
Ed Brown Products, Inc.
Eggleston, Jere D.
Entre'prise Arms, Inc.
Erhardt, Dennis
Eversull Co., Inc.
Evolution Gun Works Inc.
Eyster Heritage Gunsmiths,
Inc., Ken
F.I., Inc. - High Standard Mfg.
Co.
Ferris Firearms
Fish Mfg. Gunsmith Sptg. Co.,
Marshall
Fisher, Jerry A.
Fisher Custom Firearms
Fleming Firearms
Flynn's Custom Guns
Forkin, Ben (See Belt MTN
Arms)
Forkin Arms
Forster, Kathy
(See Custom Checkering)
Forster, Larry L.
Forthofer's Gunsmithing &
Knifemaking
Francesca, Inc.
Francotte & Cie S.A. Auguste
Fred F. Wells / Wells Sport
Store
Frontier Arms Co.,Inc.
Fullmer, Geo. M.
G.G. & G.
Galaxy Imports Ltd., Inc.
Gary Reeder Custom Guns
Gator Guns & Repair
Genecco Gun Works
Gene's Custom Guns
Gentry Custom Gunmaker,
David
George E. Mathews & Son, Inc.
Gillmann, Edwin
Gilman-Mayfield, Inc.
Gilmore Sports Concepts
Giron, Robert E.
Goens, Dale W.
Gonic Arms/North American
Arm
Gonzalez Guns, Ramon B
Goodling's Gunsmithing
Goodwin's Gun Shop
Grace, Charles E.
Grayback Wildcats
Graybill's Gun Shop
Green, Roger M.
Greg Gunsmithing Repair
GrE-Tan Rifles
Griffin & Howe, Inc.
Griffin & Howe, Inc.
Gruning Precision Inc
Guncraft Books
(See Guncraft Sports Inc.)
Guncraft Sports Inc.
Guncraft Sports, Inc.
Guns
Guns Antique & Modern DBA /
Charles E. Duffy
Gunsite Custom Shop
Gunsite Gunsmithy
(See Gunsite Custom Shop)
Gunsite Training Center
Gunsmithing Ltd.
Hagn Rifles & Actions, Martin
Hamilton, Alex B
(See Ten-Ring Precision,
Inc)
Hammans, Charles E.
Hammond Custom Guns Ltd.
Hank's Gun Shop
Hanson's Gun Center, Dick
Hanus Birdguns Bill
Harris Gunworks
Harry Lawson Co.
Hart & Son, Inc.
Hart Rifle Barrels,Inc.
Hartmann & Weiss GmbH
Harwood, Jack O.
Hawken Shop, The
(See Dayton Traister)
Hecht, Hubert J, Waffen-Hecht

Heilmann, Stephen
Heinie Specialty Products
Hensley, Gunmaker, Darwin
High Bridge Arms, Inc
High Performance International
High Precision
Highline Machine Co.
Hill, Loring F.
Hiptmayer, Armurier
Hiptmayer, Klaus
Hoag, James W.
Hodgson, Richard
Hoehn Sales, Inc.
Hoelscher, Virgil
Hoenig & Rodman
Hofer Jagdwaffen, P.
Holland's Gunsmithing
Hollis Gun Shop
Huebner, Corey O.
Hughes, Steven Dodd
Hunkeler, A
(See Buckskin Machine
Works)
Imperial Magnum Corp.
Irwin, Campbell H.
Island Pond Gun Shop
Israel Arms International, Inc.
Ivanoff, Thomas G
(See Tom's Gun Repair)
J&S Heat Treat
J.J. Roberts / Engraver
Jack Dever Co.
Jackalope Gun Shop
James Calhoon Mfg.
Jamison's Forge Works
Jarrett Rifles, Inc.
Jarvis, Inc.
Jay McCament Custom
Gunmaker
Jeffredo Gunsight
Jensen's Custom Ammunition
Jim Norman Custom
Gunstocks
Jim's Gun Shop (See
Spradlin's)
Jim's Precision, Jim Ketchum
John Norrell Arms
Jones Custom Products, Neil A.
Juenke, Vern
K. Eversull Co., Inc.
KDF, Inc.
Keith's Custom Gunstocks
Ken Eyster Heritage
Gunsmiths, Inc.
Ken Starnes Gunmaker
Ken's Gun Specialties
Ketchum, Jim (See Jim's
Precision)
Kilham & Co.
King's Gun Works
KLA Enterprises
Klein Custom Guns, Don
Kleinendorst, K. W.
Knippel, Richard
KOGOT
Korzinek Riflesmith, J.
KSN Industries Ltd
(See U.S. Importer-Israel
Arms)
L E Jurras & Assoc.
LaFrance Specialties
Lampert, Ron
LaRocca Gun Works
Larry Lyons Gunworks
Lathrop's, Inc.
Laughridge, William R
(See Cylinder & Slide Inc)
Lawson Co., Harry
Lazzeroni Arms Co.
LeFever Arms Co., Inc.
Lind Custom Guns, Al
Linebaugh Custom Sixguns
List Precision Engineering
Lock's Philadelphia Gun
Exchange
Lone Star Rifle Company
Long, George F.
Mag-Na-Port International, Inc.
Mahony, Philip Bruce
Mahony, Philip Bruce
Mahovsky's Metalife

Makinson, Nicholas
Mandall Shooting Supplies Inc.
Marent, Rudolf
Martin's Gun Shop
Martz, John V.
Mathews & Son, Inc., George E.
Mazur Restoration, Pete
McCann's Muzzle-Gun Works
McCluskey Precision Rifles
McGowen Rifle Barrels
McKinney, R.P.
(See Schuetzen Gun Co.)
McMillan Rifle Barrels
MCS, Inc.
Mercer Custom Guns
Michael's Antiques
Mid-America Recreation, Inc.
Middlebrooks Custom Shop
Miller Arms, Inc.
Miller Custom
Mills Jr., Hugh B.
Moeller, Steve
Monell Custom Guns
Montgomery Community
College
Morrison Custom Rifles, J. W.
Morrow, Bud
Mo's Competitor Supplies
(See MCS Inc)
Mowrey's Guns & Gunsmithing
Mullis Guncraft
Muzzleloaders Etcetera, Inc.
NCP Products, Inc.
Neil A. Jones Custom Products
Nelson's Custom Guns, Inc.
Nettestad Gun Works
New England Arms Co.
New England Custom Gun
Service
Newman Gunshop
Nicholson Custom
Nickels, Paul R.
Nicklas, Ted
Nitex Gun Shop
North American Shooting
Systems
Nu-Line Guns,Inc.
Oakland Custom Arms,Inc.
Old World Gunsmithing
Olson, Vic
Ottmar, Maurice
Ox-Yoke Originals, Inc.
Ozark Gun Works
P.S.M.G. Gun Co.
Pac-Nor Barreling
Pagel Gun Works, Inc.
Parker & Sons Shooting Supply
Parker Gun Finishes
Pasadena Gun Center
Paterson Gunsmithing
Paulsen Gunstocks
Peacemaker Specialists
PEM's Mfg. Co.
Pence Precision Barrels
Pennsylvania Gunsmith School
Penrod Precision
Pentheny de Pentheny
Performance Specialists
Pete Mazur Restoration
Peter Dyson & Son Ltd.
Peterson Gun Shop, Inc., A.W.
Piquette's Custom Engraving
Plum City Ballistic Range
Powell & Son (Gunmakers)
Ltd., William
Power Custom, Inc.
Professional Hunter Supplies
(See Star Custom Bull)
Quality Custom Firearms
Quality Firearms of Idaho, Inc.
R&J Gun Shop
R.A. Wells Custom Gunsmith
Ramon B. Gonzalez Guns
Ray's Gunsmith Shop
Renfrew Guns & Supplies
Ridgetop Sporting Goods
Ries, Chuck
Rifles, Inc.
Rigby & Co., John
River Road Sporting Clays

Makinson, Nicholas
RMS Custom Gunsmithing
Robert Valade Engraving
Robinson, Don
Rocky Mountain Arms, Inc.
Romain's Custom Guns, Inc.
Ron Frank Custom Classic
Arms
Ruger's Custom Guns
Rupert's Gun Shop
Ryan, Chad L.
Sanders Custom Gun Service
Savage Arms, Inc.
Schiffman, Mike
Schumakers Gun Shop
Score High Gunsmithing
Scott McDougall & Associates
Sharp Shooter Supply
Shaw, Inc., E. R.
(See Small Arms Mfg. Co.)
Shay's Gunsmithing
Shockley, Harold H.
Shooters Supply
Shootin' Shack, Inc.
Shooting Specialties
(See Titus, Daniel)
Shotguns Unlimited
Silver Ridge Gun Shop
(See Goodwin, Fred)
Simmons Gun Repair, Inc.
Singletary, Kent
Siskiyou Gun Works
(See Donnelly, C. P.)
Skeoch, Brian R.
Sklany's Machine Shop
Slezak, Jerome F.
Small Arms Mfg. Co.
Small Arms Specialists
Smith, Art
Snapp's Gunshop
Sound Technology
Speiser, Fred D.
Spencer Reblue Service
Spencer's Custom Guns
Splitfire Sporting Goods, L.L.C.
Sportsmen's Exchange &
Western Gun Traders, Inc.
Springfield, Inc.
SSK Industries
Star Custom Bullets
Steelman's Gun Shop
Steffens, Ron
Stiles Custom Guns
Storey, Dale A. (See DGS Inc.)
Stott's Creek Armory, Inc.
Sturgeon Valley Sporters
Sullivan, David S .
(See Westwind Rifles Inc.)
Swann, D. J.
Swenson's 45 Shop, A. D.
Swift River Gunworks
Szweda, Robert
(See RMS Custom
Gunsmithing)
Taconic Firearms Ltd., Perry
Lane
Talmage, William G.
Tank's Rifle Shop
Tar-Hunt Custom Rifles, Inc.
Tarnhelm Supply Co., Inc.
Taylor & Robbins
Ten-Ring Precision, Inc.
Terry K. Kopp Professional
Gunsmithing
The A.W. Peterson Gun Shop,
Inc.
The Competitive Pistol Shop
The Custom Shop
The Gun Shop
The Gun Works
The Orvis Co.
The Robar Co.'s, Inc.
The Swampfire Shop
(See Peterson Gun Shop,
Inc.)
Theis, Terry
Thompson, Randall
(See Highline Machine Co.)
Thurston Sports, Inc.
Time Precision
Tom's Gun Repair, Thomas G.
Ivanoff

Tom's Gunshop
Trevallion Gunstocks
Trulock Tool
Tucker, James C.
Turnbull Restoration, Doug
Unmussig Bullets, D. L.
Upper Missouri Trading Co.
Valade Engraving, Robert
Van Horn, Gil
Van Patten, J. W.
Van's Gunsmith Service
Vest, John
Vic's Gun Refinishing
Vintage Arms, Inc.
Virgin Valley Custom Guns
Volquartsen Custom Ltd.
Walker Arms Co., Inc.
Wallace, Terry
Wasmundt, Jim
Wayne E. Schwartz Custom
Guns
Weatherby, Inc.
Weaver Arms Corp. Gun Shop
Weber & Markin Custom
Gunsmiths
Weems, Cecil
Weigand Combat Handguns,
Inc.
Werth, T. W.
Wessinger Custom Guns &
Engraving
Western Design
(See Alpha Gunsmith
Division)
Westley Richards & Co.
Westwind Rifles, Inc., David S.
Sullivan
White Barn Wor
White Shooting Systems, Inc.
(See White Muzzleload
Wichita Arms, Inc.
Wiebe, Duane
Wild West Guns
Wild West Guns
Williams Gun Sight Co.
Williams Shootin' Iron Service,
The Lynx-Line
Williamson Precision
Gunsmithing
Wilsom Combat
Winter, Robert M.
Wise Guns, Dale
Wiseman and Co., Bill
Wood, Frank (See Classic
Guns, Inc.)
Working Guns
Wright's Gunstock Blanks
Yankee Gunsmith
Zeeryp, Russ
Custom Metalsmith
A&W Repair
Ackerman & Co.
Ahlman Guns
Alaskan Silversmith, The
Aldis Gunsmithing & Shooting
Supply
Alpha Precision, Inc.
Amrine's Gun Shop
Answer Products Co.
Antique Arms Co.
Arnold Arms Co., Inc.
Artistry in Wood
Baer Custom, Inc, Les
Baron Technology
Bear Mountain Gun & Tool
Behlert Precision, Inc.
Beitzinger, George
Bengtson Arms Co., L.
Biesen, Al
Bill Adair Custom Shop
Billings Gunsmiths Inc.
Billingsley & Brownell
Bob Rogers Gunsmithing
Bone Engraving, Ralph
Bowen Classic Arms Corp.
Brace, Larry D.
Briganti, A.J.
Broad Creek Rifle Works, Ltd.
Brown Precision, Inc.
Buckhorn Gun Works
Bull Mountain Rifle Co.

Bullberry Barrel Works, Ltd.
Burkhart Gunsmithing, Don
Carter's Gun Shop
Caywood, Shane J.
Checkmate Refinishing
Cleland's Outdoor World, Inc
Colonial Repair
Colorado Gunsmithing
  Academy
Craftguard
Crandall Tool & Machine Co.
Cullity Restoration
Custom Gun Products
Custom Single Shot Rifles
D&D Gunsmiths, Ltd.
D&H Precision Tooling
D'Arcy Echols & Co.
Dave's Gun Shop
Delorge, Ed
DGS, Inc., Dale A. Storey
Dietz Gun Shop & Range, Inc.
Dilliott Gunsmithing, Inc.
Duane's Gun Repair
  (See DGR Custom Rifles)
Duncan's Gun Works, Inc.
Erhardt, Dennis
Eversull Co., Inc.
Eyster Heritage Gunsmiths,
  Inc., Ken
Ferris Firearms
Fisher, Jerry A.
Forster, Larry L.
Forthofer's Gunsmithing &
  Knifemaking
Francesca, Inc.
Fred F. Wells / Wells Sport
  Store
Fullmer, Geo. M.
Genecco Gun Works
Gentry Custom Gunmaker,
  David
Grace, Charles E.
Grayback Wildcats
Graybill's Gun Shop
Green, Roger M.
Griffin & Howe, Inc.
Guns
Gunsmithing Ltd.
Hagn Rifles & Actions, Martin
Hamilton, Alex B
  (See Ten-Ring Precision,
  Inc)
Harry Lawson Co.
Hartmann & Weiss GmbH
Harwood, Jack O.
Hecht, Hubert J, Waffen-Hecht
Heilmann, Stephen
Highline Machine Co.
Hiptmayer, Armurier
Hiptmayer, Klaus
Hoag, James W.
Hoelscher, Virgil
Holland's Gunsmithing
Hollis Gun Shop
Island Pond Gun Shop
Ivanoff, Thomas G
  (See Tom's Gun Repair)
J J Roberts Firearm Engraver
J&S Heat Treat
J.J. Roberts / Engraver
Jamison's Forge Works
Jay McCament Custom
  Gunmaker
Jeffredo Gunsight
KDF, Inc.
Ken Eyster Heritage
  Gunsmiths, Inc., Ken
Ken Starnes Gunmaker
Ken's Gun Specialties
Kilham & Co.
Klein Custom Guns, Don
Kleinendorst, K. W.
Knippel, Richard
Lampert, Ron
Larry Lyons Gunworks
Lawson Co., Harry
List Precision Engineering
Mahovsky's Metalife
Makinson, Nicholas
Mazur Restoration, Pete
McCann Industries

McCann's Machine & Gun Shop
Mid-America Recreation, Inc.
Miller Arms, Inc.
Montgomery Community
  College
Morrison Custom Rifles, J. W.
Morrow, Bud
Mullis Guncraft
Nelson's Custom Guns, Inc.
Nettestad Gun Works
New England Custom Gun
  Service
Nicholson Custom
Nitex Gun Shop
Noreen, Peter H.
Nu-Line Guns,Inc.
Oakland Custom Arms,Inc.
Olson, Vic
Ozark Gun Works
P.S.M.G. Gun Co.
Pagel Gun Works, Inc.
Parker & Sons Shooting Supply
Parker Gun Finishes
Pasadena Gun Center
Penrod Precision
Pete Mazur Restoration
Precision Specialties
Quality Custom Firearms
R.A. Wells Custom Gunsmith
Rice, Keith
  (See White Rock Tool & Die)
Rifles, Inc.
River Road Sporting Clays
Robert Valade Engraving
Rocky Mountain Arms, Inc.
Romain's Custom Guns, Inc.
Ron Frank Custom Classic
  Arms
Sanders Custom Gun Service
Score High Gunsmithing
Simmons Gun Repair, Inc.
Singletary, Kent
Skeoch, Brian R.
Sklany's Machine Shop
Small Arms Specialists
Smith, Art
Smith, Sharmon
Snapp's Gunshop
Spencer Reblue Service
Spencer's Custom Guns
Sportsmen's Exchange &
  Western Gun Traders, Inc.
Steffens, Ron
Stiles Custom Guns
Storey, Dale A. (See DGS Inc.)
Taylor & Robbins
Ten-Ring Precision, Inc.
The A.W. Peterson Gun Shop,
  Inc.
The Custom Shop
The Gun Shop
The Robar Co.'s, Inc.
Thompson, Randall
  (See Highline Machine Co.)
Tom's Gun Repair, Thomas G.
  Ivanoff
Turnbull Restoration, Doug
Valade Engraving, Robert
Van Horn, Gil
Van Patten, J. W.
Waldron, Herman
Wallace, Terry
Weber & Markin Custom
  Gunsmiths
Werth, T. W.
Wessinger Custom Guns &
  Engraving
White Rock Tool & Die
Wiebe, Duane
Wild West Guns
Wild West Guns
Williams Shootin' Iron Service,
  The Lynx-Line
Williamson Precision
  Gunsmithing
Winter, Robert M.
Wise Guns, Dale
Wood, Frank (See Classic
  Guns, Inc.)
Wright's Gunstock Blanks
Zufall, Joseph F.

Decoys

Ad Hominem
Baekgaard Ltd.
Belding's Custom Gun Shop
Boyds' Gunstock Industries,
  Inc.
Carry-Lite, Inc.
Farm Form Decoys, Inc.
Feather, Flex Decoys
Flambeau Products Corp.
G&H Decoys,Inc.
Herter's Manufacturing Inc.
Hiti-Schuch, Atelier Wilma
Klingler Woodcarving
L.L. Bean, Inc.
Molin Industries, Tru-Nord
  Division
Murphy, R.R. Co., Inc.
North Wind Decoy Co.
Original Deer Formula Co., The.
Quack Decoy & Sporting Clays
Russ Trading Post
Sports Innovations Inc.
Tanglefree Industries
The A.W. Peterson Gun Shop,
  Inc.
Woods Wise Products

ENGRAVER, ENGRAVING TOOLS

Ackerman & Co.
Adair Custom Shop, Bill
Ahlman Guns
Alaskan Silversmith, The
Alfano, Sam
Allard, Gary/Creek Side Metal &
  Woodcrafters
Allen Firearm Engraving
Altamont Co.
American Pioneer Video
Baron Technology
Barraclough, John K.
Bates Engraving, Billy
Bill Adair Custom Shop
Billy Bates Engraving
Blair Engraving, Jim
Bleile, C. Roger
Boessler, Erich
Bone Engraving, Ralph
Brooker, Dennis
Buchsenmachermeister
Churchill, Winston G.
Clark Firearms Engraving
Collings, Ronald
Creek Side Metal &
  Woodcrafters
Cullity Restoration
Cupp, Alana, Custom Engraver
Custom Single Shot Rifles
Dayton Traister
Delorge, Ed
Dolbare, Elizabeth
Drain, Mark
Dremel Mfg. Co.
Dubber, Michael W.
Engraving Artistry
Evans Engraving, Robert
Eversull Co., Inc.
Eyster Heritage Gunsmiths,
  Inc., Ken
Firearms & Metal Engraving
Firearms Engraver's Guild of
  America
Flannery Engraving Co., Jeff W
Forty Five Ranch Enterprises
Fountain Products
Francotte & Cie S.A. Auguste
Frank Knives
Fred F. Wells / Wells Sport
  Store
French, Artistic Engraving, J. R.
Gary Reeder Custom Guns
Gene's Custom Guns
Glimm's Custom Gun
  Engraving
Golden Age Arms Co.
Gournet Artistic Engraving
Grant, Howard V.
Griffin & Howe, Inc.

GRS / Glendo Corp.
Guns
Gurney, F. R.
Gwinnell, Bryson J.
Hale, Engraver, Peter
Half Moon Rifle Shop
Hands Engraving, Barry Lee
Harris Gunworks
Harris Hand Engraving, Paul A.
Harwood, Jack O.
Hawken Shop, The
  (See Dayton Traister)
Hiptmayer, Armurier
Hiptmayer, Heidemarie
Hofer Jagdwaffen, P.
Ingle, Ralph W.
J J Roberts Firearm Engraver
J.J. Roberts / Engraver
Jantz Supply
Jeff W. Flannery Engraving Co.
Jim Blair Engraving
John J Adams & Son
  Engravers
Kamyk Engraving Co., Steve
Kane, Edward
Kehr, Roger
Kelly, Lance
Ken Eyster Heritage
  Gunsmiths, Inc.
Kenneth W. Warren Engraver
Klingler Woodcarving
Knippel, Richard
Koevenig's Engraving Service
Larry Lyons Gunworks
LeFever Arms Co., Inc.
Leibowitz, Leonard
Lindsay, Steve
Little Trees Ramble
  (See Scott Pilkington)
McCombs, Leo
McDonald, Dennis
McKenzie, Lynton
Mele, Frank
Metals Hand
  Engraver/European Hand
  Engraving
Mid-America Recreation, Inc.
Mittermeier, Inc., Frank
Montgomery Community
  College
Nelson, Gary K.
New Orleans Jewelers Supply
  Co.
Oker's Engraving
Pedersen, C. R.
Pedersen, Rex C.
Peter Hale/Engraver
Pilgrim Pewter,Inc.
  (See Bell Originals Inc. Sid)
Pilkington, Scott
  (See Little Trees Ramble)
Piquette's Custom Engraving
Potts, Wayne E.
Quality Custom Firearms
Rabeno, Martin
Ralph Bone Engraving
Reed, Dave
Reno, Wayne
Riggs, Jim
Robert Evans Engraving
Robert Valade Engraving
Rohner, Hans
Rohner, John
Rosser, Bob
Rundell's Gun Shop
Runge, Robert P.
Sam Welch Gun Engraving
Sampson, Roger
Schiffman, Mike
Sheffield Knifemakers Supply,
  Inc.
Sherwood, George
Singletary, Kent
Smith, Mark A.
Smith, Ron
Smokey Valley Rifles
Steve Kamyk Engraver
Swanson, Mark
The Gun Room
The NgraveR Co.
Theis, Terry

Thiewes, George W.
Thirion Gun Engraving, Denise
Valade Engraving, Robert
Viramontez Engraving
Vorhes, David
W.E. Brownell Checkering
  Tools
Wagoner, Vernon G.
Wallace, Terry
Warenski, Julie
Weber & Markin Custom
  Gunsmiths
Wells, Rachel
Wessinger Custom Guns &
  Engraving
Winchester Consultants
Ziegel Engineering

GUN PARTS, U.S. & FOREIGN

"Su-Press-On",Inc.
A.A. Arms, Inc.
Ahlman Guns
Amherst Arms
Antique Arms Co.
Armscorp USA, Inc.
Aro-Tek Ltd.
Auto-Ordnance Corp.
B.A.C.
Badger Shooters Supply, Inc.
Bar-Sto Precision Machine
Bear Mountain Gun & Tool
Billings Gunsmiths Inc.
Bill's Gun Repair
Bob's Gun Shop
Briese Bullet Co., Inc.
British Antiques
Brown Products, Inc., Ed
Brownells, Inc.
Bryan & Assoc.
Buffer Technologies
Cambos Outdoorsman
Cambos Outdoorsman
Cape Outfitters
Caspian Arms, Ltd.
CBC-BRAZIL
Chicasaw Gun Works
Ciener Inc., Jonathan Arthur
Cole's Gun Works
Colonial Arms, Inc.
Colonial Repair
Colt's Mfg. Co., Inc.
Cryo-Accurizing
Custom Riflestocks, Inc.,
  Michael M. Kokolus
Cylinder & Slide, Inc., William
  R. Laughridge
Delta Arms Ltd.
Dewey Mfg. Co., Inc., J.
DGR Custom Rifles
Dibble, Derek A.
Duane's Gun Repair
  (See DGR Custom Rifles)
Duffy, Charles E
  (See Guns Antique & Modern
  DBA)
E.A.A. Corp.
Elliott Inc., G. W.
EMF Co., Inc.
Enguix Import-Export
Entre'prise Arms, Inc.
European American Armory
  Corp (See E.A.A. Corp)
Evolution Gun Works Inc.
F.I., Inc. - High Standard Mfg.
  Co.
Faloon Industries, Inc.
Federal Arms Corp. of America
Fleming Firearms
Forrest Inc., Tom
Gentry Custom Gunmaker,
  David
Glimm's Custom Gun
  Engraving
Goodwin's Gun Shop
Granite Mountain Arms, Inc
Greider Precision
Groenewold, John
Gun Hunter Books
  (See Gun Hunter Trading Co)

Gun Hunter Trading Co.
Guns Antique & Modern DBA /
  Charles E. Duffy
Gunsmithing, Inc.
Hastings Barrels
Hawken Shop, The
  (See Dayton Traister)
High Performance International
  I.S.S.
Irwin, Campbell H.
Jamison's Forge Works
Jonathan Arthur Ciener, Inc.
K.K. Arms Co.
Kimber of America, Inc.
Knight's Mfg. Co.
Krico Deutschland GmbH
Lampert, Ron
LaPrade
Laughridge, William R
  (See Cylinder & Slide Inc)
Leapers, Inc.
List Precision Engineering
Lodewick, Walter H.
Logdewood Mfg.
Long, George F.
Mandall Shooting Supplies Inc.
Markell,Inc.
Martin's Gun Shop
McCormick Corp., Chip
MCS, Inc.
Merkuria Ltd.
Mid-America Recreation, Inc.
Morrow, Bud
Mo's Competitor Supplies
  (See MCS Inc)
North Star West
Northwest Arms
Nu-Line Guns,Inc.
Nygord Precision Products,
  Inc.
Olympic Arms Inc.
P.S.M.G. Gun Co.
Pacific Armament Corp
Parts & Surplus
Pennsylvania Gun Parts Inc
Performance Specialists
Peter Dyson & Son Ltd.
Peterson Gun Shop, Inc., A.W.
Quality Firearms of Idaho, Inc.
Ranch Products
Randco UK
Raptor Arms Co., Inc.
Ravell Ltd.
Retting, Inc., Martin B
Romain's Custom Guns, Inc.
Ruger (See Sturm, Ruger &
  Co., Inc.)
S&S Firearms
Sabatti S.r.l.
Samco Global Arms, Inc.
Sarco, Inc.
Scherer Supplies
Shockley, Harold H.
Shootin' Shack, Inc.
Silver Ridge Gun Shop
  (See Goodwin, Fred)
Simmons Gun Repair, Inc.
Smires, C. L.
Smith & Wesson
Southern Ammunition Co., Inc.
Sportsmen's Exchange &
  Western Gun Traders, Inc.
Springfield Sporters, Inc.
Springfield, Inc.
Steyr Mannlicher AG & CO KG
STI International
Strayer-Voigt, Inc.
Sturm Ruger & Co. Inc.
Sunny Hill Enterprises, Inc.
T&S Industries, Inc.
Tank's Rifle Shop
Tarnhelm Supply Co., Inc.
Terry K. Kopp Professional
  Gunsmithing
The A.W. Peterson Gun Shop,
  Inc.
The Gun Parts Corp.
The Gun Room Press
The Gun Shop
The Gun Shop
The Gun Works

REFERENCE

The Southern Armory
The Swampfire Shop
(See Peterson Gun Shop,
Inc.)
VAM Distribution Co LLC
Vektor USA
Vintage Arms, Inc.
W. Waller & Son, Inc.
W.C. Wolff Co.
Walker Arms Co., Inc.
Weaver Arms Corp. Gun Shop
Wescombe, Bill (See North Star
West)
Whitestone Lumber Corp.
Wild West Guns
Williams Mfg. of Oregon
Winchester Sutler, Inc., The
Wise Guns, Dale
Wisners Inc/Twin Pine Armory

GUNS & GUN PARTS, REPLICA & ANTIQUE

Ackerman & Co.
Ahlman Guns
Armi San Paolo
Auto-Ordnance Corp.
Ballard Rifle & Cartridge Co.,
LLC
Bear Mountain Gun & Tool
Billings Gunsmiths Inc.
Bob's Gun Shop
British Antiques
Buckskin Machine Works, A.
Hunkeler
Cache La Poudre Rifleworks
Cash Mfg. Co., Inc.
CBC-BRAZIL
CCL Security Products
Chambers Flintlocks Ltd., Jim
Chicasaw Gun Works
Cogar's Gunsmithing
Cole's Gun Works
Colonial Repair
Colt Blackpowder Arms Co.
Colt's Mfg. Co., Inc.
Custom Riflestocks, Inc.,
Michael M. Kokolus
Custom Single Shot Rifles
David R. Chicoine
Delhi Gun House
Delta Arms Ltd.
Dilliott Gunsmithing, Inc.
Dixie Gun Works
Dixon Muzzleloading Shop, Inc.
Ed's Gun House
Flintlocks, Etc.
George E. Mathews & Son, Inc.
Getz Barrel Co.
Golden Age Arms Co.
Goodwin's Gun Shop
Groenewold, John
Gun Hunter Books
(See Gun Hunter Trading Co)
Gun Hunter Trading Co.
Guns
Hastings Barrels
Hunkeler, A
(See Buckskin Machine
Works)
IAR Inc.
Imperial Miniature Armory
Ithaca Classic Doubles
Ken Starnes Gunmaker
Kokolus, Michael M.
(See Custom Riflestocks)
L&R Lock Co.
Leonard Day
List Precision Engineering
Lock's Philadelphia Gun
Exchange
Logdewood Mfg.
Lone Star Rifle Company
Lucas, Edward E
Mandall Shooting Supplies Inc.
Martin's Gun Shop
Mathews & Son, Inc., George E.
McKinney, R.P.
(See Schuetzen Gun Co.)
Mid-America Recreation, Inc.

Mountain State Muzzleloading
Supplies, Inc.
Mowrey Gun Works
Navy Arms Company
Neumann GmbH
North Star West
Parker & Sons Shooting Supply
Pasadena Gun Center
Pecatonica River Longrifle
PEM's Mfg. Co.
Peter Dyson & Son Ltd.
Pony Express Sport Shop
Quality Firearms of Idaho, Inc.
R.A. Wells Custom Gunsmith
Randco UK
Ravell Ltd.
Retting, Inc., Martin B
Rutgers Book Center
S&S Firearms
Samco Global Arms, Inc.
Sarco, Inc.
Shootin' Shack, Inc.
Silver Ridge Gun Shop
(See Goodwin, Fred)
Simmons Gun Repair, Inc.
Sklany's Machine Shop
Southern Ammunition Co., Inc.
Starr Trading Co., Jedediah
Stott's Creek Armory, Inc.
Taylor's & Co., Inc.
Tennessee Valley Mfg.
The A.W. Peterson Gun Shop,
Inc.
The Gun Parts Corp.
The Gun Room Press
The Gun Shop
The Gun Works
Tiger-Hunt Gunstocks
Turnbull Restoration, Doug
Uberti USA, Inc.
Upper Missouri Trading Co.
Vintage Industries, Inc.
Vortek Products, Inc.
Weber & Markin Custom
Gunsmiths
Wescombe, Bill (See North Star
West)
Whitestone Lumber Corp.
Winchester Sutler, Inc., The

GUNS, AIR

Air Arms
Air Rifle Specialists
Air Venture Airguns
AirForce Airguns
Airrow
Allred Bullet Co.
Arms Corporation of the
Philippines
BEC, Inc.
Beeman Precision Airguns
Benjamin/Sheridan Co.,
Crossman
Brass Eagle, Inc.
Brocock Ltd.
Bryan & Assoc.
BSA Guns Ltd.
Compasseco, Ltd.
Component Concepts, Inc.
Conetrol Scope Mounts
Creedmoor Sports, Inc.
Crosman Airguns
Daisy Mfg. Co.
Daystate Ltd.
Diana
(See U.S. Importer - Dynamit
Nobel-RWS, Inc.)
Domino
Dynamit Nobel-RWS, Inc.
European American Armory
Corp
(See E.A.A. Corp)
FWB
Gamo USA, Inc.
Gaucher Armes, S.A.
Great Lakes Airguns
Groenewold, John
IAR Inc.
Interarms / Howa
J.G. Anschutz GmbH & Co. KG

Labanu, Inc.
Leapers, Inc.
List Precision Engineering
Mac-1 Airgun Distributors
Marksman Products
Maryland Paintball Supply
Merkuria Ltd.
Pardini Armi Srl
Precision Airgun Sales, Inc.
Precision Sales International,
Inc.
Ripley Rifles
Robinson, Don
RWS
(See US Importer-Dynamit
Nobel-RWS, Inc.)
S.G.S. Sporting Guns Srl.
Savage Arms, Inc.
Smart Parts
Smith & Wesson
Steyr Mannlicher AG & CO KG
Stone Enterprises Ltd.
The A.W. Peterson Gun Shop,
Inc.
The Gun Room Press
The Park Rifle Co., Ltd.
Tippmann Pneumatics, Inc.
Tristar Sporting Arms, Ltd.
Trooper Walsh
UltraSport Arms, Inc.
Valor Corp.
Visible Impact Targets
Vortek Products, Inc.
Walther GmbH, Carl
Webley and Scott Ltd.
Weihrauch KG, Hermann
Whiscombe
(See U.S. Importer-Pelaire
Products)
World Class Airguns

GUNS, FOREIGN MANUFACTURER U.S. IMPORTER

Accuracy Internationl Precision
Rifles (See U.S.)
Accuracy Int'l. North America,
Inc.
Ad Hominem
Air Arms
Armas Kemen S. A.
(See U.S. Importers)
Armi Perazzi S.p.A.
Armi San Marco
(See U.S. Importers-Taylor's
& Co)
Armi Sport
(See U.S. Importers-Cape
Outfitters)
Arms Corporation of the
Philippines
Armscorp USA, Inc.
Arrieta S.L.
Astra Sport, S.A.
Atamec-Bretton
AYA
(See U.S. Importer-New
England Custom Gun Serv)
B.A.C.
B.C. Outdoors
BEC, Inc.
Benelli Armi S.p.A.
Benelli USA Corp
Beretta S.p.A., Pietro
Beretta S.U.S.A. Corp.
Bernardelli S.p.A., Vincenzo
Bersa S.A.
Bertuzzi
(See U.S. Importer-New
England Arms Co)
Bill Hanus Birdguns LLC
Blaser Jagdwaffen GmbH
Borovnik KG, Ludwig
Bosis
(See U.S. Importer-New
England Arms Co.)
Brenneke KG, Wilhelm
Browning Arms Co.
Bryan & Assoc.
BSA Guns Ltd.

Cabanas
(See U.S. Importer-Mandall
Shooting Supply
Cabela's
Cape Outfitters
CBC
Chapuis Armes
Churchill
(See U.S. Importer-Ellett
Bros.)
Cosmi Americo & Figlio s.n.c.
Crucelegui, Hermanos
(See U.S. Importer-Mandall)
Cryo-Accurizing
Cubic Shot Shell Co., Inc.
Daewoo Precision Industries
Ltd.
Dakota
(See U.S. Importer-EMF Co.,
Inc.)
Dakota Arms, Inc.
Davide Pedersoli and Co.
Diana
(See U.S. Importer - Dynamit
Nobel-RWS, Inc.)
Domino
Dumoulin, Ernest
Eagle Imports, Inc.
EAW
(See U.S. Importer-New
England Custom Gun Serv)
Ed's Gun House
Effebi SNC-Dr. Franco Beretta
EMF Co., Inc.
Euro-Imports
Eversull Co., Inc.
F.A.I.R. Tecni-Mec s.n.c. di
Isidoro Rizzini & C.
Fabarm S.p.A.
Fausti Cav. Stefano & Figlie snc
FEG
FERLIB
Fiocchi Munizioni S.p.A.
(See U.S. Importer-Fiocch)
Firearms Co Ltd. / Alpine
(See U.S. Importer-Mandall)
Firearms International
Flintlocks, Etc.
Franchi S.p.A.
FWB
Galaxy Imports Ltd., Inc.
Gamba S.p.A. Societa Armi
Bresciane Srl
Gamo
(See U.S. Importers-Arms
United Corp, Daisy M)
Garbi, Armas Urki
Gaucher Armes, S.A.
Gibbs Rifle Co., Inc.
Glock GmbH
Goergen's Gun Shop, Inc.
Gonzalez Guns, Ramon B
Grulla Armes
Hammerli Ltd.
Hammerli USA
Hartford
(See U.S. Importer-EMF Co.
Inc.)
Hartmann & Weiss GmbH
Heckler & Koch, Inc.
Hege Jagd-u. Sporthandels
GmbH
Helwan
(See U.S. Importer-
Interarms)
Holland & Holland Ltd.
Howa Machinery, Ltd.
I.A.B.
(See U.S. Importer-Taylor's
& Co. Inc.)
IAR Inc.
IGA
(See U.S. Importer-Stoeger
Industries)
Ignacio Ugartechea S.A.
Imperial Magnum Corp.
Imperial Miniature Armory
Import Sports Inc.
IMX, LLC
Inter Ordnance of America LP
Interarms / Howa

Intrac Arms International
J.G. Anschutz GmbH & Co. KG
John Rigby & Co.
JSL Ltd
(See U.S. Importer-Specialty
Shooters)
K. Eversull Co., Inc.
Kimar (See U.S. Importer-IAR,
Inc)
Korth
Krico Deutschland GmbH
Krieghoff Gun Co., H.
KSN Industries Ltd
(See U.S. Importer-Israel
Arms)
Lakefield Arms Ltd
(See Savage Arms Inc.)
Lapua Ltd.
Laurona Armas Eibar, S.A.L.
Lebeau-Courally
Lever Arms Service Ltd.
Llama Gabilondo Y Cia
London Guns Ltd.
M. Thys
(See U.S. Importer-Champlin
Firearms Inc)
Magtech Ammunition Co., Inc.
Mandall Shooting Supplies Inc.
Marocchi F.lli S.p.A
Mauser Werke Oberndorf
Waffensysteme GmbH
McCann Industries
MEC-Gar S.r.l.
Merkel Freres
Miltex, Inc
Miroku, B C/Daly, Charles
(See U.S. Importer)
Morini
(See U.S. Importers-Mandall
Shooting Supply)
New England Custom Gun
Service
New SKB Arms Co.
Norica, Avnda Otaola
Norinco
Norma Precision AB
(See U.S. Importers-
Dynamit)
Northwest Arms
OK Weber,Inc.
Para-Ordnance Mfg., Inc.
Pardini Armi Srl
Perugini Visini & Co. S.r.l.
Peters Stahl GmbH
Pietta
(See U.S. Importers-Navy
Arms Co, Taylor's)
Piotti
(See U.S. Importer-Moore &
Co, Wm. Larkin)
PMC / Eldorado Cartridge Corp.
Powell & Son (Gunmakers)
Ltd., William
Prairie Gun Works
Ramon B. Gonzalez Guns
Rigby & Co., John
Rizzini F.lli
(See U.S. Importers-Moore
& C England)
Rizzini SNC
Robinson Armament Co.
Rossi Firearms
Rottweil Compe
Rutten
(See U.S. Importer-Labanu
Inc)
RWS
(See US Importer-Dynamit
Nobel-RWS, Inc.)
S.A.R.L. G. Granger
S.I.A.C.E. (See U.S. Importer-
IAR Inc)
Sabatti S.r.l.
Sako Ltd
(See U.S. Importer-Stoeger
Industries)
San Marco
(See U.S. Importers-Cape
Outfitters-EMF)
Sarsilmaz Shotguns - Turkey
(See B.C. Outdoors)

Sauer
(See U.S. Importers-Paul
Co., The, Sigarms I)
Savage Arms (Canada), Inc.
SIG
Sigarms, Inc.
SIG-Sauer
(See U.S. Importer-Sigarms
Inc.)
SKB Shotguns
Small Arms Specialists
Societa Armi Bresciane Srl
(See U.S. Importer-Cape
Sphinx Systems Ltd.
Springfield, Inc.
Starr Trading Co., Jedediah
Steyr Mannlicher AG & CO KG
T.F.C. S.p.A.
Tanfoglio Fratelli S.r.l.
Tanner
(See U.S. Importer-Mandall
Shooting Supply)
Tar-Hunt Custom Rifles, Inc.
Taurus International Firearms
(See U.S. Importer)
Taurus S.A. Forjas
Taylor's & Co., Inc.
Techno Arms
(See U.S. Importer- Auto-
Ordnance Corp)
The A.W. Peterson Gun Shop,
Inc.
Tikka
(See U.S. Importer-Stoeger
Industries)
TOZ
(See U.S. Importer-Nygord
Precision Products)
Ugartechea S. A., Ignacio
Ultralux
(See U.S. Importer-Keng's
Firearms)
Unique/M.A.P.F.
Valtro USA, Inc
Voere-KGH m.b.H.
Walther GmbH, Carl
Weatherby, Inc.
Webley and Scott Ltd.
Weihrauch KG, Hermann
Westley Richards & Co.
Whiscombe
(See U.S. Importer-Pelaire
Products)
Wolf (See J.R. Distributing)
Zabala Hermanos S.A.

GUNS, FOREIGN-IMPORTER

Accuracy International
AcuSport Corporation
Air Rifle Specialists
American Frontier Firearms
Mfg., Inc
Auto-Ordnance Corp.
B.A.C.
B.C. Outdoors
Bell's Legendary Country Wear
Benelli USA Corp
Big Bear Arms & Sporting
Goods, Inc.
Bill Hanus Birdguns LLC
Bridgeman Products
British Sporting Arms
Browning Arms Co.
Cape Outfitters
Century International Arms,
Inc.
Champion Shooters' Supply
Champion's Choice, Inc.
Chapuis USA
Cimarron F.A. Co.
CVA
CZ USA
Dynamit Nobel-RWS, Inc.
E&L Mfg., Inc.
E.A.A. Corp.
Eagle Imports, Inc.
Ellett Bros.
EMF Co., Inc.
Euroarms of America, Inc.

Eversull Co., Inc.
Fiocchi of America Inc.
Flintlocks, Etc.
Franzen International,Inc
(See U.S. Importer for)
G.U. Inc
(See U.S. Importer for New
SKB Arms Co.)
Galaxy Imports Ltd., Inc.
Gamba, USA
Gamo USA, Inc.
Giacomo Sporting USA
Glock, Inc.
Gremmel Enterprises
Griffin & Howe, Inc.
GSI, Inc.
Guncraft Books
(See Guncraft Sports Inc.)
Guncraft Sports Inc.
Gunsite Custom Shop
Gunsite Training Center
Hammerli USA
Hanus Birdguns Bill
I.S.S.
IAR Inc.
Imperial Magnum Corp.
Imperial Miniature Armory
Import Sports Inc.
IMX, LLC
Interarms / Howa
Intrac Arms International
K. Eversull Co., Inc.
K.B.I. Inc
Kemen America
Keng's Firearms Specialty, Inc.
/ US Tactical Systems
Krieghoff International,Inc.
Labanu, Inc.
Legacy Sports International
Lion Country Supply
London Guns Ltd.
Magnum Research, Inc.
Marx, Harry
(See U.S. Importer for
FERLIB)
MCS, Inc.
MEC-Gar U.S.A., Inc.
Navy Arms Company
New England Arms Co.
Nygord Precision Products,
Inc.
OK Weber,Inc.
P.S.M.G. Gun Co.
Para-Ordnance, Inc.
Pelaire Products
Perazzi U.S.A. Inc.
Powell Agency, William
Precision Sales International,
Inc.
Quality Arms, Inc.
Rocky Mountain Armoury
S.D. Meacham
Samco Global Arms, Inc.
Sanders Custom Gun Service
Savage Arms, Inc.
Schuetzen Pistol Works
Scott Fine Guns Inc., Thad
Sigarms, Inc.
SKB Shotguns
Small Arms Specialists
Southern Ammunition Co., Inc.
Specialty Shooters Supply, Inc.
Springfield, Inc.
Stoeger Industries
Stone Enterprises Ltd.
Swarovski Optik North America
Ltd.
Tar-Hunt Custom Rifles, Inc.
Taurus Firearms, Inc.
Taylor's & Co., Inc.
The A.W. Peterson Gun Shop,
Inc.
The Gun Shop
The Orvis Co.
The Paul Co.
Track of the Wolf, Inc.
Traditions Performance
Firearms
Tristar Sporting Arms, Ltd.
Trooper Walsh

U.S. Importer-Wm. Larkin
Moore
Uberti USA, Inc.
VAM Distribution Co LLC
Vektor USA
Vintage Arms, Inc.
Westley Richards Agency USA
(See U.S. Importer)
Wingshooting Adventures
World Class Airguns

GUNS, SURPLUS, PARTS & AMMUNITION

Ahlman Guns
Alpha 1 Drop Zone
Armscorp USA, Inc.
Arundel Arms & Ammunition,
Inc., A.
B.A.C.
Bondini Paolo
Cambos Outdoorsman
Century International Arms,
Inc.
Cole's Gun Works
Conetrol Scope Mounts
Delta Arms Ltd.
Ed's Gun House
First Inc., Jack
Fleming Firearms
Forrest Inc., Tom
Garcia National Gun Traders,
Inc.
Goodwin's Gun Shop
Gun City
Gun Hunter Books
(See Gun Hunter Trading Co)
Gun Hunter Trading Co.
Hank's Gun Shop
Hege Jagd-u. Sporthandels
GmbH
Interarms / Howa
Jackalope Gun Shop
Ken Starnes Gunmaker
LaRocca Gun Works
Lever Arms Service Ltd.
Log Cabin Sport Shop
Martin's Gun Shop
Navy Arms Company
Nevada Pistol Academy, Inc.
Northwest Arms
Oil Rod and Gun Shop
Paragon Sales & Services, Inc.
Parts & Surplus
Pasadena Gun Center
Power Plus Enterprises, Inc.
Quality Firearms of Idaho, Inc.
Ravell Ltd.
Retting, Inc., Martin B
Samco Global Arms, Inc.
Sanders Custom Gun Service
Sarco, Inc.
Shootin' Shack, Inc.
Silver Ridge Gun Shop
(See Goodwin, Fred)
Simmons Gun Repair, Inc.
Sportsmen's Exchange &
Western Gun Traders, Inc.
Springfield Sporters, Inc.
T.F.C. S.p.A.
Tarnhelm Supply Co., Inc.
The A.W. Peterson Gun Shop,
Inc.
The Gun Parts Corp.
The Gun Room Press
The Gun Shop
Thurston Sports, Inc.
Vom Hoffe
(See Old Western Scrounger,
Inc., The)
Williams Shootin' Iron Service,
The Lynx-Line

GUNS, U.S. MADE

3-Ten Corp.
A.A. Arms, Inc.
Accu-Tek
Ace Custom 45's, Inc.
Acra-Bond Laminates

Ad Hominem
Airrow
Allred Bullet Co.
American Derringer Corp.
American Frontier Firearms
Mfg., Inc
AR-7 Industries, LLC
ArmaLite, Inc.
Armscorp USA, Inc.
A-Square Company, Inc.
Austin & Halleck, Inc.
Autauga Arms, Inc.
Auto-Ordnance Corp.
Baer Custom, Inc, Les
Ballard Rifle & Cartridge Co.,
LLC
Barrett Firearms Manufacturer,
Inc.
Bar-Sto Precision Machine
Benjamin/Sheridan Co.,
Crossman
Beretta S.p.A., Pietro
Beretta U.S.A. Corp.
Big Bear Arms & Sporting
Goods, Inc.
Bond Arms, Inc.
Borden Ridges Rimrock Stocks
Borden Rifles Inc
Brockman's Custom
Gunsmithing
Brown Co, E. Arthur
Brown Products, Inc., Ed
Browning Arms Co.
Bryan & Assoc.
Bushmaster Firearms
C. Sharps Arms Co.
Inc./Montana Armory
Cabela's
Calico Light Weapon Systems
Cambos Outdoorsman
Cape Outfitters
Casull Arms Corp.
CCL Security Products
Century Gun Dist. Inc.
Charter 2000
Cobra Enterprises, Inc.
Colt's Mfg. Co., Inc.
Competitor Corp. Inc.
Conetrol Scope Mounts
Connecticut Shotgun Mfg. Co.
Connecticut Valley Classics
(See CVC)
Cooper Arms
Crosman Airguns
Cryo-Accurizing
Cumberland Arms
Cumberland Mountain Arms
CVA
CVC
Daisy Mfg. Co.
Dakota Arms, Inc.
Dan Wesson Firearms
Dayton Traister
Dixie Gun Works
Downsizer Corp.
DS Arms, Inc.
E&L Mfg., Inc.
E. Arthur Brown Co.
Eagle Arms, Inc. (See ArmaLite,
Inc.)
Emerging Technologies, Inc.
(See Laseraim Technolo
Entre'prise Arms, Inc.
Essex Arms
Excel Industries Inc.
FN Manufacturing
Fort Worth Firearms
Freedom Arms, Inc.
Fulton Armory
Galena Industries AMT
Garcia National Gun Traders,
Inc.
Gary Reeder Custom Guns
Genecco Gun Works
Gentry Custom Gunmaker,
David
Gibbs Rifle Co., Inc.
Gil Hebard Guns Inc.
Gilbert Equipment Co., Inc.
Goergen's Gun Shop, Inc.
Gonzalez Guns, Ramon B

Goodwin's Gun Shop
Granite Mountain Arms, Inc
Grayback Wildcats
Griffin & Howe, Inc.
Gunsite Custom Shop
Gunsite Gunsmithy
(See Gunsite Custom Shop)
H&R 1871, Inc.
Hammerli USA
Harrington & Richardson
(See H&R 1871, Inc.)
Harris Gunworks
Hart & Son, Inc.
Hatfield Gun
Hawken Shop, The
(See Dayton Traister)
Heritage Firearms
(See Heritage Mfg., Inc.)
Heritage Manufacturing, Inc.
Hesco-Meprolight
High Precision
Hi-Point Firearms/MKS Supply
HJS Arms, Inc.
H-S Precision, Inc.
Hutton Rifle Ranch
IAR Inc.
Imperial Miniature Armory
IMX, LLC
Israel Arms International, Inc.
Ithaca Classic Doubles
Ithaca Gun Company LLC
J.P. Enterprises Inc.
J.P. Gunstocks, Inc.
Jim Norman Custom
Gunstocks
John Rigby & Co.
John's Custom Leather
K.K. Arms Co.
Kahr Arms
Kehr, Roger
Kelbly, Inc.
Kel-Tec CNC Industries, Inc.
Kimber of America, Inc.
Knight Rifles
Knight's Mfg. Co.
Kolar
KSN Industries Ltd
(See U.S. Importer-Israel
Arms)
L.A.R. Mfg., Inc.
L.W. Seecamp Co., Inc.
LaFrance Specialties
Lakefield Arms Ltd
(See Savage Arms Inc.)
Laseraim Technologies, Inc.
Lever Arms Service Ltd.
Ljutic Industries, Inc.
Lock's Philadelphia Gun
Exchange
Lomont Precision Bullets
Lone Star Rifle Company
M.O.A. Corp.
Mag-Na-Port International, Inc.
Magnum Research, Inc.
Mandall Shooting Supplies Inc.
Marlin Firearms Co.
Maverick Arms, Inc.
McBros Rifle Co.
McCann Industries
Mid-America Recreation, Inc.
Miller Arms, Inc.
MKS Supply, Inc.
(See Hi-Point Firearms)
Montana Armory, Inc
(See C. Sharps Arms Co.
Inc.)
MPI Stocks
Navy Arms Company
NCP Products, Inc.
New England Firearms
New Ultra Light Arms, LLC
Noreen, Peter H.
North American Arms, Inc.
North Star West
Northwest Arms
Nowlin Mfg. Co.
Olympic Arms Inc.
Oregon Arms, Inc.
(See Rogue Rifle Co., Inc.)
P&M Sales & Services, LLC
Parker & Sons Shooting Supply

Phillips & Rogers, Inc.
Phoenix Arms
Precision Small Arms Inc.
Professional Ordnance, Inc.
ProWare, Inc.
Ramon B. Gonzalez Guns
Rapine Bullet Mould Mfg. Co.
Raptor Arms Co., Inc.
Remington Arms Co., Inc.
Rifles, Inc.
Rigby & Co., John
Robinson Armament Co.
Rock River Arms
Rocky Mountain Arms, Inc.
Rogue Rifle Co., Inc.
Rogue River Rifleworks
Rohrbaugh
Romain's Custom Guns, Inc.
RPM
Ruger (See Sturm, Ruger &
Co., Inc.)
Russ Trading Post
Savage Arms (Canada), Inc.
Scattergun Technologies, Inc.
Searcy Enterprises
Sharps Arms Co., Inc., C.
Shiloh Rifle Mfg.
Sklany's Machine Shop
Small Arms Specialists
Smith & Wesson
Sound Technology
Springfield, Inc.
SSK Industries
STI International
Stoeger Industries
Strayer-Voigt, Inc.
Sturm Ruger & Co. Inc.
Sunny Hill Enterprises, Inc.
T&S Industries, Inc.
Taconic Firearms Ltd., Perry
Lane
Tank's Rifle Shop
Tar-Hunt Custom Rifles, Inc.
Taurus Firearms, Inc.
Texas Armory (See Bond Arms,
Inc.)
The A.W. Peterson Gun Shop,
Inc.
The Gun Room Press
The Gun Works
Thompson / Center Arms
Tristar Sporting Arms, Ltd.
U.S. Fire Arms Mfg. Co., Inc.
U.S. Repeating Arms Co., Inc.
Visible Impact Targets
Volquartsen Custom Ltd.
Wallace, Terry
Weatherby, Inc.
Wescombe, Bill (See North Star
West)
Wessinger Custom Guns &
Engraving
Whildin & Sons Ltd, E.H.
Whitestone Lumber Corp.
Wichita Arms, Inc.
Wichita Arms, Inc.
Wildey, Inc.
Wilsom Combat
Winchester Consultants
Z-M Weapons

GUNSMITH SCHOOL

American Gunsmithing
Institute
Bull Mountain Rifle Co.
Colorado Gunsmithing
Academy
Colorado School of Trades
Cylinder & Slide, Inc., William
R. Laughridge
Lassen Community College,
Gunsmithing Dept.
Laughridge, William R
(See Cylinder & Slide Inc)
Log Cabin Sport Shop
Modern Gun Repair School
Montgomery Community
College
Murray State College

North American
Correspondence Schools
The Gun Pro
Nowlin Mfg. Co.
NRI Gunsmith School
Pennsylvania Gunsmith School
Piedmont Community College
Pine Technical College
Professional Gunsmiths of
America
Smith & Wesson
Southeastern Community
College
Spencer's Custom Guns
Trinidad St. Jr Col Gunsmith
Dept.
Wright's Gunstock Blanks
Yavapai College

GUNSMITH SUPPLIES, TOOLS & SERVICES

Ace Custom 45's, Inc.
Actions by "T" Teddy Jacobson
Alaskan Silversmith, The
Aldis Gunsmithing & Shooting
Supply
Alley Supply Co.
Allred Bullet Co.
Alpec Team, Inc.
American Frontier Firearms
Mfg., Inc
American Gunsmithing
Institute
Baer Custom, Inc, Les
Bar-Sto Precision Machine
Bauska Barrels
Bear Mountain Gun & Tool
Bengtson Arms Co., L.
Biesen, Al
Biesen, Roger
Bill's Gun Repair
Blue Ridge Machinery & Tools,
Inc.
Boyds' Gunstock Industries,
Inc.
Break-Free, Inc.
Briley Mfg. Inc.
Brockman's Custom
Gunsmithing
Brown Products, Inc., Ed
Brownells, Inc.
Bryan & Assoc.
B-Square Company, Inc.
Buffer Technologies
Bull Mountain Rifle Co.
Bushmaster Firearms
C.S. Van Gorden & Son, Inc.
Carbide Checkering Tools
(See J&R Engineering)
Carter's Gun Shop
Caywood, Shane J.
CBC-BRAZIL
Chapman Manufacturing Co.
Chem-Pak Inc.
Chicasaw Gun Works
Choate Machine & Tool Co.,
Inc.
Ciener Inc., Jonathan Arthur
Colonial Arms, Inc.
Colorado School of Trades
Colt's Mfg. Co., Inc.
Conetrol Scope Mounts
Craig Custom Ltd., Research &
Development
CRR, Inc./Marble's Inc.
Cumberland Arms
Cumberland Mountain Arms
Custom Checkering Service,
Kathy Forster
Custom Gun Products
D&J Bullet Co. & Custom Gun
Shop, Inc.
D'Arcy Echols & Co.
Decker Shooting Products
Dem-Bart Checkering Tools,
Inc.
Dewey Mfg. Co., Inc., J.
Dixie Gun Works
Dixie Gun Works

PRODUCT & SERVICE DIRECTORY

Dremel Mfg. Co.
Du-Lite Corp.
Efficient Machinery Co
Entre'prise Arms, Inc.
Erhardt, Dennis
Evolution Gun Works Inc.
Faith Associates
Faloon Industries, Inc.
FERLIB
Fisher, Jerry A.
Forgreens Tool & Mfg., Inc.
Forkin, Ben (See Belt MTN Arms)
Forster, Kathy
  (See Custom Checkering)
Gentry Custom Gunmaker, David
Goodwin's Gun Shop
Grace Metal Products
Greider Precision
GrE-Tan Rifles
Gruning Precision Inc
Gunline Tools
Half Moon Rifle Shop
Hammond Custom Guns Ltd.
Hastings Barrels
Henriksen Tool Co., Inc.
High Performance International
High Precision
Hoelscher, Virgil
Holland's Gunsmithing
Ironsighter Co.
Israel Arms International, Inc.
Ivanoff, Thomas G
  (See Tom's Gun Repair)
J&R Engineering
J&S Heat Treat
Jantz Supply
Jenkins Recoil Pads, Inc.
JGS Precision Tool Mfg.
Jonathan Arthur Ciener, Inc.
Jones Custom Products, Neil A.
Kailua Custom Guns Inc.
Kasenit Co., Inc.
Kleinendorst, K. W.
Korzinek Riflesmith, J.
KSN Industries Ltd
  (See U.S. Importer-Israel Arms)
LaBounty Precision Reboring, Inc
Laurel Mountain Forge
Lea Mfg. Co.
Lee Supplies, Mark
List Precision Engineering
London Guns Ltd.
Mahovsky's Metalife
Marble Arms
  (See CRR, Inc./Marble's Inc.)
Mark Lee Supplies
Marsh, Mike
Martin's Gun Shop
McFarland, Stan
Menck, Gunsmith Inc., T.W.
Metalife Industries
  (See Mahovsky's Metalife)
Metaloy, Inc.
Michael's Antiques
Micro Sight Co.
MMC
Mo's Competitor Supplies
  (See MCS Inc)
Mowrey's Guns & Gunsmithing
Neil A. Jones Custom Products
New England Custom Gun Service
Ole Frontier Gunsmith Shop
P.M. Enterprises, Inc. / Precise Metalsmithing
Parker & Sons Shooting Supply
Parker Gun Finishes
Paulsen Gunstocks
PEM's Mfg. Co.
Perazone-Gunsmith, Brian
Peter Dyson & Son Ltd.
Power Custom, Inc.
Practical Tools, Inc.
Precise Metalsmithing Enterprises / P.M. Enterprises
Precision Specialties

R.A. Wells Custom Gunsmith
Ranch Products
Ransom International Corp.
Reardon Products
Rice, Keith
  (See White Rock Tool & Die)
Robert Valade Engraving
Rocky Mountain Arms, Inc.
Romain's Custom Guns, Inc.
Roto Carve
Royal Arms Gunstocks
Scott McDougall & Associates
Sharp Shooter Supply
Shooter's Choice Gun Care
Simmons Gun Repair, Inc.
Smith Abrasives, Inc.
Southern Bloomer Mfg. Co.
Spencer Reblue Service
Spencer's Custom Guns
Spradlin's
Starr Trading Co., Jedediah
Starrett Co., L. S.
Stiles Custom Guns
Stoney Point Products, Inc.
Sullivan, David S.
  (See Westwind Rifles Inc.)
Sunny Hill Enterprises, Inc.
T&S Industries, Inc.
T.W. Menck Gunsmith Inc.
Tank's Rifle Shop
Texas Platers Supply Co.
The A.W. Peterson Gun Shop, Inc.
The Dutchman's Firearms, Inc.
The Gun Works
The NgraveR Co.
The Robar Co.'s, Inc.
Theis, Terry
Tom's Gun Repair, Thomas G. Ivanoff
Track of the Wolf, Inc.
Trinidad St. Jr Col Gunsmith Dept.
Trulock Tool
Turnbull Restoration, Doug
United States Products Co.
Valade Engraving, Robert
Van Gorden & Son Inc., C. S.
Venco Industries, Inc.
  (See Shooter's Choice)
W.C. Wolff Co.
Warne Manufacturing Co.
Washita Mountain Whetstone Co.
Weaver Arms Corp. Gun Shop
Wessinger Custom Guns & Engraving
White Rock Tool & Die
Wilcox All-Pro Tools & Supply
Wild West Guns
Will-Burt Co.
Williams Gun Sight Co.
Williams Shootin' Iron Service, The Lynx-Line
Willow Bend
Windish, Jim
Winter, Robert M.
Wise Guns, Dale
Wright's Gunstock Blanks
Yavapai College
Ziegel Engineering

HANDGUN ACCESSORIES

"Su-Press-On",Inc.
A.A. Arms, Inc.
Ace Custom 45's, Inc.
Action Direct, Inc.
ADCO Sales, Inc.
Adventurer's Outpost
Aimpoint c/o Springfield, Inc.
Aimtech Mount Systems
Ajax Custom Grips, Inc.
Alpha 1 Drop Zone
Alpha Gunsmith Division
American Derringer Corp.
American Frontier Firearms Mfg., Inc
Arms Corporation of the Philippines

Aro-Tek Ltd.
Astra Sport, S.A.
Autauga Arms, Inc.
Baer Custom, Inc, Les
Bagmaster Mfg., Inc.
Bar-Sto Precision Machine
Behlert Precision, Inc.
Berry's Mfg., Inc.
Bill's Custom Cases
Blue and Gray Products Inc
  (See Ox-Yoke Originals)
Bond Custom Firearms
Bowen Classic Arms Corp.
Bridgeman Products
Broken Gun Ranch
Brooks Tactical Systems
Brown Products, Inc., Ed
Bushmaster Hunting & Fishing
Butler Creek Corp.
Cannon Safe, Inc.
Centaur Systems, Inc.
Central Specialties Ltd
  (See Trigger Lock Division)
Charter 2000
Cheyenne Pioneer Products
Chicasaw Gun Works
Ciener Inc., Jonathan Arthur
Clark Custom Guns, Inc.
Classic Arms Company
Conetrol Scope Mounts
Craig Custom Ltd., Research & Development
Crimson Trace Lasers
CRR, Inc./Marble's Inc.
Cylinder & Slide, Inc., William R. Laughridge
D&L Industries (See D.J. Marketing)
D.J. Marketing
Dade Screw Machine Products
Delhi Gun House
DeSantis Holster & Leather Goods, Inc.
Dixie Gun Works
Doskocil Mfg. Co., Inc.
E&L Mfg., Inc.
E. Arthur Brown Co.
E.A.A. Corp.
Ed Brown Products, Inc.
Essex Arms
European American Armory Corp (See E.A.A. Corp)
Faloon Industries, Inc.
Federal Arms Corp. of America
Fisher Custom Firearms
Fleming Firearms
Flores Publications Inc, J
  (See Action Direct Inc.)
Freedom Arms, Inc.
Frielich Police Equipment
FWB
G.G. & G.
Galati International
GALCO International Ltd.
Garcia National Gun Traders, Inc.
Garthwaite Pistolsmith, Inc., Jim
Gil Hebard Guns Inc.
Gilmore Sports Concepts
Glock, Inc.
Goodwin's Gun Shop
Gould & Goodrich
Greider Precision
Gremmel Enterprises
Gun-Alert
Gun-Ho Sports Cases
H.K.S. Products
Hafner World Wide, Inc.
Hammerli USA
Heinie Specialty Products
Henigson & Associates, Steve
Hill Speed Leather, Ernie
Hi-Point Firearms/MKS Supply
Hobson Precision Mfg. Co.
Hoppe's Div. Penguin Industries, Inc.
H-S Precision, Inc.
Hunter Co., Inc.
Impact Case Co.
J.P. Enterprises Inc.

Jarvis, Inc.
JB Custom
Jeffredo Gunsight
Jim Noble Co.
John's Custom Leather
Jonathan Arthur Ciener, Inc.
K.K. Arms Co.
Kalispel Case Line
KeeCo Impressions, Inc.
King's Gun Works
KK Air International
  (See Impact Case Co.)
L&S Technologies Inc
  (See Aimtech Mount Systems)
Lakewood Products LLC
LaserMax, Inc.
Loch Leven Industries / Convert-A-Pell
Lohman Mfg. Co., Inc.
Mag-Na-Port International, Inc.
Magnolia Sports,Inc.
Mahony, Philip Bruce
Mandall Shooting Supplies Inc.
Marble Arms
  (See CRR, Inc./Marble's Inc.)
Markell,Inc.
McCormick Corp., Chip
MEC-Gar S.r.l.
Menck, Gunsmith Inc., T.W.
Merkuria Ltd.
Middlebrooks Custom Shop
Millett Sights
Mogul Co./Life Jacket
MTM Molded Products Co., Inc.
No-Sho Mfg. Co.
Omega Sales
Outdoor Sports Headquarters, Inc.
Ox-Yoke Originals, Inc.
Pachmayr Div. Lyman Products
Pager Pal
Palmer Security Products
Parker & Sons Shooting Supply
Pearce Grip, Inc.
Perazone-Gunsmith, Brian
Phoenix Arms
Practical Tools, Inc.
Precision Small Arms Inc.
Ram-Line Blount, Inc.
Ranch Products
Ransom International Corp.
Ringler Custom Leather Co.
RPM
Seecamp Co. Inc., L. W.
Simmons Gun Repair, Inc.
Sound Technology
Southern Bloomer Mfg. Co.
Springfield, Inc.
SSK Industries
Sturm Ruger & Co. Inc.
T.F.C. S.p.A.
TacStar
Tactical Defense Institute
Tanfoglio Fratelli S.r.l.
The A.W. Peterson Gun Shop, Inc.
The Concealment Shop, Inc.
The Gun Parts Corp.
The Gun Works
The Keller Co.
The Protector Mfg. Co., Inc.
Thompson / Center Arms
Trigger Lock Division / Central Specialties Ltd.
Trijicon, Inc.
Triple-K Mfg. Co., Inc.
Truglo, Inc
Tyler Manufacturing & Distributing
United States Products Co.
Universal Sports
Valor Corp.
Volquartsen Custom Ltd.
W. Waller & Son, Inc.
W.C. Wolff Co.
Wessinger Custom Guns & Engraving

Western Design
  (See Alpha Gunsmith Division)
Whitestone Lumber Corp.
Wild West Guns
Williams Gun Sight Co.
Wilsom Combat
Ziegel Engineering

HANDGUN GRIPS

A.A. Arms, Inc.
African Import Co.
Ahrends, Kim
  (See Custom Firearms, Inc)
Ajax Custom Grips, Inc.
Altamont Co.
American Derringer Corp.
American Frontier Firearms Mfg., Inc.
American Gripcraft
Arms Corporation of the Philippines
Art Jewel Enterprises Ltd.
Baelder, Harry
Baer Custom, Inc, Les
Big Bear Arms & Sporting Goods, Inc.
Bob's Gun Shop
Boone Trading Co., Inc.
Boone's Custom Ivory Grips, Inc.
Boyds' Gunstock Industries, Inc.
Brooks Tactical Systems
Brown Products, Inc., Ed
Clark Custom Guns, Inc.
Cole-Grip
Colonial Repair
Crimson Trace Lasers
Custom Firearms (See Ahrends, Kim)
Dixie Gun Works
E.A.A. Corp.
EMF Co., Inc.
Essex Arms
European American Armory Corp (See E.A.A. Corp)
Faloon Industries, Inc.
Fibron Products, Inc.
Fisher Custom Firearms
Fitz Pistol Grip Co.
Forrest Inc., Tom
FWB
Garthwaite Pistolsmith, Inc., Jim
Goodwin's Gun Shop
Herrett's Stocks, Inc.
HIP-GRIP Barami Corp.
Hogue Grips
H-S Precision, Inc.
Huebner, Corey O.
Israel Arms International, Inc.
John Masen Co. Inc.
KeeCo Impressions, Inc.
Kim Ahrends Custom Firearms, Inc.
Korth
KSN Industries Ltd
  (See U.S. Importer-Israel Arms)
Lett Custom Grips
Linebaugh Custom Sixguns
Lyman Products Corp.
Mandall Shooting Supplies Inc.
Michaels Of Oregon
Millett Sights
N.C. Ordnance Co.
Newell, Robert H.
Northern Precision Custom Swaged Bullets
Pachmayr Div. Lyman Products
Pardini Armi Srl
Parker & Sons Shooting Supply
Perazone-Gunsmith, Brian
Pilgrim Pewter,Inc.
  (See Bell Originals Inc. Sid)
Precision Small Arms Inc.
Radical Concepts
Rosenberg & Son, Jack A
Roy's Custom Grips

Spegel, Craig
Stoeger Industries
Sturm Ruger & Co. Inc.
Sunny Hill Enterprises, Inc.
Tactical Defense Institute
Taurus Firearms, Inc.
The A.W. Peterson Gun Shop, Inc.
Tirelli
Triple-K Mfg. Co., Inc.
Tyler Manufacturing & Distributing
U.S. Fire Arms Mfg. Co., Inc.
Uncle Mike's
  (See Michaels of Oregon Co.)
Vintage Industries, Inc.
Volquartsen Custom Ltd.
Western Mfg. Co.
Whitestone Lumber Corp.
Wright's Gunstock Blanks

HEARING PROTECTORS

Aero Peltor
Ajax Custom Grips, Inc.
Brown Co, E. Arthur
Browning Arms Co.
David Clark Co., Inc.
Dillon Precision Products, Inc.
Dixie Gun Works
E-A-R, Inc.
Electronic Shooters Protection, Inc.
Gentex Corp.
Goodwin's Gun Shop
Gunsmithing, Inc.
Hoppe's Div. Penguin Industries, Inc.
Kesselring Gun Shop
Mandall Shooting Supplies Inc.
North Specialty Products
Parker & Sons Shooting Supply
Paterson Gunsmithing
Peltor, Inc. (See Aero Peltor)
R.E.T. Enterprises
Ridgeline, Inc
Rucker Dist. Inc.
Silencio/Safety Direct
Sound Technology
Tactical Defense Institute
The A.W. Peterson Gun Shop, Inc.
The Gun Room Press
Triple-K Mfg. Co., Inc.
Watson Trophy Match Bullets
Whitestone Lumber Corp.
Willson Safety Prods. Div.

HOLSTERS & LEATHER GOODS

A&B Industries,Inc
  (See Top-Line USA Inc)
A.A. Arms, Inc.
Action Direct, Inc.
Action Products, Inc.
Alessi Holsters, Inc.
Arratoonian, Andy
  (See Horseshoe Leather Products)
Autauga Arms, Inc.
Bagmaster Mfg., Inc.
Baker's Leather Goods, Roy
Bandcor Industries, Div. of Man-Sew Corp.
Bang-Bang Boutique
  (See Holster Shop, The)
Beretta S.p.A., Pietro
Bianchi International, Inc.
Brocock Ltd.
Brooks Tactical Systems
Brown, H. R.
  (See Silhouette Leathers)
Browning Arms Co.
Bull-X, Inc.
Cape Outfitters
Cathey Enterprises, Inc.
Chace Leather Products
Churchill Glove Co., James
Cimarron F.A. Co.

REFERENCE

15th EDITION **293**

Classic Old West Styles
Clements' Custom Leathercraft, Chas
Cobra Sport S.r.l.
Colonial Repair
Counter Assault
Creedmoor Sports, Inc.
Delhi Gun House
DeSantis Holster & Leather Goods, Inc.
Dillon Precision Products, Inc.
Dixie Gun Works
Ekol Leather Care
El Paso Saddlery Co.
EMF Co., Inc.
Faust Inc., T. G.
Flores Publications Inc, J (See Action Direct Inc.)
Freedom Arms, Inc.
Gage Manufacturing
GALCO International Ltd.
Garcia National Gun Traders, Inc.
Gil Hebard Guns Inc.
Gilmore Sports Concepts
GML Products, Inc.
Goodwin's Gun Shop
Gould & Goodrich
Gun Leather Limited
Gunfitters
Hafner World Wide, Inc.
HandCrafts Unltd (See Clements' Custom Leather)
Hank's Gun Shop
Heinie Specialty Products
Henigson & Associates, Steve
Hill Speed Leather, Ernie
HIP-GRIP Barami Corp.
Hobson Precision Mfg. Co.
Hogue Grips
Horseshoe Leather Products
Hume, Don
Hunter Co., Inc.
Jim Noble Co.
John's Custom Leather
K.L. Null Holsters Ltd.
Kane Products, Inc.
Kirkpatrick Leather Co.
Kolpin Mfg., Inc.
Korth
Kramer Handgun Leather
L.A.R. Mfg., Inc.
Lawrence Leather Co.
Lock's Philadelphia Gun Exchange
Lone Star Gunleather
Magnolia Sports,Inc.
Mandall Shooting Supplies Inc.
Markell,Inc.
Marksman Products
Michaels Of Oregon
Minute Man High Tech Industries
Navy Arms Company
No-Sho Mfg. Co.
Null Holsters Ltd. K.L.
October Country Muzzleloading
Ojala Holsters, Arvo
Oklahoma Leather Products,Inc.
Old West Reproductions,Inc. R.M. Bachman
Pager Pal
Parker & Sons Shooting Supply
Pathfinder Sports Leather
PWL Gunleather
Renegade
Ringler Custom Leather Co.
Rogue Rifle Co., Inc.
Safariland Ltd., Inc.
Safety Speed Holster, Inc.
Scharch Mfg., Inc.
Schulz Industries
Second Chance Body Armor
Shoemaker & Sons Inc., Tex
Silhouette Leathers
Smith Saddlery, Jesse W.
Sparks, Milt
Stalker, Inc.
Starr Trading Co., Jedediah

Strong Holster Co.
Stuart, V. Pat
Tabler Marketing
Tactical Defense Institute
Ted Blocker Holsters, Inc.
Thad Rybka Custom Leather Equipment
The A.W. Peterson Gun Shop, Inc.
The Concealment Shop, Inc.
The Eutaw Co., Inc.
The Gun Works
The Keller Co.
The Outdoor Connection,Inc.
Top-Line USA, Inc.
Torel, Inc.
Triple-K Mfg. Co., Inc.
Tristar Sporting Arms, Ltd.
Tyler Manufacturing & Distributing
Uncle Mike's (See Michaels of Oregon Co.)
Valor Corp.
Venus Industries
Walt's Custom Leather, Walt Whinnery
Watson Trophy Match Bullets
Westley Richards & Co.
Whinnery, Walt (See Walt's Custom Leather)
Wild Bill's Originals
Wilsom Combat

LABELS, BOXES & CARTRIDGE HOLDERS

Ballistic Product, Inc.
Berry's Mfg., Inc.
Brocock Ltd.
Brown Co, E. Arthur
Cabinet Mtn. Outfitters Scents & Lures
Cheyenne Pioneer Products
Del Rey Products
DeSantis Holster & Leather Goods, Inc.
Fitz Pistol Grip Co.
Flambeau Products Corp.
Goodwin's Gun Shop
Hafner World Wide, Inc.
J&J Products, Inc.
Kolpin Mfg., Inc.
Liberty Shooting Supplies
Midway Arms, Inc.
MTM Molded Products Co., Inc.
Pendleton Royal, c/o Swingler Buckland Ltd.
Ziegel Engineering

LOAD TESTING & PRODUCT TESTING

Ballistic Research
Bitterroot Bullet Co.
Bridgeman Products
Briese Bullet Co., Inc.
Buckskin Bullet Co.
Bull Mountain Rifle Co.
CFVentures
Claybuster Wads & Harvester Bullets
Clearview Products
D&H Precision Tooling
Dead Eye's Sport Center
Defense Training International, Inc.
Duane's Gun Repair (See DGR Custom Rifles)
Gonzalez Guns, Ramon B
Gun Hunter Books (See Gun Hunter Trading Co)
Gun Hunter Trading Co.
H.P. White Laboratory, Inc.
Hank's Gun Shop
Henigson & Associates, Steve
Hoelscher, Virgil
Hutton Rifle Ranch
Jackalope Gun Shop

Jensen Bullets
L E Jurras & Assoc.
Liberty Shooting Supplies
Linebaugh Custom Sixguns
Lomont Precision Bullets
Maionchi-L.M.I.
MAST Technology
McMurdo, Lynn (See Specialty Gunsmithing)
Middlebrooks Custom Shop
Modern Gun Repair School
Multiplex International
Northwest Arms
Oil Rod and Gun Shop
Plum City Ballistic Range
R.A. Wells Custom Gunsmith
Ramon B. Gonzalez Guns
Rupert's Gun Shop
Small Custom Mould & Bullet Co.
SOS Products Co. (See Buck Stix-SOS Products Co.)
Spencer's Custom Guns
Trinidad St. Jr Col Gunsmith Dept.
Vancini, Carl (See Bestload, Inc.)
Vulpes Ventures, Inc. Fox Cartridge Division
W. Square Enterprises
X-Spand Target Systems

MUZZLE-LOADING GUNS, BARRELS & EQUIPMENT

Accuracy Unlimited
Ackerman & Co.
Adkins, Luther
Allen Mfg.
Armi San Paolo
Armoury, Inc., The
Austin & Halleck, Inc.
Bauska Barrels
Beaver Lodge (See Fellowes, Ted)
Bentley, John
Big Bore Express
Birdsong & Assoc., W. E.
Black Powder Products
Blount/Outers
Blue and Gray Products Inc (See Ox-Yoke Originals)
Bridgers Best
Buckskin Bullet Co.
Buckskin Machine Works, A. Hunkeler
Butler Creek Corp.
Cabela's
Cache La Poudre Rifleworks
California Sights (See Fautheree, Andy)
Cash Mfg. Co., Inc.
CBC-BRAZIL
Chambers Flintlocks Ltd., Jim
Chicasaw Gun Works
Cimarron F.A. Co.
Claybuster Wads & Harvester Bullets
Cogar's Gunsmithing
Colonial Repair
Colt Blackpowder Arms Co.
Conetrol Scope Mounts
Cousin Bob's Mountain Products
Cumberland Arms
Cumberland Mountain Arms
Curly Maple Stock Blanks (See Tiger-Hunt)
CVA
Dangler, Homer L.
Davide Pedersoli and Co.
Dayton Traister
deHaas Barrels
Delhi Gun House
Dixie Gun Works
Dixie Gun Works
Dixon Muzzleloading Shop, Inc.
EMF Co., Inc.
Euroarms of America, Inc.

Feken, Dennis
Fellowes, Ted
Flintlocks, Etc.
Fort Hill Gunstocks
Fowler, Bob (See Black Powder Products)
Frontier
Getz Barrel Co.
Goergen's Gun Shop, Inc.
Golden Age Arms Co.
Gonic Arms/North American Arm
Goodwin's Gun Shop
Green Mountain Rifle Barrel Co., Inc.
Hastings Barrels
Hawken Shop, The (See Dayton Traister)
Hege Jagd-u. Sporthandels GmbH
Hodgdon Powder Co.
Hoppe's Div. Penguin Industries, Inc.
Hornady Mfg. Co.
House of Muskets, Inc., The
Hunkeler, A (See Buckskin Machine Works
IAR Inc.
Impact Case Co.
Ironsighter Co.
J.P. Gunstocks, Inc.
Jamison's Forge Works
Jones Co., Dale
K&M Industries, Inc.
Kalispel Case Line
Kennedy Firearms
Knight Rifles
Knight Rifles (See Modern Muzzle Loading, Inc.)
Kolar
Kwik-Site Co.
L&R Lock Co.
L&S Technologies Inc (See Aimtech Mount Systems)
Lakewood Products LLC
Legend Products Corp.
Lodgewood Mfg.
Lothar Walther Precision Tool Inc.
Lyman Products Corp.
Markesbery Muzzle Loaders, Inc.
Marlin Firearms Co.
McCann's Muzzle-Gun Works
Michaels Of Oregon
Millennium Designed Muzzleloaders
MMP
Modern Muzzleloading, Inc
Mountain State Muzzleloading Supplies, Inc.
Mowrey Gun Works
MSC Industrial Supply Co.
Mt. Alto Outdoor Products
Navy Arms Company
Newman Gunshop
North Star West
October Country Muzzleloading
Oklahoma Leather Products,Inc.
Olson, Myron
Orion Rifle Barrel Co.
Ox-Yoke Originals, Inc.
Pacific Rifle Co.
Parker & Sons Shooting Supply
Parker Gun Finishes
Pecatonica River Longrifle
Peter Dyson & Son Ltd.
Pioneer Arms Co.
Prairie River Arms
Protektor Model
Rusty Duck Premium Gun Care Products
S&S Firearms
Selsi Co., Inc.
Shiloh Creek
Simmons Gun Repair, Inc.
Sklany's Machine Shop

Smokey Valley Rifles
South Bend Replicas, Inc.
Southern Bloomer Mfg. Co.
Splitfire Sporting Goods, L.L.C.
Starr Trading Co., Jedediah
Stone Mountain Arms
Sturm Ruger & Co. Inc.
Taylor's & Co., Inc.
Tennessee Valley Mfg.
The A.W. Peterson Gun Shop, Inc.
The Eutaw Co., Inc.
The Gun Works
Thompson / Center Arms
Thompson Bullet Lube Co.
Thunder Mountain Arms
Tiger-Hunt Gunstocks
Track of the Wolf, Inc.
Traditions Performance Firearms
Truglo, Inc
Uncle Mike's (See Michaels of Oregon Co.)
Upper Missouri Trading Co.
Venco Industries, Inc. (See Shooter's Choice)
Virgin Valley Custom Guns
Voere-KGH m.b.H.
W.E. Birdsong & Assoc.
Warne Manufacturing Co.
Warren Muzzleloading Co., Inc.
Wescombe, Bill (See North Star West)
White Shooting Systems, Inc. (See White Muzzleload
Woodworker's Supply
Wright's Gunstock Blanks
Young Country Arms
Ziegel Engineering

PISTOLSMITH

A.W. Peterson Gun Shop, Inc.
Acadian Ballistic Specialties
Accuracy Unlimited
Ace Custom 45's, Inc.
Actions by "T" Teddy Jacobson
Adair Custom Shop, Bill
Ahlman Guns
Ahrends, Kim (See Custom Firearms, Inc)
Aldis Gunsmithing & Shooting Supply
Alpha Precision, Inc.
Alpine Indoor Shooting Range
Armament Gunsmithing Co., Inc.
Aro-Tek Ltd.
Arundel Arms & Ammunition, Inc., A.
Baer Custom, Inc, Les
Bain & Davis, Inc.
Banks, Ed
Bar-Sto Precision Machine
Behlert Precision, Inc.
Ben William's Gun Shop
Bengtson Arms Co., L.
Bill Adair Custom Shop
Billings Gunsmiths Inc.
Bowen Classic Arms Corp.
Broken Gun Ranch
Cannon's
Caraville Manufacturing
Chicasaw Gun Works
Clark Custom Guns, Inc.
Cleland's Outdoor World, Inc
Colonial Repair
Colorado School of Trades
Colt's Mfg. Co., Inc.
Corkys Gun Clinic
Craig Custom Ltd., Research & Development
Curtis Custom Shop
Custom Firearms (See Ahrends, Kim)
Cylinder & Slide, Inc., William R. Laughridge
D&D Gunsmiths, Ltd.
D&L Sports
David R. Chicoine
Dayton Traister

Dilliott Gunsmithing, Inc.
Ellicott Arms, Inc. / Woods Pistolsmithing
F.I., Inc. - High Standard Mfg. Co.
Ferris Firearms
Fisher Custom Firearms
Forkin, Ben (See Belt MTN Arms)
Forkin Arms
Francesca, Inc.
Frielich Police Equipment
G.G. & G.
Garthwaite Pistolsmith, Inc., Jim
Gary Reeder Custom Guns
Genecco Gun Works
Gentry Custom Gunmaker, David
George E. Mathews & Son, Inc.
Greider Precision
Guncraft Sports Inc.
Guncraft Sports, Inc.
Gunsite Custom Shop
Gunsite Gunsmithy (See Gunsite Custom Shop)
Gunsite Training Center
Hamilton, Alex B (See Ten-Ring Precision, Inc)
Hammond Custom Guns Ltd.
Hank's Gun Shop
Hanson's Gun Center, Dick
Harris Gunworks
Harwood, Jack O.
Hawken Shop, The (See Dayton Traister)
Heinie Specialty Products
High Bridge Arms, Inc
Highline Machine Co.
Hoag, James W.
Irwin, Campbell H.
Island Pond Gun Shop
Ivanoff, Thomas G (See Tom's Gun Repair)
J&S Heat Treat
Jarvis, Inc.
Jeffredo Gunsight
Jensen's Custom Ammunition
Jungkind, Reeves C.
Kaswer Custom, Inc.
Ken Starnes Gunmaker
Ken's Gun Specialties
Kilham & Co.
Kim Ahrends Custom Firearms, Inc.
King's Gun Works
La Clinique du .45
LaFrance Specialties
LaRocca Gun Works
Lathrop's, Inc.
Lawson, John G (See Sight Shop, The)
Leckie Professional Gunsmithing
Linebaugh Custom Sixguns
List Precision Engineering
Long, George F.
Mag-Na-Port International, Inc.
Mahony, Philip Bruce
Mahovsky's Metalife
Mandall Shooting Supplies Inc.
Marent, Rudolf
Marvel, Alan
Mathews & Son, Inc., George E.
McCann's Machine & Gun Shop
MCS, Inc.
Middlebrooks Custom Shop
Miller Custom
Mitchell's Accuracy Shop
MJK Gunsmithing, Inc.
Modern Gun Repair School
Montgomery Community College
Mo's Competitor Supplies (See MCS Inc)
Mowrey's Guns & Gunsmithing
Mullis Guncraft
NCP Products, Inc.
Novak's, Inc.
Nowlin Mfg. Co.

Pace Marketing, Inc.
Paris, Frank J.
Pasadena Gun Center
Peacemaker Specialists
PEM's Mfg. Co.
Performance Specialists
Peterson Gun Shop, Inc., A.W.
Pierce Pistols
Piquette's Custom Engraving
Power Custom, Inc.
Precision Specialties
Randco UK
Ries, Chuck
Rim Pac Sports, Inc.
Rocky Mountain Arms, Inc.
RPM
Ruger's Custom Guns
Sanders Custom Gun Service
Score High Gunsmithing
Scott McDougall & Associates
Shooters Supply
Shootin' Shack, Inc.
Singletary, Kent
Springfield, Inc.
SSK Industries
Swenson's 45 Shop, A. D.
Swift River Gunworks
Ten-Ring Precision, Inc.
Terry K. Kopp Professional
  Gunsmithing
The A.W. Peterson Gun Shop,
  Inc.
The Gun Shop
The Gun Works
The Robar Co.'s, Inc.
The Sight Shop
Thompson, Randall
  (See Highline Machine Co.)
Thurston Sports, Inc.
Tom's Gun Repair, Thomas G.
  Ivanoff
Turnbull Restoration, Doug
Vic's Gun Refinishing
Volquartsen Custom Ltd.
Walker Arms Co., Inc.
Walters Industries
Wardell Precision Handguns
  Ltd.
Wessinger Custom Guns &
  Engraving
White Barn Wor
Wichita Arms, Inc.
Wild West Guns
Williams Gun Sight Co.
Williamson Precision
  Gunsmithing
Wilsom Combat
Wright's Gunstock Blanks

REBORING & RERIFLING

Ahlman Guns
Bauska Barrels
BlackStar AccuMax Barrels
BlackStar Barrel Accurizing
  (See BlackStar AccuMax
Buffalo Arms Co.
Champlin Firearms, Inc.
Ed's Gun House
Fred F. Wells / Wells Sport
  Store
H&S Liner Service
Ivanoff, Thomas G
  (See Tom's Gun Repair)
Jackalope Gun Shop
LaBounty Precision Reboring,
  Inc
Mandall Shooting Supplies Inc.
NCP Products, Inc.
Pence Precision Barrels
Pro-Port Ltd.
Redman's Rifling & Reboring
Rice, Keith
  (See White Rock Tool & Die)
Ridgetop Sporting Goods
Savage Arms, Inc.
Shaw, Inc., E. R.
  (See Small Arms Mfg. Co.)
Siegrist Gun Shop
Simmons Gun Repair, Inc.

Stratco, Inc.
Terry K. Kopp Professional
  Gunsmithing
The Gun Works
Time Precision
Tom's Gun Repair, Thomas G.
  Ivanoff
Turnbull Restoration, Doug
Van Patten, J. W.
White Rock Tool & Die
Zufall, Joseph F.
Reloading Tools and
  Accessories
4-D Custom Die Co.
Advance Car Mover Co., Rowell
  Div.
American Products, Inc.
Ammo Load, Inc.
Armfield Custom Bullets
Armite Laboratories
Arms Corporation of the
  Philippines
Atlantic Rose, Inc.
Atsko/Sno-Seal, Inc.
Bald Eagle Precision Machine
  Co.
Ballistic Product, Inc.
Belltown Ltd.
Ben William's Gun Shop
Ben's Machines
Berger Bullets Ltd.
Berry's Mfg., Inc.
Blount, Inc., Sporting
  Equipment Div.
Blue Mountain Bullets
Blue Ridge Machinery & Tools,
  Inc.
Bonanza (See Forster
  Products)
Break-Free, Inc.
Brown Co, E. Arthur
BRP, Inc. High Performance
  Cast Bullets
Brynin, Milton
B-Square Company, Inc.
Buck Stix--SOS Products Co.
Buffalo Arms Co.
Bull Mountain Rifle Co.
Bullseye Bullets
C&D Special Products
  (See Claybuster Wads &
  Harves
Camdex, Inc.
Camp-Cap Products
Canyon Cartridge Corp.
Case Sorting System
CH Tool & Die Co
  (See 4-D Custom Die Co)
Chem-Pak Inc.
CheVron Bullets
Claybuster Wads & Harvester
  Bullets
CONKKO
Cook Engineering Service
Crouse's Country Cover
Cumberland Arms
Curtis Cast Bullets
Custom Products
  (See Jones Custom
  Products)
CVA
D.C.C. Enterprises
Davide Pedersoli and Co.
Davis, Don
Davis Products, Mike
Denver Instrument Co.
Dewey Mfg. Co., Inc., J.
Dillon Precision Products, Inc.
Dropkick
E&L Mfg., Inc.
Eagan, Donald V.
Eezox, Inc.
Eichelberger Bullets, Wm.
Enguix Import-Export
Euroarms of America, Inc.
E-Z-Way Systems
Federated-Fry (See Fry Metals)
Feken, Dennis
Ferguson, Bill
First Inc., Jack
Fisher Custom Firearms

Fitz Pistol Grip Co.
Flambeau Products Corp.
Flitz International Ltd.
Forster Products
Fremont Tool Works
Fry Metals
Gehmann, Walter
  (See Huntington Die
  Specialties)
Graf & Sons
Graphics Direct
Graves Co.
Green, Arthur S.
Greenwood Precision
GTB
Gun City
Hanned Precision
  (See Hanned Line, The)
Harrell's Precision
Harris Enterprises
Harrison Bullets
Haydon Shooters Supply, Russ
Heidenstrom Bullets
High Precision
Hirtenberger Aktiengesellschaft
Hoch Custom Bullet Moulds
  (See Colorado Shooter's)
Hodgdon Powder Co.
Hoehn Sales, Inc.
Hoelscher, Virgil
Holland's Gunsmithing
Hondo Ind.
Hornady Mfg. Co.
Howell Machine
Hunters Supply, Inc.
Hutton Rifle Ranch
Image Ind. Inc.
Imperial Magnum Corp.
INTEC International, Inc.
Iosso Products
J&L Superior Bullets
  (See Huntington Die Special)
Javelina Lube Products
JGS Precision Tool Mfg.
JLK Bullets
Jonad Corp.
Jones Custom Products, Neil A.
Jones Moulds, Paul
K&M Services
Kapro Mfg.Co. Inc. (See R.E.I.)
Knoell, Doug
Korzinek Riflesmith, J.
L.A.R. Mfg., Inc.
L.E. Wilson, Inc.
Lapua Ltd.
Le Clear Industries
  (See E-Z-Way Systems)
Lee Precision, Inc.
Legend Products Corp.
Liberty Metals
Liberty Shooting Supplies
Lightning Performance
  Innovations, Inc.
Lithi Bee Bullet Lube
Littleton, J. F.
Lock's Philadelphia Gun
  Exchange
Lortone Inc.
Loweth, Richard H.R.
Lyman Instant Targets, Inc.
  (See Lyman Products)
Lyman Products Corp.
MA Systems
Magma Engineering Co.
MarMik, Inc.
Marquart Precision Co.
MAST Technology
Match Prep--Doyle Gracey
Mayville Engineering Co.
  (See MEC, Inc.)
MCS, Inc.
MEC, Inc.
Midway Arms, Inc.
MI-TE Bullets
Montana Armory, Inc
  (See C. Sharps Arms Co.
  Inc.)
Mo's Competitor Supplies
  (See MCS Inc)
Mountain South

Mountain State Muzzleloading
  Supplies, Inc.
MTM Molded Products Co.,
  Inc.
Multi-Scale Charge Ltd.
MWG Co.
Navy Arms Company
Necromancer Industries, Inc.
Newman Gunshop
North Devon Firearms Services
October Country Muzzleloading
Old West Bullet Moulds
Omark Industries,Div. of
  Blount,Inc.
Original Box, Inc.
Outdoor Sports Headquarters,
  Inc.
Paco's
  (See Small Custom Mould &
  Bullet Co)
Paragon Sales & Services, Inc.
Pease Accuracy
Pinetree Bullets
Ponsness/Warren
Prairie River Arms
Prime Reloading
Professional Hunter Supplies
  (See Star Custom Bull)
Pro-Shot Products, Inc.
R.A. Wells Custom Gunsmith
R.E.I.
R.I.S. Co., Inc.
Rapine Bullet Mould Mfg. Co.
Reloading Specialties, Inc.
Rice, Keith
  (See White Rock Tool & Die)
Rochester Lead Works
Rooster Laboratories
Rorschach Precision Products
SAECO
  (See Redding Reloading
  Equipment)
Sandia Die & Cartridge Co.
Saunders Gun & Machine Shop
Saville Iron Co.
  (See Greenwood Precision)
Scot Powder Co. of Ohio, Inc.
Seebeck Assoc., R.E.
Sharp Shooter Supply
Sharps Arms Co., Inc., C.
Shiloh Creek
Shiloh Rifle Mfg.
Sierra Specialty Prod. Co.
Silver Eagle Machining
Skip's Machine
Small Custom Mould & Bullet
  Co.
Sno-Seal, Inc. (See Atsko/Sno-
  Seal)
SOS Products Co.
  (See Buck Stix-SOS
  Products Co.)
Spencer's Custom Guns
SPG LLC
Sportsman Supply Co.
SSK Industries
Stalwart Corporation
Star Custom Bullets
Starr Trading Co., Jedediah
Stillwell, Robert
Stoney Point Products, Inc.
Stratco, Inc.
Tamarack Products, Inc.
Taracorp Industries, Inc.
TCCI
TCSR
TDP Industries, Inc.
Tetra Gun Lubricants (See FTI,
  Inc.)
The Hanned Line
The Protector Mfg. Co., Inc.
Thompson / Center Arms
Timber Heirloom Products
TMI Products
  (See Haselbauer Products,
  Jerry)
Vega Tool Co.
Venco Industries, Inc.
  (See Shooter's Choice)
VibraShine, Inc.
Vibra-Tek Co.

Vihtavuori Oy/Kaltron-
  Pettibone
Vitt/Boos
W.B. Niemi Engineering
W.J. Riebe Co.
Waechter
WD-40 Co.
Webster Scale Mfg. Co.
White Rock Tool & Die
Widener's Reloading &
  Shooting Supply, Inc.
Wise Custom Guns
Woodleigh
  (See Huntington Die
  Specialties)
Yesteryear Armory & Supply
Young Country Arms

RESTS BENCH, PORTABLE AND ACCESSORIES

Adventure 16, Inc.
Armor Metal Products
Bald Eagle Precision Machine
  Co.
Bartlett Engineering
Battenfeld Technologies
Blount/Outers
Browning Arms Co.
B-Square Company, Inc.
Bull Mountain Rifle Co.
Canons Delcour
Chem-Pak Inc.
Clift Mfg., L. R.
Clift Welding Supply & Cases
Decker Shooting Products
Desert Mountain Mfg.
Efficient Machinery Co
Greenwood Precision
Harris Engineering Inc.
Hidalgo, Tony
Hoehn Sales, Inc.
Hoelscher, Virgil
Hoppe's Div. Penguin
  Industries, Inc.
Keng's Firearms Specialty, Inc.
  / US Tactical Systems
Kolpin Mfg., Inc.
Kramer Designs
Midway Arms, Inc.
Millett Sights
Protektor Model
Ransom International Corp.
Russ Haydon Shooters' Supply
Saville Iron Co.
  (See Greenwood Precision)
Sinclair International, Inc.
Stoney Point Products, Inc.
T.H.U. Enterprises, Inc.
The A.W. Peterson Gun Shop,
  Inc.
The Outdoor Connection,Inc.
Thompson Target Technology
Tonoloway Tack Drives
Varmint Masters, LLC
Wichita Arms, Inc.
Zanotti Armor, Inc.
Ziegel Engineering

SCOPES, MOUNTS, ACCESSORIES, OPTICAL EQUIPMENT

A.R.M.S., Inc.
ABO (USA) Inc
Accu-Tek
Ackerman, Bill
  (See Optical Services Co)
Action Direct, Inc.
ADCO Sales, Inc.
Adventurer's Outpost
Aimpoint c/o Springfield, Inc.
Aimtech Mount Systems
Air Rifle Specialists
Air Venture Airguns
All Rite Products, Inc.
Alley Supply Co.
Alpec Team, Inc.
Apel GmbH, Ernst

ArmaLite, Inc.
Arundel Arms & Ammunition,
  Inc., A.
B.A.C.
Baer Custom, Inc, Les
Bansner's Ultimate Rifles, LLC
Barrett Firearms Manufacturer,
  Inc.
Beaver Park Product, Inc.
BEC, Inc.
Beeman Precision Airguns
Ben William's Gun Shop
Benjamin/Sheridan Co.,
  Crossman
BKL Technologies
Blount, Inc., Sporting
  Equipment Div.
Blount/Outers
Borden Rifles Inc
Brockman's Custom
  Gunsmithing
Brocock Ltd.
Brown Co, E. Arthur
Brownells, Inc.
Brunton U.S.A.
BSA Optics
Bull Mountain Rifle Co.
Burris Co., Inc.
Bushmaster Firearms
Bushnell Sports Optics
  Worldwide
Butler Creek Corp.
Cabela's
Carl Zeiss Inc.
Center Lock Scope Rings
Chuck's Gun Shop
Clark Custom Guns, Inc.
Clearview Mfg. Co., Inc.
Compass Industries, Inc.
Compasseco, Ltd.
Concept Development Corp.
Conetrol Scope Mounts
Creedmoor Sports, Inc.
Crimson Trace Lasers
Crosman Airguns
Custom Quality Products, Inc.
D&H Prods. Co., Inc.
D.C.C. Enterprises
Daisy Mfg. Co.
Del-Sports, Inc.
DHB Products
E. Arthur Brown Co.
Eclectic Technologies, Inc.
Ed Brown Products, Inc.
Edmund Scientific Co.
Ednar, Inc.
Eggleston, Jere D.
Emerging Technologies, Inc.
  (See Laseraim Technolo
Entre'prise Arms, Inc.
Euro-Imports
Evolution Gun Works Inc.
Excalibur Electro Optics Inc
Excel Industries, Inc.
Faloon Industries, Inc.
Farr Studio, Inc.
Federal Arms Corp. of America
Freedom Arms, Inc.
Fujinon, Inc.
G.G. & G.
Galati International
Gentry Custom Gunmaker,
  David
Gil Hebard Guns Inc.
Gilmore Sports Concepts
Gonzalez Guns, Ramon B
Goodwin's Gun Shop
GSI, Inc.
Gun South, Inc. (See GSI, Inc.)
Guns
Guns Div. of D.C. Engineering,
  Inc.
Gunsmithing, Inc.
Hakko Co. Ltd.
Hammerli USA
Harris Gunworks
Harvey, Frank
Hertel & Reuss
Hiptmayer, Armurier
Hiptmayer, Klaus

REFERENCE

PRODUCT & SERVICE DIRECTORY

HiTek International
Holland's Gunsmithing
Impact Case Co.
Ironsighter Co.
Jeffredo Gunsight
Jena Eur
Jerry Phillips Optics
Jewell Triggers, Inc.
John Masen Co. Inc.
John's Custom Leather
Kahles A Swarovski Company
Kalispel Case Line
KDF, Inc.
Keng's Firearms Specialty, Inc.
/ US Tactical Systems
KenPatable Ent., Inc.
Kesselring Gun Shop
Kimber of America, Inc.
Kowa Optimed, Inc.
KVH Industries, Inc.
Kwik-Site Co.
L&S Technologies Inc
(See Aimtech Mount
Systems)
L.A.R. Mfg., Inc.
Laser Devices, Inc.
Laseraim Technologies, Inc.
LaserMax, Inc.
Leapers, Inc.
Lee Co., T. K.
Leica USA, Inc.
Leupold & Stevens, Inc.
Lightforce U.S.A. Inc.
List Precision Engineering
Lohman Mfg. Co., Inc.
Lomont Precision Bullets
London Guns Ltd.
Mac-1 Airgun Distributors
Mag-Na-Port International, Inc.
Mandall Shooting Supplies Inc.
Marksman Products
Maxi-Mount Inc.
McBros Rifle Co.
McCann's Machine & Gun Shop
McMillan Optical Gunsight Co.
MCS, Inc.
MDS
Merit Corp.
Military Armament Corp.
Millett Sights
Mirador Optical Corp.
Mitchell Optics, Inc.
MMC
Mo's Competitor Supplies
(See MCS Inc)
MWG Co.
Navy Arms Company
New England Custom Gun
Service
Nightforce (See Lightforce USA
Inc)
Nikon, Inc.
Norincoptics (See BEC, Inc.)
Olympic Optical Co.
Optical Services Co.
Orchard Park Enterprise
Oregon Arms, Inc.
(See Rogue Rifle Co., Inc.)
Ozark Gun Works
P.M. Enterprises, Inc. / Precise
Metalsmithing
Parker & Sons Shooting Supply
Parsons Optical Mfg. Co.
PECAR Herbert Schwarz GmbH
PEM's Mfg. Co.
Pentax Corp.
PMC / Eldorado Cartridge Corp.
Precise Metalsmithing
Enterprises / P.M.
Enterprises
Precision Sport Optics
Premier Reticles
R.A. Wells Custom Gunsmith
Ram-Line Blount, Inc.
Ramon B. Gonzalez Guns
Ranch Products
Rice, Keith
(See White Rock Tool & Die)
Robinson Armament Co.

Rogue Rifle Co., Inc.
Romain's Custom Guns, Inc.
S&K Scope Mounts
Sanders Custom Gun Service
Sanders Gun and Machine
Shop
Schmidt & Bender, Inc.
Schumakers Gun Shop
Scope Control, Inc.
ScopLevel
Score High Gunsmithing
Seecamp Co. Inc., L. W.
Segway Industries
Selsi Co., Inc.
Sharp Shooter Supply
Shepherd Enterprises, Inc.
Sightron, Inc.
Simmons Outdoor Corp.
Six Enterprises
Southern Bloomer Mfg. Co.
Splitfire Sporting Goods, L.L.C.
Sportsmatch U.K. Ltd.
Springfield, Inc.
SSK Industries
Stiles Custom Guns
Stoeger Industries
Stoney Point Products, Inc.
Sturm Ruger & Co. Inc.
Sunny Hill Enterprises, Inc.
Swarovski Optik North America
Ltd.
Swift Instruments, Inc.
T.K. Lee Co.
TacStar
Talley, Dave
Tasco Sales, Inc.
Tele-Optics
The A.W. Peterson Gun Shop,
Inc.
The Outdoor Connection,Inc.
Thompson / Center Arms
Thompson Target Technology
Traditions Performance
Firearms
Trijicon, Inc.
Truglo, Inc
Ultra Dot Distribution
Uncle Mike's
(See Michaels of Oregon Co.)
Unertl Optical Co., Inc.
United Binocular Co.
United States Optics
Technologies, Inc.
Valor Corp.
Virgin Valley Custom Guns
Visible Impact Targets
Voere-KGH m.b.H.
Warne Manufacturing Co.
Warren Muzzleloading Co., Inc.
WASP Shooting Systems
Watson Trophy Match Bullets
Weaver Products
Weaver Scope Repair Service
Weigand Combat Handguns,
Inc.
Wessinger Custom Guns &
Engraving
Westley Richards & Co.
White Rock Tool & Die
White Shooting Systems, Inc.
(See White Muzzleload
Whitestone Lumber Corp.
Wideview Scope Mount Corp.
Wilcox Industries Corp
Wild West Guns
Williams Gun Sight Co.
York M-1 Conversions
Zanotti Armor, Inc.

SHOOTING/
TRAINING SCHOOL

Alpine Indoor Shooting Range
American Gunsmithing
Institute
American Small Arms Academy
Auto Arms
Beretta U.S.A. Corp.
Bob's Tactical Indoor Shooting
Range & Gun Shop
Bridgeman Products

Cannon's
Chapman Academy of Practical
Shooting
Chelsea Gun Club of New York
City Inc.
Cherry Creek State Park
Shooting Center
CQB Training
Defense Training International,
Inc.
Executive Protection Institute
Ferris Firearms
Front Sight Firearms Training
Institute
G.H. Enterprises Ltd.
Gene's Custom Guns
Griffin & Howe, Inc.
Guncraft Books
(See Guncraft Sports Inc.)
Guncraft Sports Inc.
Guncraft Sports, Inc.
Gunsite Training Center
Henigson & Associates, Steve
Jensen's Custom Ammunition
Jensen's Firearms Academy
Kemen America
L.L. Bean, Inc.
Lethal Force Institute
(See Police Bookshelf)
Loch Leven Industries /
Convert-A-Pell
Mandall Shooting Supplies Inc.
McMurdo, Lynn
(See Specialty Gunsmithing)
Mendez, John A.
NCP Products, Inc.
Nevada Pistol Academy, Inc.
North American Shooting
Systems
North Mountain Pine Training
Center (See Executive)
Nowlin Mfg. Co.
Paxton Quigley's Personal
Protection Strategies
Pentheny de Pentheny
Performance Specialists
Police Bookshelf
River Road Sporting Clays
SAFE
Shoot Where You Look
Shooter's World
Shooters, Inc.
Sigarms, Inc.
Smith & Wesson
Specialty Gunsmithing
Starlight Training Center, Inc.
Tactical Defense Institute
The Firearm Training Center
The Midwest Shooting School
The Shooting Gallery
Thunden Ranch
Western Missouri Shooters
Alliance
Yankee Gunsmith
Yavapai Firearms Academy Ltd.

SIGHTS, METALLIC

100 Straight Products, Inc.
Accura-Site
(See All's, The Jim Tembelis
Co., Inc.)
Ad Hominem
Alley Supply Co.
All's, The Jim J. Tembelis Co.,
Inc.
Alpec Team, Inc.
Andela Tool & Machine, Inc.
AO Sight Systems
ArmaLite, Inc.
Aro-Tek Ltd.
Ashley Outdoors, Inc.
Aspen Outfitting Co.
Axtell Rifle Co.
B.A.C.
Baer Custom, Inc, Les
Ballard Rifle & Cartridge Co.,
LLC
BEC, Inc.
Bob's Gun Shop

Bo-Mar Tool & Mfg. Co.
Bond Custom Firearms
Bowen Classic Arms Corp.
Bradley Gunsight Co.
Brockman's Custom
Gunsmithing
Brooks Tactical Systems
Brown Co, E. Arthur
Brown Dog Ent.
Brownells, Inc.
Buffalo Arms Co.
Bushmaster Firearms
C. Sharps Arms Co.
Inc./Montana Armory
California Sights
(See Fautheree, Andy)
Cape Outfitters
Cape Outfitters
Cash Mfg. Co., Inc.
Center Lock Scope Rings
Champion's Choice, Inc.
C-More Systems
Colonial Repair
CRR, Inc./Marble's Inc.
Davide Pedersoli and Co.
DHB Products
Dixie Gun Works
DPMS (Defense Procurement
Manufacturing Services,
Inc.)
E. Arthur Brown Co.
Evolution Gun Works Inc.
Faloon Industries, Inc.
Farr Studio, Inc.
G.G. & G.
Garthwaite Pistolsmith, Inc.,
Jim
Goergen's Gun Shop, Inc.
Goodwin's Gun Shop
Guns Div. of D.C. Engineering,
Inc.
Gunsmithing, Inc.
Hank's Gun Shop
Heidenstrom Bullets
Heinie Specialty Products
Hesco-Meprolight
Hiptmayer, Armurier
Hiptmayer, Klaus
IMX, LLC
Innovative Weaponry Inc.
J.G. Anschutz GmbH & Co. KG
J.P. Enterprises Inc.
Keng's Firearms Specialty, Inc.
/ US Tactical Systems
Knight Rifles
Knight's Mfg. Co.
L.P.A. Snc
Leapers, Inc.
List Precision Engineering
London Guns Ltd.
Lyman Instant Targets, Inc.
(See Lyman Products)
Mandall Shooting Supplies Inc.
Marble Arms
(See CRR, Inc./Marble's Inc.)
MCS, Inc.
MEC-Gar S.r.l.
Meprolight (See Hesco-
Meprolight)
Merit Corp.
Mid-America Recreation, Inc.
Middlebrooks Custom Shop
Millett Sights
MMC
Modern Muzzleloading, Inc
Montana Armory, Inc
(See C. Sharps Arms Co.
Inc.)
Montana Vintage Arms
Mo's Competitor Supplies
(See MCS Inc)
Navy Arms Company
New England Custom Gun
Service
Newman Gunshop
North Pass
Novak's, Inc.
OK Weber,Inc.
One Ragged Hole
P.M. Enterprises, Inc. / Precise
Metalsmithing

Parker & Sons Shooting Supply
PEM's Mfg. Co.
Perazone-Gunsmith, Brian
Precise Metalsmithing
Enterprises / P.M.
Enterprises
RPM
Sharps Arms Co., Inc., C.
Slug Site
STI International
T.F.C. S.p.A.
Talley, Dave
Tank's Rifle Shop
The A.W. Peterson Gun Shop,
Inc.
The Gun Doctor
The Gun Works
Trijicon, Inc.
Truglo, Inc
United States Optics
Technologies, Inc.
Warne Manufacturing Co.
WASP Shooting Systems
Wichita Arms, Inc.
Wild West Guns
Williams Gun Sight Co.
Wilsom Combat
Wilsom Combat

TARGETS, BULLET
& CLAYBIRD
TRAPS

Action Target, Inc.
Air Arms
American Target
Autauga Arms, Inc.
Beeman Precision Airguns
Benjamin/Sheridan Co.,
Crossman
Beomat of America, Inc.
Birchwood Casey
Blount, Inc., Sporting
Equipment Div.
Blount/Outers
Blue and Gray Products Inc
(See Ox-Yoke Originals
Brown Precision, Inc.
Bull-X, Inc.
Champion Target Co.
Crosman Airguns
D.C.C. Enterprises
Detroit-Armor Corp.
Diamond Mfg. Co.
Federal Champion Target Co.
G.H. Enterprises Ltd.
Hiti-Schuch, Atelier Wilma
H-S Precision, Inc.
Hunterjohn
J.G. Dapkus Co., Inc.
Kennebec Journal
Kleen-Bore,Inc.
Lakefield Arms Ltd
(See Savage Arms Inc.)
Leapers, Inc.
Littler Sales Co.
Lyman Instant Targets, Inc.
(See Lyman Products)
Marksman Products
Mendez, John A.
Mountain Plains Industries
MSR Targets
Muscle Products Corp.
N.B.B., Inc.
National Target Co.
North American Shooting
Systems
Outers Laboratories Div. of
Blount, Inc. Sporting
Ox-Yoke Originals, Inc.
Palsa Outdoor Products
Passive Bullet Traps, Inc.
(See Savage Range)
PlumFire Press, Inc.
Precision Airgun Sales, Inc.
Quack Decoy & Sporting Clays
Remington Arms Co., Inc.
Rockwood Corp.

Rocky Mountain Target Co.
Savage Range Systems, Inc.
Schaefer Shooting Sports
Seligman Shooting Products
Shooters Supply
Shoot-N-C Targets
(See Birchwood Casey)
Target Shooting, Inc.
The A.W. Peterson Gun Shop,
Inc.
Thompson Target Technology
Trius Traps, Inc.
Universal Sports
Visible Impact Targets
Woods Wise Products
World of Targets
(See Birchwood Casey)
X-Spand Target Systems
Zriny's Metal Targets
(See Z's Metal Targets)

TAXIDERMY

African Import Co.
Kulis Freeze Dry Taxidermy
Montgomery Community
College
World Trek, Inc.

TRIGGERS,
RELATED
EQUIPMENT

Actions by "T" Teddy Jacobson
B&D Trading Co., Inc.
Baer Custom, Inc, Les
Behlert Precision, Inc.
Bond Custom Firearms
Boyds' Gunstock Industries,
Inc.
Bull Mountain Rifle Co.
Chicasaw Gun Works
Dayton Traister
Electronic Trigger Systems,
Inc.
Eversull Co., Inc.
FWB
Gentry Custom Gunmaker,
David
Goodwin's Gun Shop
Guns
Hart & Son, Inc.
Hawken Shop, The
(See Dayton Traister)
Hoehn Sales, Inc.
Hoelscher, Virgil
Holland's Gunsmithing
Impact Case Co.
J.P. Enterprises Inc.
Jewell Triggers, Inc.
John Masen Co. Inc.
Jones Custom Products, Neil A.
K. Eversull Co., Inc.
KK Air International
(See Impact Case Co.)
L&R Lock Co.
List Precision Engineering
London Guns Ltd.
M.H. Canjar Co.
Mahony, Philip Bruce
Master Lock Co.
Miller Single Trigger Mfg. Co.
NCP Products, Inc.
Neil A. Jones Custom Products
Nowlin Mfg. Co.
PEM's Mfg. Co.
Penrod Precision
Robinson Armament Co.
Schumakers Gun Shop
Sharp Shooter Supply
Shilen, Inc.
Simmons Gun Repair, Inc.
Spencer's Custom Guns
Tank's Rifle Shop
Target Shooting, Inc.
The A.W. Peterson Gun Shop,
Inc.
The Gun Works
Watson Trophy Match Bullets

A

A Zone Bullets, 2039 Walter Rd., Billings, MT 59105 / 800-252-3111; FAX: 406-248-1961

A&B Industries,Inc (See Top-Line USA Inc)

A&W Repair, 2930 Schneider Dr., Arnold, MO 63010 / 617-287-3725

A.A. Arms, Inc., 4811 Persimmont Ct., Monroe, NC 28110 / 704-289-5356; or 800-935-1119; FAX: 704-289-5859

A.B.S. III, 9238 St. Morritz Dr., Fern Creek, KY 40291

A.G. Russell Knives, Inc., 1920 North 26th Street, Springdale, AR 72764 / 479-751-7341; FAX: 479-751-4520 ag@agrussell.com agrussell.com

A.R.M.S., Inc., 230 W. Center St., West Bridgewater, MA 02379-1620 / 508-584-7816; FAX: 508-588-8045

A.W. Peterson Gun Shop, Inc., 4255 W. Old U.S. 441, Mt. Dora, FL 32757-3299 / 352-383-4258; FAX: 352-735-1001

ABO (USA) Inc, 615 SW 2nd Avenue, Miami, FL 33130 / 305-859-2010; FAX: 305-859-2099

AC Dyna-tite Corp., 155 Kelly St., P.O. Box 0984, Elk Grove Village, IL 60007 / 847-593-5566; FAX: 847-593-1304

Acadian Ballistic Specialties, P.O. Box 787, Folsom, LA 70437 / 504-796-0078 gunsmith@neasoft.com

Accuracy International, Foster, PO Box 111, Wilsall, MT 59086 / 406-587-7922; FAX: 406-585-9434

Accuracy Internationl Precision Rifles (See U.S.)

Accuracy Int'l. North America, Inc., PO Box 5267, Oak Ridge, TN 37831 / 423-482-0330; FAX: 423-482-0336

Accuracy Unlimited, 16036 N. 49 Ave., Glendale, AZ 85306 / 602-978-9089; FAX: 602-978-9089 frankglenn@earthlink.net

Accuracy Unlimited, 7479 S. DePew St., Littleton, CO 80123

Accura-Site (See All's, The Jim Tembelis Co., Inc.)

Accurate Arms Co., Inc., 5891 Hwy. 230 West, McEwen, TN 37101 / 931-729-4207; FAX: 931-729-4211 email@accuratecompanies.com www.accuratepowder.com

Accu-Tek, 4510 Carter Ct, Chino, CA 91710

Ace Custom 45's, Inc., 1880 1/2 Upper Turtle Creek Rd., Kerrville, TX 78028 / 830-257-4290; FAX: 830-257-5724 www.acecustom45.com

Ace Sportswear, Inc., 700 Quality Rd., Fayetteville, NC 28306 / 919-323-1223; FAX: 919-323-5392

Ackerman & Co., Box 133 US Highway Rt. 7, Pownal, VT 05261 / 802-823-9874 muskets@togsther.net

Ackerman, Bill (See Optical Services Co)

Acra-Bond Laminates, 134 Zimmerman Rd., Kalispell, MT 59901 / 406-257-9003; FAX: 406-257-9003 merlins@digisys.net; www.acrabondlaminates.com

Action Bullets & Alloy Inc, RR 1, PO Box 189, Quinter, KS 67752 / 785-754-3609; FAX: 785-754-3629 bullets@ruraltel.net

Action Direct, Inc., PO Box 770400, Miami, FL 33177 / 305-969-0056; FAX: 530-734-3760 action-direct.com

Action Products, Inc., 22 N. Mulberry St., Hagerstown, MD 21740 / 301-797-1414; FAX: 301-733-2073

Action Target, Inc., PO Box 636, Provo, UT 84603 / 801-377-8033; FAX: 801-377-8096

Actions by "T" Teddy Jacobson, 16315 Redwood Forest Ct., Sugar Land, TX 77478 / 281-277-4008; FAX: 281-277-9112; tjacobson@houston.rr.com www.actionsbyt.com

AcuSport Corporation, 1 Hunter Place, Bellefontaine, OH 43311-3001 / 513-593-7010; FAX: 513-592-5625

Ad Hominem, 3130 Gun Club Lane, RR #3, Orillia, ON L3V 6H3 CANADA / 705-689-5303; FAX: 705-689-5303

Adair Custom Shop, Bill, 2886 Westridge, Carrollton, TX 75006

ADCO Sales, Inc., 4 Draper St. #A, Woburn, MA 01801 / 781-935-1799; FAX: 781-935-1011

Adkins, Luther, 1292 E. McKay Rd., Shelbyville, IN 46176-8706 / 317-392-3795

Advance Car Mover Co., Rowell Div., P.O. Box 1, 240 N. Depot St., Juneau, WI 53039 / 414-386-4464; FAX: 414-386-4416

Adventure 16, Inc., 4620 Alvarado Canyon Rd., San Diego, CA 92120 / 619-283-6314

Adventure Game Calls, R.D. 1, Leonard Rd., Spencer, NY 14883 / 607-589-4611

Adventurer's Outpost, P.O. Box 547, Cottonwood, AZ 86326-0547 / 800-762-7471; FAX: 602-634-8781

Aero Peltor, 90 Mechanic St, Southbridge, MA 01550 / 508-764-5500; FAX: 508-764-0188

African Import Co., 22 Goodwin Rd, Plymouth, MA 02360 / 508-746-8552; FAX: 508-746-0404

AFSCO Ammunition, 731 W. Third St., P.O. Box L, Owen, WI 54460 / 715-229-2516

Ahlman Guns, 9525 W. 230th St., Morristown, MN 55052 / 507-685-4243; FAX: 507-685-4280 www.ahlmans.com

Ahrends, Inc. (See Custom Firearms, Inc), Box 203, Clarion, IA 50525 / 515-532-3449; FAX: 515-532-3926

Aimpoint c/o Springfield, Inc., 420 W. Main St, Geneseo, IL 61254 / 309-944-1702

Aimtech Mount Systems, PO Box 223, Thomasville, GA 31799 / 229-226-4313; FAX: 229-227-0222 aimtech@surfsouth.com; www.aimtech-mounts.com

Air Arms, Hailsham Industrial Park, Diplocks Way, Hailsham, E. Sussex, BN27 3JF ENGLAND / 011-0323-845853

Air Rifle Specialists, P.O. Box 138, 130 Holden Rd., Pine City, NY 14871-0138 / 607-734-7340; FAX: 607-733-3261 ars@stny.rr.com www.air-rifles.com

Air Venture Airguns, 9752 E. Flower St., Bellflower, CA 90706 / 310-867-6355

AirForce Airguns, P.O. Box 2478, Fort Worth, TX 76113 / 817-451-8966; FAX: 817-451-1613 www.airforceairguns.com

Airgun Repair Centre, 3227 Garden Meadows, Lawrenceburg, IN 47025 / 812-637-1463; FAX: 812-637-1463

Airrow, 11 Monitor Hill Rd, Newtown, CT 06470 / 203-270-6343

Aitor-Cuchilleria Del Norte S.A., Izelaieta, 17, 48260, Ermua, S SPAIN / 43-17-08-50 info@aitor.com; www.ailor.com

Ajax Custom Grips, Inc., 9130 Viscount Row, Dallas, TX 75247 / 214-630-8893; FAX: 214-630-4942

Aker International, Inc., 2248 Main St., Suite 6, Chula Vista, CA 91911 / 619-423-5182; FAX: 619-423-1363

Al Lind Custom Guns, 7821 76th Ave. SW, Lakewood, WA 98498 / 253-584-6361

Alana Cupp Custom Engraver, P.O. Box 207, Annabella, UT 84711 / 801-896-4834

Alaska Bullet Works, Inc., 9978 Crazy Horse Drive, Juneau, AK 99801 / 907-789-3834; FAX: 907-789-3433

Alaskan Silversmith, The, 2145 Wagner Hollow Rd., Fort Plain, NY 13339 / 518-993-3983 sidbell@capital.net www.sidbell.cizland.com

Aldis Gunsmithing & Shooting Supply, 502 S. Montezuma St., Prescott, AZ 86303 / 602-445-6723; FAX: 602-445-6763

Alessi Holsters, Inc., 2465 Niagara Falls Blvd., Amherst, NY 14228-3527 / 716-691-5615

Alex, Inc., Box 3034, Bozeman, MT 59772 / 406-282-7396; FAX: 406-282-7396

Alfano, Sam, 36180 Henry Gaines Rd., Pearl River, LA 70452 / 504-863-3364; FAX: 504-863-7715

All American Lead Shot Corp., P.O. Box 224566, Dallas, TX 75062

All Rite Products, Inc., 9554 Wells Circle, Suite D, West Jordan, UT 84088-6226 / 800-771-8471; FAX: 801-280-8302 www.allriteproducts.com

Allard, Gary/Creek Side Metal & Woodcrafters, Fishers Hill, VA 22626 / 703-465-3903

Allen Co., Bob, 214 SW Jackson, P.O. Box 477, Des Moines, IA 50315 / 515-283-2191; or 800-685-7020; FAX: 515-283-0779

Allen Co., Inc., 525 Burbank St., Broomfield, CO 80020 / 303-469-1857; or 800-876-8600; FAX: 303-466-7437

Allen Firearm Engraving, PO Box 155, Camp Verde, AZ 86322 / 928-567-3892; FAX: 928-567-3901 rosebudmukco@aol.com

Allen Mfg., 6449 Hodgson Rd., Circle Pines, MN 55014 / 612-429-8231

Allen Sportswear, Bob (See Allen Co., Bob)

Alley Supply Co., PO Box 848, Gardnerville, NV 89410 / 775-782-3800 FAX: 775-782-3827 jetalley@aol.com www.alleysupplyco.com

Alliant Techsystems Smokeless Powder Group, P.O. Box 6, Rt. 114, Bldg. 229, Radford, VA 24141-0096 www.alliantpowder.com

Allred Bullet Co., 932 Evergreen Drive, Logan, UT 84321 / 435-752-6983; FAX: 435-752-6983

All's, The Jim J. Tembelis Co., Inc., 216 Loper Ct., Neenah, WI 54956 / 920-725-5251; FAX: 920-725-5251

Alpec Team, Inc., 201 Ricken Backer Cir., Livermore, CA 94550 / 510-606-8245; FAX: 510-606-4279

Alpha 1 Drop Zone, 2121 N. Tyler, Wichita, KS 67212 / 316-729-0800

Alpha Gunsmith Division, 1629 Via Monserate, Fallbrook, CA 92028 / 619-723-9279; or 619-728-2663

Alpha LaFranck Enterprises, P.O. Box 81072, Lincoln, NE 68501 / 402-466-3193

Alpha Precision, Inc., 3238 Della Slaton Rd., Comer, GA 30629-2212 / 706-783-2131 jim@alphaprecisioninc.com www.alphaprecisioninc.com

Alpine Indoor Shooting Range, 2401 Government Way, Coeur d'Alene, ID 83814 / 208-676-8824; FAX: 208-676-8824

Altamont Co., 901 N. Church St., P.O. Box 309, Thomasboro, IL 61878 / 217-643-3125; or 800-626-5774; FAX: 217-643-7973

Alumna Sport by Dee Zee, 1572 NE 58th Ave., P.O. Box 3090, Des Moines, IA 50316 / 800-798-9899

Amadeo Rossi S.A., Rua: Amadeo Rossi, 143, Sao Leopoldo, RS 93030-220 BRAZIL / 051-592-5566

AmBr Software Group Ltd., P.O. Box 301, Reistertown, MD 21136-0301 / 800-888-1917; FAX: 410-526-7212

American Ammunition, 3545 NW 71st St., Miami, FL 33147 / 305-835-7400; FAX: 305-694-0037

American Derringer Corp., 127 N. Lacy Dr., Waco, TX 76705 / 800-642-7817; or 254-799-9111; FAX: 254-799-7935

American Display Co., 55 Cromwell St., Providence, RI 02907 / 401-331-2464; FAX: 401-421-1264

American Frontier Firearms Mfg., Inc, PO Box 744, Aguanga, CA 92536 / 909-763-0014; FAX: 909-763-0014

American Gas & Chemical Co., Ltd, 220 Pegasus Ave, Northvale, NJ 07647 / 201-767-7300

American Gripcraft, 3230 S Dodge 2, Tucson, AZ 85713 / 602-790-1222

American Gunsmithing Institute, 1325 Imola Ave #504, Napa, CA 94559 / 707-253-0462; FAX: 707-253-7149

American Handgunner Magazine, 591 Camino de la Reina, Ste 200, San Diego, CA 92108 / 619-297-5350; FAX: 619-297-5353

American Pioneer Video, PO Box 50049, Bowling Green, KY 42102-2649 / 800-743-4675

American Products, Inc., 14729 Spring Valley Road, Morrison, IL 61270 / 815-772-3336; FAX: 815-772-8046

American Safe Arms, Inc., 1240 Riverview Dr., Garland, UT 84312 / 801-257-7472; FAX: 801-785-8156

American Security Products Co., 11925 Pacific Ave., Fontana, CA 92337 / 909-685-9680; or 800-421-6142; FAX: 909-685-9685

American Small Arms Academy, P.O. Box 12111, Prescott, AZ 86304 / 602-778-5623

American Target, 1328 S. Jason St., Denver, CO 80223 / 303-733-0433; FAX: 303-777-0311

American Target Knives, 1030 Brownwood NW, Grand Rapids, MI 49504 / 616-453-1998

American Western Arms, Inc., 1450 S.W. 10th St., Suite 3B, Delray Beach, FL 33444 / 877-292-4867; FAX: 561-330-0881

Americase, P.O. Box 271, 1610 E. Main, Waxahachie, TX 75165 / 800-880-3629; FAX: 214-937-8373

Ames Metal Products, 4323 S. Western Blvd., Chicago, IL 60609 / 773-523-3230; or 800-255-6937; FAX: 773-523-3854

Amherst Arms, P.O. Box 1457, Englewood, FL 34295 / 941-475-2020; FAX: 941-473-1212

Ammo Load, Inc., 1560 E. Edinger, Suite G, Santa Ana, CA 92705 / 714-558-8858; FAX: 714-569-0319

Amrine's Gun Shop, 937 La Luna, Ojai, CA 93023 / 805-646-2376

Amsec, 11925 Pacific Ave., Fontana, CA 92337

Analog Devices, Box 9106, Norwood, MA 02062

Andela Tool & Machine, Inc., RD3, Box 246, Richfield Springs, NY 13439

Anderson Manufacturing Co., Inc., 22602 53rd Ave. SE, Bothell, WA 98021 / 206-481-1858; FAX: 206-481-7839

Andres & Dworsky KG, Bergstrasse 18, A-3822 Karlstein, Thaya, AUSTRIA / 0 28 44-285; FAX: 02844 28619 andres.dnorsky@wvnet.as

Angelo & Little Custom Gun Stock Blanks, P.O. Box 240046, Dell, MT 59724-0046

Answer Products Co., 1519 Westbury Drive, Davison, MI 48423 / 810-653-2911

Antique American Firearms, PO Box 71035, Dept. GD, Des Moines, IA 50325 / 515-224-6552

Antique Arms Co., 1110 Cleveland Ave., Monett, MO 65708 / 417-235-6501

AO Sight Systems, 2401 Ludelle St., Fort Worth, TX 76105 / 888-744-4880; or 817-536-0136 FAX: 817-536-3517

Apel GmbH, Ernst, Am Kirschberg 3, D-97218, Gerbrunn, GERMANY / 0 (931) 707192 info@eaw.de www.eaw.de

Aplan Antiques & Art, James O., James O., HC 80, Box 793-25, Piedmont, SD 57769 / 605-347-5016

AR-7 Industries, LLC, 998 N. Colony Rd., Meriden, CT 06450 / 203-630-3536; FAX: 203-630-3637

Arizona Ammunition, Inc., 21421 No. 14th Ave., Suite E, Phoenix, AZ 85027 / 623-516-9004; FAX: 623-516-9012 www.azammo.com

Arkansas Mallard Duck Calls, Rt. Box 182, England, AR 72046 / 501-842-3597

MANUFACTURER'S DIRECTORY

ArmaLite, Inc., P.O. Box 299, Geneseo, IL 61254 / 800-336-0184; or 309-944-6939; FAX: 309-944-6949

Armament Gunsmithing Co., Inc., 525 Rt. 22, Hillside, NJ 07205 / 908-686-0960; FAX: 718-738-5019 armamentgunsmithing@worldnet.att.net

Armas Kemen S. A. (See U.S. Importers)

Armas Urki Garbi, 12-14 20.600, Eibar (Guipuzcoa), / 43-11 38 73

Armfield Custom Bullets, 10584 County Road 100, Carthage, MO 64836 / 417-359-8480; FAX: 417-359-8497

Armi Perazzi S.p.A., Via Fontanelle 1/3, 1-25080, Botticino Mattina, / 030-2692591; FAX: 030 2692594

Armi San Marco (See U.S. Importers-Taylor's & Co I

Armi San Paolo, 172-A, I-25062, via Europa, ITALY / 030-2751725

Armi Sport (See U.S. Importers-Cape Outfitters)

Armite Laboratories, 1560 Superior Ave., Costa Mesa, CA 92627 / 213-587-7768; FAX: 213-587-5075

Armoloy Co. of Ft. Worth, 204 E. Daggett St., Fort Worth, TX 76104 / 817-332-5604; FAX: 817-335-6517

Armor (See Buck Stop Lure Co., Inc.)

Armor Metal Products, PO Box 4609, Helena, MT 59604 / 406-442-5560; FAX: 406-442-5650

Armory Publications, 17171 Bothall Way NE, #276, Seattle, WA 98155 / 206-364-7653; FAX: 206-362-9413 armorypub@aol.com www.grocities.com/armorypub

Armoury, The, Rt. 202, Box 2340, New Preston, CT 06777 / 860-868-0001; FAX: 860-868-2919

Arms & Armour Press, Wellington House, 125 Strand, London, WC2R 0BB ENGLAND / 0171-420-5555; FAX: 0171-240-7265

Arms Corporation of the Philippines, Bo. Parang Marikina, Metro Manila, PHILIPPINES / 632-941-6243; or 632-941-6244; FAX: 632-942-0682

Arms Craft Gunsmithing, 1106 Linda Dr., Arroyo Grande, CA 93420 / 805-481-2830

Arms Ingenuity Co., P.O. Box 1, 51 Canal St., Weatogue, CT 06089 / 203-658-5624

Arms Software, 4851 SW Madrona St., Lake Oswego, OR 97035 / 800-366-5559; or 503-697-0533; FAX: 503-697-3337

Arms, Programming Solutions (See Arms Software)

Armscorp USA, Inc., 4424 John Ave., Baltimore, MD 21227 / 410-247-6200; FAX: 410-247-6205 info@armscorpusa.com; www.armscorpusa.com

Arnold Arms Co., Inc., P.O. Box 1011, Arlington, WA 98223 / 800-371-1011; or 360-435-1011; FAX: 360-435-7304

Aro-Tek Ltd., 206 Frontage Rd. North, Suite C, Pacific, WA 98047 / 206-351-2984; FAX: 206-833-4483

Arratoonian, Andy (See Horseshoe Leather Products)

Arrieta S.L., Morkaiko 5, 20870, Elgoibar, SPAIN / 34-43-743150; FAX: 34-43-743154

Art Jewel Enterprises Ltd., Eagle Business Ctr., 460 Randy Rd., Carol Stream, IL 60188 / 708-260-0400

Artistry in Wood, 134 Zimmerman Rd., Kalispell, MT 59901 / 406-257-9003; FAX: 406-257-9167 merlins@digisys.net www.acrabondlaminates.com

Art's Gun & Sport Shop, Inc., 6008 Hwy. Y, Hillsboro, MO 63050

Arundel Arms & Ammunition, Inc., A., 24A Defense St., Annapolis, MD 21401 / 410-224-8683

Arvo Ojala Holsters, P.O. Box 98, N. Hollywood, CA 91603 / 818-222-9700; FAX: 818-222-0401

Ashby, David. See: ASHBY TURKEY CALLS

Ashby Turkey Calls, David L. Ashby, P.O. Box 1653, Ozark, MO 65721-1653

Ashley Outdoors, Inc., 2401 Ludelle St, Fort Worth, TX 76105 / 888-744-4880; FAX: 800-734-7939

Aspen Outfitting Co., Jon Hollinger, 9 Dean St, Aspen, CO 81611 / 970-925-3406

A-Square Company, Inc., 1230 S. Hurstbourne Parkway, Liberty Center II, Suite 220, Louisville, KY 40222 / 502-719-3006; FAX: 502-719-3030

Astra Sport, S.A., Apartado 3, 48300 Guernica, Espagne, SPAIN / 34-4-6250100; FAX: 34-4-6255186

Atamec-Bretton, 19 rue Victor Grignard, F-42026, St.-Etienne (Cedex 1, / 77-93-54-69; FAX: 33-77-93-57-98

Atlanta Cutlery Corp., 2143 Gees Mill Rd., Box 839 CIS, Conyers, GA 30207 / 800-883-0300; FAX: 404-388-0246

Atlantic Mills, Inc., 1295 Towbin Ave., Lakewood, NJ 08701-5934 / 800-242-7374

Atlantic Rose, Inc., P.O. Box 10717, Bradenton, FL 34282-0717

Atsko/Sno-Seal, Inc., 2664 Russell St., Orangeburg, SC 29115 / 803-531-1820; FAX: 803-531-2139

Auguste Francotte & Cie S.A., rue du Trois Juin 109, 4400 Herstal-Liege, BELGIUM / 32-4-248-13-18; FAX: 32-4-948-11-79

Austin & Halleck, Inc., 2150 South 950 East, Provo, UT 84606-6285 / 800-821-5783; or 801-374-9990; FAX: 801-374-9998

Austin Sheridan USA, Inc., P.O. Box 577, 36 Haddam Quarter Rd., Durham, CT 06422 / 860-349-1772; FAX: 860-349-1771; swalzer@palm.net

Autauga Arms, Inc., Pratt Plaza Mall No. 13, Prattville, AL 36067 / 800-262-9563; FAX: 334-361-2961

Auto Arms, 738 Clearview, San Antonio, TX 78228 / 512-434-5450

Automatic Equipment Sales, 627 E. Railroad Ave., Salesburg, MD 21801

Auto-Ordnance Corp., PO Box 220, Blauvelt, NY 10913 / 914-353-7770

Autumn Sales, Inc. (Blaser), 1320 Lake St., Fort Worth, TX 76102 / 817-335-1634; FAX: 817-338-0119

Avnda Otaola Norica, 16 Apartado 68, 20600, Eibar,

AWC Systems Technology, P.O. Box 41938, Phoenix, AZ 85080-1938 / 602-780-1050; FAX: 602-780-2967

Axtell Rifle Co., 353 Mill Creek Road, Sheridan, MT 59749 / 406-842-5814

AYA (See U.S. Importer-New England Custom Gun Serv

B

B & P America, 12321 Brittany Cir, Dallas, TX 75230 / 972-726-9069

B&D Trading Co., Inc., 3935 Fair Hill Rd., Fair Oaks, CA 95628 / 800-334-3790; or 916-967-9366; FAX: 916-967-4873

B.A.C., 17101 Los Modelos St., Fountain Valley, CA 92708 / 435-586-3286

B.B. Walker Co., PO Box 1167, 414 E Dixie Dr, Asheboro, NC 27203 / 910-625-1380; FAX: 910-625-8125

B.C. Outdoors, Larry McGhee, PO Box 61497, Boulder City, NV 89006 / 702-294-3056; FAX: 702-294-0413 jdalton@pmcammo.com www.pmcammo.com

B.M.F. Activator, Inc., 12145 Mill Creek Run, Plantersville, TX 77363 / 936-894-2397; or 800-527-2881; FAX: 936-894-2397

Badger Shooters Supply, Inc., P.O. Box 397, Owen, WI 54460 / 800-424-9069; FAX: 715-229-2332

Baekgaard Ltd., 1855 Janke Dr., Northbrook, IL 60062 / 708-498-3040; FAX: 708-493-3106

Baelder, Harry, Alte Goennebeker Strasse 5, 24635, Rickling, GERMANY / 04328-722732; FAX: 04328-722733

Baer Custom, Inc, Les, 29601 34th Ave, Hillsdale, IL 61257 / 309-658-2716; FAX: 309-658-2610

Baer's Hollows, P.O. Box 284, Eads, CO 81036 / 719-438-5718

Bagmaster Mfg., Inc., 2731 Sutton Ave., St. Louis, MO 63143 / 314-781-8002; FAX: 314-781-3363

Bain & Davis, Inc., 307 E. Valley Blvd., San Gabriel, CA 91776-3522 / 626-573-4241 baindavis@aol.com

Baker, Stan, 10000 Lake City Way, Seattle, WA 98125 / 206-522-4575

Baker's Leather Goods, Roy, PO Box 893, Magnolia, AR 71754 / 870-234-0344 pholsters@ipa.net

Bald Eagle Precision Machine Co., 101-A Allison St., Lock Haven, PA 17745 / 570-748-6772; FAX: 570-748-4443

Balickie, Joe, 408 Trelawney Lane, Apex, NC 27502 / 919-362-5185

Ballard, Donald. See: BALLARD INDUSTRIES

Ballard Industries, Donald Ballard Sr., PO Box 2035, Arnold, CA 95223 / 408-996-0957; FAX: 408-257-6828

Ballard Rifle & Cartridge Co., LLC, 113 W Yellowstone Ave, Cody, WY 82414 / 307-587-4914; FAX: 307-527-6097 ballard@wyoming.com

Ballistic Product, Inc., 20015 75th Ave. North, Corcoran, MN 55340-9456 / 763-494-9237; FAX: 763-494-9236 info@ballisticproducts.com www.ballisticproducts.com

Ballistic Research, 1108 W. May Ave., McHenry, IL 60050 / 815-385-0037

Ballisti-Cast, Inc., 6347 49th St. NW, Plaza, ND 58771 / 701-497-3333; FAX: 701-497-3335

Bandcor Industries, Div. of Man-Sew Corp., 6108 Sherwin Dr., Port Richey, FL 34668 / 813-848-0432

Bang-Bang Boutique (See Holster Shop, The)

Banks, Ed, 2762 Hwy. 41 N., Ft. Valley, GA 31030 / 912-987-4665

Bansner's Ultimate Rifles, LLC, P.O. Box 839, 261 E. Main St., Adamstown, PA 19501 / 717-484-2370; FAX: 717-484-0523 bansner@aol.com

Barbour, Inc., 55 Meadowbrook Dr., Milford, NH 03055 / 603-673-1313; FAX: 603-673-6510

Barnes, 4347 Tweed Dr., Eau Claire, WI 54703-6302

Barnes Bullets, Inc., P.O. Box 215, American Fork, UT 84003 / 801-756-4222; or 800-574-9200; FAX: 801-756-2465 email@barnesbullets.com barnesbullets.com

Baron Technology, 62 Spring Hill Rd., Trumbull, CT 06611 / 203-452-0515; FAX: 203-452-0663 dbaron@baronengraving.com www.baronengraving.com

Barraclough, John K., 55 Merit Park Dr., Gardena, CA 90247 / 310-324-2574

Barramundi Corp., P.O. Drawer 4259, Homosassa Springs, FL 32687 / 904-628-0200

Barrett Firearms Manufacturer, Inc., P.O. Box 1077, Murfreesboro, TN 37133 / 615-896-2938; FAX: 615-896-7313

Barry Lee Hands Engraving, 26192 E. Shore Route, Bigfork, MT 59911 / 406-837-0035

Bar-Sto Precision Machine, 73377 Sullivan Rd., PO Box 1838, Twentynine Palms, CA 92277 / 760-367-2747; FAX: 760-367-2407 barsto@eee.org www.barsto.com

Barta's Gunsmithing, 10231 US Hwy. 10, Cato, WI 54230 / 920-732-4472

Barteaux Machete, 1916 SE 50th Ave., Portland, OR 97215-3238 / 503-233-5880

Bartlett Engineering, 40 South 200 East, Smithfield, UT 84335-1645 / 801-563-5910

Basics Information Systems, Inc., 1141 Georgia Ave., Suite 515, Wheaton, MD 20902 / 301-949-1070; FAX: 301-949-5326

Bates Engraving, Billy, 2302 Winthrop Dr. SW, Decatur, AL 35603 / 256-355-3690 bbrn@aol.com

Battenfeld Technologies, 5875 W. Van Horn Tavern Rd., Columbia, MO 65203 / 573-445-9200; FAX: 573-447-4158 battenfeldtechnologies.com

Bauer, Eddie, 15010 NE 36th St., Redmond, WA 98052

Baumgartner Bullets, 3011 S. Alane St., W. Valley City, UT 84120

Bauska Barrels, 105 9th Ave. W., Kalispell, MT 59901 / 406-752-7706

Bear Archery, RR 4, 4600 Southwest 41st Blvd., Gainesville, FL 32601 / 904-376-2327

Bear Arms, 374-A Carson Road, St. Mathews, SC 29135

Bear Mountain Gun & Tool, 120 N. Plymouth, New Plymouth, ID 83655 / 208-278-5221; FAX: 208-278-5221

Beartooth Bullets, PO Box 491, Dept. HLD, Dover, ID 83825-0491 / 208-448-1865 bullets@beartoothbullets.com; beartoothbullets.com

Beaver Lodge (See Fellowes, Ted)

Beaver Park Product, Inc., 840 J St., Penrose, CO 81240 / 719-372-6744

BEC, Inc., 1227 W. Valley Blvd., Suite 204, Alhambra, CA 91803 / 626-281-5751; FAX: 626-293-7073

Beeks, Mike. See: GRAYBACK WILDCATS

Beeman Precision Airguns, 5454 Argosy Dr., Huntington Beach, CA 92649 / 714-890-4800; FAX: 714-890-4808

Behlert Precision, Inc., P.O. Box 288, 7067 Easton Rd., Pipersville, PA 18947 / 215-766-8681; or 215-766-7301; FAX: 215-766-8681

Beitzinger, George, 116-20 Atlantic Ave., Richmond Hill, NY 11419 / 718-847-7661

Belding's Custom Gun Shop, 10691 Sayers Rd., Munith, MI 49259 / 517-596-2388

Bell & Carlson, Inc., Dodge City Industrial Park, 101 Allen Rd., Dodge City, KS 67801 / 800-634-8586; or 620-225-6688; FAX: 620-225-6688 email@bellandcarlson.com www.bellandcarlson.com

Bell Reloading, Inc., 1725 Harlin Lane Rd., Villa Rica, GA 30180

Bell's Gun & Sport Shop, 3309-19 Mannheim Rd, Franklin Park, IL 60131

Bell's Legendary Country Wear, 22 Circle Dr., Bellmore, NY 11710 / 516-679-1158

Belltown Ltd., 11 Camps Rd., Kent, CT 06757 / 860-354-5750; FAX: 860-354-6764

Ben William's Gun Shop, 1151 S. Cedar Ridge, Duncanville, TX 75137 / 214-780-1807

Benchmark Knives (See Gerber Legendary Blades)

Benelli Armi S.p.A., Via della Stazione, 61029, Urbino, ITALY / 39-722-307-1; FAX: 39-722-327427

Benelli USA Corp, 17603 Indian Head Hwy, Accokeek, MD 20607 / 301-283-6981; FAX: 301-283-6988 benelliusa.com

Bengtson Arms Co., L., 6345-B E. Akron St., Mesa, AZ 85205 / 602-981-6375

Benjamin/Sheridan Co., Crossman, Rts. 5 and 20, E. Bloomfield, NY 14443 / 716-657-6161; FAX: 716-657-5405; www.crosman.com

Ben's Machines, 1151 S. Cedar Ridge, Duncanville, TX 75137 / 214-780-1807; FAX: 214-780-0316

Bentley, John, 128-D Watson Dr., Turtle Creek, PA 15145

Beomat of America, Inc., 300 Railway Ave., Campbell, CA 95008 / 408-379-4829

Beretta S.p.A., Pietro, Via Beretta, 18-25063, Gardone V.T., ITALY / 39-30-8341-1; FAX: 39-30-8341-421

Beretta U.S.A. Corp., 17601 Beretta Drive, Accokeek, MD 20607 / 301-283-2191; FAX: 301-283-0435

Berger Bullets Ltd., 5443 W. Westwind Dr., Glendale, AZ 85310 / 602-842-4001; FAX: 602-934-9083

Bernardelli, Vincenzo, P.O. Box 460243, Houston, TX 77056-8243 www.bernardelli.com

Bernardelli S.p.A., Vincenzo, 125 Via Matteotti, PO Box 74, Brescia, ITALY / 39-30-8912851-2-3; FAX: 39-30-8910249

Berry's Mfg., Inc., 401 North 3050 East St., St. George, UT 84770 / 435-634-1682; FAX: 435-634-1683 sales@berrysmfg.com www.berrysmfg.com

Bersa S.A., Benso Bonadimani, Gonzales Castillo 312, 1704, Ramos Mejia, ARGENTINA / 011-4656-2377; FAX: 011-4656-2093+

Bert Johanssons Vapentillbehor, S-430 20 Veddige, SWEDEN,

Bertuzzi (See U.S. Importer-New England Arms Co)

Better Concepts Co., 663 New Castle Rd., Butler, PA 16001 / 412-285-9000

Beverly, Mary, 3201 Horseshoe Trail, Tallahassee, FL 32312

Bianchi International, Inc., 100 Calle Cortez, Temecula, CA 92590 / 909-676-5621; FAX: 909-676-6777

Biesen, Al, 5021 Rosewood, Spokane, WA 99208 / 509-328-9340

Biesen, Roger, 5021 W. Rosewood, Spokane, WA 99208 / 509-328-9340

Big Bear Arms & Sporting Goods, Inc., 1112 Milam Way, Carrollton, TX 75006 / 972-416-8051; or 800-400-BEAR; FAX: 972-416-0771

Big Bore Bullets of Alaska, PO Box 521455, Big Lake, AK 99652 / 907-373-2673; FAX: 907-373-2673 doug.awloo.net www.awloo.com/bbb/index.

Big Bore Express, 16345 Midway Rd., Nampa, ID 83651 / 208-466-9975; FAX: 208-466-6927 bigbore.com

Big Sky Racks, Inc., P.O. Box 729, Bozeman, MT 59771-0729 / 406-586-9393; FAX: 406-585-7378

Big Spring Enterprises "Bore Stores", P.O. Box 1115, Big Spring Rd., Yellville, AR 72687 / 870-449-5297; FAX: 870-449-4446

Bilal, Mustafa, 908 NW 50th St., Seattle, WA 98107-3634 / 206-782-4164

Bilinski, Bryan. See: FIELDSPORT LTD.

Bill Austin's Calls, Box 284, Kaycee, WY 82639 / 307-738-2552

Bill Adair Custom Shop, 2886 Westridge, Carrollton, TX 75006 / 972-418-0950

Bill Hanus Birdguns LLC, PO Box 533, Newport, OR 97365 / 541-265-7433; FAX: 541-265-7400 www.billhanusbirdguns.com

Bill Wiseman and Co., P.O. Box 3427, Bryan, TX 77805 / 409-690-3456; FAX: 409-690-0156

Billeb, Stephen. See: QUALITY CUSTOM FIREARMS

Billings Gunsmiths Inc., 1841 Grand Ave., Billings, MT 59102 / 406-256-8390

Billingsley & Brownell, P.O. Box 25, Dayton, WY 82836 / 307-655-9344

Bill's Custom Cases, P.O. Box 2, Dunsmuir, CA 96025 / 530-235-0177; FAX: 530-235-4959 billscustomcases@mindspring.com

Bill's Gun Repair, 1007 Burlington St., Mendota, IL 61342 / 815-539-5786

Billy Bates Engraving, 2302 Winthrop Dr. SW, Decatur, AL 35603 / 256-355-3690 bbrn@aol.com

Birchwood Casey, 7900 Fuller Rd., Eden Prairie, MN 55344 / 800-328-6156; or 612-937-7933; FAX: 612-937-7979

Birdsong & Assoc., W. E., 1435 Monterey Rd, Florence, MS 39073-9748 / 601-366-8270

Bismuth Cartridge Co., 3500 Maple Ave., Suite 1650, Dallas, TX 75219 / 214-521-5880; FAX: 214-521-9035

Bison Studios, 1409 South Commerce St., Las Vegas, NV 89102 / 702-388-2891; FAX: 702-383-9967

Bitterroot Bullet Co., PO Box 412, 2001 Cedar Ave., Lewiston, ID 83501-0412 / 208-743-5635; FAX: 208-743-5635 brootbil@lewiston.com

BKL Technologies, PO Box 5237, Brownsville, TX 78523

Black Belt Bullets (See Big Bore Express)

Black Hills Ammunition, Inc., P.O. Box 3090, Rapid City, SD 57709-3090 / 605-348-5150; FAX: 605-348-9827

Black Hills Shooters Supply, P.O. Box 4220, Rapid City, SD 57709 / 800-289-2506

Black Powder Products, 67 Township Rd. 1411, Chesapeake, OH 45619 / 614-867-8047

Black Sheep Brand, 3220 W. Gentry Parkway, Tyler, TX 75702 / 903-592-3853; FAX: 903-592-0527

Blacksmith Corp., PO Box 280, North Hampton, OH 45349 / 800-531-2665; FAX: 937-969-8399 bcbooks@glasscity.net

BlackStar AccuMax Barrels, 11501 Brittmoore Park Drive, Houston, TX 77041 / 281-721-6040; FAX: 281-721-6041

BlackStar Barrel Accurizing (See BlackStar AccuMax

Blacktail Mountain Books, 42 First Ave. W., Kalispell, MT 59901 / 406-257-5573

Blair Engraving, Jim, PO Box 64, Glenrock, WY 82637 / 307-436-8115

Blammo Ammo, P.O. Box 1677, Seneca, SC 29679 / 803-882-1768

Blaser Jagdwaffen GmbH, D-88316, Isny Im Allgau, GERMANY

Bleile, C. Roger, 5040 Ralph Ave., Cincinnati, OH 45238 / 513-251-0249

Blount, Inc., Sporting Equipment Div., 2299 Snake River Ave., PO Box 856, Lewiston, ID 83501 / 800-627-3640; or 208-746-2351; FAX: 208-799-3904

Blount/Outers, PO Box 39, Onalaska, WI 54650 / 608-781-5800; FAX: 608-781-0368

Blue and Gray Products Inc (See Ox-Yoke Originals

Blue Book Publications, Inc., 8009 34th Ave. S. Ste. 175, Minneapolis, MN 55425 / 800-877-4867; or 612-854-5229; FAX: 612-853-1486 bluebook@bluebookinc.com www.bluebookinc.com

Blue Mountain Bullets, HC 77, PO Box 231, John Day, OR 97845 / 541-820-4594

Blue Ridge Machinery & Tools, Inc., PO Box 536-GD, Hurricane, WV 25526 / 800-872-6500; FAX: 304-562-5311 blueridgemachine@worldnet.att.net blueridgemachiney.com

BMC Supply, Inc., 26051 - 179th Ave. S.E., Kent, WA 98042

Bob Allen Co.214 SW Jackson, PO Box 477, Des Moines, IA 50315 / 800-685-7020; FAX: 515-283-0779

Bob Rogers Gunsmithing, PO Box 305, 344 S. Walnut St., Franklin Grove, IL 61031 / 815-456-2685; FAX: 815-456-2777

Bob's Gun Shop, P.O. Box 200, Royal, AR 71968 / 501-767-1970; FAX: 501-767-1970 gunparts@hsnp.com www.gun-parts.com

Bob's Tactical Indoor Shooting Range & Gun Shop, 90 Lafayette Rd., Salisbury, MA 01952 / 508-465-5561

Boessler, Erich, Am Vogeltal 3, 97702, Munnerstadt, GERMANY

Boker USA, Inc., 1550 Balsam Street, Lakewood, CO 80215 / 303-462-0662; FAX: 303-462-0668 sales@bokerusa.com bokerusa.com

Boltin, John M., PO Box 644, Estill, SC 29918 / 803-625-2185

Bo-Mar Tool & Mfg. Co., 6136 State Hwy 300, Longview, TX 75604 / 903-759-4784; FAX: 903-759-9141 marykor@earthlink.net bo-mar.com

Bonadimani, Benso. See: BERSA S.A.

Bonanza (See Forster Products), 310 E Lanark Ave, Lanark, IL 61046 / 815-493-6360; FAX: 815-493-2371

Bond Arms, Inc., PO Box 1296, Granbury, TX 76048 / 817-573-4445; FAX: 817-573-5636

Bond Custom Firearms, 8954 N. Lewis Ln., Bloomington, IN 47408 / 812-332-4519

Bondini Paolo, Via Sorrento 345, San Carlo di Cesena, ITALY / 0547-663-240; FAX: 0547-663-780

Bone Engraving, Ralph, 718 N Atlanta, Owasso, OK 74055 / 918-272-9745

Boone Trading Co., Inc., PO Box 669, Brinnon, WA 98320 / 800-423-1945; or 360-796-4330; FAX: 360-796-4511 sales@boonetrading.com boonetrading.com

Boone's Custom Ivory Grips, Inc., 562 Coyote Rd., Brinnon, WA 98320 / 206-796-4330

Boonie Packer Products, PO Box 12517, Salem, OR 97309-0517 / 800-477-3244; or 503-581-3244; FAX: 503-581-3191; booniepacker@aol.com booniepacker.com

Borden Ridges Rimrock Stocks, RR 1 Box 250 BC, Springville, PA 18844 / 570-965-2505; FAX: 570-965-2328

Borden Rifles Inc, RD 1, Box 250BC, Springville, PA 18844 / 717-965-2505; FAX: 717-965-2328

Border Barrels Ltd., Riccarton Farm, Newcastleton, SCOTLAND UK

Borovnik KG, Ludwig, 9170 Ferlach, Bahnhofstrasse 7, AUSTRIA / 042 27 24 42; FAX: 042 26 43 49

Bosis (See U.S. Importer-New England Arms Co.)

Boss Manufacturing Co., 221 W. First St., Kewanee, IL 61443 / 309-852-2131; or 800-447-4581; FAX: 309-852-0848

Bostick Wildlife Calls, Inc., P.O. Box 728, Estill, SC 29918 / 803-625-2210; or 803-625-4512

Bowen Classic Arms Corp., PO Box 67, Louisville, TN 37777 / 865-984-3583 www.bowenclassicarms.com

Bowen Knife Co., Inc., P.O. Box 590, Blackshear, GA 31516 / 912-449-4794

Bowerly, Kent, 710 Golden Pheasant Dr, Redmond, OR 97756 / 541-595-6028

Boyds' Gunstock Industries, Inc., 25376 403RD AVE, MITCHELL, SD 57301 / 605-996-5011; FAX: 605-996-9878

Brace, Larry D., 771 Blackfoot Ave., Eugene, OR 97404 / 541-688-1278; FAX: 541-607-5833

Bradley Gunsight Co., P.O. Box 340, Plymouth, VT 05056 / 860-589-0531; FAX: 860-582-6294

Brass Eagle, Inc., 7050A Bramalea Rd., Unit 19, Mississauga,, ON L4Z 1C7 CANADA / 416-848-4844

Brauer Bros., 1520 Washington Avenue., St. Louis, MO 63103 / 314-231-2864; FAX: 314-249-4952 www.brauerbros.com

Break-Free, Inc., 1035 S Linwood Ave., Santa Ana, CA 92705 / 714-953-1900; FAX: 714-953-0402

Brenneke KG, Wilhelm, PO Box 1646, 30837 Langenhagen, GERMANY / 0511-97262-0; FAX: 0511-97262-62 info@brenneke.de; www.brenneke.com

Bridgeman Products, Harry Jaffin, 153 B Cross Slope Court, Englishtown, NJ 07726 / 732-536-3604; FAX: 732-972-1004

Bridgers Best, P.O. Box 1410, Berthoud, CO 80513

Briese Bullet Co., Inc., RR1, Box 108, Tappen, ND 58487 / 701-327-4578; FAX: 701-327-4579

Brigade Quartermasters, 1025 Cobb International Blvd., Dept. VH, Kennesaw, GA 30144-4300 / 404-428-1248; or 800-241-3125; FAX: 404-426-7726

Briganti, A.J., 512 Rt. 32, Highland Mills, NY 10930 / 914-928-9573

Briley Mfg. Inc., 1230 Lumpkin, Houston, TX 77043 / 800-331-5718; or 713-932-6995; FAX: 713-932-1043

British Antiques, PO Box 35369, Tucson, AZ 85740 / 520-575-9063 britishantiques@hotmail.com

British Sporting Arms, RR1, Box 130, Millbrook, NY 12545 / 914-677-8303

Broad Creek Rifle Works, Ltd., 120 Horsey Ave., Laurel, DE 19956 / 302-875-5446; FAX: 302-875-1448 bcrw4guns@aol.com

Brockman's Custom Gunsmithing, P.O. Box 357, Gooding, ID 83330 / 208-934-5050

Brocock Ltd., 43 River Street, Digbeth, Birmingham, B5 5SA ENGLAND / 011-021-773-1200; FAX: 011-021-773-1211 sales@brocock.co.un www.brocock.co.uk

Broken Gun Ranch, 10739 126 Rd., Spearville, KS 67876 / 316-385-2587; FAX: 316-385-2597

Brooker, Dennis, Rt. 1, Box 12A, Derby, IA 50068 / 515-533-2103

Brooks Tactical Systems, 279-C Shorewood Ct., Fox Island, WA 98333 / 253-549-2866 FAX: 253-549-2703 brooks@brookstactical.com www.brookstactical.com

Brown, H. R. (See Silhouette Leathers)

Brown Co., E. Arthur, 3404 Pawnee Dr, Alexandria, MN 56308 / 320-762-8847

Brown Dog Ent., 2200 Calle Camelia, 1000 Oaks, CA 91360 / 805-497-2318; FAX: 805-497-1618

Brown Precision, Inc., 7786 Molinos Ave., Los Molinos, CA 96055 / 530-384-2506; FAX: 916-384-1638 www.brownprecision.com

Brown Products, Inc., Ed, 43825 Muldrow Trail, Perry, MO 63462 / 573-565-3261; FAX: 573-565-2791 www.edbrown.com

Brownells, Inc., 200 S. Front St., Montezuma, IA 50171 / 641-623-5401; FAX: 641-623-3896 orderdesk@brownells.com; www.brownells.com

Browning Arms Co., One Browning Place, Morgan, UT 84050 / 801-876-2711; FAX: 801-876-3331

Browning Arms Co. (Parts & Service), 3005 Arnold Tenbrook Rd., Arnold, MO 63010 / 617-287-6800; FAX: 617-287-9751

BRP, Inc. High Performance Cast Bullets, 1210 Alexander Rd., Colorado Springs, CO 80909 / 719-633-0658

Brunton U.S.A., 620 E. Monroe Ave., Riverton, WY 82501 / 307-856-6559; FAX: 307-856-1840

Bryan & Assoc., R D Sauls, PO Box 5772, Anderson, SC 29623-5772 / 864-261-6810 bryanandac@aol.com www.huntersweb.com/bryanandac

MANUFACTURER'S DIRECTORY

Brynin, Milton, P.O. Box 383, Yonkers, NY 10710 / 914-779-4333

BSA Guns Ltd., Armoury Rd. Small Heath, Birmingham, ENGLAND / 011-021-772-8543; FAX: 011-021-773-084

BSA Optics, 3911 SW 47th Ave. Ste. 914, Ft Lauderdale, FL 33314 / 954-581-2144; FAX: 954-581-3165 4inforbasaoptics.com www.bsaoptics.com

B-Square Company, Inc., ;, P.O. Box 11281, 2708 St. Louis Ave., Ft. Worth, TX 76110 / 817-923-0964; or 800-433-2909; FAX: 817-926-7012

Buchsenmachermeister, P. Hofer Jagdwaffen, Buchsenmachermeister, Kirchgasse 24 A-9170, Ferlach, AUSTRIA / 43 4227 3683; FAX: 43 4227 368330 peterhofer@hoferwaffen.com www.hoferwaffen.com

Buck Knives, Inc., 1900 Weld Blvd., P.O. Box 1267, El Cajon, CA 92020 / 619-449-1100; or 800-326-2825; FAX: 619-562-5774 8

Buck Stix--SOS Products Co., Box 3, Neenah, WI 54956

Buck Stop Lure Co., Inc., 3600 Grow Rd. NW, P.O. Box 636, Stanton, MI 48888 / 517-762-5091; FAX: 517-762-5124

Buckeye Custom Bullets, 6490 Stewart Rd., Elida, OH 45807 / 419-641-4463

Buckhorn Gun Works, 8109 Woodland Dr., Black Hawk, SD 57718 / 605-787-6472

Buckskin Bullet Co., P.O. Box 1893, Cedar City, UT 84721 / 435-586-3286

Buckskin Machine Works, A. Hunkeler, 3235 S. 358th St., Auburn, WA 98001 / 206-927-5412

Budin, Dave, Main St., Margaretville, NY 12455 / 914-568-4103; FAX: 914-586-4105

Budin, Dave. See: DEL-SPORTS, INC.

Buenger Enterprises/Goldenrod Dehumidifier, 3600 S. Harbor Blvd., Oxnard, CA 93035 / 800-451-6797; or 805-985-5828; FAX: 805-985-1534

Buffalo Arms Co., 99 Raven Ridge, Sandpoint, ID 83864 / 208-263-6953; FAX: 208-265-2096 www.buffaloarms.com

Buffalo Bullet Co., Inc., 12637 Los Nietos Rd., Unit A, Santa Fe Springs, CA 90670 / 800-423-8069; FAX: 562-944-5054

Buffalo Rock Shooters Supply, R.R. 1, Ottawa, IL 61350 / 815-433-2471

Buffer Technologies, P.O. Box 104930, Jefferson City, MO 65110 / 573-634-8529; FAX: 573-634-8522

Bull Mountain Rifle Co., 6327 Golden West Terrace, Billings, MT 59106 / 406-656-0778

Bullberry Barrel Works, Ltd., 2430 W. Bullberry Ln. 67-5, Hurricane, UT 84737 / 435-635-9866; FAX: 435-635-0348

Bullet Metals, PO Box 1238, Sierra Vista, AZ 85636 / 520-458-5321; FAX: 520-458-1421 info@theantimonyman.com; bullet_metals.com

Bullet N Press, 1210 James St., Gastonia, NC 28052 / 704-853-0265 gnpress@nemaine.com www.nemaine.com/bnpress

Bullet Swaging Supply Inc., PO Box 1056, 303 McMillan Rd, West Monroe, LA 71291 / 318-387-3266; FAX: 318-387-7779; leblackmon@colla.com

Bullseye Bullets, 1808 Turkey Creek Rd. #9, Plant City, FL 33567 / 800-741-6343 bbullets8100@aol.com

Bull-X, Inc., 520 N. Main, Farmer City, IL 61842 / 309-928-2574; or 800-248-3845; FAX: 309-928-2130

Burkhart Gunsmithing, Don, PO Box 852, Rawlins, WY 82301 / 307-324-6007

Burnham Bros., P.O. Box 1148, Menard, TX 78659 / 915-396-4572; FAX: 915-396-4574

Burris Co., Inc., PO Box 1747, 331 E. 8th St., Greeley, CO 80631 / 970-356-1670; FAX: 970-356-8702

Bushmaster Firearms, 999 Roosevelt Trail, Windham, ME 04062 / 800-998-7928; FAX: 207-892-8068 info@bushmaster.com; www.bushmaster.com

Bushmaster Hunting & Fishing, 451 Alliance Ave., Toronto, ON M6N 2J1 CANADA / 416-763-4040; FAX: 416-763-0623

Bushnell Sports Optics Worldwide, 9200 Cody, Overland Park, KS 66214 / 913-752-3400; or 800-423-3537; FAX: 913-752-3550

Buster's Custom Knives, P.O. Box 214, Richfield, UT 84701 / 801-896-5319

Butler Creek Corp., 290 Arden Dr., Belgrade, MT 59714 / 800-423-8327; or 406-388-1356; FAX: 406-388-7204

Butler Enterprises, 834 Oberting Rd., Lawrenceburg, IN 47025 / 812-537-3584

Butterfield's, 220 San Bruno Ave., San Francisco, CA 94103 / 415-861-7500; FAX: 415-861-0183 arms@butterfields.com; www.butterfields.com

Buzz Fletcher Custom Stockmaker, 117 Silver Road, P.O. Box 189, Taos, NM 87571 / 505-758-3486

C

C&D Special Products (See Claybuster Wads & Harves

C&H Research, 115 Sunnyside Dr., Box 351, Lewis, KS 67552 / 316-324-5445 www.09.net(chr)

C. Palmer Manufacturing Co., Inc., P.O. Box 220, West Newton, PA 15089 / 412-872-8200; FAX: 412-872-8302

C. Sharps Arms Co. Inc./Montana Armory, 100 Centennial Dr., PO Box 885, Big Timber, MT 59011 / 406-932-4353; FAX: 406-932-4443

C.S. Van Gorden & Son, Inc., 1815 Main St., Bloomer, WI 54724 / 715-568-2612

C.W. Erickson's L.L.C., 530 Garrison Ave NE, PO Box 522, Buffalo, MN 55313 / 73-682-3665; FAX: 763-682-4328 www.archerhunter.com

Cabanas (See U.S. Importer-Mandall Shooting Supply

Cabela's, One Cabela Drive, Sidney, NE 69160 / 308-254-5505; FAX: 308-254-8420

Cabinet Mtn. Outfitters Scents & Lures, P.O. Box 766, Plains, MT 59859 / 406-826-3970

Cache La Poudre Rifleworks, 140 N. College, Ft. Collins, CO 80524 / 303-482-6913

Calibre Press, Inc., 666 Dundee Rd., Suite 1607, Northbrook, IL 60062 / 800-323-0037; FAX: 708-498-6869

Cali'co Hardwoods, Inc., 3580 Westwind Blvd., Santa Rosa, CA 95403 / 707-546-4045; FAX: 707-546-4027 calicohardwoods@msn.com

Calico Light Weapon Systems, 1489 Greg St., Sparks, NV 89431

California Sights (See Fautheree, Andy)

Cambos Outdoorsman, 532 E. Idaho Ave., Ontario, OR 97914 / 541-889-3135; FAX: 541-889-2633

Cambos Outdoorsman, Fritz Hallberg, 532 E. Idaho Ave, Ontario, OR 97914 / 541-889-3135; FAX: 541-889-2633

Camdex, Inc., 2330 Alger, Troy, ML 48083 / 810-528-2300; FAX: 810-528-0989

Cameron's, 16690 W. 11th Ave., Golden, CO 80401 / 303-279-7365; FAX: 303-628-5413

Camillus Cutlery Co., 54 Main St., Camillus, NY 13031 / 315-672-8111; FAX: 315-672-8832

Campbell, Dick, 20000 Silver Ranch Rd., Conifer, CO 80433 / 303-697-0150; FAX: 303-697-0150

Camp-Cap Products, P.O. Box 3805, Chesterfield, MO 63006 / 314-532-4340; FAX: 314-532-4340

Cannon, Andy. See: CANNON'S

Cannon Safe, Inc., 216 S. 2nd Ave. #BLD-932, San Bernardino, CA 92400 / 310-692-0636; or 800-242-1055; FAX: 310-692-7252

Cannon's, Andy Cannon, Box 1026, 320 Main St., Polson, MT 59860 / 406-887-2048

Canons Delcour, Rue J.B. Cools, B-4040, Herstal, BELGIUM / 32.42.40.61.40; FAX: 32(0)42.40.22.88

Canyon Cartridge Corp., P.O. Box 152, Albertson, NY 11507 FAX: 516-294-8946

Cape Outfitters, 599 County Rd. 206, Cape Girardeau, MO 63701 / 573-335-4103; FAX: 573-335-1555

Caraville Manufacturing, P.O. Box 4545, Thousand Oaks, CA 91359 / 805-499-1234

Carbide Checkering Tools (See J&R Engineering

Carhartt,Inc., P.O. Box 600, 3 Parklane Blvd., Dearborn, MI 48121 / 800-358-3825; or 313-271-8460; FAX: 313-271-3455

Carl Walther GmbH, B.P. 4325, D-89033, Ulm, GERMANY

Carl Zeiss Inc., 13005 N Kingston Ave, Chester, VA 23836 / 800-441-3005; FAX: 804-530-8481

Carlson, Douglas R, Antique American Firearms, PO Box 71035, Dept GD, Des Moines, IA 50325 / 515-224-6552

Carolina Precision Rifles, 1200 Old Jackson Hwy., Jackson, SC 29831 / 803-827-2069

Carrell, William. See: CARRELL'S PRECISION FIREARMS

Carrell's Precision Firearms, William Carrell, 10346 Shadybrook Dr., Boise, ID 83704-3942

Carry-Lite, Inc., 5203 W. Clinton Ave., Milwaukee, WI 53223 / 414-355-3520; FAX: 414-355-4775

Carter's Gun Shop, 225 G St., Penrose, CO 81240 / 719-372-6240

Cartridge Transfer Group, Pete de Coux, HC 30 Box 932 G, Prescott, AZ 86305-7447 / 928-776-8285; FAX: 928-776-8276; pdbullets@commspeed.net

Cascade Bullet Co., Inc., 2355 South 6th St., Klamath Falls, OR 97601 / 503-884-9316

Cascade Shooters, 2155 N.W. 12th St., Redwood, OR 97756

Case & Sons Cutlery Co., W R, Owens Way, Bradford, PA 16701 / 814-368-4123; or 800-523-6350; FAX: 814-768-5369

Case Sorting System, 12695 Cobblestone Creek Rd., Poway, CA 92064 / 619-486-9340

Cash Mfg. Co., Inc., P.O. Box 130, 201 S. Klein Dr., Waunakee, WI 53597-0130 / 608-849-5664; FAX: 608-849-5664

Caspian Arms, Ltd., 14 North Main St., Hardwick, VT 05843 / 802-472-6454; FAX: 802-472-6709

Cast Performance Bullet Company, PO Box 153, Riverton, WY 82501 / 307-857-2940; FAX: 307-857-3132 castperform@wyoming.com castperformance.com

Casull Arms Corp., P.O. Box 1629, Afton, WY 83110 / 307-886-0200

Cathey Enterprises, Inc., P.O. Box 2202, Brownwood, TX 76804 / 915-643-2553; FAX: 915-643-3653

Cation, 2341 Alger St., Troy, MI 48083 / 810-689-0658; FAX: 810-689-7558

Caywood, Shane J., P.O. Box 321, Minocqua, WI 54548 / 715-277-3866

CBC, Avenida Humberto de Campos 3220, 09400-000, Ribeirao Pires, SP, BRAZIL / 55-11-742-7500; FAX: 55-11-459-7385

CBC-BRAZIL, 3 Cuckoo Lane, Honley, Yorkshire HD7 2BR, ENGLAND / 44-1484-661062; FAX: 44-1484-663709

CCG Enterprises, 5217 E. Belknap St., Halton City, TX 76117 / 800-819-7464

CCI Ammunition, P.O. Box 856, Lewiston, ID 83501 / 208-746-2351 www.cci_ammunition.com

CCL Security Products, 199 Whiting St, New Britain, CT 06051 / 800-733-8588

Cedar Hill Game Calls, Inc., 238 Vic Allen Rd, Downsville, LA 71234 / 318-982-5632; FAX: 318-368-2245

Centaur Systems, Inc., 1602 Foothill Rd., Kalispell, MT 59901 / 406-755-8609; FAX: 406-755-8609

Center Lock Scope Rings, 9901 France Ct., Lakeville, MN 55044 / 612-461-2114

Central Specialties Ltd (See Trigger Lock Division

Century Gun Dist. Inc., 1467 Jason Rd., Greenfield, IN 46140 / 317-462-4524

Century International Arms, Inc., 1161 Holland Dr, Boca Raton, FL 33487

CFVentures, 509 Harvey Dr., Bloomington, IN 47403-1715

CH Tool & Die Co (See 4-D Custom Die Co), 711 N Sandusky St, PO Box 889, Mt Vernon, OH 43050-0889 / 740-397-7214; FAX: 740-397-6600

Chace Leather Products, 507 Alden St., Fall River, MA 02722 / 508-678-7556; FAX: 508-675-9666

Chadick's Ltd., P.O. Box 100, Terrell, TX 75160 / 214-563-7577

Chambers Flintlocks Ltd., Jim, 116 Sams Branch Rd, Candler, NC 28715 / 828-667-8361; FAX: 828-665-0852

Champion Shooters' Supply, P.O. Box 303, New Albany, OH 43054 / 614-855-1603; FAX: 614-855-1209

Champion Target Co., 232 Industrial Parkway, Richmond, IN 47374 / 800-441-4971

Champion's Choice, Inc., 201 International Blvd., LaVergne, TN 37086 / 615-793-4066; FAX: 615-793-4070

Champlin Firearms, Inc., PO Box 3191, Woodring Airport, Enid, OK 73701 / 580-237-7388; FAX: 580-242-6922 info@champlinarms.com www.champlinarms.com

Chapman Academy of Practical Shooting, 4350 Academy Rd., Hallsville, MO 65255 / 573-696-5544; or 573-696-2266

Chapman, J Ken. See: OLD WEST BULLET MOULDS

Chapman Manufacturing Co., 471 New Haven Rd., PO Box 250, Durham, CT 06422 / 860-349-9228; FAX: 860-349-0084 sales@chapmanmfg.com www.chapmanmfg.com

Chapuis Armes, 21 La Gravoux, BP15, 42380, St. Bonnet-le-Chatea, FRANCE / (33)77.50.06.96

Chapuis USA, 416 Business Park, Bedford, KY 40006

Charter 2000, 273 Canal St, Shelton, CT 06484 / 203-922-1652

Checkmate Refinishing, 370 Champion Dr., Brooksville, FL 34601 / 352-799-5774; FAX: 352-799-2986 checkmatecustom.com

Cheddite France S.A., 99 Route de Lyon, F-26501, Bourg-les-Valence, FRANCE / 33-75-56-4545; FAX: 33-75-56-3587; export@cheddite.com

Chelsea Gun Club of New York City Inc., 237 Ovington Ave., Apt. D53, Brooklyn, NY 11209 / 718-836-9422; or 718-833-2704

Chem-Pak, Inc., PO Box 2058, Winchester, VA 22604-1258 / 800-336-9828; or 540-667-1341; FAX: 540-722-3993 info@chem-pak.com www.chem-pak.com

Cherry Creek State Park Shooting Center, 12500 E. Belleview Ave., Englewood, CO 80111 / 303-693-1765

Chet Fulmer's Antique Firearms, P.O. Box 792, Rt. 2 Buffalo Lake, Detroit Lakes, MN 56501 / 218-847-7712

CheVron Bullets, RR1, Ottawa, IL 61350 / 815-433-2471

Cheyenne Pioneer Products, PO Box 28425, Kansas City, MO 64188 / 816-413-9196; FAX: 816-455-2859 cheyennepp@aol.com www.cartridgeboxes.com

Chicago Cutlery Co., 1536 Beech St., Terre Haute, IN 47804 / 800-457-2665

Chicasaw Gun Works, 4 Mi. Mkr., Pluto Rd. Box 868, Shady Spring, WV 25918-0868 / 304-763-2848; FAX: 304-763-3725

Chipmunk (See Oregon Arms, Inc.)

Choate Machine & Tool Co., Inc., P.O. Box 218, 116 Lovers Ln., Bald Knob, AR 72010 / 501-724-6193; or 800-972-6390; FAX: 501-724-5873

Christensen Arms, 385 N. 3050 E., St. George, UT 84790 / 435-624-9535; FAX: 435-674-9293

Christie's East, 219 E. 67th St., New York, NY 10021 / 212-606-0406 christics.com

Chu Tani Ind., Inc., P.O. Box 2064, Cody, WY 82414-2064

Chuck's Gun Shop, P.O. Box 597, Waldo, FL 32694 / 904-468-2264

Chuilli, Stephen, 8895 N. Military Trl. Ste., Ste. 201E, Palm Beach Gardens, FL 33410

Churchill (See U.S. Importer-Ellett Bros.)

Churchill, Winston G., 2838 20 Mile Stream Rd., Proctorville, VT 05153 / 802-226-7772

Churchill Glove Co., James, PO Box 298, Centralia, WA 98531 / 360-736-2816; FAX: 360-330-0151

CIDCO, 21480 Pacific Blvd., Sterling, VA 22170 / 703-444-5353

Ciener Inc., Jonathan Arthur, 8700 Commerce St., Cape Canaveral, FL 32920 / 321-868-2200; FAX: 321-868-2201

Cimarron F.A. Co., P.O. Box 906, Fredericksburg, TX 78624-0906 / 210-997-9090; FAX: 210-997-0802

Cincinnati Swaging, 2605 Marlington Ave., Cincinnati, OH 45208

Clark Custom Guns, Inc., 336 Shootout Lane, Princeton, LA 71067 / 318-949-9884; FAX: 318-949-9829

Clark Firearms Engraving, P.O. Box 80746, San Marino, CA 91118 / 818-287-1652

Clarkfield Enterprises, Inc., 1032 10th Ave., Clarkfield, MN 56223 / 612-669-7140

Claro Walnut Gunstock Co., 1235 Stanley Ave., Chico, CA 95928 / 530-342-5188; FAX: 530-342-5199

Classic Arms Company, Rt 1 Box 120F, Burnet, TX 78611 / 512-756-4001

Classic Arms Corp., PO Box 106, Dunsmuir, CA 96025-0106 / 530-235-2000

Classic Old West Styles, 1060 Doniphan Park Circle C, El Paso, TX 79936 / 915-587-0684

Claybuster Wads & Harvester Bullets, 309 Sequoya Dr., Hopkinsville, KY 42240 / 800-922-6287; or 800-284-1746; FAX: 502-885-8088 50

Clean Shot Technologies, 21218 St. Andrews Blvd. Ste 504, Boca Raton, FL 33433 / 888-866-2532

Clearview Mfg. Co., Inc., 413 S. Oakley St., Fordyce, AR 71742 / 501-352-8557; FAX: 501-352-7120

Clearview Products, 3021 N. Portland, Oklahoma City, OK 73107

Cleland's Outdoor World, Inc, 10306 Airport Hwy, Swanton, OH 43558 / 419-865-4713; FAX: 419-865-5865

Clements' Custom Leathercraft, Chas, 1741 Dallas St., Aurora, CO 80010-2018 / 303-364-0403; FAX: 303-739-9824 gryphons@home.com kuntaoslcat.com

Clenzoil Worldwide Corp, Jack Fitzgerald, 25670 1st St., Westlake, OH 44145-1430 / 440-899-0482; FAX: 440-899-0483

Clift Mfg., L. R., 3821 hammonton Rd, Marysville, CA 95901 / 916-755-3390; FAX: 916-755-3393

Clift Welding Supply & Cases, 1332-A Colusa Hwy., Yuba City, CA 95993 / 916-755-3390; FAX: 916-755-3393

Cloward's Gun Shop, 4023 Aurora Ave. N, Seattle, WA 98103 / 206-632-2072

Clymer Mfg. Co., 1645 W. Hamlin Rd., Rochester Hills, MI 48309-3312 / 248-853-5555; FAX: 248-853-1530

C-More Systems, P.O. Box 1750, 7553 Gary Rd., Manassas, VA 20108 / 703-361-2663; FAX: 703-361-5881

Cobalt Mfg., Inc., 4020 Mcewen Rd Ste 180, Dallas, TX 75244-5090 / 817-382-8986; FAX: 817-383-4281

Cobra Enterprises, Inc., 1960 S. Milestone Drive, Suite F, Salt Lake City, UT 84104 FAX: 801-908-8301 www.cobrapistols@network.com

Cobra Sport S.r.l., Via Caduti Nei Lager No. 1, 56020 San Romano, Montopoli v/Arno (Pi, ITALY / 0039-571-450490; FAX: 0039-571-450492

Coffin, Charles H., 3719 Scarlet Ave., Odessa, TX 79762 / 915-366-4729; FAX: 915-366-4729

Coffin, Jim (See Working Guns)

Coffin, Jim. See: WORKING GUNS

Cogar's Gunsmithing, 206 Redwine Dr., Houghton Lake, MI 48629 / 517-422-4591

Coghlan's Ltd., 121 Irene St., Winnipeg, MB R3T 4C7 CANADA / 204-284-9550; FAX: 204-475-4127

Cold Steel Inc., 3036 Seaborg Ave. Ste. A, Ventura, CA 93003 / 800-255-4716; or 800-624-2363; FAX: 805-642-9727

Cole-Grip, 16135 Cohasset St., Van Nuys, CA 91406 / 818-782-4424

Coleman Co., Inc., 250 N. St. Francis, Wichita, KS 67201

Cole's Gun Works, Old Bank Building, Rt. 4 Box 250, Moyock, NC 27958 / 919-435-2345

Collings, Ronald, 1006 Cielta Linda, Vista, CA 92083

Colonial Arms, Inc., P.O. Box 636, Selma, AL 36702-0636 / 334-872-9455; FAX: 334-872-9540 colonialarms@mindspring.com www.colonialarms.com

Colonial Knife Co., Inc., P.O. Box 3327, Providence, RI 02909 / 401-421-1600; FAX: 401-421-2047

Colonial Repair, 47 NAVARRE ST, ROSLINDALE, MA 02131-4725 / 617-469-4951

Colorado Gunsmithing Academy, RR 3 Box 79B, El Campo, TX 77437 / 719-336-4099; or 800-754-2046; FAX: 719-336-9642

Colorado School of Trades, 1575 Hoyt St., Lakewood, CO 80215 / 800-234-4594; FAX: 303-233-4723

Colorado Sutlers Arsenal (See Cumberland States

Colt Blackpowder Arms Co., 110 8th Street, Brooklyn, NY 11215 / 718-499-4678; FAX: 718-768-8056

Colt's Mfg. Co., Inc., PO Box 1868, Hartford, CT 06144-1868 / 800-962-COLT; or 860-236-6311; FAX: 860-244-1449

Compass Industries, Inc., 104 East 25th St., New York, NY 10010 / 212-473-2614; or 800-221-9904; FAX: 212-353-0826

Compasseco, Ltd., 151 Atkinson Hill Ave., Bardtown, KY 40004 / 502-349-0910

Competition Electronics, Inc., 3469 Precision Dr., Rockford, IL 61109 / 815-874-8001; FAX: 815-874-8181

Competitor Corp. Inc., Appleton Business Center, 30 Tricnit Road Unit 16, New Ipswich, NH 03071 / 603-878-3891; FAX: 603-878-3950

Component Concepts, Inc., 530 S Springbrook Road, Newberg, OR 97132 / 503-554-8095; FAX: 503-554-9370 cci@cybcon.com www.phantomonline.com

Concept Development Corp., 16610 E. Laser Drive, Suite 5, Fountain Hills, AZ 85268-6644

Conetrol Scope Mounts, 10225 Hwy. 123 S., Seguin, TX 78155 / 210-379-3030; or 800-CONETROL; FAX: 210-379-3030

CONKKO, P.O. Box 40, Broomall, PA 19008 / 215-356-0711

Connecticut Shotgun Mfg. Co., P.O. Box 1692, 35 Woodland St., New Britain, CT 06051 / 860-225-6581; FAX: 860-832-8707

Connecticut Valley Classics (See CVC)

Conrad, C. A., 3964 Ebert St., Winston-Salem, NC 27127 / 919-788-5469

Cook Engineering Service, 891 Highbury Rd., Vict, 3133 AUSTRALIA

Cooper Arms, P.O. Box 114, Stevensville, MT 59870 / 406-777-0373; FAX: 406-777-5228

Cooper-Woodward, 3800 Pelican Rd., Helena, MT 59602 / 406-458-3800 dolymama@msn.com

Corbin Mfg. & Supply, Inc., 600 Industrial Circle, P.O. Box 2659, White City, OR 97503 / 541-826-5211; FAX: 541-826-8669

Cor-Bon Bullet & Ammo Co., 1311 Industry Rd., Sturgis, SD 57785 / 800-626-7266; FAX: 800-923-2666

Corkys Gun Clinic, 4401 Hot Springs Dr., Greeley, CO 80634-9226 / 970-330-0516

Corry, John, 861 Princeton Ct., Neshanic Station, NJ 08853 / 908-369-8019

Cosmi Americo & Figlio s.n.c., Via Flaminia 307, Ancona, ITALY / 071-888208; FAX: 39-071-887008

Coulston Products, Inc., P.O. Box 30, 201 Ferry St. Suite 212, Easton, PA 18044-0030 / 215-253-0167; or 800-445-9927; FAX: 215-252-1511

Counter Assault, 120 Industrial Court, Kalispell, MT 59901 / 406-257-4740; FAX: 406-257-6674

Cousin Bob's Mountain Products, 7119 Ohio River Blvd., Ben Avon, PA 15202 / 412-766-5114; FAX: 412-766-5114

Cox, Ed. C., RD 2, Box 192, Prosperity, PA 15329 / 412-228-4984

CP Bullets, 1310 Industrial Hwy #5-6, South Hampton, PA 18966 / 215-953-7264; FAX: 215-953-7275

CQB Training, P.O. Box 1739, Manchester, MO 63011

Craftguard, 3624 Logan Ave., Waterloo, IA 50703 / 319-232-2959; FAX: 319-232-0804

Craig Custom Ltd., Research & Development, 629 E. 10th, Hutchinson, KS 67501 / 316-669-0601

Crandall Tool & Machine Co., 19163 21 Mile Rd., Tustin, MI 49688 / 616-829-4430

Creedmoor Sports, Inc., P.O. Box 1040, Oceanside, CA 92051 / 619-757-5529

Creek Side Metal & Woodcrafters, Fishers Hill, VA 22626 / 703-465-3903

Creighton Audette, 19 Highland Circle, Springfield, VT 05156 / 802-885-2331

Crimson Trace Lasers, 8090 SW Cirrus Dr., Beverton, OR 97008 / 800-442-2406; FAX: 503-627-0166 www.crimsontrace.com

Crit'R Call (See Rocky Mountain Wildlife Products)

Crosman Airguns, Rts. 5 and 20, E. Bloomfield, NY 14443 / 716-657-6161; FAX: 716-657-5405

Crosman Blades (See Coleman Co., Inc.)

Crouse's Country Cover, P.O. Box 160, Storrs, CT 06268 / 860-423-8736

CRR, Inc./Marble's Inc., 420 Industrial Park, P.O. Box 111, Gladstone, MI 49837 / 906-428-3710; FAX: 906-428-3711

Crucelegui, Hermanos (See U.S. Importer-Mandall)

Cryo-Accurizing, 2101 East Olive, Decatur, IL 62526 / 801-395-2796; FAX: 217-423-3075

Cubic Shot Shell Co., Inc., 98 Fatima Dr., Campbell, OH 44405 / 330-755-0349

Cullity Restoration, 209 Old Country Rd., East Sandwich, MA 02537 / 508-888-1147

Cumberland Arms, 514 Shafer Road, Manchester, TN 37355 / 800-797-8414

Cumberland Mountain Arms, P.O. Box 710, Winchester, TN 37398 / 615-967-8414; FAX: 615-967-9199

Cumberland States Arsenal, 1124 Palmyra Road, Clarksville, TN 37040

Cummings Bullets, 1417 Esperanza Way, Escondido, CA 92027

Cupp, Alana, Custom Engraver, PO Box 207, Annabella, UT 84711 / 801-896-4834

Curtis Cast Bullets, 527 W. Babcock St., Bozeman, MT 59715 / 406-587-8117; FAX: 406-587-8117

Curtis Custom Shop, RR1, Box 193A, Wallingford, KY 41093 / 703-659-4265

Curtis Gun Shop (See Curtis Cast Bullets)

Custom Bullets by Hoffman, 2604 Peconic Ave., Seaford, NY 11783

Custom Calls, 607 N. 5th St., Burlington, IA 52601 / 319-752-4465

Custom Checkering Service, Kathy Forster, 2124 S.E. Yamhill St., Portland, OR 97214 / 503-236-5874

Custom Chronograph, Inc., 5305 Reese Hill Rd., Sumas, WA 98295 / 360-988-7801

Custom Firearms (See Ahrends, Kim)

Custom Gun Products, 5021 W. Rosewood, Spokane, WA 99208 / 509-328-9340

Custom Gun Stocks, 3062 Turners Bend Rd, McMinnville, TN 37110 / 615-668-3912

Custom Products (See Jones Custom Products)

Custom Quality Products, Inc., 345 W. Girard Ave., P.O. Box 71129, Madison Heights, MI 48071 / 810-585-1616; FAX: 810-585-0644

Custom Riflestocks, Inc., Michael M. Kokolus, 7005 Herber Rd., New Tripoli, PA 18066 / 610-298-3013; FAX: 610-298-2431 mkokolus@prodigy.net

Custom Single Shot Rifles, 9651 Meadows Lane, Guthrie, OK 73044 / 405-282-3634

Custom Stocking, Mike Yee, 29927 56 Pl. S., Auburn, WA 98001 / 253-839-3991

Custom Tackle and Ammo, P.O. Box 1886, Farmington, NM 87499 / 505-632-3539

Cutco Cutlery, P.O. Box 810, Olean, NY 14760 / 716-372-3111

CVA, 5988 Peachtree Corners East, Norcross, GA 30071 / 800-251-9412; FAX: 404-242-8546

CVC, 5988 Peachtree Crns East, Norcross, GA 30071

Cylinder & Slide, Inc., William R. Laughridge, 245 E. 4th St., Fremont, NE 68025 / 402-721-4277; FAX: 402-721-0263

CZ USA, PO Box 171073, Kansas City, KS 66117 / 913-321-1811; FAX: 913-321-4901

REFERENCE

D

D&D Gunsmiths, Ltd., 363 E. Elmwood, Troy, MI 48083 / 810-583-1512; FAX: 810-583-1524

D&G Precision Duplicators (See Greene Precision)

D&H Precision Tooling, 7522 Barnard Mill Rd., Ringwood, IL 60072 / 815-653-4011

D&H Prods. Co., Inc., 465 Denny Rd., Valencia, PA 16059 / 412-898-2840; or 800-776-0281; FAX: 412-898-2013

D&J Bullet Co. & Custom Gun Shop, Inc., 426 Ferry St., Russell, KY 41169 / 606-836-2663; FAX: 606-836-2663

D&L Industries (See D.J. Marketing)

D&L Sports, P.O. Box 651, Gillette, WY 82717 / 307-686-4008

D&R Distributing, 308 S.E. Valley St., Myrtle Creek, OR 97457 / 503-863-6850

D.C.C. Enterprises, 259 Wynburn Ave., Athens, GA 30601

D.D. Custom Stocks, R.H. "Dick" Devereaux, 5240 Mule Deer Dr., Colorado Springs, CO 80919 / 719-548-8468

D.J. Marketing, 10602 Horton Ave., Downey, CA 90241 / 310-806-0891; FAX: 310-806-6231

Dade Screw Machine Products, 2319 NW 7th Ave., Miami, FL 33127 / 305-573-5050

Daewoo Precision Industries Ltd., 34-3 Yeoeuido-Dong, Yeongdeungpo-GU 15th Fl., Seoul, KOREA

Daisy Mfg. Co., PO Box 220, Rogers, AR 72757 / 501-621-4210; FAX: 501-636-0573

Dakota (See U.S. Importer-EMF Co., Inc.)

Dakota Arms, Inc., 130 Industry Road, Sturgis, SD 57785 / 605-347-4686; FAX: 605-347-4459 info@dakotaarms.com; dakotaarms.com

Dakota Corp., 77 Wales St., P.O. Box 543, Rutland, VT 05701 / 802-775-6062; or 800-451-4167; FAX: 802-773-3919

Da-Mar Gunsmith's Inc., 102 1st St., Solvay, NY 13209

DAMASCUS-U.S.A., 149 Deans Farm Rd., Tyner, NC 27980 / 252-221-2010; FAX: 252-221-2009

Dan Wesson Firearms, 119 Kemper Lane, Norwich, NY 13815 / 607-336-1174; FAX: 607-336-2730

Danforth, Mikael. See: VEKTOR USA

Dangler, Homer L., 2870 Lee Marie Dr., Adrian, MI 49220 / 517-266-1997

Danner Shoe Mfg. Co., 12722 NE Airport Way, Portland, OR 97230 / 503-251-1100; or 800-345-0430; FAX: 503-251-1119

Dan's Whetstone Co., Inc., 130 Timbs Place, Hot Springs, AR 71913 / 501-767-1616; FAX: 501-767-9598 questions@danswhetstone.com danswhetstone.com

Danuser Machine Co., 550 E. Third St., P.O. Box 368, Fulton, MO 65251 / 573-642-2246; FAX: 573-642-2240

Dara-Nes, Inc. (See Nesci Enterprises, Inc.)

D'Arcy Echols & Co., PO Box 421, Millville, UT 84326 / 435-755-6842

Darlington Gun Works, Inc., P.O. Box 698, 516 S. 52 Bypass, Darlington, SC 29532 / 803-393-3931

Darwin Hensley Gunmaker, PO Box 329, Brightwood, OR 97011 / 503-622-5411

Data Tech Software Systems, 19312 East Eldorado Drive, Aurora, CO 80013

Dave Norin Schrank's Smoke & Gun, 2010 Washington St., Waukegan, IL 60085 / 708-662-4034

Dave's Gun Shop, 555 Wood Street, Powell, WY 82435 / 307-754-9724

David Clark Co., Inc., PO Box 15054, Worcester, MA 01615-0054 / 508-756-6216; FAX: 508-753-5827 sales@davidclark.com davidclark.com

David Condon, Inc., 109 E. Washington St., Middleburg, VA 22117 / 703-687-5642

David Miller Co., 3131 E Greenlee Rd, Tucson, AZ 85716 / 520-326-3117

David R. Chicoine, 1210 Jones Street, Gastonia, NC 28052 / 704-853-0265 gnpress@nemaine.com

David W. Schwartz Custom Guns, 2505 Waller St, Eau Claire, WI 54703 / 715-832-1735

Davide Pedersoli and Co., Via Artigiani 57, Gardone VT, Brescia 25063, ITALY / 030-8912402; FAX: 030-8911019 www.davide_pedersol.com

Davis, Don, 1619 Heights, Katy, TX 77493 / 713-391-3090

Davis Industries (See Cobra Enterprises, Inc.)

Davis Products, Mike, 643 Loop Dr., Moses Lake, WA 98837 / 509-765-6178; or 509-766-7281

Daystate Ltd., Birch House Lanee, Cotes Heath Staffs, ST15.022, ENGLAND / 01782-791755; FAX: 01782-791617

Dayton Traister, 4778 N. Monkey Hill Rd., P.O. Box 593, Oak Harbor, WA 98277 / 360-679-4657; FAX: 360-675-1114

DBI Books Division of Krause Publications, 700 E State St, Iola, WI 54990-0001 / 715-445-2214

D-Boone Ent., Inc., 5900 Colwyn Dr., Harrisburg, PA 17109

de Coux, Pete (See Cartridge Transfer Group)

Dead Eye's Sport Center, 76 Baer Rd., Shickshinny, PA 18655 / 570-256-7432 deadeyeprizz@aol.com

Decker Shooting Products, 1729 Laguna Ave., Schofield, WI 54476 / 715-359-5873; FAX: 715-355-7319

Deepeeka Exports Pvt. Ltd., D-78, Saket, Meerut-250-006, INDIA / 011-91-121-640363 or ; FAX: 011-91-121-640988 deepeeka@poboxes.com www.deepeeka.com

Defense Training International, Inc., 749 S. Lemay, Ste. A3-337, Ft. Collins, CO 80524 / 303-482-2520; FAX: 303-482-0548

Degen Inc. (See Aristocrat Knives)

deHaas Barrels, RR 3, Box 77, Ridgeway, MO 64481 / 816-872-6308

Del Rey Products, P.O. Box 5134, Playa Del Rey, CA 90296-5134 / 213-823-0494

Delhi Gun House, 1374 Kashmere Gate, Delhi, 0110 006 INDIA / 3940814; or 394-0974; FAX: 3917344 dgh@vsnl.com

Delorge, Ed, 6734 W. Main, Houma, LA 70360 / 985-223-0206

Del-Sports, Inc., Dave Budin, Box 685, 817 Main St., Margaretville, NY 12455 / 845-586-4103; FAX: 845-586-4105

Delta Arms Ltd., P.O. Box 1000, Delta, VT 84624-1000

Delta Enterprises, 284 Hagemann Drive, Livermore, CA 94550

Delta Frangible Ammunition LLC, PO Box 2350, Stafford, VA 22555-2350 / 540-720-5778; or 800-339-1933; FAX: 540-720-5667 dfa@dfanet.com www.dfanet.com

Dem-Bart Checkering Tools, Inc., 1825 Bickford Ave., Snohomish, WA 98290 / 360-568-7356; FAX: 360-568-1798

Denver Instrument Co., 6542 Fig St., Arvada, CO 80004 / 800-321-1135; or 303-431-7255; FAX: 303-423-4831

DeSantis Holster & Leather Goods, Inc., P.O. Box 2039, 149 Denton Ave., New Hyde Park, NY 11040-0701 / 516-354-8000; FAX: 516-354-7501

Desert Mountain Mfg., P.O. Box 130184, Coram, MT 59913 / 800-477-0762; or 406-387-5361; FAX: 406-387-5361

Detroit-Armor Corp., 720 Industrial Dr. No. 112, Cary, IL 60013 / 708-639-7666; FAX: 708-639-7694

Devereaux, R.H. "Dick" (See D.D. Custom)

Dewey Mfg. Co., Inc., J., PO Box 2014, Southbury, CT 06488 / 203-264-3064; FAX: 203-262-6907 deweyrods@worldnet.att.net www.deweyrods.com

DGR Custom Rifles, 4191 37th Ave SE, Tappen, ND 58487 / 701-327-8135

DGS, Inc., Dale A. Storey, 1117 E. 12th, Casper, WY 82601 / 307-237-2414; FAX: 307-237-2414 dalest@trib.com www.dgsrifle.com

DHB Products, P.O. Box 3092, Alexandria, VA 22302 / 703-836-2648

Diamond Machining Technology, Inc. (See DMT)

Diamond Mfg. Co., P.O. Box 174, Wyoming, PA 18644 / 800-233-9601

Diana (See U.S. Importer - Dynamit Nobel-RWS, Inc., 81 Ruckman Rd., Closter, NJ 07624 / 201-767-7971; FAX: 201-767-1589

Dibble, Derek A., 555 John Downey Dr., New Britain, CT 06051 / 203-224-2630

Dietz Gun Shop & Range, Inc., 421 Range Rd., New Braunfels, TX 78132 / 210-885-4662

Dilliott Gunsmithing, Inc., 657 Scarlett Rd., Dandridge, TN 37725 / 865-397-9204 gunsmithd@aol.com dilliottgunsmithing.com

Dillon, Ed, 1035 War Eagle Dr. N., Colorado Springs, CO 80919 / 719-598-4929; FAX: 719-598-4929

Dillon Precision Products, Inc., 8009 East Dillon's Way, Scottsdale, AZ 85260 / 480-948-8009; or 800-762-3845; FAX: 480-998-2786 sales@dillonprecision.com www.dillonprecision.com

Dina Arms Corporation, P.O. Box 46, Royersford, PA 19468 / 610-287-0266; FAX: 610-287-0266

Division Lead Co., 7742 W. 61st Pl., Summit, IL 60502

Dixie Gun Works, P.O. Box 130, Union City, TN 38281 / 731-885-0700; FAX: 731-885-0440

Dixon Muzzleloading Shop, Inc., 9952 Kunkels Mill Rd., Kempton, PA 19529 / 610-756-6271 dixonmuzzleloading.com

DKT, Inc., 14623 Vera Drive, Union, MI 49130-9744 / 800-741-7083 orders; FAX: 616-641-2015

DLO Mfg., 10807 SE Foster Ave., Arcadia, FL 33821-7304

DMT--Diamond Machining Technology Inc., 85 Hayes Memorial Dr., Marlborough, MA 01752 FAX: 508-485-3924

Dohring Bullets, 100 W. 8 Mile Rd., Ferndale, MI 48220

Dolbare, Elizabeth, P.O. Box 502, Dubois, WY 82513-0502

Domino, PO Box 108, 20019 Settimo Milanese, Milano, ITALY / 1-39-2-33512040; FAX: 1-39-2-33511587

Donnelly, C. P., 405 Kubli Rd., Grants Pass, OR 97527 / 541-846-6604

Doskocil Mfg. Co., Inc., P.O. Box 1246, 4209 Barnett, Arlington, TX 76017 / 817-467-5116; FAX: 817-472-9810

Douglas Barrels Inc., 5504 Big Tyler Rd., Charleston, WV 25313-1398 / 304-776-1341; FAX: 304-776-8560 www.benchrest.com/douglas

Downsizer Corp., PO Box 710316, Santee, CA 92072-0316 / 619-448-5510; FAX: 619-448-5780 www.downsizer.com

DPMS (Defense Procurement Manufacturing Services, Inc.), 13983 Industry Avenue, Becker, MN 55308 / 800-578-DPMS; or 763-261-5600 FAX: 763-261-5599

Dr. O's Products Ltd., P.O. Box 111, Niverville, NY 12130 / 518-784-3333; FAX: 518-784-2800

Drain, Mark, SE 3211 Kamilche Point Rd., Shelton, WA 98584 / 206-426-5452

Dremel Mfg. Co., 4915-21st St., Racine, WI 53406

Dri-Slide, Inc., 411 N. Darling, Fremont, MI 49412 / 616-924-3950

Dropkick, 1460 Washington Blvd., Williamsport, PA 17701 / 717-326-6561; FAX: 717-326-4950

DS Arms, Inc., P.O. Box 370, 27 West 990 Industrial Ave., Barrington, IL 60010 / 847-277-7258; FAX: 847-277-7259 www.dsarms.com

DTM International, Inc., 40 Joslyn Rd., P.O. Box 5, Lake Orion, MI 48362 / 313-693-6670

Duane A. Hobbie Gunsmithing, 2412 Pattie Ave, Wichita, KS 67216 / 316-264-8266

Duane's Gun Repair (See DGR Custom Rifles)

Dubber, Michael W., P.O. Box 312, Evansville, IN 47702 / 812-424-9000; FAX: 812-424-6551

Duck Call Specialists, P.O. Box 124, Jerseyville, IL 62052 / 618-498-9855

Duffy, Charles E (See Guns Antique & Modern DBA), Williams Lane, PO Box 2, West Hurley, NY 12491 /914-679-2997

Du-Lite Corp., 171 River Rd., Middletown, CT 06457 / 203-347-2505; FAX: 203-347-9404

Dumoulin, Ernest, Rue Florent Boclinville 8-10, 13-4041, Votten, BELGIUM / 41 27 78 92

Duncan's Gun Works, Inc., 1619 Grand Ave., San Marcos, CA 92069 / 760-727-0515

Duofold, Inc., RD 3 Rt. 309, Valley Square Mall, Tamaqua, PA 18252 / 717-386-2666; FAX: 717-386-3652

Dybala Gun Shop, P.O. Box 1024, FM 3156, Bay City, TX 77414 / 409-245-0866

Dykstra, Doug, 411 N. Darling, Fremont, MI 49412 / 616-924-3950

Dynalite Products, Inc., 215 S. Washington St., Greenfield, OH 45123 / 513-981-2124

Dynamit Nobel-RWS, Inc., 81 Ruckman Rd., Closter, NJ 07624 / 201-767-7971; FAX: 201-767-1589

E

E&L Mfg., Inc., 4177 Riddle By Pass Rd., Riddle, OR 97469 / 541-874-2137; FAX: 541-874-3107

E. Arthur Brown Co., 3404 Pawnee Dr., Alexandria, MN 56308 / 320-762-8847

E.A.A. Corp., P.O. Box 1299, Sharpes, FL 32959 / 407-639-4842; or 800-536-4442; FAX: 407-639-7006

Eagan, Donald V., P.O. Box 196, Benton, PA 17814 / 717-925-6134

Eagle Arms, Inc. (See ArmaLite, Inc.)

Eagle Distributing, 1750 Brielle Ave. Unit B-1, Wanamassa, NJ 07712 / 732-493-0302; FAX: 732-493-0301

Eagle Grips, Eagle Business Center, 460 Randy Rd., Carol Stream, IL 60188 / 800-323-6144; or 708-260-0400; FAX: 708-260-0486

Eagle Imports, Inc., 1750 Brielle Ave., Unit B1, Wanamassa, NJ 07712 / 908-493-0333

E-A-R, Inc., Div. of Cabot Safety Corp., 5457 W. 79th St., Indianapolis, IN 46268 / 800-327-3431; FAX: 800-488-8007

EAW (See U.S. Importer-New England Custom Gun Serv

Eckelman Gunsmithing, 3125 133rd St. SW, Fort Ripley, MN 56449 / 218-829-3176

Eclectic Technologies, Inc., 45 Grandview Dr., Suite A, Farmington, CT 06034

Ed Brown Products, Inc., P.O. Box 492, Perry, MO 63462 / 573-565-3261; FAX: 573-565-2791 www.edbrown.com

Edenpine, Inc. c/o Six Enterprises, Inc., 320 D Turtle Creek Ct., San Jose, CA 95125 / 408-999-0201; FAX: 408-999-0216

EdgeCraft Corp., S. Weiner, 825 Southwood Road, Avondale, PA 19311 / 610-268-0500; or 800-342-3255; FAX: 610-268-3545 www.edgecraft.com

Edmisten Co., P.O. Box 1293, Boone, NC 28607

Edmund Scientific Co., 101 E. Gloucester Pike, Barrington, NJ 08033 / 609-543-6250

Ednar, Inc., 2-4-8 Kayabacho, Nihonbashi Chuo-ku, Tokyo, JAPAN / 81(Japan)-3-3667-1651; FAX: 81-3-3661-8113

Ed's Gun House, Ed Kukowski, PO Box 62, Minnesota City, MN 55959 / 507-689-2925

Eezox, Inc., P.O. Box 772, Waterford, CT 06385-0772 / 800-462-3331; FAX: 860-447-3484

Effebi SNC-Dr. Franco Beretta, via Rossa, 4, 25062, ITALY / 030-2751955; FAX: 030-2180414

Efficient Machinery Co, 12878 N.E. 15th Pl., Bellevue, WA 98005 / 425-453-9318; or 800-375-8554; FAX: 425-453-9311; priemc@aol.com www.sturdybench.com

Eggleston, Jere D., 400 Saluda Ave., Columbia, SC 29205 / 803-799-3402

Eichelberger Bullets, Wm., 158 Crossfield Rd., King Of Prussia, PA 19406

Ekol Leather Care, P.O. Box 2652, West Lafayette, IN 47906 / 317-463-2250; FAX: 317-463-7004

El Paso Saddlery Co., P.O. Box 27194, El Paso, TX 79926 / 915-544-2233; FAX: 915-544-2535

Eldorado Cartridge Corp (See PMC/Eldorado

Electro Prismatic Collimators, Inc., 1441 Manatt St., Lincoln, NE 68521

Electronic Shooters Protection, Inc., 11997 West 85th Place, Arvada, CO 80005 / 800-797-7791; FAX: 303-456-7179

Electronic Trigger Systems, Inc., PO Box 13, 230 Main St. S., Hector, MN 55342 / 320-848-2760; FAX: 320-848-2760

Eley Ltd., P.O. Box 705, Witton, Birmingham, B6 7UT ENGLAND / 021-356-8899; FAX: 021-331-4173

Elite Ammunition, P.O. Box 3251, Oakbrook, IL 60522 / 708-366-9006

Elk River, Inc., 1225 Paonia St., Colorado Springs, CO 80915 / 719-574-4407

Ellett Bros., 267 Columbia Ave., P.O. Box 128, Chapin, SC 29036 / 803-345-3751; or 800-845-3711; FAX: 803-345-1820

Ellicott Arms, Inc. / Woods Pistolsmithing, 8390 Sunset Dr., Ellicott City, MD 21043 / 410-465-7979

Elliott, Inc., G. W., 514 Burnside Ave, East Hartford, CT 06108 / 203-289-5741; FAX: 203-289-3137

EMAP USA, 6420 Wilshire Blvd., Los Angeles, CA 90048 / 213-782-2000; FAX: 213-782-2867

Emerging Technologies, Inc. (See Laseraim Technolo

EMF Co., Inc., 1900 E. Warner Ave., Suite 1-D, Santa Ana, CA 92705 / 949-261-6611; FAX: 949-756-0133

Empire Cutlery Corp., 12 Kruger Ct., Clifton, NJ 07013 / 201-472-5155; FAX: 201-779-0759

English, Inc., A.G., 708 S. 12th St., Broken Arrow, OK 74012 / 918-251-3399 agenglish@wedzone.net www.agenglish.com

Engraving Artistry, 36 Alto Rd., Burlington, CT 06013 / 203-673-6837 bobburt44@hotmail.com

Enguix Import-Export, Alpujarras 58, Alzira, Valencia, SPAIN / (96) 241 43 95; FAX: (96) (241 43 95

Enhanced Presentations, Inc., 5929 Market St., Wilmington, NC 28405 / 910-799-1622; FAX: 910-799-5004

Enlow, Charles, 895 Box, Beaver, OK 73932 / 405-625-4487

Entre'prise Arms, Inc., 15861 Business Center Dr., Irwindale, CA 91706

EPC, 1441 Manatt St., Lincoln, NE 68521 / 402-476-3946

Epps, Ellwood/Isabella (See Gramps), Box 341, Washago, ON L0K 2B0 CANADA / 705-689-5348

Epps, Ellwood & Isabella. See: "GRAMPS" ANTIQUES

Erhardt, Dennis, 4508 N. Montana Ave., Helena, MT 59602 / 406-442-4533

Erma Werke GmbH, Johan Ziegler St., 13/15/FeldiglSt., D-8060 Dachau, GERMANY

Essex Arms, P.O. Box 363, Island Pond, VT 05846 / 802-723-6203; FAX: 802-723-6203

Essex Metals, 1000 Brighton St., Union, NJ 07083 / 800-282-8369

Estate Cartridge, Inc., 12161 FM 830, Willis, TX 77378 / 409-856-7277; FAX: 409-856-5486

Euber Bullets, No. Orwell Rd., Orwell, VT 05760 / 802-948-2621

Euroarms of America, Inc., PO Box 3277, Winchester, VA 22604 / 540-662-1863; FAX: 540-662-4464

Euro-Imports, 905 West Main Street, Suite E, El Cajon, CA 92020 / 619-442-7005; FAX: 619-442-7005

European American Armory Corp (See E.A.A. Corp)

Evans Engraving, Robert, 332 Vine St, Oregon City, OR 97045 / 503-656-5693

Eversull Co., Inc., 1 Tracemont, Boyce, LA 71409 / 318-793-8728; FAX: 318-793-5483 bestguns@aol.com

Evolution Gun Works Inc., 4050 B-8 Skyron Dr., Doylestown, PA 18901 / 215-348-9892; FAX: 215-348-1056

Excalibur Electro Optics Inc, P.O. Box 400, Fogelsville, PA 18051-0400 / 610-391-9105; FAX: 610-391-9220

Excel Industries Inc., 4510 Carter Ct., Chino, CA 91710 / 909-627-2404; FAX: 909-627-7817

Executive Protection Institute, PO Box 802, Berryville, VA 22611 / 540-554-2540 rwk@crosslink.com personalprotecion.com

Eyster Heritage Gunsmiths, Inc., Ken, 6441 Bishop Rd., Centerburg, OH 43011 / 740-625-6131

Eze-Lap Diamond Prods., P.O. Box 2229, 15164 West State St., Westminster, CA 92683 / 714-847-1555; FAX: 714-897-0280

E-Z-Way Systems, PO Box 4310, Newark, OH 43058-4310 / 614-345-6645; or 800-848-2072; FAX: 614-345-6600

F

F.A.I.R. Tecni-Mec s.n.c. di Isidoro Rizzini & C., Via Gitti, 41 Zona Industrial, 25060 Marcheno (Bres, ITALY / 030/861162-8610344; FAX: 030/8610179 info@fair.it www.fair.it

F.I., Inc. - High Standard Mfg. Co., 5200 Mitchelldale St., Ste. E17, Houston, TX 77092-7222 / 713-462-4200; or 800-272-7816; FAX: 713-681-5665 www.highstandard.com

Fabarm S.p.A., Via Averolda 31, 25039 Travagliato, Brescia, ITALY / 030-6863629; FAX: 030-6863684

Fagan & Co.Inc, 22952 15 Mile Rd, Clinton Township, MI 48035 / 810-465-4637; FAX: 810-792-6996

Faith Associates, PO Box 549, Flat Rock, NC 28731-0549 FAX: 828-697-6827

Faloon Industries, Inc., P.O. Box 1060, Tijeras, NM 87059 / 505-281-3783

Far North Outfitters, Box 1252, Bethel, AK 99559

Farm Form Decoys, Inc., 1602 Biovu, P.O. Box 748, Galveston, TX 77553 / 409-744-0762; or 409-765-6361; FAX: 409-765-8513

Farr Studio, Inc., 1231 Robinhood Rd., Greeneville, TN 37743 / 615-638-8825

Farrar Tool Co., Inc., 12150 Bloomfield Ave., Suite E, Santa Fe Springs, CA 90670 / 310-863-4367; FAX: 310-863-5123

Faulhaber Wildlocker, Dipl.-Ing. Norbert Wittasek, Seilergasse 2, A-1010 Wien, AUSTRIA / OM-43-1-5137001; FAX: 43-1-5137001

Faulk's Game Call Co., Inc., 616 18th St., Lake Charles, LA 70601 / 318-436-9726; FAX: 318-494-7205

Faust Inc., T. G., 544 minor St, Reading, PA 19602 / 610-375-8549; FAX: 610-375-4488

Fausti Cav. Stefano & Figlie snc, Via Martiri Dell Indipendenza, 70, Marcheno, 25060 ITALY

Fautheree, Andy, P.O. Box 4607, Pagosa Springs, CO 81157 / 970-731-5003; FAX: 970-731-5009

Feather, Flex Decoys, 4500 Doniphan Dr., Neosho, MO 64850 / 318-746-8596; FAX: 318-742-4815

Federal Arms Corp. of America, 7928 University Ave, Fridley, MN 55432 / 612-780-8780; FAX: 612-780-8780

Federal Cartridge Co., 900 Ehlen Dr., Anoka, MN 55303 / 612-323-2300; FAX: 612-323-2506

Federal Champion Target Co., 232 Industrial Parkway, Richmond, IN 47374 / 800-441-4971; FAX: 317-966-7747

Federated-Fry (See Fry Metals)

FEG, Budapest, Soroksariut 158, H-1095, HUNGARY

Feken, Dennis, Rt. 2, Box 124, Perry, OK 73077 / 405-336-5611

Felk Oil Gun Lube, 2121 Castlebridge Rd., Midlothian, VA 23113 / 804-794-3744; FAX: 208-988-4834

Fellowes, Ted, Beaver Lodge, 9245 16th Ave. SW, Seattle, WA 98106 / 206-763-1698

Ferguson, Bill, P.O. Box 1238, Sierra Vista, AZ 85636 / 520-458-5321; FAX: 520-458-9125

FERLIB, Via Costa 46, 25063, Gardone V.T., ITALY / 30-89-12-586; FAX: 30-89-12-586

Ferris Firearms, 7110 F.M. 1863, Bulverde, TX 78163 / 210-980-4424

Fibron Products, Inc., P.O. Box 430, Buffalo, NY 14209-0430 / 716-886-2378; FAX: 716-886-2394

Fieldsport Ltd., Bryan Bilinski, 3313 W South Airport Rd, Traverse Vity, MI 49684 / 616-933-0767

Fiocchi Munizioni S.p.A. (See U.S. Importer-Fiocch

Fiocchi of America Inc., 5030 Fremont Rd., Ozark, MO 65721 / 417-725-4118; or 800-721-2666; FAX: 417-725-1039

Firearms & Metal Engraving, P.O. Box 1255, Sierra Vista, AZ 85636 / 520-455-5541

Firearms Co Ltd. / Alpine (See U.S. Importer-Mandall

Firearms Engraver's Guild of America, 332 Vine St., Oregon City, OR 97045 / 503-656-5693

Firearms International, 5709 Hartsdale, Houston, TX 77036 / 713-460-2447

First Inc., Jack, 1201 Turbine Dr., Rapid City, SD 57701 / 605-343-9544; FAX: 605-343-9420

Fish Mfg. Gunsmith Sptg. Co., Marshall, Rd. Box 2439, Rt. 22 N, Westport, NY 12993 / 518-962-4897; FAX: 518-962-4897

Fisher, Jerry A., 631 Crane Mt. Rd., Big Fork, MT 59911 / 406-837-2722

Fisher Custom Firearms, 2199 S. Kittredge Way, Aurora, CO 80013 / 303-755-3710

Fitz Pistol Grip Co., P.O. Box 744, Lewiston, CA 96052-0744 / 916-778-0240

Fitzgerald, Jack. See: CLENZOIL WORLDWIDE CORP

Flambeau Products Corp., 15981 Valplast Rd., Middlefield, OH 44062 / 216-632-1631; FAX: 216-632-1581

Flannery Engraving Co., Jeff W, 11034 Riddles Run Rd, Union, KY 41091 / 606-384-3127

Flayderman & Co., Inc., PO Box 2446, Ft Lauderdale, FL 33303 / 954-761-8855

Fleming Firearms, 7720 E 126th St. N, Collinsville, OK 74021-7016 / 918-665-3624

Flintlocks, Etc., 160 Rossiter Rd., P.O. Box 181, Richmond, MA 01254 / 413-698-3822; FAX: 413-698-3866 flintetc@vgernet.net

Flitz International Ltd., 821 Mohr Ave., Waterford, WI 53185 / 414-534-5898; FAX: 414-534-2991

Flores Publications, Inc. J (See Action Direct Inc.), PO Box 830760, Miami, FL 33283 / 305-559-4652; FAX: 305-559-4652

Fluoramics, Inc., 18 Industrial Ave., Mahwah, NJ 07430 / 800-922-0075; FAX: 201-825-7035

Flynn's Custom Guns, P.O. Box 7461, Alexandria, LA 71306 / 318-455-7130

FN Manufacturing, PO Box 24257, Columbia, SC 29224 / 803-736-0522

Folks, Donald E., 205 W. Lincoln St., Pontiac, IL 61764 / 815-844-7901

Foothills Video Productions, Inc., P.O. Box 651, Spartanburg, SC 29304 / 803-573-7023; or 800-782-5358

Foredom Electric Co., Rt. 6, 16 Stony Hill Rd., Bethel, CT 06801 / 203-792-8622

Forgett, Valmore. See: NAVY ARMS COMPANY

Forgreens Tool & Mfg., Inc., PO Box 955, Robert Lee, TX 76945 / 915-453-2800; FAX: 915-453-2460

Forkin, Ben (See Belt MTN Arms)

Forkin Arms, 205 10th Avenue S.W., White Sulphur Spring, MT 59645 / 406-547-2344

Forrest Inc., Tom, PO Box 326, Lakeside, CA 92040 / 619-561-5800; FAX: 619-561-0227

Forrest Tool Co., P.O. Box 768, 44380 Gordon Lane, Mendocino, CA 95460 / 707-937-2141; FAX: 717-937-1817

Forster, Kathy (See Custom Checkering)

Forster, Larry L., PO Box 212, 220 First St. NE, Gwinner, ND 58040-0212 / 701-678-2475

Forster Products, 310 E Lanark Ave, Lanark, IL 61046 / 815-493-6360; FAX: 815-493-2371

Fort Hill Gunstocks, 12807 Fort Hill Rd., Hillsboro, OH 45133 / 513-466-2763

Fort Knox Security Products, 1051 N. Industrial Park Rd., Orem, UT 84057 / 801-224-7233; or 800-821-5216; FAX: 801-226-5493

Fort Worth Firearms, 2006-B, Martin Luther King Fwy., Ft. Worth, TX 76104-6303 / 817-536-0718; FAX: 817-535-0290

Forthofer's Gunsmithing & Knifemaking, 5535 U.S. Hwy 93S, Whitefish, MT 59937-8411 / 406-862-2674

Fortune Products, Inc., 205 Hickory Creek Rd., Marble Falls, TX 78654 / 210-693-6111; FAX: 210-693-6394

Forty Five Ranch Enterprises, Box 1080, Miami, OK 74355-1080 / 918-542-5875

Foster. See: ACCURACY INTERNATIONAL

Fountain Products, 492 Prospect Ave., West Springfield, MA 01089 / 413-781-4651; FAX: 413-733-8217

4-D Custom Die Co., 711 N. Sandusky St., PO Box 889, Mt. Vernon, OH 43050-0889 / 740-397-7214; FAX: 740-397-6600; info@ch4d.com ch4d.com

Fowler Bullets, 806 Dogwood Dr., Gastonia, NC 28054 / 704-867-3259

Fowler, Bob (See Black Powder Products)

Fox River Mills, Inc., P.O. Box 298, 227 Poplar St., Osage, IA 50461 / 515-732-3798; FAX: 515-732-5128

Foy Custom Bullets, 104 Wells Ave., Daleville, AL 36322

Francesca, Inc., 3115 Old Ranch Rd., San Antonio, TX 78217 / 512-826-2584; FAX: 512-826-8211

Franchi S.p.A., Via del Serpente 12, 25131, Brescia, ITALY / 030-3581833; FAX: 030-3581554

Francotte & Cie S.A. Auguste, rue de Trois Juin 109, 4400 Herstal-Liege, BELGIUM / 32-4-248-13-18; FAX: 32-4-948-11-79

Frank Knives, 13868 NW Keleka Pl., Seal Rock, OR 97376 / 541-563-3041; FAX: 541-563-3041

Frank Mittermeier, Inc., P.O. Box 2G, 3577 E. Tremont Ave., Bronx, NY 10465 / 718-828-3843

Franzen International,Inc (See U.S. Importer for)

Fred F. Wells / Wells Sport Store, 110 N Summit St, Prescott, AZ 86301 / 520-445-3655

Freedom Arms, Inc., P.O. Box 150, Freedom, WY 83120 / 307-883-2468; FAX: 307-883-2005

Fremont Tool Works, 1214 Prairie, Ford, KS 67842 / 316-369-2327

French, Artistic Engraving, J. R., 1712 Creek Ridge Ct, Irving, TX 75060 / 214-254-2654

Frielich Police Equipment, 211 East 21st St., New York, NY 10010 / 212-254-3045

Front Sight Firearms Training Institute, P.O. Box 2619, Aptos, CA 95001 / 800-987-7719; FAX: 408-684-2137

Frontier, 2910 San Bernardo, Laredo, TX 78040 / 956-723-5409; FAX: 956-723-1774

Frontier Arms Co.,Inc., 401 W. Rio Santa Cruz, Green Valley, AZ 85614-3932

Frontier Products Co., 2401 Walker Rd., Roswell, NM 88201-8950 / 614-262-9357

Frontier Safe Co., 3201 S. Clinton St., Fort Wayne, IN 46806 / 219-744-7233; FAX: 219-744-6678

Frost Cutlery Co., P.O. Box 22636, Chattanooga, TN 37422 / 615-894-6079; FAX: 615-894-9576

Fry Metals, 4100 6th Ave., Altoona, PA 16602 / 814-946-1611

Fujinon, Inc., 10 High Point Dr., Wayne, NJ 07470 / 201-633-5600; FAX: 201-633-5216

Fullmer, Geo. M., 2499 Mavis St., Oakland, CA 94601 / 510-533-4193

Fulmer's Antique Firearms, Chet, PO Box 792, Rt 2 Buffalo Lake, Detroit Lakes, MN 56501 / 218-847-7712

Fulton Armory, 8725 Bollman Place No. 1, Savage, MD 20763 / 301-490-9485; FAX: 301-490-9547

Furr Arms, 91 N. 970 W., Orem, UT 84057 / 801-226-3877; FAX: 801-226-3877

FWB, Neckarstrasse 43, 78727, Oberndorf a. N., GERMANY / 07423-814-0; FAX: 07423-814-89

G

G C Bullet Co. Inc., 40 Mokelumne River Dr., Lodi, CA 95240

G&H Decoys,Inc., P.O. Box 1208, Hwy. 75 North, Henryetta, OK 74437 / 918-652-3314; FAX: 918-652-3400

G.G. & G., 3602 E. 42nd Stravenue, Tucson, AZ 85713 / 520-748-7167; FAX: 520-748-7583

G.H. Enterprises Ltd., Bag 10, Okotoks, AB T0L 1T0 CANADA / 403-938-6070

G.U. Inc (See U.S. Importer for New SKB Arms Co.)

G.W. Elliott, Inc., 514 Burnside Ave., East Hartford, CT 06108 / 203-289-5741; FAX: 203-289-3137

G96 Products Co., Inc., 85 5th Ave, Bldg. #6, Paterson, NJ 07544 / 973-684-4050; FAX: 973-684-3848; g96prod@aol

Gage Manufacturing, 663 W. 7th St., A, San Pedro, CA 90731 / 310-832-3546

Gaillard Barrels, P.O. Box 21, Pathlow, SK S0K 3B0 CANADA / 306-752-3769; FAX: 306-752-5969

Gain Twist Barrel Co. Rifle Works and Armory, 707 12th Street, Cody, WY 82414 / 307-587-4919; FAX: 307-527-6097

Galati International, PO Box 10, 616 Burley Ridge Rd., Wesco, MO 65586 / 573-775-2308; FAX: 573-775-4308 support@galatiinteenation.com www.galatiinternational.com

Galaxy Imports Ltd., Inc., P.O. Box 3361, Victoria, TX 77903 / 361-573-4867; FAX: 361-576-9622 galaxy@cox_internet.com

GALCO International Ltd., 2019 W. Quail Ave., Phoenix, AZ 85027 / 602-258-8295; or 800-874-2526; FAX: 602-582-6854

Galena Industries AMT, 5463 Diaz St, Irwindale, CA 91706 / 626-856-8883; FAX: 626-856-8878

Gamba S.p.A. Societa Armi Bresciane Srl, Renato, Via Artigiani 93, ITALY / 30-8911640; FAX: 30-8911648

Gamba, USA, P.O. Box 60452, Colorado Springs, CO 80960 / 719-578-1145; FAX: 719-444-0731

Game Haven Gunstocks, 13750 Shire Rd., Wolverine, MI 49799 / 616-525-8257

Game Winner, Inc., R 1 Box Industrial Park, Opp, AL 36467 / 770-434-9210; FAX: 770-434-9215

Gamebore Division, Polywad Inc, PO Box 7916, Macon, GA 31209 / 912-477-0669

Gamo (See U.S. Importers-Arms United Corp, Daisy M

Gamo USA, Inc., 3911 SW 47th Ave., Suite 914, Ft. Lauderdale, FL 33314 / 954-581-5822; FAX: 954-581-3165 gamousa@gate.net www.gamo.com

Gander Mountain, Inc., 12400 Fox River Rd., Wilmont, WI 53192 / 414-862-6848

GAR, 590 McBride Avenue, West Paterson, NJ 07424 / 973-754-1114; FAX: 973-754-1114 garreloading@aol.com

Garbi, Armas Urki, 12-14 20.600 Eibar, Guipuzcoa, SPAIN

Garcia National Gun Traders, Inc., 225 SW 22nd Ave., Miami, FL 33135 / 305-642-2355

Garrett Cartridges Inc., PO Box 178, Chehalis, WA 98532 / 360-736-0702 garrettcartridges.com

Garthwaite Pistolsmith, Inc., Jim, Rt 2 Box 310, Watsontown, PA 17777 / 570-538-1566; FAX: 570-538-2965

Gary Goudy Classic Stocks, 1512 S. 5th St., Dayton, WA 99328 / 509-382-2726 goudy@innw.net

Gary Reeder Custom Guns, 2601 7th Avenue East, Flagstaff, AZ 86004 / 928-526-3313; FAX: 928-527-0840 gary@reedercustomguns.com www.reedercustomguns.com

Gary Schneider Rifle Barrels Inc., 12202 N. 62nd Pl., Scottsdale, AZ 85254 / 602-948-2525

Gator Guns & Repair, 7952 Kenai Spur Hwy., Kenai, AK 99611-8311

Gaucher Armes, S.A., 46 rue Desjoyaux, 42000, Saint-Etienne, FRANCE / 04-77-33-38-92; FAX: 04-77-61-95-72

GDL Enterprises, 409 Le Gardeur, Slidell, LA 70460 / 504-649-0693

Gehmann, Walter (See Huntington Die Specialties)

Genco, P.O. Box 5704, Asheville, NC 28803

Genecco Gun Works, 10512 Lower Sacramento Rd., Stockton, CA 95210 / 209-951-0706; FAX: 209-931-3872

Gene's Custom Guns, P.O. Box 10534, White Bear Lake, MN 55110 / 612-429-5105

Gentex Corp., 5 Tinkham Ave., Derry, NH 03038 / 603-434-0311; FAX: 603-434-3002 sales@derry.gentexcorp.com www.derry.gentexcorp.com

Gentner Bullets, 109 Woodlawn Ave., Upper Darby, PA 19082 / 610-352-9396

Gentry Custom Gunmaker, David, 314 N Hoffman, Belgrade, MT 59714 / 406-388-GUNS davidgent@mcn.net gentrycustom.com

George & Roy's, PO Box 2125, Sisters, OR 97759-2125 / 503-228-5424; or 800-553-3022; FAX: 503-225-9409

George E. Mathews & Son, Inc., 10224 S. Paramount Blvd., Downey, CA 90241 / 562-862-6719; FAX: 562-862-6719

George Ibberson (Sheffield) Ltd., 25-31 Allen St., Sheffield, S3 7AW ENGLAND / 0114-2766123; FAX: 0114-2738465

Gerald Pettinger Books, see Pettinger Books, Rt. 2, Box 125, Russell, IA 50238 / 641-535-2239 gpettinger@lisco.com

Gerber Legendary Blades, 14200 SW 72nd Ave., Portland, OR 97223 / 503-639-6161; or 800-950-6161; FAX: 503-684-7008

Gervais, Mike, 3804 S. Cruise Dr., Salt Lake City, UT 84109 / 801-277-7729

Getz Barrel Co., P.O. Box 88, Beavertown, PA 17813 / 717-658-7263

Giacomo Sporting USA, 6234 Stokes Lee Center Rd., Lee Center, NY 13363

Gibbs Rifle Co., Inc., 211 Lawn St, Martinsburg, WV 25401 / 304-262-1651; FAX: 304-262-1658

Gil Hebard Guns Inc., 125 Public Square, Knoxville, IL 61448 / 309-289-2700; FAX: 309-289-2233

Gilbert Equipment Co., Inc., 960 Downtowner Rd., Mobile, AL 36609 / 205-344-3322

Gillmann, Edwin, 33 Valley View Dr., Hanover, PA 17331 / 717-632-1662

Gilman-Mayfield, Inc., 3279 E. Shields, Fresno, CA 93703 / 209-221-9415; FAX: 209-221-9419

Gilmore Sports Concepts, 5949 S. Garnett, Tulsa, OK 74146 / 918-250-3810; FAX: 918-250-3845 gilmore@webzone.net www.gilmoresports.com

Giron, Robert E., 12671 Cousins Rd.., Peosta, IA 52068 / 412-731-6041

Glacier Glove, 4890 Aircenter Circle, Suite 210, Reno, NV 89502 / 702-825-8225; FAX: 702-825-6544

Glaser Safety Slug, Inc., PO Box 8223, Foster City, CA 94404 / 800-221-3489; FAX: 510-785-6685 safetyslug.com

Glass, Herb, PO Box 25, Bullville, NY 10915 / 914-361-3021

Glimm, Jerome. See: GLIMM'S CUSTOM GUN ENGRAVING

Glimm's Custom Gun Engraving, Jerome C. Glimm, 19 S. Maryland, Conrad, MT 59425 / 406-278-3574 jandlglimm@mcn.net

Glock GmbH, P.O. Box 50, A-2232, Deutsch Wagram, AUSTRIA

Glock, Inc., PO Box 369, Smyrna, GA 30081 / 770-432-1202; FAX: 770-433-8719

Glynn Scobey Duck & Goose Calls, Rt. 3, Box 37, Newbern, TN 38059 / 901-643-6241

GML Products, Inc., 394 Laredo Dr., Birmingham, AL 35226 / 205-979-4867

Gner's Hard Cast Bullets, 1107 11th St., LaGrande, OR 97850 / 503-963-8796

Goens, Dale W., P.O. Box 224, Cedar Crest, NM 87008 / 505-281-5419

Goergen's Gun Shop, Inc., 17985 538th Ave, Austin, MN 55912 / 507-433-9280; FAX: 507-433-9280

GOEX Inc., PO Box 659, Doyline, LA 71023-0659 / 318-382-9300; FAX: 318-382-9303 mfahringer@goexpowder.com; www.goexpowder.com

Golden Age Arms Co., 115 E. High St., Ashley, OH 43003 / 614-747-2488

Golden Bear Bullets, 3065 Fairfax Ave., San Jose, CA 95148 / 408-238-9515

Gonic Arms/North American Arm, 134 Flagg Rd., Gonic, NH 03839 / 603-332-8456 or 603-332-8457

Gonzalez Guns, Ramon B, PO Box 370, 93 St. Joseph's Hill Rd, Monticello, NY 12701 / 914-794-4515

Goodling's Gunsmithing, 1950 Stoverstown Road, Spring Grove, PA 17362 / 717-225-3350

Goodwin, Fred. See: GOODWIN'S GUN SHOP

Goodwin's Gun Shop, Fred Goodwin, Sherman Mills, ME 04776 / 207-365-4451

Gotz Bullets, 11426 Edgemere Ter., Roscoe, IL 61073-8232

Gould & Goodrich, 709 E. McNeil, Lillington, NC 27546 / 910-893-2071; FAX: 910-893-4742

Gourmet Artistic Engraving, Geoffroy Gournet, 820 Paxinosa Ave., Easton, PA 18042 / 610-559-0710 geoffroygournet.com

Gournet, Geoffroy. See: GOURNET ARTISTIC ENGRAVING

Grace, Charles E., 1305 Arizona Ave., Trinidad, CO 81082 / 719-846-9435

Grace Metal Products, PO Box 67, Elk Rapids, MI 49629 / 616-264-8133

Graf & Sons, 4050 S Clark St, Mexico, MO 65265 / 573-581-2266; FAX: 573-581-2875

"Gramps" Antiques, Ellwood & Isabella Epps, Box 341, Washago, ON L0K 2B0 CANADA / 705-689-5348

Granite Mountain Arms, Inc, 3145 W Hidden Acres Trail, Prescott, AZ 86305 / 520-541-9758; FAX: 520-445-6826

Grant, Howard V., Hiawatha 15, Woodruff, WI 54568 / 715-356-7146

Graphics Direct, P.O. Box 372421, Reseda, CA 91337-2421 / 818-344-9002

Graves Co., 1800 Andrews Ave., Pompano Beach, FL 33069 / 800-327-9103; FAX: 305-960-0301

Grayback Wildcats, Mike Beeks, 5306 Bryant Ave., Klamath Falls, OR 97603 / 541-884-1072

Graybill's Gun Shop, 1035 Ironville Pike, Columbia, PA 17512 / 717-684-2739

Great American Gunstock Co., 3420 Industrial Drive, Yuba City, CA 95993 / 530-671-4570; FAX: 530-671-3906

Great Lakes Airguns, 6175 S. Park Ave, New York, NY 14075 / 716-648-6666; FAX: 716-648-5279

Green, Arthur S., 485 S. Robertson Blvd., Beverly Hills, CA 90211 / 310-274-1283

Green, Roger M., P.O. Box 984, 435 E. Birch, Glenrock, WY 82637 / 307-436-9804

Green Head Game Call Co., RR 1, Box 33, Lacon, IL 61540 / 309-246-2155

Green Mountain Rifle Barrel Co., Inc., P.O. Box 2670, 153 West Main St., Conway, NH 03818 / 603-447-1095; FAX: 603-447-1099

Greenwood Precision, P.O. Box 407, Rogersville, MO 65742 / 417-725-2330

Greg Gunsmithing Repair, 3732 26th Ave. North, Robbinsdale, MN 55422 / 612-529-8103

Greg's Superior Products, P.O. Box 46219, Seattle, WA 98146

Greider Precision, 431 Santa Marina Ct., Escondido, CA 92029 / 619-480-8892; FAX: 619-480-9800

Gremmel Enterprises, 2111 Carriage Drive, Eugene, OR 97408-7537 / 541-302-3000

GrE-Tan Rifles, 29742 W.C.R. 50, Kersey, CO 80644 / 970-353-6176; FAX: 970-356-9133

Grier's Hard Cast Bullets, 1107 11th St., LaGrande, OR 97850 / 503-963-8796

Griffin & Howe, Inc., 36 W. 44th St., Suite 1011, New York, NY 10036 / 212-921-0980

Griffin & Howe, Inc., 33 Claremont Rd., Bernardsville, NJ 07924 / 908-766-2287

Grifon, Inc., 58 Guinam St., Waltham, MS 02154

Groenewold, John, PO Box 830, Mundelein, IL 60060 / 847-566-2365

GRS / Glendo Corp., P.O. Box 1153, 900 Overlander St., Emporia, KS 66801 / 316-343-1084 or 800-835-3519 glendo@glendo.com grstools.com

Grulla Armes, Apartado 453, Avda Otaloa 12, Eiber, SPAIN

Gruning Precision Inc, 7101 Jurupa Ave., No. 12, Riverside, CA 92504 / 909-689-6692; FAX: 909-689-7791 gruningprecision@earthlink.net www.gruningprecision.com

GSI, Inc., 7661 Commerce Ln., Trussville, AL 35173 / 205-655-8299

GTB, 482 Comerwood Court, San Francisco, CA 94080 / 650-583-1550

Guarasi, Robert. See: WILCOX INDUSTRIES CORP

Guardsman Products, 411 N. Darling, Fremont, MI 49412 / 616-924-3950

Gun Accessories (See Glaser Safety Slug, Inc.), PO Box 8223, Foster City, CA 94404 / 800-221-3489; FAX: 510-785-6685

Gun City, 212 W. Main Ave., Bismarck, ND 58501 / 701-223-2304

Gun Hunter Books (See Gun Hunter Trading Co), 5075 Heisig St, Beaumont, TX 77705 / 409-835-3006; FAX: 409-838-2266; gunhuntertrading@hotmail.com

Gun Hunter Trading Co., 5075 Heisig St., Beaumont, TX 77705 / 409-835-3006; FAX: 409-838-2266 gunhuntertrading@hotmail.com

Gun Leather Limited, 116 Lipscomb, Ft. Worth, TX 76104 / 817-334-0225; FAX: 800-247-0609

Gun List (See Krause Publications), 700 E State St, Iola, WI 54945 / 715-445-2214; FAX: 715-445-4087

Gun South, Inc. (See GSI, Inc.)

Gun Vault, 7339 E Acoma Dr., Ste. 7, Scottsdale, AZ 85260 / 602-951-6855

Gun-Alert, 1010 N. Maclay Ave., San Fernando, CA 91340 / 818-365-0864; FAX: 818-365-1308

Guncraft Books (See Guncraft Sports Inc.), 10737 Dutchtown Rd, Knoxville, TN 37932 / 865-966-4545; FAX: 865-966-4500 findit@guncraft.com www.usit.net/guncraft

Guncraft Sports, Inc., 10737 Dutchtown Rd., Knoxville, TN 37932 / 865-966-4545; FAX: 865-966-4500 findit@guncraft.com www.usit.net/guncraft

Guncraft Sports, Inc., Marie C. Wiest, 10737 Dutchtown Rd., Knoxville, TN 37932 / 865-966-4545; FAX: 865-966-4500 www.guncraft.com

Gunfitters, PO Box 426, Cambridge, WI 53523-0426 / 608-764-8128 gunfitters@aol.com www.gunfitters.com

Gun-Ho Sports Cases, 110 E. 10th St., St. Paul, MN 55101 / 612-224-9491

Gunline Tools, 2950 Saturn St., "O", Brea, CA 92821 / 714-993-5100; FAX: 714-572-4128

Gunnerman Books, PO Box 217, Owosso, MI 48867 / 989-729-7018

Guns, 81 E. Streetsboro St., Hudson, OH 44236 / 330-650-4563 jcpevear@aol.com

Guns Antique & Modern DBA / Charles E. Duffy, Williams Lane, West Hurley, NY 12491 / 914-679-2997

Guns Div. of D.C. Engineering, Inc., 8633 Southfield Fwy., Detroit, MI 48228 / 313-271-7111; or 800-886-7623; FAX: 313-271-7112 guns@rifletech.com www.rifletech.com

GUNS Magazine, 591 Camino de la Reina, Suite 200, San Diego, CA 92108 / 619-297-5350; FAX: 619-297-5353

Gunsite Custom Shop, P.O. Box 451, Paulden, AZ 86334 / 520-636-4104; FAX: 520-636-1236

Gunsite Gunsmithy (See Gunsite Custom Shop)

Gunsite Training Center, P.O. Box 700, Paulden, AZ 86334 / 520-636-4565; FAX: 520-636-1236

Gunsmithing Ltd., 57 Unquowa Rd., Fairfield, CT 06430 / 203-254-0436; FAX: 203-254-1535

Gunsmithing, Inc., 30 West Buchanan St., Colorado Springs, CO 80907 / 719-632-3795; FAX: 719-632-3493

Gurney, F. R., Box 13, Sooke, BC V0S 1N0 CANADA / 604-642-5282; FAX: 604-642-7859

Gwinnell, Bryson J., PO Box 1307, Kilauea, HI 96754

H&B Forge Co., Rt. 2, Geisinger Rd., Shiloh, OH 44878 / 419-895-1856

H&P Publishing, 7174 Hoffman Rd., San Angelo, TX 76905 / 915-655-5953

H&R 1871, Inc., 60 Industrial Rowe, Gardner, MA 01440 / 978-632-9393; FAX: 978-632-2300

H&S Liner Service, 515 E. 8th, Odessa, TX 79761 / 915-332-1021

H. Krieghoff Gun Co., Boschstrasse 22, D-89079, Ulm, GERMANY / 731-401820; FAX: 731-4018270

H.K.S. Products, 7841 Founion Dr., Florence, KY 41042 / 606-342-7841; or 800-354-9814; FAX: 606-342-5865

H.P. White Laboratory, Inc., 3114 Scarboro Rd., Street, MD 21154 / 410-838-6550; FAX: 410-838-2802

Hafner World Wide, Inc., PO Box 1987, Lake City, FL 32055 / 904-755-6481; FAX: 904-755-6595 hafner@isgroupe.net

Hagn Rifles & Actions, Martin, PO Box 444, Cranbrook, BC V1C 4H9 CANADA / 604-489-4861

Hakko Co. Ltd., 1-13-12, Narimasu, Itabashiku Tokyo, JAPAN / 03-5997-7870/2; FAX: 81-3-5997-7840

Hale, Engraver, Peter, 800 E Canyon Rd., Spanish Fork, UT 84660 / 801-798-8215

Half Moon Rifle Shop, 490 Halfmoon Rd., Columbia Falls, MT 59912 / 406-892-4409

Hall Manufacturing, 142 CR 406, Clanton, AL 35045 / 205-755-4094

Hall Plastics, Inc., John, P.O. Box 1526, Alvin, TX 77512 / 713-489-8709

Hallberg, Fritz. See: CAMBOS OUTDOORSMAN

Hallowell & Co., PO Box 1445, Livingston, MT 59047 / 406-222-4770; FAX: 406-222-4792 morris@hallowellco.com; hallowellco.com

Hally Caller, 443 Wells Rd., Doylestown, PA 18901 / 215-345-6354

Hamilton, Alex B (See Ten-Ring Precision, Inc)

Hammans, Charles E., PO Box 788, 2022 McCracken, Stuttgart, AR 72160-0788 / 870-673-1388

Hammerli Ltd., Seonerstrasse 37, CH-5600, SWITZERLAND / 064-50 11 44; FAX: 064-51 38 27

Hammerli USA, 19296 Oak Grove Circle, Groveland, CA 95321 FAX: 209-962-5311

Hammets VLD Bullets, P.O. Box 479, Rayville, LA 71269 / 318-728-2019

Hammond Custom Guns Ltd., 619 S. Pandora, Gilbert, AZ 85234 / 602-892-3437

Hammonds Rifles, RD 4, Box 504, Red Lion, PA 17356 / 717-244-7879

HandCrafts Unltd (See Clements' Custom Leather), 1741 Dallas St, Aurora, CO 80010-2018 / 303-364-0403; FAX: 303-739-9824 gryphons@home.com kuntaoslcat.com

Handgun Press, PO Box 406, Glenview, IL 60025 / 847-657-6500; FAX: 847-724-8831 jschroed@inter-access.com

Hands Engraving, Barry Lee, 26192 E Shore Route, Bigfork, MT 59911 / 406-837-0035

Hank's Gun Shop, Box 370, 50 West 100 South, Monroe, UT 84754 / 801-527-4456

Hanned Precision (See Hanned Line, The)

Hansen & Co. (See Hansen Cartridge Co.), 244-246 Old Post Rd, Southport, CT 06490 / 203-259-6222; FAX: 203-254-3832

Hanson's Gun Center, Dick, 233 Everett Dr, Colorado Springs, CO 80911

Hanus Birdguns Bill, PO Box 533, Newport, OR 97365 / 541-265-7433; FAX: 541-265-7400

Hanusin, John, 3306 Commercial, Northbrook, IL 60062 / 708-564-2706

Hardin Specialty Dist., P.O. Box 338, Radcliff, KY 40159-0338 / 502-351-6649

Harford (See U.S. Importer-EMF Co. Inc.)

Harper's Custom Stocks, 928 Lombrano St., San Antonio, TX 78207 / 210-732-5780

Harrell's Precision, 5756 Hickory Dr., Salem, VA 24133 / 703-380-2683

Harrington & Richardson (See H&R 1871, Inc.)

Harris Engineering Inc., Dept GD54, Barlow, KY 42024 / 502-334-3633; FAX: 502-334-3000

Harris Enterprises, P.O. Box 105, Bly, OR 97622 / 503-353-2625

Harris Gunworks, 11240 N. Cave Creek Rd., Ste. 104, Phoenix, AZ 85020 / 602-582-9627; FAX: 602-582-5178

Harris Hand Engraving, Paul A., 113 Rusty Ln, Boerne, TX 78006-5746 / 512-391-5121

Harris Publications, 1115 Broadway, New York, NY 10010 / 212-807-7100; FAX: 212-627-4678

Harrison Bullets, 6437 E. Hobart St., Mesa, AZ 85205

Harry Lawson Co., 3328 N. Richey Blvd., Tucson, AZ 85716 / 520-326-1117

Hart & Son, Inc., Robert W., 401 Montgomery St, Nescopeck, PA 18635 / 717-752-3655; FAX: 717-752-1088

Hart Rifle Barrels,Inc., PO Box 182, 1690 Apulia Rd., Lafayette, NY 13084 / 315-677-9841; FAX: 315-677-9610 hartrb@aol.com hartbarrels.com

Hartford (See U.S. Importer-EMF Co. Inc.)

Hartmann & Weiss GmbH, Rahlstedter Bahnhofstr. 47, 22143, Hamburg, GERMANY / (40) 677 55 85; FAX: (40) 677 55 92

Harvey, Frank, 218 Nightfall, Terrace, NV 89015 / 702-558-6998

Harwood, Jack O., 1191 S. Pendlebury Lane, Blackfoot, ID 83221 / 208-785-5368

Hastings Barrels, 320 Court St., Clay Center, KS 67432 / 913-632-3169; FAX: 913-632-6554

Hatfield Gun, 224 N. 4th St., St. Joseph, MO 64501

Hawk Laboratories, Inc. (See Hawk, Inc.), 849 Hawks Bridge Rd, Salem, NJ 08079 / 609-299-2700; FAX: 609-299-2800

Hawk, Inc., 849 Hawks Bridge Rd., Salem, NJ 08079 / 609-299-2700; FAX: 609-299-2800

Hawken Shop, The (See Dayton Traister)

Haydel's Game Calls, Inc., 5018 Hazel Jones Rd., Bossier City, LA 71111 / 318-746-3586; FAX: 318-746-3711

Haydon Shooters Supply, Russ, 15018 Goodrich Dr NW, Gig Harbor, WA 98329-9738 / 253-857-7557; FAX: 253-857-7884

Heatbath Corp., P.O. Box 2978, Springfield, MA 01101 / 413-543-3381

Hecht, Hubert J, Waffen-Hecht, PO Box 2635, Fair Oaks, CA 95628 / 916-966-1020

Heckler & Koch GmbH, PO Box 1329, 78722 Oberndorf, Neckar, GERMANY / 49-7423179-0; FAX: 49-7423179-2406

Heckler & Koch, Inc., 21480 Pacific Blvd., Sterling, VA 20166-8900 / 703-450-1900; FAX: 703-450-8160 www.hecklerkoch-usa.com

Hege Jagd-u. Sporthandels GmbH, P.O. Box 101461, W-7770, Ueberlingen a. Boden, GERMANY

Heidenstrom Bullets, Urdngt 1, 3937 Heroya, NORWAY

Heilmann, Stephen, PO Box 657, Grass Valley, CA 95945 / 530-272-8758; FAX: 530-274-0285 sheilmann@jps.net metalwood.com

Heinie Specialty Products, 301 Oak St., Quincy, IL 62301-2500 / 217-228-9500; FAX: 217-228-9502 rheinie@heinie.com www.heinie.com

Helwan (See U.S. Importer-Interarms)

Henigson & Associates, Steve, PO Box 2726, Culver City, CA 90231 / 310-305-8288; FAX: 310-305-1905

Henriksen Tool Co., Inc., 8515 Wagner Creek Rd., Talent, OR 97540 / 541-535-2309; FAX: 541-535-2309

Henry Repeating Arms Co., 110 8th St., Brooklyn, NY 11215 / 718-499-5600

Hensley, Gunmaker, Darwin, PO Box 329, Brightwood, OR 97011 / 503-622-5411

Heppler, Keith. See: KEITH'S CUSTOM GUNSTOCKS

Hercules, Inc. (See Alliant Techsystems, Smokeless)

Heritage / VSP Gun Books, PO Box 887, McCall, ID 83638 / 208-634-4104; FAX: 208-634-3101

Heritage Firearms (See Heritage Mfg., Inc.)

Heritage Manufacturing, Inc., 4600 NW 135th St., Opa Locka, FL 33054 or 305-685-5966; FAX: 305-687-6721 infohmi@heritagemfg.com www.heritagemfg.com

Herrett's Stocks, Inc., P.O. Box 741, Twin Falls, ID 83303 / 208-733-1498

Hertel & Reuss, Werk fr Optik und Feinmechanik GmbH, Quellhofstrasse 67, 34 127, GERMANY / 0561-83006; FAX: 0561-893308

Herter's Manufacturing Inc., 111 E. Burnett St., P.O. Box 518, Beaver Dam, WI 53916-1811 / 414-887-1765; FAX: 414-887-8444

Hesco-Meprolight, 2139 Greenville Rd., LaGrange, GA 30241 / 706-884-7967; FAX: 706-882-4683

Hesse Arms, Robert Hesse, 1126 70th Street E., Inver Grove Heights, MN 55077-2416 / 651-455-5760; FAX: 612-455-5760

Hesse, Robert. See: HESSE ARMS

Heydenberk, Warren R., 1059 W. Sawmill Rd., Quakertown, PA 18951 / 215-538-2682

Hickman, Jaclyn, Box 1900, Glenrock, WY 82637

Hidalgo, Tony, 12701 SW 9th Pl., Davie, FL 33325 / 954-476-7645

High Bridge Arms, Inc, 3185 Mission St., San Francisco, CA 94110 / 415-282-8358

High North Products, Inc., PO Box 2, Antigo, WI 54409 / 715-627-2331; FAX: 715-623-5451

High Performance International, 5734 W. Florist Ave., Milwaukee, WI 53218 / 414-466-9040

High Precision, Bud Welsh, 80 New Road, E. Amherst, NY 14051 / 716-688-6344; FAX: 716-688-0425

High Tech Specialties, Inc., P.O. Box 839, 293 E Main St., Rear, Adamstown, PA 19501 / 717-484-0405; FAX: 717-484-0523 bansner@aol.com

Highline Machine Co., Randall Thompson, 654 Lela Place, Grand Junction, CO 81504 / 970-434-4971

Hi-Grade Imports, 8655 Monterey Rd., Gilroy, CA 95021 / 408-842-9301; FAX: 408-842-2374

Hill, Loring F., 304 Cedar Rd., Elkins Park, PA 19027

Hill Speed Leather, Ernie, 4507 N 195th Ave, Litchfield Park, AZ 85340 / 602-853-9222; FAX: 602-853-9235

Hinman Outfitters, Bob, 107 N Sanderson Ave, Bartonville, IL 61607-1839 / 309-691-8132

Hi-Performance Ammunition Company, 484 State Route 366, Apollo, PA 15613 / 412-327-8100

HIP-GRIP Barami Corp., P.O. Box 252224, West Bloomfield, MI 48325-2224 / 248-738-0462; FAX: 248-738-2542 hipgripja@aol.com www.hipgrip.com

Hi-Point Firearms/MKS Supply, 8611-A North Dixie Dr., Dayton, OH 45414 / 877-425-4867; FAX: 937-454-0503 www.hi-pointfirearms.com

Hiptmayer, Armurier, RR 112 750, P.O. Box 136, Eastman, PQ J0E 1P0 CANADA / 514-297-2492

Hiptmayer, Heidemarie, RR 112 750, P.O. Box 136, Eastman, PQ J0E 1P0 CANADA / 514-297-2492

Hiptmayer, Klaus, RR 112 750, P.O. Box 136, Eastman, PQ J0E 1P0 CANADA / 514-297-2492

Hirtenberger Aktiengesellschaft, Leobersdorferstrasse 31, A-2552, Hirtenberg, / 43(0)2256 81184; FAX: 43(0)2256 81807

HiTek International, 484 El Camino Real, Redwood City, CA 94063 / 415-363-1404; or 800-54-NIGHT; FAX: 415-363-1408

Hiti-Schuch, Atelier Wilma, A-8863 Predlitz, Pirming, Y1 AUSTRIA / 0353418278

HJS Arms, Inc., P.O. Box 3711, Brownsville, TX 78523-3711 / 800-453-2767; FAX: 210-542-2767

Hoag, James W., 8523 Canoga Ave., Suite C, Canoga Park, CA 91304 / 818-998-1510

Hobson Precision Mfg. Co., 210 Big Oak Ln, Brent, AL 35034 / 205-926-4662; FAX: 205-926-3193 cahobbob@dbtech.net

Hoch Custom Bullet Moulds (See Colorado Shooter's)

Hodgdon Powder Co., 6231 Robinson, Shawnee Mission, KS 66202 / 913-362-9455; FAX: 913-362-1307

Hodgman, Inc., 1750 Orchard Rd., Montgomery, IL 60538 / 708-897-7555; FAX: 708-897-7558

Hodgson, Richard, 9081 Tahoe Lane, Boulder, CO 80301

Hoehn Sales, Inc., 2045 Kohn Road, Wright City, MO 63390 / 636-745-8144; FAX: 636-745-8144 hoehnsal@usmo.com

Hoelscher, Virgil, 1804 S. Valley View Blvd., Las Vegas, NV 89102 / 310-631-8545

Hoenig & Rodman, 6521 Morton Dr., Boise, ID 83704 / 208-375-1116

Hofer Jagdwaffen, P., Buchsenmachermeister, Kirchgasse 24, A-9170 Ferlach, AUSTRIA / 43 4227 3683; FAX: 43 4227 368330 peterhofer@hoferwaffen.com www.hoferwaffen.com

Hoffman New Ideas, 821 Northmoor Rd., Lake Forest, IL 60045 / 312-234-4075

Hogue Grips, P.O. Box 1138, Paso Robles, CA 93447 / 800-438-4747; or 805-239-2553; FAX: 805-239-2553

Holland & Holland Ltd., 33 Bruton St., London, ENGLAND / 44-171-499-4411; FAX: 44-171-408-7962

Holland's Gunsmithing, P.O. Box 69, Powers, OR 97466 / 541-439-5155; FAX: 541-439-5155

Hollinger, Jon. See: ASPEN OUTFITTING CO.

Hollis Gun Shop, 917 Rex St., Carlsbad, NM 88220 / 505-885-3782

Hollywood Engineering, 10642 Arminta St., Sun Valley, CA 91352 / 818-842-8376; FAX: 818-504-4168

Homak, 5151 W. 73rd St., Chicago, IL 60638-6613 / 312-523-3100; FAX: 312-523-9455

Home Shop Machinist The Village Press Publications, PO Box 1810, Traverse City, MI 49685 / 800-447-7367; FAX: 616-946-3289

Hondo Ind., 510 S. 52nd St., I04, Tempe, AZ 85281

Hoppe's Div. Penguin Industries, Inc., Airport Industrial Mall, Coatesville, PA 19320 / 610-384-6000

Horizons Unlimited, P.O. Box 426, Warm Springs, GA 31830 / 706-655-3603; FAX: 706-655-3603

Hornady Mfg. Co., P.O. Box 1848, Grand Island, NE 68802 / 800-338-3220; or 308-382-1390; FAX: 308-382-5761

Horseshoe Leather Products, Andy Arratoonian, The Cottage Sharow, Ripon, ENGLAND / 44-1765-605858 andy@horseshoe.co.uk www.horseshoe.co.uk

House of Muskets, Inc., The, PO Box 4640, Pagosa Springs, CO 81157 / 970-731-2295

Houtz & Barwick, P.O. Box 435, W. Church St., Elizabeth City, NC 27909 / 800-775-0337; or 919-335-4191; FAX: 919-335-1152

Howa Machinery, Ltd., Sukaguchi, Shinkawa-cho Nishikasugai-gun, Aichi 452, JAPAN

Howell Machine, 815 1/2 D St., Lewiston, ID 83501 / 208-743-7418

H-S Precision, Inc., 1301 Turbine Dr., Rapid City, SD 57701 / 605-341-3006; FAX: 605-342-8964

HT Bullets, 244 Belleville Rd., New Bedford, MA 02745 / 508-999-3338

Hubert J. Hecht Waffen-Hecht, P.O. Box 2635, Fair Oaks, CA 95628 / 916-966-1020

Huebner, Corey O., PO Box 564, Frenchtown, MT 59834 / 406-721-7168

Huey Gun Cases, PO Box 22456, Kansas City, MO 64113 / 816-444-1637; FAX: 816-444-1637 hueycases@aol.com www.hueycases.com

Hugger Hooks Co., 3900 Easley Way, Golden, CO 80403 / 303-279-0600

Hughes, Steven Dodd, PO Box 545, Livingston, MT 59047 / 406-222-9377; FAX: 406-222-9377

Hume, Don, P.O. Box 351, Miami, OK 74355 / 800-331-2686; FAX: 918-542-4340

Hungry Horse Books, 4605 Hwy. 93 South, Whitefish, MT 59937 / 406-862-7997

Hunkeler, A (See Buckskin Machine Works, 3235 S 358th St., Auburn, WA 98001 / 206-927-5412

Hunter Co., Inc., 3300 W. 71st Ave., Westminster, CO 80030 / 303-427-4626; FAX: 303-428-3980

Hunterjohn, PO Box 771457, St. Louis, MO 63177 / 314-531-7250

Hunter's Specialties Inc., 6000 Huntington Ct. NE, Cedar Rapids, IA 52402-1268 / 319-395-0321; FAX: 319-395-0326

Hunters Supply, Inc., PO Box 313, Tioga, TX 76271 / 940-437-2458; FAX: 940-437-2228 hunterssupply@hotmail.com www.hunterssupply.net

Hunting Classics Ltd., P.O. Box 2089, Gastonia, NC 28053 / 704-867-1307; FAX: 704-867-0491

Huntington Die Specialties, 601 Oro Dam Blvd., Oroville, CA 95965 / 530-534-1210; FAX: 530-534-1212

Hutton Rifle Ranch, P.O. Box 45236, Boise, ID 83711 / 208-345-8781

Hydrosorbent Products, PO Box 437, Ashley Falls, MA 01222 / 800-448-7903; FAX: 413-229-8743 orders@dehumidify.com; www.dehumidify.com

━━━ I ━━━

I.A.B. (See U.S. Importer-Taylor's & Co. Inc.)

I.D.S.A. Books, 1324 Stratford Drive, Piqua, OH 45356 / 937-773-4203; FAX: 937-778-1922

I.N.C. Inc (See Kickeez I.N.C., Inc.)

I.S.S., P.O. Box 185234, Ft. Worth, TX 76181 / 817-595-2090

I.S.W., 106 E. Cairo Dr., Tempe, AZ 85282

IAR Inc., 33171 Camino Capistrano, San Juan Capistrano, CA 92675 / 949-443-3642; FAX: 949-443-3647 sales@iar-arms.com iar-arms.com

Ide, K. See: STURGEON VALLEY SPORTERS

IGA (See U.S. Importer-Stoeger Industries)

Ignacio Ugartechea S.A., Chonta 26, Eibar, 20600 SPAIN / 43-121257; FAX: 43-121669

Illinois Lead Shop, 7742 W. 61st Place, Summit, IL 60501

Image Ind. Inc., 382 Balm Court, Wood Dale, IL 60191 / 630-766-2402; FAX: 630-766-7373

Impact Case Co., P.O. Box 9912, Spokane, WA 99209-0912 / 800-262-3322; or 509-467-3303; FAX: 509-326-5436 info@kkair.com www.kkair.com

Imperial (See E-Z-Way Systems), PO Box 4310, Newark, OH 43058-4310 / 614-345-6645; FAX: 614-345-6600 ezway@infinet.com www.jcunald.com

Imperial Magnum Corp., P.O. Box 249, Oroville, WA 98844 / 604-495-3131; FAX: 604-495-2816

Imperial Miniature Armory, 10547 S. Post Oak Road, Houston, TX 77035-3305 / 713-729-8428; FAX: 713-729-2274 miniguns@aol.com www.1800miniature.com

Imperial Schrade Corp., 7 Schrade Ct., Box 7000, Ellenville, NY 12428 / 914-647-7601; FAX: 914-647-8701 csc@schradeknives.com www.schradeknives.com

Import Sports Inc., 1750 Brielle Ave., Unit B-1, Wanamassa, NJ 07712 / 732-493-0302; FAX: 732-493-0301

IMR Powder Co., 1080 Military Turnpike, Suite 2, Plattsburgh, NY 12901 / 518-563-2253; FAX: 518-563-6916

IMX, LLC, 2169 Greenville Rd., La Grange, GA 30241 / 706-812-9841; or 877-519-3473; FAX: 706-882-9050 mpatillo@crossfirellc.com

Info-Arm, P.O. Box 1262, Champlain, NY 12919 / 514-955-0355; FAX: 514-955-0357

Ingle, Ralph W., Engraver, 112 Manchester Ct., Centerville, GA 31028 / 478-953-5824 riengraver@aol.com www.fega.com

Innovative Weaponry Inc., 2513 E. Loop 820 N., Fort Worth, TX 76118 / 817-284-0099; or 800-334-3573

INTEC International, Inc., P.O. Box 5708, Scottsdale, AZ 85261 / 602-483-1708

Inter Ordnance of America LP, 3305 Westwood Industrial Dr, Monroe, NC 28110-5204 / 704-821-8337; FAX: 704-821-8523

Interarms / Howa, PO Box 208, Ten Prince St, Alexandria, VA 22313 / 703-548-1400; FAX: 703-549-7826

Intercontinental Distributors, Ltd., PO Box 815, Beulah, ND 58523

Intrac Arms International, 5005 Chapman Hwy., Knoxville, TN 37920

Ion Industries, Inc, 3508 E Allerton Ave, Cudahy, WI 53110 / 414-486-2007; FAX: 414-486-2017

Iosso Products, 1485 Lively Blvd., Elk Grove Village, IL 60007 / 847-437-8400; FAX: 847-437-8478

Iron Bench, 12619 Bailey Rd., Redding, CA 96003 / 916-241-4623

Ironside International Publishers, Inc., 3000 S. Eaos St., Arlington, VA 22202 / 703-684-6111; FAX: 703-683-5486

Ironsighter Co., PO Box 85070, Westland, MI 48185 / 734-326-8731; FAX: 734-326-3378 www.ironsighter.com

Irwin, Campbell H., 140 Hartland Blvd., East Hartland, CT 06027 / 203-653-3901

Island Pond Gun Shop, Cross St., Island Pond, VT 05846 / 802-723-4546

Israel Arms International, Inc., 1085 Gessner Rd., Ste. F, Houston, TX 77055 / 713-789-0745; FAX: 713-914-9515 iaipro@wt.net www.israelarms.com

Ithaca Classic Doubles, Stephen Lamboy, No. 5 Railroad St., Victor, NY 14564 / 716-924-2710; FAX: 716-924-2737 ithacadoubles.com

Ithaca Gun Company LLC, 901 Rt. 34 B, King Ferry, NY 13081 / 315-364-7171; FAX: 315-364-5134 info@ithacagun.com

Ivanoff, Thomas G (See Tom's Gun Repair)

━━━ J ━━━

J J Roberts Firearm Engraver, 7808 Lake Dr, Manassas, VA 20111 / 703-330-0448; FAX: 703-264-8600 james_.roberts@angelfire.com www.angelfire.com/va2/engraver

J&D Components, 75 East 350 North, Orem, UT 84057-4719 / 801-225-7007

J&J Products, Inc., 9240 Whitmore, El Monte, CA 91731 / 818-571-5228; FAX: 800-927-8361

J&J Sales, 1501 21st Ave. S., Great Falls, MT 59405 / 406-453-7549

J&L Superior Bullets (See Huntington Die Special)

J&R Engineering, P.O. Box 77, 200 Lyons Hill Rd., Athol, MA 01331 / 508-249-9241

J&R Enterprises, 4550 Scotts Valley Rd., Lakeport, CA 95453

J&S Heat Treat, 803 S. 16th St., Blue Springs, MO 64015 / 816-229-2149; FAX: 816-228-1135

J. Dewey Mfg. Co., Inc., PO Box 2014, Southbury, CT 06488 / 203-264-3064; FAX: 203-262-6907 deweyrods@worldnet.att.net www.deweyrods.com

J. Korzinek Riflesmith, RD 2, Box 73D, Canton, PA 17724 / 717-673-8512

J.A. Blades, Inc. (See Christopher Firearms Co.)

J.A. Henckels Zwillingswerk Inc., 9 Skyline Dr., Hawthorne, NY 10532 / 914-592-7370

J.G. Dapkus Co., Inc., Commerce Circle, P.O. Box 293, Durham, CT 06422

J.G. Anschutz GmbH & Co. KG, Daimlerstr. 12, D-89079 Ulm, Ulm, GERMANY / 49 731 40120; FAX: 49 731 4012700 JGA-info@anschuetz-sport.com anschuetz-sport.com

J.I.T. Ltd., P.O. Box 230, Freedom, WY 83120 / 708-494-0937

J.J. Roberts / Engraver, 7808 Lake Dr., Manassas, VA 20111 / 703-330-0448 jjrengraver@aol.com www.angelfire.com/va2/engraver

J.P. Enterprises Inc., P.O. Box 378, Hugo, MN 55110 / 612-486-9064; FAX: 612-482-0970

J.P. Gunstocks, Inc., 4508 San Miguel Ave., North Las Vegas, NV 89030 / 702-645-0718

J.R. Williams Bullet Co., 2008 Tucker Rd., Perry, GA 31069 / 912-987-0274

J.W. Morrison Custom Rifles, 4015 W. Sharon, Phoenix, AZ 85029 / 602-978-3754

J/B Adventures & Safaris Inc., 2275 E. Arapahoe Rd., Ste. 109, Littleton, CO 80122-1521 / 303-771-0977

Jack A. Rosenberg & Sons, 12229 Cox Ln., Dallas, TX 75234 / 214-241-6302

Jack Dever Co., 8520 NW 90th St., Oklahoma City, OK 73132 / 405-721-6393 jbdever1@home.com

Jack First, Inc., 1201 Turbine Dr., Rapid City, SD 57701 / 605-343-9544; FAX: 605-343-9420

Jack Jonas Appraisals & Taki, 13952 E. Marina Dr., #604, Aurora, CO 80014

Jackalope Gun Shop, 1048 S. 5th St., Douglas, WY 82633 / 307-358-3441

Jaffin, Harry. See: BRIDGEMAN PRODUCTS

Jagdwaffen, P. See: BUCHSENMACHERMEISTER

James Calhoon Mfg., Shambo Rte. 304, Havre, MT 59501 / 406-395-4079 www.jamescalhoon.com

James Calhoon Varmint Bullets, Shambo Rt., 304, Havre, MT 59501 / 406-395-4079 www.jamescalhoon.com

James Churchill Glove Co., PO Box 298, Centralia, WA 98531 / 360-736-2816; FAX: 360-330-0151 churchillglove@localaccess.com

James Wayne Firearms for Collectors and Investors, 2608 N. Laurent, Victoria, TX 77901 / 361-578-1258; FAX: 361-578-3559

Jamison's Forge Works, 4527 Rd. 6.5 NE, Moses Lake, WA 98837 / 509-762-2659

Jantz Supply, 309 West Main Dept HD, Davis, OK 73030-0584 / 580-369-2316; FAX: 580-369-3082 jantz@brightok.net www.knifemaking.com

Jarrett Rifles, Inc., 383 Brown Rd., Jackson, SC 29831 / 803-471-3616 www.jarrettrifles.com

Jarvis, Inc., 1123 Cherry Orchard Lane, Hamilton, MT 59840 / 406-961-4392

JAS, Inc., P.O. Box 0, Rosemount, MN 55068 / 612-890-7631

Javelina Lube Products, PO Box 337, San Bernardino, CA 92402 / 714-882-5847; FAX: 714-434-6937

Jay McCament Custom Gunmaker, Jay McCament, 1730-134th St. Ct. S., Tacoma, WA 98444 / 253-531-8832

JB Custom, P.O. Box 6912, Leawood, KS 66206 / 913-381-2329

Jeff W. Flannery Engraving Co., 11034 Riddles Run Rd., Union, KY 41091 / 606-384-3127 engraving@fuse.net http://home.fuse.net/engraving/

Jeffredo Gunsight, P.O. Box 669, San Marcos, CA 92079 / 760-728-2695

Jena Eur, PO Box 319, Dunmore, PA 18512

Jenco Sales, Inc., PO Box 1000, Manchaca, TX 78652 / 800-531-5301; FAX: 800-266-2373

Jenkins Recoil Pads, Inc., 5438 E. Frontage Ln., Olney, IL 62450 / 618-395-3416

Jensen Bullets, RR 1 Box 187, Arco, ID 83213 / 208-785-5590

Jensen's Custom Ammunition, 5146 E. Pima, Tucson, AZ 85712 / 602-325-3346; FAX: 602-322-5704

Jensen's Firearms Academy, 1280 W. Prince, Tucson, AZ 85705 / 602-293-8516

Jericho Tool & Die Co., Inc., 2917 St. Hwy. 7, Bainbridge, NY 13733 / 607-563-8222; FAX: 607-563-8560 jerichotool.com www.jerichotool.com

Jerry Phillips Optics, P.O. Box L632, Langhorne, PA 19047 / 215-757-5037; FAX: 215-757-7097

Jesse W. Smith Saddlery, 0499 County Road J, Pritchett, CO 81064 / 509-325-0622

Jester Bullets, Rt. 1 Box 27, Orienta, OK 73737

Jewell Triggers, Inc., 3620 Hwy. 123, San Marcos, TX 78666 / 512-353-2999; FAX: 512-392-0543

J-Gar Co., 183 Turnpike Rd., Dept. 3, Petersham, MA 01366-9604

JGS Precision Tool Mfg., 100 Main Sumner, Coos Bay, OR 97420 / 541-267-4331; FAX: 541-267-5996

Jim Chambers Flintlocks Ltd., Rt. 1, Box 513-A, Candler, NC 28715 / 704-667-8361

Jim Garthwaite Pistolsmith, Inc., Rt. 2 Box 310, Watsontown, PA 17777 / 717-538-1566

Jim Blair Engraving, PO Box 64, Glenrock, WY 82637 / 307-436-8115

Jim Noble Co., 1305 Columbia St, Vancouver, WA 98660 / 360-695-1309; FAX: 360-695-6835 jnobleco@aol.com

Jim Norman Custom Gunstocks, 14281 Cane Rd., Valley Center, CA 92082 / 619-749-6252

Jim's Gun Shop (See Spradlin's)

Jim's Precision, Jim Ketchum, 1725 Moclips Dr., Petaluma, CA 94952 / 707-762-3014

JLK Bullets, 414 Turner Rd., Dover, AR 72837 / 501-331-4194

Johanssons Vapentillbehor, Bert, S-430 20, Veddige, SWEDEN

John Hall Plastics, Inc., P.O. Box 1526, Alvin, TX 77512 / 713-489-8709

John J. Adams & Son Engravers, 7040 VT Rt 113, Vershire, VT 05079 / 802-685-0019

John Masen Co. Inc., 1305 Jelmak, Grand Prairie, TX 75050 / 817-430-8732; FAX: 817-430-1715

John Norrell Arms, 2608 Grist Mill Rd, Little Rock, AR 72207 / 501-225-7864

John Partridge Sales Ltd., Trent Meadows Rugeley, Staffordshire, WS15 2HS ENGLAND

John Rigby & Co., 500 Linne Rd. Ste. D, Paso Robles, CA 93446 / 805-227-4236; FAX: 805-227-4723 jribgy@calinet www.johnrigbyandco.com

Johnny Stewart Game Calls, Inc., P.O. Box 7954, 5100 Fort Ave., Waco, TX 76714 / 817-772-3261; FAX: 817-772-3670

John's Custom Leather, 523 S. Liberty St., Blairsville, PA 15717 / 724-459-6802; FAX: 724-459-5996

Johnson Wood Products, 34897 Crystal Road, Strawberry Point, IA 52076 / 563-933-6504 johnsonwoodproducts@yahoo.com

Johnston Bros. (See C&T Corp. TA Johnson Brothers)

Jonad Corp., 2091 Lakeland Ave., Lakewood, OH 44107 / 216-226-3161

Jonathan Arthur Ciener, Inc., 8700 Commerce St., Cape Canaveral, FL 32920 / 321-868-2200; FAX: 321-868-2201

Jones Co., Dale, 680 Hoffman Draw, Kila, MT 59920 / 406-755-4684

Jones Custom Products, Neil A., 17217 Brookhouser Rd., Saegertown, PA 16433 / 814-763-2769; FAX: 814-763-4228

Jones, J. See: SSK INDUSTRIES

Jones Moulds, Paul, 4901 Telegraph Rd, Los Angeles, CA 90022 / 213-262-1510

JP Sales, Box 307, Anderson, TX 77830

JRP Custom Bullets, RR2 2233 Carlton Rd., Whitehall, NY 12887 / 518-282-0084 or 802-438-5548

JSL Ltd (See U.S. Importer-Specialty Shooters)

Juenke, Vern, 25 Bitterbush Rd., Reno, NV 89523 / 702-345-0225

Jungkind, Reeves C., 5001 Buckskin Pass, Austin, TX 78745-2841 / 512-442-1094

Jurras, L. See: L E JURRAS & ASSOC.

Justin Phillippi Custom Bullets, P.O. Box 773, Ligonier, PA 15658 / 412-238-9671

K

K&M Industries, Inc., Box 66, 510 S. Main, Troy, ID 83871 / 208-835-2281; FAX: 208-835-5211

K&M Services, 5430 Salmon Run Rd., Dover, PA 17315 / 717-292-3175; FAX: 717-292-3175

K. Eversull Co., Inc., 1 Tracemont, Boyce, LA 71409 / 318-793-8728; FAX: 318-793-5483 bestguns@aol.com

K.B.I. Inc., PO Box 6625, Harrisburg, PA 17112 / 717-540-8518; FAX: 717-540-8567

K.K. Arms Co., Star Route Box 671, Kerrville, TX 78028 / 210-257-4718; FAX: 210-257-4891

K.L. Null Holsters Ltd., 161 School St. NW, Hill City Station, Resaca, GA 30735 / 706-625-5643; FAX: 706-625-9392 ken@klnullholsters.com www.klnullholsters.com

Ka Pu Kapili, P.O. Box 745, Honokaa, HI 96727 / 808-776-1644; FAX: 808-776-1731

KA-BAR Knives, 1125 E. State St., Olean, NY 14760 / 800-282-0130; FAX: 716-373-6245 info@ka-bar.com www.ka-bar.com

Kahles A Swarovski Company, 2 Slater Rd., Cranston, RI 02920 / 401-946-2220; FAX: 401-946-2587

Kahr Arms, PO Box 220, 630 Route 303, Blauvelt, NY 10913 / 845-353-7770; FAX: 845-353-7833 www.kahr.com

Kailua Custom Guns Inc., 51 N. Dean Street, Coquille, OR 97423 / 541-396-5413 kailuacustom@aol.com www.kailuacustom.com

Kalispel Case Line, P.O. Box 267, Cusick, WA 99119 / 509-445-1121

Kamik Outdoor Footwear, 554 Montee de liesse, Montreal, PQ H4T 1P1 CANADA / 514-341-3950; FAX: 514-341-1861

Kamyk Engraving Co., Steve, 9 Grandview Dr, Westfield, MA 01085-1810 / 413-568-0457

Kane, Edward, P.O. Box 385, Ukiah, CA 95482 / 707-462-2937

Kane Products, Inc., 5572 Brecksville Rd., Cleveland, OH 44131 / 216-524-9962

Kapro Mfg.Co. Inc. (See R.E.I.)

Kasenit Co., Inc., 13 Park Ave., Highland Mills, NY 10930 / 914-928-9595; FAX: 914-928-7292

Kaswer Custom, Inc., 13 Surrey Drive, Brookfield, CT 06804 / 203-775-0564; FAX: 203-775-6872

KDF, Inc., 2485 Hwy. 46 N., Seguin, TX 78155 / 830-379-8141; FAX: 830-379-5420

KeeCo Impressions, Inc., 346 Wood Ave., North Brunswick, NJ 08902 / 800-468-0546

Keeler, R. H., 817 "N" St., Port Angeles, WA 98362 / 206-457-4702

Kehr, Roger, 2131 Agate Ct. SE, Lacy, WA 98503 / 360-491-0691

Keith's Bullets, 942 Twisted Oak, Algonquin, IL 60102 / 708-658-3520

Keith's Custom Gunstocks, Keith M. Heppler, 540 Banyan Circle, Walnut Creek, CA 94598 / 925-934-3509; FAX: 925-934-3143 kmheppler@hotmail.com

Kelbly, Inc., 7222 Dalton Fox Lake Rd., North Lawrence, OH 44666 / 216-683-4674; FAX: 216-683-7349

Kelley's, P.O. Box 125, Woburn, MA 01801-0125 / 800-879-7273; FAX: 781-272-7077 kels@star.net www.kelsmilitary.com

Kellogg's Professional Products, 325 Pearl St., Sandusky, OH 44870 / 419-625-6551; FAX: 419-625-6167

Kelly, Lance, 1723 Willow Oak Dr., Edgewater, FL 32132 / 904-423-4933

Kel-Tec CNC Industries, Inc., PO Box 236009, Cocoa, FL 32923 / 407-631-0068; FAX: 407-631-1169

Kemen America, 2550 Hwy. 23, Wrenshall, MN 55797 / 218-384-3670 patrickl@midwestshootingschool.com midwestshootingschool.com

Ken Eyster Heritage Gunsmiths, Inc., 6441 Bishop Rd., Centerburg, OH 43011 / 740-625-6131; FAX: 740-625-7811

Ken Starnes Gunmaker, 15940 SW Holly Hill Rd, Hillsboro, OR 97123-9033 / 503-628-0705; FAX: 503-628-6005

Keng's Firearms Specialty, Inc. / US Tactical Systems, 875 Wharton Dr., P.O. Box 44405, Atlanta, GA 30336-1405 / 404-691-7611; FAX: 404-505-8445

Kennebec Journal, 274 Western Ave., Augusta, ME 04330 / 207-622-6288

Kennedy Firearms, 10 N. Market St., Muncy, PA 17756 / 717-546-6695

Kenneth W. Warren Engraver, PO Box 2842, Wenatchee, WA 98807 / 509-663-6123; FAX: 509-665-6123

KenPatable Ent., Inc., PO Box 19422, Louisville, KY 40259 / 502-239-5447

Ken's Gun Specialties, Rt. 1, Box 147, Lakeview, AR 72642 / 501-431-5606

Ken's Kustom Kartridges, 331 Jacobs Rd., Hubbard, OH 44425 / 216-534-4595

Kent Cartridge America, Inc, PO Box 849, 1000 Zigor Rd, Kearneysville, WV 25430

Kent Cartridge Mfg. Co. Ltd., Unit 16 Branbridges Industrial Esta, Tonbridge, Kent, ENGLAND / 622-872255; FAX: 622-872645

Keowee Game Calls, 608 Hwy. 25 North, Travelers Rest, SC 29690 / 864-834-7204; FAX: 864-834-7831

Kershaw Knives, 25300 SW Parkway Ave., Wilsonville, OR 97070 / 503-682-1966; or 800-325-2891; FAX: 503-682-7168

Kesselring Gun Shop, 4024 Old Hwy. 99N, Burlington, WA 98233 / 360-724-3113; FAX: 360-724-7003 info@kesselrings.com www.kesselrings.com

Ketchum, Jim (See Jim's Precision)

Kickeez I.N.C., Inc., 301 Industrial Dr, Carl Junction, MO 64834-8806 / 419-649-2100; FAX: 417-649-2200 kickey@ipa.net

Kilham & Co., Main St., P.O. Box 37, Lyme, NH 03768 / 603-795-4112

Kim Ahrends Custom Firearms, Inc., Box 203, Clarion, IA 50525 / 515-532-3449; FAX: 515-532-3926

Kimar (See U.S. Importer-IAR,Inc)

Kimber of America, Inc., 1 Lawton St., Yonkers, NY 10705 / 800-880-2418; FAX: 914-964-9340

King & Co., PO Box 1242, Bloomington, IL 61702 / 309-473-2161

King's Gun Works, 1837 W. Glenoaks Blvd., Glendale, CA 91201 / 818-956-6010; FAX: 818-548-8606

Kingyon, Paul L. (See Custom Calls)

Kirkpatrick Leather Co., PO Box 677, Laredo, TX 78040 / 956-723-6631; FAX: 956-725-0672 mike@kirkpatrickleather.com www.kirkpatrickleather.com

KK Air International (See Impact Case Co.)

KLA Enterprises, P.O. Box 2028, Eaton Park, FL 33840 / 941-682-2829; FAX: 941-682-2829

Kleen-Bore,Inc., 16 Industrial Pkwy., Easthampton, MA 01027 / 413-527-0300; FAX: 413-527-2522 info@kleen-bore.com; www.kleen-bore.com

Klein Custom Guns, Don, 433 Murray Park Dr, Ripon, WI 54971 / 920-748-2931 daklein@charter.net

Kleinendorst, K. W., RR 1, Box 1500, Hop Bottom, PA 18824 / 717-289-4687

Klingler Woodcarving, P.O. Box 141, Thistle Hill, Cabot, VT 05647 / 802-426-3811

Knifeware, Inc., P.O. Box 3, Greenville, WV 24945 / 304-832-6878

Knight & Hale Game Calls, Box 468, Industrial Park, Cadiz, KY 42211 / 502-924-1755; FAX: 502-924-1763

Knight Rifles, 21852 hwy j46, P.O. Box 130, Centerville, IA 52544 / 515-856-2626; FAX: 515-856-2628

Knight Rifles (See Modern Muzzle Loading, Inc.)

Knight's Mfg. Co., 7750 Ninth St. SW, Vero Beach, FL 32968 / 561-562-5697; FAX: 561-569-2955

Knippel, Richard, 500 Gayle Ave Apt 213, Modesto, CA 95350-4241 / 209-869-1469

Knock on Wood Antiques, 355 Post Rd., Darien, CT 06820 / 203-655-9031

Knoell, Doug, 9737 McCardle Way, Santee, CA 92071 / 619-449-5189

Knopp, Gary. See: SUPER 6 LLC

Koevenig's Engraving Service, Box 55 Rabbit Gulch, Hill City, SD 57745 / 605-574-2239

KOGOT, 410 College, Trinidad, CO 81082 / 719-846-9406; FAX: 719-846-9406

Kokolus, Michael M. (See Custom Riflestocks)

Kolar, 1925 Roosevelt Ave, Racine, WI 53406 / 414-554-0800; FAX: 414-554-9093

Kolpin Mfg., Inc., P.O. Box 107, 205 Depot St., Fox Lake, WI 53933 / 414-928-3118; FAX: 414-928-3687

Korth, Robert-Bosch-Str. 4, P.O. Box 1320, 23909 Ratzeburg, GERMANY / 451-4991497; FAX: 451-4993230

Korth USA, 437R Chandler St., Tewksbury, MA 01876 / 978-851-8656 www.korthusa.com

Korzinek Riflesmith, J., RD 2 Box 73D, Canton, PA 17724 / 717-673-8512

Koval Knives, 5819 Zarley St., Suite A, New Albany, OH 43054 / 614-855-0777; FAX: 614-855-0945

Kowa Optimed, Inc., 20001 S. Vermont Ave., Torrance, CA 90502 / 310-327-1913; FAX: 310-327-4177

Kramer Designs, P.O. Box 129, Clancy, MT 59634 / 406-933-8658; FAX: 406-933-8658

Kramer Handgun Leather, P.O. Box 112154, Tacoma, WA 98411 / 206-564-6652; FAX: 206-564-1214

Krause Publications, Inc., 700 E. State St., Iola, WI 54990 / 715-445-2214; FAX: 715-445-4087

Krico Deutschland GmbH, Nurnbergerstrasse 6, D-90602, Pyrbaum, GERMANY / 09180-2780; FAX: 09180-2661

Krieger Barrels, Inc., N114 W18697 Clinton Dr., Germantown, WI 53022 / 414-255-9593; FAX: 414-255-9586

Krieghoff Gun Co., H., Boschstrasse 22, D-89079 Elm, GERMANY or 731-4018270

Krieghoff International,Inc., 7528 Easton Rd., Ottsville, PA 18942 / 610-847-5173; FAX: 610-847-8691

KSN Industries Ltd (See U.S. Importer-Israel Arms)

Kukowski, Ed. See: ED'S GUN HOUSE

Kulis Freeze Dry Taxidermy, 725 Broadway Ave., Bedford, OH 44146 / 216-232-8352; FAX: 216-232-7305 jkulis@kastaway.com www.kastaway.com

KVH Industries, Inc., 110 Enterprise Center, Middletown, RI 02842 / 401-847-3327; FAX: 401-849-0045

Kwik-Site Co., 5555 Treadwell St., Wayne, MI 48184 / 734-326-1500; FAX: 734-326-4120 kwiksiteco@aol.com

---

L

L E Jurras & Assoc., L. E. Jurras, PO Box 680, Washington, IN 47501 / 812-254-6170; FAX: 812-254-6170 jurasgun@rtcc.net

L&R Lock Co., 1137 Pocalla Rd., Sumter, SC 29150 / 803-775-6127; FAX: 803-775-5171

L&S Technologies Inc (See Aimtech Mount Systems)

L. Bengtson Arms Co., 6345-B E. Akron St., Mesa, AZ 85205 / 602-981-6375

L.A.R. Mfg., Inc., 4133 W. Farm Rd., West Jordan, UT 84088 / 801-280-3505; FAX: 801-280-1972

L.B.T., Judy Smith, HCR 62, Box 145, Moyie Springs, ID 83845 / 208-267-3588

L.E. Wilson, Inc., Box 324, 404 Pioneer Ave., Cashmere, WA 98815 / 509-782-1328; FAX: 509-782-7200

L.L. Bean, Inc., Freeport, ME 04032 / 207-865-4761; FAX: 207-552-2802

L.P.A. Snc, Via Alfieri 26, Gardone V.T., Brescia, ITALY / 30-891-14-81; FAX: 30-891-09-51

L.R. Clift Mfg., 3821 Hammonton Rd., Marysville, CA 95901 / 916-755-3390; FAX: 916-755-3393

L.S. Starrett Co., 121 Crescent St., Athol, MA 01331 / 617-249-3551

L.W. Seecamp Co., Inc., PO Box 255, New Haven, CT 06502 / 203-877-3429; FAX: 203-877-3429 seecamp@optonline.net

La Clinique du .45, 1432 Rougemont, Chambly,, PQ J3L 2L8 CANADA / 514-658-1144

Labanu, Inc., 2201-F Fifth Ave., Ronkonkoma, NY 11779 / 516-467-6197; FAX: 516-981-4112

LaBoone, Pat. See: THE MIDWEST SHOOTING SCHOOL

LaBounty Precision Reboring, Inc, 7968 Silver Lake Rd., PO Box 186, Maple Falls, WA 98266 / 360-599-2047; FAX: 360-599-3018

LaCrosse Footwear, Inc., P.O. Box 1328, La Crosse, WI 54602 / 608-782-3020; or 800-323-2668; FAX: 800-658-9444

LaFrance Specialties, P.O. Box 87933, San Diego, CA 92138-7933 / 619-293-3373; FAX: 619-293-7087

Lake Center Marina, PO Box 670, St. Charles, MO 63302 / 314-946-7500

Lakefield Arms Ltd (See Savage Arms Inc.)

Lakewood Products LLC, 275 June St., Berlin, WI 54923 / 800-872-8458; FAX: 920-361-7719 lakewood@dotnet.com www.lakewoodproducts.com

Lamboy, Stephen. See: ITHACA CLASSIC DOUBLES

Lampert, Ron, Rt. 1, 44857 Schoolcraft Trl., Guthrie, MN 56461 / 218-854-7345

Lamson & Goodnow Mfg. Co., 45 Conway St., Shelburne Falls, MA 03170 / 413-625-6564; or 800-872-6564; FAX: 413-625-9816 www.lamsonsharp.com

Langenberg Hat Co., P.O. Box 1860, Washington, MO 63090 / 800-428-1860; FAX: 314-239-3151

Lansky Levine, Arthur. See: LANSKY SHARPENERS

Lansky Sharpeners, Arthur Lansky Levine, PO Box 50830, Las Vegas, NV 89016 / 702-361-7511; FAX: 702-896-9511

LaPrade, PO Box 250, Ewing, VA 24248 / 423-733-2615

Lapua Ltd., P.O. Box 5, Lapua, FINLAND / 6-310111; FAX: 6-4388991

LaRocca Gun Works, 51 Union Place, Worcester, MA 01608 / 508-754-2887; FAX: 508-754-2887

Larry Lyons Gunworks, 110 Hamilton St., Dowagiac, MI 49047 / 616-782-9478

Laser Devices, Inc., 2 Harris Ct. A-4, Monterey, CA 93940 / 408-373-0701; FAX: 408-373-0903

Laseraim Technologies, Inc., P.O. Box 3548, Little Rock, AR 72203 / 501-375-2227

Laserlyte, 2201 Amapola Ct., Torrance, CA 90501

LaserMax, Inc., 3495 Winton Place, Bldg. B, Rochester, NY 14623-2807 / 800-527-3703; FAX: 716-272-5427

Lassen Community College, Gunsmithing Dept., P.O. Box 3000, Hwy. 139, Susanville, CA 96130 / 916-251-8800; FAX: 916-251-8838

Lathrop's, Inc., Inc., 5146 E. Pima, Tucson, AZ 85712 / 520-881-0266; or 800-875-4867; FAX: 520-322-5704

Laughridge, William R (See Cylinder & Slide Inc)

Laurel Mountain Forge, P.O. Box 52, Crown Point, IN 46308 / 219-548-2950; FAX: 219-548-2950

Laurona Armas Eibar, S.A.L., Avenida de Otaola 25, P.O. Box 260, Eibar 20600, SPAIN / 34-43-700600; FAX: 34-43-700616

Lawrence Brand Shot (See Precision Reloading)

Lawrence Leather Co., P.O. Box 1479, Lillington, NC 27546 / 910-893-2071; FAX: 910-893-4742

Lawson Co., Harry, 3328 N Richey Blvd., Tucson, AZ 85716 / 520-326-1117; FAX: 520-326-1117

Lawson, John. See: THE SIGHT SHOP

Lawson, John G (See Sight Shop, The)

Lazzeroni Arms Co., PO Box 26696, Tucson, AZ 85726 / 888-492-7247; FAX: 520-624-4250

Le Clear Industries (See E-Z-Way Systems), PO Box 4310, Newark, OH 43058-4310 / 614-345-6645; FAX: 614-345-6600

Lea Mfg. Co., 237 E. Aurora St., Waterbury, CT 06720 / 203-753-5116

Leapers, Inc., 7675 Five Mile Rd., Northville, MI 48167 / 248-486-1231; FAX: 248-486-1430

Leatherman Tool Group, Inc., 12106 NE Ainsworth Cir., P.O. Box 20595, Portland, OR 97294 / 503-253-7826; FAX: 503-253-7830

Lebeau-Courally, Rue St. Gilles, 386 4000, Liege, BELGIUM / 042-52-48-43; FAX: 32-042-52-20-08

Leckie Professional Gunsmithing, 546 Quarry Rd., Ottsville, PA 18942 / 215-847-8594

Ledbetter Airguns, Riley, 1804 E Sprague St, Winston Salem, NC 27107-3521 / 919-784-0676

Lee Co., T. K., 1282 Branchwater Ln., Birmingham, AL 35216 / 205-913-5222 odonmich@aol.com www.scopedot.com

Lee Precision, Inc., 4275 Hwy. U, Hartford, WI 53027 / 262-673-3075; FAX: 262-673-9273 info@leeprecision.com; www.leeprecision.com

Lee Supplies, Mark, 9901 France Ct., Lakeville, MN 55044 / 612-461-2114

LeFever Arms Co., Inc., 6234 Stokes, Lee Center Rd., Lee Center, NY 13363 / 315-337-6722; FAX: 315-337-1543

Legacy Sports International, 10 Prince St., Alexandria, VA 22314

Legend Products Corp., 21218 Saint Andrews Blvd., Boca Raton, FL 33433-2435

Leibowitz, Leonard, 1205 Murrayhill Ave., Pittsburgh, PA 15217 / 412-361-5455

Leica USA, Inc., 156 Ludlow Ave., Northvale, NJ 07647 / 201-767-7500; FAX: 201-767-8666

LEM Gun Specialties Inc. The Lewis Lead Remover, PO Box 2855, Peachtree City, GA 30269-2024 / 770-487-0556

Leonard Day, 6 Linseed Rd Box 1, West Hatfield, MA 01088-7505 / 413-337-8369

Les Baer Custom,Inc., 29601 34th Ave., Hillsdale, IL 61257 / 309-658-2716; FAX: 309-658-2610

LesMerises, Felix. See: ROCKY MOUNTAIN ARMOURY

Lethal Force Institute (See Police Bookshelf), PO Box 122, Concord, NH 03301 / 603-224-6814; FAX: 603-226-3554

Lett Custom Grips, 672 Currier Rd., Hopkinton, NH 03229-2652 / 800-421-5388; FAX: 603-226-4580 info@lettgrips.com; www.lettgrips.com

Leupold & Stevens, Inc., 14400 NW Greenbrier Pky., Beaverton, OR 97006 / 503-646-9171; FAX: 503-526-1455

Lever Arms Service Ltd., 2131 Burrard St., Vancouver, BC V6J 3H7 CANADA / 604-736-2711; FAX: 604-738-3503

Lew Horton Dist. Co., Inc., 15 Walkup Dr., Westboro, MA 01581 / 508-366-7400; FAX: 508-366-5332

Liberty Metals, 2233 East 16th St., Los Angeles, CA 90021 / 213-581-9171; FAX: 213-581-9351

Liberty Safe, 1060 N. Spring Creek Pl., Springville, UT 84663 / 800-247-5625; FAX: 801-489-6409

Liberty Shooting Supplies, P.O. Box 357, Hillsboro, OR 97123 / 503-640-5518; FAX: 503-640-5518 info@libertyshootingsupplies.com www.libertyshootingsupplies.com

Lightforce U.S.A. Inc., 19226 66th Ave. So., L-103, Kent, WA 98032 / 208-476-9814; FAX: 208-476-9814

Lightning Performance Innovations, Inc., RD1 Box 555, Mohawk, NY 13407 / 315-866-8819; FAX: 315-867-5701

Lilja Precision Rifle Barrels, PO Box 372, Plains, MT 59859 / 406-826-3084; FAX: 406-826-3083 lilja@riflebarrels.com www.riflebarrels.com

Lincoln, Dean, Box 1886, Farmington, NM 87401

Lind Custom Guns, Al, 7821 76th Ave SW, Lakewood, WA 98498 / 253-584-6361 lindcustguns@worldnot.att.net

Linder Solingen Knives, 4401 Sentry Dr., Tucker, GA 30084 / 770-939-6915; FAX: 770-939-6738

Lindsay, Steve, RR 2 Cedar Hills, Kearney, NE 68847 / 308-236-7885

Lindsley Arms Cartridge Co., P.O. Box 757, 20 College Hill Rd., Henniker, NH 03242 / 603-428-3127

Linebaugh Custom Sixguns, P.O. Box 455, Cody, WY 82414 / 307-645-3332

Lion Country Supply, P.O. Box 480, Port Matilda, PA 16870

List Precision Engineering, Unit 1 Ingley Works, 13 River Road, Barking, ENGLAND / 011-081-594-1686

Lithi Bee Bullet Lube, 1728 Carr Rd., Muskegon, MI 49442 / 616-788-4479

"Little John's" Antique Arms, 1740 W. Laveta, Orange, CA 92668

Little Trees Ramble (See Scott Pilkington)

Littler Sales Co., 20815 W. Chicago, Detroit, MI 48228 / 313-273-6889; FAX: 313-273-1099 littlerptg@aol.com

Littleton, J. F., 275 Pinedale Ave., Oroville, CA 95966 / 916-533-6084

Ljutic Industries, Inc., 732 N. 16th Ave., Suite 22, Yakima, WA 98902 / 509-248-0476; FAX: 509-576-8233 ljuticgun.net www.ljuticgun.com

Llama Gabilondo Y Cia, Apartado 290, E-01080, Victoria, spain, SPAIN

Loch Leven Industries / Convert-A-Pell, PO Box 2751, Santa Rosa, CA 95405 / 707-573-8735; FAX: 707-573-0369

Lock's Philadelphia Gun Exchange, 6700 Rowland Ave., Philadelphia, PA 19149 / 215-332-6225; FAX: 215-332-4800

Lodewick, Walter H., 2816 NE Halsey St., Portland, OR 97232 / 503-284-2554

Lodgewood Mfg., P.O. Box 611, Whitewater, WI 53190 / 262-473-5444; FAX: 262-473-6448 lodgewd@idcnet.com www.lodgewood.com

Log Cabin Sport Shop, 8010 Lafayette Rd., Lodi, OH 44254 / 330-948-1082; FAX: 330-948-4307

Logan, Harry M., Box 745, Honokaa, HI 96727 / 808-776-1644

Logdewood Mfg., PO Box 611, Whitewater, WI 53190 / 262-473-5444; FAX: 262-473-6448 lodgewd@idcnet.com

Lohman Mfg. Co., Inc., 4500 Doniphan Dr., P.O. Box 220, Neosho, MO 64850 / 417-451-4438; FAX: 417-451-2576

Lomont Precision Bullets, 278 Sandy Creek Rd, Salmon, ID 83467 / 208-756-6819; FAX: 208-756-6824 klomont.com

London Guns Ltd., Box 3750, Santa Barbara, CA 93130 / 805-683-4141; FAX: 805-683-1712

Lone Star Gunleather, 1301 Brushy Bend Dr., Round Rock, TX 78681 / 512-255-1805

Lone Star Rifle Company, 11231 Rose Road, Conroe, TX 77303 / 936-856-3363

Long, George F., 1500 Rogue River Hwy., Ste. F, Grants Pass, OR 97527 / 541-476-7552

Lortone Inc., 2856 NW Market St., Seattle, WA 98107

Lothar Walther Precision Tool Inc., 3425 Hutchinson Rd., Cumming, GA 30040 / 770-889-9998; FAX: 770-889-4919 lotharwalther@mindspring.com www.lothar-walther.com

Loweth, Richard H.R., 29 Hedgegrow Lane, Kirby Muxloe, Leics, LE9 2BN ENGLAND / (0) 116 238 6295

LPS Laboratories, Inc., 4647 Hugh Howell Rd., P.O. Box 3050, Tucker, GA 30084 / 404-934-7800

Lucas, Edward E, 32 Garfield Ave., East Brunswick, NJ 08816 / 201-251-5526

Lupton, Keith. See: PAWLING MOUNTAIN CLUB

Lyman Instant Targets, Inc. (See Lyman Products)

Lyman Products Corp., 475 Smith Street, Middletown, CT 06457-1541 / 860-632-2020; or 800-225-9626; FAX: 860-632-1699 lymansales@cshore.com www.lymanproducts.com

---

M

M. Thys (See U.S. Importer-Champlin Firearms Inc)

M.H. Canjar Co., 6510 Raleigh St., Arvada, CO 80003 / 303-295-2638; FAX: 303-295-2638

M.O.A. Corp., 2451 Old Camden Pike, Eaton, OH 45320 / 937-456-3669

MA Systems, P.O. Box 1143, Chouteau, OK 74337 / 918-479-6378

Mac-1 Airgun Distributors, 13974 Van Ness Ave., Gardena, CA 90249 / 310-327-3581; FAX: 310-327-0238 mac1@mac1airgun.com mac1airgun.com

Macbean, Stan, 754 North 1200 West, Orem, UT 84057 / 801-224-6446

Madis Books, 2453 West Five Mile Pkwy., Dallas, TX 75233 / 214-330-7168

Madis, George. See: WINCHESTER CONSULTANTS

MAG Instrument, Inc., 1635 S. Sacramento Ave., Ontario, CA 91761 / 909-947-1006; FAX: 909-947-3116

Magma Engineering Co., P.O. Box 161, 20955 E. Ocotillo Rd., Queen Creek, AZ 85242 / 602-987-9008; FAX: 602-987-0148

Mag-Na-Port International, Inc., 41302 Executive Dr., Harrison Twp., MI 48045-1306 / 586-469-6727; FAX: 586-469-0425 email@magnaport.com www.magnaport.com

Magnolia Sports,Inc., 211 W. Main, Magnolia, AR 71753 / 501-234-8410; or 800-530-7816; FAX: 501-234-8117

Magnum Power Products, Inc., P.O. Box 17768, Fountain Hills, AZ 85268

Magnum Research, Inc., 7110 University Ave. NE, Minneapolis, MN 55432 / 800-772-6168; or 763-574-1868; FAX: 763-574-0109 magnumresearch.com

---

Magnus Bullets, P.O. Box 239, Toney, AL 35773 / 256-420-8359; FAX: 256-420-8360

Mag-Pack Corp., P.O. Box 846, Chesterland, OH 44026

MagSafe Ammo Co., 4700 S US Highway 17/92, Casselberry, FL 32707-3814 / 407-834-9966; FAX: 407-834-8185

Magtech Ammunition Co. Inc., 837 Boston Rd #12, Madison, CT 06443 / 203-245-8983; FAX: 203-245-2883 rfine@mactechammunition.com www.mactech.com.br

Mahony, Philip Bruce, 67 White Hollow Rd., Lime Rock, CT 06039-2418 / 203-435-9341

Mahovsky's Metalife, R.D. 1, Box 149a Eureka Road, Grand Valley, PA 16420 / 814-436-7747

Maine Custom Bullets, RFD 1, Box 1755, Brooks, ME 04921

Maionchi-L.M.I., Via Di Coselli-Zona, Industriale Di Guamo 55060, Lucca, ITALY / 011 39-583 94291

Makinson, Nicholas, RR 3, Komoka, ON N0L 1R0 CANADA / 519-471-5462

Malcolm Enterprises, 1023 E. Prien Lake Rd., Lake Charles, LA 70601

Mallardtone Game Calls, 2901 16th St., Moline, IL 61265 / 309-762-8089

Mandall Shooting Supplies Inc., 3616 N. Scottsdale Rd., Scottsdale, AZ 85251 / 480-945-2553; FAX: 480-949-0734

Marathon Rubber Prods. Co., Inc., 1009 3rd St, Wausau, WI 54403-4765 / 715-845-6255

Marble Arms (See CRR, Inc./Marble's Inc.)

Marchmon Bullets, 8191 Woodland Shore Dr., Brighton, MI 48116

Marent, Rudolf, 9711 Tiltree St., Houston, TX 77075 / 713-946-7028

Mark Lee Supplies, 9901 France Ct., Lakeville, MN 55044 / 612-461-2114

Markell,Inc., 422 Larkfield Center 235, Santa Rosa, CA 95403 / 707-573-0792; FAX: 707-573-9867

Markesbery Muzzle Loaders, Inc., 7785 Foundation Dr., Ste. 6, Florence, KY 41042 / 606-342-5553; or 606-342-2380

Marksman Products, 5482 Argosy Dr., Huntington Beach, CA 92649 / 714-898-7535; or 800-822-8005; FAX: 714-891-0782

Marlin Firearms Co., 100 Kenna Dr., North Haven, CT 06473 / 203-239-5621; FAX: 203-234-7991

MarMik, Inc., 2116 S. Woodland Ave., Michigan City, IN 46360 / 219-872-7231; FAX: 219-872-7231

Marocchi F.lli S.p.A, Via Galileo Galilei 8, I-25068 Zanano, ITALY

Marquart Precision Co., P.O. Box 1740, Prescott, AZ 86302 / 520-445-5646

Marsh, Mike, Croft Cottage, Main St., Derbyshire, DE4 2BY ENGLAND / 01629 650 669

Marshall Enterprises, 792 Canyon Rd., Redwood City, CA 94062

Martin B. Retting Inc., 11029 Washington, Culver City, CA 90232 / 213-837-2412

Martin Hagn Rifles & Actions, P.O. Box 444, Cranbrook, BC V1C 4H9 CANADA / 604-489-4861

Martin's Gun Shop, 937 S. Sheridan Blvd., Lakewood, CO 80226 / 303-922-2184

Martz, John V., 8060 Lakeview Lane, Lincoln, CA 95648 FAX: 916-645-3815

Marvel, Alan, 3922 Madonna Rd., Jarretsville, MD 21084 / 301-557-6545

Marx, Harry (See U.S. Importer for FERLIB)

Maryland Paintball Supply, 8507 Harford Rd., Parkville, MD 21234 / 410-882-5607

MAST Technology, P.O. Box 60969, Boulder City, NV 89006

Master Lock Co., 2600 N. 32nd St., Milwaukee, WI 53245 / 414-444-2800

Match Prep--Doyle Gracey, P.O. Box 155, Tehachapi, CA 93581 / 661-822-5383; FAX: 661-823-8680

Mathews & Son, Inc., George E., 10224 S Paramount Blvd, Downey, CA 90241 / 562-862-6719; FAX: 562-862-6719

Matthews Cutlery, 4401 Sentry Dr., Tucker, GA 30084 / 770-939-6915

Mauser Werke Oberndorf Waffensysteme GmbH, Postfach 1349, 78722, Oberndorf/N., GERMANY

Maverick Arms, Inc., 7 Grasso Ave., P.O. Box 497, North Haven, CT 06473 / 203-230-5300; FAX: 203-230-5420

Maxi-Mount Inc., P.O. Box 291, Willoughby Hills, OH 44096-0291 / 440-944-9456; FAX: 440-944-9456 maximount454@yahoo.com

Mayville Engineering Co. (See MEC, Inc.)

Mazur Restoration, Pete, 13083 Drummer Way, Grass Valley, CA 95949 / 530-268-2412

McBros Rifle Co., P.O. Box 86549, Phoenix, AZ 85080 / 602-582-3713; FAX: 602-581-3825

McCament, Jay. See: JAY MCCAMENT CUSTOM GUNMAKER

McCann Industries, P.O. Box 641, Spanaway, WA 98387 / 253-537-6919; FAX: 253-537-6919 mccann.machine@worldnet.att.net www.mccannindustries.com

McCann's Machine & Gun Shop, P.O. Box 641, Spanaway, WA 98387 / 253-537-6919; FAX: 253-537-6993 mccann.machine@worldnet.att.net www.mccannindustries.com

McCann's Muzzle-Gun Works, 14 Walton Dr., New Hope, PA 18938 / 215-862-2728

McCluskey Precision Rifles, 10502 14th Ave. NW, Seattle, WA 98177 / 206-781-2776

McCombs, Leo, 1862 White Cemetery Rd., Patriot, OH 45658 / 614-256-1714

McCormick Corp., Chip, 1715 W. FM 1626 Ste. 105, Manchaca, TX 78652 / 800-328-CHIP; FAX: 512-462-0009

McDonald, Dennis, 8359 Brady St., Peosta, IA 52068 / 319-556-7940

McFarland, Stan, 2221 Idella Ct., Grand Junction, CO 81505 / 970-243-4704

McGhee, Larry. See: B.C. OUTDOORS

McGowen Rifle Barrels, 5961 Spruce Lane, St. Anne, IL 60964 / 815-937-9816; FAX: 815-937-4024

Mchalik, Gary. See: ROSSI FIREARMS

McKenzie, Lynton, 6940 N. Alvernon Way, Tucson, AZ 85718 / 520-299-5090

McKinney, R.P. (See Schuetzen Gun Co.)

McMillan Fiberglass Stocks, Inc., 1638 W. Knudsen Dr. #102, Phoenix, AZ 85027 / 602-582-9635; FAX: 602-581-3825

McMillan Optical Gunsight Co., 28638 N. 42nd St., Cave Creek, AZ 85331 / 602-585-7868; FAX: 602-585-7872

McMillan Rifle Barrels, P.O. Box 3427, Bryan, TX 77805 / 409-690-3456; FAX: 409-690-0156

McMurdo, Lynn (See Specialty Gunsmithing), PO Box 404, Afton, WY 83110 / 307-886-5535

MCS, Inc., 34 Delmar Dr., Brookfield, CT 06804 / 203-775-1013; FAX: 203-775-9462

McWelco Products, 6730 Santa Fe Ave., Hesperia, CA 92345 / 619-244-8876; FAX: 619-244-9398

MDS, P.O. Box 1441, Brandon, FL 33509-1441 / 813-653-1180; FAX: 813-684-5953

Measurement Group Inc., Box 27777, Raleigh, NC 27611

Measures, Leon. See: SHOOT WHERE YOU LOOK

MEC, Inc., 715 South St., Mayville, WI 53050 / 414-387-4500; FAX: 414-387-5802 reloaders@mayul.com www.mayvl.com

MEC-Gar S.r.l., Via Madonnina 64, Gardone V.T. Brescia, ITALY / 39-30-8912687; FAX: 39-30-8910065

MEC-Gar U.S.A., Inc., Hurley Farms Industr. Park, 115, Hurley Road 6G, Oxofrd, CT 06478 / 203-262-1525; FAX: 203-262-1719 mecgar@aol.com www.mec-gar.com

Mech-Tech Systems, Inc., 1602 Foothill Rd., Kalispell, MT 59901 / 406-755-8055

Meister Bullets (See Gander Mountain)

Mele, Frank, 201 S. Wellow Ave., Cookeville, TN 38501 / 615-526-4860

Menck, Gunsmith Inc., T.W., 5703 S 77th St, Ralston, NE 68127

Mendez, John A., P.O. Box 620984, Orlando, FL 32862 / 407-344-2791

Men-Metallwerk Elisenhuette GmbH, P.O. Box 1263, Nassau/Lahn, D-56372 GERMANY / 2604-7819

Meprolight (See Hesco-Meprolight)

Mercer Custom Guns, 216 S Whitewater Ave, Jefferson, WI 53549 / 920-674-3839

Merit Corp., PO Box 9044, Schenectady, NY 12309 / 518-346-1420 sales@meritcorporation.com www.meritcorporation.com

Merkel Freres, Strasse 7 October, 10, Suhl, GERMANY

Merkuria Ltd., Argentinska 38, 17005, Praha 7 CZECH, REPUBLIC / 422-875117; FAX: 422-809152

Metal Merchants, PO Box 186, Walled Lake, MI 48390-0186

Metalife Industries (See Mahovsky's Metalife)

Metaloy, Inc., Rt. 5, Box 595, Berryville, AR 72616 / 501-545-3611

Metals Hand Engraver/European Hand Engraving, Ste. 216, 12 South First St., San Jose, CA 95113 / 408-293-6559

Michael's Antiques, Box 591, Waldoboro, ME 04572

Michaels Of Oregon, PO Box 1690, Oregon City, OR 97045 www.michaels-oregon.com

Micro Sight Co., 242 Harbor Blvd., Belmont, CA 94002 / 415-591-0769; FAX: 415-591-7531

Microfusion Alfa S.A., Paseo San Andres N8, P.O. Box 271, Eibar, 20600 SPAIN / 34-43-11-89-16; FAX: 34-43-11-40-38

Mid-America Recreation, Inc., 1328 5th Ave., Moline, IL 61265 / 309-764-5089; FAX: 309-764-2722

Middlebrooks Custom Shop, 7366 Colonial Trail East, Surry, VA 23883 / 757-357-0881; FAX: 757-365-0442

Midway Arms, Inc., 5875 W. Van Horn Tavern Rd., Columbia, MO 65203 / 800-243-3220; or 573-445-6363; FAX: 573-446-1018

Midwest Gun Sport, 1108 Herbert Dr., Zebulon, NC 27597 / 919-269-5570

Midwest Sport Distributors, Box 129, Fayette, MO 65248

Mike Davis Products, 643 Loop Dr., Moses Lake, WA 98837 / 509-765-6178; or 509-766-7281

Military Armament Corp., P.O. Box 120, Mt. Zion Rd., Lingleville, TX 76461 / 817-965-3253

Millennium Designed Muzzleloaders, PO Box 536, Routes 11 & 25, Limington, ME 04049 / 207-637-2316

Miller Arms, Inc., P.O. Box 260 Purl St., St. Onge, SD 57779 / 605-642-5160; FAX: 605-642-5160

Miller Custom, 210 E. Julia, Clinton, IL 61727 / 217-935-9362

Miller Single Trigger Mfg. Co., Rt. 209, Box 1275, Millersburg, PA 17061 / 717-692-3704

Millett Sights, 7275 Murdy Circle, Adm. Office, Huntington Beach, CA 92647 / 714-842-5575; or 800-645-5388; FAX: 714-843-5707

Mills Jr., Hugh B., 3615 Canterbury Rd., New Bern, NC 28560 / 919-637-4631

Milstor Corp., 80-975 Indio Blvd., Indio, CA 92201 / 760-775-9998; FAX: 760-775-5229 milstor@webtv.net

Miltex, Inc, 700 S Lee St, Alexandria, VA 22314-4332 / 888-642-9123; FAX: 301-645-1430

Minute Man High Tech Industries, 10611 Canyon Rd. E., Suite 151, Puyallup, WA 98373 / 800-233-2734

Mirador Optical Corp., P.O. Box 11614, Marina Del Rey, CA 90295-7614 / 310-821-5587; FAX: 310-305-0386

Miroku, B C/Daly, Charles (See U.S. Importer)

Mitchell, Jack, c/o Geoff Gaebe, Addieville East Farm, 200 Pheasant Dr, Mapleville, RI 02839 / 401-568-3185

Mitchell Bullets, R.F., 430 Walnut St, Westernport, MD 21562

Mitchell Optics, Inc., 2072 CR 1100 N, Sidney, IL 61877 / 217-688-2219; or 217-621-3018; FAX: 217-688-2505 mitche1@attglobal.net

Mitchell's Accuracy Shop, 68 Greenridge Dr., Stafford, VA 22554 / 703-659-0165

MI-TE Bullets, 1396 Ave. K, Ellsworth, KS 67439 / 785-472-4575; FAX: 785-472-5579

Mittermeier, Inc., Frank, PO Box 2G, 3577 E Tremont Ave, Bronx, NY 10465 / 718-828-3843

Mixson Corp., 7635 W. 28th Ave., Hialeah, FL 33016 / 305-821-5190; or 800-327-0078; FAX: 305-558-9318

MJK Gunsmithing, Inc., 417 N. Huber Ct., E. Wenatchee, WA 98802 / 509-884-7683

MKS Supply, Inc. (See Hi-Point Firearms)

MMC, 5050 E. Belknap St., Haltom City, TX 76117 / 817-831-9557; FAX: 817-834-5508

MMP, 518 Buck Hollow Lane, Harrison, AR 72601 / 870-741-5019; FAX: 870-741-3104 mmp@alltel.net www.mmpsabots.com

Modern Gun Repair School, PO Box 846, Saint Albans, VT 05478 / 802-524-2223; FAX: 802-524-2053 jfwp@dlilearn.com; www.mgsinfoadlifearn.com

Modern Muzzleloading, Inc, PO Box 130, Centerville, IA 52544 / 515-856-2626

Moeller, Steve, 1213 4th St., Fulton, IL 61252 / 815-589-2300

Mogul Co./Life Jacket, 500 N. Kimball Rd., Ste. 109, South Lake, TX 76092

Molin Industries, Tru-Nord Division, P.O. Box 365, 204 North 9th St., Brainerd, MN 56401 / 218-829-2870

Monell Custom Guns, 228 Red Mills Rd., Pine Bush, NY 12566 / 914-744-3021

Moneymaker Guncraft Corp., 1420 Military Ave., Omaha, NE 68131 / 402-556-0226

Montana Armory, Inc (See C. Sharps Arms Co. Inc.), 100 Centennial Dr., PO Box 885, Big Timber, MT 59011 / 406-932-4353; FAX: 406-932-4443

Montana Outfitters, Lewis E. Yearout, 308 Riverview Dr. E., Great Falls, MT 59404 / 406-761-0859

Montana Precision Swaging, PO Box 4746, Butte, MT 59702 / 406-494-0600; FAX: 406-494-0600

Montana Vintage Arms, 2354 Bear Canyon Rd., Bozeman, MT 59715

Montgomery Community College, PO Box 787-GD, Troy, NC 27371 / 910-576-6222; or 800-839-6222; FAX: 910-576-2176; hammondp@mcc.montgomery.cc.nc.us www.montgomery.cc.nc.us

Morini (See U.S. Importers-Mandall Shooting Supply)

Morrison Custom Rifles, J. W., 4015 W Sharon, Phoenix, AZ 85029 / 602-978-3754

Morrison Precision, 6719 Calle Mango, Hereford, AZ 85615 / 520-378-6207 morprec@c2i2.com

Morrow, Bud, 11 Hillside Lane, Sheridan, WY 82801-9729 / 307-674-8360

Morton Booth Co., P.O. Box 123, Joplin, MO 64802 / 417-673-1962; FAX: 417-673-3642

Mo's Competitor Supplies (See MCS Inc)

Moss Double Tone, Inc., P.O. Box 1112, 2101 S. Kentucky, Sedalia, MO 65301 / 816-827-0827

Mountain Hollow Game Calls, Box 121, Cascade, MD 21719 / 301-241-3282

Mountain Plains Industries, 244 Glass Hollow Rd., Alton, VA 22920 / 800-687-3000; FAX: 540-456-8134

Mountain South, P.O. Box 381, Barnwell, SC 29812 / FAX: 803-259-3227

Mountain State Muzzleloading Supplies, Inc., Box 154-1, Rt. 2, Williamstown, WV 26187 / 304-375-7842; FAX: 304-375-3737

Mountain View Sports, Inc., Box 188, Troy, NH 03465 / 603-357-9690; FAX: 603-357-9691

Mowrey Gun Works, P.O. Box 246, Waldron, IN 46182 / 317-525-6181; FAX: 317-525-9595

Mowrey's Guns & Gunsmithing, 119 Fredericks St., Canajoharie, NY 13317 / 518-673-3483

MPC, P.O. Box 450, McMinnville, TN 37110-0450 / 615-473-5513; FAX: 615-473-5516

MPI Stocks, PO Box 83266, Portland, OR 97283 / 503-226-1215; FAX: 503-226-3554

MSC Industrial Supply Co., 151 Sunnyside Blvd., Plainview, NY 11803-9915 / 516-349-0330

MSR Targets, P.O. Box 1042, West Covina, CA 91793 / 818-331-7840

Mt. Alto Outdoor Products, Rt. 735, Howardsville, VA 24562

MTM Molded Products Co., Inc., 3370 Obco Ct., Dayton, OH 45414 / 937-890-7461; FAX: 937-890-1747

Mulberry House Publishing, P.O. Box 2180, Apache Junction, AZ 85217 / 888-738-1567; FAX: 480-671-1015

Mulhern, Rick, Rt. 5, Box 152, Rayville, LA 71269 / 318-728-2688

Mullins Ammunition, Rt. 2, Box 304K, Clintwood, VA 24228 / 540-926-6772; FAX: 540-926-6092

Mullis Guncraft, 3523 Lawyers Road E., Monroe, NC 28110 / 704-283-6683

Multiplex International, 26 S. Main St., Concord, NH 03301 FAX: 603-796-2223

Multipropulseurs, La Bertrandiere, 42580, FRANCE / 77 74 01 30; FAX: 77 93 19 34

Multi-Scale Charge Ltd., 3269 Niagara Falls Blvd., N. Tonawanda, NY 14120 / 905-566-1255; FAX: 905-276-6295

Mundy, Thomas A., 69 Robbins Road, Somerville, NJ 08876 / 201-722-2199

Murmur Corp., 2823 N. Westmoreland Ave., Dallas, TX 75222 / 214-630-5400

Murphy, R.R. Murphy Co., Inc. See: MURPHY, R.R. CO., INC.

Murphy, R.R. Co., Inc., R.R. Murphy Co., Inc. Murphy, P.O. Box 102, Ripley, TN 38063 / 901-635-4003; FAX: 901-635-2320

Murray State College, 1 Murray Campus St., Tishomingo, OK 73460 / 508-371-2371

Muscle Products Corp., 112 Fennell Dr., Butler, PA 16002 / 800-227-7049; or 724-283-0567; FAX: 724-283-8310 mpc@mpc_home.com www.mpc_home.com

Muzzleloaders Etcetera, Inc., 9901 Lyndale Ave. S., Bloomington, MN 55420 / 612-884-1161 muzzleloaders-etcetera.com

MWG Co., P.O. Box 971202, Miami, FL 33197 / 800-428-9394; or 305-253-8393; FAX: 305-232-1247

N

N.B.B., Inc., 24 Elliot Rd., Sterling, MA 01564 / 508-422-7538; or 800-942-9444

N.C. Ordnance Co., P.O. Box 3254, Wilson, NC 27895 / 919-237-2440; FAX: 919-243-9845

Nagel's Custom Bullets, 100 Scott St., Baytown, TX 77520-2849

Nalpak, 1937-C Friendship Drive, El Cajon, CA 92020 / 619-258-1200

Nastoff, Steve. See: NASTOFFS 45 SHOP, INC.

Nastoffs 45 Shop, Inc., Steve Nastoff, 1057 Laverne Dr., Youngstown, OH 44511

National Bullet Co., 1585 E. 361 St., Eastlake, OH 44095 / 216-951-1854; FAX: 216-951-7761

National Target Co., 4690 Wyaconda Rd., Rockville, MD 20852 / 800-827-7060; or 301-770-7060; FAX: 301-770-7892

Naval Ordnance Works, Rt. 2, Box 919, Sheperdstown, WV 25443 / 304-876-0998

Navy Arms Company, Valmore J. Forgett Jr., 815 22nd Street, Union City, NJ 07087 / 201-863-7100; FAX: 201-863-8770 info@navyarms.com www.navyarms.com

NCP Products, Inc., 3500 12th St. N.W., Canton, OH 44708 / 330-456-5130; FAX: 330-456-5234

Necessary Concepts, Inc., P.O. Box 571, Deer Park, NY 11729 / 516-667-8509; FAX: 516-667-8588

Necromancer Industries, Inc., 14 Communications Way, West Newton, PA 15089 / 412-872-8722

NEI Handtools, Inc., 51583 Columbia River Hwy., Scappoose, OR 97056 / 503-543-6776; FAX: 503-543-7865 nei@columbia-center.com www.neihandtools.com

Neil A. Jones Custom Products, 17217 Brookhouser Road, Saegertown, PA 16433 / 814-763-2769; FAX: 814-763-4228

Nelson, Gary K., 975 Terrace Dr., Oakdale, CA 95361 / 209-847-4590

Nelson, Stephen. See: NELSON'S CUSTOM GUNS, INC.

Nelson/Weather-Rite, Inc., 14760 Santa Fe Trail Dr., Lenexa, KS 66215 / 913-492-3200; FAX: 913-492-8749

Nelson's Custom Guns, Inc., Stephen Nelson, 7430 Valley View Dr. N.W., Corvallis, OR 97330 / 541-745-5232 nelsons-custom@home.com

Nesci Enterprises Inc., P.O. Box 119, Summit St., East Hampton, CT 06424 / 203-267-2588

Nesika Bay Precision, 22239 Big Valley Rd., Poulsbo, WA 98370 / 206-697-3830

Nettestad Gun Works, 38962 160th Avenue, Pelican Rapids, MN 56572 / 218-863-4301

Neumann GmbH, Am Galgenberg 6, 90575, GERMANY / 09101/8258; FAX: 09101/6356

Nevada Pistol Academy, Inc., 4610 Blue Diamond Rd., Las Vegas, NV 89139 / 702-897-1100

New England Ammunition Co., 1771 Post Rd. East, Suite 223, Westport, CT 06880 / 203-254-8048

New England Arms Co., Box 278, Lawrence Lane, Kittery Point, ME 03905 / 207-439-0593; FAX: 207-439-0525 info@newenglandarms.com www.newenglandarms.com

New England Custom Gun Service, 438 Willow Brook Rd., Plainfield, NH 03781 / 603-469-3450; FAX: 603-469-3471 bestguns@cyborportal.net www.newenglandcustom.com

New England Firearms, 60 Industrial Rowe, Gardner, MA 01440 / 508-632-9393; FAX: 508-632-2300

New Orleans Jewelers Supply Co., 206 Charters St., New Orleans, LA 70130 / 504-523-3839; FAX: 504-523-3836

New SKB Arms Co., C.P.O. Box 1401, Tokyo, JAPAN / 81-3-3943-9550; FAX: 81-3-3943-0695

New Ultra Light Arms, LLC, 1024 Grafton Rd., Morgantown, WV 26508 / 304-292-0600; FAX: 304-292-9662 newultralightarm@cs.com www.NewUltraLightArm

Newark Electronics, 4801 N. Ravenswood Ave., Chicago, IL 60640

Newell, Robert H., 55 Coyote, Los Alamos, NM 87544 / 505-662-7135

Newman Gunshop, 119 Miller Rd., Agency, IA 52530 / 515-937-5775

Nicholson Custom, 17285 Thornlay Road, Hughesville, MO 65334 / 816-826-8746

Nickels, Paul R., 4328 Seville St., Las Vegas, NV 89121 / 702-435-5318

Nicklas, Ted, 5504 Hegel Rd., Goodrich, MI 48438 / 810-797-4493

Niemi Engineering, W. B., Box 126 Center Rd, Greensboro, VT 05841 / 802-533-7180; FAX: 802-533-7141

Nightforce (See Lightforce USA Inc)

Nikon, Inc., 1300 Walt Whitman Rd., Melville, NY 11747 / 516-547-8623; FAX: 516-547-0309

Nitex Gun Shop, P.O. Box 1706, Uvalde, TX 78801 / 830-278-8843

Noreen, Peter H., 5075 Buena Vista Dr., Belgrade, MT 59714 / 406-586-7383

Norica, Avnda Otaola, 16 Apartado 68, Eibar, SPAIN

Norinco, 7A Yun Tan N, Beijing, CHINA

Norincoptics (See BEC, Inc.)

Norma Precision AB (See U.S. Importers-Dynamit)

Normark Corp., 10395 Yellow Circle Dr., Minnetonka, MN 55343-9101 / 612-933-7060; FAX: 612-933-0046

North American Arms, Inc., 2150 South 950 East, Provo, UT 84606-6285 / 800-821-5783; or 801-374-9990; FAX: 801-374-9998

North American Correspondence Schools The Gun Pro, Oak & Pawney St., Scranton, PA 18515 / 717-342-7701

MANUFACTURER'S DIRECTORY

North American Shooting Systems, P.O. Box 306, Osoyoos, BC V0H 1V0 CANADA / 604-495-3131; FAX: 604-495-2816

North Devon Firearms Services, 3 North St., Braunton, EX33 1AJ ENGLAND / 01271 813624; FAX: 01271 813624

North Mountain Pine Training Center (See Executive

North Pass, 1418 Webster Ave, Fort Collins, CO 80524 / 970-407-0426

North Specialty Products, 10091 Stageline St., Corona, CA 92883 / 714-524-1665

North Star West, P.O. Box 488, Glencoe, CA 95232 / 209-293-7010 northstarwest.com

North Wind Decoy Co., 1005 N. Tower Rd., Fergus Falls, MN 56537 / 218-736-4378; FAX: 218-736-7060

Northern Precision Custom Swaged Bullets, 329 S. James St., Carthage, NY 13619 / 315-493-1711

Northlake Outdoor Footwear, P.O. Box 10, Franklin, TN 37065-0010 / 615-794-1556; FAX: 615-790-8005

Northside Gun Shop, 2725 NW 109th, Oklahoma City, OK 73102 / 405-840-2353

Northwest Arms, 26884 Pearl Rd., Parma, ID 83660 / 208-722-6771; FAX: 208-722-1062

No-Sho Mfg. Co., 10727 Glenfield Ct., Houston, TX 77096 / 713-723-5332

Nosler, Inc., P.O. Box 671, Bend, OR 97709 / 800-285-3701; or 541-382-3921; FAX: 541-388-4667

Novak's, Inc., 1206 1/2 30th St., P.O. Box 4045, Parkersburg, WV 26101 / 304-485-9295; FAX: 304-428-6722

Now Products, Inc., PO Box 27608, Tempe, AZ 85285 / 800-662-6063; FAX: 480-966-0890

Nowlin Mfg. Co., 20622 S 4092 Rd, Claremore, OK 74017 / 918-342-0689; FAX: 918-342-0624 nowlinguns@msn.com; nowlinguns.com

NRI Gunsmith School, 4401 Connecticut Ave. NW, Washington, DC 20008

Nu-Line Guns,Inc., 1053 Caulks Hill Rd., Harvester, MO 63304 / 314-441-4500; or 314-447-4501; FAX: 314-447-5018

Null Holsters Ltd. K.L., 161 School St NW, Resaca, GA 30735 / 706-625-5643; FAX: 706-625-9392

Numrich Arms Corp., 203 Broadway, W. Hurley, NY 12491

NW Sinker and Tackle, 380 Valley Dr., Myrtle Creek, OR 97457-9717

Nygord Precision Products, Inc., P.O. Box 12578, Prescott, AZ 86304 / 928-717-2315; FAX: 928-717-2198

O

O.F. Mossberg & Sons,Inc., 7 Grasso Ave., North Haven, CT 06473 / 203-230-5300; Fax: 203-230-5420

Oakland Custom Arms,Inc., 4690 W. Walton Blvd., Waterford, MI 48329 / 810-674-8261

Oakman Turkey Calls, RD 1, Box 825, Harrisonville, PA 17228 / 717-485-4620

Obermeyer Rifled Barrels, 23122 60th St., Bristol, WI 53104 / 262-843-3537; FAX: 262-843-2129

October Country Muzzleloading, P.O. Box 969, Dept. GD, Hayden, ID 83835 / 208-772-2068; FAX: 208-772-9230 ocinfo@octobercountry.com www.octobercountry.com

Oehler Research,Inc., PO Box 9135, Austin, TX 78766 / 512-327-6900; or 800-531-5125; FAX: 512-327-6903

Oil Rod and Gun Shop, 69 Oak St., East Douglas, MA 01516 / 508-476-3687

Ojala Holsters, Arvo, PO Box 98, N Hollywood, CA 91603 / 503-669-1404

OK Weber,Inc., P.O. Box 7485, Eugene, OR 97401 / 541-747-0458; FAX: 541-747-5927 okweber@pacinfo okweber.com

Oker's Engraving, PO Box 126, Shawnee, CO 80475 / 303-838-6042

Oklahoma Ammunition Co., 3701A S. Harvard Ave., No. 367, Tulsa, OK 74135-2265 / 918-396-3187; FAX: 918-396-4270

Oklahoma Leather Products,Inc., 500 26th NW, Miami, OK 74354 / 918-542-6651; FAX: 918-542-6653

Old Wagon Bullets, 32 Old Wagon Rd., Wilton, CT 06897

Old West Bullet Moulds, J Ken Chapman, P.O. Box 519, Flora Vista, NM 87415 / 505-334-6970

Old West Reproductions,Inc. R.M. Bachman, 446 Florence S. Loop, Florence, MT 59833 / 406-273-2615; FAX: 406-273-2615

Old Western Scrounger,Inc., 12924 Hwy. A-l2, Montague, CA 96064 / 916-459-5445; FAX: 916-459-3944

Old World Gunsmithing, 2901 SE 122nd St., Portland, OR 97236 / 503-760-7681

Old World Oil Products, 3827 Queen Ave. N., Minneapolis, MN 55412 / 612-522-5037

Ole Frontier Gunsmith Shop, 2617 Hwy. 29 S., Cantonment, FL 32533 / 904-477-8074

Olson, Myron, 989 W. Kemp, Watertown, SD 57201 / 605-886-9787

Olson, Vic, 5002 Countryside Dr., Imperial, MO 63052 / 314-296-8086

Olympic Arms Inc., 620-626 Old Pacific Hwy. SE, Olympia, WA 98513 / 360-456-3471; FAX: 360-491-3447

Olympic Optical Co., P.O. Box 752377, Memphis, TN 38175-2377 / 901-794-3890; or 800-238-7120; FAX: 901-794-0676 80

Omega Sales, P.O. Box 1066, Mt. Clemens, MI 48043 / 810-469-7323; FAX: 810-469-0425

100 Straight Products, Inc., P.O. Box 6148, Omaha, NE 68106 / 402-556-1055; FAX: 402-556-1055

One Of A Kind, 15610 Purple Sage, San Antonio, TX 78255 / 512-695-3364

One Ragged Hole, P.O. Box 13624, Tallahassee, FL 32317-3624

Op-Tec, P.O. Box L632, Langhorn, PA 19047 / 215-757-5037

Optical Services Co., P.O. Box 1174, Santa Teresa, NM 88008-1174 / 505-589-3833

Orchard Park Enterprise, P.O. Box 563, Orchard Park, NY 14127 / 616-656-0356

Oregon Arms, Inc. (See Rogue Rifle Co., Inc.)

Oregon Trail Bullet Company, PO Box 529, Dept. P, Baker City, OR 97814 / 800-811-0548; FAX: 514-523-1803

Original Box, Inc., 700 Linden Ave., York, PA 17404 / 717-854-2897; FAX: 717-845-4276

Original Deer Formula Co., The., PO Box 1705, Dickson, TN 37056 / 800-874-6965; FAX: 615-446-0646 deerformula1@aol.com

Original Mink Oil, Inc., 10652 NE Holman, Portland, OR 97220 / 503-255-2814; or 800-547-5895; FAX: 503-255-2487

Orion Rifle Barrel Co., RR2, 137 Cobler Village, Kalispell, MT 59901 / 406-257-5649

Otis Technology, Inc., RR 1 Box 84, Boonville, NY 13309 / 315-942-3320

Ottmar, Maurice, Box 657, 113 E. Fir, Coulee City, WA 99115 / 509-632-5717

Outa-Site Gun Carriers, 219 Market St., Laredo, TX 78040 / 210-722-4678; or 800-880-9715; FAX: 210-726-4858

Outdoor Edge Cutlery Corp., 6395 Gunpark Dr., Unit Q, Boulder, CO 80301 / 303-652-8212; FAX: 303-652-8238

Outdoor Enthusiast, 3784 W. Woodland, Springfield, MO 65807 / 417-883-9841

Outdoor Sports Headquarters, Inc., 967 Watertower Ln., West Carrollton, OH 45449 / 513-865-5855; FAX: 513-865-5962

Outers Laboratories Div. of ATK, Route 2, P.O. Box 39, Onalaska, WI 54650 / 608-781-5800; FAX: 608-781-0368

Ox-Yoke Originals, Inc., 34 Main St., Milo, ME 04463 / 800-231-8313; or 207-943-7351; FAX: 207-943-2416

Ozark Gun Works, 11830 Cemetery Rd., Rogers, AR 72756 / 479-631-1024; FAX: 479-631-1024 ogw@hotmail.com www.eocities.com/ocarkgunworks

P

P&M Sales & Services, LLC, 4697 Tote Rd. Bldg. H-B, Comins, MI 48619 / 989-848-8364

P.A.C.T., Inc., P.O. Box 531525, Grand Prairie, TX 75053 / 214-641-0049

P.M. Enterprises, Inc. / Precise Metalsmithing, 146 Curtis Hill Rd., Chehalis, WA 98532 / 360-748-3743; FAX: 360-748-1802 precise1@quik.com

P.S.M.G. Gun Co., 10 Park Ave., Arlington, MA 02174 / 617-646-8845; FAX: 617-646-2133

Pace Marketing, Inc., P.O. Box 2039, Stuart, FL 34995 / 561-871-9682; FAX: 561-871-6552

Pachmayr Div. Lyman Products, 475 Smith St., Middletown, CT 06457 / 860-632-2020; or 800-225-9626; FAX: 860-632-1699 lymansales@cshore.com www.pachmayr.com

Pacific Armament Corp, 4813 Enterprise Way, Unit K, Modesto, CA 95356 / 209-545-2800 gunsparts@att.net

Pacific Cartridge, Inc., 2425 Salashan Loop Road, Ferndale, WA 98248 / 360-366-4444; FAX: 360-366-4445

Pacific Research Laboratories, Inc. (See Rimrock)

Pacific Rifle Co., PO Box 1473, Lake Oswego, OR 97035 / 503-538-7437

Pac-Nor Barreling, 99299 Overlook Rd., PO Box 6188, Brookings, OR 97415 / 503-469-7330; FAX: 503-469-7331

Paco's (See Small Custom Mould & Bullet Co)

Page Custom Bullets, P.O. Box 25, Port Moresby, NEW GUINEA

Pagel Gun Works, Inc., 1407 4th St. NW, Grand Rapids, MN 55744 / 218-326-3003

Pager Pal, 200 W Pleasantview, Hurst, TX 76054 / 800-561-1603; FAX: 817-285-8769 www.pagerpal.com

Paintball Games International Magazine Aceville, Castle House 97 High St., Essex, ENGLAND / 011-44-206-564840

Palmer Security Products, 2930 N. Campbell Ave., Chicago, IL 60618 / 773-267-0200; FAX: 773-267-8080 info@palmersecurity.com www.palmersecurity.com

Palsa Outdoor Products, P.O. Box 81336, Lincoln, NE 68501 / 402-488-5288; FAX: 402-488-2321

Paragon Sales & Services, Inc., 2501 Theodore St, Crest Hill, IL 60435-1613 / 815-725-9212; FAX: 815-725-8974

Para-Ordnance Mfg., Inc., 980 Tapscott Rd., Scarborough, ON M1X 1E7 CANADA / 416-297-7855; FAX: 416-297-1289

Para-Ordnance, Inc., 1919 NE 45th St., Ste 215, Ft. Lauderdale, FL 33308

Pardini Armi Srl, Via Italica 154, 55043, Lido Di Camaiore Lu, ITALY / 584-90121; FAX: 584-90122

Paris, Frank J., 17417 Pershing St., Livonia, MI 48152-3822

Parker & Sons Shooting Supply, 9337 Smoky Row Road, Strawberry Plains, TN 37871 / 865-933-3286; FAX: 865-932-8586

Parker Gun Finishes, 9337 Smokey Row Rd., Strawberry Plains, TN 37871 / 423-933-3286

Parker Reproductions, 114 Broad St., Flemington, NJ 08822 / 908-469-0100; FAX: 908-469-9692

Parsons Optical Mfg. Co., PO Box 192, Ross, OH 45061 / 513-867-0820; FAX: 513-867-8380 psscopes@concentric.net

Partridge Sales Ltd., John, Trent Meadows, Rugeley, ENGLAND

Parts & Surplus, P.O. Box 22074, Memphis, TN 38122 / 901-683-4007

Pasadena Gun Center, 206 E. Shaw, Pasadena, TX 77506 / 713-472-0417; FAX: 713-472-1322

Passive Bullet Traps, Inc. (See Savage Range)

Paterson Gunsmithing, 438 Main St., Paterson, NJ 07502 / 201-345-4100

Pathfinder Sports Leather, 2920 E. Chambers St., Phoenix, AZ 85040 / 602-276-0016

Patrick W. Price Bullets, 16520 Worthley Drive, San Lorenzo, CA 94580 / 510-278-1547

Pattern Control, 114 N. Third St., P.O. Box 462105, Garland, TX 75046 / 214-494-3551; FAX: 214-272-8447

Paul A. Harris Hand Engraving, 113 Rusty Lane, Boerne, TX 78006-5746 / 512-391-5121

Paul and Sharon Dressel, 209 N. 92nd Ave., Yakima, WA 98908 / 509-966-9233; FAX: 509-966-3365 dressels@nwinfo.net www.dressels.com

Paul D. Hillmer Custom Gunstocks, 7251 Hudson Heights, Hudson, IA 50643 / 319-988-3941

Paul Jones Moulds, 4901 Telegraph Rd., Los Angeles, CA 90022 / 213-262-1510

Paulsen Gunstocks, Rt. 71, Box 11, Chinook, MT 59523 / 406-357-3403

Pawling Mountain Club, Keith Lupton, PO Box 573, Pawling, NY 12564 / 914-855-3825

Paxton Quigley's Personal Protection Strategies, 9903 Santa Monica Blvd., 300, Beverly Hills, CA 90212 / 310-281-1762 www.defend-net.com/paxton

Payne Photography, Robert, Robert, P.O. Box 141471, Austin, TX 78714 / 512-272-4554

PC Co., 5942 Secor Rd., Toledo, OH 43623 / 419-472-6222

Peacemaker Specialists, PO Box 157, Whitmore, CA 96096 / 530-472-3438

Pearce Grip, Inc., PO Box 40367, Fort Worth, TX 76140 / 206-485-5488; FAX: 206-488-9497

Pease Accuracy, Bob, P.O. Box 310787, New Braunfels, TX 78131 / 210-625-1342

PECAR Herbert Schwarz GmbH, Kreuzbergstrasse 6, 10965, Berlin, GERMANY / 004930-785-7383; FAX: 004930-785-1934 michael.schwart@pecar-berlin.de www.pecar-berlin.de

Pecatonica River Longrifle, 5205 Nottingham Dr., Rockford, IL 61111 / 815-968-1995; FAX: 815-968-1996

Pedersen, C. R., 2717 S. Pere Marquette Hwy., Ludington, MI 49431 / 231-843-2061; FAX: 231-845-7695 fega@fega.com

Pedersen, Rex C., 2717 S. Pere Marquette Hwy., Ludington, MI 49431 / 231-843-2061; FAX: 231-845-7695 fega@fega.com

Peet Shoe Dryer, Inc., 130 S. 5th St., P.O. Box 618, St. Maries, ID 83861 / 208-245-2095; or 800-222-PEET; FAX: 208-245-5441

Peifer Rifle Co., P.O. Box 192, Nokomis, IL 62075-0192 / 217-563-7050; FAX: 217-563-7060

Pejsa Ballistics, 1314 Marquette Ave., Apt 807, Minneapolis, MN 55403 / 612-374-3337; FAX: 612-374-5383

Pelaire Products, 5346 Bonky Ct., W. Palm Beach, FL 33415 / 561-439-0691; FAX: 561-967-0052

Pell, John T. (See KOGOT)

Peltor, Inc. (See Aero Peltor)

PEM's Mfg. Co., 5063 Waterloo Rd., Atwater, OH 44201 / 216-947-3721

Pence Precision Barrels, 7567 E. 900 S., S. Whitley, IN 46787 / 219-839-4745

Pendleton Royal, c/o Swingler Buckland Ltd., 4/7 Highgate St., Birmingham, ENGLAND / 44 121 440 3060; or 44 121 446 5898; FAX: 44 121 446 4165

Pendleton Woolen Mills, P.O. Box 3030, 220 N.W. Broadway, Portland, OR 97208 / 503-226-4801

Penn Bullets, P.O. Box 756, Indianola, PA 15051

Pennsylvania Gun Parts Inc, PO Box 665, 300 Third St, East Berlin, PA 17316-0665 / 717-259-8010; FAX: 717-259-0057

Pennsylvania Gunsmith School, 812 Ohio River Blvd., Avalon, Pittsburgh, PA 15202 / 412-766-1812; FAX: 412-766-0855 pgs@pagunsmith.com www.pagunsmith.com

Penrod Precision, 312 College Ave., PO Box 307, N. Manchester, IN 46962 / 260-982-8385; FAX: 260-982-1819

Pentax Corp., 35 Inverness Dr. E., Englewood, CO 80112 / 303-799-8000; FAX: 303-790-1131

Pentheny de Pentheny, 2352 Baggett Ct., Santa Rosa, CA 95401 / 707-573-1390; FAX: 707-573-1390

Perazone-Gunsmith, Brian, Cold Spring Rd, Roxbury, NY 12474 / 607-326-4088; FAX: 607-326-3140

Perazzi U.S.A. Inc., 1010 West Tenth, Azusa, CA 91702 / 626-334-1234; FAX: 626-334-0344 perazziusa@aol.com

Performance Specialists, 308 Eanes School Rd., Austin, TX 78746 / 512-327-0119

Perugini Visini & Co. S.r.l., Via Camprelle, 126, 25080 Nuvolera, ITALY / 30-6897535; FAX: 30-6897821

Pete Elsen, Inc., 1529 S. 113th St., West Allis, WI 53214 / 414-476-4660; FAX: 414-476-5160

Pete Mazur Restoration, 13083 Drummer Way, Grass Valley, CA 95949 / 530-268-2412

Pete Rickard, Inc., 115 Roy Walsh Rd, Cobleskill, NY 12043 / 518-234-2731; FAX: 518-234-2454 rickard@telenet.net peterickard.com

Peter Dyson & Son Ltd., 3 Cuckoo Lane, Honley Huddersfield, Yorkshire, HD7 2BR ENGLAND / 44-1484-661062; FAX: 44-1484-663709 info@peterdyson.co.uk www.peterdyson.com

Peter Hale/Engraver, 800 E. Canyon Rd., Spanish Fork, UT 84660 / 801-798-8215

Peters Stahl GmbH, Stettiner Strasse 42, D-33106, Paderborn, GERMANY / 05251-750025; FAX: 05251-75611

Petersen Publishing Co. (See Emap USA), 6420 Wilshire Blvd., Los Angeles, CA 90048 / 213-782-2000; FAX: 213-782-2867

Peterson Gun Shop, Inc., A.W., 4255 W. Old U.S. 441, Mt. Dora, FL 32757-3299 / 352-383-4258; FAX: 352-735-1001

Petro-Explo Inc., 7650 U.S. Hwy. 287, Suite 100, Arlington, TX 76017 / 817-478-8888

Pettinger Books, Gerald, Rt. 2, Box 125, Russell, IA 50238 / 641-535-2239 gpettinger@lisco.com

Pflumm Mfg. Co., 10662 Widmer Rd., Lenexa, KS 66215 / 800-888-4867; FAX: 913-451-7857

PFRB Co., PO Box 1242, Bloomington, IL 61702 / 309-473-3964; FAX: 309-473-2161

Philip S. Olt Co., P.O. Box 550, 12662 Fifth St., Pekin, IL 61554 / 309-348-3633; FAX: 309-348-3300

Phillippi Custom Bullets, Justin, P.O. Box 773, Ligonier, PA 15658 / 724-238-2962; FAX: 724-238-9671 jrp@wpa.net http://www.wpa.net~jrphil

Phillips & Rogers, Inc., 100 Hilbig #C, Conroe, TX 77301 / 409-435-0011

Phoenix Arms, 1420 S. Archibald Ave., Ontario, CA 91761 / 909-947-4843; FAX: 909-947-6798

Photronic Systems Engineering Company, 6731 Via De La Reina, Bonsall, CA 92003 / 619-758-8000

Piedmont Community College, P.O. Box 1197, Roxboro, NC 27573 / 336-599-1181; FAX: 336-597-3817 www.piedmont.cc.nc.us

Pierce Pistols, 55 Sorrellwood Lane, Sharpsburg, GA 30277-9523 / 404-253-8192

Pietta (See U.S. Importers-Navy Arms Co, Taylor's

Pilgrim Pewter,Inc. (See Bell Originals Inc. Sid)

Pilkington, Scott (See Little Trees Ramble)

Pine Technical College, 1100 4th St., Pine City, MN 55063 / 800-521-7463; FAX: 612-629-6766

Pinetree Bullets, 133 Skeena St., Kitimat, BC V8C 1Z1 CANADA / 604-632-3768; FAX: 604-632-3768

Pioneer Arms Co., 355 Lawrence Rd., Broomall, PA 19008 / 215-356-5203

Piotti (See U.S. Importer-Moore & Co, Wm. Larkin)

Piquette, Paul. See: PIQUETTE'S CUSTOM ENGRAVING

Piquette's Custom Engraving, Paul R. Piquette, 80 Bradford Dr., Feeding Hills, MA 01030 / 413-789-4582; FAX: 413-786-8118 ppiquette@aol.com www.pistoldynamics.com

Plaza Cutlery, Inc., 3333 Bristol, 161 South Coast Plaza, Costa Mesa, CA 92626 / 714-549-3932

Plum City Ballistic Range, N2162 80th St., Plum City, WI 54761 / 715-647-2539

PlumFire Press, Inc., 30-A Grove Ave., Patchogue, NY 11772-4112 / 800-695-7246; FAX: 516-758-4071

PMC / Eldorado Cartridge Corp., PO Box 62508, 12801 U.S. Hwy. 95 S., Boulder City, NV 89005 / 702-294-0025; FAX: 702-294-0121 kbauer@pmcammo.com pmcammo.com

Poburka, Philip (See Bison Studios)

Pohl, Henry A. (See Great American Gun Co.

Pointing Dog Journal, Village Press Publications, P.O. Box 968, Dept. PGD, Traverse City, MI 49685 / 800-272-3246; FAX: 616-946-3289

Police Bookshelf, PO Box 122, Concord, NH 03301 / 603-224-6814; FAX: 603-226-3554

Polywad, Inc., P.O. Box 7916, Macon, GA 31209 / 912-477-0669 polywadmpb@aol.com www.polywad.com

Ponsness/Warren, P.O. Box 8, Rathdrum, ID 83858 / 208-687-2231; FAX: 208-687-2233

Pony Express Reloaders, 608 E. Co. Rd. D, Suite 3, St. Paul, MN 55117 / 612-483-9406; FAX: 612-483-9884

Pony Express Sport Shop, 16606 Schoenborn St., North Hills, CA 91343 / 818-895-1231

Potts, Wayne E., 912 Poplar St., Denver, CO 80220 / 303-355-5462

Powder Horn Ltd., PO Box 565, Glenview, IL 60025 / 305-565-6060

Powell & Son (Gunmakers) Ltd., William, 35-37 Carrs Lane, Birmingham, B4 7SX ENGLAND / 121-643-0689; FAX: 121-631-3504

Powell Agency, William, 22 Circle Dr., Bellmore, NY 11710 / 516-679-1158

Power Custom, Inc., 29739 Hwy. J, Gravois Mills, MO 65037 / 573-372-5684; FAX: 573-372-5799 rwpowers@laurie.net www.powercustom.com

Power Plus Enterprises, Inc., PO Box 38, Warm Springs, GA 31830 / 706-655-2132

Powley Computer (See Hutton Rifle Ranch)

Practical Tools, Inc., 7067 Easton Rd., P.O. Box 133, Pipersville, PA 18947 / 215-766-7301; FAX: 215-766-8681

Prairie Gun Works, 1-761 Marion St., Winnipeg, MB R2J 0K6 CANADA / 204-231-2976; FAX: 204-231-8566

Prairie River Arms, 1220 N. Sixth St., Princeton, IL 61356 / 815-875-1616; or 800-445-1541; FAX: 815-875-1402

Pranger, Ed G., 1414 7th St., Anacortes, WA 98221 / 206-293-3488

Precise Metalsmithing Enterprises / P.M. Enterprises, 146 Curtis Hill Rd., Chehalis, WA 98532 / 360-748-3743; FAX: 360-748-8102 precise1@quik.com

Precision Airgun Sales, Inc., 5247 Warrensville Ctr Rd, Maple Hts., OH 44137 / 216-587-5005; FAX: 216-587-5005

Precision Cast Bullets, 101 Mud Creek Lane, Ronan, MT 59864 / 406-676-5135

Precision Delta Corp., PO Box 128, Ruleville, MS 38771 / 662-756-2810; FAX: 662-756-2590

Precision Firearm Finishing, 25 N.W. 44th Avenue, Des Moines, IA 50313 / 515-288-8680; FAX: 515-244-3925

Precision Gun Works, 104 Sierra Rd Dept. GD, Kerrville, TX 78028 / 830-367-4587

Precision Munitions, Inc., P.O. Box 326, Jasper, IN 47547

Precision Reloading, Inc., PO Box 122, Stafford Springs, CT 06076 / 860-684-7979; FAX: 860-684-6788 info@precisionreloading.com www.precisionreloading.com

Precision Sales International, Inc., PO Box 1776, Westfield, MA 01086 / 413-562-5055; FAX: 413-562-5056 precision-sales.com

Precision Shooting, Inc., 222 McKee St., Manchester, CT 06040 / 860-645-8776; FAX: 860-643-8215 www.precisionshooting.com

Precision Small Arms Inc., 9272 Jeronimo Rd, Ste 121, Irvine, CA 92618 / 800-554-5515; or 949-768-3530; FAX: 949-768-4808 www.tcbebe.com

Precision Specialties, 131 Hendom Dr., Feeding Hills, MA 01030 / 413-786-3365; FAX: 413-786-3365

Precision Sport Optics, 15571 Producer Lane, Unit G, Huntington Beach, CA 92649 / 714-891-1309; FAX: 714-892-6920

Premier Reticles, 920 Breckinridge Lane, Winchester, VA 22601-6707 / 540-722-0601; FAX: 540-722-3522

Prescott Projectile Co., 1808 Meadowbrook Road, Prescott, AZ 86303

Preslik's Gunstocks, 4245 Keith Ln., Chico, CA 95926 / 916-891-8236

Price Bullets, Patrick W., 16520 Worthley Dr., San Lorenzo, CA 94580 / 510-278-1547

Prime Reloading, 30 Chiswick End, Meldreth, ROYSTON UK / 0763-260636

Primos, Inc., P.O. Box 12785, Jackson, MS 39236-2785 / 601-366-1288; FAX: 601-362-3274

PRL Bullets, c/o Blackburn Enterprises, 114 Stuart Rd., Ste. 110, Cleveland, TN 37312 / 423-559-0340

Pro Load Ammunition, Inc., 5180 E. Seltice Way, Post Falls, ID 83854 / 208-773-9444; FAX: 208-773-9441

Professional Gunsmiths of America, Rt 1 Box 224, Lexington, MO 64067 / 660-259-2636

Professional Hunter Supplies (See Star Custom Bull), PO Box 608, 468 Main St, Ferndale, CA 95536 / 707-786-9140; FAX: 707-786-9117 wmebride@humboldt.com

Professional Ordnance, Inc., 1070 Metric Drive, Lake Havasu City, AZ 86403 / 928-505-2420; FAX: 928-505-2141 www.professional-ordnance.com

PrOlixr Lubricants, PO Box 1348, Victorville, CA 92393 / 760-243-3129; FAX: 760-241-0148 prolix@accex.net prolixlubricant.com

Pro-Mark Div. of Wells Lamont, 6640 W. Touhy, Chicago, IL 60648 / 312-647-8200

Proofmark Corp., PO Box 610, Burgess, VA 22432 / 804-453-4337; FAX: 804-453-4337 proofmark@rivnet.net

Pro-Port Ltd., 41302 Executive Dr., Harrison Twp., MI 48045-1306 / 586-469-6727; FAX: 586-469-0425 e-mail@magnaport.com www.magnaport.com

Pro-Shot Products, Inc., P.O. Box 763, Taylorville, IL 62568 / 217-824-9133; FAX: 217-824-8861

Protektor Model, 1-11 Bridge St., Galeton, PA 16922 / 814-435-2442 hrk@penn.com www.protektormodel.com

Prototech Industries, Inc., 10532 E Road, Delia, KS 66418 / 785-771-3571; prototec@grapevine.net

ProWare, Inc., 15847 NE Hancock St., Portland, OR 97230 / 503-239-0159

PWL Gunleather, P.O. Box 450432, Atlanta, GA 31145 / 800-960-4072; FAX: 770-822-1704 covert@pwlusa.com www.pwlusa.com

Pyromid, Inc., PO Box 6466, Bend, OR 97708 / 503-548-1041; FAX: 503-923-1004

Q

Quack Decoy & Sporting Clays, 4 Ann & Hope Way, P.O. Box 98, Cumberland, RI 02864 / 401-723-8202; FAX: 401-722-5910

Quaker Boy, Inc., 5455 Webster Rd., Orchard Parks, NY 14127 / 716-662-3979; FAX: 716-662-9426

Quality Arms, Inc., Box 19477, Dept. GD, Houston, TX 77224 / 281-870-8377; FAX: 281-870-8524 arrieta2@excite.com www.gunshop.com

Quality Custom Firearms, Stepehn Billeb, 22 Vista View Drive, Cody, WY 82414 / 307-587-4278; FAX: 307-587-4297 stevebilleb@wyoming.com

Quality Firearms of Idaho, Inc., 659 Harmon Way, Middleton, ID 83644-3065 / 208-466-1631

Que Industries, Inc., PO Box 2471, Everett, WA 98203 / 425-303-9088; FAX: 206-514-3266 queinfo@queindustries.com

Queen Cutlery Co., PO Box 500, Franklinville, NY 14737 / 800-222-5233; FAX: 800-299-2618

R

R&C Knives & Such, 2136 CANDY CANE WALK, Manteca, CA 95336-9501 / 209-239-3722; FAX: 209-825-6947

R&D Gun Repair, Kenny Howell, RR1 Box 283, Beloit, WI 53511

R&J Gun Shop, 337 S. Humbolt St., Canyon City, OR 97820 / 541-575-2130 rjgunshop@highdestertnet.com

R&S Industries Corp., 8255 Brentwood Industrial Dr., St. Louis, MO 63144 / 314-781-5400 polishingcloth.com

R. Murphy Co., Inc., 13 Groton-Harvard Rd., P.O. Box 376, Ayer, MA 01432 / 617-772-3481

R.A. Wells Custom Gunsmith, 3452 1st Ave., Racine, WI 53402 / 414-639-5223

R.E. Seebeck Assoc., P.O. Box 59752, Dallas, TX 75229

R.E.I., P.O. Box 88, Tallevast, FL 34270 / 813-755-0085

R.E.T. Enterprises, 2608 S. Chestnut, Broken Arrow, OK 74012 / 918-251-GUNS; FAX: 918-251-0587

R.F. Mitchell Bullets, 430 Walnut St., Westernport, MD 21562

R.I.S. Co., Inc., 718 Timberlake Circle, Richardson, TX 75080 / 214-235-0933

R.T. Eastman Products, P.O. Box 1531, Jackson, WY 83001 / 307-733-3217; or 800-624-4311

Rabeno, Martin, 92 Spook Hole Rd., Ellenville, NY 12428 / 845-647-2121; FAX: 845-647-2121 fancygun@aol.com

Radack Photography, Lauren, 21140 Jib Court L-12, Aventura, FL 33180 / 305-931-3110

Radiator Specialty Co., 1900 Wilkinson Blvd., P.O. Box 34689, Charlotte, NC 28234 / 800-438-6947; FAX: 800-421-9525

Radical Concepts, P.O. Box 1473, Lake Grove, OR 97035 / 503-538-7437

Rainier Ballistics Corp., 4500 15th St. East, Tacoma, WA 98424 / 800-638-8722; or 206-922-7589; FAX: 206-922-7854

Ralph Bone Engraving, 718 N. Atlanta St., Owasso, OK 74055 / 918-272-9745

Ram-Line Blount, Inc., P.O. Box 39, Onalaska, WI 54650

Ramon B. Gonzalez Guns, PO Box 370, 93 St. Joseph's Hill Road, Monticello, NY 12701 / 914-794-4515

Rampart International, 2781 W. MacArthur Blvd., B-283, Santa Ana, CA 92704 / 800-976-7240; or 714-557-6405

Ranch Products, P.O. Box 145, Malinta, OH 43535 / 313-277-3118; FAX: 313-565-8536

Randall-Made Knives, P.O. Box 1988, Orlando, FL 32802 / 407-855-8075

Randco UK, 286 Gipsy Rd., Welling, DA16 1JJ ENGLAND / 44 81 303 4118

Randolph Engineering Inc., 26 Thomas Patten Dr., Randolph, MA 02368 / 781-961-6070; FAX: 781-961-0337

Randy Duane Custom Stocks, 7822 Church St., Middletown, VA 22645-9521

Range Brass Products Company, P.O. Box 218, Rockport, TX 78381

Ranger Shooting Glasses, 26 Thomas Patten Dr., Randolph, MA 02368 / 800-541-1405; FAX: 617-986-0337

Ransom International Corp., 1027 Spire Dr, Prescott, AZ 86302 / 520-778-7899; FAX: 520-778-7993 ransom@primenet.com www.ransom-intl.com

Rapine Bullet Mould Mfg. Co., 9503 Landis Lane, East Greenville, PA 18041 / 215-679-5413; FAX: 215-679-9795

Raptor Arms Co., Inc., 273 Canal St, #179, Shelton, CT 06484 / 203-924-7618; FAX: 203-924-7624

Ravell Ltd., 289 Diputacion St., 08009, Barcelona, SPAIN / 34(3) 4874486; FAX: 34(3) 4881394

Ray Riling Arms Books Co., 6844 Gorsten St., Philadelphia, PA 19119 / 215-438-2456; FAX: 215-438-5395 sales@rayrilingarmsbooks.com www.rayrilings.com

Ray's Gunsmith Shop, 3199 Elm Ave., Grand Junction, CO 81504 / 970-434-6162; FAX: 970-434-6162

Raytech Div. of Lyman Products Corp., 475 Smith Street, Middletown, CT 06457-1541 / 860-632-2020; or 800-225-9626; FAX: 860-632-1699 lymansales@cshore.com www.lymanproducts.com

RCBS Div. of Blount, 605 Oro Dam Blvd., Oroville, CA 95965 / 800-533-5000; or 916-533-5191; FAX: 916-533-1647 www.rcbs.com

Reagent Chemical & Research, Inc. (See Calico Hard)

Reardon Products, P.O. Box 126, Morrison, IL 61270 / 815-772-3155

Red Diamond Dist. Co., 1304 Snowdon Dr., Knoxville, TN 37912

Redding Reloading Equipment, 1089 Starr Rd., Cortland, NY 13045 / 607-753-3331; FAX: 607-756-8445 techline@redding-reloading.com www.redding-reloading.com

Redfield Media Resource Center, 4607 N.E. Cedar Creek Rd., Woodland, WA 98674 / 360-225-5000; FAX: 360-225-7616

Redman's Rifling & Reboring, 189 Nichols Rd., Omak, WA 98841 / 509-826-5512

Redwood Bullet Works, 3559 Bay Rd., Redwood City, CA 94063 / 415-367-6741

Reed, Dave, Rt. 1, Box 374, Minnesota City, MN 55959 / 507-689-2944

Reiswig, Wallace E. (See Claro Walnut Gunstock

Reloaders Equipment Co., 4680 High St., Ecorse, ML 48229

Reloading Specialties, Inc., Box 1130, Pine Island, MN 55463 / 507-356-8500; FAX: 507-356-8800

Remington Arms Co., Inc., 870 Remington Drive, P.O. Box 700, Madison, NC 27025-0700 / 800-243-9700; FAX: 910-548-8700

Remington Double Shotguns, 7885 Cyd Dr., Denver, CO 80221 / 303-429-6947

Renato Gamba S.p.A.-Societa Armi Bresciane Srl., Via Artigiani 93, 25063 Gardone, Val Trompia (BS), ITALY / 30-8911640; FAX: 30-8911648

Renegade, PO Box 31546, Phoenix, AZ 85046 / 602-482-6777; FAX: 602-482-1952

Renfrew Guns & Supplies, R.R. 4, Renfrew, ON K7V 3Z7 CANADA / 613-432-7080

Reno, Wayne, 2808 Stagestop Road, Jefferson, CO 80456

Republic Arms, Inc. (See Cobra Enterprises, Inc.)

Retting, Inc., Martin B, 11029 Washington, Culver City, CA 90232 / 213-837-2412

RG-G, Inc., PO Box 935, Trinidad, CO 81082 / 719-845-1436

RH Machine & Consulting Inc, PO Box 394, Pacific, MO 63069 / 314-271-8465

Rhino, P.O. Box 787, Locust, NC 28097 / 704-753-2198

Rhodeside, Inc., 1704 Commerce Dr., Piqua, OH 45356 / 513-773-5781

Rice, Keith (See White Rock Tool & Die)

Richard H.R. Loweth (Firearms), 29 Hedgegrow Lane, Kirby Muxloe, Leics. LE9 2BN, ENGLAND

Richards Micro-Fit Stocks, 8331 N. San Fernando Ave., Sun Valley, CA 91352 / 818-767-6097; FAX: 818-767-7121

Rickard, Inc., Pete, RD 1, Box 292, Cobleskill, NY 12043 / 800-282-5663; FAX: 518-234-2454

Ridgeline, Inc, Bruce Sheldon, PO Box 930, Dewey, AZ 86327-0930 / 800-632-5900; FAX: 520-632-5900

Ridgetop Sporting Goods, P.O. Box 306, 42907 Hilligoss Ln. East, Eatonville, WA 98328 / 360-832-6422; FAX: 360-832-6422

Ries, Chuck, 415 Ridgecrest Dr., Grants Pass, OR 97527 / 503-476-5623

Rifles, Inc., 873 W. 5400 N., Cedar City, UT 84720 / 801-586-5996; FAX: 801-586-5996

Rigby & Co., John, 500 Linne Rd. Ste. D, Paso Robles, CA 93446 / 805-227-4236; FAX: 805-227-4723 jrigby@calinet www.johnrigbyandco.com

Riggs, Jim, 206 Azalea, Boerne, TX 78006 / 210-249-8567

Riley Ledbetter Airguns, 1804 E. Sprague St., Winston Salem, NC 27107-3521 / 919-784-0676

Rim Pac Sports, Inc., 1034 N. Soldano Ave., Azusa, CA 91702-2135

Ringler Custom Leather Co., 31 Shining Mtn. Rd., Powell, WY 82435 / 307-645-3255

Ripley Rifles, 42 Fletcher Street, Ripley, Derbyshire, DE5 3LP ENGLAND / 011-0773-748353

River Road Sporting Clays, Bruce Barsotti, P.O. Box 3016, Gonzales, CA 93926 / 408-675-2473

Rizzini F.lli (See U.S. Importers-Moore & C England)

Rizzini SNC, Via 2 Giugno, 7/7Bis-25060, Marcheno (Brescia), ITALY

RLCM Enterprises, 110 Hill Crest Drive, Burleson, TX 76028

RMS Custom Gunsmithing, 4120 N. Bitterwell, Prescott Valley, AZ 86314 / 520-772-7626

Robert Evans Engraving, 332 Vine St., Oregon City, OR 97045 / 503-656-5693

Robert Valade Engraving, 931 3rd Ave., Seaside, OR 97138 / 503-738-7672

Robinett, R. G., P.O. Box 72, Madrid, IA 50156 / 515-795-2906

Robinson, Don, Pennsylvaia Hse, 36 Fairfax Crescent, W Yorkshire, ENGLAND / 0422-364458

Robinson Armament Co., PO Box 16776, Salt Lake City, UT 84116 / 801-355-0401; FAX: 801-355-0402 zdf@robarm.com; www.robarm.com

Robinson Firearms Mfg. Ltd., 1699 Blondeaux Crescent, Kelowna, BC V1Y 4J8 CANADA / 604-868-9596

Robinson H.V. Bullets, 3145 Church St., Zachary, LA 70791 / 504-654-4029

Rochester Lead Works, 76 Anderson Ave., Rochester, NY 14607 / 716-442-8500; FAX: 716-442-4712

Rock River Arms, 101 Noble St., Cleveland, IL 61241

Rockwood Corp., Speedwell Division, 136 Lincoln Blvd., Middlesex, NJ 08846 / 800-243-8274; FAX: 980-560-7475

Rocky Mountain Armoury, Mr. Felix LesMerises, 610 Main Street, P.O. Box 691, Frisco, CO 80443-0691 / 970-668-0136; FAX: 970-668-4484 felix@rockymountainarmoury.com

Rocky Mountain Arms, Inc., 1813 Sunset Pl, Unit D, Longmont, CO 80501 / 800-375-0846; FAX: 303-678-8766

Rocky Mountain Target Co., 3 Aloe Way, Leesburg, FL 34788 / 352-365-9598

Rocky Mountain Wildlife Products, PO Box 999, La Porte, CO 80535 / 970-484-2768; FAX: 970-484-0807 critrcall@earthlink.net www.critrcall.com

Rocky Shoes & Boots, 294 Harper St., Nelsonville, OH 45764 / 800-848-9452; or 614-753-1951; FAX: 614-753-4024

Rodgers & Sons Ltd., Joseph (See George Ibberson)

Rogue Rifle Co., Inc., P.O. Box 20, Prospect, OR 97536 / 541-560-4040; FAX: 541-560-4041

Rogue River Rifleworks, 500 Linne Road #D, Paso Robles, CA 93446 / 805-227-4706; FAX: 805-227-4723 rrrifles@calinet

Rohner, Hans, 1148 Twin Sisters Ranch Rd., Nederland, CO 80466-9600

Rohner, John, 186 Virginia Ave, Asheville, NC 28806 / 303-444-3841

Rohrbaugh, P.O. Box 785, Bayport, NY 11705 / 631-363-2843; FAX: 631-363-2681 API380@aol.com

Romain's Custom Guns, Inc., RD 1, Whetstone Rd., Brockport, PA 15823 / 814-265-1948 romwhetstone@penn.com

Ron Frank Custom Classic Arms, 7131 Richland Rd., Ft. Worth, TX 76118 / 817-284-9300; FAX: 817-284-9300 rfrank3974@aol.com

Rooster Laboratories, P.O. Box 414605, Kansas City, MO 64141 / 816-474-1622; FAX: 816-474-7622

Rorschach Precision Products, 417 Keats Cir., Irving, TX 75061 / 214-790-3487

Rosenberg & Son, Jack A, 12229 Cox Ln, Dallas, TX 75234 / 214-241-6302

Ross, Don, 12813 West 83 Terrace, Lenexa, KS 66215 / 913-492-6982

Rosser, Bob, 1824 29th Ave. So., Suite 214, Homewood, AL 35209 / 205-870-4422; FAX: 205-870-4421 bob@hand_engravers.com handengravers.com

Rossi Firearms, Gary Mchalik, 16175 NW 49th Ave, Miami, FL 33014-6314 / 305-474-0401; FAX: 305-623-7506

Roto Carve, 2754 Garden Ave., Janesville, IA 50647

Rottweil Compe, 1330 Glassell, Orange, CA 92667

Roy Baker's Leather Goods, PO Box 893, Magnolia, AR 71754 / 870-234-0344

Royal Arms Gunstocks, 919 8th Ave. NW, Great Falls, MT 59404 / 406-453-1149; FAX: 406-453-1194 royalarms@lmt.net; lmt.net/~royalarms

Roy's Custom Grips, Rt. 3, Box 174-E, Lynchburg, VA 24504 / 804-993-3470

RPM, 15481 N. Twin Lakes Dr., Tucson, AZ 85739 / 520-825-1233; FAX: 520-825-3333

Rubright Bullets, 1008 S. Quince Rd., Walnutport, PA 18088 / 215-767-1339

Rucker Dist. Inc., P.O. Box 479, Terrell, TX 75160 / 214-563-2094

Ruger (See Sturm, Ruger & Co., Inc.)

Ruger, Chris. See: RUGER'S CUSTOM GUNS

Ruger's Custom Guns, Chris Ruger, 1050 Morton Blvd., Kingston, NY 12401 / 845-336-7106; FAX: 845-336-7106 rugerscustom@outdrs.net rugergunsmith.com

Rundell's Gun Shop, 6198 Frances Rd., Clio, MI 48420 / 313-687-0559

Runge, Robert P., 1120 Helderberg Trl. #1, Berne, NY 12023-2909

Rupert's Gun Shop, 2202 Dick Rd., Suite B, Fenwick, MI 48834 / 517-248-3252

Russ Haydon Shooters' Supply, 15018 Goodrich Dr. NW, Gig Harbor, WA 98329 / 253-857-7557; FAX: 253-857-7884

Russ Trading Post, William A. Russ, 23 William St., Addison, NY 14801-1326 / 607-359-3896

Russ, William. See: RUSS TRADING POST

Rusteprufe Laboratories, 1319 Jefferson Ave., Sparta, WI 54656 / 608-269-4144; FAX: 608-366-1972 rusteprufe@centurytiel.net rusteprufe.com

Rusty Duck Premium Gun Care Products, 7785 Foundation Dr., Suite 6, Florence, KY 41042 / 606-342-5553; FAX: 606-342-5556

Rutgers Book Center, 127 Raritan Ave., Highland Park, NJ 08904 / 908-545-4344; FAX: 908-545-6686

Rutten (See U.S. Importer-Labanu Inc)

RWS (See US Importer-Dynamit Nobel-RWS, Inc.), 81 Ruckman Rd, Closter, NJ 07624 / 201-767-7971; FAX: 201-767-1589

Ryan, Chad L., RR 3, Box 72, Cresco, IA 52136 / 319-547-4384

MANUFACTURER'S DIRECTORY

S&K Scope Mounts, RD 2 Box 72E, Sugar Grove, PA 16350 / 814-489-3091; or 800-578-9862; FAX: 814-489-5466 comments@scopemounts.com www.scopemounts.com

S&S Firearms, 74-11 Myrtle Ave., Glendale, NY 11385 / 718-497-1100; FAX: 718-497-1105

S.A.R.L. G. Granger, 66 cours Fauriel, 42100, Saint Etienne, FRANCE / 04 77 25 14 73; FAX: 04 77 38 66 99

S.C.R.C., PO Box 660, Katy, TX 77492-0660 FAX: 713-578-2124

S.D. Meacham, 1070 Angel Ridge, Peck, ID 83545

S.G.S. Sporting Guns Srl., Via Della Resistenza, 37 20090, Buccinasco, ITALY / 2-45702446; FAX: 2-45702464

S.I.A.C.E. (See U.S. Importer-IAR Inc)

Sabatti S.r.l., via Alessandro Volta 90, 25063 Gardone V.T., Brescia, ITALY / 030-8912207-831312; FAX: 030-8912059

SAECO (See Redding Reloading Equipment)

Safari Press, Inc., 15621 Chemical Lane B, Huntington Beach, CA 92649 / 714-894-9080; FAX: 714-894-4949

Safariland Ltd., Inc., 3120 E. Mission Blvd., P.O. Box 51478, Ontario, CA 91761 / 909-923-7300; FAX: 909-923-7400

SAFE, PO Box 864, Post Falls, ID 83877 / 208-773-3624; FAX: 208-773-6819 staysafe@safe-llc.com; www.safe-llc.com

Safety Speed Holster, Inc., 910 S. Vail Ave., Montebello, CA 90640 / 323-723-4140; FAX: 323-726-6973 e-mail@safetyspeedholster.com www.safetyspeedholster.com

Saf-T-Lok, 5713 Corporate Way, Suite 100, W. Palm Beach, FL 33407

Sako Ltd (See U.S. Importer-Stoeger Industries)

Sam Welch Gun Engraving, Sam Welch, HC 64 Box 2110, Moab, UT 84532 / 435-259-8131

Samco Global Arms, Inc., 6995 NW 43rd St., Miami, FL 33166 / 305-593-9782; FAX: 305-593-1014 samco@samcoglobal.com; www.samcoglobal.com

Sampson, Roger, 2316 Mahogany St., Mora, MN 55051 / 612-679-4868

San Marco (See U.S. Importers-Cape Outfitters-EMF

Sanders Custom Gun Service, 2358 Tyler Lane, Louisville, KY 40205 / 502-454-3338; FAX: 502-451-8857

Sanders Gun and Machine Shop, 145 Delhi Road, Manchester, IA 52057

Sandia Die & Cartridge Co., 37 Atancacio Rd. NE, Auquerque, NM 87123 / 505-298-5729

Sarco, Inc., 323 Union St., Stirling, NJ 07980 / 908-647-3800; FAX: 908-647-9413

Sarsilmaz Shotguns - Turkey (see B.C. Outdoors)

Sauer (See U.S. Importers-Paul Co., The, Sigarms I

Sauls, R. See: BRYAN & ASSOC.

Saunders Gun & Machine Shop, R.R. 2, Delhi Road, Manchester, IA 52057

Savage Arms (Canada), Inc., 248 Water St., P.O. Box 1240, Lakefield, ON K0L 2H0 CANADA / 705-652-8000; FAX: 705-652-8431

Savage Arms, Inc., 100 Springdale Rd., Westfield, MA 01085 / 413-568-7001; FAX: 413-562-7764

Savage Range Systems, Inc., 100 Springdale RD., Westfield, MA 01085 / 413-568-7001; FAX: 413-562-1152

Saville Iron Co. (See Greenwood Precision)

Savino, Barbara J., P.O. Box 51, West Burke, VT 05871-0051

Scansport, Inc., P.O. Box 700, Enfield, NH 03748 / 603-632-7654

Scattergun Technologies, Inc., 620 8th Ave. South, Nashville, TN 37203 / 615-254-1441; FAX: 615-254-1449

Sceery Game Calls, P.O. Box 6520, Sante Fe, NM 87502 / 505-471-9110; FAX: 505-471-3476

Schaefer Shooting Sports, P.O. Box 1515, Melville, NY 11747-0515 / 516-643-5466; FAX: 516-643-2426 rschaefe@optonline.net www.schaefershooting.com

Scharch Mfg., Inc., 10325 Co. Rd. 120, Salida, CO 81201 / 719-539-7242; or 800-836-4683; FAX: 719-539-3021 scharch@chaffee.net www.scharch.com

Scherer, Liz. See: SCHERER SUPPLIES

Scherer Supplies, Liz Scherer, Box 250, Ewing, VA 24248 FAX: 423-733-2073

Schiffman, Curt, 3017 Kevin Cr., Idaho Falls, ID 83402 / 208-524-4684

Schiffman, Mike, 8233 S. Crystal Springs, McCammon, ID 83250 / 208-254-9114

Schiffman, Norman, 3017 Kevin Cr., Idaho Falls, ID 83402 / 208-524-4684

Schmidt & Bender, Inc., PO Box 134, Meriden, NH 03770 / 603-469-3565; FAX: 603-469-3471 scopes@cyberportal.net; schmidtbender.com

Schmidtke Group, 17050 W. Salentine Dr., New Berlin, WI 53151-7349

Schneider Bullets, 3655 West 214th St., Fairview Park, OH 44126

Schneider Rifle Barrels, Inc, Gary, 12202 N 62nd Pl, Scottsdale, AZ 85254 / 602-948-2525

Schroeder Bullets, 1421 Thermal Ave., San Diego, CA 92154 / 619-423-3523; FAX: 619-423-8124

Schuetzen Pistol Works, 620-626 Old Pacific Hwy. SE, Olympia, WA 98513 / 360-459-3471; FAX: 360-491-3447

Schulz Industries, 16247 Minnesota Ave., Paramount, CA 90723 / 213-439-5903

Schumakers Gun Shop, 512 Prouty Corner Lp. A, Colville, WA 99114 / 509-684-4848

Scope Control, Inc., 5775 Co. Rd. 23 SE, Alexandria, MN 56308 / 612-762-7295

ScopLevel, 151 Lindbergh Ave., Suite C, Livermore, CA 94550 / 925-449-5052; FAX: 925-373-0861

Score High Gunsmithing, 9812-A, Cochiti SE, Albuquerque, NM 087123 / 800-326-5632; or 505-292-5532; FAX: 505-292-2592

Scot Powder, Rt.1 Box 167, McEwen, TN 37101 / 800-416-3006; FAX: 615-729-4211

Scot Powder Co. of Ohio, Inc., Box GD96, Only, TN 37140 / 615-729-4207; or 800-416-3006; FAX: 615-729-4217

Scott Fine Guns Inc., Thad, PO Box 412, Indianola, MS 38751 / 601-887-5929

Scott McDougall & Associates, 7950 Redwood Dr., Suite 13, Cotati, CA 94931 / 707-546-2264; FAX: 707-795-1911 www.colt380.com

Searcy Enterprises, PO Box 584, Boron, CA 93596 / 760-762-6771; FAX: 760-762-0191

Second Chance Body Armor, P.O. Box 578, Central Lake, MI 49622 / 616-544-5721; FAX: 616-544-9824

Seebeck Assoc., R.E., P. O. Box 59752, Dallas, TX 75229

Seecamp Co. Inc., L. W., PO Box 255, New Haven, CT 06502 / 203-877-3429; FAX: 203-877-3429

Segway Industries, P.O. Box 783, Suffern, NY 10901-0783 / 914-357-5510

Seligman Shooting Products, Box 133, Seligman, AZ 86337 / 602-422-3607

Sellier & Bellot, USA Inc, PO Box 7307, Shawnee Mission, KS 66207 / 800-960-2422 or 913-664-5933; FAX: 229-723-8748

Selsi Co., Inc., P.O. Box 10, Midland Park, NJ 07432-0010 / 201-935-0388; FAX: 201-935-5851

Semmer, Charles (See Remington Double Shotguns), 7885 Cyd Dr, Denver, CO 80221 / 303-429-6947

Sentinel Arms, P.O. Box 57, Detroit, MI 48231 / 313-331-1951; FAX: 313-331-1456

Service Armament, 689 Bergen Blvd., Ridgefield, NJ 07657

Servus Footwear Co., 1136 2nd St., Rock Island, IL 61204 / 309-786-7741; FAX: 309-786-9808

SGS Importers, 1750 Brielle Ave. Unit B-1, Wanamassa, NJ 07712 / 732-493-0302; FAX: 732-493-0301

Shappy Bullets, 76 Milldale Ave., Plantsville, CT 06479 / 203-621-3704

Sharp Shooter Supply, 4970 Lehman Road, Delphos, OH 45833 / 419-695-3179

Sharps Arms Co., Inc., C., 100 Centennial, Box 885, Big Timber, MT 59011 / 406-932-4353

Shaw, Inc., E. R. (See Small Arms Mfg. Co.)

Shay's Gunsmithing, 931 Marvin Ave., Lebanon, PA 17042

Sheffield Knifemakers Supply, Inc., PO Box 741107, Orange City, FL 32774-1107 / 386-775-6453; FAX: 386-774-5754

Sheldon, Bruce. See: RIDGELINE, INC

Shepherd Enterprises, Inc., Box 189, Waterloo, NE 68069 / 402-779-2424; FAX: 402-779-4010 sshepherd@shepherdscopes.com www.shepherdscopes.com

Sherwood, George, 46 N. River Dr., Roseburg, OR 97470 / 541-672-3159

Shilen, Inc., 205 Metro Park Blvd., Ennis, TX 75119 / 972-875-5318; FAX: 972-875-5402

Shiloh Creek, Box 357, Cottleville, MO 63338 / 314-925-1842; FAX: 314-925-1842

Shiloh Rifle Mfg., 201 Centennial Dr., Big Timber, MT 59011 / 406-932-4454; FAX: 406-932-5627

Shockley, Harold H., 204 E. Farmington Rd., Hanna City, IL 61536 / 309-565-4524

Shoemaker & Sons Inc., Tex, 714 W Cienega Ave, San Dimas, CA 91773 / 909-592-2071; FAX: 909-592-2378

Shoot Where You Look, Leon Measures, Dept GD, 408 Fair, Livingston, TX 77351

Shooters Arms Manufacturing Inc., Rivergate Mall, Gen. Maxilom Ave., Cebu City 6000, PHILIPPINES / 6332-254-8478; www.shootersarms.com.ph

Shooter's Choice Gun Care, 15050 Berkshire Ind. Pky., Middlefield, OH 44062 / 440-834-8888; FAX: 440-834-3388; www.shooterschoice.com

Shooter's Edge Inc., 3313 Creekstone Dr., Fort Collins, CO 80525

Shooters Supply, 1120 Tieton Dr., Yakima, WA 98902 / 509-452-1181

Shooter's World, 3828 N. 28th Ave., Phoenix, AZ 85017 / 602-266-0170

Shooters, Inc., 5139 Stanart St., Norfolk, VA 23502 / 757-461-9152; FAX: 757-461-9155 gflocker@aol.com

Shootin' Shack, Inc., 357 Cypress Drive, No. 10, Tequesta, FL 33469 / 561-842-0990; FAX: 561-545-4861

Shooting Chrony, Inc., 3269 Niagara Falls Blvd., N. Tonawanda, NY 14120 / 905-276-6292; FAX: 416-276-6295

Shooting Specialties (See Titus, Daniel)

Shooting Star, 1715 FM 1626 Ste 105, Manchaca, TX 78652 / 512-462-0009

Shoot-N-C Targets (See Birchwood Casey)

Shotgun Sports, PO Box 6810, Auburn, CA 95604 / 530-889-2220; FAX: 530-889-9106

Shotgun Sports Magazine, dba Shootin' Accessories Ltd., P.O. Box 6810, Auburn, CA 95604 / 916-889-2220

Shotguns Unlimited, 2307 Fon Du Lac Rd., Richmond, VA 23229 / 804-752-7115

Siegrist Gun Shop, 8752 Turtle Road, Whittemore, MI 48770 / 989-873-3929

Sierra Bullets, 1400 W. Henry St., Sedalia, MO 65301 / 816-827-6300; FAX: 816-827-6300

Sierra Specialty Prod. Co., 1344 Oakhurst Ave., Los Altos, CA 94024 FAX: 415-965-1536

SIG, CH-8212 Neuhausen, SWITZERLAND

Sigarms, Inc., Corporate Park, Exeter, NH 03833 / 603-772-2302; FAX: 603-772-9082 www.sigarms.com

Sightron, Inc., 1672B Hwy. 96, Franklinton, NC 27525 / 919-528-8783; FAX: 919-528-0995 info@sightron.com www.sightron.com

Signet Metal Corp., 551 Stewart Ave., Brooklyn, NY 11222 / 718-384-5400; FAX: 718-388-7488

SIG-Sauer (See U.S. Importer-Sigarms Inc.)

Silencio/Safety Direct, 56 Coney Island Dr., Sparks, NV 89431 / 800-648-1812; or 702-354-4451; FAX: 702-359-1074

Silent Hunter, 1100 Newton Ave., W. Collingswood, NJ 08107 / 609-854-3276

Silhouette Leathers, PO Box 1161, Gunnison, CO 81230 / 303-641-6639 oldshooter@yahoo.com

Silver Eagle Machining, 18007 N. 69th Ave., Glendale, AZ 85308

Silver Ridge Gun Shop (See Goodwin, Fred)

Simmons, Jerry, 715 Middlebury St., Goshen, IN 46528-2717 / 574-533-8546

Simmons Gun Repair, Inc., 700 S. Rogers Rd., Olathe, KS 66062 / 913-782-3131; FAX: 913-782-4189

Simmons Outdoor Corp., PO Box 217, Heflin, AL 36264

Sinclair International, Inc., 2330 Wayne Haven St., Fort Wayne, IN 46803 / 260-493-1858; FAX: 260-493-2530 sales@sinclairintl.com www.sinclairintl.com

Singletary, Kent, 2915 W. Ross, Phoenix, AZ 85027 / 602-526-6836 kentscustom@hotmail.com

Siskiyou Gun Works (See Donnelly, C. P.)

Six Enterprises, 320-D Turtle Creek Ct., San Jose, CA 95125 / 408-999-0201; FAX: 408-999-0216

SKB Shotguns, 4325 S. 120th St., Omaha, NE 68137 / 800-752-2767; FAX: 402-330-8029 skb@radiks.net skbshotguns.com

Skeoch, Brian R., PO Box 279, Glenrock, WY 82637 / 307-436-9655; FAX: 307-436-9034

Skip's Machine, 364 29 Road, Grand Junction, CO 81501 / 303-245-5417

Sklany's Machine Shop, 566 Birch Grove Dr., Kalispell, MT 59901 / 406-755-4257

Slezak, Jerome F., 1290 Marlowe, Lakewood (Cleveland), OH 44107 / 216-221-1668

Slug Site, Ozark Wilds, 21300 Hwy. 5, Versailles, MO 65084 / 573-378-6430 john.ebeling.com

Small Arms Mfg. Co., 5312 Thoms Run Rd., Bridgeville, PA 15017 / 412-221-4343; FAX: 412-221-4303

Small Arms Specialists, 443 Firchburg Rd, Mason, NH 03048 / 603-878-0427; FAX: 603-878-3905 miniguns@empire.net miniguns.com

Small Custom Mould & Bullet Co., Box 17211, Tucson, AZ 85731

Smart Parts, 1203 Spring St., Latrobe, PA 15650 / 412-539-2660; FAX: 412-539-2298

Smires, C. L., 5222 Windmill Lane, Columbia, MD 21044-1328

Smith & Wesson, 2100 Roosevelt Ave., Springfield, MA 01104 / 413-781-8300; FAX: 413-731-8980

Smith, Art, 230 Main St. S., Hector, MN 55342 / 320-848-2760; FAX: 320-848-2760

Smith, Mark A., P.O. Box 182, Sinclair, WY 82334 / 307-324-7929

Smith, Michael, 2612 Ashmore Ave., Red Bank, TN 37415 / 615-267-8341

Smith, Ron, 5869 Straley, Ft. Worth, TX 76114 / 817-732-6768

Smith, Sharmon, 4545 Speas Rd., Fruitland, ID 83619 / 208-452-6329 sharmon@fmtc.com

Smith Abrasives, Inc., 1700 Sleepy Valley Rd., P.O. Box 5095, Hot Springs, AR 71902-5095 / 501-321-2244; FAX: 501-321-9232

Smith, Judy. See: L.B.T.

Smith Saddlery, Jesse W., 0499 County Road J, Pritchett, CO 81064 / 509-325-0622

Smokey Valley Rifles, E1998 Smokey Valley Rd, Scandinavia, WI 54977 / 715-467-2674

Snapp's Gunshop, 6911 E. Washington Rd., Clare, MI 48617 / 989-386-9226

Sno-Seal, Inc. (See Atsko/Sno-Seal)

Societa Armi Bresciane Srl (See U.S. Importer-Cape

SOS Products Co. (See Buck Stix-SOS Products Co.), Box 3, Neenah, WI 54956

Sotheby's, 1334 York Ave. at 72nd St., New York, NY 10021 / 212-606-7260

Sound Technology, Box 391, Pelham, AL 35124 / 205-664-5860; or 907-486-2825 rem700P@sprintmail.com; www.soundtechsilencers.com

South Bend Replicas, Inc., 61650 Oak Rd.., South Bend, IN 46614 / 219-289-4500

Southeastern Community College, 1015 S. Gear Ave., West Burlington, IA 52655 / 319-752-2731

Southern Ammunition Co., Inc., 4232 Meadow St., Loris, SC 29569-3124 / 803-756-3262; FAX: 803-756-3583

Southern Bloomer Mfg. Co., P.O. Box 1621, Bristol, TN 37620 / 615-878-6660; FAX: 615-878-8761

Southern Security, 1700 Oak Hills Dr., Kingston, TN 37763 / 423-376-6297; FAX: 800-251-9992

Sparks, Milt, 605 E. 44th St. No. 2, Boise, ID 83714-4800

Spartan-Realtree Products, Inc., 1390 Box Circle, Columbus, GA 31907 / 706-569-9101; FAX: 706-569-0042

Specialty Gunsmithing, Lynn McMurdo, P.O. Box 404, Afton, WY 83110 / 307-886-5535

Specialty Shooters Supply, Inc., 3325 Griffin Rd., Suite 9mm, Fort Lauderdale, FL 33317

Speer Bullets, PO Box 856, Lewiston, ID 83501 / 208-746-2351; www.speer-bullets.com

Spegel, Craig, PO Box 387, Nehalem, OR 97131 / 503-368-5653

Speiser, Fred D., 2229 Dearborn, Missoula, MT 59801 / 406-549-8133

Spencer Reblue Service, 1820 Tupelo Trail, Holt, MI 48842 / 517-694-7474

Spencer's Custom Guns, 4107 Jacobs Creek Dr, Scottsville, VA 24590 / 804-293-6836; FAX: 804-293-6836

SPG LLC, PO Box 1625, Cody, WY 82414 / 307-587-7621; FAX: 307-587-7695

Sphinx Systems Ltd., Gesteigtstrasse 12, CH-3800, Matten, BRNE, SWITZERLAND

Splitfire Sporting Goods, L.L.C., P.O. Box 1044, Orem, UT 84059-1044 / 801-932-7950; FAX: 801-932-7959 www.splitfireguns.com

Sport Flite Manufacturing Co., PO Box 1082, Bloomfield Hills, MI 48303 / 248-647-3747

Sporting Clays Of America, 9257 Bluckeye Rd, Sugar Grove, OH 43155-9632 / 740-746-8334; FAX: 740-746-8605

Sports Innovations Inc., P.O. Box 5181, 8505 Jacksboro Hwy., Wichita Falls, TX 76307 / 817-723-6015

Sportsman Safe Mfg. Co., 6309-6311 Paramount Blvd., Long Beach, CA 90805 / 800-266-7150; or 310-984-5445

Sportsman Supply Co., 714 E. Eastwood, P.O. Box 650, Marshall, MO 65340 / 816-886-9393

Sportsman's Communicators, 588 Radcliffe Ave., Pacific Palisades, CA 90272 / 800-538-3752

Sportsmatch U.K. Ltd., 16 Summer St., Leighton, Buzzard Beds, Bedfordshire, LU7 8HT ENGLAND / 01525-381638; FAX: 01525-851236 info@sportsmatch-uk.com www.sportsmatch-uk.com

Sportsmen's Exchange & Western Gun Traders, Inc., 560 S. C St., Oxnard, CA 93030 / 805-483-1917

Spradlin's, 457 Shannon Rd, Texos Creek, CO 81223 / 719-275-7105; FAX: 719-275-3852 spradlins@prodigy.net; www.spradlins.net

Springfield Sporters, Inc., RD 1, Penn Run, PA 15765 / 412-254-2626; FAX: 412-254-9173

Springfield, Inc., 420 W. Main St., Geneseo, IL 61254 / 309-944-5631; FAX: 309-944-3676

Spyderco, Inc., 20011 Golden Gate Canyon Rd., Golden, CO 80403 / 800-525-7770; or 800-525-7770; FAX: 303-278-2229; sales@spyderco.com www.spyderco.com

SSK Industries, J. D. Jones, 590 Woodvue Lane, Wintersville, OH 43953 / 740-264-0176; FAX: 740-264-2257

Stackpole Books, 5067 Ritter Rd., Mechanicsburg, PA 17055-6921 / 717-796-0411; FAX: 717-796-0412

Stalker, Inc., P.O. Box 21, Fishermans Wharf Rd., Malakoff, TX 75148 / 903-489-1010

Stalwart Corporation, PO Box 46, Evanston, WY 82931 / 307-789-7687; FAX: 307-789-7688

Stan De Treville & Co., 4129 Normal St., San Diego, CA 92103 / 619-298-3393

Stanley Bullets, 2085 Heatheridge Ln., Reno, NV 89509

Stanley Scruggs' Game Calls, Rt. 1, Hwy. 661, Cullen, VA 23934 / 804-542-4241; or 800-323-4828

Star Ammunition, Inc., 5520 Rock Hampton Ct., Indianapolis, IN 46268 / 800-221-5927; FAX: 317-872-5847

Star Custom Bullets, PO Box 608, 468 Main St., Ferndale, CA 95536 / 707-786-9140; FAX: 707-786-9117 wmebridge@humboldt.com

Star Machine Works, PO Box 1872, Pioneer, CA 95666 / 209-295-5000

Starke Bullet Company, P.O. Box 400, 605 6th St. NW, Cooperstown, ND 58425 / 888-797-3431

Starkey Labs, 6700 Washington Ave. S., Eden Prairie, MN 55344

Starkey's Gun Shop, 9430 McCombs, El Paso, TX 79924 / 915-751-3030

Starlight Training Center, Inc., Rt. 1, P.O. Box 88, Bronaugh, MO 64728 / 417-843-3555

Starline, Inc., 1300 W. Henry St., Sedalia, MO 65301 / 660-827-6640; FAX: 660-827-6650 info@starlinebrass.com; http://www.starlinebrass.com

Starr Trading Co., Jedediah, PO Box 2007, Farmington Hills, MI 48333 / 810-683-4343; FAX: 810-683-3282

Starrett Co., L. S., 121 Crescent St, Athol, MA 01331 / 978-249-3551; FAX: 978-249-8495

State Arms Gun Co., 815 S. Division St., Waunakee, WI 53597 / 608-849-5800

Steelman's Gun Shop, 10465 Beers Rd., Swartz Creek, MI 48473 / 810-735-4884

Steffens, Ron, 18396 Mariposa Creek Rd., Willits, CA 95490 / 707-485-0873

Stegall, James B., 26 Forest Rd., Wallkill, NY 12589

Steve Henigson & Associates, P.O. Box 2726, Culver City, CA 90231 / 310-305-8288; FAX: 310-305-1905

Steve Kamyk Engraver, 9 Grandview Dr., Westfield, MA 01085-1810 / 413-568-0457

Steves House of Guns, Rt. 1, Minnesota City, MN 55959 / 507-689-2573

Stewart Game Calls, Inc., Johnny, PO Box 7954, 5100 Fort Ave, Waco, TX 76714 / 817-772-3261; FAX: 817-772-3670

Stewart's Gunsmithing, P.O. Box 5854, Pietersburg North 0750, Transvaal, SOUTH AFRICA / 01521-89401

Steyr Mannlicher AG & CO KG, Mannlicherstrasse 1, A-4400, Steyr, AUSTRIA / 0043-7252-78621; FAX: 0043-7252-68621

STI International, 114 Halmar Cove, Georgetown, TX 78628 / 800-959-8201; FAX: 512-819-0465 www.stiguns.com

Stiles Custom Guns, 76 Cherry Run Rd, Box 1605, Homer City, PA 15748 / 712-479-9945

Stillwell, Robert, 421 Judith Ann Dr., Schertz, TX 78154

Stoeger Industries, 17603 Indian Head Hwy., Suite 200, Accokeek, MD 20607-2501 / 301-283-6300; FAX: 301-283-6986; www.stoegerindustries.com

Stoeger Publishing Co. (See Stoeger Industries)

Stone Enterprises Ltd., 426 Harveys Neck Rd., PO Box 335, Wicomico Church, VA 22579 / 804-580-5114; FAX: 804-580-8421

Stone Mountain Arms, 5988 Peachtree Corners E., Norcross, GA 30071 / 800-251-9412

Stoney Point Products, Inc., PO Box 234, 1822 N Minnesota St, New Ulm, MN 56073-0234 / 507-354-3360; FAX: 507-354-7236 stoney@newulmtel.net www.stoneypoint.com

Storage Tech, 1254 Morris Ave., N. Huntingdon, PA 15642 / 800-437-9393

Storey, Dale A. (See DGS Inc.)

Storm, Gary, P.O. Box 5211, Richardson, TX 75083 / 214-385-0862

Stott's Creek Armory, Inc., 2526 S. 475W, Morgantown, IN 46160 / 317-878-5489; FAX: 317-878-9489 www.sccalendar.com

Stratco, Inc., P.O. Box 2270, Kalispell, MT 59901 / 406-755-1221; FAX: 406-755-1226

Strayer, Sandy. See: STRAYER-VOIGT, INC.

Strayer-Voigt, Inc., Sandy Strayer, 3435 Ray Orr Blvd, Grand Prairie, TX 75050 / 972-513-0575

Streamlight, Inc., 1030 W. Germantown Pike, Norristown, PA 19403 / 215-631-0600; FAX: 610-631-0712

Strong Holster Co., 39 Grove St., Gloucester, MA 01930 / 508-281-3300; FAX: 508-281-6321

Strutz Rifle Barrels, Inc., W. C., PO Box 611, Eagle River, WI 54521 / 715-479-4766

Stuart, V. Pat, Rt.1, Box 447-S, Greenville, VA 24440 / 804-556-3845

Sturgeon Valley Sporters, K. Ide, PO Box 283, Vanderbilt, MI 49795 / 517-983-4338

Sturm Ruger & Co. Inc., 200 Ruger Rd., Prescott, AZ 86301 / 928-541-8820; FAX: 520-541-8850 www.ruger.com

"Su-Press-On",Inc., PO Box 09161, Detroit, MI 48209 / 313-842-4222

Sullivan, David S .(See Westwind Rifles Inc.)

Summit Specialties, Inc., P.O. Box 786, Decatur, AL 35602 / 205-353-0634; FAX: 205-353-9818

Sun Welding Safe Co., 290 Easy St. No.3, Simi Valley, CA 93065 / 805-584-6678; or 800-729-SAFE; FAX: 805-584-6169; sunwelding.com

Sunny Hill Enterprises, Inc., W1790 Cty. HHH, Malone, WI 53049 / 920-795-4722; FAX: 920-795-4822

Super 6 LLC, Gary Knopp, 3806 W. Lisbon Ave., Milwaukee, WI 53208 / 414-344-3343; FAX: 414-344-0304

Sure-Shot Game Calls, Inc., P.O. Box 816, 6835 Capitol, Groves, TX 77619 / 409-962-1636; FAX: 409-962-5465

Survival Arms, Inc., 273 Canal St., Shelton, CT 06484-3173 / 203-924-6533; FAX: 203-924-2581

Svon Corp., 2107 W. Blue Heron Blvd., Riviera Beach, FL 33404 / 508-881-8852

Swann, D. J., 5 Orsova Close, Eltham North Vic., 3095 AUSTRALIA / 03-431-0323

Swanndri New Zealand, 152 Elm Ave., Burlingame, CA 94010 / 415-347-6158

Swanson, Mark, 975 Heap Avenue, Prescott, AZ 86301 / 928-778-4423

Swarovski Optik North America Ltd., 2 Slater Rd., Cranston, RI 02920 / 401-946-2220; or 800-426-3089; FAX: 401-946-2587

Sweet Home, Inc., P.O. Box 900, Orrville, OH 44667-0900

Swenson's 45 Shop, A. D., 3839 Ladera Vista Rd, Fallbrook, CA 92028-9431

Swift Bullet Co., P.O. Box 27, 201 Main St., Quinter, KS 67752 / 913-754-3959; FAX: 913-754-2359

Swift Instruments, Inc., 952 Dorchester Ave., Boston, MA 02125 / 617-436-2960; FAX: 617-436-3232

Swift River Gunworks, 450 State St., Belchertown, MA 01007 / 413-323-4052

Szweda, Robert (See RMS Custom Gunsmithing)

T

T&S Industries, Inc., 1027 Skyview Dr., W. Carrollton, OH 45449 / 513-859-8414

T.F.C. S.p.A., Via G. Marconi 118, B, Villa Carcina 25069, ITALY / 030-881271; FAX: 030-881826

T.G. Faust, Inc., 544 Minor St., Reading, PA 19602 / 610-375-8549; FAX: 610-375-4488

T.H.U. Enterprises, Inc., P.O. Box 418, Lederach, PA 19450 / 215-256-1665; FAX: 215-256-9718

T.K. Lee Co., 1282 Branchwater Ln., Birmingham, AL 35216 / 205-913-5222 odonmich@aol.com www.scopedot.com

T.W. Menck Gunsmith Inc., 5703 S. 77th St., Ralston, NE 68127

Tabler Marketing, 2554 Lincoln Blvd., Suite 555, Marina Del Rey, CA 90291 / 818-755-4565; FAX: 818-755-0972

Taconic Firearms Ltd., Perry Lane, PO Box 553, Cambridge, NY 12816 / 518-677-2704; FAX: 518-677-5974

TacStar, PO Box 547, Cottonwood, AZ 86326-0547 / 602-639-0072; FAX: 602-634-8781

Tactical Defense Institute, 574 Miami Bluff Ct., Loveland, OH 45140 / 513-677-8229; FAX: 513-677-0447

Talley, Dave, P.O. Box 821, Glenrock, WY 82637 / 307-436-8724; or 307-436-9315

MANUFACTURER'S DIRECTORY

Talmage, William G., 10208 N. County Rd. 425 W., Brazil, IN 47834 / 812-442-0804

Talon Industries Inc. (See Cobra Enterprises, Inc.)

Tamarack Products, Inc., PO Box 625, Wauconda, IL 60084 / 708-526-9333; FAX: 708-526-9353

Tanfoglio Fratelli S.r.l., via Valtrompia 39, 41, Brescia, ITALY / 30-8910361; FAX: 30-8910183

Tanglefree Industries, 1261 Heavenly Dr., Martinez, CA 94553 / 800-982-4868; FAX: 510-825-3874

Tank's Rifle Shop, PO Box 474, Fremont, NE 68026-0474 / 402-727-1317; FAX: 402-721-2573 jtank@mitec.net www.tanksrifleshop.com

Tanner (See U.S. Importer-Mandall Shooting Supply)

Taracorp Industries, Inc., 1200 Sixteenth St., Granite City, IL 62040 / 618-451-4400

Target Shooting, Inc., PO Box 773, Watertown, SD 57201 / 605-882-6955; FAX: 605-882-8840

Tar-Hunt Custom Rifles, Inc., 101 Dogtown Rd., Bloomsburg, PA 17815 / 570-784-6368; FAX: 570-784-6368 www.tar-hunt.com

Tarnhelm Supply Co., Inc., 431 High St., Boscawen, NH 03303 / 603-796-2551; FAX: 603-796-2918 info@tarnhelm.com www.tarnhelm.com

Tasco Sales, Inc., 2889 Commerce Pky., Miramar, FL 33025

Taurus Firearms, Inc., 16175 NW 49th Ave., Miami, FL 33014 / 305-624-1115; FAX: 305-623-7506

Taurus International Firearms (See U.S. Importer)

Taurus S.A. Forjas, Avenida Do Forte 511, Porto Alegre, RS BRAZIL 91360 / 55-51-347-4050; FAX: 55-51-347-3065

Taylor & Robbins, P.O. Box 164, Rixford, PA 16745 / 814-966-3233

Taylor's & Co., Inc., 304 Lenoir Dr., Winchester, VA 22603 / 540-722-2017; FAX: 540-722-2018

TCCI, P.O. Box 302, Phoenix, AZ 85001 / 602-237-3823; FAX: 602-237-3858

TCSR, 3998 Hoffman Rd., White Bear Lake, MN 55110-4626 / 800-328-5323; FAX: 612-429-0526

TDP Industries, Inc., 606 Airport Blvd., Doylestown, PA 18901 / 215-345-8687; FAX: 215-345-6057

Techno Arms (See U.S. Importer- Auto-Ordnance Corp

Tecnolegno S.p.A., via A. Locatelli, 6 10, 24019 Zogno, I ITALY / 0345-55111; FAX: 0345-55155

Ted Blocker Holsters, Inc., 9396 S.W. Tigard St., Tigard, OR 97223 / 800-650-9742; FAX: 503-670-9692 www.tedblocker.com

Tele-Optics, 630 E. Rockland Rd., PO Box 6313, Libertyville, IL 60048 / 847-362-7757

Tennessee Valley Mfg., 14 County Road 521, Corinth, MS 38834 / 601-286-5014

Ten-Ring Precision, Inc., Alex B. Hamilton, 1449 Blue Crest Lane, San Antonio, TX 78232 / 210-494-3063; FAX: 210-494-3066

TEN-X Products Group, 1905 N Main St, Suite 133, Cleburne, TX 76031-1305 / 972-243-4016; or 800-433-2225; FAX: 972-243-4112

Tepeco, P.O. Box 342, Friendswood, TX 77546 / 713-482-2702

Terry K. Kopp Professional Gunsmithing, Rt 1 Box 224, Lexington, MO 64067 / 816-259-2636

Testing Systems, Inc., 220 Pegasus Ave., Northvale, NJ 07647

Tetra Gun Lubricants (See FTI, Inc.)

Tex Shoemaker & Sons, Inc., 714 W. Cienega Ave., San Dimas, CA 91773 / 909-592-2071; FAX: 909-592-2378

Texas Armory (See Bond Arms, Inc.)

Texas Platers Supply Co., 2453 W. Five Mile Parkway, Dallas, TX 75233 / 214-330-7168

Thad Rybka Custom Leather Equipment, 134 Havilah Hill, Odenville, AL 35120

Thad Scott Fine Guns, Inc., P.O. Box 412, Indianola, MS 38751 / 601-887-5929

The A.W. Peterson Gun Shop, Inc., 4255 West Old U.S. 441, Mount Dora, FL 32757-3299 / 352-383-4258

The Accuracy Den, 25 Bitterbrush Rd., Reno, NV 89523 / 702-345-0225

The Ballistic Program Co., Inc., 2417 N. Patterson St., Thomasville, GA 31792 / 912-228-5739; or 800-368-0835

The BulletMakers Workshop, RFD 1 Box 1755, Brooks, ME 04921

The Competitive Pistol Shop, 5233 Palmer Dr., Ft. Worth, TX 76117-2433 / 817-834-8479

The Concealment Shop, Inc., 617 W. Kearney St., Ste. 205, Mesquite, TX 75149 / 972-289-8997; or 800-444-7090; FAX: 972-289-4410 concealmentshop@email.msn.com www.theconcealmentshop.com

The Country Armourer, P.O. Box 308, Ashby, MA 01431-0308 / 508-827-6797; FAX: 508-827-4845

The Creative Craftsman, Inc., 95 Highway 29 North, P.O. Box 331, Lawrenceville, GA 30246 / 404-963-2112; FAX: 404-513-9488

The Custom Shop, 890 Cochrane Crescent, Peterborough, ON K9H 5N3 CANADA / 705-742-6693

The Dutchman's Firearms, Inc., 4143 Taylor Blvd., Louisville, KY 40215 / 502-366-0555

The Ensign-Bickford Co., 660 Hopmeadow St., Simsbury, CT 06070

The Eutaw Co., Inc., 7522 Old State Rd., Holly Hill, SC 29059 / 803-496-3341

The Firearm Training Center, 9555 Blandville Rd., West Paducah, KY 42086 / 502-554-5886

The Fouling Shot, 6465 Parfet St., Arvada, CO 80004

The Gun Doctor, 435 East Maple, Roselle, IL 60172 / 708-894-0668

The Gun Parts Corp., 226 Williams Lane, West Hurley, NY 12491 / 914-679-2417; FAX: 914-679-5849

The Gun Room, 1121 Burlington, Muncie, IN 47302 / 765-282-9073; FAX: 765-282-5270 bshstleguns@aol.com

The Gun Room Press, 127 Raritan Ave., Highland Park, NJ 08904 / 732-545-4344; FAX: 732-545-6686 gunbooks@rutgersgunbooks.com www.rutgersgunbooks.com

The Gun Shop, 716-A South Rogers Road, Olathe, KS 66062

The Gun Shop, 62778 Spring Creek Rd., Montrose, CO 81401

The Gun Shop, 5550 S. 900 East, Salt Lake City, UT 84117 / 801-263-3633

The Gun Works, 247 S. 2nd St., Springfield, OR 97477 / 541-741-4118; FAX: 541-988-1097 gunworks@worldnet.att.net; www.thegunworks.com

The Gunsight, 1712 North Placentia Ave., Fullerton, CA 92631

The Gunsmith in Elk River, 14021 Victoria Lane, Elk River, MN 55330 / 612-441-7761

The Hanned Line, P.O. Box 2387, Cupertino, CA 95015-2387 smith@hanned.com www.hanned.com

The Keller Co., 4215 McEwen Rd., Dallas, TX 75244 / 214-770-8585

The Lewis Lead Remover (See LEM Gun Specialties)

The Midwest Shooting School, Pat LaBoone, 2550 Hwy. 23, Wrenshall, MN 55797 / 218-384-3670 shootingschool@starband.net

The NgraveR Co., 67 Wawecus Hill Rd., Bozrah, CT 06334 / 860-823-1533

The Ordnance Works, 2969 Pidgeon Point Road, Eureka, CA 95501 / 707-443-3252

The Orvis Co., Rt. 7, Manchester, VT 05254 / 802-362-3622; FAX: 802-362-3525

The Outdoor Connection,Inc., 7901 Panther Way, Waco, TX 76712-6556 / 800-533-6076; or 254-772-5575; FAX: 254-776-3553 floyd@outdoorconnection.com www.outdoorconnection.com

The Park Rifle Co., Ltd., Unit 6a Dartford Trade Park, Power Mill Lane, Dartford DA7 7NX, ENGLAND /011-0322-222512

The Paul Co., 27385 Pressonville Rd., Wellsville, KS 66092 / 785-883-4444; FAX: 785-883-2525

The Protector Mfg. Co., Inc., 443 Ashwood Place, Boca Raton, FL 33431 / 407-394-6011

The Robar Co.'s, Inc., 21438 N. 7th Ave., Suite B, Phoenix, AZ 85027 / 623-581-2648 www.robarguns.com

The School of Gunsmithing, 6065 Roswell Rd., Atlanta, GA 30328 / 800-223-4542

The Shooting Gallery, 8070 Southern Blvd., Boardman, OH 44512 / 216-726-7788

The Sight Shop, John G. Lawson, 1802 E. Columbia Ave., Tacoma, WA 98404 / 206-474-5465

The Southern Armory, 25 Millstone Road, Woodlawn, VA 24381 / 703-238-1343; FAX: 703-238-1453

The Surecase Co., 233 Wilshire Blvd., Ste. 900, Santa Monica, CA 90401 / 800-92ARMLOC

The Swampfire Shop (See Peterson Gun Shop, Inc.)

The Wilson Arms Co., 63 Leetes Island Rd., Branford, CT 06405 / 203-488-7297; FAX: 203-488-0135

Theis, Terry, 21452 FM 2093, Harper, TX 78631 / 830-864-4438

Thiewes, George W., 14329 W. Parada Dr., Sun City West, AZ 85375

Things Unlimited, 235 N. Kimbau, Casper, WY 82601 / 307-234-5277

Thirion Gun Engraving, Denise, PO Box 408, Graton, CA 95444 / 707-829-1876

Thomas, Charles C., 2600 S. First St., Springfield, IL 62794 / 217-789-8980; FAX: 217-789-9130

Thompson / Center Arms, P.O. Box 5002, Rochester, NH 03866 / 603-332-2394; FAX: 603-332-5133 tech@tcarms.com; www.tcarms.com

Thompson Bullet Lube Co., PO Box 409, Wills Point, TX 75169 / 866-476-1500; FAX: 866-476-1500 thomlube@flash.net www.thompsonbulletlube.com

Thompson Precision, 110 Mary St., P.O. Box 251, Warren, IL 61087 / 815-745-3625

Thompson, Randall. See: HIGHLINE MACHINE CO.

Thompson Target Technology, 4804 Sherman Church Ave. S.W., Canton, OH 44710 / 330-484-6480; FAX: 330-491-1087; www.thompsontarget.com

Thompson Tool Mount, 1550 Solomon Rd., Santa Maria, CA 93455 / 805-934-1281 ttm@pronet.net thompsontoolmount.com

Thompson, Randall (See Highline Machine Co.)

3-D Ammunition & Bullets, PO Box 433, Doniphan, NE 68832 / 402-845-2285; or 800-255-6712; FAX: 402-845-6546

3-Ten Corp., P.O. Box 269, Feeding Hills, MA 01030 / 413-789-2086; FAX: 413-789-1549

Thunden Ranch, HCR 1, Box 53, Mt. Home, TX 78058 / 830-640-3138

Thunder Mountain Arms, P.O. Box 593, Oak Harbor, WA 98277 / 206-679-4657; FAX: 206-675-1114

Thurston Sports, Inc., RD 3 Donovan Rd., Auburn, NY 13021 / 315-253-0966

Tiger-Hunt Gunstocks, Box 379, Beaverdale, PA 15921 / 814-472-5161 tigerhunt4@aol.com www.gunstockwood.com

Tikka (See U.S. Importer-Stoeger Industries)

Timber Heirloom Products, 618 Roslyn Ave. SW, Canton, OH 44710 / 216-453-7707; FAX: 216-478-4723

Time Precision, 640 Federal Rd., Brookfield, CT 06804 / 203-775-8343

Tinks & Ben Lee Hunting Products (See Wellington)

Tink's Safariland Hunting Corp., P.O. Box 244, 1140 Monticello Rd., Madison, GA 30650 / 706-342-4915; FAX: 706-342-7568

Tioga Engineering Co., Inc., PO Box 913, 13 Cone St., Wellsboro, PA 16901 / 570-724-3533; FAX: 570-724-3895 tiogaeng@epix.net

Tippman Pneumatics, Inc., 3518 Adams Center Rd., Fort Wayne, IN 46806 / 219-749-6022; FAX: 219-749-6619

Tirelli, Snc Di Tirelli Primo E.C., Via Matteotti No. 359, Gardone V.T. Brescia, I ITALY / 030-8912819; FAX: 030-832240

TM Stockworks, 6355 Maplecrest Rd., Fort Wayne, IN 46835 / 219-485-5389

TMI Products (See Haselbauer Products, Jerry)

Tom Forrest, Inc., P.O. Box 326, Lakeside, CA 92040 / 619-561-5800; FAX: 619-561-0227

Tombstone Smoke'n' Deals, PO Box 31298, Phoenix, AZ 85046 / 602-905-7013; FAX: 602-443-1998

Tom's Gun Repair, Thomas G. Ivanoff, 76-6 Rt. Southfork Rd., Cody, WY 82414 / 307-587-6949

Tom's Gunshop, 3601 Central Ave., Hot Springs, AR 71913 / 501-624-3856

Tonoloway Tack Drives, HCR 81, Box 100, Needmore, PA 17238

Top-Line USA, Inc., 7920-28 Hamilton Ave., Cincinnati, OH 45231 / 513-522-2992; or 800-346-6699; FAX: 513-522-0916

Torel, Inc., 1708 N. South St., P.O. Box 592, Yoakum, TX 77995 / 512-293-2341; FAX: 512-293-3413

TOZ (See U.S. Importer-Nygord Precision Products)

Track of the Wolf, Inc., P.O. Box 6, Osseo, MN 55369-0006 / 612-424-2500; FAX: 612-424-9860

Traditions Performance Firearms, P.O. Box 776, 1375 Boston Post Rd., Old Saybrook, CT 06475 / 860-388-4656; FAX: 860-388-4657 trad@ctz.nai.net www.traditionsmuzzle.com

Trafalgar Square, P.O. Box 257, N. Pomfret, VT 05053 / 802-457-1911

Trail Visions, 5800 N. Ames Terrace, Glendale, WI 53209 / 414-228-1328

Trax America, Inc., PO Box 898, 1150 Eldridge, Forrest City, AR 72335 / 870-633-0410; or 800-232-2327; FAX: 870-633-4788 trax@ipa.net www.traxamerica.com

Treadlok Gun Safe, Inc., 1764 Granby St. NE, Roanoke, VA 24012 / 800-729-8732; or 703-982-6881; FAX: 703-982-1059

Treemaster, P.O. Box 247, Guntersville, AL 35976 / 205-878-3597

Trevallion Gunstocks, 9 Old Mountain Rd., Cape Neddick, ME 03902 / 207-361-1130

Trico Plastics, 28061 Diaz Rd., Temecula, CA 92590 / 909-676-7714; FAX: 909-676-0267 ustinfo@ustplastics.com; www.tricoplastics.com

Trigger Lock Division / Central Specialties Ltd., 220-D Exchange Dr., Crystal Lake, IL 60014 / 847-639-3900; FAX: 847-639-3972

MANUFACTURER'S DIRECTORY

Trijicon, Inc., 49385 Shafer Ave., P.O. Box 930059, Wixom, MI 48393-0059 / 810-960-7700; FAX: 810-960-7725

Trilux, Inc., P.O. Box 24608, Winston-Salem, NC 27114 / 910-659-9438; FAX: 910-768-7720

Trinidad St. Jr Col Gunsmith Dept., 600 Prospect St., Trinidad, CO 81082 / 719-846-5631; FAX: 719-846-5667

Triple-K Mfg. Co., Inc., 2222 Commercial St., San Diego, CA 92113 / 619-232-2066; FAX: 619-232-7675 sales@triplek.com www.triplek.com

Tristar Sporting Arms, Ltd., 1814 Linn St. #16, N. Kansas City, MO 64116-3627 / 816-421-1400; FAX: 816-421-4182 tristar@blity-it.net www.tristarsportingarms.com

Trius Traps, Inc., P.O. Box 25, 221 S. Miami Ave., Cleves, OH 45002 / 513-941-5682; FAX: 513-941-7970 triustraps@fuse.net triustraps.com

Trooper Walsh, 2393 N Edgewood St, Arlington, VA 22207

Trotman, Ken, 135 Ditton Walk, Unit 11, Cambridge, CB5 8PY ENGLAND / 01223-211030; FAX: 01223-212317

Tru-Balance Knife Co., P.O. Box 140555, Grand Rapids, MI 49514 / 616-453-3679

True Flight Bullet Co., 5581 Roosevelt St., Whitehall, PA 18052 / 610-262-7630; FAX: 610-262-7806

Truglo, Inc, PO Box 1612, McKinna, TX 75070 / 972-774-0300; FAX: 972-774-0323 www.truglosights.com

Trulock Tool, PO Box 530, Whigham, GA 31797 / 229-762-4678; FAX: 229-762-4050 trulockchokes@hotmail.com; trulockchokes.com

Tru-Square Metal Products Inc., 640 First St. SW, P.O. Box 585, Auburn, WA 98071 / 253-833-2310; or 800-225-1017; FAX: 253-83-2349 t-tumbler@qwest.net

Tucker, James C., PO Box 1212, Paso Robles, CA 93447-1212

Tucson Mold, Inc., 930 S. Plumer Ave., Tucson, AZ 85719 / 520-792-1075; FAX: 520-792-1075

Turnbull Restoration, Doug, 6680 Rt. 5 & 20, PO Box 471, Bloomfield, NY 14469 / 585-657-6338; FAX: 585-657-6338; turnbullrest@mindspring.com www.turnbullrestoration.com

Tuttle, Dale, 4046 Russell Rd., Muskegon, MI 49445 / 616-766-2250

Tyler Manufacturing & Distributing, 3804 S. Eastern, Oklahoma City, OK 73129 / 405-677-1487; or 800-654-8415

U

U.S. Fire Arms Mfg. Co., Inc., 55 Van Dyke Ave., Hartford, CT 06106 / 877-227-6901; FAX: 800-644-7265 usfirearms.com

U.S. Importer-Wm. Larkin Moore, 8430 E. Raintree Ste. B-7, Scottsdale, AZ 85260

U.S. Repeating Arms Co., Inc., 275 Winchester Ave., Morgan, UT 84050-9333 / 801-876-3440; FAX: 801-876-3737

U.S. Tactical Systems (See Keng's Firearms Specialty)

U.S.A. Magazines, Inc., P.O. Box 39115, Downey, CA 90241 / 800-872-2577

Uberti USA, Inc., P.O. Box 469, Lakeville, CT 06039 / 860-435-8068; FAX: 860-435-8146

Ugartechea S. A., Ignacio, Chonta 26, Eibar, SPAIN / 43-121267; FAX: 43-121669

Ultra Dot Distribution, 2316 N.E. 8th Rd., Ocala, FL 34470

Ultralux (See U.S. Importer-Keng's Firearms)

UltraSport Arms, Inc., 1955 Norwood Ct., Racine, WI 53403 / 414-554-3237; FAX: 414-554-9731

Uncle Bud's, HCR 81, Box 100, Needmore, PA 17238 / 717-294-6000; FAX: 717-294-6005

Uncle Mike's (See Michaels of Oregon Co.)

Unertl Optical Co., Inc., 103 Grand Avenue, P.O. Box 895, Mars, PA 16046-0895 / 724-625-3810; FAX: 724-625-3819; unertl@nauticom.net

Unique/M.A.P.F., 10 Les Allees, 64700, Hendaye, FRANCE / 33-59 20 71 93

UniTec, 1250 Bedford SW, Canton, OH 44710 / 216-452-4017

United Binocular Co., 9043 S. Western Ave., Chicago, IL 60620

United Cutlery Corp., 1425 United Blvd., Sevierville, TN 37876 / 865-428-2532; or 800-548-0835; FAX: 865-428-2267

United States Optics Technologies, Inc., 5900 Dale St., Buena Park, CA 90621 / 714-994-4901; FAX: 714-994-4904 www.usoptics.com

United States Products Co., 518 Melwood Ave., Pittsburgh, PA 15213-1136 / 412-621-2130; FAX: 412-621-8740 sales@us-products.com www.us-products.com

Universal Sports, PO Box 532, Vincennes, IN 47591 / 812-882-8680; FAX: 812-882-8680

Unmussig Bullets, D. L., 7862 Brentford Dr., Richmond, VA 23225 / 804-320-1165

Upper Missouri Trading Co., PO Box 100, 304 Harold St., Crofton, NE 68730-0100 / 402-388-4844

USAC, 4500-15th St. East, Tacoma, WA 98424 / 206-922-7589

Utica Cutlery Co., 820 Noyes St., Utica, NY 13503 / 315-733-4663; FAX: 315-733-6602

V

V.H. Blackinton & Co., Inc., 221 John L. Dietsch, Attleboro Falls, MA 02763-0300 / 508-699-4436; FAX: 508-695-5349

Valade Engraving, Robert, 931 3rd Ave, Seaside, OR 97138 / 503-738-7672

Valor Corp., 5555 NW 36th Ave., Miami, FL 33142 / 305-633-0127; FAX: 305-634-4536

Valtro USA, Inc, 1281 Andersen Dr., San Rafael, CA 94901 / 415-256-2575; FAX: 415-256-2576

VAM Distribution Co LLC, 1141-B Mechanicsburg Rd, Wooster, OH 44691 www.rex10.com

Van Gorden & Son Inc., C. S., 1815 Main St., Bloomer, WI 54724 / 715-568-2612

Van Horn, Gil, P.O. Box 207, Llano, CA 93544

Van Patten, J. W., P.O. Box 145, Foster Hill, Milford, PA 18337 / 717-296-7069

Vancini, Carl (See Bestload, Inc.)

Vann Custom Bullets, 330 Grandview Ave., Novato, CA 94947

Van's Gunsmith Service, 224 Route 69-A, Parish, NY 13131 / 315-625-7251

Varmint Masters, LLC, Rick Vecqueray, PO Box 6724, Bend, OR 97708 / 541-318-7306; FAX: 541-318-7306 varmintmasters@bendcable.com www.varmintmasters.net

Vecqueray, Rick. See: VARMINT MASTERS, LLC

Vega Tool Co., c/o T.R. Ross, 4865 Tanglewood Ct., Boulder, CO 80301 / 303-530-0174

Vektor USA, Mikael Danforth, 5139 Stanart St, Norfolk, VA 23502 / 888-740-0837; or 757-455-8895; FAX: 757-461-9155

Venco Industries, Inc. (See Shooter's Choice)

Venus Industries, P.O. Box 246, Sialkot-1, PAKISTAN FAX: 92 432 85579

Verney-Carron, B.P. 72, 54 Boulevard Thiers, 42002, FRANCE / 33-477791500; FAX: 33-477790702

Vest, John, 1923 NE 7th St., Redmond, OR 97756 / 541-923-8898

VibraShine, Inc., PO Box 577, Taylorsville, MS 39168 / 601-785-9854; FAX: 601-785-9874

Vibra-Tek Co., 1844 Arroya Rd., Colorado Springs, CO 80906 / 719-634-8611; FAX: 719-634-6886

Vic's Gun Refinishing, 6 Pineview Dr., Dover, NH 03820-6422 / 603-742-0013

Victory Ammunition, PO Box 1022, Milford, PA 18337 / 717-296-5768; FAX: 717-296-9298

Victory USA, P.O. Box 1021, Pine Bush, NY 12566 / 914-744-2060; FAX: 914-744-5181

Vihtavuori Oy, FIN-41330 Vihtavuori, FINLAND, / 358-41-3779211; FAX: 358-41-3771643

Vihtavuori Oy/Kaltron-Pettibone, 1241 Ellis St., Bensenville, IL 60106 / 708-350-1116; FAX: 708-350-1606

Viking Video Productions, P.O. Box 251, Roseburg, OR 97470

Vincent's Shop, 210 Antoinette, Fairbanks, AK 99701

Vincenzo Bernardelli S.p.A., 125 Via Matteotti, P.O. Box 74, Gardone V.T., Bresci, 25063 ITALY / 39-30-8912851-2-3; FAX: 39-30-8910249

Vintage Arms, Inc., 6003 Saddle Horse, Fairfax, VA 22030 / 703-968-0779; FAX: 703-968-0780

Vintage Industries, Inc., 781 Big Tree Dr., Longwood, FL 32750 / 407-831-8949; FAX: 407-831-5346

Viper Bullet and Brass Works, 11 Brock St., Box 582, Norwich, ON NOJ 1P0 CANADA

Viramontez Engraving, Ray Viramontez, 601 Springfield Dr., Albany, GA 31707 / 229-432-9683 sgtvira@aol.com

Viramontez, Ray. See: VIRAMONTEZ ENGRAVING

Virgin Valley Custom Guns, 450 E 800 N #20, Hurricane, UT 84737 / 435-635-8941; FAX: 435-635-8943 vvcguns@infowest.com www.virginvalleyguns.com

Visible Impact Targets, Rts. 5 & 20, E. Bloomfield, NY 14443 / 716-657-6161; FAX: 716-657-5405

Vitt/Boos, 1195 Buck Hill Rd., Townshend, VT 05353 / 802-365-9232

Voere-KGH m.b.H., PO Box 416, A-6333 Kufstein, Tirol, AUSTRIA / 0043-5372-62547; FAX: 0043-5372-65752

Volquartsen Custom Ltd., 24276 240th Street, PO Box 397, Carroll, IA 51401 / 712-792-4238; FAX: 712-792-2542 vcl@netins.net www.volquartsen.com

Vom Hoffe (See Old Western Scrounger, Inc., The), 12924 Hwy A-12, Montague, CA 96064 / 916-459-5445; FAX: 916-459-3944

Vorhes, David, 3042 Beecham St., Napa, CA 94558 / 707-226-9116; FAX: 707-253-7334

Vortek Products, Inc., P.O. Box 871181, Canton, MI 48187-6181 / 313-397-5656; FAX: 313-397-5656

VSP Publishers (See Heritage/VSP Gun Books), PO Box 887, McCall, ID 83638 / 208-634-4104; FAX: 208-634-3101

Vulpes Ventures, Inc. Fox Cartridge Division, PO Box 1363, Bolingbrook, IL 60440-7363 / 630-759-1229; FAX: 815-439-3945

W

W. Square Enterprises, 9826 Sagedale Dr., Houston, TX 77089 / 281-484-0935; FAX: 281-464-9940 lfdwcpdq.net www.loadammo.co,

W. Waller & Son, Inc., 2221 Stoney Brook Rd., Grantham, NH 03753-7706 / 603-863-4177 wallerandson.com

W.B. Niemi Engineering, Box 126 Center Road, Greensboro, VT 05841 / 802-533-7180 or 802-533-7141

W.C. Strutz Rifle Barrels, Inc., PO Box 611, Eagle River, WI 54521 / 715-479-4766

W.C. Wolff Co., PO Box 458, Newtown Square, PA 19073 / 610-359-9600; or 800-545-0077; mail@gunsprings.com www.gunsprings.com

W.E. Birdsong & Assoc., 1435 Monterey Rd., Florence, MS 39073-9748 / 601-366-8270

W.E. Brownell Checkering Tools, 9390 Twin Mountain Cir, San Diego, CA 92126 / 858-695-2479; FAX: 858-695-2479

W.J. Riebe Co., 3434 Tucker Rd., Boise, ID 83703

W.R. Case & Sons Cutlery Co., Owens Way, Bradford, PA 16701 / 814-368-4123; or 800-523-6350; FAX: 814-768-5369

Waechter, 43 W. South St. #1FL, Nanticoke, PA 18634 / 717-864-3967; FAX: 717-864-2669

Wagoner, Vernon G., 2325 E. Encanto St., Mesa, AZ 85213-5917 / 480-835-1307

Wakina by Pic, 24813 Alderbrook Dr., Santa Clarita, CA 91321 / 800-295-8194

Waldron, Herman, Box 475, 80 N. 17th St., Pomeroy, WA 99347 / 509-843-1404

Walker Arms Co., Inc., 499 County Rd. 820, Selma, AL 36701 / 334-872-6231; FAX: 334-872-6262

Walker Mfg., Inc., 8296 S. Channel, Harsen's Island, ML 48028

Wallace, Terry, 385 San Marino, Vallejo, CA 94589 / 707-642-7041

Walls Industries, Inc., P.O. Box 98, 1905 N. Main, Cleburne, TX 76031 / 817-645-4366; FAX: 817-645-7946

Walters Industries, 6226 Park Lane, Dallas, TX 75225 / 214-691-6973

Walters, John. See: WALTERS WADS

Walters Wads, John Walters, 500 N. Avery Dr., Moore, OK 73160 / 405-799-0376; FAX: 405-799-7727 www.tinwadman@cs.com

Walther GmbH, Carl, B.P. 4325, D-89033 Ulm, GERMANY

Walther USA, PO Box 2208, Springfield, MA 01102 / 413-747-3443 www.walther-usa.com

Walther USA, PO Box 208, Ten Prince St, Alexandria, VA 22313 / 800-372-6454; FAX: 413-747-3592

Walt's Custom Leather, Walt Whinnery, 1947 Meadow Creek Dr., Louisville, KY 40218 / 502-458-4361

WAMCO--New Mexico, P.O. Box 205, Peralta, NM 87042-0205 / 505-869-0826

Ward & Van Valkenburg, 114 32nd Ave. N., Fargo, ND 58102 / 701-232-2351

Ward Machine, 5620 Lexington Rd., Corpus Christi, TX 78412 / 512-992-1221

Wardell Precision Handguns Ltd., 48851 N. Fig Springs Rd., New River, AZ 85027-8513 / 602-465-7995

Warenski, Julie, 590 E. 500 N., Richfield, UT 84701 / 801-896-5319; FAX: 801-896-5319

Warne Manufacturing Co., 9039 SE Jannsen Rd., Clackamas, OR 97015 / 503-657-5590 or 800-683-5590; FAX: 503-657-5695

Warren & Sweat Mfg. Co., P.O. Box 350440, Grand Island, FL 32784 / 904-669-3166; FAX: 904-669-7272

Warren Muzzleloading Co., Inc., Hwy. 21 North, P.O. Box 100, Ozone, AR 72854 / 501-292-3268

Washita Mountain Whetstone Co., P.O. Box 378, Lake Hamilton, AR 71951 / 501-525-3914

Wasmundt, Jim, P.O. Box 511, Fossil, OR 97830

MANUFACTURER'S DIRECTORY

WASP Shooting Systems, Rt. 1, Box 147, Lakeview, AR 72642 / 501-431-5606

Watson Bros., 39 Redcross Way, SE1 1H6, London, ENGLAND FAX: 44-171-403-336

Watson Trophy Match Bullets, 467 Pine Loop, Frostproof, FL 33843 / 863-635-7948; or 864-244-7948 cbestbullet@aol.com

Wayne E. Schwartz Custom Guns, 970 E. Britton Rd., Morrice, MI 48857 / 517-625-4079

Wayne Firearms For Collectors & Investors

Wayne Specialty Services, 260 Waterford Drive, Florissant, MO 63033 / 413-831-7083

WD-40 Co., 1061 Cudahy Pl., San Diego, CA 92110 / 619-275-1400; FAX: 619-275-5823

Weatherby, Inc., 3100 El Camino Real, Atascadero, CA 93422 / 805-466-1767; FAX: 805-466-2527 weatherby.com

Weaver Arms Corp. Gun Shop, RR 3, P.O. Box 266, Bloomfield, MO 63825-9528

Weaver Products, P.O. Box 39, Onalaska, WI 54650 / 800-648-9624; or 608-781-5800; FAX: 608-781-0368

Weaver Scope Repair Service, 1121 Larry Mahan Dr., Suite B, El Paso, TX 79925 / 915-593-1005

Webb, Bill, 6504 North Bellefontaine, Kansas City, MO 64119 / 816-453-7431

Weber & Markin Custom Gunsmiths, 4-1691 Powick Rd., Kelowna, BC V1X 4L1 CANADA / 250-762-7575; FAX: 250-861-3655; www.weberandmarkinguns.com

Weber Jr., Rudolf, P.O. Box 160106, D-5650, GERMANY / 0212-592136

Webley and Scott Ltd., Frankley Industrial Park, Tay Rd., Birmingham, B45 0PA ENGLAND / 011-021-453-1864; FAX: 021-457-7846

Webster Scale Mfg. Co., P.O. Box 188, Sebring, FL 33870 / 813-385-6362

Weems, Cecil, 510 W Hubbard St, Mineral Wells, TX 76067-4847 / 817-325-1462

Weigand Combat Handguns, Inc., 685 South Main Rd., Mountain Top, PA 18707 / 570-868-8358; FAX: 570-868-5218; sales@jackweigand.com www.scopemount.com

Weihrauch KG, Hermann, Industriestrasse 11, 8744 Mellrichstadt, Mellrichstadt, GERMANY

Welch, Sam. See: SAM WELCH GUN ENGRAVING

Wellington Outdoors, P.O. Box 244, 1140 Monticello Rd., Madison, GA 30650 / 706-342-4915; FAX: 706-342-7568

Wells, Rachel, 110 N. Summit St., Prescott, AZ 86301 / 520-445-3655

Wells Creek Knife & Gun Works, 32956 State Hwy. 38, Scottsburg, OR 97473 / 541-587-4202; FAX: 541-587-4223

Welsh, Bud. See: HIGH PRECISION

Wenger North America/Precise Int'l, 15 Corporate Dr., Orangeburg, NY 10962 / 800-431-2996; FAX: 914-425-4700

Wenig Custom Gunstocks, 103 N. Market St., PO Box 249, Lincoln, MO 65338 / 660-547-3334; FAX: 660-547-2881 gustock@wenig.com www.wenig.com

Werth, T. W., 1203 Woodlawn Rd., Lincoln, IL 62656 / 217-732-1300

Wescombe, Bill (See North Star West)

Wessinger Custom Guns & Engraving, 268 Limestone Rd., Chapin, SC 29036 / 803-345-5677

West, Jack L., 1220 W. Fifth, P.O. Box 427, Arlington, OR 97812

Western Cutlery (See Camillus Cutlery Co.)

Western Design (See Alpha Gunsmith Division)

Western Mfg. Co., 550 Valencia School Rd., Aptos, CA 95003 / 831-688-5884 lotsabears@eathlink.net

Western Missouri Shooters Alliance, PO Box 11144, Kansas City, MO 64119 / 816-597-3950; FAX: 816-229-7350

Western Nevada West Coast Bullets, PO BOX 2270, DAYTON, NV 89403-2270 / 702-246-3941; FAX: 702-246-0836

Westley Richards & Co., 40 Grange Rd., Birmingham, ENGLAND / 010-214722953

Westley Richards Agency USA (See U.S. Importer for Westwind Rifles, Inc., David S. Sullivan, P.O. Box 261, 640 Briggs St., Erie, CO 80516 / 303-828-3823

Weyer International, 2740 Nebraska Ave., Toledo, OH 43607 / 419-534-2020; FAX: 419-534-2697

Whildin & Sons Ltd, E.H., RR 2 Box 119, Tamaqua, PA 18252 / 717-668-6743; FAX: 717-668-6745

Whinnery, Walt (See Walt's Custom Leather)

Whiscombe (See U.S. Importer-Pelaire Products)

White Barn Wor, 431 County Road, Broadlands, IL 61816

White Pine Photographic Services, Hwy. 60, General Delivery, Wilno, ON K0J 2N0 CANADA / 613-756-3452

White Rock Tool & Die, 6400 N. Brighton Ave., Kansas City, MO 64119 / 816-454-0478

White Shooting Systems, Inc. (See White Muzzleload

Whitestone Lumber Corp., 148-02 14th Ave., Whitestone, NY 11357 / 718-746-4400; FAX: 718-767-1748

Wichita Arms, Inc., 923 E. Gilbert, P.O. Box 11371, Wichita, KS 67211 / 316-265-0661; FAX: 316-265-0760

Wick, David E., 1504 Michigan Ave., Columbus, IN 47201 / 812-376-6960

Widener's Reloading & Shooting Supply, Inc., P.O. Box 3009 CRS, Johnson City, TN 37602 / 615-282-6786; FAX: 615-282-6651

Wideview Scope Mount Corp., 13535 S. Hwy. 16, Rapid City, SD 57701 / 605-341-3220; FAX: 605-341-9142 wvdon@rapidnet.com ww.jii.to

Wiebe, Duane, 5300 Merchant Cir. #2, Placerville, CA 95667 / 530-344-1357; FAX: 530-344-1357 wiebe@d-wdb.com

Wiest, Marie. See: GUNCRAFT SPORTS, INC.

Wilcox All-Pro Tools & Supply, 4880 147th St., Montezuma, IA 50171 / 515-623-3138; FAX: 515-623-3104

Wilcox Industries Corp, Robert F Guarasi, 53 Durham St, Portsmouth, NH 03801 / 603-431-1331; FAX: 603-431-1221

Wild Bill's Originals, PO Box 13037, Burton, WA 98013 / 206-463-5738; FAX: 206-465-5925

Wild West Guns, 7521 Old Seward Hwy, Unit A, Anchorage, AK 99518 / 800-992-4570; or 907-344-4500; FAX: 907-344-4005

Wilderness Sound Products Ltd., 4015 Main St. A, Springfield, OR 97478 / 800-47-0006; FAX: 541-741-0263

Wildey, Inc., 45 Angevine Rd., Warren, CT 06754-1818 / 203-355-9000; FAX: 203-354-7759

Wildlife Research Center, Inc., 1050 McKinley St., Anoka, MN 55303 / 612-427-3350; or 800-USE-LURE; FAX: 612-427-8354

Wilhelm Brenneke KG, PO Box 1646, 30837 Langenhagen, Langenhagen, GERMANY / 0511/97262-0; FAX: 0511/97262-62; info@brenneke.de www.brenneke.com

Will-Burt Co., 169 S. Main, Orrville, OH 44667

William Fagan & Co., 22952 15 Mile Rd., Clinton Township, MI 48035 / 810-465-4637; FAX: 810-792-6996

William Powell & Son (Gunmakers) Ltd., 35-37 Carrs Lane, Birmingham, B4 7SX ENGLAND / 121-643-0689; FAX: 121-631-3504

William Powell Agency, 22 Circle Dr., Bellmore, NY 11710 / 516-679-1158

Williams Gun Sight Co., 7389 Lapeer Rd., Box 329, Davison, MI 48423 / 810-653-2131; or 800-530-9028; FAX: 810-658-2140 williamsgunsight.com

Williams Mfg. of Oregon, 110 East B St., Drain, OR 97435 / 503-836-7461; FAX: 503-836-7245

Williams Shootin' Iron Service, The Lynx-Line, Rt. 2 Box 223A, Mountain Grove, MO 65711 / 417-948-0902; FAX: 417-948-0902

Williamson Precision Gunsmithing, 117 W. Pipeline, Hurst, TX 76053 / 817-285-0064; FAX: 817-280-0044

Willow Bend, PO Box 203, Chelmsford, MA 01824 / 978-256-8508; FAX: 978-256-8508

Willson Safety Prods. Div., PO Box 622, Reading, PA 19603-0622 / 610-376-6161; FAX: 610-371-7725

Wilson Combat, 2234 CR 719, Berryville, AR 72616-4573 / 800-955-4856; FAX: 870-545-3310

Wilson Case, Inc., PO Box 1106, Hastings, NE 68902-1106 / 800-322-5493; FAX: 402-463-5276 sales@wilsoncase.com; www.wilsoncase.com

Winchester Consultants, George Madis, P.O. Box 545, Brownsboro, TX 75756 / 903-852-6480; FAX: 903-852-3045; gmadis@prodigy.net

Winchester Div. Olin Corp., 427 N. Shamrock, E. Alton, IL 62024 / 618-258-3566; FAX: 618-258-3599

Winchester Sutler, Inc., The, 270 Shadow Brook Lane, Winchester, VA 22603 / 540-888-3595; FAX: 540-888-4632

Windish, Jim, 2510 Dawn Dr., Alexandria, VA 22306 / 703-765-1994

Wingshooting Adventures, 0-1845 W. Leonard, Grand Rapids, MI 49544 / 616-677-1980; FAX: 616-677-1986

Winkle Bullets, R.R. 1, Box 316, Heyworth, IL 61745

Winter, Robert M., PO Box 484, 42975-287th St., Menno, SD 57045 / 605-387-5322

Wise Custom Guns, 1402 Blanco Rd, San Antonio, TX 78212-2716 / 210-828-3388

Wise Guns, Dale, 333 W Olmos Dr, San Antonio, TX 78212 / 210-828-3388

Wiseman and Co., Bill, PO Box 3427, Bryan, TX 77805 / 409-690-3456; FAX: 409-690-0156

Wisners Inc/Twin Pine Armory, P.O. Box 58, Hwy. 6, Adna, WA 98522 / 360-748-4590; FAX: 360-748-1802

Wolf (See J.R. Distributing)

Wolf Performance Ammunition, 2201 E. Winston Rd., Ste K, Anaheim, CA 92806 / 702-837-8506; FAX: 702-837-9250

Wolfe Publishing Co., 6471 Airpark Dr., Prescott, AZ 86301 / 520-445-7810; or 800-899-7810; FAX: 520-778-5124

Wolf's Western Traders, 1250 Santa Cora Ave. #613, Chula Vista, CA 91913 / 619-482-1701 patwolf4570book@aol.com

Wolverine Footwear Group, 9341 Courtland Dr. NE, Rockford, MI 49351 / 616-866-5500; FAX: 616-866-5658

Wood, Frank (See Classic Guns, Inc.), 5305 Peachtree Ind. Blvd., Norcross, GA 30092 / 404-242-7944

Woodleigh (See Huntington Die Specialties)

Woods Wise Products, P.O. Box 681552, Franklin, TN 37068 / 800-735-8182; FAX: 615-726-2637

Woodstream, P.O. Box 327, Lititz, PA 17543 / 717-626-2125; FAX: 717-626-1912

Woodworker's Supply, 1108 North Glenn Rd., Casper, WY 82601 / 307-237-5354

Woolrich, Inc., Mill St., Woolrich, PA 17701 / 800-995-1299; FAX: 717-769-6234/6259

Working Guns, Jim Coffin, 1224 NW Fernwood Cir, Corvallis, OR 97330-2909 / 541-928-4391

World Class Airguns, 2736 Morningstar Dr., Indianapolis, IN 46229 / 317-897-5548

World of Targets (See Birchwood Casey)

World Trek, Inc., 7170 Turkey Creek Rd., Pueblo, CO 81007-1046 / 719-546-2121; FAX: 719-543-6886

Worthy Products, Inc., RR 1, P.O. Box 213, Martville, NY 13111 / 315-324-5298

Wostenholm (See Ibberson [Sheffield] Ltd., George)

Wright's Gunstock Blanks, 8540 SE Kane Rd., Gresham, OR 97080 / 503-666-1705 doyal@wrightsguns.com www.wrightsguns.com

WTA Manufacturing, PO Box 164, Kit Carson, CO 80825 / 800-700-3054; FAX: 719-962-3570

Wyant Bullets, Gen. Del., Swan Lake, MT 59911

Wyant's Outdoor Products, Inc., PO Box 9, Broadway, VA 22815

Wyoming Custom Bullets, 1626 21st St., Cody, WY 82414

Wyoming Knife Corp., 101 Commerce Dr., Ft. Collins, CO 80524 / 303-224-3454

X

X-Spand Target Systems, 26-10th St. SE, Medicine Hat, AB T1A 1P7 CANADA / 403-526-7997; FAX: 403-528-2362

Y

Yankee Gunsmith, 2901 Deer Flat Dr., Copperas Cove, TX 76522 / 817-547-8433

Yavapai College, 1100 E. Sheldon St., Prescott, AZ 86301 / 520-776-2353; FAX: 520-776-2355

Yavapai Firearms Academy Ltd., PO Box 27290, Prescott Valley, AZ 86312 / 928-772-8262 info@yfainc.corn www.yfainc.com

Yearout, Lewis E. (See Montana Outfitters), 308 Riverview Dr E, Great Falls, MT 59404 / 406-761-0859

Yee, Mike. See: CUSTOM STOCKING

Yellowstone Wilderness Supply, P.O. Box 129, W. Yellowstone, MT 59758 / 406-646-7613

Yesteryear Armory & Supply, P.O. Box 408, Carthage, TN 37030

York M-1 Conversions, 12145 Mill Creek Run, Plantersville, TX 77363 / 936-894-2397; FAX: 936-894-2397

Young Country Arms, William, 1409 Kuehner Dr #13, Simi Valley, CA 93063-4478

Z

Zabala Hermanos S.A., Lasao, 6-20690, Elgueta, Guipuzcoa, 20600 SPAIN / 943-768076; FAX: 943-768201

Zander's Sporting Goods, 7525 Hwy 154 West, Baldwin, IL 62217-9706 / 800-851-4373; FAX: 618-785-2320

Zanotti Armor, Inc., 123 W. Lone Tree Rd., Cedar Falls, IA 50613 / 319-232-9650

Zeeryp, Russ, 1601 Foard Dr., Lynn Ross Manor, Morristown, TN 37814 / 615-586-2357

Zero Ammunition Co., Inc., 1601 22nd St. SE, PO Box 1188, Cullman, AL 35056-1188 / 800-545-9376; FAX: 205-739-4683

Ziegel Engineering, 2108 Lomina Ave., Long Beach, CA 90815 / 562-596-9481; FAX: 562-598-4734 ziegel@aol.com www.ziegeleng.com

Zim's, Inc., 4370 S. 3rd West, Salt Lake City, UT 84107 / 801-268-2505

Z-M Weapons, 203 South St., Bernardston, MA 01337 / 413-648-9501; FAX: 413-648-0219

Zriny's Metal Targets (See Z's Metal Targets)

Zufall, Joseph F., P.O. Box 304, Golden, CO 80402-0304

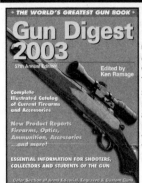

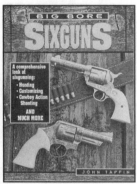

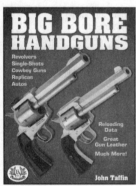